TAX FORMULA FOR INDIVIDUALS

Income (broadly conceived)	$xx,xxx
Less: Exclusions	(x,xxx)
Gross income	$xx,xxx
Less: Deductions *for* adjusted gross income	(x,xxx)
Adjusted gross income	$xx,xxx
Less: The greater of–	
Total itemized deductions	
or standard deduction	(x,xxx)
Personal and dependency exemptions	(x,xxx)
Taxable income	$xx,xxx

BASIC STANDARD DEDUCTION AMOUNTS

	Standard Deduction Amount	
Filing Status	**1995**	**1996**
Single	$3,900	$4,000
Married, filing jointly	6,550	6,700
Surviving spouse	6,550	6,700
Head of household	5,750	5,900
Married, filing separately	3,275	3,350

AMOUNT OF EACH ADDITIONAL STANDARD DEDUCTION

Filing Status	1995	1996
Single	$950	$1,000
Married, filing jointly	750	800
Surviving spouse	750	800
Head of household	950	1,000
Married, filing separately	750	800

PERSONAL AND DEPENDENCY EXEMPTION

1995	1996
$2,500	$2,550

1997 ANNUAL EDITION

WEST'S FEDERAL TAXATION:

INDIVIDUAL INCOME TAXES

1997 ANNUAL EDITION

WEST'S FEDERAL TAXATION:

INDIVIDUAL INCOME TAXES

GENERAL EDITORS

William H. Hoffman, Jr., J.D., Ph.D., C.P.A. **James E. Smith,** Ph.D., C.P.A.

Eugene Willis, Ph.D., C.P.A.

CONTRIBUTING AUTHORS

James H. Boyd,
Ph.D., C.P.A.
Arizona State University

D. Larry Crumbley,
Ph.D., C.P.A.
Texas A & M University

Steven C. Dilley,
J.D., Ph.D., C.P.A.
Michigan State University

Patrica C. Elliott,
D.B.A., C.P.A.
University of New Mexico

Mary Sue Gately,
Ph.D., C.P.A.
Texas Tech University

William H. Hoffman, Jr.,
J.D., Ph.D., C.P.A.
University of Houston

David M. Maloney,
Ph.D., C.P.A.
University of Virginia

Marilyn Phelan,
J.D., Ph.D., C.P.A.
Texas Tech University

William A. Raabe,
Ph.D., C.P.A.
University of Wisconsin-Milwaukee

Boyd C. Randall,
J.D., Ph.D.
Brigham Young University

W. Eugene Seago,
J.D., Ph.D., C.P.A.
Virginia Polytechnic Institute and State University

James E. Smith,
Ph.D., C.P.A.
College of William and Mary

Eugene Willis,
Ph.D., C.P.A.
University of Illinois at Urbana

West Publishing Company

Minneapolis/St. Paul • New York • Los Angeles • San Francisco

Copyediting: Patricia A. Lewis
Composition: Carlisle Communications, Ltd.
Text Design: LightSource Images
Cover Design: David J. Farr, *ImageSmythe*
Index: Catalyst Communication Arts

A Note On Type: Type fonts used are Palatino for text, Serif Gothic Bold for part and chapter openers display, and Helvetica Light and Black accent type.

WEST'S COMMITMENT TO THE ENVIRONMENT

In 1906, West Publishing Company began recycling materials left over from the production of books. This began a tradition of efficient and responsible use of resources. Today, 100% of our legal bound volumes are printed on acid-free, recycled paper consisting of 50% new paper pulp and 50% paper that has undergone a de-inking process. We also use vegetable-based inks to print all of our books. West recycles nearly 22,650,000 pounds of scrap paper annually—the equivalent of 187,500 trees. Since the 1960s, West has devised ways to capture and recycle waste inks, solvents, oils, and vapors created in the printing process. We also recycle plastics of all kinds, wood, glass, corrugated cardboard, and batteries, and have eliminated the use of polystyrene book packaging. We at West are proud of the longevity and the scope of our commitment to our environment.

West pocket parts and advance sheets are printed on recyclable paper and can be collected and recycled with newspapers. Staples do not have to be removed. Bound volumes can be recycled after removing the covers.

Production, Prepress, Printing and Binding by West Publishing Company.

TEXT IS PRINTED ON 10% POST CONSUMER RECYCLED PAPER

Printed with Printwise
Environmentally Advanced Water Washable Ink

By **West Publishing Company**
610 Opperman Drive
P.O. Box 64526
St. Paul, MN 55164–0526

Printed in the United States of America
03 02 01 00 99 98 97 96 8 7 6 5 4 3 2 1 0

Library of Congress Cataloging-in-Publication Data

Main entry under title:
West's Federal Taxation.
Includes index.
1. Income tax—United States—Law
I. Hoffman, William H. III. Willis, Eugene

ISBN 0–314–08817–2, 0–314–09711–2
KF6335.H63 343'.73'04 77–54355

ISSN 0270–5265
1997 ANNUAL EDITION

PREFACE

The publication of the 1997 Edition marks the twentieth year of *West's Federal Taxation* (WFT). From a single textbook on Corporations, Partnerships, Estates, and Trusts with an accompanying solutions manual, the WFT series has grown to three major textbooks and a package of 54 ancillaries. During this period, WFT has made every effort to improve the quality of the materials and has consistently added attractive innovations. With sales surpassing the one million level, WFT looks forward to continued success in the future in serving you.

This textbook is intended as a basis for a first course in Federal taxation for undergraduate or graduate accounting, business, and law students. With certain modifications in the coverage of the materials, the textbook may be used in a survey course on Federal taxation for undergraduate or graduate students. The materials may also be valuable as a tool for self-study, since they contain numerous clarifying examples adaptable to such an approach.

Tax policy considerations and historical developments are introduced in the textbook only to the extent that they shed light on the reason for a particular rule. The many simple and straightforward examples further clarify the materials by showing how a particular tax rule applies in an actual situation.

Since the original edition was issued in 1978, we have followed a policy of annually revising the text material to reflect statutory, judicial, and administrative changes in the Federal tax law and to correct any errors or other shortcomings. Not only do we encourage user input, we actively seek the advice of users as the basis for improving the textbook.

Tax legislation may be enacted in 1996 or early 1997. If any significant tax legislation is enacted during this period, we will provide you with supplements on a timely basis.

Though the primary emphasis of the textbook is on the income taxation of individuals, Chapter 20 provides an overview of the Federal taxation of other forms of business organization (corporations and partnerships). This chapter could be of particular significance to students who do not plan to take a second course in Federal taxation. For others, Chapter 20 may serve as a lead-in to *West's Federal Taxation: Corporations, Partnerships, Estates, and Trusts.*

ENHANCED PEDAGOGICAL PLAN

In the 1997 edition, we have continued to enhance the pedagogy to assist the student in the learning process and to address the recommendations of the Accounting Education Change Commission (AECC).

- *Learning Objectives.* Each chapter begins with student learning objectives for the chapter. These behavioral objectives provide the students with guidance in learning the key concepts and principles.
- *Chapter Outline.* The learning objectives are followed by a topical outline of the material in the chapter. Page references appear in the outline to provide the student with ready access to each topic.

- *Chapter Introductions.* The introductions link the material in the current chapter to previous chapters and demonstrate its relevance. Frequently, the chapter introduction includes a "real-world" illustration to help convey the relevance of the material.
- *Margin Notes.* Each of the learning objectives appears in the margin where the related material is introduced and helps to guide the student through the chapter.
- *Tax in the News.* Tax in the News items appear in each chapter as a boxed feature to enliven the text discussion. These items are drawn from today's business press and present current issues that are relevant to the chapter material.
- *Ethical Considerations.* Ethical Considerations features appear in each chapter presenting thought-provoking issues related to the chapter topics. In response to the recommendations of the AECC, they also demonstrate that many issues do not have a single correct answer. The questions raised in the Ethical Considerations were selected to provoke discussion and provide opportunities for debate (oral communication) based on the student's value system rather than to provide a defensible answer. To assist the professor in providing guidance for the discussion, the *Instructor's Guide with Lecture Notes* includes material on each Ethical Consideration. This material identifies the issues raised in the Ethical Consideration and, where appropriate, recommends a solution or alternate solutions.
- *Key Terms.* Located before the Problem Materials in each chapter is a list of key terms to assist student learning. When the key term is introduced in the chapter, it appears in bold print. The list of key terms includes page references to the chapter coverage. In addition, each key term is defined in the Glossary (Appendix C).

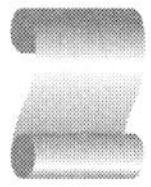

- *Communication Assignments.* In recognition of the increasing emphasis in accounting and tax education on communication, identified items in the Problem Materials now include a written communication component. Selected Problems, Cumulative Problems, and Research Problems are identified as communication assignments with a "scroll" icon. These problems ask the student to prepare a tax client letter, a memorandum for the tax files, or other written materials. The discussion of the tax research process in Chapter 2 includes an illustration of the client letter and the memo.

- *Decision-Making Problems.* The Problem Materials include decision-making problems that are designed to enhance the student's analytical skills. These problems are identified with a "scales" icon.

- *Problem Recognition Questions.* The Problem Materials include questions that are designed to require the student to identify tax issues. With this issues orientation, such questions can be multifaceted and have no single right answer. These questions are identified with a "lightbulb" icon.
- *Team Projects: Arthur Andersen Tax Challenge Cases.* This new feature at the end of the Problem Materials gives students experience working as a team to solve complex real world tax issues. The instructor can choose between two cases that can be ordered from your West representative and provided to students at no cost. Materials for the instructor can be found in the *Instructor's Guide.*

- The Research Problems heading now includes a CD-ROM icon to emphasize that solutions to all the research problems can now be prepared using *West's Federal Taxation on CD-ROM. WFT on CD-ROM* includes false leads as well as the necessary cases, Revenue Rulings, and Revenue Procedures as a way of providing a realistic environment for the tax research process.

SPECIAL FEATURES

A variety of other pedagogical devices are used to assist the student in the learning process. We recognize the importance of readability and continue to strive to make our textbook and supplements even more readable and understandable. The following features enhance the readability of the text:

- Including three levels of headings to aid in organization.
- Using bold print in the text to identify key terms the first time each term is used.
- Italicizing other key words to emphasize their importance to the student.
- Avoiding legal terminology except where it is beneficial.
- Using Concept Summaries to synthesize important concepts in chart or tabular form.
- Using Exhibits, Figures, and Tables to enhance presentations.
- Organizing the material in lists with bullets rather than presenting it in lengthy sentences.
- Using examples frequently to help the student understand the tax concept being discussed.
- Using a larger page size to provide a more open, accessible, and student-friendly textbook.

Once knowledge of the tax law has been acquired, it needs to be used. The tax minimization process, however, normally requires careful planning. Because we recognize the importance of planning procedures, most chapters include a separate section (called *Tax Planning Considerations*) illustrating the applications of these procedures to specific areas. While tax planning applications and suggestions appear throughout the chapter, this separate section at the end of the chapter calls the student's attention to the importance of tax planning.

We believe that any basic course in Federal taxation should offer the reader the opportunity to learn and utilize the methodology of tax research. This knowledge is requisite in today's environment with its increased emphasis on the concept of "learning to learn." Chapter 2 and Appendix E are devoted to this methodology. Also, most chapters contain *Research Problems* that require the use of research tools. Solutions to these Research Problems can be found in the *Instructor's Guide*. The effectiveness of the text does not, however, depend on the coverage of tax research procedures. Consequently, the treatment of this subject may be omitted without impairing the continuity of the remaining textual materials.

Although it is not our purpose to approach taxation from the standpoint of preparing tax returns, some familiarity with forms is necessary. Because 1996 forms will not be available until later in the year, most tax return problems in this edition are written for tax year 1995. The 1995 problems may be solved manually, or many may be solved using the tax return preparation software (*TurboTax* or *MacInTax*) that may be purchased by students who use this textbook.

Appendix F contains two comprehensive tax return problems written for tax year 1995. Each of these problems lends itself for use as a term project because of the sophistication required for satisfactory completion. Solutions to the problems in Appendix F appear in the *Instructor's Guide*.

For the reader's convenience, Appendix B contains a full reproduction of most of the 1995 tax forms frequently encountered in actual practice.

Most tax textbooks are published in the spring, long before tax forms for the year of publication are available from the government. We believe that students should be exposed to the most current tax forms. As a result, we develop some new problems and provide adopters with reproducible copies of these problems, along with blank tax forms and solutions on the new forms. Shortly after the beginning of 1997, adopters will receive a *Forms Problems Supplement* containing these tax return problems solved on 1996 forms.

WEST'S FEDERAL TAXATION ON CD-ROM

West is continuing to offer this text on CD-ROM. It includes the entire text of the printed version of *West's Federal Taxation: Individual Income Taxes, 1997 Edition* as well as the full text of all referenced cases, code Sections, Regulations, Revenue Procedures, and Revenue Rulings, and all tax forms, tables and schedules from the appendixes. Students can jump directly from the text they're reading to the full text of any of the references included on the disc.

We have expanded the materials on the CD-ROM so that solutions to all of the Research Problems can be prepared using the CD-ROM. In addition to adding the requisite cases, Revenue Rulings, and Revenue Procedures for the solutions, additional cases, Revenue Rulings, and Revenue Procedures are included to serve as "false leads" and provide a realistic environment for the tax research process.

Other features include "notebook" capabilities that allow students to cut and paste from the text, type in their own comments, and convert the text and notes into other word processing packages. Records of all queries are kept which allow viewing and editing of past queries. Each disc has an electronic "book-mark" feature that marks the spot where the student left off and returns to the last page that was viewed when the project is resumed. *WFT on CD-ROM* is fully supported by West's CD-ROM Customer Service Technicians and Research Attorneys. Professors and students can call for any technical or research assistance their projects require.

System requirements include an IBM or compatible PC with a 286, 386, 486, or Pentium processor; DOS version 3.3 or higher; 400K of available conventional RAM (after loading all memory-resident software including device drivers and the Microsoft CD-ROM extensions [MSCDEX]); 5 MB of available hard disc space; and a locally attached CD-ROM drive using Microsoft CD-ROM Extensions (MSCDEX) version 2.1 or higher (compatible CD-ROM drives must meet the ISO 9660 standard). To print images off the CD, 1.5MG RAM on your printer is required.

SUPPLEMENTS

West is continuing to publish the Arthur Andersen Tax Challenge Cases, a set of four capstone cases and their solutions provided to the instructor for classroom use. The cases encompass both tax compliance and tax planning and provide an opportunity for a team approach in solving tax issues and recommending tax strategies. As a technique for further integrating the cases with the textbook coverage of the tax topics in the cases, page references to two of the cases appear at the end of each chapter.

Other products in our 1997 instructional package include the following:

- The *Instructor's Guide with Lecture Notes* contains lecture notes for each chapter, materials on the Ethical Considerations found in the textbook, materials on the two Arthur Andersen Tax Challenge Cases that are page referenced to the textbook, and solutions to Research Problems and Comprehensive Tax Return problems found in the textbook. The lecture notes consist of a lecture outline that the professor can use as the basis for his or her classroom presentation. These lecture notes include not only material covered in the textbook, but also cases and other relevant material and teaching aids. The lecture notes are also available on disc in ASCII files.

- A *Solutions Manual* that has been carefully checked to ensure that it is error-free. The problems are arranged in accordance with the sequence of the material in the chapter. All problems are labeled by topical coverage in a matrix that also indicates which problems are new, modified, or unchanged in the new edition. The matrix also includes the problem number for the unchanged and modified problems in the prior edition. Approximately 20 percent of the problems in the 1997 edition are new or modified. The solutions are referenced to pages in the textbook. The solutions manual is also available on disc in ASCII files.
- A *Test Bank* with questions and solutions referenced to pages in the textbook. The questions are arranged in accordance with the sequence of the material in the chapter. To assist the professor in selecting questions for an examination, all questions are labeled by topical coverage in a matrix that also indicates which questions are new, modified, or unchanged in the new edition. The matrix includes the question number for the unchanged and modified questions in the prior edition. Approximately 20 percent of the questions in the 1997 edition are new or modified.
- *Westest*, a microcomputer test generation program for IBM PCs and compatibles and the Macintosh family of computers.
- *West CD-ROM Federal Tax Library* (Compact Disc with Read-Only Memory) provides a complete tax research library on a desktop. The Federal Tax Library is a set of compact discs with a software package that reads the discs through a PC. Each disc has a remarkable storage capacity-roughly 1,000 times more than a single-sided floppy disc. A brief list of the library contents includes the complete *Internal Revenue Code of 1986*, Regulations, 1986 Tax Reform Act with Amendments and Legislative History, Federal Court Cases on Tax (i.e., District, Circuit, and Supreme), Tax Court Cases, Revenue Rulings, and Revenue Procedures. The library is available to qualified adopters.
- A *Student Study Guide* prepared by Gerald E. Whittenburg, San Diego State University, includes a chapter review of key concepts and self-evaluation tests with solutions that are page referenced to the textbook.
- *Solutions Transparency Masters* for selected complex and cumulative problems, with a larger typeface for greater readability.
- *PowerPoint Presentation Software* allows qualified adopters to create interactive lectures and manipulate graphs, charts, and figures during in-class lectures. The package contains approximately 30 transparency masters per chapter consisting of alternate figures, outlines, and key points.
- *Teaching Transparency Masters* include most screens from the PowerPoint package reproduced as transparency masters for instructors who may wish to use traditional transparencies.
- *Teaching Transparency Acetates* contain the key charts and tables from the *Teaching Transparency Masters* package.
- A *Student Note-Taking Guide* includes selected screens from the PowerPoint package consisting of chapter outlines and key points. This unique guide provides students with the core chapter information, so they can concentrate in class on learning key concepts instead of copying basic lecture outlines and transparencies. These have been printed and bound in a manner similar to accounting working papers. The pages include all the information from the PowerPoint screens while still leaving room for student notes.
- *Instructor's Resource Notebook*—this three-ring binder can be used to house all or portions of the supplements and textbook that we will continue to offer in looseleaf form so you can reorganize the book and incorporate your supplemental materials to fit your course lectures.

- *WFT Individual Practice Sets,* 1996–97 edition, prepared by John B. Barrack, University of Georgia, is designed to cover all the common forms that a tax practitioner would use for the average client.
- Limited free use to qualified adopters of WESTLAW, a computer-assisted tax and legal research service that provides access to hundreds of valuable information sources.
- *West's Internal Revenue Code of 1986 and Treasury Regulations: Annotated and Selected 1997 Edition* by James E. Smith, College of William and Mary. This provides the opportunity for the student to be exposed to the Code and the Regulations in a single-volume book, which also contains useful annotations that help the student work with and understand the Code.
- *WFT On-line* puts the most current information in your hands as soon as it is available. Qualified adopters can log onto West Publishing's site on the World Wide Web (http://www.westpub.com/Educate/) and immediately gain access to the most recent taxation information available, including the Code and Regulations, case citations, new court rulings, and other newsworthy items. This information can then be transferred to a word-processing program for editing, printout, and classroom use while the information is still topical.

TAX PREPARATION SOFTWARE

The trend toward using the computer as an essential tool in tax practice has accelerated. To ensure that the *West's Federal Taxation* instructional package continues to set the pace in this important area, the following products are available to be used with the 1997 edition:

- *TurboTax* © Personal/1040 for DOS version 95.01 by Intuit is a commercial tax preparation package. It teaches students how to prepare over 80 forms, schedules, and worksheets, and automatically performs all mathematical calculations and data transfers. *TurboTax* also assists students with tax planning and helps them prepare "anticipated" tax returns. The *TurboTax* package, available for student purchase, includes discs bound with a 200-page workbook containing exercises and problems. The software runs on IBM PCs and compatibles with 512K memory. *MacInTax®* and *TurboTax® for Windows* are also available.

These software products are powerful, easy to learn, and easy to use. We believe that tax education can be raised to a higher level through the use of computers and well-designed software. These software packages take the drudgery out of performing the complex computations required to solve difficult tax problems.

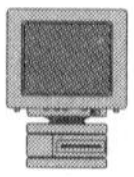

To enable students to take advantage of these new software products, the 1997 edition contains numerous tax return problems. Problems that lend themselves to computerized solutions are identified by a computer symbol.

ACKNOWLEDGMENTS

We are most appreciative of the many suggestions that we have received for revising the textbook, many of which have been incorporated in past editions and in the 1997 edition. We would also like to thank the people who have painstakingly worked through all the problems and text questions and generally acted as problem checkers to ensure the accuracy of the book and ancillary package. They are Tracey A. Anderson, Indiana University at South Bend; Caroline K. Craig, Illinois State University; Mark B. Persellin, St. Mary's University; Debra L.

Sanders, Washington State University; Randall K. Serrett, Fort Lewis College; Thomas Sternburg, University of Illinois at Urbana; and Raymond F. Wacker, Southern Illinois University at Carbondale.

Finally, this 1997 edition would not have been possible without the technical assistance of and manuscript review by Bonnie Hoffman, CPA, Freda Mulhall, CPA, and Nora Smith, M.Ed. We are indebted to them for their efforts.

William H. Hoffman, Jr.
James E. Smith
Eugene Willis

April 1, 1996

About the Editors

William H. Hoffman, Jr., earned B.A. and J.D. degrees from the University of Michigan and M.B.A. and Ph.D. degrees from The University of Texas. He is a licensed CPA and attorney in Texas. His teaching experience includes: The University of Texas (1957–1961), Louisiana State University (1961–1967), and the University of Houston (1967 to present). Professor Hoffman has addressed many tax institutes and conferences and has published extensively in professional journals. His articles appear in *The Journal of Taxation, The Tax Adviser, Taxes—The Tax Magazine, The Journal of Accountancy, The Accounting Review,* and *Taxation for Accountants.*

James E. Smith is the John S. Quinn Professor of Accounting at the College of William and Mary. He has been a member of the Accounting Faculty for twenty-five years. He received his Ph.D. degree from the University of Arizona.

Jim has served as a discussion leader for Continuing Professional Education programs for the AICPA, Federal Tax Workshops, and various state CPA societies. He has conducted programs in over 40 states for approximately 25,000 CPAs. He has been the recipient of the AICPAs' Outstanding Discussion Leader Award.

Other awards received by Jim include the Virginia Society of CPAs' Outstanding Accounting Educator Award and the James Madison University's Outstanding Accounting Educator Award. He was the President of the Administrators of Accounting Programs Group (AAPG) in 1991–1992. He was the faculty adviser for the William and Mary teams that received first place in the Arthur Andersen Tax Challenge in 1994 and 1995.

Eugene Willis is the Arthur Andersen Alumni Professor of Accountancy at the University of Illinois (Urbana-Champaign). He joined the Illinois faculty in 1975 after receiving his Ph.D. from the University of Cincinnati. He served as Acting Head of the department in 1993 and 1994 and is currently Associate Head and Director of Masters Programs. He has published articles in leading academic and professional journals, including the *Accounting Review, The Journal of the American Taxation Association, The Journal of Accountancy,* and *The Journal of Taxation.* Professor Willis is co-director of the National Tax Education Program, a continuing education program co-sponsored by the American Institute of CPAs and the University of Illinois.

Contents in Brief

CONTENTS

PART VII
Corporations and Partnerships

CHAPTER 20

Appendixes

P • A • R • T

I

Introduction and Basic Tax Model

Part I provides an introduction to taxation in the United States. Although the primary orientation of this text is income taxation, other types of taxes are also discussed briefly. The purposes of the Federal tax law are examined, and the legislative, administrative, and judicial sources of Federal tax law, including their application to the tax research process, are analyzed. Part I concludes with the introduction of the basic tax model for the individual taxpayer.

CHAPTER

1

AN INTRODUCTION TO TAXATION AND UNDERSTANDING THE FEDERAL TAX LAW

LEARNING OBJECTIVES

After completing Chapter 1, you should be able to:

1. Understand some of the history, including trends, of the Federal income tax.
2. Know some of the criteria for selecting a tax structure and understand the components of a tax structure.
3. Identify the different taxes imposed in the United States at the Federal, state, and local levels.
4. Understand the administration of the tax law including the audit process utilized by the IRS.
5. Appreciate some of the ethical guidelines involved in tax practice.
6. Recognize the economic, social, equity, and political considerations that justify various aspects of the tax law.
7. Describe the role played by the IRS and the courts in the evolution of the Federal tax system.

OUTLINE

The primary objective of this chapter is to provide an overview of the Federal tax system. Among the topics discussed are the following:

- A brief history of the Federal income tax.
- The different types of taxes imposed at the Federal, state, and local levels.
- Some highlights of tax law administration.
- Tax concepts that help explain the reasons for various tax provisions.
- The influence that the Internal Revenue Service (IRS) and the courts have had in the evolution of current tax law.

Why does a text devoted primarily to the Federal individual income tax discuss state and local taxes? A simple illustration shows the importance of non-Federal taxes.

EXAMPLE 1

Rick is employed by Flamingo Corporation in San Antonio, Texas, at a salary of $54,000. Rick's employer offers him a chance to transfer to its New York City office at a salary of $60,000. Neither Texas nor San Antonio imposes an income tax, but New York State and New York City do. A quick computation indicates that the additional income taxes (Federal, state, and local) involved approximate $4,000. ▼

Although Rick must consider many nontax factors before he decides on a job change, he should also evaluate the tax climate. How do state and local taxes compare? In this case, what appears to be a $6,000 pay increase is only $2,000 when the additional income taxes of $4,000 are taken into account.

HISTORY OF U.S. TAXATION

EARLY PERIODS

1 LEARNING OBJECTIVE
Understand some of the history, including trends, of the Federal income tax.

The concept of an income tax can hardly be regarded as a newcomer to the Western Hemisphere. An income tax was first enacted in 1634 by the English colonists in the Massachusetts Bay Colony, but the Federal government did not adopt this form of taxation until 1861. In fact, both the Federal Union and the

Confederate States of America used the income tax to raise funds to finance the Civil War. Although modest in its reach and characterized by broad exemptions and low rates, the income tax generated $376 million of revenue for the Federal government during the Civil War.

When the Civil War ended, the need for additional revenue disappeared, and the income tax was repealed. As was true before the war, the Federal government was able to finance its operations almost exclusively from customs duties (tariffs). It is interesting to note that the courts held that the Civil War income tax was not contrary to the Constitution.

When a new Federal income tax on individuals was enacted in 1894, its opponents were prepared to and did again challenge its constitutionality. The U.S. Constitution provided that "... No Capitation, or other direct, Tax shall be laid, unless in Proportion to the Census or Enumeration herein before directed to be taken." In *Pollock v. Farmers' Loan and Trust Co.*,[1] the U.S. Supreme Court found that the income tax was a direct tax that was unconstitutional because it was not apportioned among the states in proportion to their populations.

A Federal corporate income tax, enacted by Congress in 1909, fared better in the judicial system. The U.S. Supreme Court found this tax to be constitutional because it was treated as an excise tax.[2] In essence, it was a tax on the right to do business in the corporate form. As such, it was likened to a form of the franchise tax.[3] The corporate form of doing business had been developed in the late nineteenth century and was an unfamiliar concept to the framers of the U.S. Constitution. Since a corporation is an entity created under law, jurisdictions possess the right to tax its creation and operation. Using this rationale, many states still impose franchise taxes on corporations.

The ratification of the Sixteenth Amendment to the U.S. Constitution in 1913 sanctioned both the Federal individual and corporate income taxes and, as a consequence, neutralized the continuing effect of the *Pollock* decision.

REVENUE ACTS

Following ratification of the Sixteenth Amendment, Congress enacted the Revenue Act of 1913. Under this Act, the first Form 1040 was due on March 1, 1914. The law allowed various deductions and personal exemptions of $3,000 for a single individual and $4,000 for married taxpayers. Rates ranged from a low of 2 percent to a high of 6 percent. The 6 percent rate applied only to taxable income in excess of $500,000![4]

Various revenue acts were passed between 1913 and 1939. In 1939, all of these revenue laws were codified into the Internal Revenue Code of 1939. In 1954, a similar codification of the revenue law took place. The current law is entitled the Internal Revenue Code of 1986, which largely carries over the provisions of the 1954 Code. To date, the Code has been amended several times since 1986. This matter is discussed further in Chapter 2 under Origin of the Internal Revenue Code.

HISTORICAL TRENDS

The income tax has proved to be a major source of revenue for the Federal government. Figure 1–1, which contains a breakdown of the major revenue

[1] 3 AFTR 2602, 15 S.Ct. 912 (USSC, 1895). See Chapter 2 for an explanation of the citations of judicial decisions.

[2] *Flint v. Stone Tracy Co.*, 3 AFTR 2834, 31 S.Ct. 342 (USSC, 1911).

[3] See the discussion of state franchise taxes later in the chapter.

[4] This should be contrasted with the highest current tax rate of 39.6%, which applies once taxable income exceeds $263,750.

▼ FIGURE 1-1
Federal Budget Receipts—1996

Individual income taxes	39%
Corporation income taxes	10
Social insurance taxes and contributions	32
Excise taxes	3
Borrowing	12
Other	4
	100%

sources,[5] demonstrates the importance of the income tax. *Estimated* income tax collections from individuals and corporations amount to 49 percent of the total receipts.

The need for revenues to finance the war effort during World War II converted the income tax into a *mass tax*. For example, in 1939, less than 6 percent of the U.S. population was subject to the Federal income tax. In 1945, over 74 percent of the population was subject to the Federal income tax.[6]

Certain changes in the income tax law are of particular significance in understanding the Federal income tax. In 1943, Congress passed the Current Tax Payment Act, which provided for the first pay-as-you-go tax system. A pay-as-you-go income tax system requires employers to withhold for taxes a specified portion of an employee's wages. Persons with income from other than wages must make periodic (e.g., quarterly) payments to the taxing authority (the Internal Revenue Service) for estimated taxes due for the year.

One trend that has caused considerable concern has been the increased complexity of the Federal income tax laws. Often, under the name of tax reform, Congress has added to this complexity by frequently changing the tax laws. Increasingly, this has forced many taxpayers to seek the assistance of tax professionals. At this time, therefore, substantial support exists for tax law simplification.

Criteria Used in the Selection of a Tax Structure

2 Learning Objective
Know some of the criteria for selecting a tax structure and understand the components of a tax structure.

In the eighteenth century, Adam Smith identified the following *canons of taxation*, which are still considered when evaluating a particular tax structure:[7]

- *Equality*. Each taxpayer enjoys fair or equitable treatment by paying taxes in proportion to his or her income level. Ability to pay a tax is the measure of how equitably a tax is distributed among taxpayers.
- *Convenience*. Administrative simplicity has long been valued in formulating tax policy. If a tax is easily assessed and collected and its administrative costs are low, it should be favored. An advantage of the withholding (pay-as-you-go) system is its convenience for taxpayers.

[5] Budget of the United States Government for Fiscal Year 1996, Office of Management and Budget (Washington, D.C.: U.S. Government Printing Office, 1995).

[6] Richard Goode, *The Individual Income Tax* (Washington, D.C.: The Brookings Institution, 1964), pp. 2–4.

[7] *The Wealth of Nations*, Book V, Chapter II, Part II (New York: Dutton, 1910).

- *Certainty.* A tax structure is *good* if the taxpayer can readily predict when, where, and how a tax will be levied. Individuals and businesses need to know the likely tax consequences of a particular type of transaction.
- *Economy.* A *good* tax system involves only nominal collection costs by the government and minimal compliance costs on the part of the taxpayer. Although the government's cost of collecting Federal taxes amounts to less than one-half of 1 percent of the revenue collected, the complexity of our current tax structure imposes substantial taxpayer compliance costs.

By these canons, the Federal income tax is a contentious product. *Equality* is present as long as one accepts ability to pay as an ingredient of this component. *Convenience* exists due to a heavy reliance on pay-as-you-go procedures. *Certainty* probably generates the greatest controversy. In one sense, certainty is present since a mass of administrative and judicial guidelines exists to aid in interpreting the tax law. In another sense, however, certainty does not exist since many questions remain unanswered and frequent changes in the tax law by Congress lessen stability. *Economy* is present if only the collection procedure of the IRS is considered. Economy is not present, however, if one focuses instead on taxpayer compliance efforts and costs.

THE TAX STRUCTURE

TAX BASE

A tax base is the amount to which the tax rate is applied. In the case of the Federal income tax, the tax base is *taxable income.* As noted later in the chapter (Figure 1–2), taxable income is gross income reduced by certain deductions (both business and personal).

TAX RATES

Tax rates are applied to the tax base to determine a taxpayer's liability. The tax rates may be proportional or progressive. A tax is *proportional* if the rate of tax remains constant for any given income level.

EXAMPLE 2

Bill has $10,000 of taxable income and pays a tax of $3,000, or 30%. Bob's taxable income is $50,000, and the tax on this amount is $15,000, or 30%. If this constant rate is applied throughout the rate structure, the tax is proportional. ▼

A tax is *progressive* if a higher rate of tax applies as the tax base increases. The Federal income tax, Federal gift and estate taxes, and most state income tax rate structures are progressive.

EXAMPLE 3

If Cora, a married individual filing jointly, has taxable income of $10,000, her tax for 1996 is $1,500 for an average tax rate of 15%. If, however, Cora's taxable income is $50,000, her tax will be $8,787 for an average tax rate of 17.57%. The tax is progressive since higher rates are applied to greater amounts of taxable income. ▼

INCIDENCE OF TAXATION

The degree to which various segments of society share the total tax burden is difficult to assess. Assumptions must be made concerning who absorbs the burden for paying the tax. For example, since dividend payments to shareholders are not deductible by a corporation and are generally taxable to shareholders, the same income is subject to a form of double taxation. Concern over double taxation is valid to the extent that corporations are *not* able to shift the corporate tax to the consumer through higher commodity prices. Many research studies have shown a high degree of shifting of the corporate income tax. When the corporate tax can be shifted, it becomes merely a consumption tax that is borne by the ultimate purchasers of goods.

The progressiveness of the U.S. Federal income tax rate structure for individuals has varied over the years. As late as 1986, for example, there were 15 rates, ranging from 0 to 50 percent. These later were reduced to two rates of 15 and 28 percent. Currently, there are five rates, ranging from 15 to 39.6 percent.

MAJOR TYPES OF TAXES

PROPERTY TAXES

3 LEARNING OBJECTIVE
Identify the different taxes imposed in the United States at the Federal, state, and local levels.

Normally referred to as **ad valorem taxes** because they are based on value, property taxes are a tax on wealth, or capital. In this regard, they have much in common with death taxes and gift taxes discussed later in the chapter. Although property taxes do not tax income, the income actually derived (or the potential for any income) may be relevant insofar as it affects the value of the property being taxed.

Property taxes fall into *two* categories: those imposed on realty and those imposed on personalty. Both have added importance since they usually generate a deduction for Federal income tax purposes (see Chapter 10).

Ad Valorem Taxes on Realty. Property taxes on realty are exclusively within the province of the states and their local political subdivisions (e.g., cities, counties, school districts). They represent a major source of revenue for *local* governments, but their importance at the *state* level has waned over the past few years. Some states, for example, have imposed freezes on the upper revaluations of residential housing.

How realty is defined can have an important bearing on which assets are subject to tax. This is especially true in jurisdictions that do not impose ad valorem taxes on personalty. Primarily a question of state property law, **realty** generally includes real estate and any capital improvements that are classified as fixtures. Simply stated, a *fixture* is something so permanently attached to the real estate that its removal will cause irreparable damage. A built-in bookcase might well be a fixture, whereas a movable bookcase would not be a fixture. Certain items such as electrical wiring and plumbing cease to be personalty when installed in a building and become realty.

The following are some of the characteristics of ad valorem taxes on realty:

- Property owned by the Federal government is exempt from tax. Similar immunity usually is extended to property owned by state and local governments and by certain charitable organizations.
- Some states provide for lower valuations on property dedicated to agricultural use or other special uses (e.g., wildlife sanctuaries).
- Some states partially exempt the homestead portion of property from taxation. Modern homestead laws normally protect some or all of a personal residence (including a farm or ranch) from the actions of creditors pursuing claims against the owner.

- Lower taxes may apply to a residence owned by an elderly taxpayer (e.g., age 65 and older).
- When non-income-producing property (e.g., a personal residence) is converted to income-producing property (e.g., a rental house), typically the appraised value increases.
- Some jurisdictions extend immunity from tax for a specified period of time (a *tax holiday*) to new or relocated businesses.

ETHICAL CONSIDERATIONS

Tax-Exempt Status Forever?

The Orr family lives in a residence that they have owned for several years. They purchased the residence from St. John's Methodist Church, which had used the house as a parsonage for its minister.

To the Orrs' surprise, since they purchased the residence, they have not received any ad valorem property tax bills from either the city or the county. Is there a plausible reason for this? Explain.

What, if anything, should the Orrs do about the property tax matter?

Unlike the ad valorem tax on personalty (see below), the tax on realty is difficult to avoid. Since real estate is impossible to hide, a high degree of taxpayer compliance is not surprising. The only avoidance possibility that is generally available is associated with the assessed value of the property. For this reason, the assessed value of the property—particularly, a value that is reassessed upward—may be subject to controversy and litigation.

Four methods are currently in use for assessing the value of real estate:

1. Actual purchase or construction price.
2. Contemporaneous sales prices or construction costs of comparable properties.
3. Cost of reproducing a building, less allowance for depreciation and obsolescence from the time of actual construction.
4. Capitalization of income from rental property.

Because all of these methods suffer faults and lead to inequities, a combination of two or more is not uncommon. For example, when real estate values and construction costs are rising, the use of actual purchase or construction price (method 1) places the purchaser of a new home at a definite disadvantage compared with an owner who acquired similar property years before. As another illustration, if the capitalization of income (method 4) deals with property subject to rent controls (e.g., New York City), the property may be undervalued.

The history of the ad valorem tax on realty has been marked by inconsistent application due to a lack of competent tax administration and definitive guidelines for assessment procedures. In recent years, however, some significant improvements have occurred. Some jurisdictions, for example, have computerized their reassessment procedures so they will have an immediate effect on all property located within the jurisdiction. Nevertheless, the property tax area continues to be controversial.

Ad Valorem Taxes on Personalty. **Personalty** can be defined as all assets that are not realty. It may be helpful to distinguish between the *classification* of an asset

TAX IN THE NEWS

TAX IT IF YOU CAN FIND IT

The state of Florida levies a property tax on the value of intangibles. Included in the assets subject to tax are stocks, bonds, mutual funds, money market accounts, and accounts receivable. Because the tax is easily evaded, the state is attempting to have financial institutions and brokerage firms report the transactions covered. Unfortunately for the state, it has no investigatory powers beyond its borders, nor can it obtain information on stocks and bonds held in the owner's name and kept in a safe deposit box.

Other states with a comparable tax on intangibles are Georgia, Kentucky, West Virginia, and Wyoming. After a realistic assessment of the noncompliance problem, North Carolina recently repealed its tax. In an effort to improve taxpayer compliance, Michigan is reducing its tax rate on intangibles.

(realty or personalty) and the *use* to which it is put. Both realty and personalty can be either business use or personal use property. Examples include a residence (realty that is personal use), an office building (realty that is business use), surgical instruments (personalty that is business use), and regular wearing apparel (personalty that is personal use).[8]

Personalty can also be classified as tangible property or intangible property. For ad valorem tax purposes, intangible personalty includes stocks, bonds, and various other securities (e.g., bank shares).

The following generalizations may be made concerning the ad valorem taxes on personalty:

- Particularly with personalty devoted to personal use (e.g., jewelry, household furnishings), taxpayer compliance ranges from poor to zero. Some jurisdictions do not even attempt to enforce the tax on these items. For automobiles devoted to personal use, many jurisdictions have converted from value as the tax base to arbitrary license fees based on the weight of the vehicle. Some jurisdictions also consider the vehicle's age (e.g., automobiles six years or older are not subject to the ad valorem tax because they are presumed to have little, if any, value).
- For personalty devoted to business use (e.g., inventories, trucks, machinery, equipment), taxpayer compliance and enforcement procedures are measurably better.
- Which jurisdiction possesses the authority to tax movable personalty (e.g., railroad rolling stock) always has been and continues to be a troublesome issue.
- Some jurisdictions impose an ad valorem tax on intangibles.

[8] The distinction, important for ad valorem and for Federal income tax purposes, often becomes confused when personalty is referred to as "personal" property to distinguish it from "real" property. This designation does not give a complete picture of what is involved. The description "personal" residence, however, is clearer, since a residence can be identified as being realty. What is meant, in this case, is realty that is personal use property.

TRANSACTION TAXES

Transaction taxes, which characteristically are imposed at the manufacturer's, wholesaler's, or retailer's level, cover a wide range of transfers. Like many other types of taxes (e.g., income taxes, death taxes, and gift taxes), transaction taxes usually are not within the exclusive province of any level of taxing authority (Federal, state, local government). As the description implies, these levies place a tax on transfers of property and normally are determined by multiplying the value involved by a percentage rate.

Federal Excise Taxes. Long one of the mainstays of the Federal tax system, Federal **excise taxes** had declined in relative importance until recently. In late 1982, 1990, and 1993, Congress substantially increased the Federal excise taxes on such items as tobacco products, fuel and gasoline sales, telephone usage, and air travel passenger tickets. Other Federal excise taxes include the following:

- Manufacturers' excise taxes on trucks, trailers, tires, firearms, sporting equipment, coal, and the gas guzzler tax on automobiles.[9]
- Alcohol taxes.
- Luxury tax on automobiles. The tax is 10 percent of the retail price in excess of $34,000 (adjusted each year for inflation).
- Miscellaneous taxes (e.g., the tax on wagering).

The list of transactions covered, although seemingly impressive, has diminished over the years. At one time, for example, there was a Federal excise tax on admission to amusement facilities (e.g., theaters) and on the sale of such items as leather goods, jewelry, furs, and cosmetics.

When reviewing the list of both Federal and state excise taxes, one should recognize the possibility that the tax laws may be trying to influence social behavior. For example, the gas guzzler tax is intended as an incentive for the automobile companies to build cars that are fuel efficient. Since many consider alcohol and tobacco to be harmful to a person's health, why not increase their cost by imposing excise taxes and thereby discourage their use? Unfortunately, the evidence of the level of correlation between the imposition of an excise tax and consumer behavior is mixed.

State Excise Taxes. Many state and local excise taxes parallel the Federal version. Thus, all states tax the sale of gasoline, liquor, and tobacco products; however, the rates vary significantly. For gasoline products, for example, compare the 35 cents per gallon imposed by the state of Connecticut with the 8 cents per gallon levied by the state of Alaska. For tobacco sales, contrast the 2.5 cents per pack of cigarettes in effect in Virginia with the 82.5 cents per pack applicable in Washington. Given the latter situation, is it surprising that the smuggling of cigarettes for resale elsewhere is so widespread?

Other excise taxes found at some state and local levels include those on admission to amusement facilities; hotel occupancy and the rental of various other facilities; and the sale of playing cards, oleomargarine products, and prepared foods. Most states impose a transaction tax on the transfer of property that

[9] The gas guzzler tax is imposed on the manufacturers of automobiles and progresses in amount as the mileage ratings per gallon of gas decrease.

requires the recording of documents (e.g., real estate sales).[10] Some extend the tax to the transfer of stocks and other securities.

General Sales Taxes. The distinction between an excise tax and a general **sales tax** is easy to make. One is restricted to a particular transaction (e.g., the 18.4 cents per gallon Federal excise tax on the sale of gasoline), while the other covers a multitude of transactions (e.g., a 5 percent tax on *all* retail sales). In actual practice, however, the distinction is not always that clear. Some state statutes exempt certain transactions from the application of the general sales taxes (e.g., sales of food to be consumed off the premises, sales of certain medicines and drugs). Also, it is not uncommon to find that rates vary depending on the commodity involved. Many states, for example, allow preferential rates for the sale of agricultural equipment or apply different rates (either higher or lower than the general rate) to the sale of automobiles. With many of these special exceptions and classifications of rates, a general sales tax can take on the appearance of a collection of individual excise taxes.

A **use tax** is an ad valorem tax, usually at the same rate as the sales tax, on the use, consumption, or storage of tangible property. The purpose of a use tax is to prevent the avoidance of a sales tax. Every state that imposes a general sales tax levied on the consumer also has a use tax. Alaska, Delaware, Montana, New Hampshire, and Oregon have neither tax.

EXAMPLE 4

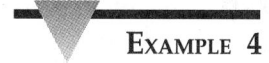

Susan resides in a jurisdiction that imposes a 5% general sales tax but lives near a state that has no sales or use tax at all. Susan purchases an automobile for $10,000 from a dealer located in the neighboring state. Has she saved $500 in sales taxes? The state use tax is designed to pick up the difference between the tax paid in another jurisdiction and what would have been paid in the state in which Susan resides. ▼

The use tax is difficult to enforce for many purchases and is therefore often avoided. In some cases, for example, it may be worthwhile to make purchases through an out-of-state mail-order business. In spite of shipping costs, the avoidance of the local sales tax that otherwise might be incurred could make the price of such products as computer components cheaper. Some states are taking steps to curtail this loss of revenue. For items such as automobiles (refer to Example 4), the use tax probably will be collected when the purchaser registers the item in his or her home state.

Local general sales taxes, over and above those levied by the state, are common. It is not unusual to find taxpayers living in the same state who pay different general sales taxes due to the location of their residence.

EXAMPLE 5

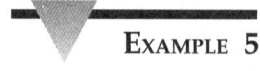

Pete and Sam both live in a state that has a general sales tax of 3%. Sam, however, resides in a city that imposes an additional general sales tax of 2%. Even though Pete and Sam live in the same state, one is subject to a rate of 3%, while the other pays a tax of 5%. ▼

Severance Taxes. **Severance taxes** are an important source of revenue for many states. These transaction taxes are based on the notion that the state has an interest in its natural resources (e.g., oil, gas, iron ore, coal). Therefore, a tax is imposed when the natural resources are extracted.

---

[10] This type of tax has much in common with the stamp tax levied by Great Britain on the American colonies during the pre–Revolutionary War period in U.S. history.

DEATH TAXES

A **death tax** is a tax on the right to transfer property or to receive property upon the death of the owner. Consequently, a death tax falls into the category of an excise tax. If the death tax is imposed on the right to pass property at death, it is classified as an **estate tax.** If it taxes the right to receive property from a decedent, it is termed an **inheritance tax.** As is typical of other types of excise taxes, the value of the property transferred provides the base for determining the amount of the death tax.

The Federal government imposes only an estate tax. State governments, however, levy inheritance taxes, estate taxes, or both.

EXAMPLE 6

At the time of her death, Wilma lived in a state that imposes an inheritance tax but not an estate tax. Mary, one of Wilma's heirs, lives in the same state. Wilma's estate is subject to the Federal estate tax, and Mary is subject to the state inheritance tax. ▼

The Federal Estate Tax. The Revenue Act of 1916 incorporated the estate tax into the tax law. Never designed to generate a large amount of revenue, the tax was originally intended to prevent large concentrations of wealth from being kept within a family for many generations. Whether this objective has been accomplished is debatable. Like the income tax, estate taxes can be reduced through various planning procedures.

The gross estate includes property the decedent owned at the time of death. It also includes life insurance proceeds when paid to the estate or when paid to a beneficiary other than the estate if the deceased-insured had any ownership rights in the policy. Quite simply, the gross estate represents property interests subject to Federal estate taxation.[11] All property included in the gross estate is valued as of the date of death or, if the alternate valuation date is elected, six months later.[12]

Deductions from the gross estate in arriving at the taxable estate include funeral and administration expenses, certain taxes, debts of the decedent, casualty losses[13] incurred during the administration of the estate, transfers to charitable organizations, and, in some cases, the marital deduction. The marital deduction is available for amounts actually passing to a surviving spouse (a widow or widower).

Once the taxable estate has been determined and certain taxable gifts have been added to it, the estate tax can be computed. From the amount derived from the appropriate tax rate schedules, various credits should be subtracted to arrive at the tax, if any, that is due.[14] Although many other credits are also available, probably the most significant is the unified transfer tax credit. The main reason for this credit is to eliminate or reduce the estate tax liability for modest estates. Currently, the amount of the credit is $192,800. Based on the estate tax rates, the credit covers a tax base of $600,000.

EXAMPLE 7

Ned made no taxable gifts before his death in 1996. If Ned's taxable estate amounts to $600,000 or less, no Federal estate tax is due because of the application of the unified transfer tax credit. Under the tax law, the estate tax on a taxable estate of $600,000 is $192,800. ▼

---

[11] For further information on these matters, see *West's Federal Taxation: Corporations, Partnerships, Estates, and Trusts.*

[12] See the discussion of the alternate valuation date in Chapter 14.

[13] For a definition of casualty losses, see the Glossary of Tax Terms in Appendix C.

[14] For tax purposes, it is always crucial to appreciate the difference between a deduction and a credit. A *credit* is a dollar-for-dollar reduction of tax liability. A *deduction*, however, only benefits the taxpayer to the extent of his or her tax bracket. An estate in a 50% tax bracket, for example, would need $2 of deductions to prevent $1 of tax liability from developing. In contrast, $1 of credit neutralizes $1 of tax liability.

State Death Taxes. As noted earlier, states usually levy an inheritance tax, an estate tax, or both. The two forms of death taxes differ according to whether the tax is imposed on the heirs or on the estate.

Characteristically, an inheritance tax divides the heirs into classes based on their relationship to the decedent. The more closely related the heir, the lower the rates imposed and the greater the exemption allowed. Some states completely exempt from taxation amounts passing to a surviving spouse.

GIFT TAXES

Like a death tax, a **gift tax** is an excise tax levied on the right to transfer property. In this case, however, the tax is imposed on transfers made during the owner's life and not at death. Also, a gift tax applies only to transfers that are not supported by full and adequate consideration.

EXAMPLE 8

Carl sells property worth $20,000 to his daughter for $1,000. Although property worth $20,000 has been transferred, only $19,000 represents a gift, since this is the portion not supported by full and adequate consideration. ▼

The Federal Gift Tax. First enacted in 1932, the Federal gift tax was intended to complement the estate tax. In the absence of a tax applicable to lifetime transfers by gift, it would be possible to avoid the estate tax and escape taxation entirely.

Only taxable gifts are subject to the gift tax. For this purpose, a taxable gift is measured by the fair market value of the property on the date of transfer less the annual exclusion of $10,000 per donee and, in some cases, less the marital deduction, which allows tax-free transfers between spouses. Each donor is allowed an annual exclusion of $10,000 for each donee.[15]

EXAMPLE 9

On December 31, 1995, Vera (a widow) gives $10,000 to each of her four married children, their spouses, and her eight grandchildren. On January 3, 1996, she repeats the same procedure. Due to the annual exclusion, Vera has not made a taxable gift, although she transferred $160,000 [$10,000 × 16 (number of donees)] in 1995 and $160,000 [$10,000 × 16 (number of donees)] in 1996 for a total of $320,000 ($160,000 + $160,000). ▼

ETHICAL CONSIDERATIONS

The Annual Exclusion for Gifts

Arlene, a wealthy widow, would like to transfer $20,000 of cash to her son, Wilbur, in 1996 without exceeding the $10,000 per donee annual exclusion. To achieve this result, Arlene devises the following scheme: she gives $10,000 to Wilbur and $10,000 to her brother, George, who gives $10,000 to Wilbur.

Will Arlene's scheme succeed? What could go wrong?

A special election applicable to married persons allows one-half of the gift made by the donor-spouse to be treated as being made by the nondonor-spouse.

[15] The purpose of the annual exclusion is to avoid the need to report and pay a tax on *modest* gifts. Without the exclusion, the IRS could face a real problem of taxpayer noncompliance.

This election to split the gifts of property made to third persons has the effect of increasing the number of annual exclusions available. Also, it allows the use of the nondonor-spouse's unified transfer tax credit and may lower the tax brackets that will apply.

The gift tax rate schedule is the same as that applicable to the estate tax. The schedule is commonly referred to as the *unified transfer tax schedule.*

The Federal gift tax is *cumulative* in effect. What this means is that the tax base for current taxable gifts includes past taxable gifts. Although a credit is allowed for prior gift taxes, the result of adding past taxable gifts to current taxable gifts is to force the donor into a higher tax bracket.[16] Like the Federal estate tax rates, the Federal gift tax rates are progressive (see Example 3 earlier in this chapter).

The unified transfer tax credit is available for all taxable gifts, and as with the Federal estate tax, the amount of this credit is $192,800. There is, however, only one unified transfer tax credit, and it applies both to taxable gifts and to the Federal estate tax. In a manner of speaking, therefore, once the unified transfer tax credit has been exhausted for Federal gift tax purposes, it is no longer available to insulate a decedent from the Federal estate tax.

In summary, transfers by gift and transfers by death are subject to the unified transfer tax. The same rates and credits apply. Further, taxable gifts are added to the taxable estate in arriving at the tax base for applying the unified transfer tax at death.

State Gift Taxes. The states currently imposing a state gift tax are Connecticut, Delaware, Louisiana, New York, North Carolina, and Tennessee. Most of the laws provide for lifetime exemptions and annual exclusions. Like the Federal gift tax, the state taxes are cumulative in effect. But unlike the Federal version, the amount of tax depends on the relationship between the donor and the donee. Like state inheritance taxes, larger exemptions and lower rates apply when the donor and donee are closely related to each other.

INCOME TAXES

Income taxes are levied by the Federal government, most states, and some local governments. The trend in recent years has been to place greater reliance on this method of taxation. This trend is not consistent with what is happening in other countries, and in this sense, our system of taxation is somewhat different.

Income taxes generally are imposed on individuals, corporations, and certain fiduciaries (estates and trusts). Most jurisdictions attempt to assure the collection of income taxes by requiring certain pay-as-you-go procedures (e.g., withholding requirements for employees and estimated tax prepayments for other taxpayers).

On occasion, Congress has seen fit to impose additional taxes on income. Such impositions were justified either by economic considerations or by special circumstances resulting from wartime conditions. During World War II, the Korean conflict, and the Vietnam conflict, excess-profits taxes were imposed in addition to the regular Federal income tax. The taxes were aimed at the profiteering that occurs when the economy is geared to the production of war materials.

Another additional income tax is the surcharge approach. During the period from April 1, 1968, to July 1, 1970, for example, taxpayers were subject to a surcharge of 10 percent of the amount of their regular income tax liability. This led

[16] For further information on the Federal gift tax, see *West's Federal Taxation: Corporations, Partnerships, Estates, and Trusts.*

▼ FIGURE 1–2
Formula for Federal Income Tax on Individuals

Income (broadly conceived)	$xx,xxx
Less: Exclusions (income that is not subject to tax)	(x,xxx)
Gross income (income that is subject to tax)	$xx,xxx
Less: Certain business deductions (usually referred to as deductions *for* adjusted gross income)	(x,xxx)
Adjusted gross income	$xx,xxx
Less: The greater of certain personal and employee deductions (usually referred to as *itemized deductions*) *or* The standard deduction (including any additional standard deduction) *and*	(x,xxx)
Less: Personal and dependency exemptions	(x,xxx)
Taxable income	$xx,xxx
Tax on taxable income (see Tax Rate Schedules in Appendix A)	$ x,xxx
Less: Tax credits (including Federal income tax withheld and other prepayments of Federal income taxes)	(xxx)
Tax due (or refund)	$ xxx

to the strange result that taxpayers had to pay, so to speak, an income tax on their income tax. Justifications for the special tax included the need to restrain what was regarded as an overactive economy, to curtail inflation, and to reduce the Federal deficit.

In light of current budget deficits, the surcharge approach has its advocates in Congress and therefore may be of more than historical interest. The advantage of the surcharge approach is that it represents a temporary solution to the problem. Thus, Congress can impose the tax on a one-shot basis without having to modify the regular income tax rates or base.

Federal Income Taxes. Chapters 3 through 19 deal with the application of the Federal income tax to individuals. The procedure for determining the Federal income tax applicable to individuals is summarized in Figure 1–2.

The application of the Federal corporate income tax does not require the computation of adjusted gross income (AGI) and does not provide for the standard deduction and personal and dependency exemptions. All allowable deductions of a corporation fall into the business-expense category. In effect, therefore, the taxable income of a corporation is the difference between gross income (net of exclusions) and deductions.

Chapter 20 summarizes the rules relating to corporations. For an in-depth treatment of the Federal income tax as it affects corporations, estates, and trusts, see *West's Federal Taxation: Corporations, Partnerships, Estates, and Trusts*, 1997 Edition, Chapters 2 through 9, 12, and 19.

State Income Taxes. All but the following states impose an income tax on individuals: Alaska, Florida, Nevada, South Dakota, Texas, Washington, and Wyoming.

Some of the characteristics of state income taxes are summarized as follows:

- With few exceptions, all states require some form of withholding procedures.

- Most states use as the tax base the income determination made for Federal income tax purposes.
- A minority of states go even further and impose a flat rate upon AGI as computed for Federal income tax purposes. Several apply a rate to the Federal income tax liability. This is often referred to as the piggyback approach to state income taxation. Although the term *piggyback* does not lend itself to precise definition, in this context, it means making use, for state income tax purposes, of what was done for Federal income tax purposes.
- Because of the tie-in to the Federal return, the state may be notified of any changes made by the IRS upon audit of a Federal return.
- Most states allow a deduction for personal and dependency exemptions. Some states substitute a tax credit for a deduction.
- A diminishing minority of states allow a deduction for Federal income taxes.
- Most states allow their residents some form of tax credit for income taxes paid to other states.
- The due date for filing generally is the same as for the Federal income tax (the fifteenth day of the fourth month following the close of the tax year).

Nearly all states have an income tax applicable to corporations. It is difficult to determine those that do not because a state franchise tax sometimes is based in part on the income earned by the corporation.[17]

Local Income Taxes. Cities imposing an income tax include, but are not limited to, Baltimore, Cincinnati, Cleveland, Detroit, Kansas City (Mo.), New York, Philadelphia, and St. Louis. The application of a city income tax is not limited to local residents.

EMPLOYMENT TAXES

Classification as an employee usually leads to the imposition of **employment taxes** and to the requirement that the employer withhold specified amounts for income taxes. The rules governing the withholding for income taxes are discussed in Chapter 13. The material that follows concentrates on the two major employment taxes: FICA (Federal Insurance Contributions Act—commonly referred to as the Social Security tax) and FUTA (Federal Unemployment Tax Act). Both taxes can be justified by social and public welfare considerations: FICA offers some measure of retirement security, and FUTA provides a modest source of income in the event of loss of employment.

Employment taxes come into play only if two conditions are satisfied. First, is the individual involved an *employee* (as opposed to *self-employed*)? The differences between an employee and a self-employed person are discussed in Chapter 9.[18] Second, if the individual involved is an employee, is he or she covered under FICA or FUTA or both? The coverage of both of these taxes is summarized in Exhibit 13–2 in Chapter 13.[19]

FICA Taxes. The **FICA tax** rates and wage base have steadily increased over the years. It is difficult to imagine that the initial rate in 1937 was only 1 percent of the first $3,000 of covered wages. Thus, the maximum tax due was only $30!

---

[17] See the discussion of franchise taxes later in the chapter.

[18] See also Circular E, Employer's Tax Guide, issued by the IRS as Publication 15.

[19] Chapter 13 deals with the self-employment tax (the Social Security and Medicare taxes for self-employed persons).

TAX IN THE NEWS

VISITORS BEWARE! THE CITY AND STATE YOU VISIT MAY NOT BE ALL THAT FRIENDLY

Even if you are not a resident, you may be subject to local and state income taxes if you earn money in that jurisdiction. Besides the nonresident who commutes (e.g., a taxpayer who lives in Connecticut but works full-time in New York City), taxpayers who perform services on an itinerant basis may be vulnerable. For example, the Dallas Cowboys are subject to the city of Philadelphia income tax every time they are hosted by the Eagles. This must be particularly distressing to Troy Aikman, who lives in a city (Dallas) and a state (Texas) that do not have an income tax.

Although these situations are commonly referred to as the application of the "jock tax," other persons besides professional athletes get hit. Particularly susceptible are entertainers, doctors, lawyers, lecturers, and anyone who generates large fees and has a high profile. Ordinary professionals are not targeted because the amount of taxes involved would not justify the collection effort.

Is it any wonder that Las Vegas, which has no city or state income tax, is such a popular place to perform highly paid services (e.g., entertainment, prize fighting)?

Currently, the FICA tax has two components: Social Security tax (old age, survivors, and disability insurance) *and* Medicare tax (hospital insurance). The Social Security tax rate is 6.2 percent for 1995 and 1996, and the Medicare tax rate is 1.45 percent for these years. The base amount for Social Security is $61,200 for 1995 and $62,700 for 1996. There is no limit on the base amount for the Medicare tax. The employer must match the employee's portion.

A spouse employed by another spouse is subject to FICA. However, children under the age of 18 who are employed in a parent's trade or business are exempted.

FUTA Taxes. The purpose of the **FUTA tax** is to provide funds that the states can use to administer unemployment benefits. This leads to the somewhat unusual situation of one tax being handled by both Federal and state governments. The end result of such joint administration is to compel the employer to observe a double set of rules. Thus, state and Federal returns must be filed and payments made to both governmental units.

In 1996, FUTA applies at a rate of 6.2 percent on the first $7,000 of covered wages paid during the year to each employee. The Federal government allows a credit for FUTA paid (or allowed under a merit rating system) to the state. The credit cannot exceed 5.4 percent of the covered wages. Thus, the amount required to be paid to the IRS could be as low as 0.8 percent (6.2% – 5.4%).

States follow a policy of reducing the unemployment tax on employers who experience stable employment. Thus, an employer with little or no employee turnover might find that the state rate drops to as low as 0.1 percent or, in some states, even to zero. The reason for the merit rating credit is that the state has to pay fewer unemployment benefits when employment is steady.

FUTA differs from FICA in the sense that the incidence of taxation falls entirely upon the employer. A few states, however, levy a special tax on employees to provide either disability benefits or supplemental unemployment compensation, or both.

OTHER U.S. TAXES

To complete the overview of the U.S. tax system, some missing links need to be covered that do not fit into the classifications discussed elsewhere in this chapter.

Federal Customs Duties. One tax that has not yet been mentioned is the tariff on certain imported goods.[20] Generally referred to as customs duties or levies, this tax, together with selective excise taxes, provided most of the revenues needed by the Federal government during the nineteenth century. In view of present times, it is remarkable to note that tariffs and excise taxes alone paid off the national debt in 1835 and enabled the U.S. Treasury to pay a surplus of $28 million to the states.

In recent years, tariffs have served the nation more as an instrument for carrying out protectionist policies than as a means of generating revenue. Thus, a particular U.S. industry might be saved from economic disaster, so the argument goes, by placing customs duties on the importation of foreign goods that can be sold at lower prices. Protectionists contend that the tariff therefore neutralizes the competitive edge held by the producer of the foreign goods.[21]

Protectionist policies seem more appropriate for less-developed countries whose industrial capacity has not yet matured. In a world where a developed country should have everything to gain by encouraging international free trade, such policies may be of dubious value. History shows that tariffs often lead to retaliatory action on the part of the nation or nations affected.

Miscellaneous State and Local Taxes. Most states impose a franchise tax on corporations. Basically, a **franchise tax** is levied on the right to do business in the state. The base used for the determination of the tax varies from state to state. Although corporate income considerations may come into play, this tax most often is based on the capitalization of the corporation (either with or without certain long-term indebtedness).

Closely akin to the franchise tax are **occupational taxes** applicable to various trades or businesses, such as a liquor store license, a taxicab permit, or a fee to practice a profession such as law, medicine, or accounting. Most of these are not significant revenue producers and fall more into the category of licenses than taxes. The revenue derived is used to defray the cost incurred by the jurisdiction in regulating the business or profession in the interest of the public good.

PROPOSED U.S. TAXES

Considerable dissatisfaction with the U.S. Federal income tax has led to several recent proposals that, to say the least, are rather drastic in nature. One proposal

[20] Less-developed countries that rely principally on one or more major commodities (e.g., oil, coffee) are prone to favor *export* duties as well.

[21] The North American Free Trade Agreement (NAFTA), enacted in 1993, substantially reduced the tariffs on trade between Canada, Mexico, and the United States. The General Agreement on Tariffs and Trade (GATT) legislation enacted in 1994 also reduced tariffs on selected commodities among 124 signatory nations.

would retain the income tax but with substantial change. Two other proposals would replace the Federal income tax with an entirely different system of taxation.

The Flat Tax. Authored by Representative Dick Armey (R, Texas), the **flat tax** would replace the current graduated income tax with one rate, 17 percent. Large personal exemptions (e.g., approximately $30,000 for a family of four) would allow many low- and middle-income taxpayers to pay no tax. All other deductions would be eliminated, and no tax would be imposed on income from investments.

Various other versions of the flat tax have been suggested that would retain selected deductions (e.g., interest on home mortgages and charitable contributions) and not exclude all investment income from taxation.

The major advantage of the flat tax is its simplicity. Everyone agrees that the current Federal income tax is unbelievably complex. Consequently, compliance costs are disproportionately high.

Value Added Tax. The **value added tax (VAT)** is one of two proposals that would replace the Federal income tax. Under the VAT, a business would pay the tax (approximately 17 percent) on all of the materials and services required to manufacture its product. In effect, the VAT taxes the increment in value as goods move through production and manufacturing stages to the marketplace. Moreover, the VAT paid by the producer will be reflected in the selling price of the goods. Thus, the VAT is a tax on consumption.

Several other countries (e.g., European Union countries) use the VAT either as a supplement to or a replacement for an income tax.

Sales Tax. A **national sales tax** is favored by Representative Bill Archer (R, Texas), who is the current chairman of the House Ways and Means Committee. This tax differs from a VAT in that it would be collected on the final sale of goods and services. Consequently, it is collected from the consumer and not from businesses adding value to the product. Like the VAT, the national sales tax is intended to replace the Federal income tax.

Critics contend that consumption taxes (both a VAT and a national sales tax) impose more of a burden on low-income taxpayers because they must spend larger proportions of their incomes on essential purchases. Representative Archer's proposal would attempt to remedy this inequity by granting some sort of credit or exemption to low-income taxpayers.

Tax Administration

INTERNAL REVENUE SERVICE

4 LEARNING OBJECTIVE
Understand the administration of the tax law including the audit process utilized by the IRS.

The responsibility for administering the Federal tax laws rests with the Treasury Department. Administratively, the IRS is part of the Department of the Treasury and is responsible for enforcing the tax laws. The Commissioner of Internal Revenue is appointed by the President and is responsible for establishing policy and supervising the activities of the entire IRS organization.

The field organization of the IRS includes the following:

- Service Centers (10) that are primarily responsible for processing tax returns, including the selection of returns for audit. The Service Center having proper jurisdiction is where taxpayers must file their Federal tax returns.

- District Directors (63) who are responsible for audits and for the collection of delinquent taxes. Each state has at least one District Director; several states (e.g., New York, California) have more.

THE AUDIT PROCESS

Selection of Returns for Audit. Due to budgetary limitations, only a small minority of returns are audited. For the fiscal year ending September 30, 1993, for example, the IRS audited only 0.92 percent of the total returns, down from 1.06 percent in the preceding fiscal year.

The IRS utilizes mathematical formulas and statistical sampling techniques to select tax returns that are most likely to contain errors and to yield substantial amounts of additional tax revenues upon audit.

Though the IRS does not openly disclose all of its audit selection techniques, the following observations may be made concerning the probability of selection for audit:

- Certain groups of taxpayers are subject to audit much more frequently than others. These groups include individuals with gross income in excess of $50,000, self-employed individuals with substantial business income and deductions, and taxpayers with prior tax deficiencies. Also vulnerable are cash businesses (e.g., cafes and small service businesses) where the potential for tax avoidance is high.

EXAMPLE 10

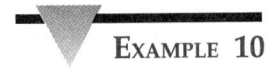

Jack owns and operates a liquor store on a cash-and-carry basis. Since all of Jack's sales are for cash, he might well be a prime candidate for an audit by the IRS. Cash transactions are easier to conceal than those made on credit. ▼

- If information returns (e.g., Form 1099, Form W–2) are not in substantial agreement with reported income, an audit can be anticipated.
- If an individual's itemized deductions are in excess of norms established for various income levels, the probability of an audit is increased.
- Filing of a refund claim by the taxpayer may prompt an audit of the return.
- Certain returns are selected on a random sampling basis under the Taxpayer Compliance Measurement Program (TCMP). The TCMP is used to develop, update, and improve the mathematical formulas and statistical sampling techniques used by the IRS.
- Information obtained from other sources (e.g., informants, news items) may lead to an audit. The tax law permits the IRS to pay rewards to persons who provide information that leads to the detection and punishment of those who violate the tax laws. The rewards may not exceed 10 percent of the taxes, fines, and penalties recovered as a result of such information.

EXAMPLE 11

After 15 years of service, Rita is discharged by her employer, Dr. Smith. Shortly thereafter, the IRS receives an anonymous letter informing it that Dr. Smith keeps two separate sets of books, one of which substantially understates his cash receipts. ▼

EXAMPLE 12

During a divorce proceeding, it is revealed that Leo, a public official, kept large amounts of cash in a shoe box at home. This information is widely disseminated by the news media and comes to the attention of the IRS. Needless to say, the IRS would be interested in knowing whether these funds originated from a taxable source and, if so, whether they were reported on Leo's income tax returns. ▼

Types of Audits. Once a return is selected for audit, the taxpayer is notified accordingly. If the issue involved is minor, the matter often can be resolved simply by correspondence (a **correspondence audit**) between the IRS and the taxpayer.

EXAMPLE 13

During 1994, Janet received dividend income from Green Corporation. In early 1995, Green Corporation reported the payment on Form 1099–DIV (an information return for reporting dividend payments), the original being sent to the IRS and a copy to Janet. When preparing her income tax return for 1994, Janet apparently overlooked this particular Form 1099–DIV and failed to include the dividend on Schedule B, Interest and Dividend Income, of Form 1040. In 1996, the IRS sends a notice to Janet calling her attention to the omission and requesting a remittance for additional tax, interest, and penalty. Janet promptly mails a check to the IRS for the requested amount, and the matter is closed. ▼

Other examinations are generally classified as either office audits or field audits. An **office audit** usually is restricted in scope and is conducted in the facilities of the IRS. In contrast, a **field audit** involves an examination of numerous items reported on the return and is conducted on the premises of the taxpayer or the taxpayer's representative.

Upon the conclusion of the audit, the examining agent issues a Revenue Agent's Report (RAR) that summarizes the findings. The RAR will result in a refund (the tax was overpaid), a deficiency (the tax was underpaid), or a *no change* (the tax was correct) finding.

Settlement Procedures. If an audit results in an assessment of additional tax and no settlement is reached with the IRS agent, the taxpayer may attempt to negotiate a settlement with the IRS. If an appeal is desired, an appropriate request must be made to the Appeals Division of the IRS. In some cases, a taxpayer may be able to obtain a percentage settlement or a favorable settlement of one or more disputed issues. The Appeals Division is authorized to settle all disputes based on the *hazard of litigation* (the probability of favorable resolution of the disputed issue or issues if litigated).

If a satisfactory settlement is not reached within the administrative appeal process, the taxpayer may wish to litigate the case in the Tax Court, a Federal District Court, or the Court of Federal Claims. However, litigation is recommended only as a last resort because of the legal costs involved and the uncertainty of the final outcome. Tax litigation considerations are discussed more fully in Chapter 2.

STATUTE OF LIMITATIONS

A **statute of limitations** is a provision in the law that offers a party a defense against a suit brought by another party after the expiration of a specified period of time. The purpose of a statute of limitations is to preclude parties from prosecuting stale claims. The passage of time makes the defense of such claims difficult since witnesses may no longer be available or evidence may have been lost or destroyed. Found at the state and Federal levels, such statutes cover a multitude of suits, both civil and criminal.

For our purposes, the relevant statutes deal with the Federal income tax. The two categories involved cover both the period of limitations applicable to the assessment of additional tax deficiencies by the IRS and the period that deals with claims for refunds by taxpayers.

Assessment by the IRS. Under the general rule, the IRS may assess (impose) an additional tax liability against a taxpayer within *three years* of the filing of the income tax return. If the return is filed early, the three-year period begins to run from the due date of the return (usually April 15 for a calendar year individual taxpayer).

If a taxpayer omits an amount of gross income in excess of 25 percent of the gross income reported on the return, the statute of limitations is increased to six years.

EXAMPLE 14

For 1991, Mark, a calendar year taxpayer, reported gross income of $400,000 on a timely filed income tax return. If Mark omitted more than $100,000 (25% × $400,000), the six-year statute of limitations would apply to the 1991 tax year. ▼

The six-year provision on assessments by the IRS applies only to the omission of income and does not cover other factors that might lead to an understatement of tax liability (e.g., overstatement of deductions and credits).

There is *no* statute of limitations on assessments of tax if *no return* is filed or if a *fraudulent* return is filed.

Limitations on Refunds. If a taxpayer believes that an overpayment of Federal income tax was made, a claim for refund should be filed with the IRS. A *claim for refund*, therefore, is a request to the IRS that it return to the taxpayer the excessive income taxes paid.[22]

A claim for refund generally must be filed within *three years* from the date the return was filed *or* within *two years* from the date the tax was paid, whichever is later. Income tax returns that are filed early are deemed to have been filed on the date the return was due.

INTEREST AND PENALTIES

Interest rates are determined quarterly by the IRS based on the existing Federal short-term rate. The rates for tax refunds (overpayments) are 1 percent below those applicable to assessments (underpayments). For the first quarter (January 1–March 31) of 1996, the rates were 8 percent for refunds and 9 percent for assessments.[23]

For assessments of additional taxes, the interest begins running on the unextended due date of the return. With refunds, however, no interest is allowed if the overpayment is refunded to the taxpayer within 45 days of the date the return is filed. For this purpose, returns filed early are deemed to have been filed on the due date.

The tax law provides various penalties for lack of compliance by taxpayers. Some of these penalties are summarized as follows:

- For a *failure to file* a tax return by the due date (including extension—see Chapter 3), a penalty of 5 percent per month (up to a maximum of 25 percent) is imposed on the amount of tax shown as due on the return. Any fraction of a month counts as a full month.

[22] The form to use by an individual in filing a claim for refund generally is Form 1040X.

[23] The rates applicable after March 31, 1996, were not available when this text went to press.

- A penalty for a *failure to pay* the tax due (as shown on the return) is imposed in the amount of 0.5 percent per month (up to a maximum of 25 percent). Again, any fraction of a month counts as a full month. During any month in which both the failure to file penalty and the failure to pay penalty apply, the failure to file penalty is reduced by the amount of the failure to pay penalty.

EXAMPLE 15

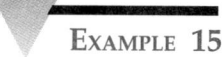

Adam files his tax return 18 days after the due date of the return. Along with the return, he remits a check for $1,000, which is the balance of the tax he owed. Disregarding the interest element, Adam's total penalties are as follows:

Failure to pay penalty (0.5% × $1,000)		$ 5
Plus:		
Failure to file penalty (5% × $1,000)	$50	
Less failure to pay penalty for the same period	(5)	
Failure to file penalty		45
Total penalties		$50

Note that the penalties for one full month are imposed even though Adam was delinquent by only 18 days. Unlike the method used to compute interest, any part of a month is treated as a whole month. ▼

- A *negligence* penalty of 20 percent is imposed if any of the underpayment was for intentional disregard of rules and regulations without intent to defraud. The penalty applies to just that portion attributable to the negligence.

EXAMPLE 16

Cindy underpaid her taxes for 1995 in the amount of $20,000, of which $15,000 is attributable to negligence. Cindy's negligence penalty is $3,000 (20% × $15,000). ▼

- Various fraud penalties may be imposed. *Fraud* is a deliberate action on the part of the taxpayer evidenced by deceit, misrepresentation, concealment, etc. For possible fraud situations, refer to Examples 11 and 12. The burden of proving fraud is on the IRS. This is in contrast to the usual deficiency assessment made by the IRS, where the burden is on the taxpayer to show that he or she does not owe any additional tax.

TAX PRACTICE

The area of tax practice is largely unregulated. Virtually anyone can aid another in complying with the various tax laws. If a practitioner is a member of a profession, such as law or public accounting, he or she must abide by certain ethical standards. Furthermore, the Internal Revenue Code imposes penalties upon the preparers of Federal tax returns who violate proscribed acts and procedures.

5 LEARNING OBJECTIVE
Appreciate some of the ethical guidelines involved in tax practice.

Ethical Guidelines. The American Institute of CPAs has issued numerous guides for CPAs engaged in tax practice. Called "Statements on Responsibilities in Tax Practice," some of these are summarized below.

- Do not take questionable positions on a client's tax return in the hope that the return will not be selected for audit by the IRS. Any positions taken

TAX IN THE NEWS

Even the Mighty Can Fall

Apparently oblivious of the fate that Pete Rose suffered, Darryl Strawberry followed the same road when he failed to report substantial amounts of income from autograph shows and promotional appearances from 1986 to 1992. Charged with tax fraud, Strawberry entered into a plea bargain that resulted in $350,000 in back taxes, interest, and penalties, six months home confinement, and three years probation.

Many criticized the result as being unduly light in that, unlike Pete Rose, Strawberry was not required to serve any time in prison. Conviction on all of the charges against Strawberry could have resulted in a prison sentence as long as 15 years.

should be supported by a good-faith belief that they have a realistic chance of being sustained if challenged. The client should be fully advised of the risks involved and of the penalties that would result if the position taken is not successful.

- A practitioner can use a client's estimates if they are reasonable under the circumstances. If the tax law requires verification (e.g., receipts), the client should be so advised. In no event should an estimate be given the appearance of greater accuracy than is the case. For example, an estimate of $1,000 should not be deducted on a return as $999.
- Every effort should be made to answer questions appearing on tax returns. A question need not be answered if the information requested is not readily available, the answer is voluminous, or the question's meaning is uncertain. The failure to answer a question on a return cannot be justified on the grounds that the answer could prove disadvantageous to the taxpayer.
- Upon learning of an error on a past tax return, advise the client to correct it. Do not, however, inform the IRS of the error. If the error is material and the client refuses to correct it, consider withdrawing from the engagement. This will be necessary if the error has a carryover effect and prevents the current year's tax liability from being determined correctly.

ETHICAL CONSIDERATIONS

A Favor for a Neighbor

Jim is a CPA who works full-time for a national accounting firm. Jim's neighbor and good friend, Lester, prepares his own income tax return for 1995.

Lester has heard that a person who has his tax return prepared by a CPA is less likely to be audited by the IRS. Consequently, Lester asks Jim to sign his return as the preparer.

Jim has known Lester for many years and considers him to be honest and well versed in business affairs. As a favor to Lester, should Jim sign the return as preparer?

Statutory Penalties Imposed on Tax Return Preparers. In addition to ethical constraints, a tax return preparer may be subject to certain statutorily sanctioned penalties, including the following:

- Various penalties involving procedural matters. Examples include failing to furnish the taxpayer with a copy of the return; endorsing a taxpayer's refund check; failing to sign the return as a preparer; failing to furnish one's identification number; and failing to keep copies of returns or maintain a client list.
- Understatement of a tax liability based on a position that lacks any realistic possibility of being sustained. If the position is not frivolous, the penalty can be avoided by disclosing it on the return.
- Any willful attempt to understate taxes. This usually results when a preparer disregards or makes no effort to obtain pertinent information from a client.

UNDERSTANDING THE FEDERAL TAX LAW

6 LEARNING OBJECTIVE
Recognize the economic, social, equity, and political considerations that justify various aspects of the tax law.

The Federal tax law is a mosaic of statutory provisions, administrative pronouncements, and court decisions. Anyone who has attempted to work with this body of knowledge would have to admit to its complexity. For the person who has to trudge through a mass of rules to find the solution to a tax problem, it may be of some consolation to know that the law's complexity can generally be explained. Whether sound or not, there is a reason for the formulation of every rule. Knowing these reasons, therefore, is a considerable step toward understanding the Federal tax law.

The Federal tax law has as its *major objective* the raising of revenue. But although the fiscal needs of the government are important, other considerations explain certain portions of the law. Economic, social, equity, and political factors also play a significant role. Added to these factors is the marked impact the IRS and the courts have had and will continue to have on the evolution of Federal tax law. These matters are treated in the remainder of the chapter, and, wherever appropriate, the discussion is referenced to subjects covered later in the text.

REVENUE NEEDS

The foundation of any tax system has to be the raising of revenue to cover the cost of government operations. Ideally, annual outlays should not exceed anticipated revenues, thereby leading to a balanced budget with no resulting deficit. Many states have achieved this objective by passing laws or constitutional amendments precluding deficit spending. Unfortunately, the Federal government has no such conclusive prohibition, and mounting annual deficits have become an increasing concern for many.

When finalizing the Tax Reform Act (TRA) of 1986, a deficit-conscious Congress was guided by the concept of **revenue neutrality.** The concept means that the changes made will neither increase nor decrease the net result reached under the prior rules. Revenue neutrality does not mean that any one taxpayer's tax liability will remain the same. Since the circumstances involved will differ, one taxpayer's increased tax liability could be another's tax savings. Although revenue-neutral tax reform does not reduce deficits, at least it does not aggravate the problem. One can expect budget deficit considerations to play an ever-increasing role in shaping future tax policy.

ECONOMIC CONSIDERATIONS

Using the tax system in an effort to accomplish economic objectives has become increasingly popular in recent years. Generally, proponents of this goal use tax legislation to amend the Internal Revenue Code and promote measures designed to help control the economy or encourage certain activities and businesses.

Control of the Economy. Congress has used depreciation write-offs as a means of controlling the economy. Theoretically, shorter asset lives and accelerated methods should encourage additional investment in depreciable property acquired for business use. Conversely, longer asset lives and the required use of the straight-line method of depreciation dampen the tax incentive for capital outlays.

Compared with past law, TRA of 1986 generally cut back on faster write-offs for property acquired after 1986. Particularly hard hit was most depreciable real estate, where asset lives were extended from 19 years to as long as 31½ years and the straight-line method was made mandatory. In 1993, the recovery period for nonresidential real property was further extended to 39 years. This last change was in the interest of revenue neutrality to compensate for the liberalization of the passive activity loss rules (see Chapter 11).

A change in the tax rate structure has a more immediate impact on the economy. With lower tax rates, taxpayers are able to retain additional spendable funds. Although TRA of 1986 lowered tax rates for most taxpayers, it also reduced or eliminated many deductions and credits. Consequently, lower rates may not lead to lower tax liabilities.

Encouragement of Certain Activities. Without passing judgment on the wisdom of any such choices, it is quite clear that the tax law does encourage certain types of economic activity or segments of the economy. For example, the favorable treatment allowed research and development expenditures can be explained by the desire to foster technological progress. Under the tax law, such expenditures can be either deducted in the year incurred or capitalized and amortized over a period of 60 months or more. In terms of the timing of the tax savings, these options usually are preferable to capitalizing the cost with a write-off over the estimated useful life of the asset created. If the asset developed has an indefinite useful life, no write-off would be available without the two options allowed by the tax law.

Is it desirable to encourage the conservation of energy resources? Considering the world energy situation and our own reliance on foreign oil, the answer to this question has to be yes. The concern over energy usage was a prime consideration in the enactment of legislation to make various tax savings for energy conservation expenditures available to taxpayers.

Is preserving the environment a desirable objective? Ecological considerations explain why the tax law permits a 60-month amortization period for costs incurred in the installation of pollution control facilities.

Is it wise to stimulate U.S. exports of goods and services? Considering the pressing and continuing problem of a deficit in the U.S. balance of payments, the answer should be clear. Along this line, Congress has created Foreign Sales Corporations (FSCs), which are designed to encourage domestic exports of goods. The FSC provisions exempt a percentage of profits from export sales from the Federal income tax. Also in an international setting, Congress has deemed it advisable to establish incentives for U.S. citizens who accept employment overseas. Such persons receive generous tax breaks through special treatment of their foreign-source income and certain housing costs.

Is saving desirable for the economy? Saving leads to capital formation and thereby makes funds available to finance home construction and industrial expansion. The tax law encourages saving by according preferential treatment to private retirement plans. Not only are contributions to Keogh (H.R. 10) plans and certain Individual Retirement Accounts (IRAs) deductible, but income from the contributions accumulates free of tax. As noted below, the encouragement of private-sector pension plans can also be justified under social considerations.

Encouragement of Certain Industries. No one can question the proposition that a sound agricultural base is necessary for a well-balanced national economy. Undoubtedly, this can explain why farmers are accorded special treatment under the Federal tax system. Among the benefits are the election to expense rather than capitalize certain soil and water conservation expenditures and fertilizers and the election to defer the recognition of gain on the receipt of crop insurance proceeds.

Encouragement of Small Business. At least in the United States, a consensus exists that what is good for small business is good for the economy as a whole. Whether valid or not, this assumption has led to a definite bias in the tax law favoring small business.

In the corporate tax area, several provisions can be explained by the desire to benefit small business. One provision permits the shareholders of a small business corporation to make a special election that generally will avoid the imposition of the corporate income tax.[24] Furthermore, such an election enables the corporation to pass through its operating losses to its shareholders.

SOCIAL CONSIDERATIONS

Some provisions of the Federal tax law, particularly those dealing with the income tax of individuals, can be explained by social considerations. Some notable examples and their rationales include the following:

- Certain benefits provided to employees through accident and health plans financed by employers are nontaxable to employees. Encouraging such plans is considered socially desirable since they provide medical benefits in the event of an employee's illness or injury.
- Most premiums paid by an employer for group term insurance covering the life of the employee are nontaxable to the employee. These arrangements can be justified on social grounds in that they provide funds for the family unit to help it adjust to the loss of wages caused by the employee's death.
- A contribution made by an employer to a qualified pension or profit sharing plan for an employee receives special treatment. The contribution and any income it generates are not taxed to the employee until the funds are distributed. Such an arrangement also benefits the employer by allowing a tax deduction when the contribution is made to the qualified plan. Private retirement plans are encouraged to supplement the subsistence income level the employee otherwise would have under the Social Security system.[25]
- A deduction is allowed for contributions to qualified charitable organizations.[26] The deduction attempts to shift some of the financial and adminis-

[24] Known as the S election, it is discussed in Chapter 20.

[25] The same rationale explains the availability of similar arrangements for self-employed persons (the H.R. 10, or Keogh, plan). See Chapter 19.

[26] The charitable contribution deduction is discussed in Chapter 10.

trative burden of socially desirable programs from the public (the government) to the private (the citizens) sector.
- A tax credit is allowed for amounts spent to furnish care for certain minor or disabled dependents to enable the taxpayer to seek or maintain gainful employment.[27] Who could deny the social desirability of encouraging taxpayers to provide care for their children while they work?
- A tax deduction is not allowed for certain expenditures deemed to be contrary to public policy. This disallowance extends to such items as fines, penalties, illegal kickbacks, bribes to government officials, and gambling losses in excess of gains. Social considerations dictate that the tax law should not encourage these activities by permitting a deduction.

Many other examples could be cited, but the conclusion would be unchanged. Social considerations do explain a significant part of the Federal tax law.

EQUITY CONSIDERATIONS

The concept of equity is relative. Reasonable persons can, and often do, disagree about what is fair or unfair. In the tax area, moreover, equity is most often tied to a particular taxpayer's personal situation. To illustrate, compare the tax positions of those who rent their personal residences with those who own their homes. Renters receive no Federal income tax benefit from the rent they pay. For homeowners, however, a large portion of the house payments they make may qualify for the Federal interest and property tax deductions. Although renters may have difficulty understanding this difference in tax treatment, the encouragement of home ownership can be justified on both economic and social grounds.

In the same vein, compare the tax treatment of a corporation with that of a partnership. Although the two businesses may be of equal size, similarly situated, and competitors in the production of goods or services, they are not treated comparably under the tax law. The corporation is subject to a separate Federal income tax; the partnership is not. Whether the differences in tax treatment can be justified logically in terms of equity is beside the point. The point is that the tax law can and does make a distinction between these business forms.

Equity, then, is not what appears fair or unfair to any one taxpayer or group of taxpayers. It is, instead, what the tax law recognizes. Some recognition of equity does exist, however, and explains part of the law. The concept of equity appears in tax provisions that alleviate the effect of multiple taxation and postpone the recognition of gain when the taxpayer lacks the ability or wherewithal to pay the tax. Provisions that mitigate the effect of the application of the annual accounting period concept and help taxpayers cope with the eroding results of inflation also reflect equity considerations.

Alleviating the Effect of Multiple Taxation. The income earned by a taxpayer may be subject to taxes imposed by different taxing authorities. If, for example, the taxpayer is a resident of New York City, income might generate Federal, state of New York, and city of New York income taxes. To compensate for this apparent inequity, the Federal tax law allows a taxpayer to claim a deduction for state and local income taxes. The deduction does not, however, neutralize the effect of multiple taxation, since the benefit derived depends on the taxpayer's Federal income tax rate. Only a tax credit, rather than a deduction, would eliminate the effects of multiple taxation on the same income.

[27] See Chapter 13.

Equity considerations can explain the Federal tax treatment of certain income from foreign sources. Since double taxation results when the same income is subject to both foreign and U.S. income taxes, the tax law permits the taxpayer to choose between a credit and a deduction for the foreign taxes paid.

The Wherewithal to Pay Concept. The **wherewithal to pay** concept recognizes the inequity of taxing a transaction when the taxpayer lacks the means with which to pay the tax. It is particularly suited to situations in which the taxpayer's economic position has not changed significantly as a result of the transaction.

An illustration of the wherewithal to pay concept is the provision of the tax law dealing with the treatment of gain resulting from the sale of a personal residence. If the proceeds are rolled over (reinvested) in another personal residence within a specified time period, the gain will not be taxed (see Chapter 15).

EXAMPLE 17

Ron sold his personal residence (cost of $60,000) for $100,000 and moved to another city. Shortly thereafter, he purchased a new personal residence for $100,000. ▼

In Example 17, Ron had a realized gain of $40,000 [$100,000 (selling price) – $60,000 (cost of residence)]. It would be inequitable to force Ron to pay a tax on this gain for two reasons. First, without disposing of the property acquired (the new residence), Ron would be hard-pressed to pay the tax. Second, his economic position has not changed significantly.

A warning is in order concerning the application of the wherewithal to pay concept. It applies only in situations specified by the tax law. Otherwise, the absence of cash and no apparent change in economic position will not prevent a transaction from being taxed.

EXAMPLE 18

Assume the same facts as in Example 17 except that the sale and purchase involved rental houses and not personal residences. Now, the sale of the first rental house results in a gain of $40,000 that is subject to tax. The fact that Ron reinvested the $100,000 in another rental house is of no consequence. ▼

Reconciling the different results reached in Examples 17 and 18 may seem difficult. But simply stated, the tax law applies the wherewithal to pay concept to the rollover on the gain from the sale of a personal residence. It does not do so when a rental house is involved, as Example 18 illustrates.

Mitigating the Effect of the Annual Accounting Period Concept. For purposes of effective administration of the tax law, all taxpayers must report to and settle with the Federal government at periodic intervals. Otherwise, taxpayers would remain uncertain as to their tax liabilities, and the government would have difficulty judging revenues and budgeting expenditures. The period selected for final settlement of most tax liabilities, in any event an arbitrary determination, is one year. At the close of each year, therefore, a taxpayer's position becomes complete for that particular year. Referred to as the annual accounting period concept, its effect is to divide each taxpayer's life, for tax purposes, into equal annual intervals.

The finality of the annual accounting period concept could lead to dissimilar tax treatment for taxpayers who are, from a long-range standpoint, in the same economic position.

EXAMPLE 19

José and Alicia, both sole proprietors, have experienced the following results during the past four years:

Profit (or Loss)		
Year	**José**	**Alicia**
1993	$50,000	$150,000
1994	60,000	60,000
1995	70,000	70,000
1996	50,000	(50,000)

Although José and Alicia have the same profit of $230,000 over the period from 1993 to 1996, the finality of the annual accounting period concept places Alicia at a definite disadvantage for tax purposes. The net operating loss procedure offers Alicia some relief by allowing her to apply some or all of her 1996 loss to the earlier profitable years (in this case, 1993). Thus, with a net operating loss carryback, Alicia is in a position to obtain a refund for some of the taxes she paid on the $150,000 profit reported for 1993. ▼

The same reasoning used to support the deduction of net operating losses can explain the special treatment the tax law accords to excess capital losses and excess charitable contributions.[28] Carryback and carryover procedures help mitigate the effect of limiting a loss or a deduction to the accounting period in which it was realized. With such procedures, a taxpayer may be able to salvage a loss or a deduction that might otherwise be wasted.

The installment method of recognizing gain on the sale of property allows a taxpayer to spread tax consequences over the payout period.[29] The harsh effect of taxing all the gain in the year of sale is thereby avoided. The installment method can also be explained by the wherewithal to pay concept since recognition of gain is tied to the collection of the installment notes received from the sale of the property. Tax consequences, then, tend to correspond to the seller's ability to pay the tax.

Coping with Inflation. Because of the progressive nature of the income tax, a wage adjustment to compensate for inflation can increase the income tax bracket of the recipient. Known as *bracket creep,* its overall impact is an erosion of purchasing power. Congress recognized this problem and began to adjust various income tax components, such as tax brackets, standard deduction amounts, and personal and dependency exemptions, through an indexation procedure. Indexation is based upon the rise in the consumer price index over the prior year.

POLITICAL CONSIDERATIONS

A large segment of the Federal tax law is made up of statutory provisions. Since these statutes are enacted by Congress, is it any surprise that political considerations influence tax law? For purposes of discussion, the effect of political considerations on the tax law is divided into the following topics: special interest legislation, political expediency situations, and state and local government influences.

[28] The tax treatment of these items is discussed in Chapters 7, 10, and 16.

[29] Under the installment method, each payment received by the seller represents both a recovery of capital (the nontaxable portion) and profit from the sale (the taxable portion). The tax rules governing the installment method are discussed in Chapter 18.

Special Interest Legislation. There is no doubt that certain provisions of the tax law can largely be explained by the political influence some pressure groups have had on Congress. Is there any other realistic reason that, for example, prepaid subscription and dues income are not taxed until earned while prepaid rents are taxed to the landlord in the year received?

An example of special interest legislation was a last minute amendment to TRA of 1986 made by former Senator Long (Louisiana) and former Representative Pickle (Austin, Texas). Under the amendment, a charitable deduction was allowed for donations to certain institutions of higher education that enabled the donor to receive choice seating at athletic events. The definition of institutions of higher education was so limited, however, that only Louisiana State University and the University of Texas were qualified recipients. Two years passed before Congress modified the tax law to neutralize this apparent preferential treatment (see Chapter 10).

Special interest legislation is not necessarily to be condemned if it can be justified on economic, social, or some other utilitarian grounds. At any rate, it is an inevitable product of our political system.

Political Expediency Situations. Various tax reform proposals rise and fall in favor with the shifting moods of the American public. That Congress is sensitive to popular feeling is an accepted fact. Therefore, certain provisions of the tax law can be explained by the political climate at the time they were enacted.

Measures that deter more affluent taxpayers from obtaining so-called preferential tax treatment have always had popular appeal and, consequently, the support of Congress. Provisions such as the alternative minimum tax, the imputed interest rules, and the limitation on the deductibility of interest on investment indebtedness can be explained on this basis.[30]

Other changes explained at least partially by political expediency include the lowering of individual income tax rates, the increase in the personal and dependency exemptions, and the increase in the amount of the earned income credit. One of the expressed objectives of legislation enacted in 1993 was to increase taxes levied on wealthy individuals by instituting new 36 and 39.6 percent rates on higher-income brackets.

State and Local Government Influences. Political considerations have played a major role in the nontaxability of interest received on state and local obligations. In view of the furor that has been raised by state and local political figures every time any modification of this tax provision has been proposed, one might well regard it as next to sacred.

Somewhat less apparent has been the influence state law has had in shaping our present Federal tax law. Such was the case with community property systems. The nine states with community property systems are Louisiana, Texas, New Mexico, Arizona, California, Washington, Idaho, Nevada, and Wisconsin. The rest of the states are classified as common law jurisdictions. The difference between common law and community property systems centers around the property rights possessed by married persons. In a common law system, each spouse owns whatever he or she earns. Under a community property system, one-half of the earnings of each spouse is considered owned by the other spouse.

EXAMPLE 20 Al and Fran are husband and wife, and their only income is the $60,000 annual salary Al receives. If they live in New Jersey (a common law state), the $60,000 salary belongs to Al.

[30] See Chapters 4, 10, and 12.

If, however, they live in Arizona (a community property state), the $60,000 is divided equally, in terms of ownership, between Al and Fran. ▼

At one time, the tax position of the residents of community property states was so advantageous that many common law states actually adopted community property systems. Needless to say, the political pressure placed on Congress to correct the disparity in tax treatment was considerable. To a large extent this was accomplished in the Revenue Act of 1948, which extended many of the community property tax advantages to residents of common law jurisdictions.

The major advantage extended was the provision allowing married taxpayers to file joint returns and compute the tax liability as if the income had been earned one-half by each spouse. This result is automatic in a community property state, since half of the income earned by one spouse belongs to the other spouse. The income-splitting benefits of a joint return are now incorporated as part of the tax rates applicable to married taxpayers. See Chapter 3.

INFLUENCE OF THE INTERNAL REVENUE SERVICE

7 LEARNING OBJECTIVE
Describe the role played by the IRS and the courts in the evolution of the Federal tax system.

The influence of the IRS is apparent in many areas beyond its role in issuing the administrative pronouncements that make up a considerable portion of our tax law. In its capacity as the protector of the national revenue, the IRS has been instrumental in securing the passage of much legislation designed to curtail the most flagrant tax avoidance practices (to close *tax loopholes*). In its capacity as the administrator of the tax law, the IRS has sought and obtained legislation to make its job easier (to attain administrative feasibility).

The IRS as Protector of the Revenue. Innumerable examples can be given of provisions in the tax law that stem from the direct influence of the IRS. Usually, such provisions are intended to prevent a loophole from being used to avoid the tax consequences intended by Congress. Working within the letter of existing law, ingenious taxpayers and their advisers devise techniques that accomplish indirectly what cannot be accomplished directly. As a consequence, legislation is enacted to close the loopholes that taxpayers have located and exploited. Some tax law can be explained in this fashion and is discussed in the chapters to follow.

In addition, the IRS has secured from Congress legislation of a more general nature that enables it to make adjustments based on the substance, rather than the formal construction, of what a taxpayer has done. One such provision permits the IRS to make adjustments to a taxpayer's method of accounting when the method used by the taxpayer does not clearly reflect income.[31]

EXAMPLE 21

Tina, a cash basis taxpayer, owns and operates a pharmacy. All drugs and other items acquired for resale (e.g., cosmetics) are charged to the purchases account and written off (expensed) for tax purposes in the year of acquisition. As this procedure does not clearly reflect income, it would be appropriate for the IRS to require that Tina establish and maintain an ending inventory account. ▼

Administrative Feasibility. Some of the tax law is justified on the grounds that it simplifies the task of the IRS in collecting the revenue and administering the law. With regard to collecting the revenue, the IRS long ago realized the importance of placing taxpayers on a pay-as-you-go basis. Elaborate withholding procedures apply to wages, while the tax on other types of income may be paid at

[31] See Chapter 18.

periodic intervals throughout the year. The IRS has been instrumental in convincing the courts that accrual basis taxpayers should pay taxes on prepaid income in the year received and not when earned. The approach may be contrary to generally accepted accounting principles, but it is consistent with the wherewithal to pay concept.

Of considerable aid to the IRS in collecting revenue are the numerous provisions that impose interest and penalties on taxpayers for noncompliance with the tax law. Provisions such as the penalties for failure to pay a tax or to file a return that is due, the negligence penalty for intentional disregard of rules and regulations, and various penalties for civil and criminal fraud serve as deterrents to taxpayer noncompliance.

One of the keys to an effective administration of our tax system is the audit process conducted by the IRS. To carry out this function, the IRS is aided by provisions that reduce the chance of taxpayer error or manipulation and therefore simplify the audit effort that is necessary. An increase in the amount of the standard deduction, for example, reduces the number of individual taxpayers who will choose the alternative of itemizing their personal deductions.[32] With fewer deductions to check, the audit function is simplified.[33]

The audit function of the IRS has also been simplified by provisions of the tax law dealing with the burden of proof. Suppose, for example, the IRS audits a taxpayer and questions a particular deduction. Who has the burden of proving the propriety of the deduction? The so-called presumption of correctness that attaches in favor of any deficiency assessed by the IRS can be explained by the nature of our tax system. The Federal income tax is a *self-assessed tax*, which means that each taxpayer is responsible for rendering an accounting to the IRS of all of his or her transactions during the year. A failure to do so means that any doubts will be resolved in favor of the IRS. Only in the case of fraud (which could involve fines and penal sanctions) does the IRS carry the burden of proof.

INFLUENCE OF THE COURTS

In addition to interpreting statutory provisions and the administrative pronouncements issued by the IRS, the Federal courts have influenced tax law in two other respects.[34] First, the courts have formulated certain judicial concepts that serve as guides in the application of various tax provisions. Second, certain key decisions have led to changes in the Internal Revenue Code.

Judicial Concepts Relating to Tax. A leading tax concept developed by the courts deals with the interpretation of statutory tax provisions that operate to benefit taxpayers. The courts have established the rule that these relief provisions are to be narrowly construed against taxpayers if there is any doubt about their application.

EXAMPLE 22 When a taxpayer has a gain on the sale of a personal residence, the gain is not subject to Federal income tax if the proceeds from the sale are reinvested in another principal residence. The tax law specifies a period of time in which the reinvestment must take place.

[32] For a discussion of the standard deduction, see Chapter 3.

[33] The same justification was given by the IRS when it proposed to Congress the $100 limitation on personal casualty and theft losses. Imposition of the limitation eliminated many casualty and theft loss deductions and, as a consequence, saved the IRS considerable audit time. Later legislation, in addition to retaining the $100 feature, limits deductible losses to those in excess of 10% of a taxpayer's adjusted gross income. See Chapter 7.

[34] A great deal of case law is devoted to ascertaining congressional intent. The courts, in effect, ask: What did Congress have in mind when it enacted a particular tax provision?

The courts have held that the nontaxability of gain is a relief provision to be narrowly construed. Thus, failure to meet the replacement period requirements, even if beyond the control of the taxpayer, will cause the gain to be taxed.[35] ▼

Important in this area is the *arm's length* concept. Particularly in dealings between related parties, transactions may be tested by looking to whether the taxpayers acted in an arm's length manner. The question to be asked is: Would unrelated parties have handled the transaction in the same way?

EXAMPLE 23

Rex, the sole shareholder of Silver Corporation, leases property to the corporation for a yearly rent of $6,000. To test whether the corporation should be allowed a rent deduction for this amount, the IRS and the courts will apply the arm's length concept. Would Silver Corporation have paid $6,000 a year in rent if it had leased the same property from an unrelated party (rather than from Rex)? Suppose it is determined that an unrelated third party would have paid an annual rent for the property of only $5,000. Under these circumstances, Silver Corporation will be allowed a deduction of only $5,000. The other $1,000 it paid for the use of the property represents a nondeductible dividend. Accordingly, Rex will be treated as having received rent income of $5,000 and dividend income of $1,000. ▼

Judicial Influence on Statutory Provisions. Some court decisions have been of such consequence that Congress has incorporated them into statutory tax law. For example, many years ago the courts found that stock dividends distributed to the shareholders of a corporation were not taxable as income. This result was largely accepted by Congress, and a provision in the tax statutes now covers the issue.

On occasion, however, Congress has reacted negatively to judicial interpretations of the tax law.

EXAMPLE 24

Nora leases unimproved real estate to Wade for 40 years. At a cost of $200,000, Wade erects a building on the land. The building is worth $100,000 when the lease terminates and Nora takes possession of the property. Does Nora have any income either when the improvements are made or when the lease terminates? In a landmark decision, a court held that Nora must recognize income of $100,000 upon the termination of the lease. ▼

Congress felt that the result reached in Example 24 was inequitable in that it was not consistent with the wherewithal to pay concept. Consequently, the tax law was amended to provide that a landlord does not recognize any income either when the improvements are made (unless made in lieu of rent) or when the lease terminates.

SUMMARY

In addition to its necessary revenue-raising objective, the Federal tax law has developed in response to several other factors:

- *Economic considerations.* The emphasis here is on tax provisions that help regulate the economy and encourage certain activities and types of businesses.
- *Social considerations.* Some tax provisions are designed to encourage (or discourage) certain socially desirable (or undesirable) practices.
- *Equity considerations.* Of principal concern in this area are tax provisions that alleviate the effect of multiple taxation, recognize the wherewithal to pay

[35] These rules are discussed further in Chapter 15.

concept, mitigate the effect of the annual accounting period concept, and recognize the eroding effect of inflation.

- *Political considerations.* Of significance in this regard are tax provisions that represent special interest legislation, reflect political expediency, and exhibit the effect of state and local law.
- *Influence of the IRS.* Many tax provisions are intended to aid the IRS in the collection of revenue and the administration of the tax law.
- *Influence of the courts.* Court decisions have established a body of judicial concepts relating to tax law and have, on occasion, led Congress to enact statutory provisions to either clarify or negate their effect.

These factors explain various tax provisions and thereby help in understanding why the tax law developed to its present state. The next step involves learning to work with the tax law, which is the subject of Chapter 2.

KEY TERMS

Ad valorem tax, 1–6
Correspondence audit, 1–20
Death tax, 1–11
Employment taxes, 1–15
Estate tax, 1–11
Excise tax, 1–9
FICA tax, 1–15
Field audit, 1–20
Flat tax, 1–18
Franchise tax, 1–17
FUTA tax, 1–16
Gift tax, 1–12
Inheritance tax, 1–11
National sales tax, 1–18
Occupational tax, 1–17
Office audit, 1–20
Personalty, 1–7
Realty, 1–6
Revenue neutrality, 1–24
Sales tax, 1–10
Severance tax, 1–10
Statute of limitations, 1–20
Use tax, 1–10
Value added tax (VAT), 1–18
Wherewithal to pay, 1–28

PROBLEM MATERIALS

DISCUSSION QUESTIONS

1. Irene, a middle management employee, is offered a pay increase by her employer. As a condition of the offer, Irene must move to another state. What tax considerations should Irene weigh before making a decision on whether to accept the offer?
2. Before the passage of the Sixteenth Amendment to the Constitution, there was no income tax in the United States. Please comment.
3. Did the passage of the Sixteenth Amendment to the U.S. Constitution have any effect on the income tax imposed on corporations? Explain.
4. A tax law that was enacted in 1953 would be part of which Internal Revenue Code (i.e., 1939, 1954, or 1986)? Explain.
5. How does the pay-as-you-go procedure apply to wage earners? To persons who have income from other than wages?
6. Analyze the Federal income tax in light of Adam Smith's canons of taxation.
7. When Gull Company constructs a climate-controlled warehouse, it is very careful to keep many of the components portable. Thus, the sprinkler system is detachable, air conditioning and heating are provided by window units, and the interior walls can be removed. What is Gull trying to accomplish?

8. When Nancy's widower father moves to a nursing home, he gives his personal residence to her. Immediately thereafter, Nancy converts the residence to rental property. Nancy has noticed a significant increase in the ad valorem taxes imposed on the property since she received it from her father. What could have caused the increase?

9. Al is considering starting a new business that will require the construction of a manufacturing facility. Jefferson County, one of the geographic locations Al is considering, has proposed a tax holiday. What does this mean?

10. Matt buys a new home for $150,000, its cost of construction plus the usual profit margin for the builder. The new home is located in a neighborhood largely developed 10 years ago when the homes sold for approximately $50,000 each. Assuming the homes of his neighbors are worth (in current values) in the vicinity of $150,000, could Matt be at a disadvantage with regard to the ad valorem tax on realty?

11. Recently, one of your friends successfully challenged a reappraisal of his personal residence by the county board of real estate tax assessors. He remarks to you that this should put him "in good shape for the next five years." What does he mean?

12. A few years ago, Al retired from his job in Alaska and moved to Florida. Before he retired, Al had the certificates for all of his stock investments placed in his name, rather than leaving them in street name. Since retirement, Al continues to use his broker in Alaska to handle any investment trades. Since this arrangement is very inconvenient, why is Al handling his investment trades in this manner?

13. What is the gas guzzler tax? What purpose does it serve?

14. While out of town on business, Paul stays at a motel with an advertised room rate of $80 per night. When checking out, Paul is charged $88. What would be a plausible reason for the extra $8 Paul had to pay?

15. Earl, a resident of Wyoming (which imposes a general sales tax), goes to Montana (which does not impose a general sales tax) to purchase his automobile. Will Earl successfully avoid the Wyoming sales tax? Explain.

16. Jean lives in Smithville (the major city in Smith County). She does all of her shopping in Madisonville (the major city in Madison County). If the cities' retail outlets are comparable, why does Jean go out of her way to shop?

17. When Alaska became a major oil producer, the state repealed its state income tax. Is there any correlation between these two events? Explain.

18. A death tax has been characterized as an excise tax. Do you agree? Why or why not?

19. Explain the difference between an inheritance tax and an estate tax.

20. What was the original objective of the Federal estate tax?

21. A decedent who leaves all of his property to his surviving spouse and to qualified charitable organizations is not subject to a Federal estate tax. Explain.

22. In 1995, Horace makes a taxable gift of $250,000 upon which he pays a Federal gift tax of $70,800. In 1996, Horace makes another taxable gift of $250,000. Will the 1996 taxable gift result in the same gift tax as the 1995 gift? Why or why not?

23. How much property can Ida, a widow, give to her two married children, their spouses, and five grandchildren over a period of 10 years without making a taxable gift?

24. When married persons elect to split a gift, what tax advantages do they enjoy?

25. Reuben, a widower, plans on making taxable gifts of $600,000 and then passing $600,000 of his property by death. Because of the unified transfer tax credit, he believes that this approach will allow him to dispose of $1,200,000 without incurring the Federal gift tax and the Federal estate tax. Do you have any comment?

26. Contrast the major differences between the Federal income tax schemes applicable to individuals and to corporations.

27. John, a nationally known vocalist, lives in Nevada. John's agent has been trying to convince him to go on tour to increase his record sales. John, however, refuses to perform anywhere but in Las Vegas clubs. What might explain John's attitude?

28. When a state uses a "piggyback" approach for its state income tax, what is the state doing?

29. Chee lives in a state that imposes an income tax. His Federal income tax return for 1994 is audited in 1996, and, as a result of several adjustments made by the IRS, Chee has to pay additional Federal income tax. Several months later, Chee is notified that his 1994 state income tax return is to be audited. Are these two incidents a coincidence or does a reasonable explanation exist?

30. Nearly all states that impose an income tax allow a credit against their tax for Federal income taxes paid. Please comment on the validity of this statement.

31. At a cocktail party you attend in early March of 1996, you overhear a guest say, "Thank heavens my Social Security tax for this year is over with." What was the guest, the CEO of a large corporation, referring to?

32. Keith, a sole proprietor, owns and operates a grocery store. Keith's wife and his 17-year-old son work in the business and are paid wages. Will the wife and son be subject to FICA? Explain.

33. Dan, the owner and operator of a construction company that builds outdoor swimming pools, releases most of his construction personnel during the winter months. Should this hurt Dan's FUTA situation? Why or why not?

34. Compare FICA and FUTA in connection with each of the following:
    a. Incidence of taxation.
    b. Justification for taxation.
    c. Rates and base involved.

35. What is a "flat tax"? What is its major advantage?

36. One of your friends contends that a value added tax (VAT) is the same as a national sales tax. Do you agree or disagree and why?

37. Mike and Laura had been engaged to be married for around five years when Mike broke the engagement and married Laura's best friend. Not long after the marriage, Mike is audited by the IRS. Please comment.

38. Norm, the owner and operator of a cash-and-carry military surplus retail outlet, has been audited many times by the IRS. When Norm mentions this fact to his next-door neighbor, an employee with Ford Motor Company, he is somewhat surprised to learn that the neighbor has never been audited by the IRS. Is there any explanation for this apparent disparity in treatment?

39. Distinguish between a field audit and an office audit by the IRS.

40. As a result of an audit by the IRS of her Federal income tax return, Sophy receives an RAR. What does this mean?

41. For tax year 1988, Linda failed to file a Federal income tax return. In 1996, the IRS notifies Linda that it wants an accounting of her tax-related transactions for tax year 1988. Linda is not concerned about the request because three years have passed since the due date (April 15, 1989) of the return. Is Linda's defense based on the statute of limitations valid? Why or why not?

42. On a Federal income tax return filed five years ago, Andy inadvertently omitted a large amount of gross income.
    a. Andy seeks your advice as to whether the IRS is barred from assessing additional income tax in the event he is audited. What is your advice?
    b. Would your advice differ if you are the person who prepared the return in question? Explain.
    c. Suppose Andy asks you to prepare his current year's return. Would you do so? Explain.

43. Jill files her income tax return 45 days after the due date of the return without obtaining an extension from the IRS. Along with the return, she remits a check for $4,000, which is the balance of the tax she owes. Disregarding the interest element, what are Jill's penalties for failure to file and for failure to pay?

44. Ed overstated deductions on his Federal income tax return for 1995. Upon audit by the IRS, it is determined that the overstatement was partially the result of negligence. As a result, Ed owes additional income taxes of $10,000 ($8,000 attributable to the negligence). What is Ed's penalty?

45. In March 1996, Jim asks you to prepare his Federal income tax returns for tax years 1993, 1994, and 1995. In discussing this matter with him, you discover that he also has not filed for tax year 1992. When you mention this fact, Jim tells you that the statute of limitations precludes the IRS from taking any action as to this year.
    a. Is Jim correct about the application of the statute of limitations? Why?
    b. If Jim refuses to file for 1992, should you prepare returns for 1993 through 1995?

46. You are preparing Ellen's Federal income tax return for 1995. Although she has no records, she estimates that she has given cash of about $500 to various charities during the year. She suggests that it would "look better" if you listed $501 as charitable contributions. What should you do?

47. What is meant by revenue-neutral tax reform?

48. How does the tax law stimulate U.S. exports of goods and services?

49. Discuss the probable justification for the following provisions of the tax law:
    a. The election permitting certain corporations to avoid the corporate income tax.
    b. A provision that excludes from gross income certain benefits furnished to employees through accident and health plans financed by employers.
    c. Nontaxable treatment for an employee for premiums paid by an employer for group term insurance covering the life of the employee.

50. The tax law encourages private retirement plans and contributions to charitable organizations. In terms of nonrevenue objectives, what is the common justification for this special tax treatment?

51. What purpose is served by allowing a deduction for home mortgage interest and property taxes?

52. Allowing a taxpayer a deduction for Federal income tax purposes for state income taxes paid eliminates the double taxation of the same income. Do you agree? Why or why not?

53. George sells a rental house for more than he paid for it. Shortly thereafter, George reinvests the proceeds in another rental house. Can George avoid the tax on any gain under the wherewithal to pay concept? Explain.

54. In what manner does the tax law mitigate the effect of the annual accounting period concept for a net operating loss?

55. How does the tax law cope with the impact of inflation?

56. Forcing accrual basis taxpayers to recognize prepaid income when received (as opposed to when earned) accomplishes what objective?

57. On his income tax return for the year, Henry claims as a deduction certain charitable contributions that he did not make. When you question him about this, he responds:
    a. "How is the IRS going to prove that I did not make these contributions?"
    b. "Even if the IRS disallows the deductions, the worst that can happen is that I will owe the same amount of tax I would have paid anyway."

    Comment on Henry's misconceptions about the tax law.

58. Edward leases real estate to Janet for a period of 20 years. Janet makes capital improvements to the property. When the lease expires, Edward reclaims the property, including the improvements made by Janet.

a. Under current law, at what point does Edward recognize income as a result of Janet's improvements?
b. Has the law in (a) always been the rule?
c. What is the justification, if any, for the current rule?

TEAM PROJECT: ARTHUR ANDERSEN TAX CHALLENGE CASES

Arthur Andersen & Co. has provided two of the cases that have been used in the Arthur Andersen Tax Challenge for use *in West's Federal Taxation: Individual Income Taxes* (or *West's Federal Taxation: Comprehensive Volume*). The Tax Challenge is a nationwide university competition to stimulate student interest in tax careers. The case studies are based on Federal tax issues confronting an individual or family with their own business, with investments made by the individual, compensation matters, itemized deductions, and related issues that impact the taxpayer's filing status and tax profile.

The Tax Challenge is a team competition with four members on each team. Thus, the cases are excellent materials for team projects in tax classes. We suggest that team members read assigned cases in their entirety at this point in the course. Because the cases require the application of knowledge gained throughout the course, it is not possible to prepare a solution early in the course. However, the length and complexity of the cases dictate that students must spend some time working on them during the entire course. To facilitate this course-long effort, we have identified topics related to each chapter and placed instructions regarding these topics in the end of chapter problem materials as appropriate.

Information related to tax issues and problems that are discussed in this chapter may be found in the

Miller case on page 4

Read and analyze the case you have been assigned and *identify* any issues and problems that are related to material covered in this chapter. If the information provided in the case is complete, prepare answers for this part of the case at this time. If you need information that is contained in later parts of the case, please write a memo summarizing the questions or problems so you can prepare a complete answer at a later date.

CHAPTER

2

WORKING WITH THE TAX LAW

LEARNING OBJECTIVES

After completing Chapter 2, you should be able to:

1. Distinguish between the statutory, administrative, and judicial sources of the tax law and understand the purpose of each source.
2. Locate and work with the appropriate tax law sources.
3. Understand the tax research process.
4. Communicate the results of the tax research process in a client letter and a tax file memorandum.
5. Apply tax research techniques and planning procedures.
6. Have an awareness of computer-assisted tax research.

OUTLINE

TAX SOURCES

1 LEARNING OBJECTIVE
Distinguish between the statutory, administrative, and judicial sources of the tax law and understand the purpose of each source.

Understanding taxation requires a mastery of the sources of the *rules of tax law.* These sources include not only legislative provisions in the form of the Internal Revenue Code, but also congressional Committee Reports, Treasury Department Regulations, other Treasury Department pronouncements, and court decisions. Thus, the *primary sources* of tax information include pronouncements from all three branches of government: legislative, executive, and judicial.

In addition to being able to locate and interpret the sources of the tax law, a tax professional must understand the relative weight of authority within these sources. The tax law is of little significance, however, until it is applied to a set of facts and circumstances. This chapter, therefore, both introduces the statutory, administrative, and judicial sources of tax law and explains how the law is applied to individual and business transactions. It also explains how to apply research techniques and use planning procedures effectively.

A large part of tax research focuses on determining the intent of Congress. Although Congress often claims simplicity as one of its goals, a cursory examination of the tax law indicates that it has not been very successful in achieving this objective. Commenting on his 48-page tax return, James Michener, the author, said "it is unimaginable in that I graduated from one of America's better colleges, yet I am totally incapable of understanding tax returns." David Brinkley, the television news commentator, observed that "settling a dispute is difficult when our tax regulations are all written in a foreign tongue whose language flows like damp sludge leaking from a sanitary landfill."

Frequently, uncertainty in the tax law causes disputes between the Internal Revenue Service (IRS) and taxpayers. Due to these *gray areas* and the complexity of the tax law, a taxpayer may have more than one alternative for structuring a business transaction. In structuring business transactions and engaging in other tax planning activities, the tax adviser must be cognizant that the objective of tax planning is not necessarily to minimize the tax liability. Instead a taxpayer should maximize his or her after-tax return, which may include maximizing nontax as well as noneconomic benefits.

TAX IN THE NEWS

Small Is Beautiful?

In income tax history, 1913 was an important year. In that year, the Sixteenth Amendment to the Constitution was ratified.

The Congress shall have power to tax and collect taxes on incomes, from whatever source derived, without apportionment among the several States, and without regard to any census or enumeration.

The first income tax legislation that definitely was constitutional was passed that same year.

Since 1913, Congress has enacted hundreds of tax bills. The *Internal Revenue Code* is now more than 2,200 pages in length. Of course, this seems short when compared to a tax service such as CCH's *Standard Federal Tax Reporter* or *RIA's United States Tax Reporter,* which fill up library shelves. As an example of how the size and complexity of the income tax have changed, consider that when CCH published its first tax guide in 1913, it was only 400 pages long.

STATUTORY SOURCES OF THE TAX LAW

Origin of the Internal Revenue Code. Before 1939, the statutory provisions relating to Federal taxation were contained in the individual revenue acts enacted by Congress. Because dealing with many separate acts was inconvenient and confusing, in 1939 Congress codified all of the Federal tax laws. Known as the Internal Revenue Code of 1939, the codification arranged all Federal tax provisions in a logical sequence and placed them in a separate part of the Federal statutes. A further rearrangement took place in 1954 and resulted in the Internal Revenue Code of 1954, which continued in effect until 1986 when it was replaced by the Internal Revenue Code of 1986. Although Congress did not recodify the law in the Tax Reform Act (TRA) of 1986, the magnitude of the changes made by TRA of 1986 did provide some rationale for renaming the Federal tax law the Internal Revenue Code of 1986.

The following observations help clarify the codification procedure:

- With some exceptions, neither the 1939 nor the 1954 Code substantially changed the tax law existing on the date of its enactment. Much of the 1939 Code, for example, was incorporated into the 1954 Code; the major change was the reorganization and renumbering of the tax provisions.
- Although the 1986 Code resulted in substantial changes, only a minority of the statutory provisions were affected.[1]
- Statutory amendments to the tax law are integrated into the Code. For example, the Technical and Miscellaneous Revenue Act of 1988, the Revenue

[1] This point is important in assessing judicial decisions interpreting provisions of the Internal Revenue Code of 1939 and the Internal Revenue Code of 1954. If the same provision was included in the Internal Revenue Code of 1986 and has not been subsequently amended, the decision has continuing validity.

Reconciliation Act of 1989, the Revenue Reconciliation Act of 1990, and the Revenue Reconciliation Act of 1993 all became part of the Internal Revenue Code of 1986. Considering the tax legislation enacted in recent years, it appears that the tax law will continue to be amended frequently.

The Legislative Process. Federal tax legislation generally originates in the House of Representatives, where it is first considered by the House Ways and Means Committee. Tax bills originate in the Senate when they are attached as riders to other legislative proposals.[2] If acceptable to the House Ways and Means Committee, the proposed bill is referred to the entire House of Representatives for approval or disapproval. Approved bills are sent to the Senate, where they are considered by the Senate Finance Committee. The next step is referral from the Senate Finance Committee to the entire Senate. Assuming no disagreement between the House and Senate, passage by the Senate results in referral to the President for approval or veto. If the bill is approved or if the President's veto is overridden, the bill becomes law and part of the Internal Revenue Code of 1986.

When the Senate version of the bill differs from that passed by the House, the Joint Conference Committee, which includes members of both the House Ways and Means Committee and the Senate Finance Committee, is called upon to resolve the differences. Major tax bills frequently have differing versions. One reason bills are often changed in the Senate is that each individual senator has considerable latitude to make amendments when the Senate as a whole is voting on a bill referred to it by the Senate Finance Committee.[3] In contrast, the entire House of Representatives either accepts or rejects what is proposed by the House Ways and Means Committee, and changes from the floor are rare. The deliberations of the Joint Conference Committee usually produce a compromise between the two versions, which is then voted on by both the House and the Senate. If both bodies accept the bill, it is referred to the President for approval or veto.

Referrals from the House Ways and Means Committee, the Senate Finance Committee, and the Joint Conference Committee are usually accompanied by Committee Reports. Because these Committee Reports often explain the provisions of the proposed legislation, they are a valuable source for ascertaining the *intent of Congress*. What Congress had in mind when it considered and enacted tax legislation is, of course, the key to interpreting such legislation by taxpayers, the IRS, and the courts. Since Regulations normally are not issued immediately after a statute is enacted, taxpayers often look to legislative history materials to determine congressional intent.

The typical legislative process for dealing with tax bills is summarized as follows:

---

[2] The Tax Equity and Fiscal Responsibility Act of 1982 originated in the Senate, and its constitutionality was unsuccessfully challenged in the courts. The Senate version of the Deficit Reduction Act of 1984 was attached as an amendment to the Federal Boat Safety Act.

[3] During the passage of the Tax Reform Act of 1986, Senate leaders tried to make the bill *amendment proof* to avoid the normal amendment process.

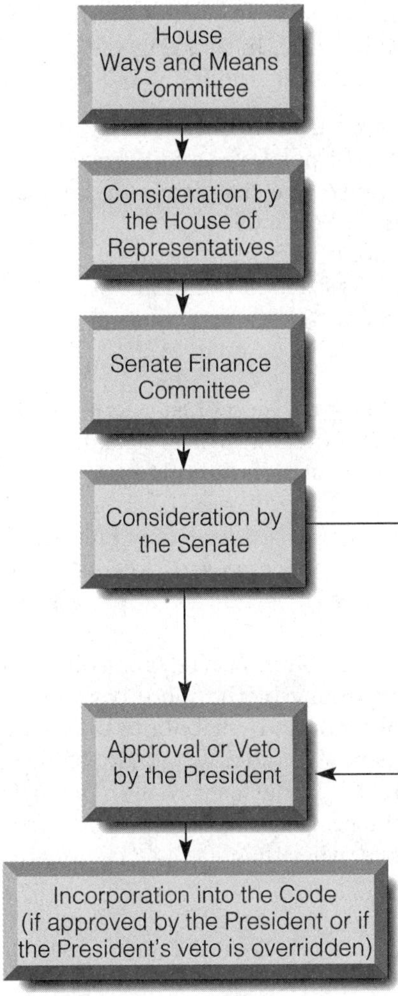

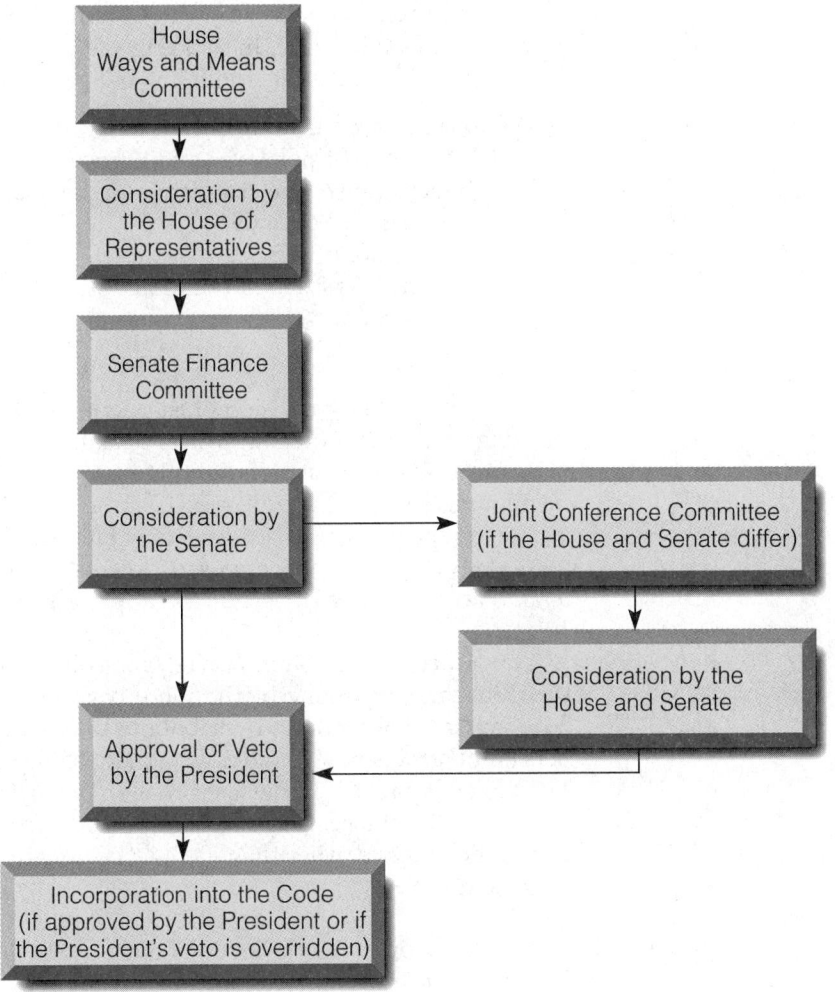

The role of the Joint Conference Committee indicates the importance of compromise in the legislative process. As an example of the practical effect of the compromise process, consider what happened to a limitation on contributions by employees to their tax-sheltered annuities in the Tax Reform Act of 1986.

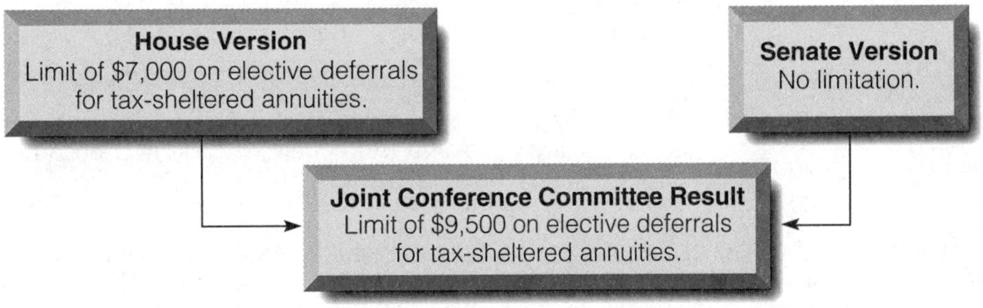

Arrangement of the Code. The Internal Revenue Code of 1986 is found in Title 26 of the U.S. Code. In working with the Code, it helps to understand the format. Note, for example, the following partial table of contents:

Subtitle A. Income Taxes
  Chapter 1. Normal Taxes and Surtaxes
    Subchapter A. Determination of Tax Liability
      Part I. Tax on Individuals
        Sections 1–5
      Part II. Tax on Corporations
        Sections 11–12

* * *

In referring to a provision of the Code, the *key* is usually the Section number. In citing Section 2(a) (dealing with the status of a surviving spouse), for example, it is unnecessary to include Subtitle A, Chapter 1, Subchapter A, Part I. Merely mentioning Section 2(a) will suffice, since the Section numbers run consecutively and do not begin again with each new Subtitle, Chapter, Subchapter, or Part. Not all Code Section numbers are used, however. Notice that Part I ends with Section 5 and Part II starts with Section 11 (at present there are no Sections 6, 7, 8, 9, and 10).[4]

Tax practitioners commonly refer to some specific areas of income tax law by their Subchapters. Some of the more common Subchapter designations include Subchapter C ("Corporate Distributions and Adjustments"), Subchapter K ("Partners and Partnerships"), and Subchapter S ("Tax Treatment of S Corporations and Their Shareholders"). In the last situation in particular, it is much more convenient to describe the subject of the applicable Code provisions (Sections 1361–1379) as S corporation status rather than as the "Tax Treatment of S Corporations and Their Shareholders."

Citing the Code. Code Sections often are broken down into subparts.[5] Section 2(a)(1)(A) serves as an example.

Broken down by content, § 2(a)(1)(A) becomes:

[4] When the 1954 Code was drafted, some Section numbers were intentionally omitted so that later changes could be incorporated into the Code without disrupting its organization. When Congress does not leave enough space, subsequent Code Sections are given A, B, C, etc., designations. A good example is the treatment of §§ 280A through 280H.

[5] Some Code Sections do not require subparts. See, for example, §§ 211 and 241.

[6] Some Code Sections omit the subsection designation and use the paragraph designation as the first subpart. See, for example, §§ 212(1) and 1221(1).

§ 2 →	Definitions and special rules (relating to the income tax imposed on individuals)
(a) →	Definition of a surviving spouse
(1) →	For purposes of § 1 (the determination of the applicable rate schedule), a surviving spouse must meet certain conditions.
(A) →	One of the conditions necessary to qualify as a surviving spouse is that the taxpayer's spouse must have died during either of his or her two taxable years immediately preceding the present taxable year.

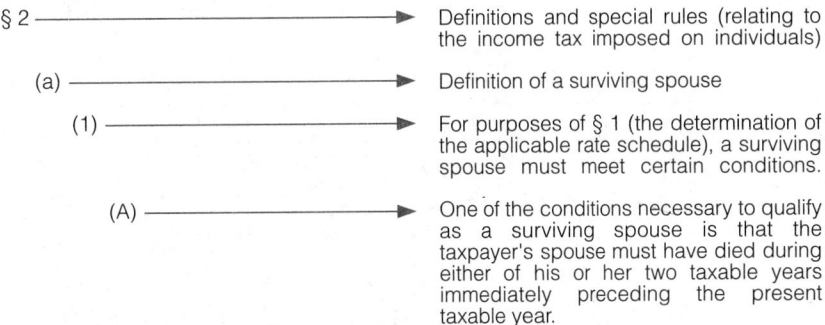

Throughout the remainder of the text, references to the Code Sections are in the form given above. The symbols "§" and "§§" are used in place of "Section" and "Sections." Unless otherwise stated, all Code references are to the Internal Revenue Code of 1986. The following table summarizes the format that will be used:

Complete Reference	Text Reference
Section 2(a)(1)(A) of the Internal Revenue Code of 1986	§ 2(a)(1)(A)
Sections 1 and 2 of the Internal Revenue Code of 1986	§§ 1 and 2
Section 2 of the Internal Revenue Code of 1954	§ 2 of the Internal Revenue Code of 1954
Section 12(d) of the Internal Revenue Code of 1939[7]	§ 12(d) of the Internal Revenue Code of 1939

Effect of Treaties. The United States signs certain tax treaties (sometimes called tax conventions) with foreign countries to render mutual assistance in tax enforcement and to avoid double taxation. The Technical and Miscellaneous Revenue Act of 1988 provided that neither a tax law nor a tax treaty takes general precedence. Thus, when there is a direct conflict, the most recent item will take precedence. A taxpayer must disclose on the tax return any position where a treaty overrides a tax law.[8] There is a $1,000 penalty per failure to disclose for individuals and a $10,000 per failure penalty for corporations.[9]

ADMINISTRATIVE SOURCES OF THE TAX LAW

The administrative sources of the Federal tax law can be grouped as follows: Treasury Department Regulations, Revenue Rulings and Revenue Procedures, and other administrative pronouncements (see Exhibit 2–1). All are issued by either the U.S. Treasury Department or one of its instrumentalities (e.g., the IRS or a District Director).

[7] § 12(d) of the Internal Revenue Code of 1939 is the predecessor to § 2 of the Internal Revenue Code of 1954 and the Internal Revenue Code of 1986. Keep in mind that the 1954 Code superseded the 1939 Code and the 1986 Code has superseded the 1954 Code. Footnote 1 of this chapter explains why references to the 1939 or 1954 code are included.

[8] § 7852(d).

[9] Reg. §§ 301.6114–1 and 301.6712–1.

▼ EXHIBIT 2–1
Administrative Sources

Source	Location	Authority**
Regulations	*Federal Register**	Force and effect of law.
Temporary Regulations	*Federal Register** *Internal Revenue Bulletin* *Cumulative Bulletin*	May be cited as a precedent.
Proposed Regulations	*Federal Register** *Internal Revenue Bulletin* *Cumulative Bulletin*	Preview of final Regulations.
Revenue Rulings Revenue Procedures Action on Decision	*Internal Revenue Bulletin* *Cumulative Bulletin*	Do not have the force and effect of law.
General Counsel's Memoranda Technical Advice Memoranda	*Tax Analysts' Tax Notes;* RIA's *Internal Memoranda of the IRS;* CCH's *IRS Position Reporter*	May not be cited as a precedent.
Letter Rulings	Research Institute of America and Commerce Clearing House looseleaf services	Applicable only to taxpayer addressed. No precedential force.

*Finalized, Temporary, and Proposed Regulations are published in soft-cover form by several publishers.
**Each of these sources may be substantial authority for purposes of the accuracy-related penalty in § 6662. Notice 90–20, 1990–1 C.B. 328.

Treasury Department Regulations. Regulations are issued by the U.S. Treasury Department under authority granted by Congress.[10] Interpretive by nature, they provide taxpayers with considerable guidance on the meaning and application of the Code. Regulations may be issued in *proposed, temporary,* or *final* form. Regulations carry considerable weight and are an important factor to consider in complying with the tax law.

Since Regulations interpret the Code, they are arranged in the same sequence as the Code. A number is added at the beginning, however, to indicate the type of tax or administrative, procedural, or definitional matter to which they relate. For example, the prefix 1 designates the Regulations under the income tax law. Thus, the Regulations under Code § 2 are cited as Reg. § 1.2 with subparts added for further identification. The numbers of these subparts often do not correspond to the numbers of the Code subsections. The prefix 20 designates estate tax Regulations; 25 covers gift tax Regulations; 31 relates to employment taxes; and 301 refers to procedure and administration. This list is not all-inclusive.

New Regulations and changes to existing Regulations are usually issued in proposed form before they are finalized. The interval between the proposal of a Regulation and its finalization permits taxpayers and other interested parties to comment on the propriety of the proposal. **Proposed Regulations** under Code § 2, for example, are cited as Prop.Reg. § 1.2. The Tax Court indicates that Proposed Regulations carry no more weight than a position advanced in a written brief

[10] § 7805.

prepared by a litigating party before the Tax Court. **Finalized Regulations** have the force and effect of law.[11]

Sometimes the Treasury Department issues **Temporary Regulations** relating to elections and other matters where speed is important. These Regulations are issued without the comment period required for Proposed Regulations. Temporary Regulations have the same authoritative value as final Regulations and may be cited as precedents. Temporary Regulations must now also be issued as Proposed Regulations and automatically expire within three years after the date of issuance.[12] Temporary Regulations and the simultaneously issued Proposed Regulations carry more weight than traditional Proposed Regulations. An example of a Temporary Regulation is Temp.Reg. § 1.417(e)–1T(d), which contains provisions for determining the present value of an employee's benefits under a defined benefit retirement plan.

Proposed, Temporary, and final Regulations are published in the *Federal Register* and are reproduced in major tax services. Final Regulations are issued as Treasury Decisions (TDs).

Regulations may also be classified as *legislative, interpretive,* or *procedural.* This classification scheme is discussed under Assessing the Validity of a Treasury Regulation later in the chapter.

Revenue Rulings and Revenue Procedures. **Revenue Rulings** are official pronouncements of the National Office of the IRS.[13] Like Regulations, they are designed to provide interpretation of the tax law. However, they do not carry the same legal force and effect as Regulations and usually deal with more restricted problems. In addition, Regulations are approved by the Secretary of the Treasury, whereas Revenue Rulings are not. Both Revenue Rulings and Revenue Procedures serve an important function by providing *guidance* to IRS personnel and taxpayers in routine tax matters. Revenue Rulings and Revenue Procedures generally apply retroactively and may be revoked or modified by subsequent rulings or procedures, Regulations, legislation, or court decisions.

Although letter rulings (discussed below) are not the same as Revenue Rulings, a Revenue Ruling often results from a specific taxpayer's request for a letter ruling. If the IRS believes that a taxpayer's request for a letter ruling deserves official publication because of its widespread impact, the holding will be converted into a Revenue Ruling and issued for the information and guidance of taxpayers, tax practitioners, and IRS personnel. Names, identifying descriptions, and money amounts are changed to disguise the identity of the taxpayer. In addition to resulting from taxpayer requests, Revenue Rulings arise from technical advice to District Offices of the IRS, court decisions, suggestions from tax practitioner groups, and various tax publications.

Revenue Procedures are issued in the same manner as Revenue Rulings, but deal with the internal management practices and procedures of the IRS. Familiarity with these procedures can increase taxpayer compliance and help the IRS administer the tax laws efficiently. A taxpayer's failure to follow a Revenue Procedure can result in unnecessary delay or cause the IRS to decline to act in a discretionary situation on behalf of the taxpayer.

---

[11] *F. W. Woolworth Co.,* 54 T.C. 1233 (1970); *Harris M. Miller,* 70 T.C. 448 (1978); and *James O. Tomerlin Trust,* 87 T.C. 876 (1986).

[12] § 7805(e).

[13] § 7805(a).

Revenue Rulings and Revenue Procedures are published weekly by the U.S. Government in the *Internal Revenue Bulletin* (I.R.B.). Semiannually, the bulletins for a six-month period are gathered together, reorganized by Code Section classification, and published in a bound volume called the *Cumulative Bulletin* (C.B.).[14] The proper form for citing Revenue Rulings and Revenue Procedures depends on whether the item has been published in the *Cumulative Bulletin* or is only available in I.R.B. form. Consider, for example, the following transition:

Temporary Citation	Rev.Rul. 95–3, I.R.B. No. 2, 8. *Explanation:* Revenue Ruling Number 3, appearing on page 8 of the 2nd weekly issue of the *Internal Revenue Bulletin* for 1995.
Permanent Citation	Rev.Rul. 95–3, 1995–1 C.B. 160. *Explanation:* Revenue Ruling Number 3, appearing on page 160 of Volume 1 of the *Cumulative Bulletin* for 1995.

Since the first volume of the 1995 *Cumulative Bulletin* was not published until December of 1995, the I.R.B. citation had to be used until that time. After the publication of the *Cumulative Bulletin*, the C.B. citation is proper. The basic portion of both citations (Rev.Rul. 95–3) indicates that this document was the 3rd Revenue Ruling issued by the IRS during 1995.

Revenue Procedures are cited in the same manner, except that "Rev.Proc." is substituted for "Rev.Rul." Some recent Revenue Procedures had the following effects:

- Announced deduction limits for cars placed in service during the year.
- Announced increases in the price of tax return copies.
- Provided a safe harbor that may be used to determine a majority of interest for a limited partnership.

Letter Rulings. Individual **(letter) rulings** are issued upon a taxpayer's request for a fee and describe how the IRS will treat a proposed transaction for tax purposes. They apply only to the taxpayer who asks for and obtains the ruling, but post-1984 letter rulings may be substantial authority for purposes of the accuracy-related penalty.[15] Though this procedure may sound like the only real way to carry out effective tax planning, the IRS limits the issuance of individual rulings to restricted, preannounced areas of taxation. The main reason the IRS will not rule in certain areas is that they involve fact-oriented situations. Thus, a ruling may not be obtained on many of the problems that are particularly troublesome for taxpayers.[16]

The law now requires the IRS to make individual rulings available for public inspection after identifying details are deleted.[17] Published digests of private letter rulings can be found in *Private Letter Rulings* (published by RIA), BNA *Daily Tax*

[14] Usually, only two volumes of the *Cumulative Bulletin* are published each year. However, when Congress has enacted major tax legislation, other volumes may be published containing the congressional Committee Reports supporting the Revenue Act. See, for example, the two extra volumes for 1984 dealing with the Deficit Reduction Act of 1984. The 1984–3 *Cumulative Bulletin,* Volume 1, contains the text of the law itself; 1984–3, Volume 2, contains the Committee Reports. There are a total of four volumes of the *Cumulative Bulletin* for 1984: 1984–1; 1984–2; 1984–3, Volume 1; 1984–3, Volume 2.

[15] Notice 90–20, 1990–1 C.B. 328. In this regard, letter rulings differ from Revenue Rulings, which are applicable to *all* taxpayers. Letter rulings may later lead to the issuance of a Revenue Ruling if the holding involved affects many taxpayers. In its Agents' Manual, the IRS indicates that letter rulings may be used as a guide with other research materials in formulating a District Office position on an issue. The IRS is required to charge a taxpayer a fee for letter rulings, determination letters, etc.

[16] Rev.Proc. 96–3, I.R.B. No. 1, 82 contains a list of areas in which the IRS will not issue advance rulings. From time to time, subsequent Revenue Procedures are issued that modify or amplify Rev.Proc. 96–3.

[17] § 6110.

Reports, and Tax Analysts & Advocates *Tax Notes. IRS Letter Rulings Reports* (published by Commerce Clearing House) contains both digests and full texts of all letter rulings. *Letter Ruling Review* (published by Tax Analysts) is a monthly publication that selects and discusses the more important of the approximately 300 letter rulings issued each month.

Letter rulings receive multidigit file numbers, which indicate the year and week of issuance as well as the number of the ruling during that week. Consider, for example, Ltr.Rul. 9532019, which deals with the employee status of inmates working in prison industries:

95	32	019
Year 1995	32nd week of issuance	Number of the ruling issued during the 32nd week

Other Administrative Pronouncements. *Treasury Decisions* (TDs) are issued by the Treasury Department to promulgate new Regulations, amend or otherwise change existing Regulations, or announce the position of the Government on selected court decisions. Like Revenue Rulings and Revenue Procedures, TDs are published in the *Internal Revenue Bulletin* and subsequently transferred to the *Cumulative Bulletin.*

The IRS publishes other administrative communications in the *Internal Revenue Bulletin* such as Announcements, Notices, LRs (Proposed Regulations), and Prohibited Transaction Exemptions.

Like letter rulings, **determination letters** are issued at the request of taxpayers and provide guidance on the application of the tax law. They differ from letter rulings in that the issuing source is the District Director rather than the National Office of the IRS. Also, determination letters usually involve completed (as opposed to proposed) transactions. Determination letters are not published and are made known only to the party making the request.

The following examples illustrate the distinction between letter rulings and determination letters:

EXAMPLE 1

The shareholders of Red Corporation and Green Corporation want assurance that the consolidation of the corporations into Blue Corporation will be a nontaxable reorganization. The proper approach would be to request the National Office of the IRS to issue a letter ruling concerning the income tax effect of the proposed transaction. ▼

EXAMPLE 2

Chris operates a barber shop in which he employs eight barbers. To comply with the rules governing income tax and payroll tax withholdings, Chris wants to know whether the barbers working for him are employees or independent contractors. The proper procedure would be to request a determination letter on their status from the appropriate District Director. ▼

The National Office of the IRS releases **Technical Advice Memoranda (TAMs)** weekly. Although TAMs and letter rulings both give the IRS's determination of an issue, they differ in several respects. Letter rulings deal with proposed transactions and are issued to taxpayers at their request. In contrast, TAMs deal with completed transactions and are often requested in relation to exempt organizations and employee plans. Futhermore, TAMs arise from questions raised by IRS personnel during audits and are issued by the National Office of the IRS to its field personnel rather than to taxpayers. TAMs are not officially published and may not be cited or used as precedent.[18] They are assigned file numbers according to the same procedure used for letter rulings. For example, TAM 9509001 refers to the 1st TAM issued during the 9th week of 1995.

Several internal memoranda that constitute the working law of the IRS now must be released. These General Counsel Memoranda (GCMs) and Technical Advice Memoranda (TAMs) are not officially published, and the IRS indicates that they may not be cited as precedents by taxpayers.[19] However, these working documents do explain the IRS's position on various issues.

ETHICAL CONSIDERATIONS

The Cost of Tax Compliance

Arthur P. Hall of the Tax Foundation points out that since 1954 the income tax code has grown from 103 sections to 698 and is now about four inches thick. An additional nine inches of Treasury Regulations explain these four inches of tax law.

Shirley Petersen, former IRS Commissioner, tells of one multinational corporation that had to file a 21,000-page tax return in 30 volumes. "They had to use a truck to deliver it to the IRS," Petersen says.

Dr. Hall continues, "Because of complexity and instability taxpayers cannot be certain about how taxation will affect a business plan or investment. At least 70 percent of the total cost of Federal tax compliance is due to the income tax, indicating that businesses paid an estimated $92.5 billion in 1994 to comply with the Federal tax."

Is it equitable that taxpayers must bear such large compliance costs in order to calculate and pay their income taxes?

JUDICIAL SOURCES OF THE TAX LAW

The Judicial Process in General. After a taxpayer has exhausted some or all of the remedies available within the IRS (i.e., no satisfactory settlement has been reached at the agent or at the Appeals Division level), the dispute can be taken to the Federal courts. The dispute is first considered by a **court of original jurisdiction** (known as a trial court) with any appeal (either by the taxpayer or the IRS) taken to the appropriate appellate court. In most situations, the taxpayer has a choice of any of *four trial courts:* a **Federal District Court,** the **U.S. Court of Federal Claims,** the **U.S. Tax Court,** or the **Small Cases Division** of the U.S. Tax Court. The trial and appellate court scheme for Federal tax litigation is illustrated in Figure 2–1.

The broken line between the U.S. Tax Court and the Small Cases Division indicates that there is no appeal from the Small Cases Division. The jurisdiction of the Small Cases Division is limited to cases involving amounts of $10,000 or less. The proceedings of the Small Cases Division are informal (e.g., no necessity for the taxpayer to be represented by a lawyer or other tax adviser). Special trial judges rather than Tax Court judges preside over these proceedings. The decisions of the Small Cases Division are not precedents for any other court decision and are not

[18] § 6110(j)(3). Post-1984 TAMs may be substantial authority for purposes of avoiding the accuracy-related penalty. Notice 90–20, 1990–1 C.B. 328.

[19] These are unofficially published by the publishers listed in Exhibit 2–1. Such internal memoranda for post-1984 may be substantial authority for purposes of the accuracy-related penalty. Notice 90–20, 1990–1 C.B. 328.

▼ **FIGURE 2–1**
Federal Judicial System

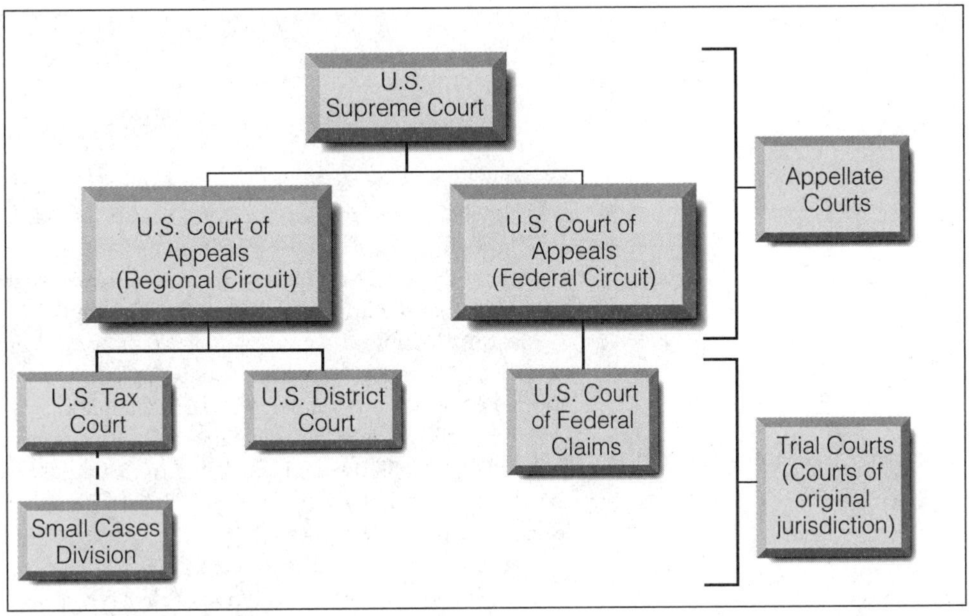

reviewable by any higher court. Proceedings can be more timely and less expensive in the Small Cases Division.

American law, following English law, is frequently *made* by judicial decisions. Under the doctrine of *stare decisis,* each case (except in the Small Cases Division) has precedential value for future cases with the same controlling set of facts. Most Federal and state appellate court decisions and some decisions of trial courts are published. More than 4 million judicial opinions have been published in the United States; over 130,000 cases are published each year.[20] Published court decisions are organized by jurisdiction (Federal or state) and level of court (trial or appellate).

A decision of a particular court is called its holding. Sometimes a decision includes dicta or incidental opinions beyond the current facts. Such passing remarks, illustrations, or analogies are not essential to the current holding. Although the holding has precedential value under *stare decisis,* dicta are not binding on a future court.

Trial Courts. The various trial courts (courts of original jurisdiction) differ in several respects:

- *Number of courts.* There is only one Court of Federal Claims and only one Tax Court, but there are many Federal District Courts. The taxpayer does not select the District Court that will hear the dispute but must sue in the one that has jurisdiction.
- *Number of judges.* Each District Court has only 1 judge, the Court of Federal Claims has 16 judges, and the Tax Court has 19 regular judges. The entire Tax Court, however, will review a case (the case is sent to court conference)

[20] Jacobstein, Mersky, and Dunn, *Fundamentals of Legal Research,* 6th ed. (Westbury, N.Y.: The Foundation Press, 1994), p. 11.

TAX IN THE NEWS

THE DOCTRINE OF *STARE DECISIS*: BASEBALL NEVER STRIKES OUT

The high court could not have cared less about the accused. The sole issue in this obscure case—stick with me—was whether the court should adhere to the doctrine of *stare decisis*. The doctrine pays great respect to precedent. It teaches, in the words of Justice Brandeis long ago, that in most matters "it is more important that the applicable rule of law be settled than that it be settled right."

Most of the time the court stands by its former decisions, even when they're terrible decisions. In the most eye-popping example of *stare decisis* gone amok, the Supreme Court has resolutely refused to abandon its incredible decision in 1922 that professional baseball is not subject to antitrust laws. Many developments have intervened. In 1955 the court held that professional boxing was subject to the law; that same year it held that traveling theater troupes are subject to the law; in 1957 it held that pro football is subject to the law; in 1971 it held that pro basketball is subject to the law.

But the court, citing the doctrine of *stare decisis*, again and again has refused to overrule its absurd opinion of 1922 that baseball is not subject to antitrust laws. Justice Harry Blackmun, writing for the court in *Flood v. Kuhn* in 1972, agreed that the situation is inconsistent and illogical, but if the long-standing aberration is to be corrected, he said, the remedy lies not with the court, but with Congress.

I like that approach to jurisprudence. *Stare decisis* is a sound doctrine. But the antitrust exemption for baseball boggles the mind. The 1922 decision, to borrow from Justice Scalia, is a weed that cries out for uprooting.

SOURCE: Taken from the Covering the Courts column by James J. Kilpatrick

only when more important or novel tax issues are involved. Most cases will be heard and decided by one of the 19 judges.

- *Location.* The Court of Federal Claims meets most often in Washington, D.C., whereas a District Court meets at a prescribed seat for the particular district. Each state has at least one District Court, and many of the more populous states have more than one. Therefore, the inconvenience and expense of traveling for the taxpayer and his or her counsel (present with many suits in the Court of Federal Claims) are largely eliminated. Although the Tax Court is officially based in Washington, D.C., the various judges travel to different parts of the country and hear cases at predetermined locations and dates. Although this procedure eases the distance problem for the taxpayer, it may mean a delay before the case comes to trial and is decided.
- *Jurisdiction of the Court of Federal Claims.* The Court of Federal Claims has jurisdiction over any claim against the United States that is based upon the Constitution, any Act of Congress, or any regulation of an executive department. Thus, the Court of Federal Claims hears nontax litigation as well as tax cases. This forum appears to be more favorable for issues having an equitable or pro-business orientation (as opposed to purely technical issues) and for those requiring extensive discovery.[21]

[21] T. D. Peyser, "The Case for Selecting the Claims Court to Litigate a Federal Tax Liability," *The Tax Executive* (Winter 1988): 149.

- *Jurisdiction of the Tax Court and District Courts.* The Tax Court hears only tax cases and is the most popular forum. The District Courts hear nontax litigation as well as tax cases. Some Tax Court justices have been appointed from IRS or Treasury Department positions. For these reasons, some people suggest that the Tax Court has more expertise in tax matters.
- *Jury trial.* The only court in which a taxpayer can obtain a jury trial is a District Court. But since juries can only decide questions of fact and not questions of law, even taxpayers who choose the District Court route often do not request a jury trial. In that event, the judge will decide all issues. Note that a District Court decision is controlling only in the district in which the court has jurisdiction.
- *Payment of deficiency.* For the Court of Federal Claims or a District Court to have jurisdiction, the taxpayer must pay the tax deficiency assessed by the IRS and sue for a refund. A taxpayer who wins (assuming no successful appeal by the Government) recovers the tax paid plus appropriate interest. For the Tax Court, however, jurisdiction is usually obtained without first paying the assessed tax deficiency. In the event the taxpayer loses in the Tax Court (and does not appeal or an appeal is unsuccessful), the deficiency must be paid with appropriate interest. With the elimination of the deduction for personal (consumer) interest, the Tax Court route of delaying payment of the deficiency can become expensive. For example, to earn 11 percent after tax, a taxpayer with a 39.6 percent marginal tax rate would have to earn 18.2 percent. By paying the tax, a taxpayer limits underpayment interest and penalties on the underpayment.
- *Termination of running of interest.* A taxpayer who selects the Tax Court may deposit a cash bond to stop the running of interest. The taxpayer must deposit both the amount of the tax and any accrued interest. If the taxpayer wins and the deposited amount is returned, the Government does not pay interest on the deposit.
- *Appeals.* Appeals from a District Court or a Tax Court decision are to the appropriate U.S. Court of Appeals. Appeals from the Court of Federal Claims go to the Court of Appeals for the Federal Circuit.
- *Bankruptcy.* When a taxpayer files a bankruptcy petition, the IRS, like other creditors, is prevented from taking action against the taxpayer. Sometimes a bankruptcy court may settle a tax claim.

Appellate Courts. The losing party can appeal a trial court decision to a **Circuit Court of Appeals.** The 11 geographical circuits, the circuit for the District of Columbia, and the Federal Circuit[22] appear in Figure 2–2. The appropriate circuit for an appeal depends upon where the litigation originated. For example, an appeal from New York goes to the Second Circuit.

If the Government loses at the trial court level (District Court, Tax Court, or Court of Federal Claims), it need not (frequently does not) appeal. The fact that an appeal is not made, however, does not indicate that the IRS agrees with the result and will not litigate similar issues in the future. The IRS may decide not to appeal for a number of reasons. First, the current litigation load may be heavy, and as a consequence, the IRS may decide that available personnel should be assigned to other, more important cases. Second, the IRS may determine that this is not a good

[22] The Court of Appeals for the Federal Circuit was created, effective October 1, 1982, by P.L. 97–164 (4/2/82) to hear decisions appealed from the Claims Court (now the Court of Federal Claims).

CONCEPT SUMMARY 2–1

Federal Judicial System: Trial Courts

Issue	U.S. Tax Court	U.S. District Court	U.S. Court of Federal Claims
Number of judges per court	19*	1	16
Payment of deficiency before trial	No	Yes	Yes
Jury trial available	No	Yes	No
Types of disputes	Tax cases only	Most criminal and civil issues	Claims against the United States
Jurisdiction	Nationwide	Location of taxpayer	Nationwide
IRS acquiescence policy	Yes	Yes	Yes
Appeal route	U.S. Court of Appeals	U.S. Court of Appeals	U.S. Court of Appeals for the Federal Circuit

*There are also 14 special trial judges and 9 senior judges.

case to appeal. Perhaps the taxpayer is in a sympathetic position or the facts are particularly strong in his or her favor. In that event, the IRS may wait to test the legal issues involved with a taxpayer who has a much weaker case. Third, if the appeal is from a District Court or the Tax Court, the Court of Appeals of jurisdiction could have some bearing on whether the IRS chooses to go forward with an appeal. Based on past experience and precedent, the IRS may conclude that the chance for success on a particular issue might be more promising in another Court of Appeals. If so, the IRS will wait for a similar case to arise in a different jurisdiction.

ETHICAL CONSIDERATIONS

Choosing Cases for Appeal

The U.S. Government loses a tax case against a prominent citizen in the U.S. District Court of Iowa. The taxpayer, a minister, had set up three separate trusts for each of his three children (i.e., a total of nine trusts). The Government argued that under Reg. § 1.641(a)–0(c) these trusts should be consolidated and treated as three trusts to stop the taxpayer from mitigating the progressive tax structure (e.g., 39.6 percent top tax bracket).

The IRS has decided to appeal a case in this multiple trust area. As one of the attorneys for the Government, you must choose between the Iowa case and a similar multiple trust conflict in the U.S. District Court of Virginia. Here the taxpayer is a CPA who has established four separate trusts for her two children (i.e., a total of eight trusts). See *Estelle Morris Trusts,*

▼ FIGURE 2-2
The Federal Courts of Appeals

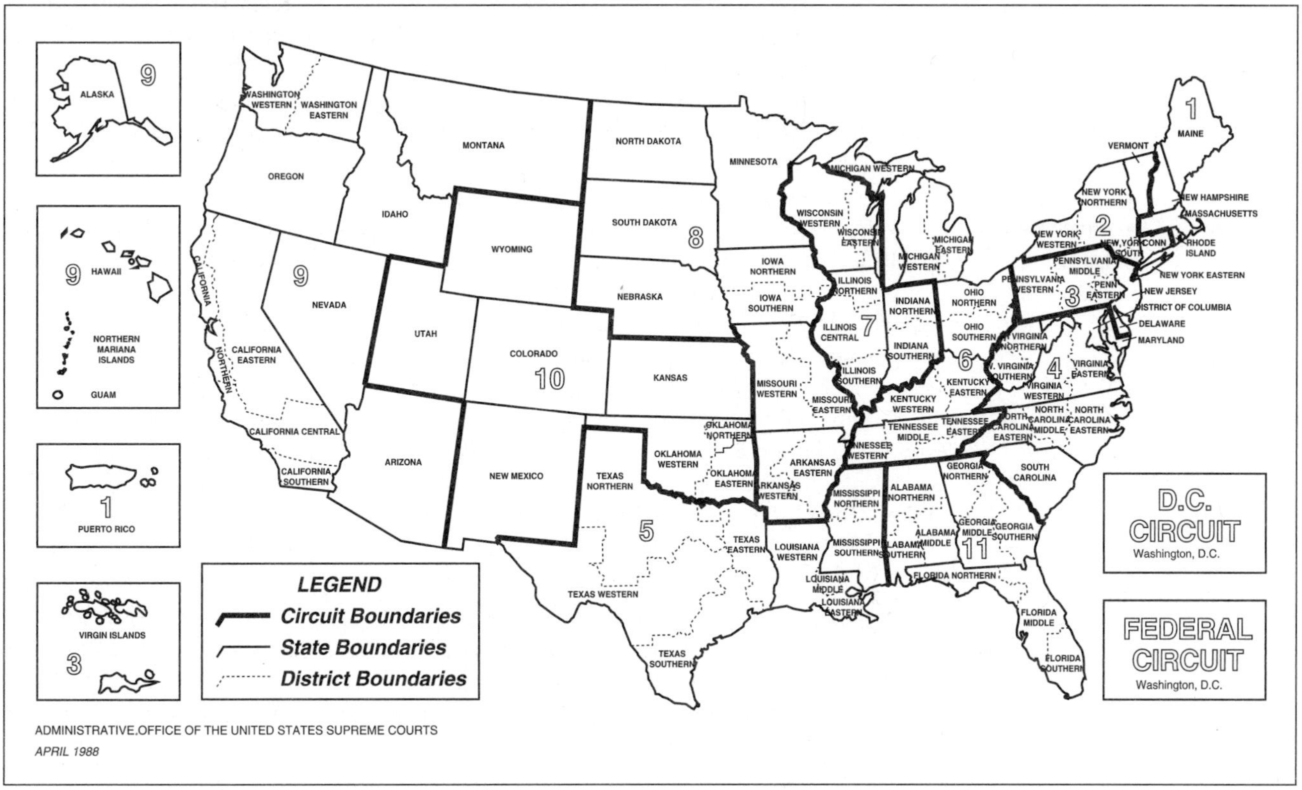

51 T.C. 20 (1968). Factors you are considering are the potential sympathy associated with the minister's profession and a lack thereof associated with the CPA, the facts indicating that the attempt at tax avoidance is more egregious in the Iowa case, and a colleague's opinion that the Virginia case is winnable. Which case will you select? Comment on the fairness of the Government's ability and willingness to select a case to appeal in this fashion.

With the establishment of the Federal Circuit at the appellate level, a taxpayer has an alternative forum to the Court of Appeals of his or her home circuit for the appeal. Appeals from both the Tax Court and the District Court go to a taxpayer's home circuit. Now, when a particular circuit has issued an adverse decision, the taxpayer may wish to select the Court of Federal Claims route, since any appeal will be to the Federal Circuit.

District Courts, the Tax Court, and the Court of Federal Claims must abide by the **precedents** set by the Court of Appeals of jurisdiction. A particular Court of Appeals need not follow the decisions of another Court of Appeals. All courts, however, must follow the decisions of the **U.S. Supreme Court.**

Because the Tax Court is a national court (it hears and decides cases from all parts of the country), the observation made in the previous paragraph has caused problems. For many years, the Tax Court followed a policy of deciding cases based on what it thought the result should be, even though its decision might be appealed to a Court of Appeals that had previously decided a similar case differently. A number of years ago this policy was changed in the *Golsen*[23] decision. Now the Tax Court will decide a case as it feels the law should be applied *only* if the Court of Appeals of appropriate jurisdiction has not yet passed on the issue or has previously decided a similar case in accord with the Tax Court's decision. If the Court of Appeals of appropriate jurisdiction has previously held otherwise, the Tax Court will conform under the *Golsen* rule even though it disagrees with the holding.

EXAMPLE 3

Emily lives in Texas and sues in the Tax Court on Issue A. The Fifth Court of Appeals is the appellate court of appropriate jurisdiction. The Fifth Court of Appeals has already decided, in a case involving similar facts but a different taxpayer, that Issue A should be resolved against the Government. Although the Tax Court feels that the Fifth Court of Appeals is wrong, under its *Golsen* policy it will render judgment for Emily. Shortly thereafter, Rashad, a resident of New York, in a comparable case, sues in the Tax Court on Issue A. Assume that the Second Court of Appeals, the appellate court of appropriate jurisdiction, has never expressed itself on Issue A. Presuming the Tax Court has not reconsidered its position on Issue A, it will decide against Rashad. Thus, it is entirely possible for two taxpayers suing in the same court to end up with opposite results merely because they live in different parts of the country. ▼

Appeal to the U.S. Supreme Court is by **Writ of Certiorari.** If the Court accepts jurisdiction, it will grant the Writ (*Cert. Granted*). Most often, it will deny jurisdiction (*Cert. Denied*). For whatever reason or reasons, the Supreme Court rarely hears tax cases. The Court usually grants certiorari to resolve a conflict among the Courts of Appeals (e.g., two or more appellate courts have assumed opposing positions on a particular issue) or where the tax issue is extremely important. The granting of a Writ of Certiorari indicates that at least four members of the Supreme Court believe that the issue is of sufficient importance to be heard by the full Court.

The *role* of appellate courts is limited to a review of the record of trial compiled by the trial courts. Thus, the appellate process usually involves a determination of whether the trial court applied the proper law in arriving at its decision. Rarely will an appellate court disturb a lower court's fact-finding determination.

Both the Code and the Supreme Court indicate that Federal appellate courts are bound by findings of facts unless they are clearly erroneous.[24] This aspect of the appellate process is illustrated by a decision of the Court of Appeals for the District of Columbia involving whether a taxpayer was engaged in an activity for profit under § 183.[25] This appeals court specifically held that the "Tax Court's findings of facts are binding on Federal courts of appeals unless clearly erroneous." The Court applauded the Tax Court for the thoroughness of its factual inquiry but could "not place the stamp of approval upon its eventual legal outcome." In reversing and remanding the decision to the Tax Court, the appellate court said that "the language of § 183, its legislative history and the applicable Treasury regulation combine to demonstrate that the court's [Tax Court's] standard is erroneous as a matter of law." The appeals court held that this taxpayer's claims of deductibility were to be evaluated by proper legal standards.

---

[23] *Jack E. Golsen*, 54 T.C. 742 (1970).

[24] §§ 7482(a) and (c). *Comm. v. Duberstein*, 60–2 USTC ¶9515, 5 AFTR2d 1626, 80 S.Ct. 1190 (USSC, 1960). See Rule 52(a) of the Federal Rules of Civil Procedure.

[25] *Dreicer v. Comm.*, 81–2 USTC ¶9683, 48 AFTR2d 5884, 665 F.2d 1292 (CA–DC, 1981).

An appeal can have any of a number of possible outcomes. The appellate court could approve (affirm) or disapprove (reverse) the lower court's finding, or it could send the case back for further consideration (remand). When many issues are involved, a mixed result is not unusual. Thus, the lower court could be affirmed (*aff'd*) on Issue A and reversed (*rev'd*) on Issue B, while Issue C is remanded (*rem'd*) for additional fact finding.

When more than one judge is involved in the decision-making process, disagreements are not uncommon. In addition to the majority view, one or more judges may concur (agree with the result reached but not with some or all of the reasoning) or dissent (disagree with the result). In any one case, of course, the majority view controls. But concurring and dissenting views can have an influence on other courts or, at some subsequent date when the composition of the court has changed, even on the same court.

Knowledge of several terms is important in understanding court decisions. The term *plaintiff* refers to the party requesting action in a court, and the *defendant* is the party against whom the suit is brought. Sometimes a court uses the terms *petitioner* and *respondent.* In general, "petitioner" is a synonym for "plaintiff," and "respondent" is a synonym for "defendant." At the trial court level, a taxpayer is normally the plaintiff (or petitioner), and the Government is the defendant (or respondent). If the taxpayer wins and the Government appeals as the new petitioner (or appellant), the taxpayer becomes the new respondent.

2 LEARNING OBJECTIVE
Locate and work with the appropriate tax law sources.

Judicial Citations—General. Having concluded a brief description of the judicial process, it is appropriate to consider the more practical problem of the relationship of case law to tax research. As previously noted, court decisions are an important source of tax law. The ability to cite and locate a case is, therefore, a must in working with the tax law. Judicial citations usually follow a standard pattern: case name, volume number, reporter series, page or paragraph number, and court (where necessary).

Judicial Citations—The U.S. Tax Court. A good starting point is with the Tax Court. The Tax Court issues two types of decisions: Regular and Memorandum. The Chief Judge decides whether the opinion is issued as a Regular or Memorandum decision. The distinction between the two involves both substance and form. In terms of substance, *Memorandum* decisions deal with situations necessitating only the application of already established principles of law. *Regular* decisions involve novel issues not previously resolved by the Court. In actual practice, however, this distinction is not always preserved. Not infrequently, Memorandum decisions will be encountered that appear to warrant Regular status and vice versa. At any rate, do not conclude that Memorandum decisions possess no value as precedents. Both represent the position of the Tax Court and, as such, can be relied upon.

The Regular and Memorandum decisions issued by the Tax Court also differ in form. Memorandum decisions are officially published in mimeograph form only. Regular decisions are published by the U.S. Government in a series entitled *Tax Court of the United States Reports.* Each volume of these *Reports* covers a six-month period (January 1 through June 30 and July 1 through December 31) and is given a succeeding volume number. But, as was true of the *Cumulative Bulletin,* there is usually a time lag between the date a decision is rendered and the date it appears in bound form. A temporary citation might be necessary to aid the researcher in locating a recent Regular decision. Consider, for example, the temporary and permanent citations for *Glen E. Miller,* a decision filed on March 29, 1995:

Temporary Citation	*Glen E. Miller,* 104 T.C. ___, No. 18 (1995). *Explanation:* Page number left blank because not yet known.
Permanent Citation	*Glen E. Miller,* 104 T.C. 378 (1995). *Explanation:* Page number now available.

Both citations tell us that the case will ultimately appear in Volume 104 of the *Tax Court of the United States Reports.* But until this volume is bound and made available to the general public, the page number must be left blank. Instead, the temporary citation identifies the case as being the 18th Regular decision issued by the Tax Court since Volume 103 ended. With this information, the decision can easily be located in either of the special Tax Court services published by Commerce Clearing House (recently acquired by the Dutch company Wolter Klower) or Research Institute of America (formerly by Prentice-Hall). Once Volume 104 is released, the permanent citation can be substituted and the number of the case dropped.

Before 1943, the Tax Court was called the Board of Tax Appeals, and its decisions were published as the *United States Board of Tax Appeals Reports* (B.T.A.). These 47 volumes cover the period from 1924 to 1942. For example, the citation *Karl Pauli,* 11 B.T.A. 784 (1928) refers to the 11th volume of the *Board of Tax Appeals Reports,* page 784, issued in 1928.

If the IRS loses in a decision, it may indicate whether it agrees or disagrees with the results reached by the court by publishing an **acquiescence** ("A" or "Acq.") or **nonacquiescence** ("NA" or "Nonacq."), respectively. Until 1991, acquiescences and nonacquiescences were published only for certain Regular decisions of the Tax Court, but the IRS has expanded its acquiescence program to include other civil tax cases where guidance is helpful. The acquiescence or nonacquiescence is published in the *Internal Revenue Bulletin* and the *Cumulative Bulletin* as an *Action on Decision.* The IRS can retroactively revoke an acquiescence.

Most often the IRS issues nonacquiescences to adverse decisions that are not appealed. A nonacquiescence provides a warning to taxpayers that a similar case cannot be settled administratively. A taxpayer will incur fees and expenses appealing within the IRS even though the IRS may be unwilling to litigate a fact pattern similar to a nonacquiesce decision.[26]

Although Memorandum decisions are not published by the U.S. Government, they are published by Commerce Clearing House (CCH) and Research Institute of America (RIA [formerly by Prentice-Hall]). Consider, for example, the three different ways that *Jack D. Carr* can be cited:

Jack D. Carr, T.C.Memo. 1985–19
The 19th Memorandum decision issued by the Tax Court in 1985.

Jack D. Carr, 49 TCM 507
Page 507 of Vol. 49 of the CCH *Tax Court Memorandum Decisions.*

Jack D. Carr, RIA T.C.Mem.Dec. ¶85,019
Paragraph 85,019 of the RIA *T.C. Memorandum Decisions.*

Note that the third citation contains the same information as the first. Thus, ¶85,019 indicates the following information about the case: year 1985, 19th T.C. Memo. decision.[27] Although the RIA citation does not specifically include a volume number, the paragraph citation indicates that the decision can be found in the 1985 volume of the RIA Memorandum decision service.

[26] G. W. Carter, "Nonacquiescence: Winning by Losing," *Tax Notes* (September 19, 1988): 1301–1307.

[27] In this text, the RIA citation for Memorandum decisions of the U.S. Tax Court is omitted. Thus, *Jack D. Carr* would be cited as 49 TCM 507, T.C.Memo. 1985–19.

Judicial Citations—The U.S. District Court, Court of Federal Claims, and Courts of Appeals. District Court, Court of Federal Claims, Court of Appeals, and Supreme Court decisions dealing with Federal tax matters are reported in both the CCH *U.S. Tax Cases* (USTC), and the RIA *American Federal Tax Reports* (AFTR) series. Federal District Court decisions, dealing with *both* tax and nontax issues, also are published by West Publishing Company in its *Federal Supplement Series*. The following examples illustrate three different ways of citing a District Court case:

> *Simons-Eastern Co. v. U.S.*, 73–1 USTC ¶9279 (D.Ct.Ga., 1972).
>
> *Explanation:* Reported in the first volume of the *U.S. Tax Cases* (USTC) published by Commerce Clearing House for calendar year 1973 (73–1) and located at paragraph 9279 (¶9279).
>
> *Simons-Eastern Co. v. U.S.*, 31 AFTR2d 73–640 (D.Ct.Ga., 1972).
>
> *Explanation:* Reported in the 31st volume of the second series of the *American Federal Tax Reports* (AFTR2d) published by RIA and beginning on page 640. The "73" preceding the page number indicates the year the case was published but is a designation used only in recent decisions.
>
> *Simons-Eastern Co. v. U.S.*, 354 F.Supp. 1003 (D.Ct.Ga., 1972).
>
> *Explanation:* Reported in the 354th volume of the *Federal Supplement Series* (F.Supp.) published by West Publishing Company and beginning on page 1003.

In all of the preceding citations, note that the name of the case is the same (Simons-Eastern Co. being the taxpayer), as is the reference to the Federal District Court of Georgia (D.Ct.Ga.) and the year the decision was rendered (1972).[28]

Decisions of the Court of Federal Claims[29] and the Courts of Appeals are published in the USTCs, AFTRs, and a West Publishing Company reporter called the *Federal Second Series* (F.2d). Volume 999, published in 1993, is the last volume of the *Federal Second Series*. It is followed by the *Federal Third Series* (F.3d). Beginning with October 1982, the Court of Federal Claims decisions are published in another West Publishing Company reporter entitled the *Claims Court Reporter*. Beginning with Volume 27 on October 30, 1992, the name of the reporter changed to the *Federal Claims Reporter* (abbreviated as *Fed.Cl.*). The following examples illustrate the different forms:

Finkbohner, Jr. v. U.S., (CA-11, 1986)
86–1 USTC ¶9393 (CCH citation)
57 AFTR2d 86–1400 (RIA citation)
788 F.2d 723 (West citation)

Apollo Computer, Inc. v. U.S., (Fed.Cl., 1994)
95–1 USTC ¶50,015 (CCH citation)
74 AFTR2d 94–7172 (RIA citation)
32 Fed.Cl. 334 (West citation)

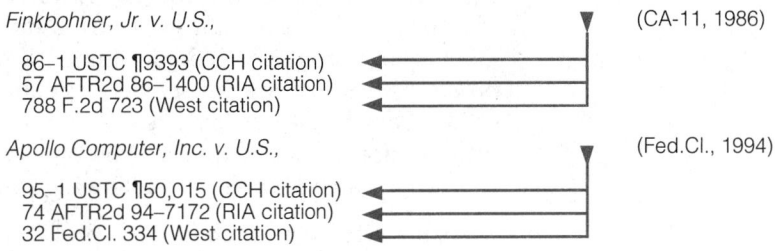

Note that *Finkbohner, Jr.* is a decision rendered by the Eleventh Court of Appeals in 1986 (CA–11, 1986), while *Apollo Computer, Inc.* was issued by the Court of Federal Claims in 1994 (Fed.Cl., 1994).

[28] In this text, the case would be cited in the following form: *Simons-Eastern Co. v. U.S.*, 73–1 USTC ¶9279, 31 AFTR2d 73–640, 354 F.Supp. 1003 (D.Ct.Ga., 1972). Prentice-Hall Information Services is now owned by Research Institute of America. Although recent volumes contain the RIA imprint, many of the older volumes continue to have the P-H imprint.

[29] Before October 29, 1992, the Court of Federal Claims was called the Claims Court. Before October 1, 1982, the Court of Federal Claims was called the Court of Claims.

Judicial Citations—The U.S. Supreme Court. Like all other Federal tax decisions (except those rendered by the Tax Court), Supreme Court decisions are published by Commerce Clearing House in the USTCs and by RIA (formerly by Prentice-Hall) in the AFTRs. The U.S. Government Printing Office also publishes these decisions in the *United States Supreme Court Reports* (U.S.) as does West Publishing Company in its *Supreme Court Reporter* (S.Ct.) and the Lawyer's Co-operative Publishing Company in its *United States Reports, Lawyer's Edition* (L.Ed.). The following illustrates the different ways the same decision can be cited:

U.S. v. The Donruss Co., (USSC, 1969)

69–1 USTC ¶9167 (CCH citation)
23 AFTR2d 69–418 (RIA citation)
89 S.Ct. 501 (West citation)
393 U.S. 297 (U.S. Government Printing Office citation)
21 L.Ed.2d 495 (Lawyer's Co-operative Publishing Co. citation)

The parenthetical reference (USSC, 1969) identifies the decision as having been rendered by the U.S. Supreme Court in 1969. In this text, the citations of Supreme Court decisions will be limited to the CCH (USTC), RIA (AFTR), and West (S.Ct.) versions. For a summary, see Concept Summary 2–2.

Working with the Tax Law— Tax Research

3 Learning Objective
Understand the tax research process.

Tax research is the method by which a tax practitioner, student, or professor determines the best available solution to a situation that possesses tax consequences. In other words, it is the process of finding a competent and professional conclusion to a tax problem. The problem may originate from completed or proposed transactions. In the case of a completed transaction, the objective of the research is to determine the tax result of what has already taken place. For example, was the expenditure incurred by the taxpayer deductible or not deductible for tax purposes? When dealing with proposed transactions, the tax research process is directed toward the determination of possible tax consequences. To the extent that tax research leads to a choice of alternatives or otherwise influences the future actions of the taxpayer, it becomes the key to effective tax planning.

Tax research involves the following procedures:

- Identifying and refining the problem.
- Locating the appropriate tax law sources.
- Assessing the validity of the tax law sources.
- Arriving at the solution or at alternative solutions with due consideration given to nontax factors.
- Effectively communicating the solution to the taxpayer or the taxpayer's representative.
- Following up on the solution (where appropriate) in light of new developments.

These procedures are diagrammed in Figure 2–3. The broken lines reflect the steps of particular interest when tax research is directed toward proposed, rather than completed, transactions.

CONCEPT SUMMARY 2–2

Judicial Sources

Court	Location	Authority
U.S. Supreme Court	S.Ct. Series (West) U.S. Series (U.S. Gov't.) L.Ed. (Lawyer's Co-op.) AFTR (RIA) USTC (CCH)	Highest authority
U.S. Courts of Appeal	Federal 3d (West) AFTR (RIA) USTC (CCH)	Next highest appellate court
Tax Court (Regular decisions)	U.S. Govt. Printing Office, RIA/CCH separate services	Highest trial court*
Tax Court (Memorandum decisions)	RIA T.C.Memo (RIA) TCM (CCH)	Less authority than regular T.C. decision
U.S. Court of Federal Claims**	Federal Claims Reporter (West) AFTR (RIA) USTC (CCH)	Similar authority as Tax Court
U.S. District Courts	F.Supp. Series (West) AFTR (RIA) USTC (CCH)	Lowest trial court
Small Cases Division of Tax Court	Not published	No precedent value

*Theoretically, the Tax Court, Court of Federal Claims, and District Courts are on the same level of authority. But some people believe that since the Tax Court hears and decides tax cases from all parts of the country (it is a national court), its decisions may be more authoritative than a Court of Federal Claims or District Court decision.
**Before October 29, 1992, the U.S. Claims Court.

IDENTIFYING THE PROBLEM

Problem identification must start with a compilation of the relevant facts involved.[30] In this regard, *all* of the facts that may have a bearing on the problem must be gathered because any omission could modify the solution to be reached. To illustrate, consider what appears to be a very simple problem.

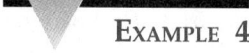

EXAMPLE 4 Early in December, Fred and Megan review their financial and tax situation with their son, Sam, and daughter-in-law, Dana. Fred and Megan are in the 28% tax bracket. Both Sam and Dana are age 21. Sam, a student at a nearby university, owns some publicly traded stock that he inherited from his grandmother. A current sale would result in approximately $7,000 of gross income. At this point, Fred and Megan provide about 55% of Sam and Dana's support. Although neither is now employed, Sam has earned $960 and Dana has earned $900. The problem: Should the stock be sold, and would the sale prohibit Fred and Megan from claiming Sam and Dana as dependents? ▼

[30] For an excellent discussion of the critical role of facts in carrying out tax research, see Ray M. Sommerfeld and G. Fred Streuling, *Tax Research Techniques*, Tax Study No. 5 (New York: The American Institute of Certified Public Accountants, 1981), Chapter 2.

▼ **FIGURE 2–3**
Tax Research Process

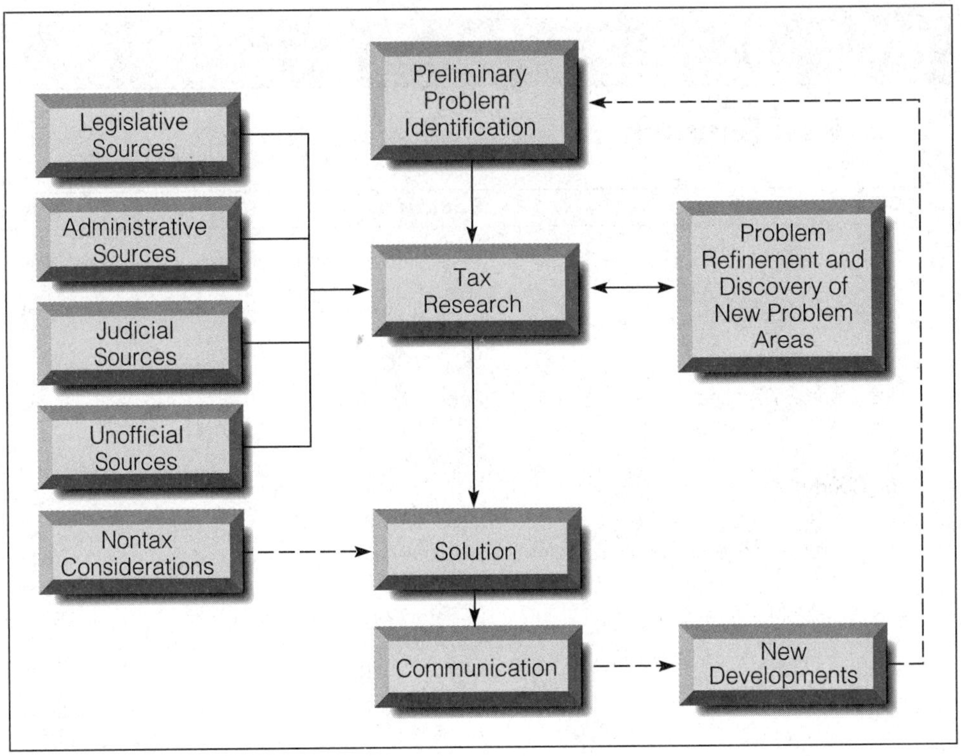

REFINING THE PROBLEM

Initial reaction is that Fred and Megan in Example 4 could *not* claim Sam and Dana as dependents if the stock is sold, since Sam would then have earned more than the exemption amount under § 151(d).[31] However, Sam is a full-time student, and § 151(c)(1)(B) allows a son or daughter who is a full-time student and is under age 24 to earn more than the exemption amount without penalizing the parents with the loss of the dependency exemption. Thus, Sam could sell the stock without penalizing the parents with respect to the gross income test. However, the $7,000 income from the sale of the stock might lead to the failure of the greater-than-50 percent support test, depending on how much Sam spends for his (or Dana's) support.

Assume, however, that further fact gathering reveals the following additional information:

- Sam does not really need to spend the proceeds from the sale of the stock.
- Sam receives a sizable portion of his own support from a scholarship.

With these new facts, additional research leads to § 152(d) and Reg. § 1.152–1(c), which indicate that a scholarship received by a student is not included for purposes of computing whether the parents furnished more than one-half of the child's support. Further, if Sam does not spend the proceeds from the sale of stock, the unexpended amount is not counted for purposes of the support test. Thus, it appears that the parents would not be denied the dependency exemptions for Sam and Dana.

[31] See the related discussion in Chapter 3.

LOCATING THE APPROPRIATE TAX LAW SOURCES

Once the problem is clearly defined, what is the next step? Although the next step is a matter of individual judgment, most tax research begins with the index volume of the tax service or a key-word search on an on-line tax service (see the subsequent discussion of Computer-Assisted Tax Research). If the problem is not complex, the researcher may bypass the tax service or on-line service and turn directly to the Internal Revenue Code and Treasury Regulations. For the beginner, the latter procedure saves time and will solve many of the more basic problems. If the researcher does not have a personal copy of the Code or Regulations, resorting to the appropriate volume(s) of a tax service will be necessary.[32] The major tax services available are as follows:

Standard Federal Tax Reporter, Commerce Clearing House.

United States Tax Reporter, Research Institute of America (entitled *Federal Taxes* prior to July 1992).

Federal Tax Coordinator 2d, Research Institute of America.

Tax Management Portfolios, Bureau of National Affairs.

Rabkin and Johnson, *Federal Income, Gift and Estate Taxation,* Matthew Bender, Inc.

CCH's Federal Tax Service, Commerce Clearing House.

Mertens Law of Federal Income Taxation, Callaghan and Co.

Working with the Tax Services. In this text, it is not feasible to teach the use of any particular tax service; this ability can be obtained only by practice.[33] However, several important observations about the use of tax services cannot be overemphasized. First, never forget to check for current developments. The main text of any service is not revised frequently enough to permit reliance on that portion as the *latest* word on any subject. Where current developments can be found depends, of course, on which service is being used. Commerce Clearing House's *Standard Federal Tax Reporter* service contains a special volume devoted to current matters. Both RIA's *U.S. Tax Reporter* and *Federal Tax Coordinator 2d* integrate the new developments into the body of the service throughout the year. Second, when dealing with a tax service synopsis of a Treasury Department pronouncement or a judicial decision, remember there is no substitute for the original source.

To illustrate, do not base a conclusion solely on a tax service's commentary on *Simons-Eastern Co. v. U.S.*[34] If the case is vital to the research, look it up. The facts of the case may be distinguishable from those involved in the problem being researched. This is not to say that the case synopsis contained in the tax service is wrong; it might just be misleading or incomplete.

Tax Periodicals. The various tax periodicals are another source of tax information. The best way to locate a journal article pertinent to a tax problem is through

[32] Several of the major tax services publish paperback editions of the Code and Treasury Regulations that can be purchased at modest prices. These editions are usually revised twice each year. For an annotated and abridged version of the Code and Regulations that is published annually, see James E. Smith, *West's Internal Revenue Code of 1986 and Treasury Regulations: Annotated and Selected* (St. Paul, Minn.: West Publishing Company, 1996).

[33] The representatives of the various tax services are prepared to provide the users of their services with printed booklets and individual instruction on the use of the materials.

[34] Refer to Footnote 28.

Commerce Clearing House's *Federal Tax Articles.* This six-volume service includes a subject index, a Code Section number index, and an author's index. The RIA (formerly P-H) tax service also has a topical "Index to Tax Articles" section that is organized using the RIA paragraph index system. Also, beginning in 1992, *The Accounting & Tax Index* is available in three quarterly issues plus a cumulative year-end volume covering all four quarters. The original *Accountant's Index* started in 1921 and ended in 1991.

The following are some of the more useful tax periodicals:

The Journal of Taxation
Warren, Gorham and Lamont
31 St. James Avenue
Boston, MA 02116

Tax Law Review
Warren, Gorham and Lamont
31 St. James Avenue
Boston, MA 02116

Trusts and Estates
6151 Powers Ferry Road NW
Atlanta, GA 30339

Oil and Gas Tax Quarterly
Matthew Bender & Co.
235 East 45th Street
New York, NY 10017

The International Tax Journal
Panel Publishers
14 Plaza Road
Greenvale, NY 11548

TAXES—The Tax Magazine
Commerce Clearing House, Inc.
4025 West Peterson Avenue
Chicago, IL 60646

National Tax Journal
5310 East Main Street
Columbus, OH 43213

The Tax Adviser
AICPA
1211 Avenue of the Americas
New York, NY 10036

The Practical Accountant
11 Penn Plaza
New York, NY 10001

Estate Planning
Warren, Gorham and Lamont
31 St. James Avenue
Boston, MA 02116

Taxation for Accountants
Warren, Gorham and Lamont
31 St. James Avenue
Boston, MA 02116

The Tax Executive
1001 Pennsylvania Avenue NW
Suite 320
Washington, D.C. 20004

Journal of Corporate Taxation
Warren, Gorham and Lamont
31 St. James Avenue
Boston, MA 02116

Journal of Taxation for Individuals
Warren, Gorham and Lamont
31 St. James Avenue
Boston, MA 02116

The Tax Lawyer
American Bar Association
750 N. Lake Shore Drive
Chicago, IL 60611

Journal of the American Taxation Association
American Accounting Association
5717 Bessie Drive
Sarasota, FL 34233

Tax Notes
6830 Fairfax Drive
Arlington, VA 22213

ASSESSING THE VALIDITY OF THE TAX LAW SOURCES

Once a source has been located, the next step is to assess it in light of the problem at hand. Proper assessment involves careful interpretation of the tax law with consideration given to its relevance and validity. In connection with validity, an important step is to check for recent changes in the tax law.

TAX IN THE NEWS

Internal Revenue Code: Interpretation Pitfalls

One author has noted 10 common pitfalls in interpreting the Code:

1. Determine the limitations and exceptions to a provision. Do not permit the language of the Code Section to carry greater or lesser weight than was intended.
2. Just because a Section fails to mention an item does not necessarily mean that the item is excluded.
3. Read definitional clauses carefully.
4. Do not overlook small words such as *and* and *or*. There is a world of difference between these two words.
5. Read the Code Section completely; do not jump to conclusions.
6. Watch out for cross-referenced and related provisions, since many Sections of the Code are interrelated.
7. At times Congress is not careful when reconciling new Code provisions with existing Sections. Conflicts among Sections, therefore, do arise.
8. Be alert for hidden definitions; terms in a particular Code Section may be defined in the same Section or in a separate Section.
9. Some answers may not be found in the Code; therefore, a researcher may have to consult the Regulations and/or judicial decisions.
10. Take careful note of measuring words such as *less than 50 percent, more than 50 percent,* and *at least 80 percent.*

SOURCE: Adapted by permission from Henry G. Wong, "Ten Common Pitfalls in Reading the Internal Revenue Code," *Journal of Business Strategy,* July-August 1972, pp. 30–33. Reprinted with permission by Faulkner & Gray, Inc., 11 Penn Plaza, New York, NY 10001.

Interpreting the Internal Revenue Code. The language of the Code can be extremely difficult to comprehend fully. For example, a subsection [§ 341(e)] relating to collapsible corporations contains *one* sentence of more than 450 words (twice as many as in the Gettysburg Address). Within this same subsection is another sentence of 300 words. Research has shown that in one-third of the conflicts reaching the Tax Court, the Court could not discern the intent of Congress by simply reading the statute. Yet the overriding attitude of the Tax Court judges is that the statute comes first. Even when the statute is unworkable, the Court will not rewrite the law.[35]

Assessing the Validity of a Treasury Regulation. It is often stated that Treasury Regulations have the force and effect of law. This statement is certainly true for most Regulations, but some judicial decisions have held a Regulation or a portion thereof invalid. When a court holds a Regulation invalid, it usually does so on the ground that the Regulation is contrary to the intent of Congress when it

[35] T. L. Kirkpatrick and W. B. Pollard, "Reliance by the Tax Court on the Legislative Intent of Congress," *The Tax Executive* (Summer 1986): 358–359.

enacted a particular Code Section. Most often the courts do not question the validity of Regulations because of the belief that "the first administrative interpretation of a provision as it appears in a new act often expresses the general understanding of the times or the actual understanding of those who played an important part when the statute was drafted."[36]

Keep the following observations in mind when assessing the validity of a Regulation:

- IRS agents must give the Code and the Regulations issued thereunder equal weight when dealing with taxpayers and their representatives.
- Proposed Regulations provide a preview of future final Regulations, but they are not binding on the IRS or taxpayers.
- In a challenge, the burden of proof is on the taxpayer to show that the Regulation is wrong. However, a court may invalidate a Regulation that varies from the language of the statute and has no support in the Committee Reports.
- If the taxpayer loses the challenge, a 20 percent negligence penalty may be imposed.[37] This accuracy-related penalty applies to any failure to make a reasonable attempt to comply with the tax law and any disregard of rules and regulations.[38]
- Final Regulations tend to be legislative, interpretive, or procedural. **Procedural Regulations** neither establish tax laws nor attempt to explain tax laws. Procedural Regulations are *housekeeping-type instructions* indicating information that taxpayers should provide the IRS as well as information about the internal management and conduct of the IRS itself.
- Some **interpretive Regulations** merely reprint or rephrase what Congress stated in the Committee Reports that were issued when the tax legislation was enacted. Such Regulations are *hard* and *solid* and almost impossible to overturn because they clearly reflect the intent of Congress. An interpretive Regulation is given less deference than a legislative Regulation, however. The Supreme Court has told lower courts to analyze Treasury Regulations carefully before accepting the Treasury's interpretation.[39]
- In some Code Sections, Congress has given the *Secretary or his delegate* the authority to prescribe Regulations to carry out the details of administration or to otherwise complete the operating rules. Under such circumstances, it could almost be said that Congress is delegating its legislative powers to the Treasury Department. Regulations issued pursuant to this type of authority truly possess the force and effect of law and are often called **legislative Regulations** (e.g., consolidated return Regulations).
- Courts tend to apply a legislative reenactment doctrine. A particular Regulation is assumed to have received congressional approval if the Regulation was finalized many years earlier and Congress has not amended the Code Section pertaining to that Regulation.

Assessing the Validity of Other Administrative Sources of the Tax Law. Revenue Rulings issued by the IRS carry less weight than Treasury Department Regulations. Revenue Rulings are important, however, in that they reflect the position of the IRS on tax matters. In any dispute with the IRS on the interpreta-

[36] *Augustus v. Comm.*, 41–1 USTC ¶9255, 26 AFTR 612, 118 F.2d 38 (CA–6, 1941).

[37] §§ 6662(a) and (b)(1).

[38] § 6662(c).

[39] *U.S. v. Vogel Fertilizer Co.*, 82–1 USTC ¶9134, 49 AFTR2d 82–491, 102 S.Ct. 821 (USSC, 1982); *National Muffler Dealers Assn., Inc.*, 79–1 USTC ¶9264, 43 AFTR2d 79–828, 99 S.Ct. 1304 (USSC, 1979).

tion of tax law, therefore, taxpayers should expect agents to follow the results reached in any applicable Revenue Rulings. A 1986 Tax Court decision, however, indicated that Revenue Rulings "typically do not constitute substantive authority for a position."[40] Most Revenue Rulings apply retroactively unless a specific statement indicates the extent to which a ruling is to be applied without retroactive effect.[41]

Actions on Decisions further tell the taxpayer the IRS's reaction to certain court decisions and Revenue Rulings. Recall that the IRS follows a practice of either acquiescing (agreeing) or nonacquiescing (not agreeing) with selected decisions. A nonacquiescence does not mean that a particular court decision is of no value, but it does indicate that the IRS will continue to litigate the issue involved.

Assessing the Validity of Judicial Sources of the Tax Law. The judicial process as it relates to the formulation of tax law has already been described. How much reliance can be placed on a particular decision depends upon the following variables:

- The level of the court. A decision rendered by a trial court (e.g., a Federal District Court) carries less weight than one issued by an appellate court (e.g., the Fifth Court of Appeals). Unless Congress changes the Code, decisions by the U.S. Supreme Court represent the last word on any tax issue.
- The legal residence of the taxpayer. If, for example, a taxpayer lives in Texas, a decision of the Fifth Court of Appeals means more than one rendered by the Second Court of Appeals. This result occurs because any appeal from a U.S. District Court or the Tax Court would be to the Fifth Court of Appeals and not to the Second Court of Appeals.[42]
- A Tax Court Regular decision carries more weight than a Memorandum decision since the Tax Court does not consider Memorandum decisions to be binding precedents.[43] Furthermore, a Tax Court *reviewed* decision carries even more weight. All of the Tax Court judges participate in a reviewed decision.
- A Circuit Court decision where certiorari has been requested and denied by the U.S. Supreme Court carries more weight than a Circuit Court decision that was not appealed. A Circuit Court decision heard *en banc* (all the judges participate) carries more weight than a normal Circuit Court case.
- Whether the decision represents the weight of authority on the issue. In other words, is it supported by the results reached by other courts?
- The outcome or status of the decision on appeal. For example, was the decision appealed and, if so, with what result?

In connection with the last two variables, the use of a citator is invaluable to tax research.[44] Citators and their use are discussed in Appendix E.

Assessing the Validity of Other Sources. *Primary sources* of tax law include the Constitution, legislative history materials, statutes, treaties, Treasury Regulations, IRS pronouncements, and judicial decisions. In general, the IRS considers

---

[40] *Nelda C. Stark*, 86 T.C. 243 (1986). See also *Ann R. Neuhoff*, 75 T.C. 36 (1980). For a different opinion, however, see *Industrial Valley Bank & Trust Co.*, 66 T.C. 272 (1976).

[41] Rev.Proc. 87–1, 1987–1 C.B. 503.

[42] Before October 1, 1982, an appeal from the then-named U.S. Court of Claims (the other trial court) was directly to the U.S. Supreme Court.

[43] *Severino R. Nico, Jr.*, 67 T.C. 647 (1977).

[44] The major citators are published by Commerce Clearing House, RIA, and Shepard's Citations, Inc.

only primary sources to constitute substantial authority. However, a researcher might wish to refer to *secondary materials* such as legal periodicals, treatises, legal opinions, General Counsel Memoranda, and written determinations. In general, secondary sources are not authority.

Until 1990, the IRS considered only primary sources to constitute substantial authority. In Notice 90–20,[45] the IRS expanded the list of substantial authority *for purposes of* the accuracy-related penalty in § 6662 to include a number of secondary materials (e.g., letter rulings, General Counsel Memoranda, the Bluebook). As under former § 6661, "authority" does not include conclusions reached in treatises, legal periodicals, and opinions rendered by tax professionals.

A letter ruling or determination letter is substantial authority only for the taxpayer to whom it is issued, except as noted above with respect to the accuracy-related penalty.

Upon the completion of major tax legislation, the staff of the Joint Committee on Taxation (in consultation with the staffs of the House Ways and Means and Senate Finance Committees) often will prepare a General Explanation of the Act, commonly known as the Bluebook because of the color of its cover. The IRS will not accept this detailed explanation as having legal effect, except as noted above with respect to the accuracy-related penalty. The Bluebook does, however, provide valuable guidance to tax advisers and taxpayers until Regulations are issued, and some letter rulings and General Counsel Memoranda of the IRS cite its explanations.

ARRIVING AT THE SOLUTION OR AT ALTERNATIVE SOLUTIONS

Example 4 raised the question of whether a taxpayer would be denied dependency exemptions for a son and a daughter-in-law if the son sold some stock near the end of the year. A refinement of the problem supplies additional information:

- Sam was a full-time student during four calendar months of the year.
- Sam and Dana anticipate filing a joint return.

Additional research leads to Regulation § 1.151–3(b), which indicates that to qualify as a student, Sam must be a full-time student during each of *five* calendar months of the year at an educational institution. Thus, proceeds from Sam's sale of the stock would cause his parents to lose at least one dependency exemption because Sam's gross income would exceed the exemption amount. The parents still might be able to claim Dana as an exemption if the support test is met.

Section 151(c)(2) indicates that a supporting taxpayer is not permitted a dependency exemption for a married dependent if the married individual files a joint return. Initial reaction is that a joint return by Sam and Dana would be disastrous to the parents. However, more research uncovers two Revenue Rulings that provide an exception if neither the dependent nor the dependent's spouse is required to file a return but does so solely to claim a refund of tax withheld. The IRS asserts that each spouse must have gross income of less than the exemption amount.[46] Therefore, if Sam sells the stock and he and Dana file a joint return, the parents would lose the dependency exemption for both Sam and Dana.

If the stock is not sold until January, both exemptions may still be available to the parents. However, under § 151(d)(2) a personal exemption is not available to a

[45] 1990–1 C.B. 328; see also Reg. § 1.6661–3(b)(2).

[46] Rev.Rul. 54–567, 1954–2 C.B. 108; Rev.Rul. 65–34, 1965–1 C.B. 86.

taxpayer who can be claimed as a dependent by another taxpayer (whether actually claimed or not). Thus, if the parents can claim Sam and Dana as dependents, Sam and Dana would lose their personal exemptions on their tax return.

COMMUNICATING TAX RESEARCH

4 LEARNING OBJECTIVE
Communicate the results of the tax research process in a client letter and a tax file memorandum.

Once satisfied that the problem has been researched adequately, the researcher may need to prepare a memo (and/or letter) setting forth the result. The form such a memo takes could depend on a number of considerations. For example, does an employer or professor recommend a particular procedure or format for tax research memos? Is the memo to be given directly to the client or will it first go to the researcher's employer? Whatever form it takes, a good research memo should contain the following elements:

- A clear statement of the issue.
- In more complex situations, a short review of the fact pattern that raises the issue.
- A review of the tax law sources (e.g., Code, Regulations, Revenue Rulings, judicial authority).
- Any assumptions made in arriving at the solution.
- The solution recommended and the logic or reasoning supporting it.
- The references consulted in the research process.

In short, a good tax memo should tell the reader what was researched, the results of that research, and the justification for the recommendation made.[47]

Illustrations of the memos for the tax file and the client letter associated with Example 4 appear in Figures 2–4, 2–5, and 2–6.

▼ FIGURE 2–4
Tax File Memorandum

August 16, 1996

TAX FILE MEMORANDUM

FROM: John J. Jones

SUBJECT: Fred and Megan Taxpayer
Engagement: Issues

Today I talked to Fred Taxpayer with respect to his August 14, 1996 letter requesting tax assistance. He wishes to know if his son, Sam, can sell stock worth $19,000 (basis = $12,000) without the parents losing the dependency exemptions for Sam and Sam's wife, Dana.

Fred Taxpayer is married to Megan, and Sam is a full-time student at a local university. Sam inherited the stock from his grandmother about five years ago. If he sells the stock, he will save the proceeds from the sale. Sam does not need to spend the proceeds if he sells the stock because he receives a $3,000 scholarship that he uses for his own support (i.e., to pay for tuition, books, and fees). Fred and Megan are in the 28% tax bracket and furnish approximately 55% of Sam and Dana's support.

ISSUE: If the stock is sold, would the sale prohibit Fred and Megan from claiming Sam and Dana as dependents? I told Fred that we would have an answer for him within two weeks.

[47] See Chapter 6 of the publication cited in Footnote 30.

▼ FIGURE 2-5
Tax File Memorandum

August 26, 1996

TAX FILE MEMORANDUM

FROM: John J. Jones

SUBJECT: Fred and Megan Taxpayer
Engagement: Conclusions

Section 152(a) provides that in order for a taxpayer to take a dependency exemption, the taxpayer must provide over 50% of the support of the potential dependent. Fred and Megan provide about 55% of the support of their son, Sam, and their daughter-in-law, Dana. If Sam should sell the stock in 1996, he would not need to spend the proceeds for support purposes (i.e., would save the proceeds). Thus, the stock sale would not affect his qualifying for the support test. In calculating the percentage of support provided by Fred and Megan, a $3,000 scholarship received by Sam is not counted in determining the amount of support Sam provides for himself [see Reg. § 1.152–1(c)].

Section 151(c)(1) provides that in order to qualify for a dependency exemption, the potential dependent's gross income must be less than the exemption amount (i.e., $2,550 in 1996). Without the stock sale, the gross income of both Sam ($960) and Dana ($900) will be below the exemption amount in 1996. The $3,000 Sam receives as a scholarship is excluded from his gross income under § 117(a) because he uses the entire amount to pay for his tuition, books, and fees at a local university.

The key issue then is whether the stock, which will generate $7,000 gain for Sam, will cause the gross income test to be violated. The gain will increase Sam's gross income to $7,960 ($7,000 + $960). However, § 151(c)(1)(B) permits a child's gross income to exceed the exemption amount if the child is a student under the age of 24. Under Reg. § 1.151–3(b), to qualify as a student, the person must be a full-time student during each of five calendar months. A telephone call to Megan provided the information that Sam was a student for only four months in 1996. Thus, since Sam is not eligible for the student exception, the sale of the stock by Sam in 1996 would result in Fred and Megan losing the dependency exemption for Sam.

The stock sale would also result in the loss of the dependency exemption for Dana if Sam and Dana file a joint return for 1996 [see § 151(c)(2)].

From a tax planning perspective, Sam should not sell the stock until 1997. This will enable Fred and Megan to claim dependency exemptions on their 1996 return for Sam and Dana. Note, however, that neither Sam nor Dana will be permitted to take a personal exemption deduction on their 1996 tax return since they are claimed as dependents on someone else's return [see § 151(d)(2)]. However, this will not produce any negative tax consequences since their tax liability will be zero if the stock is not sold in 1996.

Working with the Tax Law—Tax Planning

5 Learning Objective
Apply tax research techniques and planning procedures.

Tax research and tax planning are inseparable. The *primary* purpose of effective *tax planning* is to reduce the taxpayer's total tax bill. This statement does not mean that the course of action selected must produce the lowest possible tax under the circumstances. The minimization of tax liability must be considered in context with the legitimate business goals of the taxpayer.

A *secondary* objective of effective tax planning is to reduce or defer the tax in the current tax year. Specifically, this objective aims to accomplish one or more of the following: eradicating the tax entirely; eliminating the tax in the current year; deferring the receipt of income; converting ordinary income into capital gains; converting active to passive income; converting passive to active expense; prolif-

▼ FIGURE 2-6
Client Letter

Hoffman, Smith, and Willis, CPAs
50 Kellogg Boulevard
St. Paul, Minnesota 55164

August 30, 1996

Mr. and Ms. Fred Taxpayer
111 Boulevard
Williamsburg, Virginia 23185

Dear Mr. and Ms. Taxpayer:

This letter is in response to your request for us to review your family's financial and tax situation. Our conclusions are based upon the facts as outlined in your August 14th letter. Any change in the facts may affect our conclusions.

You provide over 50% of the support for your son, Sam, and his wife, Dana. The scholarship Sam receives is not included in determining support. If the stock is not sold, you will qualify for a dependency exemption for both Sam and Dana.

However, if the stock is sold, a gain of approximately $7,000 will result. This amount will result in the gross income requirement being violated (i.e., potential dependent's gross income must not exceed $2,550) for Sam. Therefore, you will not qualify to receive a dependency exemption for Sam. In addition, if Sam sells the stock and he and Dana file a joint return, you also will not qualify for a dependency exemption for Dana.

From a tax planning perspective, Sam should not sell the stock in 1996. Delaying the stock sale will enable you to claim dependency exemptions for both Sam and Dana. If the stock is sold, Sam and Dana should not file a joint return. This will still enable you to qualify for a dependency exemption for Dana.

Should you need more information or need to clarify our conclusions, do not hesitate to contact me.

Sincerely yours,

John J. Jones, CPA
Partner

erating taxpayers (i.e., forming partnerships and corporations or making lifetime gifts to family members); eluding double taxation; avoiding ordinary income; or creating, increasing, or accelerating deductions. However, this second objective should be approached with considerable reservation and moderation. For example, a tax election in one year may reduce taxes currently, but saddle future years with a disadvantageous tax position.

NONTAX CONSIDERATIONS

There is an honest danger that tax motivations may take on a significance that does not correspond to the true values involved. In other words, tax considerations may impair the exercise of sound business judgment by the taxpayer. Thus, the tax planning process can become a medium through which to accomplish ends that are socially and economically objectionable. All too often, planning seems to lean toward the opposing extremes of placing either too little or too much emphasis on tax considerations. The happy medium—a balance that recognizes the significance of taxes, but not beyond the point where planning detracts from the exercise of good business judgment—turns out to be the promised land that is too infrequently reached.

The remark is often made that a good rule is to refrain from pursuing any course of action that would not be followed were it not for certain tax considerations. This statement is not entirely correct, but it does illustrate the desirability of preventing business logic from being *sacrificed at the altar of tax planning.*

TAX AVOIDANCE AND TAX EVASION

A fine line exists between legal tax planning and illegal tax planning—tax avoidance versus tax evasion. **Tax avoidance** is merely tax minimization through legal techniques. In this sense, tax avoidance is the proper objective of all tax planning. Tax evasion, while also aimed at the elimination or reduction of taxes, connotes the use of subterfuge and fraud as a means to an end. Popular usage—probably because of the common goals involved—has so linked these two concepts that many individuals are no longer aware of the true distinctions between them. Consequently, some taxpayers have been deterred from properly taking advantage of planning possibilities. The now classic words of Judge Learned Hand in *Commissioner v. Newman* reflect the true values the taxpayer should have:

> Over and over again courts have said that there is nothing sinister in so arranging one's affairs as to keep taxes as low as possible. Everybody does so, rich or poor; and all do right, for nobody owes any public duty to pay more than the law demands: taxes are enforced extractions, not voluntary contributions. To demand more in the name of morals is mere cant.[48]

ETHICAL CONSIDERATIONS

Tax Avoidance

In a speech class, a philosophy student argues that tax advisers are immoral because they help people cheat the government. Each time a tax adviser shows a taxpayer a tax planning idea that reduces the client's liability, all other taxpayers have to pay more taxes. Society would be better off if all tax advisers would work at improving our environment or living conditions in the inner cities.

An accounting student argues that the primary purpose of tax planning is to reduce a taxpayer's overall liability. This advisory process can result in avoiding, deferring, or postponing the tax burden until the future. There is nothing illegal or immoral about tax avoidance. Taxpayers have every legal right to be concerned about tax avoidance and to arrange their affairs so as to pay no more taxes than the law demands. There is no difference between reducing a tax expense through the help of a tax adviser and reducing a cost of operating a business with the aid of a cost accountant.

Comment on each student's position.

FOLLOW-UP PROCEDURES

Because tax planning usually involves a proposed (as opposed to a completed) transaction, it is predicated upon the continuing validity of the advice based upon

[48] *Comm. v. Newman*, 47–1 USTC ¶9175, 35 AFTR 857, 159 F.2d 848 (CA–2, 1947).

the tax research. A change in the tax law (either legislative, administrative, or judicial) could alter the original conclusion. Additional research may be necessary to test the solution in light of current developments (refer to the broken lines at the right in Figure 2–3).

TAX PLANNING—A PRACTICAL APPLICATION

Returning to the facts of Example 4, what could be done to protect the dependency exemptions for the parents? If Sam and Dana were to refrain from filing a joint return, both could be claimed by the parents. This result assumes that the stock is not sold.

An obvious tax planning tool is the installment method. Could the securities be sold using the installment method under § 453 so that most of the gain is deferred into the next year? Under the installment method, certain gains may be postponed and recognized as the cash proceeds are received. The problem is that the installment method is not available for stock traded on an established securities market.[49]

A little more research, however, indicates that Sam can sell the stock and postpone the recognition of gain until the following year by selling short an equal number of substantially identical shares and covering the short sale in the subsequent year with the shares originally held. Selling short means that Sam sells borrowed stock (substantially identical) and repays the lender with the stock held on the date of the short sale. This *short against the box* technique would allow Sam to protect his $7,000 profit and defer the closing of the sale until the following year.[50] Further, if the original shares have been held for the required long-term holding period before the date of the short sale, Sam would be able to obtain long-term capital gain treatment.[51] Thus, some research and planning would reap tax savings for this family. Note the critical role of obtaining the correct facts in attempting to resolve the proper strategy for the taxpayers.

Throughout this text, most chapters include observations on Tax Planning Considerations. Such observations are not all-inclusive but are intended to illustrate some of the ways in which the material covered can be effectively utilized to minimize taxes.

COMPUTER-ASSISTED TAX RESEARCH

6 LEARNING OBJECTIVE
Have an awareness of computer-assisted tax research.

The computer is being used more and more frequently in the day-to-day practice of tax professionals, students, and educators. Many software vendors offer tax return software programs for individual, corporate, partnership, and fiduciary returns. The use of computers, however, is not limited to batch-processed tax returns and computer timesharing for quantitative tax and problem-solving planning and calculations.

The microcomputer has become the revolutionary tool of the present—much as the electronic calculator did in the 1970s. Electronic spreadsheets are being used to replace the 14-column worksheet. The electronic spreadsheet approach can be used for retirement planning, 1040 projections, real estate projections, partnership allocations, consolidated tax return problems, compensation planning—wherever

[49] See Chapter 18 for a discussion of installment sales.

[50] §§ 1233(a) and 1233(b)(2). See Chapter 16 for a discussion of short sales.

[51] Long-term capital gains are eligible for preferential tax treatment. In addition, if Sam had capital losses from other transactions, the capital gains and capital losses could be offset. See the discussion in Chapter 16.

projections and calculations are needed. Many public accounting firms use internally prepared tax-related programs. Microcomputer software is available for estate planning calculations.

LEXIS, a computerized legal data bank developed by Mead Data Central which was recently acquired by Reed-Elsevier, has been available since 1973 as a complement to the conventional research approach (available in many of the more than 100 graduate tax programs). WESTLAW, a competitive system from West Publishing Company, has been operational since 1975. Commerce Clearing House's legal data base is called ACCESS, and Research Institute of America's is called TAXRIA. With these data banks, one has immediate access to the current tax law, Regulations, Proposed Regulations, letter rulings, Revenue Rulings, judicial decisions, daily tax services, code commentaries, and much more. Note, however, that WESTLAW, LEXIS, ACCESS, and TAXRIA are actually document retrieval systems that cannot interpret the law.

A recent development is the proliferation of Compact Disc–Read Only Memory (CD-ROM). By employing a key-word search technique, a person can browse through a tax service, IRS publications, and other tax information. Commerce Clearing House, Research Institute of America, Tax Analysts, Tax Management, Inc., and West Publishing Company offer CD-ROM products. For example, West provides a complete Federal tax library on only nine CDs. Although CD-ROM does not offer the on-line updating provided by WESTLAW, LEXIS, ACCESS, and TAXRIA, the CDs can be replaced periodically.

Computer-assisted tax research is useful in searching for facts because human indexing centers on legal theories rather than fact patterns. Computer searching also is useful in finding new court decisions not yet in the printed indexes. Although computer searching probably does not find as many relevant cases as manual searching does, a combination of manual and computer searching can be quite effective.[52]

The latest development is the World Wide Web of the Internet, which is constantly expanding and provides a wealth of valuable information. Four broad categories of tax resources are available on the Web: gateway sites (i.e., indexes), Federal tax laws, state and foreign taxes, and secondary and commercial sites. IRS forms, state forms, tax articles, U.S. tax laws, tax treaty information, judicial and legal gateways, and Regulations are only some of the information on the Web.[53]

KEY TERMS

Acquiescence, 2–20

Circuit Court of Appeals, 2–15

Court of original jurisdiction, 2–12

Determination letters, 2–11

Federal District Court, 2–12

Finalized Regulations, 2–9

Interpretive Regulations, 2–28

Legislative Regulations 2–28

[52] See Chapter 22 of the publication cited in Footnote 20; Thomas and Weinstein, *Computer-Assisted Legal and Tax Research* (Paramus, N.J.: Prentice-Hall, 1986); and Chapter 13 of W. A. Raabe, G. E. Whittenburg, and J. C. Bost, *West's Federal Tax Research*, 3d ed. (St. Paul, Minn.: West Publishing Co., 1994).

[53] R. J. Coppins et al, "Worldwide Web: The Latest Tax Resource on the Information Superhighway," *Journal of Taxation* (August 1995): 108–118.

Letter rulings, 2–10
Nonacquiescence, 2–20
Precedents, 2–17
Procedural Regulations, 2–28
Proposed Regulations, 2–8
Revenue Procedures, 2–9
Revenue Rulings, 2–9
Small Cases Division, 2–12
Tax avoidance, 2–34
Tax research, 2–22
Technical Advice Memoranda (TAMs), 2–11
Temporary Regulations, 2–9
U.S. Court of Federal Claims, 2–12
U.S. Supreme Court, 2–17
U.S. Tax Court, 2–12
Writ of Certiorari, 2–18

PROBLEM MATERIALS

DISCUSSION QUESTIONS

1. Judicial decisions interpreting a provision of the Internal Revenue Code of 1939 or 1954 are no longer of any value in view of the enactment of the Internal Revenue Code of 1986. Assess the validity of this statement.
2. When was the last time Congress codified the tax laws?
3. Tax legislation normally originates in the House Ways and Means Committee. Assess the validity of this statement.
4. What is the function of the Joint Conference Committee of the House Ways and Means Committee and the Senate Finance Committee?
5. In which Title and Subtitle of the U.S. Code is the income tax portion of the Internal Revenue Code of 1986 found?
6. Paul Jacobs operates a small international firm named Teal, Inc. A new treaty between the United States and Ukraine conflicts with a Section of the Internal Revenue Code. Paul asks you for advice. If he follows the treaty position, does he need to disclose this on his tax return? If he is required to disclose, are there any penalties for failure to disclose? Prepare a letter in which you respond to Paul. Teal's address is 100 International Drive, Tampa, FL 33620.
7. Interpret this Regulation citation: Reg. § 1.274–2(a)(1)(i).
8. Distinguish between legislative, interpretive, and procedural Regulations.
9. Distinguish between:
   a. Treasury Regulations and Revenue Rulings.
   b. Revenue Rulings and Revenue Procedures.
   c. Revenue Rulings and letter rulings.
   d. Letter rulings and determination letters.
10. Rank the following items from the highest authority to the lowest in the Federal tax law system:
    a. Interpretive Regulation.
    b. Legislative Regulation.
    c. Letter ruling.
    d. Revenue Procedure.
    e. Internal Revenue Code.
    f. Proposed Regulation.
11. Interpret each of the following citations:
    a. Rev.Rul. 65–235, 1965–2 C.B. 88.
    b. Rev.Proc. 87–56, 1987–2 C.B. 674.
    c. Ltr.Rul. 9046036.

12. Michelle Zull calls you on the phone. She says that she has found a 1985 letter ruling that agrees with a position she wishes to take on her tax return. She asks you about the precedential value of a letter ruling. Draft a memo for the tax files outlining what you told Michelle.
13. Edith is considering writing the IRS to determine if a proposed divisive reorganization would be tax-free. Outline some relevant tax issues Edith faces in making this decision.
14. a. What are Treasury Decisions (TDs)?
    b. What purpose do they serve?
    c. Where are they published?
15. What are the major differences between letter rulings and determination letters?
16. What is a Technical Advice Memorandum (TAM)?
17. Caleb receives a ninety-day letter after his discussion with an appeals officer. He is not satisfied with the $92,000 settlement offer. Identify the relevant tax research issues facing Caleb.
18. Which of the following would be considered advantages of the Small Cases Division of the Tax Court?
    a. Appeal to the Court of Appeals for the Federal Circuit is possible.
    b. A hearing of a deficiency of $11,200 is considered on a timely basis.
    c. Taxpayer can handle the litigation without using a lawyer or certified public accountant.
    d. Taxpayer can use other Small Cases Division decisions for precedential value.
    e. The actual hearing is conducted informally.
    f. Travel time will probably be reduced.
19. List an advantage and a disadvantage of using the U.S. Tax Court as the trial court for Federal tax litigation.
20. Sam Brown is considering litigating a tax deficiency of approximately $317,000 in the court system. He asks you to provide him with a short description of his alternatives indicating the advantages and disadvantages of each. Prepare your response to Sam in the form of a letter. His address is 200 Mesa Drive, Tuscon, AZ 85714.
21. List an advantage and a disadvantage of using the U.S. Court of Federal Claims as the trial court for Federal tax litigation.
22. A taxpayer lives in Michigan. In a controversy with the IRS, the taxpayer loses at the trial court level. Describe the appeal procedure under the following different assumptions:
    a. The trial court was the Small Cases Division of the U.S. Tax Court.
    b. The trial court was the U.S. Tax Court.
    c. The trial court was a U.S. District Court.
    d. The trial court was the U.S. Court of Federal Claims.
23. Suppose the U.S. Government loses a tax case in the U.S. District Court of South Carolina but does not appeal the result. What does the failure to appeal signify?
24. Because the U.S. Tax Court is a national court, it always decides the same issue in a consistent manner. Assess the validity of this statement.
25. For the U.S. Tax Court, U.S. District Court, and the U.S. Court of Federal Claims, indicate the following:
    a. Number of regular judges per court.
    b. Availability of a jury trial.
    c. Whether the deficiency must be paid before the trial.
26. In which of the following states could a taxpayer appeal the decision of a U.S. District Court to the Fifth Court of Appeals?
    a. Arkansas.
    b. Arizona.

c. Alabama.
d. Maine.
e. Texas.

27. Explain the fact-finding determination of a Federal Court of Appeals.

28. What is the Supreme Court's policy on hearing tax cases?

29. In assessing the validity of a prior court decision, discuss the significance of the following on the taxpayer's issue:
 a. The decision was rendered by the U.S. District Court of Wyoming. Taxpayer lives in Wyoming.
 b. The decision was rendered by the U.S. Court of Federal Claims. Taxpayer lives in Wyoming.
 c. The decision was rendered by the Second Court of Appeals. Taxpayer lives in California.
 d. The decision was rendered by the U.S. Supreme Court.
 e. The decision was rendered by the U.S. Tax Court. The IRS has acquiesced in the result.
 f. Same as (e) except that the IRS has issued a nonacquiescence as to the result.

30. In the citation *Florence H. Griffith*, 35 T.C. 882 (1961), what do the 35 and the 882 refer to?

31. What is the difference between a Regular and a Memorandum decision of the U.S. Tax Court?

32. Answer the following questions based upon this citation: *Schuster's Express, Inc.*, 66 T.C. 588 (1976), *aff'd* 562 F.2d 39 (CA–2, 1977), *nonacq.*
 a. In which court did this decision first appear?
 b. Who was the plaintiff?
 c. Who was the respondent?
 d. Did the appellate court agree or disagree with the trial court?
 e. Does the Government agree with the position of the court?

33. Interpret each of the following citations:
 a. 54 T.C. 1514 (1970).
 b. 408 F.2d 1117 (CA–2, 1969).
 c. 69–1 USTC ¶9319 (CA–2, 1969).
 d. 23 AFTR2d 69–1090 (CA–2, 1969).
 e. 293 F.Supp. 1129 (D.Ct. Miss., 1967).
 f. 67–1 USTC ¶9253 (D.Ct. Miss., 1967).
 g. 19 AFTR2d 647 (D.Ct. Miss., 1967).
 h. 56 S.Ct. 289 (USSC, 1935).
 i. 36–1 USTC ¶9020 (USSC, 1935).
 j. 16 AFTR 1274 (USSC, 1935).
 k. 422 F.2d 1336 (Ct.Cls., 1970).

34. Explain the following abbreviations:

a.	CA–2	i.	USTC
b.	Cls.Ct.	j.	AFTR
c.	*aff'd.*	k.	F.3d
d.	*rev'd.*	l.	F.Supp.
e.	*rem'd.*	m.	USSC
f.	*Cert. Denied*	n.	S.Ct.
g.	*acq.*	o.	D.Ct.
h.	B.T.A.	p.	Fed.Cl.

35. Give the Commerce Clearing House citation for the following courts:
 a. Small Cases Division of the Tax Court.
 b. Federal District Court.
 c. U.S. Supreme Court.
 d. U.S. Court of Federal Claims.
 e. Tax Court Memorandum decision.

36. Where can you locate a published decision of the U.S. Court of Federal Claims?
37. Which of the following items can probably be found in the *Cumulative Bulletin*?
    a. Revenue Ruling.
    b. Small Cases Division of the U.S. Tax Court decision.
    c. Letter ruling.
    d. Revenue Procedure.
    e. Proposed Regulation.
    f. District Court decision.
    g. Senate Finance Committee Report.
    h. Acquiescences to Tax Court decisions.
    i. Tax Court Memorandum decision.
38. As part of her course work for a Masters of Tax degree, Ann is required to prepare a 30-page term paper about limited liability partnerships. Identify some relevant research steps Ann may take.
39. Where can a researcher find the current Internal Revenue Code of 1986?
40. Since a Regulation has the force and effect of tax law, can a Regulation be overturned by a court?
41. Determine the level of authority for a Tax Court Memorandum decision, a Tax Court Regular decision, and a Tax Court reviewed decision.
42. When might a researcher need to refer to a citator?
43. Which of the following would be considered differences between the Research Institute of America and Commerce Clearing House citators?
    a. Distinguishes between the various issues in a particular court decision.
    b. Lists all court decisions that cite the court decision being researched.
    c. Allows a researcher to determine the validity of a Revenue Ruling.
    d. Indicates whether a court decision is explained, criticized, followed, or overruled by a subsequent decision.
    e. Pinpoints the exact page on which a decision is cited by another case.
44. List the elements that a good tax research memo should include.
45. Defend the practice by which tax advisers such as CPAs use tax planning techniques to reduce the tax liability of their clients.
46. You inherit a tax problem that was researched five months ago. You believe the answer is correct, but you are unfamiliar with the general area. How would you find some recent articles dealing with the subject area? How do you evaluate the reliability of the authority cited in the research report? How do you determine the latest developments pertaining to the research problem?
47. In general, what type of tax information can a person find on CD-ROM?

PROBLEMS

48. Tom, an individual taxpayer, has just been audited by the IRS and, as a result, has been assessed a substantial deficiency (which has not yet been paid) in additional income taxes. In preparing his defense, Tom advances the following possibilities:
    a. Although a resident of Kentucky, Tom plans to sue in a U.S. District Court in Oregon that appears to be more favorably inclined toward taxpayers.
    b. If (a) is not possible, Tom plans to take his case to a Kentucky state court where an uncle is the presiding judge.
    c. Since Tom has found a B.T.A. decision that seems to help his case, he plans to rely on it under alternative (a) or (b).

d. If he loses at the trial court level, Tom plans to appeal either to the U.S. Court of Federal Claims or to the U.S. Second Court of Appeals because he has relatives in both Washington, D.C., and New York. Staying with these relatives could save Tom lodging expense while his appeal is being heard by the court selected.
e. Whether or not Tom wins at the trial court or appeals court level, he feels certain of success on an appeal to the U.S. Supreme Court.

Evaluate Tom's notions concerning the judicial process as it applies to Federal income tax controversies.

49. Using the legend provided, identify the governmental unit that produces the following tax sources:

Legend
T = U.S. Treasury Department
NO = National Office of the IRS
DD = District Director of the IRS
NA = Not applicable

a. Proposed Regulations.
b. Revenue Procedures.
c. Letter rulings.
d. Determination letters.
e. Technical Advice Memoranda.
f. Treasury Decisions.
g. Revenue Rulings.

50. Using the legend provided, classify each of the following statements (more than one answer per statement may be appropriate):

Legend
D = Applies to the U.S. District Court
T = Applies to the U.S. Tax Court
C = Applies to the U.S. Court of Federal Claims
A = Applies to the U.S. Court of Appeals
U = Applies to the U.S. Supreme Court
N = Applies to none of the above

a. Decides only Federal tax matters.
b. Decisions are reported in the F.3d Series.
c. Decisions are reported in the USTCs.
d. Decisions are reported in the AFTRs.
e. Appeal is by Writ of Certiorari.
f. Court meets most often in Washington, D.C.
g. A jury trial is available.
h. Trial court.
i. Appellate court.
j. Appeal is to the Federal Circuit and bypasses the taxpayer's particular circuit court.
k. Has a Small Cases Division.
l. The only trial court where the taxpayer does not have to pay the tax assessed by the IRS first.

51. Using the legend provided, classify each of the following citations as to the type of court:

Legend
T = Applies to the U.S. Tax Court
D = Applies to the U.S. District Court
C = Applies to the U.S. Court of Federal Claims
A = Applies to the U.S. Court of Appeals
U = Applies to the U.S. Supreme Court
N = Applies to none of the above

a. 388 F.2d 420 (CA–7, 1968).
b. 79 T.C. 7 (1982).
c. 54 S.Ct. 8 (USSC, 1933).
d. 3 B.T.A. 1042 (1926).
e. T.C.Memo. 1954–141.
f. 597 F.2d 760 (Ct.Cl., 1979).
g. Ltr.Rul. 9414051.
h. 465 F.Supp. 341 (D.Ct.–Okla., 1978).

52. Using the legend provided, classify each of the following tax sources:

Legend
P = Primary tax source
S = Secondary tax source
B = Both
N = Neither

a. Sixteenth Amendment to the Constitution.
b. Tax treaty between the United States and France.
c. Revenue Rulings.
d. General Counsel Memoranda (1988).
e. Tax Court Memorandum decision.
f. *Yale Law Review* article.
g. Temporary Regulations (issued 1994).
h. District Court decision.
i. Small Cases Division of the U.S. Tax Court decision.
j. Senate Finance Committee report.

53. Using the legend provided, classify each of the following citations as to publisher:

Legend	
RIA	= Research Institute of America
CCH	= Commerce Clearing House
W	= West Publishing Company
U.S.	= U.S. Government
O	= Others

a. 83–2 USTC ¶9600.
b. 52 AFTR2d 83–5954.
c. 49 T.C. 645 (1968).
d. 39 TCM 32 (1979).
e. 393 U.S. 297.
f. RIA T.C.Memo. ¶80,582.
g. 89 S.Ct. 501.
h. 2 Cl.Ct. 600.
i. 159 F.2d 848.
j. 592 F.Supp. 18.
k. Rev.Rul. 76–332, 1976–2 C.B. 81.
l. 21 L.Ed.2d 495.

RESEARCH PROBLEMS

Note: ***West's Federal Taxation on CD-ROM*** *can be used in preparing solutions to the Research Problems. Alternatively, tax research materials contained in a standard tax library can be used.*

Research Problem 1. When the same word is used at different places in the Internal Revenue Code, does the word mean the same thing?

Research Problem 2. Determine what is covered in the following subchapters in Chapter 1, Subtitle A of the Internal Revenue Code of 1986:
a. B.
b. D.
c. F.
d. K.
e. P.

Research Problem 3. A particular Code Section, which was passed in 1986, conflicts with a treaty between the United States and France, which was signed in 1991. Which source controls? Where can a researcher find tax treaties?

Research Problem 4. Determine how the term *person* is defined in the Internal Revenue Code of 1986.

Research Problem 5. Go to page 44,274 of the August 25, 1995, issue of the *Federal Register.* What action was taken by the IRS, and what was the subject matter?

Research Problem 6. What do acquiescence, acquiescence in result only, and nonacquiescence mean? What position did the IRS take with respect to *Zabolotny v. Comm.*, 7 F.3d 774 (CA–8, 1993)?

Research Problem 7. Locate the following tax services in your library and indicate the name of the publisher and whether the service is organized by topic or Code Section:
a. *United States Tax Reporter.*
b. *Standard Federal Tax Reporter.*
c. *Federal Tax Coordinator 2d.*
d. *Mertens Law of Federal Income Taxation.*
e. *Tax Management Portfolios.*
f. Rabkin & Johnson, *Federal Income, Gift & Estate Taxation.*
g. *Federal Tax Service.*

Research Problem 8. In the Tax Publications Matrix below, place an X if a court decision can be found in the publication. There may be more than one X in a row for a particular court.

Court	**U.S. Govt. Printing Office**	**West Publishing Company**				**Research Institute of America**			**Commerce Clearing House**	
		Federal Supp.	Federal 3d	Federal Claims Reporter	S.Ct.	BTA Memo	TC Memo	AFTR	TC Memo	USTC
U.S. Supreme Court										
Court of Appeals										
Court of Federal Claims										
District Court										
Tax Court (Regular decisions)										
Tax Court (Memo decisions)										
Board of Tax Appeal										
BTA Memo										

Research Problem 9. Complete the following citations:

a. *Foxman v. Comm.*, 352 F.2d 466 (CA–3, ________).
b. Rev.Rul. 79–________, 1979–1 C.B. 144.
c. *Clark v. Comm.*, 489 U.S. ________(1989).
d. Rev.Proc. 92–89, 1992–2 C.B. ________.
e. *U.S. v. Catto*, 223 F.Supp. 663 (W.D.Tex., ________).
f. *Korn Industries, Inc., v. U.S.*, 532 F.2d ________ (Ct.Cl., 1976).
g. *Miller v. Comm.*, 45 B.T.A. ________ (1941).

Research Problem 10. Answer the following questions:

a. Has Prop.Reg. § 1.482–2 been finalized?
b. What happened to *Golconda Mining Corp.*, 58 T.C. 736 (1972) on appeal?
c. Does Rev.Rul. 69–185 still represent the position of the IRS on the issue involved?

Research Problem 11. Determine the disposition of the following decisions:

a. *Kimbell-Diamond Milling Co.*, 14 T.C. 74 (1950).
b. *U.S. v. Catto*, 223 F.Supp. 663 (W.D.Tex., 1963).
c. *Schuster's Express, Inc.*, 66 T.C. 588 (1976).

Research Problem 12. Determine the reliability of the following items:

a. *Simpson v. U.S.*, 261 F.2d 497 (CA–7, 1958).
b. Rev.Proc. 83–78, 1983–2 C.B. 595.
c. *Estate of Grace E. Lang*, 64 T.C. 404 (1975).

Research Problem 13. Did the IRS agree or disagree with the following court decisions?

a. *Longue Vue Foundation*, 90 T.C. 150 (1988).
b. *Charles Crowther*, 28 T.C. 1293 (1957).
c. *Sidney Merians*, 60 T.C. 187 (1973).
d. *Zabolotny v. Comm.*, 7 F.3d 774 (CA–8, 1993).

Research Problem 14. Determine the reliability of the following decisions:

a. *Maid of The Mist Corp.*, T.C.Memo. 1977–263, 36 TCM 1068 (1977).
b. *Albert Lazisky*, 72 T.C. 495 (1979).
c. *Farm Service Cooperative*, 70 T.C. 145 (1978).
d. *Tufts v. Comm.*, 81–2 USTC ¶9574 (CA–5, 1981), *rev'g* 70 T.C. 756 (1978).

Research Problem 15. Find *Francis Levien,* 103 T.C. 120 (1994), and answer these questions.

a. Who was the petitioner (plaintiff)?
b. Who was the respondent (defendant)?
c. What was the court's holding with respect to issue one?
d. Was this a reviewed decision?
e. How many judges agreed with the majority opinion?
f. Who wrote a concurring opinion?
g. Was this decision entered under Rule 155?

Research Problem 16. During 1996, Frank lived with and supported a 20-year-old woman who was not his wife. He resides in a state that has a statute that makes it a misdemeanor for a man and woman who are not married to each other to live together. May Frank claim his *friend* as a dependent assuming he satisfies the normal tax rules for the deduction? Should Frank consider moving to another state?

Partial list of research aids:
§ 152(b)(5).
John T. Untermann, 38 T.C. 93 (1962).
S.Rept. 1983, 85th Cong., 2d Sess., reprinted in the 1958 Code Cong. & Adm. News 4791, 4804.

Research Problem 17. Using the 1985–1989 volume of CCH's *Federal Tax Articles,* locate Code Section 636, article .012. Who are the authors, in what journal does the article appear, and what principle is discussed in the article?

CHAPTER 3

Tax Determination; Personal and Dependency Exemptions; An Overview of Property Transactions

LEARNING OBJECTIVES

After completing Chapter 3, you should be able to:

1. Understand and apply the components of the Federal income tax formula.
2. Apply the rules for arriving at personal and dependency exemptions.
3. Use the proper method for determining the tax liability.
4. Identify and work with kiddie tax situations.
5. Recognize the filing requirements and the proper filing status.
6. Possess an overview of property transactions.
7. Identify tax planning opportunities associated with the individual tax formula.

OUTLINE

Individuals are subject to Federal income tax based on taxable income. This chapter explains how taxable income and the income tax of an individual taxpayer are determined.

To compute taxable income, it is necessary to understand the tax formula in Figure 3-1. Although the tax formula is rather simple, determining an individual's taxable income can be quite complex. The complexity stems from the numerous provisions that govern the determination of gross income and allowable deductions.

After computing taxable income, the appropriate rates must be applied. This requires a determination of the individual's filing status, since different rates apply for single taxpayers, married taxpayers, and heads of household. The basic tax rate structure is progressive, with rates ranging from 15 percent to 39.6 percent.[1] For

▼ **FIGURE 3-1**
Tax Formula

Income (broadly conceived)	$xx,xxx
Less: Exclusions	(x,xxx)
Gross income	$xx,xxx
Less: Deductions *for* adjusted gross income	(x,xxx)
Adjusted gross income	$xx,xxx
Less: The greater of—	
Total itemized deductions *or* the standard deduction	(x,xxx)
Personal and dependency exemptions	(x,xxx)
Taxable income	$xx,xxx

[1] The 1996 Tax Table was not available from the IRS at the date of publication of this text. The Tax Table for 1995 and the Tax Rate Schedules for 1995 and 1996 are reproduced in Appendix A. For quick reference, the 1995 and 1996 Tax Rate Schedules are also reproduced inside the front cover of this text.

comparison, the lowest rate structure, which was in effect in 1913–1915, ranged from 1 to 7 percent, and the highest, in effect during 1944–1945, ranged from 23 to 94 percent.

Once the individual's tax has been computed, prepayments and credits are subtracted to determine whether the taxpayer owes additional tax or is entitled to a refund.

When property is sold or otherwise disposed of, a gain or loss may result, which can affect the determination of taxable income. Although property transactions are covered in detail in Chapters 14–17, an understanding of certain basic concepts helps in working with some of the materials to follow. The concluding portion of this chapter furnishes an overview of property transactions, including the distinction between realized and recognized gain or loss, the classification of such gain or loss (ordinary or capital), and treatment for income tax purposes.

TAX FORMULA

1 LEARNING OBJECTIVE
Understand and apply the components of the Federal income tax formula.

Most individuals compute taxable income using the tax formula shown in Figure 3–1. Special provisions govern the computation of taxable income and the tax liability for certain minor children who have unearned income in excess of specified amounts. These provisions are discussed later in the chapter.

Before illustrating the application of the tax formula, a brief discussion of its components is helpful.

COMPONENTS OF THE TAX FORMULA

Income (Broadly Conceived). This includes all the taxpayer's income, both taxable and nontaxable. Although it is essentially equivalent to gross receipts, it does not include a return of capital or receipt of borrowed funds.

EXAMPLE 1

Dave needed money to purchase a house. He sold 5,000 shares of stock for $100,000. He had paid $40,000 for the stock. In addition, he borrowed $75,000 from a bank. Dave has taxable income of $60,000 from the sale of the stock ($100,000 selling price – $40,000 return of capital). He has no income from the $75,000 borrowed from the bank because he has an obligation to repay that amount. ▼

Exclusions. For various reasons, Congress has chosen to exclude certain types of income from the income tax base. The principal income exclusions are discussed in Chapter 5. A partial list of these exclusions is shown in Exhibit 3–1.

Gross Income. The Internal Revenue Code defines gross income broadly as "except as otherwise provided . . ., all income from whatever source derived."[2] The "except as otherwise provided" refers to exclusions. Gross income includes, but is not limited to, the items in the partial list in Exhibit 3–2. It does not include unrealized gains. Gross income is discussed in Chapters 4 and 5.

[2] § 61(a).

▼ EXHIBIT 3–1
Partial List of Exclusions from Gross Income

- Accident insurance proceeds
- Annuities (cost element)
- Bequests
- Child support payments
- Cost-of-living allowance (for military)
- Damages for personal injury or sickness
- Death benefits (up to $5,000)
- Gifts received
- Group term life insurance, premium paid by employer (for coverage up to $50,000)
- Inheritances
- Interest from state and local (i.e., municipal) bonds
- Life insurance paid on death
- Meals and lodging (if furnished for employer's convenience)
- Military allowances
- Minister's dwelling rental value allowance
- Railroad retirement benefits (to a limited extent)
- Scholarship grants (to a limited extent)
- Social Security benefits (to a limited extent)
- Veterans' benefits
- Welfare payments
- Workers' compensation benefits

▼ EXHIBIT 3–2
Partial List of Gross Income Items

- Alimony
- Annuities (income element)
- Awards
- Back pay
- Bargain purchase from employer
- Bonuses
- Breach of contract damages
- Business income
- Clergy fees
- Commissions
- Compensation for services
- Death benefits in excess of $5,000
- Debts forgiven
- Director's fees
- Dividends
- Embezzled funds
- Employee awards (in certain cases)
- Employee benefits (except certain fringe benefits)
- Estate and trust income
- Farm income
- Fees
- Gains from illegal activities
- Gains from sale of property
- Gambling winnings
- Group term life insurance, premium paid by employer (for coverage over $50,000)
- Hobby income
- Interest
- Jury duty fees
- Living quarters, meals (unless furnished for employer's convenience)
- Mileage allowance
- Military pay (unless combat pay)
- Notary fees
- Partnership income
- Pensions
- Prizes
- Professional fees
- Punitive damages (in certain cases)
- Rents
- Rewards
- Royalties
- Salaries
- Severance pay
- Strike and lockout benefits
- Supplemental unemployment benefits
- Tips and gratuities
- Travel allowance (in certain cases)
- Wages

EXAMPLE 2

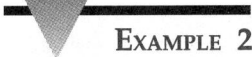

Beth received the following amounts during the year:

Salary	$30,000
Interest on savings account	900
Gift from her aunt	10,000
Prize won in state lottery	1,000
Alimony from ex-husband	12,000
Child support from ex-husband	6,000
Damages for injury in auto accident	25,000
Increase in the value of stock held for investment	5,000

Review Exhibits 3–1 and 3–2 to determine the amount Beth must include in the computation of taxable income and the amount she may exclude. Then check your answer in footnote 3.[3] ▼

Deductions for Adjusted Gross Income. Individual taxpayers have two categories of deductions: (1) deductions *for* adjusted gross income (deductions to arrive at adjusted gross income) and (2) deductions *from* adjusted gross income.

Deductions *for* adjusted gross income (AGI) include ordinary and necessary expenses incurred in a trade or business, one-half of self-employment tax paid, alimony paid, certain payments to an Individual Retirement Account, moving expenses, forfeited interest penalty for premature withdrawal of time deposits, the capital loss deduction, and others.[4] The principal deductions *for* AGI are discussed in Chapters 6, 7, 8, 9, and 11.

Adjusted Gross Income (AGI). AGI is an important subtotal that serves as the basis for computing percentage limitations on certain itemized deductions, such as medical expenses and charitable contributions. For example, medical expenses are deductible only to the extent they exceed 7.5 percent of AGI, and charitable contribution deductions may not exceed 50 percent of AGI. These limitations might be described as a 7.5 percent *floor* under the medical expense deduction and a 50 percent *ceiling* on the charitable contribution deduction.

EXAMPLE 3

Keith earned a salary of $23,000 in the current tax year. He contributed $2,000 to his Individual Retirement Account (IRA) and sustained a $1,000 capital loss on the sale of Wren Corporation stock. His AGI is computed as follows:

Gross income		
Salary		$23,000
Less: Deductions *for* AGI		
IRA contribution	$2,000	
Capital loss	1,000	(3,000)
AGI		$20,000

▼

[3] Beth must include $43,900 in computing taxable income ($30,000 salary + $900 interest + $1,000 lottery prize + $12,000 alimony). She can exclude $41,000 ($10,000 gift from aunt + $6,000 child support + $25,000 damages). The unrealized gain on the stock held for investment also is not included in gross income. Such gain will be included in gross income only when it is realized upon disposition of the stock.

[4] § 62.

EXAMPLE 4

Assume the same facts as in Example 3, and that Keith also had medical expenses of $1,800. Medical expenses may be included in itemized deductions to the extent they exceed 7.5% of AGI. In computing his itemized deductions, Keith may include medical expenses of $300 [$1,800 medical expenses – $1,500 (7.5% × $20,000 AGI)]. ▼

Itemized Deductions. As a general rule, personal expenditures are disallowed as deductions in arriving at taxable income. However, Congress has chosen to allow specified personal expenses as **itemized deductions.** Such expenditures include medical expenses, certain taxes and interest, and charitable contributions.

In addition to these personal expenses, taxpayers are allowed itemized deductions for expenses related to (1) the production or collection of income and (2) the management of property held for the production of income.[5] These expenses, sometimes referred to as *nonbusiness expenses,* differ from trade or business expenses (discussed previously). Trade or business expenses, which are deductions *for* AGI, must be incurred in connection with a trade or business. Nonbusiness expenses, on the other hand, are expenses incurred in connection with an income-producing activity that does not qualify as a trade or business. Such expenses are itemized deductions.

EXAMPLE 5

Leo is the owner and operator of a video game arcade. All allowable expenses he incurs in connection with the arcade business are deductions *for* AGI. In addition, Leo has an extensive portfolio of stocks and bonds. Leo's investment activity is not treated as a trade or business. All allowable expenses that Leo incurs in connection with these investments are itemized deductions. ▼

Itemized deductions include, but are not limited to, the expenses listed in Exhibit 3–3. See Chapter 10 for a detailed discussion of itemized deductions.

▼ EXHIBIT 3–3
Partial List of Itemized Deductions

- Medical expenses in excess of 7.5% of AGI
- State and local income taxes
- Real estate taxes
- Personal property taxes
- Interest on home mortgage
- Investment interest (to a limited extent)
- Charitable contributions (within specified percentage limitations)
- Casualty and theft losses in excess of 10% of AGI
- Miscellaneous expenses (to the extent such expenses exceed 2% of AGI)
  - Union dues
  - Professional dues and subscriptions
  - Certain educational expenses
  - Tax return preparation fee
  - Investment counsel fees
  - Unreimbursed employee business expenses (after 50% reduction for meals and entertainment)

[5] § 212.

Standard Deduction. The **standard deduction,** which is set by Congress, is a specified amount that depends on the filing status of the taxpayer. The effect of the standard deduction is to exempt a taxpayer's income, up to the specified amount, from Federal income tax liability. In the past, Congress has attempted to set the tax-free amount represented by the standard deduction approximately equal to an estimated poverty level,[6] but it has not always been consistent in doing so.

The standard deduction is the sum of two components: the *basic* standard deduction and the *additional* standard deduction.[7] Table 3–1 lists the basic standard deduction allowed for taxpayers in each filing status. All taxpayers allowed a *full* standard deduction are entitled to the applicable amount listed in Table 3–1. The standard deduction amounts are subject to adjustment for inflation each year.

Certain taxpayers are not allowed to claim *any* standard deduction, and the standard deduction is *limited* for others. These provisions are discussed later in the chapter.

A taxpayer who is age 65 or over *or* blind qualifies for an *additional standard deduction* of $800 or $1,000, depending on filing status (see amounts in Table 3–2). Two additional standard deductions are allowed for a taxpayer who is age 65 or over *and* blind. The additional standard deduction provisions also apply for a qualifying spouse who is age 65 or over or blind, but a taxpayer may not claim an additional standard deduction for a dependent.

▼ TABLE 3–1
Basic Standard Deduction Amounts

	Standard Deduction Amount	
Filing Status	**1995**	**1996**
Single	$3,900	$4,000
Married, filing jointly	6,550	6,700
Surviving spouse	6,550	6,700
Head of household	5,750	5,900
Married, filing separately	3,275	3,350

▼ TABLE 3–2
Amount of Each Additional Standard Deduction

Filing Status	1995	1996
Single	$950	$1,000
Married, filing jointly	750	800
Surviving spouse	750	800
Head of household	950	1,000
Married, filing separately	750	800

[6] S.Rep. No. 92–437, 92nd Cong., 1st Sess., 1971, p. 54. Another purpose of the standard deduction was discussed in Chapter 1 under Influence of the Internal Revenue Service—Administrative Feasibility. The size of the standard deduction has a direct bearing on the number of taxpayers who are in a position to itemize deductions. Reducing the number of taxpayers who itemize also reduces the audit effort required from the IRS. Currently, about 70% of all individual taxpayers choose to use the standard deduction.

[7] § 63(c)(1).

To determine whether to itemize, the taxpayer compares the *total* standard deduction (the sum of the basic standard deduction and any additional standard deductions) to total itemized deductions. Taxpayers are allowed to deduct the *greater* of itemized deductions or the standard deduction. Taxpayers whose itemized deductions are less than the standard deduction compute their taxable income using the standard deduction rather than itemizing.

EXAMPLE 6

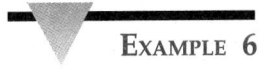

Sara, who is single, is 66 years old. She had total itemized deductions of $4,800 during 1996. Her total standard deduction is $5,000 ($4,000 basic standard deduction plus $1,000 additional standard deduction). Sara should compute her taxable income for 1996 using the standard deduction ($5,000), since it exceeds her itemized deductions ($4,800). ▼

Personal and Dependency Exemptions. Exemptions are allowed for the taxpayer, for the taxpayer's spouse, and for each dependent of the taxpayer. The exemption amount is $2,500 in 1995 and $2,550 in 1996.

APPLICATION OF THE TAX FORMULA

The tax formula shown in Figure 3–1 is illustrated in Example 7.

EXAMPLE 7

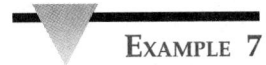

Grace, age 25, is single and has no dependents. She is a high school teacher and earned a $20,000 salary in 1996. Her other income consisted of a $1,000 prize won in a sweepstakes contest and $500 interest on municipal bonds received as a graduation gift in 1993. During 1996, she sustained a deductible capital loss of $1,000. Her itemized deductions are $4,200. Grace's taxable income for the year is computed as follows:

Income (broadly conceived)		
Salary		$20,000
Prize		1,000
Interest on municipal bonds		500
		$21,500
Less: Exclusion—		
Interest on municipal bonds		(500)
Gross income		$21,000
Less: Deduction *for* adjusted gross income—		
Capital loss		(1,000)
Adjusted gross income		$20,000
Less: The greater of—		
Total itemized deductions	$4,200	
or the standard deduction	$4,000	(4,200)
Personal and dependency exemptions		
(1 × $2,550)		(2,550)
Taxable income		$13,250

▼

The structure of the individual income tax return (Form 1040, 1040A, or 1040EZ) differs somewhat from the tax formula in Figure 3–1. On the tax return, gross income generally is the starting point in computing taxable income. With few exceptions, exclusions are not reported on the tax return.

INDIVIDUALS NOT ELIGIBLE FOR THE STANDARD DEDUCTION

The following individual taxpayers are ineligible to use the standard deduction and must therefore itemize:[8]

- A married individual filing a separate return where either spouse itemizes deductions.
- A nonresident alien.
- An individual filing a return for a period of less than 12 months because of a change in annual accounting period.

SPECIAL LIMITATIONS FOR INDIVIDUALS WHO CAN BE CLAIMED AS DEPENDENTS

Special rules apply to the standard deduction and personal exemption of an individual who can be claimed as a dependent on another person's tax return.

When filing his or her own tax return, a *dependent's* basic standard deduction is limited to the greater of $650 or the individual's earned income for the year.[9] However, if the individual's earned income exceeds the normal standard deduction, the standard deduction is limited to the appropriate standard deduction amount shown in Table 3–1. These limitations apply only to the basic standard deduction. A dependent who is 65 or over or blind or both is also allowed the additional standard deduction amount on his or her own return (refer to Table 3–2). These provisions are illustrated in Examples 8 through 11.

EXAMPLE 8

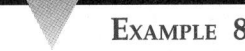

Susan, who is 17 years old and single, is claimed as a dependent on her parents' tax return. During 1996, she received $1,200 interest (unearned income) on a savings account. She also earned $500 from a part-time job. When Susan files her own tax return, her standard deduction is $650 (the greater of $650 or earned income of $500). ▼

EXAMPLE 9

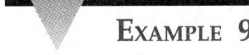

Assume the same facts as in Example 8, except that Susan is 67 years old and is claimed as a dependent on her son's tax return. In this case, when Susan files her own tax return, her standard deduction is $1,650 [$650 (the greater of $650 or earned income of $500) + $1,000 (the additional standard deduction allowed because Susan is 65 or over)]. ▼

EXAMPLE 10

Peggy, who is 16 years old and single, earned $1,000 from a summer job and had no unearned income during 1996. She is claimed as a dependent on her parents' tax return. Her standard deduction is $1,000 (the greater of $650 or earned income). ▼

EXAMPLE 11

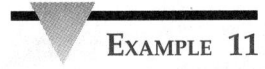

Jack, who is a 20-year-old, single, full-time college student, is claimed as a dependent on his parents' tax return. He worked as a musician during the summer of 1996, earning $4,100. Jack's standard deduction is $4,000 (the greater of $650 or $4,100 earned income, but limited to the $4,000 standard deduction for a single taxpayer). ▼

A taxpayer who claims an individual as a dependent is allowed to claim an exemption for the dependent. The dependent cannot claim a personal exemption

[8] § 63(c)(6).

[9] § 63(c)(5). The $650 amount is subject to adjustment for inflation each year. The amount was also $650 for 1995.

on his or her own return. Based on the tax formula, Jack in Example 11 would have taxable income of $100, determined as follows:

Gross income	$ 4,100
Less: Standard deduction	(4,000)
Personal exemption	(-0-)
Taxable income	$ 100

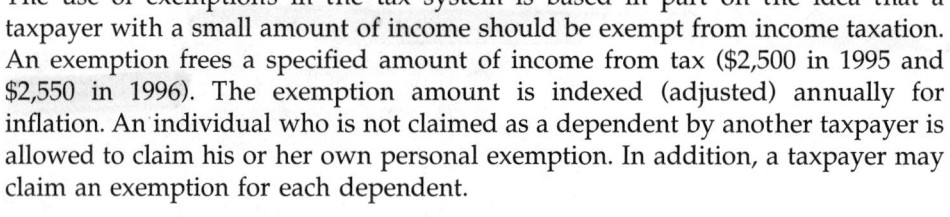

PERSONAL AND DEPENDENCY EXEMPTIONS

2 LEARNING OBJECTIVE
Apply the rules for arriving at personal and dependency exemptions.

The use of exemptions in the tax system is based in part on the idea that a taxpayer with a small amount of income should be exempt from income taxation. An exemption frees a specified amount of income from tax ($2,500 in 1995 and $2,550 in 1996). The exemption amount is indexed (adjusted) annually for inflation. An individual who is not claimed as a dependent by another taxpayer is allowed to claim his or her own personal exemption. In addition, a taxpayer may claim an exemption for each dependent.

EXAMPLE 12

Bonnie, who is single, supports her mother and father, who have no income of their own, and claims them as dependents on her tax return. Bonnie may claim a personal exemption for herself plus an exemption for each dependent. On her 1996 tax return, Bonnie may deduct $7,650 for exemptions ($2,550 per exemption × 3 exemptions). ▼

PERSONAL EXEMPTIONS

The Code provides a **personal exemption** for the taxpayer and an exemption for the spouse if a joint return is filed. However, when separate returns are filed, a married taxpayer cannot claim an exemption for his or her spouse *unless* the spouse has no gross income and is not claimed as the dependent of another taxpayer.

The determination of marital status generally is made at the end of the taxable year, except when a spouse dies during the year. Spouses who enter into a legal separation under a decree of divorce or separate maintenance before the end of the year are considered to be unmarried at the end of the taxable year. The following table illustrates the effect of death or divorce upon marital status:

	Marital Status for 1996
• Walt is the widower of Helen who died on January 3, 1996.	Walt and Helen are considered to be married for purposes of filing the 1996 return.
• Bill and Jane entered into a divorce decree that is effective on December 31, 1996.	Bill and Jane are considered to be unmarried for purposes of filing the 1996 return.

DEPENDENCY EXEMPTIONS

As indicated in Example 12, the Code allows a taxpayer to claim a dependency exemption for each eligible individual. A **dependency exemption** may be claimed for each individual for whom the following five tests are met:

- Support.
- Relationship or member of the household.
- Gross income.
- Joint return.
- Citizenship or residency.

A person who dies during the year can still be claimed as a dependent if all of the tests are met. In such a case, no proration is necessary, and the full amount of the exemption is allowed.

Support Test. Over one-half of the support of the individual must be furnished by the taxpayer. Support includes food, shelter, clothing, medical and dental care, education, etc. However, a scholarship received by a student is not included for purposes of computing whether the taxpayer furnished more than half of the child's support.[10]

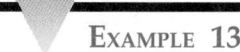

EXAMPLE 13

Hal contributed $3,400 (consisting of food, clothing, and medical care) toward the support of his son, Sam, who earned $1,500 from a part-time job and received a $2,000 scholarship to attend a local university. Assuming that the other dependency tests are met, Hal can claim Sam as a dependent since he has contributed more than half of Sam's support. The $2,000 scholarship is not included as support for purposes of this test. ▼

If the individual does not spend funds that have been received from any source, the unexpended amounts are not counted for purposes of the support test.

EXAMPLE 14

Emily contributed $3,000 to her father's support during the year. In addition, her father received $2,400 in Social Security benefits, $200 of interest, and wages of $600. Her father deposited the Social Security benefits, interest, and wages in his own savings account and did not use any of the funds for his support. Thus, the Social Security benefits, interest, and wages are not considered as support provided by Emily's father. Emily may claim her father as a dependent if the other tests are met. ▼

Capital expenditures for items such as furniture, appliances, and automobiles are included in total support if the item does, in fact, constitute support.[11]

EXAMPLE 15

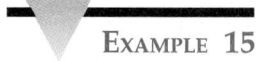

Norm purchased a television set costing $150 and gave it to his minor daughter. The television set was placed in the child's bedroom and was used exclusively by her. Norm should include the cost of the television set in determining the support of his daughter. ▼

EXAMPLE 16

Mark paid $6,000 for an automobile that was titled and registered in his name. Mark's minor son is permitted to use the automobile equally with Mark. Since Mark did not give the automobile to his son, the $6,000 cost is not includible as a support item. However, out-of-pocket operating expenses incurred by Mark for the benefit of his son are includible as support. ▼

---

[10] Reg. § 1.152–1(c).

[11] Rev.Rul. 57–344, 1957–2 C.B. 112; Rev.Rul. 58–419, 1958–2 C.B. 57.

ETHICAL CONSIDERATIONS

Claiming a Dependent

Martha is a widow and lives with her only son, Roland, and his family. Martha's only income consists of $70,000 in interest from tax-exempt bonds. She invests all of the income in stocks in her name. The stocks do not pay dividends. Martha's will provides that all of her property is to pass to Roland upon her death. Because of this expectation, Roland provides all of his mother's support. On his return, Roland claims a dependency exemption for his mother.

Is this proper procedure? After all, Martha was in a position to provide all of her support had she chosen to do so.

One exception to the support test involves a **multiple support agreement.** A multiple support agreement permits one of a group of taxpayers who furnish more than half of the support of an individual to claim a dependency exemption for that individual even if no one person provides more than 50 percent of the support.[12] Any person who contributed *more than 10 percent* of the support is entitled to claim the exemption if each person in the group who contributed more than 10 percent files a written consent. This provision frequently enables one of the children of aged dependent parents to claim an exemption when none of the children meets the 50 percent support test. Each person who is a party to the multiple support agreement must meet all other requirements (except the support requirement) for claiming the exemption. A person who does not meet the relationship or member-of-household requirement, for instance, cannot claim the dependency exemption under a multiple support agreement. It does not matter if he or she contributes more than 10 percent of the individual's support.

EXAMPLE 17

Wanda, who resides with her son, Adam, received $6,000 from various sources during 1996. This constituted her entire support for the year. She received support from the following:

	Amount	Percentage of Total
Adam, a son	$2,880	48
Bob, a son	600	10
Carol, a daughter	1,800	30
Diane, a friend	720	12
	$6,000	100

If Adam and Carol file a multiple support agreement, either may claim the dependency exemption for Wanda. Bob may not claim Wanda because he did not contribute more than 10% of her support. Bob's consent is not required in order for Adam and Carol to file a multiple support agreement. Diane does not meet the relationship or member-of-household

[12] § 152(c).

test and cannot be a party to the agreement. The decision as to who claims Wanda rests with Adam and Carol. It is possible for Carol to claim Wanda, even though Adam furnished more of Wanda's support. ▼

Each person who qualifies under the more-than-10 percent rule (except for the person claiming the exemption) must complete Form 2120 (Multiple Support Declaration) waiving the exemption. The person claiming the exemption must attach all Forms 2120 to his or her own return. Form 2120 is reproduced in Appendix B.

A second exception to the 50 percent support requirement can occur for a child of parents who are divorced or separated under a decree of separate maintenance. For decrees executed after 1984, the custodial parent is allowed to claim the exemption unless that parent agrees in writing not to claim a dependency exemption for the child.[13] Thus, claiming the exemption is dependent on whether or not a written agreement exists, *not* on meeting the support test.

EXAMPLE 18 Ira and Rita obtain a divorce decree in 1989. In 1996, their two children are in Rita's custody. Ira contributed over half of the support for each child. In the absence of a written agreement on the dependency exemptions, Rita (the custodial parent) is entitled to the exemptions in 1996. However, Ira may claim the exemptions if Rita agrees in writing. ▼

For the noncustodial parent to claim the exemption, the custodial parent must complete Form 8332 (Release of Claim to Exemption for Child of Divorced or Separated Parents). The release can apply to a single year, a number of specified years, or all future years. The noncustodial parent must attach a copy of Form 8332 to his or her return.

ETHICAL CONSIDERATIONS

Bribery to Obtain Dependency Exemptions

Will and Nora were divorced in 1993. Under the divorce decree, Will is to pay alimony and child support, and Nora has custody of their two children.

Although Will has not contributed more than 50 percent of the children's support, he would like to claim them as dependents for tax year 1996. Upon being contacted by Will, Nora agrees to waive the exemptions if she receives an extra $500 in cash. Will makes the payment, and Nora signs Form 8332 for 1996.

May Will claim the children as dependents? Have the parties acted improperly?

Relationship or Member-of-the-Household Test. To be claimed as a dependent, an individual must be either a relative of the taxpayer or a member of the taxpayer's household. The Code contains a detailed listing of the various blood and marriage relationships that qualify. Note, however, that the relationship test is met if the individual is a relative of either spouse. Once established by marriage, a relationship continues regardless of subsequent changes in marital status.

[13] § 152(e).

The following individuals may be claimed as dependents of the taxpayer if the other tests for dependency are met:[14]

- A son or daughter of the taxpayer or a descendant of either, such as a grandchild.
- A stepson or stepdaughter of the taxpayer.
- A brother, sister, stepbrother, or stepsister of the taxpayer.
- The father or mother of the taxpayer or an ancestor of either, such as a grandparent.
- A stepfather or stepmother of the taxpayer.
- A nephew or niece of the taxpayer.
- An uncle or aunt of the taxpayer.
- A son-in-law, daughter-in-law, father-in-law, mother-in-law, brother-in-law, or sister-in-law of the taxpayer.
- An individual who, for the entire taxable year of the taxpayer, has as his or her principal place of abode the home of the taxpayer and is a member of the taxpayer's household. This does not include an individual who, at any time during the taxable year, was the spouse of the taxpayer.

The following rules are also prescribed in the Code:[15]

- A legally adopted child is treated as a natural child.
- A foster child qualifies if the child's principal place of abode is the taxpayer's household.

Gross Income Test. The dependent's gross income must be less than the exemption amount ($2,550 in 1996).[16] The gross income test is measured by income that is taxable. In the case of scholarships, for example, it excludes the nontaxable portion (e.g., amounts received for books and tuition) but includes the taxable portion (e.g., amounts received for room and board).

A parent may claim a dependency exemption for his or her child, even when the child's gross income exceeds $2,550, if the parent provided over half of the child's support and the child, at year-end, is under age 19 or is a full-time student under age 24. If the parent claims a dependency exemption, the dependent child may not claim a personal exemption on his or her own income tax return.

A child is defined as a son, stepson, daughter, stepdaughter, adopted son, or adopted daughter and may include a foster child.[17] For the child to qualify as a student for purposes of the dependency exemption, he or she must be a full-time student at an educational institution during some part of five calendar months of the year.[18] This exception to the gross income test for dependent children who are under age 19 or full-time students under age 24 permits a child or college student to earn money from part-time or summer jobs without penalizing the parent with the loss of the dependency exemption.

Joint Return Test. If a dependent is married, the supporting taxpayer (e.g., the parent of a married child) generally is not permitted a dependency exemption if

---

[14] § 152(a). However, under § 152(b)(5), a taxpayer may not claim someone who is a member of his or her household as a dependent if their relationship is in violation of local law. For example, the dependency exemption was denied because the taxpayer's relationship to the person claimed as a dependent constituted *cohabitation*, a crime under applicable state law. *Cassius L. Peacock, III*, 37 TCM 177, T.C.Memo. 1978–30.

[15] § 152(b)(2).

[16] § 151(c)(1).

[17] Reg. § 1.151–3(a).

[18] Reg. §§ 1.151–3(b) and (c).

the married individual files a joint return with his or her spouse.[19] The joint return rule does not apply, however, if the following conditions are met:

- The reason for filing is to claim a refund for tax withheld.
- No tax liability would exist for either spouse on separate returns.
- Neither spouse is required to file a return.

See Table 3–4 later in the chapter and the related discussion concerning income level requirements for filing a return.

EXAMPLE 19 Paul provides over half of the support of his son Quinn. He also provides over half of the support of Vera, who is Quinn's wife. During the year, both Quinn and Vera had part-time jobs. In order to recover the taxes withheld, they file a joint return. If Quinn and Vera are not required to file a return, Paul is allowed to claim both as dependents. ▼

Citizenship or Residency Test. To be a dependent, the individual must be either a U.S. citizen, a U.S. resident, or a resident of Canada or Mexico for some part of the calendar year in which the taxpayer's tax year begins.

Phase-out of Exemptions. Several provisions of the tax law are intended to increase the tax liability of more affluent taxpayers who might otherwise enjoy some benefit from having some of their taxable income subject to the lower income tax brackets (e.g., 15 percent, 28 percent). One such provision phases out personal and dependency exemptions as AGI exceeds specified threshold amounts. For 1995 and 1996, the phase-out *begins* at the following threshold amounts:

	1995	1996
Joint returns/Surviving spouse	$172,050	$176,950
Head of household	143,350	147,450
Single	114,700	117,950
Married, filing separately	86,025	88,475

These threshold amounts are indexed for inflation each year.

Exemptions are phased out by 2 percent for each $2,500 (or fraction thereof) by which the taxpayer's AGI exceeds the threshold amounts. For a married taxpayer filing separately, the phase-out is 2 percent for each $1,250 or fraction thereof.

The allowable exemption amount can be determined with the following steps:

1. AGI – threshold amount = excess amount
2. Excess amount ÷ $2,500 = reduction factor [rounded up to the next whole increment (e.g., 18.1 = 19)] × 2 = phase-out percentage
3. Phase-out percentage (from step 2) × exemption amount = amount of exemptions phased out
4. Exemption amounts – phase-out amount = allowable exemption deduction

EXAMPLE 20 Frederico is married but files a separate return. His AGI is $108,475. He is entitled to one personal exemption.

[19] § 151(c)(2).

1. \$108,475 – \$88,475 = \$20,000 excess amount
2. [(\$20,000 ÷ \$1,250) × 2] = 32% (phase-out percentage)
3. 32% × \$2,550 = \$816 amount of exemption phased out
4. \$2,550 – \$816 = \$1,734 allowable exemption deduction ▼

Note that the exemption amount is completely phased out when the taxpayer's AGI exceeds the threshold amount by more than \$122,500 (\$61,250 for a married taxpayer filing a separate return), calculated as follows:

\$122,501 ÷ \$2,500 = 49.0004, rounded to 50 and multiplied by 2 = 100% (phase-out percentage)

EXAMPLE 21

Bill and Isabella file a joint return claiming two personal exemptions and one dependency exemption for their child. Their AGI equals \$300,950.

\$300,950 – \$176,950 = \$124,000 excess amount

Since the excess amount exceeds \$122,500, the exemptions are completely phased out. ▼

TAX DETERMINATION

TAX TABLE METHOD

3 LEARNING OBJECTIVE
Use the proper method for determining the tax liability.

Most taxpayers compute their tax using the **Tax Table.** Eligible taxpayers compute taxable income (as shown in Figure 3–1) and *must* determine their tax by reference to the Tax Table. The following taxpayers, however, may not use the Tax Table method:

- An individual who files a short period return (see Chapter 18).
- Individuals whose taxable income exceeds the maximum (ceiling) amount in the Tax Table. The 1995 Tax Table applies to taxable income below \$100,000 for Form 1040.
- An estate or trust.

The 1996 Tax Table was not available at the date of publication of this text. Therefore, the 1995 Tax Table will be used to illustrate the tax computation using the Tax Table method.

EXAMPLE 22

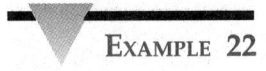

Pedro, a single taxpayer, is eligible to use the Tax Table. For 1995, he had taxable income of \$25,025. To determine Pedro's tax using the Tax Table (see Appendix A), find the \$25,000 to \$25,050 income line. The first column to the right of the taxable income column is for single taxpayers. Pedro's tax for 1995 is \$3,972. ▼

TAX RATE SCHEDULE METHOD

The **Tax Rate Schedules** contain rates of 15, 28, 31, 36, and 39.6 percent. Separate schedules are provided for the following filing statuses: single, married filing jointly, married filing separately, and head of household. The rate schedules for 1995 and 1996 are reproduced inside the front cover of this text and also in Appendix A.

The rate schedules are adjusted for inflation each year. Comparison of the 1995 and 1996 schedules for single taxpayers shows that the top amount to which the 15 percent bracket applies rose from \$23,350 in 1995 to \$24,000 in 1996. Thus,

▼ TABLE 3–3
1996 Tax Rate Schedule for Single Taxpayers

If Taxable Income Is			Of the Amount
Over	**But Not Over**	**The Tax Is:**	**Over**
$ -0-	$ 24,000	15%	$ -0-
24,000	58,150	$ 3,600.00 + 28%	24,000
58,150	121,300	13,162.00 + 31%	58,150
121,300	263,750	32,738.50 + 36%	121,300
263,750		84,020.50 + 39.6%	263,750

inflation allowed $650 ($24,000 – $23,350) more taxable income to be subject to the lowest 15 percent rate.

The 1996 rate schedule for single taxpayers is reproduced in Table 3–3. This schedule is used to illustrate the tax computations in Examples 23, 24, and 25.

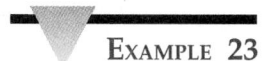

EXAMPLE 23

Pat is single and had $18,000 of taxable income in 1996. His tax is $2,700 ($18,000 × 15%). ▼

Several terms are used to describe tax rates. The rates in the Tax Rate Schedules are often referred to as *statutory* (or nominal) rates. The *marginal* rate is the highest rate that is applied in the tax computation for a particular taxpayer. In Example 23, the statutory rate and the marginal rate are both 15 percent.

EXAMPLE 24

Chris is single and had taxable income of $41,450 in 1996. Her tax is $8,486 [$3,600 + 28%($41,450 – $24,000)]. ▼

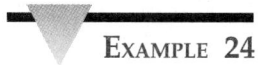

The *average* rate is equal to the tax liability divided by taxable income. In Example 24, Chris had statutory rates of 15 percent and 28 percent, and a marginal rate of 28 percent. Chris's average rate was 20.5 percent ($8,486 tax liability ÷ $41,450 taxable income).

Note that $3,600, which is the starting point in the tax computation in Example 24, is 15 percent of the $24,000 taxable income in the first bracket. Income in excess of $24,000 is taxed at a 28 percent rate. This reflects the *progressive* (or graduated) rate structure on which the U.S. income tax system is based. A tax is progressive if a higher rate of tax applies as the tax base increases.

EXAMPLE 25

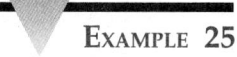

Carl is single and had taxable income of $81,900 in 1996. His tax is $20,524.50 [$13,162 + 31%($81,900 – $58,150)]. Note that the effect of this computation is to tax part of Carl's income at 15%, part at 28%, and part at 31%. An alternative computational method provides a clearer illustration of the progressive rate structure:

Tax on $24,000 at 15%	$ 3,600.00
Tax on $58,150 – $24,000 at 28%	9,562.00
Tax on $81,900 – $58,150 at 31%	7,362.50
Total	$20,524.50

▼

A special computation limits the effective tax rate on long-term capital gain. The beneficial tax treatment of long-term capital gain is discussed in detail in Chapter 16.

COMPUTATION OF NET TAXES PAYABLE OR REFUND DUE

The pay-as-you-go feature of the Federal income tax system requires payment of all or part of the taxpayer's income tax liability during the year. These payments take the form of Federal income tax withheld by employers or estimated tax paid by the taxpayer or both.[20] The payments are applied against the tax from the Tax Table or Tax Rate Schedules to determine whether the taxpayer will get a refund or pay additional tax.

Employers are required to withhold income tax on compensation paid to their employees and to pay this tax over to the government. The employer notifies the employee of the amount of income tax withheld on Form W–2 (Wage and Tax Statement). The employee should receive this form by January 31 after the year in which the income tax is withheld.

If taxpayers receive income that is not subject to withholding or income from which not enough tax is withheld, they must pay estimated tax. These individuals must file Form 1040–ES (Estimated Tax for Individuals) and pay in quarterly installments the income tax and self-employment tax estimated to be due (see Chapter 13 for a thorough discussion).

The income tax from the Tax Table or the Tax Rate Schedules is reduced first by the individual's tax credits. There is an important distinction between tax credits and tax deductions. Tax credits reduce the tax liability dollar-for-dollar. Tax deductions reduce taxable income on which the tax liability is based.

EXAMPLE 26

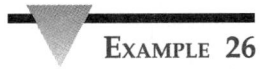

Gail is a taxpayer in the 28% tax bracket. As a result of incurring $1,000 in child care expenses (see Chapter 13 for details), she is entitled to a $200 child care credit ($1,000 child care expenses × 20% credit rate). She also contributed $1,000 to the American Cancer Society and included this amount in her itemized deductions. The child care credit results in a $200 reduction of Gail's tax liability for the year. The contribution to the American Cancer Society reduces taxable income by $1,000 and results in a $280 reduction in Gail's tax liability ($1,000 reduction in taxable income × 28% tax rate). ▼

Tax credits are discussed in Chapter 13. The following are several of the more common credits:

- Earned income credit.
- Credit for child and dependent care expenses.
- Credit for the elderly.
- Foreign tax credit.

EXAMPLE 27

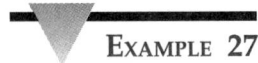

Kelly, age 30, is a head of household with two dependents. During 1996, Kelly had the following: taxable income, $30,000; income tax withheld, $3,950; estimated tax payments, $600; and credit for child care expenses, $200. Kelly's net tax payable is computed as follows:

Income tax (from 1996 Tax Rate Schedule, Appendix A)		$ 4,500
Less: Tax credits and prepayments—		
Credit for child care expenses	$ 200	
Income tax withheld	3,950	
Estimated tax payments	600	(4,750)
Net taxes payable or (refund due if negative)		$ (250)

▼

[20] § 3402 for withholding; § 6654 for estimated payments.

UNEARNED INCOME OF CHILDREN UNDER AGE 14 TAXED AT PARENTS' RATE

4 LEARNING OBJECTIVE
Identify and work with kiddie tax situations.

Before the Tax Reform Act (TRA) of 1986, a dependent child could claim an exemption on his or her own return even if claimed as a dependent by the parents. This enabled a parent to shift investment income (such as interest and dividends) to a child by transferring ownership of the assets producing the income. The child would pay no tax on the income to the extent that it was sheltered by the child's exemption.

For pre-1987 years, an additional tax motivation existed for shifting income from parents to children. Although a child's unearned income in excess of the exemption amount was subject to tax, it was taxed at the child's rate, rather than the parents' rate.

To reduce the tax savings that result from shifting income from parents to children, the net **unearned income** (commonly called investment income) of certain minor children is taxed as if it were the parents' income.[21] Unearned income includes such income as taxable interest, dividends, capital gains, rents, royalties, pension and annuity income, and income (other than earned income) received as the beneficiary of a trust. This provision, commonly referred to as the **kiddie tax,** applies to any child for any taxable year if the child has not reached age 14 by the close of the taxable year, has at least one living parent, and has unearned income of more than $1,300. The *kiddie tax* provision does not apply to a child age 14 or older. However, the limitation on the use of the standard deduction and the unavailability of the personal exemption do apply to such a child as long as he or she is eligible to be claimed as a dependent by a parent.

The term *parent* is defined in the Senate Finance Committee Report as a parent or stepparent of the child. No statutory definition exists for the term.

Net Unearned Income. Net unearned income of a dependent child is computed as follows:

Unearned income
Less: $650
Less: The greater of
- $650 of the standard deduction *or*
- The amount of allowable itemized deductions directly connected with the production of the unearned income

Equals: Net unearned income

If net unearned income is zero (or negative), the child's tax is computed without using the parent's rate. If the amount of net unearned income (regardless of source) is positive, the net unearned income will be taxed at the parent's rate. The $650 amounts in the preceding formula are subject to adjustment for inflation each year (refer to footnote 9).

Tax Determination. If a child under age 14 has net unearned income, there are two options for computing the tax on the income. A separate return may be filed for the child, or the parents may elect to report the child's income on their own return. If a separate return is filed for the child, the tax on net unearned income (referred to as the *allocable parental tax*) is computed as though the income had

[21] § 1(g).

been included on the parents' return. Form 8615 (reproduced in Appendix B) is used to compute the tax. The steps required in this computation are illustrated below.

EXAMPLE 28 Olaf and Olga have a child, Hans (age 10). In 1996, Hans received $2,800 of interest and dividend income and paid investment-related fees of $200. Olaf and Olga had $69,450 of taxable income, not including their child's investment income. Olaf and Olga do not make the parental election.

1. Determine Hans's net unearned income	
Gross income (unearned)	$ 2,800
Less: $650	(650)
Less: The greater of	
• $650 or	
• Investment expense	(650)
Equals: Net unearned income	$ 1,500
2. Determine allocable parental tax	
Parents' taxable income	$ 69,450
Plus: Hans's net unearned income	1,500
Equals: Revised taxable income	$ 70,950
Tax on revised taxable income	$ 14,653
Less: Tax on parents' taxable income	(14,233)
Allocable parental tax	$ 420
3. Determine Hans's nonparental source tax	
Hans's AGI	$ 2,800
Less: Standard deduction	(650)
Less: Personal exemption	(–0–)
Equals: Taxable income	$ 2,150
Less: Net unearned income	(1,500)
Nonparental source taxable income	$ 650
Equals: Tax ($650 × 15% rate)	$ 98
4. Determine Hans's total tax liability	
Nonparental source tax (step 3)	$ 98
Allocable parental tax (step 2)	420
Total tax	$ 518

▼

Election to Claim Certain Unearned Income on Parent's Return. If a child under age 14 is required to file a tax return and meets all of the following requirements, the parent may elect to report the child's unearned income that exceeds $1,000 on the parent's own tax return:

- Gross income is from interest and dividends only.
- Gross income is less than $5,000.
- No estimated tax has been paid in the name and Social Security number of the child, and the child is not subject to backup withholding (see Chapter 13).

If the parental election is made, the child is treated as having no gross income and then is not required to file a tax return.

The parent(s) must also pay an additional tax equal to the smaller of $75 or 15 percent of the child's gross income over $500. Parents who have substantial itemized deductions based on AGI (see Chapter 10) may find that making the parental election increases total taxes for the family unit. Taxes should be calculated both with the parental election and without it to determine the appropriate choice.

Other Provisions. If parents have more than one child subject to the tax on net unearned income, the tax for the children is computed as shown in Example 28 and then allocated to the children based on their relative amounts of income. For children of divorced parents, the taxable income of the custodial parent is used to determine the allocable parental tax. This parent is the one who may elect to report the child's unearned income. For married individuals filing separate returns, the individual with the greater taxable income is the applicable parent.

FILING CONSIDERATIONS

5 LEARNING OBJECTIVE
Recognize the filing requirements and the proper filing status.

Under the category of filing considerations, the following questions need to be resolved:

- Is the taxpayer required to file an income tax return?
- If so, which form should be used?
- When and how should the return be filed?
- In computing the tax liability, which column of the Tax Table or which Tax Rate Schedule should be used?

The first three questions are discussed under Filing Requirements, and the last is treated under Filing Status.

FILING REQUIREMENTS

General Rules. An individual must file a tax return if certain minimum amounts of gross income have been received. The general rule is that a tax return is required for every individual who has gross income that equals or exceeds the sum of the exemption amount plus the applicable standard deduction.[22] For example, a single taxpayer under age 65 must file a tax return in 1996 if gross income equals or exceeds $6,550 ($2,550 exemption plus $4,000 standard deduction). Table 3–4 lists the income levels[23] that require tax returns under the general rule and under certain special rules.

The additional standard deduction for being age 65 or older is considered in determining the gross income filing requirements. For example, note in Table 3–4 that the 1996 filing requirement for a single taxpayer age 65 or older is $7,550 ($4,000 basic standard deduction + $1,000 additional standard deduction + $2,550 exemption). However, the additional standard deduction for blindness is not taken into account. The 1996 filing requirement for a single taxpayer under age 65 and blind is $6,550 ($4,000 basic standard deduction + $2,550 exemption).

A self-employed individual with net earnings of $400 or more from a business or profession must file a tax return regardless of the amount of gross income.

[22] The gross income amounts for determining whether a tax return must be filed are adjusted for inflation each year.

[23] § 6012(a)(1).

▼ TABLE 3-4
Filing Levels

Filing Status	1995 Gross Income	1996 Gross Income
Single		
Under 65 and not blind	$ 6,400	$ 6,550
Under 65 and blind	6,400	6,550
65 or older	7,350	7,550
Married, filing joint return		
Both spouses under 65 and neither blind	$11,550	$11,800
Both spouses under 65 and one or both spouses blind	11,550	11,800
One spouse 65 or older	12,300	12,600
Both spouses 65 or older	13,050	13,400
Married, filing separate return		
All—whether 65 or older or blind	$ 2,500	$ 2,550
Head of household		
Under 65 and not blind	$ 8,250	$ 8,450
Under 65 and blind	8,250	8,450
65 or older	9,200	9,450
Qualifying widow(er)		
Under 65 and not blind	$ 9,050	$ 9,250
Under 65 and blind	9,050	9,250
65 or older	9,800	10,050

Even though an individual has gross income below the filing level amounts and therefore does not owe any tax, he or she must file a return to obtain a tax refund of amounts withheld. A return is also necessary to obtain the benefits of the earned income credit allowed to taxpayers with little or no tax liability. Chapter 13 discusses the earned income credit.

Filing Requirements for Dependents. Computation of the gross income filing requirement for an individual who can be claimed as a dependent on another person's tax return is subject to more complex rules. Such an individual must file a return if he or she has *either* of the following:

- Earned income only and gross income that is more than the total standard deduction (including any additional standard deduction) that the individual is allowed for the year.
- Unearned income only and gross income of more than $650 plus any additional standard deduction that the individual is allowed for the year.
- Both earned and unearned income and gross income of more than the larger of earned income (but limited to the applicable basic standard deduction) or $650, plus any additional standard deduction that the individual is allowed for the year.

Thus, the filing requirement for a dependent who has no unearned income is the total of the *basic* standard deduction plus any *additional* standard deduction, which includes both the additional deduction for blindness and the deduction for being age 65 or older. For example, the 1996 filing requirement for a single dependent who is under 65 and not blind is $4,000, the amount of the basic

TAX IN THE NEWS

PLEASE STOP FILING WHEN YOU DO NOT NEED TO

In Internal Revenue News Release 95–53 (August 31, 1995), the IRS is literally begging some people to stop filing income tax returns. Returns that are not required cost time and money for both the IRS and the taxpayers involved.

Many of the unnecessary filers are older taxpayers who are unaware that the annual indexation adjustments are exempting them from the filing requirement. Also, the annual filing habit developed over a lifetime of preretirement years seems hard to break.

The IRS is notifying these taxpayers by letter under its RUF (Reduce Unnecessary Filings) program.

standard deduction for 1996. The filing requirement for a single dependent under 65 and blind is $5,000 ($4,000 basic standard deduction + $1,000 additional standard deduction).

Selecting the Proper Form. The 1996 tax forms had not been released at the date of publication of this text. The following comments apply to 1995 forms. It is possible that some provisions will change for the 1996 forms.

Individual taxpayers file a return on either Form 1040 (the long form), Form 1040A (the short form), or Form 1040EZ. Taxpayers who cannot use either Form 1040EZ or Form 1040A must use Form 1040. These forms are reproduced in Appendix B. Examine the forms to determine which form is appropriate for a particular taxpayer.

When and Where to File. Tax returns of individuals are due on or before the fifteenth day of the fourth month following the close of the tax year. For the calendar year taxpayer, the usual filing date is on or before April 15 of the following year.[24] When the due date falls on a Saturday, Sunday, or legal holiday, the last day for filing falls on the next business day. If the return is mailed to the proper address with sufficient postage and is postmarked on or before the due date, it is deemed timely filed.

If a taxpayer is unable to file the return by the specified due date, a four-month extension of time can be obtained by filing Form 4868 (Application for Automatic Extension of Time to File U.S. Individual Income Tax Return).[25] Further extensions may be granted by the IRS upon a showing of good cause by the taxpayer. For this purpose, Form 2688 (Application for Extension of Time to File U.S. Individual Income Tax Return) should be used. An extension of more than six months will not be granted if the taxpayer is in the United States.

Although obtaining an extension excuses a taxpayer from a penalty for failure to file, it does not insulate against the penalty for failure to pay.[26] If more tax is owed, the filing of Form 4868 should be accompanied by an additional remittance to cover the balance due.

---

[24] § 6072(a).

[25] Reg. § 1.6081–4.

[26] For an explanation of these penalties, refer to Chapter 1.

The return should be sent or delivered to the Regional Service Center of the IRS for the area where the taxpayer lives.[27]

If an individual taxpayer needs to file an amended return (e.g., because of a failure to report income or to claim a deduction or tax credit), Form 1040X is filed. The form generally must be filed within three years of the filing date of the original return or within two years from the time the tax was paid, whichever is later.

FILING STATUS

The amount of tax will vary considerably depending on which Tax Rate Schedule is used. This is illustrated in the following example.

EXAMPLE 29

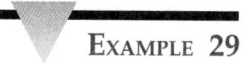

The following amounts of tax are computed using the 1996 Tax Rate Schedules for a taxpayer (or taxpayers in the case of a joint return) with $40,000 of taxable income (see Appendix A).

Filing Status	Amount of Tax
Single	$8,080
Married, filing joint return	6,000
Married, filing separate return	8,593.50
Head of household	7,020.50

▼

Rates for Single Taxpayers. A taxpayer who is unmarried or separated from his or her spouse by a decree of divorce or separate maintenance and does not qualify for another filing status must use the rates for single taxpayers. Marital status is determined as of the last day of the tax year, except when a spouse dies during the year. In that case, marital status is determined as of the date of death. State law governs whether a taxpayer is considered married, divorced, or legally separated.

Under a special relief provision, however, married persons who live apart may be able to qualify as single. Married taxpayers who are considered single under the *abandoned spouse rules* are allowed to use the head of household rates. See the discussion of this filing status under Abandoned Spouse Rules later in the chapter.

Rates for Married Individuals. The joint return (Tax Rate Schedule Y, Code § 1(a)) was originally enacted in 1948 to establish equity between married taxpayers in common law states and those in community property states. Before the joint return rates were enacted, taxpayers in community property states were in an advantageous position relative to taxpayers in common law states because they could split their income. For instance, if one spouse earned $100,000 and the other spouse was not employed, each spouse could report $50,000 of income. Splitting the income in this manner caused the total income to be subject to lower marginal tax rates. Each spouse would start at the bottom of the rate structure.

Taxpayers in common law states did not have this income-splitting option, so their taxable income was subject to higher marginal rates. This inconsistency in

[27] The Regional Service Centers and the geographical area each covers can be found in *Your Federal Income Tax,* IRS Publication 17 for 1995.

treatment was remedied by the joint return provisions. The progressive rates in the joint return Tax Rate Schedule are constructed based on the assumption that income is earned equally by the two spouses.

If married individuals elect to file separate returns, each reports only his or her own income, exemptions, deductions, and credits, and each must use the Tax Rate Schedule applicable to married taxpayers filing separately. It is generally advantageous for married individuals to file a joint return, since the combined amount of tax is lower. However, special circumstances (e.g., significant medical expenses incurred by one spouse subject to the 7.5 percent limitation) may warrant the election to file separate returns. It may be necessary to compute the tax under both assumptions to determine the most advantageous filing status.

When Congress enacted the rate structure available to those filing joint returns, it intended to favor married taxpayers. In certain situations, however, the parties would incur less tax if they were not married and filed separate returns. The additional tax that a joint return can cause, commonly called the **marriage penalty,** can develop when *both* spouses have larger taxable incomes.

EXAMPLE 30

John and Betty are employed, and each earns taxable income of $55,000. If they *are not married* and file separate returns, each has a tax liability of $12,280, or a total of $24,560 ($12,280 × 2). If they are married to each other, the filing of a joint return produces a tax of $25,980 on taxable income of $110,000 ($55,000 + $55,000). Thus, being married results in $1,420 ($25,980 – $24,560) more tax! ▼

Although some have suggested changes to lessen the impact of the marriage penalty, any remedy is apt to make the tax law more complex.

Besides the marriage penalty, a joint return can lead to another problem. This is the joint and several liability that results in the event additional taxes are due. As the Tax in the News on page 3-27 shows, a divorce could result in an ex-spouse getting hit for the full delinquency.

The Code places some limitations on deductions, credits, etc., when married individuals file separately. If either spouse itemizes deductions, the other spouse must also itemize. Married taxpayers who file separately cannot take either of the following:

- The credit for child and dependent care expenses (in most instances).
- The earned income credit.

The joint return rates also apply for two years following the death of one spouse, if the surviving spouse maintains a household for a dependent child.[28] This is referred to as **surviving spouse** status.

EXAMPLE 31

Fred dies in 1995 leaving Ethel with a dependent child. For the year of Fred's death (1995), Ethel files a joint return with Fred (presuming the consent of Fred's executor is obtained). For the next two years (1996 and 1997), Ethel, as a surviving spouse, may use the joint return rates. In subsequent years, Ethel may use the head-of-household rates if she continues to maintain a household as her home that is the domicile of the child. ▼

Rates for Heads of Household. Unmarried individuals who maintain a household for a dependent (or dependents) are entitled to use the **head-of-household** rates.[29] The tax liability using the head-of-household rates falls

[28] § 2(a).

[29] § 2(b).

TAX IN THE NEWS

Low-Income Taxpayers Also Suffer from the Marriage Penalty

The inequity of the marriage penalty is not limited to taxpayers with high incomes (see Example 30).

Consider, for example, Albert and June, each of whom has one dependent child. During 1996, Albert and June both earn wages of $10,000. Neither has any deductions *for* AGI.

Situation A shows the income tax result if Albert and June are married and file a joint return. Situation B assumes Albert and June are not married, qualify for head-of-household status, and file accordingly, with each claiming one child as a dependent. Because the Tax Tables for 1996 were not yet available, the Tax Rate Schedules were used to compute the tax.

The harsh effect of the marriage penalty is apparent. Albert and June are $2,980 better off (refunds totaling $4,304 versus $1,324) by not being married. This result is remarkable when one considers that AGI of only $20,000 is involved!

	Situation A	Situation B					
	If They Are Married	If They Are Not Married					
Their Taxes:		Albert		June		Total
Adjusted gross income	$20,000	$10,000	+	$10,000	=	$20,000
Personal and dependency exemptions	10,200	5,100	+	5,100	=	10,200
Standard deduction	6,700	5,900	+	5,900	=	11,800
Taxable income	3,100	–0–	+	–0–	=	–0–
Taxes owed	465	–0–	+	–0–	=	–0–
Earned income tax credit*	1,789	2,152	+	2,152	=	4,304
Refund	$ 1,324	$2,152	+	$2,152	=	$4,304

*See Chapter 13 for a discussion of the earned income tax credit. The credits above were calculated following the procedure utilized in Example 23 of Chapter 13.

between the liability using the joint return Tax Rate Schedule and the liability using the Tax Rate Schedule for single taxpayers.

To qualify for head-of-household rates, a taxpayer must pay more than half the cost of maintaining a household as his or her home. The household must also be the principal home of a dependent relative.[30] As a general rule, the dependent must live in the taxpayer's household for over half the year.

The general rule has two exceptions. One exception is that an *unmarried child* (child also means grandchild, stepchild, or adopted child) need not be a dependent in order for the taxpayer to qualify as a head of household.

[30] As defined in § 152(a). See § 2(b)(1)(A)(i).

TAX IN THE NEWS

THE IRS GOES AFTER ANYONE IT CAN FIND

When she was married, Elizabeth Cockrell filed joint returns with her husband. Because she never bothered to review the returns before she signed them, Elizabeth was unaware that her husband was claiming questionable tax shelters as tax deductions.

After the couple divorced, the IRS audited the returns and assessed the entire deficiency against Elizabeth. Since the IRS had made no effort to pursue her former husband, Elizabeth took the matter to court. In *Elizabeth R. Cockrell*, 66 TCM 1180, T.C.Memo. 1995–503, and in a later rehearing (T.C.Memo. 1995–551), the Tax Court found for the IRS. Although the Court was sympathetic to Elizabeth's plight, the law was clear. The IRS has no duty or obligation to look first to the spouse who was responsible for the error.

It has been suggested that Congress change the law to avoid the result reached in Elizabeth's case.*

*Elizabeth did not qualify as an "innocent spouse" under § 6013(e) because the understatements were not attributable to "grossly erroneous items."

EXAMPLE 32

Nancy maintains a household where she and Dan, her nondependent unmarried son, reside. Since Dan is not married, Nancy qualifies for the head-of-household rates. ▼

Another exception to the general rule is that head-of-household status may be claimed if the taxpayer maintains a *separate home* for his or her *parent or parents* if at least one parent qualifies as a dependent of the taxpayer.[31]

EXAMPLE 33

Rick, an unmarried individual, lives in New York City and maintains a household in Detroit for his dependent parents. Rick may use the head-of-household rates even though his parents do not reside in his New York home. ▼

Head-of-household status is not changed during the year by death of the dependent. As long as the taxpayer provided more than half of the cost of maintaining the household prior to the dependent's death, head-of-household status is preserved.

Abandoned Spouse Rules. When married persons file separate returns, several unfavorable tax consequences result. For example, the taxpayer must use the Tax Rate Schedule for married taxpayers filing separately. To mitigate such harsh treatment, Congress enacted provisions commonly referred to as the **abandoned spouse** rules. These rules allow a married taxpayer to file as a head of household if all of the following conditions are satisfied:

- The taxpayer does not file a joint return.
- The taxpayer paid more than one-half the cost of maintaining his or her home for the tax year.
- The taxpayer's spouse did not live in the home during the last six months of the tax year.

[31] § 2(b)(1)(B).

- The home was the principal residence of the taxpayer's child, stepchild, or adopted child for more than half the year.
- The taxpayer could claim the child, stepchild, or adopted child as a dependent.[32]

Gains and Losses from Property Transactions—In General

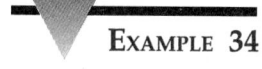

6 Learning Objective
Possess an overview of property transactions.

Gains and losses from property transactions are discussed in detail in Chapters 14 through 17. Because of their importance in the tax system, however, they are introduced briefly at this point.

When property is sold or otherwise disposed of, gain or loss may result. Such gain or loss has an effect on the income tax position of the party making the sale or other disposition when the *realized* gain or loss is *recognized* for tax purposes. Without realized gain or loss, generally, there can be no recognized gain or loss. The concept of realized gain or loss is expressed as follows:

$$\text{Amount realized from the sale} - \text{Adjusted basis of the property} = \text{Realized gain (or loss)}$$

The amount realized is the selling price of the property less any costs of disposition (e.g., brokerage commissions) incurred by the seller. Simply stated, adjusted basis of the property is determined as follows:

Cost (or other original basis) at date of acquisition[33]	
Add:	Capital additions
Subtract:	Depreciation (if appropriate) and other capital recoveries (see Chapter 8)
Equals:	Adjusted basis at date of sale or other disposition

All realized gains are recognized (taxable) unless some specific part of the tax law provides otherwise (see Chapter 15 dealing with certain nontaxable exchanges). Realized losses may or may not be recognized (deductible) for tax purposes, depending on the circumstances involved. Generally, losses realized from the disposition of personal use property (property neither held for investment nor used in a trade or business) are not recognized.

Example 34

During the current year, Ted sells his sailboat (adjusted basis of $4,000) for $5,500. Ted also sells one of his personal automobiles (adjusted basis of $8,000) for $5,000. Ted's realized gain of $1,500 from the sale of the sailboat is recognized. On the other hand, the $3,000 realized loss on the sale of the automobile is not recognized and will not provide Ted with any deductible tax benefit. ▼

Once it has been determined that the disposition of property results in a recognized gain or loss, the next step is to classify the gain or loss as capital or

[32] The dependency requirement does not apply, however, if the taxpayer could have claimed a dependency exemption except for the fact that the exemption was claimed by the noncustodial parent under a written agreement. Refer to Example 18 and the related discussion.

[33] Cost usually means purchase price plus expenses related to the acquisition of the property and incurred by the purchaser (e.g., brokerage commissions). For the basis of property acquired by gift or inheritance and other basis rules, see Chapter 14.

ordinary. Although ordinary gain is fully taxable and ordinary loss is fully deductible, the same may not hold true for capital gains and capital losses.

GAINS AND LOSSES FROM PROPERTY TRANSACTIONS—CAPITAL GAINS AND LOSSES

For tax years beginning after 1992, preferential tax treatment may apply to gains on capital assets that have been held for more than a year. The maximum rate on *net capital gain* (see Chapter 16 for details) is 28 percent. This provision could save 11.6 percent for taxpayers in the 39.6 percent bracket.

DEFINITION OF A CAPITAL ASSET

Capital assets are defined in the Code as any property held by the taxpayer *other than* property listed in § 1221. The list in § 1221 includes inventory, accounts receivable, and depreciable property or real estate used in a business. Thus, the sale or exchange of assets in these categories usually results in ordinary income or loss treatment (see Chapter 17).

EXAMPLE 35

Kelly owns a pizza parlor. During the current year, he sells two automobiles. The first automobile, which had been used as a pizza delivery car for three years, was sold at a loss of $1,000. Because this automobile is an asset used in his business, Kelly has an ordinary loss deduction of $1,000, rather than a capital loss deduction. The second automobile, which Kelly had owned for two years, was his personal car. It was sold for a gain of $800. The personal car is a capital asset. Therefore, Kelly has a capital gain of $800. ▼

The principal capital assets held by an individual taxpayer include assets held for personal (rather than business) use, such as a personal residence or an automobile, and assets held for investment purposes (e.g., corporate securities and land).

COMPUTATION OF NET CAPITAL GAINS AND LOSSES

Capital gains and losses must be classified as short term (those on assets held for one year or less) and long term (those on assets held for more than one year). Short-term capital losses (STCL) are offset against short-term capital gains (STCG). The result is either net short-term capital gain (NSTCG) or net short-term capital loss (NSTCL).

Long-term capital losses (LTCL) are offset against long-term capital gains (LTCG), and the result is either net long-term capital gain (NLTCG) or net long-term capital loss (NLTCL).

Several combinations are possible after this first round of offsetting. For example, if the taxpayer has NSTCL and NLTCG, these amounts are offset. Likewise, if the taxpayer has NLTCL and NSTCG, a similar offsetting is required. In general, the offsetting continues as long as there is gain in any category and loss in any other category.

EXAMPLE 36

In the current year, Polly has the following capital gains and losses: STCL of $4,000, STCG of $3,000, LTCG of $6,000, and LTCL of $2,000. This results in NSTCL of $1,000 ($4,000 STCL – $3,000 STCG) and NLTCG of $4,000 ($6,000 LTCG – $2,000 LTCL). The $1,000 NSTCL is used to offset the $4,000 NLTCG, resulting in an excess of NLTCG over NSTCL of $3,000. ▼

CAPITAL LOSS LIMITATION

Noncorporate Capital Losses Capital losses are first offset against capital gains (as illustrated in Example 36). If, after this offsetting, an individual taxpayer has net capital losses, such losses are deductible as a deduction *for* AGI to a maximum of $3,000 per year. Any unused amounts are carried over for an indefinite period.

EXAMPLE 37

During the year, Tina has $1,000 of NLTCL and $2,000 of NSTCL. Tina's other income is $100,000. Her capital loss deduction for the year is $3,000, consisting of the $2,000 NSTCL and $1,000 NLTCL. ▼

When a taxpayer has both short-term and long-term capital losses, and the losses together exceed $3,000, the short-term losses must be used first in applying the $3,000 limitation.

EXAMPLE 38

Matt has NSTCL of $2,500 and NLTCL of $5,000 for the year. His other income is $50,000. Matt uses the losses as follows:

NSTCL	$2,500
NLTCL	500
Maximum capital loss deduction	$3,000

The remaining NLTCL of $4,500 ($5,000 NLTCL – $500 used) may be carried forward for an indefinite period until used. See Chapter 16 for a detailed discussion of capital loss carryovers. ▼

Corporate Capital Losses. Corporate taxpayers may offset capital losses only against capital gains. Capital losses in excess of capital gains may not be used to reduce ordinary income of a corporation. A corporation's unused capital losses are subject to a carryback and carryover. Capital losses are initially carried back three years and then carried forward five years to offset capital gains that arise in those years. See Chapters 16 and 20 for a discussion of capital losses of corporate taxpayers.

TAX PLANNING CONSIDERATIONS

7 LEARNING OBJECTIVE
Identify tax planning opportunities associated with the individual tax formula.

TAKING ADVANTAGE OF TAX RATE DIFFERENTIALS

It is natural for taxpayers to be concerned about the tax rates they are paying. How does a tax practitioner communicate information about rates to clients? There are several possibilities.

The marginal rate (refer to Examples 23 through 25) provides information that can help a taxpayer evaluate a particular course of action or structure a transaction in the most advantageous manner.

EXAMPLE 39

Due to his salary, Ron is in the 28% marginal tax bracket for 1995. He is considering selling corporate stock he has held as an investment for four years for a $10,000 gain in December. If he sells the stock, his income tax increases by $2,800 ($10,000 gain × 28% marginal rate), and he has $7,200 of after-tax income ($10,000 – $2,800 tax). ▼

EXAMPLE 40

Assume the same facts as in Example 39 and that Ron plans to retire early in 1996. Upon retirement, Ron's only source of income will be nontaxable Social Security benefits and municipal bond interest. If Ron waits until 1996 to sell the stock, his tax on the gain is $1,500

($10,000 gain × 15% marginal rate), and his after-tax income is $8,500 ($10,000 gain – $1,500 tax). By being aware of the effect of marginal tax rates, Ron can save $1,300 in tax. ▼

The marginal rate analysis illustrated in Examples 39 and 40 for an income item can also help a taxpayer obtain the greatest tax benefit from a deductible expense. For example, a taxpayer who is in the 15 percent bracket this year and expects to be in the 31 percent bracket next year should, if possible, defer payment of deductible expenses until next year to maximize the tax benefit of the deduction.

A note of caution is in order with respect to shifting income and expenses between years. Congress has recognized the tax planning possibilities of such shifting and has enacted many provisions to limit a taxpayer's ability to do so. Some of these limitations on the shifting of income are discussed in Chapters 4, 5, and 18. Limitations that affect a taxpayer's ability to shift deductions are discussed in Chapters 6 through 11 and in Chapter 18.

A taxpayer's *effective rate* can be an informative measure of the effectiveness of tax planning. The effective rate is computed by dividing the taxpayer's tax liability by the total amount of income. A low effective rate can be considered an indication of effective tax planning.

One way of lowering the effective rate is to exclude income from the tax base. For example, a taxpayer might consider investing in tax-free municipal bonds rather than taxable corporate bonds. Although pre-tax income from corporate bonds is usually higher, after-tax income may be higher if the taxpayer invests in tax-free municipals.

Another way of lowering the effective rate is to make sure that the taxpayer's expenses and losses are deductible. For example, losses on investments in passive activities may not be deductible (see Chapter 11). Therefore, a taxpayer who plans to invest in an activity that will produce a loss in the early years should take steps to ensure that the business is treated as active rather than passive. Active losses are deductible while passive losses are not.

INCOME OF MINOR CHILDREN

Taxpayers can use several strategies to avoid or minimize the effect of the rules that tax the unearned income of certain minor children at the parents' rate. The kiddie tax rules do not apply once a child reaches age 14. Parents should consider giving a younger child assets that defer taxable income until the child reaches age 14. For example, U.S. government Series EE savings bonds can be used to defer income until the bonds are cashed in (see Chapter 4).

Growth stocks typically pay little in the way of dividends. However, the profit on an astute investment may more than offset the lack of dividends. The child can hold the stock until he or she reaches age 14. If the stock is sold then at a profit, the profit is taxed at the child's low rates.

Taxpayers in a position to do so can employ their children in their business and pay them a reasonable wage for the work they actually perform (e.g., light office help, such as filing). The child's earned income is sheltered by the standard deduction, and the parents' business is allowed a deduction for the wages. The kiddie tax rules have no effect on earned income, even if it is earned from the parents' business.

DEPENDENCY EXEMPTIONS

The Joint Return Test. A married person can be claimed as a dependent only if that individual does not file a joint return with his or her spouse. If a joint return has been filed, the damage may be undone if separate returns are substituted on a timely basis (on or before the due date of the return).

EXAMPLE 41

While preparing a client's 1995 income tax return on April 8, 1996, the tax practitioner discovered that the client's daughter filed a joint return with her husband in late January of 1996. Presuming the daughter otherwise qualifies as the client's dependent, the exemption is not lost if she and her husband file separate returns on or before April 15, 1996. ▼

An initial election to file a joint return must be considered carefully in any situation in which the taxpayers might later decide to amend their return and file separately. As indicated above, separate returns may be substituted for a joint return only if the amended returns are filed on or before the normal due date of the return. If the taxpayers in Example 41 attempt to file separate returns after April 15, 1996, the returns will not be accepted, and the joint return election is binding.[34]

Keep in mind that the filing of a joint return will not be fatal to the dependency exemption if the parties are filing solely to recover all income tax withholdings, are not required to file a return, and no tax liability would exist on separate returns.

The Gross Income Test. The exception to the gross income test for a person under the age of 19 or a full-time student under the age of 24 applies only to a child of the taxpayer. The term *child* is limited to a son, stepson, daughter, stepdaughter, adopted son, or adopted daughter and may include a foster child.

EXAMPLE 42

Austin provides more than 50% of the support of his son, Irvin, and his daughter-in-law, Donna, who live with him. Donna, age 22, is a full-time student and earns $3,000 from a part-time job. Irvin and Donna do not file a joint return. Austin may claim Irvin as a dependent but not Donna. Although students under the age of 24 are excepted from the gross income test, this applies only to a "child" of the taxpayer. Donna does not come within the exception because she is not Austin's child. ▼

Can the fact that the parties live in a community property state make a difference?

EXAMPLE 43

Assume the same facts as in Example 42 except that all parties live in Nevada, a community property jurisdiction. Now Austin can claim both Irvin and Donna as his dependents. Since Donna's income is only $1,500 (her half of the community), she now satisfies the gross income test (less than $2,550 for 1996). ▼

The Support Test. Adequate records of expenditures for support should be maintained in the event a dependency exemption is questioned on audit by the IRS. The maintenance of adequate records is particularly important for exemptions arising from multiple support agreements.

Relationship to the Deduction for Medical Expenses. Generally, medical expenses are deductible only if they are paid on behalf of the taxpayer, his or her spouse, and their dependents. Since deductibility may rest on dependency status, planning is important in arranging multiple support agreements.

[34] Reg. § 1.6013–1(a)(1).

EXAMPLE 44

During the year, Zelda will be supported by her two sons (Vern and Vito) and her daughter (Maria). Each will furnish approximately one-third of the required support. If the parties decide that the dependency exemption should be claimed by the daughter under a multiple support agreement, any medical expenses incurred by Zelda should be paid by Maria. ▼

In planning a multiple support agreement, take into account which of the parties is most likely to exceed the 7.5 percent limitation (see Chapter 10). In Example 44, for instance, Maria might be a poor choice if she and her family do not expect to incur many medical and drug expenses of their own.

ETHICAL CONSIDERATIONS

Manipulating Deductions

Jason and his two sisters furnish more than 50 percent of the support of their widowed mother. Their mother lives with Jason, and his sisters sign Form 2120 enabling him to claim her as a dependent. During the year, the mother incurred medical expenses that were paid by one of Jason's sisters.

In completing his income tax return for the tax year, Jason claims his mother's medical expenses along with his own. Although he did not pay the expenses, Jason reasons that he could have done so from the funds he furnished for his mother's support.

Comment on the propriety of what Jason has done.

One exception permits the deduction of medical expenses paid on behalf of someone who is not a spouse or a dependent. If the person could be claimed as a dependent *except* for the gross income or joint return test, the medical expenses are, nevertheless, deductible. For additional discussion, see Chapter 10.

KEY TERMS

Abandoned spouse, 3–27

Dependency exemption, 3–10

Head of household, 3–25

Itemized deductions, 3–6

Kiddie tax, 3–19

Marriage penalty, 3–25

Multiple support agreement, 3–12

Personal exemption, 3–10

Standard deduction, 3–7

Surviving spouse, 3–25

Tax Rate Schedules, 3–16

Tax Table, 3–16

Unearned income, 3–19

PROBLEM MATERIALS

DISCUSSION QUESTIONS

1. A friend of yours remarks that the current top rate of 39.6% is the highest the Federal income tax has ever been. Please comment.

2. Rearrange the following components to show the formula for arriving at the amount of Federal taxable income:
   a. Deductions *for* AGI.
   b. The greater of the standard deduction or itemized deductions.
   c. Income (broadly conceived).
   d. Adjusted gross income.
   e. Exclusions.
   f. Personal and dependency exemptions.
   g. Gross income.
3. To obtain funds to buy a car, Demi borrows $6,000 from a bank. Her mother gives her the purchase balance of $7,000. What is Demi's gross income?
4. During the year, Mildred's stock investment increased in value by $13,000. She also sold some stock for $4,500; the stock had cost $4,000. How do these facts affect Mildred's gross income?
5. John anticipates that his Federal income tax liability will decrease in 1996. Not only will his itemized deductions increase, but he and his wife will also become 65 years old. Is John's reasoning correct? Explain.
6. Al and Melissa are husband and wife, and both are employed. They do not live in a community property state. Since Melissa incurred most of their itemized deductions (e.g., medical, charitable), Al feels that they would save taxes if they filed separate returns. On such returns, Al would claim the standard deduction, and Melissa would itemize her deductions *from* AGI. Comment on this proposed course of action.
7. Discuss the marital status of the parties under the following circumstances:
   a. One spouse dies during the year.
   b. The spouses are divorced during the year.
8. If an individual who may qualify as a dependent does not spend funds that he or she has received (e.g., wages or Social Security benefits), are these unexpended amounts considered in applying the support test? Are they included in applying the gross income test?
9. Freda purchased a stereo system for her son Wes, age 16. The stereo was placed in Wes's room and used exclusively by him. Freda also purchased a new sports car, titled and registered in her own name, that was used 90% of the time by Wes. Should the cost of these items be considered as support in determining whether Freda may claim Wes as a dependent?
10. Carol provided 75% of the support of Debra, her niece. Debra was a full-time student during the year and earned $3,800 from a part-time job. Can Carol claim Debra as a dependent?
11. Besides what he furnishes on his own, Walter receives support from his daughter (20%) and his son (25%). Can either the daughter or the son claim Walter as a dependent under a multiple support agreement? Why or why not?
12. Steve and Lisa were divorced in 1995. Lisa was granted custody of their children. Because Steve has contributed almost all of the children's support in 1996, he plans to claim them as his dependents. Do you have any comment?
13. A taxpayer who is divorced continues to support his former mother-in-law. May he claim her as a dependent? Suppose she does not live with him. Does this make any difference?
14. Roberto, who is single, is a U.S. citizen and resident. He provides almost all of the support of his parents and two aunts, who are citizens and residents of Guatemala. Roberto's parents and aunts are seriously considering moving to and becoming residents of Mexico. Would such a move have any impact on Roberto? Why or why not?
15. What perceived abuse is the kiddie tax designed to correct?

16. A single individual age 65 or over and blind is required to file a Federal income tax return in 1996 if he or she has gross income of $7,550 or more (refer to Table 3–4).
    a. Explain how the $7,550 filing requirement was computed.
    b. In general, explain the effect of the additional standard deduction on the determination of gross income requirements for filing.

17. Ali, age 67, is married to Leila, who is age 62 and blind. Ali and Leila file a joint return. How much gross income can they earn before they are required to file an income tax return for 1996?

18. Comment on the so-called marriage penalty in connection with the following:
    a. What it is.
    b. When it is likely to occur.
    c. What income level (i.e., low, modest, high) could be vulnerable.

19. Baron and Cheryl are both professionals who have held jobs since they graduated from college five years ago. For several years, they have been engaged to be married. Both would like to tie the knot, but Cheryl is hesitant because of a "marriage penalty" she has heard about. Baron feels Cheryl's fears are unfounded and says they should be able to avoid any such penalty by filing separate returns as married persons. Comment on Baron and Cheryl's situation.

20. Ida's husband dies in 1996. Ida is planning to file as a surviving spouse for tax years 1996 through 1998. Comment regarding Ida's expectations.

21. Camille is single and lives alone in an apartment. She maintains the home where her parents live and is able to claim both of them as her dependents. When Camille files her income tax return, she uses single status. She does not claim head-of-household status because her parents do not live with her. Comment on Camille's status.

22. Several years ago, after a particularly fierce argument, Fran's husband moved out and has not been heard from or seen since. Because Fran cannot locate her husband, she has been using "married, filing separate" status when filing her income tax return. Comment on Fran's status.

23. During the current year, Andre had a $7,000 long-term capital loss on the sale of common stock he had held as an investment. In addition, he had a $3,000 loss on the sale of his personal automobile, which he had owned for a year. How do these transactions affect Andre's taxable income?

24. Ten years ago, Ann purchased a personal residence for $140,000. In the current year, she sells the residence for $105,000. Ann's friend tells her she has a recognizable loss of $35,000 from the sale. Do you agree with the friend's comment? Elaborate.

25. List some assets that are not capital assets and some that are capital assets. Why is it important to determine whether an asset is an ordinary asset or a capital asset?

26. During the current year, Kate earned a salary of $40,000. She sold 20 shares of Robin Corporation common stock that she had purchased two years ago at a loss of $2,500 and sold her personal automobile at a gain of $1,500. Compute Kate's AGI.

27. If Cole has a salary of $41,000, net short-term capital gain of $1,000, and net long-term capital losses of $8,500, what is his AGI?

28. Perry is divorced and has living with him his married daughter, Celia, and her husband, Clark. During the year, Celia earned $3,100 from a part-time job and filed a separate return to recover her withholdings. Clark has no income. Perry can prove that he provided more than 50% of Celia and Clark's support. Perry did not claim Celia as his dependent because he believed she failed the gross income test. Perry filed his return using single taxpayer status. All parties reside in California. Comment on Perry's tax position.

29. Erica and her two brothers equally furnish all of the support of their mother. Erica is married and has four children. Her brothers are single and claim the standard

deduction. Erica's mother is not in good health. What suggestions can you make regarding the tax position of the parties?

PROBLEMS

30. Compute the taxpayer's taxable income for 1996 in each of the following cases:
    a. Jack is married and files a joint return with his wife Alice. Jack and Alice have two dependent children. They have AGI of $50,000 and $8,300 of itemized deductions.
    b. Pete is an unmarried head of household with two dependents. He has AGI of $45,000 and itemized deductions of $5,200.
    c. Iris, age 22, is a full-time college student who is claimed as a dependent by her parents. She earns $4,200 from a part-time job and has interest income of $1,500.
    d. Matt, age 20, is a full-time college student who is claimed as a dependent by his parents. He earns $2,500 from a part-time job and has interest income of $4,100. His itemized deductions related to the investment income are $700.

Note: Problems 31 and 32 can be solved by referring to Figure 3–1, Exhibits 3–1 through 3–3, Tables 3–1 and 3–2, and the discussion under Deductions for Adjusted Gross Income in this chapter.

31. Compute taxable income for 1996 for Jan on the basis of the following information. Her filing status is single.

Gift received from mother	$15,000
Cash dividend received from stock investments	21,000
Interest received from savings accounts and money market deposits	9,000
Capital loss (short term)	1,300
Charitable contributions	2,000
State and local income taxes	2,900
Interest on home mortgage	5,500
Age	60

32. Compute taxable income for 1996 for Hal, who is divorced, on the basis of the following information. His filing status is head of household.

Salary	$58,000
Alimony paid	12,000
Lottery winnings	2,000
Moving expenses (deductible portion)	6,000
Theft loss (deductible portion)	5,900
State and local income taxes	1,200
Interest on home mortgage	4,100
Number of dependents	3
Age	38

33. Determine the amount of the standard deduction allowed for 1996 in each of the following independent situations. In each case, assume the taxpayer is claimed as another person's dependent.

a. Mona, age 16, has income as follows: $710 interest from a savings account and $800 from a part-time job.
b. Aaron, age 18, earns $4,300 from a part-time job.
c. Irving, age 71 and single, has income as follows: $3,100 nontaxable Social Security benefits and $1,050 from a part-time job.
d. Maureen, age 67, is single and blind and has cash dividends of $1,300 from a stock investment.

34. Determine the number of personal and dependency exemptions in each of the following independent situations:
   a. Wesley, age 45, provides all of the support of Doreen (age 70) who does not live with him. Doreen was Wesley's mother-in-law before his divorce.
   b. Carol, age 50, provides all of the support of two cousins, Rick and Jane. Jane lives with Carol but Rick does not.
   c. Ron, age 66, provides all of the support of Cynthia and Leona who live with him. Cynthia is Ron's wife, and Leona is unrelated but is a close friend of the family and a member of their church. Ron files a separate return. Neither Cynthia nor Leona has any income, and neither files a return.
   d. Nicole, age 60, provides all of the support of Alan, age 66 and blind, and Grace, age 89. Alan, Nicole's husband, died in February of the current year. Grace is Alan's mother and lives in a nursing home. Nicole files a separate return.

35. Compute the number of personal and dependency exemptions in each of the following independent situations:
   a. Roberto, a U.S. citizen and resident, contributes 100% of the support of his parents who are citizens of Mexico and live there.
   b. Pablo, a U.S. citizen and resident, contributes 100% of the support of his parents who are citizens of Guatemala. Pablo's father is a resident of Guatemala, and his mother is a legal resident of the United States.
   c. Marlena, a U.S. citizen and resident, contributes 100% of the support of her parents who are also U.S. citizens but are residents of Germany.

36. Determine the number of personal and dependency exemptions in each of the following independent situations:
   a. Warren and Terri provide more than half of the support of their children, Demi and Paul. Demi, age 18, earns $3,200 from a part-time job. Paul, age 26, earns $2,000 from a part-time job.
   b. Hortense, age 66 and widowed, furnishes more than half of the support of her father, age 88 and blind. The father receives Social Security benefits of $4,300, interest on a savings account of $2,300, and interest on tax-exempt bonds of $9,000.
   c. Dennis and Ava provide more than half of the support of their son, Henry. Henry, age 23, is a full-time student in medical school. During the year, Henry receives $3,050 in dividends from stock investments.
   d. Earl provides more than half of the support of his nephew, Brad, who lives with him. Brad, age 17 and a full-time student, earns $3,500 from a part-time job.

37. Carlos and Alicia, who are married and file a joint return, have four dependent children. They have AGI of $193,700. What is their allowable exemption deduction for 1996?

38. Fred and Eve are married and file a joint return. Fred is 66 years of age, and Eve is 65. Fred's salary for 1996 was $33,000, and Eve earned $41,000. Eve won $10,000 in the state lottery and inherited $25,000 from her aunt. Fred incurred a $2,500 capital loss on stock he sold in December; Fred had purchased the stock three months earlier. Fred and Eve provided 90% of the support for Cora, their 23-year-old daughter, who is a full-time student. Fred and Eve also provided over half of the support of Jim, who is Cora's husband. Cora and Jim did not file a joint return. Fred and Eve also provide over half of the support of Eve's mother, Abbey, who lives in a nursing home. Abbey earned interest of $2,200 on a savings account and received Social Security benefits of $6,400. Fred and Eve had total itemized deductions of $7,800. Compute taxable income for Fred and Eve for 1996.

39. Bob, age 13, is a full-time student supported by his parents who claim him on their tax return for 1996. Bob's parents present you with the following information and ask that you prepare Bob's 1996 Federal income tax return:

Wages from summer job	$2,100
Interest on savings account at First National Bank	950
Interest on City of Chicago bonds Bob received as a gift from his grandfather two years ago	750
Dividend from Owl Corporation	200

a. What is Bob's taxable income for 1996?
b. Bob's parents file a joint return for 1996 on which they report taxable income of $66,000. Compute Bob's 1996 tax liability.

40. Walter and Nancy provide 70% of the support of their daughter (age 21) and son-in-law (age 22). The son-in-law (John) is a full-time student at a local university, while the daughter (Irene) holds various part-time jobs from which she earns $3,000. Walter and Nancy engage you to prepare their tax return for 1996. During a meeting with them in late March of 1997, you learn that John and Irene do not file a joint return. What tax advice would you give based on the following assumptions:
a. All parties live in Louisiana (a community property state).
b. All parties live in New Jersey (a common law state).

41. Don is a wealthy executive who had taxable income of $200,000 in 1996. He is considering transferring title in a duplex he owns to his son Sam, age 16. Sam has no other income and is claimed as a dependent by Don. Net rent income from the duplex is $10,000 a year, which Sam will be encouraged to place in a savings account. Will the family save income taxes in 1996 if Don transfers title in the duplex to Sam? Explain.

42. Compute the 1996 tax liability for each of the following taxpayers:
a. Norm and Nancy, both age 46, are married, have two dependent children, and file a joint return. Their combined salaries totaled $75,000. They had deductions *for* AGI of $6,000 and total itemized deductions of $8,100.
b. Clark, age 45, is single and has no dependents. He had a salary of $62,000, deductions *for* AGI of $3,000, and total itemized deductions of $7,100.
c. David and Susan, both age 65, are married, have no dependents, and file a joint return. Their combined salaries were $92,000. They had deductions *for* AGI of $2,000 and itemized deductions of $17,000.

43. Chet and Eva are 68 and 65 years of age, respectively, and married. Their income consists of cash dividends ($30,000) from stock investments and interest ($24,000) from certificates of deposit. During 1996, they had a short-term capital loss of $4,000 and itemized deductions of $7,500. They provided all of the support of a nephew who lives with them. Determine their taxable income for 1996.

44. Peter, age 12, is claimed as a dependent on his parents' 1996 Federal income tax return, on which they reported taxable income of $95,000. During the summer, Peter earned $2,500 from a job as a model. His only other income consisted of $1,700 in interest on a savings account. Compute Peter's taxable income and tax liability.

45. Carmen, who is 12 years old, is claimed as a dependent on her parents' tax return. During 1996, she received $12,200 in dividends and interest and had no investment expenses related to this income. She also earned $2,000 wages from a part-time job. Compute the amount of income that is taxed at Carmen's parents' rate.

46. Ellen, who is 14 years old, is claimed as a dependent on her parents' tax return. During 1996, she received $10,000 in dividends and interest. She also earned $1,700 wages from a part-time job. Compute the amount of income that is taxed at Ellen's own rate.

47. Bruce Smith and Wanda Brown are young professionals who are employed in well-paying jobs. They have been dating each other for several years and are considering getting married in December 1996 or January 1997. For 1996, their respective AGIs are

$65,000 and $68,000. They anticipate earning the same income in 1997. In both years, they will claim the standard deduction.

Bruce and Wanda solicit your tax advice. Specifically, they wish to know what Federal income tax results from their getting married in 1996 or in 1997. Prepare a letter to Wanda (4339 Elm St., Apt. 39A, Cincinnati, OH 45221) setting forth the tax determination under each choice.

48. Which of the following individuals are required to file a tax return for 1996? Should any of these individuals file a return even if filing is not required? Why?
    a. Sam is married and files a joint return with his spouse, Lana. Both Sam and Lana are 67 years old. Their combined gross income was $13,000.
    b. Bobby is a dependent child under age 19 who received $2,000 in wages from a part-time job and $800 of dividend income.
    c. Mike is single and is 67 years old. His gross income from wages was $7,000.
    d. Marge is a self-employed single individual with gross income of $4,500 from an unincorporated business. Business expenses amounted to $4,200.

49. Which of the following taxpayers must file a Federal income tax return for 1996?
    a. Bob, age 19, is a full-time college student. He is claimed as a dependent by his parents. He earned $4,100 wages during the year.
    b. Anita, age 12, is claimed as a dependent by her parents. She earned interest of $1,200 during the year.
    c. Earl, age 16, is claimed as a dependent by his parents. He earned wages of $2,700 and interest of $1,100 during the year.
    d. Karen, age 16 and blind, is claimed as a dependent by her parents. She earned wages of $2,600 and interest of $1,200 during the year.
    e. Pat, age 17, is claimed as a dependent by her parents. She earned interest of $300 during the year. In addition, she earned $550 during the summer operating her own business at the beach, where she painted caricatures of her customers.

50. In each of the following situations, classify Darlene's filing status for tax year 1996:
    a. Darlene is a widow and maintains a household in which her two dependent children live. Darlene's husband died in 1994.
    b. Same as (a) except that Darlene's husband died in 1992 (not 1994).
    c. Darlene is single and lives alone. She maintains the household of her parents, only one of whom qualifies as her dependent.
    d. Darlene is married, but her husband disappeared for parts unknown in 1995. Darlene maintains the household in which she and her dependent children live.

51. In each of the following situations, classify Isaac's filing status for tax year 1996:
    a. Isaac lives alone. He has not seen or heard from his wife since 1995.
    b. Isaac's wife died in January 1996. He maintains the home in which he and his dependent child live.
    c. Isaac's wife died in 1992. He maintains the home in which he and his unmarried child live. The child does not qualify as Isaac's dependent.
    d. Isaac is divorced and lives alone. He also maintains a home in which his dependent child lives.

52. Henry died on January 1, 1994. He was survived by his wife, Sue, and their 19-year-old son, Mike, who was a college sophomore. Mike was a full-time student in 1995 and earned $3,000 for the year. In 1996, Mike reduced his school load and became a part-time student. He earned $5,200 in 1996. Mike continues to live with his mother, who provides over half of his support. What is Sue's filing status in 1994, 1995, and 1996?

53. Tracy, age 66, is a widow. Her husband died in 1994. Tracy maintains a home in which she and her 28-year-old son reside. Her son Gary is a piano player at a local nightclub, where he earned $12,000 during 1996. Gary contributed $3,000 of his income toward household expenses and put the remainder in a savings account that he used to return to college full-time to pursue a master's degree in music starting in August 1996. Tracy contributed $12,000 toward household expenses. What is the most favorable filing status available to Tracy for 1996, and how many exemptions may she claim?

54. Hazel, age 39, is single. She maintains a household that is the residence of her two children, Fran, age 8, and Sam, age 11. The children are claimed as dependents by their father, who provides $2,000 child support for each of them. During 1996, Hazel earned a salary of $95,000. Other items that affected her taxable income are as follows:

Total itemized deductions	$ 6,700
Capital gains	
Short-term	1,300
Long-term	3,100
Capital losses	
Short-term	(4,800)
Long-term	(4,000)
Interest income	3,100

Hazel provides all the support for her mother, Mabel, who lives in a nursing home. Mabel qualifies as Hazel's dependent.
a. Compute Hazel's AGI and taxable income for 1996.
b. What is Hazel's filing status for 1996?

55. Tina, age 61, earned a salary of $63,000 in 1996. She sold common stock that she had owned for 10 months at a loss of $1,500 and sold a pleasure boat that she had bought in 1988 at a loss of $4,000. Tina also sold an antique desk for a gain of $10,000. She acquired the desk in 1953. Compute Tina's AGI for 1996.

56. Lee is a single, cash basis calendar year taxpayer. For the years 1995 and 1996, he expects AGI of $20,000 and the following itemized deductions:

Church pledge	$2,300
Interest on home mortgage	1,200
Property taxes	500

Discuss the tax consequences of the alternatives below. Assume for purposes of this problem that the interest and taxes are deductible in the year of payment.
a. In 1995, Lee pays his church pledge for 1995 and 1996 ($2,300 for each year).
b. Lee does nothing different.

57. Gina, a cash basis taxpayer, is single and has no dependents. She provides you with the following estimates for 1995 and 1996:

	1995	1996
Adjusted gross income	$56,000	$60,000
Charitable contributions	2,200	2,400
Interest on home mortgage	1,000	850
Property taxes	700	700

Can Gina decrease taxable income over the two-year period by prepaying her 1996 charitable contributions in 1995?

CUMULATIVE PROBLEMS

58. Mike and Rosa Zapalac are married and live at 100 Royce Avenue, El Paso, TX 79968; both have jobs. Mike's Social Security number is 433–22–1111 and Rosa's is 437–00–1112. The Zapalacs have four children who live with them. Three of the children are their own, while the oldest is Rosa's child from a prior marriage.

During 1996, the Zapalacs had the following receipts:

Salaries (Mike and Rosa combined)	$71,400
Child support payments received by Rosa from her former husband	3,600
Fees earned by Mike for several days of jury duty service	90
Proceeds from garage sale	1,310
Gift of cash received from Mike's mother	4,000
Cash prize won for being the ninth caller on a radio talk show	1,000

The garage sale involved used clothing, toys, appliances, furniture, and other personal effects and household goods. The Zapalacs are quite certain that the cost of the items sold was around $5,000.

Expenses for 1996 are summarized below:

Interest on home mortgage	$5,900
Property taxes on residence	3,700
Charitable contributions	4,100

The Zapalacs furnish all of the support of Rosa's widowed mother who lives with them. The mother, although a U.S. resident, is still a citizen of Mexico. The mother helps with the household chores and takes care of the children while Rosa and Mike are at work.

The Zapalacs also furnish all of the support of Rosa's grandparents who are over 65 years of age. The grandparents live in Mexico and are Mexican citizens.

Compute the Zapalacs' taxable income for 1996. Suggested software (if available): *TurboTax* or *MacInTax*.

59. Horace Fern, age 43, lives at 321 Grant Avenue, Cheyenne, WY 82002. Horace's mother Kate (age 65) lived with him until her death in August 1995. Up to the time of her death, Kate qualified as Horace's dependent. Horace maintained the household where he and his mother lived.

Horace is a manager for Bison Lumber Company at a yearly salary of $62,000. Because his job duties will be expanded, Bison plans to increase Horace's salary by 10% starting in 1996.

During 1995, Horace paid $3,600 ($300 each month) in alimony to Janet, his ex-wife. As Janet was remarried in late December, Horace's alimony obligation has terminated.

Besides his salary, Horace received interest income of $5,800 from Western Bank and $6,200 from First Savings Bank on $200,000 in certificates of deposit (CDs) he owns. Horace received the CDs as a gift from his mother several years ago.

Except as otherwise noted, Horace's expenditures for 1995 are summarized below:

Interest on home mortgage	$3,200
Property taxes on home	1,200
Charitable contributions	1,900

Relevant Social Security numbers are as follows:

Horace Fern	520–31–4596
Kate Fern	520–32–3214
Janet Fern	520–33–4432

Federal income taxes withheld from Horace's salary amounted to $10,900. He also paid estimated tax of $400 each quarter.

Part 1—Tax Computation

Compute Horace's net tax payable or refund due for 1995. Horace does not wish to contribute to the Presidential Election Campaign Fund. If he has overpaid, he wants the amount refunded. If you use tax forms for your computations, you will need Form 1040 and Schedules A and B. Suggested software (if available): *TurboTax* or *MacInTax*.

Part 2—Tax Planning
In addition to preparing the return for 1995, Horace has asked you to advise him regarding his tax situation for 1996. He is particularly concerned about the tax effects of the following:

- The death of Kate.
- The cessation of alimony payments due to Janet's remarriage.
- The salary increase.
- Interest income on the CDs.

Write a letter to Horace in which you summarize (in approximate amounts) how much more (or less) he will owe in income taxes for 1996. Also include recommendations on what can be done to mitigate the tax consequences resulting from the investment in CDs. Assume that Horace's itemized deductions will remain constant in 1996.

RESEARCH PROBLEMS

Note: ***West's Federal Taxation on CD-ROM*** *can be used in preparing solutions to the Research Problems. Alternatively, tax research materials contained in a standard tax library can be used.*

Research Problem 1. In the state of Texas, a lawsuit was instituted charging that the state schools for the mentally retarded furnished inadequate, unsafe, and improper care, treatment, and education. As part of the settlement of this suit, the Texas Department of Mental Health offered to pay a fixed daily amount to third-party providers of these services. Under this arrangement, the taxpayers received $16,425 during the year for the care of their mentally retarded daughter. This amount covered a daily per diem for food and board, medical expenses, cost of special food, clothing, transportation, special laundry, home repairs, and other living expenses. The daughter lived with the taxpayers and during the year attended classes at a special school operated by the local school district.

Although the taxpayers did not pay for more than 50% of their daughter's support, they claimed her as a dependent for the year. The taxpayers contend that the amount they received from the state is a scholarship and, therefore, should not be taken into account in applying the support test. The IRS disagrees. What is the appropriate result?

Partial list of research aids:
§ 152(d).
Rev.Rul. 61–186, 1961–2 C.B. 30.
Rev.Rul. 64–221, 1964–2 C.B. 46.

Research Problem 2. Lori and Mike Wise were husband and wife until they were divorced in 1990. As part of the divorce settlement, Mike agreed to be liable for any income taxes that might be assessed against them by the IRS for joint returns filed in the past.

Lori and Mike filed joint returns every year they were married. For tax year 1989, however, each initially filed as "married persons filing separate." Upon further reflection, they replaced the separate returns with a joint return.

In January 1996, the IRS audits the joint return the Wises filed for tax year 1989. As a result of the audit, a deficiency of $480,000 is assessed against the taxpayers. Since Mike is not available, the full amount of the deficiency is assessed against Lori.

Lori objects to the assessment against her on three grounds. First, she maintains that she neither signed the return nor authorized the use of her signature. Second, Lori feels that the assessment should be made against Mike. After all, under the divorce decree Mike has assumed any liability for additional taxes imposed. Third, the assessment is precluded by the three-year statute of limitations.

Regarding Lori's first contention, she offers no proof other than her own statement. Also, no evidence exists that she filed a separate return for 1989.

a. Discuss the validity of each of Lori's three defenses in a letter to her. As much as possible, express your advice in nonlegal terms. Lori Wise lives at 3126 Kingsride Rd., Funston, UT 84602.
b. Prepare a memo containing legal substantiation for your position. The memo is for inclusion in your firm's client files.

Research Problem 3. Sharon Collins, although married, lives alone. She maintains a household that includes her three-year-old son. Sharon and her husband are not on good terms, but neither has ever bothered to file for legal separation or divorce. Sharon is gainfully employed and provides all of the support for herself and her son. During the year, she utilizes the services of a day care center while she works.

Presuming Sharon does not file a joint return with her husband, what is her filing status? Can she claim a child care credit on a separate return? Explain.

TEAM PROJECT: ARTHUR ANDERSEN TAX CHALLENGE CASES

For more information on the Arthur Andersen Tax Challenge Cases, please refer to Chapter 1, page 1-38.

Information related to tax issues and problems that are discussed in this chapter may be found in the

Fields case on page 1
Miller case on pages 1, 3, 4, 16

Read and analyze the case you have been assigned and *identify* any issues and problems that are related to material covered in this chapter. If the information provided in the case is complete, prepare answers for this part of the case at this time. If you need information that is contained in the later parts of the case, please write a memo summarizing the questions or problems so you can prepare a complete answer at a later date.

P • A • R • T

II

Gross Income

Part II presents the income component of the basic tax model. Included in this presentation are the determination of what is income and the statutory exclusions that are permitted in calculating gross income. Because the taxpayer's accounting method and accounting period affect when income is reported, an introductory discussion of these topics is also included.

CHAPTER

4

Gross Income: Concepts and Inclusions

LEARNING OBJECTIVES

After completing Chapter 4, you should be able to:

1. Explain the concepts of gross income and realization and distinguish between the economic, accounting, and tax concepts of gross income.
2. Describe the cash and accrual methods of accounting and the related effects of the choice of taxable year.
3. Identify who should pay the tax on a particular item of income in various situations.
4. Apply the Internal Revenue Code provisions on alimony, loans made at below-market interest rates, annuities, prizes and awards, group term life insurance, unemployment compensation, and Social Security benefits.
5. Identify tax planning strategies for minimizing gross income.

OUTLINE

Mr. Zarin lost over $2,500,000 of his own money gambling. The casino then allowed him to gamble on credit. After several months, his liability to the casino totaled more than $3,400,000. Following protracted negotiations, the casino agreed to settle its claim against Mr. Zarin for a mere $500,000. Although Mr. Zarin had paid for gambling losses of $3,000,000, the IRS had the audacity to ask him to pay tax on $2,900,000; that is, the amount the casino marked down his account.[1] Mr. Zarin undoubtedly had difficulty understanding how he could be deemed to have income in this situation.

Given an understanding of the income tax formula, though, one can see how the "free" gambling Mr. Zarin enjoyed could constitute income. The starting point in the formula is the determination of gross income rather than "net income." Once gross income is determined, the next step is to determine the allowable deductions. In Mr. Zarin's way of thinking, these steps were collapsed.

This chapter is concerned with the first step in the computation of taxable income—the determination of gross income. Questions that are addressed include the following:

- What: What is income?
- When: In which tax period is the income recognized?
- Who: Who must include the item of income in gross income?

The Code provides an all-inclusive definition of gross income in § 61. Chapter 5 presents items of income that are specifically excluded from gross income (exclusions).

[1] *Zarin v. Comm.*, 90–2 USTC ¶50,530, 66 AFTR2d 90–5679, 916 F.2d 110 (CA–3, 1990).

GROSS INCOME—WHAT IS IT?

DEFINITION

1 LEARNING OBJECTIVE
Explain the concepts of gross income and realization and distinguish between the economic, accounting, and tax concepts of gross income.

Section 61(a) of the Internal Revenue Code defines the term **gross income** as follows:

> Except as otherwise provided in this subtitle, gross income means all income from whatever source derived.

This definition is derived from the language of the Sixteenth Amendment to the Constitution.

Supreme Court decisions have made it clear that all sources of income are subject to tax unless Congress specifically excludes the type of income received:

> The starting point in all cases dealing with the question of the scope of what is included in "gross income" begins with the basic premise that the purpose of Congress was to use the full measure of its taxing power.[2]

Although at this point we know that *income* is to be broadly construed, we still do not have a satisfactory definition of the term *income.* Congress left it to the judicial and administrative branches to thrash out the meaning of income. Early in the development of the income tax law, a choice was made between two competing models: economic income and accounting income.

ECONOMIC AND ACCOUNTING CONCEPTS

The term **income** is used in the Code but is not separately defined. Thus, early in the history of our tax laws, the courts were required to interpret "the commonly understood meaning of the term which must have been in the minds of the people when they adopted the Sixteenth Amendment to the Constitution."[3] In determining the definition of income, the Supreme Court rejected the economic concept of income.

Economists measure income (**economic income**) by first determining the fair market value of the individual's net assets at the beginning and end of the year (change in net worth). Then, to arrive at economic income, this change in net worth is added to the goods and services that person actually consumed during the period. Economic income also includes imputed values for such items as the rental value of an owner-occupied home and the value of food a taxpayer might grow for personal consumption.[4]

EXAMPLE 1

Helen's economic income is calculated as follows:

Fair market value of Helen's assets on December 31, 1996	$220,000	
Less liabilities on December 31, 1996	(40,000)	
Net worth on December 31, 1996		$180,000
Fair market value of Helen's assets on January 1, 1996	$200,000	
Less liabilities on January 1, 1996	(80,000)	
Net worth on January 1, 1996		(120,000)

[2] *James v. U.S.,* 61–1 USTC ¶9449, 7 AFTR2d 1361, 81 S.Ct. 1052 (USSC, 1961).

[3] *Merchants Loan and Trust Co. v. Smietanka,* 1 USTC ¶42, 3 AFTR 3102, 41 S.Ct. 386 (USSC, 1921).

[4] See Henry C. Simons, *Personal Income Taxation* (Chicago: University of Chicago Press, 1933), Ch. 2–3.

Increase in net worth	$60,000
Consumption	
Food, clothing, and other personal expenditures	25,000
Imputed rental value of Helen's home she owns and occupies	12,000
Economic income	$97,000

▼

The need to value assets annually would make compliance with the tax law burdensome and would cause numerous controversies between the taxpayer and the IRS over valuation. In addition, using market values to determine income for tax purposes could result in liquidity problems. That is, the taxpayer's assets may increase in value even though they are not readily convertible into the cash needed to pay the tax (e.g., commercial real estate). Thus, the IRS, Congress, and the courts have rejected the economic concept of income as impractical.

In contrast, the accounting concept of income is founded on the realization principle.[5] According to this principle, income (**accounting income**) is not recognized until it is realized. For realization to occur, (1) an exchange of goods or services must take place between the accounting entity and some independent, external group, and (2) in the exchange the accounting entity must receive assets that are capable of being objectively valued. Thus, the mere appreciation in the market value of assets before a sale or other disposition is not sufficient to warrant income recognition. In addition, the imputed savings that arise when an individual creates assets for his or her own use (e.g., feed grown for a farmer's own livestock) are not income because no exchange has occurred. The courts and the IRS have ruled, however, that embezzlement proceeds and buried treasures found satisfy the realization requirement and, therefore, must be recognized as income.[6]

The Supreme Court expressed an inclination toward the accounting concept of income when it adopted the realization requirement in *Eisner v. Macomber:*

> Income may be defined as the gain derived from capital, from labor, or from both combined, provided it is understood to include profit gained through a sale or conversion of capital assets. . . . Here we have the essential matter: not a gain accruing to capital; not a *growth* or *increment* of value *in* investment; but a gain, a profit, something of exchangeable value, *proceeding from* the property, *severed from* the capital however invested or employed, and *coming in,* being *"derived"*—that is, *received* or *drawn by* the recipient for his separate use, benefit and disposal—*that is,* income derived from the property.[7]

In summary, *income* represents an increase in wealth recognized for tax purposes only upon realization.

COMPARISON OF THE ACCOUNTING AND TAX CONCEPTS OF INCOME

Although income tax rules frequently parallel financial accounting measurement concepts, differences do exist. Of major significance, for example, is the fact that unearned (prepaid) income received by an accrual basis taxpayer often is taxed in

[5] See the American Accounting Association Committee Report on the "Realization Concept," *The Accounting Review* (April 1965): 312–322.

[6] *Rutkin v. U.S.,* 52–1 USTC ¶9260, 41 AFTR2d 596, 72 S.Ct. 571 (USSC, 1952); Rev.Rul. 61, 1953–1 C.B. 17.

[7] 1 USTC ¶32, 3 AFTR 3020, 40 S.Ct. 189 (USSC, 1920).

TAX IN THE NEWS

Taxpayer Received Benefits Greater Than He Bargained For

Mr. Wentz, who had been an insurance agent for over 40 years, devised a scheme with his insurance agent whereby Mr. Wentz could receive insurance protection for one year at no cost to him. At the beginning of the year, Mr. Wentz purchased a whole life insurance policy. The insurance agent received a commission equal to 115 percent of Mr. Wentz's premiums for the first year. Then the insurance agent reimbursed Mr. Wentz the amount of the first-year premium, and at the end of the year, Mr. Wentz canceled the policy. The idea was that Mr. Wentz would get insurance protection for one year and the agent would keep the commission less the premium. The Tax Court had little trouble concluding that Mr. Wentz realized income from the transaction since he received insurance protection for one year.

After Mr. Wentz lost on the question of whether he received income, the next question was how to measure the amount of the income. Mr. Wentz argued that if he realized income, it amounted to the cost of term insurance protection for one year, which is what he expected to receive from the scam on the insurance company. The Tax Court disagreed and ruled that the income amounted to the first year's premium for a whole life policy—the amount Mr. Wentz paid before the reimbursement—which was more than twice the cost of term protection. Mr. Wentz did not want a whole life policy and would not have entered into a contract to receive such a policy without the scheme. The net result was that Mr. Wentz was required to pay more income tax than term insurance would have cost. In addition, Mr. Wentz (or his estate) probably would not have been able to enforce the insurance contract because it arose out of a fraudulent scheme.

SOURCE: *John R. Wentz,* 105 T.C. 1, No. 1 (1995).

the year of receipt. For financial accounting purposes, such prepayments are not treated as income until earned.[8] Because of this and other differences, many corporations report financial accounting income that is substantially different from the amounts reported for tax purposes (see Chapter 20, Reconciliation of Taxable Income and Accounting Income).

The Supreme Court provided an explanation for some of the variations between accounting and taxable income in a decision involving inventory and bad debt adjustments:

> The primary goal of financial accounting is to provide useful information to management, shareholders, creditors, and others properly interested; the major responsibility of the accountant is to protect these parties from being misled. The primary goal of the income tax system, in contrast, is the equitable collection of revenue. . . . Consistently with its goals and responsibilities, financial accounting has as its foundation the principle of conservatism, with its corollary that 'possible errors in measurement [should] be in the direction of understatement rather than overstatement of net income and net assets'. In view of the Treasury's markedly different goals and responsibilities, understatement of income is not destined to be its guiding light.

[8] Similar differences exist in the deduction area.

... Financial accounting, in short, is hospitable to estimates, probabilities, and reasonable certainties; the tax law, with its mandate to preserve the revenue, can give no quarter to uncertainty.[9]

FORM OF RECEIPT

Gross income is not limited to cash received. "It includes income realized in any form, whether in money, property, or services. Income may be realized [and recognized], therefore, in the form of services, meals, accommodations, stock or other property, as well as in cash."[10]

EXAMPLE 2

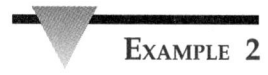

Ostrich Corporation allowed Bill, an employee, to use a company car for his vacation. Bill realized income equal to the rental value of the car for the time and mileage. ▼

EXAMPLE 3

Terry owed $10,000 on a mortgage. The creditor accepted $8,000 in full satisfaction of the debt. Terry realized income of $2,000 from retiring the debt.[11] ▼

ETHICAL CONSIDERATIONS

Unreported Income

You often see your clients at various civic meetings. During the social hour preceding a recent civic meeting, a client told you several stories about his adventures when flying. The client said he had not had to pay any airfare for his vacation in Mexico because he had used the frequent flyer points accumulated from tickets purchased by his employer. He noted, however, that he got sick in Mexico and did not enjoy his stay. Then, when he was on the plane ready to take off for home, the flight attendant announced that the flight was overbooked. The airline offered any passengers who would surrender their seats a seat on a flight to the same location that was leaving in one hour and a free round-trip ticket to any city the airline served. Your client accepted the offer and received a ticket that he used to attend his mother's funeral in Florida.

Soon after the end of the year, the client brings you the information to prepare his tax return. The information does not mention anything about the airline tickets he received. You pause to consider whether the tax system is working properly when, under the broad concept of gross income, your client may have to pay tax on the value of airfares for trips he did not enjoy. You also reflect on his likely reaction if you add these amounts to his taxable income. Evaluate this dilemma.

RECOVERY OF CAPITAL DOCTRINE

The Constitution grants Congress the power to tax income but does not define the term. Because the Constitution does not define income, it would seem that Congress could simply tax gross receipts. Although Congress does allow certain deductions, none are constitutionally required. However, the Supreme Court has held that there is no income subject to tax until the taxpayer has recovered the capital invested.[12] This concept is known as the **recovery of capital doctrine.**

---

[9] *Thor Power Tool Co. v. Comm.*, 79–1 USTC ¶9139, 43 AFTR2d 79–362, 99 S.Ct. 773 (USSC, 1979).

[10] Reg. § 1.61–1(a).

[11] Reg. § 1.61–12. See *U.S. v. Kirby Lumber Co.*, 2 USTC ¶814, 10 AFTR 458, 52 S.Ct. 4 (USSC, 1931). Exceptions to this general rule are discussed in Chapter 5.

[12] *Doyle v. Mitchell Bros. Co.*, 1 USTC ¶17, 3 AFTR 2979, 38 S.Ct. 467 (USSC, 1916).

In its simplest application, this doctrine means that sellers can reduce their gross receipts (selling price) by the adjusted basis of the property sold.[13] This net amount, in the language of the Code, is gross income.

EXAMPLE 4

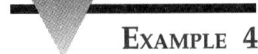

Dave sold common stock for $15,000. He had purchased the stock for $12,000. Dave's gross receipts are $15,000. This amount consists of a $12,000 recovery of capital and $3,000 of gross income. ▼

Collections on annuity contracts and installment payments received from sales of property must be allocated between recovery of capital and income. Annuities are discussed in this chapter, and installment sales are discussed in Chapter 18.

YEAR OF INCLUSION

TAXABLE YEAR

2 LEARNING OBJECTIVE
Describe the cash and accrual methods of accounting and the related effects of the choice of taxable year.

The annual accounting period or **taxable year** is a basic component of our tax system.[14] Generally, an entity must use the *calendar year* to report its income. However, a *fiscal year* (a period of 12 months ending on the last day of any month other than December) can be elected if the taxpayer maintains adequate books and records. This fiscal year option generally is not available to partnerships, S corporations, and personal service corporations, as discussed in Chapter 18.[15]

Determining the particular year in which the income will be taxed is important for determining when the tax must be paid. But the year each item of income is subject to tax can also affect the total tax liability over the entity's lifetime. This is true for the following reasons:

- With a progressive rate system, a taxpayer's marginal tax rate can change from year to year.
- Congress may change the tax rates.
- The relevant rates may change because of a change in the entity's status (e.g., a person may marry or a business may be incorporated).
- Several provisions in the Code are dependent on the taxpayer's gross income for the year (e.g., whether the person can be claimed as a dependent, as discussed in Chapter 3).

ACCOUNTING METHODS

The year an item of income is subject to tax often depends upon which acceptable **accounting method** the taxpayer regularly employs.[16] The three primary methods of accounting are (1) the cash receipts and disbursements method, (2) the accrual method, and (3) the hybrid method. Most individuals use the cash receipts and disbursements method of accounting, whereas most corporations use the accrual method. The Regulations require the accrual method for determining purchases and sales when inventory is an income-producing factor.[17] Some businesses employ a hybrid method that is a combination of the cash and accrual methods of accounting.

[13] For a definition of adjusted basis, see the Glossary of Tax Terms in Appendix C.
[14] See Accounting Periods in Chapter 18.
[15] §§ 441(a) and (d).
[16] See Accounting Methods in Chapter 18.
[17] Reg. § 1.446–1(c)(2)(i). Other circumstances in which the accrual method must be used are presented in Chapter 18.

In addition to these overall accounting methods, a taxpayer may choose to spread the gain from the sale of property over the collection periods by using the installment method of income recognition. Contractors may either spread profits from contracts over the periods in which the work is done (the percentage of completion method) or defer all profit until the year in which the project is completed (the completed contract method, which can be used only in limited circumstances).[18]

The IRS has the power to prescribe the accounting method to be used by the taxpayer. Section 446(b) grants the IRS broad powers to determine if the accounting method used *clearly reflects income*:

> Exceptions—If no method of accounting has been regularly used by the taxpayer, or *if the method used does not clearly reflect income, the computation of taxable income shall be made under such method as, in the opinion of the Secretary . . . does clearly reflect income.*

A change in the method of accounting requires the consent of the IRS.[19]

Cash Receipts Method. Under the **cash receipts method,** property or services received are included in the taxpayer's gross income in the year of actual or constructive receipt by the taxpayer or agent, regardless of whether the income was earned in that year.[20] The income received need not be reduced to cash in the same year. All that is necessary for income recognition is that property or services received have a fair market value—a cash equivalent.[21] Thus, if a cash basis taxpayer receives a note in payment for services, he or she has income in the year of receipt equal to the fair market value of the note. However, a creditor's mere promise to pay (e.g., an account receivable), with no supporting note, is not usually considered to have a fair market value.[22] Thus, the cash basis taxpayer defers income recognition until the account receivable is collected.

EXAMPLE 5

Dana, an accountant, reports her income by the cash method. In 1996, she performed an audit for Orange Corporation and billed the client for $5,000, which was collected in 1997. In 1996, Dana also performed an audit for Blue Corporation. Because of Blue's precarious financial position, Dana required Blue to issue an $8,000 secured negotiable note in payment of the fee. The note had a fair market value of $6,000. Dana collected $8,000 on the note in 1997. Dana's gross income for the two years is as follows:

	1996	1997
Fair market value of note received from Blue	$6,000	
Cash received		
From Orange on account receivable		$ 5,000
From Blue on note receivable		8,000
Less: Recovery of capital		(6,000)
Total gross income	$6,000	$ 7,000

---

[18] §§ 453(a) and (b), § 453A, and Reg. § 1.451–3. See Chapter 18 for limitations on the use of the installment method and the completed contract method.

[19] § 446(e). See Chapter 18.

[20] *Julia A. Strauss*, 2 B.T.A. 598 (1925). See the Glossary of Tax Terms in Appendix C for a discussion of the terms "cash equivalent doctrine" and "constructive receipt."

[21] Reg. §§ 1.446–1(a)(3) and (c)(1)(i).

[22] *Bedell v. Comm.*, 1 USTC ¶359, 7 AFTR 8469, 30 F.2d 622 (CA–2, 1929).

Generally, a check received is considered a cash equivalent. Thus, a cash basis taxpayer must recognize the income when the check is received. This is true even though the taxpayer receives the check after banking hours.[23]

Accrual Method. Under the **accrual method,** an item is generally included in the gross income for the year in which it is earned, regardless of when the income is collected. The income is earned when (1) all the events have occurred that fix the right to receive such income and (2) the amount to be received can be determined with reasonable accuracy.[24]

Generally, the taxpayer's rights to the income accrue when title to property passes to the buyer or the services are performed for the customer or client.[25] If the rights to the income have accrued but are subject to a potential refund claim (e.g., under a product warranty), the income is reported in the year of sale, and a deduction is allowed in subsequent years when actual claims accrue.[26]

Where the taxpayer's rights to the income are being contested (e.g., when a contractor fails to meet specifications), the year in which the income is subject to tax depends upon whether payment has been received. If payment has not been received, no income is recognized until the claim is settled. Only then is the right to the income established.[27] However, if the payment is received before the dispute is settled, the court-made **claim of right doctrine** requires the taxpayer to recognize the income in the year of receipt.[28]

EXAMPLE 6

A contractor completed a building in 1996 and presented a bill to the customer. The customer refused to pay the bill and claimed that the contractor had not met specifications. A settlement with the customer was not reached until 1997. No income would accrue to the contractor until 1997. If the customer paid for the work and then filed suit for damages, the contractor could not defer the income (the income would be taxable in 1996). ▼

The measure of accrual basis income is generally the amount the taxpayer has a right to receive. Unlike the cash basis, the fair market value of the customer's obligation is irrelevant in measuring accrual basis income.

EXAMPLE 7

Assume the same facts as in Example 5, except Dana is an accrual basis taxpayer. Dana must recognize $13,000 ($8,000 + $5,000) income in 1996, the year her rights to the income accrued. ▼

Hybrid Method. The **hybrid method** is a combination of the accrual method and the cash method. Generally, when the hybrid method is used, inventory is an income-producing factor. Therefore, the Regulations require that the accrual method be used for determining sales and cost of goods sold. In this circumstance, to simplify record keeping, the taxpayer accounts for inventory using the accrual method and uses the cash method for all other income and expense items (e.g., dividend and interest income). The hybrid method is primarily used by small businesses.

[23] *Charles F. Kahler,* 18 T.C. 31 (1952).

[24] Reg. § 1.451–1(a).

[25] *Lucas v. North Texas Lumber Co.,* 2 USTC ¶484, 8 AFTR 10276, 50 S.Ct. 184 (USSC, 1930).

[26] *Brown v. Helvering,* 4 USTC ¶1222, 13 AFTR 851, 54 S.Ct. 356 (USSC, 1933).

[27] *Burnet v. Sanford and Brooks,* 2 USTC ¶636, 9 AFTR 603, 51 S.Ct. 150 (USSC, 1931).

[28] *North American Oil Consolidated Co. v. Burnet,* 3 USTC ¶943, 11 AFTR 16, 52 S.Ct. 613 (USSC, 1932).

EXCEPTIONS APPLICABLE TO CASH BASIS TAXPAYERS

Constructive Receipt. Income that has not actually been received by the taxpayer is taxed as though it had been received—the income is constructively received—under the following conditions:

A • The amount is made readily available to the taxpayer.
B • The taxpayer's actual receipt is not subject to substantial limitations or restrictions.[29]

The rationale for the **constructive receipt** doctrine is that if the income is available, the taxpayer should not be allowed to postpone the income recognition. For instance, a taxpayer is not permitted to defer income for December services by refusing to accept payment until January. However, determining whether the income is *readily available* and whether *substantial limitations or restrictions exist* necessitates a factual inquiry that leads to a judgment call.[30] The following are some examples of the application of the constructive receipt doctrine.

EXAMPLE 8

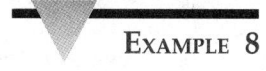

Ted is a member of a barter club. In 1996, Ted performed services for other club members and earned 1,000 points. Each point entitles him to $1 in goods and services sold by other members of the club; the points can be used at any time. In 1997, Ted exchanged his points for a new color TV. Ted must recognize $1,000 income in 1996 when the 1,000 points were credited to his account.[31] ▼

EXAMPLE 9
B

On December 31, an employer issued a bonus check to an employee but asked her to hold it for a few days until the company could make deposits to cover the check. The income was not constructively received on December 31 since the issuer did not have sufficient funds in its account to pay the debt.[32] ▼

EXAMPLE 10

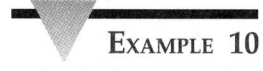

Rick owned interest coupons that matured on December 31. The coupons could be converted to cash at any bank at maturity. Thus, the income is constructively received on December 31.[33] ▼

EXAMPLE 11

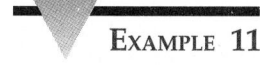

Dove Company mails dividend checks on December 31, 1996. The checks will not be received by shareholders until January. The shareholders do not realize income until 1997.[34] ▼

The constructive receipt doctrine does not reach income that the taxpayer is not yet entitled to receive even though he or she could have contracted to receive the income at an earlier date.

EXAMPLE 12

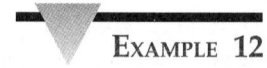

Sara offered to pay Ivan $100,000 for land in December 1996. Ivan refused but offered to sell the land to Sara on January 1, 1997, when he would be in a lower tax bracket. If Sara accepts Ivan's offer, the gain is taxed to Ivan in 1997 when the sale is completed.[35] ▼

Income set apart or made available is not constructively received if its actual receipt is subject to *substantial restrictions.* The life insurance industry has used substantial restrictions as a cornerstone for designing life insurance contracts with favorable tax features. Ordinary life insurance policies provide (1) current

[29] Reg. § 1.451–2(a).
[30] *Baxter v. Comm.*, 87–1 USTC ¶9315, 59 AFTR2d 87–1068, 816 F.2d 493 (CA–9, 1987).
[31] Rev.Rul. 80–52, 1980–1 C.B. 100.
[32] *L. M. Fischer*, 14 T.C. 792 (1950).
[33] Reg. § 1.451–2(b).
[34] Reg. § 1.451–2(b).
[35] *Cowden v. Comm.*, 61–1 USTC ¶9382, 7 AFTR2d 1160, 289 F.2d 20 (CA–5, 1961).

protection—an amount payable in the event of death—and (2) a savings feature—a cash surrender value payable to the policyholder if the policy is terminated during his or her life. The annual increase in cash surrender value is not taxable because the policyholder must cancel the policy to actually receive the increase in value. Because the cancellation requirement is a substantial restriction, the policyholder does not constructively receive the annual increase in cash surrender value.[36] Employees often receive from their employers property subject to substantial restrictions. Generally, no income is recognized until the restrictions lapse.[37]

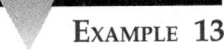

EXAMPLE 13 Carlos is a key employee of Red, Inc. The corporation gave stock with a value of $10,000 to Carlos. The stock could not be sold, however, for five years. Carlos will not be required to recognize income until the restrictions lapse at the end of five years. ▼

Original Issue Discount. Lenders frequently make loans that require a payment at maturity of more than the amount of the original loan. The difference between the amount due at maturity and the amount of the original loan is actually interest but is referred to as **original issue discount.** Under the general rules of tax accounting, the cash basis lender would not report the original issue discount as interest income until the year the amount is collected, although an accrual basis borrower would deduct the interest as it is earned. However, the Code puts the lender and borrower on parity by requiring that the original issue discount be reported when it is earned, regardless of the taxpayer's accounting method.[38] The interest "earned" is calculated by the effective interest rate method.

EXAMPLE 14 On January 1, 1996, Mark, a cash basis taxpayer, paid $82,645 for a 24-month certificate. The certificate was priced to yield 10% (the effective interest rate) with interest compounded annually. No interest was paid until maturity, when Mark received $100,000. Thus, Mark's gross income from the certificate is $17,355 ($100,000 – $82,645). Mark's income earned each year is calculated as follows:

1996 (.10 × $82,645) =	$ 8,264
1997 [.10 × ($82,645 + $8,264)] =	9,091
	$17,355

▼

The original issue discount rules do not apply to U.S. savings bonds (discussed in the following paragraphs) or to obligations with a maturity date of one year or less from the date of issue.[39] See Chapter 16 for additional discussion of the tax treatment of original issue discount.

Series E and Series EE Bonds. Certain U.S. government savings bonds (Series E before 1980 and Series EE after 1979) are issued at a discount and are redeemable for fixed amounts that increase at stated intervals. No interest payments are actually made. The difference between the purchase price and the amount received on redemption is the bondholder's interest income from the investment.

The income from these savings bonds is generally deferred until the bonds are redeemed or mature. Furthermore, Series E bonds can be exchanged within one year of their maturity date for Series HH bonds, and the interest on the Series E

[36] *Theodore H. Cohen,* 39 T.C. 1055 (1963).

[37] § 83(a). See also the discussion of Restricted Property Plans in Chapter 19.

[38] §§ 1272(a)(3) and 1273(a).

[39] § 1272(a)(2).

bonds can be further deferred until maturity of the Series HH bonds.[40] Thus, U.S. savings bonds have attractive income deferral features not available with corporate bonds and certificates of deposit issued by financial institutions.

Of course, the deferral feature of government bonds issued at a discount is not an advantage if the investor has insufficient income to be subject to tax as the income accrues. In fact, the deferral may work to the investor's disadvantage if he or she has other income in the year the bonds mature or the bunching of the bond interest into one tax year creates a tax liability. Fortunately, U.S. government bonds have a provision for these investors. A cash basis taxpayer can elect to include in gross income the annual increment in redemption value.[41]

EXAMPLE 15

Kate purchases Series EE U.S. savings bonds for $500 (face value of $1,000) on January 2 of the current year. If the bonds are redeemed during the first six months, no interest is paid. At December 31, the redemption value is $519.60.

If Kate elects to report the interest income annually, she must report interest income of $19.60 for the current year. If she does not make the election, she will report no interest income for the current year. ▼

When a taxpayer elects to report the income from the bonds on an annual basis, the election applies to all such bonds the taxpayer owns at the time of the election and to all such securities acquired subsequent to the election. A change in the method of reporting the income from the bonds requires permission from the IRS.

Amounts Received under an Obligation to Repay. The receipt of funds with an obligation to repay that amount in the future is the essence of borrowing. Because the taxpayer's assets and liabilities increase by the same amount, no income is realized when the borrowed funds are received. Because amounts paid to the taxpayer by mistake and customer deposits are often classified as borrowed funds, receipt of the funds is not a taxable event.

EXAMPLE 16

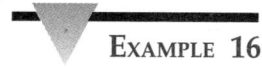

A landlord receives a damage deposit from a tenant. The landlord does not recognize income until the deposit is forfeited because the landlord has an obligation to repay the deposit if no damage occurs.[42] However, if the deposit is in fact a prepayment of rent, it is taxed in the year of receipt. ▼

EXCEPTIONS APPLICABLE TO ACCRUAL BASIS TAXPAYERS

Prepaid Income. For financial reporting purposes, advance payments received from customers are reflected as prepaid income and as a liability of the seller. However, for tax purposes, the prepaid income often is taxed in the year of receipt.

EXAMPLE 17

In December 1996, a tenant paid his January 1997 rent of $1,000. The accrual basis landlord must include the $1,000 in his 1996 income for tax purposes, although the unearned rent income is reported as a liability on the landlord's December 31, 1996, balance sheet. ▼

Taxpayers have repeatedly argued that deferral of income until it is actually earned properly matches revenues and expenses. Moreover, a proper matching of

---

[40] Treas. Dept. Circulars No. 1–80 and No. 2–80, 1980–1 C.B. 714, 715. Note that interest is paid at semiannual intervals on the Series HH bonds and must be included in income as received. Refer to Chapter 5 for a discussion of the savings bond interest exclusion.

[41] § 454(a).

[42] *John Mantell*, 17 T.C. 1143 (1952).

income with the expenses of earning the income is necessary to clearly reflect income, as required by the Code. The IRS responds that § 446(b) grants it broad powers to determine whether an accounting method clearly reflects income. The IRS further argues that generally accepted financial accounting principles should not dictate tax accounting for prepaid income because of the practical problems of collecting Federal revenues. Collection of the tax is simplest in the year the taxpayer receives the cash from the customer or client.

Over 40 years of litigation, the IRS has been only partially successful in the courts. In cases involving prepaid income from services to be performed at the demand of customers (e.g., dance lessons to be taken at any time in a 24-month period), the IRS's position has been upheld.[43] In such cases, the taxpayer's argument that deferral of the income was necessary to match the income with expenses was not persuasive because the taxpayer did not know precisely when each customer would demand services and, thus, when the expenses would be incurred. However, taxpayers have had some success in the courts when the services were performed on a fixed schedule (e.g., a baseball team's season-ticket sales).[44] In some cases involving the sale of goods, taxpayers have successfully argued that the prepayments were mere deposits[45] or in the nature of loans.[46]

Against this background of mixed results in the courts, congressional intervention, and taxpayers' strong resentment of the IRS's position, in 1971 the IRS modified its prepaid income rules, as explained in the following paragraphs.

Deferral of Advance Payments for Goods. Generally, a taxpayer can elect to defer recognition of income from *advance payments for goods* if the method of accounting for the sale is the same for tax and financial reporting purposes.[47]

EXAMPLE 18

Brown Company will ship goods only after payment for the goods has been received. In December 1996, Brown received $10,000 for goods that were not shipped until January 1997. Brown can elect to report the income for tax purposes in 1997, assuming the company reports the income in 1997 for financial reporting purposes. ▼

Deferral of Advance Payments for Services. Revenue Procedure 71–21[48] permits an accrual basis taxpayer to defer recognition of income for *advance payments for services* to be performed by the end of the tax year following the year of receipt. No deferral is allowed if the taxpayer might be required to perform any services, under the agreement, after the tax year following the year of receipt of the advance payment. In addition, prepaid rent and prepaid interest cannot be deferred under this revenue procedure.

EXAMPLE 19

Yellow Corporation, an accrual basis taxpayer, sells its services under 12-month, 18-month, and 24-month contracts. The corporation provides services to each customer every month. In April of 1996, Yellow Corporation sold the following customer contracts:

---

[43] *American Automobile Association v. U.S.*, 61–2 USTC ¶9517, 7 AFTR2d 1618, 81 S.Ct. 1727 (USSC, 1961); *Schlude v. Comm.*, 63–1 USTC ¶9284, 11 AFTR2d 751, 83 S.Ct. 601 (USSC, 1963).

[44] *Artnell Company v. Comm.*, 68–2 USTC ¶9593, 22 AFTR2d 5590, 400 F.2d 981 (CA–7, 1968). See also *Boise Cascade Corp. v. U.S.*, 76–1 USTC ¶9203, 37 AFTR2d 76–696, 530 F.2d 1367 (Ct. Cls., 1976).

[45] *Veenstra & DeHavaan Coal Co.*, 11 T.C. 964 (1948).

[46] *Consolidated-Hammer Dry Plate & Film Co. v. Comm.*, 63–1 USTC ¶9494, 11 AFTR2d 1518, 317 F.2d 829 (CA–7, 1963); *Comm. v. Indianapolis Power & Light Co.*, 90–1 USTC ¶50,007, 65 AFTR2d 90–394, 110 S.Ct. 589 (USSC, 1990).

[47] Reg. § 1.451–5(b). See Reg. § 1.451–5(c) for exceptions to this deferral opportunity. The financial accounting conformity requirement is not applicable to contractors who use the completed contract method.

[48] 1971–2 C.B. 549.

Length of Contract	Total Proceeds
12 months	$6,000
18 months	3,600
24 months	2,400

Fifteen hundred dollars of the $6,000 may be deferred (3/12 × $6,000), and $1,800 of the $3,600 may be deferred (9/18 × $3,600) because those amounts will not be earned until 1997. However, the entire $2,400 received on the 24-month contracts is taxable in the year of receipt (1996), since a part of the income will still be unearned by the end of the tax year following the year of receipt (part will be earned in 1998). ▼

In summary, Revenue Procedure 71–21 will result in conformity of tax and financial accounting in a very limited number of prepaid income cases. It is not apparent why prepaid rents and interest may not be deferred, why revenues under some service contracts may be spread over two years, and why revenues under longer service contracts must be reported in one year. Although Revenue Procedure 71–21 has reduced the number of controversies involving prepaid income, a consistent policy has not yet evolved.

Income Sources

PERSONAL SERVICES

3 Learning Objective
Identify who should pay the tax on a particular item of income in various situations.

It is a well-established principle of taxation that income from personal services must be included in the gross income of the person who performs the services. This principle was first established in a Supreme Court decision, *Lucas v. Earl*.[49] Mr. Earl entered into a binding agreement with his wife under which Mrs. Earl was to receive one-half of Mr. Earl's salary. Justice Holmes used the celebrated **fruit and tree metaphor** to explain that the fruit (income) must be attributed to the tree from which it came (Mr. Earl's services). A mere **assignment of income** does not shift the liability for the tax.

Services of an Employee. Services performed by an employee for the employer's customers are considered performed by the employer. Thus, the employer is taxed on the income from the services provided to the customer, and the employee is taxed on any compensation received from the employer.[50]

Example 20

Dr. Shontelle incorporated her medical practice and entered into a contract to work for the corporation for a salary. All patients contracted to receive their services from the corporation, and those services were provided through the corporation's employee, Dr. Shontelle. The corporation must include the patients' fees in its gross income. Dr. Shontelle must include her salary in her gross income. The corporation will be allowed a deduction for the reasonable salary paid to Dr. Shontelle (see the discussion of unreasonable compensation in Chapter 6). ▼

[49] 2 USTC ¶496, 8 AFTR 10287, 50 S.Ct. 241 (USSC, 1930).
[50] *Sargent v. Comm.*, 91–1 USTC ¶50,168, 67 AFTR2d 91–718, 929 F.2d 1252 (CA–8, 1991).

Services of a Child. In the case of a child, the Code specifically provides that amounts earned from personal services must be included in the child's gross income. This result applies even though the income is paid to other persons (e.g., the parents).[51]

INCOME FROM PROPERTY

Income from property (interest, dividends, rent) must be included in the gross income of the *owner* of the property. If a father clips interest coupons from bonds shortly before the interest payment date and gives the coupons to his son, the interest will still be taxed to the father. A father who assigns rents from rental property to his daughter will be taxed on the rent since he retains ownership of the property.[52]

Often income-producing property is transferred after income from the property has accrued but before the income is recognized under the transferor's method of accounting. The IRS and the courts have developed rules to allocate the income between the transferor and the transferee.

Interest. According to the IRS, interest accrues daily. Therefore, the interest for the period that includes the date of the transfer is allocated between the transferor and transferee based on the number of days during the period that each owned the property.

EXAMPLE 21

Floyd, a cash basis taxpayer, gave his son, Seth, bonds with a face amount of $10,000 and an 8% stated annual interest rate. The gift was made on January 31, 1996, and the interest was paid on December 31, 1996. Floyd must recognize $68 in interest income (8% × $10,000 × 31/366). Seth will recognize $732 in interest income ($800 – $68). ▼

When the transferor must recognize the income from the property depends upon the method of accounting and the manner in which the property was transferred. In the case of a gift of income-producing property, the donor must recognize his or her share of the accrued income at the time it would have been recognized had the donor continued to own the property.[53] However, if the transfer is a sale, the transferor must recognize the accrued income at the time of the sale. This results because the accrued interest will be included in the sales proceeds.

EXAMPLE 22

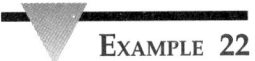

Assume the same facts as in Example 21, except the interest that was payable as of December 31 was not actually or constructively received by the bondholders until January 3, 1997. As a cash basis taxpayer, Floyd generally does not recognize interest income until it is received. If Floyd had continued to own the bonds, the interest would have been included in his 1997 gross income, the year it would have been received. Therefore, Floyd must include the $68 accrued income in his gross income as of January 3, 1997.

Further assume that Floyd sold identical bonds on the date of the gift. The bonds sold for $9,900, including accrued interest. On January 31, 1996, Floyd must recognize the

---

[51] § 73. For circumstances in which the child's unearned income is taxed at the parents' rate, see Unearned Income of Certain Minor Children Taxed at Parents' Rate in Chapter 3.

[52] *Galt v. Comm.*, 54–2 USTC ¶9457, 46 AFTR 633, 216 F.2d 41 (CA–7, 1954); *Helvering v. Horst*, 40–2 USTC ¶9787, 24 AFTR 1058, 61 S.Ct. 144 (USSC, 1940).

[53] Rev.Rul. 72–312, 1972–1 C.B. 22.

TAX IN THE NEWS

Venture Capitalist Finds Tax Benefits in Illiquid Investments

Venture capital is often available through operators of local businesses who like to invest their profits in other emerging local businesses. One disadvantage to investing in new firms is that the stock cannot be quickly converted to cash, but many of these investors are not interested in liquidity and the tax liability that comes from selling investments. As one venture capitalist commented, "I'm not interested in short-term hits. . . . I do not want to pay taxes. Paying taxes really p— me off. . . . I'll just watch the whole thing grow tax deferred."

SOURCE: Adapted from Fleming Meeks and Kate Bohner Lewis, "Blue Chips in Your Own Back Yard." *Forbes,* April 24, 1995, pp. 166 and 171.

accrued interest of $68 on the bonds sold. Thus, the selling price of the bonds is $9,832 ($9,900 – $68). ▼

Dividends. A corporation is taxed on its earnings, and the shareholders are taxed on the dividends paid to them from the corporation's after-tax earnings. The dividend can take the form of an actual dividend or a constructive dividend (e.g., shareholder use of corporate assets).

Unlike interest, dividends do not accrue on a daily basis because the declaration of a dividend is at the discretion of the corporation's board of directors. Generally, dividends are taxed to the person who is entitled to receive them—the shareholder of record as of the corporation's record date.[54] Thus, if a taxpayer sells stock after a dividend has been declared but before the record date, the dividend generally will be taxed to the purchaser.

If a donor makes a gift of stock to someone (e.g., a family member) after the declaration date but before the record date, the Tax Court has held that the donor does not shift the dividend income to the donee. The *fruit* has sufficiently ripened as of the declaration date to tax the dividend income to the donor of the stock.[55] In a similar set of facts, the Fifth Court of Appeals concluded that the dividend income should be included in the gross income of the donee (the owner at the record date). In this case, the taxpayer gave stock to a qualified charity (a charitable contribution) after the declaration date and before the record date.[56]

Example 23

On June 20, the board of directors of Black Corporation declares a $10 per share dividend. The dividend is payable on June 30, to shareholders of record on June 25. As of June 20, Maria owned 200 shares of Black Corporation's stock. On June 21, Maria sold 100 of the shares to Norm for their fair market value and gave 100 of the shares to Sam (her son). Assume both Norm and Sam are shareholders of record as of June 25. Norm (the purchaser) will be taxed on $1,000 since he is entitled to receive the dividend. However, Maria (the donor) will be taxed on the $1,000 received by Sam (the donee) because the gift was made after the declaration date of the dividend. ▼

[54] Reg. § 1.61–9(c). The record date is the cutoff for determining the shareholders who are entitled to receive the dividend.

[55] *M. G. Anton,* 34 T.C. 842 (1960).

[56] *Caruth Corporation v. U.S.,* 89–1 USTC ¶9172, 63 AFTR2d 89–716, 865 F.2d 644 (CA–5, 1989).

INCOME RECEIVED BY AN AGENT

Income received by the taxpayer's agent is considered to be received by the taxpayer. A cash basis principal must recognize the income at the time it is received by the agent.[57]

EXAMPLE 24

Jack, a cash basis taxpayer, delivered cattle to the auction barn in late December. The auctioneer, acting as the farmer's agent, sold the cattle and collected the proceeds in December. The auctioneer did not pay Jack until the following January. Jack must include the sales proceeds in his gross income for the year the auctioneer received the funds. ▼

INCOME FROM PARTNERSHIPS, S CORPORATIONS, TRUSTS, AND ESTATES

A **partnership** is not a separate taxable entity. Rather, the partnership merely files an information return (Form 1065), which serves to provide the data necessary for determining the character and amount of each partner's distributive share of the partnership's income and deductions. Each partner must then report his or her distributive share of the partnership's income and deductions for the partnership's tax year ending within or with his or her tax year. The income must be reported by each partner in the year it is earned, even if such amounts are not actually distributed to the partners. Because a partner pays tax on income as the partnership earns it, a distribution by the partnership to the partner is treated under the recovery of capital rules.[58]

EXAMPLE 25

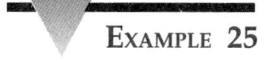

Tara owned a one-half interest in the capital and profits of T & S Company (a calendar year partnership). For tax year 1996, the partnership earned revenue of $150,000 and had operating expenses of $80,000. During the year, Tara withdrew from her capital account $2,500 per month (for a total of $30,000). For 1996, Tara must report $35,000 as her share of the partnership's profits [½ × ($150,000 – $80,000)] even though she received distributions of only $30,000. ▼

ETHICAL CONSIDERATIONS

Whether to Report Income

You are the treasurer of a scout troop. The scouts conduct car washes and use the proceeds to pay for troop members to attend summer camp. The income is allocated among the 60 troop members based on the number of hours each worked. No scout earned more than $100 for the year, and the average amount earned was $50. The IRS, if it were aware of the facts, would probably reason that the car wash operation is a partnership, and each scout is a partner. Thus, the troop would have to file a partnership tax return, and each of the 60 scouts would report his or her share of the income. From the data available, you ascertain that reporting the income would affect the liability of no more than 5 of the scouts (because of their standard deduction) and that the tax for each of the 5 scouts affected would not exceed $15.

In your opinion, the cost to the IRS and the total cost of paper consumed by the process of filing the returns would exceed the increase in IRS revenue. In addition, filing the

[57] Rev.Rul. 79–379, 1979–2 C.B. 204.

[58] § 706(a) and Reg. § 1.706–1(a)(1). For further discussion, see Chapter 20.

partnership return and reporting each partner's share would be a lot of extra work for you. Therefore, you feel that filing the return and reporting each scout's share of the income are not worth the effort. Evaluate your position from both a compliance and ethical perspective.

Contrary to the general provision that a corporation must pay tax on its income, a *small business corporation* may elect to be taxed similarly to a partnership. Thus, the shareholders, rather than the corporation, pay the tax on the corporation's income.[59] The electing corporation is referred to as an **S corporation.** Generally, the shareholder reports his or her proportionate share of the corporation's income and deductions for the year, whether or not the corporation actually makes any distributions to the shareholder.

The *beneficiaries of estates and trusts* generally are taxed on the income earned by the estates or trusts that is actually distributed or required to be distributed to them.[60] Any income not taxed to the beneficiaries is taxable to the estate or trust.

INCOME IN COMMUNITY PROPERTY STATES

General. State law in Louisiana, Texas, New Mexico, Arizona, California, Washington, Idaho, Nevada, and Wisconsin is based upon a community property system. All other states have a common law property system. The basic difference between common law and community property systems centers around the property rights of married persons. Questions about community property income most frequently arise when the husband and wife file separate returns.

Under a **community property** system, all property is deemed either to be separately owned by the spouse or to belong to the marital community. Property may be held separately by a spouse if it was acquired before marriage or received by gift or inheritance following marriage. Otherwise, any property is deemed to be community property. For Federal tax purposes, each spouse is taxed on one-half of the income from property belonging to the community.

The laws of Texas, Louisiana, Wisconsin, and Idaho distinguish between separate property and the income it produces. In these states, the income from separate property belongs to the community. Accordingly, for Federal income tax purposes, each spouse is taxed on one-half of the income. In the remaining community property states, separate property produces separate income that the owner-spouse must report on his or her Federal income tax return.

What appears to be income, however, may really represent a recovery of capital. A recovery of capital and gain realized on separate property retain their identity as separate property. Items such as nontaxable stock dividends, royalties from mineral interests, and gains and losses from the sale of property take on the same classification as the assets to which they relate.

EXAMPLE 26

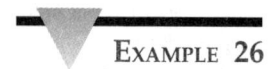

Bob and Jane are husband and wife and reside in California. Among other transactions during the year, the following occurred:

- Nontaxable stock dividend received by Jane on stock that was given to her after her marriage by her mother.
- Gain of $10,000 on the sale of unimproved land purchased by Bob before his marriage.

[59] §§ 1361(a) and 1366. For further discussion, see Chapter 20.

[60] §§ 652(a) and 662(a). For further discussion of the taxation of income from partnerships, S corporations, trusts, and estates, see *West's Federal Taxation: Corporations, Partnerships, Estates, and Trusts,* Chapters 10, 11, 12, and 19.

- Oil royalties of $15,000 from a lease Jane acquired after marriage with her separate funds.

Since the stock dividend was distributed on stock held by Jane as separate property, it also is her separate property. The same result occurs for the oil royalties Jane receives. All of the proceeds from the sale of unimproved land (including the gain of $10,000) are Bob's separate property. ▼

In all community property states, income from personal services (e.g., salaries, wages, income from a professional partnership) is generally treated as if one-half is earned by each spouse.

EXAMPLE 27

Fred and Wilma are married but file separate returns. Fred received $25,000 salary and $300 taxable interest on a savings account he established in his name. The deposits to the savings account were made from Fred's salary earned since the marriage. Wilma collected $2,000 taxable dividends on stock she inherited from her father. Wilma's gross income is computed as follows under three assumptions as to the state of residency of the couple:

	California	Texas	Common Law States
Dividends	$ 2,000	$ 1,000	$2,000
Salary	12,500	12,500	-0-
Interest	150	150	-0-
	$14,650	$13,650	$2,000

▼

Community Property Spouses Living Apart. The general rules for taxing the income from services performed by residents of community property states can create complications and even inequities for spouses who are living apart.

EXAMPLE 28

Cole and Debra were married but living apart for the first nine months of 1996 and were divorced as of October 1, 1996. In December 1996, Cole married Emily, who was married but living apart from Frank before their divorce in June 1996. Cole and Frank had no income from personal services in 1996.

Cole brought into his marriage to Emily a tax liability on one-half of Debra's earnings for the first nine months of the year. However, Emily left with Frank a tax liability on one-half of her earnings for the first six months of 1996. ▼

In circumstances such as those depicted in Example 28, the accrued tax liability could be factored into a property division being negotiated at a time when the parties do not need further complications. In other cases, an abandoned spouse could be saddled with a tax on income earned by a spouse whose whereabouts are unknown.

In 1980, Congress developed a simple solution to the many tax problems of community property spouses living apart. A spouse (or former spouse) is taxed only on his or her actual earnings from personal services if the following conditions are met:[61]

- The individuals live apart for the entire year.
- They do not file a joint return with each other.
- No portion of the earned income is transferred between the individuals.

[61] § 66.

EXAMPLE 29

Jim and Lori reside in a community property state, and both are gainfully employed. On July 1, 1996, they separated, and on June 30, 1997, they were divorced. Assuming their only source of income is wages, one-half of such income for each year is earned by June 30, and they did not file a joint return for 1996, each should report the following gross income:

	Jim's Separate Return	Lori's Separate Return
1996	One-half of Jim's wages	One-half of Jim's wages
	One-half of Lori's wages	One-half of Lori's wages
1997	All of Jim's wages	All of Lori's wages

The results would be the same if Jim or Lori married another person in 1997, except the newlyweds would probably file a joint return. ▼

The IRS may absolve from liability an *innocent spouse* who does not live apart for the entire year and files a separate return but omits his or her share of the community income received by the other spouse. To qualify for the innocent spouse relief, the taxpayer must not know or must have no reason to know of the omitted community income.

Items Specifically Included in Gross Income

4 LEARNING OBJECTIVE
Apply the Internal Revenue Code provisions on alimony, loans made at below-market interest rates, annuities, prizes and awards, group term life insurance, unemployment compensation, and Social Security benefits.

The general principles of gross income determination (discussed in the previous sections) as applied by the IRS and the courts have on occasion yielded results Congress found unacceptable. Consequently, Congress has provided more specific rules for determining the gross income from certain sources. Some of these special rules appear in §§ 71–90 of the Code.

ALIMONY AND SEPARATE MAINTENANCE PAYMENTS

When a married couple divorce or become legally separated, state law generally requires a division of the property accumulated during the marriage. In addition, one spouse may have a legal obligation to support the other spouse. The Code distinguishes between the support payments (alimony or separate maintenance) and the property division in terms of the tax consequences.

Alimony and separate maintenance payments are *deductible* by the party making the payments and are *includible* in the gross income of the party receiving the payments.[62] Thus, income is shifted from the income earner to the income beneficiary, who is better able to pay the tax on the amount received.

EXAMPLE 30

Pete and Tina were divorced, and Pete was required to pay Tina $15,000 of alimony each year. Pete earns $31,000 a year. The tax law presumes that because Tina received the $15,000, she is better able than Pete to pay the tax on that amount. Therefore, Tina must include the $15,000 in her gross income, and Pete is allowed to deduct $15,000 from his gross income. ▼

[62] §§ 71 and 215.

A transfer of property *other than cash* to a former spouse under a divorce decree or agreement is not a taxable event. The transferor is not entitled to a deduction and does not recognize gain or loss on the transfer. The transferee does not recognize income and has a cost basis equal to the transferor's basis.[63]

EXAMPLE 31 Paul transfers stock to Rosa as part of a 1996 divorce settlement. The cost of the stock to Paul is $12,000, and the stock's value at the time of the transfer is $15,000. Rosa later sells the stock for $16,000. Paul is not required to recognize gain from the transfer of the stock to Rosa, and Rosa has a realized and recognized gain of $4,000 ($16,000 – $12,000) when she sells the stock. ▼

In the case of *cash payments,* however, it is often difficult to distinguish payments under a support obligation (alimony) and payments for the other spouse's property (property settlement). In 1984, Congress developed objective rules to classify the payments.

Post-1984 Agreements and Decrees. Payments made under post-1984 agreements and decrees are *classified as alimony* only if the following conditions are satisfied:

1. The payments are in cash.
2. The agreement or decree does not specify that the payments are not alimony.
3. The payor and payee are not members of the same household at the time the payments are made.
4. There is no liability to make the payments for any period after the death of the payee.[64]

Requirement 1 simplifies the law by clearly distinguishing alimony from a property division; that is, if the payment is not in cash, it must be a property division. Requirement 2 allows the parties to determine by agreement whether or not the payments will be alimony. The prohibition on cohabitation—requirement 3—is aimed at assuring the alimony payments are associated with duplicative living expenses (maintaining two households).[65] Requirement 4 is an attempt to prevent alimony treatment from being applied to what is, in fact, a payment for property rather than a support obligation. That is, a seller's estate generally will receive payments for property due after the seller's death. Such payments after the death of the payee could not be for the payee's support.

Front-Loading. As a further safeguard against a property settlement being disguised as alimony, special rules apply to post-1986 agreements if payments in the first or second year exceed $15,000. If the change in the amount of the payments exceeds statutory limits, **alimony recapture** results to the extent of the excess alimony payments. In the *third* year, the payor must include the excess alimony payments for the first and second years in gross income, and the payee is

[63] § 1041, added to the Code in 1984 to repeal the rule of *U.S. v. Davis,* 62–2 USTC ¶9509, 9 AFTR2d 1625, 82 S.Ct. 1190 (USSC, 1962). Under the Davis rule, which applied to pre-1985 divorces, a property transfer incident to divorce was a taxable event.

[64] § 71(b)(1). This set of alimony rules can also apply to pre-1985 agreements and decrees if both parties agree in writing. The rules applicable to pre-1985 agreements and decrees are not discussed in this text.

[65] *Alexander Washington,* 77 T.C. 601 (1981) at 604.

allowed a deduction for these excess alimony payments. The recaptured amount is computed as follows:[66]

$$R = D + E$$
$$D = B - (C + \$15{,}000)$$
$$E = A - \left(\frac{B - D + C}{2} + \$15{,}000\right)$$

R = amount recaptured in Year 3 tax return

D = recapture from Year 2

E = recapture from Year 1

A, B, C = payments in the first (A), second (B), and third (C) calendar years of the agreement or decree, where $D \geqslant 0$, $E \geqslant 0$

The recapture formula provides an objective technique for determining alimony recapture. Thus, at the time of the divorce, the taxpayers can ascertain the tax consequences. The general concept is that if the alimony payments decrease by over $15,000 between years in the first three years, there will be alimony recapture with respect to the decrease in excess of $15,000 each year. This rule is applied for the change between Year 2 and Year 3 (D in the above formula). However, rather than making the same calculation for Year 2 payments versus Year 1 payments, the Code requires that the *average* of the payments in Years 2 and 3 be compared with the Year 1 payments (E in the above formula). For this purpose, revised alimony for Year 2 (alimony deducted for Year 2 minus the alimony recapture for Year 2) is used.

EXAMPLE 32

Wes and Rita were divorced in 1996. Under the agreement, Rita was to receive $50,000 in 1996, $20,000 in 1997, and nothing thereafter. The payments were to cease upon Rita's death or remarriage. In 1998, Wes must include an additional $32,500 in gross income for alimony recapture, and Rita is allowed a deduction for the same amount.

$$D = \$20{,}000 - (\$0 + \$15{,}000) = \$5{,}000$$

$$E = \$50{,}000 - \left(\frac{\$20{,}000 - \$5{,}000 + \$0}{2} + \$15{,}000\right) = \$27{,}500$$

$$R = \$5{,}000 + \$27{,}500 = \$32{,}500$$

Note that for 1996 Wes deducts alimony of $50,000 and Rita includes $50,000 in her gross income. For 1997, the amount of the alimony deduction for Wes is $20,000, and Rita's gross income from the alimony is $20,000.

If instead $50,000 were paid in 1996 and nothing is paid for the following years, $35,000 would be recaptured in 1998.

$$D = \$0 - (\$0 + \$15{,}000) = -\$15{,}000, \text{ but D must be} \geq \$0$$

$$E = \$50{,}000 - \left(\frac{\$0 - \$0 + \$0}{2} + \$15{,}000\right) = \$35{,}000$$

$$R = \$0 + \$35{,}000 = \$35{,}000$$

▼

[66] § 71(f).

CONCEPT SUMMARY 4–1

Tax Treatment of Payments and Transfers Pursuant to Post-1984 Divorce Agreements and Decrees

	Payor	Recipient
Alimony	Deduction from gross income.	Included in gross income.
Alimony recapture	Included in gross income of the third year.	Deducted from gross income of the third year.
Child support	Not deductible.	Not includible in income.
Property settlement	No income or deduction.	No income or deduction; basis for the property is the same as the transferor's basis.

For 1985 and 1986 agreements and decrees, alimony recapture is required during the second and third years if payments decrease by more than $10,000. A special formula is applied to compute the recapture amounts.[67]

Post-1984 agreements and decrees are not subject to alimony recapture if the decrease in payments is due to the death of either spouse or the remarriage of the payee. Recapture is not applicable because these events typically terminate alimony under state laws. In addition, the recapture rules do not apply to payments where the amount is contingent (e.g., a percentage of income from certain property or a percentage of the payor spouse's compensation), the payments are to be made over a period of three years or longer (unless death, remarriage, or other contingency occurs), and the contingencies are beyond the payor's control.[68]

EXAMPLE 33

Under a 1996 divorce agreement, Ed was to receive an amount equal to one-half of Nina's income from certain rental properties for 1996–1999. Payments were to cease upon the death of Ed or Nina or upon the remarriage of Ed. Ed received $50,000 in 1996 and $50,000 in 1997; in 1998, however, the property was vacant, and Ed received nothing. Nina, who deducted alimony in 1996 and 1997, is not required to recapture any alimony in 1998 because the payments were contingent. ▼

ETHICAL CONSIDERATIONS

Structuring a Divorce

In many situations, the tax laws influence how transactions are structured. The tax laws can be especially influential in structuring divorce agreements. The law seems to say that as long as one party will report as income cash received from a former spouse, the paying party can claim a deduction, even though, in reality, the paying party is purchasing the other's share of the marital property. Thus, the paying party may obtain a deduction for

[67] See § 421 of the Deficit Reduction Act of 1984 and § 1843(c)(2) of the Tax Reform Act of 1986.

[68] §§ 71(f)(5)(A) and (C).

purchasing a personal use asset (e.g., a weekend home that was formerly jointly owned). The alimony recapture provision limits the parties' ability to carry out such a transaction, but does not preclude it.

Assume that each former spouse is represented by competent tax and legal advisers and that one spouse is in a higher marginal tax bracket than the other. The divorcing couple can enter into an agreement that will increase each party's after-tax wealth at the government's expense.

One may question why the laws deliberately set forth rules that will cause a divorcing couple to engage in this arbitrage. One may also question whether a tax adviser should advise a client involved in divorce negotiations to exploit the tax laws in this manner.

Child Support. A taxpayer does not realize income from the receipt of child support payments made by his or her former spouse. This result occurs because the money is received subject to the duty to use the money for the child's benefit. The payor is not allowed to deduct the child support payments because the payments are made to satisfy the payor's legal obligation to support the child.

In many cases, it is difficult to determine whether an amount received is alimony or child support. Concerning pre-1985 decrees and agreements, the Supreme Court has ruled that if the decree or agreement does not specifically provide for child support, none of the payments will be treated as such.[69]

EXAMPLE 34

A pre-1985 divorce agreement provides that Matt is required to make periodic alimony payments of $500 per month to Grace. However, when Matt and Grace's child reaches age 21, marries, or dies (whichever occurs first), the payments will be reduced to $300 per month. Grace has custody of the child. Although it is reasonable to infer that $200 ($500 – $300) is for child support, the entire $500 is alimony because no payments are specified as child support. ▼

In 1984, Congress changed the results in Example 34 but only for post-1984 agreements and decrees. Under the revision, if the amount of the payments would be reduced upon the happening of a contingency related to a child (e.g., the child attains age 21 or dies), the amount of the future reduction in the payment is deemed child support.[70]

EXAMPLE 35

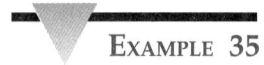

The facts are the same as in Example 34, except that the agreement is a post-1984 agreement. Child support payments are $200 each month, and alimony is $300 each month. ▼

IMPUTED INTEREST ON BELOW-MARKET LOANS

As discussed earlier in the chapter, generally no income is recognized unless it is realized. Realization generally occurs when the taxpayer performs services or sells goods and thus becomes entitled to a payment from the other party. It follows that no income is realized if the goods or services are provided at no charge. Under this interpretation of the realization requirement, before 1984, interest-free loans were used to shift income between taxpayers.

[69] *Comm. v. Lester*, 61–1 USTC ¶9463, 7 AFTR2d 1445, 81 S.Ct. 1343 (USSC, 1961).

[70] § 71(c)(2). Pre-1985 agreements can be amended so that the revision will apply [§ 422(e) of the Deficit Reduction Act of 1984].

TAX IN THE NEWS

Ex-Spouse and Federal Government Are Big Lottery Winners

In 1985, Joseph Smith and 21 co-workers each contributed one dollar toward the purchase of a lottery ticket. The group won $13.5 million. Joe's share was 21 annual payments of $30,989. In 1988, Joe was divorced, and the court awarded 85 percent of the lottery winnings to him and 15 percent to his ex-wife as an equitable distribution. Joe's ex-wife went back to court the following year and obtained a 50 percent interest in the lottery winnings. Joe was required to make payments with respect to amounts received before the revised court order so that she would receive one-half of all prior payments as well as of future payments. For 1987, Joe and his wife filed as married persons filing separate returns, and Joe included the full $30,989 in his gross income. After the court altered the award, Joe amended his 1987 return, reducing his 1987 income by the amount of his ex-wife's one-half share.

The District Court rejected Joe's claim for a tax refund, ruling that the payments were actually a distribution of marital property pursuant to divorce and were payable to the ex-wife's estate if she lived to collect the 21 payments. Therefore, Joe was required to pay tax on income his ex-wife enjoyed. Furthermore, the income paid to his ex-wife on which Joe was taxed was subject to the most expensive rate schedule for 1987—married filing a separate return—and was subject to a high marginal rate because it was "stacked" on top of his share of the winnings. Thus, Joe was left with little of his winnings.

SOURCE: *Smith v. Comm.*, 94–2 USTC ¶50,503, 75 AFTR2d 95–2253 (D.Ct.N.Y., 1994).

Example 36

Veneia (daughter) is in the 20% tax bracket and has no investment income. Kareem (father) is in the 50% tax bracket and has $200,000 in a money market account earning 10% interest. Kareem would like Veneia to receive and pay tax on the income earned on the $200,000. Because Kareem would also like to have access to the $200,000 should he need the money, he does not want to make an outright gift of the money, nor does he want to commit the money to a trust.

Before 1984, Kareem could achieve his goals as follows. He could transfer the money market account to Veneia in exchange for her $200,000 non-interest-bearing note, payable on Kareem's demand. As a result, Veneia would receive the income, and the family's taxes would be decreased by $6,000.

Decrease in Kareem's tax—(.10 × $200,000).50 =	($10,000)
Increase in Veneia's tax—(.10 × $200,000).20 =	4,000
Decrease in the family's taxes	($ 6,000)

▼

Under the 1984 amendments to the Code, Kareem in Example 36 is required to recognize **imputed interest** income.[71] Veneia is deemed to have incurred interest expense equal to Kareem's imputed interest income. Veneia's interest may be

[71] § 7872(a)(1).

deductible on her return as investment interest if she itemizes deductions (see Chapter 10). To complete the fictitious series of transactions, Kareem is then deemed to have given Veneia the amount of the imputed interest she did not pay. The gift received by Veneia is not subject to income tax (see Chapter 5), although Kareem may be subject to the gift tax (unified transfer tax) on the amount deemed given to Veneia (refer to Chapter 1).

Imputed interest is calculated using the rate the Federal government pays on new borrowings and is compounded semiannually. This Federal rate is adjusted monthly and is published by the IRS.[72] Actually, there are three Federal rates: short-term (not over three years and including demand loans), mid-term (over three years but not over nine years), and long-term (over nine years).

EXAMPLE 37 Assume the Federal rate applicable to the loan in Example 36 is 7% through June 30 and 8% from July 1 through December 31. Kareem made the loan on January 1, and the loan is still outstanding on December 31. Kareem must recognize interest income of $15,280, and Veneia has interest expense of $15,280. Kareem is deemed to have made a gift of $15,280 to Veneia.

Interest calculations	
January 1–June 30— .07($200,000) (½ year)	$ 7,000
July 1–December 31— .08($200,000 + $7,000) (½ year)	8,280
	$15,280

▼

If interest is charged on the loan but is less than the Federal rate, the imputed interest is the difference between the amount that would have been charged at the Federal rate and the amount actually charged.

EXAMPLE 38 Assume the same facts as in Example 37, except that Kareem charged 6% interest, compounded annually.

Interest at the Federal rate	$ 15,280
Less interest charged (.06 × $200,000)	(12,000)
Imputed interest	$ 3,280

▼

The imputed interest rules apply to the following *types* of below-market loans:[73]

1. Gift loans (made out of love, affection, or generosity, as in Example 36).
2. Compensation-related loans (employer loans to employees).
3. Corporation-shareholder loans (a corporation's loans to its shareholders).
4. Tax avoidance loans and other loans that significantly affect the borrower's or lender's Federal tax liability (discussed in the following paragraphs).

The effects of the first three types of loans on the borrower and lender are summarized in Concept Summary 4–2.

Tax Avoidance and Other Below-Market Loans. In addition to the three specific types of loans that are subject to the imputed interest rules, the Code

[72] §§ 7872(b)(2) and (f)(2).

[73] § 7872(c).

CONCEPT SUMMARY 4–2

Effect of Certain Below-Market Loans on the Lender and Borrower

Type of Loan		Lender	Borrower
Gift	Step 1	Interest income	Interest expense
	Step 2	Gift made	Gift received
Compensation-related	Step 1	Interest income	Interest expense
	Step 2	Compensation expense	Compensation income
Corporation to shareholder	Step 1	Interest income	Interest expense
	Step 2	Dividend paid	Dividend income

includes a catchall provision for *tax avoidance loans* and other arrangements that have a significant effect on the tax liability of the borrower or lender. The Conference Report provides the following example of an arrangement that might be subject to the imputed interest rules.[74]

EXAMPLE 39

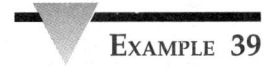

Annual dues for the Good Health Club are $400. In lieu of paying dues, a member can make a $4,000 deposit, refundable at the end of one year. The club can earn $400 interest on the deposit.

If interest were not imputed, an individual with $4,000 could, in effect, earn tax-exempt income on the deposit. That is, rather than invest the $4,000, earn $400 in interest, pay tax on the interest, and then pay $400 in dues, the individual could avoid tax on the interest by making the deposit. Thus, income and expenses are imputed as follows: interest income and nondeductible health club fees for the club member; income from fees and interest expense for the club. ▼

Many commercially motivated transactions could be swept into this other below-market loans category. However, the temporary Regulations have carved out a frequently encountered exception for customer prepayments. If the prepayments are included in the recipient's income under the recipient's method of accounting, the payments are not considered loans and, thus, are not subject to the imputed interest rules.[75]

EXAMPLE 40

Landlord, a cash basis taxpayer, charges tenants a damage deposit equal to one month's rent on residential apartments. When the tenant enters into the lease, the landlord also collects rent for the last month of the lease.

The prepaid rent for the last month of the lease is taxed in the year received and thus is not considered a loan. The security deposit is not taxed when received and is therefore a candidate for imputed interest. However, no apparent tax benefit is derived by the landlord or the tenant, and thus the security deposit should not be subject to the imputed interest provisions. But if making the deposit would reduce the rent paid by the tenant, the tenant could derive a tax benefit, much the same as the club member in Example 39. ▼

[74] H. Rep. No. 98–861, 98th Cong., 2d Sess., 1984, p. 1023.

[75] Prop. Reg. § 1.7872–2(b)(1)(i).

Exceptions and Limitations. No interest is imputed on total outstanding *gift loans* of $10,000 or less between individuals, unless the loan proceeds are used to purchase income-producing property.[76] This exemption eliminates from these complex provisions immaterial amounts that do not result in apparent shifts of income. However, if the proceeds of such a loan are used to purchase income-producing property, the limitations discussed in the following paragraphs apply instead.

On loans of $100,000 or less between individuals, the imputed interest cannot exceed the borrower's net investment income for the year (gross income from all investments less the related expenses).[77] As discussed above, one of the purposes of the imputed interest rules is to prevent high-income taxpayers from shifting income to relatives in a lower marginal bracket. This shifting of investment income is considered to occur only to the extent the borrower has investment income. Thus, the income imputed to the lender is limited to the borrower's net investment income. As a further limitation, or exemption, if the borrower's net investment income for the year does not exceed $1,000, no interest is imputed on loans of $100,000 or less. However, these limitations for loans of $100,000 or less do not apply if a principal purpose of a loan is tax avoidance. In such a case, interest is imputed, and the imputed interest is not limited to the borrower's net investment income.[78]

EXAMPLE 41

Vicki made interest-free gift loans as follows:

Borrower	Amount	Borrower's Net Investment Income	Purpose
Susan	$ 8,000	$ –0–	Education
Dan	9,000	500	Purchase of stock
Bonnie	25,000	–0–	Purchase of a business
Megan	90,000	15,000	Purchase of a residence
Olaf	120,000	–0–	Purchase of a residence

Assume that tax avoidance is not a principal purpose of any of the loans. The loan to Susan is not subject to the imputed interest rules because the $10,000 exception applies. The $10,000 exception does not apply to the loan to Dan because the proceeds were used to purchase income-producing assets. However, under the $100,000 exception, the imputed interest is limited to Dan's investment income ($500). Since the $1,000 exception also applies to this loan, no interest is imputed.

No interest is imputed on the loan to Bonnie because the $100,000 exception applies. Interest is imputed on the loan to Megan based on the lesser of (1) the borrower's $15,000 net investment income or (2) the interest as calculated by applying the Federal rate to the outstanding loan. None of the exceptions apply to the loan to Olaf because the loan was for more than $100,000.

Assume the relevant Federal rate is 10% and the loans were outstanding for the entire year. Vicki would recognize interest income, compounded semiannually, as follows:

[76] § 7872(c)(2).

[77] § 7872(d).

[78] *Deficit Reduction Tax Bill of 1984: Explanation of the Senate Finance Committee* (April 2, 1984), p. 484.

CONCEPT SUMMARY 4–3

Exceptions to the Imputed Interest Rules For Below-Market Loans

Exception	Eligible Loans	Ineligible Loans and Limitations
De minimis—aggregate loans of $10,000 or less	Gift loans	Proceeds used to purchase income-producing assets.
	Employer-employee	Principal purpose is tax avoidance.
	Corporation-shareholder	Principal purpose is tax avoidance.
Aggregate loans of $100,000 or less	Between individuals	Principal purpose is tax avoidance. For all other loans, interest is imputed to the extent of the borrower's net investment income (NII), if the borrower's NII exceeds $1,000.

Loan to Megan:	
First 6 months (.10 × $90,000 × ½ year)	$ 4,500
Second 6 months (.10 × $94,500 × ½ year)	4,725
	$ 9,225
Loan to Olaf:	
First 6 months (.10 × $120,000 × ½ year)	$ 6,000
Second 6 months (.10 × $126,000 × ½ year)	6,300
	$12,300
Total imputed interest ($9,225 + $12,300)	$21,525

▼

As with gift loans, there is a $10,000 exemption for *compensation-related loans* and *corporation-shareholder loans*. However, the $10,000 exception does not apply if tax avoidance is one of the principal purposes of a loan.[79] This vague tax avoidance standard makes practically all compensation-related and corporation-shareholder loans suspect. Nevertheless, the $10,000 exception should apply when an employee's borrowing was necessitated by personal needs (e.g., to meet unexpected expenses) rather than tax considerations.

INCOME FROM ANNUITIES

Annuity contracts generally require the purchaser (the annuitant) to pay a fixed amount for the right to receive a future stream of payments. Typically, the issuer of

[79] § 7872(c)(3).

the contract is an insurance company and will pay the annuitant a cash value if the annuitant cancels the contract. The insurance company invests the amounts received from the annuitant, and the income earned serves to increase the cash value of the policy. No income is recognized at the time the cash value of the annuity increases because the taxpayer has not actually received any income. The income is not constructively received because, generally, the taxpayer must cancel the policy to receive the increase in value (the increase in value is subject to substantial restrictions).

EXAMPLE 42 Juanita, age 50, paid $30,000 for an annuity contract that is to pay her $500 per month beginning when she reaches age 65 and continuing until her death. If Juanita should cancel the policy after one year, she would receive $30,200. The $200 increase in value is not includible in Juanita's gross income as long as she does not actually receive the $200. ▼

The tax accounting problem associated with receiving payments under an annuity contract is one of apportioning the amounts received between recovery of capital and income.

EXAMPLE 43 In 1996, Tom purchased for $15,000 an annuity intended as a source of retirement income. In 1998, when the cash value of the annuity was $17,000, Tom collected $1,000 on the contract. Is the $1,000 gross income, recovery of capital, or a combination of recovery of capital and income? ▼

The statutory solution to this problem depends upon whether the payments began before or after the annuity starting date and upon when the policy was acquired.

Collections before the Annuity Starting Date. Generally, an annuity contract specifies a date on which monthly or annual payments will begin—the annuity starting date. Often the contract will also allow the annuitant to collect a limited amount before the starting date. The amount collected may be characterized as either an actual withdrawal of the increase in cash value or a loan on the policy. In 1982, Congress changed the rules applicable to these withdrawals and loans.

Collections (including loans) equal to or less than the post–August 13, 1982, increases in cash value must be included in gross income. Amounts received in excess of post–August 13, 1982, increases in cash value are treated as a recovery of capital until the taxpayer's cost has been entirely recovered. Additional amounts are included in gross income.[80]

The taxpayer may also be subject to a penalty on early distributions of 10 percent of the income recognized. The penalty generally applies if the amount is received before the taxpayer reaches age 59½ or is disabled.[81] The early distribution penalty is deemed necessary to prevent taxpayers from using annuities as a way of avoiding the original issue discount rules. That is, the investment in the annuity earns a return that is not taxed until it is collected under the annuity rules, whereas the interest on a certificate of deposit is taxed each year as the income accrues. Thus, the annuity offers a tax advantage (deferral of income) that Congress does not want exploited.

[80] § 72(c)(3); Reg. § 1.72–9.

[81] § 72(q).

EXAMPLE 44 Jack, age 50, purchased an annuity policy for $30,000 in 1995. In 1997, when the cash value of the policy has increased to $33,000, Jack withdraws $4,000. He must recognize $3,000 of income ($33,000 cash value – $30,000 cost) and must pay a penalty of $300 ($3,000 × 10%). The remaining $1,000 is a recovery of capital and reduces Jack's basis in the annuity policy. ▼

Collections on and after the Annuity Starting Date. The annuitant is not permitted to use the recovery of capital concept to exclude all the annuity payments received until the investment in the annuity is recovered. Instead, the annuitant can exclude from income (as a recovery of capital) the proportion of each payment that the investment in the contract bears to the expected return under the contract. The *exclusion amount* is calculated as follows:

$$\frac{\text{Investment}}{\text{Expected return}} \times \text{Annuity payment} = \text{Exclusion amount}$$

The *expected return* is the annual amount to be paid to the annuitant multiplied by the number of years the payments will be received. The payment period may be fixed (a *term certain*) or for the life of one or more individuals. When payments are for life, the taxpayer must use the annuity table published by the IRS to determine the expected return (see Table 4–1). This is an actuarial table that contains life expectancies.[82] The expected return is calculated by multiplying the appropriate multiple (life expectancy) by the annual payment.

EXAMPLE 45 The taxpayer, age 54, purchased an annuity from an insurance company for $90,000. She was to receive $500 per month for life. Her life expectancy (from Table 4–1) is 29.5 years from the annuity starting date. Thus, her expected return is $500 × 12 × 29.5 = $177,000, and the exclusion amount is $3,051 [($90,000 investment/$177,000 expected return) × $6,000 annual payment]. The $3,051 is a nontaxable return of capital, and $2,949 is included in gross income. ▼

The *exclusion ratio* (investment ÷ expected return) applies until the annuitant has recovered his or her investment in the contract. Once the investment is recovered, the entire amount of subsequent payments is taxable. If the annuitant dies before recovering his or her investment, the unrecovered cost is deductible in the year the payments cease (usually the year of death).[83]

EXAMPLE 46 Assume the taxpayer in Example 45 received annuity payments for 30.5 years (366 months). For the last 12 months [366 – (12 × 29.5) = 12], the taxpayer would include $500 each month

[82] The life expectancies in Table 4–1 apply for annuity investments made on or after July 1, 1986. See *Pension and Annuity Income,* IRS Publication 575 (Rev. Nov. 87), pp. 22–24 for the IRS table to use for investments made before July 1, 1986.

[83] § 72(b).

▼ TABLE 4–1
Ordinary Life Annuities: One Life–Expected Return Multiples

Age	Multiple	Age	Multiple	Age	Multiple
5	76.6	42	40.6	79	10.0
6	75.6	43	39.6	80	9.5
7	74.7	44	38.7	81	8.9
8	73.7	45	37.7	82	8.4
9	72.7	46	36.8	83	7.9
10	71.7	47	35.9	84	7.4
11	70.7	48	34.9	85	6.9
12	69.7	49	34.0	86	6.5
13	68.8	50	33.1	87	6.1
14	67.8	51	32.2	88	5.7
15	66.8	52	31.3	89	5.3
16	65.8	53	30.4	90	5.0
17	64.8	54	29.5	91	4.7
18	63.9	55	28.6	92	4.4
19	62.9	56	27.7	93	4.1
20	61.9	57	26.8	94	3.9
21	60.9	58	25.9	95	3.7
22	59.9	59	25.0	96	3.4
23	59.0	60	24.2	97	3.2
24	58.0	61	23.3	98	3.0
25	57.0	62	22.5	99	2.8
26	56.0	63	21.6	100	2.7
27	55.1	64	20.8	101	2.5
28	54.1	65	20.0	102	2.3
29	53.1	66	19.2	103	2.1
30	52.2	67	18.4	104	1.9
31	51.2	68	17.6	105	1.8
32	50.2	69	16.8	106	1.6
33	49.3	70	16.0	107	1.4
34	48.3	71	15.3	108	1.3
35	47.3	72	14.6	109	1.1
36	46.4	73	13.9	110	1.0
37	45.4	74	13.2	111	.9
38	44.4	75	12.5	112	.8
39	43.5	76	11.9	113	.7
40	42.5	77	11.2	114	.6
41	41.5	78	10.6	115	.5

in gross income. If instead the taxpayer died after 36 months, she is eligible for a $80,847 deduction on her final tax return.

Cost of the contract	$90,000
Cost previously recovered $90,000/$177,000 × 36($500) =	(9,153)
Deduction	$80,847

▼

CONCEPT SUMMARY 4–4

Taxation of Annuities

Term	Description	Formula
A	Amount of each annuity payment under the contract.	
N	Number of expected payments based on the expected life of the annuitant.	
V	Investment in the annuity contract.	
R	Number of annuity payments actually received.	
Expected return	Total amount the annuitant is expected to collect over the life of the contract based on his or her life expectancy.	$A \times N$
Exclusion percentage	Percentage of each annuity payment that is excluded from gross income.	$\frac{V}{A \times N}$
Inclusion percentage	Percentage of each annuity payment that is included in gross income.	$1-\left(\frac{V}{A \times N}\right)$
Post–recovery of capital payments	Once R = N, the total cost has been recovered. The total amount of each subsequent payment is included in gross income.	
Annuitant's deductible loss	If the annuity payments cease before R = N, the annuitant can claim a loss.	$V-\left(\frac{V}{A \times N}\right) \times (A \times R)$

PRIZES AND AWARDS

The fair market value of prizes and awards (other than scholarships exempted under § 117, to be discussed subsequently) must be included in gross income.[84] Therefore, TV giveaway prizes, magazine publisher prizes, door prizes, and awards from an employer to an employee in recognition of performance are fully taxable to the recipient.

An exception permits a prize or award to be excluded from gross income if all of the following requirements are satisfied:

- The prize or award is received in recognition of religious, charitable, scientific, educational, artistic, literary, or civic achievement (e.g., Nobel Prize, Pulitzer Prize).
- The recipient transfers the prize or award to a qualified governmental unit or nonprofit organization.
- The recipient was selected without any action on his or her part to enter the contest or proceeding.
- The recipient is not required to render substantial future services as a condition for receiving the prize or award.[85]

Because the transfer of the property to a qualified governmental unit or nonprofit organization ordinarily would be a charitable contribution (an itemized deduction

[84] § 74.

[85] § 74(b).

as presented in Chapter 10), the exclusion produces beneficial tax consequences in the following situations:

- The taxpayer does not itemize deductions and thus would receive no tax benefit from the charitable contribution.
- The taxpayer's charitable contributions exceed the annual statutory ceiling on the deduction.
- Including the prize or award in gross income would reduce the amount of deductions the taxpayer otherwise would qualify for because of gross income limitations (e.g., the gross income test for a dependency exemption, the adjusted gross income limitation in calculating the medical expense deduction).

Another exception is provided for certain *employee achievement awards* in the form of tangible personal property (e.g., a gold watch). The awards must be made in recognition of length of service or safety achievement. Generally, the ceiling on the excludible amount for an employee is $400 per taxable year. However, if the award is a qualified plan award, the ceiling on the exclusion is $1,600 per taxable year.[86]

GROUP TERM LIFE INSURANCE

For many years, the IRS did not attempt to tax the value of life insurance protection provided to an employee by the employer. Some companies took undue advantage of the exclusion by providing large amounts of insurance protection for executives. Therefore, Congress enacted § 79, which created a limited exclusion for **group term life insurance.** Current law allows an exclusion for premiums on the first $50,000 of group term life insurance protection.

The benefits of this exclusion are available only to employees. Proprietors and partners are not considered employees. Moreover, the Regulations generally require broad-scale coverage of employees to satisfy the *group* requirement (e.g., shareholder-employees would not constitute a qualified group). The exclusion applies only to term insurance (protection for a period of time but with no cash surrender value) and not to ordinary life insurance (lifetime protection plus a cash surrender value that can be drawn upon before death).

As mentioned, the exclusion applies to the first $50,000 of group term life insurance protection. For each $1,000 of coverage in excess of $50,000, the employee must include the amounts indicated in Table 4–2 in gross income.[87]

EXAMPLE 47

Finch Corporation has a group term life insurance policy with coverage equal to the employee's annual salary. Keith, age 52, is president of the corporation and receives an annual salary of $75,000. Keith must include $144 in gross income from the insurance protection for the year.

$$\frac{\$75,000 - \$50,000}{\$1,000} \times .48 \times 12 \text{ months} = \$144$$

▼

Generally, the amount that must be included in income, computed from Table 4–2, is much less than the price an individual would pay an insurance company for the same amount of protection. Thus, even the excess coverage provides some

[86] §§ 74(c) and 274(j).

[87] Reg. § 1.79–3(d)(2).

▼ **TABLE 4–2**
Uniform Premiums for $1,000 of Group Term Life Insurance Protection

Attained Age on Last Day of Employee's Tax Year	Cost per $1,000 of Protection for One-Month Period
Under 30	8 cents
30–34	9 cents
35–39	11 cents
40–44	17 cents
45–49	29 cents
50–54	48 cents
55–59	75 cents
60–64	$1.17
65–69	$2.10
70 and over	$3.76

tax-favored income for employees when group term life insurance coverage in excess of $50,000 is desirable.

If the plan discriminates in favor of certain key employees (e.g., officers), the key employees are not eligible for the exclusion. In such a case, the key employees must include in gross income the *greater* of actual premiums paid by the employer or the amount calculated from the Uniform Premiums table in Table 4–2. The other employees are still eligible for the $50,000 exclusion and continue to use the Uniform Premiums table to compute the income from excess insurance protection.[88]

UNEMPLOYMENT COMPENSATION

The unemployment compensation program is sponsored and operated by the states and Federal government to provide a source of income for people who have been employed and are temporarily (hopefully) out of work. In a series of rulings over a period of 40 years, the IRS exempted unemployment benefits from tax. These payments were considered social benefit programs for the promotion of the general welfare. After experiencing dissatisfaction with the IRS's treatment of unemployment compensation, Congress amended the Code to provide that the benefits are taxable.[89]

SOCIAL SECURITY BENEFITS

If a taxpayer's income exceeds a specified base amount, as much as 85 percent of Social Security retirement benefits must be included in gross income. The taxable amount of benefits is determined through the application of one of two formulas that utilize a unique measure of income—*modified adjusted gross income* (*MAGI*).[90] MAGI is, generally, the taxpayer's adjusted gross income from all sources (other than Social Security) plus the foreign earned income exclusion and any tax-exempt interest income.

[88] § 79(d).
[89] § 85.
[90] § 86.

In the formulas, two sets of base amounts are established. The first set is as follows:

- $32,000 for married taxpayers who file a joint return.
- $0 for married taxpayers who do not live apart for the entire year but file separate returns.
- $25,000 for all other taxpayers.

The second set of base amounts is as follows:

- $44,000 for married taxpayers who file a joint return.
- $0 for married taxpayers who do not live apart for the entire year but file separate returns.
- $34,000 for all other taxpayers.

If MAGI plus one-half of Social Security benefits exceeds the first set of base amounts, but not the second set, the taxable amount of Social Security benefits is the *lesser* of the following:

- .50(Social Security benefits).
- .50[MAGI + .50(Social Security benefits) – first base amount].

EXAMPLE 48

A married couple with adjusted gross income of $30,000, no tax-exempt interest, and $11,000 of Social Security benefits who file jointly must include $1,750 of the benefits in gross income. This works out as the lesser of the following:

1. .50($11,000) = $5,500.
2. .50[$30,000 + .50($11,000) – $32,000] = .50($3,500) = $1,750.

If the couple's adjusted gross income were $15,000 and their Social Security benefits totaled $5,000, none of the benefits would be taxable, since .50[$15,000 + .50($5,000) – $32,000] is not a positive number. ▼

If MAGI plus one-half of Social Security benefits exceeds the second set of base amounts, the taxable amount of Social Security benefits is the *lesser* of 1 or 2 below:

1. .85(Social Security benefits).
2. Sum of:
   a. .85[MAGI + .50(Social Security benefits) – second base amount], and
   b. Lesser of:
      - Amount included through application of the first formula.
      - $4,500 ($6,000 for married filing jointly). ▼

EXAMPLE 49

A married couple who file jointly have adjusted gross income of $72,000, no tax-exempt interest, and $12,000 of Social Security benefits. Their includible Social Security benefits would be $10,200.

Include the lesser of the following:

1. .85($12,000) = $10,200.
2. Sum of:
   a. .85[$72,000 + .50($12,000) – $44,000] = $28,900, and
   b. Lesser of:
      - Amount calculated by the first formula, which is the lesser of:
        - .50($12,000) = $6,000.
        - .50[$72,000 + .50($12,000) – $32,000] = $23,000.
      - $6,000.

The sum equals $34,900 ($28,900 + $6,000). Since 85% of the Social Security benefits received is less than this amount, $10,200 is included in the couples' gross income. ▼

ETHICAL CONSIDERATIONS

Taxing Social Security Benefits

The taxation of Social Security benefits has gone through several phases. For many years, Social Security benefits were not subject to tax. Then in 1976, the Internal Revenue Code was amended to tax up to one-half of Social Security benefits received by individuals with gross income over a threshold amount (i.e., $25,000 or $32,000 depending on filing status). The apparent rationale for taxing 50 percent was that the employee had contributed half of the original payments and thus half of the benefits represented a recovery of capital.

As a result of the Revenue Reconciliation Act of 1993, taxpayers with adjusted gross income over the threshold amount (i.e., $34,000 or $44,000 depending on filing status) are required to include up to 85 percent of Social Security benefits in gross income. Under current law, as well as under pre-1993 law, if an individual dies before recovering his or her payments into the Social Security system, no loss can be claimed on the final return.

Now, two former U.S. senators (Paul Tsongas of Massachusetts and Warren Rudman of New Hampshire) are proposing that the receipt of Social Security benefits be based on the "wherewithal to pay" as part of a plan to eliminate the Federal deficit by the year 2000. Such a means-based approach would effectively result in a 100 percent inclusion for Social Security benefits combined with a 100 percent tax rate. Evaluate the trend toward increasing taxation of Social Security benefits.

TAX PLANNING CONSIDERATIONS

5 LEARNING OBJECTIVE
Identify tax planning strategies for minimizing gross income.

The materials in this chapter have focused on the following questions:

- What is income?
- When is the income recognized?
- Who is the taxpayer?

Planning strategies suggested by these materials include the following:

- Maximize economic benefits that are not included in gross income.
- Defer the recognition of income.
- Shift income to taxpayers who are in a lower marginal tax bracket.

Some specific techniques for accomplishing these strategies are discussed in the following paragraphs.

NONTAXABLE ECONOMIC BENEFITS

Home ownership is the prime example of economic income from capital that is not subject to tax. If the taxpayer uses his or her capital to purchase investments, but pays rent on a personal residence, the taxpayer would pay the rent from after-tax income. However, if the taxpayer purchases a personal residence instead of the investments, the taxpayer would give up gross income from the forgone investments in exchange for the rent savings. The savings in rent enjoyed as a result of owning the home is not subject to tax. Thus, the homeowner will have substituted nontaxable for taxable income.

TAX IN THE NEWS

INCOME TO THE IRS BUT NOT TO THE NFL

Both the print and broadcast media have reported extensively on the signing of Deion "Prime Time" Sanders to a seven-year $35 million contract by the Dallas Cowboys. The contract reportedly includes a $12,999,999 up-front signing bonus and a salary for the 1995–96 season of $178,000 (the minimum amount that can be paid to an NFL player).

The role of a tax adviser is to assist the taxpayer in reducing his or her tax liability to the minimum required by law. Therefore, from an income tax perspective, it appears that Deion's tax adviser was "asleep at the desk." Front-loading the contract to include the $13 million bonus in Deion's 1995 taxable income obviously is not sage tax planning. The standard planning approach would have been to maximize the deferral in order to reduce the current and near-term tax liability.

As it turns out, however, the driving factor was not the income tax result, but rather the NFL team salary cap of $37.2 million, which is designed to produce more equality among the various teams. The last thing that Jerry Jones, the owner of "America's Team," wants is equality—he wants continued superiority that will lead to more Super Bowl titles. Even though Deion will receive approximately $13,178,000 during the 1995–96 season, only $2,035,142 will count toward the salary cap. The bonus is amortized over the seven-year contract period at an annual amount of $1,857,142. Adding this amount to the $178,000 salary produces the $2,035,142. Under this way of thinking, Deion is a real bargain.

TAX DEFERRAL

General. Since deferred taxes are tantamount to interest-free loans from the government, the deferral of taxes is a worthy goal of the tax planner. However, the tax planner must also consider the tax rates for the years the income is shifted from and to. For example, a one-year deferral of income from a year in which the taxpayer's tax rate was 28 percent to a year in which the tax rate will be 39.6 percent would not be advisable if the taxpayer expects to earn less than a 11.6 percent after-tax return on the deferred tax dollars.

The taxpayer can often defer the recognition of income from appreciated property by postponing the event triggering realization (the final closing on a sale or exchange of property). If the taxpayer needs cash, obtaining a loan by using the appreciated property as collateral may be the least costly alternative. When the taxpayer anticipates reinvesting the proceeds, a sale may be inadvisable.

EXAMPLE 50

Ira owns 100 shares of Pigeon Company common stock with a cost of $20,000 and a fair market value of $50,000. Although the stock's value has increased substantially in the past three years, Ira thinks the growth days are over. If he sells the Pigeon stock, Ira will invest the proceeds from the sale in other common stock. Assuming Ira is in the 28% marginal tax bracket, he will have only $41,600 [$50,000 – .28($50,000 – $20,000)] to reinvest. The alternative investment must substantially outperform Pigeon in the future in order for the sale to be beneficial. ▼

Selection of Investments. Because no tax is due until a gain has been recognized, the law favors investments that yield appreciation rather than annual income.

EXAMPLE 51 Vera can buy a corporate bond or an acre of land for $10,000. The bond pays $1,000 of interest (10%) each year, and Vera expects the land to increase in value 10% each year for the next 10 years. She is in the 40% (combined Federal and state) tax bracket. Assuming the bond would mature or the land would be sold in 10 years and Vera would reinvest the interest at a 10% before-tax return, she would accumulate the following amount at the end of 10 years.

		Bond	Land
Original investment		$10,000	$10,000
Annual income	$1,000		
Less tax	(400)		
	$ 600		
Compound amount reinvested for 10 years at 6% after-tax	× 13.18	7,908	
		$17,908	
Compound amount, 10 years at 10%			× 2.59
			$25,900
Less tax on sale: 40%($25,900 – $10,000)			(6,360)
			$19,540

Therefore, the value of the deferral that results from investing in the land rather than in the bond is $1,632 ($19,540 – $17,908). ▼

Series E and EE bonds can also be purchased for long-term deferrals of income. As discussed in the chapter, Series E bonds can be exchanged for new Series HH bonds to further postpone the tax. In situations where the taxpayer's goal is merely to shift income one year into the future, bank certificates of deposit are useful tools. If the maturity period is one year or less, all interest is reported in the year of maturity. Time certificates are especially useful for a taxpayer who realizes an unusually large gain from the sale of property in one year (and thus is in a high tax bracket) but expects his or her income to be less the following year.

Cash Basis. The timing of income from services can often be controlled through the use of the cash method of accounting. Although taxpayers are somewhat constrained by the constructive receipt doctrine (they cannot turn their backs on income), seldom will customers and clients offer to pay before they are asked. The usual lag between billings and collections (e.g., December's billings collected in January) will result in a continuous deferring of some income until the last year of operations. A salaried individual approaching retirement may contract with his or her employer before the services are rendered to receive a portion of compensation in the lower tax bracket retirement years.

Prepaid Income. For the accrual basis taxpayer who receives advance payments from customers, the transactions should be structured to avoid payment of tax on income before the time the income is actually earned. Revenue Procedure

71–21 provides the guidelines for deferring the tax on prepayments for services, and Regulation § 1.451–5 provides the guidelines for deferrals on sales of goods. In addition, both cash and accrual basis taxpayers can sometimes defer income by stipulating that the payments are deposits rather than prepaid income. For example, a landlord should require an equivalent damage deposit rather than require prepayment of the last month's rent under the lease.

SHIFTING INCOME TO RELATIVES

The tax liability of a family can be minimized by shifting income from higher- to lower-bracket family members. This can be accomplished through gifts of income-producing property. Furthermore, in many cases, income can be shifted with no negative effect on the family's investment plans.

EXAMPLE 52

Adam, who is in the 28% tax bracket, would like to save for his children's education. All of the children are under 14 years of age. Adam could transfer income-producing properties to the children, and the children could each receive up to $650 of income each year (refer to Chapter 3) with no tax liability. The next $650 would be taxed at the child's tax rate. After a child has more than $1,300 income, there is no tax advantage to shifting more income to the child (because the income will be taxed at the parents' rate) until the child is 14 years old (when all income will be taxed according to the child's tax rate). ▼

The Uniform Gifts to Minors Act, a model law adopted by all states (but with some variations among the states), facilitates income shifting. Under the Act, a gift of intangibles (e.g., bank accounts, stocks, bonds, life insurance contracts) can be made to a minor but with an adult serving as custodian. Usually, a parent who makes the gift is also named as custodian. The state laws allow the custodian to sell or redeem and reinvest the principal and to accumulate or distribute the income, practically at the custodian's discretion provided there is no commingling of the child's income with the parent's property. Thus, the parent can give appreciated securities to the child, and the donor custodian can then sell the securities and reinvest the proceeds, thereby shifting both the gain and annual income to the child. Such planning is limited by the tax liability calculation provision for a child under the age of 14 (refer to Chapter 3).

U.S. government bonds (Series E and EE) can be purchased by the parent for his or her children. When this is done, the children generally should file a return and elect to report the income on the accrual basis.

EXAMPLE 53

Abby pays $7,500 for Series EE bonds in 1996 and immediately gives them to Wade (her son), who will enter college the year of original maturity of the bonds. The bonds have a maturity value of $10,000. Wade elects to report the annual increment in redemption value as income for each year the bonds are held. The first year the increase is $250, and Wade includes that amount in his gross income. If Wade has no other income, no tax will be due on the $250 bond interest, since such an amount will be more than offset by his available standard deduction. The following year, the increment is $260, and Wade includes this amount in income. Thus, over the life of the bonds, Wade will include $2,500 in income ($10,000 − $7,500), none of which will result in a tax liability, assuming he has no other income. However, if the election had not been made, Wade would be required to include $2,500 in income on the bonds in the year of original maturity, if they were redeemed as planned. This amount of income might result in a tax liability. ▼

In some cases, it may be advantageous for the child not to make the accrual election. For example, a child under age 14 with investment income of more than $1,300 each year and parents in the 28, 31, 36, or 39.6 percent tax bracket would probably benefit from deferring the tax on the savings bond interest. The child would also benefit from the use of the usually lower tax rate (rather than subjecting the income to his or her parents' tax rate) if the bonds mature after the child is age 14 or older.

ACCOUNTING FOR COMMUNITY PROPERTY

The classification of income as community or separate property becomes important when either of two events occurs:

- Husband and wife, married taxpayers, file separate income tax returns for the year.
- Husband and wife obtain a divorce and therefore have to file separate returns for the year (refer to Chapter 3).

For planning purposes, it behooves married persons to keep track of the source of income (community or separate). To be in a position to do this effectively when income-producing assets are involved, it may be necessary to distinguish between separate and community property.[91]

ALIMONY

The person making the alimony payments favors a divorce settlement that includes a provision for deductible alimony payments. On the other hand, the recipient prefers that the payments do not qualify as alimony. If the payor is in a higher tax bracket than the recipient, both parties may benefit by increasing the payments and structuring them so that they qualify as alimony.

EXAMPLE 54

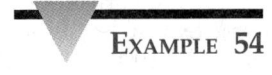

Carl and Polly are negotiating a divorce settlement. Carl has offered to pay Polly $10,000 each year for 10 years, but payments would cease upon Polly's death. Polly is willing to accept the offer, if the agreement will specify that the cash payments are not alimony. Carl is in the 36% tax bracket, and Polly's marginal rate is 15%.

If Carl and Polly agree that Carl will pay Polly $12,000 of alimony each year, both will have improved after-tax cash flows.

	Annual Cash Flows	
	Carl	Polly
Nonalimony payments	($10,000)	$10,000
Alimony payments	($12,000)	$12,000
Tax effects		
.36($12,000)	4,320	
.15($12,000)		(1,800)
After-tax cash flows	($ 7,680)	$10,200
Benefit of alimony option	$ 2,320	$ 200

Both parties benefit at the government's expense if the $12,000 alimony option is used. ▼

[91] Being able to distinguish between separate and community property is crucial to the determination of a property settlement incident to a divorce. It also is vital in the estate tax area (refer to Chapter 1) since the surviving wife's or husband's share of the community property is not included in the gross estate of the deceased spouse.

KEY TERMS

Accounting income, 4–4

Accounting method, 4–7

Accrual method, 4–9

Alimony and separate maintenance payments, 4–20

Alimony recapture, 4–21

Annuity, 4–29

Assignment of income, 4–14

Cash receipts method, 4–8

Claim of right doctrine, 4–9

Community property, 4–18

Constructive receipt, 4–10

Economic income, 4–3

Fruit and tree metaphor, 4–14

Gross income, 4–3

Group term life insurance, 4–34

Hybrid method, 4–9

Imputed interest, 4–25

Income, 4–3

Original issue discount, 4–11

Partnership, 4–17

Recovery of capital doctrine, 4–6

S corporation, 4–18

Taxable year, 4–7

PROBLEM MATERIALS

DISCUSSION QUESTIONS

1. The Internal Revenue Code contains a broad definition of gross income, but does not provide a listing of all possible types of income subject to tax. Would the tax law be improved if the Code included a complete listing of taxable sources of income?

2. Which of the following would be considered "income" for the current year by an economist but would not be gross income for tax purposes? Explain.
   a. Securities acquired two years ago for $10,000 had a value of $12,000 at the beginning of the current year and a value of $13,000 at the end of the year.
   b. An individual lives in the home he owns.
   c. A corporation obtained a loan from a bank.
   d. A shareholder paid a corporation $3,000 for property valued at $5,000.
   e. An individual owned property that was stolen. The cost of the property three years ago was $2,000, and an insurance company paid the owner $6,000 (the value of the property on the date of theft).
   f. An individual found a box of seventeenth-century Spanish coins while diving off the Virginia coast.
   g. An individual received a $200 rebate from the manufacturer upon the purchase of a new car.

3. According to economists, because our tax system does not impute income to homeowners for the rental value of their homes, the nonhomeowner who invests in securities (rather than a home) is taxed more heavily than the homeowner. This leads to overinvesting in homes. Why do you suppose the laws are not changed to tax homeowners on the rental value of their homes?

4. Evaluate the following alternative proposals for taxing the income from property:
   a. All assets would be valued at the end of the year, any increase in value that occurred during the year would be included in gross income, and any decrease in value would be deductible from gross income.
   b. No gain or loss would be recognized until the taxpayer sold or exchanged the property.
   c. Increases or decreases in the value of property traded on a national exchange (e.g., the New York Stock Exchange) would be reflected in gross income for the years the changes in value occurred. For all other assets, no gain or loss would be recognized until the property is sold or exchanged.

5. How would the realization requirement influence an investor to purchase a stock that is expected to appreciate in value but will not pay dividends rather than a stock that is not expected to appreciate but will pay a dividend?

6. Mauve Farms Corporation is an accrual basis corporation that owns and operates a farm. During the year, Mauve raised corn at a cost of $150,000. The company sold one-third of the corn for $90,000 cash and exchanged one-third for pigs with a value of $90,000. The remainder of the corn was fed to the pigs. All of the pigs were still on hand at the end of the year and had increased in value to $160,000. What is Mauve's gross income from these events?

7. Leif had owned a tract of land for several years when the local government decided to build an airport near the property. The cost of the property to Leif was $50,000. The local government paid Leif $10,000 for invasion of his airspace. What is Leif's gross income from the receipt of the $10,000?

8. What is the major tax advantage of the cash method of accounting?

9. Sparrow, Inc., receives all of its income from repairing computers. The company reports its income by the cash method. On December 31, an employee went to a customer's office and repaired a computer. The customer gave Sparrow's employee a check for $300, but the employee did not remit the check to Sparrow until January of the following year. When is Sparrow required to recognize the income?

10. Lane is a self-employed consultant who reports his income by the cash method of accounting. In December 1996, Lane received a check for $5,000 from a client. Lane misplaced the check and did not find it until January 1997, when he deposited it in his bank account. Lane uses his deposit records to compute his income. Therefore, he included the $5,000 in his 1997 gross income.
    a. In what year should Lane report the income?
    b. Why does it matter whether Lane reports the income in 1996 or 1997, so long as he actually reports it?

11. Doug, a cash basis taxpayer, operated Craig's farm under an arrangement whereby Doug would receive one-half of the grain crop, less the cost of seed and fertilizer. The seed and fertilizer cost $8,000, which was paid during the year. In October Doug harvested the crop. A portion of the grain was sold for $28,000 cash in October, and Doug received $10,000 as his share of the $28,000 in November. Also in November, more of the grain was sold for $40,000. The grain was delivered to the purchaser in November, but payment was not to be received until January of the following year. Doug also used a portion of the grain for his personal use. The cost of the personal use grain was $1,200, but it could have been sold for $2,000. In February of the following year, Doug collected the balance Craig owed to him. Identify the relevant tax issues for Doug.

12. Nora, an accrual basis taxpayer, rendered services for a customer with a poor credit rating. Nora's charge for the service was $1,000. Nora sent a bill to the customer for $1,000 but reported only $500 of income. She justified reporting only $500 as follows: "I'm being generous reporting $500. I'll be lucky if I collect anything." How much should Nora include as gross income from the contract in the current year?

13. Olga, a cash basis taxpayer, sold a bond with accrued interest of $750 for $10,250. Olga's basis in the bond was $9,000. Compute Olga's income from this transaction.

14. Leslie, a cash basis taxpayer, purchased a three-year certificate of deposit for $7,938. Upon maturity of the certificate, she will receive $10,000, which is the principal plus 8% interest compounded annually. Will Leslie's interest income be less in the first year than in the third year?

15. Taupe Car Wash, an accrual basis taxpayer, sells certificates throughout the year that entitle the holder to a free car wash at any time during the next 24 months. At the end of 1996, certificates with a total face amount of $10,000 are outstanding. When is Taupe required to include the $10,000 in gross income?

16. Quinn (father) paid $200 for an automobile that needed repairs. He worked nights and weekends to restore the car. Several individuals offered to purchase the car for $2,800.

Quinn gave the car and a list of potential buyers to Ron (son), whose college tuition was due in a few days. Ron sold the car for $2,800 and paid his tuition. Does Quinn have any taxable income from the transaction?

17. Tom Jr., a cash basis minor, performed services and was to be paid $100 in 1996. In 1996, the employer paid the $100 to Tom Sr., who deposited the money in his bank account. The following year, Tom Sr. used the $100 to buy his son a car.
    a. In whose gross income is the $100 included?
    b. When is the $100 included in gross income?

18. Isabella transferred rental properties to a corporation. Her objective was to minimize her liability for injuries that may occur on the property. The tenants continued to pay rents to Isabella. Who must include the rents in gross income?

19. Who pays the tax on (a) the income of an S corporation and on (b) the undistributed income of an estate?

20. Ted and Alice were residents of a community property state. In 1996, Ted left Alice for parts unknown. Ted and Alice were still married at year-end. How will Ted's absence complicate Alice's 1996 tax return?

21. Hank and Elaine are negotiating their divorce agreement, which requires the division of their jointly owned property. Hank has proposed that he receive the couple's house (basis of $50,000 and fair market value of $75,000) while Elaine would receive (a) securities (basis of $10,000 and fair market value of $75,000) or (b) four annual payments of $22,644 each, which is equivalent to a $75,000 loan at 8% interest. Elaine will probably sell the securities if she receives them. Elaine does not want the house. Which option should she accept?

22. A post-1984 divorce agreement between Earl and Cora provides that Earl is to pay Cora $500 per month for 13 years. Earl and Cora have a child who is 8 years old. Termination of the monthly payments will coincide with the child's attaining age 21. Can the monthly payments qualify as alimony?

23. William and Abigail, who live in San Francisco, have been experiencing problems with their marriage. They have a three-year-old daughter, April, who stays with William's parents during the day since both William and Abigail are employed. Abigail worked to support William while he attended medical school, and now she has been accepted into medical school in Mexico. Abigail has decided to divorce William and attend medical school. April will stay in San Francisco because of her strong attachment to her grandparents and because they can provide her with excellent day care. Abigail knows that William will expect her to contribute to the cost of raising April. Abigail also feels that, to finance her education, she must receive cash for her share of the property they accumulated during their marriage. In addition, she feels she should receive some reimbursement for her contribution to William's support while he was in medical school. She expects the divorce proceedings will take several months. Identify the relevant tax issues for Abigail.

24. In the case of a below-market loan between relatives, why is the lender required to recognize income although it is the borrower who appears to receive the economic benefit?

25. Mother loaned $80,000 to Son who used the money to buy a personal residence. Mother did not charge interest on the loan, although the market rate of interest was 8%. Son had investment income of $800. Do the imputed interest rules apply?

26. In the case of a corporation's interest-free loan to its controlling shareholder who is also an employee of the corporation, why would the corporation prefer that the loan be classified as an employer-employee loan rather than a corporation-shareholder loan?

27. Brad is the president of the Yellow Corporation. He and other members of his family control the corporation. Brad has a temporary need for $50,000, and the corporation has excess cash. He could borrow the money from a bank at 9%, and Yellow is earning 6% on its temporary investments. Yellow has made loans to other employees on several

occasions. Therefore, Brad is considering borrowing $50,000 from the corporation. He will repay the loan principal in two years plus interest at 5%. Identify the relevant tax issues for Brad and the Yellow Corporation.

28. At age 55, Nancy purchased an annuity for $25,000 that was to pay her $200 per month for life beginning on her 70th birthday. At that time, her life expectancy would be 16 years. Now, when Nancy is 58 years old, and the annuity policy has a value of $28,000, she needs $2,000. The annuity policy allows her to withdraw the needed funds. What are the tax consequences to Nancy of this withdrawal from the annuity policy?

29. Gail is a full-time employee of Purple Corporation. One of the fringe benefits the company offers its employees is group term life insurance protection equal to twice the employee's annual salary. Gail is 38 years old, and her annual salary is $50,000. What is Gail's gross income from the life insurance protection for the year?

30. When a taxpayer is receiving Social Security benefits, could a $1,000 increase in income from services cause the taxpayer's adjusted gross income to increase by more than $1,000?

PROBLEMS

31. Determine the effects of the following on Anne's gross income for the year:
    a. Anne bought a used sofa for $25. After she took the sofa home, she discovered $15,000 in a secret compartment. Anne was unable to determine who placed the money in the sofa. Therefore, she put the money in her bank account.
    b. Anne also discovered oil on her property during the year, and the value of the land increased from $10,000 to $3,000,000.
    c. One year later, Anne found a diamond in the sofa she had purchased. Apparently, the diamond was in the sofa when Anne purchased it. The value of the diamond was $6,000. Under state law, the diamond became Anne's property when she purchased the sofa.
    d. Anne's bank charges a $3 per month service charge. However, the fee is waived if the customer maintains an average balance for the month of at least $1,000. Anne's account exceeded the minimum deposit requirement, and as a result she was not required to pay any service charges for the year.

32. Compute the taxpayer's (1) economic income and (2) gross income for tax purposes from the following events:
    a. The taxpayer sold securities for $10,000. The securities cost $6,000 in 1992. The fair market value of the securities at the beginning of the year was $12,000.
    b. The taxpayer sold his business and received $15,000 under a covenant not to compete with the new owner.
    c. The taxpayer used her controlled corporation's automobile for her vacation. The rental value of the automobile for the vacation period was $800.
    d. The taxpayer raised vegetables in her garden. The fair market value of the vegetables was $900, and the cost of raising them was $100. She ate some of the vegetables and gave the remainder to neighbors.
    e. The local government changed the zoning ordinances so that some of the taxpayer's residential property was reclassified as commercial. Because of the change, the fair market value of the taxpayer's property increased by $10,000.
    f. During the year, the taxpayer borrowed $50,000 for two years at 9% interest. By the end of the year, interest rates had increased to 12%, and the lender accepted $49,000 in full satisfaction of the debt.

33. Kevin, a cash basis taxpayer, received the following from his employer during 1996:

    - Salary of $75,000.
    - Bonus of $10,000. In 1997, the company determined that the bonus had been incorrectly computed and required Kevin to repay $3,000.
    - Use of a company car for his vacation. Rental value for the period would have been $900. Kevin paid for the gas.

- $4,000 advance for travel expenses. Kevin had spent only $3,400 at the end of the year.

Determine the effects of these items on Kevin's gross income.

34. Which of the following investments will yield the greater after-tax value assuming the taxpayer is in the 40% tax bracket (combined Federal and state) in all years and the investments will be liquidated at the end of five years?
    a. Land that will increase in value by 10% each year.
    b. A taxable bond yielding 10% before tax, and the interest can be reinvested at 10% before tax.
    c. Common stock that will increase in value at the rate of 5% (compounded) each year and pays dividends equal to 5% of the year-end value of the stock. The dividends can be reinvested at 10% before tax.
    d. A tax-exempt state government bond yielding 8%. The interest can be reinvested at a before-tax rate of 10%, and the bond matures in 10 years.

Prepare a brief speech for your tax class in which you explain why the future value of the land will exceed the future value of the taxable bond.

Given: Compound amount of $1 and compound value of annuity payments at the end of five years:

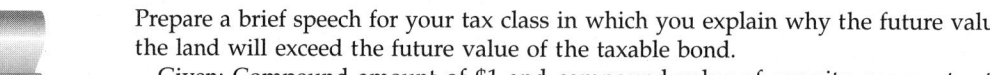

Interest Rate	$1 Compounded for 5 Years	$1 Annuity Compounded for 5 Years
6%	$1.33	$5.64
8%	1.47	5.87
10%	1.61	6.10

35. Determine the taxpayer's income for tax purposes in each of the following cases:
    a. Zelda borrowed $30,000 from the First National Bank. She was required to deliver to the bank stocks with a value of $30,000 and a cost of $10,000. The stocks were to serve as collateral for the loan.
    b. Zelda owned a lot on Sycamore Street that measured 100 feet by 100 feet. The cost of the lot to her is $10,000. The city condemned a 10-foot strip of the land so that it could widen the street. Zelda received a $2,000 condemnation award.
    c. Zelda owned land zoned for residential use only. The land cost $5,000 and had a market value of $7,000. Zelda spent $500 and several hundred hours petitioning the county supervisors to change the zoning to A–1 commercial. The value of the property immediately increased to $20,000 when the county approved the zoning change.

36. Determine the taxpayer's income for tax purposes in each of the following cases:
    a. In the current year, Seagull Corporation purchased $1,000,000 par value of its own bonds and paid the bondholders $980,000 plus $50,000 of accrued interest. The bonds had been issued 10 years ago at par and were to mature 25 years from the date of issue. Does the corporation recognize income from the purchase of the bonds?
    b. A shareholder of a corporation sold property to the corporation for $60,000 (the shareholder's cost). The value of the property on the date of sale was $50,000. Does the taxpayer have any gross income from the sale?
    c. Rex was a football coach at a state university. Because of his disappointing record, he was asked to resign and accept one-half of his pay for the remaining three years of his contract. Rex resigned, accepting $75,000.

37. Al is an attorney who conducts his practice as a sole proprietor. During the year, he received cash of $85,000 for legal services. At the beginning of the year, he had

receivables from clients of $15,000. At the end of the year, his receivables totaled $30,000. Compute Al's gross income from the practice for the year:

a. Using the cash basis of accounting.
b. Using the accrual basis of accounting.

38. The taxpayer began operating a grocery store during the year. Her only books and records are based on cash receipts and disbursements, but she has asked you to compute her gross profit from the business for tax purposes.

Sales of merchandise	$260,000
Purchases of merchandise	190,000

You determine that as of the end of the year the taxpayer has accounts payable for merchandise of $9,000 and accounts receivable from customers totaling $1,500. The cost of merchandise on hand at the end of the year was $4,000. Compute the grocery store's accrual method gross profit for the year.

39. Your client is a new partnership, Aspen Associates, which is an engineering consulting firm. Generally, Aspen bills clients for services at the end of each month. Client billings are about $50,000 each month. On average, it takes 45 days to collect the receivables. Aspen's expenses are primarily for salary and rent. Salaries are paid on the last day of each month, and rent is paid on the first day of each month. The partnership has a line of credit with a bank, which requires monthly financial statements. These must be prepared using the accrual method. Aspen's managing partner, Amanda Sims, has suggested that the firm should also use the accrual method for tax purposes and thus reduce accounting fees by $500. Write a letter to your client explaining why you believe it would be worthwhile for Aspen to file its tax return on the cash basis even though its financial statements are prepared on the accrual basis. Aspen's address is 100 James Tower, Denver, CO 80208.

40. Color Paint Shop, Inc., is an accrual basis taxpayer that paints automobiles. During the year, the company painted Samuel's car and was to receive a $1,000 payment from his insurance company. Samuel was not satisfied with the work, however, and the insurance company refused to pay. In December 1996, Color and Samuel agreed that Color would receive $600 for the work, subject to final approval by the insurance company. In the past, Color had come to terms with customers only to have the insurance company negotiate an even lesser amount. In May 1997, the insurance company reviewed the claim and paid the $600 to Color. An IRS agent thinks that Color, as an accrual basis taxpayer, should report $1,000 of income in 1996, when the work was done and then deduct a $400 loss in 1997. Prepare a memo to Susan Apple, a tax partner for whom you are working, with the recommended treatment for the disputed income.

41. Dance, Inc., is a dance studio that sells dance lessons for cash, on open account, and for notes receivable. The company also collects interest on bonds held as an investment. The company's cash receipts for the year totaled $219,000:

Cash sales	$ 70,000
Collections on accounts receivable	120,000
Collections on notes receivable	20,000
Interest on bonds	9,000
	$219,000

The balances in accounts receivable, notes receivable, and accrued interest on bonds at the beginning and end of the year were as follows:

	1–1	12–31
Accounts receivable	$24,000	$24,000
Notes receivable	9,000	13,000
Accrued interest on bonds	2,500	4,000
	$35,500	$41,000

The fair market value of the notes is equal to 60% of their face amount. There were no bad debts for the year, and all notes were for services performed during the year. Compute the corporation's gross income:

a. Using the cash basis of accounting.
b. Using the accrual basis of accounting.
c. Using a hybrid method—accrual basis for lessons and cash basis for interest income.

42. Determine the effect of the following on a cash basis taxpayer's gross income for 1996:
    a. Received his paycheck for $3,000 from his employer on December 31, 1996. He deposited the paycheck on January 2, 1997.
    b. Received a bonus of $5,000 from his employer on January 10, 1997. The bonus was for the outstanding performance of his division during 1996.
    c. Received a dividend check from IBM on November 28, 1996. He mailed the check back to IBM in December requesting that additional IBM stock be issued to him under IBM's dividend reinvestment plan.

43. Mohammed owns a life insurance policy. The cash surrender value of the policy increased $1,500 during the year. He purchased a certificate of deposit on June 30 of the current year for $44,500. The certificate matures in two years when its value will be $50,000 (interest rate of 6%). However, if Mohammed redeems the certificate before the end of the first year, he receives no interest. Mohammed also purchased a Series EE U.S. government savings bond for $7,460. The maturity value of the bond is $10,000 in six years (yield of 5%), and the redemption price of the bond increased by $400 during the year. Mohammed has owned no other savings bonds. What is Mohammed's current year gross income from the above items?

44. Pelican, Inc., an accrual basis taxpayer, sells and installs consumer appliances. Determine the effects of each of the following transactions on the company's 1996 gross income:
    a. In December 1996, the company received a $1,200 advance payment from a customer. The payment was for an appliance that Pelican specially ordered from the manufacturer. The appliance had not arrived at the end of 1996.
    b. At the end of 1996, the company installed an appliance and collected the full price of $750 for the item. However, the customer claimed the appliance was defective and asked the company for a refund. The company conceded that the appliance was defective, but claimed that the customer should collect from the manufacturer. The dispute had not been settled by the end of 1996. In early 1997, it was determined that Pelican did not install the appliance properly and the company was required to refund the full sales price.
    c. The company sold an appliance for $1,200 (plus a market rate of interest) and received the customer's note for that amount. However, because of the customer's poor credit rating, the value of the note was only $700.

45. Freda is a cash basis taxpayer. Determine her 1996 gross income from the following transactions:
    a. In 1994, Freda negotiated her 1995 salary. The employer offered to pay Freda $200,000 in 1995. Freda countered that she wanted $10,000 each month in 1995 and the remaining $80,000 in January 1996. Freda wanted the $80,000 income shifted to 1996 because she expected her 1996 tax rates to be lower. The employer agreed to Freda's terms.

b. In 1995, Freda was running short of cash and needed money for Christmas. Her employer loaned her $20,000 in November 1995. Freda signed a note for $20,000 plus 10% interest, the applicable Federal rate. In January 1996, the employer subtracted the $20,000 and $333 interest from the $80,000 due Freda and paid her $59,667.

c. On December 31, 1995, Zina offered to buy land from Freda for $30,000 (Freda's basis was $8,000). Freda refused to sell in 1995, but at that time, she contracted to sell the land to Zina in 1996 for $30,000.

46. The Heron Apartments requires its new tenants to pay the rent for the first and last months of the annual lease and a $400 damage deposit, all at the time the lease is signed. In December 1996, a tenant paid $800 for January 1997 rent, $800 for December 1997 rent, and $400 for the damage deposit. In January 1998, Heron refunded the tenant's damage deposit. What are the effects of these payments on Heron's taxable income for 1996, 1997, and 1998?
   a. Assume Heron is a cash basis taxpayer.
   b. Assume Heron is an accrual basis taxpayer.

47. Leo has asked you to review portions of his tax return. He provides you with the following information:

Gain on redemption of a 2-year 7% certificate of deposit		
Proceeds received June 30, 1996	$10,000	
Purchase price July 1, 1994	(8,735)	
Gain		$1,265
Gain on redemption of a 6-month 6% certificate of deposit		
Proceeds received March 31, 1996	$ 5,000	
Purchase price October 1, 1995	(4,855)	
Gain		145
Gain from 8% Series E savings bond		
Proceeds received September 30, 1996	$ 2,500	
Purchase price June 30, 1983	(780)	
Gain		1,720
Distributions from a family partnership		1,500

Leo's share of the partnership's earnings were $1,400. Determine Leo's 1996 gross income from the above.

48. a. Gus is a cash basis taxpayer. On September 1, 1996, Gus gave a corporate bond to his son, Hans. The bond had a face amount of $10,000 and paid $900 of interest each January 31. On December 1, 1996, Gus gave common stocks to his daughter, Dena. Dividends totaling $720 had been declared on the stocks on November 30, 1996, and were payable on January 15, 1997. Dena became the shareholder of record in time to collect the dividends. What is Gus's 1997 gross income from the bond and stocks?
   b. Gus's mother was unable to pay her bills as they came due. Gus, his employer, and his mother's creditors entered into an arrangement whereby Gus's employer would withhold $500 per month from his salary and the employer would pay the $500 to the creditors. Three thousand dollars were withheld from Gus's salary and paid to the creditors. Is Gus required to pay tax on the $3,000?

49. Tracy, a cash basis taxpayer, is employed by Eagle Corporation, also a cash basis taxpayer. Tracy is a full-time employee of the corporation and receives a salary of $60,000 per year. He also receives a bonus equal to 10% of all collections from clients he serviced during the year. Determine the tax consequences of the following events to the corporation and to Tracy:
   a. On December 31, 1996, Tracy was visiting a customer. The customer gave Tracy a $3,000 check payable to the corporation for appraisal services Tracy performed during 1996. Tracy did not deliver the check to the corporation until January 1997.
   b. The facts are the same as in (a), except that the corporation is an accrual basis taxpayer and Tracy deposited the check on December 31, but the bank did not add the deposit to the corporation's account until January 1997.

c. The facts are the same as in (a), except the customer told Tracy to hold the check until January when the customer could make a bank deposit that would cover the check.

50. Eve, Fran, and Gary each have a one-third interest in the capital and profits of the EFG Partnership. At the beginning of the year, each partner had a $50,000 balance in his or her capital account. The partnership's gross income for the year was $190,000, and its total expenses were $110,000. During the year, Eve contributed an additional $10,000 to the partnership and did not have any withdrawals from her capital account. Fran withdrew $30,000, and Gary withdrew $24,000. Compute each partner's taxable income from the partnership for the year.

51. Diego and Carmen lived together for part of the year but were divorced on December 31, 1996. Diego earned $30,000 salary from his employer during the year. Carmen's salary was $16,000. Carmen also received $8,000 in taxable dividends from stock held as separate property.
   a. If Diego and Carmen reside in Texas, how much income should each report on their separate tax returns for 1996?
   b. If amounts are withheld from their salaries, how are these amounts reported on Diego and Carmen's separate returns?
   c. If Diego and Carmen reside in a common law state, how much income should each report on their separate returns?

52. Hazel and Harry were married on June 30, 1996, and resided in Dallas, Texas. On December 31, 1996, they separated, and on March 31, 1997, they were divorced. On July 1, 1997, Harry moved to Grundy, Virginia, and remarried in December 1997. Hazel did not remarry. Hazel's and Harry's incomes for the relevant periods were as follows:

Salary	Harry	Hazel
January 1–June 30, 1996	$23,000	$15,000
July 1–December 31, 1996	24,000	16,000
January 1–March 31, 1997	25,000	18,000
April 1–December 31, 1997	40,000	20,000

In addition to the salaries listed, on January 31, 1997, Harry received $2,400 interest on savings certificates acquired on February 1, 1996. What is Hazel's gross income for 1996 and 1997 as computed on separate returns?

53. Liz and Doug were divorced on July 1 of the current year after 10 years of marriage. Their current year's income received before the divorce was as follows:

Doug's salary	$18,000
Liz's salary	25,000
Rent on apartments purchased by Liz 15 years ago	6,000
Dividends on stock Doug inherited from his mother 4 years ago	1,200
Interest on a savings account in Liz's name funded with her salary	1,800

Allocate the income to Liz and Doug assuming they live in:
   a. California.
   b. Texas.

54. Nell and Kirby Archer are in the process of negotiating their divorce agreement. What would be the tax consequences to Nell and Kirby if the following, considered individually, become part of the agreement:

a. Nell is to receive $1,000 per month until she dies or remarries. She also is to receive $500 per month for 12 years for her one-half interest in their personal residence. She paid for her one-half interest out of her earnings.
b. Nell is to receive a principal sum of $100,000. Of this amount, $50,000 is to be paid in the year of the divorce, and $5,000 per year will be paid to her in each of the following 10 years or until her death.
c. Nell is to receive stock in GM Corporation (value of $120,000 and basis of $75,000). The stock was jointly owned by Nell and Kirby. In exchange for the stock, Nell relinquished all of her rights to property accumulated during the marriage. She also is to receive $1,000 per month until her death or remarriage, but for a period of not longer than 10 years.
d. Assume that Nell and Kirby are close to agreeing on the settlement described in (c). Nell has informed you that she plans to sell the stock soon after she receives it and move into her mother's residence. Nell has asked you for a written explanation of the tax consequences of accepting the settlement described in (c). Assume Nell's marginal tax rate is 28%. Nell resides at 400 Peachtree Drive, Atlanta, GA 30303.

55. Under the terms of a post-1986 divorce agreement, Al is to receive payments from Karen as follows: $60,000 in Year 1, $45,000 in Year 2, and $20,000 each year for Years 3 through 10. Al is also to receive custody of their minor son. The payments will decrease by $5,000 per year if the son dies or when he attains age 21 and will cease upon Al's death.
   a. What will be Al's taxable alimony in Year 1?
   b. What will be the effect of the Years 2 and 3 payments on Al's taxable income?

56. Under the terms of their divorce agreement, Barry is to transfer common stock (cost of $25,000, market value of $60,000) to Sandra. Barry and Sandra have a 14-year-old child. Sandra will have custody of the child, and Barry is to pay $300 per month as child support. In addition, Sandra is to receive $1,000 per month for 10 years. However, the payments will be reduced to $750 per month when their child reaches age 21. In the first year under the agreement, Sandra receives the common stock and the correct cash payments for six months. How will the terms of the agreement affect Sandra's gross income?

57. Gus decides to buy a personal residence and goes to the bank for a $50,000 loan. The bank tells him he can borrow the funds at 8% if his father will guarantee the debt. Gus's father, Hal, owns certificates of deposit currently yielding 7%. The Federal rate is 6%. Hal is willing to do either of the following:

   - Cash in the certificates and loan Gus the funds at 7% interest.
   - Guarantee the loan for Gus.

   Hal will consider loaning the funds to Gus at an even lower interest rate, depending on the tax consequences. Hal is in the 36% marginal tax bracket. Gus, whose only source of income is his salary, is in the 15% marginal tax bracket. The interest Gus pays on the mortgage will be deductible by him. Considering only the tax consequences, which option will maximize the family's after-tax wealth?

58. On June 30, 1996, Ridge borrowed $52,000 from his employer. On July 1, 1996, Ridge used the money as follows:

Interest-free loan to Ridge's controlled corporation (operated by Ridge on a part-time basis)	$21,000
Interest-free loan to Tab (Ridge's son)	11,000
National Bank of Grundy 9% certificate of deposit ($15,260 due at maturity, June 30, 1997)	14,000
National Bank of Grundy 10% certificate of deposit ($7,260 due at maturity, June 30, 1998)	6,000
	$52,000

Ridge's employer did not charge him interest. The applicable Federal rate was 12% throughout the relevant period. Tab had investment income of $800 for the year, and he used the loan proceeds to pay medical school tuition. There were no other outstanding loans between Ridge and Tab. What are the effects of the preceding transactions on Ridge's taxable income for 1996?

59. Indicate whether the imputed interest rules should apply in the following situations:
    a. Mitch is a cash basis attorney who charges his clients based on the number of hours it takes to do the job. The bill is due upon completion of the work. However, for clients who make an initial payment when the work begins, Mitch grants a discount on the final bill. The discount is equal to 10% interest on the deposit.
    b. Local Telephone Company requires that customers make a security deposit. The deposit is refunded after the customer has established a good record for paying the telephone bill. The company pays 6% interest on the deposits.
    c. Lynn asked Kelly for a $125,000 loan to purchase a new home. Kelly made the loan and did not charge interest. Kelly never intended to collect the loan, and at the end of the year Kelly told Lynn that the debt was forgiven.

60. Vito is the sole shareholder of Vito, Inc. He is also employed by the corporation. On June 30, 1996, Vito borrowed $8,000 from Vito, Inc., and on July 1, 1997, he borrowed an additional $3,000. Both loans were due on demand. No interest was charged on the loans, and the Federal rate was 10% for all relevant dates. Vito used the money to purchase stock, and he had no investment income. Determine the tax consequences to Vito and Vito, Inc., in each of the following situations:
    a. The loans are considered employer-employee loans.
    b. The loans are considered corporation-shareholder loans.

61. Albert purchased an annuity from an insurance company for $100,000 on January 1, 1996. The annuity was to pay him $6,000 per year for life starting in January 1996. At the annuity starting date, Albert was age 65.
    a. Determine Albert's gross income from the annuity in the first year.
    b. Assume Albert lives 25 years after purchasing the contract. What would be his gross income in the twenty-fourth year?
    c. Assume Albert died in 1999, after collecting a total of $20,000. What will be the effect of the annuity on his 1999 adjusted gross income?

62. In 1996, Ahmad purchased an annuity for $50,000. He was 59 at the time he purchased the contract. Payments were to begin when Ahmad attained age 62. In 1996, when the cash surrender value had increased to $51,000, Ahmad exercised a right to receive $1,500 and accept reduced payments after age 62. In 1998, when he had a life expectancy of 22.5 years, Ahmad received his first annual $3,000 payment under the contract.
    a. What is Ahmad's income from the contract in 1996?
    b. Compute Ahmad's taxable collections under the annuity contract in 1998.

63. For each of the following, determine the amount that should be included in gross income:
    a. Joe was selected as the most valuable player in the Super Bowl. In recognition of this, he was awarded a sports car worth $60,000 and $50,000 in cash.
    b. Wanda won the Mrs. America beauty contest. She received various prizes valued at $75,000.
    c. George was awarded the Nobel Peace Prize. He took the $950,000 check he received and donated it to State University, his alma mater.

64. The LMN Partnership has a group term life insurance plan. Each partner has $100,000 protection, and each employee has protection equal to twice his or her annual salary. Employee Alice (age 44) had $90,000 insurance under the plan, and partner Kay (age 56) had $150,000 coverage. The cost of Alice's coverage for the year was $180, and the cost of Kay's protection was $950.
    a. Assuming the plan is nondiscriminatory, how much must Alice and Kay include in gross income from the insurance?
    b. Assuming the plan is discriminatory, how much must Kay include in her gross income from the insurance?

65. Herbert was employed for the first six months of the year and earned $60,000 in salary. During the next six months, he collected $7,800 of unemployment compensation, borrowed $6,000 (using his personal residence as collateral), and withdrew $1,000 from his savings account (including $60 interest). His luck was not all bad, for in December he won $800 in the lottery on a $5 ticket. Calculate Herbert's gross income.

66. Linda and Don are married and file a joint return. In 1996, they received $9,000 in Social Security benefits and $28,000 taxable pension benefits, interest, and dividends.
    a. Compute the couple's adjusted gross income on a joint return.
    b. Don would like to know whether they should sell for $100,000 a corporate bond (at no gain or loss) that pays 8% in interest each year and use the proceeds to buy a $100,000 nontaxable State of Virginia bond that will pay $6,000 in interest each year.
    c. If Linda in (a) works part-time and earns $30,000, how much would Linda and Don's adjusted gross income increase?

67. Melissa and James are married and file a joint return. They receive $11,000 in Social Security benefits, $28,000 in pension benefits (all taxable), and $10,000 of taxable interest and dividends.
    a. Assuming that Melissa and James have $15,000 in itemized deductions and personal exemptions, how much will their taxable income increase if they sell stock that cost $1,000 for $11,000?
    b. Assuming the statutory rate applied to the capital gain from the sale of the stock is 28% and the rate applied to all other income is also 28%, what are the after-tax proceeds from the sale of the stock?
    c. How might the Social Security formula influence Melissa and James's decision of whether to sell the stock for a $10,000 gain?

68. Donna does not think she has an income tax problem but would like to discuss her situation with you just to make sure she will not get hit with an unexpected tax liability. Base your suggestions on the following relevant financial information:
    a. Donna's share of the SAT Partnership income is $70,000, but none of the income can be distributed because the partnership needs the cash for operations.
    b. Donna's Social Security benefits totaled $8,400, but Donna loaned the cash received to her nephew.
    c. Donna assigned to a creditor the right to collect $1,200 interest on some bonds she owned.
    d. Donna and her husband lived together in California until September, when they separated. Donna has heard rumors that her husband had substantial gambling winnings since they separated.

CUMULATIVE PROBLEMS

69. Dan and Freida Butler, husband and wife, file a joint return. The Butlers live at 625 Oak Street, Corbin, KY 27521. Dan's Social Security number is 482–61–1231, and Freida's is 162–79–1245.

    During 1996, Dan and Freida furnished over half of the total support of each of the following individuals:
    a. Gina, their daughter, age 22, a full-time student, who was married on December 21, 1996, has no income of her own, and for 1996 did not file a joint return with her husband, who earned $4,000 during 1996.
    b. Sam, their son, age 20, who had gross income of $2,900 and who dropped out of college in February 1996.
    c. Ben Brow, Freida's brother, age 27, who is a full-time college student with gross income of $4,000.

    Dan, a radio announcer for WJJJ, earned a salary of $50,000 in 1996. Freida was employed part-time as a real estate salesperson by Corbin Realty and was paid commissions of $40,000 in 1996. Freida sold a house on December 30, 1996, and will be paid a commission of $1,500 (not included in the $40,000) on the January 10, 1997, closing date.

Dan and Freida collected $15,000 on a certificate of deposit that matured on September 30, 1996. The certificate was purchased on October 1, 1994, for $13,102, and the yield to maturity was 7%.

Other income received consisted of the following:

Dividends on CSX stock	$2,000
Interest on savings account at Second Bank	1,300

CSX had been instructed by Dan and Freida to pay the dividends directly to Freida's brother, Ben. CSX complied with their instructions.

Freida is a 10% partner in the Green Partnership. Green reported taxable income of $100,000 for 1996 and made no distributions to any of the partners in 1996.

Dan and Freida had itemized deductions as follows:

State income tax withheld	$3,100
Real estate taxes paid	2,500
Interest on home mortgage (paid to Corbin Savings and Loan)	6,400
Cash contributions to the Boy Scouts	620

Their employers withheld Federal income tax of $14,500 (Dan $8,400, Freida $6,100), and the Butlers paid estimated tax of $4,000.

Part 1—Tax Computation

Compute Dan and Freida's 1996 Federal income tax payable (or refund due). Suggested software (if available): *TurboTax* or *MacInTax*.

Part 2—Tax Planning

Dan plans to reduce his work schedule and work only halftime for WJJJ in 1997. He has been writing songs for several years and wants to devote more time to developing a career as a songwriter. Because of the uncertainty in the music business, however, he would like you to make all computations assuming he will have no income from songwriting in 1997. To make up for the loss of income, Freida plans to increase the amount of time she spends selling real estate. She estimates she will be able to earn $60,000 in 1997. Assume all other income and expense items will be approximately the same as they were in 1996. Will the Butlers have more or less disposable income (after Federal income tax) in 1997? Write a letter to the Butlers that contains your advice and prepare a memo for the tax files. Suggested software (if available): *TurboTax* or *MacInTax*.

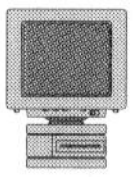

70. Sam T. Seymour would like to forget 1995 (and almost did as a result of his drinking problem). Although he received a salary of $74,000 and $600 of interest income, a divorce nearly brought him to financial ruin. The divorce was final on February 28, 1995. Under the agreement, Sam was required to do the following:

- Pay his minor daughter Pam's private school tuition of $10,800.
- Pay his ex-wife, Patricia Ann Seymour, a $40,000 lump-sum payment on March 1, 1995, and $2,000 each month thereafter through February 2001. The payments are to cease upon Patricia's death.
- Transfer to Patricia stock acquired in 1987 for $40,000 that now has a market value of $82,000.

Patricia retained custody of Pam but spent only $4,000 for Pam's support in 1995. The divorce agreement was silent as to whether Sam could claim Pam as a dependent and as to whether the cash payments to Patricia would constitute alimony.

Sam paid the tuition and made the $40,000 lump-sum payment but, because he was dismissed from his job in August 1995, was able to make only seven of the monthly payments to Patricia.

On November 1, 1995, when the applicable Federal rate was 6%, Sam was compelled to borrow $35,000 from his mother (Mollie Seymour). He gave her a non-interest-bearing second mortgage on his residence. There were no other loans outstanding between Sam and his mother.

Other information relevant to Sam's 1995 return is as follows:

a. Sam's disabled brother, Fred Seymour, lived with Sam from April through December 1995. Fred's only income was $3,600 of Social Security disability payments, and Sam contributed $4,000 toward Fred's support. No one else contributed to Fred's support. Fred's Social Security number is 245–99–4444.
b. Sam's only deductible items were home mortgage interest, $2,080; state income tax, $2,180; county property taxes, $3,000; charitable contributions, $200.
c. Sam's employer withheld $10,000 of Federal income tax.
d. Sam is 47 years old, his Social Security number is 215–71–1041, and he lives at 170 Ford Street, Gretna, TN 37929.
e. Patricia Ann Seymour's Social Security number is 712–15–9701.

Compute Sam's 1995 Federal income tax payable (or refund due). If you use tax forms for your computations, you will need Form 1040 and Schedules A and B. Suggested software (if available): *TurboTax* or *MacInTax*.

RESEARCH PROBLEMS

Note: ***West's Federal Taxation on CD-ROM*** *can be used in preparing solutions to the Research Problems. Alternatively, tax research materials contained in a standard tax library can be used.*

Research Problem 1. Edith Sanders gave common stock to her daughter, Joyce. The cost of the stock was $20,000, and its fair market value was $150,000. The uniform transfer tax on the gift was $30,000. Edith was liable for the transfer tax, but the gift was made on the condition that Joyce would pay the gift tax (i.e., a "net gift"). Joyce paid the $30,000 in accordance with the agreement.

The IRS agent contends that Edith must treat the transactions as part sale and part gift. That is, 20% of the stock ($30,000/$150,000 = .20) was sold, and the balance was given to Joyce. According to the agent, Edith must recognize taxable gain of $26,000 [$30,000 – (.20)($20,000)]. Edith is having difficulty understanding why she would be required to recognize any income since she made a gift of property and did not receive anything. Write a letter to the taxpayer that contains your advice and prepare a memo for the tax files. Edith's address is 400 Rock Street, Memphis, TN 38152.

Research Problem 2. Sam purchased a new automobile for $18,000. Sam was very pleased with himself for negotiating a low price for the automobile, so it came as a complete surprise to him when he received a $1,500 check from the manufacturer as a rebate on the new car. Sam considers the windfall the equivalent of finding money, and he asks you whether his good fortune has any tax consequences.

Research Problem 3. Debra is a cash basis taxpayer whose employer defers 10% of her annual salary until she reaches age 65. To assure that the company can pay the deferred compensation when it comes due, the company purchases an annuity policy that will be payable when Debra reaches retirement age. The company will continue to own the policy and will collect the proceeds and pay Debra. A revenue agent argues that Debra has constructively received the income as soon as her employer purchases the annuity contract. Is the revenue agent correct?

Partial list of research aids:
Rev.Rul. 72–25, 1972–1 C.B. 127; Rev.Rul 68–99, 1968–1 C.B. 193.

Research Problem 4. The Great Electric Company requires new customers to make a $100 deposit to secure future payments for electricity. After the customer has established a good payment record (usually within two years), the company refunds the deposit to the customer. If the services are terminated before refund, the deposit is usually applied against the final bill. The IRS agent insists that the company must include the deposits in gross income for the year the deposits are received. Can you find authority for excluding the deposits from income?

TEAM PROJECT: ARTHUR ANDERSEN TAX CHALLENGE CASES

For more information on the Arthur Andersen Tax Challenge Cases, please refer to Chapter 1, page 1-38.

Information related to tax issues and problems that are discussed in this chapter may be found in the

Fields case on pages 10, 18-27, 32, and 33
Miller case on pages 3, 11, 13-15, 17, 21-23, 35, and 40

Read and analyze the case you have been assigned and *identify* any issues and problems that are related to material covered in this chapter. If the information provided in the case is complete, prepare answers for this part of the case at this time. If you need information that is contained in the later parts of the case, please write a memo summarizing the questions or problems so you can prepare a complete answer at a later date.

CHAPTER

5

Gross Income: Exclusions

LEARNING OBJECTIVES

After completing Chapter 5, you should be able to:

1. Understand that statutory authority is required to exclude an item from gross income.
2. Identify the circumstances under which various items are excludible from gross income.
3. Determine the extent to which receipts can be excluded under the tax benefit rule.
4. Describe the circumstances under which income must be reported from the discharge of indebtedness.
5. Identify tax planning strategies for obtaining the maximum benefit from allowable exclusions.

OUTLINE

ITEMS SPECIFICALLY EXCLUDED FROM GROSS INCOME

Chapter 4 discussed the concepts and judicial doctrines that affect the determination of gross income. If an income item is within the all-inclusive definition of gross income, the item can be excluded only if the taxpayer can locate specific authority for doing so. Chapter 5 focuses on the exclusions Congress has authorized. These exclusions are listed in Exhibit 5–1.

Tax advisers spend countless hours trying to develop techniques to achieve tax-exempt status for income. Employee benefits planning is greatly influenced by the availability of certain types of exclusions. Taxes play an important role in employee benefits, as well as in other situations, because attaining an exclusion is another means of enhancing after-tax income. For example, for a person whose combined Federal and state marginal tax rate is 40 percent, $1.00 of tax-exempt income is equivalent to $1.66 in income subject to taxation. The tax adviser's ideal is to attach the right labels or provide the right wording to render income nontaxable without affecting the economics of the transaction.

Consider the case of an employee who is in the 28 percent marginal tax bracket and is paying $3,000 a year for health insurance. If the employer provided this protection in a manner that qualified for exclusion treatment but reduced the employee's salary by $3,000, the employee's after-tax and after-insurance income would increase at no additional cost to the employer.

▼ Exhibit 5–1
Summary of Principal Exclusions from Gross Income

1. Donative items
   Gifts, bequests, inheritances, and employee death benefits [§§ 102 and 101(b)]
   Life insurance proceeds paid by reason of death (§ 101)
   Scholarships (§ 117)
2. Personal and welfare items
   Injury or sickness payments (§ 104)
   Public assistance payments (Rev.Rul. 71–425, 1971–2 C.B. 76)
   Amounts received under insurance contracts for certain living expenses (§ 123)
   Reimbursement for the costs of caring for a foster child (§ 131)
3. Wage and salary supplements
   a. Fringe benefits
      Accident and health benefits (§§ 105 and 106)
      Lodging and meals furnished for the convenience of the employer (§ 119)
      Rental value of parsonages (§ 107)
      Employee achievement awards [§ 74(c)]
      Employer contributions to employee group term life insurance (§ 79)
      Cafeteria plans (§ 125)
      Educational assistance payments (§ 127)*
      Child or dependent care (§ 129)
      Services provided to employees at no additional cost to the employer (§ 132)
      Employee discounts (§ 132)
      Working condition and *de minimis* fringes (§ 132)
      Athletic facilities provided to employees (§ 132)
      Qualified transportation fringe (§ 132)
      Qualified moving expense reimbursement (§ 132)
      Tuition reductions granted to employees of educational institutions (§ 117)
   b. Military benefits
      Combat pay (§ 112)
      Housing, uniforms, and other benefits (§ 134)
   c. Foreign earned income (§ 911)
4. Investor items
   Interest on state and local government obligations (§ 103)
   Improvements by tenant to landlord's property (§ 109)
   Fifty percent exclusion for gain from sale of certain small business stock (§ 1202)
5. Benefits for the elderly
   Social Security benefits (except in the case of certain higher-income taxpayers) (§ 86)
   Gain from the sale of personal residence by elderly taxpayers (§ 121)
6. Other benefits
   Income from discharge of indebtedness (§ 108)
   Recovery of a prior year's deduction that yielded no tax benefit (§ 111)
   Educational savings bonds (§ 135)

*Exclusion treatment applies for tax years beginning before January 1, 1995.

Salary received to use to purchase health insurance	$ 3,000
Less: Taxes ($3,000 × 28%)	(840)
Cash available to purchase health insurance	$ 2,160
Less: Cost of health insurance	(3,000)
Excess of cost of health insurance over cash available	$ 840

Thus, the employee in this case is $840 better off with a salary reduction of $3,000 and employer-provided health insurance. The employee may still decide that the $3,000 salary is preferable. For example, if the employee has not been sick, he or she may feel that health insurance is no longer needed. Understanding the tax influence, however, does enable the employee to make a more informed choice.

Statutory Authority

1 Learning Objective
Understand that statutory authority is required to exclude an item from gross income.

Sections 101 through 150 provide the authority for excluding specific items from gross income. In addition, other exclusions are scattered throughout the Code. Each exclusion has its own legislative history and reason for enactment. Certain exclusions are intended as a form of indirect welfare payments. Other exclusions prevent double taxation of income or provide incentives for socially desirable activities (e.g., nontaxable interest on certain U.S. government bonds where the owner uses the funds for educational expenses).

In some cases, Congress has enacted exclusions to rectify the effects of judicial decisions. For example, the Supreme Court held that the fair market value of improvements (not made in lieu of rent) made by a tenant to the landlord's property should be included in the landlord's gross income upon termination of the lease.[1] The landlord was required to include the value of the improvements in gross income even though the property had not been sold or otherwise disposed of. Congress provided relief in this situation by enacting § 109, which defers taxing the value of the improvements until the property is sold.[2]

Gifts and Inheritances

2 Learning Objective
Identify the circumstances under which various items are excludible from gross income.

Beginning with the Income Tax Act of 1913 and continuing to the present, Congress has allowed the recipient of a gift to exclude the value of the property from gross income. The exclusion applies to gifts made during the life of the donor (*inter vivos* gifts) and transfers that take effect upon the death of the donor (bequests and inheritances).[3] However, as discussed in Chapter 4, the recipient of a gift of income-producing property is subject to tax on the income subsequently earned from the property. Also, as discussed in Chapter 1, the donor or the decedent's estate may be subject to gift or estate taxes on the transfer.

In numerous cases, gifts are made in a business setting. For example, a salesperson gives a purchasing agent free samples; an employee receives cash from his or her employer on retirement; a corporation makes payments to employees who were victims of a natural disaster; a corporation makes a cash payment to a deceased employee's spouse. In these and similar instances, it is frequently unclear whether the payment was a gift or whether it represents compensation for past, present, or future services.

The courts have defined a **gift** as "a voluntary transfer of property by one to another without adequate [valuable] consideration or compensation therefrom."[4]

---

[1] *Helvering v. Bruun*, 40–1 USTC ¶9337, 24 AFTR 652, 60 S.Ct. 631 (USSC, 1940).

[2] If the tenant made the improvements in lieu of rent, the value of the improvements is not eligible for exclusion.

[3] § 102.

[4] *Estate of D. R. Daly*, 3 B.T.A. 1042 (1926).

TAX IN THE NEWS

Strike Benefits Are Not Gifts

In a recent Tax Court case, striking airline pilots argued that the strike benefits they received from their union should be excluded from gross income as gifts. The benefits were funded by charges imposed on union members who worked for nonstriking airlines. The pilots argued that the benefits were nontaxable gifts from other pilots and that the union was merely a conduit for the funds. The Tax Court found that the payments were not motivated by "detached and disinterested generosity," the requisite for gift treatment. The nonstriking pilots were required to pay for the benefits, and the receipt of the benefits by the striking pilots was contingent upon their striking. Finally, unlike a gift situation, the individual financial needs of the pilots were not taken into account in setting the benefits.

SOURCE: *Richard A. Osbourne,* 69 TCM 1895, T.C.Memo. 1995–71.

If the payment is intended to be for services rendered, it is not a gift, even though the payment is made without legal or moral obligation and the payor receives no economic benefit from the transfer. To qualify as a gift, the payment must be made "out of affection, respect, admiration, charity or like impulses."[5] Thus, the cases on this issue have been decided on the basis of the donor's intent.

In a landmark case, *Comm. v. Duberstein,*[6] the taxpayer (Duberstein) received a Cadillac from a business acquaintance. Duberstein had supplied the businessman with the names of potential customers with no expectation of compensation. The Supreme Court concluded:

> . . . despite the characterization of the transfer of the Cadillac by the parties [as a gift] and the absence of any obligation, even of a moral nature, to make it, it was at the bottom a recompense for Duberstein's past service, or an inducement for him to be of further service in the future.

Duberstein was therefore required to include the fair market value of the automobile in gross income.

In the case of cash or other property *received by an employee* from his or her employer, Congress has eliminated any ambiguity. Transfers from an employer to an employee cannot be excluded as a gift unless the transfer fits into a statutory exclusion provision other than the one for gifts.[7]

Life Insurance Proceeds

GENERAL RULE

Life insurance proceeds paid to the beneficiary because of the death of the insured are exempt from income tax.[8]

---

[5] *Robertson v. U.S.,* 52–1 USTC ¶9343, 41 AFTR 1053, 72 S.Ct. 994 (USSC, 1952).

[6] 60–2 USTC ¶9515, 5 AFTR2d 1626, 80 S.Ct. 1190 (USSC, 1960).

[7] § 102(c).

[8] § 101(a).

TAX IN THE NEWS

Investors Find Death a Safe Bet

According to an Associated Press report, a new class of investments called asset-backed securities is being marketed. These investments are much like mortgage-backed securities, but are backed by life insurance policies on the terminally ill. The terminally ill patient sells his or her policy to the investment group for 70 to 80 percent of the face value. To date, the dollar value of offerings of such asset-backed securities is small, but proponents say the potential investment pool is vast and untapped.

One proponent views the securities as a form of empowerment for the terminally ill. While the idea of creating or even buying such investments at first appears callous, proponents point out that they enable the patients to improve their quality of life, buy needed medical supplies, and support themselves.

SOURCE: Associated Press, "Investors Find Death a Safe Bet," *Roanoke Times & World News*, April 21, 1995, p. A9.

Example 1

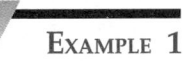

Mark purchased an insurance policy on his life and named his wife Linda as the beneficiary. Mark paid $24,000 in premiums. When he died, Linda collected the insurance proceeds of $60,000. The $60,000 is exempt from Federal income tax. ▼

Congress chose to exempt life insurance proceeds for the following reasons:

- For family members, life insurance proceeds serve much the same purpose as a nontaxable inheritance.
- In a business context (as well as in a family situation), life insurance proceeds replace an economic loss suffered by the beneficiary.

Example 2

Gold Corporation purchased a life insurance policy to cover its key employee. If the proceeds were taxable, the corporation would require more insurance coverage to pay the tax as well as to cover the economic loss of the employee. ▼

Thus, in general, Congress concluded that making life insurance proceeds exempt from income tax was a good policy.

EXCEPTIONS TO EXCLUSION TREATMENT

The income tax exclusion applies only when the insurance proceeds are received because of the death of the insured. If the owner cancels the policy and receives the cash surrender value, he or she must recognize gain to the extent of the excess of the amount received over the cost of the policy (a loss is not deductible).[9]

Another exception to exclusion treatment applies if the policy is transferred after it is issued by the insurance company. If the policy is *transferred for valuable consideration,* the insurance proceeds are includible in the gross income of the transferee to the extent the proceeds received exceed the amount paid for the policy by the transferee plus any subsequent premiums paid.

[9] *Landfield Finance Co. v. U.S.,* 69–2 USTC ¶9680, 24 AFTR2d 69–5744, 418 F.2d 172 (CA–7, 1969).

EXAMPLE 3

Adam pays premiums of $500 for an insurance policy in the face amount of $1,000 upon the life of Beth and subsequently transfers the policy to Carol for $600. On Beth's death, Carol receives the proceeds of $1,000. The amount that Carol can exclude from gross income is limited to $600 plus any premiums she paid subsequent to the transfer. ▼

The Code, however, provides four exceptions to the rule illustrated in the preceding example. These exceptions permit exclusion treatment for transfers to the following:

1. A partner of the insured.
2. A partnership in which the insured is a partner.
3. A corporation in which the insured is an officer or shareholder.
4. A transferee whose basis in the policy is determined by reference to the transferor's basis.

The first three exceptions facilitate the use of insurance contracts to fund buy-sell agreements.

EXAMPLE 4

Rick and Sam are equal partners who have an agreement that allows either partner to purchase the interest of a deceased partner for $50,000. Neither partner has sufficient cash to actually buy the other partner's interest, but each has a life insurance policy on his own life in the amount of $50,000. Rick and Sam could exchange their policies (usually at little or no taxable gain), and upon the death of either partner, the surviving partner could collect tax-free insurance proceeds. The proceeds could then be used to purchase the decedent's interest in the partnership. ▼

The fourth exception applies to policies that were transferred pursuant to a tax-free exchange or were received by gift.[10]

Investment earnings arising from the reinvestment of life insurance proceeds are generally subject to income tax. Often the beneficiary will elect to collect the insurance proceeds in installments. The annuity rules (discussed in Chapter 4) are used to apportion the installment payment between the principal element (excludible) and the interest element (includible).[11]

EMPLOYEE DEATH BENEFITS

GIFT VERSUS COMPENSATION

Frequently, an employer makes payments (**death benefits**) to a deceased employee's surviving spouse, children, or other beneficiaries. If the decedent had a nonforfeitable right to the payments (e.g., the decedent's accrued salary), the amounts are generally taxable to the recipient just the same as if the employee had lived and collected the payments. But where the employer makes voluntary payments, the gift issue arises. Generally, the IRS considers such payments to be compensation for prior services rendered by the deceased employee.[12] However, some courts have held that payments to an employee's surviving spouse or other beneficiaries are gifts if the following are true:[13]

---

[10] See the discussion of gifts in Chapter 14 and tax-free exchanges in Chapters 15 and 20.

[11] Reg. §§ 1.72–7(c)(1) and 1.101–7T.

[12] Rev.Rul. 62–102, 1962–2 C.B. 37.

[13] *Estate of Sydney J. Carter v. Comm.*, 72–1 USTC ¶9129, 29 AFTR2d 332, 453 F.2d 61 (CA–2, 1972), and the cases cited there.

- The payments were made to the surviving spouse and children rather than to the employee's estate.
- The employer derived no benefit from the payments.
- The surviving spouse and children performed no services for the employer.
- The decedent had been fully compensated for services rendered.
- Payments were made pursuant to a board of directors' resolution that followed a general company policy of providing payments for families of deceased employees (but not exclusively for families of shareholder-employees).

When all of the above conditions are satisfied, the payment is presumed to have been made *as an act of affection or charity.* When one or more of these conditions is not satisfied, the surviving spouse and children may still be deemed the recipients of a gift if the payment is made in light of the survivors' financial needs.[14]

Automatic $5,000 Exclusion. Section 101(b) attempts to eliminate or reduce controversy in this area by providing an *automatic exclusion* of the first $5,000 paid by the employer to the employee's beneficiaries by reason of the death of the employee. The maximum total exclusion on behalf of a deceased employee is $5,000 regardless of the number of employers paying the benefit. The $5,000 exclusion must be apportioned among the beneficiaries on the basis of each beneficiary's percentage of the total death benefits received. When the employer's payments exceed $5,000, the beneficiaries may still be able to exclude the entire amount received as a gift if they are able to show gratuitous intent on the part of the employer. Note that this exclusion does not apply to the decedent's accrued salary.

EXAMPLE 5 When Antonio died, his employer paid his accrued salary of $3,000 to Josefina, Antonio's widow. The employer's board of directors also authorized payments to Josefina ($4,000), Antonio's daughter ($2,000), and Antonio's son ($2,000) "in recognition of Antonio's many years of service to the company."

The $3,000 accrued salary is compensation for past services and was owed to Antonio at the time of his death. Therefore, the $3,000 is includible in gross income. The additional payments to the widow and children were not owed to Antonio. Because the payments were made in recognition of Antonio's past service, under the *Duberstein* decision, the payments are not gifts. However, the employee death benefit exclusion enables the widow and children to exclude the following amounts:

$$\text{Widow} \quad \frac{\$4,000}{\$8,000} \times \$5,000 = \$2,500$$

$$\text{Daughter} \quad \frac{\$2,000}{\$8,000} \times \$5,000 = 1,250$$

$$\text{Son} \quad \frac{\$2,000}{\$8,000} \times \$5,000 = \underline{1,250}$$

$$\underline{\underline{\$5,000}}$$

▼

Besides avoiding the gift issue in many cases, the employee death benefit exclusion is intended to allow a substitute for tax-exempt life insurance proceeds.

[14] *Simpson v. U.S.*, 58–2 USTC ¶9923, 2 AFTR2d 6036, 261 F.2d 497 (CA–7, 1958), *cert. denied*, 79 S.Ct. 724 (USSC, 1958).

SCHOLARSHIPS

GENERAL INFORMATION

Payments or benefits received by a student at an educational institution may be (1) compensation for services, (2) a gift, or (3) a scholarship. If the payments or benefits are received as compensation for services (past or present), the fact that the recipient is a student generally does not render the amounts received nontaxable.[15]

EXAMPLE 6

State University waives tuition for all graduate teaching assistants. The tuition waived is intended as compensation for services and is therefore included in the graduate assistant's gross income. ▼

As discussed earlier, gifts are not includible in gross income.

The **scholarship** rules are intended to provide exclusion treatment for education-related benefits that cannot qualify as gifts but are not compensation for services. According to the Regulations, "a scholarship is an amount paid or allowed to, or for the benefit of, an individual to aid such individual in the pursuit of study or research."[16] The recipient must be a candidate for a degree (either undergraduate or graduate) at an educational institution.[17]

EXAMPLE 7

Terry enters a contest sponsored by a local newspaper. Each contestant is required to submit an essay on local environmental issues. The prize is one year's tuition at State University. Terry wins the contest. The newspaper has a legal obligation to Terry (as contest winner). Thus, the benefits are not a gift. However, since the tuition payment aids Terry in pursuing her studies, the payment is a scholarship. ▼

A scholarship recipient may exclude from gross income the amount used for tuition and related expenses (fees, books, supplies, and equipment required for courses), provided the conditions of the grant do not require that the funds be used for other purposes.[18] Amounts received for room and board are *not* excludible and are treated as earned income for purposes of calculating the standard deduction for a taxpayer who is another taxpayer's dependent.[19]

EXAMPLE 8

Kelly received a scholarship of $9,500 from State University to be used to pursue a bachelor's degree. She spent $4,000 on tuition, $3,000 on books and supplies, and $2,500 for room and board. Kelly may exclude $7,000 ($4,000 + $3,000) from gross income. The $2,500 spent for room and board is includible in Kelly's gross income.

The scholarship was Kelly's only source of income. Her parents provided more than 50% of Kelly's support and claimed her as a dependent. Kelly's standard deduction will equal her $2,500 gross income. Thus, she has no taxable income. ▼

TIMING ISSUES

Frequently, the scholarship recipient is a cash basis taxpayer who receives the money in one tax year but pays the educational expenses in a subsequent year.

[15] Reg. § 1.117–2(a). See *C. P. Bhalla*, 35 T.C. 13 (1960), for a discussion of the distinction between a scholarship and compensation. See also *Bingler v. Johnson*, 69–1 USTC ¶9348, 23 AFTR2d 1212, 89 S.Ct. 1439 (USSC, 1969). For potential exclusion treatment, see the subsequent discussion of qualified tuition reductions.

[16] Prop.Reg. § 1.117–6(c)(3)(i).

[17] § 117(a).

[18] § 117(b).

[19] Prop.Reg. § 1.117–6(h).

The amount eligible for exclusion may not be known at the time the money is received. In that case, the transaction is held *open* until the educational expenses are paid.[20]

EXAMPLE 9

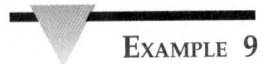

In August 1996, Sanjay received $10,000 as a scholarship for the academic year 1996–1997. Sanjay's expenditures for tuition, books, and supplies were as follows:

August–December 1996	$3,000
January–May 1997	4,500
	$7,500

Sanjay's gross income for 1997 includes $2,500 ($10,000 – $7,500) that is not excludible as a scholarship. None of the scholarship is included in his gross income in 1996. ▼

DISGUISED COMPENSATION

Some employers make scholarships available solely to the children of key employees. The tax objective of these plans is to provide a nontaxable fringe benefit to the executives by making the payment to the child in the form of an excludible scholarship. However, the IRS has ruled that the payments are generally includible in the gross income of the parent-employee.[21]

QUALIFIED TUITION REDUCTION PLANS

Employees (including retired and disabled former employees) of nonprofit educational institutions are allowed to exclude a tuition waiver from gross income, if the waiver is pursuant to a **qualified tuition reduction plan.**[22] The plan may not discriminate in favor of highly compensated employees. The exclusion applies to the employee, the employee's spouse, and the employee's dependent children. The exclusion also extends to tuition reductions granted by any nonprofit educational institution to employees of any other nonprofit educational institution (reciprocal agreements).

EXAMPLE 10

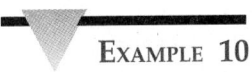

ABC University allows the dependent children of XYZ University employees to attend ABC University with no tuition charge. XYZ University grants reciprocal benefits to the children of ABC University employees. The dependent children can also attend tuition-free the university where their parents are employed. Employees who take advantage of these benefits are not required to recognize gross income. ▼

Generally, the exclusion is limited to *undergraduate* tuition waivers. However, in the case of teaching or research assistants, graduate tuition waivers may also qualify for exclusion treatment. According to the Proposed Regulations, the exclusion is limited to the value of the benefit in excess of the employee's reasonable compensation.[23] Thus, a tuition reduction that is a substitute for cash compensation cannot be excluded.

---

[20] Prop.Reg. § 1.117–6(b)(2).

[21] Rev.Rul. 75–448, 1975–2 C.B. 55. *Richard T. Armantrout*, 67 T.C. 996 (1977).

[22] § 117(d).

[23] Prop.Reg. § 1.117–6(d).

EXAMPLE 11

Susan is a graduate research assistant. She receives a $5,000 salary for 500 hours of service over a nine-month period. This pay, $10 per hour, is reasonable compensation for Susan's services. In addition, Susan receives a waiver of $6,000 for tuition. Susan may exclude the tuition waiver from gross income. ▼

ETHICAL CONSIDERATIONS

A Caring Dean

About 25 percent of the undergraduate classes in the College of Business at Amber University are taught by doctoral students. Amber recognizes that its graduates will have both research and teaching responsibilities when they graduate and become faculty members. Thus, for the first year of graduate study, the doctoral students are research assistants, and for the second year they are teaching assistants. The students currently receive fellowship grants of $16,000 each year.

The dean of the School of Business is perplexed when he learns that the doctoral students have to pay income taxes on the fellowship grants they receive as graduate assistants. He did not have to do so when he was a graduate student.

Upon checking with a tax professor in the School of Accounting, the dean learns that the fellowship grants are included in gross income as a result of a change in the tax law. After further conversations with the tax professor, the dean develops the following plan: (1) As a condition for receiving their degree, all doctoral students must be research assistants during the first year and teaching assistants during the second year. (2) The fellowship grant will be $12,000 for the first year and $20,000 for the second year with the $8,000 increment reported as compensation for services rendered. (3) A few local business people will be hired to teach part-time to provide a benchmark for the $8,000 of compensation income.

Evaluate the dean's plan both from the perspective of achieving the results he wants and from the perspective of ethical behavior.

COMPENSATION FOR INJURIES AND SICKNESS

DAMAGES

A person who suffers harm caused by another is often entitled to **compensatory damages.** The tax consequences of the receipt of damages depend on the type of harm the taxpayer has experienced. The taxpayer may seek recovery for (1) a loss of income, (2) expenses incurred, (3) property destroyed, or (4) personal injury.

Generally, reimbursement for a loss of income is taxed the same as the income replaced. The recovery of an expense is not income, unless the expense was deducted. Damages that are a recovery of the taxpayer's previously deducted expenses are generally taxable under the tax benefit rule, discussed later in this chapter.

A payment for damaged or destroyed property is treated as an amount received in a sale or exchange of the property. Thus, the taxpayer has a realized gain if the damage payments received exceed the property's basis. Damages for personal injuries receive special treatment under the Code.

Personal Injury. The legal theory of personal injury damages is that the amount received is intended "to make the plaintiff [the injured party] whole as before the injury."[24] It follows that if the damage payments received were subject to tax, the after-tax amount received would be less than the actual damages incurred and the injured party would not be "whole as before the injury."

Congress has specifically excluded from gross income the amount of any damage payments received (whether by suit or agreement) on account of personal injuries or sickness. The courts have applied the exclusion to any personal wrong committed against the taxpayer (e.g., breach of promise to marry, invasion of privacy, libel, slander, assault, battery). The exclusion also applies to compensation for loss of income (ordinarily taxable, as previously discussed) and recovery of expenses (except medical expenses deducted by the taxpayer) resulting from the personal injury.[25] According to the Supreme Court, however, the damages are taxable if under the Federal or state law establishing the taxpayer's right of recovery, the recovery is limited to the loss of income. The Supreme Court recently expanded the damages that are taxable by holding that recoveries in age-discrimination lawsuits are includible in gross income because such damages are not awarded on account of personal injury or sickness.[26]

In libel and slander cases, a single event can cause both a personal injury and damage to a business reputation. Damage to a business reputation is measured on the basis of estimated loss of income. Taxpayers argue that the amount received for loss of income in these cases is no different from the payments in other personal injury cases and thus should be excluded. According to the IRS, however, the business reputation damages are separate from the personal injury and are taxable.[27]

EXAMPLE 12

Tom, a television announcer, was dissatisfied with the manner in which Ron, an attorney, was defending the television station in a libel case. Tom stated on the air that Ron was botching the case. Ron sued Tom for slander, claiming damages for loss of income from clients and potential clients who heard Tom's statement. Ron's claim is for damages to his business reputation, and the amounts received are taxable.

Ron collected on the suit against Tom and was on his way to a party to celebrate his victory when a negligent driver, Norm, drove his truck into Ron's automobile, injuring Ron. Ron filed suit for the personal injuries and claimed as damages the loss of income for the period he was unable to work as a result of the injury. All amounts Ron received from Norm, including the reimbursement for lost income, are nontaxable because the claims are based on a personal injury. ▼

Punitive Damages. In addition to seeking compensatory damages, the injured party may seek **punitive damages,** which are often awarded to punish the defendant for gross negligence or the intentional infliction of harm. Punitive damages are includible in gross income *unless* the claim arises out of physical injury or physical sickness.[28] Thus, punitive damages received for loss of personal

---

[24] *C. A. Hawkins,* 6 B.T.A. 1023 (1928).

[25] § 104(a)(2) and Rev.Rul. 85–97, 1985–2 C.B. 50.

[26] *U.S. v. Burke,* 92–1 USTC ¶50,254, 69 AFTR2d 92–1293, 112 S.Ct. 1867 (USSC, 1992); *Comm. v. Schleier,* 95–1 USTC ¶50,309, 75 AFTR2d 95–2675, 115 S.Ct. 2159 (USSC, 1995).

[27] Rev.Rul. 85–143, 1985–2 C.B. 55, in which the IRS announced it would not follow the Ninth Court of Appeals decision in *Roemer v. Comm.,* 83–2 USTC ¶9600, 52 AFTR2d 83–5954, 716 F.2d 693 (CA–9, 1983). See also *Wade E. Church,* 80 T.C. 1104 (1983).

[28] § 104(a). Both the IRS and the courts are interpreting this provision strictly. See, for example, *Hughes A. Bagley,* 105 T.C. ____, No. 27 (1995).

TAX IN THE NEWS

Age-Bias Payments as Personal Injury

John Schmitz and Burns P. Downey were both United Airlines pilots. Both were forced into retirement at age 60. Each received about $120,000 to settle an age-discrimination class action. Neither included the $120,000 in gross income.

Last year, their financial flight paths diverged. On the same day, one Federal appeals court told Schmitz that he didn't have to pay income taxes on the settlement, while another Federal appeals court more than 2,000 miles away told Downey that he did. Caught in the lurch were hundreds of older Americans, including 70 former United pilots in the class action with Schmitz and Downey, who had received age-discrimination settlements and now, according to the IRS, owed taxes on those settlements.

In Downey's case, the Seventh Circuit Court of Appeals agreed with the IRS that the discrimination award was less like damages from a personal injury lawsuit (excludible from gross income) and more like damages from a breach of contract (includible in gross income). The Ninth Circuit Court of Appeals disagreed in deciding that Schmitz could exclude the settlement from his gross income. It concluded that the age-discrimination laws provide for jury trials and a range of damages more similar to personal injury suits than to contract actions.

Recently, Schmitz and Downey's flight paths converged with that of another former United pilot, and unfortunately, the convergence led to a crash for all of the former pilots. The Supreme Court in *Comm. v. Schleier* [95–1 USTC ¶50,309, 75 AFTR2d 95–2675, 115 S.Ct. 2159 (USSC, 1995)] ruled that former employees who successfully sue their former employers under the Age Discrimination in Employment Act of 1967 must include the damages received in gross income. In writing the majority opinion, Justice John Paul Stevens concluded that recoveries in age-discrimination lawsuits do not fit within the statutory language of § 104 of being "damages received on account of personal injuries or sickness."

SOURCE: "High Court Holds Age Discrimination Damages Are Taxable," Deloitte & Touche LLP - *Deloitte & Touche Review*, June 26, 1995, p. 5.

reputation are taxable, although the compensatory damages are excludible. Punitive damages arising out of a physical injury claim are excludible.

Example 13

Assume Ron in Example 12 also received punitive damages in each suit. The punitive damages Ron received from Norm may be excluded from gross income because the damages arose out of the physical injury claim. Ron's punitive damages received from Tom are taxable because the damages did not arise from a physical injury or sickness claim. ▼

WORKERS' COMPENSATION

State workers' compensation laws require the employer to pay fixed amounts for specific job-related injuries. The state laws were enacted so that the employee will not have to go through the ordeal of a lawsuit (and possibly not collect damages because of some defense available to the employer) to recover the damages. Although the payments are intended, in part, to compensate for a loss of future

CONCEPT SUMMARY 5–1

Taxation of Damages

Type of Claim	Taxation of Award or Settlement
Breach of contract (generally loss of income)	Taxable.
Property damages	Recovery of cost, gain to the extent of the excess over basis. A loss is deductible for business property and investment property to the extent of basis over the amount realized. A loss may be deductible for personal use property (see discussion of casualty losses in Chapter 7).
Personal injury	
Physical	All amounts (compensatory and punitive) are excluded unless previously deducted (e.g., medical expenses).
Nonphysical, general	Compensatory damages are excluded (unless previously deducted), and punitive damages are taxable.
Nonphysical, only compensation is loss of income	Taxable.

income, Congress has specifically exempted workers' compensation benefits from inclusion in gross income.[29]

ACCIDENT AND HEALTH INSURANCE BENEFITS

The income tax treatment of accident and health insurance benefits depends on whether the policy providing the benefits was purchased by the taxpayer or the taxpayer's employer. Benefits collected under an accident and health insurance policy *purchased by the taxpayer* are excludible. In this case, benefits collected under the taxpayer's insurance policy are excluded even though the payments are a substitute for income.[30]

EXAMPLE 14 Bonnie purchased a medical and disability insurance policy. The insurance company paid Bonnie $200 per week to replace wages she lost while in the hospital. Although the payments serve as a substitute for income, the amounts received are tax-exempt benefits collected under Bonnie's insurance policy. ▼

EXAMPLE 15 Joe's injury results in a partial paralysis of his left foot. He receives $5,000 for the injury from his accident insurance company under a policy he had purchased. The $5,000 accident insurance proceeds are tax-exempt. ▼

A different set of rules applies if the accident and health insurance protection was *purchased by the individual's employer,* as discussed in the following section.

---

[29] § 104(a)(1).
[30] § 104(a)(3).

Employer-Sponsored Accident and Health Plans

Congress encourages employers to provide employees, retired former employees, and their dependents with **accident and health benefits** and disability insurance plans. The *premiums* are deductible by the employer and excluded from the employee's income.[31] Although § 105(a) provides the general rule that the employee has includible income when he or she collects the insurance *benefits*, two exceptions are provided.

Section 105(b) generally excludes payments received for medical care of the employee, spouse, and dependents. However, if the payments are for expenses that do not meet the Code's definition of medical care,[32] the amount received must be included in gross income. In addition, the taxpayer must include in gross income any amounts received for medical expenses that were deducted by the taxpayer on a prior return.

Example 16

In 1996, Tab's employer-sponsored health insurance plan paid $4,000 for hair transplants that did not meet the Code's definition of medical care. Tab must include the $4,000 in his gross income for 1996. ▼

Section 105(c) excludes payments for the permanent loss or the loss of the use of a member or function of the body or the permanent disfigurement of the employee, spouse, or a dependent. Payments that are a substitute for salary (e.g., related to the period of time absent) are includible.

Example 17

Jill lost an eye in an automobile accident unrelated to her work. As a result of the accident, Jill incurred $2,000 of medical expenses, which she deducted on her return. She collected $10,000 from an accident insurance policy carried by her employer. The benefits were paid according to a schedule of amounts that varied with the part of the body injured (e.g., $10,000 for loss of an eye, $20,000 for loss of a hand). Because the payment was for loss of a *member or function of the body,* the $10,000 is excluded from income. Jill was absent from work for a week as a result of the accident. Her employer provided her with insurance for the loss of income due to illness or injury. Jill collected $500, which is includible in gross income. ▼

MEDICAL REIMBURSEMENT PLANS

In lieu of providing the employee with insurance coverage for hospital and medical expenses, the employer may agree to reimburse the employee for these expenses. The amounts received through the insurance coverage (insured plan benefits) are excluded from income under § 105 (as previously discussed). Unfortunately in terms of cost considerations, the insurance companies that issue this type of policy usually require a broad coverage of employees. An alternative is to have a plan that is not funded with insurance (a self-insured arrangement). The benefits received under a self-insured plan can be excluded from the employee's income, if the plan does not discriminate in favor of highly compensated employees.[33]

---

[31] § 106, Reg. § 1.106–1, and Rev.Rul. 82–196, 1982–1 C.B. 106.

[32] See the discussion of medical care in Chapter 10.

[33] § 105(h).

ETHICAL CONSIDERATIONS

Using a Corporation to Deduct Health Insurance

Rose is a self-employed computer consultant who has no full-time employees. She is currently paying $6,000 for health insurance, none of which is deductible as an itemized deduction because of the 7.5 percent-of-adjusted-gross-income floor on the medical expense deduction. You realize that Rose could incorporate her practice and have the corporation pay for her health insurance. She could take a salary equal to the remainder of the income from the consulting practice. Thus, the corporation would have no taxable income, and Rose would have her health insurance purchased with before-tax dollars. Would such an approach be an abuse of the tax law?

MEALS AND LODGING

FURNISHED FOR THE CONVENIENCE OF THE EMPLOYER

As discussed in Chapter 4, income can take any form, including meals and lodging. However, § 119 excludes from income the value of meals and lodging provided to the employee and the employee's spouse and dependents under the following conditions:[34]

- The meals and/or lodging are *furnished* by the employer, on the employer's *business premises,* for the *convenience of the employer.*
- In the case of lodging, the *employee* is *required* to accept the lodging as a condition of employment.

The courts have construed both of these requirements strictly.

Furnished by the Employer. The following two questions have been raised with regard to the *furnished by the employer* requirement:

- Who is considered an *employee*?
- What is meant by *furnished*?

The IRS and some courts have reasoned that because a partner is not an employee, the exclusion does not apply to a partner. However, the Tax Court and the Fifth Court of Appeals have ruled in favor of the taxpayer on this issue.[35]

The Supreme Court held that a cash meal allowance was ineligible for the exclusion because the employer did not actually furnish the meals.[36] Similarly, one court denied the exclusion where the employer paid for the food and supplied the cooking facilities but the employee prepared the meal.[37]

[34] § 119(a). The meals and lodging are also excluded from FICA and FUTA tax. *Rowan Companies, Inc. v. U.S.,* 81–1 USTC ¶9479, 48 AFTR2d 81–5115, 101 S.Ct. 2288 (USSC, 1981).

[35] Rev.Rul. 80, 1953–1 C.B. 62; *Comm. v. Doak,* 56–2 USTC ¶9708, 49 AFTR 1491, 234 F.2d 704 (CA–4, 1956); but see *G. A. Papineau,* 16 T.C. 130 (1951); *Armstrong v. Phinney,* 68–1 USTC ¶9355, 21 AFTR2d 1260, 394 F.2d 661 (CA–5, 1968).

[36] *Comm. v. Kowalski,* 77–2 USTC ¶9748, 40 AFTR2d 6128, 98 S.Ct. 315 (USSC, 1977).

[37] *Tougher v. Comm.,* 71–1 USTC ¶9398, 27 AFTR2d 1301, 441 F.2d 1148 (CA–9, 1971).

On the Employer's Business Premises. The *on the employer's business premises* requirement, applicable to both meals and lodging, has resulted in much litigation. The Regulations define business premises as simply "the place of employment of the employee."[38] Thus, the Sixth Court of Appeals held that a residence, owned by the employer and occupied by an employee, two blocks from the motel that the employee managed was not part of the business premises.[39] However, the Tax Court considered an employer-owned house across the street from the hotel that was managed by the taxpayer to be on the business premises of the employer.[40] Perhaps these two cases can be reconciled by comparing the distance from the lodging facilities to the place where the employer's business was conducted. The closer the lodging to the business operations, the more likely the convenience of the employer is served.

For the Convenience of the Employer. The *convenience of the employer* test is intended to focus on the employer's motivation for furnishing the meals and lodging rather than on the benefits received by the employee. If the employer furnishes the meals and lodging primarily to enable the employee to perform his or her duties properly, it does not matter that the employee considers these benefits to be a part of his or her compensation.

The Regulations give the following examples in which the tests for excluding meals are satisfied:[41]

- A waitress is required to eat her meals on the premises during the busy lunch and breakfast hours.
- A bank furnishes a teller meals on the premises to limit the time the employee is away from his or her booth during the busy hours.
- A worker is employed at a construction site in a remote part of Alaska. The employer must furnish meals and lodging due to the inaccessibility of other facilities.

Required as a Condition of Employment. The *employee is required to accept* test applies only to lodging. If the employee's use of the housing would serve the convenience of the employer, but the employee is not required to use the housing, the exclusion is not available.

EXAMPLE 18

VEP, a utilities company, has all of its service personnel on 24-hour call for emergencies. The company encourages its employees to live near the plant so that the employees can respond quickly to emergency calls. Company-owned housing is available rent-free. Only 10 of the employees live in the company housing because it is not suitable for families.

Although the company-provided housing serves the convenience of the employer, it is not required. Therefore, the employees who live in the company housing cannot exclude its value from gross income. ▼

In addition, if the employee has the *option* of cash or lodging, the *required* test is not satisfied.

EXAMPLE 19

Khalid is the manager of a large apartment complex. The employer gives Khalid the option of rent-free housing (value of $6,000 per year) or an additional $5,000 per year. Khalid selects the housing option. Therefore, he must include $6,000 in gross income. ▼

[38] Reg. § 1.119–1(c)(1).

[39] *Comm. v. Anderson*, 67–1 USTC ¶9136, 19 AFTR2d 318, 371 F.2d 59 (CA–6, 1966).

[40] *J. B. Lindeman*, 60 T.C. 609 (1973).

[41] Reg. § 1.119–1(f).

OTHER HOUSING EXCLUSIONS

Employees of Educational Institutions. An employee of an educational institution may be able to exclude the value of campus housing provided by the employer. Generally, the employee does not recognize income if he or she pays annual rents equal to or greater than 5 percent of the appraised value of the facility. If the rent payments are less than 5 percent of the value of the facility, the deficiency must be included in gross income.[42]

EXAMPLE 20

Swan University provides on-campus housing for its full-time faculty during the first three years of employment. The housing is not provided for the convenience of the employer. Professor Edith pays $3,000 annual rent for the use of a residence with an appraised value of $100,000 and an annual rental value of $12,000. Edith must recognize $2,000 gross income [.05($100,000) – $3,000 = $2,000] for the value of the housing provided to her. ▼

Ministers of the Gospel. Ministers of the gospel can exclude (1) the rental value of a home furnished as compensation or (2) a rental allowance paid to them as compensation, to the extent the allowance is used to rent or provide a home.[43] The housing or housing allowance must be provided as compensation for the conduct of religious worship, the administration and maintenance of religious organizations, or the performance of teaching and administrative duties at theological seminaries.

EXAMPLE 21

Pastor Bill is allowed to live rent-free in a house owned by the congregation. The annual rental value of the house is $6,000 and is provided as part of the pastor's compensation for ministerial services. Assistant Pastor Olga is paid a $4,500 cash housing allowance. She uses the $4,500 to pay rent and utilities on a home she and her family occupy. Neither Pastor Bill nor Assistant Pastor Olga is required to recognize gross income associated with the housing or housing allowance. ▼

Military Personnel. Military personnel are allowed housing exclusions under various circumstances. Authority for these exclusions generally is found in Federal laws that are not part of the Internal Revenue Code.[44]

OTHER EMPLOYEE FRINGE BENEFITS

SPECIFIC BENEFITS

In recent years, Congress has enacted exclusions to encourage employers to (1) finance and make available child care facilities, (2) provide athletic facilities for employees, and (3) finance certain employees' education. These provisions are summarized as follows:

- The employee does not have to include in gross income the value of child and dependent care services paid for by the employer and incurred to enable the employee to work. The exclusion cannot exceed $5,000 per year ($2,500 if married and filing separately). For a married couple, the annual exclusion cannot exceed the earned income of the spouse who has the lesser

[42] § 119(d).

[43] § 107 and Reg. § 1.107–1.

[44] H. Rep. No. 99–841, 99th Cong., 2d Sess., p. 548 (1986). See also § 134.

amount of earned income. For an unmarried taxpayer, the exclusion cannot exceed the taxpayer's earned income.[45]

- The value of the use of a gymnasium or other athletic facilities by employees, their spouses, and their dependent children may be excluded from an employee's gross income. The facilities must be on the employer's premises, and substantially all of the use of the facilities must be by employees and their family members.[46]
- Qualified employer-provided educational assistance (tuition, fees, books, and supplies) at the undergraduate and graduate levels is excludible from gross income. The exclusion is subject to an annual employee statutory ceiling of $5,250.[47]

CAFETERIA PLANS

Generally, if an employee is offered a choice between cash and some other form of compensation, the employee is deemed to have constructively received the cash even when the noncash option is elected. Thus, the employee has gross income regardless of the option chosen.

An exception to this constructive receipt treatment is provided under the **cafeteria plan** rules. Under such a plan, the employee is permitted to choose between cash and nontaxable benefits (e.g., group term life insurance, health and accident protection, and child care). If the employee chooses the otherwise nontaxable benefits, the cafeteria plan rules enable the benefits to remain nontaxable.[48] Cafeteria plans provide tremendous flexibility in tailoring the employee pay package to fit individual needs. Some employees (usually the younger group) prefer cash, while others (usually the older group) will opt for the fringe benefit program.

EXAMPLE 22

Hawk Corporation offers its employees (on a nondiscriminatory basis) a choice of any one or all of the following benefits:

Benefit	**Cost**
Group term life insurance	$ 200
Hospitalization insurance for family members	2,400
Child care payments	1,800
	$4,400

If a benefit is not selected, the employee receives cash equal to the cost of the benefit. Kay, an employee, has a spouse who works for another employer that provides hospitalization insurance but no child care payments. Kay elects to receive the group term life insurance, the child care payments, and $2,400 of cash. Only the $2,400 must be included in Kay's gross income. ▼

GENERAL CLASSES OF EXCLUDED BENEFITS

An employer can confer numerous forms and types of economic benefits on employees. Under the all-inclusive concept of income, the benefits are taxable

[45] § 129. The exclusion applies to the same types of expenses that, if they were paid by the employee (and not reimbursed by the employer), would be eligible for the Credit for Child and Dependent Care Expense discussed in Chapter 13.

[46] § 132(j)(4).

[47] § 127. Exclusion treatment applies for tax years beginning before January 1, 1995.

[48] § 125.

unless one of the provisions previously discussed specifically excludes the item from gross income. The amount of the income is the fair market value of the benefit. This reasoning can lead to results that Congress considers unacceptable, as illustrated in the following example.

EXAMPLE 23

Vern is employed in New York as a ticket clerk for Trans National Airlines. He has a sick mother in Miami, Florida, but has no money for plane tickets. Trans National has daily flights from New York to Miami that often leave with empty seats. The cost of a round-trip ticket is $400, and Vern is in the 28% tax bracket. If Trans National allows Vern to fly without charge to Miami, under the general gross income rules, Vern has income equal to the value of a ticket. Therefore, Vern must pay $112 tax (.28 × $400) on a trip to Miami. Because Vern does not have $112, he cannot visit his mother, and the airplane flies with another empty seat. ▼

If Trans National in Example 23 will allow employees to use resources that would otherwise be wasted, why should the tax laws interfere with the employee's decision to take advantage of the available benefit? Thus, to avoid the undesirable results that occur in Example 23 and in similar situations, as well as to create uniform rules for fringe benefits, Congress established six broad classes of nontaxable employee benefits:[49]

- No-additional-cost services.
- Qualified employee discounts.
- Working condition fringes.
- *De minimis* fringes.
- Qualified transportation fringes.
- Qualified moving expense reimbursements.

No-Additional-Cost Services. Example 23 illustrates the **no-additional-cost service** type of fringe benefit. The services will be nontaxable if all of the following conditions are satisfied:

- The employee receives services, as opposed to property.
- The employer does not incur substantial additional cost, including forgone revenue, in providing the services to the employee.
- The services are offered to customers in the ordinary course of the business in which the employee works.[50]

EXAMPLE 24

Assume that Vern in Example 23 can fly without charge only if the airline cannot fill the seats with paying customers. That is, Vern must fly on standby. Although the airplane may burn slightly more fuel because Vern is on the airplane and Vern may receive the same meal as paying customers, the additional costs would not be substantial. Thus, the trip could qualify as a no-additional-cost service.

On the other hand, assume that Vern is given a reserved seat on a flight that is frequently full. The employer would be forgoing revenue to allow Vern to fly. This forgone revenue would be a substantial additional cost, and thus the benefit would be taxable. ▼

Note that if Vern were employed in a hotel owned by Trans National, the receipt of the airline ticket would be taxable because Vern did not work in that line of business. However, the Code allows the exclusion for reciprocal benefits offered by employers in the same line of business.

[49] See, generally, § 132.

[50] Reg. § 1.132–2.

EXAMPLE 25 Grace is employed as a desk clerk for Plush Hotels, Inc. The company and Chain Hotels, Inc., have an agreement that allows any of their employees to stay without charge in either company's resort hotels during the off-season. Grace would not be required to recognize income from taking advantage of the plan by staying in a Chain Hotel. ▼

The no-additional-cost exclusion extends to the employee's spouse and dependent children and to retired and disabled former employees. In the Regulations, the IRS has conceded that partners who perform services for the partnership are employees for purposes of the exclusion.[51] (As discussed earlier in the chapter, the IRS's position is that partners are not employees for purposes of the § 119 meals and lodging exclusion.) However, the exclusion is not allowed to highly compensated employees unless the benefit is available on a nondiscriminatory basis.

Qualified Employee Discounts. When the employer sells goods or services (other than no-additional-cost benefits just discussed) to the employee for a price that is less than the price charged regular customers, the employee realizes income equal to the discount. However, the discount, referred to as a **qualified employee discount,** can be excluded from the gross income of the employee, subject to the following conditions and limitations:

- The exclusion is not available for real property (e.g., a house) or for personal property of the type commonly held for investment (e.g., common stocks).
- The property or services must be from the same line of business in which the employee works.
- In the case of *property,* the exclusion is limited to the *gross profit component* of the price to customers.
- In the case of *services,* the exclusion is limited to 20 percent of the customer price.[52]

EXAMPLE 26 Silver Corporation, which operates a department store, sells a television set to a store employee for $300. The regular customer price is $500, and the gross profit rate is 25%. The corporation also sells the employee a service contract for $120. The regular customer price for the contract is $150. The employee must recognize $75 income.

Customer price for property	$ 500
Less: Gross profit (25%)	(125)
	$ 375
Employee price	(300)
Income	$ 75
Customer price for service	$ 150
Less: 20 percent	(30)
	$ 120
Employee price	(120)
Income	$-0-

▼

EXAMPLE 27 Assume the same facts as in Example 26, except the employee is a clerk in a hotel operated by Silver Corporation. Because the line of business requirement is not met, the employee must recognize $200 income ($500 – $300) from the purchase of the television and $30 income ($150 – $120) from the service contract. ▼

[51] Reg. § 1.132–1(b).

[52] § 132(c).

As in the case of no-additional-cost benefits, the exclusion applies to employees (including service partners), employees' spouses and dependent children, and retired and disabled former employees. However, the exclusion does not apply to highly compensated individuals unless the discount is available on a nondiscriminatory basis.

ETHICAL CONSIDERATIONS

Excluding Employee Discounts

Tom works for Roadrunner Motors, a company that manufactures automobiles. Tom purchased a new automobile from Roadrunner at the company's cost of $10,000. The retail selling price for the automobile is $15,000. Sue works for Coyote, Inc., an auto dealership, which sells the car manufactured by Roadrunner. Sue purchased an automobile identical to Tom's from Coyote. The price Sue pays is equal to Coyote's cost of the automobile ($13,500). Tom and Sue each receive a salary of $40,000 per year. Considering only the above information, do Tom and Sue have equal ability to pay income taxes for the year, and does equitable treatment occur? If not, how should the tax law be changed to produce equitable treatment?

Working Condition Fringes. Generally, an employee is not required to include in gross income the cost of property or services provided by the employer if the employee could deduct the cost of those items if he or she had actually paid for them.[53] These benefits are called **working condition fringes.**

EXAMPLE 28

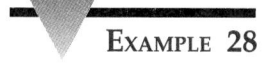

Mitch is a certified public accountant employed by an accounting firm. The employer pays Mitch's annual dues to professional organizations. Mitch is not required to include the payment of the dues in gross income because if he had paid the dues, he would have been allowed to deduct the amount as an employee business expense (as discussed in Chapter 9). ▼

In many cases, this exclusion merely avoids reporting income and an offsetting deduction. However, in two specific situations, the working condition fringe benefit rules allow an exclusion where the expense would not be deductible if paid by the employee:

- Automobile salespeople are allowed to exclude the value of certain personal use of company demonstrators (e.g., commuting to and from work).[54]
- The employee business expense would be eliminated by the 2 percent floor on miscellaneous deductions under § 67 (see Chapter 10).

Unlike the other fringe benefits discussed previously, working condition fringes can be made available on a discriminatory basis and still qualify for the exclusion.

***De Minimis* Fringes.** As the term suggests, ***de minimis* fringe** benefits are so small that accounting for them is impractical. The House Report contains the following examples of *de minimis* fringes:

[53] § 132(d).

[54] § 132(j)(3).

- The typing of a personal letter by a company secretary, occasional personal use of a company copying machine, occasional company cocktail parties or picnics for employees, occasional supper money or taxi fare for employees because of overtime work, and certain holiday gifts of property with a low fair market value are excluded.
- Subsidized eating facilities (e.g., an employees' cafeteria) operated by the employer are excluded if located on or near the employer's business premises, if revenue equals or exceeds direct operating costs, and if nondiscrimination requirements are met.

When taxpayers venture beyond the specific examples contained in the House Report and the Regulations, there is obviously much room for disagreement as to what is *de minimis.* However, note that except in the case of subsidized eating facilities, the *de minimis* fringe benefits can be granted in a manner that favors highly compensated employees.

Qualified Transportation Fringes. The Energy Policy Act of 1992 created a new category of nontaxable employee benefits called **qualified transportation fringes.** The intent was to encourage the use of mass transit for commuting to and from work. Qualified transportation fringes encompass the following transportation benefits provided by the employer to the employee:[55]

1. Transportation in a commuter highway vehicle between the employee's residence and the place of employment.
2. A transit pass.
3. Qualified parking.

Statutory dollar limits are placed on the amount of the exclusion. Categories (1) and (2) above are combined for purposes of applying the limit. In this case, the limit on the exclusion for 1996 is $65 per month. Category (3) has a separate limit. For qualified parking, the limit on the exclusion for 1996 is $165 per month. Both of these dollar limits are indexed annually for inflation.

A *commuter highway vehicle* is any highway vehicle with a seating capacity of at least 6 adults (excluding the driver). In addition, at least 80 percent of the vehicle's use must be for transporting employees between their residences and place of employment.

Qualified parking includes the following:

- Parking provided to an employee on or near the employer's business premises.
- Parking provided to an employee on or near a location from which the employee commutes to work via mass transit, in a commuter highway vehicle, or in a carpool.

Qualified transportation fringes may be provided directly by the employer or may be in the form of cash reimbursements.

EXAMPLE 29

Gray Corporation's offices are located in the center of a large city. The company pays for parking spaces to be used by the company officers. Steve, a vice president, receives $250 of such benefits each month. The parking space rental qualifies as a qualified transportation fringe. Of the $250 benefit received each month by Steve, $165 is excludible from gross

[55] § 132(f).

TAX IN THE NEWS

Federal Parking Woes

In what could be called Jimmy Carter's revenge, many Federal workers who have employer-provided parking spaces have been hit with higher tax bills since 1994. Their taxable income is boosted by the amount that the value of their parking space exceeds the tax-free ceiling on parking perks and commercial parking fees. During his tenure in the White House, President Carter created a bureaucratic backlash when he suggested that Federal workers who were parking free should pay half the commercial rate. The White House was picketed, and the President was denounced by zealous Feds who felt that the Founding Fathers intended for them to have free parking.

Amendments to the Internal Revenue Code in the Revenue Reconciliation Act of 1993 provided that workers could park tax-free only if the space would cost $155 or less per month based on local commercial fees. That limit went to $160 in 1995 and $165 in 1996 as a result of indexing for inflation. The limit applies to both Federal and private-sector employer-provided parking.

The $160 ($165 in 1966) lid is not a problem in most places. But in higher-cost cities, such as San Francisco and New York and, to a lesser extent, downtown Washington, that is a bargain rate.

Workers at the Agriculture Department headquarters, for example, recently were informed that parking would add $564 to their taxable income for 1995. VIPs with their own reserved spaces were required to add much more than $564 to their taxable income for the year, because the value of the reserved space is much higher than in a "first come, first serve" arrangement.

SOURCE: Adapted from "Fun with Parking," *Washington Post,* January 24, 1995, p. B2. Reprinted with permission.

income. The balance of $85 is included in his gross income. The same result would occur if Steve paid for the parking and was reimbursed by his employer. ▼

Qualified Moving Expense Reimbursements. The Revenue Reconciliation Act of 1993 provides that qualified moving expenses that are reimbursed or paid by the employer are excludible from gross income. A qualified moving expense is one that would be deductible under § 217. See the discussion of moving expenses in Chapter 9.

Nondiscrimination Provisions. For no-additional-cost services and qualified employee discounts, if the plan is discriminatory in favor of highly compensated employees, these key employees are denied exclusion treatment. However, the non-highly compensated employees who receive benefits from the plan can still enjoy exclusion treatment for the no-additional-cost services and qualified employee discounts.[56]

EXAMPLE 30

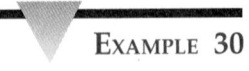

Dove Company's officers are allowed to purchase goods from the company at a 25% discount. Other employees are allowed only a 15% discount. The company's gross profit margin on these goods is 30%.

[56] § 132(j)(1).

Peggy, an officer in the company, purchased goods from the company for $750 when the price charged to customers was $1,000. Peggy must include $250 in gross income because the plan is discriminatory.

Leo, an employee of the company who is not an officer, purchased goods for $850 when the customer price was $1,000. Leo is not required to recognize income because he received a qualified employee discount. ▼

De minimis (except in the case of subsidized eating facilities) and working condition fringe benefits can be provided on a discriminatory basis. The *de minimis* benefits are not subject to tax because the accounting problems that would be created are out of proportion to the amount of additional tax that would result. A nondiscrimination test would simply add to the compliance problems. In the case of working condition fringes, the types of services required vary with the job. Therefore, a nondiscrimination test probably could not be satisfied, although usually there is no deliberate plan to benefit a chosen few. Likewise, the qualified transportation fringe and the qualified moving expense reimbursement can be provided on a discriminatory basis.

TAXABLE FRINGE BENEFITS

If the fringe benefits cannot qualify for any of the specific exclusions or do not fit into any of the general classes of excluded benefits, the taxpayer must recognize gross income equal to the fair market value of the benefits. Obviously, problems are frequently encountered in determining values. The IRS has issued extensive Regulations addressing the valuation of personal use of an employer's automobiles and meals provided at an employer-operated eating facility.[57]

If a fringe benefit plan discriminates in favor of highly compensated employees, generally those employees are not allowed to exclude the benefits they receive that other employees do not enjoy. However, the highly compensated employees, as well as the other employees, are generally allowed to exclude the nondiscriminatory benefits.[58]

EXAMPLE 31

MED Company has a medical reimbursement plan that reimburses officers for 100% of their medical expenses, but reimburses all other employees for only 80% of their medical expenses. Cliff, the president of the company, was reimbursed $1,000 during the year for medical expenses. Cliff must include $200 in gross income [(1 – .80) × $1,000 = $200]. Mike, an employee who is not an officer, received $800 (80% of his actual medical expenses) under the medical reimbursement plan. None of the $800 is includible in his gross income. ▼

FOREIGN EARNED INCOME

A U.S. citizen is generally subject to U.S. tax on his or her income regardless of the income's geographic origin. The income may also be subject to tax in the foreign country, and thus the taxpayer must carry a double tax burden. Out of a sense of

[57] Reg. § 1.61–2 T(j). Generally, the income from the personal use of the employer's automobile is based on the lease value of the automobile (what it would have cost the employee to lease the automobile). Meals are valued at 150% of the employer's direct costs (e.g., food and labor) of preparing the meals.

[58] §§ 79(d), 105(h), 127(b)(2), and 132(j)(1). See the discussion of the term "highly compensated employee" in Chapter 19.

CONCEPT SUMMARY 5–2

General Classes of Excluded Benefits

Benefit	Description and Examples	Coverage Allowed	Effect of Discrimination
1. No-additional-cost services	The employee takes advantage of the employer's excess capacity (e.g., free passes for airline employees).	Current, retired, and disabled employees; their spouses and dependent children; spouses of deceased employees. Partners are treated as employees.	No exclusion for highly compensated employees.
2. Qualified discounts on goods	The employee is allowed to purchase the employer's merchandise at a price that is not less than the employer's cost.	Same as (1) above.	Same as (1) above.
3. Qualified discounts on services	The employee is allowed a discount (maximum of 20%) on services the employer offers to customers.	Same as (1) above.	Same as (1) above.
4. Working condition fringes	Expenses paid by the employer that would be deductible if paid by the employee (e.g., a mechanic's tools). Also, includes auto salesperson's use of a car held for sale.	Current employees, partners, directors, and independent contractors.	No effect.
5. *De minimis* items	Expenses so immaterial that accounting for them is not warranted (e.g., occasional supper money, personal use of the copy machine).	*Any recipient* of a fringe benefit.	No effect.
6. Qualified transportation fringes	Transportation benefits provided by the employer to employees including commuting in a commuter highway vehicle, a transit pass, and qualified parking.	Current employees.	No effect.
7. Qualified moving expense reimbursements	Qualified moving expenses that are paid or reimbursed by the employer. A qualified moving expense is one that would be deductible under § 217.	Current employees.	No effect.

fairness and to encourage U.S. citizens to work abroad (so that exports might be increased), Congress has provided alternative forms of relief from taxes on foreign earned income. The taxpayer can elect *either* (1) to include the foreign income in his or her taxable income and then claim a credit for foreign taxes paid or (2) to exclude the foreign earnings from his or her U.S. gross income (the **foreign earned**

income exclusion).[59] The foreign tax credit option is discussed in Chapter 13, but as is apparent from the following discussion, most taxpayers will choose the exclusion.

Foreign earned income consists of the earnings from the individual's personal services rendered in a foreign country (other than as an employee of the U.S. government). To qualify for the exclusion, the taxpayer must be either of the following:

- A bona fide resident of the foreign country (or countries).
- Present in a foreign country (or countries) for at least 330 days during any 12 consecutive months.[60]

EXAMPLE 32

Sandra's trips to and from a foreign country in connection with her work were as follows:

Arrived in Foreign Country	Arrived in United States
March 10, 1995	February 1, 1996
March 7, 1996	June 1, 1996

During the 12 consecutive months ending on March 10, 1996, Sandra was present in the foreign country for at least 330 days (366 days less 29 days in February and 7 days in March 1996). Therefore, all income earned in the foreign country through March 10, 1996, is eligible for the exclusion. The income earned from March 11, 1996, through May 31, 1996, is also eligible for the exclusion because Sandra was present in the foreign country for 330 days during the 12 consecutive months ending on May 31, 1996. ▼

The exclusion is *limited* to $70,000 per year. For married persons, both of whom have foreign earned income, the exclusion is computed separately for each spouse. Community property rules do not apply (the community property spouse is not deemed to have earned one-half of the other spouse's foreign earned income). A taxpayer who is present in the country for less than the entire year must compute the maximum exclusion on a daily basis ($70,000 divided by the number of days in the entire year and multiplied by the number of days present in the foreign country during the year).

EXAMPLE 33

Keith qualifies for the foreign earned income exclusion. He was present in France for all of 1996 except for 7 days in December, when he was in the United States. Keith's salary for 1996 is $90,000. If Keith had been in France for all of the 366 days in 1996, he would have been able to exclude $70,000. However, since he was not present in the foreign country for 7 days, his exclusion is limited to $68,661 as follows:

$$\$70{,}000 \times \frac{359 \text{ days in foreign country}}{366 \text{ days in the year}} = \$68{,}661$$

▼

In addition to the exclusion for foreign earnings, the *reasonable housing costs* incurred by the taxpayer and the taxpayer's family in a foreign country in excess of a base amount may be excluded from gross income. The base amount is 16

59 § 911(a).

60 § 911(d). For the definition of resident, see Reg. § 1.871–2(b). Under the Regulations, a taxpayer is not a resident if he or she is there for a definite period (e.g., until completion of a construction contract).

percent of the U.S. government pay scale for a GS–14 (Step 1) employee, which varies from year to year.[61]

As previously mentioned, the taxpayer may elect to include the foreign earned income in gross income and claim a credit (an offset against U.S. tax) for the foreign tax paid. The credit alternative may be advantageous if the individual's foreign earned income far exceeds the excludible amount so that the foreign taxes paid exceed the U.S. tax on the amount excluded. However, once an election is made, it applies to all subsequent years unless affirmatively revoked. A revocation is effective for the year of the change and the four subsequent years.

Interest on Certain State and Local Government Obligations

At the time the Sixteenth Amendment was ratified by the states, there was some question as to whether the Federal government possessed the constitutional authority to tax interest on state and local government obligations. Taxing such interest was thought to violate the doctrine of intergovernmental immunity in that the tax would impair the state and local governments' ability to finance their operations.[62] Thus, interest on state and local government obligations was specifically exempted from Federal income taxation.[63] However, the Supreme Court recently concluded that there is no constitutional prohibition against levying a nondiscriminatory Federal income tax on state and local government obligations.[64] Nevertheless, currently the statutory exclusion still exists.

Obviously, the exclusion of the interest reduces the cost of borrowing for state and local governments. A taxpayer in the 36 percent tax bracket requires only a 5.12 percent yield on a tax-exempt bond to obtain the same after-tax income as a taxable bond paying 8 percent interest [5.12% ÷ (1 – .36) = 8%].

The lower cost for the state and local governments is more than offset by the revenue loss of the Federal government. Also, tax-exempt interest is considered to be a substantial loophole for the very wealthy. For these reasons, bills have been introduced in Congress calling for Federal government subsidies to state and local governments that voluntarily choose to issue taxable bonds. Under the proposals, the tax-exempt status of existing bonds would not be eliminated.

The current exempt status applies solely to state and local government bonds. Thus, income received from the accrual of interest on a condemnation award or an overpayment of state income tax is fully taxable.[65] Nor does the exemption apply to gains on the sale of tax-exempt securities.

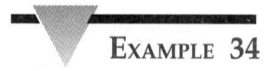

Example 34 Megan purchases State of Virginia bonds for $10,000 on July 1, 1995. The bonds pay $400 interest each June 30th and December 31st. On March 31, 1996, Megan sells the bonds for $10,500 plus $200 accrued interest. Megan must recognize a $500 gain ($10,500 – $10,000), but the $200 accrued interest is exempt from taxation. ▼

---

[61] § 911(c).

[62] *Pollock v. Farmer's Loan & Trust Co.*, 3 AFTR 2602, 15 S.Ct. 912 (USSC, 1895).

[63] § 103(a).

[64] *South Carolina v. Baker III*, 88–1 USTC ¶9284, 61 AFTR2d 88–995, 108 S.Ct. 1355 (USSC, 1988).

[65] *Kieselbach v. Comm.*, 43–1 USTC ¶9220, 30 AFTR 370, 63 S.Ct. 303 (USSC, 1943); *U.S. Trust Co. of New York v. Anderson*, 3 USTC ¶1125, 12 AFTR 836, 65 F.2d 575 (CA–2, 1933).

State and local governments have developed sophisticated financial schemes to attract new industry. For example, local municipalities have issued bonds to finance the construction of plants to be leased to private enterprise. Because the financing could be arranged with low-interest municipal obligations, the plants could be leased at a lower cost than the private business could otherwise obtain. However, Congress has placed limitations on the use of tax-exempt securities to finance private business.[66]

DIVIDENDS

GENERAL INFORMATION

A *dividend* is a payment to a shareholder with respect to his or her stock. Dividends to shareholders are taxable only to the extent the payments are made from *either* the corporation's *current earnings and profits* (similar to net income per books) or its *accumulated earnings and profits* (similar to retained earnings per books).[67] Distributions that exceed earnings and profits are treated as a nontaxable recovery of capital and reduce the shareholder's basis in the stock. Once the shareholder's basis is reduced to zero, any subsequent distributions are taxed as capital gains (see Chapter 14).[68]

Some payments are frequently referred to as dividends but are not considered dividends for tax purposes:

- Dividends received on deposits with savings and loan associations, credit unions, and banks are actually interest (a contractual rate paid for the use of money).
- Patronage dividends paid by cooperatives (e.g., for farmers) are rebates made to the users and are considered reductions in the cost of items purchased from the association. The rebates are usually made after year-end (after the cooperative has determined whether it has met its expenses) and are apportioned among members on the basis of their purchases.
- Mutual insurance companies pay dividends on unmatured life insurance policies that are considered rebates of premiums.
- Shareholders in a mutual investment fund are allowed to report as capital gains their proportionate share of the fund's gains realized and distributed. The capital gain and ordinary income portions are reported on the Form 1099 that the fund supplies its shareholders each year.

STOCK DIVIDENDS

When a corporation issues a simple stock dividend (e.g., common stock issued to common shareholders), the shareholder has merely received additional shares that represent the same total investment. Thus, the shareholder does not realize income.[69] However, if the shareholder has the *option* of receiving either cash or stock in the corporation, the individual realizes gross income whether he or she

[66] See § 103(b).

[67] § 316(a).

[68] § 301(c). See Chapter 4, *West's Federal Taxation: Corporations, Partnerships, Estates, and Trusts,* for a detailed discussion of corporate distributions.

[69] *Eisner v. Macomber,* 1 USTC ¶32, 3 AFTR 3020, 40 S.Ct. 189 (USSC, 1920); § 305(a).

receives stock or cash.[70] A taxpayer who elects to receive the stock could be deemed to be in constructive receipt of the cash he or she has rejected.[71] However, the amount of the income in this case is the value of the stock received, rather than the cash the shareholder has rejected. See Chapter 14 for a detailed discussion of stock dividends.

EDUCATIONAL SAVINGS BONDS

The cost of a college education has risen dramatically during the past 10 years, increasing at a rate almost twice the change in the general price level. The U.S. Department of Education estimates that by the year 2007, the cost of attending a publicly supported university for four years will exceed $60,000. For a private university, the cost is expected to exceed $200,000.[72] Consequently, Congress has attempted to assist low- to middle-income parents in saving for their children's college education.

The assistance is in the form of an interest income exclusion on **educational savings bonds.**[73] The interest on Series EE U.S. government savings bonds may be excluded from gross income if the bond proceeds are used to pay qualified higher education expenses. The exclusion applies only if both of the following requirements are satisfied:

- The savings bonds are issued after December 31, 1989.
- The savings bonds are issued to an individual who is at least 24 years old at the time of issuance.

The exclusion is not available for a married couple who file separate returns.

The redemption proceeds must be used to pay qualified higher education expenses. *Qualified higher education expenses* consist of tuition and fees paid to an eligible educational institution for the taxpayer, spouse, or dependent. In calculating qualified higher education expenses, the tuition and fees paid are reduced by excludible scholarships and veterans' benefits received. If the redemption proceeds (both principal and interest) exceed the qualified higher education expenses, only a pro rata portion of the interest will qualify for exclusion treatment.

EXAMPLE 35

Tracy's redemption proceeds from qualified savings bonds during the taxable year were $6,000 (principal of $4,000 and interest of $2,000). Tracy's qualified higher education expenses were $5,000. Since the redemption proceeds exceed the qualified higher education expenses, only $1,667 ($5,000/$6,000 × $2,000) of the interest is excludible. ▼

The exclusion is limited by the application of the wherewithal to pay concept. That is, once the modified adjusted gross income exceeds a threshold amount, the phase-out of the exclusion begins. *Modified adjusted gross income* (*MAGI*) is adjusted gross income prior to the § 911 foreign earned income exclusion and the educational savings bond exclusion. The threshold amounts are adjusted for inflation

[70] § 305(b).

[71] Refer to the discussion of constructive receipt in Chapter 4.

[72] See generally, Knight and Knight, "New Ways to Manage Soaring Tuition Costs," *Journal of Accountancy* (March 1989): 207.

[73] § 135.

each year. For 1996, the phase-out begins at $43,500 ($65,250 on a joint return).[74] The phase-out is completed when MAGI exceeds the threshold amount by more than $15,000 ($30,000 on a joint return). The otherwise excludible interest is reduced by the amount calculated as follows:

$$\frac{\text{MAGI} - \$43{,}500}{\$15{,}000} \times \begin{array}{l}\text{Excludible interest}\\ \text{before phase-out}\end{array} = \begin{array}{l}\text{Reduction in}\\ \text{excludible interest}\end{array}$$

On a joint return, $65,250 is substituted for $43,500 (in 1996), and $30,000 is substituted for $15,000.

EXAMPLE 36 Assume the same facts as in Example 35, except that Tracy's MAGI for 1996 is $50,000. The phase-out will result in Tracy's interest exclusion being reduced by $722 [($50,000 – $43,500)/ $15,000 × $1,667]. Therefore, Tracy's exclusion is $945 ($1,667 – $722). ▼

TAX BENEFIT RULE

3 LEARNING OBJECTIVE
Determine the extent to which receipts can be excluded under the tax benefit rule.

Generally, if a taxpayer obtains a deduction for an item in one year and in a later year recovers all or a portion of the prior deduction, the recovery is included in gross income in the year received.[75]

EXAMPLE 37 A taxpayer deducted as a loss a $1,000 receivable from a customer when it appeared the amount would never be collected. The following year, the customer paid $800 on the receivable. The taxpayer must report the $800 as income in the year it is received. ▼

However, the § 111 **tax benefit rule** provides that no income is recognized upon the recovery of a deduction, or the portion of a deduction, that did not yield a tax benefit in the year it was taken. If the taxpayer in Example 37 had no tax liability in the year of the deduction (e.g., itemized deductions and personal exemptions exceeded adjusted gross income), the recovery would be partially or totally excluded from income in the year of the recovery.[76]

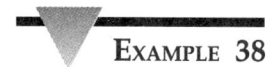

EXAMPLE 38 Before deducting a $1,000 loss from an uncollectible business receivable, Ali had taxable income of $200, computed as follows:

Adjusted gross income	$ 13,300
Itemized deductions and personal exemptions	(13,100)
Taxable income	$ 200

The business bad debt deduction yields only a $200 tax benefit. That is, taxable income is reduced by only $200 (to zero) as a result of the bad debt deduction. Therefore, if the customer makes a payment on the previously deducted receivable in a subsequent year, only the first $200 is a recovery of a prior deduction and thus is taxable. Any additional amount collected is nontaxable because only $200 of the loss yielded a reduction in taxable income. ▼

[74] The indexed amounts for 1995 are $42,300 and $63,450. A drafting error in the Revenue Reconciliation Act of 1993 allows inflation adjustments only for periods subsequent to 1992 (rather than for periods subsequent to 1989). If a proposed technical correction is enacted, the indexed amounts for 1996 would be $49,450 and $74,200.

[75] § 111(a).

[76] Itemized deductions are discussed in Chapter 10.

INCOME FROM DISCHARGE OF INDEBTEDNESS

4 LEARNING OBJECTIVE
Describe the circumstances under which income must be reported from the discharge of indebtedness.

A transfer of appreciated property (fair market value is greater than adjusted basis) in satisfaction of a debt is an event that triggers the realization of income. The transaction is treated as a sale of the appreciated property followed by payment of the debt.[77] Foreclosure by a creditor is also treated as a sale or exchange of the property.[78]

EXAMPLE 39

Juan owed the State Bank $100,000 on an unsecured note. Juan satisfied the note by transferring to the bank common stock with a basis of $60,000 and a fair market value of $100,000. Juan must recognize $40,000 gain on the transfer. Juan also owed the bank $50,000 on a note secured by land. When Juan's basis in the land was $20,000 and the land's fair market value was $50,000, the bank foreclosed on the loan and took title to the land. Juan must recognize a $30,000 gain on the foreclosure. ▼

In some cases, a creditor will not exercise his or her right of foreclosure and will even forgive a portion of the debt to assure the vitality of the debtor. In such cases, the debtor realizes income from discharge of indebtedness.

EXAMPLE 40

Brown Corporation is unable to meet the mortgage payments on its factory building. Both the corporation and the mortgage holder are aware of the depressed market for industrial property in the area. Foreclosure would only result in the creditor's obtaining unsalable property. To improve Brown Corporation's financial position and thus improve Brown's chances of obtaining the additional credit from other lenders necessary for survival, the creditor agrees to forgive all amounts past due and to reduce the principal amount of the mortgage. ▼

Generally, the income realized by the debtor from the forgiveness of a debt is taxable.[79] A similar debt discharge (produced by a different creditor motivation) associated with personal use property is illustrated in Example 41.

EXAMPLE 41

In 1991, Joyce borrowed $60,000 from National Bank to purchase her personal residence. Joyce agreed to make monthly principal and interest payments for 15 years. The interest rate on the note was 7%. In 1996, when the balance on the note had been reduced through monthly payments to $48,000, the bank offered to accept $45,000 in full settlement of the note. The bank made the offer because interest rates had increased to 11%. Joyce accepted the bank's offer. As a result, Joyce must recognize $3,000 ($48,000 – $45,000) income.[80] ▼

The following discharge of indebtedness situations are subject to special treatment:[81]

1. Creditors' gifts.
2. Discharges under Federal bankruptcy law.
3. Discharges that occur when the debtor is insolvent.
4. Discharge of the farm debt of a solvent taxpayer.
5. Discharge of **qualified real property business indebtedness.**

[77] Reg. § 1.1001–2(a).
[78] *Estate of Delman v. Comm.*, 73 T.C. 15 (1979).
[79] *U.S. v. Kirby Lumber Co.*, 2 USTC ¶814, 10 AFTR 458, 52 S.Ct. 4 (USSC, 1931), codified in § 61(a)(12).
[80] Rev.Rul. 82–202, 1982–1 C.B. 35.
[81] §§ 108 and 1017.

6. A seller's cancellation of the buyer's indebtedness.
7. A shareholder's cancellation of the corporation's indebtedness.
8. Forgiveness of loans to students.

If the creditor reduces the debt as an act of *love, affection or generosity,* the debtor has simply received a nontaxable gift (situation 1). Rarely will a gift be found to have occurred in a business context. A businessperson may settle a debt for less than the amount due, but as a matter of business expediency (e.g., high collection costs or disputes as to contract terms) rather than generosity.[82]

In situations 2, 3, 4, and 5, the Code allows the debtor to reduce his or her basis in the assets by the realized gain from the discharge.[83] Thus, the realized gain is merely deferred until the assets are sold (or depreciated). Similarly, in situation 6 (a price reduction), the debtor reduces the basis in the specific assets financed by the seller.[84]

A shareholder's cancellation of the corporation's indebtedness to him or her (situation 7) usually is considered a contribution of capital to the corporation. Thus, the corporation's paid-in capital is increased, and its liabilities are decreased by the same amount.[85]

Many states make loans to students on the condition that the loan will be forgiven if the student practices a profession in the state upon completing his or her studies. The amount of the loan that is forgiven (situation 8) is excluded from gross income.[86]

Tax Planning Considerations

The present law excludes certain types of economic gains from taxation. Therefore, taxpayers may find tax planning techniques helpful in obtaining the maximum benefits from the exclusion of such gains. Following are some of the tax planning opportunities made available by the exclusions described in this chapter.

LIFE INSURANCE

5 Learning Objective
Identify tax planning strategies for obtaining the maximum benefit from allowable exclusions.

Life insurance offers several favorable tax attributes. As discussed in Chapter 4, the annual increase in the cash surrender value of the policy is not taxable (because no income has been actually or constructively received). By borrowing on the policy's cash surrender value, the owner can actually receive the policy's increase in value in cash but without recognizing income.

EMPLOYEE BENEFITS

Generally, employees view accident and health insurance, as well as life insurance, as necessities. Employees can obtain group coverage at much lower rates than individuals would have to pay for the same protection. Premiums paid by the employer can be excluded from the employees' gross income. Because of the exclusion, employees will have a greater after-tax and after-insurance income if the employer pays a lower salary but also pays the insurance premiums.

Example 42

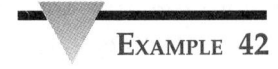

Pat receives a salary of $30,000. The company has group insurance benefits, but Pat was required to pay his own premiums as follows:

---

[82] *Comm. v. Jacobson,* 49–1 USTC ¶9133, 37 AFTR 516, 69 S.Ct. 358 (USSC, 1949).

[83] §§ 108(a), (c), (e), and (g). Note that § 108(b) provides that other tax attributes (e.g., net operating loss) will be reduced by the realized gain from the debt discharge prior to the basis adjustment unless the taxpayer elects to apply the basis adjustment first.

[84] § 108(e)(5).

[85] § 108(e)(6).

[86] § 108(f).

Hospitalization and medical insurance	$1,400
Term life insurance ($30,000 coverage)	200
Disability insurance	400
	$2,000

To simplify the analysis, assume Pat's tax rate on income is 28%. After paying taxes of $8,400 (.28 × $30,000) and $2,000 for insurance, Pat has $19,600 ($30,000 – $8,400 – $2,000) for his other living needs.

If Pat's employer reduced Pat's salary by $2,000 (to $28,000) but paid his insurance premiums, Pat's tax liability would be only $7,840 ($28,000 × .28). Thus, Pat would have $20,160 ($28,000 – $7,840) to meet his other living needs. The change in the compensation plan would save Pat $560 ($20,160 – $19,600). ▼

Similarly, employees must often incur expenses for child care and parking. The employee can have more income for other uses if the employer pays these costs for the employee but reduces the employee's salary by the cost of the benefits.

The use of cafeteria plans has increased dramatically in recent years. These plans allow employees to tailor their benefits to meet their individual situations. Thus, where both spouses in a married couple are working, duplications of benefits can be avoided and other needed benefits can often be added. If less than all of the employee's allowance is spent, the employee can receive cash.

The meals and lodging exclusion enables employees to receive from their employer what they ordinarily must purchase with after-tax dollars. Although the requirements that the employee live and take his or her meals on the employer's premises limit the tax planning opportunities, the exclusion is an important factor in the employee's compensation in certain situations, (e.g., hotels, motels, restaurants, farms, and ranches).

The employees' discount provision is especially important for manufacturers and wholesalers. Employees of manufacturers can avoid tax on the manufacturer's, wholesaler's, and retailer's markups. The wholesaler's employees can avoid tax on an amount equal to the wholesale and retail markups.

It should be recognized that the exclusion of benefits is generally available only to employees. Proprietors and partners must pay tax on the same benefits their employees receive tax-free. By incorporating and becoming an employee of the corporation, the former proprietor or partner can also receive these tax-exempt benefits. Thus, the availability of employee benefits is a consideration in the decision to incorporate.

INVESTMENT INCOME

Tax-exempt state and local government bonds are almost irresistible investments for many high-income taxpayers. To realize the maximum benefit from the exemption, the investor can purchase zero coupon bonds. Like Series EE U.S. government savings bonds, these investments pay interest only at maturity. The advantage of the zero coupon feature is that the investor can earn tax-exempt interest on the accumulated principal and interest. If the investor purchases a bond that pays the interest each year, the interest received may be such a small amount that an additional tax-exempt investment cannot be made. In addition, reinvesting the interest may entail transaction costs (broker's fees). The zero coupon feature avoids these problems.

Series EE U.S. government savings bonds can earn tax-exempt interest if the bond proceeds are used for qualified higher education expenses. Many taxpayers can foresee these expenditures being made for their children's educations. In deciding whether to invest in the bonds, however, the investor must take into account the income limitations for excluding the interest from gross income.

KEY TERMS

Accident and health benefits, 5–15

Cafeteria plan, 5–19

Compensatory damages, 5–11

De minimis fringes, 5–22

Death benefits, 5–7

Educational savings bonds, 5–30

Foreign earned income exclusion, 5–26

Gift, 5–4

Life insurance proceeds, 5–5

No-additional-cost service, 5–20

Punitive damages, 5–12

Qualified employee discount, 5–21

Qualified real property business indebtedness, 5–32

Qualified transportation fringes, 5–23

Qualified tuition reduction plan, 5–10

Scholarship, 5–9

Tax benefit rule, 5–31

Working condition fringes, 5–22

PROBLEM MATERIALS

DISCUSSION QUESTIONS

1. In 1993, Grape Corporation constructed a building on property it leased on a long-term basis. In 1995, Grape went bankrupt and forfeited the improvements to the owner of the land. In 1996, the owner sold the land. When does the landlord realize income from the improvements made by Grape?

2. Hazel made gifts to her three nephews. The first nephew, Al, received $10,000 cash during Hazel's lifetime. The second nephew, Bob, received $10,000 as a bequest when Hazel died. The third nephew, Carl, was the beneficiary of a $10,000 life insurance policy that Hazel purchased for $4,000. Are Al, Bob, and Carl required to include the amounts they received in gross income?

3. Violet Company gave $500 to each household in the community that had suffered a flood loss. The purpose of the payments was to help the flood victims. If some of the recipients are employees of Violet Company, can the employees exclude the payments from gross income?

4. Matt's truck was stalled on the side of the road. Abby stopped to help and called Al, who agreed to repair the truck for $75. Matt paid Al $75 and Abby $25. The payment to Al was made because of a contractual obligation and therefore is not a gift. The payment to Abby was not made because of a contractual obligation. Does this mean that the payment Abby received is a gift?

5. What are the two principal tax benefits of buying life insurance that has a cash surrender value?

6. Daryl took out a $10,000 life insurance policy on the life of his brother, Dave, a daredevil stunt driver. Daryl's other brother, Larry, similarly took out a $10,000 policy on Dave. Larry could not keep up with the premium payments and sold the policy to Dave's new wife for "what he had in it" (i.e., premium payments of $1,000.) If Dave were to die now, how much of the insurance proceeds of $10,000 would be taxable to Daryl, to Larry, and to Dave's wife?

7. Black Corporation purchased a $1 million insurance policy on the life of the company's president. The company paid $100,000 of premiums, the president died, and the company collected the face amount of the policy. How much must Black Corporation include in gross income?

8. Gilda, a cash basis taxpayer, died while employed by Swan Corporation. Swan paid Gilda's husband $3,000 in sales commissions that Gilda had earned. The company also paid him $7,000 pursuant to a policy of making payments to the spouse of a deceased employee. Swan used the proceeds of a life insurance policy it owned on Gilda's life to make the payment to her husband. Is any of the $10,000 Gilda's husband received subject to income tax?

9. Yellow Company provides its employees with $10,000 group term life insurance. Red Company does not provide insurance but generally gives the family of a deceased employee $10,000. Compare the tax consequences of the insured and uninsured plans.

10. James received an academic scholarship to State University. Under the scholarship agreement, he received tuition ($1,500), books ($400), and room and board ($5,000). What is James's gross income from the scholarship?

11. José is a graduate assistant at State University. He receives $7,000 a year in salary. In addition, tuition of $4,000 is waived. The tuition waiver is available to all full- and part-time employees. The fair market value of José's services is $11,000. How much is José required to include in his gross income?

12. Sara was the victim of sexual harassment and collected the following from her employer: $15,000 for lost wages and $50,000 in punitive damages. How much of the damage award of $65,000 must Sara include in her gross income?

13. Holly works in a factory and earns $400 per week. Jill usually works in an office, but she was unable to work for one week because of an infected paper cut sustained at work. Jill collected $400 in workers' compensation as a result of her injury. Is the $400 Holly and Jill each received treated the same for income tax purposes?

14. Pam was hit by an automobile driven by a person under the influence of alcohol. Although Pam's injuries were minor (she did not go to the hospital or visit a doctor), she has recurring nightmares about the accident. Over the past 12 months, she has spent more than $6,000 for psychological therapy. Although she had problems before the accident, the recurring nightmares brought her to the realization that she needed professional help. Pam has not filed a lawsuit, but the driver of the automobile, who is very wealthy, "wants to do the right thing." The driver has offered Pam $30,000 as a settlement. He believes that this is more than she is entitled to under the law, but feels a great deal of remorse about all of the grief he has caused her. Pam is concerned about the tax consequences of the settlement offer. What are the relevant tax issues raised by these facts?

15. Wes purchases an accident and health insurance plan that was advertised in the Sunday newspaper. The annual premiums are $400. During the year, Wes received payments of $1,200 under the plan.
    a. How much of the $1,200 must Wes include in his gross income?
    b. Would the tax consequences differ if the $1,200 represented amounts paid by the insurance company to replace lost wages while Wes was hospitalized?

16. What nontaxable fringe benefits are available to employees that are not available to partners and proprietors?

17. How does one determine if the meals and lodging supplied by the employer are to serve a valid business purpose? Is the tax treatment of meals and lodging affected if the employer advertises that the meals and lodging provided are one of the employees' fringe benefits?

18. Paula is employed by a telemarketing firm that pays a fixed amount for unlimited long-distance telephone calls. Employees are allowed to use the toll-free line for 5

minutes each month at no charge to the employee. The normal charge for the calls Paula made during the year was $75. How much is Paula required to include in gross income?

19. Gary is employed by Pelican, Inc., an automobile manufacturing company. Pelican sells Gary a new automobile at company cost of $12,000. The price charged a dealer would have been $14,000, and the retail price of the automobile is $17,000. What is Gary's gross income from the purchase of the automobile?

20. Jane works at a bakery and is allowed to take home bread that could not be sold during the day. The bakery gives the day-old bread to the employees because it has no other use for the goods. Is Jane required to recognize income as a result of receiving the bread?

21. Eagle Life Insurance Company pays its employees $.25 per mile for driving their personal automobiles to and from work. The company reimburses each employee who rides the bus $45 a month for the cost of a pass. Tom collected $60 for his automobile mileage, and Ted received $45 as reimbursement for the cost of a bus pass.
    a. What are the effects of the above on Tom and Ted's gross income?
    b. Assume that Tom and Ted are in the 28% marginal tax bracket, and the actual before-tax cost for Tom to drive to and from work is $.25 per mile. What are Tom and Ted's after-tax costs of commuting to and from work?

22. Zack works for Blue Pest Control, which offers a discount on its extermination services to its employees: officers receive a 50% discount, and all other employees receive a 30% discount. Zack, who is not an officer, had the company treat his home for termites and paid $280 for the service that is normally priced at $400. Zack's supervisor, an officer, had her home treated for carpenter ants and paid $500 for the service that is normally priced at $1,000. How much, if any, will Zack and his supervisor have to include in gross income for the services they received?

23. Flamingo, Inc., has implemented employee benefit plans in each of five broad classes of employee fringe benefits: (1) no-additional-cost services, (2) qualified employee discounts, (3) working condition fringes, (4) *de minimis* fringes, and (5) qualified transportation fringes. Eligibility requirements discriminate in favor of the company's officers. Which of the following items best describes the tax effect of each of the five classes of employee fringe benefits for an officer in Flamingo?
    a. None of the benefit is taxable.
    b. Only the discriminatory portion of the benefit is taxable.
    c. All of the benefit is taxable.

    Support your answer with discussion.

24. Several of Egret Company's employees have asked the company to create a hiking trail that employees could use during their lunch hours. The company owns vacant land that is being held for future expansion, but would have to spend approximately $50,000 if it were to make a trail. Nonemployees would be allowed to use the facility as part of the company's effort to build strong community support. What are the relevant tax issues for the employees?

25. Marla worked for Robin Industries, Inc., and earned $58,000 in 1996. She spent 345 days out of the United States during 1996 working in a foreign country. Marla wants to exclude her foreign-earned income from U.S. taxation if possible. Does Marla qualify for doing so? If she does, how much of her income will be taxable in the United States?

26. Falcon Corporation is opening a branch in Kazonbi, an African country that does not levy an income tax on citizens of foreign countries. Carl, a U.S. citizen, is considering two offers from his employer, Falcon Corporation. He can work for 6 months in Kazonbi and 6 months in the United States and receive a salary of $4,000 per month, or he can work in Kazonbi for 12 months at the same monthly salary. Carl would like to spend as much time in the United States as possible and prefers the first alternative. However, he asks your advice as to how income taxes might affect his decision.

27. Donna and George are married, file a joint return, and are in the 36% marginal tax bracket. They would like to save for their child's education. What would be the advantage of buying State of Virginia bonds as compared to buying Series EE U.S. government bonds?

28. Maria owned 100 shares of common stock in Roadrunner Corporation when the company declared a 100% stock dividend. She did not have the option to receive cash. Is the fair market value of the 100 shares received by Maria included in her gross income?

29. What special tax benefits are available to students and their parents?

30. In 1996, Mary received a $2,000 sales commission. However, in 1997, her employer discovered that Mary should have received only a $1,500 commission in 1996. Therefore, the employer withheld $500 from Mary's 1997 commission. Mary's standard deduction and personal exemption for 1996 exceeded her gross income. What effect would the tax benefit rule have on Mary's gross income for 1997?

31. How does the tax treatment of a corporation's income generated by the retirement of bonds for less than book value (issue price plus amortized discount or less amortized premium) differ from the income derived from a shareholder's forgiveness of the corporation's indebtedness?

32. Ida purchased a farm. She gave the seller $50,000 cash and an 8% note for $150,000. When the principal on the note had been reduced to $120,000, the seller agreed to accept $100,000 in retirement of the debt. The creditor made the offer because interest rates had increased substantially. Ida was not undergoing bankruptcy and was not insolvent. Did Ida realize income from retiring the debt and, if so, is she required to include the amount in her gross income?

33. Harry has experienced financial difficulties as a result of his struggling business. He has been behind on his mortgage payments for the last six months. The mortgage holder, who is a friend of Harry's, has offered to accept $80,000 in full payment of the $100,000 owed on the mortgage and payable over the next 10 years. The interest rate of the mortgage is 7%, and the market rate is now 8%. What tax issues are raised by the creditor's offer?

PROBLEMS

34. Determine whether the following may be excluded from gross income as gifts, bequests, scholarships, prizes, or life insurance proceeds:
    a. Uncle told Nephew, "Come live with me and take care of me in my old age and you can have all my property after my death." Nephew complied with Uncle's request. Uncle's will made Nephew sole beneficiary of the estate.
    b. Uncle told Nephew, "If you study hard and make the dean's list this year, I will pay your tuition for the following year." Nephew made the dean's list, and Uncle paid the tuition.
    c. Uncle told Nephew, "If you make the dean's list this year, I will pay you $500." Nephew made the dean's list, and Uncle paid the $500.
    d. Diane cashed in her life insurance contract and collected $10,000. She had paid premiums totaling $7,000.
    e. Fred received $500 from his employer to pay the medical expenses of Fred's child. The payment was not part of a medical reimbursement plan, and the employer made the payment out of compassion.

35. Determine the taxable life insurance proceeds in the following cases:
    a. When José died, his wife collected $50,000 on a group term insurance policy purchased by José's employer. José had never included the premiums in gross income.
    b. The Cardinal Software Company purchased an insurance policy on the life of a key employee. The company paid $50,000 in premiums and collected $500,000 of insurance proceeds.

c. When Barbara died, she and her husband owed $15,000 on a loan. Under the terms of the loan, Barbara was required to purchase life insurance to pay the creditor the amount due at the date of Barbara's death. The creditor collected from the life insurance company the amount due at the time of Barbara's death. Is the creditor required to recognize income from the collection of the life insurance proceeds?

36. The Egret Company, which is in the 40% (combined Federal and state) marginal tax bracket, estimated that if its current president should die, the company would incur $200,000 in costs to find a suitable replacement. In addition, profits on various projects the president is responsible for would likely decrease by $300,000. The president has recommended that Egret purchase a $500,000 life insurance policy. How much insurance should the company carry on the life of its president to compensate for the after-tax loss that would result from the president's death, assuming the $200,000 costs of finding a president are deductible and the lost profits would have been taxable?

37. Determine whether the taxpayer has gross income in each of the following situations:
    a. Jim is a waiter in a restaurant. The rule of thumb is that a customer should leave the waiter a tip equal to 15% of the customer's bill for food and beverages. Jim collected $6,000 in tips during the year.
    b. Tara works at a grocery store, bagging groceries and carrying them to the customers' automobiles. Her employer posts a sign saying that the employees are paid by the hour and the customer is not expected to tip them. Tara received $1,800 in tips from customers.
    c. Sheila worked at a hotel. Her home was damaged by a fire. Sheila's employer allowed her to stay at the hotel for no charge until she could return to her home. The normal charge for the room Sheila occupied during this period was $500, and the hotel had several vacant rooms.

38. Donald died at age 35. He was married and had four minor children. Donald's employer, Lark Painting Company, made payments to his wife as follows:

Donald's accrued salary at date of death	$4,000
Family death benefits under long-standing company policy ($2,000 is paid to the spouse and $1,500 is paid to each child of a deceased employee)	2,000
A payment authorized by the board of directors to help his wife pay debts accumulated by Donald	7,000

In addition, Donald's wife was the beneficiary of her husband's life insurance policy of $50,000. Lark Painting Company had paid for the policy. Donald had excluded all of the premiums paid by the employer from gross income as group term life insurance. His wife left the insurance proceeds with the insurance company and elected to receive an annuity of $4,000 each year for life. Her life expectancy is 40 years. She collected one $4,000 payment at the end of the current year. A joint return was filed in the year of Donald's death. Which of the above amounts must be included in gross income?

39. Walt made the all-state football team during his junior and senior years in high school. He accepted an athletic scholarship from State University. The scholarship provided the following:

Tuition and fees	$4,000
Room and board	2,500
Books and supplies	500

Determine the effect of the scholarship on Walt's gross income.

40. Alejandro was awarded an academic scholarship to State University. He received $5,000 in August and $6,000 in December 1996. Alejandro had enough personal savings to pay all expenses as they came due. Alejandro's expenditures for the relevant period were as follows:

Tuition, August 1996	$2,900
Tuition, December 1996	3,200
Room and board	
August–December 1996	3,000
January–May 1997	2,400
Books and educational supplies	
August–December 1996	800
January–May 1997	950

Determine the effect on Alejandro's gross income for 1996 and 1997.

41. Determine the taxpayer's taxable damages in each of the following cases:
    a. Orange Corporation collected $500,000 for damages to its business reputation.
    b. Don collected $100,000 in lost wages caused by age discrimination by his employer. Under the relevant law, a successful plaintiff can recover only lost wages.
    c. Kirby was injured in an automobile accident and collected $10,000 for loss of the use of his left arm, $15,000 for pain and suffering, $9,000 in lost wages, $5,000 for medical expenses, and $10,000 of punitive damages. Kirby had deducted none of the medical expenses.
    d. Nell received $10,000 of damages for invasion of her privacy by a photographer and $5,000 of punitive damages.
    e. Joanne received compensatory damages of $50,000 and punitive damages of $200,000 from a cosmetic surgeon who botched her nose job.

42. Tom was accused of shoplifting. He sued the store and collected $1,000 for actual damages to his personal reputation and $10,000 in punitive damages for the outrageous behavior by the store's security guard. Tom's wife, Jane, slipped on a banana peel in the same store and collected $5,000 in medical expenses she incurred (the expenses were not deducted on their return) and $1,500 in lost wages (wages she would have earned if she had not been injured). Must any of these amounts be included in Tom and Jane's income reported on a joint return?

43. Rex, age 45, is an officer of Blue Company, which provided him with the following nondiscriminatory fringe benefits in 1996:
    a. Hospitalization insurance for Rex and his dependents. The cost of coverage for Rex was $450, and the additional cost for Rex's dependents was $400.
    b. Reimbursement of $700 from an uninsured medical reimbursement plan available to all employees.
    c. Group term life insurance protection of $120,000. (Each employee received coverage equal to twice his or her annual salary.)
    d. Salary continuation payments of $2,600 while Rex was hospitalized for an illness.

    While Rex was ill, he collected $1,600 on a salary continuation insurance policy he had purchased. Determine the amounts Rex must include in gross income.

44. The UVW Union and HON Corporation are negotiating contract terms. Assume the union members are in the 28% marginal tax bracket and all benefits are provided on a nondiscriminatory basis. Write a letter to the UVW Union members explaining the tax consequences of the options discussed below. The union's address is 905 Spruce Street, Washington, D.C. 20227.
    a. The company would impose a $100 deductible on medical insurance benefits. Most employees incur more than $100 each year in medical expenses.
    b. Employees would get an additional paid holiday with the same annual income (the same pay but less work).
    c. An employee who did not need health insurance (because the employee's spouse works and receives family coverage) would be allowed to receive the cash value of the coverage.

45. Sally and Bill are married and file joint returns. In 1996, Bill, an accountant, has a salary of $75,000, and Sally receives a salary of $25,000 as an apartment manager. What are the tax consequences of the following benefits that Bill and Sally's employers provide?
    a. Bill receives a reimbursement of $5,000 for child care expenses. Sally and Bill have three children who are not yet school age.
    b. Bill and Sally are provided a free membership at a local fitness and exercise club that allows them to attend three aerobic exercise sessions per week. The value of this type of membership is $450.
    c. Bill is provided free parking at work. The value of the parking is $1,500 per year.
    d. Sally is provided with a free apartment. Living in this apartment is a condition of her employment. Similar apartments rent for $1,000 per month.

46. Determine the taxpayer's gross income for each of the following:
    a. Alice is the manager of a plant. The company owns a house one mile from the plant (rental value of $6,000) that Alice is allowed to occupy.
    b. Pam works for an insurance company that allows employees to eat in the cafeteria for $.50 a meal. Generally, the cost to the insurance company of producing a meal is $5.00, and a comparable meal could be purchased for $4.00. Pam ate 150 meals in the cafeteria during the year.
    c. Wade is a Methodist minister and receives a housing allowance of $600 per month from his church. Wade is buying his home and uses the $600 to make house payments ($450) and to pay utilities ($150).
    d. Floyd is a college professor and lives in campus housing. He is not charged rent. The fair market value of the house is $100,000, and the annual rental value is $7,200.

47. Does the taxpayer recognize gross income in the following situations?
    a. Ann is a registered nurse working in a community hospital. She is not required to take her lunch on the hospital premises, but she can eat in the cafeteria at no charge. The hospital adopted this policy to encourage employees to stay on the premises and be available in case of emergencies. During the year, Ann ate most of her meals on the premises. The total value of those meals was $750.
    b. Ira is the manager of a hotel. His employer will allow him to live in one of the rooms rent-free or to receive a $600 per month cash allowance for rent. Ira elected to live in the hotel.
    c. Seth is a forest ranger and lives in his employer's cabin in the forest. He is required to live there, and because there are no restaurants nearby, the employer supplies Seth with groceries that he cooks and eats on the premises.
    d. Rocky is a partner in the BAR Ranch (a partnership). He is the full-time manager of the ranch. BAR has a business purpose for Rocky's living on the ranch.

48. Betty is considering taking an early retirement offered by her employer. She would receive $1,500 per month, indexed for inflation. However, she would no longer be able to use the company's health facilities, and she would be required to pay her hospitalization insurance of $6,000 each year. Betty and her husband will file a joint return and take the standard deduction. She currently receives a salary of $37,500 a year, and her employer pays for all of her hospitalization insurance. If she retires, Betty would not be able to use her former employer's exercise facilities because of the commuting distance. She would like to continue to exercise, however, and will therefore join a health club at a cost of $50 per month. Betty and her husband have other sources of income and are in and will remain in the 28% marginal tax bracket. She currently pays Social Security taxes of 7.65% on her salary, but her retirement pay would not be subject to this tax. She will earn about $9,000 a year from a part-time job. Betty would like to know whether she should accept the early retirement offer.

49. Sparrow, Inc., has a wide variety of fringe benefits available to its employees. However, not all of the employees actually need the benefits. For example, some employees have working spouses whose employers provide health insurance benefits for the employee's families. In addition, Sparrow reimburses up to $5,000 for child care costs, but not all of the employees have children. Sparrow's management has asked you to write a

memo explaining how the company can accommodate the varying needs of its employees at the lowest after-tax cost to the employee. Sparrow's address is 300 Harbor Drive, Vermillion, SD 57069.

50. Ed is employed by FUN Bowling Lanes, Inc. Determine Ed's gross income in each of the following situations:
   a. Ed's children are allowed to use the lanes without charge. Each child can also bring a friend without charge. This benefit is available to all employees. During the year, the children bowled 100 games, and the usual charge was $1.50 per game. Friends of Ed's children bowled 90 games.
   b. The company has a lunch counter. Ed is allowed to take home the leftover donuts each night. The company's cost was $450, and the value of the donuts Ed took home was $100.
   c. The company pays Ed's subscription to *Bowling Lanes Management,* a monthly journal.

51. Thrush Corporation has 10 employees and is considering offering group hospitalization benefits. The average cost is $3,000 per employee per year. Three of the employees are shareholders and are in the 40% (combined Federal and state) income tax bracket; they currently pay for their own health insurance. The corporation is in the 34% marginal tax bracket. The remaining 7 employees who are not shareholders are considering taking a $1,500 per year pay cut in exchange for the hospitalization benefits. These employees are in the 30% (combined Federal and state) income tax bracket.
   a. Evaluate this proposal for the 7 employees.
   b. Write a memo explaining the after-tax effects on the employees and the corporation of providing health insurance to all employees. Thrush's address is 500 Fern Avenue, Scranton, PA 18509.

52. Snowbird Corporation would like you to review its employee fringe benefits program with regard to the effects of the plan on the company's president (Polly), who is also the majority shareholder:
   a. All employees receive free tickets to State University football games. Polly is seldom able to attend the games and usually gives her tickets to her nephew. The cost of Polly's tickets for the year was $75.
   b. The company pays all parking fees for its officers but not for other employees. The company paid $1,200 for Polly's parking for the year.
   c. Employees are allowed to use the copy machine for personal purposes as long as the privilege is not abused. Polly is president of a trade association and made extensive use of the copy machine to prepare mailings to members of the association. The cost of the copies was $900.
   d. The company is in the household moving business. Employees are allowed to ship goods without charge whenever there is excess space on a truck. Polly purchased a dining room suite for her daughter. Company trucks delivered the furniture to the daughter. Normal freight charges would have been $600.
   e. The company has a storage facility for household goods. Officers are allowed a 20% discount on charges for storing their goods. All other employees are allowed a 10% discount. Polly's discounts for the year totaled $400.

53. Eli works for a company that operates a cruise ship. All employees are allowed to take a one-week cruise each year at no cost to the employee. The employee is provided with a room, meals, and general recreation on the ship. Determine the tax consequences of Eli accepting a trip under the following assumptions:
   a. Eli must travel on a standby basis; that is, Eli can travel only if the ship is not completely booked. The room Eli occupies has maid service, and the sheets and towels are changed each day.
   b. Eli takes his meals with the other customers who pay a fixed amount for the cruise that includes meals and lodging.
   c. The recreation consists of the use of the pool, dancing, and bingo games.
   d. All guests must pay for their drinks and snacks between meals, but Eli and the other employees are given a 20% discount.

e. Employees at Eli's level and above are provided with free parking at the pier. Parking for the week would cost $70. This group comprises about 25% of all employees of the company.

54. George, a U.S. citizen, is employed by Pelican, Inc., a global company. His salary for both 1996 and 1997 is $80,000. George's first foreign assignment is to St. Petersburg, Russia, and began on March 1, 1996. He spent 15 days in the United States in December and returned to St. Petersburg and worked there until February 28, 1997. He went back to St. Petersburg one more time, spending the month of May 1997 there to train his successor. What is the amount of salary that George must include in his gross income for 1996 and 1997, assuming he claims the maximum exclusion?

55. Determine Hazel's gross income from the following receipts for the year:

Gain on sale of Augusta County bonds	$ 600
Interest on U.S. government savings bonds	900
Interest on state income tax refund	150
Interest on Augusta County bonds	900
Patronage dividend from Potato Growers Cooperative	1,700

The patronage dividend was received in March of the current year for amounts paid and deducted in the previous year as expenses of Hazel's profitable cash basis farming business.

56. Determine Jack's gross income from the following items:
   a. Jack owns 100 shares of Roadrunner Company common stock. The company has a dividend reinvestment plan. Under the plan, Jack can receive an $18 cash dividend or an additional share of stock with a fair market of $18. Jack elected to take the stock.
   b. Jack owns 100 shares of Bat Corporation. The company declared a dividend, and Jack was to receive an additional share of the company's common stock with a fair market value of $18. Jack did not have the option to receive cash. However, a management group announced a plan to repurchase all available shares for $18 each. The offer was part of a takeover defense.
   c. Jack also collected $125 on a corporate debenture. The corporation had been in bankruptcy for several years. Jack had correctly deducted the cost of the bond in a prior year because the bankruptcy judge had informed the bondholders they would not receive anything in the final liquidation. Later the company collected on an unanticipated claim and had the funds to make partial payment on the bonds.

57. Lynn Schwartz recently inherited $25,000. She is considering using the money to finance a college education for her 5-year-old child. Lynn does not expect her gross income to ever exceed $40,000 a year. She is very concerned with the safety of the principal and has decided to invest the $25,000 in Series EE U.S. government savings bonds. The bonds earn 5% interest each year. At the end of 13 years, when Lynn's child is 18 and ready to go to college, the bonds will be worth $44,375. This would pay a substantial portion of the cost of a 4-year college education at that time. Write a letter to Lynn advising her as to whether the Series EE bonds will be an appropriate investment for financing her child's college education, including whether the bonds should be purchased in Lynn's name or in the child's name (with Lynn as custodian). Lynn's address is 100 Myrtle Cove, Fairfield, CT 06432.

58. How does the tax benefit rule apply in the following cases?
   a. In 1996, Wilma paid Vera $5,000 for locating a potential client. The deal fell through, and in 1997, Vera refunded the $5,000 to Wilma.
   b. In 1996, Wilma paid an attorney $300 for services in connection with a title search. Because the attorney was negligent, Wilma incurred some additional costs in acquiring the land. In 1997, the attorney refunded his $300 fee to Wilma.
   c. In 1996, Wilma received a $90 dividend with respect to 1996 premiums on her life insurance policy.

d. In 1997, a cash basis farmer received a $400 patronage dividend with respect to 1996 purchases of cattle feed.

59. Mary and her two sisters, Cary and Gladys, were injured in a car accident in 1996, and each sustained injuries requiring $1,200 in medical expenses. Because the claim was not settled until 1997, each sister had completed her 1996 income tax return before the settlement. Mary does not itemize deductions. Cary does itemize deductions, but the $1,200 medical expense did not exceed the 7.5%-of-AGI threshold; consequently, the deduction did not result in a reduction of her tax liability. Gladys also itemizes deductions. Because of other medical expenses, the $1,200 expense pushed her $800 over the 7.5%-of-AGI threshold. Therefore, Gladys benefited from the deduction by having her taxes reduced. In 1997, each sister received a $1,200 insurance settlement for her injuries. How much of the $1,200 settlement received does each sister need to include in gross income?

60. Fran, who is in the 36% tax bracket, recently collected $100,000 on a life insurance policy she carried on her father. She currently owes $120,000 on her personal residence and $120,000 on business property. National Bank holds the mortgage on both pieces of property and has agreed to accept $100,000 in complete satisfaction of either mortgage. The interest rate on the mortgages is 8%, and both mortgages are payable over 10 years. What would be the tax consequences of each of the following alternatives, assuming Fran currently deducts the mortgage interest on her tax return?
  a. Retire the mortgage on the residence.
  b. Retire the mortgage on the business property.

  Which alternative should Fran select?

61. Robin Company is experiencing financial troubles and is considering negotiating the following with its creditors. Determine the tax consequences to Robin of the following plan:
  a. The Motor Finance Company will cancel $1,500 in accrued interest. Robin had deducted the interest in the prior year. Motor Finance Company will also reduce the principal on the note by $1,000. The note financed the purchase of equipment from a local dealer.
  b. The Trust Land Company, which sold Robin land and buildings, will reduce the mortgage on the building by $15,000.
  c. Ridge, the sole shareholder in the corporation, will cancel a $50,000 receivable from the corporation in exchange for additional stock.

CUMULATIVE PROBLEMS

62. Oliver W. Hand was divorced from Sandra D. Hand on May 12, 1995. On September 6, 1996, Oliver married Beulah Crane. Oliver and Beulah will file a joint return for 1996. Oliver's Social Security number is 262–60–3814. Beulah's number is 259–68–4184, and she will adopt "Hand" as her married name. The Hands live at 210 Mason Drive, Atlanta, GA 30304. Sandra's Social Security number is 219–74–1361.

  Oliver is 50 and is employed by Atom, Inc., as an electrical engineer. His salary for 1996 was $60,000. Beulah is 35 and earned $37,000 as a marriage counselor in 1996. She was employed by Family Counselors, Inc.

  The divorce agreement required Oliver to make 132 monthly payments to Sandra. The payments are $1,200 per month for 84 months, at which time the payments decrease to $1,000 per month. Oliver and Sandra have a 14-year-old daughter, Daisy Hand. If Daisy should die before she attains age 21, Oliver's remaining payments to Sandra would be reduced to $1,000 per month. Sandra was granted custody of Daisy and can document that she provided $2,000 of support for Daisy. Oliver made 12 payments in 1996.

  Oliver's employer provided him with group term life insurance coverage in the amount of $100,000 in 1996.

Beulah's employer provided Beulah with free parking in a parking garage adjacent to the office building where Beulah works. The monthly charge to the general public is $65.

Oliver received dividends of $40 on Red Corporation stock he owned before marriage, and Beulah received dividends of $50 on her separately owned White Corporation stock. They received dividends of $600 on jointly owned Blue Corporation stock, which they acquired after marriage. Oliver and Beulah live in a common law state.

Combined itemized deductions for Oliver and Beulah in 1996 were as follows:

State income taxes withheld		
Oliver	$3,200	
Beulah	1,200	$4,400
Real estate taxes on residence		1,500
Home mortgage interest (paid to Atlanta Federal Savings and Loan)		4,020
Cash contributions to church		900

In 1996, Beulah received a refund of 1995 state income taxes of $700. She had deducted state income taxes withheld as an itemized deduction on her 1995 return. Oliver received a $500 refund on his 1995 state income taxes. He had used the standard deduction in 1995.

Additional information:

- Oliver's employer withheld Federal income tax of $10,650 and $4,590 of FICA (Social Security) tax. Beulah's employer withheld $4,580 of Federal income tax and $2,831 of FICA tax.

Part 1—Tax Computation

Compute the Hands' net tax payable (or refund due) for 1996. Suggested software (if available): *TurboTax* or *MacInTax.*

Part 2—Tax Planning

Assume the Hands came to you in early December of 1996 seeking tax planning advice for 1996 and 1997. They provide you with the following information:

a. All the facts previously presented will be essentially the same in 1997 except for the items described in (b), (c), (d), and (e).
b. Oliver inherited $100,000 from his mother on December 1. He will use part of his inheritance to pay off the mortgage on the Hands' residence on January 3, 1997. Consequently, there will be no mortgage interest expense in 1997.
c. Oliver expects a 4% salary increase in 1997, and Beulah expects a 10% increase.
d. The Hands have pledged to contribute $2,400 to their church in 1997 (as opposed to $900 contributed in 1996). However, they could use Oliver's inherited funds to pay the pledge before the end of 1996 if you advise them to do so to achieve an overall tax savings.
e. The Hands acquired 100 shares of ABC Corporation stock on July 5, 1996, at a total cost of $2,000. The value of the stock has increased rapidly, and it is now worth $5,000. The Hands plan to sell the stock and ask whether they should sell it in 1996 or wait until 1997.

Advise the Hands as to the appropriate tax planning strategy for 1996 and 1997. Support your recommendations by computing their tax liabilities for 1996 and 1997 considering the various available alternatives. Suggested software (if available): *TurboTax* or *MacInTax.*

63. Archie S. Monroe (Social Security number 363–33–1411) is 35 years old and is married to Annie B. Monroe (Social Security number 259–68–4284). The Monroes live at 215

Adams Dr., Thor, VA 24317. They file a joint return and have two dependent children (Barry and Betty). In 1996, Archie and Annie had the following transactions:

a. Salary received by Archie from Allen Steel Company (Archie is vice president).	$84,000
b. Interest received on jointly owned State of Nebraska bonds.	9,000
c. Group term life insurance premiums paid by Archie's employer (coverage of $72,000).	250
d. Annual increment in the value of Series EE government savings bonds (the Monroes have not previously included the accrued amounts in gross income).	450
e. Taxable dividends received from Dove Steel Company, a U.S. corporation (the stock was jointly owned). Of the $6,300 in dividends, $1,000 was mailed on December 31, 1996, and received by Archie and Annie on January 4, 1997.	6,300
f. Award received by Annie for outstanding community service in Thor.	1,000
g. Proceeds from sale of Pigeon, Inc., stock on November 3, 1996. The adjusted basis of the stock, which had been purchased on June 1, 1996, is $5,000.	7,000
h. Alimony payments to Archie's former wife (Rosa T. Monroe, Social Security number 800–60–2580) under a divorce decree.	12,000
i. Itemized deductions:	
State income tax	2,150
Real estate tax on residence	2,300
Interest on personal residence (paid to Thor Federal Savings)	3,800
Cash contribution to church	900
j. Federal income tax withheld.	12,500

Part 1—Tax Computation

Compute the Monroes' net tax payable (or refund due) for 1996. Suggested software (if available): *TurboTax* or *MacInTax*.

Part 2—Tax Planning

The Monroes plan to sell 200 shares of AXE stock they purchased on July 12, 1984, at a cost of $20,000. The stock is worth $11,000 in December 1996, and the Monroes' broker predicts a continued decline in value. Annie plans to resume her career as a model in 1997, and her earnings will move the Monroes into the 31% bracket. How much Federal income tax will the Monroes save for 1996 if they sell the stock in 1996? Should they sell the stock in 1996 or 1997? Write a letter to the Monroes that contains your advice and prepare a memo for the tax files. Suggested software (if available): *TurboTax* or *MacInTax*.

RESEARCH PROBLEMS

Note: ***West's Federal Taxation on CD-ROM*** *can be used in preparing solutions to the Research Problems. Alternatively, tax research materials contained in a standard tax library can be used.*

Research Problem 1. David is the minister at the First Baptist Church. As part of his compensation, David receives an $800 per month housing allowance. David is purchasing his residence, and he uses the $800 each month to make mortgage and property tax payments. The mortgage interest and property taxes are deducted (as itemized deductions) on David's tax return. The examining IRS agent thinks David would be enjoying a double benefit if the housing allowance is excluded and the itemized deductions are allowed. In addition, the agent contends that the housing allowance exclusion should apply only where the church provides the residence or the minister uses the funds to pay rent. Therefore, the agent maintains that David should include in gross income the $800 received each month. David has asked your assistance in this matter. Write a letter to David that contains your advice and prepare a memo for the tax files.

Research Problem 2. Dan was recently hired as manager of Fertile Farm, Inc. Dan is required to live in the employer's house on the farm. Dan and the employer are trying to decide how to arrange terms with the electric company. The employer would like the utility account to be in Dan's name, but with the employer reimbursing Dan $200 each month. The $200 should be adequate to cover all charges. The employer requests this arrangement because the previous manager established the account in the company's name and left town without paying the bill. Dan has asked your tax advice on the matter.

Partial list of research aids:
Rev.Rul. 68–579, 1968–2 C.B. 61.

Research Problem 3. Mega City was experiencing cash flow problems. Therefore, the city offered property owners a 3% discount if they would pay their property taxes six months before the due date. Electric Utilities, Inc., took advantage of the offer and received a $65,000 discount. The company deducted the undiscounted amount of the taxes and excluded the discount from gross income. The company reasons that the discount represents interest on local government obligations and thus is nontaxable under § 103. Evaluate the company's position.

Research Problem 4. Snipe Company is closing one of its plants. The company's management is very concerned about employee morale at other plants. To minimize the damage to employee relations, the company has decided to pay the costs of "outplacement services" for the employees of the plant to be closed. The services include the use of a consultant in writing resumés, identifying potential employers, and writing to those employers. The company has asked your advice as to whether the employees would be required to include the costs of the services in their gross incomes.

TEAM PROJECT: ARTHUR ANDERSEN TAX CHALLENGE CASES

For more information on the Arthur Andersen Tax Challenge Cases, please refer to Chapter 1, page 1-38.

Information related to tax issues and problems that are discussed in this chapter may be found in the

Fields case on pages 9, 23, and 25
Miller case on pages 2, 3, 11, 13, 14, 15, 22, and 29

Read and analyze the case you have been assigned and *identify* any issues and problems that are related to material covered in this chapter. If the information provided in the case is complete, prepare answers for this part of the case at this time. If you need information that is contained in the later parts of the case, please write a memo summarizing the questions or problems so you can prepare a complete answer at a later date.

P • A • R • T

III

DEDUCTIONS

Part III presents the deduction component of the basic tax model. Deductions are classified as business versus nonbusiness, "for" versus "from," employee versus employer, active versus passive, and reimbursed versus unreimbursed. The effect of each of these classifications is analyzed. The presentation includes not only the deductions that are permitted, but also limitations and disallowances associated with deductions. Because deductions can exceed gross income, the treatment of losses is also included.

CHAPTER

6

Deductions and Losses: In General

LEARNING OBJECTIVES

After completing Chapter 6, you should be able to:

1. Differentiate between deductions *for* and *from* adjusted gross income and understand the relevance of the differentiation.
2. Describe the cash and accrual methods of accounting.
3. Apply the Internal Revenue Code deduction disallowance provisions associated with the following: public policy limitations, political activities, excessive executive compensation, investigation of business opportunities, hobby losses, vacation home rentals, payment of others' expenses, personal expenditures, capital expenditures, related-party transactions, and expenses related to tax-exempt income.
4. Identify tax planning opportunities for maximizing deductions and minimizing the disallowance of deductions.

CLASSIFICATION OF DEDUCTIBLE EXPENSES

1 LEARNING OBJECTIVE
Differentiate between deductions *for* and *from* adjusted gross income and understand the relevance of the differentiation.

The tax law has an all-inclusive definition of income; that is, income from whatever source derived is includible in gross income. Income cannot be excluded unless there is a specific statement to that effect in the Internal Revenue Code.

Similarly, deductions are disallowed unless a specific provision in the tax law permits them. The inclusive definition of income and the exclusive definition of deductions may not seem fair to taxpayers, but it is the structure of the tax law.

The courts have held that whether and to what extent deductions are allowed depends on legislative grace.[1] In other words, any exclusions from income and all deductions are gifts from Congress!

It is important to classify deductible expenses as **deductions for adjusted gross income** (AGI) or **deductions from adjusted gross income.** Deductions *for* AGI can be claimed whether or not the taxpayer itemizes. Deductions *from* AGI result in a tax benefit only if they exceed the taxpayer's standard deduction. If itemized deductions (*from* AGI) are less than the standard deduction, they provide no tax benefit.

EXAMPLE 1

Steve is a self-employed CPA. Ralph is one of Steve's employees. During the year, Steve and Ralph incur the following expenses:

	Steve	Ralph
Dues in American Institute of CPAs and Virginia Society of CPAs	$ 400	$ 300
Subscriptions to professional journals	500	200
Registration fees for tax conferences	800	800
	$1,700	$1,300

[1] *New Colonial Ice Co. v. Helvering*, 4 USTC ¶1292, 13 AFTR 1180, 54 S.Ct. 788 (USSC, 1934).

Steve does not reimburse any of his employees for dues, subscriptions, or educational programs.

Steve's expenses are classified as a deduction *for* AGI. Therefore, he can deduct the $1,700 on his Federal income tax return. Ralph's expenses are classified as deductions *from* AGI. Ralph will be able to benefit from the $1,300 of expenses on his Federal income tax return only if he itemizes deductions. If he takes the standard deduction instead, the $1,300 of expenses will have no effect on the calculation of his taxable income. Even if Ralph does itemize deductions, he must reduce the $1,300 of expenses, which are classified as miscellaneous itemized deductions, by 2% of his AGI. As this example illustrates, whether a deduction is classified as *for* AGI or *from* AGI can affect the benefit the taxpayer receives from the deduction. ▼

Deductions *for* AGI are also important in determining the *amount* of itemized deductions because many itemized deductions are limited to amounts in excess of specified percentages of AGI. Examples of itemized deductions that are limited by AGI are medical expenses and personal casualty losses. Itemized deductions that are deductible only to the extent that they exceed a specified percentage of AGI are increased when AGI is decreased. Likewise, when AGI is increased, these itemized deductions are decreased.

EXAMPLE 2

Tina earns a salary of $20,000 and has no other income. She itemizes deductions during the current year. Medical expenses for the year are $1,800. Since medical expenses are deductible only to the extent they exceed 7.5% of AGI, Tina's medical expense deduction is $300 [$1,800 – (7.5% × $20,000)]. If Tina had a $2,000 deduction *for* AGI, her medical expense deduction would be $450 [$1,800 – (7.5% × $18,000)], or $150 more. If the $2,000 deduction was *from* AGI, her medical expense deduction would remain $300 since AGI is unchanged. ▼

DEDUCTIONS FOR ADJUSTED GROSS INCOME

To understand how deductions of individual taxpayers are classified, it is necessary to examine the role of § 62. The purpose of § 62 is to classify various deductions as deductions *for* AGI. It does not provide the statutory authority for taking the deduction. For example, § 212 allows individuals to deduct expenses attributable to income-producing property. Section 212 expenses that are attributable to rents or royalties are classified as deductions *for* AGI. Likewise, a deduction for trade or business expenses is allowed by § 162. These expenses are classified as deductions *for* AGI.

If a deduction is not listed in § 62, it is an itemized deduction, *not* a deduction *for* AGI. Following is a *partial* list of the items classified as deductions *for* AGI by § 62:

- Expenses attributable to a trade or business carried on by the taxpayer. A trade or business does not include the performance of services by the taxpayer as an employee.
- Expenses incurred by a taxpayer in connection with the performance of services as an employee if the expenses are reimbursed and other conditions are satisfied.
- Deductions that result from losses on the sale or exchange of property by the taxpayer.
- Deductions attributable to property held for the production of rents and royalties.
- The deduction for payment of alimony.
- Certain contributions to pension, profit sharing, and annuity plans of self-employed individuals.

TAX IN THE NEWS

America's Team

A political football is in the air with respect to tax reform, and it appears almost everybody wants to play. The "football" is the Federal income tax system.

Numerous players, both Democrats and Republicans, are trying out for the team. The prospects include Rep. Bill Archer (chairman of the House Ways and Means Committee), Sen. Pete Domenici, Rep. Dick Armey (House Majority Leader), and Rep. Dick Gephardt (House Minority Leader). Even Newt Gingrich (Speaker of the House) is weighing what position he would like to play. Other members of Congress are expected to jockey for positions on the team. On the sidelines now but hoping to participate are Jack Kemp and Bill Bradley.

A debate is raging over the rules of the game. Should the current income tax system be reformed or should it be replaced? Should the replacement be a flat tax, a consumption tax, or a value added tax? It is almost impossible to read a newspaper or turn on the TV without encountering a discussion of someone's tax proposal. Archer has stated, "I want to tear the income tax out by its roots," and Armey has said, "America needs nothing less than a completely new tax system." Not only are the players willing to take on the reform of the Federal income tax system, but some would like to go even further and repeal the Sixteenth Amendment to the U.S. Constitution.

A key element in all of the proposals is simplicity. One method advocated for advancing simplicity is the elimination of deductions (a foundation of the flat tax proposals). As the legislative process goes forward, it will be interesting to observe the lobbying and debate over deductions and other components of the current Federal income tax system and to see what results finally emerge from the process.

- The deduction for certain retirement savings allowed by § 219 (e.g., IRAs).
- The penalty imposed on premature withdrawal of funds from time savings accounts or deposits.
- The deduction for moving expenses.

These items are covered in detail in various chapters in the text.

ITEMIZED DEDUCTIONS

The Code defines itemized deductions as the deductions allowed other than "the deductions allowable in arriving at adjusted gross income."[2] Thus, if a deduction is not properly classified as a deduction *for* AGI, then it is classified as an itemized deduction.

Section 212 Expenses. Section 212 allows deductions for ordinary and necessary expenses paid or incurred for the following:

- The production or collection of income.
- The management, conservation, or maintenance of property held for the production of income.
- Expenses paid in connection with the determination, collection, or refund of any tax.

[2] § 63(d).

Section 212 expenses related to rent and royalty income are deductions *for* AGI.[3] Expenses paid in connection with the determination, collection, or refund of taxes related to the income of sole proprietorships, rents and royalties, or farming operations are deductions *for* AGI. All other § 212 expenses are itemized deductions (deductions *from* AGI). For example, investment-related expenses (e.g., safe deposit box rentals) are deductible as itemized deductions attributable to the production of investment income.[4]

Deductible Personal Expenses. Taxpayers are allowed to deduct certain expenses that are primarily personal in nature. These expenses, which generally are not related to the production of income, are deductions *from* AGI (itemized deductions). Some of the more frequently encountered deductions in this category include the following:

- Contributions to qualified charitable organizations (not to exceed a specified percentage of AGI).
- Medical expenses (in excess of 7.5 percent of AGI).
- Certain state and local taxes (e.g., real estate taxes and state and local income taxes).
- Personal casualty losses (in excess of an aggregate floor of 10 percent of AGI and a $100 floor per casualty).
- Certain personal interest (e.g., mortgage interest on a personal residence).

Itemized deductions are discussed in detail in Chapter 10.

TRADE OR BUSINESS EXPENSES AND PRODUCTION OF INCOME EXPENSES

Section 162(a) permits a deduction for all ordinary and necessary expenses paid or incurred in carrying on a trade or business. These include reasonable salaries paid for services, expenses for the use of business property, and one-half of self-employment taxes paid (see Chapter 13). Such expenses are deducted *for* AGI.

It is sometimes difficult to determine whether an expenditure is deductible as a trade or business expense. The term "trade or business" is not defined in the Code or Regulations, and the courts have not provided a satisfactory definition. It is usually necessary to ask one or more of the following questions to determine whether an item qualifies as a trade or business expense:

- Was the use of the particular item related to a business activity? For example, if funds are borrowed for use in a business, the interest is deductible as a business expense.
- Was the expenditure incurred with the intent to realize a profit or to produce income? For example, expenses in excess of the income from raising horses are not deductible if the activity is classified as a personal hobby rather than a trade or business.
- Were the taxpayer's operation and management activities extensive enough to indicate the carrying on of a trade or business?

Section 162 *excludes* the following items from classification as trade or business expenses:

- Charitable contributions or gifts.
- Illegal bribes and kickbacks and certain treble damage payments.
- Fines and penalties.

[3] § 62(a)(4).

[4] Reg. § 1.212–1(g).

A bribe paid to a domestic official is not deductible if it is illegal under the laws of the United States. Foreign bribes are deductible unless they are unlawful under the Foreign Corrupt Practices Act of 1977.[5]

Ordinary and Necessary Requirement. The terms **ordinary and necessary** are found in both §§ 162 and 212. To be deductible, any trade or business expense must be "ordinary and necessary." In addition, compensation for services must be "reasonable" in amount.

Many expenses that are necessary are *not* ordinary. Neither "ordinary" nor "necessary" is defined in the Code or Regulations. The courts have held that an expense is *necessary* if a prudent businessperson would incur the same expense and the expense is expected to be appropriate and helpful in the taxpayer's business.[6]

EXAMPLE 3

Pat purchased a manufacturing concern that had just been adjudged bankrupt. Because the business had a poor financial rating, Pat satisfied some of the obligations to employees and outside salespeople incurred by the former owners. Pat had no legal obligation to pay these debts, but felt this was the only way to keep salespeople and employees. The Second Court of Appeals found that the payments were necessary in that they were both appropriate and helpful.[7] However, the Court held that the payments were *not* ordinary but were in the nature of capital expenditures to build a reputation. Therefore, no deduction was allowed. ▼

An expense is *ordinary* if it is normal, usual, or customary in the type of business conducted by the taxpayer and is not capital in nature.[8] However, an expense need not be recurring to be deductible as ordinary.

EXAMPLE 4

Albert engaged in a mail-order business. The post office judged that his advertisements were false and misleading. Under a fraud order, the post office stamped "fraudulent" on all letters addressed to Albert's business and returned them to the senders. Albert spent $30,000 on legal fees in an unsuccessful attempt to force the post office to stop. The legal fees (though not recurring) were ordinary business expenses because they were normal, usual, or customary in the circumstances.[9] ▼

For § 212 deductions, the law requires that expenses bear a reasonable and proximate relationship to (1) the production or collection of income or to (2) the management, conservation, or maintenance of property held for the production of income.[10]

EXAMPLE 5

Wendy owns a small portfolio of investments, including 10 shares of Hawk, Inc., common stock worth $1,000. She incurred $350 in travel expenses to attend the annual shareholders' meeting at which she voted her 10 shares against the current management group. No deduction is permitted because a 10-share investment is insignificant in value in relation to the travel expenses incurred.[11] ▼

[5] § 162(c)(1).
[6] *Welch v. Helvering*, 3 USTC ¶1164, 12 AFTR 1456, 54 S.Ct. 8 (USSC, 1933).
[7] *Dunn and McCarthy, Inc. v. Comm.*, 43–2 USTC ¶9688, 31 AFTR 1043, 139 F.2d 242 (CA–2, 1943).
[8] *Deputy v. DuPont*, 40–1 USTC ¶9161, 23 AFTR 808, 60 S.Ct. 363 (USSC, 1940).
[9] *Comm. v. Heininger*, 44–1 USTC ¶9109, 31 AFTR 783, 64 S.Ct. 249 (USSC, 1943).
[10] Reg. § 1.212–1(d).
[11] *J. Raymond Dyer*, 36 T.C. 456 (1961).

Reasonableness Requirement. The Code refers to **reasonableness** solely with respect to salaries and other compensation for services.[12] But the courts have held that for any business expense to be ordinary and necessary, it must also be reasonable in amount.[13]

What constitutes reasonableness is a question of fact. If an expense is unreasonable, the excess amount is not allowed as a deduction. The question of reasonableness generally arises with respect to closely held corporations where there is no separation of ownership and management.

Transactions between the shareholders and the closely held company may result in the disallowance of deductions for excessive salaries and rent expense paid by the corporation to the shareholders. The courts will view an unusually large salary in light of all relevant circumstances and may find that the salary is reasonable despite its size.[14] If excessive payments for salaries and rents are closely related to the percentage of stock owned by the recipients, the payments are generally treated as dividends.[15] Since dividends are not deductible by the corporation, the disallowance results in an increase in the corporate taxable income. Deductions for reasonable salaries will not be disallowed *solely* because the corporation has paid insubstantial portions of its earnings as dividends to its shareholders.

EXAMPLE 6

Sparrow Corporation, a closely held corporation, is owned equally by Lupe, Carlos, and Ramon. The company has been highly profitable for several years and has not paid dividends. Lupe, Carlos, and Ramon are key officers of the company, and each receives a salary of $200,000. Salaries for similar positions in comparable companies average only $100,000. Amounts paid the owners in excess of $100,000 may be deemed unreasonable, and, if so, a total of $300,000 in salary deductions by Sparrow is disallowed. The disallowed amounts are treated as dividends rather than salary income to Lupe, Carlos, and Ramon because the payments are proportional to stock ownership. Salaries are deductible by the corporation, but dividends are not. ▼

100k × 3

BUSINESS AND NONBUSINESS LOSSES

Section 165 provides for a deduction for losses not compensated for by insurance. As a general rule, deductible losses of individual taxpayers are limited to those incurred in a trade or business or in a transaction entered into for profit. Individuals are also allowed to deduct losses that are the result of a casualty. Casualty losses include, but are not limited to, fire, storm, shipwreck, and theft. See Chapter 7 for a further discussion of this topic. Deductible personal casualty losses are reduced by $100 per casualty, and the aggregate of all personal casualty losses is reduced by 10 percent of AGI. A personal casualty loss is an itemized deduction. See Concept Summary 6–2 on p. 6–32 for the classification of expenses.

REPORTING PROCEDURES

All deductions *for* and *from* AGI wind up on pages 1 and 2 of Form 1040. All deductions *for* AGI are reported on page 1. The last line on page 1 is adjusted gross income.

---

[12] § 162(a)(1).

[13] *Comm. v. Lincoln Electric Co.*, 49–2 USTC ¶9388, 38 AFTR 411, 176 F.2d 815 (CA–6, 1949).

[14] *Kennedy, Jr. v. Comm.*, 82–1 USTC ¶9186, 49 AFTR2d 82–628, 671 F.2d 167 (CA–6, 1982), *rev'g* 72 T.C. 793 (1979).

[15] Reg. § 1.162–8.

The first item on page 2 is also adjusted gross income. Itemized deductions are entered next, followed by the deduction for personal and dependency exemptions. The result is taxable income.

Most of the deductions *for* AGI on page 1 originate on supporting schedules. Examples include business expenses (Schedule C) and rent, royalty, partnership, and fiduciary deductions (Schedule E). Other deductions *for* AGI, such as IRAs, Keogh retirement plans, and alimony, are entered directly on page 1 of Form 1040.

All itemized deductions on page 2 are carried over from Schedule A. Some Schedule A deductions originate on other forms. Examples include home mortgage interest, investment interest, noncash charitable contributions in excess of $500, casualty losses, and unreimbursed employee expenses.

Form 1040 becomes a summary of the detailed information entered on the other schedules and forms. See Figure 6–1.

▼ FIGURE 6–1
Format of Form 1040

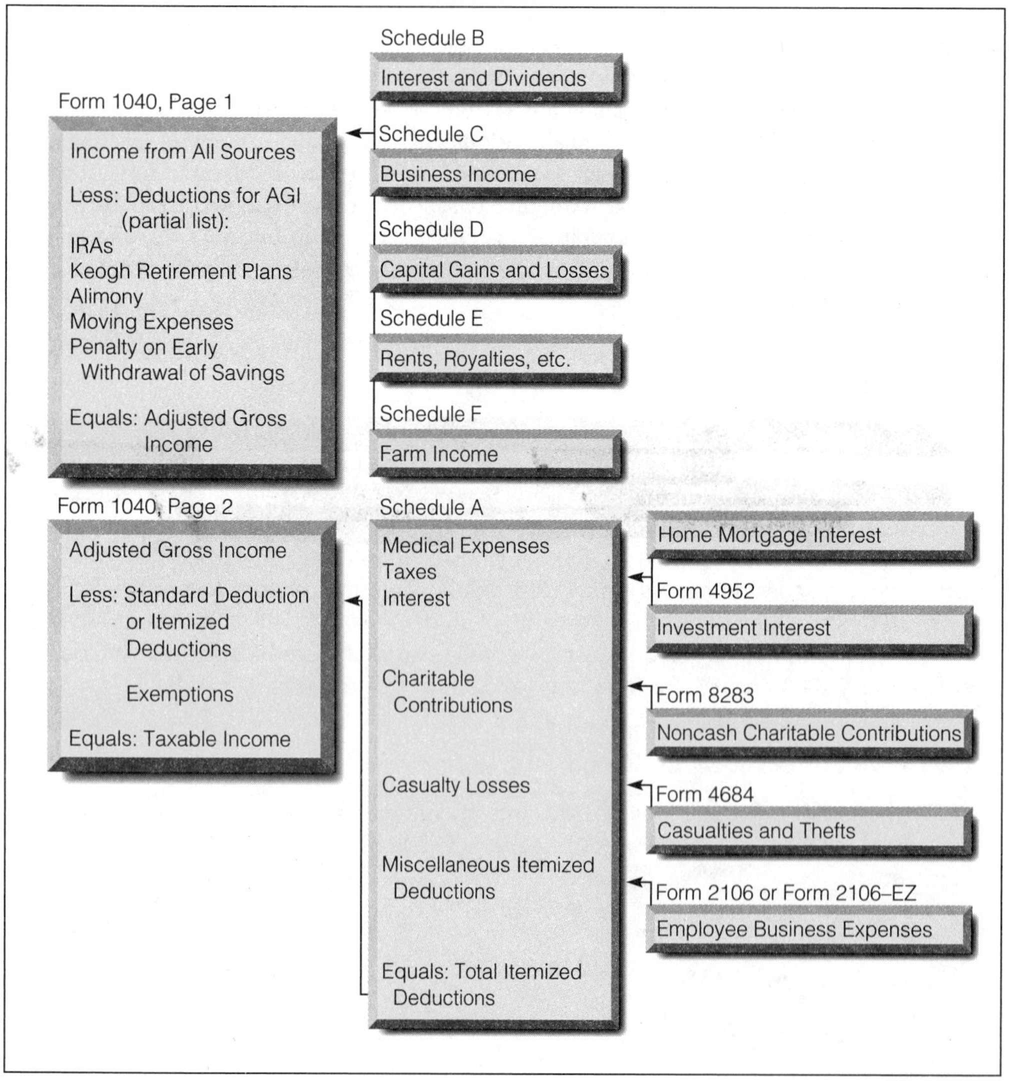

Deductions and Losses—Timing of Expense Recognition

IMPORTANCE OF TAXPAYER'S METHOD OF ACCOUNTING

2 LEARNING OBJECTIVE
Describe the cash and accrual methods of accounting.

A taxpayer's **accounting method** is a major factor in determining taxable income. The method used determines when an item is includible in income and when an item is deductible on the tax return. Usually, the taxpayer's regular method of record keeping is used for income tax purposes.[16] The taxing authorities do not require uniformity among all taxpayers. They do require that the method used clearly reflect income and that items be handled consistently.[17] The most common methods of accounting are the cash method and the accrual method.

Throughout the portions of the Code dealing with deductions, the phrase "paid or incurred" is used. *Paid* refers to the cash basis taxpayer who gets a deduction only in the year of payment. *Incurred* concerns the accrual basis taxpayer who obtains the deduction in the year in which the liability for the expense becomes certain (refer to Chapter 4).

CASH METHOD REQUIREMENTS

The expenses of cash basis taxpayers are deductible only when they are actually paid with cash or other property. Promising to pay or issuing a note does not satisfy the actually paid requirement.[18] However, the payment can be made with borrowed funds. At the time taxpayers charge expenses on their credit cards, they are allowed to claim the deduction. They are deemed to have simultaneously borrowed money from the credit card issuer and constructively paid the expenses.[19]

Although the cash basis taxpayer must have actually or constructively paid the expense, payment does not assure a current deduction. Cash basis and accrual basis taxpayers cannot take a current deduction for capital expenditures except through amortization, depletion, or depreciation over the life (actual or statutory) of the asset. The Regulations set forth the general rule that an expenditure that creates an asset having a useful life that extends substantially beyond the end of the tax year must be capitalized.[20] ← 1 yr rule

EXAMPLE 7

John, a cash basis taxpayer, rents property from Carl. On July 1, 1996, John paid $2,400 rent for the 24 months ending June 30, 1998. The prepaid rent extends 18 months after the close of the tax year—substantially beyond the year of payment. Therefore, John must capitalize the prepaid rent and amortize the expense on a monthly basis. His deduction for 1996 is $600. ▼

The Tax Court and the IRS took the position that an asset that will expire or be consumed by the end of the tax year following the year of payment must be prorated. The Ninth Court of Appeals held that such expenditures are currently deductible, however, and the Supreme Court apparently concurs (the one-year rule for prepaid expenses).[21]

---

[16] § 446(a).

[17] §§ 446(b) and (e); Reg. § 1.446–1(a)(2).

[18] *Page v. Rhode Island Trust Co., Exr.*, 37–1 USTC ¶9138, 19 AFTR 105, 88 F.2d 192 (CA–1, 1937).

[19] Rev.Rul. 78–39, 1978–1 C.B. 73. See also Rev.Rul. 80–335, 1980–2 C.B. 170, which applies to pay-by-phone arrangements.

[20] Reg. § 1.461–1(a).

[21] *Zaninovich v. Comm.*, 80–1 USTC ¶9342, 45 AFTR2d 80–1442, 616 F.2d 429 (CA–9, 1980), *rev'g* 69 T.C. 605 (1978). Cited by the Supreme Court in *Hillsboro National Bank v. Comm.*, 83–1 USTC ¶9229, 51 AFTR2d 83–874, 103 S.Ct. 1134 (USSC, 1983).

EXAMPLE 8

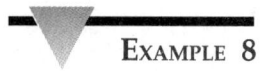

Assume the same facts as in Example 7 except that John was required to pay only 12 months rent in 1996. He paid $1,200 on July 1, 1996. The entire $1,200 would be deductible in 1996. ▼

The payment must be required, not a voluntary prepayment, to obtain the current deduction under the one-year rule.[22] The taxpayer must also demonstrate that allowing the current deduction will not result in a material distortion of income. Generally, the deduction will be allowed if the item is recurring or was made for a business purpose rather than to manipulate income.[23]

As Chapter 18 explains, not all taxpayers are allowed to use the cash method.[24]

ACCRUAL METHOD REQUIREMENTS

The period in which an accrual basis taxpayer can deduct an expense is determined by applying the *all events test* and the *economic performance test*. A deduction cannot be claimed until (1) all the events have occurred to create the taxpayer's liability and (2) the amount of the liability can be determined with reasonable accuracy. Once these requirements are satisfied, the deduction is permitted only if economic performance has occurred. The economic performance test is met only when the service, property, or use of property giving rise to the liability is actually performed for, provided to, or used by the taxpayer.[25]

EXAMPLE 9

On December 22, 1996, Chris's entertainment business sponsored a jazz festival in a rented auditorium at a local college. His business is responsible for cleaning up the auditorium after the festival and for reinstalling seats that were removed so more people could attend the festival. Since the college is closed over the Christmas holidays, the company hired by Chris to perform the work did not begin these activities until January 2, 1997. The cost to Chris is $1,200. Chris cannot deduct the $1,200 until 1997, when the services are performed. ▼

An exception to the economic performance requirements allows certain *recurring items* to be deducted if the following conditions are met:

- The item is recurring in nature and is treated consistently by the taxpayer.
- Either the accrued item is not material, or accruing it results in better matching of income and expenses.
- All the events have occurred that determine the fact of the liability and the amount of the liability can be determined with reasonable accuracy.
- Economic performance occurs within a reasonable period (but not later than 8½ months after the close of the taxable year).[26]

EXAMPLE 10

Rick, an accrual basis, calendar year taxpayer, entered into a monthly maintenance contract during the year. He makes a monthly accrual at the end of every month for this service and pays the fee sometime between the first and fifteenth of the following month when services are performed. The amount involved is immaterial, and all the other tests are met. The December 1996 accrual is deductible even though the service is performed on January 12, 1997. ▼

---

[22] *Bonaire Development Co. v. Comm.*, 82–2 USTC ¶9428, 50 AFTR2d 82–5167, 679 F.2d 159 (CA–9, 1982).

[23] *Keller v. Comm.*, 84–1 USTC ¶9194, 53 AFTR2d 84–663, 725 F.2d 1173 (CA–8, 1984), *aff'g* 79 T.C. 7 (1982).

[24] § 448.

[25] § 461(h).

[26] § 461(h)(3)(A).

EXAMPLE 11

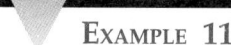

Rita, an accrual basis, calendar year taxpayer, shipped merchandise sold on December 30, 1996, via Greyhound Van Lines on January 2, 1997, and paid the freight charges at that time. Since Rita reported the sale of the merchandise in 1996, the shipping charge should also be deductible in 1996. This procedure results in a better matching of income and expenses. ▼

Reserves for estimated expenses (frequently employed for financial accounting purposes) generally are not allowed for tax purposes because the economic performance test cannot be satisfied.

EXAMPLE 12

Blackbird Airlines is required by Federal law to test its engines after 3,000 flying hours. Aircraft cannot return to flight until the tests have been conducted. An unrelated aircraft maintenance company does all of the company's tests for $1,500 per engine. For financial reporting purposes, the company accrues an expense based upon $.50 per hour of flight and credits an allowance account. The actual amounts paid for maintenance are offset against the allowance account. For tax purposes, the economic performance test is not satisfied until the work has been done. Therefore, the reserve method cannot be used for tax purposes. ▼

Disallowance Possibilities

3 LEARNING OBJECTIVE
Apply the Internal Revenue Code deduction disallowance provisions associated with the following: public policy limitations, political activities, excessive executive compensation, investigation of business opportunities, hobby losses, vacation home rentals, payment of others' expenses, personal expenditures, capital expenditures, related-party transactions, and expenses related to tax-exempt income.

The tax law provides for the disallowance of certain types of expenses. Without specific restrictions in the tax law, taxpayers might attempt to deduct certain items that in reality are personal expenditures. For example, specific tax rules are provided to determine whether an expenditure is for trade or business purposes or related to a personal hobby.

Certain disallowance provisions are a codification or extension of prior court decisions. After the courts denied deductions for payments considered to be in violation of public policy, the tax law was changed to provide specific authority for the disallowance of these deductions. Discussions of specific disallowance provisions in the tax law follow.

PUBLIC POLICY LIMITATION

Justification for Denying Deductions. The courts developed the principle that a payment that is in violation of public policy is not a necessary expense and is not deductible.[27] Although a bribe or fine, may be appropriate, helpful, and even contribute to the profitability of an activity, the courts held that to allow such expenses would frustrate clearly defined public policy. A deduction would dilute the effect of the penalty since the government would be indirectly subsidizing a taxpayer's wrongdoing.

Accordingly, the IRS was free to restrict deductions if, in its view, the expenses were contrary to public policy. But since the law did not explain which actions violated public policy, taxpayers often had to go to court to determine whether or not their expense fell into this category.

Furthermore, the public policy doctrine could be arbitrarily applied in cases where no clear definition had emerged. To solve these problems, Congress enacted legislation that attempts to limit the use of the doctrine. Under the legislation,

[27] *Tank Truck Rentals, Inc. v. Comm.*, 58–1 USTC ¶9366, 1 AFTR2d 1154, 78 S.Ct. 507 (USSC, 1958).

deductions are disallowed for certain specific types of expenditures that are considered contrary to public policy:

- Bribes and kickbacks including those associated with Medicare or Medicaid (in the case of foreign bribes and kickbacks, only if the payments violate the U.S. Foreign Corrupt Practices Act of 1977).
- Fines and penalties paid to a government for violation of law.

EXAMPLE 13

Brown Corporation, a moving company, consistently loads its trucks with weights in excess of the limits allowed by state law. The additional revenue more than offsets the fines levied. The fines are for a violation of public policy and are not deductible. ▼

- Two-thirds of the treble damage payments made to claimants resulting from violation of the antitrust law.[28]

To be disallowed, the bribe or kickback must be illegal under either Federal or state law and must also subject the payer to a criminal penalty or the loss of license or privilege to engage in a trade or business. For a bribe or kickback that is illegal under state law, a deduction is denied only if the state law is generally enforced.

EXAMPLE 14

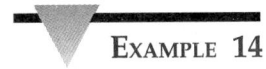

During the year, Keith, an insurance salesman, paid $5,000 to Karen, a real estate broker. The payment represented 20% of the commissions Keith earned from customers referred by Karen. Under state law, the splitting of commissions by an insurance salesperson is an act of misconduct that could warrant a revocation of the salesperson's license. Keith's $5,000 payments to Karen are not deductible provided the state law is generally enforced. ▼

ETHICAL CONSIDERATIONS

Obtaining Zoning Variances

Tex is a real estate developer. He has a contract with a major retailer to handle its land acquisitions in the southeastern part of the state. One of Tex's major responsibilities is to secure the requisite zoning to enable the retailer to build and operate its retail outlets. Typically, obtaining proper zoning is more of a procedural activity than a strategic activity.

Tex has identified a site he would like to acquire for the retailer in a small historic city surrounded by two counties with substantially greater populations. Tex and the retailer have agreed that it is imperative that the site be in the city rather than in one of the counties. The city has very restrictive zoning for commercial properties, and the retailer will have to obtain several zoning variances.

Tex's normal strategy in such a situation is to hire the leading law firm in the community to represent him in dealing with the property owner, the city planning commission, and the city council. In this instance, however, the senior partner in the major law firm is also the city mayor, so Tex adopts the following strategy. He hires another law firm as his representative on this acquisition, but so as not to antagonize the mayor and potentially adversely affect the city council's approval of the zoning variances, he pays a $10,000 retainer to the mayor's law firm to serve as his legal representative on any real estate acquisitions during the next 12-month period in the two adjoining counties. Tex deducts the $10,000 payment as an ordinary and necessary business expense. He is successful in securing the zoning

[28] §§ 162(c), (f), and (g).

variances and acquires the site for the retailer. During the following 12-month period, Tex does not need to use the services of the mayor's law firm.

What is Tex trying to achieve and will he be successful?

Legal Expenses Incurred in Defense of Civil or Criminal Penalties. To deduct legal expenses, the taxpayer must be able to show that the origin and character of the claim are directly related to a trade or business, an income-producing activity, or the determination, collection, or refund of a tax. Personal legal expenses are not deductible. Thus, legal fees incurred in connection with a criminal defense are deductible only if the crime is associated with the taxpayer's trade or business or income-producing activity.[29]

EXAMPLE 15

Debra, a financial officer of Blue Corporation, incurred legal expenses in connection with her defense in a criminal indictment for evasion of Blue's income taxes. Debra may deduct her legal expenses because she is deemed to be in the trade or business of being an executive. The legal action impairs her ability to conduct this business activity.[30] ▼

Deductible legal expenses associated with the following are deductible *for* AGI:

- Ordinary and necessary expenses incurred in connection with a trade or business.
- Ordinary and necessary expenses incurred in conjunction with rental or royalty property held for the production of income.

All other deductible legal expenses are deductible *from* AGI. For example, legal expenses generally are deductible *from* AGI if they are for fees for tax advice relative to the preparation of an individual's income tax return. Contrast this with the deduction *for* classification of legal fees for tax advice relative to the preparation of the portion of the tax return for a sole proprietor's trade or business (Schedule C) or an individual's rental or royalty income (Schedule E).

Expenses Relating to an Illegal Business. The usual expenses of operating an illegal business (e.g., a numbers racket) are deductible.[31] However, § 162 disallows a deduction for fines, bribes to public officials, illegal kickbacks, and other illegal payments.

EXAMPLE 16

Sam owns and operates an illegal gambling establishment. In connection with this activity, he had the following expenses during the year:

Rent ✓	$ 60,000
Payoffs to the police	40,000
Depreciation on equipment ✓	100,000
Wages ✓	140,000
Interest ✓	30,000
Criminal fines	50,000
Illegal kickbacks	10,000
Total	$430,000

[29] *Comm. v. Tellier*, 66–1 USTC ¶9319, 17 AFTR2d 633, 86 S.Ct. 1118 (USSC, 1966).

[30] Rev.Rul. 68–662, 1968–2 C.B. 69.

[31] *Comm. v. Sullivan*, 58–1 USTC ¶9368, 1 AFTR2d 1158, 78 S.Ct. 512 (USSC, 1958).

All of the usual expenses (rent, depreciation, wages, and interest) are deductible; payoffs, fines, and kickbacks are not deductible. Of the $430,000 spent, $330,000 is deductible and $100,000 is not. ▼

An exception applies to expenses incurred in illegal trafficking in drugs.[32] *Drug dealers* are not allowed a deduction for ordinary and necessary business expenses incurred in their business. In arriving at gross income from the business, however, dealers may reduce total sales by the cost of goods sold.[33] In this regard, no distinction is made between legal and illegal businesses in calculating gross income. Treating cost of goods sold as a negative income item rather than as a deduction item produces the unseemly result that a drug dealer's taxable income is reduced by cost of goods sold.

POLITICAL CONTRIBUTIONS AND LOBBYING ACTIVITIES

Political Contributions. Generally, no business deduction is permitted for direct or indirect payments for political purposes.[34] Historically, the government has been reluctant to accord favorable tax treatment to business expenditures for political purposes. Allowing deductions might encourage abuses and enable businesses to have undue influence upon the political process.

Lobbying Expenditures. Prior to the effect of the Revenue Reconciliation Act of 1993 (RRA of 1993), a deduction was allowed for certain expenses incurred to influence legislation (appearances before or statements filed with legislative bodies or individual legislators). For the expense to qualify as a deductible lobbying expenditure, the proposed legislation had to be of direct interest to the taxpayer. A direct interest existed if the legislation would, or could reasonably be expected to, affect the trade or business of the taxpayer. No deduction was allowed for expenses incurred to influence the public on legislative matters or for any political campaign.

RRA of 1993 generally repeals this lobbying deduction.[35] Any lobbying expenses incurred in attempting to influence state or Federal legislation or the actions of certain high-ranking public officials (e.g., the President, Vice-President, cabinet-level officials, and the two most senior officials in each agency of the executive branch) are no longer deductible. The disallowance also applies to a pro rata portion of the membership dues of trade associations and other groups that are used for lobbying activities.

EXAMPLE 17

Egret Company pays a $10,000 annual membership fee to the Free Trade Group, a trade association for plumbing wholesalers. The trade association estimates that 70% of its dues are allocated to lobbying activities. Thus, Egret Company's deduction is limited to $3,000 ($10,000 × 30%). ▼

There are three exceptions to this repeal of the lobbying expenses deduction. An exception is provided for influencing local legislation (e.g., city and county governments). Second, the disallowance provision does not apply to activities devoted solely to monitoring legislation. Third, a *de minimis* exception is provided for annual in-house expenditures (lobbying expenses other than those paid to

---

[32] § 280E.

[33] Reg. § 1.61–3(a). Gross income is defined as sales minus cost of goods sold. Thus, while § 280E prohibits any deductions for drug dealers, it does not modify the normal definition of gross income.

[34] § 276.

[35] § 162(e).

TAX IN THE NEWS

Lobbyists Work and Sue to Work

The Revenue Reconciliation Act of 1993 generally eliminated the ability of businesses to deduct the amounts paid to lobbyists to lobby for them. Subsequently, eleven nonprofit trade groups and professional societies filed a lawsuit in the U.S. District Court in Washington, D.C., alleging that their rights of free speech, petition, and association were threatened by the new statutory provision contained in § 162(e). While denying the request for an injunction on procedural grounds, the district court judge left the door open by commenting that he did not agree with the way Congress wrote the law or the way the IRS implemented it. As a result, the American Society of Association Executives has filed a lawsuit seeking to invalidate § 162(e) and recover its initial payment to the IRS.

In a different vein, lobbyists are still finding work even though their clients cannot deduct the amounts paid for lobbying services. For example, the *Wall Street Journal* reported that some lobbyists were concerned that Congress might not extend the research activities credit beyond its June 30, 1995, expiration date. One lobbyist, however, confided that he had an even bigger fear--that Congress might extend the provision permanently, rather than temporarily, and thus hurt his lobbying business.

SOURCE: Adapted from "Lobbyists Try Again to Shoot Down Part of the 1993 Tax Law," *Wall Street Journal*, June 7, 1995, p. A1.

professional lobbyists or any portion of dues used by associations for lobbying) if such expenditures do not exceed $2,000. If the in-house expenditures exceed $2,000, none of the in-house expenditures can be deducted.

EXCESSIVE EXECUTIVE COMPENSATION

Prior to the effect of RRA of 1993, there was no statutory dollar limit on the deduction for executive compensation. The only limitation was the reasonableness requirement (discussed earlier in this chapter) for shareholder-employees of closely held corporations.

RRA of 1993 includes the so-called millionaires provision, which applies to publicly held corporations.[36] The provision does not limit the amount of compensation that can be paid to an employee. Instead, it limits the amount the employer can deduct for the compensation of a covered executive to $1 million annually. Covered employees include the chief executive officer and the four other most highly compensated officers.

Employee compensation *excludes* the following:

- Commissions based on individual performance.
- Certain performance-based compensation based on company performance according to a formula approved by a board of directors compensation committee (comprised solely of two or more outside directors) and by

[36] A publicly held corporation, for this provision, is a corporation that has at least one class of stock registered under the Securities Act of 1934.

TAX IN THE NEWS

EXCESSIVE EXECUTIVE CONPENSATION: WIN ONE AND LOSE ONE

Revisions to the original Proposed Regulations on excessive executive compensation are beneficial to the taxpayer on one point and detrimental on another, according to Bill Dunn, a specialist in executive compensation with the National Tax Services Office of Coopers & Lybrand.

On the favorable side, one example in the revisions appears to provide an open door with respect to the definition of a "substantial uncertainty." The original Proposed Regulations provided that when a performance goal is substantially uncertain, it is considered preestablished (a requirement of the Proposed Regulations) if it is written no later than 90 days after the goal period begins. The example indicates that performance goals based on corporate profitability are substantially uncertain even when the company has a profitable history. Thus, the goal could be the maintenance of the current level of earnings rather than improvements in earnings.

On the unfavorable side, the definition of a corporate outside director is restricted. An outside director is now defined as one who does not receive remuneration from the company in a nondirector capacity. Gone for providers of professional services is the provision in the original Proposed Regulations that did not count as remuneration payments up to $60,000 or 5 percent of the company's gross income, whichever was less. The elimination of this threshold will make it more difficult for attorneys, accountants, management consultants, investment bankers, and other providers of professional services to qualify for compensation committees.

SOURCE: Information from "Executive Compensation Amendments Ease Deduction Worries," *Washington Perspective,* January 1995, Coopers & Lybrand, L.L.P., p. 2.

shareholder vote. The performance attainment must be certified by this compensation committee.

- Payments to tax-qualified retirement plans.
- Payments that are excludible from the employees' gross income (e.g., certain fringe benefits).

INVESTIGATION OF A BUSINESS

Investigation expenses are expenses paid or incurred to determine the feasibility of entering a new business or expanding an existing business. They include such costs as travel, engineering and architectural surveys, marketing reports, and various legal and accounting services. How such expenses are treated for tax purposes depends on a number of variables, including the following:

- The current business, if any, of the taxpayer.
- The nature of the business being investigated.
- The extent to which the investigation has proceeded.
- Whether or not the acquisition actually takes place.

If the taxpayer is in a business the *same as or similar to* that being investigated, all investigation expenses are deductible in the year paid or incurred. The tax result is the same whether or not the taxpayer acquires the business being investigated.[37]

EXAMPLE 18 Terry, an accrual basis sole proprietor, owns and operates three motels in Georgia. In the current year, Terry incurs expenses of $8,500 in investigating the possibility of acquiring several additional motels located in South Carolina. The $8,500 is deductible in the current year whether or not Terry acquires the motels in South Carolina. ▼

When the taxpayer is *not* in a business that is the same as or similar to the one being investigated, the tax result depends on whether the new business is acquired. If the business is not acquired, all investigation expenses generally are nondeductible.[38]

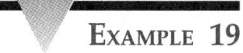

EXAMPLE 19 Lynn, a retired merchant, incurs expenses in traveling from Rochester, New York, to California to investigate the feasibility of acquiring several auto care centers. If no acquisition takes place, none of the expenses are deductible. ▼

If the taxpayer is *not* in a business that is the same as or similar to the one being investigated and actually acquires the new business, the expenses must be capitalized. At the election of the taxpayer, the expenses may be amortized over a period of 60 months or more, beginning with the month in which the business is started.[39]

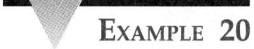

EXAMPLE 20 Tina owns and operates 10 restaurants located in various cities throughout the Southeast. She travels to Atlanta to discuss the acquisition of an auto dealership. In addition, she incurs legal and accounting costs associated with the potential acquisition. After incurring total investigation costs of $12,000, she acquires the auto dealership on October 1, 1996.

Tina must capitalize the $12,000 of investigation expenses for the auto dealership. If she elects to amortize the expenses over 60 months, she can deduct $600 ($12,000 × 3/60) in 1996. ▼

HOBBY LOSSES

Business or investment expenses are deductible only if the taxpayer can show that the activity was entered into for the purpose of making a profit. Certain activities may have either profit-seeking or personal attributes, depending upon individual circumstances. Examples include raising horses and operating a farm used as a weekend residence. While personal losses are not deductible, losses attributable to profit-seeking activities may be deducted and used to offset a taxpayer's other income. For this reason, the tax law limits the deductibility of **hobby losses.**

General Rules. If an individual can show that an activity has been conducted with the intent to earn a profit, losses from the activity are fully deductible. The hobby loss rules apply only if the activity is not engaged in for profit. Hobby expenses are deductible only to the extent of hobby income.[40]

The Regulations stipulate that the following nine factors should be considered in determining whether an activity is profit-seeking or a hobby:[41]

---

[37] *York v. Comm.*, 58–2 USTC ¶9952, 2 AFTR2d 6178, 261 F.2d 421 (CA–4, 1958).

[38] Rev.Rul. 57–418, 1957–2 C.B. 143; *Morton Frank*, 20 T.C. 511 (1953); and *Dwight A. Ward*, 20 T.C. 332 (1953).

[39] § 195.

[40] § 183(b)(2).

[41] Reg. §§ 1.183–2(b)(1) through (9).

- Whether the activity is conducted in a businesslike manner.
- The expertise of the taxpayers or their advisers.
- The time and effort expended.
- The expectation that the assets of the activity will appreciate in value.
- The taxpayer's previous success in conducting similar activities.
- The history of income or losses from the activity.
- The relationship of profits earned to losses incurred.
- The financial status of the taxpayer (e.g., if the taxpayer does not have substantial amounts of other income, this may indicate that the activity is engaged in for profit).
- Elements of personal pleasure or recreation in the activity.

The presence or absence of a factor is not by itself determinative of whether the activity is profit-seeking or a hobby. Rather, the decision is a subjective one that is based on an analysis of the facts and circumstances.

Presumptive Rule of § 183. The Code provides a rebuttable presumption that an activity is profit-seeking if the activity shows a profit in at least three of any five prior consecutive years.[42] If the activity involves horses, a profit in at least two of seven consecutive years meets the presumptive rule. If these profitability tests are met, the activity is presumed to be a trade or business rather than a personal hobby. In this situation, the IRS bears the burden of proving that the activity is personal rather than trade or business related.

EXAMPLE 21

Camille, an executive for a large corporation, is paid a salary of $200,000. Her husband is a collector of antiques. Several years ago, he opened an antique shop in a local shopping center and spends most of his time buying and selling antiques. He occasionally earns a small profit from this activity but more frequently incurs substantial losses. If the losses are business related, they are fully deductible against Camille's salary income on a joint return. In resolving this issue, consider the following:

- Initially determine whether the antique activity has met the three-out-of-five years profit test.
- If the presumption is not met, the activity may nevertheless qualify as a business if the taxpayer can show that the intent is to engage in a profit-seeking activity. It is not necessary to show actual profits.
- Attempt to fit the operation within the nine criteria prescribed in the Regulations and listed above. These criteria are the factors considered in trying to rebut the § 183 presumption. ▼

Determining the Amount of the Deduction. If an activity is deemed to be a hobby, the expenses are deductible only to the extent of the gross income from the hobby. These expenses must be deducted in the following order:

- Amounts deductible under other Code sections without regard to the nature of the activity, such as property taxes and home mortgage interest.
- Amounts deductible under other Code sections if the activity had been engaged in for profit, but only if those amounts do not affect adjusted basis. Examples include maintenance, utilities, and supplies.
- Amounts that affect adjusted basis and would be deductible under other Code sections if the activity had been engaged in for profit.[43] Examples include depreciation, amortization, and depletion.

[42] § 183(d).

[43] Reg. § 1.183–1(b)(1).

These deductions are deductible *from* AGI as itemized deductions to the extent they exceed 2 percent of AGI.[44] If the taxpayer uses the standard deduction rather than itemizing, all hobby loss deductions are wasted.

EXAMPLE 22

Jim, the vice president of an oil company, has AGI of $80,000. He decides to pursue painting in his spare time. He uses a home studio, comprising 10% of the home's square footage. During the current year, Jim incurs the following expenses:

Frames	$ 350
Art supplies	300
Fees paid to models	1,000
Home studio expenses:	
Total property taxes	900
Total home mortgage interest	10,000
Depreciation on 10% of home	500
Total home maintenance and utilities	3,600

During the year, Jim sold paintings for a total of $3,200. If the activity is held to be a hobby, Jim is allowed deductions as follows:

Gross income		$ 3,200
Deduct: Taxes and interest (10% of $10,900)		(1,090)
Remainder		$ 2,110
Deduct: Frames	$ 350	
Art supplies	300	
Models' fees	1,000	
Maintenance and utilities (10%)	360	(2,010)
Remainder		$ 100
Depreciation ($500, but limited to $100)		(100)
Net income		$ -0-

Jim includes the $3,200 of income in AGI, making his AGI $83,200. The taxes and interest are itemized deductions, deductible in full. The remaining $2,110 of expenses are reduced by 2% of his AGI ($1,664); so the net deduction is $446. Since the property taxes and home mortgage interest are deductible anyway, the net effect is a $2,754 ($3,200 less $446) increase in taxable income. ▼

EXAMPLE 23

If Jim's activity in Example 22 is held to be a business, he could deduct expenses totaling $2,510 ($2,010 plus $500 of depreciation) *for* AGI, in addition to the $1,090 of taxes and interest. All these expenses would be trade or business expenses deductible *for* AGI. His reduction in AGI would be as follows:

Gross income		$ 3,200
Less: Taxes and interest	$1,090	
Other business expenses	2,010	
Depreciation	500	(3,600)
Reduction in AGI		$ (400)

As is the case in Example 22, Jim can deduct the remaining property taxes and home mortgage interest of $9,810 ($10,900 – $1,090) as itemized deductions. ▼

[44] Reg. § 1.67–1T(a)(1)(iv) and Rev.Rul. 75–14, 1975–1 C.B. 90.

RENTAL OF VACATION HOMES

Restrictions on the deductions allowed for part-year rentals of personal **vacation homes** were written into the law to prevent taxpayers from deducting essentially personal expenses as rental losses. Many taxpayers who owned vacation homes had formerly treated the homes as rental property and generated rental losses as deductions *for* AGI. For example, a summer cabin would be rented for 2 months per year, used for vacationing for 1 month, and left vacant the rest of the year. The taxpayer would then deduct 11 months' depreciation, utilities, maintenance, etc., as rental expenses, resulting in a rental loss. Section 280A eliminates this treatment by allowing deductions on residences used primarily for personal purposes only to the extent of the income generated. Only a break-even situation is allowed; no losses can be deducted.

There are three possible tax treatments for residences used for both personal and rental purposes. The treatment depends upon the *relative time* the residence is used for personal purposes versus rental use.

Primarily Personal Use. If the residence is *rented* for *less than 15 days* in a year, it is treated as a personal residence. The rent income is excluded from gross income, and mortgage interest and real estate taxes are allowed as itemized deductions, as with any personal residence.[45] No other expenses (e.g., depreciation, utilities, maintenance) are deductible. Although this provision exists primarily for administrative convenience, a bill was introduced in Congress in 1994 that would have repealed this exclusion from gross income.

EXAMPLE 24

Dixie owns a vacation cottage on the lake. During the current year, she rented it for $1,600 for two weeks, lived in it two months, and left it vacant the remainder of the year. The year's expenses amounted to $6,000 mortgage interest expense, $500 property taxes, $1,500 utilities and maintenance, and $2,400 depreciation. Since the property was not rented for at least 15 days, the income is excluded, the mortgage interest and property tax expenses are itemized deductions, and the remaining expenses are nondeductible personal expenses. ▼

ETHICAL CONSIDERATIONS

Renting for One More Day

June is a widow who lives in Williamsburg, Virginia. For the past five years (since the death of her husband), she has rented her home for one week to a professional golfer who is participating in the A–B Golf Classic. The rent income is $1,500. During this week, June visits her sister in Charlotte. A neighbor who is a CPA advises June that she does not need to report the $1,500 on her Federal income tax return because she did not rent her house for more than two weeks during the year.

In 1996, June has the opportunity to rent the house for $2,800 for an additional week in December to the golfer and his family who would like to spend Christmas in Williamsburg. She checks with her CPA neighbor to verify she will not have to include the rent income in her gross income. June agrees to rent her house and to visit her sister through New Year's Day.

The golfer and his family arrived on December 20 and were scheduled to depart on December 27. On December 26, the golfer's wife calls June at her sister's, explains that their two-year-old child is ill, and asks if they can rent for an additional day until the child

[45] § 280A(g).

feels better. June says yes, of course, but indicates she will not accept any rent for the additional day.

When June returns home on January 2, 1997, she finds the check on her kitchen counter is for $3,200 rather than for $2,800. The check is enclosed in a Christmas card from the golfer and his family.

On her 1996 Federal income tax return, June does not report any rent income or deduct any rental expenses. According to her records, she rented her house for exactly two weeks.

Can you justify June's treatment of the rent income and expenses?

Primarily Rental Use. If the residence is *rented* for 15 days or more in a year and is *not used* for personal purposes for more than the greater of (1) 14 days or (2) 10 percent of the total days rented, the residence is treated as rental property.[46] The expenses must be allocated between personal and rental days if there are any personal use days during the year. The deduction of the expenses allocated to rental days can exceed rent income and result in a rental loss. The loss may be deductible under the passive activity loss rules (discussed in Chapter 11).

EXAMPLE 25

Assume instead that Dixie in Example 24 rented the cottage for 120 days and lived in it for 13 days. The cottage is primarily rental use since she rented it for 15 days or more and did not use it for personal purposes for more than 14 days. ▼

EXAMPLE 26

Assume instead that Dixie in Example 24 rented the cottage for 200 days and lived in it for 19 days. The cottage is primarily rental use since she rented it for 15 days or more and did not use it for personal purposes for more than 20 days (10% of the rental days). ▼

EXAMPLE 27

Assume instead that Dixie in Example 24 used the cottage for 12 days and rented it for 48 days for $4,800. Since she rented the cottage for 15 days or more but did not use it for more than 14 days, the cottage is treated as rental property. The expenses must be allocated between personal and rental days.

	Percentage of Use	
	Rental	**Personal**
	80%	**20%**
Income	$4,800	$ -0-
Expenses		
Mortgage interest ($6,000)	($4,800)	($1,200)
Property taxes ($500)	(400)	(100)
Utilities and maintenance ($1,500)	(1,200)	(300)
Depreciation ($2,400)	(1,920)	(480)
Total expenses	($8,320)	($2,080)
Rental loss	($3,520)	$ -0-

Dixie deducts the $3,520 rental loss *for* AGI (assuming she meets the passive activity loss rules, discussed in Chapter 11). She also has an itemized deduction for property taxes of $100 associated with the personal use. The mortgage interest of $1,200 associated with the personal use is not deductible as an itemized deduction because the cottage is not a

[46] § 280A(d) and Prop.Reg. § 1.280A–3(c).

qualified residence (qualified residence interest) for this purpose (see Chapter 10). The portion of utilities and maintenance and depreciation attributable to personal use is not deductible. ▼

Personal/Rental Use. If the residence is rented for 15 days or more in a year *and* is used for personal purposes for more than the greater of (1) 14 days or (2) 10 percent of the total days rented, it is treated as a personal/rental use residence. The expenses must be allocated between personal days and rental days. Expenses are allowed only to the extent of rent income.

EXAMPLE 28

Assume instead that Dixie in Example 24 rented the property for 30 days and lived in it for 30 days. The residence is classified as personal/rental use property since she used it more than 14 days and rented it for 15 days or more. The expenses must be allocated between rental use and personal use, and the rental expenses are allowed only to the extent of rent income. ▼

If a residence is classified as personal/rental use property, the expenses that are deductible anyway (e.g., real estate taxes and mortgage interest) must be deducted first. If a positive net income results, otherwise nondeductible expenses that do not affect adjusted basis (e.g., maintenance, utilities, insurance) are allowed next. Finally, if any positive balance remains, depreciation is allowed.

Expenses must be allocated between personal and rental days before the limits are applied. The courts have held that real estate taxes and mortgage interest, which accrue ratably over the year, are allocated on the basis of 365 days.[47] The IRS, however, disagrees and allocates real estate taxes and mortgage interest on the basis of total days of use.[48] Other expenses (utilities, maintenance, depreciation, etc.) are allocated on the basis of total days used.

EXAMPLE 29

Sue rents her vacation home for 60 days and lives in the home for 30 days. The limitations on personal/rental use residences apply. Sue's gross rent income is $10,000. For the entire year (not a leap year), the real estate taxes are $2,190; her mortgage interest expense is $10,220; utilities and maintenance expense equals $2,400; and depreciation is $9,000. Using the IRS approach, these amounts are deductible in this specific order:

Gross income	$10,000
Deduct: Taxes and interest (60/90 × $12,410)	(8,273)
Remainder to apply to rental operating expenses and depreciation	$ 1,727
Deduct: Utilities and maintenance (60/90 × $2,400)	(1,600)
Balance	$ 127
Deduct: Depreciation (60/90 × $9,000 = $6,000 but limited to above balance)	(127)
Net rent income	$ -0-

The nonrental use portion of real estate taxes and mortgage interest ($4,137 in this case) is deductible if the taxpayer elects to itemize (see Chapter 10). The personal use portion of utilities, maintenance, and depreciation is not deductible in any case. Also note that the basis of the property is not reduced by the $5,873 depreciation not allowed ($6,000 – $127) because of the above limitation. (See Chapter 14 for a discussion of the reduction in basis for depreciation allowed or allowable.) ▼

[47] *Bolton v. Comm.*, 82–2 USTC ¶9699, 51 AFTR2d 83–305, 694 F.2d 556 (CA–9, 1982).

[48] Prop.Reg. § 1.280A–3(d)(4).

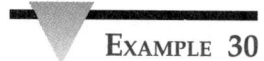

EXAMPLE 30 Using the court's approach in allocating real estate taxes and mortgage interest, Sue, in Example 29, would have this result:

Gross income	$10,000
Deduct: Taxes and interest (60/365 × $12,410)	(2,040)
Remainder to apply to rental operating expenses and depreciation	$ 7,960
Deduct: Utilities and maintenance (60/90 × $2,400)	(1,600)
Balance	$ 6,360
Deduct: Depreciation (60/90 × $9,000, but limited to $6,360)	(6,000)
Net rent income	$ 360

Sue can deduct $10,370 ($12,410 paid – $2,040 deducted as expense in computing net rent income) of personal use mortgage interest and real estate taxes as itemized deductions. ▼

Note the contrasting results in Examples 29 and 30. The IRS's approach (Example 29) results in no rental gain or loss and an itemized deduction for real estate taxes and mortgage interest of $4,137. In Example 30, Sue has net rent income of $360 and $10,370 of itemized deductions. The court's approach decreases her taxable income by $10,010 ($10,370 itemized deductions less $360 net rent income). The IRS's approach reduces her taxable income by only $4,137.

EXAMPLE 31 Assume instead that Sue in Example 29 had not lived in the home at all during the year. The house is rental property. The rental loss is calculated as follows:

Gross income	$10,000
Expenses	
Taxes and interest	($12,410)
Utilities and maintenance	(2,400)
Depreciation	(9,000)
Total expenses	($23,810)
Rental loss	($13,810)

Whether any of the rental loss would be deductible depends upon whether Sue actively participated in the rental activity and met the other requirements for passive activity losses (discussed in Chapter 11). ▼

Conversion to Rental Property. A related issue is whether or not a taxpayer's *primary residence* is subject to the preceding rules if it is converted to rental property. If the vacation home rules apply, a taxpayer who converts his or her personal residence to rental property during the tax year, without any tax avoidance motive, could have the allowable deductions limited to the rent income. This would occur if the personal use exceeded the greater of 14 days or 10 percent of rental days test (a likely situation). The Code, however, provides that during a *qualified rental period,* any personal use days are not counted as personal use days in terms of classifying the use of the residence as *personal/rental use* rather than as *primarily rental use.*[49] In effect, the deduction for expenses of the property incurred during a qualified rental period is not subject to the personal use test of the vacation home rules. A qualified rental period is a consecutive period of 12 or more months. The period begins or ends in the taxable year in which the residence

[49] § 280A(d).

CONCEPT SUMMARY 6–1

Vacation/Rental Home

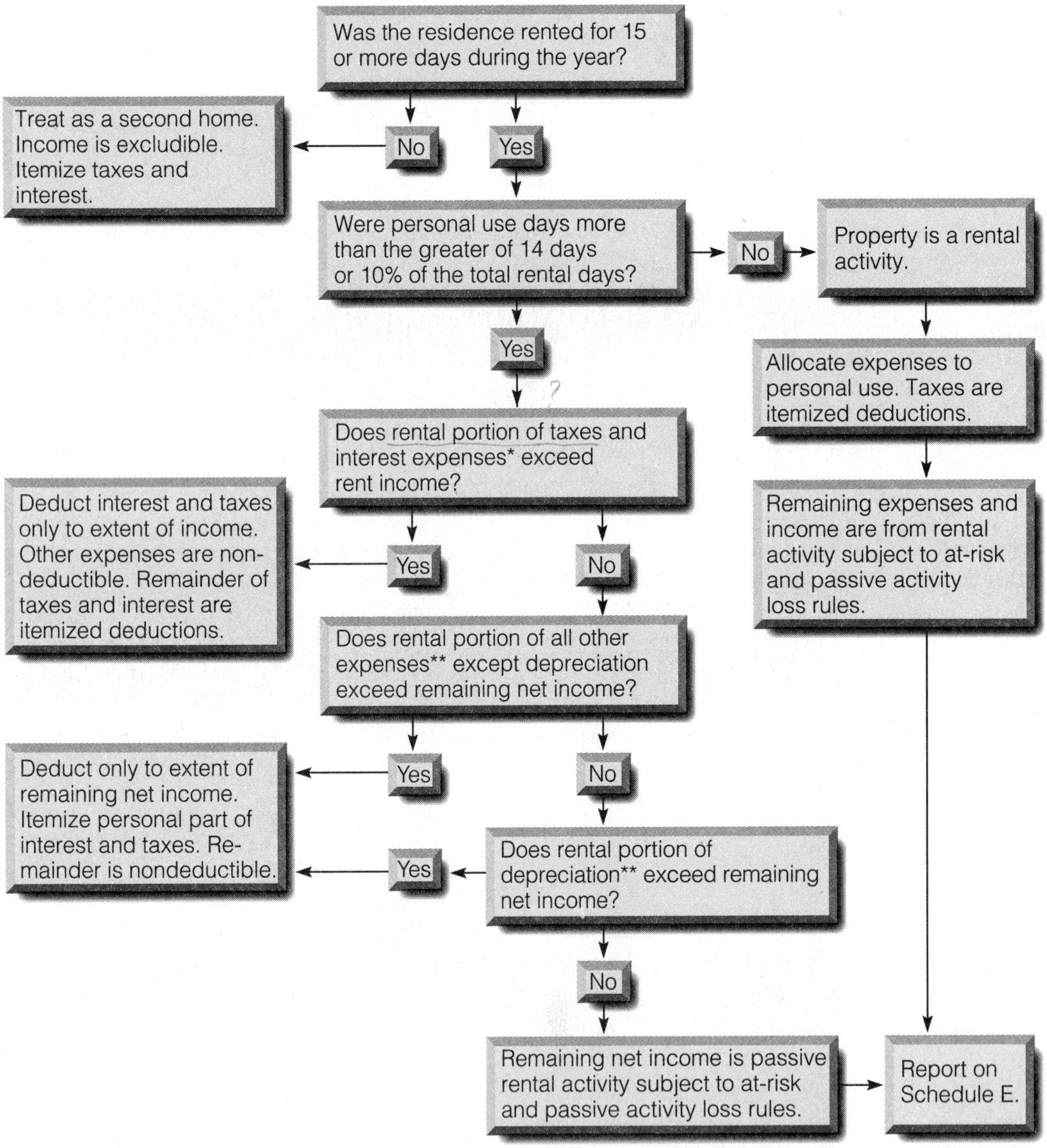
Was the residence rented for 15 or more days during the year?
No
Yes
Treat as a second home. Income is excludible. Itemize taxes and interest.
Were personal use days more than the greater of 14 days or 10% of the total rental days?
No
Property is a rental activity.
Allocate expenses to personal use. Taxes are itemized deductions.
Remaining expenses and income are from rental activity subject to at-risk and passive activity loss rules.
Yes
Does rental portion of taxes and interest expenses* exceed rent income?
Yes
Deduct interest and taxes only to extent of income. Other expenses are non-deductible. Remainder of taxes and interest are itemized deductions.
No
Does rental portion of all other expenses** except depreciation exceed remaining net income?
Yes
Deduct only to extent of remaining net income. Itemize personal part of interest and taxes. Remainder is nondeductible.
No
Does rental portion of depreciation** exceed remaining net income?
Yes
No
Remaining net income is passive rental activity subject to at-risk and passive activity loss rules.
Report on Schedule E.

*Allocated on the basis of 365 (366 in a leap year) days (court) or total days of use (IRS).
**Allocated on the basis of total days of use.

is rented or held for rental at a fair price. The residence must not be rented to a related party. If the property is sold before the 12-month period expires, the qualified rental period is the actual time rented.

EXAMPLE 32

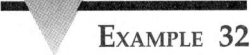

Rhonda converts her residence to rental property on May 1 and rents it for the remainder of 1996 for $5,600 and for all of 1997 for $8,400. The house would be classified as personal/rental use property (personal use days during 1996 are greater than both 14 days and 10%

of rental days) except that this is a qualified rental period. Therefore, Rhonda's deduction for rental expenses is not limited to the gross income of $5,600 in 1996. ▼

See Concept Summary 6–1 for a summary of the vacation home rules.

EXPENDITURES INCURRED FOR TAXPAYER'S BENEFIT OR TAXPAYER'S OBLIGATION

An expense must be incurred for the taxpayer's benefit or arise from the taxpayer's obligation. An individual cannot claim a tax deduction for the payment of the expenses of another individual.

EXAMPLE 33

During the current year, Fred pays the interest on his son, Vern's, home mortgage. Neither Fred nor Vern can take a deduction for the interest paid. Fred is not entitled to a deduction because the mortgage is not his obligation. Vern cannot claim a deduction because he did not pay the interest. The tax result would have been more favorable had Fred made a cash gift to Vern and let him pay the interest. Then Vern could have deducted the interest, and Fred might not have been liable for any gift taxes depending upon the amount involved. A deduction would have been created with no cash difference to the family. ▼

One exception to this disallowance rule is the payment of medical expenses for a dependent. Such expenses are deductible by the payer subject to the normal rules that limit the deductibility of medical expenses (see Chapter 10).[50]

ETHICAL CONSIDERATIONS

How the Payment Is Made

Dan and Jeff both have sons who graduated from college recently and are employed by the same company in a rural community where rental housing is not readily available. Each father loans his son $10,000; the sons combine their resources and use the $20,000 as a down payment on a house that they buy together.

During 1996, the sons make all the mortgage payments on their house until December when they are furloughed from their jobs. Dan gives his son $900 to use to pay his share of the mortgage payment, and Jeff pays $900 directly to the mortgage company for his son. In each of these $900 amounts, $800 represents interest on the mortgage.

Over lunch recently, Dan and Jeff were discussing their sons' real estate investment and the $900 mortgage payment each father had funded. Jeff indicated that since he had paid the mortgage payment directly, he was going to deduct the $800 of interest on his Form 1040. After this conversation, Dan concludes that, in substance, he and Jeff have done the same thing. Accordingly, Dan calls his son and tells him that he wants to deduct the $800 on his tax return. Though Dan's son is not pleased, he agrees to permit his father to take the deduction and says he will not deduct the mortgage interest on his own return.

Evaluate the propriety of the position taken by Dan.

DISALLOWANCE OF PERSONAL EXPENDITURES

Section 262 states that "except as otherwise expressly provided in this chapter, no deduction shall be allowed for personal, living, or family expenses." To justify a

[50] § 213(a).

deduction, an individual must be able to identify a particular section of the Code that sanctions the deduction (e.g., charitable contributions, medical expenses). Sometimes the character of a particular expenditure is not easily determined.

EXAMPLE 34 During the current year, Howard pays $1,500 in legal fees and court costs to obtain a divorce from his wife, Vera. Involved in the divorce action is a property settlement that concerns the disposition of income-producing property owned by Howard. In a similar situation, the Tax Court held that the taxpayer could not deduct any such costs.[51] "Although fees primarily related to property division concerning his income-producing property, they weren't ordinary and necessary expenses paid for conservation or maintenance of property held for production of income. Legal fees incurred in defending against claims that arise from a taxpayer's marital relationship aren't deductible expenses regardless of possible consequences on taxpayer's income-producing property." ▼

The IRS has clarified the issue of the deduction of legal fees incurred in connection with a divorce.[52] To be deductible, an expense must relate solely to tax advice in a divorce proceeding. For example, legal fees attributable to the determination of dependency exemptions of children are deductible if the fees are distinguishable from the general legal fees incurred in obtaining a divorce. Other examples are the costs of creating a trust to make periodic alimony payments and the determination of the tax consequences of a property settlement. Therefore, it is advisable to request an itemization of attorney's fees to substantiate a deduction for the tax-related amounts.

DISALLOWANCE OF DEDUCTIONS FOR CAPITAL EXPENDITURES

The Code specifically disallows a deduction for "any amount paid out for new buildings or for permanent improvements or betterments made to increase the value of any property or estate."[53] The Regulations further define capital expenditures to include those expenditures that add to the value or prolong the life of property or adapt the property to a new or different use.[54] Incidental repairs and maintenance of the property are not capital expenditures and can be deducted as ordinary and necessary business expenses. Repairing a roof is a deductible expense, but replacing a roof is a capital expenditure subject to depreciation deductions over its useful life. The tune-up of a delivery truck is an expense; a complete overhaul probably is a capital expenditure.

Capitalization versus Expense. When an expenditure is capitalized rather than expensed, the deduction is at best deferred and at worst lost forever. Although an immediate tax benefit for a large cash expenditure is lost, the cost may be deductible in increments over a longer period of time.

If the expenditure is for a tangible asset that has an ascertainable life, it is capitalized and may be deducted as depreciation (or cost recovery) over the life of the asset (for depreciation) or over a statutory period (for cost recovery under either ACRS or MACRS).[55] Land is not subject to depreciation (or cost recovery) since it does not have an ascertainable life.

---

[51] *Harry H. Goldberg*, 29 TCM 74, T.C.Memo. 1970–27.

[52] Rev.Rul. 72–545, 1972–2 C.B. 179.

[53] § 263(a)(1).

[54] Reg. § 1.263(a)–1(b).

[55] See Chapter 8 for the discussion of depreciation and cost recovery.

EXAMPLE 35

Stan purchased a prime piece of land located in an apartment-zoned area. Stan paid $500,000 for the property, which had an old but usable apartment building on it. He immediately had the building demolished at a cost of $100,000. The $500,000 purchase price and the $100,000 demolition costs must be capitalized, and the basis of the land is $600,000. Since land is a nondepreciable asset, no deduction is allowed. More favorable tax treatment might result if Stan rented the apartments in the old building for a period of time to attempt to establish that there was no intent to demolish the building. If Stan's attempt is successful, it might be possible to allocate a substantial portion of the original purchase price of the property to the building (a depreciable asset). When the building is later demolished, any remaining adjusted basis can be deducted as an ordinary (§ 1231) loss. (See Chapter 17 for a discussion of the treatment of § 1231 assets.) ▼

If the expenditure is for an intangible asset (e.g., copyright, patent, covenant not to compete, goodwill), the capitalized expenditure can be amortized. Prior to the effect of RRA of 1993, only intangible assets with ascertainable lives (e.g., copyright, patent, covenant not to compete) could be amortized. Intangible assets with indeterminate lives (e.g., goodwill) could not be amortized. The amortization period generally was the life of the asset, and the amortization method was the straight-line method.

RRA of 1993 provides that intangibles acquired after August 10, 1993, are to be amortized over a 15-year period using the straight-line method.[56] This statutory change can produce both positive and negative results. On the positive side, goodwill is now subject to amortization. On the negative side, intangibles with an actual life shorter than 15 years must be amortized over the longer 15-year statutory period (e.g., a covenant not to compete with a 5-year life).

TRANSACTIONS BETWEEN RELATED PARTIES

The Code places restrictions on the recognition of gains and losses from **related-party transactions.** Without these restrictions, relationships created by birth, marriage, and business would provide endless possibilities for engaging in financial transactions that produce tax savings with no real economic substance or change. For example, to create an artificial loss, a wife could sell investment property to her husband at a loss and deduct the loss on their joint return. Her husband could then hold the asset indefinitely, and the family would sustain no real economic loss. A complex set of laws has been designed to eliminate such possibilities.

Losses. The Code provides for the disallowance of any "losses from sales or exchanges of property . . . directly or indirectly" between related parties.[57] When the property is subsequently sold to a nonrelated party, any gain recognized is reduced by the loss previously disallowed. Any disallowed loss not used by the related-party buyer to offset his or her recognized gain on a subsequent sale or exchange to an unrelated party is permanently lost.

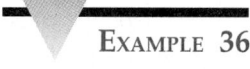

EXAMPLE 36

Freida sells common stock with a basis of $1,000 to her son, Bill, for $800. Bill sells the stock several years later for $1,100. Freida's $200 loss is disallowed upon the sale to Bill, and only $100 of gain ($1,100 selling price – $800 basis – $200 disallowed loss) is taxable to him upon the subsequent sale. ▼

[56] § 197.

[57] § 267(a)(1).

EXAMPLE 37

George sells common stock with a basis of $1,050 to his son, Ray, for $800. Ray sells the stock eight months later to an unrelated party for $900. Ray's gain of $100 ($900 selling price – $800 basis) is not recognized because of George's previously disallowed loss of $250. Note that the offset may result in only partial tax benefit upon the subsequent sale (as in this case). If the property had not been transferred to Ray, George could have recognized a $150 loss upon the subsequent sale to the unrelated party ($1,050 basis – $900 selling price). ▼

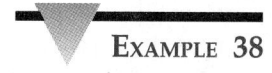

EXAMPLE 38

Pete sells common stock with a basis of $1,000 to an unrelated third party for $800. Pete's son repurchased the same stock in the market on the same day for $800. The $200 loss is not allowed because the transaction is an indirect sale between related parties.[58] ▼

Unpaid Expenses and Interest. The law prevents related taxpayers from engaging in tax avoidance schemes where one related taxpayer uses the accrual method of accounting and the other uses the cash basis. An accrual basis, closely held corporation, for example, could borrow funds from a cash basis individual shareholder. At the end of the year, the corporation would accrue and deduct the interest, but the cash basis lender would not recognize interest income since no interest had been paid. Section 267 specifically defers the deduction of the accruing taxpayer until the recipient taxpayer must include it in income; that is, when it is actually paid to the cash basis taxpayer. This *matching* provision applies to interest as well as other expenses, such as salaries and bonuses.

This deduction deferral provision does not apply if both of the related taxpayers use the accrual method or both use the cash method. Likewise, it does not apply if the related party reporting income uses the accrual method and the related party taking the deduction uses the cash method.

Relationships and Constructive Ownership. Section 267 operates to disallow losses and defer deductions only between related parties. Losses or deductions generated by similar transactions with an unrelated party are allowed. *Related parties* include the following:

- Brothers and sisters (whether whole, half, or adopted), spouse, ancestors (parents, grandparents), and lineal descendants (children, grandchildren) of the taxpayer.
- A corporation owned more than 50 percent (directly or indirectly) by the taxpayer.
- Two corporations that are members of a controlled group.
- A series of other complex relationships between trusts, corporations, and individual taxpayers.

Constructive ownership provisions are applied to determine whether the taxpayers are related. Under these provisions, stock owned by certain relatives or related entities is *deemed* to be owned by the taxpayer for purposes of applying the loss and expense deduction disallowance provisions. A taxpayer is deemed to own not only his or her stock but the stock owned by his or her lineal descendants, ancestors, brothers and sisters or half-brothers and half-sisters, and spouse. The taxpayer is also deemed to own his or her proportionate share of stock owned by any partnership, corporation, estate, or trust of which he or she is a member. An individual is deemed to own any stock owned, directly or indirectly, by his or her partner. However, constructive ownership by an individual of the partnership's and the other partner's shares does not extend to the individual's spouse or other relatives (no double attribution).

[58] *McWilliams v. Comm.*, 47–1 USTC ¶9289, 35 AFTR 1184, 67 S.Ct. 1477 (USSC, 1947).

EXAMPLE 39

The stock of Sparrow Corporation is owned 20% by Ted, 30% by Ted's father, 30% by Ted's mother, and 20% by Ted's sister. On July 1 of the current year, Ted loaned $10,000 to Sparrow Corporation at 8% annual interest, principal and interest payable on demand. For tax purposes, Sparrow uses the accrual basis, and Ted uses the cash basis. Both are on a calendar year. Since Ted is deemed to own the 80% owned by his parents and sister, he constructively owns 100% of Sparrow Corporation. If the corporation accrues the interest within the taxable year, no deduction can be taken until payment is made to Ted. ▼

SUBSTANTIATION REQUIREMENTS

The tax law is built on a voluntary system. Taxpayers file their tax returns, report income and take deductions to which they are entitled, and pay their taxes through withholding or estimated tax payments during the year. The taxpayer has the burden of proof for substantiating expenses deducted on the returns and must retain adequate records. Upon audit, the IRS will disallow any undocumented or unsubstantiated deductions. These requirements have resulted in numerous conflicts between taxpayers and the IRS.

Some events throughout the year should be documented as they occur. For example, it is generally advisable to receive a pledge payment statement from one's church, in addition to a canceled check (if available) for proper documentation of a charitable contribution.[59] In addition, for charitable contributions made after December 31, 1993, a donor must obtain a receipt from the donee for contributions of $250 or more. Other types of deductible expenditures may require receipts or some other type of support.

Specific and *more stringent* rules for deducting travel, entertainment, and gift expenses are discussed in Chapter 9. Certain mixed-use (both personal and business use) and listed property are also subject to the adequate records requirement (discussed in Chapter 8).

EXPENSES AND INTEREST RELATING TO TAX-EXEMPT INCOME

Certain income, such as interest on municipal bonds, is tax-exempt.[60] The law also allows the taxpayer to deduct expenses incurred for the production of income.[61] Deduction disallowance provisions, however, make it impossible to make money at the expense of the government by excluding interest income and deducting interest expense.[62]

EXAMPLE 40

Sandy, a taxpayer in the 36% bracket, purchased $100,000 of 6% municipal bonds. At the same time, she used the bonds as collateral on a bank loan of $100,000 at 8% interest. A positive cash flow would result from the tax benefit as follows:

Cash paid out on loan	($8,000)
Cash received from bonds	6,000
Tax savings from deducting interest expense (36% of $8,000 interest expense)	2,880
Net positive cash flow	$ 880

▼

[59] Rev.Proc. 92–71, 1992–2 C.B. 437, addresses circumstances where checks are not returned by a financial institution or where electronic transfers are made.

[60] § 103.

[61] § 212.

[62] § 265.

To eliminate the possibility illustrated in Example 40, the Code specifically disallows as a deduction the expenses of producing tax-exempt income. Interest on any indebtedness incurred or continued to purchase or carry tax-exempt obligations also is disallowed.

Judicial Interpretations. It is often difficult to show a direct relationship between borrowings and investment in tax-exempt securities. Suppose, for example, that a taxpayer borrows money, adds it to existing funds, buys inventory and stocks, then later sells the inventory and buys municipal bonds. A series of transactions such as these can completely obscure any connection between the loan and the tax-exempt investment. One solution would be to disallow interest on any debt to the extent that the taxpayer holds any tax-exempt securities. This approach would preclude individuals from deducting part of their home mortgage interest if they owned any municipal bonds. The law was not intended to go to such extremes. As a result, judicial interpretations have tried to be reasonable in disallowing interest deductions.

In one case, a company used municipal bonds as collateral on short-term loans to meet seasonal liquidity needs.[63] The Court disallowed the interest deduction on the grounds that the company could predict its seasonal liquidity needs. The company could anticipate the need to borrow the money to continue to carry the tax-exempt securities. The same company *was* allowed an interest deduction on a building mortgage, even though tax-exempt securities it owned could have been sold to pay off the mortgage. The Court reasoned that short-term liquidity needs would have been impaired if the tax-exempt securities were sold. Furthermore, the Court ruled that carrying the tax-exempt securities bore no relationship to the long-term financing of a construction project.

EXAMPLE 41

In January of the current year, Gayle borrowed $100,000 at 8% interest. She used the loan proceeds to purchase 5,000 shares of stock in White Corporation. In July, she sold the stock for $120,000 and reinvested the proceeds in City of Denver bonds, the income from which is tax-exempt. Assuming the $100,000 loan remained outstanding throughout the entire year, Gayle cannot deduct the interest attributable to the period in which she held the bonds. ▼

TAX PLANNING CONSIDERATIONS

TIME VALUE OF TAX DEDUCTIONS

4 LEARNING OBJECTIVE
Identify tax planning opportunities for maximizing deductions and minimizing the disallowance of deductions.

Cash basis taxpayers often have the ability to make early payments for their expenses at the end of the tax year. This permits the payments to be deducted currently instead of in the following tax year. In view of the time value of money, a tax deduction this year may be worth more than the same deduction next year. Before employing this strategy, the taxpayer must consider next year's expected income and tax rates and whether a cash-flow problem may develop from early payments. Thus, the time value of money as well as tax rate changes must be considered when an expense can be paid and deducted in either of two years.

EXAMPLE 42

Jena pledged $5,000 to her church's special building fund. She can make the contribution in December 1996 or January 1997. Jena is in the 36% tax bracket in 1996, and in the 31% bracket in 1997. She itemizes in both years. Assume Jena's discount rate is 8%. If she takes the deduction in 1996, she saves $365 ($1,800 – $1,435), due to the decrease in the tax rates and the time value of money.

[63] *The Wisconsin Cheeseman, Inc. v. U.S.*, 68–1 USTC ¶9145, 21 AFTR2d 383, 388 F.2d 420 (CA–7, 1968).

	1996	1997
Contribution	$5,000	$5,000
Tax bracket	.36	.31
Tax savings	$1,800	$1,550
Discounted @ 8%	1.0	.926
Savings in present value	$1,800	$1,435

▼

EXAMPLE 43

Assume the same facts as in Example 42, except that Jena is in the 31% bracket in both 1996 and 1997. By taking the deduction in 1996, Jena saves $115 ($1,550 – $1,435), due to the time value of money.

	1996	1997
Contribution	$5,000	$5,000
Tax bracket	.31	.31
Tax savings	$1,550	$1,550
Discounted @ 8%	1.0	.926
Savings in present value	$1,550	$1,435

▼

UNREASONABLE COMPENSATION

In substantiating the reasonableness of a shareholder-employee's compensation, an internal comparison test is sometimes useful. If it can be shown that nonshareholder-employees and shareholder-employees in comparable positions receive comparable compensation, it is indicative that compensation is not unreasonable.

Another possibility is to demonstrate that the shareholder-employee has been underpaid in prior years. For example, the shareholder-employee may have agreed to take a less-than-adequate salary during the unprofitable formative years of the business. He or she would expect the "postponed" compensation to be paid in later, more profitable years. The agreement should be documented, if possible, in the corporate minutes.

Keep in mind that in testing for reasonableness, the *total* pay package must be considered. Look at all fringe benefits or perquisites, such as contributions by the corporation to a qualified pension plan. Even though those amounts are not immediately available to the covered shareholder-employee, they must be taken into account.

EXCESSIVE EXECUTIVE COMPENSATION

With the $1 million limit on the deduction of compensation of covered employees, many corporations and their executives must engage in additional tax planning. Previously, concerns over the deductibility of compensation related primarily to closely held corporations. The $1 million limit applies specifically to publicly held corporations. In many instances, it is now necessary for these corporations to restructure the compensation packages of their top executives in order to deduct payments in excess of $1 million. Opportunities include compensation payable on a commission basis, certain other performance-based compensation, payments to qualified retirement plans, and payments that are excludible fringe benefits.

CONCEPT SUMMARY 6–2

Classification of Expenses

Expense Item	Deductible For AGI	Deductible From AGI	Not Deductible	Applicable Code §
Investment expenses				
Rent and royalty	X			§ 62(a)(4)
All other investments		X[4]		§ 212
Employee expenses				
Commuting expenses			X	§ 262
Travel and transportation[1]		X[4,5]		§ 162(a)(2)
Reimbursed expenses[1]	X			§ 62(a)(2)(A)
Moving expenses	X			§ 62(a)(15)
Entertainment[1]		X[4,5]		§ 162(a)
All other employee expenses[1]		X[4,5]		§ 162(a)
Certain expenses of performing artists	X			§ 62(a)(2)(B)
Trade or business expenses	X			§§ 162 and 62(a)(1)
Casualty losses				
Business	X			§ 165(c)(1)
Personal		X[6]		§ 165(c)(3)
Tax determination				
Collection or refund expenses	X[8]	X[4]		§§ 212 and 62(a)(1) or (4)
Bad debts	X			§§ 166 and 62(a)(1) or (3)
Medical expenses		X[7]		§ 213
Charitable contributions		X		§ 170
Taxes				
Trade or business	X			§§ 162 and 62(a)(1)
Personal taxes				
Real property		X		§ 164(a)(1)
Personal property		X		§ 164(a)(2)
State and local income		X		§ 164(a)(3)
Investigation of a business[2]	X			§§ 162 and 62(a)(1)
Interest				
Business	X			§§ 162 and 62(a)(1)
Personal		X[3]	X[9]	§ 163(a), (d), and (h)
All other personal expenses			X	§ 262

1. Deduction *for* AGI if reimbursed, an adequate accounting is made, and employee is required to repay excess reimbursements.
2. Provided certain criteria are met.
3. Subject to the excess investment interest and the qualified residence interest provisions.
4. Subject (in the aggregate) to a 2%-of-AGI floor imposed by § 67.
5. Only 50% of meals and entertainment are deductible.
6. Subject to a 10%-of-AGI floor and a $100 floor.
7. Subject to a 7.5%-of-AGI floor.
8. Only the portion relating to business, rental, or royalty income or losses.
9. Other personal interest is disallowed.

SHIFTING DEDUCTIONS

Taxpayers should manage their obligations to avoid the loss of a deduction. Deductions can be shifted among family members, depending upon which member makes the payment. For example, a father buys a condo for his daughter and puts the title in both names. The taxpayer who makes the payment gets the deduction for the property taxes. If the condo is owned by the daughter only and her father makes the payment, neither is entitled to a deduction. In this case, the father should make a cash gift to the daughter who then makes the payment to the taxing authority.

HOBBY LOSSES

To demonstrate that an activity has been entered into for the purpose of making a profit, a taxpayer should treat the activity as a business. The business should engage in advertising, use business letterhead stationery, and maintain a business phone.

If a taxpayer's activity earns a profit in three out of five consecutive years, the presumption is that the activity is engaged in for profit. It may be possible for a cash basis taxpayer to meet these requirements by timing the payment of expenses or the receipt of revenues. The payment of certain expenses incurred before the end of the year might be made in the following year. The billing of year-end sales might be delayed so that collections are received in the following year.

Keep in mind that the three-out-of-five-years rule under § 183 is not absolute. All it does is shift the presumption. If a profit is not made in three out of five years, the losses may still be allowed if the taxpayer can show that they are due to the nature of the business. For example, success in artistic or literary endeavors can take a long time. Also, due to the present state of the economy, even full-time farmers and ranchers are often unable to show a profit. How can one expect a part-time farmer or rancher to do so?

Merely satisfying the three-out-of-five-years rule does not guarantee that a taxpayer is automatically home free. If the three years of profits are insignificant relative to the losses of other years, or if the profits are not from the ordinary operation of the business, the taxpayer is vulnerable. The IRS may still be able to establish that the taxpayer is not engaged in an activity for profit.

EXAMPLE 44

Ashley had the following gains and losses in an artistic endeavor:

1992	($ 50,000)
1993	(65,000)
1994	400
1995	200
1996	125

Under these circumstances, the IRS might try to overcome the presumption. ▼

If Ashley in Example 44 could show conformity with the factors enumerated in the Regulations or could show evidence of business hardships (e.g., injury, death, or illness), the government cannot override the presumption.[64]

[64] *Faulconer, Sr. v. Comm.*, 84–2 USTC ¶9955, 55 AFTR2d 85–302, 748 F.2d 890 (CA–4, 1984), *rev'g* 45 TCM 1084, T.C.Memo. 1983–165.

CAPITAL EXPENDITURES

RRA of 1993 has modified the planning strategy associated with goodwill and covenants not to compete. Prior to RRA of 1993, on the sale of a sole proprietorship where the sales price exceeded the fair market value of the tangible assets and stated intangible assets, a natural tax conflict typically existed between the seller and the buyer. The seller's preference was for the excess amount to be allocated to goodwill. Goodwill is a capital asset whereas a covenant not to compete produces ordinary income treatment (see Chapter 16). The buyer's preference was for the excess amount to be allocated to a covenant not to compete because it could be amortized over the covenant life whereas goodwill was not eligible for amortization.

RRA of 1993 provides that both a covenant and goodwill are to be amortized over a statutory 15-year period. Therefore, the tax results for the buyer are the same. The seller's motive was not affected by the change in the law. Therefore, the seller and buyer, in negotiating the sales price, should factor in the tax benefit to the seller of having the excess amount labeled goodwill rather than a covenant not to compete. Of course, if the noncompetition aspects of a covenant are important to the buyer, part of the excess amount can be assigned to a covenant.

KEY TERMS

Accounting method, 6–9

Deductions *for* adjusted gross income, 6–2

Deductions *from* adjusted gross income, 6–2

Hobby losses, 6–17

Ordinary and necessary, 6–6

Reasonableness, 6–7

Related-party transactions, 6–27

Vacation home, 6–20

PROBLEM MATERIALS

DISCUSSION QUESTIONS

1. "All income must be reported and all deductions are allowed unless specifically disallowed in the Code." Discuss.
2. Discuss the difference in the tax treatment of deductions *for* and deductions *from* AGI.
3. Does an expenditure that is classified as a deduction *from* AGI produce the same tax benefit as an expenditure that is classified as a deduction *for* AGI?
4. Classify each of the following expenditures as a deduction *for* AGI, a deduction *from* AGI, or not deductible:
   a. Pete gives $1,000 to his mother for her birthday.
   b. Janet gives $1,000 to the First Baptist Church.
   c. Alex pays Dr. Dafashy $1,000 for medical services rendered.
   d. Susan pays alimony of $1,000 to Herman.
   e. Rex contributes $1,000 to his pension plan.
5. Classify each of the following expenditures as a deduction *for* AGI, a deduction *from* AGI, or not deductible:
   a. Amos contributes $500 to his H.R. 10 plan (i.e., a retirement plan for a self-employed individual).
   b. Keith pays $500 of child support to his former wife, Renee, for the support of their son, Chris.
   c. Judy pays $500 for professional dues that are reimbursed by her employer.

d. Ted pays $500 as the monthly mortgage payment on his personal residence. Of this amount, $100 represents a payment on principal, and $400 represents an interest payment.
e. Lynn pays $500 to a moving company for moving her household goods to Detroit where she is starting a new job.

6. Larry and Susan each invest $10,000 in separate investment activities. They each incur deductible expenses of $800 associated with their respective investments. Explain why Larry's expenses are properly classified as deductions *from* AGI (itemized deductions) and Susan's expenses are appropriately classified as deductions *for* AGI.

7. List the three items that § 162 specifically excludes from classification as a trade or business expense.

8. Define and contrast the "ordinary" and "necessary" tests for business expenses.

9. Wendy, a machinist employed by Silver Airlines, owns 25 shares of Silver Airlines stock. Silver has 900,000 shares of stock outstanding. Wendy spends $800 to travel to Chicago for Silver's annual meeting. Her expenses would have been $500 more, but she was permitted to fly free on Silver. She attended both days of the shareholders' meeting and actively participated. What are the tax consequences of the trip for Wendy?

10. Sam and Vera are the owners of a corporation. To reduce the corporation's taxable income, they pay a $1,000 salary each month to their 7-year-old daughter, Peg. Why is this salary disallowed as a deduction?

11. Which of the following losses are deductible?
    a. Loss on the sale of a factory building used in a trade or business.
    b. Loss on the sale of a truck held for personal use.
    c. Loss from the destruction by a tornado of a warehouse used in a trade or business.
    d. Loss on the destruction by fire of the taxpayer's residence.
    e. Loss on the sale of Lavender Corporation stock held as an investment.

12. Distinguish between the timing for the recording of a deduction under the cash method versus the accrual method.

13. Landry, a cash basis taxpayer, decides to reduce his taxable income for 1996 by buying $10,000 worth of supplies on December 28, 1996. The supplies will be used up in 1997.
    a. Can Landry deduct this expenditure in 1996?
    b. Would your answer differ if Landry bought the supplies because a supplier was going out of business and had given him a significant discount on the supplies?

14. What is the "actually paid" requirement for the deduction of an expense by a cash basis taxpayer? Does actual payment ensure a deduction?

15. What is the significance of the all events and economic performance tests?

16. James provides a one-year warranty on the vacuum cleaners manufactured by his company. Claims under the warranty typically amount to 2% of sales. Can James use the reserve method to account for the warranty expense?

17. Are any bribes or kickbacks deductible?

18. Ted is an agent for an airline manufacturer and is negotiating a sale with a representative of the U.S. government and with a representative of a developing country. Ted's company has sufficient capacity to handle only one of the orders. Both orders will have the same contract price. Ted believes that if his employer will authorize a $500,000 payment to the representative of the foreign country, he can guarantee the sale. He is not sure that he can obtain the same result with the U.S. government. Identify the relevant tax issues for Ted.

19. Edna obtains a divorce from Ralph for which she incurs legal fees of $10,000. Distinguish between the types of expenses associated with the divorce that are deductible by Edna and those that are not deductible.

20. Stuart, an insurance salesman, is arrested for allegedly robbing a convenience store. He hires an attorney who is successful in getting the charges dropped. Is the attorney's fee deductible?

21. Linda operates a drug-running operation. Which of the following expenses she incurs can reduce taxable income?
    a. Bribes paid to border guards.
    b. Salaries to employees.
    c. Price paid for drugs purchased for resale.
    d. Kickbacks to police.
    e. Rent on an office.

22. Gordon anticipates that being positively perceived by the individual who is elected mayor will be beneficial for his business. Therefore, he contributes to the campaigns of both the Democratic and the Republican candidates. The Republican candidate is elected mayor. Can Gordon deduct any of the political contributions he made?

23. Melissa, the owner of a sole proprietorship that has 20 employees, does not provide health insurance for her employees. She is going to spend $1,500 lobbying in opposition to health care legislation that would require her to provide employee health insurance. Discuss the tax advantages and disadvantages of her paying the $1,500 to a professional lobbyist rather than spending the $1,500 on in-house lobbying expenditures.

24. What limits exist on the deductibility of executive compensation? Do the limits apply to all types of business entities? Are there any exceptions to the limitations?

25. What is the significance of one's present occupation in the deductibility of expenses incurred in investigating another business?

26. Amanda had been raising quarter horses for three years. Each year, her losses were about $15,000. She projects that her losses for the current year will be about $10,000. However, if she sells a promising mare before the end of the year, the $10,000 projected loss can be converted into a $4,000 projected profit. Without the perceived need to produce a current-year profit, Amanda would prefer to keep the mare for breeding purposes. Identify the relevant tax issues for Amanda.

27. Discuss the tax treatment of the rental of a vacation home if it is:
    a. Rented 10 days during the year.
    b. Rented 130 days during the year; used personally for 12 days.
    c. Rented for 250 days; used personally for 40 days.

28. Karen and Andy own a beach house. They have an agreement with a rental agent to rent it up to 200 days per year. For the past three years, the agent has been successful in renting it for 200 days. Karen and Andy use the beach house for one week during the summer and one week during Thanksgiving. Their daughter, Sarah, a college student, has asked if she and some friends can use the beach house for the week of spring break. Advise Karen and Andy how they should respond and identify any relevant tax issues.

29. Contrast the differing results obtained in a personal/rental situation by allocating property taxes and mortgage interest on the IRS's basis and the court's basis. Which method would the taxpayer prefer?

30. Hank was transferred from Phoenix to North Dakota on March 1 of the current year. He immediately put his home in Phoenix up for rent. The home was rented May 1 to November 30 and was vacant during the month of December. It was rented again on January 1 for six months. What expenses, if any, can Hank deduct on his return? Which deductions are *for* AGI and which ones are *from* AGI?

31. Erika would like to help her daughter Hillary and son-in-law James with what she hopes are short-term financial problems. This assistance will be in the form of paying their monthly mortgage payments for the past six months. If the payments are not made, the mortgage company will foreclose on their residence. Erika's preference is to make the payments directly to the mortgage company. However, she is willing to give the money to Hillary and James who then would pay the arrearages. Advise Erika on which option, if any, offers preferential tax treatment to her.

32. Explain which, if any, legal fees incurred obtaining a divorce are deductible. Are they deductible *for* or *from* AGI?

33. Igor repaired the roof on his factory at a cost of $1,500 in the current year. During the same year, Raisa replaced the roof on her small rental house for $1,500. Both taxpayers are on the cash basis. Are their expenditures treated the same on their tax returns? Why or why not?

34. Discuss the reasons for the disallowance of losses between related parties. Would it make any difference if a parent sold stock to an unrelated third party and the child repurchased the same number of shares of the stock in the market the same day?

35. Tara sold 100 shares of Eagle Company stock to Frank, her brother, for $8,000. She had originally paid $7,100 for the stock. Frank later sold the stock for $6,000 on the open market. What are the tax consequences to Tara and Frank? Would your answer differ if Tara had sold the stock to Frank for $6,500?

36. Helen owns 20% of Black Corporation; 20% of Black's stock is owned by Sara, Helen's mother; 15% is owned by Richard, Helen's brother; the remaining 45% is owned by unrelated parties. Helen is on the cash basis, and Black Corporation is on the accrual basis. On December 31, 1996, Black accrued Helen's salary of $5,000 and paid it on April 4, 1997. Both are on a calendar year. What is the tax effect to Helen and Black?

PROBLEMS

37. Sandra is an attorney. She incurs the following expenses when she and her employee, Fred, attend the American Bar Association convention in San Francisco:

Conference registration:	
Sandra	$200
Fred	200
Airline tickets from Pittsburgh to San Francisco:	
Sandra	700
Fred	400
Lodging in San Francisco:	
Sandra	450
Fred	250

Calculate the effect of these expenses on Sandra's AGI.

38. Ted, Agnes, and Steve each own one-third of the stock of Swan, Inc. Each is actively employed in the activities of the business and is paid an annual salary as follows:

Ted (president)	$200,000
Agnes (vice-president)	175,000
Steve (chief financial officer)	150,000

The industry average for salaries is $25,000 less for each position. The salaries have remained relatively constant for the past three years. Swan's taxable income for the past three years has been in the $800,000 to $900,000 range. Calculate the amount of salary expense that Swan can deduct associated with these salaries.

39. Sam and his wife Vera own all of the stock of Thrush, Inc. Vera is the president and Sam is the vice-president. Vera and Sam are paid salaries of $400,000 and $300,000, respectively, each year. They consider the salaries to be reasonable based on a comparison with salaries paid for comparable positions in comparable companies. They project Thrush's taxable income for next year, before their salaries, to be $800,000. They decide to place their four teenage children on the payroll and to pay them total salaries of $100,000. The children will each work about five hours per week for Thrush.

a. What are Sam and Vera trying to achieve by hiring the children?
b. Calculate the tax consequences of hiring the children on Thrush, Inc., and on Sam and Vera's family.

40. Falcon, Inc., paid salaries of $400,000 to its employees during the year, which was its first year of operations. At the end of the year, Falcon had unpaid salaries of $30,000.
    a. Calculate the salary deduction if Falcon is a cash basis taxpayer.
    b. Calculate the salary deduction if Falcon is an accrual basis taxpayer.

41. Doris is the owner of a sole proprietorship that uses the cash method. She leases an office building for $24,000 for an 18-month period on October 1, 1996. In order to obtain this favorable lease rate, she pays the $24,000 at the inception of the lease. How much rent expense may Doris deduct on her 1996 tax return?

42. Duck, Inc., an accrual basis corporation, sponsored a rock concert on December 29, 1996. Gross receipts were $300,000. The following expenses were incurred and paid as indicated:

Expense		**Payment Date**
Rental of coliseum	$ 25,000	December 21, 1996
Cost of goods sold:		
Food	30,000	December 30, 1996
Souvenirs	60,000	December 30, 1996
Performers	100,000	January 5, 1997
Cleaning of coliseum	10,000	February 1, 1997

Since the coliseum was not scheduled to be used again until January 15, the company with which Duck had contracted did not actually perform the cleanup until January 8–10, 1997.

Calculate Duck's net income from the concert for tax purposes for 1996.

43. Doug incurred and paid the following expenses during the year:
    - $50 for a ticket for running a red light while he was commuting to work.
    - $100 for a ticket for parking in a handicapped parking space.
    - $200 to an attorney to represent him for the two aforesaid tickets.
    - $500 to an attorney to draft a lease agreement with a tenant for a one-year lease on an apartment that Doug owns.

    Determine the amount that Doug can deduct for each of these payments.

44. Marcia, an attorney with a leading New York law firm, is convicted of failing to file Federal income tax returns for 1993–1995. Her justification for failing to do so was the pressures of her profession (80–90 hour workweeks). She is assessed taxes, interest, and penalties of $90,000 by the IRS. In addition, she incurs related legal fees of $60,000. Determine the amount that Marcia can deduct, and classify it as a deduction *for* or a deduction *from* AGI.

45. David runs an illegal numbers racket. His gross income was $500,000. He incurred the following expenses:

Illegal kickbacks	$20,000
Salaries	80,000
Rent	24,000
Utilities and telephone	9,000
Bribes to police	25,000
Interest	6,000
Depreciation on equipment	12,000

a. What is his net income from this business that is includible in taxable income?
b. If the business was an illegal drug operation, would your answer differ?

46. Edward, an attorney, is hired by a major accounting firm to represent it and its clients in dealing with members of the U.S. Congress. The accounting firm is supporting liability reform that would limit the "joint and several" liability of professionals such as attorneys and CPAs. During the year, Edward is paid $10,000 for this representation. The firm also reimburses Edward $2,500 for meal and entertainment expenses incurred in meeting with members of Congress and their staffs. In addition, the firm pays Edward $5,000 for his work in opposing legislation that would adversely affect several of its major clients. What is the amount of these payments that the firm may deduct?

47. Amber, Inc., a publicly held corporation, currently pays its president an annual salary of $900,000. In addition, it contributes $20,000 annually to a defined contribution pension plan for him. As a means of increasing company profitability, the board of directors decides to increase the president's compensation. Two proposals are being considered. Under the first proposal, the salary and pension contribution for the president would be increased by 30%. Under the second proposal, Amber would implement a performance-based compensation program that is projected to provide about the same amount of additional compensation and pension contribution for the president.
a. Evaluate the alternatives from the perspective of Amber, Inc.
b. Prepare a letter to Amber's board of directors that contains your recommendations. Address the letter to the board chairperson, Agnes Riddle, whose address is 100 James Tower, Cleveland, OH 44106.

48. Jenny, the owner of a very successful restaurant chain, is exploring the possibility of expanding the chain into a city in the neighboring state. She incurs $20,000 of expenses associated with this investigation. Based on the regulatory environment for restaurants in the city, she decides not to do so. During the year, she also investigates opening a hotel that will be part of a national hotel chain. Her expenses for this are $15,000. The hotel begins operations on December 1. Determine the amount that Jenny can deduct in the current year for investigating these two businesses.

49. Tim traveled to a neighboring state to investigate the purchase of two restaurants. His expenses included travel, legal, accounting, and miscellaneous expenses. The total was $12,000. He incurred the expenses in March and April 1996.
a. What can Tim deduct in 1996 if he was in the restaurant business and did not acquire the two restaurants?
b. What can Tim deduct in 1996 if he was in the restaurant business and acquired the two restaurants and began operating them on July 1, 1996?
c. What can Tim deduct in 1996 if he did not acquire the two restaurants and was not in the restaurant business?
d. What can he deduct in 1996 if he acquired the two restaurants, but was not in the restaurant business when he acquired them? Operations began on July 1, 1996.

50. Alfred conducts an activity that is appropriately classified as a hobby. The activity produces the following revenues and expenses:

Revenue	$10,000
Property taxes	3,000
Materials and supplies	2,000
Utilities	1,000
Advertising	2,500
Insurance	500
Depreciation	4,000

Without regard to this activity, Alfred's AGI is $40,000. Determine how much income Alfred must report, the amount of the expenses he is permitted to deduct, and his AGI.

51. Samantha is an executive with an AGI of $100,000 before consideration of income or loss from her miniature horse business. Her income comes from winning horse shows, stud fees, and sales of yearlings. Her home is on 20 acres, 18 of which she uses to

pasture the horses and upon which she has erected stables, paddocks, fences, tack houses, and so forth.

Samantha uses an office in her home that is 10% of the square footage of the house. She uses the office exclusively for keeping records of breeding lines, histories, and show and veterinary records. Her records show the following income and expenses for the current year:

Income from fees, prizes, and sales	$22,000
Expenses	
Entry fees	1,000
Feed and veterinary bills	4,000
Supplies	900
Publications and dues	500
Travel to horse shows (no meals)	2,300
Salaries and wages of employees	8,000
Depreciation on horse equipment	3,000
Depreciation on horse farm improvements	7,000
Depreciation on 10% of home	1,000
Total home mortgage interest	24,000
Total property taxes on home	2,200
Total property taxes on horse farm improvements	800

The mortgage interest is only on her home. The horse farm improvements are not mortgaged.

How must Samantha treat the income and expenses of the operation if the miniature horse activity is held to be a hobby?

52. How would your answer in Problem 51 differ if the horse operation was held to be a business?

53. Louis makes macramé animals in his spare time. He sold $5,000 worth of animals during the year and incurred expenses as follows:

Supplies	$2,800
Depreciation on business property	1,900
Advertising	800

How are these items treated if the endeavor is a hobby? A business?

54. In 1996, Anna rented her vacation home for 60 days, used it personally for 20 days, and left it vacant for 286 days. She had the following income and expenses:

Rent income	$ 6,000
Expenses	
Real estate taxes	2,000
Interest on mortgage	9,000
Utilities	600
Repairs	1,000
Roof replacement	12,000
Depreciation	8,000

Compute Anna's net rent income or loss and the amounts she can itemize on her tax return, using the court's approach in allocating property taxes and interest.

55. How would your answer in Problem 54 differ using the IRS's method of allocating property taxes and interest?

56. How would your answer in Problem 54 differ if Anna had rented the house for 90 days and had used it personally for 12 days?

57. Chee, single, age 40, had the following income and expenses in 1996:

Income	
Salary	$ 43,000
Rental of vacation home (rented 60 days, used personally 60 days, vacant 246 days)	4,000
Municipal bond interest	2,000
Dividend from General Motors	400
Expenses	
Interest	
On home mortgage	8,400
On vacation home	4,758
On loan used to buy municipal bonds	3,100
Taxes	
Property tax on home	2,200
Property tax on vacation home	1,098
State income tax	3,300
Charitable contributions	1,100
Tax return preparation fee	300
Utilities and maintenance on vacation home	2,600
Depreciation on rental 50% of vacation home	3,500

Calculate Chee's taxable income for 1996 before personal exemptions.

58. During the current year, Robert pays the following amounts associated with his own residence and that of his daughter, Anne:

• Property taxes:	
On home owned by Robert	$3,000
On home owned by Anne	1,500
• Mortgage interest:	
Associated with Robert's home	8,000
Associated with Anne's home	4,500
• Repairs to:	
Robert's home	1,200
Anne's home	700
• Utilities:	
Robert's home	2,700
Anne's home	1,600
• Replacement of roof:	
Robert's home	4,000

a. Which of these expenses can Robert deduct?
b. Which of these expenses can Anne deduct?
c. Are the deductions *for* AGI or *from* AGI (itemized)?
d. How could the tax consequences be improved?

59. Lee incurred the following expenses in the current tax year. Indicate, in the spaces provided, whether each expenditure is deductible *for* AGI, *from* AGI, or not deductible.

	Deductible		Not
Expense Item	**For AGI**	**From AGI**	**Deductible**
a. Lee's personal medical expenses	______	______	______
b. Lee's dependent daughter's medical expenses	______	______	______
c. Real estate taxes on rental property	______	______	______
d. Real estate taxes on Lee's personal residence	______	______	______
e. Real estate taxes on daughter's personal residence	______	______	______
f. Lee's state income taxes	______	______	______
g. Interest on rental property mortgage	______	______	______
h. Interest on Lee's personal residence mortgage	______	______	______
i. Interest on daughter's personal residence mortgage	______	______	______
j. Interest on business loans	______	______	______
k. Charitable contributions	______	______	______
l. Depreciation on rental property	______	______	______
m. Utilities & maintenance on:			
(1) Rental property	______	______	______
(2) Lee's home	______	______	______
(3) Daughter's home	______	______	______
n. Depreciation on auto used in Lee's business	______	______	______
o. Depreciation on Lee's personal auto	______	______	______
p. Depreciation on daughter's personal auto	______	______	______

60. Janet Saxon sold stock (basis of $40,000) to her brother, Fred, for $32,000.
    a. What are the tax consequences to Janet?
    b. What are the tax consequences to Fred if he later sells the stock for $42,000? For $28,000? For $36,000?
    c. Write a letter to Janet in which you inform her of the tax consequences if she sells the stock to Fred for $32,000 and explain how a sales transaction could be structured that would produce better tax consequences for her. Janet's address is 32 Country Lane, Lawrence, KS 66045.

61. The Robin Corporation is owned as follows:

Irene	20%
Paul, Irene's husband	20%
Sylvia, Irene's mother	15%
Ron, Irene's father	25%
Quinn, an unrelated party	20%

Robin is on the accrual basis, and Irene and Paul are on the cash basis. Irene and Paul each loaned the Robin Corporation $10,000 out of their separate funds. On December 31,

1996, Robin accrued interest at 7% on both loans. The interest was paid on February 4, 1997. What is the tax treatment of this interest expense/income to Irene, Paul, and Robin?

62. What is Kim's constructive ownership of Wren Corporation, given the following information?

Shares owned by Kim	900
Shares owned by Sam, Kim's uncle	600
Shares owned by Barbara, Kim's partner	30
Shares owned by Vera, Kim's granddaughter	670
Shares owned by unrelated parties	800

63. Chris has a brokerage account and buys on the margin, which resulted in an interest expense of $8,000 during the year. Income generated through the brokerage account was as follows:

Municipal interest	$30,000
Taxable dividends and interest	70,000

How much investment interest can Chris deduct?

64. Jay's sole proprietorship has the following assets

	Basis	Fair Market Value
Cash	$ 10,000	$ 10,000
Accounts receivable	18,000	18,000
Inventory	25,000	30,000
Patent	22,000	40,000
Land	50,000	75,000
	$125,000	$173,000

The building in which Jay's business is located is leased. The lease expires at the end of the year.

Jay is age 70 and would like to retire. He expects to be in the 36% tax bracket. Jay is negotiating the sale of the business with Lois, a key employee. They have agreed on the fair market value of the assets, as indicated above, and agree the total purchase price should be about $200,000.

a. Advise Jay regarding how the sale should be structured.
b. Advise Lois regarding how the purchase should be structured.
c. What might they do to achieve an acceptable compromise?

CUMULATIVE PROBLEMS

65. John and Mary Jane Sanders are married, filing jointly. Their address is 204 Shoe Lane, Blacksburg, VA 24061. They are expecting their first two children (twins) in early 1997. John's salary in 1996 was $85,000, from which $14,000 of Federal income tax and $3,500 of state income tax were withheld. Mary Jane made $40,000 and had $5,000 of Federal income tax and $2,000 of state income tax withheld.

John makes alimony payments of $15,000 per year to June, his former wife. He also makes child support payments of $10,000 for his son, Rod, who lives with June except for one month in the summer when he visits John and Mary Jane.

Mary Jane's father lived with them until his death in October. His only source of income was Social Security benefits of $4,800. Of this amount, he deposited $2,800 in a savings account. The remainder of his support, including funeral expenses of $5,000, was provided by John and Mary Jane.

They had $2,000 of savings account interest and $1,500 of dividends during the year. They made charitable contributions of $3,000 during the year and paid an additional $700 in state income taxes in 1996 upon filing their 1995 state income tax return. Their deductible home mortgage interest was $8,200, and their property taxes came to $2,100. They had no other deductible expenses.

Part 1—Tax Computation
Calculate their tax (or refund) due for 1996. Suggested software (if available): *TurboTax* or *MacInTax*.

Part 2—Tax Planning
Assume that they come to you for advice in December 1996. John has learned that he will receive a $25,000 bonus. He wants to know if he should take it in December 1996 or in January 1997. Mary Jane will quit work on December 31 to stay home with the twins. Their itemized deductions will decrease by $2,000 because Mary Jane will not have state income taxes withheld. Write a letter to John and Mary Jane that contains your advice and prepare a memo for the tax files. Suggested software (if available): *TurboTax* or *MacInTax*.

66. Helen Archer, age 30, is single and lives at 120 Sanborne Avenue, Springfield, IL 60740. Her Social Security number is 648–11–9981. Helen has been divorced from her former husband, Albert, for three years. She has a son, Jason, who is age 8. His Social Security number is 648–98–3471. Helen does not wish to contribute $3 to the Presidential Election Campaign Fund.

Helen, an advertising executive, earned a salary of $75,000 in 1995. Her employer withheld $10,200 in Federal income tax, $3,200 in state income tax, and the appropriate amount of FICA tax.

Helen has legal custody of Jason. Jason lives with his father during summer vacation. Albert indicates that his expenses for Jason are $6,000. Helen can document that she spent $4,500 for Jason's support during 1995.

Helen's mother died on January 7, 1995. Helen inherited assets worth $200,000 from her mother. As the sole beneficiary of her mother's life insurance policy, Helen received insurance proceeds of $100,000. Her mother's cost basis for the life insurance policy was $40,000. Helen's favorite aunt gave her $10,000 for her thirtieth birthday in October.

On November 8, 1995, Helen sells for $19,000 Amber, Inc. stock that she had inherited from her father on December 5, 1991. His cost basis for the stock was $12,000, and the stock was worth $20,000 at the time of his death. (See Chapter 14 for basis of inherited property.) On December 1, 1995, Helen sold Falcon, Inc., stock for $15,000. She had acquired the stock on July 2, 1995, for $9,000.

An examination of Helen's records reveals the following information:

- Received interest income of $3,500 from First Savings Bank.
- Received dividend income of $1,200 from Amber, Inc.
- Received $1,700 of interest income on City of Springfield school bonds.
- Received alimony of $40,000 from Albert.

From her checkbook records, she determines that she made the following payments during 1995.

- Charitable contributions of $1,500 to First Presbyterian Church and $800 to the American Red Cross.
- Mortgage interest on her residence of $6,500.
- Property taxes of $1,900 on her residence and $800 on her car.
- Sales taxes of $1,700.
- Estimated Federal income taxes of $17,000 and estimated state income taxes of $1,000.
- Medical expenses of $4,000 for her and $500 for Jason. Eight hundred dollars of her medical expenses were reimbursed by her medical insurance policy in December.

Calculate Helen's net tax payable or refund due for 1995. If you use tax forms, you will need Form 1040 and Schedules A, B, and D. Suggested software (if available): *TurboTax* or *MacInTax*.

RESEARCH PROBLEMS

Note: ***West's Federal Taxation on CD-ROM*** *can be used in preparing solutions to the Research Problems. Alternatively, tax research materials contained in a standard tax library can be used.*

Research Problem 1. Noel is an employee of the U.S. Immigration Service and is stationed at Dorval International Airport in Montreal. Noel received a Living Quarters Allowance (LQA) of $10,000. An LQA is a stipend provided to qualifying Federal employees stationed abroad who are not otherwise provided with housing and is excludible from gross income under § 912(1)(C).

Noel and Janet, his spouse, purchased a house in Montreal and lived in it during the tax year. They deducted mortgage interest of $9,000 and property taxes of $2,000. A Revenue Agent disallowed a portion of these deductions under § 265 (Expenses and Interest Relating to Tax-Exempt Income). The disallowed amount was the portion that was allocable to the tax-exempt LQA. Advise Noel on the appropriate treatment of the disallowed property taxes and mortgage interest.

Research Problem 2. Gray Chemical Company manufactured pesticides that were toxic. Over the course of several years, the toxic waste contaminated the air and water around the company's plant. Several employees suffered toxic poisoning, and the Environmental Protection Agency cited the company for violations. In court, the judge found Gray guilty and imposed fines of $15 million. The company voluntarily set up a charitable fund for the purpose of bettering the environment and funded it with $8 million. The company incurred legal expenses in setting up the foundation and defending itself in court. The court reduced the fine from $15 million to $7 million.

Gray Chemical Company deducted the $8 million paid to the foundation and the legal expenses incurred. The IRS disallowed both deductions on the grounds that the payment was, in fact, a fine and in violation of public policy.

Gray's president, Ted Jones, has contacted you regarding the deductibility of the $7 million fine, the $8 million payment to the foundation, and the legal fees. Write a letter to Mr. Jones that contains your advice and prepare a memo for the tax files. Gray's address is 200 Lincoln Center, Omaha, NE 68182.

Partial list of research aids:
§ 162(a) and (f).
Reg. § 1.162–21(b).

Research Problem 3. Rex and Agnes Harrell purchased a beach house at Duck, North Carolina, in early 1995. Although they intended to use the beach house occasionally for recreational purposes, they also planned to rent it through the realty agency that had handled the purchase in order to help pay the mortgage payments, property taxes, and maintenance costs. Rex is a surgeon, and Agnes is a counselor.

The beach house was in need of substantial repairs. Rather than hiring a contractor, Rex and Agnes decided they would make the repairs themselves. During both high school and college, Rex had worked summers in construction. In addition, he had taken an advanced course in woodworking and related subjects from a local community college several years ago.

During 1995, according to a log maintained by the Harrells, they occupied the beach house on 38 days and rented it on 49 days. The log also indicated that on 24 of the 38 days that they occupied the beach house, one or both of them were engaged in work on the beach house. Their two teenage children were with them on all of these days, but did not help with the work being done. On their 1995 income tax return, Rex and Agnes, who filed a joint return, treated the beach house as a rental property and deducted a pro rata share of the property taxes, mortgage interest, utilities, maintenance and repairs, and depreciation in determining their net loss from the beach home. A Revenue Agent has limited the deductions to the rent income. He contends that the 14-day personal use provision was exceeded and that many of the alleged repairs were capital expenditures. Advise the Harrells on how they should respond to the IRS.

Research Problem 4. Sam and Vera were engaged to be married. While Vera was on a four-day business trip to Madison County, she met Tex. They fell in love and were married the following week in Las Vegas. Vera returned the engagement ring to Sam who was devastated. He sued Vera for breach of promise to marry. Can Sam deduct the attorney's fees associated with the lawsuit?

TEAM PROJECT: ARTHUR ANDERSEN TAX CHALLENGE CASES

For more information on the Arthur Andersen Tax Challenge Cases, please refer to Chapter 1, page 1-38.

Information related to tax issues and problems that are discussed in this chapter may be found in the

Miller case on pages 1, 11-12 and 31

Read and analyze the case you have been assigned and *identify* any issues and problems that are related to material covered in this chapter. If the information provided in the case is complete, prepare answers for this part of the case at this time. If you need information that is contained in the later parts of the case, please write a memo summarizing the questions or problems so you can prepare a complete answer at a later date.

CHAPTER

7

Deductions and Losses: Certain Business Expenses and Losses

LEARNING OBJECTIVES

After completing Chapter 7, you should be able to:

1. Determine the amount, classification, and timing of the bad debt deduction.
2. Understand the tax treatment of worthless securities including § 1244 stock.
3. Distinguish between deductible and nondeductible losses of individuals.
4. Identify a casualty and determine the amount, classification, and timing of casualty and theft losses.
5. Recognize and apply the alternative tax treatments for research and experimental expenditures.
6. Determine the amount of the net operating loss and recognize the impact of the carryback and carryover provisions.
7. Identify tax planning opportunities in deducting certain business expenses, business losses, and personal losses.

OUTLINE

Working with the tax formula for individuals requires the proper classification of items that are deductible *for* adjusted gross income (AGI) and items that are deductions *from* AGI (itemized deductions). Business expenses and losses, discussed in this chapter, are reductions of gross income to arrive at the taxpayer's AGI. Expenses and losses incurred in connection with a transaction entered into for profit and attributable to rents and royalties are deducted *for* AGI. All other expenses and losses incurred in connection with a transaction entered into for profit are deducted *from* AGI.

The situation of Robert P. Groetzinger provides an interesting insight into the importance of the proper classification for the individual taxpayer. In January 1978, Groetzinger terminated his employment with a private company and devoted virtually all of his working time to pari-mutuel wagering on dog races. He had no other profession or employment, and his only sources of income, apart from his gambling winnings, were interest, dividends, and sales from investments. During the tax year in question, he went to the track six days a week and devoted 60 to 80 hours per week to preparing and making wagers on his own account.

The tax question that this case presents is whether Groetzinger's gambling activities constitute a trade or business. If the gambling is a trade or business, his gambling losses are deductions *for* AGI. If the gambling activity is not a trade or business, the losses are itemized deductions, and Groetzinger's taxes increase by $2,142.[1]

Deductible losses on personal use property are deducted as an itemized deduction. Itemized deductions are deductions *from* AGI. While the general coverage of itemized deductions is in Chapter 10, casualty and theft losses on personal use property are discussed in this chapter.

In determining the amount and timing of the deduction for bad debts, proper classification is again important. A business bad debt is classified as a deduction *for* AGI, and a nonbusiness bad debt is classified as a short-term capital loss.

---

[1] *Groetzinger v. Comm.*, 85–2 USTC ¶9622, 56 AFTR2d 85–5683, 771 F.2d 269 (CA–7, 1985).

Other topics discussed in Chapter 7 are research and experimental expenditures and the net operating loss deduction.

Bad Debts

1 **Learning Objective**
Determine the amount, classification, and timing of the bad debt deduction.

If a taxpayer sells goods or provides services on credit and the account receivable subsequently becomes worthless, a **bad debt** deduction is permitted only if income arising from the creation of the account receivable was previously included in income.[2] No deduction is allowed, for example, for a bad debt arising from the sale of a product or service when the taxpayer is on the cash basis because no income is reported until the cash has been collected. Permitting a bad debt deduction for a cash basis taxpayer would amount to a double deduction because the expenses of the product or service rendered are deducted when payments are made to suppliers and to employees, or at the time of the sale.

Example 1

Tracy, an individual engaged in the practice of accounting, performed accounting services for Pat for which she charged $8,000. Pat never paid the bill, and his whereabouts are unknown.

If Tracy is an accrual basis taxpayer, the $8,000 is included in income when the services are performed. When it is determined that Pat's account will not be collected, the $8,000 is expensed as a bad debt.

If Tracy is a cash basis taxpayer, the $8,000 is not included in income until payment is received. When it is determined that Pat's account will not be collected, the $8,000 is not deducted as a bad debt expense since it was never recognized as income. ▼

A bad debt can also result from the nonrepayment of a loan made by the taxpayer or from purchased debt instruments.

SPECIFIC CHARGE-OFF METHOD

Taxpayers (other than certain financial institutions) may use only the **specific charge-off method** in accounting for bad debts. Certain financial institutions are allowed to use the **reserve method** for computing deductions for bad debts.

A taxpayer using the specific charge-off method may claim a deduction when a specific business debt becomes either partially or wholly worthless or when a specific nonbusiness debt becomes wholly worthless.[3] For the business debt, the taxpayer must satisfy the IRS that the debt is partially worthless and must demonstrate the amount of worthlessness.

If a business debt previously deducted as partially worthless becomes totally worthless in a future year, only the remainder not previously deducted can be deducted in the future year.

In the case of total worthlessness, a deduction is allowed for the entire amount in the year the debt becomes worthless. The amount of the deduction depends on the taxpayer's basis in the bad debt. If the debt arose from the sale of services or products and the face amount was previously included in income, that amount is deductible. If the taxpayer purchased the debt, the deduction is equal to the amount the taxpayer paid for the debt instrument.

---

[2] Reg. § 1.166–1(e).

[3] § 166(a) and Reg. § 1.166.

One of the more difficult tasks is determining if and when a bad debt is worthless. The loss is deductible only in the year of partial or total worthlessness for business debts and only in the year of total worthlessness for nonbusiness debts. Legal proceedings need not be initiated against the debtor when the surrounding facts indicate that such action will not result in collection.

EXAMPLE 2

In 1994, Jill loaned $1,000 to Kay, who agreed to repay the loan in two years. In 1996, Kay disappeared after the note became delinquent. If a reasonable investigation by Jill indicates that she cannot find Kay or that a suit against Kay would not result in collection, Jill can deduct the $1,000 in 1996. ▼

Bankruptcy is generally an indication of at least partial worthlessness of a debt. Bankruptcy may create worthlessness before the settlement date. If this is the case, the deduction may be taken in the year of worthlessness.

EXAMPLE 3

In Example 2, assume Kay filed for personal bankruptcy in 1995 and that the debt is a business debt. At that time, Jill learned that unsecured creditors (including Jill) were ultimately expected to receive 20¢ on the dollar. In 1996, settlement is made and Jill receives only $150. She should deduct $800 ($1,000 loan – $200 expected settlement) in 1995 and $50 in 1996 ($200 balance – $150 proceeds). ▼

If a receivable has been written off as uncollectible during the current tax year and is subsequently collected during the current tax year, the write-off entry is reversed. If a receivable has been written off as uncollectible, the collection of the receivable in a later tax year may result in income being recognized. Income will result if the deduction yielded a tax benefit in the year it was taken. See Examples 37 and 38 in Chapter 5.

BUSINESS VERSUS NONBUSINESS BAD DEBTS

A **nonbusiness bad debt** is a debt unrelated to the taxpayer's trade or business either when it was created or when it became worthless. The nature of a debt depends on whether the lender was engaged in the business of lending money or whether there is a proximate relationship between the creation of the debt and the lender's trade or business. The use to which the borrowed funds are put by the debtor is of no consequence. Loans to relatives or friends are the most common type of nonbusiness bad debt.

EXAMPLE 4

José loaned his friend, Esther, $1,500. Esther used the money to start a business, which subsequently failed. Even though proceeds of the loan were used in a business, the loan is a nonbusiness bad debt because the business was Esther's, not José's. ▼

The distinction between a business bad debt and a nonbusiness bad debt is important. A **business bad debt** is deductible as an ordinary loss in the year incurred, whereas a nonbusiness bad debt is always treated as a short-term capital loss. Thus, regardless of the age of a nonbusiness bad debt, the deduction may be of limited benefit due to the capital loss limitations on deductibility in any one year. The maximum amount of a net short-term capital loss that an individual can deduct against ordinary income in any one year is $3,000 (see Chapter 16 for a detailed discussion). Although no deduction is allowed when a nonbusiness bad debt is partially worthless, the taxpayer is entitled to deduct the net amount of the loss upon final settlement.

CONCEPT SUMMARY 7–1

Specific Charge-Off Method

Expense deduction and account write-off	The expense arises and the write-off takes place when a specific business account becomes either partially or wholly worthless or when a specific nonbusiness account becomes wholly worthless.
Recovery of accounts previously written off	If the account recovered was written off during the current taxable year, the write-off entry is reversed. If the account recovered was written off during a previous taxable year, income is created subject to the tax benefit rule.

The following example is an illustration of business bad debts adapted from the Regulations.[4]

EXAMPLE 5

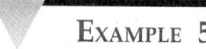

In 1995, Leif sold his business but retained a claim (note or account receivable) against Bob. The claim became worthless in 1996. Leif's loss is treated as a business bad debt because the debt was created in the conduct of his former trade or business. Leif is accorded business bad debt treatment even though he was holding the note as an investor and was no longer in a trade or business when the claim became worthless. ▼

The nonbusiness bad debt provisions are *not* applicable to corporations. It is assumed that any loans made by a corporation are related to its trade or business. Therefore, any bad debts of a corporation are business bad debts.

LOANS BETWEEN RELATED PARTIES

Loans between related parties (especially family members) raise the issue of whether the transaction was a *bona fide* loan or a gift. The Regulations state that a bona fide debt arises from a debtor-creditor relationship based on a valid and enforceable obligation to pay a fixed or determinable sum of money. Thus, individual circumstances must be examined to determine whether advances between related parties are gifts or loans. Some considerations are these:

- Was a note properly executed?
- Was there a reasonable rate of interest?
- Was collateral provided?
- What collection efforts were made?
- What was the intent of the parties?

EXAMPLE 6

Lana loans $2,000 to her widowed mother for an operation. Lana's mother owns no property and is not employed, and her only income consists of Social Security benefits. No note is issued for the loan, no provision for interest is made, and no repayment date is mentioned. In the current year, Lana's mother dies leaving no estate. Assuming the loan is not repaid, Lana cannot take a deduction for a nonbusiness bad debt because the facts indicate that no debtor-creditor relationship existed. ▼

[4] Reg. § 1.166–5(d).

TAX IN THE NEWS

Family Bad Debts Can Be Deducted under the Right Circumstances

A father who lived in Tennessee loaned his daughter $37,500 for a skating rink business. Although the loan was not evidenced by a note with a market rate of interest and a specified repayment schedule, the father had a long history of making such loans to his relatives and of being repaid (e.g., 8 other loans between 1985 and 1988). The daughter was a skater and thought she would be qualified to run this type of business. The daughter repaid $2,000, but the business failed two years later. No subsequent payments were made, and the daughter declared bankruptcy under Chapter 7 the following year.

The father deducted the $35,500 on his income tax return as a nonbusiness bad debt. According to the IRS, the father made no attempt to collect the debt. Therefore, since this was a family situation, the IRS disallowed the deduction.

The Tax Court sided with the father. Since the daughter declared bankruptcy, attempts by the father to collect would have been futile. Buttressing the father's position even prior to the bankruptcy was his familiarity with the daughter's business affairs (i.e., the amount of her outstanding debts, her frequent requests to borrow additional funds, and her landlord's seizure of her business assets). He knew that even if he tried to collect, he would be unsuccessful. In addition, the fact that he had made loans to other family members that had been repaid supported his position that he expected to be repaid.

SOURCE: *Loy E. Bowman*, T.C. Memo. 1995–259, 69 TCM 2886.

LOSS OF DEPOSITS IN INSOLVENT FINANCIAL INSTITUTIONS

Qualified individuals can *elect* to deduct losses on deposits in qualified financial institutions as personal casualty losses in the year in which the amount of the loss can be reasonably estimated. If the election is made to treat a loss on a deposit as a personal casualty loss, no bad debt deduction for the loss is allowed.[5] As a personal casualty loss, the loss is subject to the $100 per event floor and the 10 percent-of-AGI aggregate floor. Both floors limiting casualty losses are explained later in the chapter. The amount of loss to be recognized under the election is the difference between (1) the taxpayer's basis in the deposit and (2) a reasonable estimate of the amount to be received.

A *qualified individual* is any individual other than:

- An owner of 1 percent or more of the value of the stock of the institution in which the loss was sustained.
- An officer of the institution.
- Certain relatives and other persons who are tax-related to such owners and officers.

A *qualified financial institution* is a commercial bank, thrift institution, insured credit union, or any similar institution chartered and supervised under Federal or

[5] § 165(l).

CONCEPT SUMMARY 7–2

Bad Debt Deductions

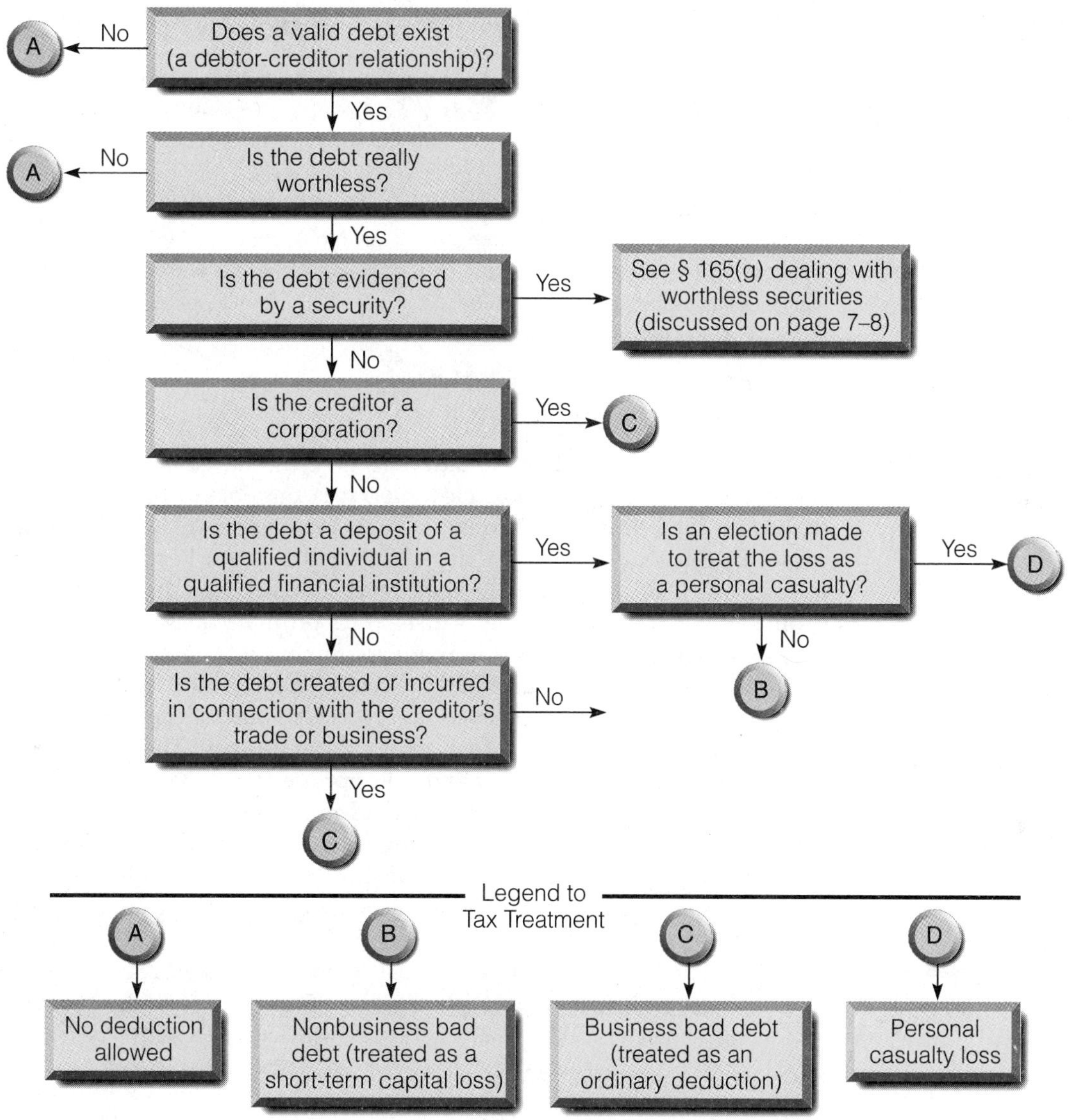

state law. A *deposit*, for purposes of this provision, is any deposit, withdrawal certificate, or withdrawable or repurchasable share of or in a qualified financial institution. The term *insolvent* generally denotes a situation where the liabilities exceed the fair market value of the assets.

If the individual does not elect to deduct the loss as a casualty loss, it is treated as a nonbusiness bad debt and, hence, as a short-term capital loss. As a short-term capital loss, it is subject to the capital loss limitation rules (see the discussion in Chapter 16).

WORTHLESS SECURITIES

2 LEARNING OBJECTIVE
Understand the tax treatment of worthless securities including § 1244 stock.

A loss is allowed for securities that become *completely* worthless during the year (**worthless securities**).[6] Such securities are shares of stock, bonds, notes, or other evidence of indebtedness issued by a corporation or government. The losses generated are treated as capital losses deemed to have occurred on the *last day* of the taxable year. By treating the loss as having occurred on the last day of the taxable year, a loss that would otherwise have been classified as short term (if the date of worthlessness was used) may be classified as a long-term capital loss. Capital losses may be of limited benefit due to the $3,000 capital loss limitation.

EXAMPLE 7

Ali, a calendar year taxpayer, owns stock in Owl Corporation (a publicly held company). The stock was acquired as an investment on November 30, 1995, at a cost of $5,000. On April 1, 1996, the stock became worthless. Since the stock is deemed to have become worthless as of December 31 of 1996, Ali has a capital loss from an asset held for 13 months (a long-term capital loss). ▼

SMALL BUSINESS STOCK

The general rule is that shareholders receive capital gain or loss treatment upon the sale or exchange of stock. However, it is possible to receive an ordinary loss deduction if the loss is sustained on **small business stock (§ 1244 stock).** This loss could arise from a sale of the stock or from the stock becoming worthless. Only *individuals*[7] who acquired the stock *from* the corporation are eligible to receive ordinary loss treatment under § 1244. The ordinary loss treatment is limited to $50,000 ($100,000 for married individuals filing jointly) per year. Losses on § 1244 stock in excess of the statutory limits receive capital loss treatment.

The corporation must meet certain requirements for the loss on § 1244 stock to be treated as an *ordinary*—rather than a capital—loss. The major requirement is that the total amount of money and other property received by the corporation for stock as a contribution to capital (or paid-in surplus) does not exceed $1 million. The $1 million test is made at the time the stock is issued. Section 1244 stock can be common or preferred stock. Section 1244 applies only to losses. If § 1244 stock is sold at a gain, the Section has no application, and the gain is capital gain.

EXAMPLE 8

On July 1, 1994, Iris, a single individual, purchased 100 shares of Eagle Corporation common stock for $100,000. The Eagle stock qualified as § 1244 stock. On June 20, 1996, Iris sold all of the Eagle stock for $20,000. Because the Eagle stock is § 1244 stock, Iris would have $50,000 of ordinary loss and $30,000 of long-term capital loss. ▼

LOSSES OF INDIVIDUALS

3 LEARNING OBJECTIVE
Distinguish between deductible and nondeductible losses of individuals.

An individual may deduct the following losses under § 165(c):

- Losses incurred in a trade or business.
- Losses incurred in a transaction entered into for profit.
- Losses caused by fire, storm, shipwreck, or other casualty or by theft.

[6] § 165(g).
[7] The term "individuals" for this purpose includes a partnership but not a trust or an estate.

An individual taxpayer may deduct losses to property used in the taxpayer's trade or business or losses to property used in a transaction entered into for profit. Examples include a loss on property used in a proprietorship, a loss on property held for rent, or a loss on stolen bearer bonds. Note that an individual's losses on property used in a trade or business or on transactions entered into for profit are not limited to losses caused by fire, storm, shipwreck, or other casualty or by theft.

An individual taxpayer suffering losses from damage to nonbusiness property can deduct only those losses attributable to fire, storm, shipwreck, or other casualty or theft. Although the meaning of the terms *fire, storm, shipwreck,* and *theft* is relatively free from dispute, the term *other casualty* needs further clarification. It means casualties analogous to fire, storm, or shipwreck. The term also includes accidental loss of property provided the loss qualifies under the same rules as any other casualty. These rules are that the loss must result from an event that is (1) identifiable; (2) damaging to property; and (3) sudden, unexpected, and unusual in nature.

A *sudden event* is one that is swift and precipitous and not gradual or progressive. An *unexpected event* is an event that is ordinarily unanticipated and occurs without the intent of the individual who suffers the loss. An *unusual event* is one that is extraordinary and nonrecurring and does not commonly occur during the activity in which the taxpayer was engaged when the destruction occurred.[8] Examples include hurricanes, tornadoes, floods, storms, shipwrecks, fires, auto accidents, mine cave-ins, sonic booms, and vandalism. Weather that causes damages (drought, for example) must be unusual and severe for the particular region. Damage must be to the taxpayer's property to qualify as a **casualty loss.**

A taxpayer can take a deduction for a casualty loss from an automobile accident only if the damage was not caused by the taxpayer's willful act or willful negligence.

EXAMPLE 9

Ted parks his car on a hill and fails to set the brake properly and to curb the wheels. As a result of Ted's negligence, the car rolls down the hill and is damaged. The repairs to Ted's car should qualify for casualty loss treatment since Ted's act of negligence appears to be simple rather than willful. ▼

EVENTS THAT ARE NOT CASUALTIES

4 LEARNING OBJECTIVE
Identify a casualty and determine the amount, classification, and timing of casualty and theft losses.

Not all acts of God are treated as casualty losses for income tax purposes. Because a casualty must be sudden, unexpected, and unusual, progressive deterioration (such as erosion due to wind or rain) is not a casualty because it does not meet the suddenness test.

Examples of nonsudden events that generally do not qualify as casualties include disease and insect damages. When the damage was caused by termites over a period of several years, some courts have disallowed a casualty loss deduction.[9] On the other hand, some courts have held that termite damage over periods of up to 15 months after infestation constituted a sudden event and was, therefore, deductible as a casualty loss.[10] Despite the existence of some judicial support for the deductibility of termite damage as a casualty loss, the current position of the IRS is that termite damage is not deductible.[11]

[8] Rev.Rul. 72–592, 1972–2 C.B. 101.

[9] *Fay v. Helvering*, 41–2 USTC ¶9494, 27 AFTR 432, 120 F.2d 253 (CA–2, 1941); *U.S. v. Rogers*, 41–1 USTC ¶9442, 27 AFTR 423, 120 F.2d 244 (CA–9, 1941).

[10] *Rosenberg v. Comm.*, 52–2 USTC ¶9377, 42 AFTR 303, 198 F.2d 46 (CA–8, 1952); *Shopmaker v. U.S.*, 54–1 USTC ¶9195, 45 AFTR 758, 119 F. Supp. 705 (D.Ct.Mo., 1953).

[11] Rev.Rul. 63–232, 1963–2 C.B. 97.

Other examples of events that are not casualties are losses resulting from a decline in value rather than an actual loss of the property. No loss was allowed where the taxpayer's home declined in value as a result of a landslide that destroyed neighboring homes but did no actual damage to the taxpayer's home.[12] Similarly, a taxpayer was allowed a loss for the actual flood damage to his property but not for the decline in market value due to the property's being flood-prone.[13]

THEFT LOSSES

Theft includes, but is not necessarily limited to, larceny, embezzlement, and robbery.[14] Theft does not include misplaced items.[15]

Theft losses are computed like other casualty losses (discussed in the following section), but the *timing* for recognition of the loss differs. A theft loss is deducted in the year of discovery, not the year of the theft (unless, of course, the discovery occurs in the same year as the theft). If, in the year of the discovery, a claim exists (e.g., against an insurance company) and there is a reasonable expectation of recovering the adjusted basis of the asset from the insurance company, no deduction is permitted.[16] If, in the year of settlement, the recovery is less than the asset's adjusted basis, a partial deduction may be available. If the recovery is greater than the asset's adjusted basis, gain may be recognized.

EXAMPLE 10

Keith's new sailboat, which he uses for personal purposes, was stolen from the storage marina in December 1994. He discovered the loss on June 3, 1995, and filed a claim with his insurance company that was settled on January 30, 1996. Assuming there is a reasonable expectation of full recovery, no deduction is allowed in 1995. A partial deduction may be available in 1996 if the actual insurance proceeds are less than the lower of the fair market value or the adjusted basis of the asset. (Loss measurement rules are discussed later in this chapter.) ▼

ETHICAL CONSIDERATIONS

Deducting a Theft Loss

Theft losses of personal use assets are itemized deductions in the year of discovery. The taxpayer must show that the property was actually stolen. Losses due to mislaying or losing property cannot be deducted. If there is no positive proof that a theft occurred, all of the details and evidence should be presented. If the reasonable inferences point to a theft, the Tax Court has allowed a deduction. If the inferences point to a mysterious (unexplained) disappearance, however, the deduction will be disallowed.

A taxpayer went shopping in a major city, riding the subway to and from the city. During the day, he purchased items using money from his wallet. When he arrived home, his wallet was missing. He is considering claiming a theft loss deduction for the wallet and the money it contained.

---

12 *H. Pulvers v. Comm.*, 69–1 USTC ¶9222, 23 AFTR2d 69–678, 407 F.2d 838 (CA–9, 1969).

13 *S. L. Solomon*, 39 TCM 1282, T.C.Memo. 1980–87.

14 Reg. § 1.165–8(d).

15 *Mary Francis Allen*, 16 T.C. 163 (1951).

16 Reg. §§ 1.165–1(d)(2) and 1.165–8(a)(2).

WHEN TO DEDUCT CASUALTY LOSSES

General Rule. Generally, a casualty loss is deducted in the year the loss occurs. However, no casualty loss is permitted if a reimbursement claim with a *reasonable prospect of full recovery* exists.[17] If the taxpayer has a partial claim, only part of the loss can be claimed in the year of the casualty, and the remainder is deducted in the year the claim is settled.

EXAMPLE 11

Chee's new sailboat was completely destroyed by fire in 1996. Its cost and fair market value were $10,000. Chee's only claim against the insurance company was on a $7,000 policy that was not settled by year-end. The following year, 1997, Chee settled with the insurance company for $6,000. Chee is entitled to a $3,000 deduction in 1996 and a $1,000 deduction in 1997. If Chee held the sailboat for personal use, the $3,000 deduction in 1996 would be reduced first by $100 and then by 10% of Chee's 1996 AGI. The $1,000 deduction in 1997 would be reduced by 10% of Chee's 1997 AGI (see the following discussion on the $100 and 10% floors). ▼

If a taxpayer receives reimbursement for a casualty loss sustained and deducted in a previous year, an amended return is not filed for that year. Instead, the taxpayer must include the reimbursement in gross income on the return for the year in which it is received to the extent that the previous deduction resulted in a tax benefit.

EXAMPLE 12

Fran had a deductible casualty loss of $5,000 on her 1995 tax return. Fran's taxable income for 1995 was $60,000. In June 1996, Fran was reimbursed $3,000 for the prior year's casualty loss. Fran would include the entire $3,000 in gross income for 1996 because the deduction in 1995 produced a tax benefit. ▼

Disaster Area Losses. An exception to the general rule for the time of deduction is allowed for **disaster area losses,** which are casualties sustained in an area designated as a disaster area by the President of the United States.[18] In such cases, the taxpayer may *elect* to treat the loss as having occurred in the taxable year immediately *preceding* the taxable year in which the disaster actually occurred. The rationale for this exception is to provide immediate relief to disaster victims in the form of accelerated tax benefits.

If the due date, plus extensions, for the prior year's return has not passed, a taxpayer makes the election to claim the disaster area loss on the prior year's tax return. If the disaster occurs after the prior year's return has been filed, it is necessary to file either an amended return or a refund claim. In any case, the taxpayer must show clearly that such an election is being made.

Disaster loss treatment also applies in the case of a personal residence that has been rendered unsafe for use as a residence because of a disaster. This provision applies when, within 120 days after the President designates the area as a disaster area, the state or local government where the residence is located orders the taxpayer to demolish or relocate the residence.[19]

---

[17] Reg. § 1.165–1(d)(2)(i).
[18] § 165(h).
[19] § 165(k).

TAX IN THE NEWS

Is 1995 the Year of the 'Hurricane?

Is 1995 the Year of the Hurricane? Based on the frequency of the storms and the severity of the damage, many residents of the Caribbean would respond yes.

Hurricane Marilyn left St. Thomas in shambles. This was the fourth storm to hit the Caribbean islands in a four-week period. In addition to a death toll of nine on St. Thomas, Marilyn destroyed 25 percent of the houses on the island and damaged most of the rest. Yachts were blown onto the highways and cars into the sea. Roofs were nowhere to be seen on houses where only the walls were left standing. St. Thomas lost electricity, telephone service, and water.

President Clinton declared the U.S. Virgin Islands and Puerto Rico disaster areas. This declaration made the islands eligible for federal emergency relief and for disaster area treatment for Federal income tax purposes. Taxpayers suffering losses have the option of deducting the losses on their 1994 or 1995 Federal income tax returns.

MEASURING THE AMOUNT OF LOSS

Amount of Loss. The rules for determining the amount of a loss depend in part on whether business use, income-producing use, or personal use property was involved. Another factor that must be considered is whether the property was partially or completely destroyed.

If business property or property held for the production of income (e.g., rental property) is *completely destroyed*, the loss is equal to the adjusted basis of the property at the time of destruction.

EXAMPLE 13

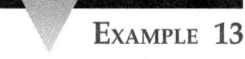

Vicki's automobile, which was used only for business purposes, was destroyed by fire. Vicki had unintentionally allowed her insurance coverage to expire. The fair market value of the automobile was $9,000 at the time of the fire, and its adjusted basis was $10,000. Vicki is allowed a loss deduction of $10,000 (the basis of the automobile). The $10,000 loss is a deduction *for* AGI. ▼

A different measurement rule applies for *partial destruction* of business property and income-producing property and for *partial* or *complete destruction* of personal use property. In these situations, the loss is the *lesser* of the following:

- The adjusted basis of the property.
- The difference between the fair market value of the property before the event and the fair market value immediately after the event.

EXAMPLE 14

Kelly's uninsured automobile, which was used only for business purposes, was damaged in a wreck. At the date of the wreck, the fair market value of the automobile was $12,000, and its adjusted basis was $9,000. After the wreck, the automobile was appraised at $4,000. Kelly's loss deduction is $8,000 (the lesser of the adjusted basis or the decrease in fair market value). The $8,000 loss is a deduction *for* AGI. ▼

The deduction for the loss of property that is part business and part personal must be computed separately for the business portion and the personal portion.

Any insurance recovery reduces the loss for business, production of income, and personal use losses. In fact, a taxpayer may realize a gain if the insurance proceeds exceed the amount of the loss. Chapter 17 discusses the treatment of net gains and losses on business property and income-producing property.

A taxpayer is not permitted to deduct a casualty loss for damage to insured personal use property unless he or she files a *timely insurance claim* with respect to the damage to the property. This rule applies to the extent that any insurance policy provides for full or partial reimbursement for the loss.[20]

Generally, an appraisal before and after the casualty is needed to measure the amount of the loss. However, the *cost of repairs* to the damaged property is acceptable as a method of establishing the loss in value provided the following criteria are met:

- The repairs are necessary to restore the property to its condition immediately before the casualty.
- The amount spent for such repairs is not excessive.
- The repairs do not extend beyond the damage suffered.
- The value of the property after the repairs does not, as a result of the repairs, exceed the value of the property immediately before the casualty.[21]

ETHICAL CONSIDERATIONS

Deducting the Cost of Repairs

Twenty years ago, Mary purchased a home for $140,000. The house was fairly new and fully landscaped. On July 15, of the current year, a severe storm blew down several large pine trees in front of the home. Mary paid a local nursery $4,000 to replace the trees with comparable trees. Because Mary's homeowners insurance excludes damage to trees, Mary intends to deduct $4,000 as a casualty loss on her Federal income tax return.

Reduction for $100 and 10 Percent-of-AGI Floors. The amount of the loss for personal use property must be further reduced by a $100 *per event* floor and a 10 percent-of-AGI *aggregate* floor.[22] The $100 floor applies separately to each casualty and applies to the entire loss from each casualty (e.g., if a storm damages both a taxpayer's residence and automobile, only $100 is subtracted from the total amount of the loss). The losses are then added together, and the total is reduced by 10 percent of the taxpayer's AGI. The resulting loss is the taxpayer's itemized deduction for casualty and theft losses.

EXAMPLE 15

Rocky, who had AGI of $30,000, was involved in a motorcycle accident. His motorcycle, which was used only for personal use and had a fair market value of $12,000 and an adjusted basis of $9,000, was completely destroyed. He received $5,000 from his insurance company. Rocky's casualty loss deduction is $900 [$9,000 basis – $5,000 insurance – $100 floor – $3,000 (.10 × $30,000 AGI)]. The $900 casualty loss is an itemized deduction (*from* AGI). ▼

[20] § 165(h)(4)(E).

[21] Reg. § 1.165–7(a)(2)(ii).

[22] § 165(c)(3).

When a nonbusiness casualty loss is spread between two taxable years because of the *reasonable prospect of recovery* doctrine, the loss in the second year is not reduced by the $100 floor. This result occurs because this floor is imposed per event and has already reduced the amount of the loss in the first year. However, the loss in the second year is still subject to the 10 percent floor based on the taxpayer's second-year AGI (refer to Example 11).

Taxpayers who suffer qualified disaster area losses can elect to deduct the losses in the year preceding the year of occurrence. The disaster loss is treated as having occurred in the preceding taxable year. Hence, the 10 percent of AGI floor is determined by using the AGI of the year for which the deduction is claimed.[23]

Multiple Losses. The rules for computing loss deductions where multiple losses have occurred are explained in Examples 16 and 17.

EXAMPLE 16

During the year, Tim had the following casualty losses:

Asset	Adjusted Basis	Fair Market Value of Asset: Before the Casualty	Fair Market Value of Asset: After the Casualty	Insurance Recovery
A	$900	$600	$–0–	$400
B	300	800	250	100

Assets A and B were used in Tim's business at the time of the casualty. The following losses are allowed:

Asset A: $500. The complete destruction of a business asset results in a deduction of the adjusted basis of the property (reduced by any insurance recovery) regardless of the asset's fair market value.

Asset B: $200. The partial destruction of a business (or personal use) asset results in a deduction equal to the lesser of the adjusted basis ($300) or the decline in value ($550), reduced by any insurance recovery ($100).

Both Asset A and Asset B losses are deductions *for* AGI. The $100 floor and the 10%-of-AGI floor do not apply because the assets are business assets. ▼

EXAMPLE 17

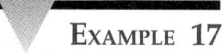

During the year, Emily had AGI of $20,000 and the following casualty losses:

Asset	Adjusted Basis	Fair Market Value of Asset: Before the Casualty	Fair Market Value of Asset: After the Casualty	Insurance Recovery
A	$ 900	$ 600	$ –0–	$200
B	2,500	4,000	1,000	–0–
C	800	400	100	250

Assets A, B, and C were held for personal use, and the losses to these three assets are from three different casualties. The loss for each asset is computed as follows:

[23] § 165(i).

Asset A: $300. The lesser of the adjusted basis of $900 or the $600 decline in value, reduced by the insurance recovery of $200, minus the $100 floor.

Asset B: $2,400. The lesser of the adjusted basis of $2,500 or the $3,000 decline in value, minus the $100 floor.

Asset C: $0. The lesser of the adjusted basis of $800 or the $300 decline in value, reduced by the insurance recovery of $250, minus the $100 floor.

Emily's itemized casualty loss deduction for the year is $700:

Asset A loss	$ 300
Asset B loss	2,400
Asset C loss	-0-
Total loss	$ 2,700
Less: 10% of AGI (10% × $20,000)	(2,000)
Itemized casualty loss deduction	$ 700

▼

STATUTORY FRAMEWORK FOR DEDUCTING LOSSES OF INDIVIDUALS

Casualty and theft losses incurred by an individual in connection with a trade or business are deductible *for* AGI.[24] These losses are not subject to the $100 per event and the 10 percent-of-AGI limitations.

Casualty and theft losses incurred by an individual in a transaction entered into for profit are not subject to the $100 per event and the 10 percent-of-AGI limitations. If these losses are attributable to rents or royalties, the deduction is *for* AGI.[25] However, if these losses are not connected with property held for the production of rents and royalties, they are deductions *from* AGI. More specifically, these losses are classified as other miscellaneous itemized deductions. An example of this type of loss would be the theft of a security. The aggregate of certain miscellaneous itemized deductions is subject to a 2 percent-of-AGI floor (explained in Chapter 9).

Casualty and theft losses attributable to personal use property are subject to the $100 per event and the 10 percent-of-AGI limitations. These losses are itemized deductions, but they are not subject to the 2 percent-of-AGI floor.[26]

PERSONAL CASUALTY GAINS AND LOSSES

If a taxpayer has personal casualty and theft gains as well as losses, a special set of rules applies for determining the tax consequences. A **personal casualty gain** is the recognized gain from a casualty or theft of personal use property. A **personal casualty loss** for this purpose is a casualty or theft loss of personal use property after the application of the $100 floor. A taxpayer who has both gains and losses for the taxable year must first net (offset) the personal casualty gains and personal casualty losses. If the gains exceed the losses, the gains and losses are treated as gains and losses from the sale of capital assets. The capital gains and losses are short term or long term, depending on the period the taxpayer held each of the

[24] § 62(a)(1).
[25] § 62(a)(4).
[26] § 67(b)(3).

assets. In the netting process, personal casualty and theft gains and losses are not netted with the gains and losses on business and income-producing property.

EXAMPLE 18

During the year, Cliff had the following personal casualty gains and losses (after deducting the $100 floor):

Asset	Holding Period	Gain or (Loss)
A	Three months	($ 300)
B	Three years	(2,400)
C	Two years	3,200

Cliff would compute the tax consequences as follows:

Personal casualty gain	$ 3,200
Personal casualty loss ($300 + $2,400)	(2,700)
Net personal casualty gain	$ 500

Cliff would treat all of the gains and losses as capital gains and losses and would have the following:

Short-term capital loss (Asset A)	$ 300
Long-term capital loss (Asset B)	2,400
Long-term capital gain (Asset C)	3,200

▼

If personal casualty losses exceed personal casualty gains, all gains and losses are treated as ordinary items. The gains—and the losses to the extent of gains—are treated as ordinary income and ordinary loss in computing AGI. Losses in excess of gains are deducted as itemized deductions to the extent the losses exceed 10 percent of AGI.[27]

EXAMPLE 19

During the year, Hazel had AGI of $20,000 and the following personal casualty gain and loss (after deducting the $100 floor):

Asset	Holding Period	Gain or (Loss)
A	Three years	($2,700)
B	Four months	200

Hazel would compute the tax consequences as follows:

Personal casualty loss	($2,700)
Personal casualty gain	200
Net personal casualty loss	($2,500)

Hazel would treat the gain and the loss as ordinary items. The $200 gain and $200 of the loss would be included in computing AGI. Hazel's itemized deduction for casualty losses would be computed as follows:

[27] § 165(h).

Concept Summary 7–3

Casualty Gains and Losses

	Business Use or Income-Producing Property	Personal Use Property
Event creating the loss	Any event.	Casualty or theft.
Amount	The lesser of the decline in fair market value or the adjusted basis, but always the adjusted basis if the property is totally destroyed.	The lesser of the decline in fair market value or the adjusted basis.
Insurance	Insurance proceeds received reduce the amount of the loss.	Insurance proceeds received (or for which there is an unfiled claim) reduce the amount of the loss.
$100 floor	Not applicable.	Applicable per event.
Gains and losses	Gains and losses are netted (see detailed discussion in Chapter 17).	Personal casualty and theft gains and losses are netted.
Gains exceeding losses		The gains and losses are treated as gains and losses from the sale of capital assets.
Losses exceeding gains		The gains—and the losses to the extent of gains—are treated as ordinary items in computing AGI. The losses in excess of gains, to the extent they exceed 10% of AGI, are itemized deductions.

Casualty loss in excess of gain ($2,700 – $200)	$ 2,500
Less: 10% of AGI (10% × $20,000)	(2,000)
Itemized deduction	$ 500

▼

Research and Experimental Expenditures

5 Learning Objective
Recognize and apply the alternative tax treatments for research and experimental expenditures.

Section 174 covers the treatment of research and experimental expenditures. The Regulations define **research and experimental expenditures** as follows:

> . . . all such costs incident to the development of an experimental or pilot model, a plant process, a product, a formula, an invention, or similar property, and the improvement of already existing property of the type mentioned. The term does not include expenditures such as those for the ordinary testing or inspection of materials or products for quality control or those for efficiency surveys, management studies, consumer surveys, advertising, or promotions.[28]

[28] Reg. § 1.174–2(a)(1).

Expenses in connection with the acquisition or improvement of land or depreciable property are not research and experimental expenditures. Rather, they increase the basis of the land or depreciable property. However, depreciation on a building used for research may be a research and experimental expense. Only the depreciation that is a research and experimental expense (not the cost of the asset) is subject to the three alternatives discussed below.

The law permits the following *three alternatives* for the handling of research and experimental expenditures:

- Expensed in the year paid or incurred.
- Deferred and amortized.
- Capitalized.

If the costs are capitalized, a deduction is not available until the research project is abandoned or is deemed worthless. Since many products resulting from research projects do not have a definite and limited useful life, a taxpayer should ordinarily elect to write off the expenditures immediately or to defer and amortize them. It is generally preferable to elect an immediate write-off of the research expenditures because of the time value of the tax deduction.

The law also provides for a research activities credit. The credit amounts to 20 percent of certain research and experimental expenditures.[29] (The credit is discussed more fully in Chapter 13.)

EXPENSE METHOD

A taxpayer can elect to expense all of the research and experimental expenditures incurred in the current year and all subsequent years. The consent of the IRS is not required if the method is adopted for the first taxable year in which such expenditures were paid or incurred. Once the election is made, the taxpayer must continue to expense all qualifying expenditures unless a request for a change is made to, and approved by, the IRS. In certain instances, a taxpayer may incur research and experimental expenditures before actually engaging in any trade or business activity. In such instances, the Supreme Court has applied a liberal standard of deductibility and permitted a deduction in the year of incurrence.[30]

DEFERRAL AND AMORTIZATION METHOD

Alternatively, research and experimental expenditures may be deferred and amortized if the taxpayer makes an election.[31] Under the election, research and experimental expenditures are amortized ratably over a period of not less than 60 months. A deduction is allowed beginning with the month in which the taxpayer first realizes benefits from the experimental expenditure. The election is binding, and a change requires permission from the IRS.

EXAMPLE 20

Gold Corporation decided to develop a new line of adhesives. The project was begun in 1996. Gold incurred the following expenses in 1996 in connection with the project:

---

[29] § 41. See the information in Chapter 13 on the termination date for the research activities credit.

[30] *Snow v. Comm.*, 74–1 USTC ¶9432, 33 AFTR2d 74–1251, 94 S.Ct. 1876 (USSC, 1974).

[31] § 174(b)(2).

Salaries	$25,000
Materials	8,000
Depreciation on machinery	6,500

Gold incurred the following expenses in 1997 in connection with the project:

Salaries	$18,000
Materials	2,000
Depreciation on machinery	5,700

The benefits from the project will be realized starting in March 1998. If Gold Corporation elects a 60-month deferral and amortization period, there will be no deduction prior to March 1998, the month benefits from the project begin to be realized. The deduction for 1998 would be $10,867, computed as follows:

Salaries ($25,000 + $18,000)	$43,000
Materials ($8,000 + $2,000)	10,000
Depreciation ($6,500 + $5,700)	12,200
Total	$65,200
$65,200 × (10 months/60 months) =	$10,867

▼

The option to treat research and experimental expenditures as deferred expense is usually employed when a company does not have sufficient income to offset the research and experimental expenses. Rather than create net operating loss carryovers that might not be utilized because of the 15-year limitation on such carryovers, the deferral and amortization method may be used. The deferral of research and experimental expenditures should also be considered if the taxpayer expects higher tax rates in the future.

Net Operating Losses

6 Learning Objective
Determine the amount of the net operating loss and recognize the impact of the carryback and carryover provisions.

The requirement that every taxpayer file an annual income tax return (whether on a calendar year or a fiscal year) may result in certain inequities for taxpayers who experience cyclical patterns of income or expense. Inequities result from the application of a progressive rate structure to taxable income determined on an annual basis. A **net operating loss (NOL)** in a particular tax year would produce no tax benefit if the Code did not provide for the carryback and carryforward of such losses to profitable years.

Example 21

Juanita has a business and realizes the following taxable income or loss over a five-year period: Year 1, $50,000; Year 2, ($30,000); Year 3, $100,000; Year 4, ($200,000); and Year 5, $380,000. She is married and files a joint return. Hubert also has a business and has a taxable income pattern of $60,000 every year. He, too, is married and files a joint return. Note that both Juanita and Hubert have total taxable income of $300,000 over the five-year period. Assume there is no provision for carryback or carryover of NOLs. Juanita and Hubert would have the following five-year tax bills:

TAX IN THE NEWS

A Better Banana in the Works

Setting their sights for the first time on a mainstay of tropical agriculture, two biotechnology companies yesterday announced a collaboration to genetically engineer a better banana. Oakland-based DNA Plant Technology Corporation and Zeneca Plant Science, a subsidiary of Britain's Zeneca Group Plc, said they will develop a banana that resists spoilage, so that it can be allowed to ripen on the tree longer and still survive shipping. Currently, bananas are harvested while still green to allow them to be shipped to distant markets without turning mushy. The bananas are then ripened artificially.

DNA Plant and Zeneca plan to develop a banana that produces less ethylene, a natural plant hormone that triggers the ripening process. With delayed ripening, the banana can be left on the tree longer, enhancing its flavor and nutrition and improving the economics of production. The companies will work on the more exotic varieties, such as "red" bananas, which are sweeter than the standard variety, and "ice cream" bananas, which are smoother and creamier, as well as the Cavendish banana, the most popular variety.

The collaboration will meld DNA Plant's technology for switching genes on and off and Zeneca's work in identifying ethylene genes. In an effort to avoid a patent battle, the two companies agreed in April to share their genetic technologies. The size of the $3 billion U.S. banana market and the fact that their technology could be easily applied to bananas convinced the companies to target the banana business.

Under the agreement, the companies will share research costs and jointly own the resulting technology. They do not expect to start selling a bio-engineered banana until 1998.

SOURCE: Alex Barnum, "A Better Banana Is in the Works—More Desirable Fruit Sought," *San Francisco Chronicle*, July 8, 1994, p. B1.

Year	Juanita's Tax	Hubert's Tax
1	$ 8,787	$11,587
2	-0-	11,587
3	22,880	11,587
4	-0-	11,587
5	125,480	11,587
	$157,147	$57,935

The computation of tax is made without regard to any NOL benefit. Rates applicable to 1996 are used to compute the tax.

Even though Juanita and Hubert realized the same total taxable income ($300,000) over the five-year period, Juanita had to pay taxes of $157,147, while Hubert paid taxes of only $57,935. ▼

To provide partial relief from this inequitable tax treatment, a deduction is allowed for NOLs.[32] This provision permits NOLs for any one year to be offset against taxable income of other years. The NOL provision is intended as a form of relief for business income and losses. Thus, only losses from the operation of a trade or business (or profession), casualty and theft losses, or losses from the confiscation of a business by a foreign government can create an NOL. In other words, a salaried individual with itemized deductions and personal exemptions in excess of gross income is not permitted to deduct the excess amounts as an NOL. On the other hand, a personal casualty loss is treated as a business loss and can therefore create (or increase) an NOL for an individual.

CARRYBACK AND CARRYOVER PERIODS

General Rules. An NOL must be applied initially to the three taxable years preceding the year of the loss (unless an election is made not to carry the loss back at all). It is carried first to the third prior year, then to the second prior year, then to the immediately preceding tax year (or until used up). If the loss is not fully used in the carryback period, it must be carried forward to the first year after the loss year, and then forward to the second, third, etc., year after the loss year. The carryover period is 15 years. A loss sustained in 1996 is used in this order: 1993, 1994, 1995, 1997 through 2011.

If the loss is being carried to a preceding year, an amended return is filed on Form 1040X, or a quick refund claim is filed on Form 1045. In any case, a refund of taxes previously paid is requested. When the loss is carried forward, the current return shows an NOL deduction for the prior year's loss.

Sequence of Use of NOLs. Where there are NOLs in two or more years, the rule is always to use the earliest year's loss first until it is completely absorbed. The later years' losses can then be used until they also are absorbed or lost. Thus, one year's return could show NOL carryovers from two or more years. Each loss is computed and applied separately.

Election to Forgo Carryback. A taxpayer can *irrevocably elect* not to carry back an NOL to any of the three prior years. In that case, the loss is available as a carryover for 15 years. A taxpayer would make the election if it is to his or her tax advantage. For example, a taxpayer might be in a low marginal tax bracket in the carryback years but expect to be in a high marginal tax bracket in future years. Therefore, it would be to the taxpayer's advantage to use the NOL to offset income in years when the tax rate is high rather than use it when the tax rate is relatively low.

COMPUTATION OF THE NET OPERATING LOSS

Since the NOL provisions apply solely to business-related losses, certain adjustments must be made so that the loss more closely resembles the taxpayer's *economic* loss. The required adjustments for corporate taxpayers are usually insignificant because a corporation's tax loss is generally similar to its economic loss. However, in computing taxable income, individual taxpayers are allowed deductions for such items as personal and dependency exemptions and itemized deductions that do not reflect actual business-related economic losses.

[32] § 172.

To arrive at the NOL for an individual, taxable income must be adjusted by adding back the following items:[33]

1. No deduction is allowed for personal and dependency exemptions. These amounts do not reflect economic, or business, outlays and hence must be added back.
2. The NOL carryover or carryback from another year is not allowed in the computation of the current year's NOL.
3. Capital losses and nonbusiness deductions are limited in determining the current year's NOL. These limits are as follows:
   a. The excess of nonbusiness capital losses over nonbusiness capital gains must be added back.
   b. The excess of nonbusiness deductions over the sum of nonbusiness income and *net* nonbusiness capital gains must be added back. *Net nonbusiness capital gains* are the excess of nonbusiness capital gains over nonbusiness capital losses. *Nonbusiness income* includes such passive items as dividends and interest. It does not include such items as salaries, rents, and gains and losses on the sale or exchange of business assets. *Nonbusiness deductions* are total itemized deductions less personal casualty and theft losses.

      A taxpayer who does not itemize deductions computes the excess of nonbusiness deductions over nonbusiness income by substituting his or her standard deduction for total itemized deductions.
   c. The excess of business capital losses over the sum of business capital gains and the excess of nonbusiness income and net nonbusiness capital gains over nonbusiness deductions must be added back.
   d. The add-back for net nonbusiness capital losses and excess business capital losses does not include net capital losses not included in the current year computation of taxable income because of the capital loss limitation provisions (discussed in Chapter 16).

The capital loss and nonbusiness deduction limits are illustrated in Examples 22 through 25.

EXAMPLE 22

For 1996, taxpayer and spouse have $6,000 of nonbusiness capital losses and $4,000 of nonbusiness capital gains. They must add back $2,000 ($6,000 – $4,000) in determining the excess of nonbusiness capital losses over nonbusiness capital gains. ▼

EXAMPLE 23

For 1996, taxpayer and spouse have $2,000 of nonbusiness capital gains, $1,000 of nonbusiness capital losses, $2,000 of interest income, and no itemized deductions. They must add back $3,700 {$6,700 standard deduction – [$2,000 interest income + $1,000 ($2,000 – $1,000) net nonbusiness capital gains]}. Note that, in this example, there is no excess of nonbusiness capital losses over nonbusiness capital gains. ▼

EXAMPLE 24

For 1996, taxpayer and spouse have $2,000 of nonbusiness capital gains, $1,000 of nonbusiness capital losses, $9,000 of interest income, $9,500 of itemized deductions (none of which are personal casualty and theft losses), $4,000 of business capital losses, and $1,000 of business capital gains. They must add back $2,500 {$4,000 business capital losses – [$1,000 business capital gains + ($9,000 nonbusiness income + $1,000 net nonbusiness capital gains – $9,500 nonbusiness deductions)]}. Note that, in this example, there is no excess of nonbusiness capital losses over nonbusiness capital gains, nor is there an excess of nonbusiness deductions over the sum of nonbusiness income and net nonbusiness capital gains. ▼

[33] § 172(d); Reg. § 1.172–3(a).

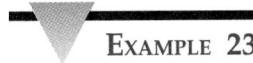

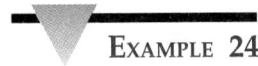

EXAMPLE 25

For 1996, taxpayer and spouse have $2,000 of nonbusiness capital gains, $3,000 of nonbusiness capital losses, $8,000 of interest income, $9,000 of itemized deductions (none of which are personal casualty and theft losses), $8,000 of business capital losses, and $4,000 of business capital gains. They must add back $1,000 ($9,000 – $8,000), the excess of nonbusiness deductions over nonbusiness income, and $3,000, the excess of combined capital losses. Because of the capital loss limitations, only $3,000 of the loss would have been used in computing taxable income for the year. ▼

Example 26 illustrates the computation of an NOL.

EXAMPLE 26

James opened a retail store in 1995 and experienced an NOL of $185 for that year. James had no taxable income for 1992, 1993, or 1994. James is married, has no dependents, and files a joint return. For 1996, James and his wife had the following taxable income:

Gross income from the business	$ 67,000	
Less: Business expenses	(71,000)	($ 4,000)
Salary from a part-time job		875
Interest on savings account		525
Nonbusiness long-term capital gain		1,000
NOL carryover from 1995		(185)
Net loss on rental property		(100)
Adjusted gross income		($ 1,885)
Less: Itemized deductions		
Interest expense	$ 3,000	
Taxes	4,300	
Casualty loss	2,000	
Total itemized deductions		(9,300)
Exemptions (2 × $2,550)		(5,100)
Taxable income		($16,285)

James's NOL is computed as follows:

Taxable income				($16,285)
Add:				
Net operating loss from 1995			$ 185	
Personal exemptions (2)			5,100	
Excess of nonbusiness deductions over nonbusiness income				
Total itemized deductions		$ 9,300		
Less: Casualty loss		(2,000)		
		$ 7,300		
Less: Interest	$ 525			
Less: Long-term capital gain	1,000	(1,525)	5,775	11,060
Net operating loss				($ 5,225)

The NOL can be thought of as follows:

Business loss	($ 4,000)
Rental loss	(100)
Casualty loss	(2,000)
Salary income	875
Net operating loss	($ 5,225)

▼

ETHICAL CONSIDERATIONS

Net Operating Losses

Adam is aware that the net operating loss carryback and carryover provisions enable him to carry back current period losses for 3 years and to carry the losses forward for 15 years. He also is aware of the time value of money concept. In addition, he recognizes that certain adjustments must be made in converting negative taxable income into an NOL.

Adam discusses with you, his accountant, the projections for his new business for the next five years, which show losses in the first two years, profits in the subsequent three years, and a cumulative profit of $90,000 for the five-year period. Adam indicates that if he delays certain transactions (by modifying the contract dates) from Years 1 and 2 into Years 3 and 4, he can convert the losses for the first two years into small profits with the cumulative projected profits for the five years remaining at $90,000. He raises the issues with you of the benefit and appropriateness of doing so.

RECOMPUTATION OF TAX LIABILITY FOR YEAR TO WHICH NET OPERATING LOSS IS CARRIED

When an NOL is carried back to a nonloss year, the taxable income and income tax for the carryback year must be recomputed by including the NOL as a deduction *for* AGI. Several deductions (such as medical expenses and charitable contributions) are based on the amount of AGI. When an NOL is carried back, all such deductions *except* the charitable contributions deduction must be recomputed on the basis of the new AGI after the NOL has been applied. The deduction for charitable contributions is determined without regard to any NOL carryback but with regard to any other modification affecting AGI. Furthermore, any tax credits limited by or based upon the tax must be recomputed, based on the recomputed tax.

EXAMPLE 27

Peggy sustained an NOL of $11,000 in 1997. Because Peggy had no taxable income in 1994 or 1995, the loss is carried back to 1996. For 1996, the joint income tax return of Peggy and her husband was as follows:

Salary income		$10,000
Dividends		4,000
Net long-term capital gain		1,400
Adjusted gross income		$15,400
Itemized deductions		
Charitable contributions	$2,700	
Interest	4,800	
Taxes	1,420	(8,920)
Exemptions (2 × $2,550)		(5,100)
Taxable income		$ 1,380
Tax (married filing jointly)		$ 207

Peggy's new tax liability for the carryback year is computed as follows:

Adjusted gross income		$ 15,400
Less: Net operating loss		(11,000)
Recomputed adjusted gross income		$ 4,400
Itemized deductions		
Charitable contributions	$2,700	
Interest	4,800	
Taxes	1,420	(8,920)
Exemptions (2 × $2,550)		(5,100)
Recomputed taxable income		$ (9,620)
Tax		$ -0-
Tax originally paid and refund claim		$ 207

▼

CALCULATION OF THE REMAINING NET OPERATING LOSS

After computing the amount of the refund claim for the initial carryback year, it is then necessary to determine the extent to which any NOL remains to carry over to future years. The amount of this carryover loss is the excess of the NOL over the taxable income of the year to which the loss is being applied. However, the taxable income of the year to which the loss is being applied must be determined with the following *modifications:*

- No deduction is allowed for excess capital losses over capital gains.
- No deduction is allowed for the NOL that is being carried back. However, deductions are allowed for NOLs occurring before the loss year.
- Any deductions claimed that are based on or limited by AGI must be determined after making the preceding adjustments. However, charitable contributions do not take into account any NOL carryback.
- No deduction is allowed for personal and dependency exemptions.

EXAMPLE 28 Referring to the facts in Example 27, the NOL carryover from 1996 available for future years would be ($4,520), computed as follows:

Salary income		$10,000
Dividends		4,000
Net long-term capital gain		1,400
Adjusted gross income		$15,400
Itemized deductions		
Charitable contributions	$2,700	
Interest	4,800	
Taxes	1,420	(8,920)
Exemptions (not allowed)		-0-
Modified taxable income		$ 6,480
Net operating loss		($11,000)
Modified taxable income		6,480
Net operating loss to carry forward		($ 4,520)

▼

Since the ending figure is negative, it represents the NOL remaining to carry over to 1998 or later years.

CONCEPT SUMMARY 7–4

Computation of Net Operating Loss

Taxable income shown on the return
Add back:

1. Personal and dependency exemptions.
2. Net operating loss carryover or carryback from another year.
3. The excess of nonbusiness capital losses over nonbusiness capital gains.
4. The excess of nonbusiness deductions over the sum of nonbusiness income plus *net* nonbusiness capital gains.
5. The excess of business capital losses over the sum of business capital gains plus the excess of nonbusiness income and *net* nonbusiness capital gains over nonbusiness deductions. The add-back from the total of items 3 and 5 will not exceed $3,000 because of the capital loss limitation rules.

Equals the net operating loss

TAX PLANNING CONSIDERATIONS

7 LEARNING OBJECTIVE
Identify tax planning opportunities in deducting certain business expenses, business losses, and personal losses.

TAX CONSEQUENCES OF THE *GROETZINGER* CASE

In the *Groetzinger* case discussed earlier in the chapter, the court established that the appropriate tests for determining if gambling is a trade or business are whether an individual engages in gambling full-time in good faith, with regularity, and for the production of income as a livelihood, and not as a mere hobby. The court held that Robert Groetzinger satisfied the tests because of his constant and large-scale effort. Skill was required and was applied. He did what he did for a livelihood, though with less than successful results. His gambling was not a hobby, a passing fancy, or an occasional bet for amusement. Therefore, his gambling was a trade or business, and hence, he was able to deduct his gambling losses *for* AGI. If the court had ruled that Groetzinger's gambling was not a trade or business, his gambling losses would have been limited to his gambling winnings and would have been classified as itemized deductions.

DOCUMENTATION OF RELATED-TAXPAYER LOANS, CASUALTY LOSSES, AND THEFT LOSSES

Since non-bona fide loans between related taxpayers may be treated as gifts, adequate documentation is needed to substantiate a bad debt deduction if the loan subsequently becomes worthless. Documentation should include proper execution of the note (legal form) and the establishment of a bona fide purpose for the loan. In addition, it is desirable to stipulate a reasonable rate of interest and a fixed maturity date.

Since a theft loss is not permitted for misplaced items, a loss should be documented by a police report and evidence of the value of the property (e.g., appraisals, pictures of the property, newspaper clippings). Similar documentation of the value of property should be provided to support a casualty loss deduction because the amount of loss is measured, in part, by the decline in fair market value of the property.

Casualty loss deductions must be reported on Form 4684 (see Appendix B).

SMALL BUSINESS STOCK

Because § 1244 limits the amount of loss classified as ordinary loss on a yearly basis, a taxpayer might maximize the benefits of § 1244 by selling the stock in more than one taxable year. The result could be that the losses in any one taxable year would not exceed the § 1244 limits on ordinary loss.

EXAMPLE 29

Mitch, a single individual, purchased small business stock in 1994 for $150,000 (150 shares at $1,000 per share). On December 20, 1996, the stock is worth $60,000 (150 shares at $400 per share). Mitch wants to sell the stock at this time. Mitch earns a salary of $80,000 a year, has no other capital transactions, and does not expect any in the future. If Mitch sells all of the small business stock in 1996, his recognized loss will be $90,000 ($60,000 – $150,000). The loss will be characterized as a $50,000 ordinary loss and a $40,000 long-term capital loss. In computing taxable income for 1996, Mitch could deduct the $50,000 ordinary loss but could deduct only $3,000 of the capital loss. The remainder of the capital loss could be carried over and used in future years subject to the $3,000 limitation if Mitch has no capital gains. If Mitch sells 82 shares in 1996, he will recognize an ordinary loss of $49,200 [82 × ($1,000 – $400)]. If Mitch then sells the remainder of the shares in 1997, he will recognize an ordinary loss of $40,800 [68 × ($1,000 – $400)]. Mitch could deduct the $49,200 ordinary loss in computing 1996 taxable income and the $40,800 ordinary loss in computing 1997 taxable income. ▼

CASUALTY LOSSES

A special election is available for taxpayers who sustain casualty losses in an area designated by the President as a disaster area. This election affects only the timing, not the calculation, of the deduction. The deduction can be taken in the year before the year in which the loss occurred. Thus, an individual can take the deduction on the 1995 return for a loss occurring between January 1 and December 31, 1996. The benefit, of course, is a faster refund (or reduction in tax). It will also be advantageous to carry the loss back if the taxpayer's tax rate in the carryback year is higher than the tax rate in the year of the loss.

To find out if an event qualifies as a disaster area loss, one can look in any of the major tax services, the Weekly Compilation of Presidential Documents, or the *Internal Revenue Bulletin.*

NET OPERATING LOSSES

In certain instances, it may be advisable for a taxpayer to elect not to carry back an NOL. For an individual, the benefits from the loss carryback could be scaled down or lost due to the economic adjustments that must be made to taxable income for the year to which the loss is carried. For example, a taxpayer should attempt to minimize the number of taxable years to which an NOL is carried. The more years to which the NOL is applied, the more benefits are lost from adjustments for items such as personal and dependency exemptions.

The election not to carry back the loss might also be advantageous if there is a disparity in marginal tax rates applicable to different tax years.

EXAMPLE 30 Abby sustained an NOL of $10,000 in Year 4. Her marginal tax bracket in Year 1 was 15%. In Year 5, however, she expects her bracket to be 39.6% due to a large profit she will make on a business deal. If Abby carries her loss back, her refund will be $1,500 (15% × $10,000). If she elects not to carry it back to Year 1 but chooses, instead, to carry it forward, her savings will be $3,960 (39.6% × $10,000). Even considering the time value of an immediate tax refund, Abby appears to be better off using the carryover approach. ▼

KEY TERMS

Bad debt, 7–3

Business bad debt, 7–4

Casualty loss, 7–9

Disaster area losses, 7–11

Net operating loss (NOL), 7–20

Nonbusiness bad debt, 7–4

Personal casualty gain, 7–15

Personal casualty loss, 7–15

Research and experimental expenditures, 7–17

Reserve method, 7–3

Section 1244 stock, 7–8

Small business stock, 7–8

Specific charge-off method, 7–3

Theft loss, 7–10

Worthless securities, 7–8

PROBLEM MATERIALS

DISCUSSION QUESTIONS

1. Explain whether a bad debt deduction is allowed for a debt arising from the sale of inventory by an accrual basis taxpayer.
2. Discuss whether legal proceedings must be brought against a debtor in order to show that a debt is worthless.
3. Discuss the tax treatment for the recovery of an account receivable previously written off as uncollectible.
4. Bill made a loan to a friend three years ago to help the friend purchase an automobile. Bill's friend has notified him that the car has been sold and the most he will be able to repay is 50% of the loan. Discuss the possibility of Bill taking a bad debt deduction for half of the loan.
5. Discuss the difference between business and nonbusiness bad debts. How is the distinction determined? How is each treated on the return?
6. What factors are to be considered in determining whether a bad debt arising from a loan between related parties is, in fact, a bad debt?
7. Discuss a taxpayer's options for the tax treatment of a loss incurred on a deposit in a qualified financial institution. Also note the consequences of each option.
8. Macy owns § 1244 stock in a corporation. The stock becomes completely worthless during the current year. Discuss the tax consequences of Macy's worthless § 1244 stock.
9. Discuss the ordinary loss limitations on the sale of § 1244 stock and the advantages of such a characterization.
10. Discuss whether a taxpayer can take a deduction for a casualty loss from an accident caused by the taxpayer's negligence.

11. Jim discovers that his sea wall, which protects his personal residence from the ocean, has been extensively damaged by the ocean. Discuss whether he may take a deduction for the damage to the wall.

12. Discuss the provision for determining the year in which a theft loss is deductible.

13. What is a disaster area loss? Why might a taxpayer benefit from making the disaster area loss election?

14. Discuss the tax consequences of property being partially destroyed in determining the amount of a casualty loss assuming no insurance proceeds are received.

15. How is a personal casualty loss computed? A business casualty loss? What effect do insurance proceeds have on both types of losses?

16. Discuss the tax consequences of not making an insurance claim when insured business property is subject to a loss.

17. Discuss the circumstances under which the cost of repairs to the damaged property can be used to measure the amount of a casualty loss.

18. Discuss the reduction of personal casualty losses by the $100 and 10%-of-AGI floors.

19. If a taxpayer is required to spread a personal casualty loss between two years under the reasonable prospect of recovery doctrine, how will the $100 per event floor and the 10%-of-AGI limitation be treated?

20. Bonnie sustained a loss on a duplex damaged by fire. She owns the duplex and lives in one unit. She rents out the other unit to a tenant. Discuss the tax treatment of the loss on Bonnie's individual tax return.

21. Discuss the tax treatment of a loss resulting from the theft of a security from an individual.

22. When casualty losses exceed casualty gains, only the amount of the casualty loss in excess of casualty gains is subject to the 10%-of-AGI floor. Discuss the significance of netting losses against gains in this manner rather than having the entire casualty loss subject to the 10%-of-AGI floor.

23. Monte opened a personal savings account at First National Bank many years ago. Last year, First National's banking license was revoked. In January of this year, Monte was informed that First National had been put into compulsory liquidation. The liquidation was precipitated by the embezzlement of funds by First National's former president. In February Monte submitted a claim for $12,459 to the liquidators of First National. In May of the current year, the liquidators advised Monte that they would keep him informed as to the progress of the liquidation and his prospects of recovery. The letter also stated that claimants would be notified if the liquidators were unable to agree to their claims. In November of the current year, Monte was notified that at the present time the liquidators could not predict with any degree of certainty how much of their funds depositors might eventually recover. Identify the relevant tax issues for Monte.

24. Fred and Diane purchased their home many years ago. The property included a large black oak tree approximately 80 feet in height and about 100 years old. The tree was the dominant feature of the front yard, where it stood alone next to the street. Because of the age and stature of the tree, Fred and Diane had it inspected regularly by a tree expert. In August of the current year, Fred noticed that the entire top or crown of the tree had turned brown. Because none of the leaves on other trees in the area had turned brown, Fred called the tree expert to inspect the tree. The inspection showed that the tree had been attacked by woodborers and was beyond saving and effectively dead. Identify the relevant tax issues for Fred and Diane.

25. Why do most taxpayers elect to write off research and experimental expenditures rather than capitalize and amortize such amounts? Are there some situations in which the capitalization and amortization approach would be preferable?

26. If a business does not elect to expense or amortize research expenditures, what is the possibility of writing off such expenditures?

27. Power and Light, a public utility company, planned a research and development project. To obtain a construction permit to expand its facilities, the company filed an application with state regulatory agencies and conducted various studies to support its application as required by the agencies. Because the taxpayer's expansion involved both the construction of a nuclear power plant and the installation of an ultrahigh voltage electric transmission line, the agencies required that the company conduct several types of environmental impact studies for site selection. The studies measured specific site conditions and the resulting environmental impact of the construction and operation of the project. The company conducted part of the studies directly and used a research organization to conduct the remainder of the studies on its behalf. Identify the relevant tax issues for Power and Light.

28. Why can the sale of small business stock (§ 1244 stock) at a loss create or increase an NOL?

29. Discuss the periods to which NOLs may be carried. Can the taxpayer elect not to carry an NOL back to any one year? What possible benefit might result from not carrying a loss back to a particular year?

30. Why are such items as nonbusiness deductions and personal and dependency exemptions not allowed in computing the NOL?

31. If an individual has no nonbusiness capital transactions for the year, discuss the treatment of the excess of nonbusiness income over nonbusiness deductions with respect to the NOL.

32. Discuss the recomputation of the tax liability for the year to which an NOL is carried.

33. Discuss the calculation of the NOL remaining after a carryback to a particular tax year.

PROBLEMS

34. Several years ago John Johnson loaned his friend Sara $20,000 to help her make a business investment. In May of the current year, Sara filed for bankruptcy, and John was notified that he could expect to receive no more than 60 cents on the dollar. As of the end of the current year, John has not received any payments. John has contacted you about the possibility of taking a bad debt deduction of $8,000 for the current year.

    Write a letter to John that contains your advice as to whether he can claim a bad debt deduction of $8,000 for the current year. Also, prepare a memo for the tax files. John's address is 100 Tyler Lane, Erie, PA 16563.

35. In 1994, Jack loaned his mother $10,000. In 1996, his mother told him that she would try and pay him $1,000. In 1997, Jack's mother filed for bankruptcy and told Jack that she would be unable to pay him anything. Determine Jack's possible deductions with respect to the loan.

36. In 1995, Wilma deposited $117,500 with a commercial bank. On July 1, 1996, Wilma was notified that the bank was insolvent, and subsequently she received only $100,000 of the deposit. Wilma also has a salary of $5,000, long-term capital gain of $12,000, and itemized deductions (other than casualty and theft) of $7,000. Determine whether Wilma should elect to treat the loss on the deposit as a personal casualty loss or as a bad debt.

37. Zenith, a single taxpayer, had the following items for 1996:

    - Salary of $75,000.
    - Gain of $15,000 on the sale of § 1244 stock acquired three years ago.
    - Loss of $60,000 on the sale of § 1244 stock acquired two years ago.
    - Stock acquired on December 20, 1995, for $2,500 became worthless on April 3, 1996.

    Determine Zenith's AGI for 1996.

38. Mary, a single taxpayer, purchased 10,000 shares of § 1244 stock several years ago at a cost of $20 per share. In November of the current year, Mary received an offer to sell the stock for $12 per share. She has the option of either selling all of the stock now or selling half of the stock now and half of the stock in January of next year. Mary will receive a salary of $80,000 for the current year and $90,000 next year. Mary will have long-term capital gains of $8,000 for the current year and $10,000 next year. If Mary's goal is to minimize her AGI for the two years, determine whether Mary should sell all of her stock this year or half of her stock this year and half next year.

39. When Helen returned from a vacation in Hawaii on November 8, 1996, she discovered that a burglar had stolen her silver, stereo, and color television. In the process of removing these items, the burglar damaged some furniture that originally cost $1,400. Helen's silver cost $12,000 and was valued at $16,500; the stereo system cost $8,400 and was valued at $6,200; the television cost $840 and was worth $560. Helen filed a claim with her insurance company and was reimbursed in the following amounts on December 20, 1996.

the lesser of the FMV or basis

Silver	$2,800
Stereo	5,600
Television	490

The insurance company disputed the reimbursement claimed by Helen for the damaged furniture, but she protested and was finally paid $280 on January 30, 1997. The repairs to the furniture totaled $1,550. Helen's AGI for 1996 was $20,000, and it was $500 for 1997. How much can Helen claim as a casualty and theft loss? In which year?

40. Olaf owns a 500-acre farm in Minnesota. A tornado hit the area and destroyed a farm building and some farm equipment and damaged a barn. Fortunately for Olaf, the tornado occurred after he had harvested his corn crop. Applicable information is as follows:

Item	Adjusted Basis	FMV Before	FMV After	Insurance Proceeds
Building	$80,000	$100,000	$ -0-	$60,000
Equipment	60,000	50,000	-0-	25,000
Barn	90,000	120,000	90,000	25,000

Because of the extensive damage caused by the tornado, the President designated the area as a disaster area.

Olaf, who files a joint return with his wife Anna, had $90,000 of taxable income last year. Their taxable income for the current year, excluding the loss from the tornado, is $220,000.

Determine the amount of Olaf and Anna's loss and the year in which they should take the loss.

41. On January 7 of the current year, Wade dropped off to sleep while driving home from a business trip. Luckily, he was only slightly injured in the resulting accident, but his car was completely destroyed.

Wade had purchased the car new two years ago and had driven it 64,000 miles at the time of the accident. Of these miles, 28,000 were business miles; the remaining miles were personal miles. The car cost $7,200 new. Wade has taken $1,985 of depreciation for the business use of the car. The fair market value at the time of the accident was $4,000. Wade carried zero deductible collision insurance on the car. He made no claim on his insurance policy because he was afraid that his insurance premiums would increase if he did.

After Wade's release from the hospital the day after the accident, he could not find his wallet (cost $65, fair replacement value $30) or its contents, which included $350 in cash and $500 in traveler's checks. The traveler's checks were replaced by the issuing company. He also was unable to locate the stone from his diamond ring. The stone cost his wife $2,500 when purchased nine years ago and was worth $6,400 at the time of the loss.

a. Determine the amount of Wade's deductible loss *for* AGI.
b. Determine the amount of the loss deductible *from* AGI, assuming AGI for the year is $25,000.

42. On November 1 of the current year, Sam Smith was involved in an accident with his personal use automobile. Sam had purchased the car for $25,000. The automobile had a fair market value of $19,000 before the accident and $12,000 after the accident. The car was covered by an insurance policy that had a $1,000 deductible clause. Sam is afraid that the policy will be canceled if he makes a claim for the damages. Therefore, he is considering not filing a claim. Sam believes that the casualty loss deduction will help mitigate the loss of the insurance reimbursement. Sam's AGI for the current year is $25,000.

Write a letter to Sam that contains your advice with respect to the tax consequences of filing versus not filing a claim for the insurance reimbursement for the damages to his car. Also, prepare a memo for the tax files. Sam's address is 450 Colonel's Way, Warrensburg, MO 64093.

43. Green Corporation, a manufacturing company, decided to develop a new line of fireworks. Because of the danger involved, Green purchased an isolated parcel of land for $300,000 and constructed a building for $1,220,000. The building was to be used for research and experimentation in creating the new fireworks. The project was begun in 1996. Green had the following expenses in 1996 in connection with the project:

Salaries	$160,000
Utilities	20,000
Materials	40,000
Insurance	50,000
Cost of market survey to determine profit potential for new fireworks line	20,000
Depreciation on the building	30,000

Green had the following expenses in 1997 in connection with the project:

Salaries	$200,000
Utilities	30,000
Materials	40,000
Insurance	30,000
Depreciation on the building	31,000

The benefits from the project will be realized starting in June 1998.

a. If Green Corporation elects to expense research and experimental expenditures, determine the amount of the deduction for 1996, 1997, and 1998.
b. If Green Corporation elects a 60-month deferral and amortization period, determine the amount of the deduction for 1996, 1997, and 1998.

44. Rex and Rosa, who file a joint return, had the following items for their 1996 tax return:

- Rex's salary—$50,000.
- Rosa's salary—$52,000.
- Dividends from domestic corporations—$15,000.

- Interest on savings account—$1,000.
- During the year, a fire completely destroyed an apartment building owned by Rex and Rosa. The building was worth $400,000 at the time of the fire, and Rex and Rosa had a basis for the building of $390,000. The building was insured for 60% of its fair market value.
- Other itemized deductions—$20,000.

a. What is Rex and Rosa's taxable income for 1996?
b. What is Rex and Rosa's NOL for 1996?

45. Carol, a single taxpayer, had the following items of income and expense during 1996:

Gross receipts from business	$240,000
Business expenses	300,000
Carol's salary	30,000
Interest from Blue Company bonds	24,000
Itemized deductions	15,000

a. Determine the amount of Carol's 1996 taxable income.
b. Determine the amount of Carol's 1996 NOL.

46. Gus, who is married and files a joint return, owns a grocery store. In 1996, his gross sales were $286,000 and operating expenses were $310,000. Other items on his 1996 return were as follows:

Nonbusiness capital gains (short-term)	$10,000
Nonbusiness capital losses (long-term)	9,000
Itemized deductions	10,000
Ordinary nonbusiness income	4,000
Salary from part-time job	10,000

During the years 1993 and 1994, Gus had no taxable income. In 1995, Gus had taxable income of $24,100 computed as follows:

Net business income		$60,000
Interest income		2,000
Adjusted gross income		$62,000
Less: Itemized deductions		
Charitable contributions of $40,000, limited to 50% of AGI	$31,000	
Medical expenses of $6,550, limited to the amount in excess of 7.5% of AGI ($6,550 – $4,650)	1,900	
Total itemized deductions		(32,900)
Exemptions (2 × 2,500)		(5,000)
Taxable income		$24,100

a. What is Gus's 1996 NOL?
b. Determine Gus's recomputed taxable income for 1995.

47. During 1996, Rick and his wife Sara had the following items of income and expense to report:

• Gross receipts from business	$400,000
• Business expenses	525,000
• Interest income from bank savings accounts	8,000

• Sara's salary	50,000
• Long-term capital gain on stock held as an investment	4,000
• Itemized deductions	15,000

a. Assuming Rick and Sara file a joint return, what is their taxable income for 1996?
b. What is the amount of Rick and Sara's NOL for 1996?

48. Assume that in addition to the information in Problem 47, Rick had no taxable income for the years 1993 and 1994 and $6,700 of taxable income for 1995 computed as follows:

Salary		$ 25,000
Capital loss		(1,000)
Adjusted gross income		$ 24,000
Less: Itemized deductions		
Charitable contributions of $20,000, limited to 50% of AGI	$12,000	
Medical expenses of $2,100, limited to the amount in excess of 7.5% of AGI ($2,100 – $1,800)	300	
Total itemized deductions		(12,300)
Exemptions (2 × $2,500)		(5,000)
Taxable income		$ 6,700

Determine the amount of Rick and Sara's 1996 NOL to be carried forward to 1997.

49. Robert and Susan Reid had an NOL of $50,000 in 1996. They had no taxable income for the years 1993 and 1994 and $18,400 of taxable income for 1995 computed as follows:

Salary		$ 50,000
Capital loss		(2,000)
Adjusted gross income		$ 48,000
Less: Itemized deductions		
Charitable contributions of $40,000, limited to 50% of AGI	$24,000	
Medical expenses of $4,200, limited to the amount in excess of 7.5% of AGI ($4,200 – $3,600)	600	
Total itemized deductions		(24,600)
Exemptions (2 × $2,500)		(5,000)
Taxable income		$ 18,400

Write a letter to Robert and Susan informing them of the amount of the remaining NOL to be carried forward if the loss is applied against the 1995 taxable income. Also, prepare a memo for the tax files. Their address is 201 Jerdone Avenue, Conway, SC 29526.

50. Fran is single and had the following income and deductions for 1996:

Business receipts	$ 90,000
Business expenses	130,000
Dividends from domestic corporations	20,000
Interest received from bank savings account	6,000
Itemized deductions	10,000
1995 NOL carried to 1996	25,000

a. What is Fran's taxable income for 1996?
b. What is Fran's NOL for 1996?

51. Soong, single and age 32, had the following items for the tax year 1996:

- Salary of $40,000.
- Interest income from U.S. government bonds of $2,000.
- Dividends from a foreign corporation of $500.
- Sale of small business § 1244 stock on October 20, 1996, for $10,000. The stock had been acquired two years earlier for $65,000.
- Business bad debt of $3,000.
- Nonbusiness bad debt of $5,000.
- Sale of small business § 1244 stock on November 12, 1996, for $4,000. The stock had been acquired on June 5, 1996, for $800.
- Sale of common stock on December 4, 1996, for $40,000. The stock was acquired four years ago for $18,000.
- Total itemized deductions of $8,000.

Determine Soong's NOL for 1996.

52. Nell, single and age 38, had the following income and expense items in 1996:

Nonbusiness bad debt	$ 6,000
Business bad debt	2,000
Nonbusiness long-term capital gain	4,000
Nonbusiness short-term capital loss	3,000
Salary	40,000
Interest income	1,000

Determine Nell's AGI for 1996.

53. Assume that in addition to the information in Problem 52, Nell had the following items in 1996:

Personal casualty gain on an asset held for four months	$10,000
Personal casualty loss on an asset held for two years	1,000

Determine Nell's AGI for 1996.

54. Assume that in addition to the information in Problems 52 and 53, Nell had the following items in 1996:

Personal casualty loss on an asset held for five years	$50,000
Interest expense on home mortgage	3,000

Determine Nell's taxable income and NOL for 1996.

55. Jed, age 55, is married with no children. During 1996, Jed had the following income and expense items:
a. Three years ago, Jed loaned a friend $10,000 to help him purchase a new car. In June of the current year, Jed learned that his friend had been declared bankrupt and had left the country. There is no possibility that Jed will ever collect any of the $10,000.
b. In December of last year, Jed purchased some stock for $5,000. In March of the current year, the company was declared bankrupt, and Jed was notified that his shares of stock were worthless.
c. Several years ago, Jed purchased some § 1244 stock for $120,000. This year, he sold the stock for $30,000.

d. In July of this year, Jed sold some land that he had held for two years for $60,000. He had originally paid $42,000 for the land.
e. Jed received $40,000 of interest income from State of Minnesota bonds.
f. In September, Jed's home was damaged by an earthquake. Jed's basis in his home was $430,000. The value of the home immediately before the quake was $610,000. After the quake, the home was worth $540,000. Because earthquake damage was an exclusion on Jed's homeowners insurance policy, he received no insurance recovery.
g. Jed received a salary of $80,000.
h. Jed made a charitable contribution of $4,000.

If Jed files a joint return for 1996, determine his NOL for the year.

CUMULATIVE PROBLEMS

56. Ned Wilson, age 60, single, and retired, has no dependents. Ned lives at 231 Wander Lane, Salt Lake City, UT 84201. Ned's Social Security number is 985–12–3774. During 1996, Ned had the following income and expense items:

a. On January 27, 1995, Ned deposited $8,000 in a savings account at the ABC Financial Company. The savings account bore interest at 15%, compounded semiannually. Ned received a $600 interest payment on July 27, 1995, but received no interest payments thereafter. The finance company filed for bankruptcy on January 12, 1996. Ned received a $710 check in final settlement of his account from the bankruptcy trustee on December 20, 1996.
b. On January 1, 1996, a fire severely damaged a two-story building owned by Ned, who occupied the second story of the building as a residence and had recently opened a hardware store on the ground level. The following information is available with respect to the incident:

		Fair Market Value	
Asset	**Adjusted Basis**	**Before**	**After**
Building	$70,000	$130,000	$50,000
Inventory	35,000	55,000	None
Store equipment	3,000	2,500	None
Home furnishings	12,600	7,000	800
Personal auto	8,900	7,800	7,600

Ned's fire insurance policy paid the following amounts for damages covered by the policy:

Building	$50,000	(policy maximum)
Inventory	30,000	
Store equipment	None	
Home furnishings	1,000	(policy maximum)
Personal auto	None	

Assume all of the destroyed property was acquired on December 15, 1995.

c. On March 1, 1991, Ned loaned a neighboring businessman $17,000. The debtor died of a heart attack on June 21, 1996. Ned had no security and was unable to collect anything from the man's estate.
d. Ned received $125,000 of interest income from Salt Lake City Bank.
e. On March 3, 1996, Ned sold a piece of real estate he had been holding for speculation for $90,000. Ned had bought the land July 18, 1981, for $52,800.

f. Ned made a charitable contribution of $13,000.
g. Ned made four quarterly estimated tax payments of $7,000 each.

Part 1—Tax Computation
Compute Ned's 1996 Federal income tax payable (or refund due), assuming he deducts the lost deposit as a bad debt. Suggested software (if available): *TurboTax* or *MacInTax.*

Part 2—Tax Planning
Determine whether Ned should elect to treat the deposit in ABC Financial Company as a casualty loss rather than as a bad debt. Suggested software (if available): *TurboTax* or *MacInTax.*

57. Jane Smith, age 40, is single and has no dependents. She is employed as a legal secretary by Legal Services, Inc. She owns and operates Typing Services located near the campus of San Jose State University at 1986 Campus Drive. She is a cash basis taxpayer. Jane lives at 2020 Oakcrest Road, San Jose, CA 95134. Jane's Social Security number is 123–89–6666. Jane indicates that she wishes to designate $3 to the Presidential Election Campaign Fund. During 1995, Jane had the following income and expense items:
a. $50,000 salary from Legal Services, Inc.
b. $20,000 gross receipts from her typing services business.
c. $700 cash dividend from Buffalo Mining Company, a Canadian corporation.
d. $1,000 Christmas bonus from Legal Services, Inc.
e. $60,000 life insurance proceeds on the death of her sister.
f. $5,000 check given to her by her wealthy aunt.
g. $100 won in a bingo game.
h. Expenses connected with the typing service:

Office rent	$7,000
Supplies	4,400
Utilities and telephone	4,680
Wages to part-time typists	5,000
Payroll taxes	500
Equipment rentals	3,000

i. $9,000 interest expense on a home mortgage (paid to San Jose Savings and Loan).
j. $5,000 fair market value of silverware stolen from her home by a burglar on October 12, 1995. Jane had paid $4,000 for the silverware on July 1, 1986. She was reimbursed $1,500 by her insurance company.
k. Jane had loaned $2,100 to a friend, Joan Jensen, on June 3, 1992. Joan declared bankruptcy on August 14, 1995, and was unable to repay the loan.
l. Legal Services, Inc., withheld Federal income tax of $8,500 and the required amount of FICA tax.
m. Alimony of $10,000 received from her former husband, Ted Smith.
n. Interest income of $800 on City of San Jose bonds.
o. Jane made estimated tax payments of $1,000.

Part 1—Tax Computation
Compute Jane Smith's 1995 Federal income tax payable (or refund due). If you use tax forms for your computations, you will need Forms 1040 and 4684 and Schedules A, C, and D. Suggested software (if available): *TurboTax* or *MacInTax.*

Part 2—Tax Planning
In 1996, Jane plans to continue her job with Legal Services, Inc. Therefore, items a, d, and l will recur in 1996. Jane plans to continue her typing services business (refer to item b) and expects gross receipts of $26,000. She projects that all business expenses (refer to item h) will increase by 10%, except for office rent, which, under the terms of her lease, will remain the same as in 1995. Items e, f, g, j, and k will not recur in 1996. Items c, i, m, and n will be approximately the same as in 1995.

Jane would like you to compute the minimum amount of estimated tax she will have to pay for 1996 so that she will not have to pay any additional tax upon filing her 1996

Federal income tax return. Write a letter to Jane that contains your advice and prepare a memo for the tax files. Suggested software (if available): *TurboTax* or *MacInTax*.

RESEARCH PROBLEMS

Note: ***West's Federal Taxation on CD-ROM*** *can be used in preparing solutions to the Research Problems. Alternatively, tax research materials contained in a standard tax library can be used.*

Research Problem 1. While Ralph was in the process of obtaining a divorce, his wife, without Ralph's knowledge, had the furniture removed from his apartment. Discuss whether Ralph would be entitled to a tax deduction for the loss of the furniture.

Partial list of research aids:
Landis G. Brown, 30 TCM 257, T.C.Memo. 1971–60.
Jerry L. Goode, 42 TCM 1209, T.C.Memo. 1981–548.

Research Problem 2. Janice Jones is single and a very successful executive. For the past five years, her taxable income has exceeded $160,000. Lately, Janice has been seeing a lot of Jim Johnson. Jim suffered a financial setback a few years ago, and as a result, he has $500,000 of NOL carryforwards. Janice wants to know if she marries Jim and they file a joint return, will she be able to use Jim's NOL carryforwards to offset her income? Discuss the potential tax consequences.

Research Problem 3. George Johnson, a Minnesota resident, parked his car on a lake while he was watching an iceboat race. During the race, the ice beneath his car unexpectedly gave way, and the car sank to the bottom of the lake. Write a letter to George advising him as to whether he can claim a casualty loss for the damage to the car. Also, prepare a memo for the tax files. George's address is 100 Apple Lane, St. Paul, MN 55123.

Research Problem 4. John Smith was engaged to be married to Nancy Brown. In contemplation of marriage, Nancy deposited $20,000 in a bank account for John, to be used after their marriage. Sometime thereafter, the engagement was broken off, and John used the $20,000 for himself. Nancy has attempted to collect the $20,000 from John without success, and now John has filed for bankruptcy. Discuss the possibility of Nancy's claiming the $20,000 as a nonbusiness bad debt on her income tax return.

TEAM PROJECT: ARTHUR ANDERSEN TAX CHALLENGE CASES

For more information on the Arthur Andersen Tax Challenge Cases, please refer to Chapter 1, page 1-38.

Information related to tax issues and problems that are discussed in this chapter may be found in the

Fields case on pages 2, 11, and 23

Read and analyze the case you have been assigned and *identify* any issues and problems that are related to material covered in this chapter. If the information provided in the case is complete, prepare answers for this part of the case at this time. If you need information that is contained in the later parts of the case, please write a memo summarizing the questions or problems so you can prepare a complete answer at a later date.

CHAPTER

8

DEPRECIATION, COST RECOVERY, AMORTIZATION, AND DEPLETION

LEARNING OBJECTIVES

After completing Chapter 8, you should be able to:

1. Understand the rationale for the cost consumption concept and identify the relevant time periods for depreciation, ACRS, and MACRS.
2. Determine the amount of cost recovery under ACRS and MACRS.
3. Recognize when and how to make the § 179 expensing election, calculate the amount of the deduction, and apply the effect of the election in making the MACRS calculation.
4. Identify listed property and apply the deduction limitations on listed property and on luxury automobiles.
5. Determine when and how to use the alternative depreciation system (ADS).
6. Identify intangible assets that are eligible for amortization and calculate the amount of the deduction.
7. Determine the amount of depletion expense including being able to apply the alternative tax treatments for intangible drilling and development costs.
8. Perform the reporting procedures for cost recovery.
9. Identify tax planning opportunities for cost recovery, amortization, and depletion.

OUTLINE

1 **LEARNING OBJECTIVE** Understand the rationale for the cost consumption concept and identify the relevant time periods for depreciation, ACRS, and MACRS.

The Internal Revenue Code provides for a deduction for the consumption of the cost of an asset through depreciation, cost recovery, amortization, or depletion. These deductions are applications of the recovery of capital doctrine (discussed in Chapter 4).

A distinction is made between tangible and intangible property. Tangible property is any property with physical substance (e.g., equipment, buildings), while intangible property lacks such substance (e.g., goodwill, patents).

The **depreciation** rules were completely overhauled by the Economic Recovery Tax Act of 1981 (ERTA). Hence, *most* property placed in service after December 31, 1980, is subject to the accelerated **cost recovery** system (ACRS). However, property placed in service before January 1, 1981, that is still in use, as well as *certain* property placed in service after December 31, 1980, is subject to the pre-ERTA depreciation rules. The Tax Reform Act (TRA) of 1986 completely revised the ACRS rules for property placed in service after December 31, 1986 (MACRS). Therefore, a knowledge of all of the depreciation and cost recovery rules may be needed as Example 1 illustrates.

EXAMPLE 1

The Brown Company owns machinery purchased in 1980. The machinery has a 17-year useful life. The business also owns equipment purchased in 1986 that has a 15-year cost recovery life. In 1990, the business purchased a computer. To compute the depreciation and cost recovery for 1996, Brown will use the pre-ERTA depreciation rules for the machinery, the pre-TRA of 1986 cost recovery rules (ACRS) for the equipment, and the post-TRA of 1986 cost recovery rules (MACRS) for the computer. ▼

This chapter initially focuses on the ACRS and MACRS rules.[1] The chapter then concludes with a discussion of the amortization of intangible property and the depletion of natural resources.

ACRS was one of many provisions in ERTA that were intended to stimulate the economy. The following features of ACRS result in accelerated write-offs:

- Cost recovery periods are shorter than the estimated useful lives required under the pre-1981 depreciation system.

[1] § 168. Pre-ERTA depreciation rules under § 167 are covered in Appendix H.

Concept Summary 8–1

Depreciation and Cost Recovery: Relevant Time Periods

System	Date Property Is Placed in Service
§ 167 depreciation	Before January 1, 1981, and *certain* property placed in service after December 31, 1980.
Original accelerated cost recovery system (ACRS)	After December 31, 1980, and before January 1, 1987.
Modified accelerated cost recovery system (MACRS)	After December 31, 1986.

- The use of salvage value, required under the pre-1981 depreciation system, is eliminated under ACRS.
- For many assets, the methods for computing ACRS deductions are more generous than the allowable methods for computing depreciation.

For assets placed in service after 1986, ACRS is replaced with MACRS. The basic effect of MACRS is to somewhat dampen the economic stimulus effect of ACRS. MACRS cost recovery periods are generally longer than ACRS cost recovery periods. In addition, the cost recovery methods available under MACRS are, in most cases, not as generous as the methods available under ACRS.

Overview

Taxpayers may write off the cost of certain assets that are used in a trade or business or held for the production of income. A write-off may take the form of depreciation (or cost recovery), depletion, or amortization. Tangible assets, other than natural resources, are *depreciated.* Natural resources, such as oil, gas, coal, and timber, are *depleted.* Intangible assets, such as copyrights and patents, are *amortized.* Generally, no write-off is allowed for an asset that does not have a determinable useful life.

ACRS and MACRS provide separate cost recovery tables for realty (real property) and personalty (personal property). Realty generally includes land and buildings permanently affixed to the land. Write-offs are not available for land because it does not have a determinable useful life. Cost recovery allowances for real property, other than land, are based on recovery lives specified in the law. The IRS provides tables that specify cost recovery allowances for most types of realty.

Personalty is defined as any asset that is not realty.[2] Personalty includes furniture, machinery, equipment, and many other types of assets. Do not confuse personalty (or personal property) with *personal use* property. Personal use property is any property (realty or personalty) that is held for personal use rather than for use in a trade or business or an income-producing activity. Write-offs are not allowed for personal use assets.

[2] Refer to Chapter 1 for a further discussion.

In summary, both realty and personalty can be either business use/income-producing property or personal use property. Examples include a residence (realty that is personal use), an office building (realty that is business use), a dump truck (personalty that is business use), and regular wearing apparel (personalty that is personal use). It is imperative that this distinction between the *classification* of an asset (realty or personalty) and the *use* to which the asset is put (business or personal) be understood.

Accelerated Cost Recovery System (ACRS and MACRS)

GENERAL CONSIDERATIONS

2 LEARNING OBJECTIVE Determine the amount of cost recovery under ACRS and MACRS.

Under the **accelerated cost recovery system (ACRS),** the cost of an asset is recovered over a predetermined period that is generally shorter than the useful life of the asset or the period the asset is used to produce income. The ACRS system was designed to encourage investment, improve productivity, and simplify the law and its administration. However, the pre-ACRS depreciation rules will continue to apply in the following situations:

- Property placed in service after 1980 whose life is not based on years (e.g., units-of-production method).
- The remaining depreciation on property placed in service by the taxpayer before 1981.
- Personal property acquired after 1980 if the property was owned or used during 1980 by the taxpayer or a related person (antichurning rule).[3]
- Property that is amortized (e.g., leasehold improvements).

The basis for cost recovery generally is the adjusted cost basis used to determine gain if property is sold or otherwise disposed of. The basis is reduced by the amount of the cost recovery deducted.

Cost Recovery Allowed or Allowable. The basis of cost recovery property must be reduced by the cost recovery allowed and by not less than the allowable amount. The *allowed* cost recovery is the cost recovery actually taken, whereas the *allowable* cost recovery is the amount that could have been taken under the applicable cost recovery method. If the taxpayer does not claim any cost recovery on property during a particular year, the basis of the property must still be reduced by the amount of cost recovery that should have been deducted (the allowable cost recovery).

EXAMPLE 2

On March 15, Jack paid $10,000 for a copier to be used in his business. The copier is five-year property. Jack elected to use the straight-line method of cost recovery, but did not take cost recovery in years three or four. Therefore, the allowed cost recovery (cost recovery actually deducted) and the allowable cost recovery are as follows:

[3] § 168(f). The antichurning rules may also require the use of pre-TRA of 1986 ACRS rules on property placed in service after December 31, 1986 (property that otherwise would be subject to MACRS).

	Cost Recovery Allowed	Cost Recovery Allowable
Year 1	$1,000	$1,000
Year 2	2,000	2,000
Year 3	–0–	2,000
Year 4	–0–	2,000
Year 5	2,000	2,000
Year 6	1,000	1,000

If Jack sold the copier for $800 in year seven, he would recognize an $800 gain ($800 amount realized – $0 adjusted basis) because the adjusted basis of the copier is zero. ▼

Cost Recovery Basis for Personal Use Assets Converted to Business or Income-Producing Use. If personal use assets are converted to business or income-producing use, the basis for cost recovery and for loss is the *lower* of the adjusted basis or the fair market value at the time the property was converted. As a result of this lower-of-basis rule, losses that occurred while the property was personal use property will not be recognized for tax purposes through the cost recovery of the property.

EXAMPLE 3

Hans acquires a personal residence for $120,000. Four years later, when the fair market value is only $100,000, he converts the property to rental use. The basis for cost recovery is $100,000, since the fair market value is less than the adjusted basis. The $20,000 decline in value is deemed to be personal (since it occurred while the property was held for personal use) and therefore nondeductible. ▼

ETHICAL CONSIDERATIONS

Deducting Depreciation on a Converted Truck

Bill purchased a new truck several years ago and has always used the truck for personal use. This year Bill started a business and used the truck almost exclusively for business. Because he has not taken any depreciation on his truck and because the cost of a new truck is significantly more than he paid for his truck, Bill wants to use the original cost of the truck for purposes of determining depreciation on his tax return. Evaluate the equity and the appropriateness of Bill's perspective.

ELIGIBLE PROPERTY UNDER ACRS OR MACRS

Assets used in a trade or business or for the production of income are eligible for cost recovery if they are subject to wear and tear, decay or d[illegible]ral causes, or obsolescence. Assets that do not decline in v[illegible]sis or that do not have a determinable useful life (e.g., lar[illegible]ot eligible for cost recovery.

PERSONALTY: RECOVERY PERIODS AND ME[illegible]

Classification of Property: ACRS. ACRS provides [illegible] personalty (and certain realty) is recovered over 3, 5, 10, [illegible] classified by recovery period as follows:

TAX IN THE NEWS

A Seventeenth-Century Ruggeri Bass Violin Is a Tool of Trade Rather Than a Work of Art

On September 16, 1995, the *Wall Street Journal* reported that the U.S. Third Circuit Court of Appeals affirmed a Tax Court decision, holding that a valuable bass violin could be depreciated when it is used as a tool of trade by a professional musician. The depreciation was allowed even though the instrument actually increased in value while the musician owned it. The key factor appears to be that the taxpayer viewed the instrument as a tool of his trade that was subject to normal wear and tear and not as a work of art.

The petitioner, Brian P. Liddle, who was a very accomplished professional musician with the Philadelphia Orchestra, purchased the violin for $28,000 on November 8, 1984. The violin was built in the seventeenth century by Franceso Ruggeri. Ruggeri studied stringed instrument construction under Nicolo Amati, who also instructed Antonio Stradivari. His other contemporaries included the craftsmen Guadanini and Guarneri. These artisans were members of the so-called Cremonese School of instrument makers.

3 years.................. Autos, light-duty trucks, R & D equipment, racehorses over 2 years old and other horses over 12 years old, and personalty with an ADR* midpoint life of 4 years or less.[4]

5 years.................. Most other equipment except long-lived public utility property. Also includes single-purpose agricultural structures and petroleum storage facilities, which are designated as § 1245 property under the law.

10 years................. Public utility property with an ADR midpoint life greater than 18 but not greater than 25 years, burners and boilers using coal as a primary fuel if used in a public utility power plant and if replacing or converting oil- or gas-fired burners or boilers, railroad tank cars, mobile homes, and realty with an ADR midpoint life of 12.5 years or less (e.g., theme park structures).

15 years................. Public utility property with an ADR midpoint life exceeding 25 years (except certain burners and boilers using coal as a primary fuel).

*ADR refers to the Asset Depreciation Range system.

Taxpayers who own 10-year or 15-year ACRS property continue to compute cost recovery allowances under the ACRS rules. However, all cost has already been recovered on any 3-year or 5-year ACRS property.

Taxpayers had the choice of using (1) the straight-line method over the regular or optional (see below) recovery period or (2) a prescribed accelerated method over the regular recovery period. These two methods are both part of the ACRS system, but a convenient name is not provided for either method. Hereafter, the straight-line method will be referred to as the *optional* (or *elective*) *straight-line*

[4] Rev.Proc. 83–35, 1983–1 C.B. 745 is the source for the ADR midpoint lives.

method. The method using percentages prescribed in the Code will be referred to as the *statutory percentage method.*

The rates to be used in computing the deduction under the statutory percentage method are shown in Table 8–1 (all tables are located at the end of the chapter prior to the Problem Materials) and are based on the 150 percent declining-balance method, using the **half-year convention**[5] and an assumption of zero salvage value. The rates in the cost recovery tables at the end of the chapter reflect the relevant methods, conventions, and assumptions.

EXAMPLE 4

Green Utilities acquired 15-year public utility property in 1985 at a cost of $100,000. The property was placed in service on September 1, 1985. Green's cost recovery allowance for 1996 is determined from Table 8–1. The cost recovery percentage for 1996 (recovery year 12) is 6%, and the cost recovery allowance is $6,000 ($100,000 cost × 6%). ▼

Note that in 1985, Green got a half-year's cost recovery deduction (since the half-year convention is reflected in the percentages in Table 8–1) although it held the property only four months.

In the year that personal property is disposed of, no cost recovery is allowed.

EXAMPLE 5

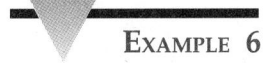

Assume the same facts as in the previous example and that the property is sold in May 1997. Green is not allowed a cost recovery deduction for the property in 1997. ▼

Reduction of Basis for Investment Tax Credit. For personalty placed in service after 1982 and before January 1, 1986, taxpayers were required to reduce the basis of the property for the ACRS write-off by one-half the amount of the investment tax credit taken on the property.[6] The investment tax credit was not allowed on realty.

EXAMPLE 6

Beige Electric Company acquired property on September 4, 1985, for $100,000. The property was 15-year ACRS property, and Beige claimed a $10,000 investment tax credit ($100,000 × 10% investment tax credit rate). The basis of the property was reduced by $5,000 (one-half of the $10,000 investment tax credit). Therefore, the basis for cost recovery was $95,000. The cost recovery for 1996 is $5,700 [$95,000 × 6% (Table 8–1)]. ▼

As an alternative to reducing the basis of the property, a taxpayer could elect to take a *reduced* investment tax credit. Under this election, the investment tax credit was 8 percent (rather than 10 percent) for recovery property other than three-year property and 4 percent (instead of 6 percent) for three-year property. In Example 6, if the reduced investment tax credit election were made, Beige's cost recovery basis would be $100,000 rather than $95,000.

TRA of 1986 generally repealed the investment tax credit for property placed in service after December 31, 1985. Therefore, the reduction of basis for the investment tax credit does not apply to such property.

Classification of Property: MACRS. The general effect of TRA of 1986 was to lengthen asset lives. The **modified accelerated cost recovery system (MACRS)** provides that the cost recovery basis of eligible personalty (and certain realty) is recovered over 3, 5, 7, 10, 15, or 20 years. Property is classified by recovery period under MACRS as follows (see Exhibit 8–1 for examples):[7]

[5] The half-year convention assumes all property is placed in service at mid-year and thus provides for a half-year's cost recovery.

[6] § 48(q).

[7] § 168(e).

▼ EXHIBIT 8–1
Cost Recovery Periods: MACRS

Class of Property	Examples
3-year	Tractor units for use over-the-road. Any horse that is not a racehorse and is more than 12 years old at the time it is placed in service. Any racehorse that is more than 2 years old at the time it is placed in service. Breeding hogs. Special tools used in the manufacturing of motor vehicles such as dies, fixtures, molds, and patterns.
5-year	Automobiles and taxis. Light and heavy general-purpose trucks. Buses. Trailers and trailer-mounted containers. Typewriters, calculators, and copiers. Computers and peripheral equipment. Breeding and dairy cattle.
7-year	Office furniture, fixtures, and equipment. Breeding and work horses. Agricultural machinery and equipment. Single-purpose agricultural or horticultural structures. Railroad track.
10-year	Vessels, barges, tugs, and similar water transportation equipment. Assets used for petroleum refining or for the manufacture of grain and grain mill products, sugar and sugar products, or vegetable oils and vegetable oil products.
15-year	Land improvements. Assets used for industrial steam and electric generation and/or distribution systems. Assets used in the manufacture of cement. Assets used in pipeline transportation. Electric utility nuclear production plant. Municipal wastewater treatment plant.
20-year	Farm buildings except single-purpose agricultural and horticultural structures. Gas utility distribution facilities. Water utilities. Municipal sewer.

3-year 200% class...... ADR midpoints of 4 years and less.[8] Excludes automobiles and light trucks. Includes racehorses more than 2 years old and other horses more than 12 years old.

5-year 200% class...... ADR midpoints of more than 4 years and less than 10 years, adding automobiles, light trucks, qualified technological equipment, renewable energy and biomass properties that are small power production facilities, research and experimentation property, semiconductor manufacturing equipment, and computer-based central office switching equipment.

[8] Rev.Proc. 87–56, 1987–2 C.B. 674 is the source for the ADR midpoint lives.

7-year 200% class...... ADR midpoints of 10 years and more and less than 16 years, adding single-purpose agricultural or horticultural structures and property with no ADR midpoint not classified elsewhere. Includes railroad track and office furniture, fixtures, and equipment.

10-year 200% class..... ADR midpoints of 16 years and more and less than 20 years.

15-year 150% class..... ADR midpoints of 20 years and more and less than 25 years, including sewage treatment plants, and telephone distribution plants and comparable equipment used for the two-way exchange of voice and data communications.

20-year 150% class..... ADR midpoints of 25 years and more, other than real property with an ADR midpoint of 27.5 years and more, and including sewer pipes.

Accelerated depreciation is allowed for these six MACRS classes of property. Two hundred percent declining-balance is used for the 3-, 5-, 7-, and 10-year classes, with a switchover to straight-line depreciation when it yields a larger amount. One hundred and fifty percent declining-balance is allowed for the 15- and 20-year classes, with an appropriate straight-line switchover.[9]

Taxpayers may *elect* the straight-line method to compute cost recovery allowances for each of these classes of property. Certain property is not eligible for accelerated cost recovery and must be depreciated under an alternative depreciation system (ADS). Both the straight-line election and ADS are discussed later in the chapter.

The original ACRS system gave the taxpayer a half-year of cost recovery for the tax year an asset was placed in service but allowed the taxpayer to recover the balance of the cost recovery basis over the years remaining in the property's recovery period. No cost recovery deduction was permitted for the year of disposition or retirement of the property. Thus, conceptually, the taxpayer was considered to have placed property in service at the beginning of the recovery period but was allowed only a half-year's worth of cost recovery for the year it was placed in service.

By contrast, MACRS views property as placed in service in the middle of the first year.[10] Thus, for example, the statutory recovery period for three-year property begins in the middle of the year an asset is placed in service and ends three years later. In practical terms, this means that taxpayers must wait an extra year to recover the cost of depreciable assets. That is, the actual write-off periods are 4, 6, 8, 11, 16, and 21 years. MACRS also allows for a half-year of cost recovery in the year of disposition or retirement.

The procedure for computing the cost recovery allowance under MACRS is the same as under the original ACRS method. The cost recovery basis is multiplied by the percentages that reflect the applicable cost recovery method and the applicable convention. The percentages are shown in Table 8–2.

EXAMPLE 7

Kareem acquires a five-year class asset on April 10, 1996, for $30,000. Kareem's cost recovery deduction for 1996 is $6,000 [$30,000 × .20 (Table 8–2)]. ▼

EXAMPLE 8

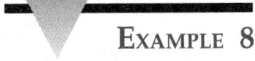

Assume the same facts as in Example 7, and that Kareem disposes of the asset on March 5, 1998. Kareem's cost recovery deduction for 1998 is $2,880 [$30,000 × ½ × .192 (Table 8–2)]. ▼

[9] § 168(b).

[10] § 168(d)(4)(A).

Mid-Quarter Convention. Under the original ACRS rules for personal property, the half-year convention was used no matter when property was acquired during the year. Thus, if a substantial dollar amount of assets was acquired late in the tax year, the half-year convention still applied. The law now contains a provision to curtail the benefits of such a tax strategy. If more than 40 percent of the value of property other than eligible real estate (see Realty: Recovery Periods and Methods: MACRS for a discussion of eligible real estate) is placed in service during the last quarter of the year, a **mid-quarter convention** applies.[11] Property acquisitions are then grouped by the quarter they were acquired for cost recovery purposes. Acquisitions during the first quarter are allowed 10.5 months of cost recovery; the second quarter, 7.5 months; the third quarter, 4.5 months; and the fourth quarter, 1.5 months. The percentages are shown in Table 8–3.

EXAMPLE 9

Silver Corporation acquires the following five-year class property in 1996:

Property Acquisition Dates	Cost
February 15	$ 200,000
July 10	400,000
December 5	600,000
Total	$1,200,000

If Silver Corporation uses the statutory percentage method, the cost recovery allowances for the first two years are computed as indicated below. Since more than 40% ($600,000/$1,200,000 = 50%) of the acquisitions are in the last quarter, the mid-quarter convention applies.

1996		
February 15	[$200,000 × .35 (Table 8–3)]	$ 70,000
July 10	($400,000 × .15)	60,000
December 5	($600,000 × .05)	30,000
Total		$160,000
1997		
February 15	[$200,000 × .26 (Table 8–3)]	$ 52,000
July 10	($400,000 × .34)	136,000
December 5	($600,000 × .38)	228,000
Total		$416,000

When property to which the mid-quarter convention applies is disposed of, the property is treated as though it were disposed of at the midpoint of the quarter. Hence, in the quarter of disposition, cost recovery is allowed for one-half of the quarter.

EXAMPLE 10

Assume the same facts as in Example 9, except that Silver Corporation sells the $400,000 asset on November 30 of 1997. The cost recovery allowance for 1997 is computed as follows:

[11] § 168(d)(3).

February 15	[$200,000 × .26 (Table 8–3)]	$ 52,000
July 10	[$400,000 × .34 × (3.5/4)]	119,000
December 5	($600,000 × .38)	228,000
Total		$399,000

▼

REALTY: RECOVERY PERIODS AND METHODS

ACRS. Under the original ACRS rules, realty was assigned a 15-year recovery period. Real property other than low-income housing is depreciated using the 175 percent declining-balance method, with a switchover to straight-line depreciation when it yields a larger amount. Low-income housing is depreciated using the 200 percent declining-balance method, with an appropriate straight-line switchover. In either case, zero salvage value is assumed. Statutory percentages for real property are shown in Table 8–4, which contains rates for low-income housing as well as for other 15-year real estate. As explained later in the chapter, taxpayers were allowed to elect the straight-line method for real property.

The half-year convention does not apply to 15-year real property. As a result, Table 8–4 is structured differently from Tables 8–1 and 8–2. The cost recovery deduction for 15-year real property is based on the month the asset is placed in service rather than on the half-year convention. No cost recovery is allowed for the month in which an asset is disposed of if the asset is disposed of before the end of the recovery period.

EXAMPLE 11

Alicia purchased a warehouse for $100,000 on January 1, 1984. The cost recovery allowance for the years 1984 through 1996, using the statutory percentage method, is as follows (see Table 8–4 for percentages).

1984—$12,000 (12% × $100,000)
1985—$10,000 (10% × $100,000)
1986—$9,000 (9% × $100,000)
1987—$8,000 (8% × $100,000)
1988—$7,000 (7% × $100,000)
1989—$6,000 (6% × $100,000)
1990—$6,000 (6% × $100,000)
1991—$6,000 (6% × $100,000)
1992—$6,000 (6% × $100,000)
1993—$5,000 (5% × $100,000)
1994—$5,000 (5% × $100,000)
1995—$5,000 (5% × $100,000)
1996—$5,000 (5% × $100,000)

▼

EXAMPLE 12

Assume the same facts as in Example 11, except the property is low-income housing. Cost recovery deductions using the statutory percentage method for 1984 through 1996 are as follows (see Table 8–4 for percentages):

1984—$13,000 (13% × $100,000)
1985—$12,000 (12% × $100,000)
1986—$10,000 (10% × $100,000)
1987—$9,000 (9% × $100,000)
1988—$8,000 (8% × $100,000)
1989—$7,000 (7% × $100,000)

1990—$6,000 (6% × $100,000)
1991—$5,000 (5% × $100,000)
1992—$5,000 (5% × $100,000)
1993—$5,000 (5% × $100,000)
1994—$4,000 (4% × $100,000)
1995—$4,000 (4% × $100,000)
1996—$4,000 (4% × $100,000) ▼

The Deficit Reduction Act of 1984 changed the recovery period for real property to 18 years. This applies generally to property placed in service after March 15, 1984. However, the 15-year recovery period was retained for low-income housing as well as for other real property placed in service before March 16, 1984.

Eighteen-year real property placed in service after June 22, 1984, is subject to a **mid-month convention.**[12] This means that real property placed in service at any time during a particular month is treated as if it were placed in service in the middle of the month. This allows for one-half month's cost recovery for the month the property is placed in service. If the property is disposed of before the end of the recovery period, one-half month's cost recovery is permitted for the month of disposition regardless of the specific date of disposition. Statutory percentages for 18-year real property with a mid-month convention are shown in Table 8–5.

EXAMPLE 13

Rex purchased a building for $300,000 and placed it in service on August 21, 1984. The first year's cost recovery using the statutory percentage method is $12,000 [$300,000 × 4% (Table 8–5)]. ▼

EXAMPLE 14

Assume the same facts as in Example 13 and that Rex disposes of the building on May 3, 1996. The cost recovery in the year of disposition is $4,500 ($300,000 × 4% × 4.5/12). ▼

Public Law 99–121 extended the minimum recovery period for real property (except low-income housing) from 18 years to 19 years. This applies to property placed in service after May 8, 1985, and before January 1, 1987. Statutory percentages for 19-year real property are shown in Table 8–6. Because the percentages are determined using a mid-month convention, the computation of cost recovery is mechanically the same as for 18-year property with the mid-month convention.

MACRS. Under MACRS, the cost recovery period for residential rental real estate is 27.5 years, and the straight-line method is used for computing the cost recovery allowance. **Residential rental real estate** includes property where 80 percent or more of the gross rental revenues are from nontransient dwelling units (e.g., an apartment building). Hotels, motels, and similar establishments are not residential rental property. Low-income housing is classified as residential rental real estate. Nonresidential real estate has a recovery period of 31.5 years (39 years for such property placed in service after May 12, 1993) and is also depreciated using the straight-line method.[13]

[12] A transitional rule, which provides for a full-month convention, is effective for property placed in service after March 15, 1984, and before June 23, 1984. The cost recovery tables for property placed in service during this period are not included in this chapter.

[13] §§ 168(b), (c), and (e).

CONCEPT SUMMARY 8–2

Statutory Percentage Method under ACRS and MACRS

ACRS

	Personal Property	Real Property: 15-Year	Real Property: 18-Year	Real Property: 19-Year
Convention	Half-year	Full-month	Mid-month	Mid-month
Cost recovery deduction in the year of disposition	None	Full-month up to month of disposition	Half-month for month of disposition	Half-month for month of disposition

MACRS

	Personal Property	Real Property*
Convention	Half-year or mid-quarter	Mid-month
Cost recovery deduction in the year of disposition	Half-year for year of disposition or half-quarter for quarter of disposition	Half-month for month of disposition

*Straight-line method must be used.

Some items of real property are not treated as real estate for purposes of MACRS. For example, single-purpose agricultural structures are in the 7-year MACRS class. Land improvements are in the 15-year MACRS class.

All eligible real estate is depreciated using the mid-month convention. Regardless of when during the month the property is placed in service, it is deemed to have been placed in service at the middle of the month. In the year of disposition, a mid-month convention is also used.

Cost recovery is computed by multiplying the applicable rate (Table 8–7) by the cost recovery basis.

EXAMPLE 15

Ann acquired a building on April 1, 1993, for $800,000. If the building is classified as residential rental real estate, the cost recovery allowance for 1996 is $29,088 (.03636 × $800,000). If the building is classified as nonresidential real estate, the 1996 cost recovery allowance is $25,400 (.03175 × $800,000). (See Table 8–7 for percentages.) ▼

As part of the deficit reduction legislation of the Clinton administration (Revenue Reconciliation Act of 1993), nonresidential real estate placed in service after May 12, 1993, is subject to a 39-year recovery period. Property placed in service before 1994 that was subject to a binding contract to construct or purchase, as of May 12, 1993, may still be treated as 31.5-year property under the prior rules.

EXAMPLE 16

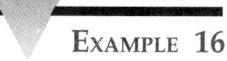

Assume the same facts as in Example 15, except Ann acquired the nonresidential building on November 19, 1996. The 1996 cost recovery allowance is $2,568 [$800,000 × .00321 (Table 8–7)]. ▼

STRAIGHT-LINE ELECTION UNDER ACRS AND MACRS

ACRS. Under ACRS, taxpayers could *elect* to write off an asset using the straight-line method rather than the statutory percentage method. The straight-line recovery period could be the same as the prescribed recovery period under the statutory percentage method, or a longer period. The allowable straight-line recovery periods for each class of property are summarized as follows:

3-year property	3, 5, or 12 years
5-year property	5, 12, or 25 years
10-year property	10, 25, or 35 years
15-year property	15, 35, or 45 years
18-year real property and low-income housing (placed in service after March 15, 1984)	18, 35, or 45 years
19-year real property and low-income housing (placed in service after May 8, 1985)	19, 35, or 45 years

If the straight-line option was elected for personal property, the half-year convention applies in computing the cost recovery deduction. The effect of electing the straight-line method for personal property is to extend the statutory recovery period by one year (e.g., three to four and five to six years). There is no cost recovery deduction in the year of the disposition of the property.

EXAMPLE 17

On May 6, 1986, Owl Utilities paid $20,000 for coal-fired boilers to replace gas-fired boilers (10-year property). Owl elected to compute the cost recovery allowance using the optional straight-line method and the regular cost recovery period. Owl's cost recovery allowance for 1986 was $1,000 ($20,000 basis × 10% straight-line rate × ½ year). The cost recovery allowance for 1996 is $1,000 ($20,000 basis × 10% straight-line rate × ½ year). These cost recovery allowances reflect the half-year convention for the first and last years of the cost recovery period. ▼

For each class of personal property, the straight-line election applied to *all* assets in a *particular class* that were placed in service during the year for which the election was made. The election applies for the entire recovery period of these assets. The election is not binding for personal property of the same class placed in service in another tax year.

Under the straight-line option for 15-year *real* property, the first year's cost recovery deduction and the cost recovery deduction for the year of disposition are computed on the basis of the number of months the property was in service during the year.

EXAMPLE 18

Kate acquired a store building on October 1, 1983, at a cost of $150,000. She elected the straight-line method using a recovery period of 15 years. Kate's cost recovery deduction for 1983 was $2,500 [($150,000 ÷ 15) × 3/12]. ▼

EXAMPLE 19

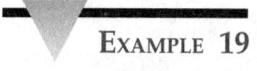

Assume the same facts as in Example 18 and that Kate disposes of the asset on September 30, 1996. Kate's cost recovery deduction for 1996 is $7,500 [($150,000 ÷ 15) × 9/12]. ▼

Under the straight-line option for 18-year or 19-year real property, the cost recovery allowances in the year the property is placed in service and in the year of disposition are computed in the same manner (except for the use of different rates) as under the statutory percentage method. Note that 18-year and 19-year real property use a mid-month convention, whereas 15-year real property uses a full-month convention. Table 8–8 contains the applicable percentages to be used under the straight-line option for 19-year real property. (The tables that contain the percentages for 18-year real property using the straight-line method over 18, 35, and 45 years and 19-year real property using the straight-line method over 35 and 45 years are not reproduced in this text.)

EXAMPLE 20

Ned acquired 19-year real property on October 1, 1986, at a cost of $150,000. He elected the straight-line method of cost recovery. Ned's cost recovery deduction for 1986 was $1,650 [$150,000 × 1.1% (Table 8–8)]. ▼

EXAMPLE 21

Assume the same facts as in Example 20 and that Ned disposes of the asset on September 20, 1996. Ned's cost recovery deduction for 1996 is $5,631 [($150,000 × 5.3% × 8.5/12) (Table 8–8)]. ▼

The straight-line election for 15-year, 18-year, or 19-year real property may be made on a *property-by-property* basis within the same year.

MACRS. Although MACRS requires straight-line depreciation for all eligible real estate as previously discussed, the taxpayer may *elect* to use the straight-line method for personal property.[14] The property is depreciated using the class life (recovery period) of the asset with a half-year convention or a mid-quarter convention, whichever is applicable. The election is available on a class-by-class and year-by-year basis. The percentages for the straight-line election with a half-year convention appear in Table 8–9.

EXAMPLE 22

Terry acquires a 10-year class asset on August 4, 1996, for $100,000. He elects the straight-line method of cost recovery. Terry's cost recovery deduction for 1996 is $5,000 ($100,000 × .050). His cost recovery deduction for 1997 is $10,000 ($100,000 × .100). (See Table 8–9 for percentages.) ▼

ELECTION TO EXPENSE ASSETS

3 LEARNING OBJECTIVE
Recognize when and how to make the § 179 expensing election, calculate the amount of the deduction, and apply the effect of the election in making the MACRS calculation.

Section 179 (Election to Expense Certain Depreciable Business Assets) permits the taxpayer to elect to write off up to $17,500[15] of the acquisition cost of *tangible personal property* used in a trade or business. Amounts that are expensed under § 179 may not be capitalized and depreciated. The **§ 179 expensing** election is an annual election and applies to the acquisition cost of property placed in service that year. The immediate expense election is not available for real property or for property used for the production of income.[16]

EXAMPLE 23

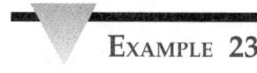

Kelly acquires machinery (five-year class) on February 1, 1996, at a cost of $40,000 and elects to expense $17,500 under § 179. Kelly's statutory percentage cost recovery deduction for 1996 is $4,500 [($40,000 cost − $17,500 expensed) × .200]. (See Table 8–2 for percentage.) Kelly's total deduction for 1996 is $22,000 ($17,500 + $4,500). ▼

Annual Limitations. Two additional limitations apply to the amount deductible under § 179. First, the ceiling amount on the deduction is reduced dollar-for-

[14] § 168(b)(5).

[15] This amount was $10,000 for property placed in service in tax years beginning before January 1, 1993.

[16] §§ 179(b) and (d). The amount shown is per taxpayer, per year. On a joint return, the statutory amounts apply to the couple. If the taxpayers are married and file separate returns, each spouse is eligible for 50% of the statutory amount.

CONCEPT SUMMARY 8–3

Straight-Line Election under ACRS and MACRS

ACRS

	Personal Property	Real Property: 15-Year	Real Property: 18-Year	Real Property: 19-Year
Convention	Half-year	Full-month	Mid-month	Mid-month
Cost recovery deduction in the year of disposition	None	Full-month up to month of disposition	Half-month for month of disposition	Half-month for month of disposition
Elective or mandatory	Elective	Elective	Elective	Elective
Breadth of election	Class by class	Property by property	Property by property	Property by property

MACRS

	Personal Property	Real Property
Convention	Half-year or mid-quarter	Mid-month
Cost recovery deduction in the year of disposition	Half-year for year of dispositon or half-quarter for quarter of disposition	Half-month for month of disposition
Elective or mandatory	Elective	Mandatory
Breadth of election	Class by class	

dollar when property (other than eligible real estate) placed in service during the taxable year exceeds $200,000. Second, the amount expensed under § 179 cannot exceed the aggregate amount of taxable income derived from the conduct of any trade or business by the taxpayer. Taxable income of a trade or business is computed without regard to the amount expensed under § 179. Any § 179 expensed amount in excess of taxable income is carried forward to future taxable years and added to other amounts eligible for expensing (and is subject to the ceiling rules for the carryforward years).

EXAMPLE 24 Jill owns a computer service and operates it as a sole proprietorship. In 1996, she will net $11,000 before considering any § 179 deduction. If Jill spends $204,000 on new equipment, her § 179 expense deduction is computed as follows:

§ 179 deduction before adjustment	$17,500
Less: Dollar limitation reduction ($204,000 – $200,000)	(4,000)
Remaining § 179 deduction	$13,500
Business income limitation	$11,000
§ 179 deduction allowed	$11,000
§ 179 deduction carryforward ($13,500 – $11,000)	$ 2,500

▼

Effect on Basis. The basis of the property for cost recovery purposes is reduced by the § 179 amount after it is adjusted for property placed in service in excess of $200,000. This adjusted amount does not reflect any business income limitation.

EXAMPLE 25

Assume the same facts as in Example 24 and that the new equipment is five-year class property. Jill's statutory percentage cost recovery deduction for 1996 is $38,100 [($204,000 – $13,500) × .200]. (See Table 8–2 for percentage.) ▼

ETHICAL CONSIDERATIONS

Section 179 and Limited Personal Use

Sam, a salesman, purchased a new computer near the end of last year. Sam used the computer during the remainder of the year only in connection with his business. On his tax return for last year, Sam expensed the computer under § 179. During the current year, Sam continued to use the computer in his business. However, he also allowed his children to use the computer for their school work. Sam has not maintained a log showing business and personal use of the computer for the current year. He feels that because the computer was expensed last year, no further accounting for it on his tax return is necessary.

Conversion to Personal Use. Conversion of the expensed property to personal use at any time results in recapture income (see Chapter 17). A property is converted to personal use if it is not used predominantly in a trade or business. Regulations provide for the mechanics of the recapture.[17]

BUSINESS AND PERSONAL USE OF AUTOMOBILES AND OTHER LISTED PROPERTY

4 LEARNING OBJECTIVE
Identify listed property and apply the deduction limitations on listed property and on luxury automobiles.

Limits exist on ACRS and MACRS deductions for automobiles and other listed property that are used for both personal and business purposes.[18] If the listed property is *predominantly used* for business, the taxpayer is allowed to use the statutory percentage method to recover the cost. In cases where the property is *not predominantly used* for business, the cost is recovered using a straight-line recovery.

Listed property includes the following:

- Any passenger automobile.
- Any other property used as a means of transportation.
- Any property of a type generally used for purposes of entertainment, recreation, or amusement.
- Any computer or peripheral equipment, with the exception of equipment used exclusively at a regular business establishment, including a qualifying home office.
- Any cellular telephone or other similar telecommunications equipment.
- Any other property specified in the Regulations.[19]

17 Reg. § 1.179–1(e).
18 § 280F.
19 § 280F(d)(4).

TAX IN THE NEWS

A Ferrari as Medical Equipment

Babies do not always arrive during office hours. Obstetricians frequently need to get to the delivery room quickly. The question is whether "quickly" requires a red Ferrari sports car.

On August 26, 1995, the *Newport News Daily Press* reported that a Chesapeake obstetrician purchased a red Ferrari and then wrote off the cost on his corporate tax return. On the return, the doctor claimed the purchase price was for an ultrasound machine and treated the amount as a business expense. From the *Daily Press* and other local media reports, it is unclear whether the $85,000 amount was expensed or whether it was capitalized and deducted as cost recovery.

Automobiles and Other Listed Property Used Predominantly in Business. For listed property to be considered as predominantly used in business, its business usage must exceed 50 percent.[20] The use of listed property for production of income does not qualify as business use for purposes of the more-than-50 percent test. However, if the more-than-50 percent test is met, both production of income and business use percentages are used to compute the cost recovery deduction.

Example 26 On September 1, 1996, Shontelle places in service listed five-year recovery property. The property cost $10,000. If Shontelle uses the property 40% for business and 25% for the production of income, the property is not considered as predominantly used for business. The cost is recovered using straight-line cost recovery. If, however, Shontelle uses the property 60% for business and 25% for the production of income, the property is considered as used predominantly for business. Therefore, she may use the statutory percentage method. Shontelle's cost recovery allowance for the year is $1,700 ($10,000 × .200 × 85%). ▼

The method for determining the percentage of business usage for listed property is specified in the Regulations. The Regulations provide that for automobiles a mileage-based percentage is to be used. Other listed property is to use the most appropriate unit of time (e.g., hours) the property is actually used (rather than available for use).[21]

The law places special limitations on the cost recovery deduction for passenger automobiles. These statutory dollar limits were imposed on passenger automobiles because of the belief that the tax system was being used to underwrite automobiles whose cost and luxury far exceeded what was needed for their business use.

A *passenger automobile* is any four-wheeled vehicle manufactured for use on public streets, roads, and highways with an unloaded gross vehicle weight rating of 6,000 pounds or less.[22] This definition specifically excludes vehicles used directly in the business of transporting people or property for compensation such as taxicabs, ambulances, hearses, and trucks and vans as prescribed by the Regulations.

[20] § 280F(b)(4).

[21] Reg. § 1.280F–6T(e).

[22] § 280F(d)(5).

The following limits apply to the cost recovery deductions for passenger automobiles for 1996:[23]

Year	Recovery Limitation
1	$3,060
2	4,900
3	2,950
Succeeding years until the cost is recovered	1,775

These limits are imposed before any percentage reduction for personal use. In addition, the limitation in the first year includes any amount the taxpayer elects to expense under § 179.[24] If the passenger automobile is used partly for personal use, the personal use percentage is ignored for the purpose of determining the unrecovered cost available for deduction in later years.

EXAMPLE 27

On July 1, 1996, Dan places in service an automobile that cost $20,000. The car is always used 80% for business and 20% for personal use. The cost recovery for the automobile would be as follows:

1996—$2,448[$20,000 × 20% (limited to $3,060) × 80%]
1997—$3,920[$20,000 × 32% (limited to $4,900) × 80%]
1998—$2,360[$20,000 × 19.2% (limited to $2,950) × 80%]
1999—$1,420[$20,000 × 11.52% (limited to $1,775) × 80%]
2000—$1,420[$20,000 × 11.52% (limited to $1,775) × 80%]
2001—$1,420[$5,540 unrecovered cost ($20,000 – $14,460*) (limited to $1,775) × 80%]

*($3,060 + $4,900 + $2,950 + $1,775 + $1,775). Although the statutory percentage method appears to restrict the deduction to $922 [$20,000 × 5.76% (limited to $1,775) × 80%], the unrecovered cost of $5,540 (limited to $1,775) multiplied by the business usage percentage is deductible. At the start of 1999 (year 4), there is an automatic switch to the straight-line cost recovery method. Under this method, the unrecovered cost up to the maximum allowable limit ($1,775) is deductible in the last year of the recovery period (2001 or year 6). Because the limit may restrict the deduction, any remaining unrecovered cost is deductible in the next or succeeding year(s), subject to the maximum allowable yearly limit ($1,775), multiplied by the business usage percentage.

The total cost recovery for the years 1996–2001 is $12,988. ▼

The cost recovery limitations are maximum amounts. If the regular calculation produces a lesser amount of cost recovery, the lesser amount is used.

EXAMPLE 28

On April 2, 1996, Gail places in service an automobile that cost $10,000. The car is always used 70% for business and 30% for personal use. The cost recovery allowance for 1996 is $1,400 ($10,000 × 20% × 70%), which is less than $2,142 ($3,060 × 70%). ▼

Note that the cost recovery limitations apply *only* to passenger automobiles and not to other listed property.

Automobiles and Other Listed Property Not Used Predominantly in Business. The cost of listed property that does not pass the more-than-50 percent business usage test in the year the property is placed in service must be

[23] § 280F(a)(2). The 1995 indexed amounts are $3,060, $4,900, $2,950, and $1,775.

[24] § 280F(d)(1).

recovered using the straight-line method.[25] The straight-line method to be used is that required under the alternative depreciation system (explained later in the chapter). This system requires a straight-line recovery period of five years for automobiles. However, even though the straight-line method is used, the cost recovery allowance for passenger automobiles cannot exceed the dollar limitations.

EXAMPLE 29

On July 27, 1996, Fred places in service an automobile that cost $20,000. The auto is used 40% for business and 60% for personal use. The cost recovery allowance for 1996 is $800 [$20,000 × 10% (Table 8–11) × 40%]. ▼

EXAMPLE 30

Assume the same facts as in Example 29, except that the auto cost $50,000. The cost recovery allowance for 1996 is $1,224 [$50,000 × 10% (Table 8–11) = $5,000 (limited to $3,060) × 40%]. ▼

If the listed property fails the more-than-50 percent business usage test, the straight-line method must be used for the remainder of the property's life. This applies even if at some later date the business usage of the property increases to more than 50 percent. Even though the straight-line method must continue to be used, however, the amount of cost recovery will reflect the increase in business usage.

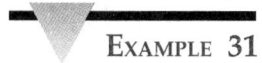

EXAMPLE 31

Assume the same facts as in Example 29, except that in 1997, Fred uses the auto 70% for business and 30% for personal use. Fred's cost recovery allowance for 1997 is $2,800 [$20,000 × 20% (Table 8–11) × 70%]. ▼

Change from Predominantly Business Use. If the business use percentage of listed property falls to 50 percent or lower after the year the property is placed in service, the property is subject to *cost recovery recapture.* The amount required to be recaptured and included in the taxpayer's return as ordinary income is the excess cost recovery.

Excess cost recovery is the excess of the cost recovery deduction taken in prior years using the statutory percentage method over the amount that would have been allowed if the straight-line method had been used since the property was placed in service.[26]

EXAMPLE 32

Seth purchased a car on January 22, 1996, at a cost of $20,000. Business usage was 80% in 1996, 70% in 1997, 40% in 1998, and 60% in 1999. Statutory percentage cost recovery deductions in 1996 and 1997 are $2,448 (80% × $3,060) and $3,430 (70% × $4,900), respectively. Seth's excess cost recovery to be recaptured as ordinary income in 1998 is $1,478, calculated as follows:

1996	
Statutory percentage allowance	$ 2,448
Straight-line ($20,000 × 10% × 80%)	(1,600)
Excess	$ 848

[25] § 280F(b)(2).

[26] § 280F(b)(3).

1997	
Statutory percentage allowance	$ 3,430
Straight-line ($20,000 × 20% × 70%)	(2,800)
1997 excess	$ 630
1996 excess	848
Total excess	$ 1,478

▼

After the business usage of the listed property drops below the more-than-50 percent level, the straight-line method must be used for the remaining life of the property.

EXAMPLE 33

Assume the same facts as in Example 32. Seth's cost recovery allowance for the years 1998 and 1999 would be $1,180 and $1,065, computed as follows:

1998—$1,180	[($20,000 × 20%) limited to $2,950 × 40%]
1999—$1,065	[($20,000 × 20%) limited to $1,775 × 60%]

▼

Leased Automobiles. A taxpayer who leases a passenger automobile must report an *inclusion amount* in gross income. The inclusion amount is computed from an IRS table for each taxable year for which the taxpayer leases the automobile. The purpose of this provision is to prevent taxpayers from circumventing the cost recovery dollar limitations by leasing, instead of purchasing, an automobile.

The dollar amount of the inclusion is based on the fair market value of the automobile and is prorated for the number of days the auto is used during the taxable year. The prorated dollar amount is then multiplied by the business and income-producing usage percentage to determine the amount to be included in gross income.[27] The taxpayer deducts the lease payments, multiplied by the business and income-producing usage percentage. The net effect is that the annual deduction for the lease payment is reduced by the inclusion amount.

EXAMPLE 34

On April 1, 1996, Jim leases and places in service a passenger automobile worth $40,000. The lease is to be for a period of five years. During the taxable years 1996 and 1997, Jim uses the automobile 70% for business and 30% for personal use. Assuming the dollar amounts from the IRS table for 1996 and 1997 are $188 and $412, Jim must include $99 in gross income for 1996 and $288 for 1997, computed as follows:

1996	$188 × (275/366) × 70% = $99
1997	$412 × (365/365) × 70% = $288

In addition, Jim can deduct 70% of the lease payments each year because this is the business use percentage. ▼

Substantiation Requirements. Listed property is now subject to the substantiation requirements of § 274. This means that the taxpayer must prove the business usage as to the amount of expense or use, the time and place of use, the business purpose for the use, and the business relationship to the taxpayer of persons using the property. Substantiation requires adequate records or sufficient

[27] Reg. § 1.280F–7T(a).

CONCEPT SUMMARY 8–4

Listed Property Cost Recovery

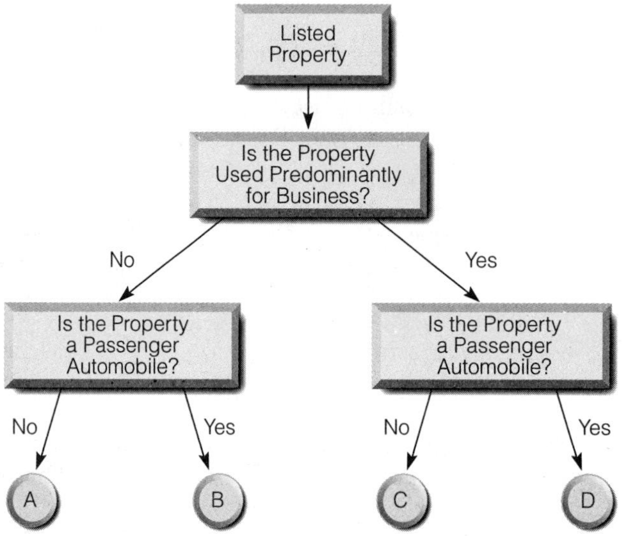

Legend to Tax Treatment

A Straight-line cost recovery reduced by the personal use percentage.

B Straight-line cost recovery subject to the recovery limitations ($3,060, $4,900, $2,950, $1,775) and reduced by the personal use percentage.

C Statutory percentage cost recovery reduced by the personal use percentage.

D Statutory percentage cost recovery subject to the recovery limitations ($3,060, $4,900, $2,950, $1,775) and reduced by the personal use percentage.

evidence corroborating the taxpayer's statement. However, these substantiation requirements do not apply to vehicles that, by reason of their nature, are not likely to be used more than a *de minimis* amount for personal purposes.[28]

ALTERNATIVE DEPRECIATION SYSTEM (ADS)

5 LEARNING OBJECTIVE
Determine when and how to use the alternative depreciation system (ADS).

The **alternative depreciation system (ADS)** must be used for the following:[29]

- To calculate the portion of depreciation treated as an alternative minimum tax (AMT) adjustment for purposes of the corporate and individual AMT (see Chapters 12 and 20).
- To compute depreciation allowances for property for which any of the following is true:
  - Used predominantly outside the United States.
  - Leased or otherwise used by a tax-exempt entity.

[28] §§ 274(d) and (i).

[29] § 168(g).

  - Financed with the proceeds of tax-exempt bonds.
  - Imported from foreign countries that maintain discriminatory trade practices or otherwise engage in discriminatory acts.

- To compute depreciation allowances for earnings and profits purposes (see Chapter 20).

In general, ADS depreciation is computed using straight-line recovery without regard to salvage value. However, for purposes of the AMT, depreciation of personal property is computed using the 150 percent declining-balance method with an appropriate switch to the straight-line method.

The taxpayer must use the half-year or the mid-quarter convention, whichever is applicable, for all property other than eligible real estate. The mid-month convention is used for eligible real estate. The applicable ADS rates are found in Tables 8–10, 8–11, and 8–12.

The recovery periods under ADS are as follows:[30]

- The ADR midpoint life for property that does not fall into any of the following listed categories.
- Five years for qualified technological equipment, automobiles, and light-duty trucks.
- Twelve years for personal property with no class life.
- Forty years for all residential rental property and all nonresidential real property.

Taxpayers may *elect* to use the 150 percent declining-balance method to compute the regular income tax rather than the 200 percent declining-balance method that is available for personal property. Hence, if the election is made, there will be no difference between the cost recovery for computing the regular income tax and the AMT. However, taxpayers who make this election must use the ADS recovery periods in computing the cost recovery for the regular income tax, and the ADS recovery periods generally are longer than the regular recovery periods under MACRS.

The following are examples of the classification of property by class life for the ADS recovery periods:[31]

3-year	Special tools used in the manufacture of motor vehicles, breeding hogs.
5-year	Automobiles, light general-purpose trucks.
7-year	Breeding and dairy cattle.
9.5-year	Computer-based telephone central office switching equipment.
10-year	Office furniture, fixtures, and equipment, railroad track.
12-year	Racehorses more than 2 years old at the time they are placed in service.

EXAMPLE 35

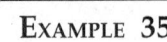

On March 1, 1996, Abby purchases computer-based telephone central office switching equipment for $80,000. If Abby uses statutory percentage cost recovery (assuming no § 179 election), the cost recovery allowance for 1996 is $16,000 [$80,000 × 20% (Table 8–2, 5-year class property)]. If Abby elects to use ADS 150% declining-balance cost recovery (assuming no § 179 election), the cost recovery allowance for 1996 is $6,312 [$80,000 × 7.89% (Table 8–10, 9.5-year class property)]. ▼

[30] The class life for certain properties described in § 168(e)(3) is specially determined under § 168(g)(3)(B).

[31] Rev.Proc. 87–56, 1987–2 C.B. 674 is the source for the recovery periods.

In lieu of depreciation under the regular MACRS method, taxpayers may *elect* straight-line under ADS for property that qualifies for the regular MACRS method. The election is available on a class-by-class and year-by-year basis for property other than eligible real estate. The election for eligible real estate is on a property-by-property basis. One reason for making this election is to avoid a difference between deductible depreciation and earnings and profits depreciation.

EXAMPLE 36

Polly acquires an apartment building on March 17, 1996, for $700,000. She takes the maximum cost recovery allowance for determining taxable income. Polly's cost recovery allowance for computing 1996 taxable income is $20,153 [$700,000 × .02879 (Table 8–7)]. However, Polly's cost recovery for computing her earnings and profits is only $13,853 [$700,000 × .01979 (Table 8–12)]. ▼

AMORTIZATION § 197

6 LEARNING OBJECTIVE
Identify intangible assets that are eligible for amortization and calculate the amount of the deduction.

software is amortized over 3 year period.

Prior to the Revenue Reconciliation Act of 1993 (RRA of 1993), the tax treatment of intangible assets had become a source of much controversy between taxpayers and the IRS. Disputes arose as to whether a covenant not to compete (an amortizable asset) was separate and distinct from goodwill and going-concern value (a nonamortizable asset) or merely a transfer of goodwill.

Under RRA of 1993, taxpayers can claim an **amortization** deduction on intangible assets called "amortizable § 197 intangibles." The amount of the deduction is determined by amortizing the adjusted basis of such intangibles ratably over a 15-year period beginning in the month in which the intangible is acquired.[32]

An *amortizable § 197 intangible* is any § 197 intangible acquired after August 10, 1993, and held in connection with the conduct of a trade or business or for the production of income. Section 197 intangibles include goodwill and going-concern value, franchises (except sports franchises), trademarks, and trade names. Covenants not to compete, copyrights, and patents are also included if they are acquired in connection with the acquisition of a business. Generally, self-created

TAX IN THE NEWS

ACCOUNTING FOR LOTUS

After International Business Machines Corporation announced that it would acquire Lotus Development Corporation in 1995, analysts predicted that IBM would take a one-time after-tax charge of $900 million and write off an additional $1.8 billion over five years to account for the acquisition. After the one-time charge, IBM was expected to write off the remaining goodwill as quickly as possible. This amount, representing the excess of the purchase price over the stated value of Lotus's assets, was estimated at around $1.8 billion.

SOURCE: Information from Laurie Hays, "IBM Is Expected to Record a Charge of $900 Million for Lotus Acquisition," *Wall Street Journal*, June 14, 1995, p. B6.

[32] § 197(a).

intangibles are not § 197 intangibles. The 15-year amortization period applies regardless of the actual useful life of an amortizable § 197 intangible. No other depreciation or amortization deduction is permitted with respect to any amortizable § 197 intangible except those permitted under the 15-year amortization rules.

EXAMPLE 37

On June 1, 1996, Sally purchased and began operating the Falcon Cafe. Of the purchase price, $90,000 is correctly allocated to goodwill. The deduction for amortization for 1996 is $3,500 [($90,000/15) × (7/12)]. ▼

ETHICAL CONSIDERATIONS

Allocating Intangible Assets When a Business Is Sold

Marge and Stan are negotiating Stan's purchase of Marge's business. Both are in the 36 percent tax bracket. They have agreed that the tangible assets of the business are worth $100,000. Marge's adjusted basis for these assets is $70,000. The only other asset of the business is the going-concern value. Marge believes that this asset is worth about $50,000. Stan believes that it is worth somewhat less, probably about $40,000.

Marge and Stan are handling their own negotiations since they do not believe in wasting money on attorneys or CPAs when such professional services are not required. Stan knows from an MBA class he took five years ago that goodwill is not deductible, but that a covenant not to compete can be deducted over the covenant period. Stan believes that Marge, who is age 67 and in poor health, is going to retire. In order to maximize the tax benefits to himself, Stan increases his offer from $140,000 to $145,000 (i.e., "we'll split the difference") if Marge will agree to sign a five-year covenant with $45,000 of the $145,000 purchase price allocated to the covenant. Marge, who believes that the tax consequences of the sale ($145,000 amount realized – $70,000 adjusted basis = $75,000 recognized gain) will be the same regardless of whether the $45,000 is for goodwill or for a covenant, accepts the offer. Evaluate the decisions made by Marge and Stan.

DEPLETION

7 LEARNING OBJECTIVE
Determine the amount of depletion expense including being able to apply the alternative tax treatments for intangible drilling and development costs.

Natural resources (e.g., oil, gas, coal, gravel, timber) are subject to **depletion,** which is simply a form of depreciation applicable to natural resources. Land generally cannot be depleted.

The owner of an interest in the natural resource is entitled to deduct depletion. An owner is one who has an economic interest in the property.[33] An economic interest requires the acquisition of an interest in the resource in place and the receipt of income from the extraction or severance of that resource. Like depreciation, depletion is a deduction *for* adjusted gross income.

Although all natural resources are subject to depletion, oil and gas wells are used as an example in the following paragraphs to illustrate the related costs and issues.

In developing an oil or gas well, the producer must make four types of expenditures.

[33] Reg. § 1.611–1(b).

- Natural resource costs.
- Intangible drilling and development costs.
- Tangible asset costs.
- Operating costs.

Natural resources are physically limited, and the costs to acquire them (e.g., oil under the ground) are, therefore, recovered through depletion. Costs incurred in making the property ready for drilling such as the cost of labor in clearing the property, erecting derricks, and drilling the hole are **intangible drilling and development costs (IDC).** These costs generally have no salvage value and are a lost cost if the well is dry. Costs for tangible assets such as tools, pipes, and engines are capital in nature. These costs must be capitalized and recovered through depreciation (cost recovery). Costs incurred after the well is producing are operating costs. These costs would include expenditures for such items as labor, fuel, and supplies. Operating costs are deductible when incurred (on the accrual basis) or when paid (on the cash basis).

The expenditures for depreciable assets and operating costs pose no unusual problems for producers of natural resources. The tax treatment of depletable costs and intangible drilling and development costs is quite a different matter.

INTANGIBLE DRILLING AND DEVELOPMENT COSTS (IDC)

Intangible drilling and development costs (IDC) can be handled in one of two ways at the option of the taxpayer. They can be *either* charged off as an expense in the year in which they are incurred *or* capitalized and written off through depletion. The taxpayer makes the election in the first year such expenditures are incurred either by taking a deduction on the return or by adding them to the depletable basis. No formal statement of intent is required. Once made, the election is binding on both the taxpayer and the IRS for all such expenditures in the future. If the taxpayer fails to make the election to expense IDC on the original timely filed return the first year such expenditures are incurred, an automatic election to capitalize them has been made and is irrevocable.

As a general rule, it is more advantageous to expense IDC. The obvious benefit of an immediate write-off (as opposed to a deferred write-off through depletion) is not the only advantage. Since a taxpayer can use percentage depletion, which is calculated without reference to basis (see Example 41), the IDC may be completely lost as a deduction if they are capitalized.

DEPLETION METHODS

There are two methods of calculating depletion: cost and percentage. Cost depletion can be used on any wasting asset (and is the only method allowed for timber). Percentage depletion is subject to a number of limitations, particularly for oil and gas deposits. Depletion should be calculated both ways, and generally the method that results in the *larger* deduction is used. The choice between cost and percentage depletion is an annual election.

Cost Depletion.

Cost depletion is determined by using the adjusted basis of the asset.[34] The basis is divided by the estimated recoverable units of the asset (e.g., barrels, tons) to arrive at the depletion per unit. The depletion per unit then is multiplied by the number of units sold (*not* the units produced) during the year

[34] § 612.

to arrive at the cost depletion allowed. Cost depletion, therefore, resembles the units-of-production method of calculating depreciation.

EXAMPLE 38 On January 1, 1996, Pablo purchased the rights to a mineral interest for $1,000,000. At that time, the remaining recoverable units in the mineral interest were estimated to be 200,000. The depletion per unit is $5 [$1,000,000 (adjusted basis) ÷ 200,000 (estimated recoverable units)]. If during the year 60,000 units were mined and 25,000 were sold, the cost depletion would be $125,000 [$5 (depletion per unit) × 25,000 (units sold)]. ▼

If the taxpayer later discovers that the original estimate was incorrect, the depletion per unit for future calculations must be redetermined based on the revised estimate.[35]

EXAMPLE 39 Assume the same facts as in Example 38. In 1997, Pablo realizes that an incorrect estimate was made. The remaining recoverable units now are determined to be 400,000. Based on this new information, the revised depletion per unit is $2.1875 [$875,000 (adjusted basis) ÷ 400,000 (estimated recoverable units)]. Note that the adjusted basis is the original cost ($1,000,000) reduced by the depletion claimed in 1996 ($125,000). If 30,000 units are sold in 1997, the depletion for the year would be $65,625 [$2.1875 (depletion per unit) × 30,000 (units sold)]. ▼

Percentage Depletion. **Percentage depletion** (also referred to as statutory depletion) is a specified percentage provided for in the Code. The percentage varies according to the type of mineral interest involved. A sample of these percentages is shown in Exhibit 8–2. The rate is applied to the gross income from the property, but in no event may percentage depletion exceed 50 percent of the taxable income from the property before the allowance for depletion.[36]

EXAMPLE 40 Assuming gross income of $100,000, a depletion rate of 22%, and other expenses relating to the property of $60,000, the depletion allowance is determined as follows:

Gross income	$100,000
Less: Other expenses	(60,000)
Taxable income before depletion	$ 40,000
Depletion allowance [the lesser of $22,000 (22% × $100,000) or $20,000 (50% × $40,000)]	(20,000)
Taxable income after depletion	$ 20,000

The adjusted basis of the property is reduced by $20,000, the depletion allowed. If the other expenses had been only $55,000, the full $22,000 could have been deducted, and the adjusted basis would have been reduced by $22,000. ▼

Note that percentage depletion is based on a percentage of the gross income from the property and makes no reference to cost. Thus, when percentage depletion is used, it is possible to deduct more than the original cost of the property. If percentage depletion is used, however, the adjusted basis of the property (for computing cost depletion) must be reduced by the amount of percentage depletion taken until the adjusted basis reaches zero.

---

[35] § 611(a).

[36] § 613(a). Special rules apply for certain oil and gas wells under § 613A (e.g., the 50% ceiling is replaced with a 100% ceiling, and the percentage depletion may not exceed 65% of the taxpayer's taxable income from all sources before the allowance for depletion).

▼ EXHIBIT 8–2
Sample of Percentage Depletion Rates

22% Depletion	
Cobalt	Sulfur
Lead	Tin
Nickel	Uranium
Platinum	Zinc
15% Depletion	
Copper	Oil and gas
Gold	Oil shale
Iron	Silver
14% Depletion	
Borax	Magnesium carbonates
Calcium carbonates	Marble
Granite	Potash
Limestone	Slate
10% Depletion	
Coal	Perlite
Lignite	Sodium chloride
5% Depletion	
Gravel	Pumice
Peat	Sand

Effect of Intangible Drilling Costs on Depletion. The treatment of IDC has an effect on the depletion deduction in two ways. If the costs are capitalized, the basis for cost depletion is increased. As a consequence, the cost depletion is increased. If IDC are expensed, they reduce the taxable income from the property. This reduction may result in application of the provision that limits depletion to 50 percent (100 percent for certain oil and gas wells) of taxable income before deducting depletion.

EXAMPLE 41

Iris purchased the rights to an oil interest for $1,000,000. The recoverable barrels were estimated to be 200,000. During the year, 50,000 barrels were sold for $2,000,000. Regular expenses amounted to $800,000, and IDC were $650,000. If the IDC are capitalized, the depletion per unit is $8.25 ($1,000,000 + $650,000 ÷ 200,000 barrels), and the following taxable income results:

Gross income	$2,000,000
Less: Expenses	(800,000)
Taxable income before depletion	$1,200,000
Cost depletion ($8.25 × 50,000) = $412,500	
Percentage depletion (15% × $2,000,000) = $300,000	
Greater of cost or percentage depletion	(412,500)
Taxable income	$ 787,500

If the IDC are expensed, the taxable income is $250,000, calculated as follows:

Gross income	$ 2,000,000
Less: Expenses, including IDC	(1,450,000)
Taxable income before depletion	$ 550,000
Cost depletion [($1,000,000 ÷ 200,000 barrels) × 50,000 barrels] = $250,000	
Percentage depletion (15% of $2,000,000 = $300,000, limited to 100% of $550,000 taxable income before depletion) = $300,000	
Greater of cost or percentage depletion	(300,000)
Taxable income	$ 250,000

For further restrictions on the use or availability of the percentage depletion method, see § 613.

Reporting Procedures

8 Learning Objective
Perform the reporting procedures for cost recovery.

Sole proprietors engaged in a business should file a Schedule C, Profit or Loss from Business, to accompany Form 1040. Schedule C for 1995 is presented because the 1996 form was not yet available.

The top part of page 1 requests certain key information about the taxpayer (e.g., name, address, Social Security number) and the business methods involved (e.g., accounting method and inventory method used). Part I provides for the reporting of items of income. If the business requires the use of inventories and the computation of cost of goods sold (see Chapter 18 for when this is necessary), Part III must be completed and the cost of goods sold amount transferred to line 4 of Part I.

Part II allows for the reporting of deductions. Some of the deductions discussed in Chapters 7 and 8 and their location on the form are bad debts (line 9), depletion (line 12), and depreciation (line 13). Other expenses (line 27) include those items not already covered (see lines 8–26). An example would be research and experimental expenditures.

If depreciation is claimed, it should be supported by completing Form 4562. Form 4562 for 1995 is presented because the 1996 form was not yet available. The amount listed on line 21 of Form 4562 is then transferred to line 13 of Part II of Schedule C.

Example 42

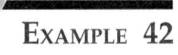

Thomas Andrews, Social Security number 123–45–6789, was employed as an accountant until July 1994, when he opened his own practice. His address is 279 Mountain View, Ogden, UT 84201. Andrews keeps his books on the accrual basis and had the following revenue and business expenses in 1995:

a. Revenue from accounting practice, $80,000.
b. Bad debts, $2,000.
c. Automobile expenses, $3,000.
d. Insurance, $800.
e. Office supplies, $4,000.
f. Rent, $12,000.

g. Furniture and fixtures acquired on July 15, 1994, for $8,000. Andrews used the statutory percentage cost recovery method.
h. Business automobile acquired on May 20, 1994, for $10,000. Andrews used the statutory percentage cost recovery method. The automobile, which was driven 12,000 miles during 1995, was used only for business purposes.
i. Microcomputer acquired on May 7, 1995, for $21,500. Andrews elects § 179 and uses the statutory percentage cost recovery method.

Andrews would report the above information on Schedule C and Form 4562 as illustrated on the following pages. ▼

TAX PLANNING CONSIDERATIONS

COST RECOVERY

Cost recovery schedules should be reviewed annually for possible retirements, abandonments, and obsolescence.

EXAMPLE 43

An examination of the cost recovery schedule of Eagle Company reveals the following:

- Asset A was abandoned when it was discovered that the cost of repairs would be in excess of the cost of replacement. Asset A had an adjusted basis of $3,000.
- Asset J became obsolete this year, at which point, its adjusted basis was $8,000.

Assets A and J should be written off for an additional expense of $11,000 ($3,000 + $8,000). ▼

9 LEARNING OBJECTIVE
Identify tax planning opportunities for cost recovery, amortization, and depletion.

Because of the deductions for cost recovery, interest, and ad valorem property taxes, investments in real estate can be highly attractive. In figuring the economics of such investments, one should be sure to take into account any tax savings that result.

EXAMPLE 44

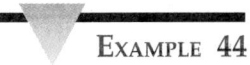

In early January 1995, Vern purchased residential rental property for $170,000 (of which $20,000 was allocated to the land and $150,000 to the building). Vern made a down payment of $25,000 and assumed the seller's mortgage for the balance. Under the mortgage agreement, monthly payments of $1,000 are required and are applied toward interest, taxes, insurance, and principal. Since the property was already occupied, Vern continued to receive rent of $1,200 per month from the tenant. Vern actively participates in this activity and hence comes under the special rule for a rental real estate activity with respect to the limitation on passive activity losses (refer to Chapter 11). Vern is in the 31% tax bracket.

During 1996, Vern's expenses were as follows:

Interest	$10,000
Taxes	800
Insurance	1,000
Repairs and maintenance	2,200
Depreciation ($150,000 × .03636)	5,454
Total	$19,454

The deductible loss from the rental property is computed as follows:

Rent income ($1,200 × 12 months)	$ 14,400
Less expenses (see above)	(19,454)
Net loss	($ 5,054)

Form **4562**

Department of the Treasury
Internal Revenue Service (99)

Depreciation and Amortization
(Including Information on Listed Property)

▶ See separate instructions. ▶ Attach this form to your return.

OMB No. 1545-0172
1995
Attachment Sequence No. **67**

Name(s) shown on return	Business or activity to which this form relates	Identifying number
Thomas Andrews	*Accounting Services*	*123-45-6789*

Part I **Election To Expense Certain Tangible Property (Section 179) (Note:** *If you have any "Listed Property," complete Part V before you complete Part I.*)

1	Maximum dollar limitation. If an enterprise zone business, see page 1 of the instructions	1	$17,500
2	Total cost of section 179 property placed in service during the tax year. See page 2 of the instructions	2	*$21,500*
3	Threshold cost of section 179 property before reduction in limitation	3	$200,000
4	Reduction in limitation. Subtract line 3 from line 2. If zero or less, enter -0-	4	*–0–*
5	Dollar limitation for tax year. Subtract line 4 from line 1. If zero or less, enter -0-. If married filing separately, see page 2 of the instructions	5	*$17,500*

	(a) Description of property	(b) Cost	(c) Elected cost
6			
7	Listed property. Enter amount from line 27	7	

8	Total elected cost of section 179 property. Add amounts in column (c), lines 6 and 7	8	*$17,500*
9	Tentative deduction. Enter the smaller of line 5 or line 8	9	*$17,500*
10	Carryover of disallowed deduction from 1994. See page 2 of the instructions	10	
11	Taxable income limitation. Enter the smaller of taxable income (not less than zero) or line 5 (see instructions)	11	*$17,500*
12	Section 179 expense deduction. Add lines 9 and 10, but do not enter more than line 11	12	*$17,500*
13	Carryover of disallowed deduction to 1996. Add lines 9 and 10, less line 12 ▶	13	

Note: *Do not use Part II or Part III below for listed property (automobiles, certain other vehicles, cellular telephones, certain computers, or property used for entertainment, recreation, or amusement). Instead, use Part V for listed property.*

Part II **MACRS Depreciation For Assets Placed in Service ONLY During Your 1995 Tax Year (Do Not Include Listed Property.)**

Section A—General Asset Account Election

14 If you are making the election under section 168(i)(4) to group any assets placed in service during the tax year into one or more general asset accounts, check this box. See page 2 of the instructions ▶ ☐

(a) Classification of property	(b) Month and year placed in service	(c) Basis for depreciation (business/investment use only—see instructions)	(d) Recovery period	(e) Convention	(f) Method	(g) Depreciation deduction
Section B—General Depreciation System (GDS) (See page 2 of the instructions.)						
15a 3-year property						
b 5-year property		*4,000*	*5-Year*	*HY*	*200DB*	*800*
c 7-year property						
d 10-year property						
e 15-year property						
f 20-year property						
g Residential rental property			27.5 yrs.	MM	S/L	
			27.5 yrs.	MM	S/L	
h Nonresidential real property			39 yrs.	MM	S/L	
				MM	S/L	
Section C—Alternative Depreciation System (ADS) (See page 4 of the instructions.)						
16a Class life					S/L	
b 12-year			12 yrs.		S/L	
c 40-year			40 yrs.	MM	S/L	

Part III **Other Depreciation (Do Not Include Listed Property.)** (See page 4 of the instructions.)

17	GDS and ADS deductions for assets placed in service in tax years beginning before 1995	17	*1,959*
18	Property subject to section 168(f)(1) election	18	
19	ACRS and other depreciation	19	

Part IV **Summary** (See page 4 of the instructions.)

20	Listed property. Enter amount from line 26	20	*3,200*
21	**Total.** Add deductions on line 12, lines 15 and 16 in column (g), and lines 17 through 20. Enter here and on the appropriate lines of your return. Partnerships and S corporations—see instructions	21	*23,459*
22	For assets shown above and placed in service during the current year, enter the portion of the basis attributable to section 263A costs	22	

For Paperwork Reduction Act Notice, see page 1 of the separate instructions. Cat. No. 12906N Form **4562** (1995)

Form 4562 (1995) Page **2**

Part V Listed Property—Automobiles, Certain Other Vehicles, Cellular Telephones, Certain Computers, and Property Used for Entertainment, Recreation, or Amusement

Note: *For any vehicle for which you are using the standard mileage rate or deducting lease expense, complete **only** 23a, 23b, columns (a) through (c) of Section A, all of Section B, and Section C if applicable.*

Section A—Depreciation and Other Information (Caution: *See page 5 of the instructions for limitations for automobiles.*)

23a Do you have evidence to support the business/investment use claimed? ☒ **Yes** ☐ **No** | **23b** If "Yes," is the evidence written? ☒ **Yes** ☐ **No**

(a) Type of property (list vehicles first)	(b) Date placed in service	(c) Business/ investment use percentage	(d) Cost or other basis	(e) Basis for depreciation (business/investment use only)	(f) Recovery period	(g) Method/ Convention	(h) Depreciation deduction	(i) Elected section 179 cost
24 Property used more than 50% in a qualified business use (See page 5 of the instructions.):								
Automobile	*5/20/94*	*100* %	*10,000*	*10,000*	*5-YR*	*200DB-HY*	*3,200*	
		%						
		%						
25 Property used 50% or less in a qualified business use (See page 5 of the instructions.):								
		%				S/L –		
		%				S/L –		
		%				S/L –		
26 Add amounts in column (h). Enter the total here and on line 20, page 1						**26**	*3,200*	
27 Add amounts in column (i). Enter the total here and on line 7, page 1							**27**	

Section B—Information on Use of Vehicles

Complete this section for vehicles used by a sole proprietor, partner, or other "more than 5% owner," or related person.
If you provided vehicles to your employees, first answer the questions in Section C to see if you meet an exception to completing this section for those vehicles.

	(a) Vehicle 1		(b) Vehicle 2		(c) Vehicle 3		(d) Vehicle 4		(e) Vehicle 5		(f) Vehicle 6	
28 Total business/investment miles driven during the year (DO NOT include commuting miles)	*12,000*											
29 Total commuting miles driven during the year	*-0-*											
30 Total other personal (noncommuting) miles driven	*-0-*											
31 Total miles driven during the year. Add lines 28 through 30.												
	Yes	**No**	**Yes**	**No**	**Yes**	**No**	**Yes**	**No**	**Yes**	**No**	**Yes**	**No**
32 Was the vehicle available for personal use during off-duty hours?		*X*										
33 Was the vehicle used primarily by a more than 5% owner or related person?	*X*											
34 Is another vehicle available for personal use?	*X*											

Section C—Questions for Employers Who Provide Vehicles for Use by Their Employees

*Answer these questions to determine if you meet an exception to completing Section B for vehicles used by employees who **are not** more than 5% owners or related persons.*

	Yes	No
35 Do you maintain a written policy statement that prohibits all personal use of vehicles, including commuting, by your employees?		
36 Do you maintain a written policy statement that prohibits personal use of vehicles, except commuting, by your employees? See page 6 of the instructions for vehicles used by corporate officers, directors, or 1% or more owners		
37 Do you treat all use of vehicles by employees as personal use?		
38 Do you provide more than five vehicles to your employees, obtain information from your employees about the use of the vehicles, and retain the information received?		
39 Do you meet the requirements concerning qualified automobile demonstration use? See page 6 of the instructions . .		

Note: *If your answer to 35, 36, 37, 38, or 39 is "Yes," you need not complete Section B for the covered vehicles.*

Part VI Amortization

(a) Description of costs	(b) Date amortization begins	(c) Amortizable amount	(d) Code section	(e) Amortization period or percentage	(f) Amortization for this year
40 Amortization of costs that begins during your 1995 tax year:					
41 Amortization of costs that began before 1995				**41**	
42 **Total.** Enter here and on "Other Deductions" or "Other Expenses" line of your return . . .				**42**	

Printed on recycled paper

SCHEDULE C (Form 1040)

Department of the Treasury
Internal Revenue Service (99)

Profit or Loss From Business

(Sole Proprietorship)

▶ Partnerships, joint ventures, etc., must file Form 1065.

▶ Attach to Form 1040 or Form 1041. ▶ See Instructions for Schedule C (Form 1040).

OMB No. 1545-0074

1995

Attachment Sequence No. **09**

Name of proprietor: *Thomas Andrews*

Social security number (SSN): *123 45 6789*

A Principal business or profession, including product or service (see page C-1): *Accounting Services*

B Enter principal business code (see page C-6) ▶

C Business name. If no separate business name, leave blank. *Andrews Accounting Services*

D Employer ID number (EIN), if any

E Business address (including suite or room no.) ▶ *270 Mountain View*
City, town or post office, state, and ZIP code *Ogden, UT 84201*

F Accounting method: (1) ☐ Cash (2) ☒ Accrual (3) ☐ Other (specify) ▶

G Method(s) used to value closing inventory: (1) ☐ Cost (2) ☐ Lower of cost or market (3) ☐ Other (attach explanation) (4) ☒ Does not apply (if checked, skip line H)

		Yes	No
H	Was there any change in determining quantities, costs, or valuations between opening and closing inventory? If "Yes," attach explanation		
I	Did you "materially participate" in the operation of this business during 1995? If "No," see page C-2 for limit on losses	*X*	

J If you started or acquired this business during 1995, check here ▶ ☐

Part I Income

		Line	Amount
1	Gross receipts or sales. **Caution:** *If this income was reported to you on Form W-2 and the "Statutory employee" box on that form was checked, see page C-2 and check here* ▶ ☐	1	*80,000*
2	Returns and allowances	2	
3	Subtract line 2 from line 1	3	*80,000*
4	Cost of goods sold (from line 40 on page 2)	4	
5	**Gross profit.** Subtract line 4 from line 3	5	*80,000*
6	Other income, including Federal and state gasoline or fuel tax credit or refund (see page C-2)	6	
7	**Gross income.** Add lines 5 and 6 ▶	7	*80,000*

Part II Expenses. Enter expenses for business use of your home **only** on line 30.

	Line	Amount		Line	Amount
8 Advertising	8		19 Pension and profit-sharing plans	19	
9 Bad debts from sales or services (see page C-3)	9	*2,000*	20 Rent or lease (see page C-4): a Vehicles, machinery, and equipment	20a	
10 Car and truck expenses (see page C-3)	10	*3,000*	b Other business property	20b	*12,000*
11 Commissions and fees	11		21 Repairs and maintenance	21	
12 Depletion	12		22 Supplies (not included in Part III)	22	
13 Depreciation and section 179 expense deduction (not included in Part III) (see page C-3)	13	*23,459*	23 Taxes and licenses	23	
14 Employee benefit programs (other than on line 19)	14		24 Travel, meals, and entertainment: a Travel	24a	
15 Insurance (other than health)	15	*800*	b Meals and entertainment		
16 Interest:			c Enter 50% of line 24b subject to limitations (see page C-4)		
a Mortgage (paid to banks, etc.)	16a		d Subtract line 24c from line 24b	24d	
b Other	16b		25 Utilities	25	
17 Legal and professional services	17		26 Wages (less employment credits)	26	
18 Office expense	18	*4,000*	27 Other expenses (from line 46 on page 2)	27	

		Line	Amount
28	**Total expenses** before expenses for business use of home. Add lines 8 through 27 in columns ▶	28	*45,259*
29	Tentative profit (loss). Subtract line 28 from line 7	29	*34,741*
30	Expenses for business use of your home. Attach **Form 8829**	30	
31	**Net profit or (loss).** Subtract line 30 from line 29. • If a profit, enter on **Form 1040, line 12,** and ALSO on **Schedule SE, line 2** (statutory employees, see page C-5). Estates and trusts, enter on Form 1041, line 3. • If a loss, you MUST go on to line 32.	31	*34,741*

32 If you have a loss, check the box that describes your investment in this activity (see page C-5).
- If you checked 32a, enter the loss on **Form 1040, line 12,** and ALSO on **Schedule SE, line 2** (statutory employees, see page C-5). Estates and trusts, enter on Form 1041, line 3.
- If you checked 32b, you MUST attach **Form 6198.**

32a ☐ All investment is at risk.
32b ☐ Some investment is not at risk.

But what is Vern's overall position for the year when the tax benefit of the loss is taken into account? Considering just the cash intake and outlay, it is summarized as follows:

Intake—		
Rent income	$14,400	
Tax savings [31% (income tax bracket) × $5,054 (loss from the property)]	1,567	$ 15,967
Outlay—		
Mortgage payments ($1,000 × 12 months)	$12,000	
Repairs and maintenance	2,200	(14,200)
Net cash benefit		$ 1,767

▼

It should be noted, however, that should Vern cease being an active participant in the rental activity, the passive activity loss rules would apply, and Vern could lose the current period benefit of the loss.

AMORTIZATION

When a business is purchased, goodwill and covenants not to compete are both subject to a statutory amortization period of 15 years. Therefore, the purchaser does not derive any tax benefits when part of the purchase price is assigned to a covenant rather than to goodwill.

Thus, from the purchaser's perspective, bargaining for a covenant should be based on legal rather than tax reasons. Note, however, that from the seller's perspective, goodwill is a capital asset and the covenant is an ordinary income asset.

Since the amortization period for both goodwill and a covenant is 15 years, the purchaser may want to attempt to minimize these amounts if the purchase price can be assigned to assets with shorter lives (e.g., inventory, receivables, and personalty). Conversely, the purchaser may want to attempt to maximize these amounts if part of the purchase price will otherwise be assigned to assets with longer recovery periods (e.g., realty) or to assets not eligible for cost recovery (e.g., land).

DEPLETION

Since the election to use the cost or percentage depletion method is an annual election, a taxpayer can use cost depletion (if higher) until the basis is exhausted and then switch to percentage depletion in the following years.

EXAMPLE 45

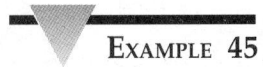

Assume the following facts for Melissa:

Remaining depletable basis	$ 11,000
Gross income (10,000 units)	100,000
Expenses (other than depletion)	30,000

Since cost depletion is limited to the basis of $11,000 and if the percentage depletion is $22,000 (assume a 22% rate), Melissa would choose the latter. Her basis is then reduced to zero. In future years, however, she can continue to take percentage depletion since percentage depletion is taken without reference to the remaining basis. ▼

The election to expense intangible drilling and development costs is a one-time election. Once the election is made to either expense or capitalize the intangible drilling and development costs, it is binding on all future expenditures. The permanent nature of the election makes it extremely important for the taxpayer to determine which treatment will provide the greatest tax advantage. (Refer to Example 41 for an illustration of the effect of using the two different alternatives for a given set of facts.)

TABLES

Summary of Tables

Table 8–1	Original ACRS statutory percentage table for personalty. Applicable depreciation method: 150 percent declining-balance switching to straight-line. Applicable recovery periods: 3, 5, 10, 15 years. Applicable convention: half-year.
Table 8–2	Modified ACRS statutory percentage table for personalty. Applicable depreciation methods: 200 or 150 percent declining-balance switching to straight-line. Applicable recovery periods: 3, 5, 7, 10, 15, 20 years. Applicable convention: half-year.
Table 8–3	Modified ACRS statutory percentage table for personalty. Applicable depreciation method: 200 percent declining-balance switching to straight-line. Applicable recovery periods: 3, 5, 7 years. Applicable convention: mid-quarter.
Table 8–4	Original ACRS statutory percentage table for realty. Applicable depreciation methods: 200 or 175 percent declining-balance switching to straight-line. Applicable recovery period: 15 years. Applicable convention: full-month.
Table 8–5	Original ACRS statutory percentage table for realty. Applicable depreciation method: 175 percent declining-balance switching to straight-line. Applicable recovery period: 18 years. Applicable convention: mid-month.
Table 8–6	Original ACRS statutory percentage table for realty. Applicable depreciation method: 175 percent declining-balance switching to straight-line. Applicable recovery period: 19 years. Applicable convention: mid-month.
Table 8–7	Modified ACRS straight-line table for realty. Applicable depreciation method: straight-line. Applicable recovery periods: 27.5, 31.5, 39 years. Applicable convention: mid-month.
Table 8–8	Original ACRS optional straight-line table for realty. Applicable depreciation method: straight-line. Applicable recovery period: 19 years. Applicable convention: mid-month.
Table 8–9	Modified ACRS optional straight-line table for personalty. Applicable depreciation method: straight-line. Applicable recovery periods: 3, 5, 7, 10, 15, 20 years. Applicable convention: half-year.
Table 8–10	Alternative minimum tax declining-balance table for personalty. Applicable depreciation method: 150 percent declining-balance switching to straight-line. Applicable recovery periods: 3, 5, 9.5, 10 years. Applicable convention: half-year.
Table 8–11	Alternative depreciation system straight-line table for personalty. Applicable depreciation method: straight-line. Applicable recovery periods: 5, 9.5, 12 years. Applicable convention: half-year.
Table 8–12	Alternative depreciation system straight-line table for realty. Applicable depreciation method: straight-line. Applicable recovery period: 40 years. Applicable convention: mid-month.

▼ TABLE 8–1
ACRS Statutory Percentages for Property Other Than 15-Year Real Property, 18-Year Real Property, or 19-Year Real Property Assuming Half-Year Convention

For Property Placed in Service after December 31, 1980, and before January 1, 1987

Recovery Year	The Applicable Percentage for the Class of Property Is: 3-Year	5-Year	10-Year	15-Year Public Utility
1	25	15	8	5
2	38	22	14	10
3	37	21	12	9
4		21	10	8
5		21	10	7
6			10	6
7			9	6
8			9	6
9			9	6
10			9	6
11				6
12				6
13				6
14				6
15				6

▼ TABLE 8–2
MACRS Accelerated Depreciation for Personal Property Assuming Half-Year Convention

For Property Placed in Service after December 31, 1986

Recovery Year	3-Year (200% DB)	5-Year (200% DB)	7-Year (200% DB)	10-Year (200% DB)	15-Year (150% DB)	20-Year (150% DB)
1	33.33	20.00	14.29	10.00	5.00	3.750
2	44.45	32.00	24.49	18.00	9.50	7.219
3	14.81*	19.20	17.49	14.40	8.55	6.677
4	7.41	11.52*	12.49	11.52	7.70	6.177
5		11.52	8.93*	9.22	6.93	5.713
6		5.76	8.92	7.37	6.23	5.285
7			8.93	6.55*	5.90*	4.888
8			4.46	6.55	5.90	4.522
9				6.56	5.91	4.462*
10				6.55	5.90	4.461
11				3.28	5.91	4.462
12					5.90	4.461
13					5.91	4.462
14					5.90	4.461
15					5.91	4.462
16					2.95	4.461
17						4.462
18						4.461
19						4.462
20						4.461
21						2.231

*Switchover to straight-line depreciation.

▼ TABLE 8–3
MACRS Accelerated Depreciation for Personal Property Assuming Mid-Quarter Convention

For Property Placed in Service after December 31, 1986 (Partial Table*)

Recovery Year	First Quarter	Second Quarter	Third Quarter	Fourth Quarter
		3-Year		
1	58.33	41.67	25.00	8.33
2	27.78	38.89	50.00	61.11
		5-Year		
Recovery Year	**First Quarter**	**Second Quarter**	**Third Quarter**	**Fourth Quarter**
1	35.00	25.00	15.00	5.00
2	26.00	30.00	34.00	38.00
		7-Year		
Recovery Year	**First Quarter**	**Second Quarter**	**Third Quarter**	**Fourth Quarter**
1	25.00	17.85	10.71	3.57
2	21.43	23.47	25.51	27.55

*The figures in this table are taken from the official tables that appear in Rev.Proc.87–57, 1987–2 C.B. 687. Because of their length, the complete tables are not presented.

▼ TABLE 8–4
ACRS Statutory Percentages for 15-Year Real Property

For Property Placed in Service after December 31, 1980, and before January 1, 1987: 15-Year Real Property—Low Income Housing

If the Recovery Year Is:	And the Month in the First Recovery Year the Property Is Placed in Service Is: 1	2	3	4	5	6	7	8	9	10	11	12
	The Applicable Percentage Is (Use the Column for the Month in the First Year the Property Is Placed in Service):											
1	13	12	11	10	9	8	7	6	4	3	2	1
2	12	12	12	12	12	12	12	13	13	13	13	13
3	10	10	10	10	11	11	11	11	11	11	11	11
4	9	9	9	9	9	9	9	9	10	10	10	10
5	8	8	8	8	8	8	8	8	8	8	8	9
6	7	7	7	7	7	7	7	7	7	7	7	7
7	6	6	6	6	6	6	6	6	6	6	6	6
8	5	5	5	5	5	5	5	5	5	5	6	6
9	5	5	5	5	5	5	5	5	5	5	5	5
10	5	5	5	5	5	5	5	5	5	5	5	5
11	4	5	5	5	5	5	5	5	5	5	5	5
12	4	4	4	5	4	5	5	5	5	5	5	5
13	4	4	4	4	4	4	5	4	5	5	5	5
14	4	4	4	4	4	4	4	4	4	5	4	4
15	4	4	4	4	4	4	4	4	4	4	4	4
16	—	—	1	1	2	2	2	3	3	3	4	4

▼ TABLE 8–4 (Continued)

For Property Placed in Service after December 31, 1980, and before March 16, 1984: 15-Year Real Property—Other Than Low-Income Housing

1	12	11	10	9	8	7	6	5	4	3	2	1
2	10	10	11	11	11	11	11	11	11	11	11	12
3	9	9	9	9	10	10	10	10	10	10	10	10
4	8	8	8	8	8	8	9	9	9	9	9	9
5	7	7	7	7	7	7	8	8	8	8	8	8
6	6	6	6	6	7	7	7	7	7	7	7	7
7	6	6	6	6	6	6	6	6	6	6	6	6
8	6	6	6	6	6	6	5	6	6	6	6	6
9	6	6	6	6	5	6	5	5	5	6	6	6
10	5	6	5	6	5	5	5	5	5	5	6	5
11	5	5	5	5	5	5	5	5	5	5	5	5
12	5	5	5	5	5	5	5	5	5	5	5	5
13	5	5	5	5	5	5	5	5	5	5	5	5
14	5	5	5	5	5	5	5	5	5	5	5	5
15	5	5	5	5	5	5	5	5	5	5	5	5
16	—	—	1	1	2	2	3	3	4	4	4	5

▼ TABLE 8–5

ACRS Cost Recovery Table for 18-Year Real Property

For Property Placed in Service after June 22, 1984, and before May 9, 1985: 18-Year Real Property (18-Year 175% Declining Balance) (Assuming Mid-Month Convention)

If the Recovery Year Is:	And the Month in the First Recovery Year the Property Is Placed in Service Is: 1	2	3	4	5	6	7	8	9	10	11	12
	The Applicable Percentage Is (Use the Column for the Month in the First Year the Property Is Placed in Service):											
1	9	9	8	7	6	5	4	4	3	2	1	0.4
2	9	9	9	9	9	9	9	9	9	10	10	10.0
3	8	8	8	8	8	8	8	8	9	9	9	9.0
4	7	7	7	7	7	8	8	8	8	8	8	8.0
5	7	7	7	7	7	7	7	7	7	7	7	7.0
6	6	6	6	6	6	6	6	6	6	6	6	6.0
7	5	5	5	5	6	6	6	6	6	6	6	6.0
8	5	5	5	5	5	5	5	5	5	5	5	5.0
9	5	5	5	5	5	5	5	5	5	5	5	5.0
10	5	5	5	5	5	5	5	5	5	5	5	5.0
11	5	5	5	5	5	5	5	5	5	5	5	5.0
12	5	5	5	5	5	5	5	5	5	5	5	5.0
13	4	4	4	5	4	4	5	4	4	4	5	5.0
14	4	4	4	4	4	4	4	4	4	4	4	4.0
15	4	4	4	4	4	4	4	4	4	4	4	4.0
16	4	4	4	4	4	4	4	4	4	4	4	4.0
17	4	4	4	4	4	4	4	4	4	4	4	4.0
18	4	3	4	4	4	4	4	4	4	4	4	4.0
19		1	1	1	2	2	2	3	3	3	3	3.6

▼ TABLE 8-6
ACRS Cost Recovery Table for 19-Year Real Property

For Property Placed in Service after May 8, 1985, and before January 1, 1987
19-Year Real Property (19-Year 175% Declining Balance)
(Assuming Mid-Month Convention)

If the Recovery Year Is:	And the Month in the First Recovery Year the Property Is Placed in Service Is: 1	2	3	4	5	6	7	8	9	10	11	12
	The Applicable Percentage Is (Use the Column for the Month in the First Year the Property Is Placed in Service):											
1	8.8	8.1	7.3	6.5	5.8	5.0	4.2	3.5	2.7	1.9	1.1	0.4
2	8.4	8.5	8.5	8.6	8.7	8.8	8.8	8.9	9.0	9.0	9.1	9.2
3	7.6	7.7	7.7	7.8	7.9	7.9	8.0	8.1	8.1	8.2	8.3	8.3
4	6.9	7.0	7.0	7.1	7.1	7.2	7.3	7.3	7.4	7.4	7.5	7.6
5	6.3	6.3	6.4	6.4	6.5	6.5	6.6	6.6	6.7	6.8	6.8	6.9
6	5.7	5.7	5.8	5.9	5.9	5.9	6.0	6.0	6.1	6.1	6.2	6.2
7	5.2	5.2	5.3	5.3	5.3	5.4	5.4	5.5	5.5	5.6	5.6	5.6
8	4.7	4.7	4.8	4.8	4.8	4.9	4.9	5.0	5.0	5.1	5.1	5.1
9	4.2	4.3	4.3	4.4	4.4	4.5	4.5	4.5	4.5	4.6	4.6	4.7
10	4.2	4.2	4.2	4.2	4.2	4.2	4.2	4.2	4.2	4.2	4.2	4.2
11	4.2	4.2	4.2	4.2	4.2	4.2	4.2	4.2	4.2	4.2	4.2	4.2
12	4.2	4.2	4.2	4.2	4.2	4.2	4.2	4.2	4.2	4.2	4.2	4.2
13	4.2	4.2	4.2	4.2	4.2	4.2	4.2	4.2	4.2	4.2	4.2	4.2
14	4.2	4.2	4.2	4.2	4.2	4.2	4.2	4.2	4.2	4.2	4.2	4.2
15	4.2	4.2	4.2	4.2	4.2	4.2	4.2	4.2	4.2	4.2	4.2	4.2
16	4.2	4.2	4.2	4.2	4.2	4.2	4.2	4.2	4.2	4.2	4.2	4.2
17	4.2	4.2	4.2	4.2	4.2	4.2	4.2	4.2	4.2	4.2	4.2	4.2
18	4.2	4.2	4.2	4.2	4.2	4.2	4.2	4.2	4.2	4.2	4.2	4.2
19	4.2	4.2	4.2	4.2	4.2	4.2	4.2	4.2	4.2	4.2	4.2	4.2
20	0.2	0.5	0.9	1.2	1.6	1.9	2.3	2.6	3.0	3.3	3.7	4.0

▼ TABLE 8–7
MACRS Straight-Line Depreciation for Real Property Assuming Mid-Month Convention*

For Property Placed in Service after December 31, 1986: 27.5-Year Residential Real Property

The Applicable Percentage Is (Use the Column for the Month in the First Year the Property Is Placed in Service): if sold in Feb. 1.5/12 (3.636)

Recovery Year(s)	1	2	3	4	5	6	7	8	9	10	11	12
1	3.485	3.182	2.879	2.576	2.273	1.970	1.667	1.364	1.061	0.758	0.455	0.152
2–18	3.636	3.636	3.636	3.636	3.636	3.636	3.636	3.636	3.636	3.636	3.636	3.636
19–27	3.637	3.637	3.637	3.637	3.637	3.637	3.637	3.637	3.637	3.637	3.637	3.637
28	1.970	2.273	2.576	2.879	3.182	3.485	3.636	3.636	3.636	3.636	3.636	3.636
29	0.000	0.000	0.000	0.000	0.000	0.000	0.152	0.455	0.758	1.061	1.364	1.667

For Property Placed in Service after December 31, 1986, and before May 13, 1993: 31.5-Year Nonresidential Real Property commercial – warehouse's

The Applicable Percentage Is (Use the Column for the Month in the First Year the Property Is Placed in Service):

Recovery Year(s)	1	2	3	4	5	6	7	8	9	10	11	12
1	3.042	2.778	2.513	2.249	1.984	1.720	1.455	1.190	0.926	0.661	0.397	0.132
2–19	3.175	3.175	3.175	3.175	3.175	3.175	3.175	3.175	3.175	3.175	3.175	3.175
20–31	3.174	3.174	3.174	3.174	3.174	3.174	3.174	3.174	3.174	3.174	3.174	3.174
32	1.720	1.984	2.249	2.513	2.778	3.042	3.175	3.175	3.175	3.175	3.175	3.175
33	0.000	0.000	0.000	0.000	0.000	0.000	0.132	0.397	0.661	0.926	1.190	1.455

For Property Placed in Service after May 12, 1993: 39-Year Nonresidential Real Property

warehouses

The Applicable Percentage Is (Use the Column for the Month in the First Year the Property Is Placed in Service):

Recovery Year(s)	1	2	3	4	5	6	7	8	9	10	11	12
1	2.461	2.247	2.033	1.819	1.605	1.391	1.177	0.963	0.749	0.535	0.321	0.107
2–39	2.564	2.564	2.564	2.564	2.564	2.564	2.564	2.564	2.564	2.564	2.564	2.564
40	0.107	0.321	0.535	0.749	0.963	1.177	1.391	1.605	1.819	2.033	2.247	2.461

*The official tables contain a separate row for each year. For ease of presentation, certain years are grouped in these tables. In some instances, this will produce a difference of .001 for the last digit when compared with the official tables.

▼ TABLE 8–8
ACRS Cost Recovery Table for 19-Year Real Property: Optional Straight-Line

For Property Placed in Service after May 8, 1985, and before January 1, 1987: 19-Year Real Property for Which an Optional 19-Year Straight-Line Method Is Elected (Assuming Mid-Month Convention)

If the Recovery Year Is:	And the Month in the First Recovery Year the Property Is Placed in Service Is: 1	2	3	4	5	6	7	8	9	10	11	12
	The Applicable Percentage Is (Use the Column for the Month in the First Year the Property Is Placed in Service):											
1	5.0	4.6	4.2	3.7	3.3	2.9	2.4	2.0	1.5	1.1	.7	.2
2	5.3	5.3	5.3	5.3	5.3	5.3	5.3	5.3	5.3	5.3	5.3	5.3
3	5.3	5.3	5.3	5.3	5.3	5.3	5.3	5.3	5.3	5.3	5.3	5.3
4	5.3	5.3	5.3	5.3	5.3	5.3	5.3	5.3	5.3	5.3	5.3	5.3
5	5.3	5.3	5.3	5.3	5.3	5.3	5.3	5.3	5.3	5.3	5.3	5.3
6	5.3	5.3	5.3	5.3	5.3	5.3	5.3	5.3	5.3	5.3	5.3	5.3
7	5.3	5.3	5.3	5.3	5.3	5.3	5.3	5.3	5.3	5.3	5.3	5.3
8	5.3	5.3	5.3	5.3	5.3	5.3	5.3	5.3	5.3	5.3	5.3	5.3
9	5.3	5.3	5.3	5.3	5.3	5.3	5.3	5.3	5.3	5.3	5.3	5.3
10	5.3	5.3	5.3	5.3	5.3	5.3	5.3	5.3	5.3	5.3	5.3	5.3
11	5.3	5.3	5.3	5.3	5.3	5.3	5.3	5.3	5.3	5.3	5.3	5.3
12	5.3	5.3	5.3	5.3	5.3	5.3	5.3	5.3	5.3	5.3	5.3	5.3
13	5.3	5.3	5.3	5.3	5.3	5.3	5.3	5.3	5.3	5.3	5.3	5.3
14	5.2	5.2	5.2	5.2	5.2	5.2	5.2	5.2	5.2	5.2	5.2	5.2
15	5.2	5.2	5.2	5.2	5.2	5.2	5.2	5.2	5.2	5.2	5.2	5.2
16	5.2	5.2	5.2	5.2	5.2	5.2	5.2	5.2	5.2	5.2	5.2	5.2
17	5.2	5.2	5.2	5.2	5.2	5.2	5.2	5.2	5.2	5.2	5.2	5.2
18	5.2	5.2	5.2	5.2	5.2	5.2	5.2	5.2	5.2	5.2	5.2	5.2
19	5.2	5.2	5.2	5.2	5.2	5.2	5.2	5.2	5.2	5.2	5.2	5.2
20	.2	.6	1.0	1.5	1.9	2.3	2.8	3.2	3.7	4.1	4.5	5.0

▼ TABLE 8–9
MACRS Straight-Line Depreciation for Personal Property Assuming Half-Year Convention*

For Property Placed in Service after December 31, 1986

MACRS Class	% First Recovery Year	Other Recovery Years: Years	%	Last Recovery Year: Year	%
3-year	16.67	2–3	33.33	4	16.67
5-year	10.00	2–5	20.00	6	10.00
7-year	7.14	2–7	14.29	8	7.14
10-year	5.00	2–10	10.00	11	5.00
15-year	3.33	2–15	6.67	16	3.33
20-year	2.50	2–20	5.00	21	2.50

*The official table contains a separate row for each year. For ease of presentation, certain years are grouped in this table. In some instances, this will produce a difference of .01 for the last digit when compared with the official table.

▼ TABLE 8–10
Alternative Minimum Tax: 150% Declining-Balance Assuming Half-Year Convention

For Property Placed in Service after December 31, 1986 (Partial Table*)

Recovery Year	3-Year 150%	5-Year 150%	9.5-Year 150%	10-Year 150%
1	25.00	15.00	7.89	7.50
2	37.50	25.50	14.54	13.88
3	25.00**	17.85	12.25	11.79
4	12.50	16.66**	10.31	10.02
5		16.66	9.17**	8.74**
6		8.33	9.17	8.74
7			9.17	8.74
8			9.17	8.74
9			9.17	8.74
10			9.16	8.74
11				4.37

*The figures in this table are taken from the official table that appears in Rev.Proc. 87–57, 1987–2 C.B. 687. Because of its length, the complete table is not presented.
**Switchover to straight-line depreciation.

▼ TABLE 8–11
ADS Straight-Line for Personal Property Assuming Half-Year Convention

For Property Placed in Service after December 31, 1986 (Partial Table*)

Recovery Year	5-Year Class	9.5-Year Class	12-Year Class
1	10.00	5.26	4.17
2	20.00	10.53	8.33
3	20.00	10.53	8.33
4	20.00	10.53	8.33
5	20.00	10.52	8.33
6	10.00	10.53	8.33
7		10.52	8.34
8		10.53	8.33
9		10.52	8.34
10		10.53	8.33
11			8.34
12			8.33
13			4.17

*The figures in this table are taken from the official table that appears in Rev.Proc. 87–57, 1987–2 C.B. 687. Because of its length, the complete table is not presented. The tables for the mid-quarter convention also appear in Rev.Proc. 87–57.

▼ TABLE 8–12
ADS Straight-Line for Real Property Assuming Mid-Month Convention

For Property Placed in Service after December 31,1986

Recovery Year	Month Placed in Service 1	2	3	4	5	6	7	8	9	10	11	12
1	2.396	2.188	1.979	1.771	1.563	1.354	1.146	0.938	0.729	0.521	0.313	0.104
2–40	2.500	2.500	2.500	2.500	2.500	2.500	2.500	2.500	2.500	2.500	2.500	2.500
41	0.104	0.312	0.521	0.729	0.937	1.146	1.354	1.562	1.771	1.979	2.187	2.396

KEY TERMS

Accelerated cost recovery system (ACRS), 8–4

Alternative depreciation system (ADS), 8–22

Amortization, 8–24

Cost depletion, 8–26

Cost recovery, 8–2

Depletion, 8–25

Depreciation, 8–2

Half-year convention, 8–7

Intangible drilling and development costs (IDC), 8–26

Listed property, 8–17

Mid-month convention, 8–12

Mid-quarter convention, 8–10

Modified accelerated cost recovery system (MACRS), 8–7

Percentage depletion, 8–27

Residential rental real estate, 8–12

Section 179 expensing, 8–15

PROBLEM MATERIALS

DISCUSSION QUESTIONS

1. Distinguish between cost recovery, amortization, and depletion.
2. Discuss whether personal use property is subject to cost recovery.
3. Distinguish between allowed and allowable cost recovery.
4. If a personal use asset is converted to business use, why is it necessary to compute cost recovery on the lower of fair market value or adjusted basis at the date of conversion?
5. Discuss whether a parking lot that is used in a business is subject to cost recovery.
6. Discuss the half-year convention as it is used in the ACRS rules.
7. On January 1, 1986, Aaron, a calendar year taxpayer, purchased a machine (15-year property). In June 1996, Aaron traded the old machine for a new machine (15-year property). Aaron paid $500,000 cash in addition to the first machine as a trade-in for the second machine. Identify the relevant tax issues for Aaron.
8. Discuss the half-year convention as it is used in the MACRS rules.
9. Discuss when the mid-quarter convention must be used.
10. Discuss the computation of cost recovery in the year of sale of an asset when the mid-quarter convention is being used.
11. What is the cost recovery period for nonresidential realty placed in service in 1996?
12. Discuss the mid-month convention as it is used in the MACRS rules.

13. Alan is engaged in the sale of rental warehouse space and related services. When he sought a bank loan to expand one of his warehouses, the lender required Alan to abate the problem of exposed and damaged asbestos-containing pipe insulation in the warehouse. Accordingly, Alan incurred costs of $200,000 to employ an asbestos contractor to remedy the problem. The contractor rewrapped and encapsulated the damaged or punctured areas of asbestos-containing pipe insulation and removed insulation that was too damaged to be rewrapped. The pipes requiring encapsulation amounted to less than 25% of the total pipes in the warehouse. Identify the relevant tax issues for Alan.

14. Discuss the applicable conventions if a taxpayer elects to use straight-line cost recovery for property placed in service after December 31, 1986.

15. If a taxpayer makes a straight-line election under MACRS, discuss the possibility of taking a cost recovery deduction, for personal and real property, in the year of disposition.

16. Discuss whether an election made one year to use straight-line cost recovery under ACRS for personal property of a particular class is binding for property of the same class placed in service in another tax year.

17. Discuss whether an election to use straight-line cost recovery under MACRS can be applied on an asset-by-asset basis.

18. Discuss whether the § 179 expensing election can be used for an apartment building.

19. Discuss the limitation on the § 179 amount that can be expensed and its impact on the basis of the property.

20. John was employed as a financial officer for an investment bank. By the middle of the year, John realized that he was going to be terminated by the bank. Therefore, he began preparing for a career in financial consulting as a sole practitioner. John became interested in consulting for a marina, but believing that boat owners formed a close fraternity, he decided that he could obtain such work only by acquiring a boat himself. Accordingly, he purchased a 23-foot Sea Ray Boat for $25,000. During the year, John used the boat only once to visit marinas on the lake to discuss potential employment as a consultant. A few days after this one excursion, John injured his back and was unable to use the boat for the remainder of the year. John was unsuccessful in his attempts to obtain a consulting position with any of the marinas.
At the beginning of the year, John also purchased a new car to be used for personal purposes. After John was terminated from the bank in September, he began using the car for business purposes.
Identify the relevant tax issues for John.

21. What are the tax consequences of listed property failing to meet the predominantly business use test?

22. Discuss what factors are used in determining whether the more-than-50% business use test has been satisfied.

23. If a taxpayer does not pass the more-than-50% business use test on an automobile, discuss whether the statutory dollar limitations on cost recovery are applicable.

24. Discuss the tax consequences that result when a passenger automobile, which failed the more-than-50% business usage test during the first two years, satisfies the test for the third year.

25. Discuss whether § 179 should be elected for a passenger automobile.

26. Explain the reason for the inclusion amount with respect to leased passenger automobiles.

27. Explain how an inclusion amount is determined with respect to leased passenger automobiles.

28. Discuss the substantiation requirements for listed property.

29. Explain the amortization period of a § 197 intangible if the actual useful life is less than 15 years.

30. What is the amortization period for self-created goodwill?

31. Discuss the options for handling intangible drilling and development costs.

32. Briefly discuss the differences between cost depletion and percentage depletion.

PROBLEMS

33. On January 1, 1992, Black Company acquired an asset (three-year property) for $10,000 for use in its business. In the years 1992 and 1993, Black took $3,333 and $4,445 of cost recovery. The allowable cost recovery for the years 1994 and 1995 was $1,481 and $741, but Black did not take the deductions. In those years, Black had net operating losses, and the company wanted to "save" the deductions for later years. On January 1, 1996, the asset was sold for $2,000. Calculate the gain or loss on the sale of the asset in 1996.

34. Eve acquired a personal residence in 1991 for $70,000. In January 1996, when the fair market value was $80,000, she converted the residence to rental property.
   a. Calculate the amount of cost recovery that can be taken in 1996.
   b. What would your answer be if the property were worth only $50,000 in 1996?

35. Jim acquired a 15-year class asset on March 1, 1986, for $40,000. He did not elect immediate expensing under § 179. On November 10, 1996, Jim sells the asset.
   a. Determine Jim's cost recovery for 1986.
   b. Determine Jim's cost recovery for 1996.

36. Walt purchased a tugboat for use in his business on March 15, 1996, for $500,000. He does not elect immediate expensing under § 179. On February 16, 2002, Walt sells the tug.
   a. Determine Walt's cost recovery for 1996.
   b. Determine Walt's cost recovery for 2002.

37. Juan acquires a five-year class asset on December 2, 1996, for $100,000. This is the only asset acquired by Juan during the year. He does not elect immediate expensing under § 179. On July 15, 1997, Juan sells the asset.
   a. Determine Juan's cost recovery for 1996.
   b. Determine Juan's cost recovery for 1997.

38. Debra acquired a building for $300,000 (exclusive of land) on January 1, 1984. Calculate the cost recovery using the statutory percentage method for 1984 and 1996 if:
   a. The real property is low-income housing.
   b. The real property is a factory building.

39. On December 2, 1984, Wade purchased and placed in service a warehouse. The warehouse cost $800,000. Wade used the statutory percentage cost recovery method. On July 7, 1996, Wade sold the warehouse.
   a. Determine Wade's cost recovery for 1984.
   b. Determine Wade's cost recovery for 1996.

40. On November 1, 1996, Sam purchases and places in service a building that is used as a warehouse. The cost of the building is $2.5 million. Determine Sam's cost recovery for 1996.

41. Pat acquires a warehouse on November 1, 1996, at a cost of $4,500,000. On January 30, 2007, Pat sells the warehouse. Calculate Pat's cost recovery for 1996. For 2007.

42. James acquired an apartment building on March 10, 1996, for $1,300,000. Calculate James's cost recovery for 1996.

43. Lori, who is single, acquired a new copier (five-year class property) on March 2, 1996, for $30,000. Lori's taxable income derived from her business (without regard to the amount expensed under § 179) is $100,000. If Lori elects immediate expensing under § 179, determine her total deduction, with respect to the copier, for 1996.

44. Jack owns a small business that he operates as a sole proprietor. In 1996, Jack will net $9,000 of business income before consideration of any § 179 deduction. Jack spends $208,000 on new equipment in 1996. If Jack also has $3,000 of § 179 deduction carryforwards from 1995, determine his § 179 expense deduction for 1996 and the amount of any carryforward.

45. Olga is the proprietor of a small business. In 1996, her business income, before consideration of any § 179 deduction, is $5,000. Olga spends $203,000 on new equipment and furniture for 1996. If Olga elects to take the § 179 deduction on a desk that cost $20,000 (included in the $203,000), determine her total cost recovery for 1996 with respect to the desk.

46. On March 10, 1996, Yoon purchased three-year class property for $20,000. On December 15, 1996, Yoon purchased five-year class property for $50,000.
   a. Calculate Yoon's cost recovery for 1996, assuming he does not make the § 179 election or use straight-line cost recovery.
   b. Calculate Yoon's cost recovery for 1996, assuming he does elect to use § 179 and does not elect to use straight-line cost recovery.
   c. Assuming Yoon's marginal tax rate is 36%, determine his tax benefit from electing § 179.

47. On July 1, 1996, Wilma places in service a computer (five-year class property). The computer cost $20,000. Wilma used the computer 65% for business. The remainder of the time, she used the computer for personal purposes. If Wilma does not elect § 179, determine her cost recovery deduction for the computer for 1996.

48. John Johnson is considering acquiring an automobile at the beginning of 1996 that he will use 100% of the time as a taxi. The purchase price of the automobile is $25,000. John has heard of cost recovery limits on automobiles and wants to know how much of the $25,000 he can deduct in the first year. Write a letter to John in which you present your calculations. Also, prepare a memo for the tax files. John's address is 100 Morningside, Clinton, MS 39058.

5yr.

49. On February 16, 1996, Ron purchased and placed into service a new car. The purchase price was $18,000. Ron drove the car 12,000 miles during the remainder of the year, 9,000 miles for business and 3,000 miles for personal use. Ron used the statutory percentage method of cost recovery. Calculate the total deduction Ron may take for 1996 with respect to the car.

50. On June 5, 1996, Leo purchased and placed in service a $19,000 car. The business use percentage for the car is always 100%. Compute Leo's cost recovery deduction in 2002.

51. On June 14, 1996, Helen purchased and placed in service a new car. The purchase price was $16,000. The car was used 75% for business and 25% for personal use in both 1996 and 1997. In 1998, the car was used 40% for business and 60% for personal use. Compute the cost recovery deduction for the car in 1998 and the cost recovery recapture.

52. In 1996, Paul purchased a computer (five-year property) for $120,000. The computer was used 60% for business, 20% for income production, and 20% for personal use. In 1997, the usage changed to 40% for business, 30% for income production, and 30% for personal use. Compute the cost recovery deduction for 1997 and any cost recovery recapture. Assume Paul did not make a § 179 election on the computer in 1996.

53. Sally purchased a computer (five-year property) for $3,000. Sally could use the computer 100% of the time in her business, or she could allow her family to also use the computer. Sally estimates that if her family uses the computer, the business use will be 40% and the personal use will be 60%. Determine the tax cost to Sally, in the year of acquisition, of allowing her family to use the computer. Assume that Sally would not elect § 179 limited expensing and that her marginal tax rate is 31%.

54. Midway through 1996, Abdel leases and places in service a passenger automobile. The lease will run for five years, and the payments are $430 per month. During 1996, Abdel uses the car 70% for business use and 30% for personal use. Assuming the inclusion dollar amount from the IRS table is $76, determine the tax consequences to Abdel from the lease for the year 1996.

55. Use the information given in Problem 54, but assume the inclusion dollar amount is $167. Abdel uses the car 60% for business use and 40% for personal use in 1997. Determine Abdel's tax consequences from the lease in 1997.

56. Dennis Harding is considering acquiring an automobile that he will use 100% for business. The purchase price of the automobile would be $30,500. If Dennis leased the car for five years, the lease payments would be $350 per month. Dennis will acquire the car on January 1, 1996. The inclusion dollar amounts from the IRS table for the next five years are $111, $244, $363, $435, and $503. Dennis desires to know the effect on his adjusted gross income of purchasing versus leasing the car for the next five years. Write a letter to Dennis and present your calculations. Also, prepare a memo for the tax files. His address is 150 Avenue I, Memphis, TN 38112.

57. On March 5, 1996, Nell purchased equipment for $60,000. The equipment is 7-year class property and has an ADS midpoint of 9.5 years. Determine Nell's cost recovery deduction for computing 1996 taxable income using the straight-line method under the alternative depreciation system and assuming she does not make a § 179 election.

58. In 1996, Muhammad purchased a light-duty truck for $12,000. The truck is used 100% for business. Muhammad did not make a § 179 election with respect to the truck. If Muhammad uses the statutory percentage method, determine his cost recovery deduction for 1996 for computing taxable income and for computing his alternative minimum tax.

59. In June 1996, Cardinal, Inc., purchased and placed in service railroad track costing $600,000.
    a. Calculate Cardinal's cost recovery deduction for 1996 for computing taxable income, assuming Cardinal does not make the § 179 election or use straight-line cost recovery.
    b. Calculate Cardinal's cost recovery deduction for 1996 for computing taxable income, assuming Cardinal does not make the § 179 election but does elect to use ADS 150% declining-balance cost recovery.

60. Jamie purchased $60,000 of office furniture for her business in June of the current year. Jamie understands that if she elects to use the alternative depreciation system to compute her regular income tax, there will be no difference between the cost recovery for computing the regular income tax and the AMT. Jamie wants to know the *regular* income tax cost, after three years, of using ADS rather than MACRS. Assume that Jamie does not elect § 179 limited expensing and that her marginal tax rate is 31%.

61. On August 1, 1996, Jake acquired a dental practice from Bob for $250,000. The purchase price was allocated $200,000 to the tangible assets of the practice and $50,000 to the goodwill. Determine Jake's deduction for the amortization of the goodwill for 1996.

62. Mike Saxon is negotiating the purchase of a business. The final purchase price has been agreed upon, but the allocation of the purchase price to the assets is still being discussed. Appraisals on a warehouse range from $1,200,000 to $1,500,000. If a value of $1,200,000 is used for the warehouse, the remainder of the purchase price, $800,000, will be allocated to goodwill. If $1,500,000 is allocated to the warehouse, goodwill will be $500,000. Mike wants to know what effect each alternative will have on cost recovery and amortization during the first year. Under the agreement, Mike will take over the business on January 1 of next year. Write a letter to Mike in which you present your calculations and recommendation. Also, prepare a memo for the tax files. Mike's address is 200 Rolling Hills Drive, Shavertown, PA 18708.

63. Wes acquired a mineral interest during the year for $5 million. A geological survey estimated that 250,000 tons of the mineral remained in the deposit. During the year, 80,000 tons were mined, and 45,000 tons were sold for $6 million. Other expenses amounted to $4 million. Assuming the mineral depletion rate is 22%, calculate Wes's lowest taxable income.

64. Chris purchased an oil interest for $2,000,000. Recoverable barrels were estimated to be 500,000. During the year, 120,000 barrels were sold for $3,840,000, regular expenses (including cost recovery) were $1,240,000, and IDC were $1,000,000. Calculate Chris's taxable income under the expensing and capitalization methods of handling IDC.

CUMULATIVE PROBLEMS

65. John Smith, age 31, is single and has no dependents. At the beginning of 1996, John started his own excavation business and named it Earth Movers. John lives at 1045 Center Street, Lindon, UT, and his business is located at 381 State Street, Lindon, UT. The zip code for both addresses is 84059. John's Social Security number is 321–09–6456, and the business identification number is 98–1234567. John is a cash basis taxpayer. During 1996, John had the following items in connection with his business:

Fees for services	$275,000
Building rental expense	32,000
Office furniture and equipment rental expense	5,000
Office supplies	1,500
Utilities	4,000
Salary for secretary	25,000
Salary for equipment operators	75,000
Payroll taxes	9,000
Fuel and oil for the equipment	20,000
Purchase of three front-end loaders on January 15, 1996, for $175,000. John made the election under § 179.	175,000
Purchase of a new dump truck on January 18, 1996	30,000

During 1996, John had the following additional items:

Interest income from First National Bank	$ 9,000
Dividends from Exxon	1,500
Quarterly estimated tax payments	11,500

On October 8, 1996, John inherited IBM stock from his Aunt Mildred. John had been her favorite nephew. According to the data provided by the executor of Aunt Mildred's estate, the stock had been valued for estate tax purposes at $70,000. John is considering selling the IBM stock for $75,000 on December 29, 1996, and using $60,000 of the proceeds to purchase an Acura NSX. He would use the car 100% for business. John wants to know what effect these transactions would have on his 1996 adjusted gross income.

Write a letter to John in which you present your calculations. Also, prepare a memo for the tax files. Suggested software (if available): *TurboTax* or *MacInTax*.

66. Bob Brown, age 30, is single and has no dependents. He was employed as a barber until May 1995 by Hair Cuts, Inc. In June 1995, Bob opened his own styling salon, the Style Shop, located at 465 Willow Drive, St. Paul, MN 55455. Bob is a cash basis taxpayer. He lives at 1021 Snelling Avenue, St. Paul, MN 55455. His Social Security number is 321–56–7102. Bob does not wish to designate $3 to the Presidential Election Campaign Fund. During 1995, Bob had the following income and expense items:

a. $25,000 salary from Hair Cuts, Inc.
b. $3,000 Federal income tax withheld by Hair Cuts, Inc.

c. $50,000 gross receipts from his own hair styling business.
d. Expenses connected with Bob's hair styling business:
   - $900 laundry and cleaning
   - $7,000 rent
   - $2,000 supplies
   - $800 utilities and telephone
e. Bob purchased and installed a fancy barber chair (five-year class property) on June 3, 1995. The chair cost $8,000. Bob did not make the § 179 election.
f. Bob purchased and installed furniture and fixtures (seven-year class property) on June 5, 1995. These items cost $20,000. Bob did make the § 179 election.
g. Bob's itemized deductions are as follows:

Property taxes on his residence	$2,000
Mortgage interest on his residence	4,000
State income taxes	2,500
Charitable contributions	1,500

h. Bob made estimated tax payments of $5,500.

Compute Bob Brown's 1995 Federal income tax payable (or refund due). If you use tax forms for your computations, you will need Forms 1040 and 4562 and Schedules A, C, and SE. Suggested software (if available): *TurboTax* or *MacInTax*..

RESEARCH PROBLEMS

Note: ***West's Federal Taxation on CD-ROM*** *can be used in preparing solutions to the Research Problems. Alternatively, tax research materials contained in a standard tax library can be used.*

Research Problem 1. Harry Pickart, who is one of your clients, is considering building a golf course in the resort area of Sun River, Oregon. Because the land is unimproved, all of the sand traps, greens, fairways, and tees will need to be constructed. Write a letter to Harry that contains your advice on whether any deductions can be taken for the landscaping improvements. Also, prepare a memo for the tax files. His mailing address is P.O. Box 100, Sun River, OR 97600.

Research Problem 2. Doug operates a restaurant in a small town. In May of the current year, Doug had a new septic tank installed for the restaurant. The town plans to construct a sewage system in five years. At that time, Doug will be required to be connected to the town system, and his septic tank will be obsolete. Doug believes that depreciation should represent wear, tear, and obsolescence, and, hence, he believes he should use a five-year life for the depreciation of the septic tank. Discuss the proper period and method for depreciating the septic tank.

Partial list of research aids:
J. O. Miller, 56 TCM 1242, T.C.Memo. 1989–66.
Rev.Proc. 87–56, 1987–2 C.B. 674.

Research Problem 3. Sandra purchased the following personal property during 1996:

Date	Asset	Cost
June 1	Machine A	$20,000
July 10	Machine B	10,000
November 15	Machine C	25,000

Sandra elects to take the § 179 expense on Machine C. Discuss what convention Sandra must use to determine her cost recovery deduction for 1996.

Research Problem 4. Gabriella is a professor of violin at the University of Minnesota. She is also a concert violinist. Gabriella purchased her violin for $80,000. Discuss whether Gabriella's violin is of a character subject to cost recovery using MACRS with the violin being classified as five-year property.

Research Problem 5. Alfred acquires $50,000 of machinery and equipment for his sole proprietorship. In addition, the Golden Partnership, in which Alfred is a 20% partner, acquires $100,000 of machinery and equipment during the year. Both Alfred's sole proprietorship and Golden Partnership would like to elect the maximum § 179 limited expensing for the tax year. The net income of the partnership is $300,000, and the sole proprietorship has net income of $150,000. Advise Alfred of the amount of § 179 deductions he can take on his income tax return and the source (i.e., sole proprietorship, partnership, or both).

TEAM PROJECT: ARTHUR ANDERSEN TAX CHALLENGE CASES

For more information on the Arthur Andersen Tax Challenge Cases, please refer to Chapter 1, page 1-38.

Information related to tax issues and problems that are discussed in this chapter may be found in the

Fields case on page 20

Read and analyze the case you have been assigned and *identify* any issues and problems that are related to material covered in this chapter. If the information provided in the case is complete, prepare answers for this part of the case at this time. If you need information that is contained in the later parts of the case, please write a memo summarizing the questions or problems so you can prepare a complete answer at a later date.

CHAPTER

9

DEDUCTIONS: EMPLOYEE EXPENSES

LEARNING OBJECTIVES

After completing Chapter 9, you should be able to:

1. Distinguish between employee and self-employed status.
2. Recognize deductible transportation expenses.
3. Know how travel expenses are treated.
4. Determine the moving expense deduction.
5. Differentiate between deductible and nondeductible education expenses.
6. Understand how entertainment expenses are treated.
7. Identify other employee expenses.
8. Appreciate the difference between accountable and nonaccountable employee plans.
9. Work with the limitations on miscellaneous itemized deductions.
10. Develop tax planning ideas related to employee business expenses.

OUTLINE

Considering the large number of taxpayers affected, the tax treatment of job-related expenses is unusually complex. To resolve this matter in a systematic fashion, a number of key questions must be asked:

- Is the taxpayer an *employee* or *self-employed?*
- If an employee, what expenses *qualify* as deductions?
- How are the expenses that qualify *classified* for tax purposes?
- To the extent the expenses are classified as deductions *from* AGI, are they subject to any *limitation?*

Once these questions have been posed and answered, the chapter considers various planning procedures available to maximize the deductibility of employee expenses.

EMPLOYEE VERSUS SELF-EMPLOYED

1 LEARNING OBJECTIVE
Distinguish between employee and self-employed status.

The determination of employment status is already controversial and can be expected to become an even greater problem in the future. Businesses are increasingly relying on the services of self-employed persons (i.e., **independent contractors**) for numerous reasons. Unlike employees, self-employed persons do not have to be included in various fringe benefit programs (e.g., group term life insurance) and retirement plans. Since they are not covered by FICA and FUTA (see Chapter 1), these payroll costs are avoided.

The IRS is very much aware of the tendency of businesses to wrongly classify workers as self-employed rather than as employees. In terms of tax consequences, employment status also makes a great deal of difference to the persons who perform the services. Expenses of self-employed taxpayers, to the extent allowable, are classified as deductions *for* AGI and are reported on Schedule C (Profit or Loss From Business) of Form 1040.[1] With the exception of reimbursement under an accountable plan (see later in the chapter), expenses of employees are deductions *from* AGI. They are reported on Form 2106 (Employee Business Expenses) and Schedule A (Itemized Deductions) of Form 1040.[2]

But when does an employer-employee relationship exist? Such a relationship exists when the employer has the right to specify the end result and the ways and means by which that result is to be attained.[3] An employee is subject to the will and control of the employer with respect not only to what shall be done but also to how it shall be done. If the individual is subject to the direction or control of another only to the extent of the end result but not as to the means of accomplishment, an employer-employee relationship does not exist. An example is the preparation of a taxpayer's return by an independent CPA.

Certain factors indicate an employer-employee relationship. They include (1) the right to discharge without legal liability the person performing the service, (2) the furnishing of tools or a place to work, and (3) payment based on time spent rather than the task performed. Each case is tested on its own merits, and the right to control the means and methods of accomplishment is the definitive test. Generally, physicians, lawyers, dentists, contractors, subcontractors, and others who offer services to the public are not classified as employees.

EXAMPLE 1

Arnold is a lawyer whose major client accounts for 60% of his billings. He does the routine legal work and income tax returns at the client's request. He is paid a monthly retainer in addition to amounts charged for extra work. Arnold is a self-employed individual. Even though most of his income comes from one client, he still has the right to determine how the end result of his work is attained. ▼

EXAMPLE 2

Ellen is a lawyer hired by Arnold to assist him in the performance of services for the client mentioned in Example 1. Ellen is under Arnold's supervision; he reviews her work and pays her an hourly fee. Ellen is an employee of Arnold. ▼

EXAMPLE 3

Frank is a licensed practical nurse who works as a private-duty nurse. He is under the supervision of the patient's doctor and is paid by the patient. Frank is not an employee of either the patient (who pays him) or the doctor (who supervises him). The ways and means of attaining the end result (care of the patient) are under his control. ▼

Employees in a special category are also allowed to file Schedule C to report income and deduct expenses *for* AGI. These employees are called **statutory employees** because they are not common law employees under the rules explained above. The wages or commissions paid to statutory employees are not subject to Federal income tax withholding but are subject to Social Security tax.[4]

[1] §§ 62(a)(1) and 162(a). See Appendix B for a reproduction of Schedule C.

[2] See Appendix B for a reproduction of Form 2106 and Schedule A.

[3] Reg. § 31.3401(c)–(1)(b).

[4] See Circular E, *Employer's Tax Guide* (IRS Publication 15), for further discussion of statutory employees.

Employee Expenses—In General

Once the employment relationship is established, employee expenses fall into one of the following categories:

- Transportation.
- Travel.
- Moving.
- Education.
- Entertainment.
- Other.

These expenses are discussed below in the order presented.

Keep in mind, however, that these expenses are not necessarily limited to employees. A deduction for business transportation, for example, is equally available to taxpayers who are self-employed.

Transportation Expenses

QUALIFIED EXPENDITURES

2 LEARNING OBJECTIVE
Recognize deductible transportation expenses.

An employee may deduct unreimbursed employment-related transportation expenses as an itemized deduction *from* AGI. **Transportation expenses** include only the cost of transporting the employee from one place to another when the employee is *not* away from home *in travel status.* Such costs include taxi fares, automobile expenses, tolls, and parking.

Commuting Expenses. Commuting between home and one's place of employment is a personal, nondeductible expense. The fact that one employee drives 30 miles to work and another employee walks six blocks is of no significance.[5]

EXAMPLE 4

Geraldo is employed by Sparrow Corporation. He drives 22 miles each way to work. The 44 miles he drives each workday are nondeductible commuting expenses. ▼

The rule that disallows a deduction for commuting expenses has several exceptions. An employee who uses an automobile to transport heavy tools to work and who otherwise would not drive to work is allowed a deduction, but only for the additional costs incurred to transport the work implements. Additional costs are those exceeding the cost of commuting by the same mode of transportation without the tools. For example, the rental of a trailer for transporting tools is deductible, but the expenses of operating the automobile generally are not deductible.[6] The Supreme Court has held that a deduction is permitted only when the taxpayer can show that the automobile would not have been used without the necessity to transport tools or equipment.[7]

Another exception is provided for an employee who has a second job. The expenses of getting from one job to another are deductible. If the employee goes home between jobs, the deduction is based on the distance between jobs.

---

[5] *Tauferner v. U.S.*, 69–1 USTC ¶9241, 23 AFTR2d 69–1025, 407 F.2d 243 (CA–10, 1969).

[6] Rev.Rul. 75–380, 1975–2 C.B. 59.

[7] *Fausner v. Comm.*, 73–2 USTC ¶9515, 32 AFTR2d 73–5202, 93 S.Ct. 2820 (USSC, 1973).

EXAMPLE 5

In the current year, Cynthia holds two jobs, a full-time job with Blue Corporation and a part-time job with Wren Corporation. During the 250 days that she works (adjusted for weekends, vacation, and holidays), Cynthia customarily leaves home at 7:30 A.M. and drives 30 miles to the Blue Corporation plant, where she works until 5:00 P.M. After dinner at a nearby cafe, Cynthia drives 20 miles to Wren Corporation and works from 7:00 to 11:00 P.M. The distance from the second job to Cynthia's home is 40 miles. Her deduction is based on 20 miles (the distance between jobs). ▼ deductible

If the taxpayer is required to incur a transportation expense to travel between work stations, that expense is deductible.

EXAMPLE 6

Thomas, a general contractor, drives from his home to his office, then drives to three building sites to perform his required inspections, and finally drives home. The costs of driving to his office and driving home from the last inspection site are nondeductible commuting expenses. The other transportation costs are deductible. ▼

Likewise, the commuting costs from home to a temporary work station and from the temporary work station to home are deductible.[8]

EXAMPLE 7

Vivian works for a firm in downtown Denver and commutes to work. She occasionally works in a customer's office. On one such occasion, Vivian drove directly to the customer's office, a round-trip distance from her home of 40 miles. She did not go into her office, which is a 52-mile round-trip. Her mileage for going to and from the temporary work station is deductible. ▼

Also deductible is the reasonable travel cost between the general working area and a temporary work station outside that area.[9] What constitutes the general working area depends on the facts and circumstances of each situation. Furthermore, if an employee customarily works on several temporary assignments in a localized area, that localized area becomes the regular place of employment. Transportation from home to these locations becomes a personal, nondeductible commuting expense.

EXAMPLE 8

Sam, a building inspector in Minneapolis, regularly inspects buildings for building code violations for his employer, a general contractor. During one busy season, the St. Paul inspector became ill, and Sam was required to inspect several buildings in St. Paul. The expenses for transportation for the trips to St. Paul are deductible. ▼

COMPUTATION OF AUTOMOBILE EXPENSES

A taxpayer has two choices in computing automobile expenses. The actual operating cost, which includes depreciation (cost recovery), gas, oil, repairs, licenses, and insurance, may be used. Records must be kept that detail the automobile's personal and business use. Only the percentage allocable to business transportation and travel is allowed as a deduction. Complex rules for the computation of depreciation (discussed in Chapter 8) apply if the actual expense method is used.

Use of the **automatic mileage method** is the second alternative. For 1996 the deduction is based on 31 cents per mile for all business miles.[10] Parking fees and

[8] Rev.Rul. 90–23, 1990–1 C.B. 28 as amplified by Rev.Rul. 94–47, 1994–2 C.B. 18.

[9] Rev.Rul. 190, 1953–2 C.B. 303 as amplified by Rev.Rul. 94–47, 1994–2 C.B. 18.

[10] Rev.Proc. 95–54, I.R.B. No. 52, 27. The rate was 30 cents a mile for 1995.

tolls are allowed in addition to expenses computed using the automatic mileage method.

Generally, a taxpayer may elect either method for any particular year. However, the following restrictions apply:

- The vehicle must be owned by the taxpayer.
- If two or more vehicles are in use (for business purposes) at the *same* time (not alternately), a taxpayer may not use the automatic mileage method.
- A basis adjustment is required if the taxpayer changes from the automatic mileage method to the actual operating cost method. Depreciation is considered allowed for the business miles in accordance with the following schedule for the most recent five years:

Year	Rate per Mile
1996	12 cents
1995	12 cents
1994	12 cents
1993	11.5 cents
1992	11.5 cents

EXAMPLE 9

Tim purchased his automobile in 1993 for $15,000. It is used 90% for business purposes. Tim drove the automobile for 10,000 business miles in 1995; 8,500 miles in 1994; and 6,000 miles in 1993. At the beginning of 1996, the basis of the business portion is $10,590.

Cost ($15,000 × 90%)	$13,500
Less depreciation:	
1995 (10,000 miles × 12 cents)	(1,200)
1994 (8,500 miles × 12 cents)	(1,020)
1993 (6,000 × 11.5 cents)	(690)
Adjusted business basis 1/1/96	$10,590

▼

- Use of the automatic mileage method in the first year the auto is placed in service is considered an election to exclude the auto from the MACRS method of depreciation (discussed in Chapter 8).
- A taxpayer may not switch to the automatic mileage method if the MACRS statutory percentage method or the election to expense under § 179 has been used.

TRAVEL EXPENSES

DEFINITION OF TRAVEL EXPENSES

3 LEARNING OBJECTIVE
Know how travel expenses are treated.

An itemized deduction is allowed for unreimbursed travel expenses related to a taxpayer's employment. **Travel expenses** are more broadly defined in the Code than are transportation expenses. Travel expenses include transportation expenses and meals and lodging while away from home in the pursuit of a trade or business. Meals cannot be lavish or extravagant under the circumstances. Transportation expenses (as previously discussed) are deductible even though the taxpayer is not away from home. A deduction for travel expenses is available only if the taxpayer is away from his or her tax home. Travel expenses also include reasonable laundry and incidental expenses.

AWAY-FROM-HOME REQUIREMENT

The crucial test for the deductibility of travel expenses is whether or not the employee is away from home overnight. "Overnight" need not be a 24-hour period, but it must be a period substantially longer than an ordinary day's work and must require rest, sleep, or a relief-from-work period.[11] A one-day business trip is not travel status, and meals and lodging for such a trip are not deductible.

Temporary Assignments. The employee must be away from home for a temporary period. If the taxpayer-employee is reassigned to a new post for an indefinite period of time, that new post becomes his or her tax home. *Temporary* indicates that the assignment's termination is expected within a reasonably short period of time. The position of the IRS is that the tax home is the business location, post, or station of the taxpayer. Thus, travel expenses are not deductible if a taxpayer is reassigned for an indefinite period and does not move his or her place of residence to the new location.

EXAMPLE 10

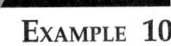

Malcolm's employer opened a branch office in San Diego. Malcolm was assigned to the new office for three months to train a new manager and to assist in setting up the new office. He tried commuting from his home in Los Angeles for a week and decided that he could not continue driving several hours a day. He rented an apartment in San Diego, where he lived during the week. He spent weekends with his wife and children at their home in Los Angeles. Malcolm's rent, meals, laundry, incidentals, and automobile expenses in San Diego are deductible. To the extent that Malcolm's transportation expense related to his weekend trips home exceeds what his cost of meals and lodging would have been, the excess is personal and nondeductible. ▼

EXAMPLE 11

Assume that Malcolm in Example 10 was transferred to the new location to become the new manager permanently. His wife and children continued to live in Los Angeles until the end of the school year. Malcolm is no longer "away from home" because the assignment is not temporary. His travel expenses are not deductible. ▼

To curtail controversy in this area, the Code specifies that a taxpayer "*shall not* be treated as *temporarily* away from home during any period of employment if such period exceeds 1 year."[12]

Determining the Tax Home. Under ordinary circumstances, determining the location of a taxpayer's tax home does not present a problem. The tax home is the area in which the taxpayer derives his or her principal source of income. When the taxpayer has more than one place of employment, the tax home is based on the amount of time spent in each area..

It is possible for a taxpayer never to be away from his or her tax home. In other words, the tax home follows the taxpayer.[13] Thus, all meals and lodging remain personal and are not deductible.

---

[11] *U.S. v. Correll,* 68–1 USTC ¶9101, 20 AFTR2d 5845, 88 S.Ct. 445 (USSC, 1967); Rev.Rul. 75–168, 1975–1 C.B. 58.

[12] § 162(a). Added by the Comprehensive National Energy Policy Act of 1992.

[13] *Moses Mitnick,* 13 T.C. 1 (1949).

EXAMPLE 12 Bill is employed as a long-haul truck driver. He is single, stores his clothes and other belongings at his parents' home, and stops there for periodic visits. Most of the time, Bill is on the road, sleeping in his truck and in motels. It is likely that Bill is never in travel status, as he is not away from home. Consequently, none of his meals and lodging are deductible. ▼

RESTRICTIONS ON TRAVEL EXPENSES

The possibility always exists that taxpayers will attempt to treat vacation or pleasure travel as deductible business travel. To prevent such practices, the law contains restrictions on certain travel expenses.

Conventions. For travel expenses to be deductible, a convention must be directly related to the taxpayer's trade or business.[14]

EXAMPLE 13 Dr. Hill, a pathologist who works for a hospital in Ohio, travels to Las Vegas to attend a two-day session on recent developments in estate planning. No deduction is allowed for Dr. Hill's travel expenses. ▼

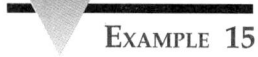

EXAMPLE 14 Assume the same facts as in Example 13 except that the convention deals entirely with recent developments in forensic medicine. Under these circumstances, a travel deduction is allowed. ▼

If the proceedings of the convention are videotaped, the taxpayer must attend convention sessions to view the videotaped materials along with other participants. This requirement does not disallow deductions for costs (other than travel, meals, and entertainment) of renting or using videotaped materials related to business.

EXAMPLE 15 A CPA is unable to attend a convention at which current developments in taxation are discussed. She pays $200 for videotapes of the lectures and views them at home later. The $200 is an itemized deduction if the CPA is an employee. If she is self-employed, the $200 is a deduction *for* AGI. ▼

The Code places stringent restrictions on the deductibility of travel expenses of the taxpayer's spouse or dependent.[15] Generally, the accompaniment by the spouse or dependent must serve a bona fide business purpose, and the expenses must be otherwise deductible.

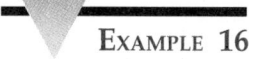

EXAMPLE 16 Assume the same facts as in Example 14 with the additional fact that Dr. Hill is accompanied by Mrs. Hill. Mrs. Hill is not employed, but possesses secretarial skills and takes notes during the proceedings. No deduction is allowed for Mrs. Hill's travel expenses. ▼

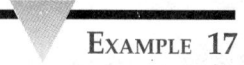

EXAMPLE 17 Modify the facts in Example 16 to make Mrs. Hill a nurse trained in pathology, who is employed by Dr. Hill as his assistant. Now, Mrs. Hill's travel expenses qualify as deductions. ▼

Education. Travel as a form of education is not deductible.[16] If, however, the education qualifies as a deduction, the travel involved is allowed.

---

[14] § 274(h)(1).
[15] § 274(m)(3).
[16] § 274(m)(2).

EXAMPLE 18

Greta, a German teacher, travels to Germany to maintain general familiarity with the language and culture. No travel expense deduction is allowed. ▼

EXAMPLE 19

Jean-Claude, a scholar of French literature, travels to Paris to do specific library research that cannot be done elsewhere and to take courses that are offered only at the Sorbonne. The travel costs are deductible, assuming that the other requirements for deducting education expenses (discussed later in the chapter) are met. ▼

COMBINED BUSINESS AND PLEASURE TRAVEL

To be deductible, travel expenses need not be incurred in the performance of specific job functions. Travel expenses incurred in attending a professional convention are deductible by an employee if attendance is connected with services as an employee. For example, an employee of a law firm can deduct travel expenses incurred in attending a meeting of the American Bar Association.

Domestic Travel. Travel deductions have been used in the past by persons who claimed a tax deduction for what was essentially a personal vacation. As a result, several provisions have been enacted to govern deductions associated with combined business and pleasure trips. If the business/pleasure trip is from one point in the United States to another point in the United States, the transportation expenses are deductible only if the trip is *primarily for business.*[17] If the trip is primarily for pleasure, no transportation expenses qualify as a deduction. Meals, lodging, and other expenses are allocated between business and personal days.

EXAMPLE 20

In the current year, Hana travels from Seattle to New York primarily for business. She spends five days conducting business and three days sightseeing and attending shows. Her plane and taxi fare amounts to $560. Her meals amount to $100 per day, and lodging and incidental expenses are $150 per day. She can deduct the transportation charges of $560, since the trip is primarily for business (five days of business versus three days of sightseeing). Meals are limited to five days and are subject to the 50% cutback (discussed later in the chapter) for a total of $250 [5 days × ($100 × 50%)], and other expenses are limited to $750 (5 days × $150). If Hana is an employee, the unreimbursed travel expenses are miscellaneous itemized deductions. ▼

EXAMPLE 21

Assume Hana goes to New York for a two-week vacation. While there, she spends several hours renewing acquaintances with people in her company's New York office. Her transportation expenses are not deductible. ▼

Foreign Travel. When the trip is *outside the United States,* special rules apply.[18] Transportation expenses must be allocated between business and personal unless (1) the taxpayer is away from home for seven days or less *or* (2) less than 25 percent of the time was for personal purposes. No allocation is required if the taxpayer has no substantial control over arrangements for the trip or the desire for a vacation is not a major factor in taking the trip. If the trip is primarily for pleasure, no transportation charges are deductible. Days devoted to travel are considered business days. Weekends, legal holidays, and intervening days are considered business days, provided that both the preceding and succeeding days were business days.

---

[17] Reg. § 1.162–2(b)(1).

[18] § 274(c) and Reg. § 1.274–4.

EXAMPLE 22

In the current year, Robert takes a trip from New York to Japan primarily for business purposes. He is away from home from June 10 through June 19. He spends three days vacationing and seven days conducting business (including two travel days). His air fare is $2,500, his meals amount to $100 per day, and lodging and incidental expenses are $160 per day. Since Robert is away from home for more than seven days and more than 25% of his time is devoted to personal purposes, only 70% (7 days business/10 days total) of the transportation is deductible. His deductions are as follows:

Transportation (70% × $2,500)		$1,750
Lodging ($160 × 7)		1,120
Meals ($100 × 7)	$ 700	
Less: 50% cutback (discussed later)	(350)	350
Total		$3,220

If Robert is gone the same period of time but spends only two days (rather than three) vacationing, no allocation of transportation is required. Since the pleasure portion of the trip is less than 25% of the total, all of the air fare qualifies for the travel deduction. ▼

Certain restrictions are imposed on the deductibility of expenses paid or incurred to attend conventions located outside the North American area. The expenses are disallowed unless it is established that the meeting is directly related to a trade or business of the taxpayer. Disallowance also occurs unless the taxpayer shows that it is as reasonable for the meeting to be held in a foreign location as within the North American area.

The foreign convention rules do not operate to bar a deduction to an employer if the expense is compensatory in nature. For example, a trip to Rome won by a top salesperson is included in the gross income of the employee and is fully deductible by the employer.

MOVING EXPENSES

4 LEARNING OBJECTIVE
Determine the moving expense deduction.

In 1993, Congress significantly changed the tax treatment of moving expenses. Major changes included, but are not limited to, the following:

- Expansion of the distance test (see below) from 35 miles to 50 miles.
- Elimination of any deduction for move-related meals.
- Deletion of a deduction for certain indirect moving expenses (e.g., house-hunting and temporary living expenses).
- Reclassification of moving expenses to deductions *for* AGI rather than deductions *from* AGI.

The changes applied to expenses incurred after 1993.

Moving expenses are deductible for moves in connection with the commencement of work at a new principal place of work.[19] Both employees and self-employed individuals can deduct these expenses. To be eligible for a moving expense deduction, a taxpayer must meet two basic tests: distance and time.

[19] § 217(a).

DISTANCE TEST

To meet the distance test, the taxpayer's new job location must be at least 50 miles farther from the taxpayer's old residence than the old residence was from the former place of employment. In this regard, the location of the new residence is not relevant. This eliminates a moving deduction for taxpayers who purchase a new home in the same general area without changing their place of employment. Those who accept a new job in the same general area as the old job location are also eliminated.

EXAMPLE 23

Harry is permanently transferred to a new job location. The distance from Harry's former home to his new job (80 miles) exceeds the distance from his former home to his old job (30 miles) by at least 50 miles. Harry has met the distance test for a moving expense deduction. (See the following diagram.)

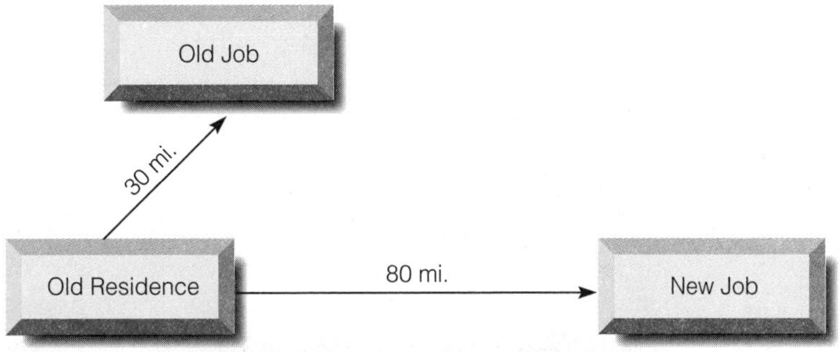

If Harry is not employed before the move, his new job must be at least 50 miles from his former residence. In this instance, Harry has met the distance test if he was not previously employed. ▼

TIME TEST

To meet the time test, an employee must be employed on a full-time basis at the new location for 39 weeks in the 12-month period following the move. If the taxpayer is a self-employed individual, he or she must work in the new location for 78 weeks during the next two years. The first 39 weeks must be in the first 12 months. The time test is suspended if the taxpayer dies, becomes disabled, or is discharged or transferred by the new employer through no fault of the employee.

A taxpayer might not be able to meet the 39-week test by the due date of the tax return for the year of the move. For this reason, two alternatives are allowed. The taxpayer can take the deduction in the year the expenses are incurred, even though the 39-week test has not been met. If the taxpayer later fails to meet the test, either (1) the income of the following year is increased by an amount equal to the deduction previously claimed for moving expenses, or (2) an amended return is filed for the year of the move. The second alternative is to wait until the test is met and then file an amended tax return for the year of the move.

TREATMENT OF MOVING EXPENSES

What Is Included. "Qualified" moving expenses include *reasonable* expenses of:

- Moving household goods and personal effects.
- Traveling from the former residence to the new place of residence.

For this purpose, *traveling* includes lodging, but not meals, for the taxpayer and members of the household.[20] It does not include the cost of moving servants or others who are not members of the household. The taxpayer can elect to use actual auto expenses (no depreciation is allowed) or the automatic mileage method. In this case, moving expense mileage is limited in 1996 to 10 cents per mile (nine cents in 1995) for each car. These expenses are also limited by the reasonableness standard. For example, if one moves from Texas to Florida via Maine and takes six weeks to do so, the transportation and lodging must be allocated between personal and moving expenses.

EXAMPLE 24

Jill is transferred by her employer from the Atlanta office to the San Francisco office. In this connection, she spends the following amounts:

Cost of moving furniture	$2,800
Transportation	700
Meals	200
Lodging	300

Jill's total qualified moving expense is $3,800 ($2,800 + $700 + $300). ▼

The moving expense deduction is allowed regardless of whether the employee is transferred by the existing employer or is employed by a new employer. It is allowed if the employee moves to a new area and obtains employment or switches from self-employed status to employee status (and vice versa). The moving expense deduction is also allowed if an individual is unemployed before obtaining employment in a new area.

How Treated. Qualified moving expenses that are paid (or reimbursed) by the employer are not reported as part of the gross income of the employee.[21] Moving expenses that are paid (or reimbursed) by the employer and are not qualified moving expenses are included in the employee's gross income and are not deductible. The employer is responsible for allocating the reimbursement between the qualified and nonqualified moving expenses. Reimbursed qualified moving expenses are separately stated on the Form W–2 given to the employee for the year involved. Qualified moving expenses that are not reimbursed and those of self-employed taxpayers are deductions *for* AGI.[22]

Form 3903 is used to report the details of the moving expense deduction if the employee is not reimbursed or a self-employed person is involved.

EDUCATION EXPENSES

GENERAL REQUIREMENTS

5 LEARNING OBJECTIVE
Differentiate between deductible and nondeductible education expenses.

An employee can deduct expenses incurred for education (**education expenses**) as ordinary and necessary business expenses provided the expenses are incurred for either of two reasons:

1. To maintain or improve existing skills required in the present job.
2. To meet the express requirements of the employer or the requirements imposed by law to retain his or her employment status.

[20] § 217(b).
[21] §§ 132(a)(6) and (g).
[22] § 62(a)(15).

Education expenses are *not* deductible if the education is for either of the following purposes:

1. To meet the minimum educational standards for qualification in the taxpayer's existing job.
2. To qualify the taxpayer for a new trade or business.[23]

Fees incurred for professional qualification exams (the bar exam, for example) and fees for review courses (such as a CPA review course) are not deductible.[24] If the education incidentally results in a promotion or raise, the deduction still can be taken as long as the education maintained and improved existing skills and did not qualify a person for a new trade or business. A change in duties is not always fatal to the deduction if the new duties involve the same general work. For example, the IRS has ruled that a practicing dentist's education expenses incurred to become an orthodontist are deductible.[25]

REQUIREMENTS IMPOSED BY LAW OR BY THE EMPLOYER FOR RETENTION OF EMPLOYMENT

Teachers are permitted to deduct education expenses if additional courses are required by the employer or are imposed by law. Many states require a minimum of a bachelor's degree and a specified number of additional courses to retain a teaching job. In addition, some public school systems have imposed a master's degree requirement and require teachers to make satisfactory progress toward a master's degree in order to keep their positions. If the required education is the minimum degree required for the job, no deduction is allowed.

A taxpayer classified as an Accountant I who went back to school to obtain a bachelor's degree was not allowed to deduct the expenses. Although some courses tended to maintain and improve his existing skills in his entry-level position, the degree was the minimum requirement for his job.[26]

Expenses incurred for education required by law for various professions will also qualify for deduction.

EXAMPLE 25 In order to satisfy the State Board of Public Accountancy rules for maintaining her CPA license, Nancy takes an auditing course sponsored by a local college. The cost of the education is deductible. ▼

ETHICAL CONSIDERATIONS

Employer-Imposed Education Requirement

Justin, a CPA, is the owner and operator of Condor Corporation. Condor provides accounting and tax services for a number of regular businesses. These services are provided by Justin and two long-time employees, Martha and Alan. Martha and Alan have expressed a desire to attend a local college part-time and earn bachelor of accounting degrees.

[23] Reg. §§ 1.162–5(b)(2) and (3).
[24] Reg. § 1.212–1(f) and Rev.Rul. 69–292, 1969–1 C.B. 84.
[25] Rev.Rul. 74–78, 1974–1 C.B. 44.
[26] Reg. § 1.162–5(b)(2)(iii) Example (2); *Collin J. Davidson*, 43 TCM 743, T.C.Memo. 1982–119.

When Justin hears about the college plans that Martha and Alan have made, he adopts the following resolution for Condor Corporation: "Employees performing accounting and tax services for clients must possess or be pursuing a bachelor's degree in accounting."

What is Justin trying to accomplish with the resolution? Will it work? Is this ethical behavior?

MAINTAINING OR IMPROVING EXISTING SKILLS

The "maintaining or improving existing skills" requirement in the Code has been difficult for both taxpayers and the courts to interpret. For example, a business executive is permitted to deduct the costs of obtaining an M.B.A. on the grounds that the advanced management education is undertaken to maintain and improve existing management skills. The executive is eligible to deduct the costs of specialized, nondegree management courses that are taken for continuing education or to maintain or improve existing skills. Expenses incurred by the executive to obtain a law degree are not deductible, however, because the education constitutes training for a new trade or business. The Regulations deny a self-employed accountant a deduction for expenses relating to law school.[27]

CLASSIFICATION OF SPECIFIC ITEMS

Education expenses include books, tuition, typing, and transportation (e.g., from the office to night school) and travel (e.g., meals and lodging while away from home at summer school).

EXAMPLE 26

Bill, who holds a bachelor of education degree, is a secondary education teacher in the Los Angeles school system. The school board recently raised its minimum education requirement for new teachers from four years of college training to five. A grandfather clause allows teachers with only four years of college to continue to qualify if they show satisfactory progress toward a graduate degree. Bill enrolls at the University of California and takes three graduate courses. His unreimbursed expenses for this purpose are as follows:

Books and tuition	$2,600
Lodging while in travel status (June-August)	1,150
Meals while in travel status	800
Laundry while in travel status	220
Transportation	600

Bill has an itemized deduction as follows:

Books and tuition	$2,600
Lodging	1,150
Meals less 50% cutback (see below)	400
Laundry	220
Transportation	600
	$4,970

▼

[27] Reg. § 1.162–5(b)(3)(ii) Example (1).

OTHER PROVISIONS DEALING WITH EDUCATION

The focus of this chapter is on the deduction aspects of certain items. For education, however, two important provisions involve the income aspects. One deals with the exclusion of certain scholarships from gross income.[28] The other deals with the exclusion from gross income of employer amounts provided under certain educational assistance programs.[29] Both of these provisions are discussed in Chapter 5.

ENTERTAINMENT EXPENSES

6 LEARNING OBJECTIVE
Understand how entertainment expenses are treated.

Many taxpayers attempt to deduct personal entertainment expenses as business expenses. For this reason, the tax law restricts the deductibility of entertainment expenses. The Code contains strict record-keeping requirements and provides restrictive tests for the deduction of certain types of **entertainment expenses.**

DOLLAR LIMITATIONS

Currently, only 50 percent of meal and entertainment expenses are allowed as a deduction.[30] The limitation applies in the context of both employment and self-employment status. The 50 percent cutback is effective for tax years beginning after 1993 (previously the cutback was 20 percent). Although the cutback can apply to either the employer or the employee, it will not apply twice. The cutback applies to the one who really pays (economically) for the meals or entertainment.

EXAMPLE 27

Jane, an employee of Pelican Corporation, entertains one of her clients. If Pelican Corporation does not reimburse Jane, she is subject to the cutback adjustment. If, however, Pelican Corporation reimburses Jane (or pays for the entertainment directly), Pelican suffers the cutback. ▼

What Is Covered. Transportation expenses are not affected by this provision—only meals and entertainment. The cutback also applies to taxes and tips relating to meals and entertainment. Cover charges, parking fees at an entertainment location, and room rental fees for a meal or cocktail party are also subject to the 50 percent rule.

EXAMPLE 28

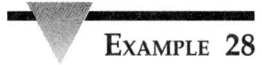

Joe pays a $30 cab fare to meet his client for dinner. The meal costs $120, and Joe leaves a $20 tip. His deduction is $100 (($120 + $20) × 50% + $30 cab fare). ▼

What Is Not Covered. The cutback rule has a number of exceptions. One exception covers the case where the full value of the meals or entertainment is included in the compensation of the employee (or independent contractor).[31]

EXAMPLE 29

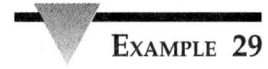

Myrtle wins an all-expense-paid trip to Europe for selling the most insurance for her company during the year. Her employer treats this trip as additional compensation to Myrtle. The cutback adjustment does not apply to the employer. ▼

[28] § 117.
[29] § 127.
[30] § 274(n).
[31] §§ 274(e)(2) and (9).

TAX IN THE NEWS

Will the 50 Percent Cutback Last?

A survey conducted by American Express Travel Related Services found that approximately 30 percent of the companies polled say that they have taken steps to curb dining expenses. Most of the companies in the 30 percent group are small and medium-size businesses and claim they are responding to the increase in the disallowance cutback for meals. When only 50 percent of the cost of business meals is deductible, these expenses are difficult for concerns with modest profit margins to absorb.

Recently, at least four bills have been introduced in Congress to help remedy the situation. Two bills would restore the 20 percent cutback rule, while the others would delete any cutback whatsoever. Even if the rule is changed, it seems doubtful that the cutback would be completely deleted in view of the revenue loss (estimated at $30 billion over a five-year period).

Another exception applies to meals and entertainment in a subsidized eating facility or where the *de minimis* fringe benefit rule is met (see Chapter 5).[32]

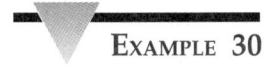

Example 30 General Hospital has an employee cafeteria on the premises for its doctors, nurses, and other employees. The cafeteria operates at cost. The cutback rule does not apply to General Hospital. ▼

Example 31 Canary Corporation gives a ham, a fruitcake, and a bottle of wine to each employee at year-end. Since the *de minimis* fringe benefit exclusion applies to business gifts of packaged foods and beverages, their *full* cost is deductible by Canary. ▼

A somewhat similar exception applies to employer-paid recreational activities for employees (e.g., the annual Christmas party or spring picnic).[33]

CLASSIFICATION OF EXPENSES

Entertainment expenses are categorized as follows: those *directly related* to business and those *associated with* business.[34] Directly related expenses are related to an actual business meeting or discussion. These expenses are distinguished from entertainment expenses that are incurred to promote goodwill, such as maintaining existing customer relations. To obtain a deduction for directly related entertainment, it is not necessary to show that actual benefit resulted from the expenditure as long as there was a reasonable expectation of benefit. To qualify as directly related, the expense should be incurred in a clear business setting. If there is little possibility of engaging in the active conduct of a trade or business due to the nature of the social facility, it is difficult to qualify the expenditure as directly related to business.

[32] § 274(n)(2).
[33] § 274(e)(4).
[34] § 274(a)(1)(A).

Expenses associated with, rather than directly related to, business entertainment must serve a specific business purpose, such as obtaining new business or continuing existing business. These expenditures qualify only if the expenses directly precede or follow a bona fide business discussion. Entertainment occurring on the same day as the business discussion meets the test.

RESTRICTIONS UPON DEDUCTIBILITY

Business Meals. Any business meal is deductible only if the following are true:[35]

- The meal is directly related to or associated with the active conduct of a trade or business.
- The expense is not lavish or extravagant under the circumstances.
- The taxpayer (or an employee) is present at the meal.

A business meal with a business associate or customer is not deductible unless business is discussed before, during, or after the meal. This requirement is not intended to disallow the deduction for a meal consumed while away from home on business.

EXAMPLE 32

Lacy travels to San Francisco for a business convention. She pays for dinner with three colleagues and is not reimbursed by her employer. They do not discuss business. She can deduct 50% of the cost of her meal. However, she cannot deduct the cost of her colleagues' meals. ▼

The *clear business purpose* test requires that meals be directly related to or associated with the active conduct of a business. A meal is not deductible if it serves no business purpose.

ETHICAL CONSIDERATIONS

Reciprocal Entertaining

Walter (an attorney), Susan (an insurance broker), Richard (a realtor), and Nancy (a banker) are all good friends and do business with each other. Richard's accountant suggests that each might derive a substantial tax benefit if they went to lunch together as often as possible and rotated the tab. Do you believe the procedure suggested by Richard's accountant is proper? Why or why not?

The taxpayer or an employee must be present at the business meal for the meal to be deductible.[36] An independent contractor who renders significant services to the taxpayer is treated as an employee.

EXAMPLE 33

Lance, a party to a contract negotiation, buys dinner for other parties to the negotiation but does not attend the dinner. No deduction is allowed. ▼

[35] § 274(k).

[36] § 274(k)(1)(B).

Club Dues. In 1993, Congress amended the Code to provide: "No deduction shall be allowed . . . for amounts paid or incurred for membership in any club organized for business, pleasure, recreation, or other social purpose."[37] Although this prohibition seems quite broad, the IRS does not intend to deny a deduction for dues to clubs whose primary purpose is public service and community volunteerism (e.g., Kiwanis, Lions, Rotary).

Even though dues no longer are deductible, actual entertainment at a club may qualify.

EXAMPLE 34 During the current year, Vincent spent $1,400 on business lunches at the Lakeside Country Club. The annual membership fee was $6,000, and Vincent used the facility 60% of the time for business. Presuming the lunches meet the business meal test, Vincent may claim $700 (50% × $1,400) as a deduction. None of the club dues are deductible. ▼

Ticket Purchases for Entertainment. A deduction for the cost of a ticket for an entertainment activity is limited to the face value of the ticket.[38] This limitation is applied before the 50 percent rule. The face value of a ticket includes any tax. Under this rule, the excess payment to a scalper for a ticket is not deductible. Similarly, the fee to a ticket agency for the purchase of a ticket is not deductible.

Expenditures for the rental or use of a luxury skybox at a sports arena in excess of the face value of regular tickets are disallowed as deductions. If a luxury skybox is used for entertainment that is directly related to or associated with business, the deduction is limited to the face value of nonluxury box seats. All seats in the luxury skybox are counted, even when some seats are unoccupied.

The taxpayer may also deduct stated charges for food and beverages under the general rules for business entertainment. The deduction for skybox seats, food, and beverages is limited to 50 percent of cost.

EXAMPLE 35 In the current year, Condor Company pays $6,000 to rent a 10-seat skybox at City Stadium for three football games. Nonluxury box seats at each event range in cost from $25 to $35 a seat. In March, a Condor representative and five clients use the skybox for the first game. The entertainment follows a bona fide business discussion, and Condor spends $86 for food and beverages during the game. The deduction for the first sports event is as follows:

Food and beverages	$ 86
Deduction for seats ($35 × 10 seats)	350
Total entertainment expense	$436
50% limitation	×.50
Deduction	$218

▼

Business Gifts. Business gifts are deductible to the extent of $25 per donee per year.[39] An exception is made for gifts costing $4 or less (e.g., pens with the employee's or company's name on them) or promotional materials. Such items are not treated as business gifts subject to the $25 limitation. In addition, incidental costs such as engraving of jewelry and nominal charges for gift-wrapping, mailing, and delivery are not included in the cost of the gift in applying the limitation. Gifts to superiors and employers are not deductible.

Records must be maintained to substantiate business gifts.

[37] § 274(a)(3).
[38] § 274(l).
[39] § 274(b)(1).

Other Employee Expenses

OFFICE IN THE HOME

7 Learning Objective
Identify other employee expenses.

Employees and self-employed individuals are not allowed a deduction for **office in the home expenses** unless a portion of the residence is used *exclusively* on a *regular basis* as either:

- The principal place of business for any trade or business of the taxpayer.
- A place of business used by clients, patients, or customers.

Employees must meet an additional test: The use must be for the *convenience of the employer* rather than merely being "appropriate and helpful."[40]

The precise meaning of "principal place of business" was resolved by the U.S. Supreme Court. In a divided opinion, the Court established a two-pronged test.[41] First, determine the relative importance of the activities performed at each business location (i.e., inside and outside the personal residence). Second, compare the time spent at each business location.

Example 36

Dr. Smith is a self-employed anesthesiologist. During the year, he spends 30 to 35 hours per week administering anesthesia and postoperative care to patients in three hospitals, none of which provides him with an office. He also spends two to three hours per day in a room in his home that he uses exclusively as an office. He does not meet patients there, but he performs a variety of tasks related to his medical practice (e.g., contacting surgeons, bookkeeping, reading medical journals). None of Dr. Smith's expenses of the office in the home are deductible because the hospital procedures (i.e., administering to patients) are more important than those done at home. Also, more business time is spent outside the home than inside. ▼

Example 37

Lori is a salesperson. Her only office is a room in her home that she uses regularly and exclusively to set up appointments, store product samples, and write up orders and other reports for the companies whose products she sells. Lori makes most of her sales to customers by telephone or mail from her home office. She spends an average of 30 hours a week working at home and 12 hours a week visiting prospective customers to deliver products and occasionally take orders. Under these circumstances, Lori qualifies for the office in the home deduction. Visiting customers is less important to the business than the activities conducted in Lori's office.[42] ▼

The exclusive use requirement means that a specific part of the home must be used *solely* for business purposes. A deduction, if permitted, requires an allocation of total expenses of operating the home between business and personal use based on floor space or number of rooms.

Even if the taxpayer meets the above requirements, the allowable home office expenses cannot exceed the gross income from the business less all other business expenses attributable to the activity. Furthermore, the home office expenses that are allowed as itemized deductions anyway (e.g., mortgage interest and real estate taxes) must be deducted first. All home office expenses of an employee are miscellaneous itemized deductions, except those (such as interest and taxes) that

---

[40] § 280A(c)(1).

[41] *Comm. v. Soliman*, 93–1 USTC ¶50,014, 71 AFTR2d 93–463, 113 S.Ct. 701 (USSC, 1993) *rev'g*. 91–1 USTC ¶50,291, 67 AFTR2d 91–1112, 935 F.2d 52 (CA–4, 1991) and 94 T.C. 20 (1990).

[42] Notice 93–12, 1993–1 C.B. 298 amplified by Rev.Rul. 94–24, 1994–1 C.B. 87.

TAX IN THE NEWS

HAS THE SUPREME COURT GONE TOO FAR?

In the *Soliman* decision, the U.S. Supreme Court severely restricted the deductibility of an office in the home. Did the Court go too far? Representative Peter Hoagland (D-Neb.) and Senator Orrin Hatch (R-Utah) seem to think so, since they are co-sponsoring legislation that would relax the rules. Under the proposed bills, a home office deduction would be allowed in circumstances where management activities carried on from the home office are a significant part of the entire business.

qualify as other personal itemized deductions. Home office expenses of a self-employed individual are trade or business expenses and are deductible *for* AGI.

Any disallowed home office expenses are *carried forward* and used in future years subject to the same limitations.

EXAMPLE 38

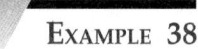

Rick is a certified public accountant employed by a regional CPA firm as a tax manager. He operates a separate business in which he refinishes furniture in his home. For this business, he uses two rooms in the basement of his home exclusively and regularly. The floor space of the two rooms constitutes 10% of the floor space of his residence. Gross income from the business totals $8,000. Expenses of the business (other than home office expenses) are $6,500. Rick incurs the following home office expenses:

Real property taxes on residence	$4,000
Interest expense on residence	7,500
Operating expenses of residence	2,000
Depreciation on residence (based on 10% business use)	250

Rick's deductions are determined as follows:

Business income		$ 8,000
Less: Other business expenses		(6,500)
		$ 1,500
Less: Allocable taxes ($4,000 × 10%)	$400	
Allocable interest ($7,500 × 10%)	750	(1,150)
		$ 350
Allocable operating expenses of the residence ($2,000 × 10%)		(200)
		$ 150
Allocable depreciation ($250, limited to remaining income)		(150)
		$ -0-

Rick has a carryover of $100 (the unused excess depreciation). Because he is self-employed, the allocable taxes and interest ($1,150), the other deductible office expenses ($200 + $150), and $6,500 of other business expenses are deductible *for* AGI. ▼

Form 8829 (Expenses for Business Use of Your Home) is available from the IRS for computation of the office in the home deduction.

The home office limitation cannot be circumvented by leasing part of one's home to an employer, using it as a home office, and deducting the expenses as a rental expense under § 212.

MISCELLANEOUS EMPLOYEE EXPENSES

Deductible miscellaneous employee expenses include special clothing and its upkeep, union dues, and professional expenses. Also deductible are professional dues, professional meetings, and employment agency fees for seeking employment in the same trade or business, whether or not a new job is secured.

To be deductible, *special clothing* must be both specifically required as a condition of employment and not adaptable for regular wear. For example, a police officer's uniform is not suitable for off-duty activities. An exception is clothing used to the extent that it takes the place of regular clothing (e.g., military uniforms).

EXAMPLE 39

Captain Roberts is on active duty in the U.S. Marines. The cost of his regular uniforms is not deductible since such clothing is suitable for regular wear. Military regulations, however, generally preclude marines from wearing battle fatigues when they are off the military base. The cost of the fatigues, to the extent it exceeds any clothing allowance, qualifies as a deduction. ▼

The current position of the IRS is that expenses incurred in *seeking employment* are deductible if the taxpayer is seeking employment in the same trade or business. The deduction is allowed whether or not the attempts to secure employment are successful. An unemployed taxpayer can take a deduction providing there has been no substantial lack of continuity between the last job and the search for a new one. No deduction is allowed for persons seeking their first job or seeking employment in a new trade or business.

The basic cost of one *telephone* in the home is not deductible, even if used for business. Any long-distance or toll charges relating to business are deductible.

CONTRIBUTIONS TO INDIVIDUAL RETIREMENT ACCOUNTS

An important and popular deduction *for* AGI is the amount contributed to an Individual Retirement Account (IRA). This amount may be as great as $2,000 per year for an individual (or $2,250 for spousal IRAs). IRAs are covered in detail in Chapter 19.

CLASSIFICATION OF EMPLOYEE EXPENSES

8 LEARNING OBJECTIVE
Appreciate the difference between accountable and nonaccountable employee plans.

The classification of employee expenses depends on whether they are reimbursed by the employer under an accountable plan. If so, then they are not reported by the employee at all. In effect, therefore, this result is equivalent to treating the expenses as deductions *for* AGI.[43] If the expenses are reimbursed under a nonaccountable plan or are not reimbursed at all, then they are classified as deductions *from* AGI and can only be claimed if the employee-taxpayer itemizes. An exception is made for moving expenses and the employment-related expenses of a qualified performing artist.[44] Here, deduction *for* AGI classification is allowed.

[43] § 62(a)(2).

[44] As defined in § 62(b).

For classification purposes, therefore, the difference between accountable and nonaccountable plans is significant.

ACCOUNTABLE PLANS

In General. An **accountable plan** requires the employee to satisfy these two requirements:

- Adequately account for (substantiate) the expenses. An employee renders an *adequate accounting* by submitting a record, with receipts and other substantiation, to the employer.[45]
- Return any excess reimbursement or allowance. An "excess reimbursement or allowance" is any amount that the employee does not adequately account for as an ordinary and necessary business expense.

Substantiation. The law provides that no deduction is allowed for any travel, entertainment, business gift, or listed property (automobiles, computers) expenditure unless properly substantiated by adequate records. The records should contain the following information:[46]

- The amount of the expense.
- The time and place of travel or entertainment (or date of gift).
- The business purpose of the expense.
- The business relationship of the taxpayer to the person entertained (or receiving the gift).

This means the taxpayer must maintain an account book or diary in which the above information is recorded at the time of the expenditure. Documentary evidence, such as itemized receipts, is required to support any expenditure for lodging while traveling away from home and for any other expenditure of $75 or more. If a taxpayer fails to keep adequate records, each expense must be established by a written or oral statement of the exact details of the expense and by other corroborating evidence.[47]

EXAMPLE 40

Bertha has travel expenses substantiated only by canceled checks. The checks establish the date, place, and amount of the expenditure. Because neither the business relationship nor the business purpose is established, the deduction is disallowed.[48] ▼

EXAMPLE 41

Dwight has travel and entertainment expenses substantiated by a diary showing the time, place, and amount of the expenditure. His oral testimony provides the business relationship and business purpose; however, since he has no receipts, any expenditures of $75 or more are disallowed.[49] ▼

Deemed Substantiation. In lieu of reimbursing actual expenses for travel away from home, many employers reduce their paperwork by adopting a policy of reimbursing employees with a *per diem* allowance, a flat dollar amount per day of business travel. Of the substantiation requirements listed above, the *amount* of the expense is proved, or *deemed substantiated*, by using such a per diem allowance

---

[45] Reg. § 1.162–17(b)(4).
[46] § 274(d).
[47] Reg. § 1.274–5T(c)(3).
[48] *William T. Whitaker*, 56 TCM 47, T.C.Memo. 1988–418.
[49] *W. David Tyler*, 43 TCM 927, T.C.Memo. 1982–160.

TAX IN THE NEWS

NO THANKS FOR THE FAVOR

A taxpayer must have documentary evidence (i.e., a receipt) when a travel or entertainment item is $75 or more. The threshold amount used to be $25 or more but was recently changed to reduce taxpayers' recordkeeping burden. The change, announced in Notice 95–50 (I.R.B. No. 42, 8), is effective for expenditures incurred on or after October 1, 1995.

Many businesses that previously followed the IRS receipt threshold for purposes of reimbursing their employees will not conform to the change. In effect, they will retain the prior $25 rule. Companies fear that if they adopt the change, what used to be a $24.95 lunch will become a $74.95 lunch.

or reimbursement procedure. The amount of expenses that is deemed substantiated is equal to the lesser of the per diem allowance or the amount of the Federal per diem rate.

The regular Federal per diem rate is the highest amount that the Federal government will pay to its employees for lodging and meals[50] while in travel status away from home in a particular area. The rates are different for different locations.[51]

The use of the standard Federal per diem for meals constitutes an adequate accounting. Employees and self-employed persons can use the standard meal allowance instead of deducting the actual cost of daily meals, even if not reimbursed. There is no standard lodging allowance, however.

Only the amount of the expense is considered substantiated under the deemed substantiated method. The other substantiation requirements must be provided: place, date, business purpose of the expense, and the business relationship of the parties involved.

NONACCOUNTABLE PLANS

A **nonaccountable plan** is one in which an adequate accounting or return of excess amounts, or both, is not required. All reimbursements of expenses are reported in full as wages on the employee's Form W–2. Any allowable expenses are deductible in the same manner as are unreimbursed expenses.

Unreimbursed Employee Expenses. Unreimbursed employee expenses are treated in a straightforward manner. Meals and entertainment expenses are subject to the 50 percent limit. Total unreimbursed employee business expenses are usually reported as miscellaneous itemized deductions subject to the 2 percent-of-AGI floor (see below). If the employee could have received, but did not seek, reimbursement for whatever reason, none of the employment-related expenses are deductible.

[50] The meals per diem rate also covers incidental expenses, including laundry and cleaning of clothing and tips for waiters. Taxi fares and telephone calls are not included.

[51] Each current edition of *Per Diem Rates* (IRS Publication 1542) contains the list and amounts for that year.

ETHICAL CONSIDERATIONS

The Frugal Employee

Wally is employed by Harrier Corporation as a regional sales manager. As such, he does a great deal of entertaining of both sales representatives and key clients. Harrier has a policy of reimbursing its employees for these expenses upon the rendition of an adequate accounting.

Wally does not submit all of his entertainment expenses, however, because he wants higher management to think he is frugal and efficient in utilizing company funds. Wally has no reason to believe that the company would have refused to reimburse the expenses he has not submitted. Harrier Corporation has never turned down any of Wally's expense vouchers.

On his Federal income tax return, Wally deducts the expenses not reimbursed. The return reflects nothing as to the reimbursed expenses.

Has Wally handled this tax matter properly? Why?

Failure to Comply with Accountable Plan Requirements. An employer may have an accountable plan and require employees to return excess reimbursements or allowances, but an employee may fail to follow the rules of the plan. In that case, the expenses and reimbursements are subject to nonaccountable plan treatment.

REPORTING PROCEDURES

The reporting requirements range from no reporting at all (accountable plans when all requirements are met) to the use of some or all of the following forms: Form W–2 (Wage and Tax Statement), Form 2106 (Employee Business Expenses) or Form 2106–EZ (Unreimbursed Employee Business Expenses), and Schedule A (Itemized Deductions) for nonaccountable plans and unreimbursed employee expenses.

Reimbursed employee expenses that are adequately accounted for under an accountable plan are deductible *for* AGI on Form 2106. Allowed excess expenses, expenses reimbursed under a nonaccountable plan, and unreimbursed expenses are deductible *from* AGI on Schedule A, subject to the 2 percent-of-AGI floor.

When a reimbursement under an accountable plan is paid in separate amounts relating to designated expenses such as meals or entertainment, no problem arises. The reimbursements and expenses are reported as such on the appropriate forms. If the reimbursement is made in a single amount, an allocation must be made to determine the appropriate portion of the reimbursement that applies to meals and entertainment and to other employee expenses.

EXAMPLE 42

Elizabeth, who is employed by Green Company, had AGI of $42,000. During the year, she incurred $2,000 of transportation and lodging expense and $1,000 of meals and entertainment expense, all fully substantiated. Elizabeth received $1,800 reimbursement under an accountable plan. The reimbursement rate that applies to meals and entertainment is 33.33% ($1,000 meals and entertainment expense/$3,000 total expenses). Thus, $600 ($1,800 × 33.33%) of the reimbursement applies to meals and entertainment, and $1,200 ($1,800 – $600) applies to transportation and lodging. Elizabeth's itemized deduction consists of the $800 ($2,000 total – $1,200 reimbursement) of unreimbursed transportation and lodging expenses and $400 ($1,000 – $600) of unreimbursed meal and entertainment expenses as follows:

Transportation and lodging	$ 800
Meals and entertainment ($400 × 50%)	200
Total (reported on Form 2106)	$1,000
Less: 2% of $42,000 AGI (see limitation discussed below)	(840)
Deduction (reported on Schedule A)	$ 160

In summary, Elizabeth reports $3,000 of expenses and the $1,800 reimbursement on Form 2106 and $160 as a miscellaneous itemized deduction on Schedule A. ▼

Limitations on Itemized Deductions

9 **Learning Objective**
Work with the limitations on miscellaneous itemized deductions.

Many itemized deductions, such as medical expenses and charitable contributions, are subject to limitations expressed as a percentage of AGI. These limitations may be expressed as floors or ceilings. These limitations are discussed in Chapter 10.

MISCELLANEOUS ITEMIZED DEDUCTIONS SUBJECT TO THE 2 PERCENT FLOOR

Certain miscellaneous itemized deductions, including most *unreimbursed employee business expenses,* are aggregated and then reduced by 2 percent of AGI.[52] Expenses subject to the 2 percent floor include the following:

- All § 212 expenses, except expenses of producing rent and royalty income (refer to Chapter 6).
- All unreimbursed employee expenses (after the 50 percent reduction, if applicable) except moving.
- Professional dues and subscriptions.
- Union dues and work uniforms.
- Employment-related education expenses.
- Malpractice insurance premiums.
- Expenses of job hunting (including employment agency fees and resumé-writing expenses).
- Home office expenses of an employee or outside salesperson.
- Legal, accounting, and tax return preparation fees.
- Hobby expenses (up to hobby income).
- Investment expenses, including investment counsel fees, subscriptions, and safe deposit box rental.
- Custodial fees relating to income-producing property or an IRA or a Keogh plan.
- Any fees paid to collect interest or dividends.
- Appraisal fees establishing a casualty loss or charitable contribution.

MISCELLANEOUS ITEMIZED DEDUCTIONS NOT SUBJECT TO THE 2 PERCENT FLOOR

Certain miscellaneous itemized deductions, including the following, are not subject to the 2 percent floor:

[52] § 67.

- Impairment-related work expenses of handicapped individuals.
- Gambling losses to the extent of gambling winnings.
- Certain terminated annuity payments.

EXAMPLE 43

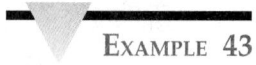

Ted, who has AGI of $20,000, has the following miscellaneous itemized deductions:

Gambling losses (to extent of gains)	$ 1,200
Tax return preparation fees	300
Unreimbursed employee transportation	200
Professional dues and subscriptions	260
Safe deposit box rental	30

Ted's itemized deductions are as follows:

Deduction not subject to 2% floor (gambling losses)		$1,200
Deductions subject to 2% floor ($300 + $200 + $260 + $30)	$ 790	
Less 2% of AGI	(400)	390
Total miscellaneous itemized deductions		$1,590

If instead Ted's AGI is $40,000, the floor is $800 (2% of $40,000), and he cannot deduct any expenses subject to the 2% floor. ▼

TAX PLANNING CONSIDERATIONS

SELF-EMPLOYED INDIVIDUALS

10 LEARNING OBJECTIVE
Develop tax planning ideas related to employee business expenses.

Some taxpayers have the flexibility to be classified as either employees or self-employed individuals. Examples include real estate agents and direct sellers. These taxpayers should carefully consider all factors and not automatically assume that self-employed status is preferable.

It is advantageous to deduct one's business expenses *for* AGI and avoid the 2 percent floor. However, a self-employed individual may have higher expenses, such as local gross receipts taxes, license fees, franchise fees, personal property taxes, and occupation taxes. The record-keeping and filing requirements can be quite burdensome.

One of the most expensive considerations is the Social Security tax versus the self-employment tax. For an employee in 1996, for example, the Social Security tax applies at a rate of 6.2 percent on a base amount of wages of $62,700, and the Medicare tax applies at a rate of 1.45 percent with no limit on the base amount. For self-employed persons, the rate, but not the base amount, for each tax doubles. Even though a deduction *for* AGI is allowed for one-half of the self-employment tax paid, an employee and a self-employed individual are not in the same tax position on equal amounts of earnings. The self-employment tax is explained in Chapter 13. For the applicability of these taxes to employees, see Chapter 1.

After analyzing all these factors, a taxpayer may decide that employee status is preferable to self-employed status.

SHIFTING DEDUCTIONS BETWEEN EMPLOYER AND EMPLOYEE

An employee can avoid the 2 percent floor for employee business expenses. Typically, an employee incurs travel and entertainment expenses in the course of employment. The employer gets the deduction if it reimburses the employee, and the employee gets the deduction *for* AGI. An adequate accounting must be made, and excess reimbursements cannot be kept.

TRANSPORTATION AND TRAVEL EXPENSES

Adequate detailed records of all transportation and travel expenses should be kept. Since the regular mileage allowance is 31 cents per mile, a new, expensive automobile used primarily for business may generate a higher expense based on actual cost. The election to expense part of the cost of the automobile under § 179, MACRS depreciation, insurance, repairs and maintenance, automobile club dues, and other related costs may result in automobile expenses greater than the automatic mileage allowance.

If a taxpayer wishes to sightsee or vacation on a business trip, it would be beneficial to schedule business on both a Friday and a Monday to turn the weekend into business days for allocation purposes. It is especially crucial to schedule appropriate business days when foreign travel is involved.

MOVING EXPENSES

Persons who retire and move to a new location incur personal nondeductible moving expenses. If the retired person accepts a full-time job in the new location before moving, the moving expenses are deductible.

EXAMPLE 44

At the time of his retirement from the national office of a major accounting firm, Gordon had an annual salary of $220,000. He moves from New York City to Seattle to retire. To qualify for the moving expense deduction, Gordon accepts a full-time teaching position at a Seattle junior college at an annual salary of $15,000. If Gordon satisfies the 39-week test, his moving expenses are deductible. The disparity between the two salaries (previous and current) is of no consequence. ▼

EDUCATION EXPENSES

Education expenses are treated as nondeductible personal items unless the individual is employed or is engaged in a trade or business. A temporary leave of absence for further education is one way to reasonably assure that the taxpayer is still qualified, even if a full-time student. An individual was permitted to deduct education expenses even though he resigned from his job, returned to school full-time for two years, and accepted another job in the same field upon graduation. The Court held that the student had merely suspended active participation in his field.[53]

If the time out of the field is too long, educational expense deductions will be disallowed. For example, a teacher who left the field for four years to raise her child and curtailed her employment searches and writing activities was denied a deduction. She was not actively engaged in the trade or business of being an educator.[54]

To secure the deduction, an individual should arrange his or her work situation to preserve employee or business status.

ENTERTAINMENT EXPENSES

Proper documentation of expenditures is essential because of the strict recordkeeping requirements and the restrictive tests that must be met. For example, documentation that consists solely of credit card receipts and canceled checks may be inadequate to substantiate the business purpose and business relationship.[55]

---

[53] *Stephen G. Sherman*, 36 TCM 1191, T.C.Memo. 1977–301.

[54] *Brian C. Mulherin*, 42 TCM 834, T.C.Memo. 1981–454; *George A. Baist*, 56 TCM 778, T.C.Memo. 1988–554.

[55] *Kenneth W. Guenther*, 54 TCM 382, T.C.Memo. 1987–440.

Taxpayers should maintain detailed records of amounts, time, place, business purpose, and business relationships. A credit card receipt details the place, date, and amount of the expense. A notation made on the receipt of the names of the person(s) attending, the business relationship, and the topic of discussion should constitute proper documentation.

Associated with or goodwill entertainment is not deductible unless a business discussion is conducted immediately before or after the entertainment. Furthermore, a business purpose must exist for the entertainment. Taxpayers should arrange for a business discussion before or after such entertainment. They must provide documentation of the business purpose, such as obtaining new business from a prospective customer.

Unreimbursed meals and entertainment are subject to the 50 percent rule in addition to the 2 percent floor. Consequently, the procedure of negotiating a salary reduction, as discussed below under Unreimbursed Employee Business Expenses, is even more valuable to the taxpayer.

UNREIMBURSED EMPLOYEE BUSINESS EXPENSES

The 2 percent floor for unreimbursed employee business expenses offers a tax planning opportunity for married couples. If one spouse has high miscellaneous expenses subject to the floor, it may be beneficial for the couple to file separate returns. If they file jointly, the 2 percent floor is based on the incomes of both. Filing separately lowers the reduction to 2 percent of only one spouse's income.

Other provisions of the law should be considered, however. For example, filing separately could cost a couple losses of up to $25,000 from self-managed rental units under the passive activity loss rules (discussed in Chapter 11).

Another possibility is to negotiate a salary reduction with one's employer in exchange for the 100 percent reimbursement of employee expenses. The employee is better off because the 2 percent floor does not apply. The employer is better off because certain expense reimbursements are not subject to Social Security and other payroll taxes.

17 109 16 107 15 81 12 65 6 5 44 42

KEY TERMS

Accountable plan, 9–22

Automatic mileage method, 9–5

Education expenses, 9–12

Entertainment expenses, 9–15

Independent contractor, 9–2

Moving expenses, 9–10

Nonaccountable plan, 9–23

Office in the home expenses, 9–19

Statutory employees, 9–3

Transportation expenses, 9–4

Travel expenses, 9–6

PROBLEM MATERIALS

DISCUSSION QUESTIONS

research?

1. Why might a business prefer to classify a worker as an independent contractor (i.e., self-employed) rather than as an employee?
2. What difference does it make if an individual's expenses are classified as employment-related expenses or as expenses from self-employment?

3. Discuss the factors that may indicate an employer-employee relationship.

4. Walter is employed by an accounting firm in downtown Birmingham. Occasionally during tax season, Walter tries to save time by not going first to his office. Instead, he goes directly from his home to the client's business location. Are any of Walter's automobile expenses deductible? Explain.

5. Dawn just purchased a new automobile for use in her business. For the first few years, she plans to use the automatic mileage method for tax purposes. Then she plans to switch to the actual operating cost method and depreciate the original cost of the automobile. Is Dawn's understanding of the tax rules correct? Why or why not?

6. Distinguish between transportation expenses and travel expenses.

7. Under the "away-from-home" requirement, what is the significance of the "overnight" concept? What does "overnight" require?

8. Jim works in St. Louis. On Tuesday morning he flies to San Francisco for a business meeting. After the meeting, Jim has lunch by himself and then flies back to St. Louis that same evening. Is the cost of Jim's lunch deductible? Why or why not?

9. Refer to the facts set forth in Example 12 (page 9–8 of the text). What are some of the things Bill might do to avoid the potential tax disaster he faces?

10. Dr. Fuerst, a practicing orthodontist in Buffalo, travels to New York City to attend a two-day convention on experimental orthodontia procedures. Mr. Fuerst accompanies his wife since he prepares their tax return and knows how to properly prepare the required substantiation for the trip. Comment on the deductibility of the trip.

11. If any pleasure is involved, then the travel deduction is not allowed. Comment on the validity of this statement.

12. Josephine took a combined business and pleasure trip to Europe. She traveled to London from New York on Friday, vacationed on Saturday and Sunday, conducted business on Monday, got snowed in at the airport on Tuesday, traveled to Paris on Wednesday, relaxed on Thursday (a legal holiday), conducted business on Friday, went sightseeing on Saturday and Sunday, picked up business samples and papers on Monday, and flew back to New York on Tuesday. What portion of her air fare can she deduct?

13. What is the distance test for moving expenses?

14. For moving expenses to be deductible, a time test must be met.
    a. What is this test?
    b. Does it matter whether the taxpayer is employed or self-employed? Why?
    c. When, if ever, is the time test suspended?

15. What difference does it make whether a taxpayer is improving existing skills or acquiring new ones for the purpose of the education deduction? On what general tax principle is the justification for this rule based?

16. What expenses can qualify for the education deduction?

17. In each of the following situations, indicate whether there is a cutback adjustment and, if so, to whom it applies (i.e., employer or employee).
    a. The employer expects certain employees to entertain their key customers. The employer does not reimburse the employees for these costs.
    b. Same as (a) except that the employees are reimbursed for these costs.
    c. Each year the employer awards its top salesperson an expense-paid trip to the Cayman Islands.
    d. The employer has a cafeteria for its employees where meals are furnished at cost.
    e. The employer sponsors an annual Fourth of July picnic for its employees.
    f. Every Christmas, the employer gives each employee a turkey.

18. Discuss the difference between entertainment that is *directly related to* business and entertainment that is *associated with* business.

19. Discuss the requirements for the deductibility of business meals.

20. Currently, which club dues are deductible? Not deductible?
21. Sandra pays annual dues to belong to the Wichita Country Club. In addition to social and leisure activities, she also utilizes the facilities for business lunches. Presuming adequate substantiation, are any of Sandra's expenses involving the club deductible? Explain.
22. What limits are imposed on the deduction of expenses for tickets purchased for business entertainment? How are such expenses treated on an employee's return if they are reimbursed? Not reimbursed?
23. To what extent may a taxpayer take a deduction for business gifts to a business associate? To an employee? To a superior?
24. Lieutenant Hebert is on active duty with the U.S. Navy. To what extent, if any, is the cost of her uniforms deductible?
25. Cynthia, a CPA, is currently employed by a public accounting firm. On a part-time basis, she earns a law degree. After attending a bar review course, she takes and passes the state bar exam. Currently, she is incurring costs in seeking employment with a law firm. Comment on the deductibility to Cynthia of each of the following expenditures:
    a. The cost of attending law school.
    b. The cost of the bar review course.
    c. The cost of seeking employment with a law firm.
26. What constitutes an adequate accounting to an employer?
27. What tax return reporting procedures must be followed by an employee under the following circumstances?
    a. Expenses and reimbursements are equal under an accountable plan.
    b. Reimbursements at the appropriate Federal per diem rate exceed expenses, and an adequate accounting is made to the employer.
    c. Expenses exceed reimbursements under a nonaccountable plan.
28. Kim has just graduated from college and is interviewing for a position in marketing. Crane Corporation has offered her a job as a sales representative that will require extensive travel and entertainment but provide valuable experience. Under the offer, she has two options: a salary of $48,000 and she absorbs all expenses; a salary of $35,000 and Crane reimburses for all expenses. Crane assures Kim that the $13,000 difference in the two options will be adequate to cover the expenses incurred. What issues should have an impact on Kim's choice?
29. Jeff has been practicing as a physician in Boston. Shortly, he plans to sell his practice to his partners and retire in Taos, New Mexico. Besides the sale of his practice, what should be some of Jeff's concerns?
30. Martha is an associate with a law firm in New York City. Although she already has a J.D. degree, she feels a master of laws from New York University would improve her promotion potential. Although she can earn the degree on a part-time basis, Martha is inclined to shorten her career interruption as much as possible. What should be some of Martha's concerns?

PROBLEMS

31. To support his family, Horace holds two jobs during 1996. The relevant distances are as follows:

	Miles
Residence to main job	40
Main job to second job	30
Second job to residence	45

During the 260 days he worked, Horace drove the family car from his residence to the main job. After eight hours, Horace then drove to the second job and worked for four hours. On his way back to the residence, he stopped for dinner. He paid $390 for parking at the second job and $1,100 for dinners. What, if any, is Horace's deduction for the year?

32. Alec has two jobs in 1996. He drives 40 miles to his first job. The distance from the first job to the second is 32 miles. During 1996, Alec worked 200 days at both jobs. On 150 days, he drove from the first job to the second job. On the remaining 50 days, he drove home (40 miles) and then to the second job (42 miles). Presuming the automatic mileage method is used, how much qualifies as a deduction?

33. Erlyne purchased a new automobile for $17,000 in 1993. She used it 70% for business purposes, driving 13,000 business miles in 1993, 11,000 business miles in 1994, 9,000 business miles in 1995, and 8,000 business miles in 1996.

    Erlyne used the automatic mileage method for all years. What is the adjusted basis of the business portion of her automobile on January 1, 1997?

34. Louis took a business trip from Chicago to Seattle. He spent two days in travel, conducted business for eight days, and visited friends for five days. He incurred the following expenses:

Air fare	$ 950
Lodging	2,400
Meals	1,200
Entertainment of clients	800

Louis received no reimbursements. What amount can he deduct?

35. Nadine took a business trip of 10 days. Seven days were spent on business (including travel time) and 3 days were personal. Her unreimbursed expenses were as follows:

Air fare	$3,200
Lodging (per day)	300
Meals (per day)	210
Entertainment of clients	900

a. How much can Nadine deduct if the trip is within the United States?
b. How much can she deduct if the trip is outside the United States?

36. Hal, an investment counselor, attended a conference on the impact of the new tax law on investment choices. His unreimbursed expenses were as follows:

Air fare	$350
Lodging	450
Meals	330
Tuition and fees	410

a. How much can Hal deduct on his return? Are the expenses *for* or *from* AGI?
b. Would your answer differ if Hal were a self-employed physician?

37. Ricardo, a professor of Spanish history, went to Spain during the year to research documents available only in Spain. His time on the trip was spent entirely on business. No vacation days were involved, and Ricardo kept adequate records. Ricardo received no reimbursements for the following carefully documented expenses:

Air fare and other transportation	$2,600
Hotels	1,800
Meals	1,200

a. What can Ricardo deduct if he has AGI of $40,000 and no other miscellaneous itemized deductions? Are the deductions *for* or *from* AGI?
b. Would your answer differ if Ricardo had gone to Spain to soak up the culture and brush up on his Spanish?

38. Monica travels from her office in Boston to Lisbon, Portugal, on business. Her absence of 13 days was spent as follows:

Thursday	Depart for and arrive at Lisbon
Friday	Business transacted
Saturday and Sunday	Vacationing
Monday through Friday	Business transacted
Saturday and Sunday	Vacationing
Monday	Business transacted
Tuesday	Depart Lisbon and return to office in Boston

a. For tax purposes, how many days has Monica spent on business?
b. What difference does it make?
c. Could Monica have spent more time than she did vacationing on the trip without loss of existing tax benefits? Explain.

39. During 1996, Eric changed jobs and moved from San Francisco to Rochester, New York. Eric had the following expenses in connection with the move:

Cost of moving household effects	$3,600
Transportation	1,200
Meals	400
Lodging	600

Presume the time test is satisfied and Eric is not reimbursed for these expenses.
a. What, if any, is Eric's deduction?
b. How is the deduction, if any, classified?

40. To satisfy a newly imposed school board requirement, Arthur spends part of the summer at a college pursuing a master of education degree. Arthur, a high school math teacher, spent the following amounts:

Books and tuition	$2,200
Lodging while in travel status	1,500
Meals while in travel status	1,100
Laundry while in travel status	300
Transportation	700

a. How much of these amounts may Arthur deduct?
b. How is the deduction classified?

41. Warren is a self-employed CPA whose practice primarily involves tax matters. During the year, he attended a three-day tax seminar and incurred the following expenses:

Lodging	$305
Meals	250
Course registration (including materials)	520
Transportation	105

Since the seminar was conducted out-of-town, Warren had to obtain lodging.

Warren is convinced that obtaining a J.D. degree would improve his skills as a CPA engaged in tax practice. Consequently, he enrolls as a part-time student at a local law school and begins taking courses. During the current year, he spent $2,850 for tuition and $420 for books and supplies.

How much can Warren deduct for these transactions?

42. Dorothy is an employee of Cardinal Corporation, a commercial property broker involved in the leasing of office space. She takes a client to dinner and incurs the following expenses:

Taxi (to and from restaurant)	$ 32
Cover charge	40
Meal cost	160
Tip	30

Assume the event is adequately substantiated.
a. If Dorothy is not reimbursed, how much can she claim as a deduction?
b. If Dorothy is reimbursed (under an adequate accounting), how much can Cardinal Corporation claim?

43. Crane Corporation spends $15,000 to purchase a 12-seat skybox for six professional football games. Regular seats at these games normally sell for $30 each. At one game, an employee of Crane entertained eight clients; Crane furnished food and beverages for the event at a cost of $142. The game was preceded by a bona fide business discussion, and all expenses are adequately substantiated.
a. How much may Crane Corporation deduct for this event?
b. Would the answer change if the employee took 11 clients (rather than 8) to the game, and all seats were occupied? Explain.

44. During 1996, Kevin, the assistant manager of a truck leasing firm, made gifts that cost the following amounts:

To Darlene (Kevin's secretary) for Christmas ($2 was for gift wrapping)	$27
To George (Kevin's boss) on his birthday	25
To Susan (a key client) for Christmas	30
To John (a key client) for Christmas	20

Presuming Kevin has adequate substantiation and is not reimbursed, how much can he deduct?

45. Ruth is a professor who consults on the side. She uses one-fifth of her home exclusively for her consulting business, and clients regularly meet her there. Ruth is single and under 65. Her AGI (before considering consulting income) is $50,000. Other relevant data follow:

Income from consulting business	$5,000
Consulting expenses other than home office	2,400
Total costs relating to home	
Interest and taxes	6,000
Utilities	2,000
Maintenance and repairs	600
Depreciation (business part only)	1,500

Calculate Ruth's AGI for 1996.

46. Paige incurred the following expenses related to her employment as a chief executive officer:

Lodging while away from home	$2,800
Meals while away from home	1,200
Entertainment while away from home	2,000
Dues, subscriptions, and books	1,000
Transportation expenses	4,000

Her AGI was $100,000, and she received $6,600 under her employer's accountable plan. What are Paige's deductions *for* and *from* AGI?

47. Kenneth received $4,400 in reimbursements under an accountable plan after he had made an adequate accounting to his employer. His expenses were as follows:

Transportation expenses	$3,200
Meals	1,400
Lodging and incidentals	2,300
Dues, phone, and subscriptions	100
Entertainment	1,000

How much can Kenneth deduct *for* and *from* AGI? Assume he had AGI of $50,000 and no other miscellaneous itemized deductions.

48. Thelma, who is age 42 and single, earned a salary of $60,000. She had other income consisting of interest of $2,000, dividends of $1,600, and long-term capital gains of $4,000.

Thelma incurred the following expenses during the year:

Transportation	$2,300
Meals	1,600
Dues and subscriptions	800
Entertainment of clients	300
Total	$5,000

Thelma received reimbursements of $3,000 under an accountable plan. Calculate her AGI and itemized employee business expenses.

49. Kyle and Sharon are married, have no dependents, and are full-time employees. Both work for employers who do not reimburse for job-related costs but expect the employee to absorb the expenses. Kyle and Sharon's expenses for 1996 are as follows:

Kyle's union dues	$610
Kyle's safety items (e.g., work shoes, glasses, gloves)	340
Kyle's lab clothing	405
Laundry of Kyle's lab clothing	120
Sharon's business lunches with clients	1,340
Sharon's professional dues and journals	610
Sharon's taxi fares to and from work (when personal car was being repaired)	160
Other itemized deductions (e.g., interest on home mortgage, property taxes, charitable contributions)	10,200

If Kyle and Sharon file a joint return and have AGI of $72,000, what is their taxable income?

CUMULATIVE PROBLEMS

50. Debra Bond, age 42 and single, is the personnel manager of the northwest regional office of Olympia Insurance Company. Her Social Security number is 432–60–1000. Debra lives in her own home at 524 Wilcrest Drive, Seattle, WA 98122. Lisa Wall, Debra's 20-year-old niece, lives with her and is a full-time student at a local college. Except for a $3,600 nontaxable scholarship Lisa receives for tuition, Debra provides all of her niece's support. Lisa's Social Security number is 444–11–5555.

Olympia Insurance usually does not reimburse its employees for employment-related expenses. Instead, it estimates the expected expenses of each class of employees and sets their base salary accordingly. During 1996, Debra had the following employment-related expenses:

- Mileage of 5,350 on personal auto (includes 3,100 miles for commuting). Parking and toll charges (not related to commuting) are $190.
- Business lunches for potential hires are $1,424. Taxi fares of $132 are not included in this amount.
- Debra attended a three-day seminar on improving managerial skills by using a team approach. The sessions were held at a convention center in Portland, Oregon. Debra's expenses are summarized below:

Transportation	$210
Registration (includes course materials)	750
Meals	290
Hotel	375

- Dues to professional organizations of $205 and subscriptions to professional journals of $310.

In 1996, Debra earned wages of $61,200 (not including any bonus). Usually, Olympia Insurance follows a policy of issuing a bonus to its employees. The bonus for any one year is determined and paid in January of the following year. Debra's bonus for 1995 (received in January of 1996) was $5,900, while her bonus for 1996 (received in January of 1997) was $6,100.

In 1996, Debra had a certificate of deposit with Bank of America that earned $1,400 in interest and received cash dividends of $1,150 from Chevron stock she owns. She also received a check for $120 from Aetna Insurance Company as an adjustment on the homeowners insurance premium she paid in 1995. The carrier had mistakenly overcharged Debra by $120.

Expenditures incurred by Debra in 1996 include the following:

Interest on home mortgage	$6,900
Property taxes on personal residence	2,600
Charitable contributions	1,450
Political contribution to reelect representative to Congress	200

Compute Debra's taxable income for 1996. Suggested software (if available): *TurboTax* or *MacInTax*.

51. George M. and Martha J. Jordan have no dependents and are both under age 65. George is a statutory employee of Consolidated Jobbers (business code is 2634), and his Social Security number is 582–99–4444. Martha is an executive with General Corporation, and her Social Security number is 241–88–6642. The Jordans live at 321 Oak Street, Lincoln, NV 89553. They both want to contribute to the Presidential Election Campaign Fund.

In 1995, George earned $49,000 in commissions. His employer withholds FICA but not Federal income taxes. George paid $10,000 in estimated taxes. Martha earned $62,000, from which $9,000 was withheld for Federal income taxes and the appropriate amount was withheld for FICA taxes. Neither George nor Martha received any expense reimbursements.

George uses his two-year-old car (purchased on January 3, 1993) on sales calls and keeps a log of all miles driven. In 1995, he drove 36,000 miles, 24,554 of them for business. He made several out-of-state sales trips, incurring transportation costs of $1,600, meals of $800, and lodging costs of $750. During the year, he also spent $1,400 taking customers to lunch.

Martha incurred the following expenses related to her work: taxi fares of $125, business lunches of $615, and a yearly commuter train ticket of $800. During the year, Martha received $1,200 in interest from the employees' credit union, $100,000 life insurance proceeds upon the death of her mother in December, and $500 in dividends from General Motors. She contributed $2,000 to her Individual Retirement Account. Neither George nor Martha is covered by an employee retirement plan. Martha gave a gift valued at $500 to the president of her firm upon his promotion to that position.

The Jordans had additional expenditures as follows:

Charitable contributions (cash)	$1,200
Medical and dental expenses	1,400
Real property taxes	1,200
Home mortgage interest	9,381
Tax return preparation fee	150

Part 1—Tax Computation
Compute the Jordans' Federal income tax payable or refund due, assuming they file a joint income tax return for 1995. If they have a refund due, they want the amount refunded. You will need Form 1040, Form 2106, and Schedules A, B, and C. Suggested software (if available): *TurboTax* or *MacInTax*.

Part 2—Tax Planning
Martha and George ask your help in deciding what to do with the $100,000 Martha inherited in 1995. They are considering two conservative investment alternatives:

- Invest in 8% long-term U.S. bonds.
- Invest in 6.5% municipal bonds.

a. Calculate the best alternative for next year. Assume that Martha and George will have the same income and deductions in 1996, except for the income from the investment they choose. In computing the tax, use the tax rate schedules for 1996.
b. What other factors should the Jordans take into account?
c. Write a memo to the Jordans, explaining their alternatives.

Suggested software (if available): *TurboTax* or *MacInTax*.

RESEARCH PROBLEMS

Note: ***West's Federal Taxation on CD-ROM*** *can be used in preparing solutions to the Research Problems. Alternatively, tax research materials contained in a standard tax library can be used.*

Research Problem 1. Hawk Corporation is a consulting business with a national market for its services. Many of Hawk's employees do a great deal of traveling. In this regard, the company has an informal policy of reimbursing its employees for air travel at coach fare rates. However, some of Hawk's employees travel first class, and several use their own private planes.

Hawk Corporation does not want to discourage those employees who fly first class or use private planes. Further, it would like to do everything possible to improve the income tax position of these employees. The company fully expects the affected employees to claim as a deduction the excess of their travel cost over the coach reimbursement received.

Do you have any suggestions as to what Hawk Corporation can do to help those employees who do not fly coach on business trips?

Partial list of research aids:
Rev.Rul. 57–502, 1957–2 C.B. 118.
Rev.Rul. 70–558, 1970–2 C.B. 35.
Robert N. Noyce, 97 T.C. 670 (1991).

Research Problem 2. Alan, a heart specialist, left his job in Texas to accept a position in a California medical center. In addition to seeing patients, he was required to work on the hospital's heart transplant project under the supervision of Dr. Hume. Dr. Hume was an impossible boss, who had already had two other doctors removed from the team. Dr. Hume had Alan terminated from the project after 35 weeks of employment. Will Alan be able to deduct his moving expenses?

Research Problem 3. Rick Beam has been an independent sales representative for various textile manufacturers for many years. His products consist of soft goods, such as tablecloths, curtains, and drapes. Rick's customers are clothing store chains, department stores, and smaller specialty stores. The employees of these companies who are responsible for purchasing merchandise are known as buyers. These companies generally prohibit their buyers from accepting gifts from manufacturers' sales representatives.

Each year Rick gives cash gifts (never more than $25) to most of the buyers who are his customers. Generally, he cashes a large check in November and gives the money personally to the buyers around Christmas. Rick says, "This is one of the ways that I maintain my relationship with my buyers." He maintains adequate substantiation of all the gifts.

Rick's deductions for these gifts have been disallowed by the IRS, based on Code § 162(c)(2). Rick is confused and comes to you, a CPA, for advice.

a. Write a letter to Rick concerning his tax position on this issue.
b. Prepare a memo for your files supporting the advice you have given.

Research Problem 4. Lyle has been a schoolteacher since he earned his bachelor of education degree 10 years ago. In 1993, the governing board of his school district passed a resolution requiring all teachers to begin pursuing an advanced degree in education. Because of this new requirement, Lyle spent the summer of 1994 taking graduate courses in education at a major university. For the summer activity, Lyle *estimates* his expenses to be:

Books	$ 220
Tuition	3,200
Room and board	1,800
Transportation	1,500

Lyle kept no receipts and made no record of these expenses. When he files his income tax return for 1994, Lyle claims all of these expenses on Schedule C of Form 1040.

In the event Lyle is audited by the IRS, comment on his vulnerability.

Partial list of research aids:
§§ 274(d), 6001, and 6662(b)(1).
Cohan v. Comm., 2 USTC ¶489, 8 AFTR 10552, 39 F.2d 540 (CA–2, 1930).
William F. Sanford, 50 T.C. 823 (1968).

CHAPTER

10

DEDUCTIONS AND LOSSES: CERTAIN ITEMIZED DEDUCTIONS

LEARNING OBJECTIVES

After completing Chapter 10, you should be able to:

1. Distinguish between deductible and nondeductible personal expenses.
2. Define medical expenses and compute the medical expense deduction.
3. Contrast deductible taxes and nondeductible fees, licenses, etc.
4. Understand the Federal tax treatment of state and local income taxes.
5. Distinguish between deductible and nondeductible interest and apply the appropriate limitations to deductible interest.
6. Understand charitable contributions and their related measurement problems and percentage limitations.
7. List the business and personal expenditures that are deductible either as miscellaneous itemized deductions or as other itemized deductions.
8. Recognize the limitation on certain itemized deductions applicable to high-income taxpayers.
9. Identify tax planning procedures that can maximize the benefit of itemized deductions.

OUTLINE

General Classification of Expenses

1 Learning Objective
Distinguish between deductible and nondeductible personal expenses.

As a general rule, the deduction of personal expenditures is disallowed by § 262 of the Code. However, Congress has chosen to allow certain personal expenditures to be deducted as itemized deductions. Personal expenditures that are deductible as itemized deductions include medical expenses, certain taxes, mortgage interest, investment interest, and charitable contributions. These expenditures and other personal expenditures that are allowed as itemized deductions are covered in this chapter. Any personal expenditures not specifically allowed as itemized deductions by the tax law are nondeductible.

Allowable itemized deductions are deductible *from* AGI in arriving at taxable income if the taxpayer elects to itemize. The election to itemize is appropriate when total itemized deductions exceed the standard deduction based on the taxpayer's filing status (refer to Chapter 3).[1]

Medical Expenses

GENERAL REQUIREMENTS

2 Learning Objective
Define medical expenses and compute the medical expense deduction.

Medical expenses paid for the care of the taxpayer, spouse, and dependents are allowed as an itemized deduction to the extent the expenses are not reimbursed. The **medical expense** deduction is limited to the amount by which such expenses *exceed* 7.5 percent of the taxpayer's AGI.

[1] The total standard deduction is the sum of the basic standard deduction and the additional standard deduction (refer to Chapter 3). Chapter 3 also describes the situations in which a taxpayer is not eligible for the standard deduction.

TAX IN THE NEWS

AVERAGE ITEMIZED DEDUCTIONS

Are your itemized deductions close to average for your income level? Actually, if you're a typical taxpayer, you take the standard deduction instead of itemizing. In 1993, when the standard deduction was $3,700 for single taxpayers, $6,200 for married taxpayers filing jointly, and $5,450 for heads of household, about 70 percent of individual taxpayers took the standard deduction.

The IRS recently released statistics on the approximately 30 percent of individual taxpayers who did itemize in 1993—a year that saw itemized deductions rise 1.1 percent over 1992. Statistics for the most popular deductions are listed in the following table. The table omits medical expenses because few taxpayers have medical expenses in excess of the 7.5 percent floor. Similarly, casualty losses (subject to a 10 percent floor) and miscellaneous itemized deductions (subject to a 2 percent floor) are omitted.

AGI	Taxes	Contributions	Interest	Total
$ 30,000–39,999	$ 2,772	$ 1,384	$ 5,503	$ 9,659
40,000–49,999	3,322	1,541	5,738	10,601
50,000–74,999	4,442	1,739	6,618	12,799
75,000–99,999	6,220	2,319	8,282	16,821
100,000–199,999	10,035	3,427	11,389	24,851
200,000–499,999	22,655	8,207	17,772	48,634
500,000–999,999	52,462	20,635	27,605	100,702
1,000,000+	173,490	108,883	60,427	342,800

These statistics reveal some interesting aspects of the U.S. lifestyle. For one thing, taxpayers at all income levels—even those with AGI of more than $1 million—owe money. For another, taxpayers with AGI below $40,000 are more charitable than wealthier taxpayers. Those with AGI of $30,000 to $39,999 contribute 3.95 percent of their median income; least generous are taxpayers with AGI of $100,000 to $199,999, who contribute only 2.28 percent of their median income. Above this level, the contribution percentage rises but never reaches the 3.95 percent of those at the $30,000–$39,999 level.

Finally, consider what taxpayers have left after meeting the expenses reflected in the table. A single taxpayer with income of $35,000, for example, would have only $25,341 left after paying typical itemized deductions for that income level ($35,000 – $9,659 itemized deductions). After paying $3,246 of this amount as Federal income taxes, the taxpayer would have $22,095 left for other expenses. Some of the proposed flat tax schemes, which eliminate itemized deductions but allow a single large standard deduction, would result in zero Federal income tax for taxpayers at this income level.

SOURCE: Information from "Tax Report: A Special Summary and Forecast of Federal and State Tax Developments," *Wall Street Journal*, June 21, 1995, p. A1.

EXAMPLE 1

During the year, Iris had medical expenses of $4,800, of which $1,000 was reimbursed by her insurance company. If her AGI for the year is $40,000, the itemized deduction for medical expenses is limited to $800 [$4,800 – $1,000 = $3,800 – (7.5% × $40,000)]. ▼

MEDICAL EXPENSES DEFINED

The term *medical care* includes expenditures incurred for the "diagnosis, cure, mitigation, treatment, or prevention of disease, or for the purpose of affecting any structure or function of the body."[2] A *partial* list of deductible and nondeductible medical items appears in Exhibit 10–1.

A medical expense does not have to relate to a particular ailment to be deductible. Since the definition of medical care is broad enough to cover preventive measures, the cost of periodic physical and dental exams qualifies even for a taxpayer in good health.

Amounts paid for unnecessary *cosmetic surgery* are not deductible medical expenses. However, if cosmetic surgery is deemed necessary, it is deductible as a medical expense. Cosmetic surgery is necessary when it ameliorates (1) a deformity arising from a congenital abnormality, (2) a personal injury, or (3) a disfiguring disease.

EXAMPLE 2

Art, a calendar year taxpayer, paid $11,000 to a plastic surgeon for a face lift. Art, age 75, merely wanted to improve his appearance. The $11,000 does not qualify as a medical expense since the surgery was unnecessary. ▼

EXAMPLE 3

As a result of a serious automobile accident, Marge's face is disfigured. The cost of restorative cosmetic surgery is deductible as a medical expense. ▼

ETHICAL CONSIDERATIONS

Necessary or Unnecessary Cosmetic Surgery?

Steven, age 37, had his nose broken in a high school football game 20 years ago. As a result, his nose is slightly crooked. In addition, he thinks his nose is too long. In March, he scheduled an appointment with Dr. Keane to discuss surgery to improve his appearance, primarily to shorten his nose. Dr. Keane presented him with computer simulations showing several different possibilities for the size and shape of his nose. Steven picked a nose that was much shorter and completely straight.

Steven called his CPA to ask if the cost of the surgery would be deductible. His CPA told him that unnecessary cosmetic surgery is not deductible, but hinted that most doctors can come up with a medical reason that would make such surgery deductible.

Steven discussed the tax issue with Dr. Keane on his next visit, and the doctor indicated that the surgery would be necessary to repair Steven's deviated septum, which was caused by his football injury. Dr. Keane said that he would be willing to write a letter for Steven's files, stating that the surgery was medically necessary. Is Steven justified in taking a deduction for the cosmetic surgery?

[2] § 213(d)(1)(A).

▼ **EXHIBIT 10–1**
Examples of Deductible and Nondeductible Medical Expenses

Deductible	Nondeductible
Medical (including dental, mental, and hospital) care	Funeral, burial, or cremation expenses
Prescription drugs	Nonprescription drugs (except insulin)
Special equipment	Bottled water
Wheelchairs	Toiletries, cosmetics
Crutches	Diaper service, maternity clothes
Artificial limbs	Programs for the *general* improvement of health
Eyeglasses (including contact lenses)	Weight reduction
Hearing aids	Health spas
Transportation for medical care	Stop-smoking clinics
Medical and hospital insurance premiums	Social activities (e.g., dancing and swimming lessons)
Cost of alcohol and drug rehabilitation	Unnecessary cosmetic surgery

The cost of care in a *nursing home or home for the aged,* including meals and lodging, can be included in deductible medical expenses if the primary reason for being in the home is to get medical care. If the primary reason for being there is personal, any costs for medical or nursing care can be included in deductible medical expenses, but the cost of meals and lodging must be excluded.[3]

EXAMPLE 4

Norman has a chronic heart ailment. His family decides to place Norman in a nursing home equipped to provide medical and nursing care facilities. Total nursing home expenses amount to $15,000 per year. Of this amount, $4,500 is directly attributable to medical and nursing care. Since Norman is in need of significant medical and nursing care and is placed in the facility primarily for this purpose, all $15,000 of the nursing home costs are deductible (subject to the 7.5% floor). ▼

Tuition expenses of a dependent at a special school may be deductible as a medical expense. The cost of medical care can include the expenses of a special school for a mentally or physically handicapped individual. The deduction is allowed if a principal reason for sending the individual to the school is the school's special resources for alleviating the infirmities. In this case, the cost of meals and lodging, in addition to the tuition, is a proper medical expense deduction.[4]

EXAMPLE 5

Jason's daughter Marcia attended public school through the seventh grade. Because Marcia was a poor student, she was examined by a psychiatrist who diagnosed an organic problem that created a learning disability. Upon the recommendation of the psychiatrist, Marcia is enrolled in a private school so that she can receive individual attention. The school has no special program for students with learning disabilities and does not provide special medical treatment. The expense related to Marcia's attendance is not deductible as a medical expense. The cost of any psychiatric care, however, qualifies as a medical expense. ▼

[3] Reg. § 1.213–1(e)(1)(v).

[4] *Donald R. Pfeifer,* 37 TCM 816, T.C.Memo. 1978–189. Also see Rev.Rul. 78–340, 1978–2 C.B. 124.

Example 5 shows that the recommendation of a physician does not automatically make the expenditure deductible.

CAPITAL EXPENDITURES FOR MEDICAL PURPOSES

Some examples of *capital expenditures* for medical purposes are swimming pools if the taxpayer does not have access to a neighborhood pool and air conditioners if they do not become permanent improvements (e.g., window units).[5] Other examples include dust elimination systems,[6] elevators,[7] and a room built to house an iron lung. These expenditures are medical in nature if they are incurred as a medical necessity upon the advice of a physician, the facility is used primarily by the patient alone, and the expense is reasonable.

Capital expenditures normally are adjustments to basis and are not deductible. However, both a capital expenditure for a permanent improvement and expenditures made for the operation or maintenance of the improvement may qualify as medical expenses. If a capital expenditure qualifies as a medical expense, the allowable cost is deductible in the year incurred. Although depreciation is required for most other capital expenditures, it is not required for capital expenditures for medical purposes.

A capital improvement that ordinarily would not have a medical purpose qualifies as a medical expense if it is directly related to prescribed medical care and is deductible to the extent that the expenditure *exceeds* the increase in value of the related property. Appraisal costs related to capital improvements are also deductible, but not as medical expenses. These costs are expenses incurred in the determination of the taxpayer's tax liability.[8]

EXAMPLE 6

Fred is afflicted with heart disease. His physician advises him to install an elevator in his residence so he will not be required to climb the stairs. The cost of installing the elevator is $3,000, and the increase in the value of the residence is determined to be only $1,700. Therefore, $1,300 ($3,000 – $1,700) is deductible as a medical expense. Additional utility costs to operate the elevator and maintenance costs are deductible as medical expenses as long as the medical reason for the capital expenditure continues to exist. ▼

The full cost of certain home-related capital expenditures incurred to enable a *physically handicapped* individual to live independently and productively qualifies as a medical expense. Qualifying costs include expenditures for constructing entrance and exit ramps to the residence, widening hallways and doorways to accommodate wheelchairs, installing support bars and railings in bathrooms and other rooms, and adjusting electrical outlets and fixtures.[9] These expenditures are subject to the 7.5 percent floor only, and the increase in the home's value is deemed to be zero.

MEDICAL EXPENSES INCURRED FOR SPOUSE AND DEPENDENTS

In computing the medical expense deduction, a taxpayer may include medical expenses for a spouse and for a person who was a dependent at the time the

[5] Rev.Rul. 55–261, 1955–1 C.B. 307, modified by Rev.Rul. 68–212, 1968–1 C.B. 91.

[6] *F. S. Delp*, 30 T.C. 1230 (1958).

[7] *Riach v. Frank*, 62–1 USTC ¶9419, 9 AFTR2d 1263, 302 F.2d 374 (CA–9, 1962).

[8] § 212(3).

[9] For a complete list of the items that qualify, see Rev.Rul. 87–106, 1987–2 C.B. 67.

expenses were paid or incurred. Of the five requirements that normally apply in determining dependency status,[10] neither the gross income nor the joint return test applies in determining dependency status for medical expense deduction purposes.

EXAMPLE 7

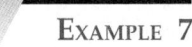

Ernie (age 22) is married and a full-time student at a university. During the year, Ernie incurred medical expenses that were paid by Matilda (Ernie's mother). She provided more than half of Ernie's support for the year. Even if Ernie files a joint return with his wife, Matilda may claim the medical expenses she paid for him. Matilda would combine Ernie's expenses with her own before applying the 7.5% floor. ▼

For *divorced persons* with children, a special rule applies to the noncustodial parent. The noncustodial parent may claim any medical expenses he or she pays even though the custodial parent claims the children as dependents. This rule applies if the dependency exemptions could have been shifted to the noncustodial parent by the custodial parent's waiver (refer to Chapter 3).

EXAMPLE 8

Irv and Joan are divorced in 1995, and Joan is awarded custody of their child, Keith. During 1996, Irv makes the following payments to Joan: $3,600 for child support and $2,500 for Keith's medical bills. Together, Irv and Joan provide more than half of Keith's support. Even though Joan claims Keith as a dependent, Irv can combine the medical expenses that he pays for Keith with his own. ▼

TRANSPORTATION, MEAL, AND LODGING EXPENSES FOR MEDICAL TREATMENT

Payments for transportation to and from a point of treatment for medical care are deductible as medical expenses (subject to the 7.5 percent floor). Transportation expenses for medical care include bus, taxi, train, or plane fare, charges for ambulance service, and out-of-pocket expenses for the use of an automobile. A mileage allowance of ten cents per mile[11] may be used instead of actual out-of-pocket automobile expenses. Whether the taxpayer chooses to claim out-of-pocket automobile expenses or the ten cents per mile automatic mileage option, related parking fees and tolls can also be deducted. The cost of meals while en route to obtain medical care is not deductible.

A deduction is also allowed for the transportation expenses of a parent who must accompany a child who is receiving medical care or for a nurse or other person giving assistance to a person who is traveling to get medical care and cannot travel alone.

A deduction is allowed for lodging while away from home for medical expenses if the following requirements are met:[12]

- The lodging is primarily for and essential to medical care.
- Medical care is provided by a doctor in a licensed hospital or a similar medical facility (e.g., a clinic).
- The lodging is not lavish or extravagant under the circumstances.
- There is no significant element of personal pleasure, recreation, or vacation in the travel away from home.

The deduction for lodging expenses included as medical expenses cannot exceed $50 *per* night for *each* person. The deduction is allowed not only for the patient but

[10] Refer to Chapter 3 for discussion of these requirements.

[11] For 1995, the amount is nine cents.

[12] § 213(d)(2).

also for a person who must travel with the patient (e.g., a parent traveling with a child who is receiving medical care).

EXAMPLE 9

Herman, a resident of Winchester, Kentucky, is advised by his family physician that Martha, Herman's dependent and disabled mother, needs specialized treatment for her heart condition. Consequently, Herman and Martha fly to Cleveland, Ohio, where Martha receives the therapy at a heart clinic on an out-patient basis. Expenses in connection with the trip are as follows:

Round trip airfare ($250 each)	$500
Lodging in Cleveland for two nights ($60 each per night)	240

Herman's medical expense deduction for transportation is $500, and his medical expense deduction for lodging is $200 ($50 per night per person). Because Martha is disabled, it is assumed that his accompanying her is justified. ▼

No deduction is allowed for the cost of meals unless they are part of the medical care and are furnished at a medical facility. When allowable, such meals are not subject to the 50 percent limit.

AMOUNTS PAID FOR MEDICAL INSURANCE PREMIUMS

Medical insurance premiums are included with other medical expenses subject to the 7.5 percent floor. Premiums paid by the taxpayer under a group plan or an individual plan are included as medical expenses. If an employer pays all or part of the taxpayer's medical insurance premiums, the amount paid by the employer is not included in gross income by the employee. Likewise, the premium is not included in the employee's medical expenses.

If a taxpayer is *self-employed,* 30 percent of insurance premiums paid for medical coverage is deductible as a *business* expense (*for* AGI). Any excess can be treated as a *medical* expense. The deduction *for* AGI is allowed for premiums paid on behalf of the taxpayer, the taxpayer's spouse, and dependents of the taxpayer. The deduction is not allowed to any taxpayer who is eligible to participate in a subsidized health plan maintained by any employer of the taxpayer or of the taxpayer's spouse. Premiums paid for medical insurance coverage of *employees* are deductible as business expenses.

EXAMPLE 10

Ellen, a sole proprietor of a restaurant, has two dependent children. During the year, she paid health insurance premiums of $1,800 for her own coverage and $1,000 for coverage of her two children. Ellen can deduct $840 ($2,800 × 30%) as a business deduction (for AGI) in computing net income from her business. She can include the remaining $1,960 ($2,800 − $840) as a medical expense (subject to the 7.5% floor) in computing itemized deductions. ▼

YEAR OF DEDUCTION

Regardless of a taxpayer's method of accounting, medical expenses are deductible only in the year *paid.* In effect, this places all individual taxpayers on a cash basis as far as the medical expense deduction is concerned. One exception, however, is allowed for deceased taxpayers. If the medical expenses are paid within one year from the day following the day of death, they can be treated as being paid at the time they were *incurred.*[13] Thus, such expenses may be reported on the final

[13] § 213(c).

income tax return of the decedent or on earlier returns if incurred before the year of death.

No current deduction is allowed for payment of medical care to be rendered in the future unless the taxpayer is under an obligation to make the payment.[14] Whether an obligation to make the payment exists depends upon the policy of the physician or the institution furnishing the medical care.

EXAMPLE 11

Upon the recommendation of his regular dentist, in late December 1996 Gary consults Dr. Smith, a prosthodontist, who specializes in crown and bridge work. Dr. Smith tells Gary that he can do the restorative work for $12,000. To cover his lab bill, however, Dr. Smith requires that 40% of this amount be prepaid. Accordingly, Gary pays $4,800 in December 1996. The balance of $7,200 is paid when the work is completed in July 1997. Under these circumstances, the qualifying medical expenses are $4,800 for 1996 and $7,200 in 1997. The result would be the same even if Gary prepaid the full $12,000 in 1996. ▼

REIMBURSEMENTS

If medical expenses are reimbursed in the same year as paid, no problem arises. The reimbursement merely reduces the amount that would otherwise qualify for the medical expense deduction. But what happens if the reimbursement occurs in a later year than the expenditure? In computing casualty losses, any reasonable prospect of recovery must be considered (refer to Chapter 7). For medical expenses, however, any expected reimbursement is disregarded in measuring the amount of the deduction. Instead, the reimbursement is accounted for separately in the year in which it occurs.

Under the *tax benefit rule,* a taxpayer who receives an insurance reimbursement for medical expenses deducted in a previous year might have to include the reimbursement in gross income in the year of receipt. However, a taxpayer who did not itemize deductions in the year the expenses were paid did not receive a tax benefit and is *not* required to include a reimbursement in gross income.

The tax benefit rule applies to reimbursements if the taxpayer itemized deductions in the previous year. In this case, the taxpayer may be required to report some or all of the medical expense reimbursement in income in the year the reimbursement is received. Under the tax benefit rule, the taxpayer must include the reimbursement in income up to the amount of the deductions that decreased taxable income in the earlier year.

EXAMPLE 12

Homer had AGI of $20,000 for 1996. He was injured in a car accident and paid $1,300 for hospital expenses and $700 for doctor bills. Homer also incurred medical expenses of $600 for his dependent child. In 1997, Homer was reimbursed $650 by his insurance company for the medical expenses attributable to the car accident. His deduction for medical expenses in 1996 is computed as follows:

Hospitalization	$ 1,300
Bills for doctor's services	700
Medical expenses for dependent	600
Total	$ 2,600
Less: 7.5% of $20,000	(1,500)
Medical expense deduction (assuming Homer itemizes his deductions)	$ 1,100

[14] *Robert S. Basset,* 26 T.C. 619 (1956).

Assume that Homer would have elected to itemize his deductions even if he had no medical expenses in 1996. If the reimbursement for medical care had occurred in 1996, the medical expense deduction would have been only $450 [$2,600 (total medical expenses) – $650 (reimbursement) – $1,500 (floor)], and Homer would have paid more income tax.

Since the reimbursement was made in a subsequent year, Homer would include $650 in gross income for 1997. If Homer had not itemized in 1996, he would not include the $650 reimbursement in 1997 gross income because he would have received no tax benefit in 1996. ▼

TAXES

3 LEARNING OBJECTIVE Contrast deductible taxes and nondeductible fees, licenses, etc.

A deduction is allowed for certain state and local taxes paid or accrued by a taxpayer.[15] The deduction was created to relieve the burden of multiple taxes upon the same source of revenue.

DEDUCTIBILITY AS A TAX

A distinction must be made between a tax and a fee, since fees are not deductible unless incurred as an ordinary and necessary business expense or as an expense in the production of income. The IRS has defined a tax as follows:

> A tax is an enforced contribution exacted pursuant to legislative authority in the exercise of taxing power, and imposed and collected for the purpose of raising revenue to be used for public or governmental purposes, and not as payment for some special privilege granted or service rendered. Taxes are, therefore, distinguished from various other contributions and charges imposed for particular purposes under particular powers or functions of the government. In view of such distinctions, the question whether a particular contribution or charge is to be regarded as a tax depends upon its real nature.[16]

Accordingly, fees for dog licenses, automobile inspection, automobile titles and registration, hunting and fishing licenses, bridge and highway tolls, drivers' licenses, parking meter deposits, postage, etc., are not deductible if personal in nature. These items, however, could be deductible if incurred as a business expense or for the production of income. Deductible and nondeductible taxes are summarized in Exhibit 10–2.[17]

PROPERTY TAXES

State, local, and foreign taxes on real property are generally deductible only by the person upon whom the tax is imposed. Deductible personal property taxes must be *ad valorem* (assessed in relation to the value of the property). Therefore, a motor vehicle tax based on weight, model, year, and horsepower is not an ad valorem tax. However, a tax based on value and other criteria may qualify in part.

EXAMPLE 13 A state imposes a motor vehicle registration tax on 4% of the value of the vehicle plus 40 cents per hundredweight. Belle, a resident of the state, owns a car having a value of $4,000 and weighing 3,000 pounds. Belle pays an annual registration fee of $172. Of this amount,

[15] § 164.

[16] Rev.Rul. 57–345, 1957–2 C.B. 132, and Rev.Rul. 70–622, 1970–2 C.B. 41.

[17] Most deductible taxes are listed in § 164, while the nondeductible items are included in § 275.

▼ **EXHIBIT 10–2**
Deductible and Nondeductible Taxes

Deductible	Nondeductible
State, local, and foreign real property taxes	Federal income taxes
State and local personal property taxes	FICA taxes imposed on employees
State, local, and foreign income taxes	Employer FICA taxes paid on domestic household workers
The environmental tax	Estate, inheritance, and gift taxes
	General sales taxes
	Federal, state, and local excise taxes (e.g., gasoline, tobacco, spirits)
	Foreign income taxes if the taxpayer chooses the foreign tax credit option
	Taxes on real property to the extent such taxes are to be apportioned and treated as imposed on another taxpayer

$160 (4% of $4,000) is deductible as a personal property tax. The remaining $12, based on the weight of the car, is not deductible. ▼

Assessments for Local Benefits. As a general rule, real property taxes do not include taxes assessed for local benefits since such assessments tend to increase the value of the property (e.g., special assessments for streets, sidewalks, curbing, and other similar improvements). A taxpayer was denied a deduction for the cost of a new sidewalk (relative to a personal residence), even though the construction was required by the city and the sidewalk may have provided an incidental benefit to the public welfare.[18] Such assessments are added to the adjusted basis of the taxpayer's property.

Apportionment of Real Property Taxes between Seller and Purchaser. Real estate taxes for the entire year are apportioned between the buyer and seller on the basis of the number of days the property was held by each during the real property tax year. This apportionment is required whether the tax is paid by the buyer or the seller or is prorated according to the purchase agreement. It is the apportionment that determines who is entitled to deduct the real estate taxes in the year of sale. In making the apportionment, the assessment date and the lien date are disregarded. The date of sale counts as a day the property is owned by the buyer.

EXAMPLE 14

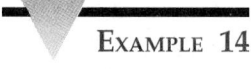

A county's real property tax year runs from April 1 to March 31. Susan, the owner on April 1, 1996, of real property located in the county, sells the real property to Bob on June 30, 1996. Bob owns the real property from June 30, 1996, through March 31, 1997. The tax for the real property tax year April 1, 1996, through March 31, 1997, is $730. The portion of the real property tax treated as imposed upon Susan, the seller, is $180 (90/365 × $730, April 1 through June 29, 1996), and $550 (275/365 × $730, June 30, 1996, through March 31, 1997) of the tax is treated as imposed upon Bob, the purchaser. ▼

If the actual real estate taxes are not prorated between the buyer and seller as part of the purchase agreement, adjustments are required. The adjustments are necessary to determine the amount realized by the seller and the adjusted basis of

[18] *Erie H. Rose*, 31 TCM 142, T.C. Memo. 1972–39; Reg. § 1.164–4(a).

the property to the buyer. If the buyer pays the entire amount of the tax, he or she has, in effect, paid the seller's portion of the real estate tax and has therefore paid more for the property than the actual purchase price. Thus, the amount of real estate tax that is apportioned to the seller (for Federal income tax purposes) and paid by the buyer is added to the buyer's adjusted basis. The seller must increase the amount realized on the sale by the same amount.

EXAMPLE 15

Seth sells real estate on October 3, 1996, for $50,000. The buyer, Wilma, pays the real estate taxes of $1,098 for the 1996 calendar year (a leap year), which is the real estate property tax year. Of the real estate taxes, $828 (for 276 days) is apportioned to and is deductible by the seller, Seth, and $270 (for 90 days) of the taxes is deductible by Wilma. The buyer has, in effect, paid Seth's real estate taxes of $828 and has therefore paid $50,828 for the property. Wilma's basis is increased to $50,828, and the amount realized by Seth from the sale is increased to $50,828. ▼

The opposite result occurs if the seller (rather than the buyer) pays the real estate taxes. In this case, the seller reduces the amount realized from the sale by the amount that has been apportioned to the buyer. The buyer is required to reduce his or her adjusted basis by a corresponding amount.

EXAMPLE 16

Ruth sells real estate to Butch for $50,000 on October 3, 1996. While Ruth held the property, she paid the real estate taxes of $1,098 for the calendar year, which is the real estate property tax year. Although Ruth paid the entire $1,098 of real estate taxes, $270 of that amount is apportioned to Butch and is therefore deductible by him. The effect is that the buyer, Butch, has paid only $49,730 for the property. The amount realized by Ruth, the seller, is reduced by $270, and Butch reduces his basis in the property to $49,730. ▼

STATE AND LOCAL INCOME TAXES

4 LEARNING OBJECTIVE
Understand the Federal tax treatment of state and local income taxes.

The position of the IRS is that state and local income taxes imposed upon an individual are deductible only as itemized deductions, even if the taxpayer's sole source of income is from a business, rents, or royalties.

Cash basis taxpayers are entitled to deduct state income taxes withheld by the employer in the year the taxes are withheld. In addition, estimated state income tax payments are deductible in the year the payment is made by cash basis taxpayers even if the payments relate to a prior or subsequent year.[19] If the taxpayer overpays state income taxes because of excessive withholdings or estimated tax payments, the refund received is included in gross income of the following year to the extent that the deduction reduced the tax liability in the prior year.

EXAMPLE 17

Leona, a cash basis, unmarried taxpayer, had $800 of state income tax withheld during 1996. Additionally in 1996, Leona paid $100 that was due when she filed her 1995 state income tax return and made estimated payments of $300 on her 1996 state income tax. When Leona files her 1996 Federal income tax return in April 1997, she elects to itemize deductions, which amount to $5,500, including the $1,200 of state income tax payments and withholdings, all of which reduce her tax liability.

As a result of overpaying her 1996 state income tax, Leona receives a refund of $200 early in 1997. She will include this amount in her 1997 gross income in computing her

---

[19] Rev.Rul. 71–190, 1971–1 C.B. 70. See also Rev.Rul. 82–208, 1982–2 C.B. 58, where a deduction is not allowed when the taxpayer cannot, in good faith, reasonably determine that there is additional state income tax liability.

Federal income tax. It does not matter whether Leona received a check from the state for $200 or applied the $200 toward her 1997 state income tax. ▼

INTEREST

5 LEARNING OBJECTIVE
Distinguish between deductible and nondeductible interest and apply the appropriate limitations to deductible interest.

A deduction for interest has been allowed since the income tax law was enacted in 1913. Despite its long history of congressional acceptance, the interest deduction has been one of the most controversial areas in the tax law. The controversy centered around the propriety of allowing the deduction of interest charges for the purchase of consumer goods and services and interest on borrowings used to acquire investments (investment interest). Personal (consumer) interest is not deductible. This includes credit card interest, interest on car loans, and any other interest that is not investment interest, home mortgage interest, or business interest. **Investment interest** and **qualified residence** (home mortgage) **interest** continue to be deductible, subject to limits discussed below.

ALLOWED AND DISALLOWED ITEMS

The Supreme Court has defined *interest* as compensation for the use or forbearance of money.[20] The general rule permits a deduction for interest paid or accrued within the taxable year on indebtedness.[21]

Investment Interest. Taxpayers frequently borrow funds that they use to acquire investment assets. When the interest expense is large relative to the income from the investments, substantial tax benefits could result. Congress has therefore limited the deductibility of interest on funds borrowed for the purpose of purchasing or continuing to hold investment property. Investment interest expense is *now* limited to net investment income for the year.[22]

Investment income is gross income from interest, dividends, annuities, and royalties not derived in the ordinary course of a trade or business. Income from a passive activity and income from a real estate activity in which the taxpayer actively participates are not included in investment income (see Chapter 11).

Net capital gain attributable to the disposition of property producing the types of income just enumerated or from property held for investment purposes is *not* included in investment income unless the taxpayer elects to do so.

EXAMPLE 18

Terry incurred $13,000 of interest expense related to her investments during the year. Her investment income included $4,000 of interest, $2,000 of dividends, and a $5,000 net capital gain on the sale of securities. Her investment income for purposes of computing the investment income limitation is $6,000 ($4,000 interest + $2,000 dividends). ▼

Taxpayers may *elect* to include the capital gains as investment income, but only if they agree to reduce capital gains qualifying for the alternative tax computation for net capital gain (see Chapter 16) by an equivalent amount.

Net investment income is the excess of investment income over investment expenses. Investment expenses are those deductible expenses directly connected with the production of investment income. Investment expenses *do not* include

[20] *Old Colony Railroad Co. v. Comm.*, 3 USTC ¶880, 10 AFTR 786, 52 S.Ct. 211 (USSC, 1932).

[21] § 163(a).

[22] § 63(d).

interest expense. When investment expenses fall into the category of miscellaneous itemized deductions that are subject to the 2 percent-of-AGI floor, some may not enter into the calculation of net investment income because of the floor.

EXAMPLE 19

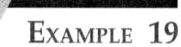

Gina has AGI of $80,000, which includes dividends and interest income of $18,000. Besides investment interest expense, she paid $3,000 of city ad valorem property tax on stocks and bonds and had the following miscellaneous itemized expenses:

Safe deposit box rental (to hold investment securities)	$ 120
Investment counsel fee	1,200
Unreimbursed business travel	850
Uniforms	600

Before Gina can determine her investment expenses for purposes of calculating net investment income, those miscellaneous expenses that are not investment expenses are disallowed before any investment expenses are disallowed under the 2%-of-AGI floor. This is accomplished by selecting the *lesser* of the following:

1. The amount of investment expenses included in the total of miscellaneous itemized deductions subject to the 2%-of-AGI floor.
2. The amount of miscellaneous expenses deductible after the 2%-of-AGI rule is applied.

The amount under item 1 is $1,320 [$120 (safe deposit box rental) + $1,200 (investment counsel fee)]. The item 2 amount is $1,170 [$2,770 (total of miscellaneous expenses) – $1,600 (2% of $80,000 AGI)].

Then, Gina's investment expenses are calculated as follows:

Deductible miscellaneous deductions investment expense (the lesser of item 1 or item 2)	$1,170
Plus: Ad valorem tax on investment property	3,000
Total investment expenses	$4,170

Gina's net investment income is $13,830 ($18,000 investment income – $4,170 investment expenses). ▼

After net investment income is determined, deductible investment interest expense can be calculated.

EXAMPLE 20

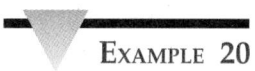

Adam is a single person employed by a law firm. His investment activities for the year are as follows:

Net investment income	$30,000
Investment interest expense	44,000

Adam's investment interest deduction is $30,000. ▼

The amount of investment interest disallowed is carried over to future years. In Example 20, therefore, the amount that is carried over to the following year is $14,000 ($44,000 investment interest expense – $30,000 allowed). No limit is placed on the length of the carryover period. The investment interest expense deduction is determined by completing Form 4952 (see Appendix B).

Qualified Residence Interest. *Qualified residence interest* is interest paid or accrued during the taxable year on indebtedness (subject to limitations) *secured* by any property that is a qualified residence of the taxpayer. Qualified residence interest falls into two categories: (1) interest on acquisition indebtedness and (2) interest on home equity loans. Before discussing each of these categories, however, the term qualified residence must be defined.

A *qualified residence* includes the taxpayer's principal residence and one other residence of the taxpayer or spouse. The *principal residence* is one that meets the requirement for nonrecognition of gain upon sale under § 1034 (see Chapter 15). The *one other residence*, or second residence, refers to one that is used as a residence if not rented or, if rented, meets the requirements for a personal residence under the rental of vacation home rules (refer to Chapter 6). A taxpayer who has more than one second residence can make the selection each year of which one is the qualified second residence. A residence includes, in addition to a house in the ordinary sense, cooperative apartments, condominiums, and mobile homes and boats that have living quarters (sleeping accommodations and toilet and cooking facilities).

Although in most cases interest paid on a home mortgage would be fully deductible, there are limitations.[23] Interest paid or accrued during the tax year on aggregate **acquisition indebtedness** of $1 million or less ($500,000 for married persons filing separate returns) is deductible as qualified residence interest. Acquisition indebtedness refers to amounts incurred in acquiring, constructing, or substantially improving a qualified residence of the taxpayer.

Qualified residence interest also includes interest on **home equity loans.** These loans utilize the personal residence of the taxpayer as security. Because the funds from home equity loans can be used for personal purposes (e.g., auto purchases, medical expenses), what would otherwise have been nondeductible consumer interest becomes deductible qualified residence interest.

However, interest is deductible only on the portion of a home equity loan that does not exceed the *lesser of*:

- The fair market value of the residence, reduced by the acquisition indebtedness, *or*
- $100,000 ($50,000 for married persons filing separate returns).

EXAMPLE 21

Larry owns a personal residence with a fair market value of $150,000 and an outstanding first mortgage of $120,000. Therefore, his equity in his home is $30,000 ($150,000 − $120,000). Larry issues a lien on the residence and in return borrows $15,000 to purchase a new family automobile. All interest on the $135,000 of debt is treated as qualified residence interest. ▼

EXAMPLE 22

Leon and Pearl, married taxpayers, took out a mortgage on their home for $200,000 in 1983. In March of the current year, when the home had a fair market value of $400,000 and they owed $195,000 on the mortgage, Leon and Pearl took out a home equity loan for $120,000. They used the funds to purchase a boat to be used for recreational purposes. The boat, which does not have living quarters, does not qualify as a personal residence. On a joint return, Leon and Pearl can deduct all of the interest on the first mortgage since it is acquisition indebtedness. Of the $120,000 home equity loan, only the interest on the first $100,000 is deductible. The interest on the remaining $20,000 is not deductible because it exceeds the statutory ceiling of $100,000. ▼

Interest Paid for Services. Mortgage loan companies commonly charge a fee for finding, placing, or processing a mortgage loan. Such fees are often called

[23] § 163(h)(3).

points and are expressed as a percentage of the loan amount. Borrowers often have to pay points to obtain the necessary financing. To qualify as deductible interest, the points must be considered compensation to a lender solely for the use or forbearance of money. The points cannot be a form of service charge or payment for specific services if they are to qualify as deductible interest.[24]

Points must be capitalized and are amortized and deductible ratably over the life of the loan. A special exception permits the purchaser of a personal residence to deduct qualifying points in the year of payment.[25] The exception also covers points paid to obtain funds for home improvements.

EXAMPLE 23

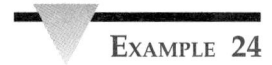

During 1996, Thelma purchased a new residence for $130,000 and paid points of $2,600 to obtain mortgage financing. At Thelma's election, the $2,600 can be claimed as an interest deduction for tax year 1996. ▼

Points paid to *refinance* an existing home mortgage cannot be immediately expensed, but must be capitalized and amortized as interest expense over the life of the new loan.[26]

EXAMPLE 24

Sandra purchased her residence four years ago, obtaining a 30-year mortgage at an annual interest rate of 12%. In the current year, Sandra refinances the mortgage in order to reduce the interest rate to 9%. To obtain the refinancing, she had to pay points of $2,600. The $2,600 paid comes under the usual rule applicable to points. The $2,600 must be capitalized and amortized over the life of the mortgage. ▼

The rules governing the deductibility of points *paid by a seller* to help a buyer finance the purchase of the residence were changed in 1994.[27] Under prior rules, such points were not deductible by the buyer, but were treated by the seller as a reduction of the selling price of the property.

The IRS changed its position on this issue, retroactive to tax years beginning after December 31, 1990. In effect, points paid by the seller are treated as an adjustment to the price of the residence, and the buyer is treated as having used cash to pay the points that were paid by the seller. A buyer may deduct seller-paid points in the tax year in which they are paid if several conditions are met. Refer to Revenue Procedure 94–27 for a complete list of these conditions (see footnote 27 for citation).

Prepayment Penalty. When a mortgage or loan is paid off in full in a lump sum before its term (early), the lending institution may require an additional payment of a certain percentage applied to the unpaid amount at the time of prepayment. This is known as a prepayment penalty and is considered to be interest (e.g., personal, qualified residence, investment) in the year paid. The general rules for deductibility of interest also apply to prepayment penalties.

Interest Paid to Related Parties. Nothing prevents the deduction of interest paid to a related party as long as the payment actually took place and the interest meets the requirements for deductibility. Recall from Chapter 6 that a special rule for related taxpayers applies when the debtor uses the accrual basis and the related creditor is on the cash basis. If this rule is applicable, interest that has been accrued but not paid at the end of the debtor's tax year is not deductible until payment is made and the income is reportable by the cash basis recipient.

[24] Rev.Rul. 67–297, 1967–2 C.B. 87.
[25] § 461(g)(2).
[26] Rev.Rul. 87–22, 1987–1 C.B. 146.
[27] Rev.Proc. 94–27, 1994–1 C.B. 613.

Tax-Exempt Securities. The tax law provides that no deduction is allowed for interest on debt incurred to purchase or carry tax-exempt securities.[28] A major problem for the courts has been to determine what is meant by the words *to purchase or carry*. Refer to Chapter 6 for a detailed discussion of these issues.

RESTRICTIONS ON DEDUCTIBILITY AND TIMING CONSIDERATIONS

Taxpayer's Obligation. Allowed interest is deductible if the related debt represents a bona fide obligation for which the taxpayer is liable.[29] Thus, a taxpayer may not deduct interest paid on behalf of another individual. For interest to be deductible, both the debtor and creditor must intend for the loan to be repaid. Intent of the parties can be especially crucial between related parties such as a shareholder and a closely held corporation. A shareholder may not deduct interest paid by the corporation on his or her behalf.[30] Likewise, a husband may not deduct interest paid on his wife's property if he files a separate return, except in the case of qualified residence interest. If both husband and wife consent in writing, either the husband or the wife may deduct the allowed interest on the principal residence and one other residence.

Time of Deduction. Generally, interest must be paid to secure a deduction unless the taxpayer uses the accrual method of accounting. Under the accrual method, interest is deductible ratably over the life of the loan.

EXAMPLE 25

On November 1, 1996, Ramon borrows $1,000 to purchase appliances for a rental house. The loan is payable in 90 days at 12% interest. On the due date in January 1997, Ramon pays the $1,000 note and interest amounting to $30. Ramon can deduct the accrued portion ($\frac{2}{3} \times \$30 = \$20$) of the interest in 1996 only if he is an accrual basis taxpayer. Otherwise, the entire amount of interest ($30) is deductible in 1997. ▼

Prepaid Interest. Accrual method reporting is imposed on cash basis taxpayers for interest prepayments that extend beyond the end of the taxable year.[31] Such payments must be allocated to the tax years to which the interest payments relate. These provisions are intended to prevent cash basis taxpayers from *manufacturing* tax deductions before the end of the year by prepaying interest.

CLASSIFICATION OF INTEREST EXPENSE

Whether interest is deductible *for* AGI or as an itemized deduction *(from)* depends on whether the indebtedness has a business, investment, or personal purpose. If the indebtedness is incurred in relation to a business (other than performing services as an employee) or for the production of rent or royalty income, the interest is deductible *for* AGI. If the indebtedness is incurred for personal use, such as qualified residence interest, any deduction allowed is reported on Schedule A of Form 1040 if the taxpayer elects to itemize. If the taxpayer is an employee who incurs debt in relation to his or her employment, the interest is considered to be personal, or consumer, interest. Business expenses appear on Schedule C of Form 1040, and expenses related to rents or royalties are reported on Schedule E.

If a taxpayer deposits money in a certificate of deposit (CD) that has a term of one year or less and the interest cannot be withdrawn without penalty, the full

[28] § 265(a)(2).

[29] *Arcade Realty Co.*, 35 T.C. 256 (1960).

[30] *Continental Trust Co.*, 7 B.T.A. 539 (1927).

[31] § 461(g)(1).

Concept Summary 10–1

Deductibility of Personal, Investment, and Mortgage Interest

Type	Deductible	Comments
Personal (consumer) interest	No	Includes any interest that is not home mortgage interest, investment interest, or business interest. Examples include car loans, credit cards, etc.
Investment interest (*not* related to rental or royalty property)	Yes	Itemized deduction; limited to net investment income for the year; disallowed interest can be carried over to future years.
Investment interest (related to rental or royalty property)	Yes	Deduction *for* AGI; limited to net investment income for the year; disallowed interest can be carried over to future years.
Qualified residence interest on acquisition indebtedness	Yes	Deductible as an itemized deduction; limited to indebtedness of $1 million.
Qualified residence interest on home equity indebtedness	Yes	Deductible as an itemized deduction; limited to indebtedness equal to lesser of $100,000 or FMV of residence minus acquisition indebtedness.

amount of the interest must still be included in income, even though part of the interest is forfeited due to an early withdrawal. However, the taxpayer will be allowed a deduction *for* AGI as to the forfeited amount.

Charitable Contributions

6 Learning Objective
Understand charitable contributions and their related measurement problems and percentage limitations.

Individuals and corporations are allowed to deduct contributions made to qualified *domestic* organizations.[32] Contributions to qualified charitable organizations serve certain social welfare needs and thus relieve the government of the cost of providing these needed services to the community.

The **charitable contribution** provisions are among the most complex in the tax law. To determine the amount deductible as a charitable contribution, several important questions must be answered:

- What constitutes a charitable contribution?
- Was the contribution made to a qualified organization?
- When is the contribution deductible?
- What record-keeping and reporting requirements apply to charitable contributions?
- How is the value of donated property determined?
- What special rules apply to contributions of property that has increased in value?
- What percentage limitations apply to the charitable contribution deduction?

These questions are addressed in the sections that follow.

[32] § 170.

CRITERIA FOR A GIFT

A *charitable contribution* is defined as a gift made to a qualified organization.[33] The major elements needed to qualify a contribution as a gift are a donative intent, the absence of consideration, and acceptance by the donee. Consequently, the taxpayer has the burden of establishing that the transfer was made from motives of *disinterested generosity* as established by the courts.[34] This test is quite subjective and has led to problems of interpretation (refer to the discussion of gifts in Chapter 5).

Benefit Received Rule. When a donor derives a tangible benefit from a contribution, he or she cannot deduct the value of the benefit.

EXAMPLE 26

Ralph purchases a ticket at $100 for a special performance of the local symphony (a qualified charity). If the price of a ticket to a symphony concert is normally $35, Ralph is allowed only $65 as a charitable contribution. ▼

An exception to this benefit rule provides for the deduction of an automatic percentage of the amount paid for the right to purchase athletic tickets from colleges and universities.[35] Under this exception, 80 percent of the amount paid to or for the benefit of the institution qualifies as a charitable contribution deduction.

EXAMPLE 27

Janet donates $500 to State University's athletic department. The payment guarantees that she will have preferred seating on the 50-yard line. Subsequently, Janet buys four $35 game tickets. Under the exception to the benefit rule, she is allowed a $400 (80% of $500) charitable contribution deduction for the taxable year.

If, however, Janet's $500 donation includes four $35 tickets, that portion [$140 ($35 × 4)] and the remaining portion of $360 ($500 – $140) are treated as separate amounts. Thus, Janet is allowed a charitable contribution deduction of $288 (80% of $360). ▼

Contribution of Services. No deduction is allowed for a contribution of one's services to a qualified charitable organization. However, unreimbursed expenses related to the services rendered may be deductible. For example, the cost of a uniform (without general utility) that is required to be worn while performing services may be deductible, as are certain out-of-pocket transportation costs incurred for the benefit of the charity. In lieu of these out-of-pocket costs for an automobile, a standard mileage rate of 12 cents per mile is allowed.[36] Deductions are permitted for transportation, reasonable expenses for lodging, and the cost of meals while away from home incurred in performing the donated services. The travel may not involve a significant element of personal pleasure, recreation, or vacation.[37]

EXAMPLE 28

Grace, a delegate representing her church in Miami, Florida, travels to a two-day national meeting in Denver, Colorado, in February. After the meeting, Grace spends two weeks at a nearby ski resort. Under these circumstances, none of the transportation, meals, or lodging is deductible since the travel involved a significant element of personal pleasure, recreation, or vacation. ▼

---

[33] § 170(c).

[34] *Comm. v. Duberstein*, 60–2 USTC ¶9515, 5 AFTR2d 1626, 80 S.Ct. 1190 (USSC, 1960).

[35] § 170(l).

[36] § 170(i).

[37] § 170(j).

Nondeductible Items. In addition to the benefit received rule and the restrictions placed on contribution of services, the following items may *not* be deducted as charitable contributions:

- Dues, fees, or bills paid to country clubs, lodges, fraternal orders, or similar groups.
- Cost of raffle, bingo, or lottery tickets.
- Cost of tuition.
- Value of blood given to a blood bank.
- Donations to homeowners associations.
- Gifts to individuals.
- Rental value of property used by a qualified charity.

QUALIFIED ORGANIZATIONS

To be deductible, a contribution must be made to one of the following organizations:[38]

- A state or possession of the United States or any subdivisions thereof.
- A corporation, trust, or community chest, fund, or foundation that is situated in the United States and is organized and operated exclusively for religious, charitable, scientific, literary, or educational purposes or for the prevention of cruelty to children or animals.
- A veterans' organization.
- A fraternal organization operating under the lodge system.
- A cemetery company.

The IRS publishes a list of organizations that have applied for and received tax-exempt status under § 501 of the Code.[39] This publication is updated frequently and may be helpful in determining if a gift has been made to a qualifying charitable organization.

Because gifts made to needy individuals are not deductible, a deduction will not be permitted if a gift is received by a donee in an individual capacity rather than as a representative of a qualifying organization.

TIME OF DEDUCTION

A charitable contribution generally is deducted in the year the payment is made. This rule applies to both cash and accrual basis individuals. A contribution is ordinarily deemed to have been made on the delivery of the property to the donee. For example, if a gift of securities (properly endorsed) is made to a qualified charitable organization, the gift is considered complete on the day of delivery or mailing. However, if the donor delivers the certificate to his or her bank or broker or to the issuing corporation, the gift is considered complete on the date the stock is transferred on the books of the corporation.

A contribution made by check is considered delivered on the date of mailing. Thus, a check mailed on December 31, 1996, is deductible on the taxpayer's 1996 tax return. If the contribution is charged on a bank credit card, the date the charge is made determines the year of deduction.

---

[38] § 170(c).

[39] Although this *Cumulative List of Organizations,* IRS Publication 78 (available by purchase from the Superintendent of Documents, U.S. Government Printing Office, Washington, DC 20402), may be helpful, qualified organizations are not required to be listed. Not all organizations that qualify are listed in this publication.

RECORD-KEEPING AND VALUATION REQUIREMENTS

Record-Keeping Requirements. No deduction is allowed for contributions of $250 or more unless the taxpayer obtains *written substantiation* of the contribution from the charitable organization. The substantiation must specify the amount of cash and a description (but not value) of any property other than cash contributed. The substantiation must be obtained before the earlier of (1) the due date (including extensions) of the return for the year the contribution is claimed or (2) the date such return is filed.[40]

Additional information is required if the value of the donated property is over $500 but not over $5,000. Also, the taxpayer must file Section A of Form 8283 (Noncash Charitable Contributions) for such contributions.

For noncash contributions with a claimed value in excess of $5,000 ($10,000 in the case of nonpublicly traded stock), the taxpayer must obtain a qualified appraisal and must file Section B of Form 8283. This schedule must show a summary of the appraisal and must be attached to the taxpayer's return. Failure to comply with these reporting rules may result in disallowance of the charitable contribution deduction. Additionally, significant overvaluation exposes the taxpayer to rather stringent penalties.

Valuation Requirements. Property donated to a charity is generally valued at fair market value at the time the gift is made. The Code and Regulations give very little guidance on the measurement of the fair market value except to say, "The fair market value is the price at which the property would change hands between a willing buyer and a willing seller, neither being under any compulsion to buy or sell and both having reasonable knowledge of relevant facts."

Generally, charitable organizations do not attest to the fair market value of the donated property. Nevertheless, the taxpayer must maintain reliable written evidence of the following information concerning the donation:

- The fair market value of the property and how that value was determined.
- The amount of the reduction in the value of the property (if required) for certain appreciated property and how that reduction was determined.
- Terms of any agreement with the charitable organization dealing with the use of the property and potential sale or other disposition of the property by the organization.
- A signed copy of the appraisal if the value of the property was determined by appraisal. Only for a contribution of art with an aggregate value of $20,000 or more must the appraisal be attached to the taxpayer's return.

LIMITATIONS ON CHARITABLE CONTRIBUTION DEDUCTION

In General. The potential charitable contribution deduction is the total of all donations, both money and property, that qualify for the deduction. After this determination is made, the actual amount of the charitable contribution deduction that is allowed for individuals for the tax year is limited as follows:

- If the qualifying contributions for the year total 20 percent or less of AGI, they are fully deductible.
- If the qualifying contributions are more than 20 percent of AGI, the deductible amount may be limited to either 20 percent, 30 percent, or 50

[40] § 170(f)(8).

percent of AGI, depending on the type of property given and the type of organization to which the donation is made.

- In any case, the maximum charitable contribution deduction may not exceed 50 percent of AGI for the tax year.

To understand the complex rules for computing the amount of a charitable contribution, it is necessary to understand the distinction between capital gain property and ordinary income property. In addition, it is necessary to understand when the 50 percent, 30 percent, and 20 percent limitations apply. If a taxpayer's contributions for the year exceed the applicable percentage limitations, the excess contributions may be carried forward and deducted during a five-year carryover period. These topics are discussed in the sections that follow.

Ordinary Income Property. **Ordinary income property** is any property that, if sold, will result in the recognition of ordinary income. The term includes inventory for sale in the taxpayer's trade or business, a work of art created by the donor, and a manuscript prepared by the donor. It also includes, *for purposes of the charitable contribution calculation,* a capital asset held by the donor for less than the required holding period for long-term capital gain treatment. To the extent that disposition of property results in the recognition of ordinary income due to the recapture of depreciation, it is ordinary income property.[41]

If ordinary income property is contributed, the deduction is equal to the fair market value of the property less the amount of ordinary income that would have been reported if the property were sold. In most instances, the deduction is limited to the adjusted basis of the property to the donor.

EXAMPLE 29

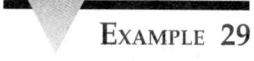

Tim owned stock in White Corporation that he donated to a university on May 1, 1996. Tim had purchased the stock for $2,500 on March 3, 1996, and the stock had a value of $3,600 when he made the donation. Since he had not held the property long enough to meet the long-term capital gain requirement, Tim would have recognized a short-term capital gain of $1,100 if he had sold the property. Since short-term capital gain property is treated as ordinary income property for charitable contribution purposes, Tim's charitable contribution deduction is limited to the property's adjusted basis of $2,500 ($3,600 – $1,100 = $2,500). ▼

In Example 29, suppose the stock had a fair market value of $2,300 (rather than $3,600) when it was donated to charity. Because the fair market value now is less than the adjusted basis, the charitable contribution deduction is $2,300.

Capital Gain Property. **Capital gain property** is any property that would have resulted in the recognition of long-term capital gain or § 1231 gain if the property had been sold by the donor. As a general rule, the deduction for a contribution of capital gain property is equal to the fair market value of the property.

Two major exceptions disallow the deductibility of the appreciation on long-term capital gain property. One exception concerns certain private foundations. Private foundations are organizations that traditionally do not receive their funding from the general public (e.g., the Ford Foundation). Generally, foundations fall into two categories: operating and nonoperating. A private *operating* foundation is one that spends substantially all of its income in the active conduct

[41] For a more complete discussion of the difference between ordinary income and capital gain property, see Chapter 16.

of the charitable undertaking for which it was established.[42] Other private foundations are *nonoperating* foundations. However, if a private nonoperating foundation distributes the contributions it receives according to special rules within two and one-half months following the year of the contribution, the organization is treated the same as public charities and private operating foundations. Often, only the private foundation knows its status (operating or nonoperating) for sure, and the status can change from year to year.

If capital gain property is contributed to a private nonoperating foundation, the taxpayer must reduce the contribution by the long-term capital gain that would have been recognized if the property had been sold at its fair market value. The effect of this provision is to limit the deduction to the property's adjusted basis.

EXAMPLE 30

Walter purchases stock for $800 on January 1, 1975, and donates it to a private nonoperating foundation on June 21, 1996, when it is worth $2,000. Walter's charitable contribution is $800 ($2,000 – $1,200), the stock's basis. ▼

If, in Example 30, Walter had donated the stock to either a public charity or a private operating foundation, his charitable contribution would be $2,000, the fair market value of the stock.

A second exception applying to capital gain property relates to *tangible personalty.* Tangible personalty is all property that is not realty (land and buildings) and does not include intangible property such as stock or securities. If tangible personalty is contributed to a public charity such as a museum, church, or university, the charitable deduction may have to be reduced. The amount of the reduction is the long-term capital gain that would have been recognized if the property had been sold for its fair market value. The reduction is required *if* the property is put to an unrelated use. The term *unrelated use* means a use that is unrelated to the exempt purpose or function of the charitable organization.

A taxpayer in this instance must establish that the property is not in fact being put to an unrelated use by the donee. The taxpayer must also establish that at the time of the contribution it was reasonable to anticipate that the property would not be put to an unrelated use. For a contribution of personalty to a museum, if the work of art is the kind of art normally retained by the museum, it is reasonable for a donor to anticipate that the work of art will not be put to an unrelated use. This is the case even if the object is later sold or exchanged by the museum.[43]

EXAMPLE 31

Myrtle contributes a Picasso painting, for which she paid $20,000, to a local museum. She had owned the painting for four years. It had a value of $30,000 at the time of the donation. The museum displayed the painting for two years and subsequently sold it for $50,000. The charitable contribution is $30,000. It is not reduced by the unrealized appreciation since the painting was put to a related use even though it was later sold by the museum. ▼

Fifty Percent Ceiling. Contributions made to public charities may not exceed 50 percent of an individual's AGI for the year. Excess contributions may be carried over to the next five years. The 50 percent ceiling on contributions applies to the following types of public charities:

- A church or a convention or association of churches.
- An educational organization that maintains a regular faculty and curriculum.
- A hospital or medical school.

[42] § 4942.

[43] Reg. § 1.170A–4(b)(3)(ii)(b).

TAX IN THE NEWS

GET RID OF YOUR OLD STUFF AND TAKE A TAX DEDUCTION

Most taxpayers have closets, attics, and garages cluttered with items they will never use. However, there is an easy way to convert these items into tax savings. Many charities, such as Goodwill and the Salvation Army, have thrift stores in which they sell used merchandise. Taxpayers can take charitable contribution deductions equal to the fair market value of most items they donate to charitable organizations. However, it is sometimes difficult to determine the value of used items. William Lewis, a CPA, claims to have the solution for this problem. Lewis has scouted 34 thrift shops in 12 states to compile a list of prices for 750 articles of used clothing and household items and has published these values in a book, *Cash for Your Used Clothing.* He is so confident about the accuracy of the values reported in his book that he will pay any penalties assessed if the IRS rejects these values.

SOURCE: Kristin Davis, "Don't Miss These Tax Savers," *Kiplinger's Personal Finance Magazine,* December 1995, pp. 40–42. Reprinted by permission of *Kiplinger's Personal Finance Magazine.*

- An organization supported by the government that holds property or investments for the benefit of a college or university.
- A Federal, state, or local governmental unit.
- An organization normally receiving a substantial part of its support from the public or a governmental unit.

In the remaining discussion of charitable contributions, public charities and private foundations (both operating and nonoperating) that qualify for the 50 percent ceiling will be referred to as *50 percent organizations.*

The 50 percent ceiling also applies to contributions to the following organizations:

- All private operating foundations.
- Certain private nonoperating foundations that distribute the contributions they receive to public charities and private operating foundations within two and one-half months following the year they receive the contribution.
- Certain private nonoperating foundations in which the contributions are pooled in a common fund and the income and principal sum are paid to public charities.

Thirty Percent Ceiling. A 30 percent ceiling applies to contributions of cash and ordinary income property to private nonoperating foundations that are not 50 percent organizations. The 30 percent ceiling also applies to contributions of appreciated capital gain property to 50 percent organizations unless the taxpayer makes a special election (see below).

In the event the contributions for any one tax year involve both 50 percent and 30 percent property, the allowable deduction comes first from the 50 percent property.

EXAMPLE 32

During the year, Lisa made the following donations to her church: cash of $2,000 and unimproved land worth $30,000. Lisa had purchased the land four years ago for $22,000 and held it as an investment. Therefore, it is long-term capital gain property. Lisa's AGI for the year is $50,000. Disregarding percentage limitations, Lisa's potential deduction is $32,000 [$2,000 (cash) + $30,000 (fair market value of land)].

In applying the percentage limitations, however, the *current* deduction for the land is limited to $15,000 [30% (limitation applicable to long-term capital gain property) × $50,000 (AGI)]. Thus, the total deduction is $17,000 ($2,000 cash + $15,000 land). Note that the total deduction does not exceed $25,000, which is 50% of Lisa's AGI. ▼

Under a special election, a taxpayer may choose to forgo a deduction of the appreciation on capital gain property. Referred to as the *reduced deduction election,* this enables the taxpayer to move from the 30 percent limitation to the 50 percent limitation.

EXAMPLE 33

Assume the same facts as in Example 32, except that Lisa makes the reduced deduction election. Now the deduction becomes $24,000 [$2,000 (cash) + $22,000 (basis in land)] because both donations fall under the 50% limitation. Thus, by making the election, Lisa has increased her charitable contribution deduction by $7,000 [$24,000 − $17,000 (Example 32)]. ▼

Although the reduced deduction election appears attractive, it should be considered carefully. The election sacrifices a deduction for the appreciation on long-term capital gain property that might eventually be allowed. Note that in Example 32, the potential deduction was $32,000, yet in Example 33 only $24,000 is allowed. The reason the potential deduction is decreased by $8,000 ($32,000 − $24,000) is that no carryover is allowed for the amount sacrificed by the election.

Twenty Percent Ceiling. A 20 percent ceiling applies to contributions of appreciated long-term capital gain property to private nonoperating foundations that are not 50 percent organizations.

Contribution Carryovers. Contributions that exceed the percentage limitations for the current year can be carried over for five years. In the carryover process, such contributions do not lose their identity for limitation purposes. Thus, if the contribution originally involved 30 percent property, the carryover will continue to be classified as 30 percent property in the carryover year.

EXAMPLE 34

Assume the same facts as in Example 32. Because only $15,000 of the $30,000 value of the land was deducted in the current year, the balance of $15,000 may be carried over to the following year. But the carryover will still be treated as long-term capital gain property and is subject to the 30%-of-AGI limitation. ▼

In applying the percentage limitations, current charitable contributions must be claimed first before any carryovers can be considered. If carryovers involve more than one year, they are utilized in a first-in, first-out order.

7 LEARNING OBJECTIVE
List the business and personal expenditures that are deductible either as miscellaneous itemized deductions or as other itemized deductions.

MISCELLANEOUS ITEMIZED DEDUCTIONS

No deduction is allowed for personal, living, or family expenses.[44] However, a taxpayer may incur a number of expenditures related to employment. If an

[44] § 262.

Concept Summary 10–2

Determining the Deduction for Contributions of Appreciated Property by Individuals

If the Type of Property Contributed Is:	And the Property Is Contributed to:	The Contribution Is Measured by:	But the Deduction Is Limited to:
1. Capital gain property	A 50% organization	Fair market value of the property	30% of AGI
2. Ordinary income property	A 50% organization	The basis of the property*	50% of AGI
3. Capital gain property (and the property is tangible personal property put to an unrelated use by the donee)	A 50% organization	The basis of the property*	50% of AGI
4. Capital gain property (and the reduced deduction is elected)	A 50% organization	The basis of the property	50% of AGI
5. Capital gain property	A private nonoperating foundation that is not a 50% organization	The basis of the property*	The lesser of: 1. 20% of AGI 2. 50% of AGI minus other contributions to 50% organizations

*If the fair market value of the property is less than the adjusted basis (i.e., the property has declined in value instead of appreciating), the fair market value is used.

employee or outside salesperson incurs unreimbursed business expenses or expenses that are reimbursed under a nonaccountable plan, including travel and transportation, the expenses are deductible as **miscellaneous itemized deductions.**[45] Certain other expenses also fall into the special category of miscellaneous itemized deductions. Some are deductible only if, in total, they exceed 2 percent of the taxpayer's AGI. These miscellaneous itemized deductions include (but are not limited to) the following:

- Professional dues to membership organizations.
- Uniforms or other clothing that cannot be used for normal wear.
- Fees incurred for the preparation of one's tax return or fees incurred for tax litigation before the IRS or the courts.
- Job-hunting costs.
- Fee paid for a safe deposit box used to store papers and documents relating to taxable income-producing investments.
- Investment expenses that are deductible under § 212 as discussed in Chapter 6.

[45] Actors and performing artists who meet certain requirements are not subject to this rule.

- Appraisal fees to determine the amount of a casualty loss or the fair market value of donated property.
- Hobby losses up to the amount of hobby income (see Chapter 6).
- Unreimbursed employee expenses (see Chapter 9).

Certain employee business expenses that are reimbursed are not itemized deductions, but are deducted *for* AGI. Employee business expenses are discussed in depth in Chapter 9.

ETHICAL CONSIDERATIONS

Job Hunting in Ski Country: A Deductible Expense?

Julio, an avid skier, manages the ski department of a sporting goods store in Indianapolis. He has been taking ski vacations in Colorado for several years and has decided to find a job in Colorado and move there. Julio just learned that he can deduct job-hunting costs on his Federal income tax return. One of his customers, who is a CPA, told Julio that transportation costs can be deducted if the primary purpose of the trip is to hunt for a job. According to the CPA, other travel costs must be allocated between job-hunting days and personal days. Julio plans to fly to Colorado on Sunday, have job interviews each morning from Monday through Thursday, and ski each afternoon after the job interviews are concluded. He will ski all day Friday and Saturday and fly back to Indianapolis on Saturday night. Is Julio justified in taking a deduction for job-hunting expenses this year? Will he be justified in taking future deductions if he is unable to find a job this year and continues his job-hunting trips each year for the next several years?

Other Miscellaneous Deductions

Certain expenses and losses do not fall into any category of itemized deductions already discussed but are nonetheless deductible. The following expenses and losses are deductible on line 27 of Schedule A as Other Miscellaneous Deductions.

- Gambling losses up to the amount of gambling winnings.
- Impairment-related work expenses of a handicapped person.
- Federal estate tax on income in respect of a decedent.
- Deduction for repayment of amounts under a claim of right if more than $3,000 (discussed in Chapter 18).
- The unrecovered investment in an annuity contract when the annuity ceases by reason of death, discussed in Chapter 4.

Unlike the expenses and losses discussed previously under Miscellaneous Itemized Deductions, the above expenses and losses are not subject to the 2 percent-of-AGI floor.

Comprehensive Example of Schedule A

Harry and Jean Brown, married filing jointly, had the following transactions for the current year:

• Medicines that required a prescription	$ 430
• Doctor and dentist bills paid and not reimbursed	2,120
• Medical insurance premium payments	1,200
• Contact lenses	175
• Transportation for medical purposes (425 miles × 9 cents/mile + $4.75 parking)	43
• State income tax withheld	620
• Real estate taxes	1,580
• Interest paid on qualified residence mortgage	2,840
• Charitable contributions in cash	860
• Transportation in performing charitable services (860 miles × 12 cents/mile + $15.80 parking and tolls)	119
• Unreimbursed employee expenses (from a Form 2106)	870
• Tax return preparation	150
• Professional expenses (dues and publications)	135
• Safe deposit box (used for keeping investment documents and tax records)	35

The Browns' AGI is $40,000. Their completed 1995 Schedule A on the following page reports itemized deductions totaling $7,377.

Overall Limitation on Certain Itemized Deductions

8 Learning Objective
Recognize the limitation on certain itemized deductions applicable to high-income taxpayers.

Congress has enacted several provisions limiting tax benefits for high-income taxpayers. These limitations include the exemption phase-out (refer to Chapter 3) and a phase-out of itemized deductions. The phase-out of itemized deductions (also referred to as a cutback adjustment) applies to taxpayers whose AGI exceeds $117,950 ($58,975 for married taxpayers filing separately).[46] The limitation applies to the following frequently encountered itemized deductions:[47]

- Taxes.
- Home mortgage interest, including points.
- Charitable contributions.
- Unreimbursed employee expenses subject to the 2 percent-of-AGI floor.
- All other expenses subject to the 2 percent-of-AGI floor.

The following deductions are *not* subject to the limitation on itemized deductions:

- Medical and dental expenses.
- Investment interest expense.
- Nonbusiness casualty and theft losses.
- Gambling losses.

[46] For 1995, the limitation applied if AGI exceeded $114,700 ($57,350 for married taxpayers filing separately).

[47] Other deductions subject to the limitation include Federal estate tax on income in respect of a decedent, certain amortizable bond premiums, the deduction for repayment of certain amounts, certain unrecovered investments in an annuity, and impairment-related work expenses.

SCHEDULES A&B (Form 1040)

Department of the Treasury Internal Revenue Service (99)

Schedule A—Itemized Deductions

(Schedule B is on back)

▶ Attach to Form 1040. ▶ See Instructions for Schedules A and B (Form 1040).

OMB No. 1545-0074

1995

Attachment Sequence No. **07**

Name(s) shown on Form 1040: *Harry and Jean Brown*

Your social security number: *371 : 30 : 3987*

Section	Line	Description	Box	Amount	Line	Total
Medical and Dental Expenses		**Caution:** *Do not include expenses reimbursed or paid by others.*				
	1	Medical and dental expenses (see page A-1)	1	*3,968*		
	2	Enter amount from Form 1040, line 32. [2] *40,000*				
	3	Multiply line 2 above by 7.5% (.075)	3	*3,000*		
	4	Subtract line 3 from line 1. If line 3 is more than line 1, enter -0-			4	*968*
Taxes You Paid (See page A-1.)	5	State and local income taxes	5	*620*		
	6	Real estate taxes (see page A-2)	6	*1,580*		
	7	Personal property taxes	7			
	8	Other taxes. List type and amount ▶	8			
	9	Add lines 5 through 8			9	*2,200*
Interest You Paid (See page A-2.)	10	Home mortgage interest and points reported to you on Form 1098	10	*2,840*		
	11	Home mortgage interest not reported to you on Form 1098. If paid to the person from whom you bought the home, see page A-3 and show that person's name, identifying no., and address ▶	11			
Note: Personal interest is not deductible.	12	Points not reported to you on Form 1098. See page A-3 for special rules	12			
	13	Investment interest. If required, attach Form 4952. (See page A-3.)	13			
	14	Add lines 10 through 13			14	*2,840*
Gifts to Charity If you made a gift and got a benefit for it, see page A-3.	15	Gifts by cash or check. If you made any gift of $250 or more, see page A-3	15	*860*		
	16	Other than by cash or check. If any gift of $250 or more, see page A-3. If over $500, you **MUST** attach Form 8283	16	*119*		
	17	Carryover from prior year	17			
	18	Add lines 15 through 17			18	*979*
Casualty and Theft Losses	19	Casualty or theft loss(es). Attach Form 4684. (See page A-4.)			19	
Job Expenses and Most Other Miscellaneous Deductions	20	Unreimbursed employee expenses—job travel, union dues, job education, etc. If required, you **MUST** attach Form 2106 or 2106-EZ. (See page A-5.) ▶ *Form 2106 $870*	20	*870*		
	21	Tax preparation fees	21	*150*		
(See page A-5 for expenses to deduct here.)	22	Other expenses—investment, safe deposit box, etc. List type and amount ▶ *Professional expenses, $135; safe deposit box, $35*	22	*170*		
	23	Add lines 20 through 22	23	*1,190*		
	24	Enter amount from Form 1040, line 32. [24] *40,000*				
	25	Multiply line 24 above by 2% (.02)	25	*800*		
	26	Subtract line 25 from line 23. If line 25 is more than line 23, enter -0-			26	*390*
Other Miscellaneous Deductions	27	Other—from list on page A-5. List type and amount ▶			27	
Total Itemized Deductions	28	Is Form 1040, line 32, over $114,700 (over $57,350 if married filing separately)? **NO.** Your deduction is not limited. Add the amounts in the far right column for lines 4 through 27. Also, enter on Form 1040, line 34, the **larger** of this amount or your standard deduction. **YES.** Your deduction may be limited. See page A-5 for the amount to enter.			28	*7,377*

nursing care, unreimbursed medical exp. tax benefit — General itemized deduction — no limitations — CA — Miscellaneous — qualifying residents, motor boats, 3rd home, Winnebago - not over $1M and interest on home equity loan doesn't exceed of the lesser value — pts from 1st time acquiring the house - refinancing pts is amortized. — must have 2% AGI — investment exp - inv. income (dividends) — if received something in return; the amount must be reduced to amount given — limited to 2% AGI by overall limitations — phase out? — can take a loss up to gambling earnings

Taxpayers subject to the limitation must reduce itemized deductions by the lesser of:

- 3 percent of the amount by which AGI exceeds $117,950 ($58,975 if married filing separately).
- 80 percent of itemized deductions that are affected by the limit.

The overall limitation is applied after applying all other limitations to itemized deductions that are affected by the overall limitation. Other limitations apply to charitable contributions, certain meals and entertainment expenses, and certain miscellaneous itemized deductions.

EXAMPLE 35

Herman, who is single, had AGI of $200,000 for 1996. He incurred the following expenses and losses during the year:

Medical expenses before 7.5%-of-AGI limitation	$16,000
State and local income taxes	3,200
Real estate taxes	2,800
Home mortgage interest	7,200
Charitable contributions	2,000
Casualty loss before 10% limitation (after $100 floor)	21,500
Unreimbursed employee expenses subject to 2%-of-AGI limitation	4,300
Gambling losses (Herman had $3,000 gambling income)	7,000

Herman's itemized deductions *before* the overall limitation are computed as follows:

Medical expenses [$16,000 − (7.5% × $200,000)]	$ 1,000
State and local income taxes	3,200
Real estate taxes	2,800
Home mortgage interest	7,200
Charitable contributions	2,000
Casualty loss [$21,500 − (10% × $200,000)]	1,500
Unreimbursed employee expenses ($4,300 − (2% × $200,000)]	300
Gambling losses ($7,000 loss limited to $3,000 of gambling income)	3,000
Total itemized deductions before overall limitation	$21,000

Herman's itemized deductions subject to the overall limitation are as follows:

State and local income taxes	$ 3,200
Real estate taxes	2,800
Home mortgage interest	7,200
Charitable contributions	2,000
Unreimbursed employee expenses	300
Total	$15,500

Herman must reduce this amount by the smaller of the following:

• 3% ($200,000 AGI − $117,950)	$2,462
• 80% of itemized deductions subject to limitation ($15,500 × .80)	12,400

Therefore, the amount of the reduction is $2,462, and Herman has $18,538 of deductible itemized deductions, computed as follows:

Deductible itemized deductions subject to overall limitation ($15,500 − $2,462)	$13,038
Itemized deductions not subject to overall limitation:	
Medical expenses	1,000
Casualty loss	1,500
Gambling losses	3,000
Deductible itemized deductions	$18,538

▼

TAX PLANNING CONSIDERATIONS

9 LEARNING OBJECTIVE
Identify tax planning procedures that can maximize the benefit of itemized deductions.

EFFECTIVE UTILIZATION OF ITEMIZED DEDUCTIONS

Since an individual may use the standard deduction in one year and itemize deductions in another year, it is frequently possible to obtain maximum benefit by shifting itemized deductions from one year to another. For example, if a taxpayer's itemized deductions and the standard deduction are approximately the same for each year of a two-year period, the taxpayer should use the standard deduction in one year and shift itemized deductions (to the extent permitted by law) to the other year. The individual could, for example, prepay a church pledge for a particular year to shift the deduction to the current year or avoid paying end-of-the-year medical expenses to shift the deduction to the following year.

UTILIZATION OF MEDICAL DEDUCTIONS

When a taxpayer anticipates that medical expenses will approximate the percentage floor, much might be done to generate a deductible excess. Any of the following procedures can help build a deduction by the end of the year:

- Incur the obligation for needed dental work or have needed work carried out.[48] Orthodontic treatment, for example, may have been recommended for a member of the taxpayer's family.
- Have elective remedial surgery that may have been postponed from prior years (e.g., tonsillectomies, vasectomies, correction of hernias, hysterectomies).
- Incur the obligation for capital improvements to the taxpayer's personal residence recommended by a physician (e.g., an air filtration system to alleviate a respiratory disorder).

[48] Prepayment of medical expenses does not generate a current deduction unless the taxpayer is under an obligation to make the payment.

TAX IN THE NEWS

The President's Tax Return

President Bill Clinton and First Lady Hillary Rodham Clinton were entitled to a $14,418 refund on their 1994 Federal income tax return, resulting in Federal income taxes of $40,895. Gross income included President Clinton's $200,000 salary and $63,900 of investment income from a blind trust established by the Clintons when the President took office. Also included was a $1,421 royalty from a video of Arsenio Hall highlights, which featured President Clinton playing the saxophone in an appearance on Hall's show during the presidential campaign.

The Clintons made charitable contributions of $30,125 in 1994, compared to $17,000 in 1993. They paid $10,000 in legal and accounting fees for preparation of their 1994 tax return. They will be able to claim this amount as an itemized deduction on their 1995 return, subject to the 2 percent floor for miscellaneous itemized deductions. Because of their income level, the Clintons are also subject to the 3 percent overall floor for itemized deductions.

Vice President Al Gore and his wife Tipper reported considerably more income, which included the Vice President's $171,500 salary and $259,013 of royalties from his book *Earth in the Balance: Ecology and the Human Spirit.*

SOURCE: Information from John F. Harris, "Clintons' Income Tax Return Provides Good and Bad News,"

As an aid to taxpayers who may experience temporary cash-flow problems at the end of the year, the use of bank credit cards is deemed to be payment for purposes of timing the deductibility of charitable and medical expenses.

EXAMPLE 36 On December 13, 1996, Marge (a calendar year taxpayer) purchases two pairs of prescription contact lenses and one pair of prescribed orthopedic shoes for a total of $305. These purchases are separately charged to Marge's credit card. On January 6, 1997, Marge receives her statement containing these charges and makes payment shortly thereafter. The purchases are deductible as medical expenses in the year charged (1996) and not in the year the account is settled (1997). ▼

Recognizing which expenditures qualify for the medical deduction also may be crucial to exceeding the percentage limitations.

EXAMPLE 37 Mortimer employs Lana (an unrelated party) to care for his incapacitated and dependent mother. Lana is not a trained nurse but spends approximately one-half of the time performing nursing duties (e.g., administering injections and providing physical therapy) and the rest of the time doing household chores. An allocable portion of Lana's wages that Mortimer pays (including the employer's portion of FICA taxes) qualifies as a medical expense. ▼

To assure a deduction for the entire cost of nursing home care for an aged dependent, it is helpful if the transfer of the individual to the home is for medical reasons and is recommended by a doctor. In addition, the nursing home facilities should be adequate to provide the necessary medical and nursing care. To assure a deduction for all of the nursing home expenses, it is necessary to show that the individual was placed in the home for required medical care rather than for personal or family considerations.

Proper documentation is required to substantiate medical expenses. The taxpayer should keep all receipts for credit card or other charge purchases of medical services and deductible drugs as well as all cash register receipts. In addition, medical transportation mileage should be recorded.

If a taxpayer or a dependent of the taxpayer must be institutionalized in order to receive adequate medical care, it may be good tax planning to make a lump-sum payment that will cover medical treatment for future periods. It is advisable to negotiate a contract with the institution so that the expense is fixed and the payment is not a mere deposit.

TIMING THE PAYMENT OF DEDUCTIBLE TAXES

It is sometimes possible to defer or accelerate the payment of certain deductible taxes, such as state income tax, real property tax, and personal property tax. For instance, the final installment of estimated state income tax is generally due after the end of a given tax year. Accelerating the payment of the final installment could result in larger itemized deductions for the current year.

EXAMPLE 38

Jenny, who is single, expects to have itemized deductions of $3,900 in 1996 and $2,500 in 1997. She plans to pay $900 as the final installment on her 1996 estimated state income tax, which is due on January 15, 1997. If Jenny does not pay the final installment until 1997, she will not itemize in either 1996 or 1997. However, if she pays the final installment in December 1996, her itemized deductions will be $4,800 ($3,900 + $900) in 1996, and she will benefit from itemizing. ▼

PROTECTING THE INTEREST DEDUCTION

Although the deductibility of prepaid interest by a cash basis taxpayer has been severely restricted, a notable exception allows a deduction for points paid by the buyer to obtain financing for the purchase or improvement of a principal residence in the year of payment. However, such points must actually be paid by the taxpayer obtaining the loan and must represent a charge for the use of money. It has been held that points paid from the mortgage proceeds do not satisfy the payment requirement.[49] Also, the portion of the points attributable to service charges does not represent deductible interest.[50] Taxpayers financing home purchases or improvements usually should direct their planning toward avoiding these two hurdles to immediate deductibility.

In rare instances, a taxpayer may find it desirable to forgo the immediate expensing of points in the year paid. Instead, it could prove beneficial to capitalize the points and write them off as interest expense over the life of the mortgage.

EXAMPLE 39

Geraldine purchases a home on December 15, 1996, for $95,000 with $30,000 cash and a 15-year mortgage of $65,000 financed by the Greater Metropolis National Bank. Geraldine pays two points in addition to interest allocated to the period from December 15 until December 31, 1996, at an annual rate of 10%. Since Geraldine does not have enough

[49] *Alan A. Rubnitz*, 67 T.C. 621 (1977). Seller-paid points may also be deductible by the buyer under the provisions of Rev.Proc. 94–27, cited in footnote 27.

[50] *Donald L. Wilkerson*, 70 T.C. 240 (1978).

itemized deductions to exceed the standard deduction for 1996, she should elect to capitalize the interest expense by amortizing the points over 15 years. In this instance, Geraldine would deduct $86.67 for 1997, as part of her qualified residence interest expense [$1,300 (two points) divided by 15 years], if she elects to itemize that year. ▼

Because personal (consumer) interest is not deductible, taxpayers should consider making use of home equity loans. Recall that these loans utilize the personal residence of the taxpayer as security. Since the tracing rules do not apply to home equity loans, the funds from these loans can be used for personal purposes (e.g., auto loans, education). By making use of home equity loans, therefore, what would have been nondeductible consumer interest becomes deductible qualified residence interest.

ASSURING THE CHARITABLE CONTRIBUTION DEDUCTION

For a charitable contribution deduction to be available, the recipient must be a qualified charitable organization. Sometimes the mechanics of how the contribution is carried out can determine whether or not a deduction results.

EXAMPLE 40

Fumiko wants to donate $5,000 to her church's mission in Kobe, Japan. In this regard, she considers three alternatives:

1. Send the money directly to the mission.
2. Give the money to her church with the understanding that it is to be passed on to the mission.
3. Give the money directly to the missionary in charge of the mission who is currently in the United States on a fund-raising trip.

If Fumiko wants to obtain a deduction for the contribution, she should choose alternative 2. A direct donation to the mission (alternative 1) is not deductible because the mission is a foreign charity. A direct gift to the missionary (alternative 3) does not comply since an individual cannot be a qualified charity for income tax purposes.[51] ▼

When making noncash donations, the type of property chosen can have decided implications in determining the amount, if any, of the deduction.

EXAMPLE 41

Samantha wants to give $60,000 in value to her church in some form other than cash. In this connection, she considers four alternatives:

1. Stock held for two years as an investment with a basis of $100,000 and a fair market value of $60,000.
2. Stock held for five years as an investment with a basis of $10,000 and a fair market value of $60,000.
3. The rent-free use for a year of a building that normally leases for $5,000 a month.
4. A valuable stamp collection held as an investment and owned for 10 years with a basis of $10,000 and a fair market value of $60,000. The church plans to sell the collection if and when it is donated.

Alternative 1 is ill-advised as the subject of the gift. Even though Samantha would obtain a deduction of $60,000, she would forgo the potential loss of $40,000 that would be

[51] *Thomas E. Lesslie*, 36 TCM 495, T.C.Memo. 1977–111.

recognized if the property were sold.[52] Alternative 2 makes good sense since the deduction still is $60,000 and none of the $50,000 of appreciation that has occurred must be recognized as income. Alternative 3 yields no deduction at all and is not a wise choice. Alternative 4 involves tangible personalty that the recipient does not plan to use. As a result, the amount of the deduction is limited to $10,000, the stamp collection's basis.[53] ▼

ETHICAL CONSIDERATIONS

Charitable Motivations and Tax Considerations

Billy owns a principal residence in Columbia, South Carolina, and a vacation home in Myrtle Beach. Billy has retired and plans to move permanently to the vacation house in Myrtle Beach, which is worth $350,000 (adjusted basis of $90,000). He enters into a contract to sell his Columbia residence, which he has owned for 10 years, for $200,000. His adjusted basis in the house is $120,000.

Billy, a devout supporter of his church, then calls his CPA, tells her that he plans to donate the $200,000 to his church, and inquires about the tax consequences. The CPA tells Billy that he has made a bad tax move because he will have to pay tax on the $80,000 gain and that he could have taken a $200,000 charitable contribution deduction without reporting any gain if he had donated the house directly to the church.

Billy, who sold the Columbia residence subject to approval by a building inspector, then proposes two actions he can take to ensure that the sale will fall through. Plan 1 is to secretly give the building inspector a gift and indicate that he'd like a negative inspection report. Plan 2 is to point out some hard-to-detect architectural flaws that he knows about to the building inspector. What advice should the CPA give to Billy? Should the CPA prepare Billy's return if Billy follows through with either plan?

For property transfers (particularly real estate), the ceiling limitations on the amount of the deduction allowed in any one year (50 percent, 30 percent, or 20 percent of AGI, as the case may be) could be a factor to take into account. With proper planning, donations can be controlled to stay within the limitations and therefore avoid the need for a carryover of unused charitable contributions.

EXAMPLE 42

Andrew wants to donate a tract of unimproved land held as an investment to the University of Maryland (a qualified charitable organization). The land has been held for six years and has a current fair market value of $300,000 and a basis to Andrew of $50,000. Andrew's AGI for the current year is estimated to be $200,000, and he expects much the same for the next few years. In the current year, he deeds (transfers) an undivided one-fifth interest in the real estate to the university. ▼

What has Andrew in Example 42 accomplished for income tax purposes? In the current year, he will be allowed a charitable contribution deduction of $60,000 ($\frac{1}{5}$ × $300,000), which will be within the applicable limitation of AGI (30% ×

[52] *LaVar M. Withers*, 69 T.C. 900 (1978).

[53] No reduction of appreciation is necessary in alternative 2 since stock is intangible property and not tangible personalty.

TAX IN THE NEWS

CAN YOU BELIEVE THIS NOW THAT YOU'VE READ THE CHAPTER?

The IRS is required to provide estimated preparation times for the various forms and schedules that taxpayers must file. The estimated times for Schedule A—Itemized Deductions are as follows:

Record keeping	2 hr, 32 min
Learning about the law or the form	26 min
Preparing the form	1 hr, 10 min
Copying, assembling, and sending the form to the IRS	27 min
Total time for Schedule A	4 hr, 35 min

All taxpayers who have interest or dividend income of $400 or more and elect to itemize deductions must complete Form 1040, Schedule A, and Schedule B (Interest and Dividend Income), which constitute a relatively simple tax return. The IRS estimates that filing such a return requires 16 hours and 22 minutes.

SOURCE: 1994 Instructions for Form 1040, Internal Revenue Service (Washington, D.C.: U.S. Government Printing Office, 1995).

$200,000). Presuming no other charitable contributions for the year, Andrew has avoided the possibility of a carryover. In future years, Andrew can arrange donations of undivided interests in the real estate to stay within the bounds of the percentage limitations. The only difficulty with this approach is the need to revalue the real estate each year before the donation, since the amount of the deduction is based on the fair market value of the interest contributed at the time of the contribution.

It may be wise to avoid a carryover of unused charitable contributions, if possible, because that approach may be dangerous in several respects. First, the carryover period is limited to five years. Depending on the taxpayer's projected AGI rather than actual AGI, some of the amount carried over may expire without tax benefit after the five-year period has ended. Second, unused charitable contribution carryovers do not survive the death of the party making the donation and as a consequence are lost.

EXAMPLE 43

Tiffany dies in October 1996. In completing her final income tax return for 1996, Tiffany's executor determines the following information: AGI of $104,000 and a donation by Tiffany to her church of stock worth $60,000. Tiffany had purchased the stock two years ago for $50,000 and held it as an investment. Tiffany's executor makes the reduced deduction election and, as a consequence, claims a charitable contribution deduction of $50,000. With the election, the potential charitable contribution deduction of $50,000 ($60,000 – $10,000) is less than the 50% ceiling of $52,000 ($104,000 × 50%). If the executor had not made the election, the potential charitable contribution deduction of $60,000 would have been reduced by the 30% ceiling to $31,200 ($104,000 × 30%). No carryover of the $28,800 ($60,000 – $31,200) would have been available. ▼

KEY TERMS

Acquisition indebtedness, 10–15

Capital gain property, 10–22

Charitable contribution, 10–18

Home equity loans, 10–15

Investment income, 10–13

Investment interest, 10–13

Medical expense, 10–2

Miscellaneous itemized deductions, 10–26

Net investment income, 10–13

Ordinary income property, 10–22

Points, 10–16

Qualified residence interest, 10–13

PROBLEM MATERIALS

DISCUSSION QUESTIONS

1. Dan, a self-employed individual taxpayer, prepared his own income tax return for the past year and asked you to check it over for accuracy. Your review indicates that Dan failed to claim certain business entertainment expenses.
   a. Will the correction of this omission affect the amount of medical expenses Dan can deduct? Explain.
   b. Would it matter if Dan were employed rather than self-employed?
2. Nina is in perfect health. During the current year, however, she pays $450 for an annual physical exam and $80 for a dental checkup. Do these expenses qualify for the medical deduction? Why or why not?
3. Nathan sustained serious facial damage in a skiing accident. To restore his physical appearance, he had cosmetic surgery. At the same time, he also had surgery to remove wrinkles from under his eyes caused by age. Can Nathan claim the cost of these procedures as a medical expense?
4. What are the criteria for determining whether the cost of a nursing home can qualify as a medical expense?
5. Hugo has a history of heart disease. Upon the advice of his doctor, he installs an elevator in his residence so he does not have to climb stairs. Is this a valid medical expense? If it is, how much of the expense is deductible?
6. Susan, a sole proprietor of an antique shop, has two dependent children. During the year, she paid health insurance premiums of $1,400 for her own coverage and $1,800 for coverage of her children. How will these premium payments affect Susan's taxable income computation?
7. Tim took his disabled mother, Sharon, from Green Bay to Milwaukee for surgery at a clinic on an outpatient basis. They stayed in a motel near the clinic for two days after the surgery for postoperative evaluations. Discuss the extent to which transportation, meals, and lodging costs incurred by Tim and his mother are deductible as medical expenses (ignore the 7.5% floor).
8. If Ida's medical expense deduction was $500 in 1996 and the amount reduced her tax liability, how would a $300 insurance reimbursement be treated if received in 1997? Received in 1996? What if Ida had not itemized deductions in 1996 and received the $300 reimbursement in 1997?
9. By December 1, Anna had medical expenses of $5,000, of which $1,000 was reimbursed by her insurance company. She expects her AGI for the year to be $60,000 and her other

itemized deductions to be $5,300. Can you suggest any tax planning ideas that will enable Anna to increase her medical expense deduction for the year?

10. Susan and Anna, who are sisters, both itemize deductions. Susan, who lives in Arizona, can deduct part of the cost of licensing her automobile. Anna, who lives in Illinois, cannot deduct any part of her automobile license fees. Explain.

11. The city required Heather to pay $3,000 for the cost of a new sidewalk in front of her personal residence. What effect will this $3,000 have on Heather from a tax perspective?

12. Joe sold his personal residence to Emma on July 1, 1996. He had paid real property taxes on March 1, 1996, the due date for property taxes for 1996. How will Joe's payment affect his deduction for property taxes in 1996? Will Joe's payment of the taxes have any effect on Emma's itemized deductions for 1996? What other tax or financial effects will Joe's payment of the taxes have on either party?

13. Edna, a calendar year, cash basis taxpayer, overpaid her 1996 state income tax by $800. Edna chose to apply the overpayment toward her state income taxes for 1997 and did not claim a refund. She itemized deductions in 1996. Does Edna have to report the $800 as income in 1997?

14. Donald owns a principal residence in Chicago, a vacation lodge in New Mexico, and a yacht (with living quarters) on Lake Michigan. All three properties have mortgages on which Donald pays interest. Discuss any limitations that apply to Donald's mortgage interest deduction, and suggest any strategy Donald should consider to maximize his deduction.

15. Ed borrows $20,000 and purchases an automobile. Jack borrows $20,000 to purchase a diamond engagement ring for his fiancée. Ed qualifies for an interest deduction on the amount he borrowed, but Jack does not. Can you offer any explanation for the difference?

16. As to the deductibility of "points," comment on the following:
    a. Those paid by the seller.
    b. Those paid to finance the purchase of a rental house.
    c. Those relating to the rendering of personal services.
    d. When capitalization and amortization might be advisable.
    e. Points paid from the mortgage proceeds.

17. Ellen borrows $50,000 from her parents for a down payment on a condominium. She paid interest of $4,200 in 1994, $0 in 1995, and $11,000 in 1996. The IRS disallows the deduction. Can you offer any explanation for the disallowance?

18. To dissuade his pastor from resigning and taking a position with a larger church, Michael, an ardent leader of the congregation, gives the pastor a new car. Is the cost of the car deductible by Michael as a charitable contribution?

19. Lola purchased a ticket to a fund-raising banquet and dance for the Pittsburgh Symphony, a public charity. The ticket cost $250, and the normal cost of such an event is $50. How much can Lola deduct as a charitable contribution?

20. Bill pays tuition to a parochial school run by his church so that his children can attend the school. The church is a qualified charity. Can Bill deduct any portion of the tuition payments as a charitable contribution?

21. Zane donated property that cost $1,000 and was worth $3,000 to a charity. Under what circumstances will Zane be allowed to deduct $3,000 for this charitable contribution? Under what circumstances will he be limited to a $1,000 deduction?

22. What is capital gain property? What tax treatment is required if capital gain property is contributed to a private nonoperating foundation? To a public charity? What difference does it make if the contribution is tangible personalty and it is put to a use unrelated to the donee's business?

23. During the year, Shirley donated five dresses to the Salvation Army. She had purchased the dresses three years ago at a cost of $1,200 and worn them as personal attire. Because the dresses are long-term capital assets, Shirley plans to deduct $1,200 on her income tax return. Comment on Shirley's understanding of the tax law governing charitable contributions.

24. A local opthalmologist's advertising campaign included a certificate for a free radial keratotomy for the lucky winner of a drawing. Ahmad held the winning ticket, which was drawn in December 1995. Ahmad had no vision problems and was uncertain what he should do with the prize. In February 1996, Ahmad's daughter, who lives with his former wife, was diagnosed with a vision problem that could be treated either with prescription glasses or a radial keratotomy. The divorce decree requires that Ahmad pay for all medical expenses incurred for his daughter. Identify the relevant tax issues for Ahmad.

25. The Skins Game, which involves four of the top golfers on the PGA Tour, is held each year on the weekend after Thanksgiving. Total prize money amounts to $510,000, and the leading money winner also receives an automobile as a prize. The announcers point out that 10% of the money won by each player goes to charity. In addition, on some holes, the winner of the hole receives the keys to an automobile, which goes to the player's favorite charity. Identify the relevant tax issues for the players. Consider the following possibilities with respect to the car won by the leading money winner: (1) he might keep the car for his own use and sell his present car; (2) he might sell the new car; (3) he might give the car to a friend or relative; (4) he might donate the car to charity; or (5) he might give the car to his caddy.

26. Henry is a television evangelist. In August 1995, the IRS ruled that his organization was no longer a qualified charitable organization because of violations of the tax law. Miguel donated $10,000 to Henry's organization in September 1995. At the time, he did not know that Henry's organization had been disqualified as a charitable organization. In 1996, Henry was jailed for mail fraud. Miguel has filed a civil suit demanding return of the $10,000 plus $100,000 in damages. Identify the relevant tax issues for Miguel.

PROBLEMS

27. Bill and Nancy are married and together have AGI of $60,000. They have no dependents and filed a joint return. Each pays $900 for hospitalization insurance. During the year, they paid the following amounts for medical care: $6,200 in doctor and dentist bills and hospital expenses and $800 for prescribed medicine and drugs. In December, they received an insurance reimbursement of $1,200 for hospitalization. Determine the deduction allowable for medical expenses paid during the year.

28. Frank, a widower, had a serious stroke and is no longer capable of caring for himself. He has three sons, all of whom live in different states. Because they are unable to care for Frank in their homes, his sons have placed him in a nursing home equipped to provide medical and nursing care facilities. Total nursing home expenses amount to $45,000 per year. Of this amount, $18,000 is directly attributable to medical and nursing care. Frank's Social Security benefits are used to pay for $12,000 of the nursing home charges. He has no other income. His sons plan to split the remaining medical expenses equally.
    a. What portion of the nursing home charges is potentially deductible as a medical expense?
    b. Can you provide Frank's sons with a tax planning idea for maximizing the deduction for his medical expenses?

29. Ken developed a severe asthmatic condition, and his physician advised him to install a special air conditioning, heating, and filtration system in his home. The cost of installing the system was $6,000, and the increase in the value of the residence was determined to be $2,000. Ken's AGI for the year was $30,000.

a. How much of the expenditure can Ken deduct as a medical expense?
b. Assume the same facts as in (a), except that Ken was paralyzed in an automobile accident and the expenditures were incurred to build entrance and exit ramps and widen the hallways in his home to accommodate his wheelchair. How much of the expenditure can Ken deduct as a medical expense?

30. Julia had medical expenses of $9,000 and AGI of $100,000 in 1996. She had other itemized deductions of $8,200 for the year. Julia expects that her insurance company will reimburse her for all of her medical expenses in January 1997. What is the maximum amount Julia can deduct as itemized deductions for 1996? If she deducts the maximum allowable amount in 1996, will this affect her taxable income in 1997? What factors should Julia consider in deciding whether to deduct the medical expenses in 1996?

31. During the current year, Sara incurred and paid the following expenses for Seth (her son), Emma (her mother), and herself:

Surgery for Seth	$3,200
Trout Valley Academy charges for Seth:	
Tuition	9,000
Room, board, and other expenses	6,600
Psychiatric treatment	7,200
Doctor bills for Emma	2,700
Prescription drugs for Sara, Seth, and Emma	1,300
Insulin for Emma	950
Nonprescription drugs for Sara, Seth, and Emma	800
Charges at Riverview Nursing Home for Emma:	
Medical care	6,500
Lodging	8,200
Meals	3,300

Seth qualifies as Sara's dependent, and Emma would also qualify except that she receives $6,100 of taxable retirement benefits from her former employer. Seth's psychiatrist recommended Trout Valley Academy because of its small class sizes and specialized psychiatric treatment program that is needed to treat Seth's illness. Emma is a paraplegic and diabetic, and Riverview offers the type of care that she requires.

Upon the recommendation of a physician, Sara has an air filtration system installed in her personal residence. She suffers from severe allergies. In connection with this equipment, Sara incurs and pays the following amounts during the year:

Filtration system and cost of installation	$6,800
Increase in utility bills due to the system	550
Cost of certified appraisal	370

The system has an estimated useful life of 10 years. The appraisal was to determine the value of Sara's residence with and without the system. The appraisal states that the system increased the value of Sara's residence by $1,000. Ignoring the 7.5% floor, what is the total of Sara's expenses that qualifies for the medical expense deduction?

32. Henry, a resident of Decatur, Illinois, is advised by his family physician that his dependent son needs surgery for benign tumors in his leg. Henry and his son travel to Rochester, Minnesota, for treatment at the Mayo Clinic, which specializes in this type of surgery. Henry incurred the following costs:

Round-trip airfare ($320 each)	$640
Henry's hotel in Rochester for four nights ($80 per night)	320
Henry's meals while in Rochester	88

Compute Henry's medical expenses for the trip (subject to the 7.5% floor).

33. In Clay County, the real property tax year is the calendar year. The real property tax becomes a personal liability of the owner of real property on January 1 in the current real property tax year, 1996. The tax is payable on July 1, 1996. On May 30, 1996, Joe sells his house to Celia for $280,000. On July 1, 1996, Celia pays the entire real estate tax of $7,320 for the year ending December 31, 1996.
   a. How much of the property taxes may Joe deduct?
   b. How much of the property taxes may Celia deduct?

34. Assume the same facts as in Problem 33.
   a. What is Celia's basis for the residence?
   b. How much did Joe realize from the sale of the residence?

35. Roland uses the cash method of accounting and lives in a state that imposes an income tax (including withholding from wages). On April 14, 1996, he files his state return for 1995, paying an additional $500 in state income taxes. During 1996, his withholdings for state income tax purposes amount to $3,700. On April 13, 1997, he files his state return for 1996 claiming a refund of $900. Roland receives the refund on August 3, 1997.
   a. If Roland itemizes deductions, how much may he claim as a deduction for state income taxes on his Federal return for calendar year 1996 (filed in April 1997)?
   b. How will the refund of $900 received in 1997 be treated for Federal income tax purposes?

36. Sandra incurred $19,500 of interest expense related to her investments in 1996. Her investment income included $6,000 of interest, $4,000 of dividends, and a $7,500 net capital gain on the sale of securities.
   a. What is the maximum amount that Sandra can treat as investment income for the year?
   b. What other tax factors should Sandra consider in deciding whether to elect to include net capital gain in her investment income?

37. Maria has AGI of $72,000, which includes dividends and interest income of $16,200. In addition to investment interest expense of $14,000, she paid $2,700 of city ad valorem property tax on stocks and bonds and had the following miscellaneous itemized expenses:

Safe deposit box rental (to hold investment securities)	$ 108
Investment counsel fee	1,080
Professional dues and subscriptions	765
Tax return preparation fees	540

Determine Maria's investment expense deduction and discuss the treatment of any portion of the investment interest expense that is disallowed due to the investment interest limitation.

38. Veronica borrowed $200,000 to acquire a parcel of land to be held for investment purposes. During the year, she paid interest of $20,000 on the loan. She had AGI of $50,000 for the year. Other items related to Veronica's investments include the following:

Investment income	$10,200
Long-term gain on sale of stock	4,000
Investment counsel fees	1,500

Veronica is unmarried and elected to itemize her deductions. She had no miscellaneous deductions other than the investment counsel fees. Determine Veronica's investment interest deduction.

39. Sid and Sara, married taxpayers, took out a mortgage on their home for $100,000 in 1987. In March of the current year, when the home had a fair market value of $200,000

and they owed $85,000 on the mortgage, Sid and Sara took out a home equity loan for $110,000. They used the funds to purchase a motor home to be used for recreational purposes. What is the maximum amount on which they can deduct home equity interest?

40. Ella purchased her residence five years ago, obtaining a 20-year mortgage at an annual interest rate of 11%. On January 2, 1996, Ella refinanced with a 15-year mortgage in order to reduce the interest rate to 8.25%. To obtain the refinancing, she was required to pay points of $3,000. How much, if any, of the $3,000 points can Ella deduct in 1996?

41. Ron and Tom are equal owners in Robin Corporation. On July 1, 1996, each loans the corporation $30,000 at annual interest of 10%. Ron and Tom are brothers. Both shareholders are on the cash method of accounting, while Robin Corporation is on the accrual method. All parties use the calendar year for tax purposes. On June 30, 1997, Robin repays the loans of $60,000 together with the specified interest of $6,000.
   a. How much of the interest can Robin Corporation deduct in 1996? In 1997?
   b. When is the interest taxed to Ron and Tom?

42. Erin donates $1,000 to State University's athletic department. The payment guarantees that Erin will have preferred seating on the 50-yard line.
   a. Assume Erin subsequently buys four $50 game tickets. How much can she deduct as a charitable contribution to the university's athletic department?
   b. Assume that Erin's $1,000 donation includes four $50 tickets. How much can she deduct as a charitable contribution to the university's athletic department?

43. Tim owned stock in White Corporation that he donated to a university (a qualified charitable organization) on May 1, 1996.
   a. What is the amount of Tim's deduction assuming that he had purchased the stock for $2,500 on March 3, 1996, and the stock had a value of $3,600 when he made the donation.
   b. Assume the same facts as in (a), except that Tim had purchased the stock for $2,500 on March 3, 1995.
   c. Assume the same facts as in (a), except that the stock had a fair market value of $2,300 (rather than $3,600) when it was donated to the university.

44. Darby contributed a painting to an art museum in 1996. She had owned the painting for 20 years, and it had a value of $120,000 at the time of the donation. The museum displayed the painting in its impressionist gallery.
   a. Assume that Darby's AGI is $230,000 and her basis for the painting is $80,000. Would you recommend that she make the reduced deduction election?
   b. Assume that Darby's AGI is $230,000 and her basis for the painting is $115,000. Would you recommend that she make the reduced deduction election?

45. During the year, Al made the following contributions to his church:

Cash	$20,000
Stock in Thrush Corporation (a publicly traded corporation)	30,000

The stock in Thrush Corporation was acquired as an investment three years ago at a cost of $10,000. Al's AGI is $70,000.
   a. What is Al's charitable contribution deduction?
   b. How are excess amounts, if any, treated?

46. Mae died in 1996. Before she died, Mae made a gift of stock in Eagle Corporation (a publicly traded corporation) to her church. The stock was worth $70,000 and had been acquired as an investment two years ago at a cost of $56,000. In the year of her death, Mae had AGI of $110,000. In completing her final income tax return, how should Mae's executor handle the charitable contribution?

47. On December 30, 1996, Roberta purchased four tickets to a charity ball sponsored by the city of San Diego for the benefit of underprivileged children. Each ticket cost $200 and

had a fair market value of $35. On the same day as the purchase, Roberta gave the tickets to the minister of her church for personal use by his family. At the time of the gift of the tickets, Roberta pledged $4,000 to the building fund of her church. The pledge was satisfied by check dated December 31, 1996, but not mailed until January 3, 1997.

a. Presuming Roberta is a cash basis and calendar year taxpayer, how much can she deduct as a charitable contribution for 1996?
b. Would the amount of the deduction be any different if Roberta is an accrual basis taxpayer? Explain.

48. In December each year, Sandy Wren contributes 10% of her gross income to her church. Sandy, who is in the 36% marginal tax bracket, is considering the following alternatives as charitable contributions in December 1996:

	Fair Market Value
1. Cash donation	$12,000
2. Unimproved land held for six years ($2,000 basis)	12,000
3. Purple Corporation stock held for eight months ($2,000 basis)	12,000
4. Silver Corporation stock held for two years ($17,000 basis)	12,000

Sandy has asked you to help her decide which of these potential contributions will be most advantageous taxwise. Rank the four alternatives, and write a letter to Sandy communicating your advice to her. Her address is 1201 Baywatch Drive, Chicago, IL 60606.

49. Classify each of the following independent expenditures as nondeductible *(ND)* items, business *(dfor)* deductions, or itemized *(dfrom)* deductions. (*Note:* In many cases, it may be necessary to refer to the materials in earlier chapters of the text.)

a. Interest allowed on home mortgage accrued by a cash basis taxpayer.
b. State income taxes paid by a sole proprietor of a business.
c. Subscription to the *Wall Street Journal* paid by a vice president of a bank and not reimbursed by her employer.
d. Automobile mileage for attendance at weekly church services.
e. Street-paving assessment paid to the county by a homeowner.
f. Speeding ticket paid by the owner-operator of a taxicab.
g. Interest and taxes paid by the owner of residential rental property.
h. Business entertainment expenses (properly substantiated) paid by a self-employed taxpayer.
i. State and Federal excise taxes on tobacco paid by a self-employed taxpayer who gave his clients cigars as Christmas presents. The business gifts were properly substantiated and under $25 each.
j. State and Federal excise taxes on cigarettes purchased by a heavy smoker for personal consumption.
k. Federal excise taxes on the purchase of gasoline for use in the taxpayer's personal automobile.
l. Theft loss of personal jewelry worth $300 but which originally cost $75.
m. Maternity clothing purchased by a taxpayer who is pregnant.
n. Medical expenses paid by an employer on behalf of an employee.
o. Qualified residence interest paid by a taxpayer on a loan obtained to build an artist studio in his personal residence. Assume that the taxpayer's art activities are classified as a hobby.
p. Assume the same facts as in (o) except that the art activities are classified as a trade or business.

50. Manuel and Rosa Garcia, both age 45, are married and have no dependents. They have asked you to advise them whether they should file jointly or separately in 1996. They present you with the following information:

	Manuel	Rosa	Joint
Salary	$40,000		
Business net income		$100,000	
Interest income	400	1,200	$2,200
Deductions *for* AGI	2,000	13,000	
Medical expenses	9,500	600	
State income tax	800	2,000	
Real estate tax			3,400
Mortgage interest			5,200
Unreimbursed employee expenses	1,100		

If they file separately, Manuel and Rosa will split the real estate tax and mortgage interest deductions equally. Write Manuel and Rosa a letter in which you make and explain a recommendation on filing status for 1996. Manuel and Rosa reside at 5904 Stevens Avenue, Durham, NC 27707.

51. For calendar year 1996, Clyde and Trisha file a joint return reflecting AGI of $160,000. Their itemized deductions are as follows:

Medical expenses	$12,000
Casualty loss (not covered by insurance)	17,000
Interest on home mortgage	15,000
Property taxes on home	13,000
Charitable contributions	14,000
State income tax	10,000

After all necessary adjustments are made, what is the amount of itemized deductions Clyde and Trisha may claim?

52. Kareem and Veneia are married and file a joint return. For 1996, they have AGI of $305,520. Their itemized deductions for the year total $39,000 and consist of the following:

Medical expenses	$32,000	phase out limitation
Interest on home mortgage	3,000	
State income tax	4,000	

After all necessary adjustments are made, what is the amount of itemized deductions Kareem and Veneia may claim?

53. Ben and Laura are married and file a joint return. For 1996, they have AGI of $358,450, which included net investment income of $41,000 before deducting investment interest. Compute Ben and Laura's allowable itemized deductions for 1996 based on the following information:

Investment interest	$11,000
Casualty loss (after applicable limitations)	8,000
Qualified residence interest	5,400
Property taxes	4,700
Charitable contributions	2,900
State income taxes	5,300

54. Andy, who is single, had AGI of $180,000 for 1996. He incurred the following expenses and losses during the year:

Medical expenses before 7.5%-of-AGI limitation	$15,000
State and local income taxes	2,600
Real estate taxes	3,400
Home mortgage interest	6,600
Charitable contribution	3,500
Casualty loss before 10% limitation (after $100 floor)	20,600
Unreimbursed employee expenses subject to 2%-of-AGI limitation	4,100
Gambling losses (Andy had $3,500 gambling income)	7,000

Calculate Andy's allowable itemized deductions for the year.

CUMULATIVE PROBLEMS

55. Alice and Bruce Byrd are married taxpayers, ages 47 and 45, who file a joint return. Their Social Security numbers are 034–48–4382 and 016–50–9556, respectively. They live at 473 Revere Avenue, Ames, MA 01850. Alice is the office manager for a dental clinic and earns an annual salary of $45,000. Bruce is the manager of a fast-food outlet owned and operated by Plymouth Corporation. His annual salary is $36,000.

The Byrds have two children, Cynthia (age 23 and S.S. no. 017–44–9126) and John (age 22 and S.S. no. 017–27–4148), who live with them. Both children are full-time students at a nearby college. Alice's mother, Myrtle Jones (age 74 and S.S. no. 016–15–8266), also lives with them. Her sole source of income is from Social Security benefits, which she deposits in a savings account.

During 1995, a particularly harsh storm struck the Ames area. As a result, the Byrds suffered severe flood damage to the basement and foundation of their personal residence, which was purchased in 1986 at a cost of $80,000. Based on an appraisal, the fair market value of the house was $115,000 before the storm and $90,000 after. The Byrds' homeowner's insurance policy does not cover damage due to flooding. The cost of the appraisal was $300.

During 1995, the Byrds furnished one-third of the total support of Bruce's widower father, Sam Byrd (age 70 and S.S. no. 034–82–8583). Sam lives alone and receives the rest of his support from Bruce's sister and brother (one-third each). They have signed a multiple support agreement allowing Bruce to claim Sam as a dependent for 1995. Sam died in November, and Bruce received life insurance proceeds of $270,000 on December 28.

The Byrds had the following expenses relating to their personal residence during 1995:

Property taxes	$2,400
Interest on home mortgage	5,900
Repairs to roof	1,000
Utilities	2,800
Fire and theft insurance	1,100

Medical expenses for 1995 include:

Medical insurance premiums	$3,100
Doctor bill for Sam incurred in 1994 and not paid until 1995	1,600
Operation for Sam	3,900

The operation for Sam represents the one-third Bruce contributed toward his father's support.

Other relevant information follows:

- On December 1, 1995, Myrtle gave Alice and Bruce a tract of undeveloped land (basis of $30,000 and fair market value of $90,000).

- Alice and Bruce had $2,452 ($1,252 for Alice and $1,200 for Bruce) withheld from their salaries for state income taxes. When they filed their 1994 state return in 1995, they paid additional tax of $280.
- During 1995, Alice and Bruce attended a dinner dance sponsored by the Ames Police Disability Association (a qualified charitable organization). The Byrds paid $100 for the tickets. Cost of comparable entertainment would normally be $40. The Byrds contributed $1,700 to their church and gave used clothing (cost of $800 and fair market value of $300) to the Salvation Army. All donations are supported by receipts.
- In 1995, the Byrds received interest income of $1,450 from a savings account they maintained.
- Alice's employer requires that all employees wear uniforms to work. During 1995, Alice spent $290 on new uniforms and $102 on laundry charges. Bruce paid $120 for an annual subscription to the *Journal of Franchise Management*. Neither Alice's nor Bruce's employers reimburse for employee expenses.
- Alice and Bruce had $6,032 ($3,086 for Alice and $2,946 for Bruce) of Federal income tax withheld in 1995 and paid no estimated Federal income tax. Neither Alice nor Bruce wishes to designate $3 to the Presidential Election Campaign Fund.

Part 1—Tax Computation
Compute net tax payable or refund due for Alice and Bruce Byrd for 1995. If they have overpaid, the amount is to be refunded. If you use tax forms for your computations, you will need Form 1040, Schedules A and B, and Form 4684. Suggested software (if available): *TurboTax* or *MacInTax*.

Part 2—Tax Planning
Alice and Bruce are planning some significant changes for 1996. They have provided you with the following information and asked you to project their taxable income and tax liabiliy for 1996.

Myrtle became seriously ill in December 1995 and is no longer able to care for herself. As a result, Alice plans to take a one-year leave of absence from work during 1996 to care for her. The Byrds will use $70,000 of the life insurance proceeds they received as a result of Sam's death and pay off their mortgage in early January 1996. They will invest the remaining $200,000 in short-term certificates of deposit (CDs) and use the interest for living expenses during 1996. They expect to earn total interest of $13,500 on the CDs. Bruce has been awarded a 5% raise for 1996, and withholdings on his salary will increase accordingly.

The Byrds will not incur any additional costs related to the flood damage or Sam's medical problem. Alice will not work at all during 1996, so none of her job-related expenses or withholdings will continue. The Byrds do not expect to owe additional state income tax when they file their 1995 return, but they do expect their charitable contributions and medical insurance premiums to continue at the 1995 level. Assume all other income and deduction items will continue at the same level in 1996 unless you have information that indicates otherwise.

56. Paul and Donna Decker are married taxpayers, ages 44 and 42, who file a joint return for 1996. The Deckers live at 1121 College Avenue, Carmel, IN 46032. Paul is an assistant manager at Carmel Motor Inn, and Donna is a teacher at Carmel Elementary School. They present you with W–2 Forms that reflect the following information:

	Paul	Donna
Salary	$35,000	$38,000
Federal tax withheld	6,092	5,400
State income tax withheld	700	760
FICA (Social Security) withheld	2,678	2,907
Social Security numbers	222–11–4567	333–11–9872

Donna is the custodial parent of two children from a previous marriage who reside with the Deckers through the school year. The children, Larry and Jane Parker, reside with their father, Bob, during the summer. Relevant information for the children follows:

	Larry	**Jane**
Age	11	9
Social Security numbers	305–11–4567	303–11–9872
Months spent with Deckers	9	9

Under the divorce decree, Bob pays child support of $150 per month per child during the nine months the children live with the Deckers. Bob says he spends $200 per month per child during the three summer months they reside with him. Donna and Paul can document that they provide $1,800 support per child per year. The divorce decree is silent as to which parent can claim the exemption for the children.

In August, Paul and Donna added a suite to their home to provide more comfortable accommodations for Hannah Snyder (263–33–4738), Donna's mother, who had moved in with them in February 1995 after the death of Donna's father. Not wanting to borrow money for this addition, Paul sold 300 shares of Acme Corporation stock for $50 per share on May 3, 1996, and used the proceeds of $15,000 to cover construction costs. The Deckers had purchased the stock on April 27, 1995, for $22 per share. They received dividends of $550 on the jointly owned stock a month before the sale.

Hannah, who is 66 years old, received $7,200 in Social Security benefits during the year, of which she gave the Deckers $1,700 to use toward household expenses and deposited the remainder in her personal savings account. The Deckers determine that they have spent $1,500 of their own money for food, clothing, medical expenses, and other items for Hannah. They do not know what the rental value of Hannah's suite would be, but they estimate it would be at least $300 per month.

The Deckers received $2,100 interest on City of Indianapolis bonds they had bought in 1994. Paul had heard from a friend that municipal bonds were paying good rates and that municipal bond interest was not taxable. To finance the purchase of the bonds, he borrowed $20,000 from the bank and paid $1,760 interest during 1996. Other interest paid during the year included the following:

Home mortgage interest (paid to Carmel Federal Savings & Loan)	$4,890
Interest on an automobile loan (paid to Carmel National Bank)	920
Interest on Citibank Visa card	855

Donna's uncle died on November 11, 1996, and left her 50 shares of Thrush Corporation stock worth $70 per share. Her uncle's basis in the stock was $34 per share. Donna received $530 in dividends on the stock in December 1996.

In July, Paul hit a submerged rock while boating. Fortunately, he was thrown from the boat, landed in deep water, and was uninjured. However, the boat, which was uninsured, was destroyed. Paul had paid $18,000 for the boat in June 1995, and its value was appraised at $14,500 on the date of the accident.

The Deckers paid doctor and hospital bills of $4,100 and were reimbursed $1,600 by their insurance company. They spent $780 for prescription drugs and medicines and $1,440 for premiums on their health insurance policy. They have filed additional claims of $700 with their insurance company and have been told they will receive payment for that amount in January 1997. Included in the amounts paid for doctor and hospital bills were payments of $360 for Hannah and $750 for the children.

Additional information of potential tax consequence follows:

Real estate taxes paid	$1,900
Cash contributions to church	800
Appraised value of books donated to public library	450
Paul's unreimbursed employee expenses to attend hotel management convention:	
Airfare	340
Hotel	130
Meals	95
Registration fee	100
Refund of state income tax for 1995 (the Deckers itemized on their 1995 return)	910

Compute net tax payable or refund due for the Deckers for 1996. If they have overpaid, the amount is to be credited toward their taxes for 1997. Suggested software (if available): *TurboTax* or *MacInTax*.

RESEARCH PROBLEMS

Note: ***West's Federal Taxation on CD-ROM*** *can be used in preparing solutions to the Research Problems. Alternatively, tax research materials contained in a standard tax library can be used.*

Research Problem 1. Jane suffers from a degenerative spinal disorder. Her physician recommended the installation of a swimming pool at her residence for her use to prevent the onset of permanent paralysis. Jane's residence had a market value of approximately $500,000 before the swimming pool was installed. The swimming pool was built, and an appraiser estimated that the value of Jane's home increased by $98,000 because of the addition.

The pool cost $194,000, and Jane claimed a medical deduction of $96,000 on her tax return. Upon audit of the return, the IRS determined that an adequate pool should have cost $70,000 and would increase the property value by only $31,000. Thus, the IRS claims that Jane should be entitled to a deduction of only $39,000.

a. Is there any ceiling limitation on the amount deductible as a medical expense?
b. Can capital expenditures be deducted as medical expenses?
c. What is the significance of a "minimum adequate facility"? Should aesthetic or architectural qualities be considered in this determination?

Research Problem 2. Tom and Mary Smith, whose son was found murdered in a parking lot, offered a $100,000 reward for the city police to use to obtain for information leading to the arrest and conviction of the murderer. As a result of the reward, a person who had overheard the murderer telling a friend about the crime reported the conversation to the police. The murderer was arrested and convicted, and the Smiths contributed the money to the police department. Can the Smiths treat this payment as a charitable contribution?

Research Problem 3. George Fields contributed $2,700 to the United Way (a qualified public charity) in 1995. The contribution was made through his employer's charitable fund drive, and his employer withheld $225 per month from each of George's monthly payroll checks. George filed his Federal income tax return on April 10, 1996. In June 1996, he was discussing the contribution with a friend who told him that charitable contribution deductions of $250 or more are not allowed unless the taxpayer obtains a written substantiation from the donee organization by the earlier of the due date for the return or the date on which the return was filed. George has not obtained any written substantiation from the donee. George, who lives at 3602 Sunbury Avenue, New York, NY 10012, has called and asked you if he can (or should) do anything to ensure that the deduction will not be disallowed. Write George a letter to advise him on this issue, and prepare a memo for your firm's tax files.

Research Problem 4. Falcon Corporation is the owner and operator of a large daily metropolitan newspaper. For at least 80 years, Falcon has collected and maintained a "clippings library." The library is a collection of past news items from Falcon's and other newspapers. The 7,800,000 items are well-preserved, cataloged, and cross-listed under various categories. Falcon estimates that it has spent in excess of $10 million compiling and organizing the library. However, since this amount was deducted as incurred, the income tax basis of the library is zero. The fair market value of the library is $3 million.

Falcon Corporation contributes the clippings library to the state historical society (a qualified organization) and claims a charitable contribution deduction of $3 million. Upon audit, the IRS disallows the entire amount of the deduction because the basis of the property is zero. Who is correct?

Partial list of research aids:
§§ 170(e)(1)(A) and 1221(3).

Research Problem 5. The city of Cincinnati wished to establish a scenic corridor along portions of Interstate 75, but did not have the funds to purchase all of the land involved and to make the necessary improvements (e.g., terracing and other landscaping). Likewise, the city was fearful of any personal liability that might result from the operation of the scenic corridor. If, however, state funding could be obtained to cover the improvements and liability costs, the project would be carried out. State funding was possible but not probable.

In 1994, all but one of the property owners affected by the project donated the necessary land to the city. The city purchased the land of the one owner who refused to make a donation. The city agreed to return the land to the donors in the event the project was not carried out. By 1996, it became certain that state funding would not be forthcoming. Therefore, the city returned the land to the donors, except for the parcel it had purchased.

William Baird, one of the donors, claimed a charitable deduction for the fair market value of the land transferred in 1994. Upon audit of William's 1994 income tax return, the IRS disallowed the deduction and assessed the penalty for overvaluation. Is the IRS correct?

a. Write a letter to William that contains your tax advice. His address is 405 Westwood, Cincinnati, OH 45999.
b. Prepare a memo for your firm's tax files.

Partial list of research aids:
§ 6659 [now § 6662(b)(3)].
Reg. § 1.170A–1(e).
Ronald W. McCrary, 92 T.C. 827 (1989).

TEAM PROJECT: ARTHUR ANDERSEN TAX CHALLENGE CASES

For more information on the Arthur Andersen Tax Challenge Cases, please refer to Chapter 1, page 1-38.

Information related to tax issues and problems that are discussed in this chapter may be found in the

Fields case on pages 1, 2, 13-17, 19, 21-27, 31
Miller case on pages 2, 3, 11-15, 24-27, 29-30, 34, 38

Read and analyze the case you have been assigned and *identify* any issues and problems that are related to material covered in this chapter. If the information provided in the case is complete, prepare answers for this part of the case at this time. If you need information that is contained in the later parts of the case, please write a memo summarizing the questions or problems so you can prepare a complete answer at a later date.

CHAPTER

11

PASSIVE ACTIVITY LOSSES

LEARNING OBJECTIVES

After completing Chapter 11, you should be able to:

1. Discuss tax shelters and the reasons for at-risk and passive loss limitations.
2. Explain the at-risk limitation.
3. Describe how the passive loss rules limit deductions for losses.
4. Identify taxpayers who are subject to the passive loss limits.
5. Discuss the definition of passive activities.
6. Apply the rules for identifying an activity.
7. Analyze and apply the tests for material participation.
8. Understand the nature of rental activities under the passive loss rules.
9. Recognize the relationship between the at-risk and passive activity limitations.
10. Discuss the special treatment available to real estate activities.
11. Determine the proper tax treatment upon the disposition of a passive activity.
12. Suggest tax planning strategies to minimize the effect of the passive loss limitations.

OUTLINE

THE TAX SHELTER PROBLEM

1 LEARNING OBJECTIVE
Discuss tax shelters and the reasons for at-risk and passive loss limitations.

Before Congress enacted legislation to reduce or eliminate their effectiveness, **tax shelters** were popular investments for tax avoidance purposes because they could generate deductions and other benefits that could be used to offset income from other sources. Because of the tax avoidance potential of many tax shelters, they were attractive to wealthy taxpayers in high income tax brackets. Many tax shelters merely provided an opportunity for "investors" to buy deductions and credits in ventures that were not expected to generate a profit, even in the long run.

Although it may seem odd that a taxpayer would intentionally invest in an activity that was designed to produce losses, there is a logical explanation. The typical tax shelter operated as a partnership and relied heavily on nonrecourse financing.[1] Accelerated depreciation and interest expense deductions generated large losses in the early years of the activity. At the very least, the tax shelter deductions deferred the recognition of any net income from the venture until the activity was sold. In the best of situations, the investor could realize additional tax savings by offsetting other income (e.g., salary, interest, and dividends) with deductions flowing from the tax shelter. Ultimately, the sale of the investment would result in capital gain. The following examples illustrate what was possible *before* Congress enacted legislation to curb tax shelter abuses.

EXAMPLE 1

Bob, who earned a salary of $100,000 as a business executive and dividend income of $15,000, invested $20,000 for a 10% interest in a cattle-breeding tax shelter. Through the use of $800,000 of nonrecourse financing and available cash of $200,000, the partnership acquired a herd of an exotic breed of cattle costing $1 million. Depreciation, interest, and other deductions related to the activity resulted in a loss of $400,000, of which Bob's share was $40,000. Bob was allowed to deduct the $40,000 loss, even though he had invested and stood to lose only $20,000 if the investment turned sour. The net effect of the $40,000 deduction from the partnership was that a portion of Bob's salary and dividend income was "sheltered," and as a result, he was required to calculate his tax liability on only $75,000 of income [$115,000 (salary and dividends) − $40,000 (deduction)] rather than $115,000. If this deduction were available under current law and if Bob was in the 39.6% income tax bracket, this deduction would generate a tax savings of $15,840 ($40,000 × 39.6%) in the first year alone! ▼

A review of Example 1 shows that the taxpayer took a *two-for-one* write-off ($40,000 deduction, $20,000 investment). In the heyday of tax shelters, promoters often promised *multiple* write-offs for the investor.

[1] Nonrecourse debt is an obligation for which the borrower is not personally liable. An example of nonrecourse debt is a liability on real estate acquired by a partnership without the partnership or any of the partners assuming any liability for the mortgage. The acquired property generally is pledged as collateral for the loan.

TAX IN THE NEWS

THE FEDS MAY ASK TAX SHELTERS TO REGISTER

Investment bankers and other tax advisers who devise intricate tax-saving deals for clients often require them to sign confidentiality agreements. Representative Bill Archer, the Texas Republican who heads the House Ways and Means Committee, supports requiring advisers to register such deals confidentially with the IRS as "tax shelters." Tax advisers say such pacts are meant to keep competitors from learning of complex tax strategies, but the House budget committee suggests that many also conceal various "inappropriate corporate tax benefits" that cost the government billions.

This requirement would be in addition to the current law that requires investment promoters to register as tax shelters deals that yield inordinate tax benefits relative to the amount invested. Many corporate tax advisers say the idea is too intrusive and would be too time-consuming. Penalty rules already require taxpayers to alert the IRS on their returns if they take overly aggressive positions.

SOURCE: Information from *Wall Street Journal*, May 24, 1995, p. A1.

The first major provision aimed at tax shelters was the **at-risk limitation.** Its objective is to limit a taxpayer's deductions to the amount at risk, that is, the amount the taxpayer stands to lose if the investment turns out to be a financial disaster.

EXAMPLE 2

Returning to the facts of Example 1, under the current at-risk rules Bob would be allowed to deduct $20,000 (i.e., the amount that he could lose if the business failed). This deduction would reduce his other income and as a result, Bob would have to report only $95,000 of income ($115,000 − $20,000). The remaining nondeductible $20,000 loss and any future losses flowing from the partnership would be suspended under the at-risk rules and would be deductible in the future only as his at-risk amount increased. ▼

The second major attack on tax shelters came with the passage of the passive activity loss rules. These rules were intended to halt an investor's ability to benefit from the mismatching of an entity's expenses and income that often occurs in the early years of the business. Congress observed that despite the at-risk limitations, investors could still deduct losses flowing from an entity and thereby defer their tax liability on other income. In effect, passive activity rules have essentially made the term *tax shelter* obsolete. Now such ventures where investors are not involved in the day-to-day operations of the business are generally referred to as passive investments, or *passive activities,* rather than tax shelters.

The **passive loss** rules require the taxpayer to segregate all income and losses into three categories: active, passive, and portfolio. In general, the passive loss limits disallow the deduction of passive losses against active or portfolio income, even when the taxpayer is at risk to the extent of the loss. Normally, passive losses can only offset passive income.

EXAMPLE 3

Returning to the facts of Example 1, the passive activity loss rules further restrict Bob's ability to claim the $20,000 tax deduction shown in Example 2. Because Bob is a passive investor and does not materially participate in any meaningful way in the activities of the cattle-breeding operation, the $20,000 loss allowed under the at-risk rules is disallowed under the passive loss rules. The passive loss is disallowed because Bob does not generate any passive income that could absorb his passive loss. Further, his salary (active income) and dividends (portfolio income) cannot be used to absorb any of the passive loss. Consequently, Bob's current year taxable income must reflect his nonpassive income of $115,000, and he receives no current benefit for his share of the partnership loss. However, all is not lost because Bob's share of the entity's loss is *suspended;* it is carried forward and can be deducted in the future when he has passive income or sells his interest in the activity. ▼

This chapter explores the nature of the at-risk limits and passive activity loss rules and their impact on investors. An interesting consequence of these rules is that now investors evaluating potential investments must consider mainly the economics of the venture instead of the tax benefits or tax avoidance possibilities that an investment may generate.

AT-RISK LIMITS

2 LEARNING OBJECTIVE
Explain the at-risk limitation.

The at-risk provisions limit the deductibility of losses from business and income-producing activities. These provisions, which apply to individuals and closely held corporations, are designed to prevent taxpayers from deducting losses in excess of their actual economic investment in an activity. In the case of an S corporation or a partnership, the at-risk limits apply at the owner level. Under the at-risk rules, a taxpayer's deductible loss from an activity for any taxable year is limited to the amount the taxpayer has at risk at the end of the taxable year (the amount the taxpayer could actually lose in the activity).

While the amount at risk generally vacillates over time, the initial amount considered at risk consists of the following:[2]

- The amount of cash and the adjusted basis of property contributed to the activity by the taxpayer.
- Amounts borrowed for use in the activity for which the taxpayer is personally liable or has pledged as security property not used in the activity.

This amount generally is increased each year by the taxpayer's share of income and is decreased by the taxpayer's share of losses and withdrawals from the activity. In addition, because general partners are jointly and severally liable for recourse debts of the partnership, their at-risk amounts are increased when the partnership increases its debt and are decreased when the partnership reduces its debt. However, a taxpayer generally is not considered at risk with respect to borrowed amounts if either of the following is true:

- The taxpayer is not personally liable for repayment of the debt (e.g., nonrecourse debt).
- The lender has an interest (other than as a creditor) in the activity.

An important exception provides that in the case of an activity involving the holding of real property, a taxpayer is considered at risk for his or her share of any *qualified nonrecourse financing* that is secured by real property used in the activity.[3]

[2] § 465(b)(1).

[3] § 465(b)(6).

Concept Summary 11–1

Calculation of At-Risk Amount

Increases to a taxpayer's at-risk amount:

- Cash and the adjusted basis of property contributed to the activity.
- Amounts borrowed for use in the activity for which the taxpayer is personally liable or has pledged as security property not used in the activity.
- Taxpayer's share of amounts borrowed for use in the activity that is qualified nonrecourse financing.
- Taxpayer's share of the activity's income.

Decreases to a taxpayer's at-risk amount:

- Withdrawals from the activity.
- Taxpayer's share of the activity's loss.
- Taxpayer's share of any reductions of debt for which recourse against the taxpayer exists or reductions of qualified nonrecourse debt.

Subject to the passive activity rules discussed later in the chapter, a taxpayer may deduct a loss as long as his or her at-risk amount is positive. However, once the at-risk amount is exhausted, any remaining loss cannot be deducted until a later year. Any losses disallowed for any given taxable year by the at-risk rules may be deducted in the first succeeding year in which the rules do not prevent the deduction—that is, when and to the extent of a positive at-risk amount.

EXAMPLE 4

In 1996, Sue invests $40,000 in an oil partnership that, by the use of nonrecourse loans, spends $60,000 on deductible intangible drilling costs applicable to her interest. Assume Sue's interest in the partnership is subject to the at-risk limits but is not subject to the passive loss limits. Since Sue has only $40,000 of capital at risk, she cannot deduct more than $40,000 against her other income and must reduce her at-risk amount to zero ($40,000 at-risk amount – $40,000 loss deducted). The nondeductible loss of $20,000 ($60,000 loss generated – $40,000 loss allowed) can be carried over to 1997. ▼

EXAMPLE 5

In 1997, Sue has taxable income of $15,000 from the oil partnership and invests an additional $10,000 in the venture. Her at-risk amount is now $25,000 ($0 beginning balance + $15,000 taxable income + $10,000 additional investment). This enables Sue to deduct the carryover loss and requires her to reduce her at-risk amount to $5,000 ($25,000 at-risk amount – $20,000 carryover loss allowed). ▼

An additional complicating factor is that previously allowed losses must be recaptured to the extent the at-risk amount is reduced below zero.[4] That is, previous losses that were allowed must be offset by the recognition of enough income to bring the at-risk amount up to zero. This rule applies in such situations as when the amount at risk is reduced below zero by distributions to the taxpayer or when the status of indebtedness changes from recourse to nonrecourse.

[4] § 465(e).

ETHICAL CONSIDERATIONS

Manipulating the At-Risk Limits

At a social function, you encounter your friend Juan. You have known for some time that Juan has an investment in a venture that could make him subject to the at-risk rules. Not wanting to appear "nosy," you make an oblique reference to his investment. He laughs and says, "That hasn't been a problem. At the end of every year, I make a contribution to the partnership to raise my at-risk basis, and then on January 2 of the following year, I get that money back. This approach has worked well for me every year, and the IRS has never caught on. As I've always said, 'there's more than one way to skin a cat.' " As a respected tax accountant in the community, you frown on such techniques with your clients and will not sign tax returns that involve such manipulation. However, Juan is not one of your clients. How do you respond to Juan's confession?

PASSIVE LOSS LIMITS

CLASSIFICATION AND IMPACT OF PASSIVE INCOME AND LOSSES

3 LEARNING OBJECTIVE
Describe how the passive loss rules limit deductions for losses.

Classification. The passive loss rules require income and losses to be classified into three categories: active, passive, and portfolio. **Active income** includes, but is not limited to, the following:

- Wages, salary, commissions, bonuses, and other payments for services rendered by the taxpayer.
- Profit from a trade or business in which the taxpayer is a material participant.
- Gain on the sale or other disposition of assets used in an active trade or business.
- Income from intangible property if the taxpayer's personal efforts significantly contributed to the creation of the property.

Portfolio income includes, but is not limited to, the following:

- Interest, dividends, annuities, and royalties not derived in the ordinary course of a trade or business.
- Gain or loss from the disposition of property that produces portfolio income or is held for investment purposes.

Section 469 provides that income or loss from the following activities is treated as *passive:*

- Any trade or business or income-producing activity in which the taxpayer does not materially participate.
- Subject to certain exceptions, all rental activities, whether the taxpayer materially participates or not.

Although the Code defines rental activities as passive activities, several exceptions allow losses from certain real estate rental activities to be offset against nonpassive

TAX IN THE NEWS

Knowledge of Tax Laws Is a Key to Real Estate Success

One often hears the sage investment advice to "buy low and sell high," or to "buy cheap, and, as much as possible, use other people's money." These tips, though often difficult to implement, can lead to rich rewards. To realize the full benefits of investing, however, whether in stocks and bonds or in real estate, an investor needs to know and be able to apply the tax law.

For example, due to the passive activity loss rules, a taxpayer who wishes to participate in a real estate investment should avoid being a passive investor. Becoming personally involved may be a better approach. Not only can actual participation by the owner lead to favorable tax results, but the fees and commissions of brokers and middlemen can be avoided.

People who buy real estate through partnerships often find the odds stacked against them. Not only is a lot of their money skimmed off the top in fees, but if the cost of the property is highly inflated or highly leveraged, many of the depreciation and interest deductions may be disallowed due to the operation of the passive activity loss rules. Thus, for some taxpayers, the answer to successful real estate investing is to participate actively in the operation of the real estate, avoid high fees, make a profit, and avoid the passive activity loss rules.

SOURCE: Information from John R. Hayes, "A Nice Little Sideline," *Forbes*, July 17, 1995, p. 306.

(active or portfolio) income. The exceptions are discussed under Special Passive Activity Rules for Real Estate Activities later in the chapter.

General Impact. Deductions or expenses generated by passive activities can only be deducted to the extent of income from all of the taxpayer's passive income. Any excess may not be used to offset income from active sources or portfolio income. Instead, any unused passive losses are suspended and carried forward to future years to offset passive income generated in those years. Otherwise, suspended losses may be used only when a taxpayer disposes of his or her entire interest in an activity. In that event, all current and suspended losses related to the activity may offset active and portfolio income.

Example 6 Kim, a physician, earned $150,000 from her full-time practice. She also received $10,000 in dividends and interest on various portfolio investments, and her share of a passive loss from a tax shelter not limited by the at-risk rules was $60,000. Because the loss is a passive loss, it is not deductible against her other income. The loss is suspended and is carried over to the future. If Kim has passive income from this investment, or from other passive investments, in the future, she can offset the suspended loss against that passive income. If she does not have passive income to offset this suspended loss in the future, she will be allowed to offset the loss against other types of income when she eventually disposes of the passive activity. ▼

Impact of Suspended Losses. When a taxpayer disposes of his or her entire interest in a passive activity, the actual economic gain or loss on the investment, including any suspended losses, can finally be determined. As a result, under the passive loss rules, upon a fully taxable disposition, any overall loss realized from the activity by the taxpayer is recognized and can be offset against any income.

A fully taxable disposition generally involves a sale of the property to a third party at arm's length and thus, presumably, for a price equal to the property's fair market value. Gain recognized upon a transfer of an interest in a passive activity generally is treated as passive and is first offset by the suspended losses from that activity.

EXAMPLE 7

Rex sells an apartment building with an adjusted basis of $100,000 for $180,000. In addition, he has suspended losses of $60,000 associated with that building. His total gain, $80,000, and his taxable gain, $20,000, are calculated as follows:

Net sales price	$ 180,000
Less: Adjusted basis	(100,000)
Total gain	$ 80,000
Less: Suspended losses	(60,000)
Taxable gain (passive)	$ 20,000

▼

If current and suspended losses of the passive activity exceed the gain realized or if the sale results in a realized loss, the sum of

- any loss from the activity for the tax year (including losses suspended in the activity disposed of), plus
- any loss realized on the disposition

in excess of

- net income or gain for the tax year from all passive activities (without regard to the activity disposed of)

is treated as a loss that is not from a passive activity.

EXAMPLE 8

Dean sells an apartment building with an adjusted basis of $100,000 for $150,000. In addition, he has current and suspended losses of $60,000 associated with that building and has no other passive activities. His total gain, $50,000, and his deductible loss, $10,000, are calculated as follows:

Net sales price	$ 150,000
Less: Adjusted basis	(100,000)
Total gain	$ 50,000
Less: Suspended losses	(60,000)
Deductible loss	($ 10,000)

The $10,000 deductible loss is offset against Dean's ordinary income and portfolio income. ▼

Carryovers of Suspended Losses. In the above examples, it was assumed that the taxpayer had an interest in only one passive activity, and as a result, the suspended loss was related exclusively to the activity that was disposed of. Taxpayers often own interests in more than one activity, however, and in that case, any suspended losses must be allocated among the activities in which the taxpayer has an interest. The allocation to an activity is made by multiplying the disallowed passive activity loss from all activities by the following fraction:

$$\frac{\text{Loss from activity}}{\text{Sum of losses for taxable year from all activities having losses}}$$

EXAMPLE 9 Diego has investments in three passive activities with the following income and losses for 1995:

Activity A	($30,000)
Activity B	(20,000)
Activity C	25,000
Net passive loss	($25,000)
Allocated to:	
Activity A ($25,000 × $30,000/$50,000)	$15,000
Activity B ($25,000 × $20,000/$50,000)	10,000
Total suspended losses	($25,000)

▼

Suspended losses are carried over indefinitely and are offset in the future against any passive income from the activities to which they relate.[5]

EXAMPLE 10 Assume the same facts as in Example 9 and that Activity A produces $10,000 of income in 1996. Of the suspended loss of $15,000 from 1995 for Activity A, $10,000 is offset against the income from this activity. If Diego sells Activity A in early 1997, then the remaining $5,000 suspended loss is used in determining his final gain or loss. ▼

Passive Credits. Credits arising from passive activities are limited in much the same way as passive losses. Passive credits can be utilized only against regular tax attributable to passive income,[6] which is calculated by comparing the tax on all income (including passive income) with the tax on income excluding passive income.

EXAMPLE 11 Sam owes $50,000 of tax, disregarding net passive income, and $80,000 of tax, considering both net passive and other taxable income (disregarding the credits in both cases). The amount of tax attributable to the passive income is $30,000.

Tax due (before credits) including net passive income	$ 80,000
Less: Tax due (before credits) without including net passive income	(50,000)
Tax attributable to passive income	$ 30,000

▼

Sam in the preceding example can claim a maximum of $30,000 of passive activity credits; the excess credits are carried over. These passive activity credits (such as the low-income housing credit and rehabilitation credit) can only be used against the *regular* tax attributable to passive income. If a taxpayer has a net loss from passive activities during a given year, no credits can be used. Likewise, if a

[5] § 469(b).

[6] § 469(d)(2).

taxpayer has net passive income but the alternative minimum tax applies to that year, no passive activity credits can be used. (The alternative minimum tax is discussed in Chapter 12.)

Carryovers of Passive Credits. Tax credits attributable to passive activities can be carried forward indefinitely much like suspended passive losses. Unlike passive losses, however, passive credits are lost forever when the activity is disposed of in a taxable transaction where loss is recognized. Credits are allowed on dispositions only when there is sufficient tax on passive income to absorb them.

EXAMPLE 12

Alicia sells a passive activity for a gain of $10,000. The activity had suspended losses of $40,000 and suspended credits of $15,000. The $10,000 gain is offset by $10,000 of the suspended losses, and the remaining $30,000 of suspended losses is deductible against Alicia's active and portfolio income. The suspended credits are lost forever because the sale of the activity did not generate any tax. This is true even if Alicia has positive taxable income or is subject to the alternative minimum tax. ▼

EXAMPLE 13

If Alicia in Example 12 had realized a $100,000 gain on the sale of the passive activity, the $15,000 of suspended credits could have been used to the extent of regular tax attributable to the net passive income.

Gain on sale	$100,000
Less: Suspended losses	(40,000)
Net gain	$ 60,000

If the tax attributable to the net gain of $60,000 is $15,000 or more, the entire $15,000 of suspended credits can be used. If the tax attributable to the gain is less than $15,000, the excess of the suspended credit over the tax attributable to the gain is lost forever. ▼

When a taxpayer has adequate regular tax liability from passive activities to trigger the use of suspended credits, the credits lose their character as passive credits. They are reclassified as regular tax credits and made subject to the same limits as other credits (discussed in Chapter 13).

ETHICAL CONSIDERATIONS

An Opportunity to Share with Those Less Fortunate

Henry, a 50-year-old pipe fitter, had been playing the same numbers in the state lottery every week for the past 15 years and finally struck it rich, winning a jackpot of $15 million. Once the news of Henry's good fortune made the newspapers and television, he was inundated with advice on how he should spend his wealth. One such caller, Sally, tried to persuade Henry to buy an interest in a low-income housing venture in the local community that would produce a $50,000 tax credit for him every year for the next 10 years. Henry's uncle, a CPA, pointed out a potential problem with the investment: because Henry would be a passive investor in the venture, he may not be able to benefit from the tax credits unless he also generated passive income. Henry had no idea what his uncle was talking about, but assured his uncle that he did not anticipate generating any passive income in the future.

When Henry relayed his uncle's misgivings concerning the potential investment, Sally responded that "in the grand scheme of things," the tax considerations were irrelevant.

Instead, she claimed that Henry should be more concerned about sharing his newfound wealth with his low-income neighbors who would benefit from finally having decent, affordable housing. Sally insisted that Henry had a responsibility to assist those less fortunate than himself and said that unless he made investments such as this, he could never hope to spend all of his money. How would you advise Henry in his dealings with Sally?

TAXPAYERS SUBJECT TO THE PASSIVE LOSS RULES

4 LEARNING OBJECTIVE
Identify taxpayers who are subject to the passive loss limits.

The passive loss rules apply to individuals, estates, trusts, closely held C corporations, and personal service corporations.[7] Passive income or loss from investments in S corporations or partnerships (see Chapter 20) flows through to the owners, and the passive loss rules are applied at the owner level.

Personal Service Corporations. Application of the passive loss limitations to **personal service corporations** is intended to prevent taxpayers from sheltering personal service income by creating personal service corporations and acquiring passive activities at the corporate level.

EXAMPLE 14

Five tax accountants, who earn a total of $1 million a year in their individual practices, form a personal service corporation. Shortly after its formation, the corporation invests in a passive activity that produces a $200,000 loss during the year. Because the passive loss rules apply to personal service corporations, the corporation may not deduct the $200,000 loss. ▼

Determination of whether a corporation is a *personal service corporation* is based on rather broad definitions. A personal service corporation is a corporation that meets *both* of the following conditions:

- The principal activity is the performance of personal services.
- Such services are substantially performed by owner-employees.

Generally, personal service corporations include those in the fields of health, law, engineering, architecture, accounting, actuarial science, performing arts, and consulting.[8] A corporation is treated as a personal service corporation if more than 10 percent of the stock (by value) is held by owner-employees.[9] A shareholder is treated as an owner-employee if he or she is an employee or shareholder on *any day* during the testing period.[10] For these purposes, shareholder status and employee status do not even have to occur on the same day.

Closely Held Corporations. Application of the passive loss rules to closely held (non-personal service) corporations is also intended to prevent individuals from incorporating to avoid the passive loss limitations. A corporation is classified as a **closely held corporation** if at any time during the taxable year, more than 50 percent of the value of its outstanding stock is owned, directly or indirectly, by or for not more than five individuals. Closely held corporations (other than personal service corporations) may offset passive losses against *active* income, but not against portfolio income.

7 § 469(a).
8 § 448(d)(2).
9 § 469(j)(2).
10 § 269A(b)(2).

EXAMPLE 15

Silver Corporation, a closely held (non-personal service) C corporation, has $500,000 of passive losses from a rental activity, $400,000 of active income, and $100,000 of portfolio income. The corporation may offset $400,000 of the $500,000 passive loss against the $400,000 of active business income, but may not offset the remainder against the $100,000 of portfolio income. Thus, $100,000 of the passive loss is suspended ($500,000 passive loss − $400,000 offset against active income). ▼

Application of the passive loss limitations to closely held corporations prevents taxpayers from transferring their portfolio investments to such corporations in order to offset passive losses against portfolio income.

PASSIVE ACTIVITIES DEFINED

5 LEARNING OBJECTIVE
Discuss the definition of passive activities.

Section 469 specifies that the following types of activities are to be treated as passive:

- Any trade or business or income-producing activity in which the taxpayer does not materially participate.
- Subject to certain exceptions, all rental activities.

To understand the meaning of the term *passive activity* and the impact of the rules, one must address the following issues, each of which is the subject of statutory or administrative guidance:

- What constitutes an activity?
- What is meant by material participation?
- When is an activity a rental activity?

Even though guidance is available to help the taxpayer deal with these issues, their resolution is anything but simple.

6 LEARNING OBJECTIVE
Apply the rules for identifying an activity.

Identification of an Activity. Identifying what constitutes an activity is a necessary first step in applying the passive loss limitations. Taxpayers who are involved in complex business operations need to be able to determine whether a given segment of their overall business operations constitutes a separate activity or is to be treated as part of a single activity. Proper treatment is necessary in order to determine whether income or loss from an activity is active or passive.

EXAMPLE 16

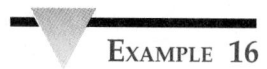

Ben owns a business with two separate departments. Department A generates net income of $120,000, and Department B generates a net loss of $95,000. Ben participates for 700 hours in the operations of Department A and for 100 hours in Department B. If Ben is allowed to treat both departments as a single activity, he can offset the $95,000 loss from Department B against the $120,000 income from Department A. ▼

EXAMPLE 17

Assume the same facts as in the previous example. If Ben is required to treat each department as a separate activity, because he is a material participant in Department A (having devoted 700 hours to it) the $120,000 profit is active income. However, he is not considered a material participant in Department B (100 hours), and the $95,000 loss is a passive loss. Ben cannot offset the $95,000 passive loss from Department B against the $120,000 of active income from Department A. (A complete discussion of the material participation rules follows.) ▼

Recall that on the disposition of a passive activity, a taxpayer is allowed to offset suspended losses from the activity against other types of income. Therefore, identifying what constitutes an activity is of crucial importance for this purpose too.

TAX IN THE NEWS

A Vacation Home Does Not Necessarily Mean a Vacation from the Tax Law

Many purchasers of vacation homes think they will be able to make ownership more affordable by opening their doors to renters and deducting the related mortgage interest expense and real estate taxes. Sometimes taxpayers also count on deducting a portion of maintenance expenses and depreciation. However, these taxpayers will likely find the tax rules that apply to vacation homes more than they counted on. Indeed, anyone looking for a complicated area of the tax law need look no further than the rules that apply to vacation rental property.

Depending on who uses the property and for how long, the property is classified as either personal-use property, rental property, or a combination of the two. Often the best approach from a tax perspective is for the owners to qualify for the rental classification by limiting their personal use to 14 days or less (or less than 10 percent of the rental days). Then all of the expenses, after allocating any that related to the owners' personal use, may be deductible against the taxpayers' other income. But the rub is that the deduction of any resulting net loss is limited by the passive activity loss rules.

Because rental property is treated as a passive activity, any losses typically are deductible only against passive income. For taxpayers with adjusted gross incomes of $150,000 or less, however, up to $25,000 of real estate rental losses may be deductible against nonpassive income. Even with these limitations, this result is the best that the owners can hope for if they rent the property out for more than a limited period of time.

SOURCE: Information from Albert B. Crenshaw, "That Vacation Hideaway Offers No Rest on Taxes," *Washington Post*, July 2, 1995, p. H1. Reprinted with permission.

Example 18 Linda owns a business with two departments. Department A had a net loss of $125,000 in the current year, and Department B had a $70,000 net loss. She disposes of Department B during the year. Assuming Linda is allowed to treat the two departments as separate passive activities, she can offset the passive loss from Department B against other types of income in the following order: gain from disposition of the passive activity, other passive income, and nonpassive income. This treatment leaves her with a suspended loss of $125,000 from Department A. If Departments A and B are treated as components of the same activity, however, on the disposal of Department B, its $70,000 net loss would be suspended along with the other $125,000 of suspended losses of the activity. ▼

The current rules used to delineate what constitutes an activity for purposes of the passive loss limitations are provided in Regulations.[11] These guidelines state that, in general, a taxpayer can treat one or more trade or business activities or rental activities as a single activity if those activities form an *appropriate economic unit* for measuring gain or loss. To determine what ventures form an appropriate economic unit, all of the relevant facts and circumstances must be considered. Taxpayers may use any reasonable method in applying the facts and circum-

[11] Reg. § 1.469–4.

stances. However, the following five factors are given the greatest weight in determining whether activities constitute an appropriate economic unit. It is not necessary to meet all of these conditions in order to treat multiple activities as a single activity.

- Similarities and differences in types of business conducted in the various trade or business or rental activities.
- The extent of common control over the various activities.
- The extent of common ownership of the activities.
- The geographical location of the different units.
- Interdependencies among the activities.

The following examples, adapted from the Regulations, illustrate the application of the general rules for grouping activities.[12]

EXAMPLE 19

George owns a men's clothing store and a video game parlor in Chicago. He also owns a men's clothing store and a video game parlor in Milwaukee. Reasonable methods of applying the facts and circumstances test may result in any of the following groupings:

- All four activities may be grouped into a single activity.
- The clothing stores may be grouped into an activity, and the video parlors may be grouped into a separate activity.
- The Chicago activities may be grouped into an activity, and the Milwaukee activities may be grouped into a separate activity.
- Each of the four activities may be treated as a separate activity. ▼

EXAMPLE 20

Sharon is a partner in a business that sells snack items to drugstores. She also is a partner in a partnership that owns and operates a warehouse. Both partnerships, which are under common control, are located in the same industrial park. The predominant part of the warehouse business is warehousing items for the snack business, and it is the only warehousing business in which Sharon is involved. Sharon should treat the snack business and the warehousing business as a single activity. ▼

Regrouping of Activities. Taxpayers should carefully consider all tax factors in deciding how to group their activities. Once activities have been grouped, they cannot be regrouped unless the original grouping was clearly inappropriate or there has been a material change in the facts and circumstances. If a regrouping is necessary for either of these reasons, the taxpayer is required to disclose to the IRS all information relevant to the regrouping.

The Regulations also grant the IRS the right to regroup activities when both of the following conditions exist.[13]

- The taxpayer's grouping fails to reflect one or more appropriate economic units.
- One of the primary purposes of the taxpayer's grouping is to avoid the passive loss limitations.

The following example, adapted from the Regulations, illustrates a situation where the IRS would exercise its prerogative to regroup a taxpayer's activities.

EXAMPLE 21

Baker, Edwards, Andrews, Clark, and Henson are physicians who operate their own separate practices. Each of the physicians owns interests in activities that generate passive

---

[12] Reg. § 1.469–4(c)(3).

[13] Reg. § 1.469–4(f).

losses, so they devise a plan to set up an entity that will generate passive income. They form the BEACH Partnership to acquire and operate X-ray equipment, and each receives a limited partnership interest. They select an unrelated person to operate the X-ray business as a general partner, and none of the limited partners participates in the activity. Substantially all of the services provided by BEACH are provided to the physicians who own limited partnership interests, and fees are set at a level that assures a profit for BEACH. Each physician treats his medical practice and his interest in the partnership as separate activities and offsets losses from passive investments against the passive income from the partnership. The IRS would interpret the physicians' separate groupings as attempts to avoid the passive loss limitations and would regroup each medical practice and the services performed by the partnership as an appropriate economic unit. ▼

Special Grouping Rules for Rental Activities. Two rules deal specifically with the grouping of rental activities. These provisions are designed to prevent taxpayers from grouping rental activities, which are generally passive, with other businesses in a way that would result in a tax advantage.

First, a rental activity may be grouped with a trade or business activity only if one activity is insubstantial in relation to the other. That is, the rental activity must be insubstantial in relation to the trade or business activity, or the trade or business activity must be insubstantial in relation to the rental activity. The Regulations provide no clear guidelines as to the meaning of insubstantial.[14]

EXAMPLE 22

Schemers, a firm of CPAs, owns a building in downtown Washington, D.C., in which they conduct their practice of public accounting. The firm also rents space on the street level of the building to several retail establishments. Of the total revenue generated by the firm, 95% is associated with the practice of public accounting, and 5% is related to the rental operation. It is likely that the rental activity would be considered insubstantial relative to the accounting practice and the two ventures could be grouped as one nonrental activity. This grouping could be advantageous to the firm, particularly if the rental operation generated a loss! ▼

Second, taxpayers generally may not treat an activity involving the rental of real property and an activity involving the rental of personal property as a single activity.

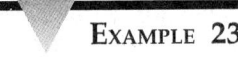

7 LEARNING OBJECTIVE
Analyze and apply the tests for material participation.

Material Participation. If an individual taxpayer materially participates in a nonrental trade or business activity, any loss from that activity is treated as an active loss that can be offset against active income. If a taxpayer does not materially participate, however, the loss is treated as a passive loss, which can only be offset against passive income. Therefore, controlling whether a particular activity is treated as active or passive is an important part of the tax strategy of a taxpayer who owns an interest in one or more businesses. Consider the following examples.

EXAMPLE 23

Dewayne, a corporate executive, earns a salary of $200,000 per year. In addition, he owns a separate business in which he participates. The business produces a loss of $100,000 during the year. If Dewayne materially participates in the business, the $100,000 loss is an active loss that may be offset against his active income from his corporate employer. If he does not materially participate, the loss is passive and is suspended. Dewayne may use the suspended loss in the future only when he has passive income or disposes of the activity. ▼

[14] Reg. § 1.469–4(d).

EXAMPLE 24 Kay, an attorney, earns $250,000 a year in her law practice. She owns interests in two activities, A and B, in which she participates. Activity A, in which she does *not* materially participate, produces a loss of $50,000. Kay has not yet met the material participation standard for Activity B, which produces income of $80,000. However, she can meet the material participation standard if she spends an additional 50 hours in Activity B during the year. Should Kay attempt to meet the material participation standard for Activity B? If she continues working in Activity B and becomes a material participant, the $80,000 income from the activity is *active,* and the $50,000 passive loss from Activity A must be suspended. A more favorable tax strategy is for Kay to *not meet* the material participation standard for Activity B, thus making the income from that activity passive. This enables her to offset the $50,000 passive loss from Activity A against the passive income from Activity B. ▼

It is possible to devise numerous scenarios in which the taxpayer could control the tax outcome by increasing or decreasing his or her participation in different activities. Examples 23 and 24 demonstrate some of the possibilities. The conclusion reached in most analyses of this type is that taxpayers will benefit by having profitable activities classified as passive, so that any passive losses can be used to offset passive income. If the activity produces a loss, however, the taxpayer will benefit if it is classified as active so the loss is not subject to the passive loss limitations.

As discussed above, a nonrental trade or business in which a taxpayer owns an interest must be treated as a passive activity unless the taxpayer materially participates. The Staff of the Joint Committee on Taxation explained the importance of the material participation standard as follows:

> Congress believed that there were several reasons why it was appropriate to examine the materiality of a taxpayer's participation in an activity in determining the extent to which such taxpayer should be permitted to use tax benefits from the activity. A taxpayer who materially participated in an activity was viewed as more likely than a passive investor to approach the activity with a significant nontax economic profit motive, and to form a sound judgment as to whether the activity had genuine economic significance and value. A material participation standard identified an important distinction between different types of taxpayer activities. It was thought that, in general, the more passive investor seeks a return on capital invested, including returns in the form of reductions in the taxes owed on unrelated income, rather than an ongoing source of livelihood. A material participation standard reduced the importance, for such investors, of the tax-reduction features of an investment, and thus increased the importance of the economic features in an investor's decision about where to invest his funds.[15]

Even if the concept or the implication of being a material participant is clear, the precise meaning of the term **material participation** can be vague. As enacted, § 469 required a taxpayer to participate on a *regular, continuous, and substantial* basis in order to be a material participant. In many situations, however, it was difficult or impossible to gain any assurance that this nebulous standard was met.

In response to this dilemma, Temporary Regulations[16] providing seven tests were issued to help taxpayers cope with these issues. Material participation is

[15] *General Explanation of the Tax Reform Act of 1986 ("Blue Book"),* prepared by The Staff of the Joint Committee on Taxation, May 4, 1987, H.R. 3838, 99th Cong., p. 212.

[16] Temp. and Prop.Reg § 1.469–5T(a). The Temporary Regulations are also Proposed Regulations. Temporary Regulations have the same effect as final Regulations. Refer to Chapter 2 for a discussion of the different categories of Regulations.

achieved by meeting any one of the tests. These tests can be divided into three categories:

- Tests based on current participation.
- Tests based on prior participation.
- Test based on facts and circumstances.

Tests Based on Current Participation. The first four tests are quantitative tests that require measurement, in hours, of the taxpayer's participation in the activity during the year.

1. *Does the individual participate in the activity for more than 500 hours during the year?*

The purpose of the 500-hour requirement is to restrict deductions from the types of trade or business activities Congress intended to treat as passive activities. The 500-hour standard for material participation was adopted for the following reasons:[17]

- Few investors in traditional tax shelters devote more than 500 hours a year to such an investment.
- The IRS believes that income from an activity in which the taxpayer participates for more than 500 hours a year should not be treated as passive.

2. *Does the individual's participation in the activity for the taxable year constitute substantially all of the participation in the activity of all individuals (including nonowner employees) for the year?*

EXAMPLE 25

Ned, a physician, operates a separate business in which he participates for 80 hours during the year. He is the only participant and has no employees in the separate business. Ned meets the material participation standard of Test 2. If he had employees, it would be difficult to apply Test 2, because the Temporary Regulations do not define the term *substantially all.* ▼

3. *Does the individual participate in the activity for more than 100 hours during the year, and is the individual's participation in the activity for the year not less than the participation of any other individual (including nonowner employees) for the year?*

EXAMPLE 26

Adam, a college professor, owns a separate business in which he participates 110 hours during the year. He has an employee who works 90 hours during the year. Adam meets the material participation standard under Test 3, but probably does not meet it under Test 2 because his participation is only 55% of the total participation. It is unlikely that 55% would meet the *substantially all* requirement of Test 2. ▼

Tests 2 and 3 are included because the IRS recognizes that the operation of some activities does not require more than 500 hours of participation during the year.

4. *Is the activity a significant participation activity for the taxable year, and does the individual's aggregate participation in all significant participation activities during the year exceed 500 hours?*

[17] T.D. 8175, 1988–1 C.B. 191.

A **significant participation activity** is a trade or business in which the individual's participation exceeds 100 hours during the year. This test treats taxpayers whose aggregate participation in several significant participation activities exceeds 500 hours as material participants. Test 4 thus accords the same treatment to an individual who devotes an aggregate of more than 500 hours to several significant participation activities as to an individual who devotes more than 500 hours to a single activity.

EXAMPLE 27

Mike owns five different businesses. He participated in each activity during the year as follows:

Activity	Hours of Participation
A	110
B	140
C	120
D	150
E	100

Activities A, B, C, and D are significant participation activities, and Mike's aggregate participation in those activities is 520 hours. Therefore, Activities A, B, C, and D are not treated as passive activities. Activity E is not a significant participation activity (not more than 100 hours), so it is not included in applying the 500-hour test. Activity E is treated as a passive activity, unless Mike meets one of the other material participation tests for that activity. ▼

EXAMPLE 28

Assume the same facts as in the previous example, except that Activity A does not exist. All of the activities are now treated as passive. Activity E is not counted in applying the more-than-500-hour test, so Mike's aggregate participation in significant participation activities is 410 hours (140 in Activity B + 120 in Activity C + 150 in Activity D). He could meet the significant participation test for Activity E by participating for one more hour in the activity. This would cause Activities B, C, D, and E to be treated as nonpassive activities. However, before deciding whether to participate for at least one more hour in Activity E, Mike should assess how the participation would affect his overall tax liability. ▼

Tests Based on Prior Participation. Tests 5 and 6 are based on material participation in prior years. Under these tests, a taxpayer who is no longer a participant in an activity can continue to be *classified* as a material participant. The IRS takes the position that material participation in a trade or business for a long period of time is likely to indicate that the activity represents the individual's principal livelihood, rather than a passive investment. Consequently, withdrawal from the activity, or reduction of participation to the point where it is not material, does not change the classification of the activity from active to passive.

5. *Did the individual materially participate in the activity for any 5 taxable years (whether consecutive or not) during the 10 taxable years that immediately precede the taxable year?*

EXAMPLE 29

Dawn, who owns a 50% interest in a restaurant, was a material participant in the operations of the restaurant from 1990 through 1994. She retired at the end of 1994 and is no longer involved in the restaurant except as an investor. Dawn will be treated as a material participant in the restaurant in 1995. Even if she does not become involved in the restaurant as a material participant again, she will continue to be treated as a material participant in 1996, 1997, 1998, and 1999. In 2000 and later years, Dawn's share of income or loss from the restaurant will be classified as passive unless she materially participates in those years. ▼

6. *Is the activity a personal service activity, and did the individual materially participate in the activity for any three preceding taxable years (whether consecutive or not)?*

As indicated above, the material participation standards differ for personal service activities and other businesses. An individual who was a material participant in a personal service activity for *any three years* prior to the taxable year continues to be treated as a material participant after withdrawal from the activity.

EXAMPLE 30

Evan, a CPA, retires from the EFG Partnership after working full-time in the partnership for 30 years. As a retired partner, he will continue to receive a share of the profits of the firm for the next 10 years, even though he will not participate in the firm's operations. Evan also owns an interest in a passive activity that produces a loss for the year. He continues to be treated as a material participant in the EFG Partnership, and his income from the partnership is active income. Therefore, he is not allowed to offset the loss from his passive investment against the income from the EFG Partnership. ▼

Facts and Circumstances Test. Test 7 is a facts and circumstances test to determine whether the taxpayer has materially participated.

7. *Based on all the facts and circumstances, did the individual participate in the activity on a regular, continuous, and substantial basis during the year?*

The Temporary Regulations do not define what constitutes regular, continuous, and substantial participation except to say that the taxpayer's activities will *not* be considered material participation under Test 7 in the following three circumstances:[18]

- The taxpayer satisfies the participation standards (whether or not a *material participant*) of any Code section other than § 469.
- The taxpayer manages the activity, unless
  - no other person receives compensation for management services, and
  - no individual spends more hours during the tax year managing the activity than does the taxpayer.
- The taxpayer participates in the activity for 100 hours or less during the tax year.

A part of the Temporary Regulations has been reserved for further development of this test. Presumably, additional guidelines will be issued in the future. For the time being, taxpayers should rely on Tests 1 through 6 in determining whether the material participation standards have been met.

Participation Defined. Participation generally includes any work done by an individual in an activity that he or she owns. Participation does not include work if it is of a type not customarily done by owners *and* if one of its principal purposes is to avoid the disallowance of passive losses or credits. Also, work done in an

[18] Temp. and Prop.Reg. § 1.469–5T(b)(2).

individual's capacity as an investor (e.g., reviewing financial reports in a non-managerial capacity) is not counted in applying the material participation tests. However, participation by an owner's spouse counts as participation by the owner.[19]

EXAMPLE 31

Tom, who is a partner in a CPA firm, owns a computer store that has operated at a loss during the year. In order to offset this loss against the income from his CPA practice, Tom would like to avoid having the computer business classified as a passive activity. Through December 15, he has worked 400 hours in the business in management and selling activities. During the last two weeks of December, he works 80 hours in management and selling activities and 30 hours doing janitorial chores. Also during the last two weeks in December, Tom's wife participates 40 hours as a salesperson. She has worked as a salesperson in the computer store in prior years, but has not done so during the current year. If any of Tom's work is of a type not customarily done by owners *and* if one of its principal purposes is to avoid the disallowance of passive losses or credits, it is not counted in applying the material participation tests. It is likely that Tom's 480 hours of participation in management and selling activities will count as participation, but the 30 hours spent doing janitorial chores will not. However, the 40 hours of participation by his wife will count, and Tom will qualify as a material participant under the more-than-500-hour rule (480 + 40 = 520). ▼

Limited Partners. A *limited* partner is one whose liability to third-party creditors of the partnership is limited to the amount the partner has invested in the partnership. Such a partnership must have at least one *general* partner, who is fully liable in an individual capacity for the debts of the partnership to third parties. Generally, a *limited partner* is not considered a material participant unless he or she qualifies under Test 1, 5, or 6 in the above list. However, a *general partner* may qualify as a material participant by meeting any of the seven tests. If an unlimited, or general, partner also owns a limited interest in the same limited partnership, all interests are treated as a general interest.[20]

8 LEARNING OBJECTIVE
Understand the nature of rental activities under the passive loss rules.

Rental Activities Defined. As discussed previously, § 469 specifies that, subject to certain exceptions, all rental activities are to be treated as passive activities.[21] A **rental activity** is defined as any activity where payments are received principally for the use of tangible (real or personal) property.[22] Importantly, an activity that is classified as a rental activity is subject to the passive activity loss rules, even if the taxpayer involved is a material participant.

EXAMPLE 32

Sarah owns an apartment building and spends an average of 60 hours a week in its operation. Assuming that the apartment building operation is classed as a rental activity, it is automatically subject to the passive activity rules, even though Sarah spends more than 500 hours a year in its operation. ▼

As suggested, Temporary Regulations provide that in certain circumstances activities involving rentals of real and personal property are *not* to be *treated* as rental activities.[23]

[19] Temp. and Prop.Reg. § 1.469–5T(f)(3).
[20] Temp. and Prop.Reg. § 1.469–5T(e)(3)(ii).
[21] § 469(c)(2).
[22] § 469(j)(8).
[23] Temp. and Prop.Reg. § 1.469–1T(e)(3)(ii).

EXAMPLE 33

Dan owns a videotape business. Because the average period of customer use is seven days or less, Dan's videotape business is not treated as a rental activity. ▼

The fact that Dan's videotape business in the previous example is not treated as a rental activity does not necessarily mean that it is classified as a nonpassive activity. Instead, the videotape business is treated as a trade or business activity subject to the material participation standards. If Dan is a material participant, the business is treated as active. If he is not a material participant, it is treated as a passive activity.

Therefore, activities covered by any of the following six exceptions provided by the Temporary Regulations are not *automatically* treated as passive activities because they would not be classified as rental activities. Instead, the activities are subject to the material participation tests.

1. *The average period of customer use for the property is seven days or less.*

Under this exception, activities involving the short-term use of tangible property such as automobiles, videocassettes, tuxedos, tools, and other such property are not treated as rental activities. The provision also applies to short-term rentals of hotel or motel rooms.

This exception is based on the presumption that a person who rents property for seven days or less is generally required to provide *significant services* to the customer. Providing such services supports a conclusion that the person is engaged in a service business rather than a rental business.

2. *The average period of customer use for the property is 30 days or less, and the owner of the property provides significant personal services.*

For longer-term rentals, the presumption that significant services are provided is not automatic, as it is in the case of the seven-day exception. Instead, the taxpayer must be able to *prove* that significant personal services are rendered in connection with the activity. Therefore, an understanding of what constitutes significant personal services is necessary in order to apply the rule.

Significant personal services include only services provided by *individuals.* This provision excludes such items as telephone and cable television services. Four additional categories of *excluded services* are not considered significant personal services:[24]

- Services necessary to permit the lawful use of the property.
- Services performed in connection with the construction of improvements to the property.
- Services performed in connection with the performance of repairs that extend the property's useful life for a period substantially longer than the average period for which the property is used by customers.
- Services similar to those commonly provided in connection with long-term rentals of high-grade commercial or residential real property (including cleaning and maintenance of common areas, routine repairs, trash collection, elevator service, and security at entrances or perimeters).

3. *The owner of the property provides extraordinary personal services. The average period of customer use is of no consequence in applying this test.*

[24] Temp. and Prop.Reg. § 1.469–1T(e)(3)(iv).

Extraordinary personal services are services provided by individuals where the customers' use of the property is incidental to their receipt of the services. For example, a patient's use of a hospital bed is incidental to his or her use of medical services. Another example is the use of a boarding school's dormitory, which is incidental to the scholastic services received.

4. *The rental of the property is treated as incidental to a nonrental activity of the taxpayer.*

Rentals of real property incidental to a nonrental activity are not considered a passive activity. The Temporary Regulations provide that the following rentals are not passive activities.[25]

- *Property held primarily for investment.* This occurs where the principal purpose for holding the property is the expectation of gain from the appreciation of the property and the gross rent income is less than 2 percent of the lesser of (1) the unadjusted basis or (2) the fair market value of the property.

EXAMPLE 34

Ramon invests in vacant land for the purpose of realizing a profit on its appreciation. He leases the land during the period it is held. The unadjusted basis is $250,000, and the fair market value is $350,000. The lease payments are $4,000 per year. Because gross rent income is less than 2% of $250,000, the activity is not a rental activity. ▼

- *Property used in a trade or business.* This occurs where the property is owned by a taxpayer who is an owner of the trade or business using the rental property. The property must also have been used in the trade or business during the year or during at least two of the five preceding taxable years. The 2 percent test above also applies in this situation.

EXAMPLE 35

A farmer owns land with an unadjusted basis of $250,000 and a fair market value of $350,000. He used it for farming purposes in 1994 and 1995. In 1996, he leased the land to another farmer for $4,000. The activity is not a rental activity. ▼

- *Property held for sale to customers.* If property is held for sale to customers and rented during the year, the rental of the property is not a rental activity. If, for instance, an automobile dealer rents automobiles held for sale to customers to persons who are having their own cars repaired, the activity is not a rental activity.

- *Lodging rented for the convenience of an employer.* If an employer provides lodging for an employee incidental to the employee's performance of services in the employer's trade or business, no rental activity exists.

- A partner who rents property to a partnership that is used in the partnership's trade or business does not have a rental activity.

These rules were written to prevent taxpayers from converting active or portfolio income into a passive activity for the purpose of offsetting other passive losses.

5. *The taxpayer customarily makes the property available during defined business hours for nonexclusive use by various customers.*

[25] Temp. and Prop.Regs. §§ 1.469–1T(e)(3)(vi)(B) through (E).

EXAMPLE 36

Pat is the owner-operator of a public golf course. Some customers pay daily greens fees each time they use the course, while others purchase weekly, monthly, or annual passes. The golf course is open every day from sunrise to sunset, except on certain holidays and on days when the course is closed due to inclement weather conditions. Pat is not engaged in a rental activity, regardless of the average period customers use the course. ▼

6. *The property is provided for use in an activity conducted by a partnership, S corporation, or joint venture in which the taxpayer owns an interest.*

EXAMPLE 37

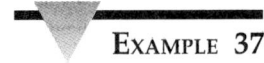

Joe, a partner in the Skyview Partnership, contributes the use of a building to the partnership. The partnership has net income of $30,000 during the year, of which Joe's share is $10,000. Unless the partnership is engaged in a rental activity, none of Joe's income from the partnership is income from a rental activity. ▼

INTERACTION OF THE AT-RISK AND PASSIVE ACTIVITY LIMITS

9 LEARNING OBJECTIVE
Recognize the relationship between the at-risk and passive activity limitations.

The determination of whether a loss is suspended under the passive loss rules is made after application of the at-risk rules, as well as other provisions relating to the measurement of taxable income. A loss that is not allowed for the year because the taxpayer is not at risk with respect to it is suspended under the at-risk provision and not under the passive loss rules. Further, a taxpayer's basis is reduced by deductions (e.g., depreciation) even if the deductions are not currently usable because of the passive loss rules.

EXAMPLE 38

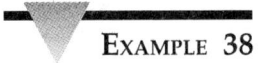

Jack's adjusted basis in a passive activity is $10,000 at the beginning of 1995. His loss from the activity in 1995 is $4,000. Since Jack had no passive activity income, the $4,000 cannot be deducted. At year-end, Jack has an adjusted basis and an at-risk amount of $6,000 in the activity and a suspended passive loss of $4,000. ▼

EXAMPLE 39

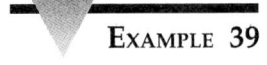

Jack in Example 38 had a loss of $9,000 in the activity in 1996. Since the $9,000 exceeds his at-risk amount ($6,000) by $3,000, that $3,000 loss is disallowed by the at-risk rules. If Jack has no passive activity income, the remaining $6,000 is suspended under the passive activity rules. At year-end, he has a $3,000 loss suspended under the at-risk rules, $10,000 of suspended passive losses, and an adjusted basis and an at-risk amount in the activity of zero. ▼

EXAMPLE 40

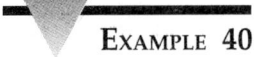

Jack in Example 39 realized a $1,000 gain in 1997. Because the $1,000 increases his at-risk amount, $1,000 of the $3,000 unused loss can be reclassified as a passive loss. If he has no other passive income, the $1,000 income is offset by $1,000 of suspended passive losses. At the end of 1997, Jack has no taxable passive income, $2,000 ($3,000 – $1,000) of unused losses under the at-risk rules, $10,000 of (reclassified) suspended passive losses ($10,000 + $1,000 of reclassified unused at-risk losses – $1,000 of passive losses offset against passive gains), and an adjusted basis and an at-risk amount in the activity of zero. ▼

EXAMPLE 41

In 1998, Jack had no gain or loss from the activity in Example 40. He contributed $5,000 more to the passive activity. Because the $5,000 increases his at-risk amount, the $2,000 of losses suspended under the at-risk rules is reclassified as a passive loss. Jack gets no passive loss deduction in 1998. At year-end, he has no suspended losses under the at-risk rules, $12,000 of suspended passive losses ($10,000 + $2,000 of reclassified suspended at-risk losses), and an adjusted basis and an at-risk amount of $3,000 ($5,000 additional investment – $2,000 of reclassified losses). ▼

SPECIAL PASSIVE ACTIVITY RULES FOR REAL ESTATE ACTIVITIES

10 LEARNING OBJECTIVE
Discuss the special treatment available to real estate activities.

The passive loss limits contain two exceptions related to real estate activities. These exceptions allow all or part of real estate rental losses to be offset against active or portfolio income, even though the activity is a passive activity.

Material Participation in a Real Property Trade or Business. After 1993, losses from real estate rental activities are *not* treated as passive losses for certain real estate professionals.[26] To qualify for nonpassive treatment, a taxpayer must satisfy both of the following requirements:

- More than half of the personal services that the taxpayer performs in trades or businesses are performed in real property trades or businesses in which the taxpayer materially participates.
- The taxpayer performs more than 750 hours of services in these real property trades or businesses as a material participant.

Taxpayers who do not satisfy the above requirements must continue to treat losses from real estate rental activities as passive losses.

EXAMPLE 42

During the current year, Della performed personal service activities as follows: 900 hours as a personal financial planner, 550 hours in a real estate development and leasing business, and 600 hours in real estate rental activities. Any loss Della incurred in either real estate activity will *not* be subject to the passive loss rules, since more than 50% of her personal services were devoted to real property trades or businesses, and her material participation in those real estate activities exceeded 750 hours. Thus, any loss from the real estate rental activity could offset active and portfolio sources of income. ▼

On a joint return, the requirements for nonpassive treatment of losses must be met by one spouse or the other. That is, the spouses cannot combine their services in order to meet the requirements. Services performed by an employee are not treated as being related to a real estate trade or business unless the employee performing the services has at least a 5 percent ownership interest in the employer. Additionally, a closely held regular corporation may also qualify for the passive loss relief if more than 50 percent of its gross receipts for the year are derived from real property trades or businesses in which it materially participates.

Rental Real Estate Activities. The second exception is more significant in that it is not restricted to real estate professionals. This exception allows individuals to deduct up to $25,000 of losses on real estate rental activities against active and portfolio income.[27] The potential annual $25,000 deduction is reduced by 50 percent of the taxpayer's AGI in excess of $100,000. Thus, the entire deduction is phased out at $150,000. If married individuals file separately, the $25,000 deduction is reduced to zero unless they lived apart for the entire year. If they lived apart for the entire year, the loss amount is $12,500 each, and the phase-out begins at $50,000. AGI for purposes of the phase-out is calculated without regard to IRA deductions, Social Security benefits, and net losses from passive activities.

To qualify for the $25,000 exception, a taxpayer must meet the following requirements.[28]

[26] § 469(c)(7).
[27] § 469(i).
[28] § 469(i)(6).

- Actively participate in the real estate rental activity.
- Own 10 percent or more (in value) of all interests in the activity during the entire taxable year (or shorter period during which the taxpayer held an interest in the activity).

The difference between *active participation* and *material participation* is that the former can be satisfied without regular, continuous, and substantial involvement in operations as long as the taxpayer participates in making management decisions in a significant and bona fide sense. In this context, relevant management decisions include such decisions as approving new tenants, deciding on rental terms, and approving capital or repair expenditures.

The $25,000 allowance is available after all active participation rental losses and gains are netted and applied to other passive income. If a taxpayer has a real estate rental loss in excess of the amount that can be deducted under the real estate rental exception, that excess is treated as a passive loss.

EXAMPLE 43

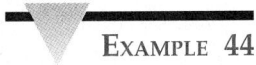

Brad, who has $90,000 of AGI before considering rental activities, has $85,000 of losses from a real estate rental activity in which he actively participates. He also actively participates in another real estate rental activity from which he has $25,000 of income. He has other passive income of $36,000. The net rental loss of $60,000 is offset by the $36,000 of passive income, leaving $24,000 that can be deducted against other income. ▼

The $25,000 offset allowance is an aggregate of both deductions and credits in deduction equivalents. The deduction equivalent of a passive activity credit is the amount of deductions that reduces the tax liability for the taxable year by an amount equal to the credit.[29] A taxpayer with $5,000 of credits and a tax bracket of 28 percent would have a deduction equivalent of $17,857 ($5,000 ÷ 28%).

If the total deduction and deduction equivalent exceed $25,000, the taxpayer must allocate on a pro rata basis, first among the losses (including real estate rental activity losses suspended in prior years) and then to credits in the following order: (1) credits other than rehabilitation credits, (2) rehabilitation credits, and (3) low-income housing credits.

EXAMPLE 44

Kevin is an active participant in a real estate rental activity that produces $8,000 of income, $26,000 of deductions, and $1,500 of credits. Kevin, who is in the 28% tax bracket, may deduct the net passive loss of $18,000 ($8,000 – $26,000). After deducting the loss, he has an available deduction equivalent of $7,000 ($25,000 – $18,000 passive loss). Therefore, the maximum amount of credits that he may claim is $1,960 ($7,000 × 28%). Since the actual credits are less than this amount, Kevin may claim the entire $1,500 credit. ▼

EXAMPLE 45

Kelly, who is in the 28% tax bracket, is an active participant in three separate real estate rental activities. The relevant tax results for each activity are as follows:

- Activity A: $20,000 of losses.
- Activity B: $10,000 of losses.
- Activity C: $4,200 of credits.

Kelly's deduction equivalent from the credits is $15,000 ($4,200 ÷ 28%). Therefore, the total passive deductions and deduction equivalents are $45,000 ($20,000 + $10,000 + $15,000), which exceeds the maximum allowable amount of $25,000. Consequently, Kelly must allocate pro rata first from among losses and then from among credits. Deductions from losses are limited as follows:

[29] § 469(j)(5).

- Activity A {$25,000 × [$20,000 ÷ ($20,000 + $10,000)]} = $16,667.
- Activity B {$25,000 × [$10,000 ÷ ($20,000 + $10,000)]} = $8,333.

Since the amount of passive deductions exceeds the $25,000 maximum, the deduction balance of $5,000 and passive credit of $4,200 must be carried forward. Kelly's suspended losses and credits by activity are as follows:

		Activity		
	Total	**A**	**B**	**C**
Allocated losses	$30,000	$ 20,000	$10,000	$ -0-
Allocated credits	4,200	-0-	-0-	4,200
Utilized losses	(25,000)	(16,667)	(8,333)	-0-
Suspended losses	5,000	3,333	1,667	-0-
Suspended credits	4,200	-0-	-0-	4,200

▼

ETHICAL CONSIDERATIONS

Applying the Rules on Rental Real Estate

Ted, a management consultant, owns an apartment complex that produces a profit of $60,000 in the current year. He earned $120,000 in his consulting business and had a $40,000 loss on a passive activity (not real estate). Ted worked for 800 hours at the apartment complex during the year, but characterizes the $60,000 profit as passive income so he can utilize the $40,000 passive loss. He claims that he is doing nothing wrong because the law is designed only to protect the passive loss deduction of real estate professionals and is not applicable to profits.

Further, Ted thinks that he is justified in classifying the loss as passive because of the nature of the work he performed during the time devoted to managing the apartments. Ted feels certain that of the 800 hours, between 300 and 400 hours were spent coaching and supporting about 20 underprivileged children living in the apartment complex as part of a year-round sports program. Ted says that his involvement not only benefits the children, but will make the apartment a more desirable place to live and thus could also benefit him economically in the long run. He sees the hours devoted to the sports program as an integral part of his job in managing the apartment complex, but feels that they should not count in determining whether the activity is passive. Ted asks you to prepare his return. What actions will you take?

DISPOSITIONS OF PASSIVE INTERESTS

11 LEARNING OBJECTIVE
Determine the proper tax treatment upon the disposition of a passive activity.

Recall from an earlier discussion that if a taxpayer disposes of an entire interest in a passive activity, any suspended losses (and in certain cases, suspended credits) may be utilized when calculating the final economic gain or loss on the investment. In addition, if a loss ultimately results, that loss can be offset against other types of income. However, the consequences may differ if the activity is disposed of in a transaction that is other than a fully taxable transaction. The following discusses the treatment of suspended passive losses in other types of dispositions.

Disposition of a Passive Activity at Death. A transfer of a taxpayer's interest in an activity by reason of the taxpayer's death results in suspended losses being allowed (to the decedent) to the extent they exceed the amount, if any, of the step-up in basis allowed.[30] Suspended losses are lost to the extent of the amount of the basis increase. The losses allowed generally are reported on the final return of the deceased taxpayer.

EXAMPLE 46

A taxpayer dies with passive activity property having an adjusted basis of $40,000, suspended losses of $10,000, and a fair market value at the date of the decedent's death of $75,000. The increase (i.e., step-up) in basis (see Chapter 14) is $35,000 (fair market value at date of death in excess of adjusted basis). None of the $10,000 suspended loss is deductible by either the decedent or the beneficiary. The suspended losses ($10,000) are lost because they did not exceed the step-up in basis ($35,000). ▼

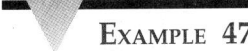

EXAMPLE 47

A taxpayer dies with passive activity property having an adjusted basis of $40,000, suspended losses of $10,000, and a fair market value at the date of the decedent's death of $47,000. Since the step-up in basis would be only $7,000 ($47,000 – $40,000), the suspended losses allowed are limited to $3,000 ($10,000 suspended loss at time of death – $7,000 increase in basis). The $3,000 loss available to the decedent is reported on the decedent's final income tax return. ▼

Disposition of a Passive Activity by Gift. In a disposition of a taxpayer's interest in a passive activity by gift, the suspended losses are added to the basis of the property.[31]

EXAMPLE 48

A taxpayer makes a gift of passive activity property having an adjusted basis of $40,000, suspended losses of $10,000, and a fair market value at the date of the gift of $100,000. The taxpayer cannot deduct the suspended losses in the year of the disposition. However, the suspended losses transfer with the property and are added to the adjusted basis of the property. ▼

Installment Sale of a Passive Activity. An installment sale of a taxpayer's entire interest in a passive activity triggers the recognition of the suspended losses.[32] The losses are allowed in each year of the installment obligation in the ratio that the gain recognized in each year bears to the total gain on the sale.

EXAMPLE 49

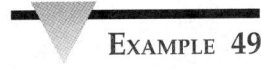

Stan sold his entire interest in a passive activity for $100,000. His adjusted basis in the property was $60,000. If he uses the installment method, his gross profit ratio is 40% ($40,000/$100,000). If Stan received a $20,000 down payment, he would recognize a gain of $8,000 (40% of $20,000). If the activity had a suspended loss of $25,000, Stan would deduct $5,000 [($8,000 ÷ $40,000) × $25,000] of the suspended loss in the first year. ▼

Passive Activity Changes to Active. If a formerly passive activity becomes an active one, suspended losses are allowed to the extent of income from the now active business.[33] If any of the suspended loss remains, it continues to be treated as a loss from a passive activity. The excess suspended loss can be deducted from passive income or carried over to the next tax year and deducted to the extent of income from the now active business in the succeeding year(s). The activity must continue to be the same activity.

Nontaxable Exchange of a Passive Activity. In a nontaxable exchange of a passive investment, the taxpayer keeps the suspended losses, which generally

[30] § 469(g)(2).
[31] § 469(j)(6).
[32] § 469(g)(3).
[33] § 469(f).

CONCEPT SUMMARY 11–2

Passive Activity Loss Rules: General Concepts

What is the fundamental passive activity rule?	Passive activity losses may be deducted only against passive activity gains. Losses not allowed are suspended and used in future years.
Who is subject to the passive activity rules?	Individuals. Estates. Trusts. Personal service corporations. Closely held C corporations.
What is a passive activity?	Trade or business or income-producing activity in which the taxpayer does not materially participate during the year, or rental activities, subject to certain exceptions, regardless of the taxpayer's level of participation.
What is an activity?	One or more trade or business or rental activities that comprises an appropriate economic unit.
How is an appropriate economic unit determined?	Based on a reasonable application of the relevant facts and circumstances.
What is material participation?	In general, the taxpayer participates in a regular, continuous, and substantial basis. More specifically, when the taxpayer meets the conditions of one of the seven tests provided in the Regulations.
What is a rental activity?	In general, an activity where payments are received for the use of tangible property. More specifically, a rental activity that does *not* meet one of the six exceptions provided in the Regulations. Special rules apply to rental real estate.

become deductible when the acquired property is sold. If the activity of the old and new property are the same, suspended losses can be used.

EXAMPLE 50

A taxpayer exchanged a duplex for a limited partnership interest in a § 721 nonrecognition transaction (see Chapter 20 for details). The suspended losses from the duplex are not deductible until the limited partnership interest is sold. Two separate activities exist: a real estate rental activity and a limited partnership activity. If the taxpayer had continued to own the duplex and the duplex had future taxable income, the suspended losses would have become deductible before the time of disposition. ▼

EXAMPLE 51

In a § 1031 nontaxable exchange (see Chapter 15 for details), a taxpayer exchanged a duplex for an apartment building. The suspended losses from the duplex are deductible against future taxable income of the apartment building. The same activity exists. ▼

TAX PLANNING CONSIDERATIONS

12 LEARNING OBJECTIVE
Suggest tax planning strategies to minimize the effect of the passive loss limitations.

UTILIZING PASSIVE LOSSES

Taxpayers who have passive activity losses (PALs) should adopt a strategy of generating passive activity income that can be sheltered by existing passive losses. One approach is to buy an interest in a passive activity that is generating income (referred to as passive income generators, or PIGs). Then the PAL can be offset against income from the PIG. From a tax perspective, it would be foolish to buy a loss-generating passive activity (PAL) unless one has other passive income (PIG) to shelter or the activity is rental real estate that can qualify for the $25,000 exception or the exception available to real estate professionals.

A taxpayer with existing passive losses might consider buying rental property. If a large down payment is made and the straight-line method of MACRS (discussed in Chapter 8) is elected, a positive net income could be realized. The income would be sheltered by other passive losses, depreciation expense would be spread out evenly and preserved for future years, and depreciation recapture (discussed in Chapter 17) would be avoided upon the sale of the property. Future gain realized upon the sale of the rental property could be sheltered by existing suspended passive losses.

Taxpayers with passive losses should consider all other trades or businesses in which they have an interest. If they show that they do not materially participate in the activity, the activity becomes a passive activity. Any income generated could be sheltered by existing passive losses and suspended losses. Family partnerships in which certain members do not materially participate would qualify. The silent partner in any general partnership engaged in a trade or business would also qualify.

As the chapter has shown, the passive loss rules can have a dramatic effect on a taxpayer's ability to claim passive losses currently. However, several steps can be taken to mitigate their impact:

- Replace passive activity debt with home equity indebtedness.
- Carefully select the year in which a passive activity is to be disposed of at a gain, as it can be to the taxpayer's advantage to wait until sufficient passive losses have been generated to completely offset the gain recognized on the asset's disposition.
- Keep accurate records of all sources of income and losses, particularly any suspended passive losses and credits and the activities to which they relate, so that their potential tax benefit will not be lost.

Finally, because of the restrictive nature of the passive activity loss rules, it may be advantageous for a taxpayer to use a vacation home enough to convert it to a second residence. This would enable all of the qualified interest to be deducted without limitation. However, this strategy would lead to the loss of other deductions, such as repairs, maintenance, and insurance.

KEY TERMS

Active income, 11–6

At-risk limitation, 11–3

Closely held corporation, 11–11

Extraordinary personal services, 11–22

Material participation, 11–16

Passive loss, 11–3

Personal service corporation, 11–11

Portfolio income, 11–6

Rental activity, 11–20

Significant participation activity, 11–18

Tax shelters, 11–2

PROBLEM MATERIALS

DISCUSSION QUESTIONS

1. Congress has passed two major provisions to inhibit taxpayers' ability to use tax shelters to reduce or defer Federal income tax. Explain.

2. Alice invested $100,000 for a 25% interest in a partnership in which she is not a material participant. The partnership borrowed $200,000 from a bank and used the proceeds to

acquire a building. What is Alice's at-risk amount if the $200,000 was borrowed on a recourse loan?

3. Eric invested $40,000 for a 20% interest in a partnership in which he is not a material participant. The partnership borrowed $200,000 from a bank and used the proceeds to acquire machinery. What is Eric's at-risk amount if the $200,000 was borrowed on a nonrecourse loan?

4. List some events that increase and decrease an investor's at-risk amount, and discuss some strategies that a taxpayer can employ to increase the at-risk amount in order to claim a higher deduction for losses.

5. Roy invested $30,000 in a cattle-feeding operation that used nonrecourse notes to purchase $300,000 in feed, which was fed to the cattle and expensed. His share of the expense was $54,000. How much can Roy deduct?

6. Explain the meaning of the terms *active income, portfolio income,* and *passive income.*

7. Manuel owns an interest in an activity that produces a $100,000 loss during the year. Would he generally prefer to have the activity classified as active or passive? Discuss.

8. Kim owns an interest in an activity that produces $100,000 of income during the year. Would Kim generally prefer to have the activity classified as active or passive? Discuss.

9. Felicia owns a passive activity that she acquired several years ago. She has incurred losses on the activity since its acquisition. This is the only passive activity she has ever owned. How will these passive losses affect Felicia's taxable income when she disposes of the activity?

10. What is a suspended loss? Why is it important to allocate suspended losses in cases where a taxpayer has interests in more than one passive activity?

11. Upon a taxable disposition of a passive activity, the taxpayer can utilize any suspended losses and credits related to that activity. Do you agree? Explain.

12. Discuss whether the passive loss rules apply to the following: individuals, closely held regular corporations, S corporations, partnerships, and personal service corporations.

13. Gray Corporation has $100,000 of active income and a $55,000 passive loss for the year. Under what circumstances is the corporation prohibited from deducting the loss? Under what circumstances is the corporation allowed to deduct the loss?

14. Hi-Tech Consulting, Inc., is a corporation owned by four engineers, all of whom work full-time for the corporation. The corporation has eight other full-time employees, all on the clerical staff. Hi-Tech provides consulting services to inventors. The corporation has invested in a passive activity that produced a $60,000 loss during the current year. Can Hi-Tech deduct the loss this year? Explain.

15. The Regulations set forth a *facts and circumstances test* for determining what constitutes an activity. Describe this test and comment on the significance of the term *appropriate economic unit.*

16. What factors are given the greatest weight in determining whether activities constitute an appropriate economic unit?

17. Discuss what constitutes a passive activity.

18. Under what circumstances may the IRS regroup activities in a different way than the taxpayer has grouped them? Give an example of a situation to which the regrouping rule would be applied.

19. The Regulations prohibit grouping rental activities in certain circumstances. Discuss these rules.

20. What is the significance of the term *material participation?* Why is the extent of a taxpayer's participation in an activity important in determining whether a loss from the activity is deductible or nondeductible?

21. Why did the IRS adopt the more-than-500-hour standard for material participation?

22. Keith, a physician, operates a separate business that he acquired nine years ago. He participated for 90 hours in the business during the current year, and the business incurred a loss of $20,000. Under what circumstances will the loss be deductible as an active loss?

23. Jan, an attorney, operates a separate business that she acquired nine years ago. She has one part-time employee in the business. Jan participated for 130 hours in the business during the current year, and the business incurred a loss of $20,000. Under what circumstances will the loss be deductible as an active loss?

24. Zelda, a professor, operates three separate businesses on the side. She participates for less than 500 hours in each business. Each business incurs a loss during the year. Are there any circumstances under which Zelda may treat the losses as active?

25. Last year, Paul retired as a partner in a CPA firm he founded 30 years ago. He continues to share in the profits, although he no longer participates in the activities of the firm. Paul also owns an interest in a passive activity that produced a loss of $50,000 in the current year. Can Paul offset the passive loss against his income from the CPA firm?

26. Rene retired from public accounting after a long and successful career of 45 years. As part of her retirement package, she continues to share in the profits and losses of the firm, albeit at a lower rate than when she was working full-time. Because Rene wants to stay busy during her retirement years, she has invested and works in a local hardware business, operated as a partnership. Unfortunately, the business has recently gone through a slump and has not been generating profits. Identify relevant tax issues for Rene.

27. Some types of work are counted in applying the material participation standards, and some types are not counted. Discuss and give examples of each type.

28. During the current year, Alan is determined to make better use of the tax losses that tend to flow from the various businesses that he owns. He is particularly sensitive to the limitations that the passive loss rules place on the deductibility of losses because of the disaster that occurred last year: his accountant informed him that he would not be able to claim any of the losses on his income tax return because of his lack of material participation. He has even suggested to his wife that she may have to put in some time at the businesses if his goals are to be accomplished. Identify the tax issues that Alan faces.

29. Ira, who is a limited partner in Zelcova Gardens, is informed that his portion of the entity's current loss is $10,000. Given that Ira is a limited partner, may one assume that his share of the partnership loss is a passive loss?

30. What are *significant personal services,* and what role do they play in determining whether a rental activity is treated as a passive activity?

31. What are *extraordinary personal services,* and what is their importance in determining whether a rental activity is treated as a passive activity?

32. Some rental operations involving tangible personal property automatically are treated as passive activities, and others are treated as passive only if the owner does not meet the material participation standards. How can one differentiate between the two categories?

33. How is passive activity defined in the Code, and what aspects of the definition have been clarified by the Temporary Regulations?

34. Laura owns an apartment building and a videotape rental business. She participates for more than 500 hours in the operations of each activity. Are the businesses active or passive?

35. Hilda incurred a loss of $60,000 on a real estate rental activity during the current year. Under what circumstances can Hilda treat the entire loss as nonpassive?

36. Since his college days, Charles has developed an entrepreneurial streak. After testing his wings in his family's grocery business, he has decided to start several ventures on his own. Even though Charles is independently wealthy, he is looking forward to working, even if for a limited amount of time, in each of the ventures. He plans to "drop in" on the businesses from time to time between personal trips to Europe, the Caribbean, and the South Pacific. As of the end of the year, he has established computer software stores in Dayton, Austin, and Seattle; bagel bakeries in Albany, Athens, and Tallahassee; and mountain bike and ski rental shops in small towns in Vermont, West Virginia, Colorado, and California. Identify the tax issues facing Charles.

37. In the current year, George and Susie White, both successful CPAs, made a cash investment for a limited partnership interest in a California avocado grove. In addition to the cash generated from the investors, the grove's management borrowed a substantial sum to purchase assets necessary for its operation. The Whites' investment adviser told them that their share of the tax loss in the first year alone would be in excess of their initial cash investment, followed by several more years of losses. They feel confident that their interest in the avocado grove is a sound investment. Identify the tax issues facing the Whites.

38. Under what circumstances can a closely held C (regular) corporation treat rental real estate losses as nonpassive?

39. Can an employer treat services performed by an employee as being related to a real estate trade or business?

40. Matt owns a small apartment building that generated a loss during the year. Under what circumstances can Matt deduct a loss from the rental activity, and what limitations apply?

41. In connection with passive activities, what is a *deduction equivalent?* How is a deduction equivalent computed?

42. Betty and Steve received a substantial windfall due to a recent inheritance. Because they have always loved spending time at the beach, they plan to devote some of the newly available cash to a beach-related investment. Their analysis identifies two possibilities that seem to be logical given their particular situation. They could purchase a beach cottage and use it for both personal and rental purposes; or they could pool their money with Steve's brother and purchase several cottages, one of which would be held strictly for personal use, while the others would be held solely for rental use. Identify the tax issues facing Betty and Steve.

PROBLEMS

43. In the current year, Lionel invested $20,000 for an interest in a partnership in which he is a material participant. His share of the partnership loss for the year was $25,000. Discuss the tax treatment of Lionel's share of the loss, and compute his at-risk amount.

44. Last year, Fred invested $50,000 in a limited partnership that has a working interest in an oil well (not a passive activity). During that initial year of his investment, his share of the partnership loss was $35,000. In the current year, his share of the partnership loss was $25,000. How much can Fred deduct in the prior and current years?

45. In the current year, Bill Parker (54 Oak Drive, St. Paul, MN 55162) is considering making an investment of $60,000 in Best Choice Partnership. The prospectus provided by Bill's broker indicates that the partnership investment is not a passive activity and that Bill's share of the entity's loss in the current year will likely be $40,000, while his share of the partnership loss next year will probably be $25,000. Write a letter to Bill in which you indicate how the losses would be treated for tax purposes in the current and next years.

46. Carmen wishes to invest $25,000 in a relatively safe venture and has discovered two alternatives that would produce the following reportable income and loss over the next three years:

Year	Alternative 1 Income (Loss)	Alternative 2 Income (Loss)
1	($15,000)	($30,000)
2	(15,000)	20,000
3	45,000	25,000

She is interested in the after-tax effects of these alternatives over a three-year horizon. Assume that Carmen's investment portfolio produces sufficient passive income to offset any potential passive loss that may arise from these alternatives, that her cost of capital is 8% (the present value factors are 0.92593, 0.85734, and 0.79383), that she is in the 28% tax bracket, that each investment alternative possesses equal growth potential, and that each alternative exposes her to comparable financial risk. In addition, assume that in the loss years for each alternative, there is no cash flow from or to the investment (i.e., the loss is due to depreciation), while in those years when the income is positive, cash flows to Carmen equal the amount of the income. Based on these facts, compute the present value of these two investment alternatives and determine which option Carmen should choose.

47. Tina acquired passive Activity A in January 1991 and Activity B in September 1992. Until 1995, Activity A was profitable. Activity A produced a loss of $200,000 in 1995 and a loss of $100,000 in 1996. Tina has passive income from Activity B of $20,000 in 1995 and $40,000 in 1996. After offsetting passive income, how much of the net losses may she deduct?

48. In 1991, Kay acquired an interest in a partnership in which she is not a material participant. The partnership was profitable until 1995. Kay's basis in her partnership interest at the beginning of 1995 was $40,000. In 1995, Kay's share of the partnership loss was $35,000. In 1996, her share of the partnership income was $15,000. How much can Kay deduct in 1995 and 1996?

49. Ray acquired an interest in a bakery three years ago. The loss from the activity was $50,000 in the current year. He had AGI of $140,000 before considering the loss from the bakery. Ray is not a material participant in the bakery. What is his AGI after considering this activity?

50. Sarah has $100,000 that she wishes to invest, and she is considering the following two options:

- Option A—Investment in Bluebird Equity Mutual fund, which would be expected to produce dividends of $8,000 per year.
- Option B—Investment in Redbird Limited Partnership (buys, sells, and operates avocado groves). Sarah's share of the partnership's income and loss over the next three years is expected to be:

Year	Income (Loss)
1	($ 8,000)
2	(2,000)
3	34,000

Sarah is interested in the after-tax effects of these alternatives over a three-year horizon. Assume that Sarah's investment portfolio produces no passive income, that her cost of capital is 8% (the present value factors are 0.92593, 0.85734, and 0.79383), that she is in the 31% tax bracket, that each investment alternative possesses equal growth potential, and that each alternative exposes her to comparable financial risk. Based on these facts, compute the present value of these two investment alternatives and determine which option Sarah should choose.

51. Emily has $100,000 that she wishes to invest, and she is considering the following two options:

- Option A—Investment in Redbird Equity Mutual fund, which would be expected to produce dividends of $8,000 per year.
- Option B—Investment in Cardinal Limited Partnership (buys, sells, and operates wine vineyards). Emily's share of the partnerhip's income and loss over the next three years is expected to be:

Year	Income (Loss)
1	($ 8,000)
2	(2,000)
3	34,000

Emily is interested in the after-tax effects of these alternatives over a three-year horizon. Assume that Emily's investment portfolio produces ample passive income to offset any passive losses that may be generated, that her cost of capital is 8% (the present value factors are 0.92593, 0.85734, and 0.79383), that she is in the 31% tax bracket, that each investment alternative possesses equal growth potential, and that each alternative exposes her to comparable financial risk. Based on these facts, compute the present value of these two investment alternatives and determine which option Emily should choose.

52. Hazel has two investments in nonrental passive activities. Activity A, which was acquired seven years ago, was profitable until the current year. Activity B was acquired this year. Currently, Hazel's share of the loss from Activity A is $10,000, and her share of the loss from Activity B is $6,000. What is the total of Hazel's suspended losses from these activities as of the end of the current year?

53. Leanne has investments in four passive activity partnerships purchased several years ago. Last year, the income and losses were as follows:

Activity	Income (Loss)
A	$60,000
B	(60,000)
C	(30,000)
D	(10,000)

In the current year, she sold her interest in Activity D for a $20,000 gain. Activity D, which had been profitable until last year, had a current loss of $3,000. How will the sale of Activity D affect Leanne's taxable income in the current year?

54. Green, Inc., a closely held personal service corporation, has $100,000 of passive losses in the current year. In addition, Green has $80,000 of active business income and $20,000 of portfolio income. How much of the passive loss may Green use to offset other types of income this year?

55. White, Inc., earned $400,000 from operations in the current year. White also received $36,000 in dividends and interest on various portfolio investments. During the year, White paid $150,000 to acquire a 20% interest in a passive activity that produced a $200,000 loss.

a. How will this affect White's taxable income, assuming the corporation is a personal service corporation?
b. How will this affect White's taxable income, assuming the corporation is a closely held, non-personal service corporation?

56. Green Corporation, a closely held, non-personal service corporation, earned active income of $50,000 in the current year. Green received $60,000 in dividends during the year. In addition, Green incurred a loss of $80,000 from an investment in a passive activity acquired last year. What is Green's net income for the current year after considering the passive investment?

57. Greg Reynolds (66 Hanover Street, Cincinnati, OH 45230), a syndicated radio talk show host, earns a $400,000 salary in the current year. He works approximately 30 hours per week in this job, which leaves him time to participate in several businesses he acquired in the current year. He owns a movie theater and a drugstore in Cincinnati. He also owns a movie theater and a drugstore in Indianapolis and a drugstore in Louisville. A preliminary analysis on December 1 of the current year shows projected income and losses for the various businesses as follows:

	Income (Loss)
Cincinnati movie theater (95 hours participation)	$56,000
Cincinnati drugstore (140 hours participation)	(89,000)
Indianapolis movie theater (90 hours participation)	34,000
Indianapolis drugstore (170 hours participation)	(41,000)
Louisville drugstore (180 hours participation)	(15,000)

Greg has full-time employees at each of the five businesses listed above. Consider all possible groupings for Greg's activities. Write a letter to him suggesting the grouping method and other strategies that will provide the greatest tax advantage. Greg does not know much about the tax law, so you should provide a concise, nontechnical explanation.

58. Ann acquired an activity four years ago. The loss from the activity was $50,000 in the current year. She had AGI of $140,000 before considering the loss from the activity. The activity is a service station, and Ann is a material participant. What is her AGI after considering this activity?

59. Lee acquired a 20% interest in the ABC Partnership for $60,000 in 1991. The partnership was profitable until 1996, and Lee's amount at risk in the partnership interest was $120,000 at the end of 1995. ABC incurred a loss of $400,000 in 1996 and reported income of $200,000 in 1997. Assuming Lee is not a material participant in ABC, how much of his loss from ABC Partnership is deductible in 1996 and 1997, respectively?

60. Ken has a $40,000 loss from an investment in a partnership in which he does not participate. He paid $30,000 for his interest in the partnership. How much of the loss is disallowed by the at-risk rules? How much is disallowed by the passive loss rules?

61. Last year, Fran invested $20,000 for an interest in a partnership in which she is a material participant. Her share of the partnership's loss for the year was $25,000. In the current year, Fran's share of the partnership's income is $15,000. What is the effect on her taxable income for the current year?

62. Soong, a physician, earned $200,000 from his practice. He also received $18,000 in dividends and interest on various portfolio investments. During the year, he paid $45,000 to acquire a 20% interest in a partnership that produced a $300,000 loss.
a. Compute Soong's AGI assuming he does not participate in the operations of the partnership.
b. Compute Soong's AGI assuming he is a material participant in the operations of the partnership.

63. Sam invested $150,000 in a passive activity five years ago. On January 1, 1995, his amount at risk in the activity was $30,000. His shares of the income and losses in the activity were as follows:

Year	Income (Loss)
1995	($40,000)
1996	(30,000)
1997	50,000

How much can Sam deduct in 1995 and 1996? What is his taxable income from the activity in 1997? Keep in mind the at-risk rules as well as the passive loss rules.

64. Joe Cook (125 Hill Street, Charleston, WV 25311) acquired an activity four years ago. The loss from the activity was $50,000 in the current year. He had AGI of $140,000 before considering the loss from the activity. The activity is an apartment building, and Joe is an active participant. Write a letter to Joe in which you explain what his AGI is after the loss is considered.

65. Beth acquired an activity four years ago. The loss from the activity was $50,000 in the current year. She had AGI of $140,000 before considering the loss from the activity. The activity is an apartment building, and Beth is not an active participant. What is her AGI after considering the activity?

66. During the current year, Donald worked 1,200 hours as a computer consultant, 600 hours in a real estate development business, and 500 hours in real estate rental activities. He earned $60,000 as a computer consultant, but lost $18,000 in the development business and $26,000 in the real estate rental business. How should Donald treat the losses on his current Federal income tax return?

67. During the current year, Maria Castro worked 1,200 hours as a computer consultant, 320 hours in a real estate development business, and 400 hours in real estate rental activities. Jorge, her husband, worked 250 hours in the real estate development business and 180 hours in the real estate rental business. Maria earned $60,000 as a computer consultant, but the Castros lost $18,000 in the development business and $26,000 in the real estate rental business. How should they treat the losses on their joint current Federal income tax return?

68. Hal and Wanda are married with no dependents and live together in Ohio, which is not a community property state. Since Wanda has large medical expenses, they seek your advice about filing separately to save taxes. Their income and expenses for 1996 are as follows:

Hal's salary	$ 36,000
Wanda's salary	44,000
Dividends and interest (joint)	1,500
Rental loss from actively managed apartments (joint)	(24,000)
Wanda's unreimbursed medical expenses	6,300
All other itemized deductions:*	
Hal	8,000
Wanda	2,000

*None subject to limitations.

Determine whether Hal and Wanda should file jointly or separately for 1996.

69. Lucy and Leon have owned a beach cottage on the New Jersey shore for several years and have always used it as a family retreat. When they acquired the property, they had no intentions of renting it, but because their family circumstances have changed, they

are considering using the cottage for only two weeks a year and renting it for the remainder of the year. Their AGI is currently approximately $80,000 per year, and they are in the 36% tax bracket (combined Federal and state). Their financial records indicate that interest and real estate taxes have totaled $8,000 per year, and Lucy and Leon expect these expenditures to continue at this level into the foreseeable future. In addition, if they rent the property, their *incremental* revenue and expenses are projected to be:

Rent income	$20,000
Rental commissions	3,000
Maintenance expenses	12,000
Depreciation expense	10,000
	($ 5,000)

If they do convert the cottage to rental property, they insist that they will be actively involved in key rental and maintenance decisions. Given the tax effects of converting the property to rental use, would the cash flow resulting from renting the property be enough to meet the $12,000 annual mortgage payment? This is an important factor in Lucy and Leon's decision.

70. Ida, who has AGI of $80,000 before considering rental activities, is active in three separate real estate rental activities and is in the 28% tax bracket. She had $12,000 of losses from Activity A, $18,000 of losses from Activity B, and income of $10,000 from Activity C. She also had $2,100 of tax credits from Activity A. Calculate her deductions and credits allowed and the suspended losses and credits.

71. Ella has $105,000 of losses from a real estate rental activity in which she actively participates. She has other rental income of $25,000 and other passive income of $32,000. How much rental loss can Ella deduct against active and portfolio income (ignoring the at-risk rules)? Does she have any suspended losses to carry over?

72. Faye died owning an interest in a passive activity property with an adjusted basis of $160,000, suspended losses of $16,000, and a fair market value of $170,000. What can be deducted on her final income tax return?

73. Last year, Nina gave her son a passive activity with an adjusted basis of $100,000. Fair market value of the activity was $180,000, and the activity had suspended losses of $25,000. In the current year, her son realized income of $12,000 from the passive activity. What is the effect on Nina and her son last year and in the current year?

74. Tonya sold a passive activity in the current year for $150,000. Her adjusted basis was $50,000. She used the installment method of reporting the gain. The activity had suspended losses of $12,000. Tonya received $60,000 in the year of sale. What is her gain? How much of the suspended losses can she deduct?

75. If Tonya in Problem 74 had no suspended losses, was in the 28% tax bracket, and had $10,000 of suspended tax credits attributable to the activity, how much of the credits could she use in the current year?

RESEARCH PROBLEMS

Note: ***West's Federal Taxation on CD-ROM*** *can be used in preparing solutions to the Research Problems. Alternatively, tax research materials contained in a standard tax library can be used.*

Research Problem 1. Leon Lane (77 Lakeview Drive, Salt Lake City, UT 84109) is a married individual who files a separate return for the taxable year. He is employed full-time as an attorney. Leon, who also owns an interest in a minor league baseball team, does no work in connection with the activity during the year. He anticipates that the activity will result in a loss for the taxable year. Leon pays his wife to work as an office receptionist in connection with the activity for an average of 20 hours a week during the year. Write a letter to Leon and explain whether he will be allowed to deduct his share of the loss from the activity.

Research Problem 2. Bill owns an interest in a small engine repair shop in which he works 425 hours during the year. He has four full-time employees at the repair shop. Bill also owns an apartment building to which he devotes 1,300 hours during the year. He has no employees for the apartment activity. Are these activities active or passive? In your response, consider the impact of the significant participation activity rules.

Research Problem 3. Having become relatively affluent due to their success as respected dentists, George and Julie Sharp (1203 Peach Street, Atlanta, GA 30305) decided to invest $100,000 of their excess cash in a nearby resort community. Their investment gave them ownership rights in a cottage that normally would be rented out to vacationers for six-day periods by Paradise Resorts, Inc. While the Sharps were legally the sole owners of the cottage, they were required to allow Paradise Resorts to market their cottage's availability and maintain the unit. George and Julie were also allowed to use the cottage rent-free every year for no more than 14 days.

During the first year, Paradise Resorts reported that the Sharps' loss from the property was $25,000. During that period, the Sharps had accumulated documentation showing that they had spent 300 hours of their time on activities such as the following: preparing an annual budget for their cottage investment, marketing Paradise Resorts in conversations with their friends and at their country club, attending the annual business meeting of Paradise Resorts with the other cottage owners, and receiving and depositing net revenues received from rental of their cottage.

As the Sharps' tax adviser, how would you recommend that they report their loss from this investment on their tax return? Write a memo to the tax files in which your recommendation is documented.

TEAM PROJECT: ARTHUR ANDERSEN TAX CHALLENGE CASES

For more information on the Arthur Andersen Tax Challenge Cases, please refer to Chapter 1, page 1-38.

Information related to tax issues and problems that are discussed in this chapter may be found in the

Fields case on pages 10, 35-37

Read and analyze the case you have been assigned and *identify* any issues and problems that are related to material covered in this chapter. If the information provided in the case is complete, prepare answers for this part of the case at this time. If you need information that is contained in the later parts of the case, please write a memo summarizing the questions or problems so you can prepare a complete answer at a later date.

P•A•R•T

IV

Special Tax Computation Methods, Payment Procedures, and Tax Credits

Part IV presents several topics that relate to the theme of tax liability determination. The taxpayer must calculate the tax liability in accordance with the basic tax formula and also in accordance with the tax formula for the alternative minimum tax (AMT). The basic tax formula was presented in Part I, and the AMT formula is covered in Part IV. Tax credits reduce the amount of the calculated tax liability. The specific procedures for the timing of the payment of the tax liability are also discussed.

CHAPTER

12

ALTERNATIVE MINIMUM TAX

LEARNING OBJECTIVES

After completing Chapter 12, you should be able to:

1. Explain the rationale for the alternative minimum tax (AMT).
2. Understand the formula for computing the AMT for individuals.
3. Identify the adjustments made in calculating the AMT.
4. Identify the tax preferences that are included in calculating the AMT.
5. Apply the formula for computing the AMT and illustrate Form 6251.
6. Describe the role of the AMT credit in the alternative minimum tax structure.
7. Understand the basic features of the corporate AMT.
8. Identify tax planning opportunities to minimize the AMT.

OUTLINE

1 LEARNING OBJECTIVE
Explain the rationale for the alternative minimum tax (AMT).

Bob and Carol are unmarried individuals who work for the same employer and have the same amount of gross income and the same amount of deductions. Bob's tax return is prepared by Adam, and Carol's tax return is prepared by Eve. While discussing their tax liability one day at lunch, Carol is dismayed to learn that she paid $15,000 more in Federal income taxes than Bob did for the tax year. Carol meets with Eve that evening. Eve reviews Carol's tax return and assures her that her tax liability was properly calculated.

The above events raise a number of interesting questions for Bob and Carol that can be answered after completing this chapter. Why didn't Bob and Carol have the same tax liability? Were both tax returns properly prepared? Should Carol consider replacing her tax return preparer Eve with Adam? Is it possible and/or desirable for Carol to file an amended return? Should Bob do anything?

The tax law contains many incentives that are intended to influence the economic and social behavior of taxpayers (refer to Chapter 1). Some taxpayers have been able to take advantage of enough of these incentives to avoid or minimize any liability for Federal income tax. Although these taxpayers were reducing taxes legally, Congress became concerned about the inequity that results when taxpayers with substantial economic incomes can avoid paying any income tax. The **alternative minimum tax (AMT)** was enacted as a backup to the regular income tax. The rationale for the AMT was expressed as follows:

> [T]he minimum tax should serve one overriding objective: to ensure that no taxpayer with substantial economic income can avoid significant tax liability by using exclusions, deductions, and credits. Although these provisions may provide incentives for worthy goals, they become counterproductive when taxpayers are allowed to use them to avoid virtually all tax liability. The ability of high-income taxpayers to pay little or no tax undermines respect for the entire tax system and, thus, for the incentive provisions themselves. In addition, even aside from public perceptions . . . it is inherently unfair for high-income taxpayers to pay little or no tax due to their ability to utilize tax preferences.[1]

The individual AMT is discussed in the first part of this chapter. The corporate AMT is similar to the individual AMT, but differs in several important ways. Details of the corporate AMT are presented in the last part of the chapter.

---

[1] *General Explanation of the Tax Reform Act of 1986 ("Blue Book"),* prepared by The Staff of the Joint Committee on Taxation, May 4, 1987, H.R. 3838, 99th Cong., pp. 432–433.

Individual Alternative Minimum Tax

AMT Formula for Alternative Minimum Taxable Income (AMTI)

2 Learning Objective
Understand the formula for computing the AMT for individuals.

The AMT is separate from, but parallel to, the regular income tax system.[2] Most income and expense items are treated the same way for both regular income tax and AMT purposes. For example, a taxpayer's salary is included in computing taxable income and is also included in alternative minimum taxable income (AMTI). Alimony paid is allowed as a deduction *for* AGI for both regular income tax and AMT purposes. Certain itemized deductions, such as gambling losses, are allowed for both regular income tax and AMT purposes.

On the other hand, some income and expense items are treated differently for regular income tax and AMT purposes. For example, interest income on bonds issued by state, county, or local governments is *excluded* in computing taxable income. However, interest on such bonds is *included* in computing AMTI if the bonds are private activity bonds issued after August 7, 1986. The deduction for personal and dependency exemptions is *allowed* for regular income tax purposes, but is *disallowed* for AMT purposes.

In other cases, certain items are considered in both the regular income tax and AMT computations, but the amounts are different. For example, the completed contract method can be used to report income from some long-term contracts for regular income tax purposes, but the percentage of completion method is required for AMT purposes. Thus, the amount of income included in taxable income will differ from the amount included in AMTI. Depreciation is allowed as a deduction for both regular income tax and AMT purposes, but the *amount* of the regular income tax deduction will be different from the amount of the AMT deduction. Medical expenses are deductible in calculating both taxable income and AMTI, but the floor on the deduction is different.

The parallel but separate nature of the AMT means that AMTI will differ from taxable income. It is possible to compute AMTI by direct application of the AMT provisions, using the following formula:

Gross income computed by applying the AMT rules

Minus: Deductions computed by applying the AMT rules

Equals: AMTI before tax preferences

Plus: Tax preferences

Equals: Alternative minimum taxable income

While the direct approach for computing AMTI appears quite logical, both the tax law and the tax forms provide a very different approach. Both of these use taxable income as the starting point for computing AMTI, as shown in Figure 12–1. This indirect approach for computing AMTI is analogous to the indirect approach used in calculating a net operating loss.

The purpose of the AMT formula is to *reconcile* taxable income to AMTI. This reconciliation is similar to a bank reconciliation, which reconciles a checkbook balance to a bank balance by considering differences between the depositor's records and the bank's records. The reconciliation of taxable income to AMTI is accomplished by entering reconciling items to account for differences between regular income tax provisions and AMT provisions. These reconciling items are

[2] § 55.

▼ **FIGURE 12–1**
Alternative Minimum Taxable Income (AMTI) Formula

Taxable income
Plus: Positive AMT adjustments
Minus: Negative AMT adjustments
Equals: Taxable income after AMT adjustments
Plus: Tax preferences
Equals: Alternative minimum taxable income

referred to as **AMT adjustments** or **tax preferences.** *Adjustments* can be either positive or negative, as shown in the formula in Figure 12–1. Tax preferences are always positive.

Adjustments. The concept of AMT adjustments was introduced in the Tax Reform Act of 1986. Most adjustments relate to *timing differences* that arise because of *separate* regular income tax and AMT treatments. Adjustments that are caused by timing differences will eventually *reverse;* that is, positive adjustments will be offset by negative adjustments in the future, and vice versa.[3]

For example, **circulation expenditures** can give rise to a timing difference that requires an AMT adjustment. For regular income tax purposes, circulation expenditures can be deducted in the year incurred. For AMT purposes, however, circulation expenditures must be deducted over a three-year period. This difference in treatment will be used to illustrate the role of adjustments in the formula for computing AMTI.

EXAMPLE 1

Bob had taxable income of $100,000 in 1995. In computing taxable income, he deducted $30,000 of circulation expenditures incurred in 1995. Bob's allowable deduction for AMT purposes was only $10,000. Therefore, an AMT adjustment was required in 1995 as follows:

Taxable income		$100,000
+AMT adjustment:		
Circulation expenditures deducted for regular income tax purposes	$ 30,000	
–Circulation expenditures allowed for AMT purposes	(10,000)	
Positive adjustment		20,000
=AMTI before tax preferences		$120,000
+Tax preferences		-0-
AMTI		$120,000

Analysis of this computation shows that the allowable AMT deduction is $20,000 less than the allowable regular income tax deduction. Therefore, AMTI will be $20,000 greater than taxable income. This is accomplished by entering a positive AMT adjustment of $20,000. ▼

EXAMPLE 2

Assume that Bob from Example 1 has taxable income of $95,000 in 1996. He is allowed to deduct $10,000 of circulation expenditures for AMT purposes, but is not allowed a deduction for regular income tax purposes because all $30,000 was deducted in 1995. Therefore, a *negative* AMT adjustment is required.

[3] § 56.

Taxable income		$ 95,000
–AMT adjustment:		
Circulation expenditures allowed for regular income tax purposes	$ –0–	
Circulation expenditures deducted for AMT purposes	(10,000)	
Negative adjustment		(10,000)
=AMTI before tax preferences		$ 85,000
+Tax preferences		–0–
AMTI		$ 85,000

Analysis of this computation shows that the allowable AMT deduction is $10,000 more than the allowable regular income tax deduction. Therefore, AMTI will be $10,000 less than taxable income. This is accomplished by entering a negative AMT adjustment of $10,000. ▼

As noted previously, timing differences eventually reverse. Therefore, total positive adjustments will be offset by total negative adjustments with respect to a particular item.

EXAMPLE 3

Refer to Examples 1 and 2. The difference in regular income tax and AMT treatments of circulation expenditures will result in AMT adjustments over a three-year period.

Year	Income Tax Deduction	AMT Deduction	AMT Adjustment
1995	$30,000	$10,000	+$20,000
1996	–0–	10,000	–10,000
1997	–0–	10,000	–10,000
Total	$30,000	$30,000	$ –0–

As the last column illustrates, if positive and negative AMT adjustments with respect to a particular item are caused by a timing difference, they will eventually net to zero. ▼

The adjustments for circulation expenditures and other items are discussed in detail under AMT Adjustments.

Although most adjustments relate to timing differences, there are exceptions. See the subsequent discussion of such items under Itemized Deductions. Adjustments that do not relate to timing differences result in a permanent difference between taxable income and AMTI.

Tax Preferences. Some deductions and exclusions allowed to taxpayers for regular income tax purposes provide extraordinary tax savings. Congress has chosen to single out these items, which are referred to as tax preferences.[4] The AMT is designed to take back all or part of the tax benefits derived through the use of preferences in the computation of taxable income for regular income tax purposes. This is why taxable income, which is the starting point in computing AMTI, is increased by tax preference items. The effect of adding these preference items is to disallow for *AMT purposes* those preferences that were allowed in the

[4] § 57.

▼ **FIGURE 12–2**
Alternative Minimum Tax Formula

Regular taxable income
Plus or minus: Adjustments
Equals: Taxable income after AMT adjustments
Plus: Tax preferences
Equals: Alternative minimum taxable income
Minus: Exemption
Equals: Alternative minimum tax base
Times: 26% or 28% rate
Equals: Tentative minimum tax before foreign tax credit
Minus: Alternative minimum tax foreign tax credit
Equals: Tentative minimum tax
Minus: Regular tax liability*
Equals: Alternative minimum tax (if amount is positive)

*This is the regular tax liability for the year reduced by any allowable foreign tax credit.

regular income tax computation. Tax preferences include the following items, which are discussed in detail under AMT Preferences:

- Percentage depletion in excess of the property's adjusted basis.
- Excess intangible drilling costs reduced by 65 percent of the net income from oil, gas, and geothermal properties.
- Interest on certain private activity bonds.
- Excess of accelerated over straight-line depreciation on real property placed in service before 1987.
- Excess of accelerated over straight-line depreciation on *leased* personal property placed in service before 1987.
- Excess of amortization allowance over depreciation on pre-1987 certified pollution control facilities.
- Fifty percent exclusion from gross income associated with gains on the sale of certain small business stock.

AMT FORMULA: OTHER COMPONENTS

To convert AMTI to AMT, other formula components including the exemption, rates, credit, and regular tax liability must be considered. The impact of each of these components is depicted in the AMT formula in Figure 12–2.

The relationship between the regular tax liability and the tentative AMT is key to the AMT formula. If the regular tax liability exceeds tentative AMT, then the AMT is zero. If the tentative AMT exceeds the regular tax liability, the amount of the excess is the AMT. In essence, the taxpayer will pay whichever tax liability is greater—that calculated using the regular income tax rules or that calculated using the AMT rules. However, both the tax law and Form 6251 adopt this excess approach with the taxpayer paying the regular tax liability plus any AMT.

EXAMPLE 4

Anna, an unmarried individual, has regular taxable income of $100,000. She has positive adjustments of $40,000 and tax preferences of $25,000. Calculate her AMT for 1996.

Anna's regular tax liability is $26,136. Her AMT is calculated as follows:

Taxable income (TI)	$100,000
Plus: Adjustments	40,000
Equals: TI after AMT adjustments	$140,000
Plus: Tax preferences	25,000
Equals: AMTI	$165,000
Minus: AMT exemption ($33,750 − $13,125)	(20,625)*
Equals: AMT base	$144,375
Times: AMT rate	× 26%
Equals: Tentative AMT	$ 37,538
Minus: Regular tax liability	(26,136)
Equals: AMT	$ 11,402

*Discussed below under Exemption Amount.

Anna will pay the IRS a total of $37,538, consisting of her regular tax liability of $26,136 plus her AMT of $11,402. ▼

Exemption Amount. The exemption amount can be thought of as a materiality provision. As such, it enables a taxpayer with a small amount of positive adjustments and tax preferences to avoid being subject to the burden of the AMT.

The *initial* exemption amount is $45,000 for married taxpayers filing joint returns, $33,750 for single taxpayers, and $22,500 for married taxpayers filing separate returns.[5] However, the exemption is *phased out* at a rate of 25 cents on the dollar when AMTI exceeds these levels:

- $112,500 for single taxpayers.
- $150,000 for married taxpayers filing jointly.
- $75,000 for married taxpayers filing separately.

The phase-out of the exemption amount is an application of the wherewithal to pay concept. As a taxpayer's income level increases, so does his or her ability to pay income taxes.

The following example explains the calculation of the phase-out of the AMT exemption.

EXAMPLE 5

Hugh, who is single, has AMTI of $192,500 for the year. His $33,750 initial exemption amount is reduced by $20,000 [($192,500 − $112,500) × 25% phase-out rate]. Hugh's AMT exemption is $13,750 ($33,750 exemption − $20,000 reduction). ▼

The following table shows the beginning and end of the AMT exemption phase-out range for each filing status.

		Phase-out	
Status	**Exemption**	**Begins at**	**Ends at**
Married, joint	$45,000	$150,000	$330,000
Single or head of household	33,750	112,500	247,500
Married, separate	22,500	75,000	165,000

[5] § 55(d).

AMT Rate Schedule. A graduated, two-tier AMT rate schedule applies to noncorporate taxpayers. A 26 percent rate applies to the first $175,000 of the AMT base ($87,500 for married, filing separately), and a 28 percent rate applies to the AMT base in excess of $175,000 ($87,500 for married, filing separately).[6]

Regular Tax Liability. The AMT is equal to the tentative minimum tax minus the *regular tax liability*. In most cases, the regular tax liability is equal to the amount of tax from the Tax Table or Tax Rate Schedules decreased by any foreign tax credit allowable for regular income tax purposes. Only the foreign tax credit is allowed as a reduction of the tentative minimum tax. Therefore, taxpayers who pay AMT lose the benefit of all other nonrefundable credits. Furthermore, the foreign tax credit cannot offset more than 90 percent of the tentative minimum tax.

In an AMT year, the taxpayer's total tax liability is equal to the tentative minimum tax (refer to Figure 12–2). The tentative minimum tax consists of two potential components: the regular tax liability and the AMT. The disallowance of credits does not affect a taxpayer's total liability in an AMT year. However, it does decrease the amount of the AMT and, as a consequence, reduces the minimum tax credit (discussed subsequently) available to be carried forward. Thus, for AMT purposes, the government denies all the credits (except the foreign tax credit) that apply in computing the regular income tax liability.

It is also possible that taxpayers who have adjustments and preferences but *do not pay* AMT will lose the benefit of some or all of their nonrefundable credits. This result occurs because a taxpayer may claim nonrefundable credits only to the extent that his or her regular tax liability exceeds the tentative minimum tax.[7]

EXAMPLE 6

Vern has total nonrefundable credits of $10,000, regular tax liability of $33,000, and tentative minimum tax of $25,000. He can claim only $8,000 of the nonrefundable credits in the current year. The disallowed $2,000 credit is lost unless a carryover provision applies. ▼

ETHICAL CONSIDERATIONS

Minimizing the Tax Liability

Billy, a single individual, projects his taxable income for 1996 to be approximately $300,000. He also has positive adjustments and tax preferences of $200,000. Billy anticipates taxable income for 1997 to be about the same with no adjustments or tax preferences for AMT purposes. He is evaluating several proposed transactions that would have the effect of reducing his 1996 tax liability.

One such transaction involves an office building for which he is currently negotiating a lease. The starting date for the lease will be July 1, 1996. The annual rent is going to be around $20,000 with an 18-month prepayment clause. Though Billy favors a five-year lease, a real estate agent has suggested that he lease the office building for an 18-month period with a 42-month renewal option. The real estate agent indicates that there are tax advantages (i.e., Billy can deduct the $30,000 of rent paid at the inception of the lease) as well as business reasons for structuring the transaction this way.

Billy takes the agent's advice and calculates his projected tax liability for 1996 with the 18-month lease with the renewal option and with the five-year lease. Based on his calculations, his regular income tax liability and AMT under each option would be as follows:

[6] § 55(b)(1).

[7] § 26(a).

	18-Month Lease	5-Year Lease
Regular income tax liability	$ 86,496	$ 94,416
AMT	41,604	39,284
Total	$128,100	$133,700

Is it appropriate for Billy to avoid taxes in this manner? Is is wise? Would you be willing to prepare and sign Billy's tax return showing the lease transaction as proposed by the real estate agent?

AMT ADJUSTMENTS

3 LEARNING OBJECTIVE
Identify the adjustments made in calculating the AMT.

Direction of Adjustments. It is necessary to determine not only the amount of an adjustment, but also whether the adjustment is positive or negative. Careful study of Example 3 reveals the following pattern with regard to *deductions:*

- If the deduction allowed for regular income tax purposes exceeds the deduction allowed for AMT purposes, the difference is a positive adjustment.
- If the deduction allowed for AMT purposes exceeds the deduction allowed for regular income tax purposes, the difference is a negative adjustment.

Conversely, the direction of an adjustment attributable to an *income* item can be determined as follows:

- If the income reported for regular income tax purposes exceeds the income reported for AMT purposes, the difference is a negative adjustment.
- If the income reported for AMT purposes exceeds the income reported for regular income tax purposes, the difference is a positive adjustment.

Circulation Expenditures. For regular income tax purposes, circulation expenditures, other than those the taxpayer elects to charge to a capital account, may be expensed in the year incurred.[8] These expenditures include expenses incurred to establish, maintain, or increase the circulation of a newspaper, magazine, or other periodical.

Circulation expenditures are not deductible in the year incurred for AMT purposes. In computing AMTI, these expenditures must be capitalized and amortized ratably over the three-year period beginning with the year in which the expenditures were made.[9]

The AMT adjustment for circulation expenditures is the amount expensed for regular income tax purposes minus the amount that can be amortized for AMT purposes. The adjustment can be either positive or negative (refer to Examples 1, 2, and 3). A taxpayer can avoid the AMT adjustments for circulation expenditures by electing to write off the expenditures over a three-year period for regular income tax purposes.[10]

Depreciation of Post-1986 Real Property. For real property placed in service after 1986 (MACRS property), AMT depreciation is computed under the

[8] § 173(a).
[9] § 56(b)(2)(A)(i).
[10] § 59(e)(2)(A).

alternative depreciation system (ADS), which uses the straight-line method over a 40-year life. The depreciation lives for regular tax purposes are 27.5 years for residential rental property and 39 years for all other real property.[11] The difference between AMT depreciation and regular income tax depreciation is treated as an adjustment in computing the AMT. The differences will be positive during the regular income tax life of the asset because the cost is written off over a shorter period for regular income tax purposes. For example, during the 27.5-year income tax life of residential real property, the regular income tax depreciation will exceed the AMT depreciation because AMT depreciation is computed over a 40-year period.

Table 8–7 is used to compute regular income tax depreciation on real property placed in service after 1986. For AMT purposes, depreciation on real property placed in service after 1986 is computed under the ADS (refer to Table 8–12).

EXAMPLE 7

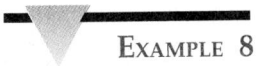

In January 1996, Sara placed in service a residential building that cost $100,000. Depreciation for 1996 for regular income tax purposes is $3,485 ($100,000 cost × 3.485% from Table 8–7). For AMT purposes, depreciation is $2,396 ($100,000 cost × 2.396% from Table 8–12). In computing AMTI for 1996, Sara has a positive adjustment of $1,089 ($3,485 regular income tax depreciation – $2,396 AMT depreciation). ▼

After real property has been held for the entire depreciation period for regular income tax purposes, the asset will be fully depreciated. However, the depreciation period under the ADS is 41 years due to application of the half-year convention, so depreciation will continue for AMT purposes. This causes negative adjustments after the property has been fully depreciated for regular income tax purposes.

EXAMPLE 8

Assume the same facts as in the previous example, and compute the AMT adjustment for 2024 (the twenty-ninth year of the asset's life). Regular income tax depreciation is zero (refer to Table 8–7). AMT depreciation is $2,500 ($100,000 cost × 2.500% from Table 8–12). Therefore, Sara has a negative AMT adjustment of $2,500 ($0 regular income tax depreciation – $2,500 AMT depreciation). ▼

After real property is fully depreciated for both regular income tax and AMT purposes, the positive and negative adjustments that have been made for AMT purposes will net to zero.

Depreciation of Post-1986 Personal Property. For most personal property placed in service after 1986 (MACRS property), the modified ACRS (MACRS) deduction for regular income tax purposes is based on the 200 percent declining-balance method with a switch to straight-line when that method produces a larger depreciation deduction for the asset. Refer to Table 8–2 for computing regular income tax depreciation.

For AMT purposes, the taxpayer must use the ADS. This method is based on the 150 percent declining-balance method with a similar switch to straight-line for all personal property.[12] Refer to Table 8–10 for percentages to be used in computing AMT depreciation.

All personal property placed in service after 1986 may be taken into consideration in computing one net adjustment. Using this netting process, the AMT adjustment for a tax year is the difference between the total MACRS depreciation

[11] The 39-year life generally applies to nonresidential real property placed in service on or after May 13, 1993.

[12] § 56(a)(1).

for all personal property computed for regular income tax purposes and the total ADS depreciation computed for AMT purposes. When the total of MACRS deductions exceeds the total of ADS deductions, the amount of the adjustment is positive. When the total of ADS deductions exceeds the total of MACRS deductions, the adjustment for AMTI is negative.

The MACRS deduction for personal property is larger than the ADS deduction in the early years of an asset's life. However, the ADS deduction is larger in the later years. This is so because ADS lives (based on class life) are longer than MACRS lives (based on recovery period).[13] Over the ADS life of the asset, the same amount of depreciation is deducted for both regular income tax and AMT purposes. In the same manner as other timing adjustments, the AMT adjustments for depreciation will net to zero over the ADS life of the asset.

The taxpayer may elect to use the ADS for regular income tax purposes. If this election is made, no AMT adjustment is required because the depreciation deduction is the same for regular income tax and for the AMT. The election eliminates the burden of maintaining two sets of tax depreciation records.

Pollution Control Facilities. For regular income tax purposes, the cost of certified pollution control facilities may be amortized over a period of 60 months. For AMT purposes, the cost of these facilities placed in service after 1986 must be depreciated under the ADS over the appropriate class life, determined as explained above for depreciation of post-1986 property.[14] The required adjustment for AMTI is equal to the difference between the amortization deduction allowed for regular income tax purposes and the depreciation deduction computed under the ADS. The adjustment may be positive or negative.

Expenditures Requiring 10-Year Write-off for AMT Purposes. Certain expenditures that may be deducted in the year incurred for regular income tax purposes must be written off over a 10-year period for AMT purposes. These rules apply to (1) mining exploration and development costs and (2) research and experimental expenditures.

In computing taxable income, taxpayers are allowed to deduct certain mining exploration and development expenditures. The deduction is allowed for expenditures paid or incurred during the taxable year for exploration (ascertaining the existence, location, extent, or quality of a deposit or mineral) and for development of a mine or other natural deposit, other than an oil or gas well.[15] Mining development expenditures are expenses paid or incurred after the existence of ores and minerals in commercially marketable quantities has been disclosed.

For AMT purposes, however, mining exploration and development costs must be capitalized and amortized ratably over a 10-year period.[16] The AMT adjustment for mining exploration and development costs that are expensed is equal to the amount expensed minus the allowable expense if the costs had been capitalized and amortized ratably over a 10-year period. This provision does not apply to costs relating to an oil or gas well.

EXAMPLE 9

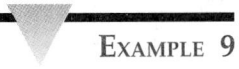

In 1996, Eve incurs $150,000 of mining exploration expenditures and deducts this amount for regular income tax purposes. For AMT purposes, these mining exploration expenditures must be amortized over a 10-year period. Eve must make a positive adjustment for AMTI of $135,000 ($150,000 allowed for regular income tax – $15,000 for AMT) for 1996, the first

[13] Class lives and recovery periods are established for all assets in Rev.Proc. 87–56, 1987–2 C.B. 674.

[14] § 56(a)(5).

[15] §§ 617(a) and 616(a).

[16] § 56(a)(2).

year. In each of the next nine years for AMT purposes, Eve is required to make a negative adjustment of $15,000 ($0 allowed for regular income tax – $15,000 for AMT). ▼

To avoid the AMT adjustments for mining exploration and development costs, a taxpayer may elect to write off the expenditures over a 10-year period for regular income tax purposes.[17]

Similar rules apply to computation of the adjustment for research and experimental expenditures.

Use of Completed Contract Method of Accounting. For a long-term contract, taxpayers are required to use the percentage of completion method for AMT purposes.[18] However, in limited circumstances, taxpayers can use the completed contract method for regular income tax purposes.[19] Thus, a taxpayer recognizes a different amount of income for regular income tax purposes than for AMT purposes. The resulting AMT adjustment is equal to the difference between income reported under the percentage of completion method and the amount reported using the completed contract method. The adjustment can be either positive or negative, depending on the amount of income recognized under the different methods.

A taxpayer can avoid an AMT adjustment on long-term contracts by using the percentage of completion method for regular income tax purposes rather than the completed contract method.

Incentive Stock Options. **Incentive stock options (ISOs)** are granted by employers to help attract new personnel and retain those already employed. At the time an ISO is granted, the employer corporation sets an option price for the corporate stock. If the value of the stock increases during the option period, the employee can obtain stock at a favorable price by exercising the option. Employees are generally restricted as to when they can dispose of stock acquired under an ISO (e.g., a certain length of employment may be required). Therefore, the stock may not be freely transferable until some specified period has passed. See Chapter 19 for details regarding ISOs.

The exercise of an ISO does not increase regular taxable income.[20] However, for AMT purposes, the excess of the fair market value of the stock over the exercise price is treated as an adjustment in the first taxable year in which the rights in the stock are freely transferable or are not subject to a substantial risk of forfeiture.[21]

EXAMPLE 10

In 1994, Manuel exercised an ISO that had been granted by his employer, Gold Corporation. Manuel acquired 1,000 shares of Gold stock for the option price of $20 per share. The stock became freely transferable in 1996. The fair market value of the stock at the date of exercise was $50 per share. For AMT purposes, Manuel has a positive gain adjustment of $30,000 ($50,000 fair market value – $20,000 option price) for 1996. The transaction does not affect regular taxable income in 1994 or 1996. ▼

No adjustment is required if the taxpayer exercises the option and disposes of the stock in the same tax year because the bargain element gain is reported for both regular income tax and AMT purposes in that tax year.

[17] §§ 59(e)(2)(D) and (E).

[18] § 56(a)(3).

[19] See Chapter 18 for a detailed discussion of the completed contract and percentage of completion methods of accounting.

[20] § 421(a).

[21] § 56(b)(3).

The regular income tax basis of stock acquired through exercise of ISOs is different from the AMT basis. The regular income tax basis of the stock is equal to its cost, whereas the AMT basis is equal to the fair market value on the date the options are exercised. Consequently, the gain or loss upon disposition of the stock is different for regular income tax purposes and AMT purposes.

EXAMPLE 11

Assume the same facts as in the previous example and that Manuel sells the stock for $60,000 in 1998. His gain for regular income tax purposes is $40,000 ($60,000 amount realized – $20,000 regular income tax basis). For AMT purposes, the gain is $10,000 ($60,000 amount realized – $50,000 AMT basis). Therefore, Manuel has a $30,000 negative adjustment in computing AMT in 1998 ($40,000 regular income tax gain – $10,000 AMT gain). Note that the $30,000 negative adjustment upon disposition in 1998 offsets the $30,000 positive adjustment upon exercise of the ISO in 1996. ▼

Adjusted Gain or Loss. When property is sold during the year or a casualty occurs to business or income-producing property, gain or loss reported for regular income tax may be different than gain or loss determined for the AMT. This difference occurs because the adjusted basis of the property for AMT purposes must reflect any current and prior AMT adjustments for the following:[22]

- Depreciation.
- Circulation expenditures.
- Research and experimental expenditures.
- Mining exploration and development costs.
- Amortization of certified pollution control facilities.

A negative gain or loss adjustment is required if:

- the gain for AMT purposes is less than the gain for regular income tax purposes;
- the loss for AMT purposes is more than the loss for regular income tax purposes; or
- a loss is computed for AMT purposes and a gain is computed for regular income tax purposes.

Otherwise, the AMT gain or loss adjustment is positive.

EXAMPLE 12

In January 1996, Kate paid $100,000 for a duplex acquired for rental purposes. Regular income tax depreciation in 1996 was $3,485 ($100,000 cost × 3.485% from Table 8–7). AMT depreciation was $2,396 ($100,000 cost × 2.396% from Table 8–12). For AMT purposes, Kate made a positive adjustment of $1,089 ($3,485 regular income tax depreciation – $2,396 AMT depreciation). ▼

EXAMPLE 13

Kate sold the duplex on December 20, 1997, for $105,000. Regular income tax depreciation for 1997 is $3,485 [($100,000 cost × 3.636% from Table 8–7) × 11.5/12]. AMT depreciation for 1997 is $2,396 [($100,000 cost × 2.500% from Table 8–12) × 11.5/12]. Kate's positive AMT adjustment for 1997 is $1,089 ($3,485 regular income tax depreciation – $2,396 AMT depreciation). ▼

Because depreciation on the duplex differs for regular income tax and AMT purposes, the adjusted basis is different for regular income tax and AMT purposes. Consequently, the gain or loss on disposition of the duplex is different for regular income tax and AMT purposes.

[22] § 56(a)(7).

EXAMPLE 14

The adjusted basis of Kate's duplex for regular income tax purposes is $93,030 ($100,000 cost – $3,485 depreciation for 1996 – $3,485 depreciation for 1997). For AMT purposes, the adjusted basis is $95,208 ($100,000 cost – $2,396 depreciation for 1996 – $2,396 depreciation for 1997). The regular income tax gain is $11,970 ($105,000 amount realized – $93,030 regular income tax basis). The AMT gain is $9,792 ($105,000 amount realized – $95,208 AMT basis). Because the regular income tax and AMT gain on the sale of the duplex differ, Kate must make a negative AMT adjustment of $2,178 ($11,970 regular income tax gain – $9,792 AMT gain). Note that this negative adjustment offsets the $2,178 total of the two positive adjustments for depreciation ($1,089 in 1996 + $1,089 in 1997). ▼

Passive Activity Losses. Losses on passive activities are not deductible in computing either the regular income tax or the AMT. This does not, however, eliminate the possibility of adjustments attributable to passive activities.

The rules for computing taxable income differ from the rules for computing AMTI. It follows, then, that the rules for computing a loss for regular income tax purposes differ from the AMT rules for computing a loss. Therefore, any *passive loss* computed for regular income tax purposes may differ from the passive loss computed for AMT purposes.[23]

EXAMPLE 15

Soong acquired two passive activities in 1996. He received net passive income of $10,000 from Activity A and had no AMT adjustments or preferences in connection with the activity. Activity B had gross income of $27,000 and operating expenses (not affected by AMT adjustments or preferences) of $19,000. Soong claimed MACRS depreciation of $20,000 for Activity B; depreciation under the ADS would have been $15,000. In addition, Soong deducted $10,000 of percentage depletion in excess of basis. The following comparison illustrates the differences in the computation of the passive loss for regular income tax and AMT purposes for Activity B.

	Regular Income Tax	AMT
Gross income	$ 27,000	$ 27,000
Deductions:		
Operating expenses	($ 19,000)	($ 19,000)
Depreciation	(20,000)	(15,000)
Depletion	(10,000)	-0-
Total deductions	($ 49,000)	($ 34,000)
Passive loss	($ 22,000)	($ 7,000)

Because the adjustment for depreciation ($5,000) applies and the preference for depletion ($10,000) is not taken into account in computing AMTI, the regular income tax passive activity loss of $22,000 for Activity B is reduced by these amounts, resulting in a passive activity loss of $7,000 for AMT purposes. ▼

For regular income tax purposes, Soong would offset the $10,000 of net passive income from Activity A with $10,000 of the passive loss from Activity B. For AMT purposes, he would offset the $10,000 of net passive income from Activity A with the $7,000 passive activity loss allowed from Activity B, resulting in passive activity income of $3,000. Thus, in computing AMTI, Soong makes a positive

[23] See Chapter 11.

passive loss adjustment of $3,000 [$10,000 (passive activity loss allowed for regular income tax) – $7,000 (passive activity loss allowed for the AMT)]. To avoid duplication, the AMT adjustment for depreciation and the preference for depletion are *not* reported separately. They are accounted for in determining the AMT passive loss adjustment.

EXAMPLE 16

Assume the same facts as in the previous example. For regular income tax purposes, Soong has a suspended passive loss of $12,000 [$22,000 (amount of loss) – $10,000 (used in 1996)]. This suspended passive loss can offset passive income in the future or can offset active or portfolio income when Soong disposes of the loss activity (refer to Chapter 11). For AMT purposes, Soong's suspended passive loss is $0 [$7,000 (amount of loss) – $7,000 (amount used in 1996)]. ▼

Alternative Tax Net Operating Loss Deduction. In computing taxable income, taxpayers are allowed to deduct net operating loss (NOL) carryovers and carrybacks (refer to Chapter 7). The regular income tax NOL must be modified, however, in computing AMTI. The starting point in computing the **alternative tax NOL deduction (ATNOLD)** is the NOL computed for regular income tax purposes. The regular income tax NOL is then modified for AMT adjustments and tax preferences with the result being the ATNOLD. Thus, preferences and adjustment items that have benefited the taxpayer in computing the regular income tax NOL are added back, thereby reducing or eliminating the ATNOLD.[24]

EXAMPLE 17

In 1996, Adam incurred an NOL of $100,000. Adam had no AMT adjustments, but his deductions included tax preferences of $18,000. His ATNOLD carryback to 1993 is $82,000 ($100,000 regular income tax NOL – $18,000 tax preferences deducted in computing the NOL). ▼

In Example 17, if the adjustment was not made to the regular income tax NOL, the $18,000 in tax preference items deducted in 1996 would have the effect of reducing AMTI in the year (or years) the 1996 NOL is utilized. This would weaken the entire concept of the AMT.

A ceiling exists on the amount of the ATNOLD that can be deducted in the carryback or carryforward year. The deduction is limited to 90 percent of AMTI (before the ATNOLD) for the carryback or carryforward year.

EXAMPLE 18

Assume the same facts as in the previous example. Adam's AMTI (before the ATNOLD) in 1993 is $90,000. Therefore, of the $82,000 ATNOLD carried back to 1993 from 1996, only $81,000 ($90,000 × 90%) can be used in recalculating the 1993 AMT. The unused $1,000 of 1996 ATNOLD is now carried to 1994 for use in recalculating the 1994 AMT. ▼

A taxpayer who has an ATNOLD that is carried back or over to another year must use the ATNOLD against AMTI in the carryback or carryforward year even if the regular income tax, rather than the AMT, applies.

EXAMPLE 19

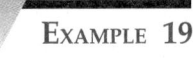

Matt's ATNOLD for 1997 (carried over from 1996) is $10,000. AMTI before considering the ATNOLD is $25,000. If Matt's regular income tax exceeds the AMT, the AMT does not apply. Nevertheless, Matt's ATNOLD of $10,000 is "used up" in 1997 and is not available for carryover to a later year. ▼

[24] § 56(a)(4).

TAX IN THE NEWS

AMT Turns Winning into Losing

A taxpayer who was discharged (i.e., fired) by his employer filed a wrongful discharge suit against the employer. The taxpayer was successful and was awarded taxable back pay and benefits of $250,000. In winning the taxable part of the judgment, he incurred attorney's fees of $245,100.

In filing his Form 1040, the taxpayer included the $250,000 in gross income net of the $245,100 (i.e., included a net $4,900 in gross income). Thus, although he was required to pay $245,100 in attorney's fees, he did receive a tax benefit by reducing his gross income.

Unfortunately, the Tax Court agreed with the IRS that the attorney's fees are appropriately classified as miscellaneous itemized deductions (*Kenneth J. Alexander*, 69 TCM 1792, T.C.Memo. 1995–51). Classifying the attorney's fees in this manner resulted in an AMT of $57,441.

For regular income tax purposes, the NOL can be carried back 3 years and forward 15 years. However, the taxpayer may elect to forgo the 3-year carryback. These rules generally apply to the ATNOLD as well, except that the election to forgo the 3-year carryback is available for the ATNOLD only if the taxpayer elected it for the regular income tax NOL.

Itemized Deductions. Most of the itemized deductions that are allowed for regular income tax purposes are allowed for AMT purposes. Itemized deductions that are allowed for AMT purposes include the following:

- Casualty losses.
- Gambling losses.
- Charitable contributions.
- Medical expenses in excess of 10 percent of AGI.
- Estate tax on income in respect of a decedent.
- Qualified interest.

Taxes (state, local, foreign income, and property taxes) and miscellaneous itemized deductions that are subject to the 2 percent-of-AGI floor are not allowed in computing AMT.[25] A positive AMT adjustment in the total amount of the regular income tax deduction for each is required.

If the taxpayer's gross income includes the recovery of any tax deducted as an itemized deduction for regular income tax purposes, a negative AMT adjustment in the amount of the recovery is allowed for AMTI purposes.[26] For example, state, local, and foreign income taxes can be deducted for regular income tax purposes, but cannot be deducted in computing AMTI. Because of this, any refund of such taxes from a prior year is not included in AMTI. Therefore, in calculating AMTI, the taxpayer must make a negative adjustment for an income tax refund that has been included in computing regular taxable income. Under the tax benefit rule, a tax refund is included in taxable income to the extent that the taxpayer obtained a tax benefit by deducting the tax in a prior year.

[25] § 56(b)(1)(A).

[26] § 56(b)(1)(D).

Cutback Adjustment. The 3 percent cutback adjustment that applies to regular income tax itemized deductions of certain high-income taxpayers (refer to Chapter 10) does not apply in computing AMT.[27] The effect of the 3 percent cutback adjustment is to disallow a portion of the taxpayer's itemized deductions for regular income tax purposes. Because this cutback adjustment does not apply for AMT purposes, taxable income, which is the starting point for computing AMTI, must be reduced by the amount of the disallowed deductions. Although this reduction has the same effect on AMTI as a negative adjustment, it is not shown on Form 6251 as such. Instead, it is shown on a separate line (line 18) as a subtraction from taxable income.

Medical Expenses. The rules for determining the AMT deductions for medical expenses are sufficiently complex to require further explanation. For regular income tax purposes, medical expenses are deductible to the extent they exceed 7.5 percent of AGI. However, for AMT purposes, medical expenses are deductible only to the extent they exceed 10 percent of AGI.[28]

EXAMPLE 20

Joann incurred medical expenses of $16,000 in 1996. She had AGI of $100,000 for the year. Her AMT adjustment for medical expenses is computed as follows:

	Regular Income Tax	AMT
Medical expenses incurred	$16,000	$ 16,000
Less reduction:		
$100,000 AGI × 7.5%	(7,500)	
$100,000 AGI × 10%		(10,000)
Medical expense deduction	$ 8,500	$ 6,000

Joann's AMT adjustment for medical expenses is $2,500 ($8,500 regular income tax deduction – $6,000 AMT deduction). ▼

Interest in General. The AMT itemized deduction allowed for interest expense includes only qualified housing interest and investment interest to the extent of net investment income that is included in the determination of AMTI.[29] Any interest that is deducted in calculating the regular income tax that is not permitted in calculating the AMT is treated as a positive adjustment.

In computing regular taxable income, taxpayers who itemize can deduct the following types of interest (refer to Chapter 10):

- Qualified residence interest.
- Investment interest, subject to the investment interest limitations (discussed under Investment Interest below).

Housing Interest. Under current regular income tax rules, taxpayers who itemize can deduct *qualified residence interest* on up to two residences. The deduction is limited to interest on acquisition indebtedness up to $1 million and home equity indebtedness up to $100,000. Acquisition indebtedness is debt that is incurred in

[27] § 56(b)(1)(F).

[28] § 56(b)(1)(B).

[29] § 56(b)(1)(C).

acquiring, constructing, or substantially improving a qualified residence of the taxpayer and is secured by the residence. Home equity indebtedness is indebtedness secured by a qualified residence of the taxpayer, but does not include acquisition indebtedness.

EXAMPLE 21

Gail, who used the proceeds of a mortgage to acquire a personal residence, paid mortgage interest of $112,000 in 1996. Of this amount, $14,000 is attributable to acquisition indebtedness in excess of $1 million. For regular income tax purposes, Gail may deduct mortgage interest of $98,000 ($112,000 total – $14,000 disallowed). ▼

The mortgage interest deduction for AMT purposes is limited to *qualified housing interest,* rather than *qualified residence interest.* Qualified housing interest includes only interest incurred to acquire, construct, or substantially improve the taxpayer's principal residence and such interest on one other qualified dwelling used for personal purposes. A home equity loan qualifies only if it meets the definition of qualified housing interest, which frequently is not the case. When additional mortgage interest is incurred (e.g., a mortgage refinancing), interest paid is deductible as qualified housing interest for AMT purposes only if:

- The proceeds are used to acquire or substantially improve a qualified residence.
- Interest on the prior loan was qualified housing interest.
- The amount of the loan was not increased.

A positive AMT adjustment is required in the amount of the difference between qualified *residence* interest allowed as an itemized deduction for regular income tax purposes and qualified *housing* interest allowed in the determination of AMTI.

Investment Interest. Investment interest is deductible for regular income tax purposes and for AMT purposes to the extent of qualified net investment income.

EXAMPLE 22

For the year, Dan had net investment income of $16,000 before deducting investment interest. He incurred investment interest expense of $30,000 during the year. His investment interest deduction is $16,000. ▼

Even though investment interest is deductible for both regular income tax and AMT purposes, an adjustment is required if the amount of investment interest deductible for regular income tax purposes differs from the amount deductible for AMT purposes. For example, an adjustment will arise if proceeds from a home equity loan are used to purchase investments. Interest on a home equity loan is deductible as qualified residence interest for regular income tax purposes, but is not deductible for AMT purposes unless the proceeds are used to acquire or substantially improve a qualified residence. For AMT purposes, however, interest on a home equity loan is deductible as investment interest expense if proceeds from the loan are used for investment purposes.

To determine the AMT adjustment for investment interest expense, it is necessary to compute the investment interest deduction for both regular income tax and AMT purposes. This computation is illustrated in the following example.

EXAMPLE 23

Tom had $20,000 interest income from corporate bonds and $5,000 dividends from preferred stock. He reported the following amounts of investment income for regular income tax and AMT purposes:

	Regular Income Tax	AMT
Corporate bond interest	$20,000	$20,000
Preferred stock dividends	5,000	5,000
Net investment income	$25,000	$25,000

Tom incurred investment interest expense of $10,000 related to the corporate bonds. He also incurred $4,000 interest on a home equity loan and used the proceeds of the loan to purchase preferred stock. For regular income tax purposes, this $4,000 is deductible as qualified residence interest. His *investment* interest expense for regular income tax and AMT purposes is computed below:

	Regular Income Tax	AMT
To carry corporate bonds	$10,000	$10,000
On home equity loan to carry preferred stock	-0-	4,000
Total investment interest expense	$10,000	$14,000

Investment interest expense is deductible to the extent of net investment income. Because the amount deductible for regular income tax purposes ($10,000) differs from the amount deductible for AMT purposes ($14,000), an AMT adjustment is required. The adjustment is computed as follows:

AMT deduction for investment interest expense	$14,000
Regular income tax deduction for investment interest expense	(10,000)
Negative AMT adjustment	$4,000

▼

As discussed subsequently under AMT Preferences, the interest on private activity bonds is a tax preference for AMT purposes. Such interest can also affect the calculation of the AMT investment interest deduction in that it is included in the calculation of net investment income.

Other Adjustments. The standard deduction is not allowed as a deduction in computing AMTI.[30] Although a person who does not itemize is rarely subject to the AMT, it is possible. In such a case, the taxpayer is required to enter a positive adjustment for the standard deduction in computing the AMT.

The personal and dependency exemption amount deducted for regular income tax purposes is not allowed in computing AMT.[31] Therefore, taxpayers must enter a positive AMT adjustment for the personal and dependency exemption amount claimed in computing the regular income tax. A separate exemption (see Exemption Amount) is allowed for AMT purposes. To allow both the regular income tax exemption amount and the AMT exemption amount would result in extra benefits for taxpayers.

EXAMPLE 24

Eli, who is single, has no dependents and does not itemize deductions. He earned a salary of $106,550 in 1996. Based on this information, Eli's taxable income for 1996 is $100,000 ($106,550 – $4,000 standard deduction – $2,550 exemption). ▼

30 § 56(b)(1)(E).

31 § 56(b)(1)(E).

EXAMPLE 25 Assume the same facts as in Example 24. In addition, assume Eli's tax preferences for the year totaled $150,000. Eli's AMTI is $256,550 ($100,000 taxable income + $4,000 adjustment for standard deduction + $2,550 adjustment for exemption + $150,000 tax preferences). ▼

AMT PREFERENCES

4 LEARNING OBJECTIVE
Identify the tax preferences that are included in calculating the AMT.

Percentage Depletion. Congress originally enacted the percentage depletion rules to provide taxpayers with incentives to invest in the development of specified natural resources. Percentage depletion is computed by multiplying a rate specified in the Code times the gross income from the property (refer to Chapter 8). The percentage rate is based on the type of mineral involved. The basis of the property is reduced by the amount of depletion taken until the basis reaches zero. However, once the basis of the property reaches zero, taxpayers are allowed to continue taking percentage depletion deductions. Thus, over the life of the property, depletion deductions may greatly exceed the cost of the property.

The percentage depletion preference is equal to the excess of the regular income tax deduction for percentage depletion over the adjusted basis of the property at the end of the taxable year.[32] Basis is determined without regard to the depletion deduction for the taxable year. This preference item is figured separately for each piece of property for which the taxpayer is claiming depletion.

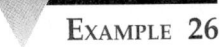

EXAMPLE 26 Kim owns a mineral property that qualifies for a 22% depletion rate. The basis of the property at the beginning of the year is $10,000. Gross income from the property for the year is $100,000. For regular income tax purposes, Kim's percentage depletion deduction (assume it is not limited by taxable income from the property) is $22,000. For AMT purposes, Kim has a tax preference of $12,000 ($22,000 – $10,000). ▼

Intangible Drilling Costs. In computing the regular income tax, taxpayers are allowed to deduct certain intangible drilling and development costs in the year incurred, although such costs are normally capital in nature (refer to Chapter 8). The deduction is allowed for costs incurred in connection with oil and gas wells and geothermal wells.

For AMT purposes, excess intangible drilling costs (IDC) for the year are treated as a preference.[33] The preference for excess IDC is computed as follows:

IDC expensed in the year incurred

Minus: Deduction if IDC were capitalized and amortized over 10 years

Equals: Excess of IDC expense over amortization

Minus: 65% of net oil and gas and geothermal income

Equals: Tax preference item

EXAMPLE 27 Ben, who incurred IDC of $50,000 during the year, elected to expense that amount. His net oil and gas income for the year was $60,000. Ben's tax preference for IDC is $6,000 [($50,000 IDC – $5,000 amortization) – (65% × $60,000 income)]. ▼

A taxpayer can avoid the preference for IDC by electing to write off the expenditures over a 10-year period for regular income tax purposes.

---

[32] § 57(a)(1). Note the preference label does not apply to percentage depletion on oil and gas wells for independent producers and royalty owners as defined in § 613A(c).

[33] § 57(a)(2).

Interest on Private Activity Bonds. Income from private activity bonds is not included in taxable income, and expenses related to carrying such bonds are not deductible for regular income tax purposes. However, interest on private activity bonds is included as a preference in computing AMTI. Therefore, expenses incurred in carrying the bonds are offset against the interest income in computing the tax preference.[34]

The Code contains a lengthy, complex definition of private activity bonds.[35] In general, **private activity bonds** are bonds issued by states or municipalities with more than 10 percent of the proceeds being used for private business use. For example, a bond issued by a city whose proceeds are used to construct a factory that is leased to a private business at a favorable rate is a private activity bond.

ETHICAL CONSIDERATIONS

Taxability of Bond Interest: Regular Income Tax versus AMT

Jason, who is single and in the 31 percent tax bracket, recently inherited $1 million of bonds from his mother. Rather than changing investments, Jason decides to retain the investment in municipal bonds for the time being.

The Form 1099 he received from the municipality has confused Jason about the tax treatment of the bond interest. He thought that all municipal bonds were tax-exempt, but from an article that he read recently, he is now aware that certain such bonds are not tax-exempt for Federal income tax purposes. Rereading the article, Jason notes that bonds classified as private activity bonds are excludible from gross income for regular income tax purposes but are a tax preference for AMT purposes. Jason has asked the issuer for clarification on the status of the bonds, but has received no answer. He checks his mother's tax return for the past three years and finds that none of her returns included a Form 6251.

Since he wants to file his return this week, Jason has to decide how to report the bond interest. He knows that he is going to be subject to the AMT with some of his income being taxed at the 28 percent rate. He is considering resolving his dilemma by not treating the bonds as private activity bonds. His justification for his position is that his mother was an astute businesswoman and she did not report the bond interest on her tax returns as private activity bond interest. If Jason does not treat the bonds as private activity bonds, the bond interest will not be subject to either the regular income tax or the AMT. Evaluate Jason's proposal.

Depreciation. For real property and leased personal property placed in service before 1987, there is an AMT preference for the excess of accelerated depreciation over straight-line depreciation.[36] However, examination of the cost recovery tables for pre-1987 real property (refer to Chapter 8) reveals that from the eighth year on, accelerated depreciation will not exceed straight-line depreciation. Consequently, taxpayers no longer have preferences attributable to pre-1987 real property.

Accelerated depreciation on pre-1987 leased personal property was computed using specified ACRS percentages (refer to Table 8–1, Chapter 8). AMT depreciation was based on the straight-line method, which was computed using the

[34] § 57(a)(5).

[35] § 141.

[36] § 57(a)(6).

TAX IN THE NEWS

RECEIVING PREFERENTIAL TREATMENT AND AVOIDING THE AMT

Museums were among the leading beneficiaries of a change in the tax law that made it easier to give appreciated long-term capital gain property to charity. Since a law change enacted in August 1993, taxpayers who donate appreciated assets to qualified charities no longer have an AMT preference equal to the amount by which the assets' fair market value exceeds their adjusted basis. The repeal of the preference had an immediate impact. By December 1993, the Metropolitan Museum of Art in New York City had already received several valuable donations of art and expected to receive several more in the near future.

Among the donors to museums in the wake of the preference's repeal was the accounting firm of KPMG Peat Marwick, which donated its collection of American crafts to the Renwick Gallery of the National Museum of American Art at the Smithsonian Institution. Had the firm donated the collection before the repeal, the preference would have been passed through to the partners and appeared on their individual tax returns.

half-year convention, no salvage value, and a longer recovery period.[37] As a result, in the early years of the life of the asset, the cost recovery allowance used in computing the regular income tax was greater than the straight-line depreciation deduction allowed in computing AMT. The excess depreciation was treated as a tax preference item. For all leased personal property placed in service before 1987 (3-year, 5-year, and 10-year), except for 15-year public utility property, the cost recovery period has expired. Since there is no excess depreciation, there is no tax preference for AMT purposes.

EXAMPLE 28 Paul acquired personal property on January 1, 1986, at a cost of $30,000. The property, which was placed in service as leased personal property on January 1, was 10-year ACRS property. Paul's 1986 depreciation deduction for regular income tax purposes was $2,400 ($30,000 cost × 8% rate from Table 8–1). For AMT purposes, the asset was depreciated over the AMT life of 15 years using the straight-line method with the half-year convention. Thus, AMT depreciation for 1986 was $1,000 [($30,000 ÷ 15) × ½ year convention]. Paul's tax preference for 1986 was $1,400 ($2,400 – $1,000). ACRS depreciation for 1996 is $0 ($30,000 × 0% ACRS rate), and straight-line depreciation is $2,000 ($30,000 ÷ 15). Thus, Paul's tax preference for 1996 is $0 since there is no excess depreciation. ▼

The preference item for excess depreciation on leased personal property is figured separately for each piece of property. No preference is reported in the year the taxpayer disposes of the property.

Fifty Percent Exclusion for Certain Small Business Stock. Fifty percent of the gain on the sale of certain small business stock is excludible from gross income for regular income tax purposes. The excluded amount is a tax preference for AMT purposes.[38]

[37] The specified lives for AMT purposes are 5 years for 3-year property, 8 years for 5-year property, 15 years for 10-year property, and 22 years for 15-year property.

[38] § 57(a)(7).

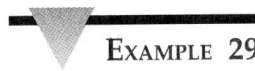

5 LEARNING OBJECTIVE
Apply the formula for computing the AMT and illustrate Form 6251.

ILLUSTRATION OF THE AMT COMPUTATION

The computation of the AMT is illustrated in the following example.

EXAMPLE 29

Hans Sims, who is single, had taxable income for 1996 as follows:

Salary		$ 92,000
Interest		8,000
Adjusted gross income		$100,000
Less itemized deductions:		
Medical expenses ($17,500 – 7.5% of $100,000 AGI)[a]	$10,000	
State income taxes	4,000	
Interest[b]		
Home mortgage (for qualified housing)	20,000*	
Investment interest	3,300*	
Contributions (cash)	5,000*	
Casualty losses ($14,000 – 10% of $100,000 AGI)	4,000*	(46,300)
		$ 53,700
Less exemption		(2,550)
Taxable income		$ 51,150

[a]Total medical expenses were $17,500, reduced by 7.5% of AGI, resulting in an itemized deduction of $10,000. However, for AMT purposes, the reduction is 10%, which leaves an AMT itemized deduction of $7,500 ($17,500 – 10% of $100,000 AGI). Therefore, an adjustment of $2,500 ($10,000 – $7,500) is required for medical expenses disallowed for AMT purposes.

[b]In this illustration, all interest is deductible in computing AMTI. Qualified housing interest is deductible. Investment interest ($3,300) is deductible to the extent of net investment income included in the minimum tax base. For this purpose, the $8,000 of interest income is treated as net investment income.

Deductions marked by an asterisk are allowed as *alternative minimum tax itemized deductions,* and AMT adjustments are required for the other itemized deductions. Thus, adjustments are required for state income taxes and for medical expenses to the extent the medical expenses deductible for regular income tax purposes are not deductible in computing AMT (see note a above). In addition to the items that affected taxable income, Hans had $35,000 interest on private activity bonds (an exclusion tax preference). AMTI is computed as follows:

Taxable income	$ 51,150
Plus: Adjustments	
State income taxes	4,000
Medical expenses (see note a above)	2,500
Personal exemption	2,550
Plus: Tax preference (interest on private activity bonds)	35,000
Equals: AMTI	$ 95,200
Minus: AMT exemption	(33,750)
Equals: Minimum tax base	$ 61,450
Times: AMT rate	× 26%
Equals: Tentative AMT	$ 15,977
Minus: Regular income tax on taxable income	(11,202)
Equals: AMT	$ 4,775

▼

CONCEPT SUMMARY 12–1

AMT Adjustments and Preferences for Individuals

Adjustments	Positive	Negative	Both*
Circulation expenditures			*X*
Depreciation of post-1986 real property			*X*
Depreciation of post-1986 personal property			*X*
Pollution control facilities			*X*
Mining exploration and development costs			*X*
Research and experimental expenditures			*X*
Completed contract method			*X*
Incentive stock options	*X***		
Adjusted gain or loss			*X*
Passive activity losses			*X*
Alternative tax NOLD			*X*
Itemized deductions:			
Medical expenses	*X*		
State income tax	*X*		
Property tax on realty	*X*		
Property tax on personalty	*X*		
Miscellaneous itemized deductions	*X*		
Tax benefit rule for state income tax refund		*X*	
Cutback adjustment		*X*	
Qualified residence interest that is not qualified housing interest	*X*		
Qualified residence interest that is AMT investment interest	*X*	*X*	
Private activity bond interest that is AMI investment interest		*X*	
Standard deduction	*X*		
Personal exemptions and dependency deductions	*X*		
Preferences			
Percentage depletion in excess of adjusted basis	*X*		
Intangible drilling costs	*X*		
Private activity bond interest income	*X*		
Depreciation on pre-1987 leased personal property	*X*		
§ 1202 exclusion for certain small business stock	*X*		

*Timing differences.
**While the adjustment is a positive adjustment, the AMT basis for the stock is increased by the amount of the positive adjustment.

The solution to Example 29 is also presented on Form 6251. Though this example is for 1996, 1995 tax forms are used because the 1996 tax forms were not available at the time of this writing.

Note that the $2,550 personal exemption amount is a positive adjustment in the Example 29 solution, but does not appear as an adjustment in Form 6251. This

Form **6251**
Department of the Treasury
Internal Revenue Service

Alternative Minimum Tax—Individuals

▶ See separate instructions.
▶ Attach to Form 1040, Form 1040NR, or Form 1040-T.

OMB No. 1545-0227
1995
Attachment Sequence No. **32**

Name(s) shown on Form 1040: *Hans Sims*
Your social security number:

Part I Adjustments and Preferences

1	If you itemized deductions on Schedule A (Form 1040) (or you entered the amount from Form 1040-T, Section B, line t, on Form 1040-T, line 20), go to line 2. Otherwise, enter your standard deduction from Form 1040, line 34 (or Form 1040-T, line 20), and go to line 6	1	
2	Medical and dental. Enter the smaller of Schedule A (Form 1040), line 4 **or** 2½% of Form 1040, line 32 (Form 1040-T filers, enter the smaller of Section B, line c **or** 2½% of Form 1040-T, line 16)	2	*2,500*
3	Taxes. Enter the amount from Schedule A (Form 1040), line 9 (or the total of lines d through g of Form 1040-T, Section B)	3	*4,000*
4	Certain interest on a home mortgage not used to buy, build, or improve your home	4	
5	Miscellaneous itemized deductions. Enter the amount from Schedule A (Form 1040), line 26 (or Form 1040-T, Section B, line r)	5	
6	Refund of taxes. Enter any tax refund from Form 1040, line 10 or line 21 (or Form 1040-T, line 4 or line 9)	6	( )
7	Investment interest. Enter difference between regular tax and AMT deduction	7	
8	Post-1986 depreciation. Enter difference between regular tax and AMT depreciation	8	
9	Adjusted gain or loss. Enter difference between AMT and regular tax gain or loss	9	
10	Incentive stock options. Enter excess of AMT income over regular tax income	10	
11	Passive activities. Enter difference between AMT and regular tax income or loss	11	
12	Beneficiaries of estates and trusts. Enter the amount from Schedule K-1 (Form 1041), line 8	12	
13	Tax-exempt interest from private activity bonds issued after 8/7/86	13	*35,000*
14	Other. Enter the amount, if any, for each item and enter the total on line 14.		
	a Charitable contributions ____ h Loss limitations ____		
	b Circulation expenditures ____ i Mining costs ____		
	c Depletion ____ j Patron's adjustment ____		
	d Depreciation (pre-1987) ____ k Pollution control facilities ____		
	e Installment sales ____ l Research and experimental ____		
	f Intangible drilling costs ____ m Tax shelter farm activities ____		
	g Long-term contracts ____ n Related adjustments ____	14	
15	**Total Adjustments and Preferences.** Combine lines 1 through 14 ▶	15	*41,500*

Part II Alternative Minimum Taxable Income

16	Enter the amount from **Form 1040, line 35 (or Form 1040-T, line 21).** If less than zero, enter as a (loss) ▶	16	*53,700*
17	Net operating loss deduction, if any, from Form 1040, line 21. Enter as a positive amount	17	
18	If Form 1040, line 32 (or Form 1040-T, line 16), is over $114,700 (over $57,350 if married filing separately), and you itemized deductions, enter the amount, if any, from line 9 of the worksheet for Schedule A (Form 1040), line 28 (or line 9 of the worksheet for Section B, line t, of Form 1040-T)	18	( )
19	Combine lines 15 through 18 ▶	19	*95,200*
20	Alternative tax net operating loss deduction. See page 5 of the instructions	20	
21	**Alternative Minimum Taxable Income.** Subtract line 20 from line 19. (If married filing separately and line 21 is more than $165,000, see page 5 of the instructions.) ▶	21	*95,200*

Part III Exemption Amount and Alternative Minimum Tax

22 **Exemption Amount.** (If this form is for a child under age 14, see page 6 of the instructions.)

If your filing status is:	And line 21 is not over:	Enter on line 22:
Single or head of household	$112,500	$33,750
Married filing jointly or qualifying widow(er)	150,000	45,000
Married filing separately	75,000	22,500

If line 21 is **over** the amount shown above for your filing status, see page 6 of the instructions.

22	Exemption Amount	22	*33,750*
23	Subtract line 22 from line 21. If zero or less, enter -0- here and on lines 26 and 28 ▶	23	*61,450*
24	If line 23 is $175,000 or less ($87,500 or less if married filing separately), multiply line 23 by 26% (.26). Otherwise, multiply line 23 by 28% (.28) and subtract $3,500 ($1,750 if married filing separately) from the result	24	*15,977*
25	Alternative minimum tax foreign tax credit. See page 6 of the instructions	25	
26	Tentative minimum tax. Subtract line 25 from line 24 ▶	26	*15,977*
27	Enter your tax from Form 1040, line 38 (plus any amount from Form 4970 included on Form 1040, line 39), minus any foreign tax credit from Form 1040, line 43 (Form 1040-T filers, enter the amount from Form 1040-T, line 26)	27	*11,202*
28	**Alternative Minimum Tax.** (If this form is for a child under age 14, see page 7 of the instructions.) Subtract line 27 from line 26. If zero or less, enter -0-. Enter here and on Form 1040, line 48 (or Form 1040-T, line 31) ▶	28	*4,775*

For Paperwork Reduction Act Notice, see separate instructions. *Printed on recycled paper* Cat. No. 13600G Form **6251** (1995)

difference occurs because line 16 of Form 6251 includes the amount from line 35 of Form 1040. Line 35 of Form 1040 is taxable income before the deduction for personal and dependency exemptions.

AMT CREDIT

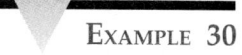

6 LEARNING OBJECTIVE
Describe the role of the AMT credit in the alternative minimum tax structure.

As discussed previously, timing differences give rise to adjustments to the minimum tax base. In later years, the timing differences reverse, as was illustrated in several of the preceding examples. To provide equity for the taxpayer when timing differences reverse, the regular income tax liability may be reduced by a tax credit for prior years' minimum tax liability attributable to timing differences. The **alternative minimum tax credit** may be carried over indefinitely. Therefore, there is no need to keep track of when the minimum tax credit arose.[39]

EXAMPLE 30

Assume the same facts as in Example 3. Also assume that in 1995, Bob paid AMT as a result of the $20,000 positive adjustment arising from the circulation expenditures. In 1996, $10,000 of the timing difference reverses, resulting in regular taxable income that is $10,000 greater than AMTI. Because Bob has already paid AMT as a result of the write-off of circulation expenditures, he is allowed an AMT credit in 1996. The AMT credit can offset Bob's regular income tax liability in 1996 to the extent that his regular income tax liability exceeds his tentative AMT. ▼

The AMT credit is applicable only for the AMT that results from timing differences. It is not available in connection with **AMT exclusions,** which represent permanent differences rather than timing differences between the regular income tax liability and the AMT. These AMT exclusions include the following:

- The standard deduction.
- Personal exemptions.
- Medical expenses, to the extent deductible for regular income tax purposes but not deductible in computing AMT.
- Other itemized deductions not allowable for AMT purposes, including miscellaneous itemized deductions, taxes, and interest expense.
- Excess percentage depletion.
- Tax-exempt interest on specified private activity bonds.

EXAMPLE 31

Don, who is single, has zero taxable income for 1996. He also has positive timing adjustments of $300,000 and AMT exclusions of $100,000. His AMT base is $400,000 because his AMT exemption is phased out completely due to the level of AMTI. Don's tentative AMT is $108,500 [($175,000 × 26% AMT rate) + ($225,000 × 28% AMT rate)]. ▼

To determine the amount of AMT credit to carry over, the AMT must be recomputed reflecting only the AMT exclusions and the AMT exemption amount.

EXAMPLE 32

Assume the same facts as in the previous example. If there had been no positive timing adjustments for the year, Don's tentative AMT would have been $17,225 [($100,000 AMT exclusions − $33,750 exemption) × 26% AMT rate]. Don may carry over an AMT credit of $91,275 ($108,500 AMT − $17,225 related to AMT exclusions) to 1997 and subsequent years. ▼

[39] § 53.

Corporate Alternative Minimum Tax

7 Learning Objective
Understand the basic features of the corporate AMT.

The AMT applicable to corporations is similar to that applicable to noncorporate taxpayers. However, there are several important differences:

- The corporate AMT rate is 20 percent versus a top rate of 28 percent for noncorporate taxpayers.[40]
- The AMT exemption for corporations is $40,000 reduced by 25 percent of the amount by which AMTI exceeds $150,000.[41]
- Tax preferences applicable to noncorporate taxpayers are also applicable to corporate taxpayers, but some adjustments differ (see below).

Although there are computational differences, the corporate AMT and the noncorporate AMT have the identical objective: to force taxpayers who are more profitable than their taxable income reflects to pay additional tax. The formula for determining the corporate AMT appears in Figure 12–3.

AMT ADJUSTMENTS

Adjustments Applicable to Individuals and Corporations. The following adjustments that were discussed in connection with the individual AMT also apply to the corporate AMT:

- Excess of MACRS over ADS depreciation on real and personal property placed in service after 1986.

▼ FIGURE 12–3
AMT Formula for Corporations

Taxable income
Plus: Income tax NOL deduction
Plus or minus: AMT adjustments
Plus: Tax preferences
Equals: AMTI before ATNOLD
Minus: ATNOLD (limited to 90% of AMTI before ATNOLD)
Equals: AMTI
Minus: Exemption
Equals: AMT base
Times: 20% rate
Equals: Tentative minimum tax before AMT foreign tax credit
Minus: AMT foreign tax credit (limited to 90% of AMT before AMT foreign tax credit)
Equals: Tentative minimum tax
Minus: Regular tax liability before credits minus regular foreign tax credit
Equals: AMT if positive

[40] § 55(b)(1)(B).

[41] §§ 55(d)(2) and (3).

TAX IN THE NEWS

Who Pays Corporate AMT?

During 1995, the question of whether the corporate AMT should be repealed was the subject of much debate. Among the issues discussed were the amount of revenue generated, the related compliance costs, and the number of corporations subject to the AMT.

According to a Government Accounting Office report, only about 30,000 of the 2.1 million corporations potentially subject to the AMT (i.e., less than 1.5 percent) paid any AMT for the period 1987–1992. Approximately 2,000 corporations paid 85 percent of the corporate AMT during that period.

Proponents of the corporate AMT claimed these statistics showed that the corporations that should be paying the AMT (i.e., large corporations) are doing so. Opponents claimed the same statistics supported their position that the compliance costs borne by the mass of corporations do not justify the continuation of this tax system. Truly, "beauty is in the eye of the beholder."

- Pollution control facilities placed in service after 1986 (AMT requires ADS depreciation over the asset's ADR life; 60-month amortization is allowed for regular income tax purposes).
- Mining and exploration expenditures (AMT requires amortization over 10 years versus immediate expensing allowed for regular income tax purposes).
- Income on long-term contracts (AMT requires percentage of completion method; completed contract method is allowed in limited circumstances for regular income tax purposes).
- Dispositions of assets (if gain or loss for AMT purposes differs from gain or loss for regular income tax purposes).
- Allowable ATNOLD (which cannot exceed 90 percent of AMTI before deduction for ATNOLD).

Adjustments Applicable Only to Corporations. Three AMT adjustments are applicable only to corporations:[42]

- The adjusted current earnings (ACE) adjustment.
- The Merchant Marine capital construction fund adjustment.
- The adjustment for special deductions allowed to Blue Cross/Blue Shield organizations.

The latter two adjustments apply to specific types of corporations and are not discussed in the chapter. On the other hand, the **ACE adjustment** generally applies to all corporations[43] and is expected to have a significant impact on both tax and financial accounting.

Corporations are subject to an AMT adjustment equal to 75 percent of the excess of ACE over AMTI before the ACE adjustment.[44] Historically, the government has not required conformity between tax accounting and financial account-

---

[42] § 56(c).

[43] The ACE adjustment does not apply to S corporations. § 56(g)(6).

[44] § 56(g).

CONCEPT SUMMARY 12–2

Determining the ACE Adjustment*

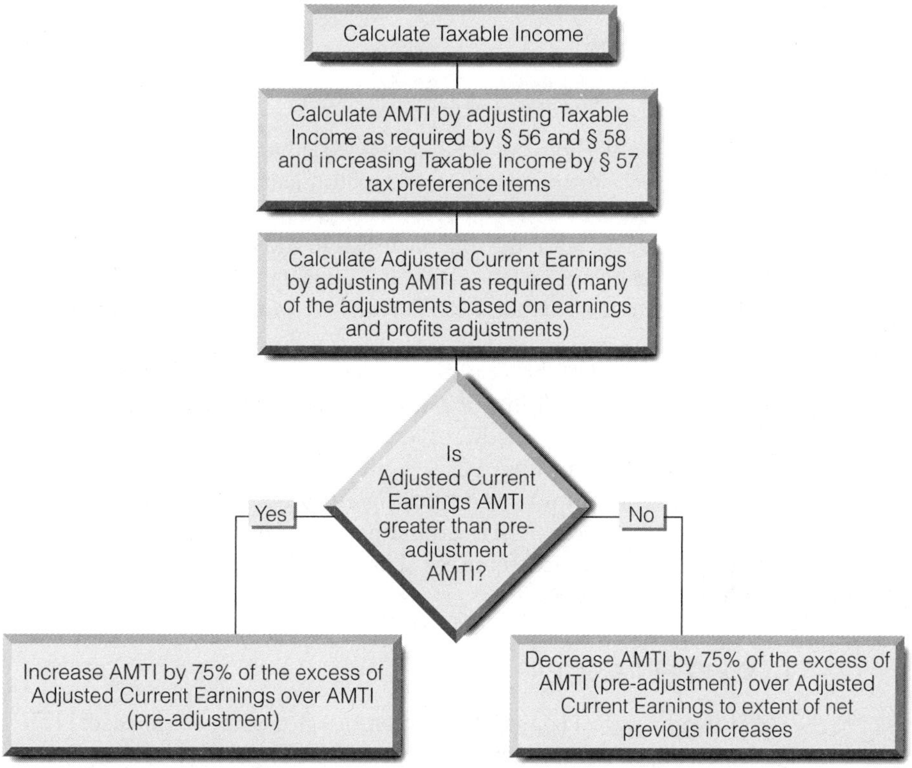

*Adapted from "Corporate Alternative Minimum Tax: The Impact of Current Earnings Adjustment on Oil and Gas Companies" by Gallun and Zachry, which appeared in the September 1989 issue of the *Oil and Gas Tax Quarterly*, published and copyrighted 1989 by Matthew Bender & Co,. and appears here with their permission.

ing. For many years, the only *direct* conformity requirement was that a corporation that used the LIFO method for tax accounting also had to use LIFO for financial accounting.[45] Through the ACE adjustment, Congress is *indirectly* imposing a conformity requirement on corporations. While a corporation may still choose to use different methods for tax and financial accounting purposes, it may no longer be able to do so without incurring AMT as a result of the ACE adjustment. Thus, a corporation may incur AMT not only because of specifically targeted adjustments and preferences, but also as a result of any methods that cause ACE to exceed AMTI before the ACE adjustment.

The ACE adjustment can be either a positive or a negative amount. AMTI is increased by 75 percent of the excess of ACE over unadjusted AMTI. Or AMTI is reduced by 75 percent of the excess of unadjusted AMTI over ACE. The negative adjustment is limited to the aggregate of the positive adjustments under ACE for prior years, reduced by the previously claimed negative adjustments. See Concept Summary 12–2. Thus, the ordering of the timing differences is crucial because any

[45] § 472(c).

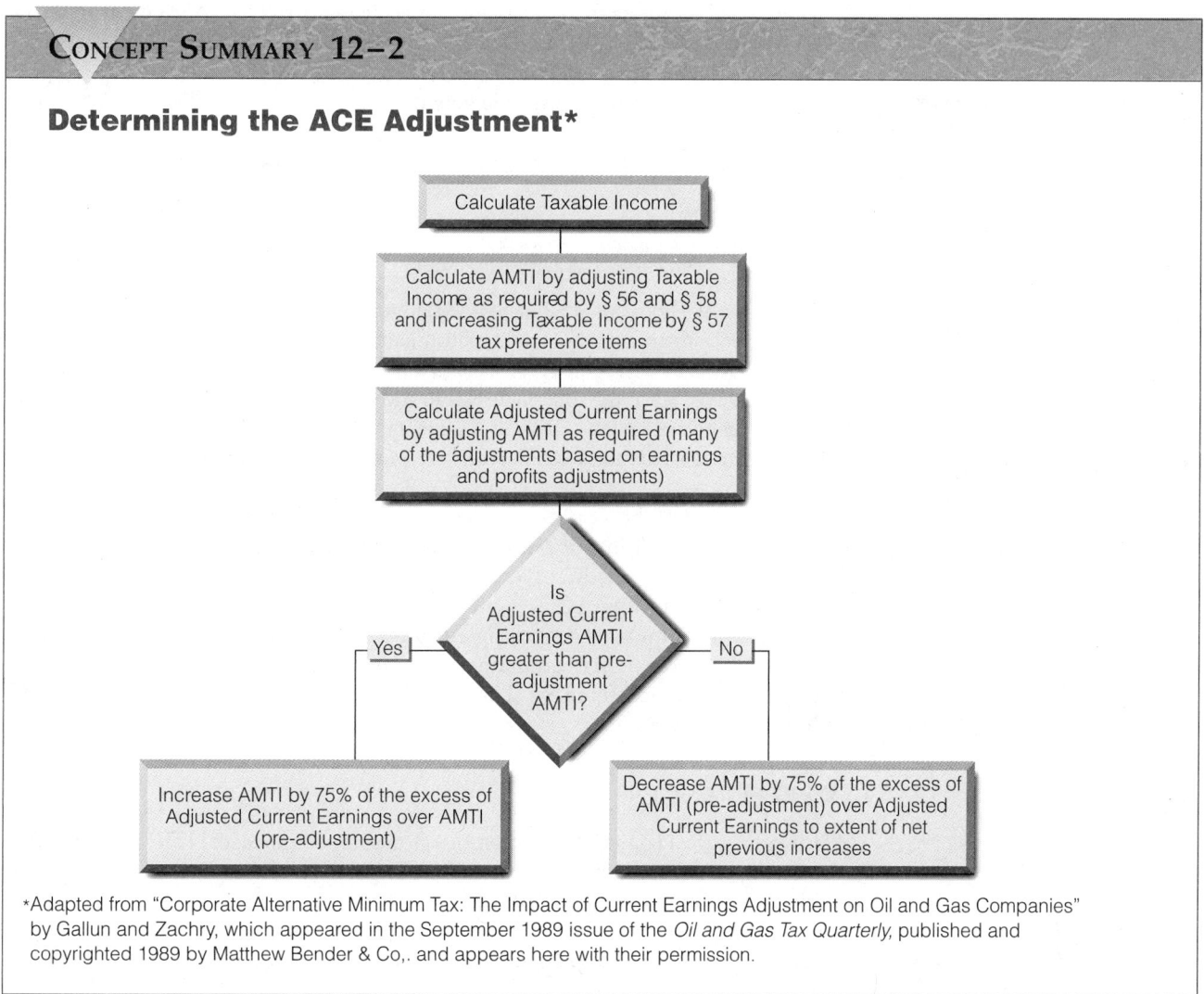

lost negative adjustment is permanent. Unadjusted AMTI is AMTI without the ACE adjustment or the ATNOLD.[46]

EXAMPLE 33

A calendar year corporation has the following data:

	1995	1996	1997
Pre-adjusted AMTI	$3,000	$3,000	$3,100
Adjusted current earnings	4,000	3,000	2,000

In 1995, because ACE exceeds unadjusted AMTI by $1,000, $750 (75% × $1,000) is included as a positive adjustment to AMTI. No adjustment is necessary for 1996. As unadjusted AMTI exceeds ACE by $1,100 in 1997, there is a potential negative adjustment to AMTI of $825 ($1,100 × 75%). Since the total increases to AMTI for prior years equal $750 and there are no previously claimed negative adjustments, only $750 of the potential negative adjustment reduces AMTI for 1997. Further, $75 of the negative amount is lost forever. ▼

ACE should not be confused with current earnings and profits. Although many items are treated in the same manner, certain variations exist. For example, Federal income taxes, deductible in computing earnings and profits, are not deductible in determining ACE.

The starting point for computing ACE is AMTI, which is defined as regular taxable income after AMT adjustments (other than the ATNOLD and ACE adjustments) and tax preferences. The resulting figure is adjusted for several items in order to arrive at ACE.

TAX PREFERENCES

AMTI includes designated tax preference items. In some cases, this has the effect of subjecting nontaxable income to the AMT. Tax preference items that apply to individuals also apply to corporations.

EXAMPLE 34

The following information applies to Brown Corporation (a calendar year taxpayer) for 1996:

Taxable income	$200,000
Mining exploration costs	50,000
Percentage depletion claimed (the property has a zero adjusted basis)	70,000
Interest on City of Elmira (Michigan) private activity bonds	30,000

Brown Corporation's AMTI for 1996 is determined as follows:

Taxable income		$200,000
Adjustments:		
Excess mining exploration costs [$50,000 (amount expensed) – $5,000 (amount allowed over a 10-year amortization period)]		45,000
Tax preferences:		
Excess depletion	$70,000	
Interest on private activity bonds	30,000	100,000
AMTI		$345,000

▼

46 §§ 56(g)(1) and (2).

EXEMPTION

The tentative AMT is 20 percent of AMTI that exceeds the corporation's exemption amount. The exemption amount for a corporation is $40,000 reduced by 25 percent of the amount by which AMTI exceeds $150,000.

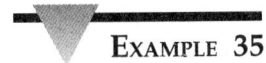

EXAMPLE 35

Blue Corporation has AMTI of $180,000. The exemption amount is reduced by $7,500 [25% × ($180,000 – $150,000)], and the amount remaining is $32,500 ($40,000 – $7,500). Thus, Blue Corporation's AMT base (refer to Figure 12–3) is $147,500 ($180,000 – $32,500). ▼

Note that the exemption phases out entirely when AMTI reaches $310,000.

OTHER ASPECTS OF THE AMT

Foreign tax credits can be applied against only 90 percent of tentative AMT liability. The 90 percent limit does not apply to certain corporations meeting specified requirements for tax years beginning after March 31, 1990.

All of a corporation's AMT is available for carryover as a minimum tax credit. This is so regardless of whether the adjustments and preferences originate from timing differences or AMT exclusions.

EXAMPLE 36

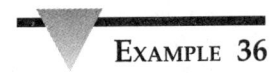

In Example 34, the AMTI exceeds $310,000, so no exemption is allowed. The tentative minimum tax is $69,000 (20% of $345,000). The regular income tax liability is $61,250, and the AMT liability is $7,750 ($69,000 – $61,250). The amount of the minimum tax credit carryover is $7,750, which is all of the current year's AMT. ▼

TAX PLANNING CONSIDERATIONS

8 LEARNING OBJECTIVE
Identify tax planning opportunities to minimize the AMT.

RESPONDING TO BOB AND CAROL

The chapter began with a set of circumstances involving Bob and Carol that raised a number of interesting questions. By now, the student should have arrived at a logical reason for the difference in Bob and Carol's tax liabilities and expect the following to happen to Bob.

Bob contacts Adam, his tax return preparer, and explains in an excited voice that he has received a bill from the IRS for $15,000 plus interest associated with the underpayment of his tax liability. Adam has Bob fax him a copy of the IRS deficiency notice. He checks Bob's tax file and then calls Bob to explain that Bob does owe the IRS the $15,000 plus interest. Somehow Bob's tax return was prepared without including a Form 6251 (the alternative minimum tax). Adam suggests that Bob stop by his office later that afternoon to discuss the disposition of the matter further.

AVOIDING PREFERENCES AND ADJUSTMENTS

Several strategies and elections are available to help taxpayers avoid having preferences and adjustments.

- A taxpayer who is in danger of incurring AMT liability should not invest in tax-exempt private activity bonds unless doing so makes good investment sense. Any AMT triggered by interest on private activity bonds reduces the yield on an investment in the bonds. Other tax-exempt bonds or taxable corporate bonds might yield a better after-tax return.
- A taxpayer may elect to expense certain costs in the year incurred or to capitalize and amortize the costs over some specified period. The decision should be based on the present discounted value of after-tax cash flows under the available alternatives. Costs subject to elective treatment include

circulation expenditures, mining exploration and development costs, and research and experimental expenditures.

CONTROLLING THE TIMING OF PREFERENCES AND ADJUSTMENTS

The AMT exemption often keeps items of tax preference from being subject to the AMT. To use the AMT exemption effectively, taxpayers should avoid bunching preferences and positive adjustments in any one year. To avoid this bunching, taxpayers should attempt to control the timing of such items when possible.

TAKING ADVANTAGE OF THE AMT/REGULAR TAX RATE DIFFERENTIAL

A taxpayer who cannot avoid triggering the AMT in a given year can usually save taxes by taking advantage of the rate differential between the AMT and the regular income tax.

EXAMPLE 37

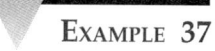

Peter, a real estate dealer who expects to be in the 31% tax bracket in 1997, is subject to the AMT in 1996. He is considering the sale of a parcel of land (inventory) at a gain of $100,000. If he sells the land in 1997, he will have to pay tax of $31,000 ($100,000 gain × regular income tax rate). However, if he sells the land in 1996, he will pay tax of $26,000 ($100,000 gain × 26% AMT rate). Thus, accelerating the sale into 1996 will save Peter $5,000 in tax. ▼

EXAMPLE 38

Cora, who expects to be in the 39.6% tax bracket in 1997, is subject to the AMT in 1996. She is going to contribute $10,000 in cash to her alma mater, State University. If Cora makes the contribution in 1997, she will save tax of $3,960 ($10,000 contribution × 39.6% regular income tax rate). However, if she makes the contribution in 1996, she will save tax of $2,600 ($10,000 contribution × 26% AMT rate). Thus, deferring the contribution until 1997 will save Cora $1,360 in tax. ▼

This deferral/acceleration strategy should be considered for any income or expenses where the taxpayer can control the timing. This strategy applies to corporations as well as to individuals.

KEY TERMS

ACE adjustment, 12–28

Alternative minimum tax (AMT), 12–2

Alternative minimum tax credit, 12–26

Alternative tax NOL deduction (ATNOLD), 12–15

AMT adjustments, 12–4

AMT exclusions, 12–26

Circulation expenditures, 12–4

Incentive stock options (ISOs), 12–12

Private activity bonds, 12–21

Tax preferences, 12–4

PROBLEM MATERIALS

DISCUSSION QUESTIONS

1. Since there is a regular income tax, why is there a need for an AMT?
2. How can the AMT be calculated without using taxable income from the regular income tax as the starting point?
3. What is the difference between AMT adjustments and tax preferences?
4. Identify which of the following are tax preferences:
   a. Fifty percent exclusion associated with gains on the sale of certain small business stock.
   b. Exclusion on the receipt of property by gift.
   c. Exclusion associated with payment of premiums by the employer on group term life insurance for coverage not in excess of $50,000.
   d. Percentage depletion in excess of the property's adjusted basis.
   e. Tax-exempt interest on certain private activity bonds.
5. Identify which of the following are tax preferences:
   a. Exclusion on the receipt of property by inheritance.
   b. Exclusion to employee on the employer's contribution to the employee's pension plan.
   c. Excess of deduction for circulation expenditures for regular income tax purposes over the deduction for AMT purposes.
   d. Excess of amortization allowance over depreciation on pre-1987 certified pollution control facilities.
   e. Excess of accelerated over straight-line depreciation on real property placed in service before 1987.
6. Describe the tax formula for the AMT.
7. Discuss the relationship between the regular income tax liability and the AMT.
8. For the exemption amount, indicate the following:
   a. Purpose for the exemption.
   b. Amount of the exemption.
   c. Reason for the phase-out of the exemption.
9. What are the AMT rates for an individual taxpayer? To what levels of income do the rates apply?
10. How do nonrefundable tax credits affect the calculation of the AMT?
11. Tom, who owns and operates a sole proprietorship, acquired machinery and placed it in service in February 1996. If Tom has to pay AMT in 1996, will he be required to make an AMT adjustment for depreciation on the machinery? Explain.
12. How can an individual taxpayer avoid having an AMT adjustment for mining exploration and development costs?
13. Rick, who is single, incurs mining exploration and development costs associated with his energy company. He would expense the costs in the current year in order to reduce his regular income tax, but is aware that this would create a positive adjustment for AMT purposes. His AGI is large enough to reduce the AMT exemption amount to zero. Therefore, he is considering electing to amortize the mining exploration and development costs over 10 years to avoid having to pay any AMT. Advise Rick.
14. Certain taxpayers have the option of using either the percentage of completion method or the completed contract method for reporting profit on long-term contracts. What impact could the AMT have on this decision?
15. Megan, a corporate executive, plans to exercise an incentive stock option granted by her employer to purchase 100 shares of the corporation's stock for an option price of $20 per share. The stock is currently selling for $65 per share.

a. Explain the possible consequences of this action on Megan's regular income tax and AMT.

b. Would your response differ if Megan exercises the option and disposes of the stock in the same tax year?

16. Desiree purchased a building several years ago for $100,000. She sells the building in the current tax year. Explain why her recognized gain or loss for regular income tax purposes is different from her recognized gain or loss for AMT purposes.

17. Carol is going to be subject to the AMT. She owns investment land and is considering disposing of it before the end of 1996 and investing in other realty. Based on an appraisal of the land's value, the realized gain would be $20,000. Ed has offered to purchase the land from Carol, and Abby has offered to trade her other realty that would qualify for § 1031 like-kind exchange treatment. The land has a $25,000 greater AMT adjusted basis. What are the relevant tax issues that Carol faces in making her decision?

18. Passive activity losses are not deductible in computing either taxable income or AMTI. Explain why an adjustment for passive activity losses may be required for AMT purposes.

19. What effect do adjustments and preferences have on the calculation of the ATNOLD?

20. The following itemized deductions are allowed for regular income tax purposes: medical expenses, state and local income taxes, real estate taxes, personal property taxes, home mortgage interest, investment interest, charitable contributions of cash, charitable contributions of long-term capital gain property, casualty losses, unreimbursed employee business expenses, and gambling losses. Which of these itemized deductions can result in an AMT adjustment?

21. Matt, who is single, has always elected to itemize deductions rather than take the standard deduction. In prior years, his itemized deductions always exceeded the standard deduction by a substantial amount. As a result of paying off the mortgage on his residence, he projects that his itemized deductions for 1996 will exceed the standard deduction by only $500. Matt anticipates that the amount of his itemized deductions will remain about the same in the foreseeable future. Matt's AGI is $150,000. He is investing the amount of his former mortgage payment each month in tax-exempt bonds. A friend recommends that Matt buy a beach house in order to increase his itemized deductions. What are the relevant tax issues for Matt?

22. In computing the alternative tax itemized deduction for interest, it is possible that some interest allowed as an itemized deduction for regular income tax purposes will not be allowed. Explain.

23. Could computation of the AMT ever require an adjustment for the standard deduction or personal and dependency exemptions? Explain.

24. Alvin owns a mineral deposit that qualifies for the 15% percentage depletion rate. Under what circumstances will the depletion deduction for regular income tax purposes and AMT purposes not be the same?

25. During the year, Fran earned $18,000 interest on private activity bonds and incurred interest expense of $7,000 in connection with the bonds. How will this affect Fran's taxable income? AMT?

26. What is the purpose of the AMT credit? Briefly describe how the credit is computed.

27. Discuss the similarities and differences between the individual AMT and the corporate AMT.

28. Some observers believe the ACE adjustment will cause corporations to change some of the methods they use for financial accounting and tax accounting purposes. Comment.

29. Is it ever advisable for a taxpayer to accelerate income into an AMT year? Explain and give an example of how this acceleration might be accomplished.

30. Is it ever advisable for a taxpayer to defer deductions from an AMT year into a non-AMT year where the regular income tax applies? Explain and give an example of how such a deferral might be accomplished.

PROBLEMS

31. Use the following data to calculate Rachel's AMT base:

Taxable income	$200,000
Positive AMT adjustments	40,000
Negative AMT adjustments	30,000
AMT preferences	15,000

Rachel is not married.

32. Arthur East, an unmarried individual who is age 66, has taxable income of $100,000. He has AMT positive adjustments of $60,000 and tax preferences of $40,000.
    a. What is Arthur's AMT?
    b. What is the total amount of Arthur's tax liability?
    c. Draft a letter to Arthur explaining why he must pay more than the regular income tax liability. Arthur's address is 100 Colonel's Way, Conway, SC 29526.

33. Calculate the AMT for the following cases. The taxpayer has regular taxable income of $500,000 and does not have any credits.

	Tentative AMT	
Filing Status	**Case 1**	**Case 2**
Single	$190,000	$175,000
Married, filing jointly	190,000	175,000

34. Calculate the exemption amount for the following cases for a single taxpayer, a married taxpayer filing jointly, and a married taxpayer filing separately.

Case	AMTI
1	$100,000
2	200,000
3	400,000

35. Leona has nonrefundable credits of $25,000 for 1996. Her regular income tax liability before credits is $35,000, and her tentative AMT is $15,000.
    a. What is the amount of Leona's AMT?
    b. What is the amount of Leona's regular income tax liability after credits?

36. Angela, who is single, incurs circulation expenditures of $123,000 during 1996. She is in the process of deciding whether to expense the $123,000 or to capitalize it and elect to deduct it over a three-year period. Angela already knows that she will be subject to the AMT for 1996 at the 28% rate. Angela is in the 31% bracket for regular income tax purposes this year and expects to remain in that bracket in the future. Advise Angela on whether she should elect the three-year write-off rather than expensing the $123,000 in 1996.

37. Vito owns and operates a news agency (as a sole proprietorship). During 1996, he incurred expenses of $60,000 to increase circulation of newspapers and magazines that his agency distributes. For regular income tax purposes, he elected to expense the $60,000 in 1996. In addition, he incurred $30,000 in circulation expenditures in 1997 and again elected expense treatment. What AMT adjustments will be required in 1996 and 1997 as a result of the circulation expenditures?

38. Lance is a landlord who owns two apartment buildings. He acquired Longwood Acres on February 21, 1986, for $300,000, with $60,000 of the cost allocated to the land. He acquired Colony Square on April 5, 1992, for $800,000, and $200,000 of the cost was allocated to land. Neither apartment complex is low-income housing. Lance elected to write off the cost of each building as fast as possible. What is the effect of depreciation (cost recovery) on Lance's AMTI for 1996?

39. In March 1996, Helen Carlon acquired equipment for her business at a cost of $140,000. The equipment is 5-year class property for regular income tax purposes and 9.5-year class property for AMT purposes.
    a. If Helen depreciates the equipment using the method that will produce the greatest deduction for 1996, what is the amount of the AMT adjustment?
    b. How can Helen reduce the AMT adjustment to $0? What circumstances would motivate her to do so?
    c. Draft a letter to Helen regarding the choice of depreciation methods. Helen's address is 500 Monticello Avenue, Glendale, AZ 85306.

40. In 1996, Gary incurred $180,000 of mining and exploration expenditures. He elects to deduct the expenditures as quickly as the tax law allows for regular income tax purposes.
    a. How will Gary's treatment of mining and exploration expenditures affect his regular income tax and AMT computations for 1996?
    b. How can Gary avoid having AMT adjustments related to the mining and exploration expenditures?
    c. What factors should Gary consider in deciding whether to deduct the expenditures in the year incurred?

41. Rust Company is a real estate construction company with average annual gross receipts of $3 million. Rust uses the completed contract method on a contract that requires 18 months to complete. The contract is for $500,000 with estimated costs of $300,000. At the end of 1996, $180,000 of costs have been incurred. The contract is completed in 1997 with the total costs being $295,000. Determine the amount of adjustments for AMT purposes for 1996 and 1997.

42. In 1994, Diego exercised an incentive stock option, acquiring 1,000 shares of stock at an option price of $65 per share. The fair market value of the stock at the date of exercise was $92 per share. In 1996, the rights in the stock become freely transferable and are not subject to a substantial risk of forfeiture. Diego sells the 1,000 shares of stock in 1997 for $100 per share. How do these transactions affect Diego's AMTI in 1994, 1996 and 1997?

43. In 1996, Lori exercised an incentive stock option that had been granted by her employer, Black Corporation. Lori acquired 100 shares of Black stock for the option price of $175 per share. The rights in the stock become freely transferable and not subject to a substantial risk of forfeiture in 1996. The fair market value of the stock at the date of exercise was $210 per share. Lori sells the stock for $320 per share in 1996. What is the amount of her AMT adjustment in 1996, and what is her recognized gain on the sale for regular income tax purposes and AMT purposes?

44. Bobby sells an apartment building for $400,000. His adjusted basis is $250,000 for regular income tax purposes and $312,000 for AMT purposes.
    a. Calculate Bobby's gain for regular income tax purposes.
    b. Calculate Bobby's gain for AMT purposes.
    c. Calculate Bobby's AMT adjustment, if any.

45. Freda acquired a passive activity in 1996. Gross income from operations of the activity was $150,000. Operating expenses, not including depreciation, were $135,000. Regular income tax depreciation of $37,500 was computed under MACRS. AMT depreciation, computed under ADS, was $24,000. Compute Freda's passive loss deduction and passive loss suspended for regular income tax purposes and for AMT purposes.

46. Wolfgang had the following itemized deductions for 1996:

Medical expenses [$5,000 – (7.5% × $50,000)]	$ 1,250
State income taxes	3,000
Charitable contributions	5,000
Home mortgage interest on his personal residence	6,000
Casualty loss	1,500
Miscellaneous itemized deductions [$3,500 – 2%($50,000)]	2,500
	$19,250

a. Calculate Wolfgang's itemized deductions for AMT purposes.
b. What is the amount of the AMT adjustment?

47. Tom, who is single, owns a personal residence in the city. He also owns a cabin near a ski resort in the mountains. He uses the cabin as a vacation home. In February 1996, he borrowed $60,000 on a home equity loan and used the proceeds to pay off credit card obligations and other debt. During 1996, he paid the following amounts of interest:

On his personal residence	$12,000
On the cabin	4,800
On the home equity loan	5,000
On credit card obligations	1,200

What amount, if any, must Tom recognize as an AMT adjustment in 1996?

48. Walter and Edith, who are married with two dependents, had AGI of $110,000 in 1996. Their AGI included net investment income of $10,000 and gambling income of $2,500. They incurred the following expenses during the year, all of which resulted in itemized deductions for income tax purposes:

Medical expenses (before 7.5%-of-AGI floor)	$9,500
State income taxes	2,800
Personal property tax	900
Real estate tax	9,100
Interest on personal residence	8,600
Interest on home equity loan (proceeds were used to buy a new fishing boat)	1,800
Investment interest expense	2,600
Charitable contribution (cash)	4,200
Unreimbursed employee expenses (before 2%-of-AGI floor)	3,800

What is the amount of Walter and Edith's AMT adjustment for itemized deductions in 1996, and is it positive or negative?

49. Assume the same facts as in the preceding problem and that Walter and Edith also earned interest of $5,000 on private activity bonds. They borrowed the money to buy these bonds and paid interest of $3,900 on the loan. Determine the effect on AMTI.

50. During the current year, Yoon earned $10,000 in dividends on corporate stock and incurred $13,000 of investment interest expense related to his stock holdings. Yoon also earned $5,000 interest on private activity bonds during the year and incurred interest expense of $3,500 in connection with the bonds. How much investment interest expense can Yoon deduct for regular income tax and AMT purposes for the year?

51. Bill, who is single with no dependents, had AGI of $100,000 in 1996. His AGI included net investment income of $15,000 and gambling income of $1,100. Bill incurred the following expenses during the year, all of which resulted in itemized deductions for income tax purposes:

Medical expenses (before 7.5%-of-AGI floor)	$11,000
State income taxes	3,200
Personal property tax	2,000
Real estate tax	8,400
Interest on personal residence	12,200
Interest on vacation home (never rented to others)	3,800
Interest on home equity loan (proceeds were used to buy a new automobile)	2,700
Investment interest expense	3,300
Charitable contribution	5,000
Casualty loss (after $100 floor, before 10%-of-AGI floor)	13,000
Unreimbursed employee expenses (before 2%-of-AGI floor)	2,400
Gambling losses	900

What is the amount of Bill's AMT adjustment for itemized deductions in 1996, and is it positive or negative?

52. Peggy, who is single and has no dependents, had taxable income of $102,000 and tax preferences of $72,500 in 1996. She did not itemize deductions for regular income tax purposes. Compute Peggy's AMT exemption and AMTI for 1996.

53. Carl, who is single, has no dependents and does not itemize deductions. He had a personal exemption of $2,550 and taxable income of $82,000 in 1996. His tax preferences totaled $118,000. What is Carl's AMTI for 1996?

54. Emily owns a coal mine that had a basis of $12,000 at the beginning of the year. The property qualifies for a 15% depletion rate. Gross income from the property was $140,000, and net income before the percentage depletion deduction was $60,000. What is Emily's tax preference for excess depletion?

55. Rita incurred and expensed intangible drilling costs (IDC) of $70,000. Her net oil and gas income was $60,000. What is the amount of Rita's tax preference item for IDC?

56. Pat, who is single and has no dependents, had a salary of $90,000 in 1996. She had interest and dividend income of $6,000, gambling income of $4,000, and $40,000 interest income from private activity bonds. Pat presents the following additional information:

Medical expenses (before 7.5%-of-AGI floor)	$12,000
State income taxes	4,100
Real estate taxes	2,800
Mortgage interest on residence	3,100
Investment interest expense	1,800
Gambling losses	5,100

Compute Pat's tentative minimum tax for 1996 (rounded to the nearest dollar).

57. Jack, who is single with no dependents and does not itemize, provides you with the following information for 1996:

Short-term capital loss	$ 5,000
Long-term capital gain	25,000
Municipal bond interest received on private activity bonds acquired in 1990	9,000
Dividends from General Motors	1,500
Excess of FMV over cost of incentive stock options (the rights became freely transferable and not subject to a substantial risk of forfeiture in 1996)	35,000

What is the total amount of Jack's tax preference items and AMT adjustments for 1996?

58. Rosa, who is single, had taxable income of $100,000 for 1996. She had positive AMT adjustments of $50,000, negative AMT adjustments of $15,000, and tax preference items of $57,500.

a. Compute her AMTI.
b. Compute Rosa's tentative minimum tax.

59. Tara, who is single, has no dependents and does not itemize. She has the following items relative to her tax return for 1996:

Bargain element from the exercise of an incentive stock option (no restrictions apply to the stock)	$ 45,000
Accelerated depreciation on leased equipment acquired before 1987 (straight-line depreciation would have yielded $26,000)	41,000
Percentage depletion in excess of property's adjusted basis	50,000
Taxable income for regular income tax purposes	121,000

a. Determine Tara's AMT adjustments and preferences for 1996.
b. Calculate the AMT (if any) for 1996.

60. Beth, who is single, has the following items for 1996:

Income	
Salary	$105,000
Interest from bank	12,000
Interest on corporate bonds	7,000
Dividends	6,000
Short-term capital gain	8,000
Expenses	
Unreimbursed employee business expenses (no meals or entertainment)	4,000
Total medical expenses	24,000
State income taxes	6,500
Real property taxes	6,800
Home mortgage (qualified housing) interest	7,200
Casualty loss on vacation home	
Decline in value	20,000
Adjusted basis	70,000
Insurance proceeds	12,000
Tax preferences	116,000

Compute Beth's tax liability for 1996 before credits or prepayments.

61. Lynn is single and has no dependents. Based on the financial information presented below, compute Lynn's AMT for 1996.

Income:	
Salary	$33,000
Taxable interest on corporate bonds	1,800
Dividend income	1,900
Business income	64,000
Expenditures:	
Medical expenses	$12,000
State income taxes	6,000
Real estate taxes	8,500
Mortgage (qualified housing) interest	9,200
Investment interest	5,500
Cash contributions to various charities	2,900

Additional information:

a. The $64,000 business income is from Acme Office Supplies Company, a sole proprietorship Lynn owns and operates. Acme claimed MACRS depreciation of $3,175 on real property used in the business. ADS depreciation on the property would have been $2,500.

b. Lynn received interest of $30,000 on City of Columbus private activity bonds.

62. Bonnie, who is single, had taxable income of $0 in 1996. She has positive timing adjustments of $200,000 and AMT exclusion items of $100,000 for the year. What is the amount of Bonnie's AMT credit for carryover to 1997?

63. Browne Corporation, a calendar year taxpayer, has AMTI (before the ACE adjustment) of $600,000 for 1996. Browne's ACE is $1,500,000. What is Browne's tentative minimum tax for 1996?

64. Gray Corporation (a calendar year corporation) reports the following information for the years listed below:

	1995	1996	1997
Unadjusted AMTI	$3,000	$2,000	$5,000
Adjusted current earnings	4,000	3,000	2,000

Compute the ACE adjustment for each year.

65. In each of the following independent situations, determine the tentative AMT:

	AMTI (Before the Exemption Amount)
Quincy Corporation	$150,000
Redland Corporation	160,000
Tanzen Corporation	320,000

66. For 1996, Brown Corporation (a calendar year taxpayer) had the following transactions:

Taxable income	$100,000
Depreciation for regular income tax purposes on realty in excess of ADS (placed in service in 1989)	150,000
Excess amortization of certified pollution control facilities	10,000
Tax-exempt interest on municipal bonds (funds were used for nongovernmental purposes)	30,000
Percentage depletion in excess of the property's adjusted basis	60,000

a. Determine Brown Corporation's AMTI for 1996.
b. Determine the AMT base (refer to Figure 12–3).
c. Determine the tentative minimum tax.
d. What is the amount of the AMT?

CUMULATIVE PROBLEMS

67. Ron, age 38, is divorced and has no dependents. He pays alimony of $20,000 per year to his former wife, Kate. Ron's Social Security number is 444–11–2222, and Kate's is 555–67–2222. Ron's address is 201 Front Street, Missoula, MT 59812. He is independently wealthy as a result of having inherited sizable holdings in real estate and corporate stocks and bonds. Ron is a minister at First Methodist Church, but he accepts no salary from the church. However, he does reside in the church's parsonage free of charge. The rental value of the parsonage is $400 a month. The church also provides him a cash grocery allowance of $100 a week. Examination of Ron's financial records provides the following information for 1996:

a. On January 16, 1996, Ron sold 2,000 shares of stock for a gain of $40,000. The stock was acquired four months ago.

b. He received $60,000 of interest on private activity bonds in 1996.
c. He received gross rent income of $145,000 from an apartment complex he owns and manages.
d. Expenses related to the apartment complex, which he acquired in 1983, were $230,000.
e. Ron's dividend and interest income (on a savings account) totaled $26,000.
f. On October 9, 1994, Ron exercised his rights under Egret Corporation's incentive stock option plan. For an option price of $20,000, he acquired stock worth $45,000. The stock became freely transferable in 1996.
g. Ron had the following potential itemized deductions *from* AGI:

- $3,000 fair market value of stock contributed to Methodist church (basis of stock was $1,000). He owned the stock for five years.
- $3,000 interest on consumer purchases.
- $1,600 state and local taxes.
- $7,000 medical expenses (before 7.5% floor).

Compute Ron's tax liability, including AMT if applicable, before prepayments or credits, for 1996.

68. Robert M. and Jane R. Armstrong live at 1802 College Avenue, Carmel, IN 46302. They are married and file a joint return for 1995. The Armstrongs have two dependent children, Ellen J. and Sean M., who are 10-year-old twins. Ellen's Social Security number is 333–42–3368, and Sean's is 333–42–3369.

Robert (224–36–9987) is a factory foreman, and Jane (443–56–3421) is a computer systems analyst. The Armstrongs' W–2 forms for 1995 reflect the following information:

	Robert	Jane
Salary (Indiana Foundry, Inc.)	$55,000	
Salary (Carmel Computer Associates)		$74,000
Federal income tax withheld	6,600	13,600
Social Security wages	55,000	61,200
Social Security withheld	3,410	3,795
Medicare wages	55,000	74,000
Medicare tax withheld	798	1,073
State wages	55,000	74,000
State income tax withheld	1,650	2,220

In addition to their salaries, the Armstrongs had the following income items in 1995:

Interest income (Carmel Sanitation District Bonds)	$14,500
Interest income (Carmel National Bank)	1,000
Dividend income (Able Computer Corporation)	2,500
Gambling income	2,000

Jane inherited $200,000 from her grandfather in January and invested the money in the Carmel Sanitation District Bonds, which are private activity bonds.

The Armstrongs incurred the following expenses during 1995:

Medical expenses (doctor and hospital bills)	$17,000
Real property tax on personal residence	4,500
Mortgage interest on personal residence (reported on Form 1098)	4,000
Investment interest expense	1,900
Contributions to Salvation Army	20,000
Gambling losses	1,750

On March 1, Robert and Jane contributed Ace stock to the Carmel Salvation Army, a public charity. They had acquired the stock on February 9, 1979, for $1,500. The stock was listed on the New York Stock Exchange at a value of $20,000 on the date of the contribution.

Robert received a gift of 25 acres of land from his Uncle Sam on May 15. The appraised value of the land at the date of the gift was $63,000, and Uncle Sam's adjusted basis was $10,000. Uncle Sam was not required to pay any gift tax.

Use Forms 1040, 4952, 6251, and 8283 and Schedules A and B to compute the AMT for Robert and Jane Armstrong for 1995. Suggested software (if available): *TurboTax* or *MacInTax*. Write a letter to the Armstrongs indicating whether they have a refund or balance due for 1995, and suggest possible tax planning strategies for 1996.

RESEARCH PROBLEMS

Note: ***West's Federal Taxation on CD-ROM*** *can be used in preparing solutions to the Research Problems. Alternatively, tax research materials contained in a standard tax library can be used.*

Research Problem 1. Tony is a full-time gambler whose only source of income is money that he wins from his gambling activities. The IRS contends that Tony's gambling losses should be treated as itemized deductions for purposes of computing the AMT. Tony argues that the gambling losses should be treated as trade or business expenses. Write a letter to Tony that contains your advice on the classification of the gambling losses. Also prepare a memo for the tax files. Tony's address is 200 Cole Lane, Wichita Falls, TX 76308.

Research Problem 2. Carol owns two warehouses that were placed in service before 1987. Accelerated depreciation for 1996 on Warehouse A was $12,000, and straight-line depreciation would have been $8,000. On Warehouse B, accelerated depreciation was $6,000, and straight-line depreciation would have been $7,500. What was the amount of Carol's tax preference for excess depreciation in 1996?

Research Problem 3. Stuart is a journalist for a metropolitan newspaper. He has a degree in journalism from a major midwestern university.

For the past 10 years, Stuart has prepared his own income tax return. He finds doing so to be challenging and stimulating and believes that he pays lower taxes than he would if he hired a tax return preparer.

His 1995 return is audited. Although it included an AMT form (Form 6251), Stuart had not prepared it properly. Data from his Form 1040 were transferred to the wrong line in several places. In other cases, positive adjustments were not included because Stuart had failed to calculate them (e.g., did not recalculate itemized deductions for AMT purposes and did not have a positive adjustment for the personal exemption). Based on the IRS's calculation, a deficiency of $3,000 was assessed. Stuart's response to the IRS is that Form 6251 is ambiguous and misleading and, therefore, he should not be liable for the AMT. Evaluate Stuart's argument.

Partial list of research aids:
William M. Christine, 66 TCM 1025, T.C.Memo. 1993–473.

Research Problem 4. On his 1995 Federal income tax return, Walter deducted state income taxes of $8,000 for amounts withheld and estimated tax payments made in 1995. When he filed his 1995 state income tax return in April 1996, he discovered that he had overpaid his state income taxes by $1,500. Rather than having the $1,500 refunded to him, he treated it as a 1996 estimated tax payment. The year 1995 was not an AMT year for Walter.

In preparing his 1996 Federal income tax return, Walter is confused about how he should treat the $1,500 in calculating his Federal income tax liability. He knows that under the § 111 tax benefit rule, he should include the $1,500 in gross income in calculating his taxable income. However, since he is going to be subject to the AMT, he is uncertain as to how he should treat the $1,500 in calculating AMT. He thinks that the amount could be treated as a negative adjustment in converting taxable income to AMTI if 1995 had been an AMT year. Since it was not, Walter is unsure of the treatment.

Advise Walter on the appropriate treatment of the $1,500 in calculating his 1996 Federal income tax liability.

TEAM PROJECT: ARTHUR ANDERSEN TAX CHALLENGE CASES

For more information on the Arthur Andersen Tax Challenge Cases, please refer to Chapter 1, page 1-38.

Information related to tax issues and problems that are discussed in this chapter may be found in the

Miller case on pages 3, 19, 21, 39, 41

Read and analyze the case you have been assigned and *identify* any issues and problems that are related to material covered in this chapter. If the information provided in the case is complete, prepare answers for this part of the case at this time. If you need information that is contained in the later parts of the case, please write a memo summarizing the questions or problems so you can prepare a complete answer at a later date.

CHAPTER

13

Tax Credits and Payment Procedures

LEARNING OBJECTIVES

After completing Chapter 13, you should be able to:

1. Explain how tax credits are used as a tool of Federal tax policy.
2. Distinguish between refundable and nonrefundable credits and understand the order in which they can be used by taxpayers.
3. Describe various business-related tax credits.
4. Describe several other tax credits that are available primarily to individual taxpayers.
5. Understand the tax withholding and payment procedures applicable to employers.
6. Understand the payment procedures applicable to self-employed persons.
7. Identify tax planning opportunities related to tax credits and payment procedures.

OUTLINE

As explained in Chapter 1, Federal tax law often serves other purposes besides merely raising revenue for the government. Evidence of equity, social, and economic considerations, among others, is found throughout the tax law. These considerations also bear heavily in the area of **tax credits.** Consider the following examples:

EXAMPLE 1

Paul and Peggy, husband and wife, are both employed outside the home. Their combined salaries are $50,000. However, after paying for child care expenses of $2,000 on behalf of their daughter, Polly, the net economic benefit from both spouses working is $48,000. The child care expenses are, in a sense, business related in that they would not have been incurred if both spouses did not work outside the home. If no tax benefits are associated with the child care expenditures, $50,000 is subject to tax.

Another couple, Alicia and Diego, also have a child, John. Diego stays at home to care for John (the value of those services is $2,000) while Alicia earns a $48,000 salary. Because the value of Diego's services rendered is not subject to tax, only Alicia's earnings of $48,000 are subject to tax. ▼

The credit for child and dependent care expenses is allowed to mitigate the inequity felt by working taxpayers who must pay for child care services in order to work outside the home.

EXAMPLE 2

Olaf is a retired taxpayer who received $10,000 of Social Security benefits as his only source of income in 1996. His Social Security benefits are excluded from gross income. Therefore, Olaf's income tax is $0. In 1996, Olga, a single taxpayer 66 years of age, has, as her sole source of income, $10,000 from a pension plan funded by her former employer. Assuming Olga has no itemized deductions or deductions *for* AGI, her income tax for 1996 (before credits) is $368, based on the following computation:

Pension plan benefits	$10,000
Less: Basic standard deduction	(4,000)
Additional standard deduction	(1,000)
Personal exemption	(2,550)
Taxable income	$ 2,450
Income tax (at 15%)	$ 368

▼

The tax credit for elderly or disabled taxpayers was enacted to mitigate this inequity.

EXAMPLE 3

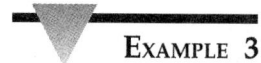

Jane is a single parent who depends on the government's "safety net" for survival—she receives Aid for Dependent Children in the amount of $10,000 per year. However, she very much wishes to work. Jane has located a job that will pay $10,500 per year and has found an individual to care for her child at no cost. But, with the $803.25 ($10,500 × 7.65%) payroll deduction for Social Security and Medicare taxes, the economic benefit from working is less than remaining reliant on the government ($9,696.75 as compared to $10,000). ▼

To help offset the effect of Social Security and Medicare taxes on wages of the working poor and to provide an incentive to work, the earned income credit is used to increase the after-tax earnings of qualified individuals. In addition, the earned income credit helps offset the regressive nature of certain taxes, such as the Social Security and Medicare taxes, which impose a relatively larger burden on low-income taxpayers than on more affluent taxpayers.

These three tax credits and many of the other important tax credits available to individuals and other types of taxpayers are a major focus of this chapter. The chapter begins by discussing important tax policy considerations relevant to tax credits. Tax credits are categorized as being either refundable or nonrefundable. The distinction between refundable and nonrefundable credits is important because it may affect the taxpayer's ability to enjoy a tax benefit from a particular credit.

Next an overview of the priority of tax credits is presented. The credit portion of the chapter continues with a discussion of the credits available to businesses and to individual taxpayers and the ways in which credits enter into the calculation of the tax liability.

The Federal tax system has long been based on the pay-as-you-go concept. That is, taxpayers or their employers are required to make regular deposits with the Federal government during the year as payment toward the tax liability that will be determined at the end of the tax year. These deposits are in effect refundable credits. In addition to presenting the procedures used in calculating these payments and the special problems self-employed persons encounter in estimating their payments, the penalties on underpayment are discussed.

TAX POLICY CONSIDERATIONS

1 LEARNING OBJECTIVE
Explain how tax credits are used as a tool of Federal tax policy.

Congress has generally used tax credits to achieve social or economic objectives or to provide equity for different types of taxpayers. For example, the disabled access credit, enacted in 1990, was intended to meet a social objective: to encourage taxpayers to renovate older buildings so they would be in compliance with the Americans with Disabilities Act. This Act requires businesses and institutions to make their facilities more accessible to persons with various types of disabilities. In another example, the foreign tax credit, which has been a part of the law for decades, has as its purpose the economic and equity objectives of mitigating the burden of multiple taxation of a single flow of income.

A tax credit should not be confused with an income tax deduction. Certain expenditures of individuals (e.g., business expenses) are permitted as deductions from gross income in arriving at adjusted gross income (AGI). Additionally, individuals are allowed to deduct certain nonbusiness and investment-related expenses *from* AGI. While the tax benefit received from a tax deduction depends on the tax rate, a tax credit is not affected by the tax rate of the taxpayer.

EXAMPLE 4

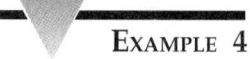

Assume Congress wishes to encourage a certain type of expenditure. One way to accomplish this objective is to allow a tax credit of 25% for such expenditures. Another way is to allow an itemized deduction for the expenditures. Assume Abby's tax rate is 15%, while Bill's tax rate is 39.6%. In addition, assume that Carmen does not incur enough qualifying expenditures to itemize deductions. The following tax benefits are available to each taxpayer for a $1,000 expenditure:

	Abby	Bill	Carmen
Tax benefit if a 25% credit is allowed	$250	$250	$250
Tax benefit if an itemized deduction is allowed	150	396	–0–

As these results indicate, tax credits provide benefits on a more equitable basis than do tax deductions. Equally apparent is that the deduction approach in this case benefits only taxpayers who itemize deductions, while the credit approach benefits all taxpayers who make the specified expenditure. ▼

For many years, Congress has used the tax credit provisions of the Code liberally in implementing tax policy. Although budget constraints and economic considerations often have dictated the repeal of some credits, other credits, such as those applicable to expenses incurred for child and dependent care, have been kept to respond to important social policy considerations. Other credits, such as the one available to low-income workers, have been retained based on economic and equity considerations. Finally, as the myriad of tax proposals that are always before Congress make clear, the use of tax credits as a tax policy tool continues to evolve as economic and political circumstances change.

OVERVIEW AND PRIORITY OF CREDITS

2 LEARNING OBJECTIVE
Distinguish between refundable and nonrefundable credits and understand the order in which they can be used by taxpayers.

REFUNDABLE VERSUS NONREFUNDABLE CREDITS

As illustrated in Exhibit 13–1, certain credits are refundable while others are nonrefundable. **Refundable credits** are paid to the taxpayer even if the amount of the credit (or credits) exceeds the taxpayer's tax liability.

EXAMPLE 5

Ted, who is single, had taxable income of $21,000 in 1996. His income tax from the 1996 Tax Rate Schedule is $3,150. During 1996, Ted's employer withheld income tax of $3,500. Ted is entitled to a refund of $350 because the credit for tax withheld on wages is a refundable credit. ▼

Nonrefundable credits are not paid if they exceed the taxpayer's tax liability.

EXAMPLE 6

Tina is single, age 67, and retired. Her taxable income for 1996 is $1,320, and the tax on this amount is $198. Tina's tax credit for the elderly is $225. This credit can be used to reduce her net tax liability to zero, but it will not result in a refund, even though the credit ($225) exceeds Tina's tax liability ($198). This result occurs because the tax credit for the elderly is a nonrefundable credit. ▼

Some nonrefundable credits, such as the foreign tax credit, are subject to carryover provisions if they exceed the amount allowable as a credit in a given year. Other nonrefundable credits, such as the tax credit for the elderly (refer to

▼ EXHIBIT 13–1
Partial Listing of Refundable and Nonrefundable Credits

Refundable Credits

Taxes withheld on wages
Earned income credit

Nonrefundable Credits

Credit for child and dependent care expenses
Credit for the elderly or disabled
Foreign tax credit
General business credit, which is the sum of the following:

- Tax credit for rehabilitation expenditures
- Business energy credits
- Research activities credit*
- Low-income housing credit
- Disabled access credit

*Not available after June 30, 1995.

Example 6), are not subject to carryover provisions and are lost if they exceed the limitations. Because some credits are subject to carryover provisions while others are not, the order in which credits are offset against the tax liability is important. The Code provides that nonrefundable credits are to be offset against a taxpayer's income tax liability in the order shown in Exhibit 13–1.

GENERAL BUSINESS CREDIT

As shown in Exhibit 13–1, the **general business credit** is comprised of a number of other credits, each of which is computed separately under its own set of rules. The general business credit combines these credits into one amount to limit the amount of business credits that can be used to offset a taxpayer's income tax liability. The idea behind combining the credits is to prevent a taxpayer from completely avoiding his or her income tax liability in any one year by offsetting it with business credits that would otherwise be available.

Two special rules apply to the general business credit. First, any unused credit must be carried back 3 years, then forward 15 years. Second, for any tax year, the general business credit is limited to the taxpayer's *net income tax* reduced by the greater of:[1]

- The *tentative minimum tax.*
- 25 percent of *net regular tax liability* that exceeds $25,000.[2]

In order to understand the general business credit limitation, several terms need defining:

[1] § 38(c).

[2] This amount is $12,500 for married taxpayers filing separately unless one of the spouses is not entitled to the general business credit.

- *Net income tax* is the sum of the regular tax liability and the alternative minimum tax reduced by certain nonrefundable tax credits.
- *Tentative minimum tax* for this purpose is reduced by the foreign tax credit allowed.
- *Regular tax liability* is determined from the appropriate tax table or tax rate schedule, based on taxable income. However, the regular tax liability does not include certain taxes (e.g., alternative minimum tax).
- *Net regular tax liability* is the regular tax liability reduced by certain nonrefundable credits (e.g., credit for child and dependent care expenses, foreign tax credit).

EXAMPLE 7

Floyd's general business credit for the current year is $70,000. His net income tax is $150,000, tentative minimum tax is $130,000, and net regular tax liability is $150,000. He has no other tax credits. Floyd's general business credit allowed for the tax year is computed as follows:

Net income tax	$ 150,000
Less: The greater of	
• $130,000 (tentative minimum tax)	
• $31,250 [25% × ($150,000 – $25,000)]	(130,000)
Amount of general business credit allowed for tax year	$ 20,000

Floyd then has $50,000 ($70,000 – $20,000) of unused general business credits that may be carried back or forward as discussed below. ▼

TREATMENT OF UNUSED GENERAL BUSINESS CREDITS

Unused general business credits are initially carried back three years (to the earliest year in the sequence first) and are applied to reduce the tax liability during these years. Thus, the taxpayer may receive a tax refund as a result of the carryback. Any remaining unused credits are then carried forward 15 years.[3]

A FIFO method is applied to the carryovers, carrybacks, and utilization of credits earned during a particular year. The oldest credits are used first in determining the amount of the general business credit. The FIFO method minimizes the potential for loss of a general business credit benefit due to the expiration of credit carryovers, since the earliest years are used before the current credit for the taxable year.

EXAMPLE 8

This example illustrates the use of general business credit carryovers.

General business credit carryovers		
1993	$ 4,000	
1994	6,000	
1995	2,000	
Total carryovers	$12,000	
1996 general business credit		$40,000
Total credit allowed in 1996 (based on tax liability)	$50,000	
Less: Utilization of carryovers		
1993	(4,000)	

[3] § 39(a)(1).

1994	(6,000)	
1995	(2,000)	
Remaining credit allowed	$38,000	
Applied against		
1996 general business credit		(38,000)
1996 unused amount carried forward to 1997		$ 2,000

▼

Specific Business-Related Tax Credit Provisions

3 **Learning Objective**
Describe various business-related tax credits.

Each component of the general business credit is determined separately under its own set of rules. The components are explained here in the order listed in Exhibit 13–1.

TAX CREDIT FOR REHABILITATION EXPENDITURES

Taxpayers are allowed a tax credit for expenditures incurred to rehabilitate industrial and commercial buildings and certified historic structures. The **rehabilitation expenditures credit** is intended to discourage businesses from moving from older, economically distressed areas (e.g., inner city) to newer locations and to encourage the preservation of historic structures. The current operating features of this credit follow:[4]

Rate of the Credit for Rehabilitation Expenses	Nature of the Property
10%	Nonresidential buildings and residential rental propert other than certified historic structures, originally placed in service before 1936
20%	Nonresidential and residential certified historic structures

When taking the credit, the basis of a rehabilitated building must be red by the full rehabilitation credit allowed.[5]

Example 9

Juan spent $60,000 to rehabilitate a building (adjusted basis of $40,000) that had ori been placed in service in 1932. He is allowed a credit of $6,000 (10% × $60,0 rehabilitation expenditures. Juan then increases the basis of the building by $54,000 (rehabilitation expenditures) – $6,000 (credit allowed)]. If the building were a structure, the credit allowed would be $12,000 (20% × $60,000), and the b depreciable basis would increase by $48,000 [$60,000 (rehabilitation expenditures) (credit allowed)]. ▼

To qualify for the credit, buildings must be substantially rehab building has been *substantially rehabilitated* if qualified rehabilitation ex exceed the greater of:

[4] § 47.

[5] § 50(c).

- The adjusted basis of the property before the rehabilitation expenc
- $5,000.

Qualified rehabilitation expenditures do not include the cost of acqu building, the cost of facilities related to a building (such as a parking lot), a cost of enlarging an existing building. Stringent rules apply concerning retention of internal and external walls.

Recapture of Tax Credit for Rehabilitation Expenditures. The rehabilit tion credit taken must be recaptured if the rehabilitated property is disposed o prematurely or if it ceases to be qualifying property. The **rehabilitation expenditures credit recapture** is based on a holding period requirement of five years and is added to the taxpayer's regular tax liability in the recapture year. In addition, the recapture amount is *added* to the adjusted basis of the rehabilitation expenditures for purposes of determining the amount of gain or loss realized on the property's disposition.

The portion of the credit recaptured is a specified percentage of the credit that was taken by the taxpayer. This percentage is based on the period the property was held by the taxpayer, as shown in Table 13–1.

EXAMPLE 10

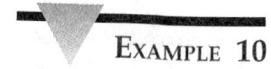

On March 15, 1993, Rashad placed in service $30,000 of rehabilitation expenditures on a building qualifying for the 10% credit. A credit of $3,000 ($30,000 × 10%) was allowed, and the basis of the building was increased by $27,000 ($30,000 – $3,000). The building was sold on December 15, 1996. Rashad must recapture a portion of the rehabilitation credit based on the schedule in Table 13–1. Because he held the rehabilitated property for more than three years but less than four, 40% of the credit, or $1,200, must be added to his 1996 tax liability. Also, the adjusted basis of the rehabilitation expenditures is increased by the $1,200 recapture amount. ▼

▼ **TABLE 13–1**
Recapture Calculation for Rehabilitation Expenditures Credit

If the Property Is Held for	The Recapture Percentage Is
Less than 1 year	100
One year or more but less than 2 years	80
Two years or more but less than 3 years	60
Three years or more but less than 4 years	40
Four years or more but less than 5 years	20
Five years or more	0

ETHICAL CONSIDERATIONS

Using the Rehabilitation Expenditures Credit

The tax credit for rehabilitation expenditures is available to help offset the costs related to substantially rehabilitating certain buildings. The credit is calculated on the rehabilitation expenditures incurred and not on the acquisition cost of the building itself.

You are a developer who buys, sells, and does construction work on real estate in the inner city of your metropolitan area. A potential customer approaches you about acquiring one of your buildings that easily could qualify for the 20 percent rehabilitation credit on historic structures. The stated sales price of the structure is $100,000 (based on appraisals

ranging from $80,000 to $120,000), and the rehabilitation expenditures, if the job is done correctly, would be about $150,000.

Your business has been slow recently due to the sluggish real estate market in your area, and the potential customer makes the following proposal: if you reduce the sales price of the building to $75,000, he will pay you $175,000 to perform the rehabilitation work. Although the buyer's total expenditures would be the same, he would benefit from this approach by obtaining a larger tax credit ($25,000 increased rehabilitation costs × 20% = $5,000).

It has been a long time since you have sold any of your real estate. How will you respond?

BUSINESS ENERGY CREDITS

For many years, **business energy credits** have been allowed to encourage the conservation of natural resources and the development of alternative energy sources (to oil and natural gas). Over the years, some of these credits have expired while new ones have been added. The most important business energy credits that remain are the 10 percent credits for solar energy property and geothermal property.

RESEARCH ACTIVITIES CREDIT

To encourage research and experimentation, usually described as research and development (R & D), a credit is allowed for certain qualifying expenditures paid or incurred through June 30, 1995. Many commentators expect Congress will extend this credit in future legislation. The **research activities credit** is the *sum* of two components: an incremental research activities credit and a basic research credit.[6]

Incremental Research Activities Credit. The incremental research activities credit applies at a 20 percent rate to the *excess* of qualified research expenses for the taxable year (the credit year) over the base amount. These components of the credit are explained below.

In general, *research expenditures* qualify if the research relates to discovering technological information that is intended for use in the development of a new or improved business component of the taxpayer. Such expenses qualify fully if the research is performed in-house (by the taxpayer or employees). If the research is conducted by persons outside the taxpayer's business (under contract), only 65 percent of the amount paid qualifies for the credit.[7]

EXAMPLE 11

Sungho incurs the following research expenditures for the tax year.

In-house wages, supplies, computer time	$50,000
Paid to Cutting Edge Scientific Foundation for research	30,000

Sungho's qualified research expenditures are $69,500 [$50,000 + ($30,000 × 65%)]. ▼

Beyond the general guidelines described above, the Code does not give specific examples of qualifying research. However, the credit is *not* allowed for research that falls into certain categories, including the following:[8]

[6] § 41.

[7] § 41(b)(3)(A).

[8] § 41(d).

TAX IN THE NEWS

Considering the Impact of Nonpermanent Tax Credits

Over the years, Congress has enacted a number of tax credits in an attempt to encourage certain types of taxpayer behavior. Some of these credits, such as the foreign tax credit and the credit for child and dependent care expenses, have had long, uninterrupted histories. Other tax credits, however, have been enacted for only limited periods of time. For example, before it was recently made permanent, the low-income housing credit was normally extended for 12 to 24 months; then either just before or after its expiration, Congress would enact new legislation extending the provision once again. The research activities credit has also repeatedly been extended on a temporary basis, only to expire at a later date.

Among other problems that arise, the uncertain lives of such credits make planning by taxpayers very difficult. With the research activities credit having expired for qualifying purchases made after June 30, 1995, taxpayers who might be encouraged by the presence of the credit may hesitate to make a qualifying expenditure until the credit is reenacted. Yet, even if Congress were to make these tax credits permanent, some parties would object: among those most adversely affected would be those persons who lobby Congress!

- Research conducted after the beginning of commercial production of the business component.
- Surveys and studies such as market research, testing, and routine data collection.
- Research conducted *outside* the United States.
- Research in the social sciences, arts, or humanities.

The *base amount* for the credit year is determined by multiplying the taxpayer's fixed base percentage by the average gross receipts for the four preceding taxable years. The fixed base percentage depends on whether the taxpayer is an existing firm or a start-up company. For purposes of the incremental research activities credit, an *existing firm* is one that both incurred qualified research expenditures *and* had gross receipts during each of at least three years from 1984 to 1988. A *start-up company* is one that did not have both of the above during each of at least three years in the same 1984–1988 period.

For existing firms, the fixed base percentage is the ratio of total qualified research expenses for the 1984–1988 period to total gross receipts for this same period. Gross receipts are net of sales returns and allowances. The fixed base percentage cannot exceed a maximum ratio of .16, or 16 percent. A start-up company is *assigned* a fixed base percentage ratio of .03, or 3 percent, for each of its first five tax years after 1993. For subsequent years, the base percentage is calculated based on the taxpayer's actual experience.

To calculate the incremental research activities credit available for 1995, the following template may be used. Essentially, the steps lead to the multiplication of the excess or incremental research expenditures incurred by the tax credit rate.

1. Calculate the fixed base percentage for the period 1984–1988 (aggregate research expenses ÷ aggregate gross receipts).	________
2. Calculate the average gross receipts for the four preceding years.	________
3. Multiply the line 2 amount by the lesser of the line 1 amount or 16%.	________
4. Subtract from the qualified research expenditures for the credit year the line 3 amount or, if greater, 50% of the credit year's qualified research expenditures. This is the excess research expenditures incurred.	________
5. Multiply the line 4 amount by 20%. This is the incremental research activities credit.	________

EXAMPLE 12

Jack, a calendar year taxpayer, has both gross receipts (net of sales returns and allowances) and qualified research expenses as follows:

	Gross Receipts	Qualified Research Expenses
1984	$150,000	$25,000
1985	300,000	45,000
1986	400,000	30,000
1987	350,000	35,000
1988	450,000	50,000
1989	425,000	60,000
1990	430,000	62,000
1991	450,000	65,000
1992	450,000	50,000
1993	500,000	55,000
1994	650,000	73,000
1995	700,000	80,000

Using the template above, calculate Jack's incremental research activities credit.

1. Calculate the fixed base percentage for the period 1984–1988 (aggregate research expenses ÷ aggregate gross receipts). ($185,000 ÷ $1,650,000)	11.21%
2. Calculate the average gross receipts for the four preceding years. [($450,000 + $450,000 + $500,000 + $650,000) ÷ 4]	$512,500
3. Multiply the line 2 amount by the lesser of the line 1 amount or 16%. ($512,500 × 11.21%)	$ 57,451
4. Subtract from the qualified research expenditures for the credit year the line 3 amount or, if greater, 50% of the credit year's qualified research expenditures. This is the excess research expenditures incurred. ($80,000 – $57,451)	$ 22,549
5. Multiply the line 4 amount by 20%. This is the incremental research activities credit.	$ 4,510

▼

As indicated in the template, a special rule limits the credit available for taxpayers who have incurred small amounts of research and experimentation costs during the base period. The rule provides that in no event shall the base amount be less than 50 percent of qualified research expenses for the credit year.

EXAMPLE 13 Assume the same facts as in Example 12, except that qualified research and experimentation expenses in 1995 were $200,000. Incremental research and experimentation expenditures eligible for the credit are $100,000, and the tax credit is computed as follows:

1. Calculate the fixed base percentage for the period 1984–1988 (aggregate research expenses ÷ aggregate gross receipts). ($185,000 ÷ $1,650,000)	11.21%
2. Calculate the average gross receipts for the four preceding years. [($450,000 + $450,000 + $500,000 + $650,000) ÷ 4]	$512,500
3. Multiply the line 2 amount by the lesser of the line 1 amount or 16%. ($512,500 × 11.21%)	$ 57,451
4. Subtract from the qualified research expenditures for the credit year the line 3 amount or, if greater, 50% of the credit year's qualified research expenditures. This is the excess research expenditures incurred. ($200,000 – $100,000)	$100,000
5. Multiply the line 4 amount by 20%. This is the incremental research activities credit.	$ 20,000

▼

Qualified research and experimentation expenditures are not only eligible for the 20 percent credit, but can also be *expensed* in the year incurred.[9] In this regard, a taxpayer has two choices:[10]

- Use the full credit and reduce the expense deduction for research expenses by 100 percent of the credit.
- Retain the full expense deduction and reduce the credit by the product of 50 percent of the credit times the maximum corporate tax rate.

As an alternative to the expense deduction, the taxpayer may *capitalize* the research expenses and *amortize* them over 60 months or more. In this case, the amount capitalized and subject to amortization is reduced by the full amount of the credit *only* if the credit exceeds the amount allowable as a deduction.

EXAMPLE 14 Assume the same facts as in Example 13, which shows that the potential incremental research activities credit is $20,000. The expense that the taxpayer can deduct and the credit amount are as follows:

	Credit Amount	Deduction Amount
• Full credit and reduced deduction		
$20,000 – $0	$20,000	
$200,000 – $20,000		$180,000
• Reduced credit and full deduction		
$20,000 – [(.50 × $20,000) × .35]	16,500	
$200,000 – $0		200,000
• Full credit and capitalize and elect to amortize costs over 60 months		
$20,000 – $0	20,000	
$200,000/60 × 12		40,000

▼

[9] § 174. Also refer to the discussion of rules for deducting research and experimental expenditures in Chapter 7.

[10] § 280C(c).

Basic Research Credit. Corporations (other than S corporations or personal service corporations) are allowed an additional 20 percent credit for basic research payments through June 30, 1995, in *excess* of a base amount. Like the incremental research activities credit, many commentators expect Congress will extend this credit in future legislation. This credit is not available to individual taxpayers. *Basic research payments* are defined as amounts paid in cash to a qualified basic research organization, such as a college or university or a tax-exempt organization operated primarily to conduct scientific research.

Basic research is defined generally as any original investigation for the advancement of scientific knowledge not having a specific commercial objective. The definition excludes basic research conducted outside the United States and basic research in the social sciences, arts, or humanities. This reflects the intent of Congress to encourage high-tech research in the United States.

The calculation of this additional credit for basic research expenditures is complex and is based on expenditures in excess of a specially defined base amount.[11] The portion of the basic research expenditures not in excess of the base amount is treated as a part of the qualifying expenditures for purposes of the regular credit for incremental research activities.

EXAMPLE 15

Orange Corporation, a qualifying corporation, pays $75,000 to a university for basic research. Assume that Orange's base amount for the basic research credit is $50,000. The basic research activities credit allowed is $5,000 [($75,000 – $50,000) × 20%]. The $50,000 of basic research expenditures that equals the base amount are treated as research expenses for purposes of the regular incremental research activities credit. ▼

LOW-INCOME HOUSING CREDIT

To encourage building owners to make affordable housing available for low-income individuals, Congress has made a credit available to owners of qualified low-income housing projects.[12]

More than any other, the **low-income housing credit** is influenced by nontax factors. For example, certification of the property by the appropriate state or local agency authorized to provide low-income housing credits is required. These credits are issued based on a nationwide allocation.

The amount of the credit is based on the qualified basis of the property. The qualified basis depends on the number of units rented to low-income tenants. Tenants are low-income tenants if their income does not exceed a specified percentage of the area median gross income. The amount of the credit is determined by multiplying the qualified basis by the applicable percentage; the credit is allowed over a 10-year period if the property continues to meet the required conditions.

EXAMPLE 16

Sarah spends $100,000 to build a qualified low-income housing project completed January 1, 1996. The entire project is rented to low-income families. The credit rate for property placed in service during January 1996 is 8.40%.[13] Sarah may claim a credit of $8,400 ($100,000 × 8.40%) in 1996 and in each of the following nine years. Generally, first-year

[11] § 41(e).
[12] § 42.
[13] Rev.Rul. 96–6, I.R.B. No. 2, 8. The rate is subject to adjustment every month by the IRS.

credits are prorated based on the date the project is placed in service. A full year's credit is taken in each of the next nine years, and any remaining first-year credit is claimed in the eleventh year. ▼

Recapture of a portion of the credit may be required if the number of units set aside for low-income tenants falls below a minimum threshold, if the taxpayer disposes of the property or the interest in it, or if the taxpayer's amount at risk decreases.

ETHICAL CONSIDERATIONS

A Win-Win Situation or an Incalculable Loss?

John and Susie rent a unit at an apartment complex owned by Mitch Brown, who has been Susie's friend since they attended business school together. One day Mitch told John and Susie about the thousands of tax dollars that he has saved by claiming the low-income housing credit for his investment in the apartment complex. Susie was pleased that Mitch had reduced his tax burden because she believes that the government rarely uses its resources wisely. Inadvertently, though, Mitch let slip that the complex "qualified" for the credit only because he overstated the percentage of low-income tenants living in the facility. Mitch admitted that by claiming that John and Susie were low-income tenants (even though they weren't), the percentage of low-income tenants was just enough for Mitch to "qualify" for the credit. Mitch said that because John and Susie were his friends, he was passing along some of his tax savings to them in the form of lower rent.

John and Susie know that if they report Mitch, he will not only lose the economic benefit of the credit, but he will also have legal troubles. Further, if Mitch were to be sentenced to prison for the tax fraud, his children would necessarily become guardians of the state. In addition, John and Susie would have to pay higher rent. Evaluate the courses of action available to John and Susie.

DISABLED ACCESS CREDIT

The **disabled access credit** is designed to encourage small businesses to make their businesses more accessible to disabled individuals. The credit is available for any eligible access expenditures paid or incurred by an eligible small business. The credit is calculated at the rate of 50 percent of the eligible expenditures that exceed \$250 but do not exceed \$10,250. Thus, the maximum amount for the credit is \$5,000 (\$10,000 × 50%).[14]

An *eligible small business* is one that during the previous year either had gross receipts of \$1 million or less or had no more than 30 full-time employees. An eligible business can include a sole proprietorship, partnership, regular corporation, or S corporation.

Eligible access expenditures are generally any reasonable and necessary amounts that are paid or incurred to make certain changes to facilities. These changes must involve the removal of architectural, communication, physical, or transportation barriers that would otherwise make a business inaccessible to disabled and handicapped individuals. Examples of qualifying projects include installing ramps, widening doorways, and adding raised markings on elevator control

[14] § 44.

buttons. However, eligible expenditures do *not* include amounts that are paid or incurred in connection with any facility that has been placed into service after the enactment (November 5, 1990) of the provision.

To the extent a disabled access credit is available, no deduction or credit is allowed under any other provision of the tax law. The adjusted basis for depreciation is reduced by the amount of the credit.

EXAMPLE 17

This year Red, Inc., an eligible business, made $11,000 of capital improvements to business realty that had been placed in service in June 1990. The expenditures were intended to make Red's business more accessible to the disabled and were considered eligible expenditures for purposes of the disabled access credit. The amount of the credit is $5,000 [($10,250 – $250) × 50%]. Although $11,000 of eligible expenditures were incurred, only the excess of $10,250 over $250 qualifies for the credit. Further, the depreciable basis of the capital improvement is $6,000 because the basis must be reduced by the amount of the credit [$11,000 (cost) – $5,000 (amount of the credit)]. ▼

OTHER TAX CREDITS

EARNED INCOME CREDIT

4 LEARNING OBJECTIVE
Describe several other tax credits that are available primarily to individual taxpayers.

The **earned income credit,** which has been a part of the law for many years, consistently has been justified as a means of providing tax equity to the working poor. More recently, the credit has also been designed to help offset regressive taxes that are a part of our tax system, such as the gasoline and Social Security taxes. In addition, the credit has been intended to encourage economically disadvantaged individuals to become contributing members of the workforce.[15] Not only is the current version of the earned income credit more generous than in previous years, it is also touted as being easier to compute.

In 1996, the earned income credit is determined by multiplying a maximum amount of earned income by the appropriate credit percentage (see Table 13–2). Generally, earned income includes employee compensation and net earnings from self-employment but excludes items such as interest, dividends, pension benefits, and alimony. If a taxpayer has children, the credit percentage used in the calculation depends on the number of qualifying children. Thus, in 1996, the maximum earned income credit for a taxpayer with one qualifying child is $2,152 ($6,330 × 34%) and $3,556 ($8,890 × 40%) for a taxpayer with two or more qualifying children. However, the maximum earned income credit is phased out completely if the taxpayer's earned income or AGI exceeds certain thresholds as shown in Table 13–2. To the extent that the greater of earned income or AGI exceeds $11,610 in 1996, the difference, multiplied by the appropriate phase-out percentage, is subtracted from the maximum earned income credit.

EXAMPLE 18

In 1996, Grace, who otherwise qualifies for the earned income credit, receives wages of $14,000 and has no other income. She has one qualifying child. Grace's earned income credit is $2,152 ($6,330 × 34%) reduced by $382 [($14,000 – $11,610) × 15.98%]. Thus, Grace's earned income credit is $1,770. If Grace has two or more qualifying children, the calculation would produce a credit of $3,556 ($8,890 × 40%) reduced by $503 [($14,000 – $11,610) × 21.06%]. Thus, Grace's earned income credit would be $3,053. ▼

[15] § 32.

▼ **TABLE 13–2**
Earned Income Credit and Phase-out Percentages

Tax Year	Number of Qualifying Children	Maximum Earned Income	Credit Percentage	Phase-out Begins	Phase-out Percentage	Phase-out Ends
1996	One child	$6,330	34	$11,610	15.98	$25,078
	Two or more children	8,890	40	11,610	21.06	28,495
1995	One child	6,160	34	11,290	15.98	24,396
	Two or more children	8,640	36	11,290	20.22	26,673

Earned Income Credit Table. It is not necessary to compute the credit as was done in Example 18. As part of the tax simplification process, the IRS issues an Earned Income Credit Table for the determination of the appropriate amount of the earned income credit. This table and a worksheet are included in the instructions to both Form 1040 and Form 1040A.

Eligibility Requirements. *Eligibility* for the credit may depend not only on the taxpayer meeting the earned income and AGI thresholds, but on whether he or she has a qualifying child. A *qualifying child* must meet the following tests:

- *Relationship test.* The individual must be a son, daughter, descendant of the taxpayer's son or daughter, stepson, stepdaughter, or an eligible foster child of the taxpayer. A legally adopted child of the taxpayer is considered the same as a child by blood.
- *Residency test.* The qualifying child must share the taxpayer's principal place of abode, which must be located within the United States, for more than one-half of the tax year of the taxpayer. Temporary absences (e.g., due to illness or education) are disregarded for purposes of this test. For foster children, however, the child must share the taxpayer's home for the entire year.
- *Age test.* The child must not have reached the age of 19 (24 in the case of a full-time student) as of the end of the tax year. In addition, a child who is permanently and totally disabled at any time during the year is considered to meet the age test.

In addition to being available for taxpayers with qualifying children, the earned income credit is also available to certain *workers without children.* However, this provision is available only to taxpayers aged 25 through 64 who cannot be claimed as a dependent on another taxpayer's return. The credit is calculated on a maximum earned income of $4,220 times 7.65 percent and reduced by 7.65 percent of earned income over $5,280. This credit is phased out completely at $9,500.

▼ EXAMPLE 19

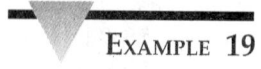

Walt, who is single, 28 years of age, and is not claimed as a dependent on anyone else's return, earns $6,500 during 1996. Even though he does not have any qualifying children, he qualifies for the earned income credit. His credit is $323 ($4,220 × 7.65%) reduced by $93 [($6,500 − $5,280) × 7.65%]. Thus, Walt's earned income credit is $230. If, instead, Walt's earned income is $4,900, his earned income credit is $323. In this situation, there is no phase-out of the maximum credit because his earned income is not in excess of $5,280. ▼

Advance Payment. The earned income credit is a form of negative income tax (a refundable credit for taxpayers who do not have a tax liability). An eligible

TAX IN THE NEWS

"EARNED INCOME CREDIT" OR "EASY INCOME FOR CHEATS"?

The earned income credit was designed to mitigate the effects of the regressive tax system on low-income taxpayers and to encourage individuals to seek work rather than welfare. Currently, however, the benefits the credit provides are being underused and abused.

To be considered a success, the earned income credit would have to be used by those persons it is intended to help. For example, workers who have a qualifying child and income below a certain amount are allowed to receive advance payment of the credit. However, less than 1 percent of qualifying Americans take advantage of this advance payment opportunity. Some commentators contend that the provisions, which have been changed 10 times since 1976, have become overly complex, difficult to comply with, and almost unusable by the low-income workers the credit is intended to aid. Estimates show that 14 percent of persons qualifying for the credit fail to claim it.

On the other hand, others who don't qualify have found the lure of the credit too good to pass up. In a recent IRS study, one-half of the electronically filed returns that claimed the earned income credit contained errors suspected to be intentional. In fact, some of the tax fraud schemes involving the credit have been initiated by persons in prison. One IRS investigation uncovered a scam operating out of the Maine Correctional Center. A dozen current and former inmates were indicted for improperly seeking refunds for earned income credit claims. Another taxpayer convicted of cheating the government by improperly using the credit testified before Congress that the earned income tax credit could stand for easy income for cheats!"

individual may elect to receive advance payments of the earned income credit from his or her employer (rather than receiving the credit from the IRS upon filing the tax return). The amount that can be received in advance is limited to 60 percent of the credit that is available to a taxpayer with only one qualifying child. If this election is made, the taxpayer must file a certificate of eligibility (Form W–5) with his or her employer and *must* file a tax return for the year the income is earned.

TAX CREDIT FOR ELDERLY OR DISABLED TAXPAYERS

The credit for the elderly was originally enacted in 1954 as the retirement income credit to provide tax relief on retirement income for individuals who were not receiving substantial benefits from tax-free Social Security payments.[16]

Currently, the **tax credit for the elderly or disabled** applies to the following:

- Taxpayers age 65 or older.
- Taxpayers under age 65 who are retired with a permanent and total disability and who have disability income from a public or private employer on account of the disability.

[16] § 22. This credit is not subject to indexation.

The *maximum* allowable credit is $1,125 (15% × $7,500 of qualifying income), but the credit will be less for a taxpayer who receives Social Security benefits or has AGI exceeding specified amounts. Under these circumstances, the base used in the credit computation is reduced. Many taxpayers receive Social Security benefits or have AGI high enough to reduce the base for the credit to zero.

The eligibility requirements and the tax computation are somewhat complicated. Consequently, an individual may elect to have the IRS compute his or her tax and the amount of the tax credit.

The credit generally is based on an initial amount (referred to as the *base amount*) and the filing status of the taxpayer in accordance with Table 13–3. To qualify for the credit, married taxpayers who live together must file a joint return. For taxpayers under age 65 who are retired on permanent and total disability, the base amounts could be less than those shown in Table 13–3 because these amounts are limited to taxable disability income.

This initial base amount is *reduced* by (1) Social Security, Railroad Retirement, and certain excluded pension benefits and (2) one-half of the taxpayer's AGI in excess of a threshold amount, which is a function of the taxpayer's filing status. The credit may be calculated using the procedure presented in the following template:

Base amount ($3,750, $5,000, or $7,500—see Table 13–3)		______
Less: Qualifying nontaxable benefits	______	
One-half of excess of AGI over: $7,500 for single, head of household, or surviving spouse taxpayers; $10,000 for married taxpayers; $5,000 for married taxpayers filing separately	______	
Total reductions		______
Balance subject to credit		______
Multiply balance subject to credit by 15%—this is the tax credit allowed		______

EXAMPLE 20 Paul and Peggy, husband and wife, are both over age 65 and received Social Security benefits of $2,400 in the current year. On a joint return, they reported AGI of $14,000.

Base amount ($3,750, $5,000, or $7,500—see Table 13–3)		$ 7,500
Less: Qualifying nontaxable benefits	$2,400	
One-half of excess of AGI over: $7,500 for single, head of household, or surviving spouse taxpayers; $10,000 for married taxpayers; $5,000 for married taxpayers filing separately	2,000	
Total reductions		(4,400)
Balance subject to credit		$ 3,100
Multiply balance subject to credit by 15%—this is the tax credit allowed		$ 465

▼

Schedule R of Form 1040 (see Appendix B) is used to calculate and report the credit.

TABLE 13–3
Base Amounts for Tax Credit for Elderly or Disabled Taxpayers

Status	Base Amount
Single, head of household, or surviving spouse	$5,000
Married, joint return, only one spouse qualified	5,000
Married, joint return, both spouses qualified	7,500
Married, separate returns, spouses live apart the entire year	3,750 each

FOREIGN TAX CREDIT

Both individual taxpayers and corporations may claim a tax credit for foreign income tax paid on income earned and subject to tax in another country or a U.S. possession.[17] As an alternative, a taxpayer may claim a deduction instead of a credit.[18] In most instances, the **foreign tax credit (FTC)** is advantageous since it provides a direct offset against the tax liability.

The purpose of the FTC is to mitigate double taxation since income earned in a foreign country is subject to both U.S. and foreign taxes. However, the ceiling limitation formula may result in some form of double taxation or taxation at rates in excess of U.S. rates when the foreign tax rates are higher than the U.S. rates. This is a distinct possibility because U.S. tax rates are lower than those of many foreign countries.

Other special tax treatments applicable to taxpayers working outside the United States include the foreign earned income exclusion (refer to Chapter 5) and limitations on deducting expenses of employees working outside the United States (refer to Chapter 9). Recall from the earlier discussion that a taxpayer may not take advantage of *both* the FTC and the foreign earned income exclusion.

Computation. Taxpayers are required to compute the FTC based upon an overall limitation.[19] The FTC allowed is the *lesser* of the foreign taxes imposed or the *overall limitation* determined according to the following formula:

$$\frac{\text{Foreign-source taxable income}}{\text{Worldwide taxable income}} \times \begin{array}{c}\text{U.S. tax}\\ \text{before FTC}\end{array}$$

For individual taxpayers, worldwide taxable income in the overall limitation formula is determined *before* personal and dependency exemptions are deducted.

EXAMPLE 21

In 1996, Carlos, a calendar year taxpayer, has $10,000 of income from Country Y, which imposes a 15% tax, and $20,000 from Country Z, which imposes a 50% tax. He has taxable income of $59,800 from within the United States, is married filing a joint return, and claims two dependency exemptions. Thus, although Carlos's taxable income for purposes of determining U.S. tax is $89,800, taxable income amounts used in the limitation formula are not reduced by personal and dependency exemptions. Thus, for this purpose, taxable income is $100,000 [$89,800 + (4 × $2,550)]. Assume that Carlos's U.S. tax before the credit is $19,931. Overall limitation:

$$\frac{\text{Foreign-source taxable income}}{\text{Worldwide taxable income}} = \frac{\$30,000}{\$100,000} \times \$19,931 = \$5,979$$

In this case, $5,979 is allowed as the FTC because this amount is less than the $11,500 of foreign taxes imposed [$1,500 (Country Y) + $10,000 (Country Z)]. ▼

[17] Section 27 provides for the credit, but the qualifications and calculation procedure for the credit are contained in §§ 901–908.

[18] § 164.

[19] § 904.

Thus, the overall limitation may result in some of the foreign income being subjected to double taxation. Unused FTCs [e.g., the $5,521 ($11,500 – $5,979) from Example 21] can be carried back two years and forward five years.[20]

Only foreign income taxes, war profits taxes, and excess profits taxes (or taxes paid in lieu of such taxes) qualify for the credit. In determining whether or not a tax is an income tax, U.S. criteria are applied. Thus, value added taxes (VAT), severance taxes, property taxes, and sales taxes do not qualify because they are not regarded as taxes on income. Such taxes may be deductible, however.

CREDIT FOR CHILD AND DEPENDENT CARE EXPENSES

A credit is allowed to taxpayers who incur employment-related expenses for child or dependent care.[21] The **credit for child and dependent care expenses** is a specified percentage of expenses incurred to enable the taxpayer to work or to seek employment. Expenses on which the credit for child and dependent care expenses is based are subject to limitations.

Eligibility. To be eligible for the credit, an individual must maintain a household for either of the following:

- A dependent under age 13.
- A dependent or spouse who is physically or mentally incapacitated.

Generally, married taxpayers must file a joint return to obtain the credit. The credit may also be claimed by the custodial parent for a nondependent child under age 13 if the noncustodial parent is allowed to claim the child as a dependent under a pre-1985 divorce agreement or under a waiver in the case of a post-1984 agreement.

Eligible Employment-Related Expenses. Eligible expenses include amounts paid for household services and care of a qualifying individual that are incurred to enable the taxpayer to be employed. Child and dependent care expenses include expenses incurred in the home, such as payments for a housekeeper. Out-of-the-home expenses incurred for the care of a dependent under the age of 13 also qualify for the credit. In addition, out-of-the-home expenses incurred for an older dependent or spouse who is physically or mentally incapacitated qualify for the credit if that person regularly spends at least eight hours each day in the taxpayer's household. This makes the credit available to taxpayers who keep handicapped older children and elderly relatives in the home instead of institutionalizing them. Out-of-the-home expenses incurred for services provided by a dependent care center will qualify only if the center complies with all applicable laws and regulations of a state or unit of local government.

Child care payments to a relative are eligible for the credit unless the relative is a dependent of the taxpayer or the taxpayer's spouse or is a child (under age 19) of the taxpayer.

EXAMPLE 22

Wilma is an employed mother of an eight-year-old child. She pays her mother, Rita, $1,500 per year to care for the child after school. Wilma does not claim Rita as a dependent. Wilma pays her daughter Eleanor, age 17, $900 for the child's care during the summer. Of these amounts, only the $1,500 paid to Rita qualifies as employment-related child care expenses. ▼

[20] § 904(c) and Reg. § 1.904–2(g), Example 1.

[21] § 21.

Earned Income Ceiling. The total for qualifying employment-related expenses is limited to an individual's earned income. For married taxpayers, this limitation applies to the spouse with the *lesser* amount of earned income. Special rules are provided for taxpayers with nonworking spouses who are disabled or are full-time students. If a nonworking spouse is physically or mentally disabled or is a full-time student, he or she is *deemed* to have earned income for purposes of this limitation. The deemed amount is $200 per month if there is one qualifying individual in the household or $400 per month if there are two or more qualifying individuals in the household. In the case of a student-spouse, the student's income is *deemed* to be earned only for the months that the student is enrolled on a full-time basis at an educational institution.

Calculation of the Credit. In general, the credit is equal to a percentage of *unreimbursed* employment-related expenses up to $2,400 for one qualifying individual and $4,800 for two or more individuals. The credit rate varies between 20 percent and 30 percent, depending on the taxpayer's AGI. The following chart shows the applicable percentage for taxpayers as AGI increases:

Adjusted Gross Income		
Over	But Not Over	Applicable Rate of Credit
$ 0	$10,000	30%
10,000	12,000	29%
12,000	14,000	28%
14,000	16,000	27%
16,000	18,000	26%
18,000	20,000	25%
20,000	22,000	24%
22,000	24,000	23%
24,000	26,000	22%
26,000	28,000	21%
28,000	No limit	20%

EXAMPLE 23

Nancy, who has two children under age 13, worked full-time while her spouse, Ron, was attending college for 10 months during the year. Nancy earned $21,000 and incurred $5,000 of child care expenses. Ron is *deemed* to be fully employed and to have earned $400 for each of the 10 months (or a total of $4,000). Since Nancy and Ron have AGI of $21,000, they are allowed a credit rate of 24%. Nancy and Ron are limited to $4,000 in qualified child care expenses (the lesser of $4,800 or $4,000). Therefore, they are entitled to a tax credit of $960 (24% × $4,000) for the year. ▼

Dependent Care Assistance Program. Recall from Chapter 5 that a taxpayer is allowed an exclusion from gross income for a limited amount reimbursed for child or dependent care expenses. However, the taxpayer is not allowed both an exclusion from income and a child and dependent care credit on the same amount. The $2,400 and $4,800 ceilings for allowable child and dependent care expenses are reduced dollar for dollar by the amount of reimbursement.[22]

[22] § 21(c).

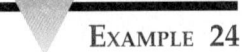

EXAMPLE 24 Assume the same facts as in Example 23, except that of the $5,000 paid for child care, Nancy was reimbursed $2,500 by her employer under a qualified dependent care assistance program. Under the employer's plan, the reimbursement reduces Nancy's taxable wages. Thus, Nancy and Ron have AGI of $18,500 ($21,000 – $2,500). The maximum amount of child care expenses for two or more dependents of $4,800 is reduced by the $2,500 reimbursement, resulting in a tax credit of $575 [25% × ($4,800 – $2,500)]. ▼

Reporting Requirements. The credit is claimed by completing and filing Form 2441, Credit for Child and Dependent Care Expenses (see Appendix B).

ETHICAL CONSIDERATIONS

Using the Credit for Child and Dependent Care Expenses

Your friends, Bob and Carol, have hired a child care provider to come into their home for three hours a day to care for their child while they both are at work. The child care provider, Delores, charges $1,800 for her services for the year. Bob and Carol learn that up to $2,400 of qualifying expenditures will generate a credit for child and dependent care expenses and that qualifying expenditures can include payments for housecleaning services. As a result, they ask Delores whether she would be interested in working several hours more per week, after Bob returns from work, for the sole purpose of cleaning the house. Delores seems interested. For Bob and Carol, the net cost of the additional services would be $480 [$600 – ($600 × 20%)] due to the availability of the tax credit.

You learn of Bob and Carol's opportunity, but think it is unfair. If you hired Delores to perform similar housecleaning services, your net cost would be $600 and not $480 because you do not qualify for the credit. You are not sure that Bob and Carol should "take advantage" of the system in this way. How do you suppose Bob and Carol will feel, or should feel, about this "abuse" if you approach them?

PAYMENT PROCEDURES

5 LEARNING OBJECTIVE Understand the tax withholding and payment procedures applicable to employers.

The tax law contains elaborate rules that require the prepayment of various Federal taxes. Consistent with the pay-as-you-go approach to the collection of taxes, these rules carry penalties for lack of compliance.[23] Prepayment procedures fall into two major categories: those applicable to employers and those applicable to self-employed persons. For employers, both payroll taxes (FICA and FUTA) and income taxes may be involved. With self-employed taxpayers, the focus is on the income tax and the self-employment tax.

PROCEDURES APPLICABLE TO EMPLOYERS

Employment taxes include FICA (Federal Insurance Contributions Act) and FUTA (Federal Unemployment Tax Act). The employer usually is responsible for with-

[23] See, for example, § 3403 (employer liable for any taxes withheld and not paid over to the IRS), § 6656 (up to 15% penalty on amounts withheld and not paid over), and § 6654 (penalty for failure by an individual to pay estimated income taxes).

CONCEPT SUMMARY 13–1

Tax Credits

Credit	Computation	Comments
Tax withheld on wages (§ 31)	Amount is reported to employee on W–2 form.	Refundable credit.
Earned income (§ 32)	Amount is determined by reference to Earned Income Credit Table published by IRS. Computations of underlying amounts in Earned Income Credit Table are illustrated in Example 18.	Refundable credit. A form of negative income tax to assist low-income taxpayers. Earned income and AGI must be less than certain threshold amounts. Generally, one or more qualifying children must reside with the taxpayer.
Child and dependent care (§ 21)	Rate ranges from 20% to 30% depending on AGI. Maximum base for credit is $2,400 for one qualifying individual, $4,800 for two or more.	Nonrefundable personal credit. No carryback or carryforward. Benefits taxpayers who incur employment-related child or dependent care expenses in order to work or seek employment. Eligible dependents include children under age 13 or dependent (any age) or spouse who is physically or mentally incapacitated.
Elderly or disabled (§ 22)	15% of sum of base amount minus reductions for (a) Social Security and other nontaxable benefits and (b) excess AGI. Base amount is fixed by law (e.g., $5,000 for a single taxpayer).	Nonrefundable personal credit. No carryback or carryforward. Provides relief for taxpayers not receiving substantial tax-free retirement benefits.
Foreign tax (§ 27)	Foreign income/total worldwide taxable income × U.S. tax = overall limitation. Lesser of foreign taxes imposed or overall limitation.	Nonrefundable credit. Unused credits may be carried back two years and forward five years. Purpose is to prevent double taxation of foreign income.
General business (§ 38)	May not exceed net income tax minus the greater of tentative minimum tax or 25% of net regular tax liability that exceeds $25,000.	Nonrefundable credit. Components include tax credit for rehabilitation expenditures, business energy credits, research activities credit, low-income housing credit, and disabled access credit. Unused credit may be carried back 3 years and forward 15 years. FIFO method applies to carryovers, carrybacks, and credits earned during current year.
Investment (§ 46)	Qualifying investment times energy percentage or rehabilitation percentage, depending on type of property. Part of general business credit and subject to its limitations.	Nonrefundable credit. Part of general business credit and therefore subject to same carryback, carryover, and FIFO rules. Energy percentage is 10%. Regular rehabilitation rate is 10%; rate for certified historic structures is 20%.

Credit	Computation	Comments
Research activities (§ 41)	Incremental credit is 20% of excess of computation year expenditures minus the base amount. Basic research credit is allowed to certain corporations for 20% of cash payments to qualified organizations that exceed a specially calculated base amount. To qualify for the credit, research expenditures must be made prior to June 30, 1995.	Nonrefundable credit. Part of general business credit and therefore subject to same carryback, carryover, and FIFO rules. Purpose is to encourage high-tech research in the United States.
Low-income housing (§ 42)	Appropriate rate times eligible basis (portion of project attributable to low-income units).	Nonrefundable credit. Part of general business credit and therefore subject to same carryback, carryover, and FIFO rules. Credit is available each year for 10 years. Recapture may apply. Purpose is to encourage construction of housing for low-income individuals.
Disabled access (§ 44)	Credit is 50% of eligible access expenditures that exceed $250, but do not exceed $10,250. Maximum credit is $5,000.	Nonrefundable credit. Part of general business credit and therefore subject to same carryback, carryover, and FIFO rules. Available only to eligible small businesses. Purpose is to encourage small businesses to become more accessible to disabled individuals.

holding the employee's share of FICA (commonly referred to as Social Security tax) and appropriate amounts for income taxes. In addition, the employer must match the FICA portion withheld and fully absorb the cost of FUTA. The sum of the employment taxes and the income tax withholdings must be paid to the IRS at specified intervals.

The key to employer compliance in this area involves the resolution of the following points:

- Ascertaining which employees and wages are covered by employment taxes and are subject to withholding for income taxes.
- Arriving at the amount to be paid and/or withheld.
- Reporting and paying employment taxes and income taxes withheld to the IRS on a timely basis through the use of proper forms.

Coverage Requirements. Circular E, Employer's Tax Guide (Publication 15) and Employer's Supplemental Tax Guide (Publication 15-A), issued by the IRS contain a discussion or listing of which employees and which wages require withholdings for income taxes and employment taxes. Excerpts from these publications appear in Exhibit 13–2. In working with Exhibit 13–2, consider the following observations:

- The designation "Exempt" in the income tax withholding column does not mean that the amount paid is nontaxable to the employee. It merely relieves the employer from having to withhold.

▼ EXHIBIT 13–2
Withholding Classifications

Special Classes of Employment and Special Types of Payments	**Treatment under Different Employment Taxes**		
	Income Tax Withholding	**Social Security and Medicare**	**Federal Unemployment**
Family employees:			
a. Child employed by parent (or by partnership consisting only of parents) in a trade or business.	Withhold	Exempt until age 18	Exempt until age 21
b. Spouse employed by spouse.	Withhold	Taxable if in course of spouse's business	Exempt
c. Parent employed by a child.	Withhold	Taxable if in course of the child's business.	Exempt
Household employees (domestic service in private homes; farmers, see Circular A).	Exempt (withhold if both employer and employee voluntarily agree).	Taxable if paid $1,000 or more in cash in calendar year. Exempt if performed by an individual under age 18 during any portion of the calendar year and is not the principal occupation of the employee.	Taxable if employer paid cash wages of $1,000 or more (for all household employees) in any quarter in the current or preceding calendar year.
Interns working in hospitals.	Withhold	Taxable	Exempt
Meals and lodging.	a. Meals—Subject to withholding and taxable unless furnished for employer's convenience and on the employer's premises. b. Lodging—Subject to withholding and taxable unless furnished on employer's premises, for the employer's convenience, and as a condition of employment.		
Ministers of churches performing duties as such.	Exempt (withhold if both employer and employee voluntarily agree).	Exempt	Exempt
Moving expense reimbursement:			
a. Qualified expenses.	Exempt, unless you have knowledge that the employee deducted the expenses in a prior year.		
b. Nonqualified expenses.	Withhold	Taxable	Taxable
Newspaper carriers under age 18.	Exempt (withhold if both employer and employee voluntarily agree).	Exempt	Exempt
Severance pay or dismissal.	Withhold	Taxable	Taxable
Tips, if less than $20 in a month.	Exempt	Exempt	Exempt
Worker's compensation.	Exempt	Exempt	Exempt

▼ TABLE 13–4
FICA Rates and Base

	Social Security Tax				Medicare Tax				
	Percent	**×**	**Base Amount**	**+**	**Percent**	**×**	**Base Amount**	**=**	**Maximum Tax**
1990	6.20%	×	$51,300	+	1.45%	×	$ 51,300	=	$3,924.45
1991	6.20%	×	53,400	+	1.45%	×	125,000	=	5,123.30
1992	6.20%	×	55,500	+	1.45%	×	130,200	=	5,328.90
1993	6.20%	×	57,600	+	1.45%	×	135,000	=	5,528.70
1994	6.20%	×	60,600	+	1.45%	×	Unlimited	=	Unlimited
1995	6.20%	×	61,200	+	1.45%	×	Unlimited	=	Unlimited
1996	6.20%	×	62,700	+	1.45%	×	Unlimited	=	Unlimited
1997 on	6.20%	×	*	+	1.45%	×	Unlimited	=	Unlimited

*Not yet determined.

EXAMPLE 25

Lee works for Yellow Corporation and has the type of job where tips are not common but do occur. If Lee's total tips amount to less than $20 per month, Yellow Corporation need not withhold Federal income taxes on the tips. Nevertheless, Lee must include the tips in his gross income. ▼

- In some cases, income tax withholding is not required but is voluntary. This is designated "Exempt (withhold if both employer and employee voluntarily agree)."

EXAMPLE 26

Pat is employed as a gardener by a wealthy family. In the past, he has encountered difficulty in managing his finances so as to be in a position to pay the income tax due every April 15. To ease the cash-flow problem that develops in April, Pat asks his employer to withhold income taxes from his wages. ▼

- The Social Security and Medicare (FICA) column refers to the employer's share. The same is true of the Federal Unemployment (FUTA) column since the employee does not contribute to this tax.

Amount of FICA Taxes. The FICA tax is comprised of two components: Social Security tax (old age, survivors, and disability insurance) *and* Medicare tax (hospital insurance). The tax rates and wage base under FICA have increased both frequently and substantially over the years. There appears to be every reason to predict that the rates and/or base amount will continue to rise in the future. As Table 13–4 shows, the top base amount differs for the Medicare portion and for the Social Security portion. Also note that Table 13–4 represents the employee's share of the tax. The employer must match the employee's portion.

Withholdings from employees must continue until the maximum base amount is reached. In 1996, for example, FICA withholding ceases for the Social Security portion (6.2 percent) once the employee has earned wages subject to FICA in the amount of $62,700. For the Medicare portion (1.45 percent), however, the employer is required to withhold on all wages without limit. This contrasts with years prior to 1994 when a maximum base existed for the Medicare portion also.

EXAMPLE 27

In 1996, Keshia earned a salary of $140,000 from her employer. Therefore, FICA taxes withheld from her salary are $3,887 ($62,700 × 6.2%) plus $2,030 ($140,000 × 1.45%) for a total of $5,917. In addition to paying the amount withheld from Keshia's salary to the government, her employer will also have to pay $5,917. ▼

In at least two situations, it is possible for an employee to have paid excess FICA taxes.

EXAMPLE 28

During 1996, Kevin changed employers in the middle of the year and earned $40,000 (all of which was subject to FICA) from each job. As a result, each employer withheld $3,060 [(6.2% × $40,000) + (1.45% × $40,000)] for a total of $6,120. Although each employer acted properly, Kevin's total FICA tax liability for the year is only $5,047 [(6.2% × $62,700) + (1.45% × $80,000)]. Thus, Kevin has overpaid his share of FICA taxes by $1,073 [$6,120 (amount paid) – $5,047 (amount of correct liability)]. He should claim this amount as a tax credit when filing his income tax return for 1996. The tax credit will reduce any income tax Kevin might owe or, possibly, generate a tax refund. ▼

EXAMPLE 29

During 1996, Lori earned $60,000 from her regular job and $20,000 from a part-time job (all of which was subject to FICA). As a result, one employer withheld $4,590 [(6.2% × $60,000) + (1.45% × $60,000)] while the other employer withheld $1,530 [(6.2% × $20,000) + (1.45% × $20,000)] for a total of $6,120. Lori's total FICA tax liability for the year is only $5,047 [(6.2% × $62,700) + (1.45% × $80,000)]. Thus, Lori has overpaid her share of FICA taxes by $1,073 [$6,120 (amount paid) – $5,047 (amount of correct liability)]. She should claim this amount as a tax credit when filing her income tax return for 1996. ▼

In Examples 28 and 29, the employee was subject to overwithholding. In both cases, however, the employee was able to obtain a credit for the excess withheld. The same result does not materialize for the portion paid by the employer. Since this amount is not refundable, in some situations employers may pay more FICA taxes than the covered employees.

The mere fact that a husband and wife are both employed does not, by itself, result in overwithholding of FICA taxes.

EXAMPLE 30

During 1996, Jim and Betty (husband and wife) are both employed, and each earns wages subject to FICA of $40,000. Accordingly, each has $3,060 FICA withheld [(6.2% × $40,000) + (1.45% × $40,000)] for a total of $6,120. Since neither spouse paid FICA tax on wages in excess of $62,700 (Social Security tax) [see Table 13–4], there is no overwithholding. ▼

A spouse employed by another spouse is subject to FICA. However, children under the age of 18 who are employed in a parent's trade or business are exempted.

Amount of Income Tax Withholding. Arriving at the amount to be withheld for income tax purposes is not so simple. It involves three basic steps:[24]

- Have the employee complete Form W–4, Employee's Withholding Allowance Certificate.
- Determine the employee's payroll period.
- Compute the amount to be withheld, usually using either the wage-bracket tables or the percentage method.

Form W–4 reflects the employee's marital status and **withholding allowances.** Generally, it need not be filed with the IRS and is retained by the employer as part of the payroll records.

[24]The withholding provisions are contained in §§ 3401 and 3402. These Sections will not be referenced specifically in the discussion that follows.

TAX IN THE NEWS

THE "NANNY TAX" PROVISIONS HAVE FINALLY ARRIVED

Beginning with the 1995 tax filing season, taxpayers will finally see the changes that were inspired by the Zoe Baird fiasco--the embarrassing situation when President Clinton's would-be attorney general learned that payroll taxes were due and payable quarterly on behalf of household help.

The recent changes in the tax law have not only raised the threshold before which employment taxes are due, but have simplified the payment procedures for any tax liability actually payable to the government. Before the legislation, if a taxpayer paid more than $50 per calendar quarter for any kind of household help, a special filing and tax payment were required. Now a taxpayer need not file or pay employment tax unless the domestic worker earns more than $1,000 during the year. In addition, the actual filing is now much simpler, involving only the completion of a new line appearing on the employer's regular income tax return. The entire process has been made relatively pain-free--except for paying the tax totaling 15.3 percent of the employee's wages.

The employer need not verify the number of exemptions claimed. Any misinformation in the form will be attributed to the employee. However, if the employer has reason to believe that the employee made a false statement, the IRS District Director should be notified. In the meantime, the Form W–4 should be honored. Employees are subject to both civil and criminal penalties for filing false withholding statements.

On the current Form W–4 an employee may claim *withholding allowances* for the following: personal exemptions for self and spouse (unless either is claimed as a dependent of another person) and dependency exemptions. One *special withholding allowance* may be claimed if the employee is single and has only one job, if the employee is married and has only one job and the spouse is not employed, or if wages from a second job or a spouse's wages (or both) are $1,000 or less. An additional allowance is available if the employee expects to file using the head-of-household status or if the employee expects to claim a credit for child and dependent care expenses on qualifying expenditures of at least $1,500. An employee who plans to itemize deductions or claim adjustments to income (e.g., alimony, deductible IRA contributions) should use the worksheet provided on Form W–4 to determine the correct number of additional allowances.

To avoid having too little tax withheld, some employees may find it necessary to reduce their withholding allowances. This might be the case for an employee who has more than one job or who has other sources of income that are not subject to adequate withholding. Likewise, a married employee who has a working spouse or more than one job might wish to claim fewer allowances.

If both spouses of a married couple are employed, they may allocate their total allowances between themselves as they see fit. The same allocation procedure is required if a taxpayer has more than one job. In no event should the same allowance be claimed more than once at the same time. It is permissible to declare *fewer* allowances than the taxpayer is entitled to in order to increase the amount of withholding. Doing so, however, does not affect the number of exemptions allowable on the employee's income tax return. An employee is also permitted to have the employer withhold a certain dollar amount in addition to the required amount. This additional dollar amount can be arbitrary or calculated in accordance with a worksheet and tables on Form W–4.

EXAMPLE 31

Carl, who earns $15,000, is married to Carol, who earns $25,000. They have three dependent children and will claim the standard deduction. Together they should be entitled to five allowances [2 (for personal exemptions) + 3 (for dependency exemptions)]. The special withholding allowance is not available since both spouses earn more than $1,000. If Carl is the spouse first employed and his Form W–4 reflects five allowances, Carol's Form W–4 should report none. They could, however, reallocate their allowances between them as long as the total claimed does not exceed five. ▼

The period of service for which an employee is paid is known as the *payroll period*. Daily, weekly, biweekly, semimonthly, and monthly periods are the most common arrangements. If an employee has no regular payroll period, he or she is considered to be paid on a daily basis.

Once the allowances are known (as reflected on Form W–4) and the payroll period determined, the amount to be withheld for Federal income taxes can be computed. The computation usually is made by using the wage-bracket tables or the percentage method.

Wage-bracket tables are available for daily, weekly, biweekly, semimonthly, and monthly payroll periods for single (including heads of household) and married taxpayers. An extract of the tables dealing with married persons on a monthly payroll period is reproduced in Table 13–5.

The data in Table 13–5 are for the period after December 31, 1995. Example 32 illustrates the use of withholding tables.

EXAMPLE 32

Tom is married and has three dependent children and no additional allowances for itemized deductions, adjustments to income, or credit for child and dependent care expenses. In his job with Pink Corporation, he earns $2,770 in May 1996. Assuming Tom's wife is not employed and all available allowances are claimed on Form W–4, Pink should withhold $145 a month from his wages. This amount is taken from the six allowances column in the $2,760–$2,800 wage bracket. The six allowances result from personal exemptions (two) plus the special withholding allowance (one) plus dependency exemptions (three). ▼

Although the wage-bracket table requires few, if any, calculations, the percentage method is equally acceptable. Its use may be necessary for payroll periods where no wage-bracket tables are available (quarterly, semiannual, and annual payroll periods) and where wages paid exceed the amount allowed for use of the wage-bracket tables. The percentage method is particularly useful when payroll computations are computerized. This method, however, requires the use of a conversion chart based on one withholding allowance. That is, the amount of one allowance is equal to the exemption amount divided by the number of payroll periods in a year. For example, the amount of one allowance for a taxpayer who is paid weekly is $49.04 ($2,550/52 payroll periods)--see Table 13–6.

To use the percentage method, proceed as follows:

Step 1. Multiply the amount of one allowance (as specified in the conversion chart in Table 13–6) by the employee's total allowances (taken from Form W–4).

Step 2. Subtract the product reached in step 1 from the employee's wages. The remainder is called "amount of wages."

Step 3. Using the result derived in step 2, compute the income tax withholding under the proper percentage-method table.

▼ **TABLE 13–5**
Withholding Table

MARRIED Persons– **MONTHLY** Payroll Period

(For Wages Paid in 1996)

If the wages are-		And the number of withholding allowances claimed is–										
At least	But less than	0	1	2	3	4	5	6	7	8	9	10
		The amount of income tax to be withheld is–										
$0	$540	$0	$0	$0	$0	$0	$0	$0	$0	$0	$0	$0
540	560	2	0	0	0	0	0	0	0	0	0	0
560	580	5	0	0	0	0	0	0	0	0	0	0
580	600	8	0	0	0	0	0	0	0	0	0	0
600	640	13	0	0	0	0	0	0	0	0	0	0
640	680	19	0	0	0	0	0	0	0	0	0	0
680	720	25	0	0	0	0	0	0	0	0	0	0
720	760	31	0	0	0	0	0	0	0	0	0	0
760	800	37	5	0	0	0	0	0	0	0	0	0
800	840	43	11	0	0	0	0	0	0	0	0	0
840	880	49	17	0	0	0	0	0	0	0	0	0
880	920	55	23	0	0	0	0	0	0	0	0	0
920	960	61	29	0	0	0	0	0	0	0	0	0
960	1,000	67	35	3	0	0	0	0	0	0	0	0
1,000	1,040	73	41	9	0	0	0	0	0	0	0	0
1,040	1,080	79	47	15	0	0	0	0	0	0	0	0
1,080	1,120	85	53	21	0	0	0	0	0	0	0	0
1,120	1,160	91	59	27	0	0	0	0	0	0	0	0
1,160	1,200	97	65	33	1	0	0	0	0	0	0	0
1,200	1,240	103	71	39	7	0	0	0	0	0	0	0
1,240	1,280	109	77	45	13	0	0	0	0	0	0	0
1,280	1,320	115	83	51	19	0	0	0	0	0	0	0
1,320	1,360	121	89	57	25	0	0	0	0	0	0	0
1,360	1,400	127	95	63	31	0	0	0	0	0	0	0
1,400	1,440	133	101	69	37	5	0	0	0	0	0	0
1,440	1,480	139	107	75	43	11	0	0	0	0	0	0
1,480	1,520	145	113	81	49	17	0	0	0	0	0	0
1,520	1,560	151	119	87	55	23	0	0	0	0	0	0
1,560	1,600	157	125	93	61	29	0	0	0	0	0	0
1,600	1,640	163	131	99	67	35	3	0	0	0	0	0
1,640	1,680	169	137	105	73	41	9	0	0	0	0	0
1,680	1,720	175	143	111	79	47	15	0	0	0	0	0
1,720	1,760	181	149	117	85	53	21	0	0	0	0	0
1,760	1,800	187	155	123	91	59	27	0	0	0	0	0
1,800	1,840	193	161	129	97	65	33	1	0	0	0	0
1,840	1,880	199	167	135	103	71	39	7	0	0	0	0
1,880	1,920	205	173	141	109	77	45	13	0	0	0	0
1,920	1,960	211	179	147	115	83	51	19	0	0	0	0
1,960	2,000	217	185	153	121	89	57	25	0	0	0	0
2,000	2,040	223	191	159	127	95	63	31	0	0	0	0
2,040	2,080	229	197	165	133	101	69	37	6	0	0	0
2,080	2,120	235	203	171	139	107	75	43	12	0	0	0
2,120	2,160	241	209	177	145	113	81	49	18	0	0	0
2,160	2,200	247	215	183	151	119	87	55	24	0	0	0
2,200	2,240	253	221	189	157	125	93	61	30	0	0	0
2,240	2,280	259	227	195	163	131	99	67	36	4	0	0
2,280	2,320	265	233	201	169	137	105	73	42	10	0	0
2,320	2,360	271	239	207	175	143	111	79	48	16	0	0
2,360	2,400	277	245	213	181	149	117	85	54	22	0	0
2,400	2,440	283	251	219	187	155	123	91	60	28	0	0
2,440	2,480	289	257	225	193	161	129	97	66	34	2	0
2,480	2,520	295	263	231	199	167	135	103	72	40	8	0
2,520	2,560	301	269	237	205	173	141	109	78	46	14	0
2,560	2,600	307	275	243	211	179	147	115	84	52	20	0
2,600	2,640	313	281	249	217	185	153	121	90	58	26	0
2,640	2,680	319	287	255	223	191	159	127	96	64	32	0
2,680	2,720	325	293	261	229	197	165	133	102	70	38	6
2,720	2,760	331	299	267	235	203	171	139	108	76	44	12
2,760	2,800	337	305	273	241	209	177	145	114	82	50	18
2,800	2,840	343	311	279	247	215	183	151	120	88	56	24
2,840	2,880	349	317	285	253	221	189	157	126	94	62	30
2,880	2,920	355	323	291	259	227	195	163	132	100	68	36
2,920	2,960	361	329	297	265	233	201	169	138	106	74	42
2,960	3,000	367	335	303	271	239	207	175	144	112	80	48
3,000	3,040	373	341	309	277	245	213	181	150	118	86	54
3,040	3,080	379	347	315	283	251	219	187	156	124	92	60
3,080	3,120	385	353	321	289	257	225	193	162	130	98	66
3,120	3,160	391	359	327	295	263	231	199	168	136	104	72
3,160	3,200	397	365	333	301	269	237	205	174	142	110	78
3,200	3,240	403	371	339	307	275	243	211	180	148	115	84

▼ TABLE 13–6
Conversion Chart for 1996

Payroll Period	Amount of One Allowance
Daily	$ 9.81
Weekly	49.04
Biweekly	98.08
Semimonthly	106.25
Monthly	212.50
Quarterly	637.50
Semiannual	1,275.00
Annual	2,550.00

The table used in applying the percentage method for those with monthly payroll periods is reproduced in Table 13–7. An illustration of the percentage method follows.

EXAMPLE 33

Assume the same facts as in Example 32, except that Tom's income tax withholding is determined using the percentage method.

Step 1. $212.50 (amount of one allowance for a monthly payroll period) × 6 (total allowances) = $1,275.

Step 2. $2,770 (monthly salary) – $1,275 (step 1) = $1,495 (amount of wages).

Step 3. Referring to Table 13–7: 15% × $960 (excess of step 2 amount over $535) = $144. ▼

▼ TABLE 13–7
Table for Percentage Method of Withholding*

TABLE 4–MONTHLY Payroll Period

(a) SINGLE person (including head of household)–

If the amount of wages (after subtracting withholding allowances) is:		The amount of income tax to withhold is:	
Not over $219		$0	
Over–	**But not over–**		**of excess over–**
$219	–$2,121 . .	15%	–$219
$2,121	–$4,477 . .	$285.30 plus 28%	–$2,121
$4,477	–$10,229 . .	$944.98 plus 31%	–$4,477
$10,229	–$22,100 . .	$2,728.10 plus 36%	–$10,229
$22,100		$7,001.68 plus 39.6%	–$22,100

(b) MARRIED person–

If the amount of wages (after subtracting withholding allowances) is:		The amount of income tax to withhold is:	
Not over $535		$0	
Over–	**But not over–**		**of excess over–**
$535	–$3,688 . . .	15%	–$535
$3,688	–$7,473 . . .	$472.95 plus 28%	–$3,688
$7,473	–$12,654 . .	$1,532.75 plus 31%	–$7,473
$12,654	–$22,325 . .	$3,138.86 plus 36%	–$12,654
$22,325.		$6,620.42 plus 39.6%	–$22,325

*This table is for wages paid in 1996.

Note that the wage-bracket tables yield an amount for income tax withholding of $145 (refer to Example 32) while the percentage method results in $144 (refer to Example 33). The difference occurs because the wage-bracket table amounts are derived by computing the withholding on the median wage within each bracket.

Reporting and Payment Procedures. Proper handling of employment taxes and income tax withholdings requires considerable compliance effort on the part of the employer. Among the Federal forms that have to be filed are the following:

Form Designation	Title
SS–4	Application for Employer Identification Number
W–2	Wage and Tax Statement
W–3	Transmittal of Wage and Tax Statements
940 or 940 EZ	Employer's Annual Federal Unemployment (FUTA) Tax Return
941	Employer's Quarterly Federal Tax Return

Form SS–4 is the starting point since it provides the employer with an identification number that must be used on all of the other forms filed with the IRS and the Social Security Administration. The number issued consists of nine digits and is hyphenated between the second and third digits (e.g., 72–1987316).

Form W–2 furnishes essential information to employees concerning wages paid, FICA, and income tax withholdings. Copies of Form W–2 are distributed to several parties for various purposes: to enable the employee to complete his or her income tax return, to inform the Social Security Administration of the amount of FICA wages earned by the employee, and to serve as a permanent record for the employer and employee of the payroll information contained on the form. Form W–2 must be furnished to an employee not later than January 31 of the following year. If an employee leaves a place of employment before the end of the year, Form W–2 can be given to him or her at any time after employment ends prior to the following January 31. However, if the terminated employee asks for Form W–2, it must be given to him or her within 30 days after the request or the final wage payment, whichever is later.

Form W–3 must accompany the copies of Forms W–2 filed by the employer with the Social Security Administration. Its basic purpose is to summarize and reconcile the amounts withheld for FICA and income taxes from *all* employees.

Form 940 (or Form 940 EZ) constitutes the employer's annual accounting for FUTA purposes. Generally, it must be filed on or before January 31 of the following year and must be accompanied by the payment of any undeposited FUTA due the Federal government.

Regardless of whether or not deposits[25] are required, most employers must settle their employment taxes every quarter. To do this, Form 941 must be filed on or before the last day of the month following the end of each calendar quarter.

Backup Withholding. Some types of payments made to individuals by banks or businesses are subject to backup withholding under certain conditions. Backup withholding is designed to ensure that income tax is collected on interest and other payments reported on a Form 1099. If backup withholding applies, the payer must withhold 31 percent of the amount paid. Backup withholding applies when the taxpayer does not give the business or bank his or her identification number in the required manner and in other situations.[26]

6 LEARNING OBJECTIVE
Understand the payment procedures applicable to self-employed persons.

PROCEDURES APPLICABLE TO SELF-EMPLOYED PERSONS

Although the following discussion largely centers on self-employed taxpayers, some of the procedures may be applicable to employed persons. In many cases, for

[25] Deposit requirements are specified in each current issue of Circular E, *Employer's Tax Guide,* IRS Publication 15. Under current rules, most employers must make deposits on a monthly or semiweekly basis.

[26] § 3406(a).

example, employed persons may be required to pay estimated tax if they have income other than wages that is not subject to withholding. An employee may conduct a second trade or business in a self-employment capacity. Depending on the circumstances, the second job may require the payment of a self-employment tax. In addition, taxpayers whose income consists primarily of rentals, dividends, or interest (this list is not all-inclusive) may be required to pay estimated tax.

Estimated Tax for Individuals. **Estimated tax** is the amount of tax (including alternative minimum tax and self-employment tax) an individual expects to owe for the year after subtracting tax credits and income tax withheld. Any individual who has estimated tax for the year of $500 or more *and* whose withholding does not equal or exceed the required annual payment (discussed below) must make quarterly payments.[27] Otherwise, a penalty may be assessed. No quarterly payments are required (no penalty will apply on an underpayment) if the taxpayer's estimated tax is under $500. No penalty will apply if the taxpayer had no tax liability for the preceding tax year *and* the preceding tax year was a taxable year of 12 months *and* the taxpayer was a citizen or resident for the entire preceding tax year. In this regard, having no tax liability is not the same as having no additional tax to pay.

The required annual payment must first be computed. This is the *smaller* of the following amounts:

- Ninety percent of the tax shown on the current year's return.
- One hundred percent of the tax shown on the preceding year's return (the return must cover the full 12 months of the preceding year). The 100 percent requirement is increased to 110 percent if the AGI on the preceding year's return exceeds $150,000 ($75,000 if married filing separately).

In general, one-fourth of this required annual payment is due on April 15, June 15, and September 15 of the tax year and January 15 of the following year.

An equal part of withholding is deemed paid on each due date. Thus, the quarterly installment of the required annual payment reduced by the applicable withholding is the estimated tax to be paid. Payments are to be accompanied by the payment voucher for the appropriate date from Form 1040–ES.

Married taxpayers may make joint estimated tax payments even though a joint income tax return is not subsequently filed. In such event, the estimated tax payments may be applied against the separate return liability of the spouses as they see fit. If a husband and wife cannot agree on a division of the estimated tax payments, the Regulations provide that the payments are to be allocated in proportion to the tax liability on the separate returns.

Penalty on Underpayments. A nondeductible penalty is imposed on the amount of underpayment of estimated tax. The rate for this penalty is the same as the rate for underpayments of tax and is adjusted quarterly to reflect changes in the average prime rate.

An *underpayment* occurs when any installment (the sum of estimated tax paid and income tax withheld) is less than 25 percent of the required annual payment. The penalty is applied to the amount of the underpayment for the period of the underpayment.[28]

EXAMPLE 34

Marta made the following payments of estimated tax for 1996 and had no income tax withheld:

[27] § 6654(c)(1).

[28] § 6654(b)(2).

April 15, 1996	$1,400
June 17, 1996	2,300
September 16, 1996	1,500
January 15, 1997	1,800

Marta's actual tax for 1996 is $8,000, and her tax in 1995 was $10,000. Therefore, each installment should have been at least $1,800 [($8,000 × 90%) × 25%]. Of the payment on June 17, $400 will be credited to the unpaid balance of the first quarterly installment due on April 15,[29] thereby effectively stopping the underpayment penalty for the first quarterly period. Of the remaining $1,900 payment on June 17, $100 is credited to the September 16 payment, resulting in this third quarterly payment being $200 short. Then $200 of the January 15 payment is credited to the September 16 shortfall, ending the period of underpayment for that portion due. The January 15, 1997, installment is now underpaid by $200, and a penalty will apply from January 15, 1997, to April 15, 1997 (unless paid sooner). Marta's underpayments for the periods of underpayment are as follows:

1st installment due:	$400 from April 15–June 17
2nd installment due:	Paid in full
3rd installment due:	$200 from September 16, 1996–January 15, 1997
4th installment due:	$200 from January 15–April 15, 1997

▼

If a possible underpayment of estimated tax is indicated, Form 2210 (see Appendix B) should be filed to compute the penalty due or to justify that no penalty applies.

Self-Employment Tax. The tax on self-employment income is levied to provide Social Security and Medicare benefits (old age, survivors, and disability insurance and hospital insurance) for self-employed individuals. Individuals with net earnings of $400 or more from self-employment are subject to the **self-employment tax.**[30] For 1996, the self-employment tax is 15.3 percent on self-employment income up to $62,700 and 2.9 percent on self-employment income in excess of $62,700. In other words, for 1996 the self-employment tax is 12.4 percent of self-employment earnings up to $62,700 (for the Social Security portion) *plus* 2.9 percent of the total amount of self-employment earnings (for the Medicare portion)--see Table 13–8.

▼ TABLE 13–8
Self-Employment Tax: Social Security and Medicare Portions

Year		Tax Rate	Ceiling Amount
1996	Social Security portion	12.4%	$62,700
	Medicare portion	2.9%	Unlimited
	Aggregate rate	15.3%	
1995	Social Security portion	12.4%	$61,200
	Medicare portion	2.9%	Unlimited
	Aggregate rate	15.3%	

[29] Payments are credited to unpaid installments in the order in which the installments are required to be paid. § 6654(b)(3).

[30] § 6017.

▼ FIGURE 13–1
1996 Self-Employment Tax Worksheet

1. Net earnings from self-employment.	______
2. Multiply line 1 by 92.35%.	______
3. If the amount on line 2 is $62,700 or less, multiply the line 2 amount by 15.3%. This is the self-employment tax.	______
4. If the amount on line 2 is more than $62,700, multiply the excess of line 2 over $62,700 by 2.9% and add $9,593.10. This is the self-employment tax.	______

Currently, self-employed taxpayers are allowed a deduction from net earnings from self-employment, at one-half of the self-employment rate, for purposes of determining self-employment tax[31] *and* an income tax deduction for one-half the amount of self-employment tax paid.[32]

Determining the amount of self-employment tax to be paid for 1996 involves completing the steps in Figure 13–1. The result of step 3 or 4 is the amount of self-employment tax to be paid. For *income tax purposes,* the amount to be reported is net earnings from self-employment before the deduction for one-half of the self-employment tax. Then the taxpayer is allowed a deduction *for* AGI of one-half of the self-employment tax.

EXAMPLE 35

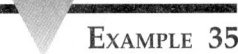

Using the format in Figure 13–1, the self-employment tax is determined for two taxpayers with net earnings from self-employment for 1996 as follows: Ned, $55,000 and Terry, $80,000.

Ned's Self-Employment Tax Worksheet

1. Net earnings from self-employment.	$55,000.00
2. Multiply line 1 by 92.35%.	$50,792.50
3. If the amount on line 2 is $62,700 or less, multiply the line 2 amount by 15.3%. This is the self-employment tax.	$ 7,771.25
4. If the amount on line 2 is more than $62,700, multiply the excess over $62,700 by 2.9% and add $9,593.10. This is the self-employment tax.	______

Terry's Self-Employment Tax Worksheet

1. Net earnings from self-employment.	$80,000.00
2. Multiply line 1 by 92.35%.	$73,880.00
3. If the amount on line 2 is $62,700 or less, multiply the line 2 amount by 15.3%. This is the self-employment tax.	______
4. If the amount on line 2 is more than $62,700, multiply the excess over $62,700 by 2.9% and add $9,593.10. This is the self-employment tax.	$ 9,917.32

For income tax purposes, Ned has net earnings from self-employment of $55,000 and a deduction *for* AGI of $3,885.63 (one-half of $7,771.25). Terry has net earnings from self-employment of $80,000 and a deduction *for* AGI of $4,958.66 (one-half of $9,917.32). Both taxpayers benefit from the deduction for one-half of the self-employment tax paid. ▼

[31] § 1402(a)(12).
[32] § 164(f).

▼ **FIGURE 13–2**
1995 Self-Employment Tax Worksheet

1. Net earnings from self-employment.	______
2. Multiply line 1 by 92.35%.	______
3. If the amount on line 2 is $61,200 or less, multiply the line 2 amount by 15.3%. This is the self-employment tax.	______
4. If the amount on line 2 is more than $61,200, multiply the excess of line 2 over $61,200 by 2.9% and add $9,363.60. This is the self-employment tax.	______

For 1995, the self-employment tax computations are similar to those for 1996. The only difference is that the tax base was lower for 1995 than it is for 1996 (see Table 13–8 and Figure 13–2).

If an individual also receives wages subject to FICA tax, the ceiling amount of the Social Security portion on which the self-employment tax is computed is reduced. Thus, self-employment tax may be reduced if a self-employed individual also receives FICA wages in excess of the ceiling amount.

EXAMPLE 36

In 1996, Kelly had $42,000 of net earnings from the conduct of a bookkeeping service (trade or business activity). She also received wages as an employee amounting to $25,000 during the year. The amount of Kelly's self-employment income subject to the Social Security portion (12.4%) is $37,700, producing a tax of $4,674.80 ($37,700 × 12.4%). All of Kelly's net self-employment earnings are subject to the Medicare portion of the self-employment tax of 2.9%. Therefore, the self-employment tax on this portion is $1,124.82 ($38,787 × 2.9%).

	Social Security Portion
Ceiling amount	$ 62,700
Less: FICA wages	(25,000)
Net ceiling	$ 37,700
Net self-employment income ($42,000 × 92.35%)	$ 38,787
Lesser of net ceiling or net self-employment income	$ 37,700

▼

Net earnings from self-employment include gross income from a trade or business less allowable trade or business deductions, the distributive share of any partnership income or loss derived from a trade or business activity, and net income from the rendering of personal services as an independent contractor. Gain or loss from the disposition of property (including involuntary conversions) is excluded from the computation of self-employment income unless the property involved is inventory.

Director's fees, which are paid to a nonemployee, are also considered self-employment income because a director is considered to be engaged in a trade or business activity. However, director's fees received on a deferred basis are not subject to the self-employment tax until the fees are paid or constructively received and thus are subject to the income tax.

EXAMPLE 37

Tara, a former treasurer, is retired from Emerald Company but is retained as a corporate director. She performs these duties in 1996 under a deferred arrangement whereby she will be paid $12,000 in 1998, at which time she will be 70 years old. In 1996, the year earned, none of the director's fees are subject to self-employment tax. For income tax purposes and for self-employment tax purposes, the $12,000 of director's fees are subject to tax in 1998, the year received. ▼

EXAMPLE 38

Assume the same facts as in Example 37, except that Tara is not retired. In addition to the director's fees, she is paid a salary of $150,000 in her capacity as treasurer of the company. Because her salary exceeds the Social Security portion wage base ($62,700) for FICA tax purposes, the director's fees are not subject to the Social Security portion of the self-employment tax if they were paid in 1996. If not paid until 1998, the director's fees will be subject to both portions of the self-employment tax in 1998 unless Tara's salary in 1998 exceeds the Social Security wage base. Thus, she will need to consider both the income tax deferral consequences and the self-employment tax consequences for the year the director's fees are to be paid. ▼

An employee who performs services on a part-time basis as an independent contractor or an employee who is engaged in a separate trade or business activity may be subject to the self-employment tax.

TAX PLANNING CONSIDERATIONS

FOREIGN TAX CREDIT

A U.S. citizen or resident working abroad (commonly referred to as an *expatriate*) may elect to take either a foreign tax credit or the foreign earned income exclusion. In cases where the income tax of a foreign country is higher than the U.S. income tax, the credit choice usually is preferable. If the reverse is true, electing the foreign earned income exclusion probably reduces the overall tax burden.

7 LEARNING OBJECTIVE
Identify tax planning opportunities related to tax credits and payment procedures.

Unfortunately, the choice between the credit and the earned income exclusion is not without some limitations. The election of the foreign earned income exclusion, once made, can be revoked for a later year. However, once revoked, the earned income exclusion will not be available for a period of five years unless the IRS consents to an earlier date. This will create a dilemma for expatriates whose job assignments over several years shift between low- and high-bracket countries.

EXAMPLE 39

In 1995, Ira, a calendar year taxpayer, is sent by his employer to Saudi Arabia (a low-tax country). For 1995, therefore, Ira elects the foreign earned income exclusion. In 1996, Ira's employer transfers him to France (a high-tax country). Accordingly, he revokes the foreign earned income exclusion election for 1996 and chooses instead to use the foreign tax credit. If Ira is transferred back to Saudi Arabia (or any other low-tax country) within five years, he no longer may utilize the foreign earned income exclusion. ▼

CREDIT FOR CHILD AND DEPENDENT CARE EXPENSES

A taxpayer may incur employment-related expenses that also qualify as medical expenses (e.g., a nurse is hired to provide in-the-home care for an ill and incapacitated dependent parent). Such expenses may be either deducted as medical expenses (subject to the 7.5 percent limitation) or utilized in determining the credit for child and dependent care expenses. If the credit for child and dependent care expenses is chosen and the employment-related expenses exceed the limitation ($2,400, $4,800, or earned income, as the case may be), the excess may be considered a medical expense. If, however, the taxpayer chooses to deduct qualified employment-related expenses as medical expenses, any portion that is not deductible because of the 7.5 percent limitation may not be used in computing the credit for child and dependent care expenses.

EXAMPLE 40

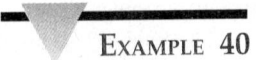

Alicia, a single taxpayer, has the following tax position for the current tax year.

Adjusted gross income		$30,000
Potential itemized deductions *from* AGI—		
Other than medical expenses	$3,500	
Medical expenses	6,000	$ 9,500

All of Alicia's medical expenses were incurred to provide nursing care for her disabled father while she was working. The father lives with Alicia and qualifies as her dependent. ▼

What should Alicia do in this situation? One approach would be to use $2,400 of the nursing care expenses to obtain the maximum credit for child and dependent care expenses allowed of $480 (20% × $2,400). The balance of these expenses should be claimed as medical expenses. After a reduction of 7.5 percent of AGI, this would produce a medical expense deduction of $1,350 [$3,600 (remaining medical expenses) – (7.5% × $30,000)].

Another approach would be to claim the full $6,000 as a medical expense and forgo the credit for child and dependent care expenses. After the 7.5 percent adjustment of $2,250 (7.5% × $30,000), a deduction of $3,750 remains.

The choice, then, is between a credit of $480 plus a deduction of $1,350 or a credit of $0 plus a deduction of $3,750. Which is better, of course, depends on the relative tax savings involved.

One of the traditional goals of *family tax planning* is to minimize the total tax burden within the family unit. With proper planning and implementation, the credit for child and dependent care expenses can be used to help achieve this goal. For example, payments to certain relatives for the care of qualifying dependents and children qualify for the credit if the care provider is *not* a dependent of the taxpayer or the taxpayer's spouse or is *not* a child (under age 19) of the taxpayer. Thus, if the care provider is in a lower tax bracket than the taxpayer, the following benefits result:

- Income is shifted to a lower-bracket family member.
- The taxpayer qualifies for the credit for child and dependent care expenses.

In addition, the goal of minimizing the family income tax liability can be enhanced in some other situations, but only if the credit's limitations are recognized and avoided. For example, tax savings may still be enjoyed even if the qualifying expenditures incurred by a cash basis taxpayer have already reached the annual ceiling ($2,400 or $4,800). To the extent that any additional payments can be shifted into future tax years, the benefit from the credit may be preserved on these excess expenditures.

EXAMPLE 41

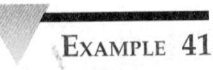

Andre, a calendar year and cash basis taxpayer, has spent $2,400 by December 1 on qualifying child care expenditures for his dependent 11-year-old son. The $200 that is due the care provider for child care services rendered in December does not generate a tax credit benefit if the amount is paid in the current year because the $2,400 ceiling has been reached. However, if the payment can be delayed until the next year, the total credit over the two-year period for which Andre is eligible may be increased. ▼

A similar shifting of expenditures to a subsequent year may be wise if the potential credit otherwise generated would exceed the tax liability available to absorb the credit.

ADJUSTMENTS TO INCREASE WITHHOLDING

The penalty for underpayment of estimated tax by individuals is computed for each quarter of the tax year. A taxpayer can play *catch-up* to a certain extent. Each quarterly payment is credited to the unpaid portion of any previous required installment. Thus, the penalty stops on that portion of the underpayment for the previous quarter. Since income tax withheld is assumed to have been paid evenly throughout the year and is allocated equally among the four installments in computing any penalty, a taxpayer who would otherwise be subject to a penalty for underpayment should increase withholdings late in the year. This can be done by changing the number of allowances claimed on Form W–4 or by special arrangement with the employer to increase the amount withheld.

A similar way to avoid (or reduce) a penalty for underpayment is to have the employer continue Social Security withholding beyond the base amount.

EXAMPLE 42

Rose, a calendar year taxpayer, earns $72,000 from her job. In late August 1996, she realizes that she will be subject to a penalty for underpayment of estimated tax due to income from outside sources. Consequently, she instructs her employer to continue FICA withholdings for the rest of 1996. If this is done, an extra $9,300 [$72,000 (annual salary) – $62,700 (base amount of the Social Security portion for 1996)] will be subject to the 6.2% Social Security portion of the FICA tax [7.65% (total FICA rate) – 1.45% (Medicare portion of the FICA rate)]. Thus, Rose generates an additional $577 (6.2% × $9,300) that will be deemed withheld ratably during 1996. ▼

ADJUSTMENTS TO AVOID OVERWITHHOLDING

Publication 505, Tax Withholding and Estimated Tax, contains worksheets that taxpayers may use to take advantage of special provisions for avoiding overwithholding. Extra exemptions for withholding purposes are allowed if the taxpayer has unusually large itemized deductions, deductions *for* AGI, or tax credits. Net losses from Schedules C, D, E, and F may be considered in computing the number of extra withholding exemptions. Net operating loss carryovers may also be considered in the computation. A taxpayer who is entitled to extra withholding exemptions for any of these reasons should file a new Form W–4, Employee's Withholding Allowance Certificate, with his or her employer.

KEY TERMS

Business energy credits, 13–9

Credit for child and dependent care expenses, 13–20

Disabled access credit, 13–14

Earned income credit, 13–15

Employment taxes, 13–22

Estimated tax, 13–33

Foreign tax credit (FTC), 13–19

General business credit, 13–5

Low-income housing credit, 13–13

Nonrefundable credits, 13–4

Refundable credits, 13–4

Rehabilitation expenditures credit, 13–7

Rehabilitation expenditures credit recapture, 13–8

Research activities credit, 13–9

Self-employment tax, 13–34

Tax credits, 13–2

Tax credit for the elderly or disabled, 13–17

Withholding allowances, 13–27

PROBLEM MATERIALS

DISCUSSION QUESTIONS

1. Would an individual taxpayer receive greater benefit from deducting an expenditure or from taking a credit equal to 25% of the expenditure?

2. What is a refundable credit? Give examples. What is a nonrefundable credit? Give examples.

3. Discuss the order in which credits are offset against the tax liability. Why is the order in which credits are utilized important?

4. In determining the maximum amount of general business credit allowed an individual taxpayer for a tax year, net income tax, tentative minimum tax, regular tax liability, and net regular tax liability are important concepts.
   a. Define each term.
   b. Using these terms, state the general business credit limitation for an individual taxpayer for the current year.

5. John graduated from college several years ago with high hopes and expectations of enjoying a very successful business career. Almost as soon as he completed his final exams, he borrowed over $250,000 from a local bank (the loan was guaranteed by his parents) in order to make several "hot" investments. The investments, as expected, spun off huge tax losses and tax credits in their early years. More recently, however, John has begun to have doubts as to the wisdom of these investments as they have not begun to generate profits as promised. As a result, he is contemplating selling the investments, at yet another loss. Because his investments have not as yet produced any profits to support his lifestyle, he has been forced to live at home with his parents. Identify the relevant tax issues.

6. Vic is considering the purchase and renovation of an old building. He has heard about the tax credit for rehabilitation expenditures but does not know the specific rules applicable to the credit. He has asked you to explain the most important details to him. What will you tell Vic?

7. If property on which the tax credit for rehabilitation expenditures was claimed is prematurely disposed of or ceases to be qualified property, how is the tax liability affected in the year of the disposition or disqualification?

8. What credit provisions in the tax law were enacted to encourage technological development in the United States?

9. Explain the alternatives a taxpayer has in claiming the deduction and credit for research and experimentation expenditures incurred.

10. Explain the purpose of the disabled access credit and describe the general characteristics of its computation.

11. Identify several examples of the type of structural changes to a building that qualify for the disabled access credit.

12. Which of the following taxpayers are eligible for the earned income credit for the current tax year?
    a. Joe and Marie are married and have a 15-year-old dependent child living with them. Joe earns $8,000 and Marie earns $8,500.
    b. Alan, a single parent, supports his 20-year-old daughter who is a full-time college student. Alan earns $15,000 and has no other income.
    c. Paula, an unmarried 26-year-old taxpayer, earns $8,000 and has no other income. She claims a dependency exemption for her aunt under a multiple support agreement.

13. Is the earned income credit a form of a negative income tax? Why or why not?

14. Individuals who receive substantial Social Security benefits are usually not eligible for the tax credit for the elderly or disabled because these benefits effectively eliminate the base upon which the credit is computed. Explain.

15. What purpose is served by the overall limitation to the foreign tax credit?

16. Do all foreign taxes qualify for the U.S. foreign tax credit? Explain.

17. In general, when would an individual taxpayer find it more beneficial to take advantage of the foreign earned income exclusion rather than the foreign tax credit in computing his or her income tax liability?

18. Ten years ago, Suzanne opened a high-tech business that had its headquarters and research operations in Seattle and its manufacturing facility in Singapore. Because of the competitive nature of the business, Suzanne's firm was forced to pour millions of dollars into research activities involving the most recent technology. Fortunately, the research paid off as evidenced by the astounding 40% annual increase in the business's sales over the past two years. Identify the relevant tax issues.

19. Sally was recently called into the partner's office and offered a one-year assignment in her public accounting firm's Prague office. Realizing Sally will face incremental expenses while in Prague, such as for foreign income taxes and rent, the firm will try to make her "whole" from a financial perspective by increasing her salary to help offset the expenses she will incur while living overseas. If Sally takes the assignment, she will likely rent her personal residence and sell several major tangible assets such as her personal automobile. Identify the relevant tax issues.

20. Gary and Gail are married and have a dependent child eight years of age. Gary earned $15,000 during the current year. Gail, a full-time student for the entire year, was not employed. Gary and Gail believe they are not entitled to the credit for child and dependent care expenses because Gail was not employed. Is this correct? Explain your answer.

21. Polly and her spouse, Leo, file a joint return and expect to report AGI of $125,000 in the current year. Polly's employer offers a child and dependent care reimbursement plan that allows up to $2,500 of qualifying expenses to be reimbursed in exchange for a $2,500 reduction in the employee's salary. Because Polly and Leo have one minor child requiring child care that costs $2,500 each year, she is wondering if she should sign up for the program instead of taking advantage of the credit for child and dependent care expenses. Assuming Polly and Leo are in the 31% tax bracket, analyze the effect of the two alternatives. How would your answer differ if Polly and Leo's AGI was $10,000 instead of $95,000?

22. Discuss the rationale underlying the enactment of the following tax credits:
    a. Tax credit for rehabilitation expenditures.
    b. Low-income housing credit.
    c. Disabled access credit.
    d. Earned income credit.
    e. Foreign tax credit.
    f. Credit for child and dependent care expenses.

23. Sam and Martha have two preschool-age children. On several occasions during the current year, Sam and Martha took out-of-town trips due to Sam's business. While Sam and Martha were out of town, a 14-year-old neighbor cared for the children during the day; at night, they stayed with their grandparents. Sam and Martha had a neighborhood teenager mow their lawn, but only once, because of the damage he did to Martha's flower garden. On a later out-of-town trip, they hired a professional lawn service to mow the lawn. Identify the relevant tax issues.

24. If the employer is not required to withhold income taxes on an item of income paid to an employee, does this mean that the item is nontaxable? Explain.

25. At a social function you attended in early July of 1996, you overhear a guest, the CEO of a corporation, remark, "Thank goodness this is the end of FICA for a while!" Interpret this remark.

26. Keith, a sole proprietor, owns and operates a grocery store. Keith's wife and his 17-year-old son work in the business and are paid wages. Will the wife and son be subject to FICA? Explain.

27. Although Vicki is entitled to four allowances, she claimed just one on her Form W–4.
   a. Why would Vicki claim fewer allowances than she is entitled to?
   b. Is this procedure permissible?
   c. Will this affect the number of exemptions Vicki can claim on her Federal income tax return?

28. Under what circumstances will the special withholding allowance be allowed for purposes of determining income tax withholding?

29. Describe the exposure (i.e., wage base and tax rate) that a self-employed individual has to the self-employment tax for 1996.

30. You read that self-employed taxpayers get a double deduction for one-half of the self-employment tax, not only as a deduction in computing the self-employment tax but also as a deduction *for* AGI. Is this true? Explain.

PROBLEMS

31. Dan has a tentative general business credit of $85,000 for the current year. His net regular tax liability before the general business credit is $95,000; tentative minimum tax is $90,000. Compute Dan's allowable general business credit for the current year.

32. Tan Corporation has the following general business credit carryovers:

1992	$10,000
1993	30,000
1994	10,000
1995	40,000
Total carryovers	$90,000

If the general business credit generated by activities during 1996 equals $90,000 and the total credit allowed during the current year is $160,000 (based on tax liability), what amounts of the current general business credit and carryovers are utilized against the 1996 income tax liability? What is the amount of unused credit carried forward to 1997?

33. In January 1996, Mike acquired an office building in downtown Athens, Georgia, for $300,000; the building was originally constructed in 1932. Of the $300,000 cost, $25,000 was allocated to the land. Mike immediately placed the building into service but quickly realized that substantial renovation would be required to keep and attract new tenants. The renovations, costing $350,000, were of the type that qualify for the rehabilitation credit. The improvements were completed in October 1996.
   a. Compute Mike's rehabilitation tax credit for the year of acquisition.
   b. Determine the cost recovery for 1996.
   c. What is the basis in the property at the end of its first year of use by Mike?

34. In the current year, Diane Lawson (123 Sunview Avenue, Jacksonville, FL 32231) acquires a qualifying historic structure for $250,000 (excluding the cost of land) with full intentions of substantially rehabilitating the building. Write a letter to Diane and a memo to the tax files explaining the computation that determines the rehabilitation tax credit available to her and the impact on the depreciable basis, assuming either $245,000 or $255,000 is incurred for the rehabilitation project. Because Diane must decide whether to pursue the renovation plan costing $245,000 or the one costing $255,000, you should indicate in the letter and the memo the differences in cash flow to Diane arising from the tax consequences associated with the two renovation projects.

35. Matt, a calendar year taxpayer, furnishes the following information. Gross receipts are net of returns and allowances.

	Gross Receipts	Qualified Research Expenses
1995	$180,000	$30,000
1994	170,000	50,000
1993	160,000	35,000
1992	120,000	45,000
1991	120,000	50,000
1990	130,000	35,000
1989	125,000	30,000
1988	120,000	45,000
1987	135,000	40,000
1986	110,000	20,000
1985	95,000	-0-
1984	80,000	30,000

a. Using the template in the text, determine Matt's incremental research activities credit for 1995.
b. Matt is in the 28% tax bracket. Determine which approach to the research expenditures and the research activities credit (other than capitalization and subsequent amortization) would provide the greatest tax benefit to Matt.

36. Assume the same facts as in the previous problem, except that Matt incurs $60,000 of qualified research expenditures in 1995. Using the template in the text, compute the incremental research activities credit for 1995.

37. Rose Corporation is an eligible small business for purposes of the disabled access credit. During the year, Rose Corporation makes the following expenditures on a structure originally placed in service in 1984:

Removal of architectural barriers	$4,250
Acquired equipment for disabled persons	3,000
	$7,250

In addition, $3,500 was expended on a building placed in service in the current year, to ensure easy accessibility by disabled individuals. Calculate the amount of the disabled access credit available to Rose Corporation.

38. Ahmed Zinna (16 Southside Drive, Charlotte, NC 28204), one of your clients, owns two retail establishments in downtown Charlotte, North Carolina, and has come to you seeking advice concerning the tax consequences of complying with the Americans with Disabilities Act. He understands that he needs to install various features at his stores (e.g., ramps, doorways, and restrooms that are handicapped accessible) to make them more accessible to disabled individuals. He inquires whether any tax credits will be available to help offset the cost of the necessary changes. He estimates the cost of the planned changes to his facilities as follows:

Location	Projected Cost
Oak Street	$ 4,000
Maple Avenue	12,000

He reminds you that the Oak Street store was constructed in 1995 while the Maple Avenue store is in a building that was constructed in 1902. Ahmed operates his business as a sole proprietorship and has approximately eight employees at each location. Write a letter to Ahmed in which you summarize your conclusions concerning the tax consequences of his proposed capital improvements.

39. Which of the following individuals qualify for the earned income credit for 1996?
   a. Eduardo is single, 19 years of age, and has no dependents. His income consists of $8,000 of wages.
   b. Kate maintains a household for a dependent 12-year-old son and is eligible for head-of-household tax rates. Her income consists of $10,500 of salary and $300 of taxable interest.
   c. Keith and Susan are married and file a joint return. Keith and Susan have no dependents. Their combined income consists of $18,500 of salary and $100 of taxable interest. Adjusted gross income is $18,600.
   d. George is a 26-year-old single taxpayer. He has no dependents and generates earnings of $9,000.

40. Irene, who qualifies for the earned income credit, has two qualifying children who live with her. Irene earns a salary of $14,500 during 1996. Calculate Irene's earned income credit for the year.

41. Vern, a widower, lives in an apartment with his three minor children (ages 3, 4, and 5) whom he supports. Vern earned $19,500 during 1996. He contributed $500 to an IRA and uses the standard deduction. Calculate the amount, if any, of Vern's earned income credit.

42. Joyce, a widow, lives in an apartment with her two minor children (ages 8 and 10) whom she supports. Joyce earns $25,000 during 1996. She uses the standard deduction.
   a. Calculate the amount, if any, of Joyce's earned income credit.
   b. During the year, Joyce is offered a new job that has greater future potential than her current job. If she accepts the job offer, her earnings for the year would be $28,500; however, she will not qualify for the earned income credit. Using after-tax cash-flow calculations, determine whether Joyce should accept the new job offer.

43. Hank, age 67, and Thelma, age 66, are married retirees who received the following income and retirement benefits during the current year:

Fully taxable pension from Hank's former employer	$ 8,000
Dividends and interest	2,500
Social Security benefits	4,000
	$14,500

Assume Hank and Thelma file a joint return, have no deductions *for* AGI, and do not itemize. Are they eligible for the tax credit for the elderly? If so, calculate the amount of the credit, assuming the credit is not limited by their tax liability.

44. Kim, a U.S. citizen and resident, owns and operates a novelty goods business. During 1996, Kim has taxable income of $100,000, made up as follows: $50,000 from foreign sources and $50,000 from U.S. sources. In calculating taxable income, the standard deduction is used. The income from foreign sources is subject to foreign income taxes of $26,000. For 1996, Kim files a joint return claiming his three children as dependents.
   a. Assuming Kim chooses to claim the foreign taxes as an income tax credit, what is his income tax liability for 1996?
   b. Recently, Kim has become disenchanted with the location of his business and is considering moving his foreign operation to a different country. Based on his research, if he moves his business to his country of choice, all relevant revenues and costs would remain approximately the same except that the income taxes payable to that country would be only $10,000. Given that all of the foreign income taxes paid are available to offset the U.S. tax liability (whether he operates in a high-tax or a low-tax foreign jurisdiction), what impact will this have on his decision regarding the potential move?

45. Blue Corporation, a U.S. corporation, is a manufacturing concern that sells most of its products in the United States. It does, however, do some business in Europe through various branches. During 1996, Blue Corporation had taxable income of $500,000, of

which $350,000 was U.S.-sourced and $150,000 was foreign-sourced. Foreign income taxes paid are $45,000. Blue Corporation's U.S. income tax liability before any foreign tax credit is $170,000. What is Blue Corporation's U.S. income tax net of the allowable foreign tax credit?

46. Pat and Jeri are husband and wife, and both are gainfully employed. They have three children under the age of 13. During the current year, Pat earned $60,000, while Jeri earned $4,900. In order for them to work, they paid $5,800 to various unrelated parties to care for their children. Assuming Pat and Jeri file a joint return, what, if any, is their credit for child and dependent care expenses for the current year?

47. Jim and Jill are husband and wife and have two dependent children under the age of 13. They both are gainfully employed and during the current year earned salaries as follows: $12,000 (Jim) and $4,500 (Jill). To care for their children while they work, they pay Megan (Jim's mother) $5,600. Megan does not qualify as a dependent of Jim and Jill. Assuming Jim and Jill file a joint return, what, if any, is their credit for child and dependent care expenses?

48. Kevin and Jane are husband and wife and have one dependent child, age 9. Kevin is a full-time student for all of the current year, while Jane earns $18,000 as a nurse's aid. In order to provide care for their child while Kevin attends classes and Jane works, they pay Sara (Jane's 17-year-old sister) $2,300. Sara is not a dependent of Kevin and Jane. Assuming Kevin and Jane file a joint return, what, if any, is their credit for child and dependent care expenses?

49. In each of the following independent situations, determine the amount of FICA that should be withheld from the employee's 1996 salary by the employer:
    a. Harry earns a $50,000 salary, files a joint return, and claims four withholding allowances.
    b. Hazel earns a $70,000 salary, files a joint return, and claims four withholding allowances.
    c. Tracy earns a $150,000 salary, files a joint return, and claims four withholding allowances.
    d. Alicia's 17-year-old son, Carlos, earns $10,000 at the family business.

50. During 1996, Greg Cruz (1401 Orangedale Road, Troy, MI 48084) worked for Maple Corporation and Gray Company. He earned $60,000 at Maple Corporation where he was a full-time employee. Greg also worked part-time for Gray Company for wages of $30,000.
    a. Did Greg experience an overwithholding of FICA taxes? Write a letter to Greg and a memo for the tax files in which you explain your conclusion.
    b. Did Maple Corporation and Gray Company overpay the employer's portion of FICA? Explain.

51. In each of the following independent situations, determine the maximum withholding allowances permitted Eli (an employee) on Form W–4:
    a. Eli is single with no dependents.
    b. Eli is married to a nonemployed spouse, and they have no dependents.
    c. Eli is married to Vera, an employed spouse, and they have three dependent children. On the Form W–4 that she filed with the employer, Vera claimed zero allowances.
    d. Assume the same facts as in (c), except that Eli and Vera fully support Eli's mother, who lives with them. The mother (age 70 and blind) qualifies as their dependent. (Refer to Chapter 3.)
    e. Eli is single with no dependents but works for two employers, one on a full-time basis and the other on a part-time basis. The Form W–4 filed with the first employer (the full-time job) reflects two withholding exemptions. The wages from each job exceed $1,000.
    f. Assume the same facts as in (e), except that Eli is married to a nonemployed spouse.

52. Norm is married to a nonemployed spouse and has four dependents. He is employed by Beige Corporation and is paid a monthly salary of $2,620 ($31,440 per year). Using these facts, determine the amount to be withheld by Beige Corporation for Federal

income tax purposes under the wage-bracket tables and under the percentage method for 1996.

53. During 1996, Helen, the owner of a store, had the following income and expenses:

Gross profit on sales	$63,000
Income from part-time job (subject to FICA)	24,000
Business expenses (related to store)	15,000
Fire loss on store building	1,200
Dividend income	200
Long-term capital gain on the sale of a stock investment	2,000

Compute Helen's self-employment tax using the format illustrated in the text.

54. In 1996, Fran has self-employed earnings of $150,000. Compute Fran's self-employment tax liability and the allowable income tax deduction for the self-employment tax paid using the format illustrated in the text.

CUMULATIVE PROBLEMS

55. Hal and Wanda Atkins, ages 38 and 36, are married and file a joint return. Their Social Security numbers are 123–32–1232 and 456–65–4321, respectively. Hal and Wanda's household includes Sam, their 10-year-old son, and Fred, who is Hal's 76-year-old father. Sam's Social Security number is 789–87–6543, and Fred's Social Security number is 123–87–1232. Fred is very ill and has been confined to bed for most of the year. He has no income of his own and is fully supported by Hal and Wanda. Hal and Wanda had the following income and expenses during 1996:

Hal's wages	$ 8,000
Wanda's salary	14,000
Interest from First National Bank	50
Unemployment compensation received by Hal, who was laid off for five months during the year	5,500
Dividends received on January 3, 1997; the corporation mailed the check on December 31, 1996	350
Amounts paid to Nora, Hal's niece, for household help and caring for Sam and Fred while Hal and Wanda were working	5,000
Unreimbursed travel expenses (including meals of $200) incurred by Wanda in connection with her job	1,250
Total itemized deductions (not including any potential deductions mentioned elsewhere in the problem)	6,600
Federal income taxes withheld by their employers	700

Compute net tax payable or refund due for Hal and Wanda for 1996. Suggested software (if available): *TurboTax* or *MacInTax*.

56. Beth R. Jordan lives at 2322 Skyview Road, Mesa, AZ 85202. She is a tax accountant with Mesa Manufacturing Company. She also writes computer software programs for tax practitioners and has a part-time tax practice. Beth, age 35, is single and has no dependents. Her Social Security number is 111–35–2222. She wants to contribute $3 to the Presidential Election Campaign Fund.

During 1995, Beth earned a salary of $50,000 from her employer. She received interest of $290 from Home Federal Savings and Loan and $335 from Home State Bank. She received dividends of $500 from Gray Corporation, $400 from Blue Corporation, and $300 from Orange Corporation.

Beth received a $1,200 income tax refund from the state of Arizona on May 12, 1995. On her 1994 Federal income tax return, she reported total itemized deductions of $6,700, which included $2,000 of state income tax withheld by her employer.

Fees earned from her part-time tax practice in 1995 totaled $3,800. She paid $400 to have the tax returns processed by a computerized tax return service.

On February 1, 1995, Beth bought 500 shares of Gray Corporation common stock for $17.60 a share. On July 16, Beth sold the stock for $15 a share.

Beth bought a used utility vehicle for $3,000 on June 5, 1995. She purchased the vehicle from her brother-in-law, who was unemployed and was in need of cash. On November 2, 1995, she sold the vehicle to a friend for $3,400.

On January 2, 1984, Beth acquired 100 shares of Blue Corporation common stock for $30 a share. She sold the stock on December 19, 1995, for $75 a share.

During 1995, Beth received royalties of $14,000 on a software program she had written. Beth incurred the following expenditures in connection with her software-writing activities:

Cost of microcomputer (100% business use)	$7,000
Cost of printer (100% business use)	2,000
Furniture	3,000
Supplies	650
Fee paid to computer consultant	3,500

Beth elected to expense the maximum portion of the cost of the microcomputer, printer, and furniture allowed under the provisions of § 179. This equipment and furniture were placed in service on January 15, 1995.

Although her employer suggested that Beth attend a convention on current developments in corporate taxation, Beth was not reimbursed for the travel expenses of $1,420 she incurred in attending the convention. The $1,420 included $200 for the cost of meals.

During 1995, Beth paid $300 for prescription medicines and $2,875 in doctor bills, hospital bills, and medical insurance premiums. Her employer withheld state income tax of $1,954. Beth paid real property taxes of $1,766 on her home. Interest on her home mortgage was $3,845, and interest to credit card companies was $320. Beth contributed $20 each week to her church and $10 each week to the United Way. Professional dues and subscriptions totaled $350.

Beth's employer withheld Federal income taxes of $9,500 during 1995. Beth paid estimated taxes of $1,600. What is the amount of Beth's net tax payable or refund due for 1995? If Beth has a tax refund due, she wants to have it credited toward her 1996 income tax. If you use tax forms for your solution, you will need Forms 1040, 2106, and 4562 and Schedules A, B, C, D, and SE. Suggested software (if available): *TurboTax* or *MacInTax*.

RESEARCH PROBLEMS

Note: ***West's Federal Taxation on CD-ROM*** *can be used in preparing solutions to the Research Problems. Alternatively, tax research materials contained in a standard tax library can be used.*

Research Problem 1. Matthew Mark, who is the pastor of your church, asks your advice concerning a tax issue that was briefly discussed on the evening television news. According to the news story, the fair rental value of a home provided to a minister is excluded in calculating income tax. This exclusion is clearly provided by § 107. However, Mark did not understand whether the fair rental value of the home should be included in the base for computing the self-employment tax. Mark admitted that he had never included the rental value in computing his self-employment tax and said that "such taxation just wouldn't be right because the home is clearly excluded from income tax." How do you respond to your pastor?

Partial list of research aids:
§§ 107(1) and 1402(a)(8).

Research Problem 2. Sandy and John Via (12 Maple Avenue, Albany, NY 12205) are married, file a joint Federal income tax return, and have a 12-year-old son and a 10-year-old daughter. Sandy is currently in the U.S. Air Force and has been stationed in Germany for the entire year. John and their children have remained in the United States where John picks up work only on an irregular basis. In working on their Federal income tax return for 1995, John wonders if they qualify for the earned income credit. Sandy's income consists of salary of $18,000 (taxable) and food and lodging provided by the Air Force, valued at $4,000 (not taxable), while John's earnings for the current year total $5,000. John approaches you and asks your advice. Write a letter to Sandy and John that contains your conclusion and prepare a memo for the tax files.

Research Problem 3. Isabella, a lover of early twentieth-century American history and architecture, discovers a 1920s house in a downtown district of Atlanta during a recent visit. She decides not only to purchase and renovate this particular home, but also to move the structure to her hometown of Little Rock, Arkansas, so her community can enjoy its architectural features. Also, being aware of the availability of the tax credit for rehabilitation expenditures incurred on old structures, she wants to maximize her use of the provision once the renovation work begins in Arkansas. Comment on whether the renovation expenditures incurred will qualify for the tax credit for rehabilitation expenditures.

Research Problem 4. On graduating from the University of the Southeast with a Ph.D. in neurology, Sally learns that she has been awarded a postdoctoral fellowship from the university. This grant will enable her to pursue further study in her area of expertise dealing with the potential regeneration of atrophied nerve tissue. Besides the honor that the fellowship represents, Sally is excited about the opportunity to continue her studies, completely independent of the grantor. There is no requirement that Sally provide any services to the university in exchange for the grant. As she has been informed by the university's business office that she will receive a Form 1099–MISC at year-end reporting the grant proceeds as "nonemployee compensation," Sally is fully aware that the grant will be subject to Federal income taxation. However, the business office does not mention any exposure to the self-employment tax. Since the research grant proceeds will be reported to the IRS as "nonemployee compensation," Sally wonders whether she will be subject to the self-employment tax. What do you tell her?

TEAM PROJECT: ARTHUR ANDERSEN TAX CHALLENGE CASES

For more information on the Arthur Andersen Tax Challenge Cases, please refer to Chapter 1, page 1-38.

Information related to tax issues and problems that are discussed in this chapter may be found in the

Fields case on pages 1, 2, 3, 12, 19, 26, 33
Miller case on pages 1, 12-15

Read and analyze the case you have been assigned and *identify* any issues and problems that are related to material covered in this chapter. If the information provided in the case is complete, prepare answers for this part of the case at this time. If you need information that is contained in the later parts of the case, please write a memo summarizing the questions or problems so you can prepare a complete answer at a later date.

P • A • R • T

V

PROPERTY TRANSACTIONS

Part V presents the tax treatment of sales, exchanges, and other dispositions of property. Included are the determination of the realized gain or loss, recognized gain or loss, and the classification of the recognized gain or loss as capital or ordinary. The topic of basis is evaluated both in terms of its effect on the calculation of the gain or loss and in terms of the determination of the basis of any contemporaneous or related subsequent acquisitions of property.

CHAPTER

14

PROPERTY TRANSACTIONS: DETERMINATION OF GAIN OR LOSS AND BASIS CONSIDERATIONS

LEARNING OBJECTIVES

After completing Chapter 14, you should be able to:

1. Understand the computation of realized gain or loss on property dispositions.
2. Distinguish between realized and recognized gain or loss.
3. Apply the recovery of capital doctrine.
4. Explain how basis is determined for various methods of asset acquisition.
5. Describe various loss disallowance provisions.
6. Identify tax planning opportunities related to selected property transactions.

OUTLINE

This chapter and the following three chapters are concerned with the income tax consequences of property transactions (the sale or other disposition of property). The following questions are considered with respect to the sale or other disposition of property:

- Is there a realized gain or loss?
- If so, is the gain or loss recognized?
- If the gain or loss is recognized, is it ordinary or capital?
- What is the basis of any replacement property that is acquired?

EXAMPLE 1

Alice owns a house that she received from her mother seven months ago. Her mother's cost for the house was $75,000. Alice is considering selling the house to her favorite nephew, Dan, for $75,000. Alice anticipates she will have no gain or loss on the transaction. She comes to you for advice.

As Alice's tax adviser, you need answers to the following questions:

- You are aware that Alice's mother died around the time Alice indicates she received the house from her mother. Did Alice receive the house by gift prior to her mother's death? If so, what was the mother's adjusted basis? If instead Alice inherited the house from her mother, what was the fair market value of the house on the date of her mother's death?
- Was the house Alice's principal residence during the period she owned it and was it her principal residence prior to receiving it from her mother?
- How long did Alice's mother own the house?
- What is the fair market value of the house?
- Does Alice intend for the transaction with Dan to be a sale or part sale and part gift?
- What does Alice intend to do with the sale proceeds?

Once you have the answers to these questions, you can advise Alice on the tax consequences of the proposed transaction. ▼

Chapters 14 and 15 discuss the determination of realized and recognized gain or loss and the basis of property. Chapters 16 and 17 cover the classification of the recognized gain or loss as ordinary or capital.

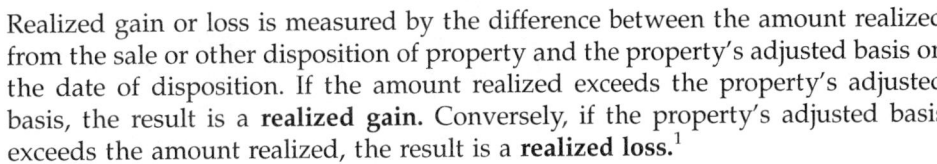

DETERMINATION OF GAIN OR LOSS

REALIZED GAIN OR LOSS

1 LEARNING OBJECTIVE
Understand the computation of realized gain or loss on property dispositions.

Realized gain or loss is measured by the difference between the amount realized from the sale or other disposition of property and the property's adjusted basis on the date of disposition. If the amount realized exceeds the property's adjusted basis, the result is a **realized gain.** Conversely, if the property's adjusted basis exceeds the amount realized, the result is a **realized loss.**[1]

EXAMPLE 2

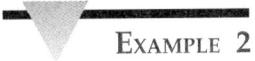

Tab sells Swan Corporation stock with an adjusted basis of $3,000 for $5,000. Tab's realized gain is $2,000. If Tab had sold the stock for $2,000, he would have had a $1,000 realized loss. ▼

Sale or Other Disposition. The term *sale or other disposition* is defined broadly in the tax law and includes virtually any disposition of property. Thus, transactions such as trade-ins, casualties, condemnations, thefts, and bond retirements are treated as dispositions of property. The most common disposition of property is through a sale or exchange. The key factor in determining whether a disposition has taken place usually is whether an identifiable event has occurred[2] as opposed to a mere fluctuation in the value of the property.[3]

EXAMPLE 3

Lori owns Tan Corporation stock that cost $3,000. The stock has appreciated in value by $2,000 since Lori purchased it. Lori has no realized gain since mere fluctuation in value is not a disposition or identifiable event for tax purposes. Nor would Lori have a realized loss had the stock declined in value by $2,000. ▼

Amount Realized. The **amount realized** from a sale or other disposition of property is the sum of any money received plus the fair market value of other property received. The amount realized also includes any real property taxes treated as imposed on the seller that are actually paid by the buyer.[4] The reason for including these taxes in the amount realized is that by paying the taxes, the purchaser is, in effect, paying an additional amount to the seller of the property.

The amount realized also includes any liability on the property disposed of, such as a mortgage debt, if the buyer assumes the mortgage or the property is sold subject to the mortgage.[5] The amount of the liability is included in the amount realized even if the debt is nonrecourse and the amount of the debt is greater than the fair market value of the mortgaged property.[6]

EXAMPLE 4

Barry sells property on which there is a mortgage of $20,000 to Cole for $50,000 cash. Barry's amount realized from the sale is $70,000 if Cole assumes the mortgage or takes the property subject to the mortgage. ▼

[1] § 1001(a) and Reg. § 1.1001–1(a).
[2] Reg. § 1.1001–1(c)(1).
[3] *Lynch v. Turrish,* 1 USTC ¶18, 3 AFTR 2986, 38 S.Ct. 537 (USSC, 1918).
[4] § 1001(b) and Reg. § 1.1001–1(b). Refer to Chapter 10 for a discussion of this subject.
[5] *Crane v. Comm.,* 47–1 USTC ¶9217, 35 AFTR 776, 67 S.Ct. 1047 (USSC, 1947). Although a legal distinction exists between the direct assumption of a mortgage and taking property subject to a mortgage, the tax consequences in calculating the amount realized are the same.
[6] *Comm. v. Tufts,* 83–1 USTC ¶9328, 51 AFTR2d 83–1132, 103 S.Ct. 1826 (USSC, 1983).

TAX IN THE NEWS

What Is the Amount Realized?

Determining the "amount realized" may be difficult, but usually can be done. The statutory definition is as follows: the sum of any money received plus the fair market value of property received. In a foreclosure sale, the amount realized includes the indebtedness discharged as the result of the foreclosure. In a real-world situation, however, the facts may not be nearly as clear as they are in a textbook situation.

In a recent case [*Wicker v. Comm.* 95–1 USTC ¶50,182, 75 AFTR2d 95–1701 (CA–8, 1995)], the Court of Appeals affirmed a Tax Court decision regarding the inability to calculate the "amount realized." In the case, both the IRS and the taxpayer could be viewed as losers or as winners, depending on one's perspective. The taxpayer had claimed a loss on his return associated with the foreclosure of mortgaged properties (i.e., the creditor accepted the mortgaged properties in exchange for the mortgage, with the properties being sold at a foreclosure sale). The IRS's position was that the foreclosure transaction produced a gain.

Because there was no evidence as to whether the loan was recourse or nonrecourse or the amount of the proceeds from the foreclosure sale, the Court concluded that the amount realized from the foreclosure could not be determined. Without a determination of the amount realized, it was not possible to ascertain if the foreclosure resulted in a gain or loss.

The **fair market value** of property received in a sale or other disposition has been defined by the courts as the price at which property will change hands between a willing seller and a willing buyer when neither is compelled to sell or buy.[7] Fair market value is determined by considering the relevant factors in each case.[8] An expert appraiser is often required to evaluate these factors in arriving at fair market value. When the fair market value of the property received cannot be determined, the value of the property surrendered may be used.[9]

In calculating the amount realized, selling expenses such as advertising, commissions, and legal fees relating to the disposition are deducted. The amount realized is the net amount received directly or indirectly by the taxpayer from the disposition of property in the form of cash or anything else of value.

Adjusted Basis. The **adjusted basis** of property disposed of is the property's original basis adjusted to the date of disposition.[10] Original basis is the cost or other basis of the property on the date the property is acquired by the taxpayer. *Capital additions* increase and *recoveries of capital* decrease the original basis so that on the date of disposition the adjusted basis reflects the unrecovered cost or other basis of the property.[11] Adjusted basis is determined as follows:

[7] *Comm. v. Marshman*, 60–2 USTC ¶9484, 5 AFTR2d 1528, 279 F.2d 27 (CA–6, 1960).

[8] *O'Malley v. Ames*, 52–1 USTC ¶9361, 42 AFTR 19, 197 F.2d 256 (CA–8, 1952).

[9] *U.S. v. Davis*, 62–2 USTC ¶9509, 9 AFTR2d 1625, 82 S.Ct. 1190 (USSC, 1962).

[10] § 1011(a) and Reg. § 1.1011–1.

[11] § 1016(a) and Reg. § 1.1016–1.

Cost (or other adjusted basis) on date of acquisition
+ Capital additions
− Capital recoveries
= Adjusted basis on date of disposition

Capital Additions. Capital additions include the cost of capital improvements and betterments made to the property by the taxpayer. These expenditures are distinguishable from expenditures for the ordinary repair and maintenance of the property that are neither capitalized nor added to the original basis (refer to Chapter 6). The latter expenditures are deductible in the current taxable year if they are related to business or income-producing property. Amounts representing real property taxes treated as imposed on the seller but paid or assumed by the buyer are part of the cost of the property.[12] Any liability on property that is assumed by the buyer is also included in the buyer's original basis of the property. The same rule applies if property is acquired subject to a liability. Amortization of the discount on bonds increases the adjusted basis of the bonds.[13]

Capital Recoveries. The following are examples of capital recoveries:

1. *Depreciation and cost recovery allowances.* The original basis of depreciable property is reduced by the annual depreciation charges (or cost recovery allowances) while the property is held by the taxpayer. The amount of depreciation that is subtracted from the original basis is the greater of the *allowed* or *allowable* depreciation on an annual basis.[14] In most circumstances, the allowed and allowable depreciation amounts are the same (refer to Chapter 8).
2. *Casualties and thefts.* A casualty or theft may result in the reduction of the adjusted basis of property.[15] The adjusted basis is reduced by the amount of the deductible loss. In addition, the adjusted basis is reduced by the amount of insurance proceeds received. However, the receipt of insurance proceeds may result in a recognized gain rather than a deductible loss. The gain increases the adjusted basis of the property.[16]

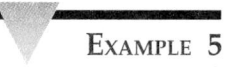

EXAMPLE 5

An insured truck used in a trade or business is destroyed in an accident. The adjusted basis is $8,000, and the fair market value is $6,500. Insurance proceeds of $6,500 are received. The amount of the casualty loss is $1,500 ($6,500 insurance proceeds − $8,000 adjusted basis). The adjusted basis is reduced by the $1,500 casualty loss and the $6,500 of insurance proceeds received. ▼

EXAMPLE 6

An insured truck used in a trade or business is destroyed in an accident. The adjusted basis is $6,500, and the fair market value is $8,000. Insurance proceeds of $8,000 are received. The amount of the casualty gain is $1,500 ($8,000 insurance proceeds − $6,500 adjusted basis). The adjusted basis is increased by the $1,500 casualty gain and is reduced by the $8,000 of insurance proceeds received ($6,500 basis before casualty + $1,500 casualty gain − $8,000 insurance proceeds = $0 basis). ▼

3. *Certain corporate distributions.* A corporate distribution to a shareholder that is not taxable is treated as a return of capital, and it reduces the basis of the

---

[12] Reg. §§ 1.1001–1(b)(2) and 1.1012–1(b). Refer to Chapter 10 for a discussion of this subject.

[13] See Chapter 16 for a discussion of bond discount and the related amortization.

[14] § 1016(a)(2) and Reg. § 1.1016–3(a)(1)(i).

[15] Refer to Chapter 7 for the discussion of casualties and thefts.

[16] Reg. § 1.1016–6(a).

shareholder's stock in the corporation.[17] For example, if a corporation makes a cash distribution to its shareholders and has no earnings and profits, the distributions are treated as a return of capital. Once the basis of the stock is reduced to zero, the amount of any subsequent distributions is a capital gain if the stock is a capital asset. These rules are illustrated in Example 21 of Chapter 20.

4. *Amortizable bond premium.* The basis in a bond purchased at a premium is reduced by the amortizable portion of the bond premium.[18] Investors in taxable bonds may *elect* to amortize the bond premium, but the premium on tax-exempt bonds *must be* amortized.[19] The amount of the amortized premium on taxable bonds is permitted as an interest deduction. Therefore, the election produces the opportunity for an annual interest deduction to offset ordinary income in exchange for a larger capital gain or smaller capital loss on the disposition of the bond. No such interest deduction is permitted for tax-exempt bonds.

The amortization deduction is allowed for taxable bonds because the premium is viewed as a cost of earning the taxable interest from the bonds. The reason the basis of taxable bonds is reduced is that the amortization deduction is a recovery of the cost or basis of the bonds. The basis of tax-exempt bonds is reduced even though the amortization is not allowed as a deduction. No amortization deduction is permitted on tax-exempt bonds since the interest income is exempt from tax and the amortization of the bond premium merely represents an adjustment of the effective amount of such income.

EXAMPLE 7

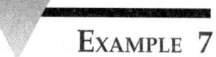

Antonio purchases Eagle Corporation taxable bonds with a face value of $100,000 for $110,000, thus paying a premium of $10,000. The annual interest rate is 7%, and the bonds mature 10 years from the date of purchase. The annual interest income is $7,000 (7% × $100,000). If Antonio elects to amortize the bond premium, the $10,000 premium is deducted over the 10-year period. Antonio's basis for the bonds is reduced each year by the amount of the amortization deduction. Note that if the bonds were tax-exempt, amortization of the bond premium and the basis adjustment would be mandatory. However, no deduction would be allowed for the amortization. ▼

RECOGNIZED GAIN OR LOSS

2 LEARNING OBJECTIVE
Distinguish between realized and recognized gain or loss.

Recognized gain is the amount of the realized gain included in the taxpayer's gross income.[20] A **recognized loss,** on the other hand, is the amount of a realized loss that is deductible for tax purposes.[21] As a general rule, the entire amount of a realized gain or loss is recognized.[22]

Concept Summary 14–1 summarizes the realized gain or loss and recognized gain or loss concepts.

NONRECOGNITION OF GAIN OR LOSS

In certain cases, a realized gain or loss is not recognized upon the sale or other disposition of property. One of the exceptions to the recognition of gain or loss

[17] § 1016(a)(4) and Reg. § 1.1016–5(a).

[18] § 1016(a)(5) and Reg. § 1.1016–5(b). The accounting treatment of bond premium amortization is the same as for tax purposes. The amortization results in a decrease in the bond investment account.

[19] § 171(c).

[20] § 61(a)(3) and Reg. § 1.61–6(a).

[21] § 165(a) and Reg. § 1.165–1(a).

[22] § 1001(c) and Reg. § 1.1002–1(a).

CONCEPT SUMMARY 14–1

Recognized Gain or Loss

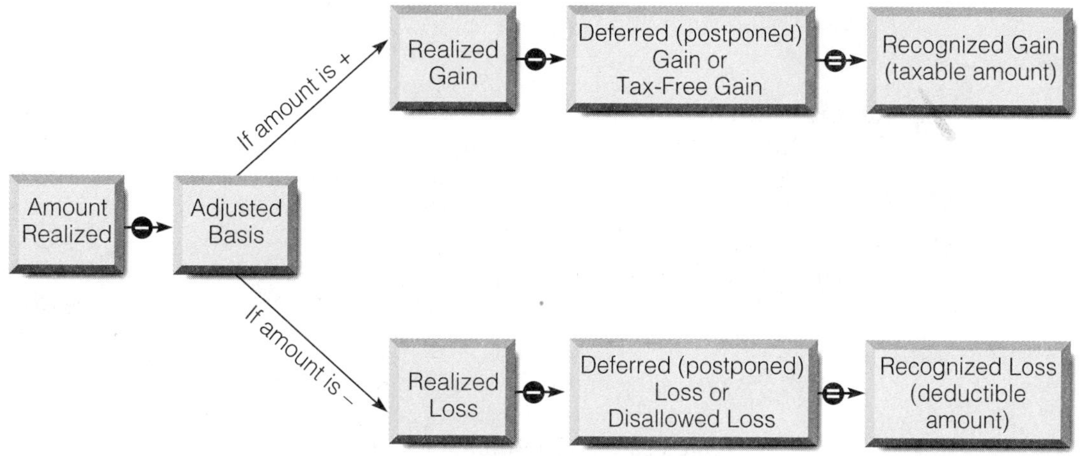

involves nontaxable exchanges, which are covered in Chapter 15. Additional exceptions include losses realized upon the sale, exchange, or condemnation of personal use assets (as opposed to business or income-producing property) and gains realized upon the sale of a residence by taxpayers 55 years of age or older (see Chapter 15). In addition, realized losses from the sale or exchange of business or income-producing property between certain related parties are not recognized.[23]

Sale, Exchange, or Condemnation of Personal Use Assets. A realized loss from the sale, exchange, or condemnation of personal use assets (e.g., a personal residence or an automobile not used at all for business or income-producing purposes) is not recognized for tax purposes. An exception exists for casualty or theft losses from personal use assets (see Chapter 7). In contrast, any gain realized from the sale or other disposition of personal use assets is, generally, fully taxable.

EXAMPLE 8

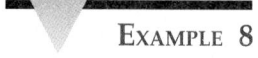

Freda sells an automobile, which is held exclusively for personal use, for $6,000. The adjusted basis of the automobile is $5,000. Freda has a realized and recognized gain of $1,000. ▼

EXAMPLE 9

Freda sells the automobile in Example 8 for $4,000. She has a realized loss of $1,000, but the loss is not recognized. ▼

RECOVERY OF CAPITAL DOCTRINE

3 LEARNING OBJECTIVE
Apply the recovery of capital doctrine.

Doctrine Defined. The **recovery of capital doctrine** is very significant and pervades all the tax rules relating to property transactions. The doctrine derives its roots from the very essence of the income tax—a tax on income. Therefore, as

[23] § 267(a)(1).

a general rule, a taxpayer is entitled to recover the cost or other original basis of property acquired and is not taxed on that amount.

The cost or other original basis of depreciable property is recovered through annual depreciation deductions. The basis is reduced as the cost is recovered over the period the property is held. Therefore, when property is sold or otherwise disposed of, it is the adjusted basis (unrecovered cost or other basis) that is compared to the amount realized from the disposition to determine realized gain or loss.

Relationship of the Recovery of Capital Doctrine to the Concepts of Realization and Recognition. If a sale or other disposition results in a realized gain, the taxpayer has recovered more than the adjusted basis of the property. Conversely, if a sale or other disposition results in a realized loss, the taxpayer has recovered less than the adjusted basis.

The general rules for the relationship between the recovery of capital doctrine and the realized and recognized gain and loss concepts are summarized as follows:

Rule 1. A realized gain that is *never recognized* results in the *permanent recovery* of more than the taxpayer's cost or other basis for tax purposes. For example, all or a portion of the realized gain on the sale of a personal residence by taxpayers 55 years of age or older can be excluded from gross income under § 121.

Rule 2. A realized gain on which *recognition is postponed* results in the *temporary recovery* of more than the taxpayer's cost or other basis for tax purposes. For example, an exchange of like-kind property under § 1031, an involuntary conversion under § 1033, and a replacement of a personal residence under § 1034 are all eligible for postponement treatment.

Rule 3. A realized loss that is *never recognized* results in the *permanent recovery* of less than the taxpayer's cost or other basis for tax purposes. For example, a loss on the sale of an automobile held for personal use is not deductible.

Rule 4. A realized loss on which *recognition is postponed* results in the *temporary recovery* of less than the taxpayer's cost or other basis for tax purposes. For example, the realized loss on the exchange of like-kind property under § 1031 is postponed.

These rules are illustrated in discussions to follow in this and the next chapter.

Basis Considerations

DETERMINATION OF COST BASIS

4 Learning Objective
Explain how basis is determined for various methods of asset acquisition.

The basis of property is generally the property's cost. Cost is the amount paid for the property in cash or other property.[24] This general rule follows logically from the recovery of capital doctrine; that is, the cost or other basis of property is to be recovered tax-free by the taxpayer.

A *bargain purchase* of property is an exception to the general rule for determining basis. A bargain purchase may result when an employer transfers

[24] § 1012 and Reg. § 1.1012–1(a).

property to an employee at less than the property's fair market value (as compensation for services) or when a corporation transfers property to a shareholder at less than the property's fair market value (a dividend). The basis of property acquired in a bargain purchase is the property's fair market value.[25] If the basis of the property were not increased by the bargain amount, the taxpayer would be taxed on this amount again at disposition.

EXAMPLE 10

Wade buys a machine from his employer for $10,000 on December 30, 1996. The fair market value of the machine is $15,000. Wade must include the $5,000 difference between cost and the fair market value of the machine in gross income for the taxable year 1996. The bargain element represents additional compensation to Wade. His basis for the machine is $15,000, the machine's fair market value. ▼

Identification Problems. Cost identification problems are frequently encountered in securities transactions. For example, the Regulations require that the taxpayer adequately identify the particular stock that has been sold.[26] A problem arises when the taxpayer has purchased separate lots of stock on different dates or at different prices and cannot adequately identify the lot from which a particular sale takes place. In this case, the stock is presumed to come from the first lot or lots purchased (a FIFO presumption).[27] When securities are left in the custody of a broker, it may be necessary to provide specific instructions and receive written confirmation as to which securities are being sold.

EXAMPLE 11

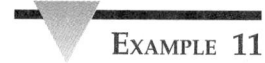

Polly purchases 100 shares of Olive Corporation stock on July 1, 1994, for $5,000 ($50 a share) and another 100 shares of Olive stock on July 1, 1995, for $6,000 ($60 a share). She sells 50 shares of the stock on January 2, 1996. The cost of the stock sold, assuming Polly cannot adequately identify the shares, is $50 a share, or $2,500. This is the cost Polly will compare to the amount realized in determining the gain or loss from the sale. ▼

Allocation Problems. When a taxpayer acquires *multiple assets in a lump-sum purchase,* the total cost must be allocated among the individual assets.[28] Allocation is necessary because some of the assets acquired may be depreciable (e.g., buildings) and others not (e.g., land). In addition, only a portion of the assets acquired may be sold, or some of the assets may be capital or § 1231 assets that receive special tax treatment upon subsequent sale or other disposition. The lump-sum cost is allocated on the basis of the fair market values of the individual assets acquired.

EXAMPLE 12

Harry purchases a building and land for $800,000. Because of the depressed nature of the industry in which the seller was operating, Harry was able to negotiate a very favorable purchase price. Appraisals of the individual assets indicate that the fair market value of the building is $600,000 and that of the land is $400,000. Harry's basis for the building is $480,000 ($600,000/$1,000,000 × $800,000), and his basis for the land is $320,000 ($400,000/$1,000,000 × $800,000). ▼

If a business is purchased and **goodwill** is involved, a special allocation rule applies. Initially, the purchase price is assigned to the assets, excluding goodwill, to the extent of their total fair market value. This assigned amount is allocated among the assets on the basis of the fair market value of the individual assets

[25] Reg. §§ 1.61–2(d)(2)(i) and 1.301–1(j).
[26] Reg. § 1.1012–1(c)(1).
[27] *Kluger Associates, Inc.*, 69 T.C. 925 (1978).
[28] Reg. § 1.61–6(a).

acquired. Goodwill is then assigned the residual amount of the purchase price. The resultant allocation is applicable to both the buyer and the seller.[29]

EXAMPLE 13

Rocky sells his business to Paul. They agree that the values of the individual assets are as follows:

Inventory	$ 50,000
Building	500,000
Land	200,000
Goodwill	150,000

After negotiations, Rocky and Paul agree on a sales price of $1 million. Applying the residual method with respect to goodwill results in the following allocation of the $1 million purchase price:

Inventory	$ 50,000
Building	500,000
Land	200,000
Goodwill	250,000

The residual method requires that all of the excess of the purchase price over the fair market value of the assets ($1,000,000 – $900,000 = $100,000) be allocated to goodwill. Without this requirement, the purchaser could allocate the excess pro rata to all of the assets, including goodwill, based on their respective fair market values. This would have resulted in only $166,667 [$150,000 + ($150,000 ÷ $900,000 × $100,000)] being assigned to goodwill. ▼

In the case of *nontaxable stock dividends,* the allocation depends upon whether the dividend is a common stock dividend on common stock or a preferred stock dividend on common stock. If the dividend is common on common, the cost of the original common shares is allocated to the total shares owned after the dividend.[30]

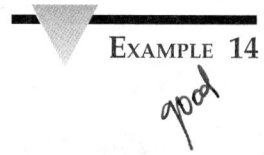

EXAMPLE 14

Susan owns 100 shares of Sparrow Corporation common stock for which she paid $1,100. She receives a 10% common stock dividend, giving her a new total of 110 shares. Before the stock dividend, Susan's basis was $11 per share ($1,100 ÷ 100 shares). The basis of each share after the stock dividend is $10 ($1,100 ÷ 110 shares). ▼

If the dividend is preferred stock on common, the cost of the original common shares is allocated between the common and preferred shares on the basis of their relative fair market values on the date of distribution.[31]

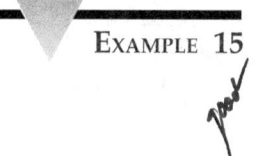

EXAMPLE 15

Fran owns 100 shares of Cardinal Corporation common stock for which she paid $1,000. She receives a stock dividend of 50 shares of preferred stock on her common stock. The fair market values on the date of distribution of the preferred stock dividend are $30 a share for common stock and $40 a share for preferred stock. Thus, the total fair market value is $3,000 ($30 × 100) for common stock and $2,000 ($40 × 50) for preferred stock. The basis of Fran's common stock after the dividend is $600, or $6 a share ($3,000/$5,000 × $1,000), and the basis of the preferred stock is $400, or $8 a share ($2,000/$5,000 × $1,000). ▼

[29] § 1060.

[30] §§ 305(a) and 307(a). The holding period of the new shares includes the holding period of the old shares. § 1223(5) and Reg. § 1.1223–1(e). See Chapter 16 for a discussion of the importance of the holding period.

[31] Reg. § 1.307–1(a).

In the case of *nontaxable stock rights,* the basis of the rights is zero unless the taxpayer elects or is required to allocate a portion of the cost of the stock to the rights. If the fair market value of the rights is 15 percent or more of the fair market value of the stock, the taxpayer is required to allocate. If the value of the rights is less than 15 percent of the fair market value of the stock, the taxpayer may elect to allocate.[32] The result is that either the rights will have no basis or the cost of the stock on which the rights are received will be allocated between the stock and rights on the basis of their relative fair market values.

EXAMPLE 16

Donald receives nontaxable stock rights with a fair market value of $1,000. The fair market value of the stock on which the rights were received is $8,000 (cost $10,000). Donald does not elect to allocate. The basis of the rights is zero. If he exercises the rights, the basis of the new stock is the exercise (subscription) price. ▼

EXAMPLE 17

Assume the same facts as in Example 16, except the fair market value of the rights is $3,000. Donald must allocate because the value of the rights is 15% or more of the value of the stock ($3,000/$8,000 = 37.5%). The basis of the rights is $2,727 ($3,000/$11,000 × $10,000), and the basis of the stock is $7,273 ($8,000/$11,000 × $10,000). If Donald exercises the rights, the basis of the new stock is the exercise (subscription) price plus the basis of the rights. If he sells the rights, he recognizes gain or loss to the extent of the difference between the amount realized and the basis of the rights. This allocation rule applies only when the rights are exercised or sold. Therefore, if the rights are allowed to lapse (expire), they have no basis, and the basis of the original stock is the stock's cost, $10,000. ▼

The holding period of nontaxable stock rights includes the holding period of the stock on which the rights were distributed. However, if the rights are exercised, the holding period of the newly acquired stock begins with the date the rights are exercised.[33] The significance of the holding period for capital assets is discussed in Chapter 16.

GIFT BASIS

When a taxpayer receives property as a gift, there is no cost to the recipient. Thus, under the cost basis provision, the donee's basis would be zero. However, this would violate the statutory intent that gifts are not subject to the income tax. With a zero basis, a sale by the donee would result in all of the amount realized being treated as realized gain. Therefore, a basis is assigned to the property received depending on the following:[34]

- The date of the gift.
- The basis of the property to the donor.
- The amount of the gift tax paid.
- The fair market value of the property.

Gift Basis Rules if No Gift Tax Is Paid. Property received by gift can be referred to as *dual basis* property; that is, the basis for gain and the basis for loss might not be the same amount. The present basis rules for gifts of property are as follows:

---

[32] § 307(b).

[33] § 1223(5) and Reg. §§ 1.1223–1(e) and (f).

[34] § 102(a).

- If the donee subsequently disposes of gift property in a transaction that results in a gain, the basis to the donee is the same as the donor's adjusted basis.[35] The donee's basis in this case is referred to as the *gain basis.* Therefore, a *realized gain* results if the amount realized from the disposition exceeds the donee's gain basis.

EXAMPLE 18

Melissa purchased stock in 1995 for $10,000. She gave the stock to her son, Joe, in 1996, when the fair market value was $15,000. Assume no gift tax is paid on the transfer and Joe subsequently sells the property for $15,000. Joe's basis is $10,000, and he has a realized gain of $5,000. ▼

- If the donee subsequently disposes of gift property in a transaction that results in a loss, the basis to the donee is the *lower* of the donor's adjusted basis or fair market value on the date of the gift. The donee's basis in this case is referred to as the *loss basis.* Therefore, a *realized loss results* if the amount realized from the disposition is less than the donee's loss basis.

EXAMPLE 19

Burt purchased stock in 1995 for $10,000. He gave the stock to his son, Cliff, in 1996, when the fair market value was $7,000. Assume no gift tax is paid on the transfer. Cliff later sells the stock for $6,000. Cliff's basis is $7,000 (fair market value is less than donor's adjusted basis of $10,000), and the realized loss from the sale is $1,000 ($6,000 amount realized – $7,000 basis). ▼

The amount of the loss basis will *differ* from the amount of the gain basis only if at the date of the gift the adjusted basis of the property exceeds the property's fair market value. Note that the loss basis rule prevents the donee from receiving a tax benefit from the decline in value while the donor held the property. Therefore, in Example 19, Cliff has a loss of only $1,000 rather than a loss of $4,000. The $3,000 difference represents the decline in value while Burt held the property. Ironically, however, the gain basis rule may eventually result in the donee's being subject to income tax on the appreciation that occurred while the donor held the property, as illustrated in Example 18.

If the amount realized from sale or other disposition is *between* the basis for loss and the basis for gain, no gain or loss is realized.

EXAMPLE 20

Assume the same facts as in Example 19, except that Cliff sold the stock for $8,000. The application of the gain basis rule produces a loss of $2,000 ($8,000 – $10,000). The application of the loss basis rule produces a gain of $1,000 ($8,000 – $7,000). Therefore, Cliff recognizes neither a gain nor a loss because the amount realized is between the gain basis and the loss basis. ▼

Adjustment for Gift Tax. If gift taxes are paid by the donor, the donee's gain basis may exceed the adjusted basis of the property to the donor. This occurs only if the fair market value of the property at the date of the gift is greater than the donor's adjusted basis (the property has appreciated in value). The portion of the gift tax paid that is related to the appreciation is added to the donor's basis in

[35] § 1015(a) and Reg. § 1.1015–1(a)(1). See Reg. § 1.1015–1(a)(3) for cases in which the facts necessary to determine the donor's adjusted basis are unknown. Refer to Example 24 for the effect of depreciation deductions by the donee.

calculating the donee's gain basis for the property. In this circumstance, the following formula is used for calculating the donee's gain basis:[36]

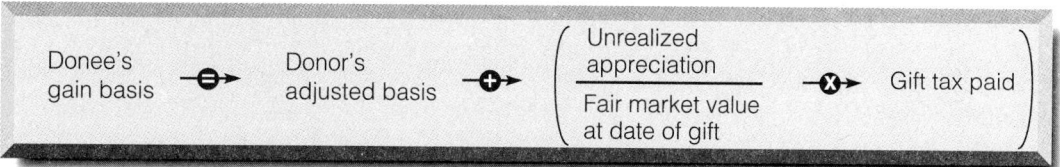

$$\text{Donee's gain basis} = \text{Donor's adjusted basis} + \left(\frac{\text{Unrealized appreciation}}{\text{Fair market value at date of gift}} \times \text{Gift tax paid} \right)$$

EXAMPLE 21

Bonnie made a gift of stock to Peggy in 1996, when the fair market value of the stock was $40,000. Bonnie had purchased the stock in 1982 for $10,000. Because the unrealized appreciation is $30,000 ($40,000 fair market value − $10,000 adjusted basis) and the fair market value is $40,000, three-fourths ($30,000/$40,000) of the gift tax paid is added to the basis of the property. If Bonnie paid gift tax of $4,000, Peggy's basis in the property is $13,000 [$10,000 + $3,000 (¾ of the $4,000 gift tax)]. ▼

EXAMPLE 22

Don made a gift of stock to Matt in 1996, when the fair market value of the stock was $40,000. Gift tax of $4,000 was paid by Don, who had purchased the stock in 1982 for $45,000. Because there is no unrealized appreciation at the date of the gift, none of the gift tax paid is added to Don's basis in calculating Matt's gain basis. Therefore, Matt's gain basis is $45,000. ▼

For *gifts made before 1977,* the full amount of the gift tax paid is added to the donor's basis. However, the ceiling on this total is the fair market value of the property at the date of the gift. Thus, in Example 21, if the gift had been made before 1977, the basis of the property would be $14,000 ($10,000 + $4,000). In Example 22, the gain basis would still be $45,000 ($45,000 + $0).

Holding Period. The **holding period** for property acquired by gift begins on the date the donor acquired the property if the gain basis rule applies.[37] The holding period starts on the date of the gift if the loss basis rule applies.[38] The significance of the holding period for capital assets is discussed in Chapter 16.

The following example summarizes the basis and holding period rules for gift property:

EXAMPLE 23

Jill acquires 100 shares of Wren Corporation stock on December 30, 1982, for $40,000. On January 3, 1996, when the stock has a fair market value of $38,000, Jill gives it to Dennis and pays gift tax of $4,000. The basis is not increased by a portion of the gift tax paid because the property has not appreciated in value at the time of the gift. Therefore, Dennis's gain basis is $40,000. Dennis's basis for determining loss is $38,000 (fair market value) because the fair market value on the date of the gift is less than the donor's adjusted basis.

- If Dennis sells the stock for $45,000, he has a recognized gain of $5,000. The holding period for determining whether the capital gain is short term or long term begins on December 30, 1982, the date Jill acquired the property.

---

[36] § 1015(d)(6).

[37] § 1223(2) and Reg. § 1.1223–1(b).

[38] Rev.Rul. 59–86, 1959–1 C.B. 209.

- If Dennis sells the stock for $36,000, he has a recognized loss of $2,000. The holding period for determining whether the capital loss is short term or long term begins on January 3, 1996, the date of the gift.
- If Dennis sells the property for $39,000, there is no gain or loss since the amount realized is less than the gain basis of $40,000 and more than the loss basis of $38,000. ▼

ETHICAL CONSIDERATIONS

Looking a Gift Horse in the Eye

Walter rarely sees his Uncle George because George is a devoted world traveler. On February 10, 1996, Walter received an envelope that George had mailed to him from Angola on December 23, 1995. The envelope contained 1,000 shares of stock of Lavender, Inc., and a Christmas card from George.

Walter is engaged to be married in December 1996. To finance the wedding (he and his fiancée have agreed that this is his responsibility) and the honeymoon, and to pay for the engagement ring, Walter sells the stock in October 1996 for $45,000.

In early April 1997, the accountant who is preparing Walter's tax return tells him that she needs to know his uncle's adjusted basis for the stock and the amount of any gift tax paid. Since Walter is unable to contact his uncle by April 15, 1997, he requests a filing extension on Form 4868. He does mail a letter to Uncle George requesting this information and thanking him for the gift. Walter is able to ascertain from a stock service that during the past 10 years, the stock price has ranged from $10 per share to $50 per share.

On August 10, 1997, Uncle George unexpectedly calls from Bosnia. He says he has not filed any type of Federal tax return in years. He thinks he won the stock in a poker game in Monaco about 15 years ago when another player used it to cover a $15,000 bet.

Walter wants to file his tax return by the August 15, 1997, due date. He does not think it is a good idea to tell the tax return preparer how his uncle acquired the stock or about his uncle's not filing tax returns. So he calls the accountant and tells her that his uncle's basis for the stock is $15,000 and that no gift taxes were paid.

Evaluate Walter's behavior.

Basis for Depreciation. The basis for depreciation on depreciable gift property is the donee's gain basis.[39] This rule is applicable even if the donee later sells the property at a loss and uses the loss basis rule in calculating the amount of the realized loss.

EXAMPLE 24

Vito gave a machine to Tina in 1996, when the adjusted basis was $32,000 (cost of $40,000 – accumulated depreciation of $8,000) and the fair market value was $26,000. No gift tax was paid. Tina's gain basis at the date of the gift is $32,000, and her loss basis is $26,000. During 1996, Tina deducts depreciation (cost recovery) of $10,240 ($32,000 × 32%). Therefore, at the end of 1996, Tina's gain basis and loss basis are calculated as follows:

[39] § 1011 and Reg. §§ 1.1011–1 and 1.167(g)–1.

	Gain Basis	Loss Basis
Donor's basis or fair market value	$ 32,000	$ 26,000
Depreciation	(10,240)	(10,240)
	$ 21,760	$ 15,760

▼

PROPERTY ACQUIRED FROM A DECEDENT

General Rules. The basis of property acquired from a decedent is generally the property's fair market value at the date of death (referred to as the *primary valuation amount*).[40] The property's basis is the fair market value six months after the date of death if the executor or administrator of the estate *elects* the alternate valuation date for estate tax purposes. This amount is referred to as the *alternate valuation amount.*

EXAMPLE 25

Linda and various other family members inherited property from Linda's father, who died in 1996. At the date of death, her father's adjusted basis for the property Linda inherited was $35,000. The property's fair market value at date of death was $50,000. The alternate valuation date was not elected. Linda's basis for income tax purposes is $50,000. This is commonly referred to as a *stepped-up basis.* ▼

EXAMPLE 26

Assume the same facts as in Example 25, except the property's fair market value at date of death was $20,000. Linda's basis for income tax purposes is $20,000. This is commonly referred to as a *stepped-down basis.* ▼

If an estate tax return does not have to be filed because the estate is below the threshold amount for being subject to the estate tax, the alternate valuation date and amount are not available. Even if an estate tax return is filed and the executor elects the alternate valuation date, the six months after death date is available only for property that the executor has not distributed before this date. Any property distributed or otherwise disposed of by the executor during this six-month period will have an adjusted basis to the beneficiary equal to the fair market value on the date of distribution or other disposition.[41]

The alternate valuation date can be *elected only* if the election results in both the value of the gross estate and the estate tax liability being reduced below the amounts they would have been if the primary valuation date had been used. This provision prevents the alternate valuation election from being used to increase the basis of the property to the beneficiary for income tax purposes without simultaneously increasing the estate tax liability (because of estate tax deductions or credits).[42]

EXAMPLE 27

Nancy inherited all the property of her father, who died in 1996. Her father's adjusted basis for the property at date of death was $35,000. The property's fair market value was $750,000 at date of death and $760,000 six months after death. The alternate valuation date cannot be elected because the value of the gross estate has increased during the six-month period. Nancy's basis for income tax purposes is $750,000. ▼

[40] § 1014(a).
[41] § 2032(a)(1) and Rev.Rul. 56–60, 1956–1 C.B. 443.
[42] § 2032(c).

TAX IN THE NEWS

Carryover Basis versus Stepped-Up Basis

According to the old saying, "what goes around comes around." A good example is the proposal to replace the stepped-up basis (i.e., fair market value) for inherited property with a carryover basis.

The Tax Reform Act of 1976 amended the Code to provide that a beneficiary's basis for inherited property would be a carryover basis. The provision had a future effective date. Prior to that date, Senator Harry F. Byrd, Jr., of Virginia (now retired) was successful in attaching a rider to the Crude Oil Windfall Profit Tax Act of 1980, which repealed the carryover basis provision.

Several proposals to resurrect carryover basis for inherited property surfaced during the debates over the Revenue Reconciliation Act of 1993. Those who support carryover basis point out that it would make the basis rules for gifts during life and transfers at death symmetrical and would generate additional revenue. Opponents counter that the inherited property may be subject to the Federal estate tax and that determining the decedent's basis for the property may be difficult in many instances.

The proposals for carryover basis were not included in the Revenue Reconciliation Act of 1993. But the question still remains: Is carryover basis an issue whose time has come?

Example 28 Assume the same facts as in Example 27, except the property's fair market value six months after death was $745,000. If the executor elects the alternate valuation date, Nancy's basis for income tax purposes is $745,000. ▼

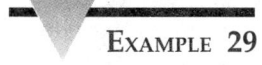

Example 29 Assume the same facts as in the previous example, except the property is distributed four months after the date of the decedent's death. At the distribution date, the property's fair market value is $747,500. Since the executor elected the alternate valuation date, Nancy's basis for income tax purposes is $747,500. ▼

For inherited property, both unrealized appreciation and decline in value are taken into consideration in determining the basis of the property for income tax purposes. Contrast this with the carryover basis rules for property received by gift.

Deathbed Gifts. The Code contains a provision designed to eliminate a tax avoidance technique referred to as *deathbed gifts*. If the time period between the date of the gift of appreciated property and the date of the donee's death is not longer than one year, the usual basis rule (stepped-up basis) for inherited property may not apply. The adjusted basis of such property inherited by the donor or his or her spouse from the donee shall be the same as the decedent's adjusted basis for the property rather than the fair market value at the date of death or the alternate valuation date.[43]

[43] § 1014(e).

EXAMPLE 30

Ned gives stock to his uncle, Vern, in 1996. Ned's basis for the stock is $1,000, and the fair market value is $9,000. No gift tax is paid. Eight months later, Ned inherits the stock from Vern. At the date of Vern's death, the fair market value of the stock is $12,000. Ned's adjusted basis for the stock is $1,000. ▼

ETHICAL CONSIDERATIONS

Helping a Friend Increase Basis

Holly owns stock with an adjusted basis of $2,500 and a fair market value of $9,500. Holly expects the stock to continue to appreciate. Alice, Holly's best friend, has recently been operated on for cancer. Alice's physicians have told her that her life expectancy is between six months and one and a half years.

One day at lunch, the two friends were discussing their tax situations (both feel they pay too much), when Alice mentioned that she had read a newspaper article about a tax planning opportunity that might be suitable for Holly. Holly would make a gift of the appreciated stock to Alice. In her will, Alice would bequeath the stock to Holly. Since Alice is confident that she will live longer than a year, the basis of the stock to Holly would be the fair market value on the date of Alice's death. Alice would "feel good" because she had helped Holly "beat the tax system."

You are Holly's tax adviser. How will you respond to Alice's proposal to Holly?

Survivor's Share of Property. Both the decedent's share and the survivor's share of *community property* have a basis equal to fair market value on the date of the decedent's death.[44] This result applies to the decedent's share of the community property because the property flows to the surviving spouse from the estate (fair market value basis for inherited property). Likewise, the surviving spouse's share of the community property is deemed to be acquired by bequest, devise, or inheritance from the decedent. Therefore, it also has a basis equal to fair market value.

EXAMPLE 31

Floyd and Vera reside in a community property state. They own community property (200 shares of Crow stock) that was acquired in 1974 for $100,000. Assume that Floyd dies in 1996, when the securities are valued at $300,000. One-half of the Crow stock is included in Floyd's estate. If Vera inherits Floyd's share of the community property, the basis for determining gain or loss is $300,000, determined as follows:

Vera's one-half of the community property (stepped up from $50,000 to $150,000 due to Floyd's death)	$150,000
Floyd's one-half of the community property (stepped up from $50,000 to $150,000 due to inclusion in his gross estate)	150,000
Vera's new basis	$300,000

▼

In a *common law* state, only one-half of jointly held property of spouses (tenants by the entirety or joint tenants with rights of survivorship) is includible in

[44] § 1014(b)(6). See the listing of community property states in Chapter 4.

the estate.[45] In such a case, no adjustment of the basis is permitted for the excluded property interest (the surviving spouse's share).

EXAMPLE 32

Assume the same facts as in the previous example, except that the property is jointly held by Floyd and Vera who reside in a common law state. Also assume that Floyd purchased the property and made a gift of one-half of the property when the stock was acquired, with no gift tax being paid. Only one-half of the Crow stock is included in Floyd's estate. Vera's basis for determining gain or loss in the excluded half is not adjusted upward for the increase in value to date of death. Therefore, Vera's basis is $200,000, determined as follows:

Vera's one-half of the jointly held property (carryover basis of $50,000)	$ 50,000
Floyd's one-half of the jointly held property (stepped up from $50,000 to $150,000 due to inclusion in his gross estate)	150,000
Vera's new basis	$200,000

Holding Period of Property Acquired from a Decedent. The holding period of property acquired from a decedent is *deemed to be long term* (held for the required long-term holding period). This provision applies regardless of whether the property is disposed of at a gain or a loss.[46]

DISALLOWED LOSSES

5 LEARNING OBJECTIVE
Describe various loss disallowance provisions.

Related Taxpayers. Section 267 provides that realized losses from sales or exchanges of property, directly or indirectly, between certain related parties are not recognized. This loss disallowance provision applies to several types of related-party transactions. The most common involve (1) members of a family and (2) transactions between an individual and a corporation in which the individual owns, directly or indirectly, more than 50 percent in value of the corporation's outstanding stock. Section 707 provides a similar loss disallowance provision if the related parties are a partner and a partnership in which the partner owns, directly or indirectly, more than 50 percent of the capital interests or profits interests in the partnership. The rules governing the relationships covered by § 267 were discussed in Chapter 6. See Chapter 15 for the discussion of the special rules under § 1041 for property transfers between spouses or incident to divorce.

If income-producing or business property is transferred to a related taxpayer and a loss is disallowed, the basis of the property to the recipient is the property's cost to the transferee. However, if a subsequent sale or other disposition of the property by the original transferee results in a realized gain, the amount of gain is reduced by the loss that was previously disallowed.[47] This *right of offset* is not applicable if the original sale involved the sale of a personal use asset (e.g., the sale of a personal residence between related taxpayers). Likewise, this right of offset is available only to the original transferee (the related-party buyer).

EXAMPLE 33

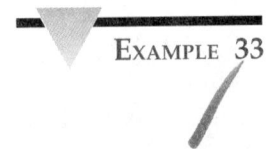

Pedro sells business property with an adjusted basis of $50,000 to his daughter, Josefina, for its fair market value of $40,000.

- Pedro's realized loss of $10,000 is not recognized.
- How much gain will Josefina recognize if she sells the property for $52,000? Josefina recognizes a $2,000 gain. Her realized gain is $12,000 ($52,000 less her basis of $40,000), but she can offset Pedro's $10,000 loss against the gain.

[45] § 2040(b).
[46] § 1223(11).
[47] § 267(d) and Reg. § 1.267(d)–1(a).

- How much gain will Josefina recognize if she sells the property for $48,000? Josefina recognizes no gain or loss. Her realized gain is $8,000 ($48,000 less her basis of $40,000), but she can offset $8,000 of Pedro's $10,000 loss against the gain. Note that Pedro's loss can only offset Josefina's gain. It cannot create a loss for Josefina.
- How much loss will Josefina recognize if she sells the property for $38,000? Josefina recognizes a $2,000 loss, the same as her realized loss ($38,000 less $40,000 basis). Pedro's loss does not increase Josefina's loss. His loss can be offset only against a gain. Since Josefina has no realized gain, Pedro's loss cannot be used and is never recognized. This example assumes that the property is business or income producing to Josefina. If not, her $2,000 loss is personal and is not recognized. ▼

The loss disallowance rules are designed to achieve two objectives. First, the rules prevent a taxpayer from directly transferring an unrealized loss to a related taxpayer in a higher tax bracket who could receive a greater tax benefit from the recognition of the loss. Second, the rules eliminate a substantial administrative burden on the Internal Revenue Service as to the appropriateness of the selling price (fair market value or not). The loss disallowance rules are applicable even where the selling price is equal to fair market value and can be validated (e.g., listed stocks).

The holding period of the buyer for the property is not affected by the holding period of the seller. That is, the buyer's *holding period* includes only the period of time he or she has held the property.[48]

ETHICAL CONSIDERATIONS

Transactions between Spouses

Ted and Lisa, both age 53, have been married for 10 years. At the time of their marriage, they both had substantial assets, so they signed a premarital agreement, establishing that their assets would not be commingled and that each would retain separate title to his or her respective assets.

As a result of their marriage, Ted and Lisa's Federal tax liability has been larger than it would have been if they were single (i.e., the marriage penalty). Ted and Lisa each own a 50 percent interest in some undeveloped land. Ted believes that they will be successful in having the land rezoned from residential to commercial. The rezoning could result in as much as a fourfold increase in the fair market value of the land. Based on her conversations with two members of the Planning Commission, Lisa has serious doubts that the rezoning request will be approved.

Ted has offered to buy Lisa's interest in the land for $300,000. Lisa's adjusted basis is $500,000. The land has declined in value since Ted and Lisa purchased it in accordance with a general decline in residential real estate values in the area.

Lisa's CPA informs her that her realized loss of $200,000 on the sale would be disallowed under § 267 as a transaction between related parties. He also informs her that if the land appreciates as a result of the rezoning, Ted, but not Lisa, could use her disallowed loss from the sale to Ted to reduce his recognized gain on a subsequent sale of the land.

From Lisa's perspective, this is the last straw. Their marriage is producing too many negative tax consequences. She proposes to Ted that they get a divorce "for tax purposes" and continue to live together as man and wife. Only Lisa, Ted, their CPA, and their attorney will be aware that they are no longer married.

Evaluate the necessity for Lisa's proposal and the likelihood of its success.

[48] §§ 267(d) and 1223(2) and Reg. § 1.267(d)–1(c)(3).

Wash Sales. Section 1091 stipulates that in certain cases, a realized loss on the sale or exchange of stock or securities is not recognized. Specifically, if a taxpayer sells or exchanges stock or securities and within 30 days before *or* after the date of the sale or exchange acquires substantially identical stock or securities, any loss realized from the sale or exchange is not recognized because the transaction is a **wash sale.**[49] The term *acquire* means acquire by purchase or in a taxable exchange and includes an option to purchase substantially identical securities. *Substantially identical* means the same in all important particulars. Corporate bonds and preferred stock are normally not considered substantially identical to the corporation's common stock. However, if the bonds and preferred stock are convertible into common stock, they may be considered substantially identical under certain circumstances.[50] Attempts to avoid the application of the wash sales rules by having a related taxpayer repurchase the securities have been unsuccessful.[51] The wash sales provisions do *not* apply to gains.

Recognition of the loss is disallowed because the taxpayer is considered to be in substantially the same economic position after the sale and repurchase as before the sale and repurchase. This disallowance rule does not apply to taxpayers engaged in the business of buying and selling securities.[52] Investors, however, are not allowed to create losses through wash sales to offset income for tax purposes.

Realized loss that is not recognized is added to the *basis* of the substantially identical stock or securities whose acquisition resulted in the nonrecognition of loss.[53] In other words, the basis of the replacement stock or securities is increased by the amount of the unrecognized loss. If the loss were not added to the basis of the newly acquired stock or securities, the taxpayer would never recover the entire basis of the old stock or securities.

The basis of the new stock or securities includes the unrecovered portion of the basis of the formerly held stock or securities. Therefore, the *holding period* of the new stock or securities begins on the date of acquisition of the old stock or securities.[54]

EXAMPLE 34

Bhaskar owns 100 shares of Green Corporation stock (adjusted basis of $20,000), 50 shares of which he sells for $8,000. Ten days later, he purchases 50 shares of the same stock for $7,000. Bhaskar's realized loss of $2,000 ($8,000 amount realized – $10,000 adjusted basis of 50 shares) is not recognized because it resulted from a wash sale. Bhaskar's basis in the newly acquired stock is $9,000 ($7,000 purchase price + $2,000 unrecognized loss from the wash sale). ▼

The taxpayer may acquire less than the number of shares sold in a wash sale. In this case, the loss from the sale is prorated between recognized and unrecognized loss on the basis of the ratio of the number of shares acquired to the number of shares sold.[55]

CONVERSION OF PROPERTY FROM PERSONAL USE TO BUSINESS OR INCOME-PRODUCING USE

As discussed previously, losses from the sale of personal use assets are not recognized for tax purposes, but losses from the sale of business and income-producing assets are deductible. Can a taxpayer convert a personal use asset that

[49] § 1091(a) and Reg. §§ 1.1091–1(a) and (f).

[50] Rev.Rul. 56–406, 1956–2 C.B. 523.

[51] *McWilliams v. Comm.*, 47–1 USTC ¶9289, 35 AFTR 1184, 67 S.Ct. 1477 (USSC, 1947).

[52] Reg. § 1.1091–1(a).

[53] § 1091(d) and Reg. § 1.1091–2(a).

[54] § 1223(4) and Reg. § 1.1223–1(d).

[55] § 1091(b) and Reg. § 1.1091–1(c).

has declined in value to business (or income-producing) use and then sell the asset to recognize a business (or income-producing) loss? The tax law prevents this by specifying that the *original basis for loss* on personal use assets converted to business or income-producing use is the *lower* of the property's adjusted basis or fair market value on the date of conversion.[56] The *gain basis* for converted property is the property's adjusted basis on the date of conversion. The tax law is not concerned with gains on converted property because gains are recognized regardless of whether property is business, income producing, or personal use.

EXAMPLE 35

Diane's personal residence has an adjusted basis of $75,000 and a fair market value of $60,000. Diane converts the personal residence to rental property. Her basis for loss is $60,000 (lower of $75,000 adjusted basis and fair market value of $60,000). The $15,000 decline in value is a personal loss and can never be recognized for tax purposes. Diane's basis for gain is $75,000. ▼

The basis for loss is also the *basis for depreciating* the converted property.[57] This is an exception to the general rule that provides that the basis for depreciation is the gain basis (e.g., property received by gift). This exception prevents the taxpayer from recovering a personal loss indirectly through depreciation of the higher original basis. After the property is converted, both its basis for loss and its basis for gain are adjusted for depreciation deductions from the date of conversion to the date of disposition. These rules apply only if a conversion from personal to business or income-producing use has actually occurred.

EXAMPLE 36

At a time when his personal residence (adjusted basis of $40,000) is worth $50,000, Keith converts one-half of it to rental use. The property is not MACRS recovery property. At this point, the estimated useful life of the residence is 20 years, and there is no estimated salvage value. After renting the converted portion for five years, Keith sells the property for $44,000. All amounts relate only to the building; the land has been accounted for separately. Keith has a $2,000 realized gain from the sale of the personal use portion of the residence and a $7,000 realized gain from the sale of the rental portion. These gains are computed as follows:

	Personal Use	Rental
Original basis for gain and loss—adjusted basis on date of conversion (fair market value is greater than the adjusted basis)	$20,000	$20,000
Depreciation—five years	None	5,000
Adjusted basis—date of sale	$20,000	$15,000
Amount realized	22,000	22,000
Realized gain	$ 2,000	$ 7,000

▼

As discussed in Chapter 15, Keith may be able to defer recognition of part or all of the $2,000 gain from the sale of the personal use portion of the residence under § 1034. The $7,000 gain from the rental portion is recognized.

[56] Reg. § 1.165–9(b)(2).
[57] Reg. § 1.167(g)–1.

EXAMPLE 37

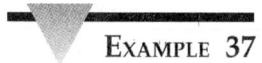

Assume the same facts as in the previous example, except that the fair market value on the date of conversion is $30,000 and the sales proceeds are $16,000. Keith has a $12,000 realized loss from the sale of the personal use portion of the residence and a $3,250 realized loss from the sale of the rental portion. These losses are computed as follows:

	Personal Use	Rental
Original basis for loss—fair market value on date of conversion (fair market value is less than the adjusted basis)	*	$15,000
Depreciation—five years	None	3,750
Adjusted basis—date of sale	$20,000	$11,250
Amount realized	8,000	8,000
Realized loss	$12,000	$ 3,250

*Not applicable.

The $12,000 loss from the sale of the personal use portion of the residence is not recognized. The $3,250 loss from the rental portion is recognized. ▼

ADDITIONAL COMPLEXITIES IN DETERMINING REALIZED GAIN OR LOSS

Amount Realized. The calculation of the amount realized may appear to be one of the least complex areas associated with property transactions. However, because numerous positive and negative adjustments may be required, the calculation of this amount can be complex and confusing. In addition, the determination of the fair market value of the items received by the taxpayer can be difficult. The following example provides insight into various items that can have an impact on the amount realized.

EXAMPLE 38

Ridge sells an office building and the associated land on October 1, 1996. Under the terms of the sales contract, Ridge is to receive $600,000 in cash. The purchaser is to assume Ridge's mortgage of $300,000 on the property. To enable the purchaser to obtain adequate financing to pay the $600,000, Ridge is to pay the $15,000 in points charged by the lender. The broker's commission on the sale is $45,000. The purchaser agrees to pay the $12,000 in property taxes for the entire year. The amount realized by Ridge is calculated as follows:

Selling price		
Cash	$600,000	
Mortgage assumed by purchaser	300,000	
Seller's property taxes paid by purchaser ($12,000 × 9/12)	9,000	$909,000
Less		
Broker's commission	$ 45,000	
Points paid by seller	15,000	(60,000)
Amount realized		$849,000

▼

Adjusted Basis. Three types of items tend to complicate the determination of adjusted basis. First, the applicable tax provisions for calculating the adjusted basis are dependent on how the property was acquired (e.g., purchase, taxable exchange, nontaxable exchange, gift, inheritance). Second, if the asset is subject to depreciation, cost recovery, amortization, or depletion, adjustments must be made to the basis during the time period the asset is held by the taxpayer. Upon disposition of the asset, the taxpayer's records for both of these items may be deficient. For example, the donee does not know the amount of the donor's basis or the amount of gift tax paid by the donor, or the taxpayer does not know how much depreciation he or she has deducted. Third, the complex positive and negative adjustments encountered in calculating the amount realized are also involved in calculating the adjusted basis.

EXAMPLE 39

Jane purchased a personal residence in 1990. The purchase price and the related closing costs were as follows:

Purchase price	$125,000
Recording costs	140
Title fees and title insurance	815
Survey costs	115
Attorney's fees	750
Appraisal fee	60

Other relevant tax information for the house during the time Jane owned it follows:

- Constructed a swimming pool for medical reasons. The cost was $10,000, of which $3,000 was deducted as a medical expense.
- Added a solar heating system. The cost was $15,000.
- Deducted home office expenses of $6,000. Of this amount, $3,200 was for depreciation.

The adjusted basis for the house is calculated as follows:

Purchase price	$125,000
Recording costs	140
Title fees and title insurance	815
Survey costs	115
Attorney's fees	750
Appraisal fee	60
Swimming pool ($10,000 – $3,000)	7,000
Solar heating system	15,000
	$148,880
Less: Depreciation deducted on home office	(3,200)
Adjusted basis	$145,680

SUMMARY OF BASIS ADJUSTMENTS

Some of the more common items that either increase or decrease the basis of an asset appear in Concept Summary 14–2.

In discussing the topic of basis, a number of specific techniques for determining basis have been presented. Although the various techniques are responsive to and mandated by transactions occurring in the marketplace, they do possess enough common characteristics to be categorized as follows:

- The basis of the asset may be determined by reference to the asset's cost.
- The basis of the asset may be determined by reference to the basis of another asset.
- The basis of the asset may be determined by reference to the asset's fair market value.

CONCEPT SUMMARY 14–2

Adjustments to Basis

Item	Effect	Refer to Chapter	Explanation
Amortization of bond discount.	Increase	16	Amortization is mandatory for certain taxable bonds and elective for tax-exempt bonds.
Amortization of bond premium.	Decrease	14	Amortization is mandatory for tax-exempt bonds and elective for taxable bonds.
Amortization of covenant not to compete.	Decrease	16	Covenant must be for a definite and limited time period. The amortization period is a statutory period of 15 years.
Amortization of intangibles.	Decrease	8	Even goodwill is now subject to amortization.
Assessment for local benefits.	Increase	10	To the extent not deductible as taxes (e.g., assessment for streets and sidewalks that increase the value of the property versus one for maintenance or repair or for meeting interest charges).
Bad debts.	Decrease	7	Only the specific charge-off method is permitted.
Capital additions.	Increase	14	Certain items, at the taxpayer's election, can be capitalized or deducted (e.g., selected medical expenses).
Casualty.	Decrease	7	For a casualty loss, the amount of the adjustment is the summation of the deductible loss and the insurance proceeds received. For a casualty gain, the amount of the adjustment is the insurance proceeds received reduced by the recognized gain.
Condemnation.	Decrease	15	See casualty explanation.
Cost recovery.	Decrease	8	§ 168 is applicable to tangible assets placed in service after 1980 whose useful life is expressed in terms of years.
Depletion.	Decrease	8	Use the greater of cost or percentage depletion. Percentage depletion can still be deducted when the basis is zero.
Depreciation.	Decrease	8	§ 167 is applicable to tangible assets placed in service before 1981 and to tangible assets not depreciated in terms of years.
Easement.	Decrease		If the taxpayer does not retain any use of the land, all of the basis is allocable to the easement transaction. However, if only part of the land is affected by the easement, only part of the basis is allocable to the easement transaction.
Improvements by lessee to lessor's property.	Increase	5	Adjustment occurs only if the lessor is required to include the fair market value of the improvements in gross income under § 109.
Imputed interest.	Decrease	18	Amount deducted is not part of the cost of the asset.
Inventory: lower of cost or market.	Decrease	18	Not available if the LIFO method is used.
Limited expensing under § 179.	Decrease	8	Occurs only if the taxpayer elects § 179 treatment.

Item	Effect	Refer to Chapter	Explanation
Medical capital expenditure permitted as a medical expense.	Decrease	10	Adjustment is the amount of the deduction (the effect on basis is to increase it by the amount of the capital expenditure net of the deduction).
Real estate taxes: apportionment between the buyer and seller.	Increase or decrease	10	To the extent the buyer pays the seller's pro rata share, the buyer's basis is increased. To the extent the seller pays the buyer's pro rata share, the buyer's basis is decreased.
Rebate from manufacturer.	Decrease		Since the rebate is treated as an adjustment to the purchase price, it is not included in the buyer's gross income.
Stock dividend.	Decrease	5	Adjustment occurs only if the stock dividend is nontaxable. While the basis per share decreases, the total stock basis does not change.
Stock rights.	Decrease	14	Adjustment to stock basis occurs only for nontaxable stock rights and only if the fair market value of the rights is at least 15% of the fair market value of the stock or, if less than 15%, the taxpayer elects to allocate the basis between the stock and the rights.
Theft.	Decrease	7	See casualty explanation.

- The basis of the asset may be determined by reference to the basis of the asset to another taxpayer.

Tax Planning Considerations

TAX CONSEQUENCES OF ALICE'S PROPOSED TRANSACTION

6 Learning Objective
Identify tax planning opportunities related to selected property transactions.

In Example 1 earlier in the chapter, Alice's tax adviser asked a number of questions in order to advise her on a proposed transaction. Alice provided the following answers:

- Alice inherited the house from her mother. The fair market value of the house at the date of her mother's death, based on the estate tax return, was $200,000. Based on an appraisal, the house is worth $230,000. Alice's mother lived in the house for 48 years. According to the mother's attorney, her adjusted basis for the house was $75,000.
- As a child, Alice lived in the house for 10 years. She has not lived there during the 35 years she has been married.
- The house has been vacant during the seven months that Alice has owned it. She has been trying to decide whether she should sell it for its fair market value or sell it to her nephew for $75,000. Alice has suggested a $75,000 price for the sale to Dan because she believes this is the amount at which she will have no gain or loss.
- Alice intends to invest the $75,000 in stock.

You advise Alice that her adjusted basis for the house is the $200,000 fair market value on the date of her mother's death. If Alice sells the house for $230,000 (assuming no selling expenses), she would have a recognized gain of $30,000 ($230,000 amount realized − $200,000 adjusted basis). The house is a capital asset, and her holding period is long term since she inherited the house.

Thus, the gain would be classified as a long-term capital gain. If, instead, Alice sells the house to her nephew for $75,000, she will have a part sale and part gift. The realized gain on the sale of $9,783 is recognized.

Amount realized	$ 75,000
Less: Adjusted basis	(65,217)*
Realized gain	$ 9,783
Recognized gain	$ 9,783

*[($75,000/$230,000) × $200,000] = $65,217.

The gain is classified as a long-term capital gain. Alice is then deemed to have made a gift to Dan of $155,000 ($230,000 − $75,000).

With this information, Alice can make an informed selection between the two options.

COST IDENTIFICATION AND DOCUMENTATION CONSIDERATIONS

When multiple assets are acquired in a single transaction, the contract price must be allocated for several reasons. First, some of the assets may be depreciable while others are not. From the different viewpoints of the buyer and the seller, this may produce a tax conflict that needs to be resolved. That is, the seller prefers a high allocation for nondepreciable assets, whereas the purchaser prefers a high allocation for depreciable assets (see Chapters 16 and 17). Second, the seller needs to know the amount realized on the sale of the capital assets and the ordinary income assets so that the recognized gains and losses can be classified as capital or ordinary. For example, an allocation to goodwill or to a covenant not to compete (see Chapters 8, 16, and 17) produces different tax consequences to the seller. Third, the buyer needs the adjusted basis of each asset to calculate the realized gain or loss on a subsequent sale or other disposition of each asset.

SELECTION OF PROPERTY FOR MAKING GIFTS

A donor can achieve several tax advantages by making gifts of appreciated property. Income tax on the unrealized gain that would have occurred had the donor sold the property is avoided by the donor. A portion of this amount can be permanently avoided because the donee's adjusted basis is increased by part or all of any gift tax paid by the donor. Even without this increase in basis, the income tax liability on the sale of the property by the donee can be less than the income tax liability that would have resulted from the donor's sale of the property, if the donee is in a lower tax bracket than the donor. In addition, any subsequent appreciation during the time the property is held by the lower tax bracket donee results in a tax savings on the sale or other disposition of the property. Such gifts of appreciated property can be an effective tool in family tax planning.

Taxpayers should generally not make gifts of depreciated property (property that, if sold, would produce a realized loss) because the donor does not receive an income tax deduction for the unrealized loss element. In addition, the donee receives no benefit from this unrealized loss upon the subsequent sale of the property because of the loss basis rule. The loss basis rule provides that the donee's basis is the lower of the donor's basis or fair market value at the date of the gift. If the donor anticipates that the donee will sell the property upon receiving it, the donor should sell the property and take the loss deduction, assuming the loss is deductible. The donor can then give the proceeds from the sale to the donee.

SELECTION OF PROPERTY FOR MAKING BEQUESTS

A decedent's will should generally make bequests of appreciated property. Doing so enables both the decedent and the heir to avoid income tax on the unrealized gain because the recipient takes the fair market value as his or her basis.

Taxpayers generally should not make bequests of depreciated property (property that, if sold, would produce a realized loss) because the decedent does not receive an income tax deduction for the unrealized loss element. In addition, the heir will receive no benefit from this unrealized loss upon the subsequent sale of the property.

EXAMPLE 40

On the date of her death, Marta owned land held for investment purposes. The land had an adjusted basis of $600,000 and a fair market value of $100,000. If Marta had sold the property before her death, the recognized loss would have been $500,000. If Ramon inherits the property and sells it for $60,000, the recognized loss will be $40,000 (the decline in value since Marta's death). In addition, regardless of the period of time Ramon holds the property, the holding period is long term (see Chapter 16). ▼

From an income tax perspective, it is preferable to transfer appreciated property as a bequest rather than as a gift. This results because inherited property receives a step-up in basis, whereas property received by gift has a carryover basis to the donee. However, in making this decision, the estate tax consequences of the bequest should also be weighed against the gift tax consequences of the gift.

DISALLOWED LOSSES

Section 267 Disallowed Losses. Taxpayers should be aware of the desirability of avoiding transactions that activate the loss disallowance provisions for related parties. This is so even in light of the provision that permits the related-party buyer to offset his or her realized gain by the related-party seller's disallowed loss. Even with this offset, several inequities exist. First, the tax benefit associated with the disallowed loss ultimately is realized by the wrong party (the related-party buyer rather than the related-party seller). Second, the tax benefit of this offset to the related-party buyer does not occur until the buyer disposes of the property. Therefore, the longer the time period between the purchase and disposition of the property by the related-party buyer, the less the economic benefit. Third, if the property does not appreciate to at least its adjusted basis to the related-party seller during the time period the related-party buyer holds it, part or all of the disallowed loss is permanently lost. Fourth, since the right of offset is available only to the original transferee (the related-party buyer), all of the disallowed loss is permanently lost if the original transferee subsequently transfers the property by gift or bequest.

EXAMPLE 41

Tim sells property with an adjusted basis of $35,000 to Wes, his brother, for $25,000, the fair market value of the property. The $10,000 realized loss to Tim is disallowed by § 267. If Wes subsequently sells the property to an unrelated party for $37,000, he has a recognized gain of $2,000 (realized gain of $12,000 reduced by disallowed loss of $10,000). Therefore, from the perspective of the family unit, the original $10,000 realized loss ultimately is recognized. However, if Wes sells the property for $29,000, he has a recognized gain of $0 (realized gain of $4,000 reduced by disallowed loss of $4,000 necessary to offset the realized gain). From the perspective of the family unit, $6,000 of the realized loss of $10,000 is permanently wasted ($10,000 realized loss – $4,000 offset permitted). ▼

Wash Sales. The wash sales provisions can be avoided if the security is replaced within the statutory time period with a similar rather than a substantially identical security. For example, the sale of Bethlehem Steel common stock and a purchase of Inland Steel common stock is not treated as a wash sale. Such a procedure can enable the taxpayer to use an unrealized capital loss to offset a recognized capital gain. The taxpayer can sell the security before the end of the taxable year, offset the recognized capital loss against the capital gain, and invest the sales proceeds in a similar security.

Because the wash sales provisions do not apply to gains, it may be desirable to engage in a wash sale before the end of the taxable year. This recognized capital gain may be used to offset capital losses or capital loss carryovers from prior years. Since the basis of the replacement stock or securities will be the purchase price, the taxpayer in effect has exchanged a capital gain for an increased basis for the stock or securities.

KEY TERMS

Adjusted basis, 14–4

Amount realized, 14–3

Fair market value, 14–4

Goodwill, 14–9

Holding period, 14–13

Realized gain, 14–3

Realized loss, 14–3

Recognized gain, 14–6

Recognized loss, 14–6

Recovery of capital doctrine, 14–7

Wash sale, 14–20

PROBLEM MATERIALS

DISCUSSION QUESTIONS

1. Upon the sale or other disposition of property, what four questions should be considered for income tax purposes?
2. A realized gain occurs when the amount realized is greater than the adjusted basis, and a realized loss occurs when the adjusted basis is greater than the amount realized. Evaluate this statement.
3. Which of the following would be treated as a "sale or other disposition"?
   a. Sale for cash.
   b. Sale on credit.
   c. Exchange.
   d. Involuntary conversion.
   e. Bond retirement.
4. Ivan invests in land and Grace invests in taxable bonds. The land appreciates by $5,000 each year, and the bonds earn interest of $5,000 each year. After holding the land and bonds for five years, Ivan and Grace sell them. There is a $25,000 realized gain on the sale of the land and no realized gain or loss on the sale of the bonds. Are the tax consequences to Ivan and Grace the same for each of the five years? Explain.

5. Carol and Dave each purchase 100 shares of stock of Burgundy, Inc., a publicly owned corporation, in July for $10,000 each. Carol sells her stock on December 31 for $14,000. Since Burgundy's stock is listed on a national exchange, Dave is able to ascertain that his shares are worth $14,000 on December 31. Does the tax law treat the appreciation in value of the stock differently for Carol and Dave? Explain.

6. If a taxpayer sells property for cash, the amount realized consists of the net proceeds from the sale. For each of the following, indicate the effect on the amount realized:
   a. The property is sold on credit.
   b. A mortgage on the property is assumed by the buyer.
   c. The buyer acquires the property subject to a mortgage of the seller.
   d. The seller pays real property taxes that are treated as imposed on the purchaser.
   e. Stock that has a basis to the purchaser of $6,000 and a fair market value of $10,000 is received by the seller as part of the consideration.

7. If the buyer pays real property taxes that are treated as imposed on the seller, what are the effects on the seller's amount realized and the buyer's adjusted basis for the property? If the seller pays real property taxes that are treated as imposed on the buyer, what are the effects on the seller's amount realized and the buyer's adjusted basis for the property?

8. Tom is negotiating to buy some land. Under the first option, Tom will give Sandra $70,000 and assume her mortgage on the land for $30,000. Under the second option, Tom will give Sandra $100,000, and she will immediately pay off the mortgage. Tom would like for his basis for the land to be as high as possible. Given this objective, which option should Tom select?

9. Edith purchases land from Gail. Edith gives Gail $40,000 in cash and agrees to pay Gail an additional $80,000 one year later plus interest at 8%.
   a. What is Edith's adjusted basis for the land at the date purchased?
   b. What is Edith's adjusted basis for the land one year later?

10. The taxpayer owns land and a building with an adjusted basis of $50,000 and a fair market value of $250,000. The property is subject to a mortgage of $400,000. Since the taxpayer is in arrears on the mortgage payments, the creditor is willing to accept the property in return for canceling the amount of the mortgage.
    a. How can the adjusted basis of the property be less than the amount of the mortgage?
    b. If the creditor's offer is accepted, what are the effects on the amount realized, the adjusted basis, and the realized gain or loss?
    c. Does it matter in (b) if the mortgage is recourse or nonrecourse?

11. Discuss the relationship between the adjusted basis and capital additions and between the adjusted basis and capital recoveries.

12. On August 16, 1996, Todd acquires land and a building for $300,000 to use in his sole proprietorship. Of the purchase price, $200,000 is allocated to the building, and $100,000 is allocated to the land. Cost recovery of $1,926 is deducted in 1996 for the building.
    a. What is the adjusted basis for the land and the building at the acquisition date?
    b. What is the adjusted basis for the land and the building at the end of 1996?

13. Abby owns stock in Orange Corporation and Blue Corporation. She receives a $1,000 distribution from both corporations. The instructions from Orange state that the $1,000 is a dividend. The instructions from Blue state that the $1,000 is not a dividend. What could cause the instructions to differ as to the tax consequences?

14. A taxpayer who acquires a taxable bond at a premium may elect to amortize the premium, whereas a taxpayer who acquires a tax-exempt bond at a premium must amortize the premium. Why would a taxpayer make the amortization election for taxable bonds? What effect does the mandatory amortization of tax-exempt bonds have on taxable income?

15. Kara owns two assets that she is considering selling. One has appreciated in value by $3,000, and the other has declined in value by $3,000. Both assets are held for personal use. Kara believes that she should sell both assets in the same taxable year so that the loss of $3,000 can offset the gain of $3,000. Advise Kara regarding the tax consequences.

16. Ron sold a sailboat for a $5,000 loss in the current year because he was diagnosed as having skin cancer. His spouse wants him to sell his Harley Davidson motorcycle because her brother broke his leg while riding his motorcycle. Since Ron no longer has anyone to ride with, he is seriously considering accepting his wife's advice. Because the motorcycle is a classic, Ron has received two offers. Each offer would result in a $5,000 gain. Joe would like to purchase the motorcycle before Christmas, and Jeff would like to purchase it after New Year's. Identify the relevant tax issues Ron faces in making his decision.

17. Lee owns a life insurance policy that will pay $100,000 to Rita, his spouse, on his death. At the date of Lee's death, he had paid total premiums on the policy of $65,000. In accordance with § 101(a)(1), Rita excludes the $100,000 of insurance proceeds. Discuss the relationship, if any, between the § 101 exclusion and the recovery of capital doctrine.

18. Helene purchases a one-acre lot from her employer, a real estate developer, for $75,000. Explain how Helene's adjusted basis for the lot on the date of the purchase could be $100,000.

19. Discuss the differences in tax treatment for allocating basis to nontaxable stock dividends when the form of the dividend is a common stock dividend on common stock versus a preferred stock dividend on common stock.

20. Discuss the differences in tax treatment when stock rights are allocated a cost basis and when stock rights have no cost basis. When does each of these situations occur?

21. Why does the Code contain both a gain basis rule and a loss basis rule for gift property? Under what circumstances will these rules produce different basis amounts?

22. Simon, who is retired, owns Teal, Inc., stock that has declined in value since he purchased it. He has decided to give the stock to his nephew, Fred, who is a high school teacher, or to sell the stock and give the proceeds to Fred. Because nearly all of his wealth is invested in tax-exempt bonds, Simon is in the 15% tax bracket. Fred will use the cash or the proceeds from his sale of the stock to make the down payment on the purchase of a house. Based on a recent conversation, Simon is aware that Fred is in the 28% bracket. Identify the tax issues relevant to Simon in deciding whether to give the stock or the sale proceeds to Fred.

23. Howard receives a gift of appreciated land from Del. Del pays gift taxes on the transfer. Discuss how the formula for calculating Howard's basis for the land differs depending on whether the gift was made:
    a. Before 1977.
    b. After 1976.

24. Discuss the differences in tax treatment between property sold before death and inherited property. Why is this important?

25. Gary makes a gift of an appreciated building to Carmen. She dies three months later, and Gary inherits the building from her. During the period that Carmen held the building, she deducted depreciation and made a capital expenditure. What effect might these items have on Gary's basis for the inherited building?

26. Immediately before his death in 1996, Kirby sells securities (adjusted basis of $100,000) for their fair market value of $20,000. The sale was not to a related party. The securities were community property, and Kirby is survived by his wife, Zina, who inherits all of his property.
    a. Did Kirby act wisely? Why or why not?
    b. Suppose the figures are reversed (sale for $100,000 of property with an adjusted basis of $20,000). Would the sale be wise? Why or why not?

27. Thelma inherited land from her Aunt Sadie on June 7, 1996. The land appreciated in value by 100% during the six months that Aunt Sadie owned it. The value has remained stable during the three months that Thelma has owned it, and she expects it to continue to do so in the near future. Although she would like to sell the land, Thelma has decided to delay the sale for another three months so that the gain will qualify for long-term capital gain treatment. Evaluate Thelma's understanding of the relevant tax issues.

28. What are related-party transactions, and why are they important?

29. What is a wash sale? Why isn't a realized loss recognized on a wash sale? How is the recovery of capital doctrine maintained?

30. Ava owned a residence whose adjusted basis (i.e., cost) was $20,000 greater than its fair market value. She knew that if she sold the house, the $20,000 realized loss would not be recognized. Therefore, she decided that she would rent it for a year and then sell it in order to be able to deduct the realized loss. Evaluate Ava's understanding of the relevant tax issues.

PROBLEMS

31. Anne sold her home for $260,000 in 1996. Selling expenses were $15,000. She had purchased it in 1990 for $190,000. During the period of ownership, Anne had:

- Deducted $50,500 office-in-home expenses, which included $14,500 in depreciation. (Refer to Chapter 9.)
- Deducted a casualty loss of residential trees destroyed by a hurricane. The total loss was $19,000 (after the $100 floor and the 10%-of-AGI floor), and Anne's insurance company reimbursed her for $13,500. (Refer to Chapter 7.)
- Paid street paving assessment of $7,000 and added sidewalks for $11,000.
- Installed an elevator for medical reasons. The total cost was $20,000, and Anne deducted $12,000 as medical expenses. (Refer to Chapter 10.)
- Received $7,500 from a utility company for an easement to install underground utility lines across the property.

What is Anne's realized gain?

32. Kareem bought a rental house at the beginning of 1991 for $80,000, of which $10,000 is allocated to the land and $70,000 to the building. Early in 1993, he had a tennis court built in the backyard at a cost of $5,000. Kareem has deducted $32,200 for depreciation on the house and $1,300 for depreciation on the court. At the beginning of 1996, he sells the house and tennis court for $125,000 cash.
   a. What is Kareem's realized gain or loss?
   b. If an original mortgage of $20,000 is still outstanding and the buyer assumes the mortgage in addition to the cash payment, what is Kareem's realized gain or loss?
   c. If the buyer takes the property subject to the mortgage, what is Kareem's realized gain or loss?

33. Norm is negotiating the sale of a tract of his land to Pat. Use the following classification scheme to classify each of the items contained in the proposed sales contract:

Legend		
DARN	=	Decreases amount realized by Norm
IARN	=	Increases amount realized by Norm
DABN	=	Decreases adjusted basis to Norm
IABN	=	Increases adjusted basis to Norm
DABP	=	Decreases adjusted basis to Pat
IABP	=	Increases adjusted basis to Pat

a. Norm is to receive cash of $50,000.
b. Norm is to receive Pat's note payable for $25,000, payable in three years.
c. Pat assumes Norm's mortgage of $5,000 on the land.
d. Pat agrees to pay the realtor's sales commission of $8,000.
e. Pat agrees to pay the property taxes on the land for the entire year. If each party paid his or her respective share, Norm's share would be $1,000, and Pat's share would be $3,000.
f. Pat pays legal fees of $500.
g. Norm pays legal fees of $750.

34. Gayla owns a building (adjusted basis of $366,500 on January 1, 1996) that she rents to Len who operates a restaurant in the building. The municipal health department closed the restaurant for two months during 1996 because of health code violations. Under MACRS, the cost recovery deduction for 1996 would be $12,000. However, Gayla deducted cost recovery only for the 10 months the restaurant was open since she waived the rent income during the two-month period the restaurant was closed.
   a. What is the amount of the cost recovery deduction that Gayla should report on her 1996 income tax return?
   b. Calculate the adjusted basis of the building at the end of 1996.

35. Nell owns a personal use automobile that has an adjusted basis of $18,000. The fair market value of the automobile is $14,500. Nell's AGI is $40,000.
   a. Calculate the realized and recognized loss if Nell sells the automobile for $14,500.
   b. Calculate the realized and recognized loss if Nell exchanges the automobile for another automobile worth $14,500.
   c. Calculate the realized and recognized loss if the automobile is stolen and Nell receives insurance proceeds of $14,500.

36. Mitch's automobile, which is used exclusively in his business, is stolen. The adjusted basis is $30,000, and the fair market value is $33,000. Mitch's AGI is $50,000.
   a. If Mitch receives insurance proceeds of $33,000, what effect do the theft and the receipt of the insurance proceeds have on the adjusted basis of the automobile?
   b. If the automobile is not insured, what effect do the theft and the absence of insurance have on the adjusted basis of the automobile?

37. Aaron owns stock in Dove Corporation. His adjusted basis for the stock is $30,000. During the year, he receives a distribution from the corporation of $25,000 that is labeled a return of capital (i.e., Dove has no earnings and profits).
   a. Determine the tax consequences to Aaron.
   b. Assume instead that the amount of the distribution is $40,000. Determine the tax consequences to Aaron.

38. Chee purchases Tan, Inc., bonds for $110,000 on January 2, 1996. The face value of the bonds is $100,000, the maturity date is December 31, 2000, and the annual interest rate is 8%. Chee will amortize the premium only if he is required to do so. Chee sells the bonds on July 1, 1998, for $109,000.
   a. Determine the interest income Chee should report for 1996.
   b. Calculate Chee's recognized gain or loss on the sale of the bonds in 1998.

39. Which of the following would definitely result in a recognized gain or loss?
   a. Kay sells her lakeside cabin, which has an adjusted basis of $100,000, for $150,000.
   b. Adam sells his personal residence, which has an adjusted basis of $150,000, for $100,000.
   c. Carl's personal residence is on the site of a proposed airport and is condemned by the city. Carl receives $55,000 for the house, which has an adjusted basis of $65,000.
   d. Olga's land is worth $40,000 at the end of the year. Olga had purchased the land six months earlier for $25,000.
   e. Vera's personal use vehicle is stolen. Her adjusted basis is $22,000. She receives a check from the insurance company for $23,000. Vera has decided that in the future she will use mass transit rather than owning an automobile.
   f. Jerry sells used clothing, adjusted basis of $500, to a thrift store for $50.

40. Tiffany sells the following assets during the year. All are held for personal use.
- Car with an adjusted basis of $19,000 for $7,000.
- Used clothing with an adjusted basis of $600 for $100.
- Sailboat with an adjusted basis of $3,500 for $4,500.

Calculate Tiffany's realized and recognized gain or loss.

41. Hubert's personal residence is condemned as part of an urban renewal project. His adjusted basis for the residence is $160,000. He receives condemnation proceeds of $150,000 and invests the proceeds in stock.
   a. Calculate Hubert's realized and recognized gain or loss.
   b. If the condemnation proceeds are $180,000, what are Hubert's realized and recognized gain or loss?
   c. What are Hubert's realized and recognized gain or loss in (a) if the house was rental property?

42. Walt Barnes is a real estate agent for Governor's Farms, a residential real estate development. Because of his outstanding sales performance, Walt is permitted to buy a lot that normally would sell for $125,000 for $100,000. Walt is the only real estate agent for Governor's Farms who is permitted to do so.
   a. Does Walt have gross income from the transaction?
   b. What is Walt's adjusted basis for the land?
   c. Write a letter to Walt informing him of the tax consequences of his acquisition of the lot. His address is 100 Tower Road, San Diego, CA 92182.

43. Karen makes the following purchases and sales of stock:

Transaction	Date	Number of Shares	Company	Price per Share
Purchase	1–1–94	300	MDG	$ 75
Purchase	6–1–94	150	GRU	300
Purchase	11–1–94	60	MDG	70
Sale	12–3–94	180	MDG	70
Purchase	3–1–95	120	GRU	375
Sale	8–1–95	90	GRU	330
Sale	1–1–96	150	MDG	90
Sale	2–1–96	75	GRU	500

Assuming that Karen is unable to identify the particular lots that are sold with the original purchase, what is the realized gain or loss on each type of stock as of:
   a. 7–1–94.
   b. 12–31–94.
   c. 12–31–95.
   d. 7–1–96.

44. Frank purchases 100 shares of Bluebird Corporation stock on June 3, 1996, for $150,000. On August 25, 1996, Frank purchases an additional 50 shares of Bluebird stock for $60,000. According to market quotations, Bluebird stock is selling for $1,100 per share on December 31, 1996. Frank sells 60 shares of Bluebird stock on March 1, 1997, for $51,000.
   a. What is the adjusted basis of Frank's Bluebird stock on December 31, 1996?
   b. What is Frank's recognized gain or loss from the sale of Bluebird stock on March 1, 1997, assuming the shares sold are from the shares purchased on June 3, 1996?
   c. What is Frank's recognized gain or loss from the sale of Bluebird stock on March 1, 1997, assuming Frank cannot adequately identify the shares sold?

45. Paula Andrews purchases the assets of a sole proprietorship from Seth. The adjusted basis of each of the assets on Seth's books and the fair market value of each asset as agreed to by Paula and Seth are as follows:

Asset	Seth's Adjusted Basis	FMV
Accounts receivable	$ -0-	$ 10,000
Notes receivable	15,000	20,000
Machinery and equipment	85,000	100,000
Building	100,000	300,000
Land	200,000	350,000

The purchase price is $900,000.

a. Calculate Seth's realized and recognized gain.
b. Determine Paula's basis for each of the assets.
c. Write a letter to Paula informing her of the tax consequences of the purchase. Her address is 300 Riverside Drive, Cincinnati, OH 45207.

46. Adrenna owns 1,000 shares of Dove, Inc., common stock for which her adjusted basis is $50,000. She receives a nontaxable stock dividend of 200 shares of Dove, Inc., preferred stock. The fair market value of the common shares is $60 per share, and the fair market value of the preferred shares is $20 per share.
    a. What is Adrenna's basis per share for the common stock before the stock dividend?
    b. What is Adrenna's basis per share for the common stock and the preferred stock after the stock dividend?
    c. Assume instead that the 200 shares received were additional shares of common stock with a fair market value of $60 per share. What is Adrenna's basis per share for the common stock?

47. Shontelle owns 1,000 shares of Gray Corporation stock with a basis of $15,000 and a fair market value of $20,000. She receives nontaxable stock rights to purchase additional shares. The rights have a fair market value of $2,000.
    a. What is the basis of the stock and the basis of the stock rights?
    b. What is the holding period for the stock rights?
    c. What is the recognized gain or loss if the stock rights are sold for $2,000?
    d. What is the recognized gain or loss if the stock rights are allowed to lapse?

48. Rick received various gifts over the years. He has decided to dispose of the following assets that he received as gifts:
    a. In 1949, he received land worth $25,000. The donor's adjusted basis was $30,000. Rick sells the land for $87,000 in 1996.
    b. In 1955, he received stock in Gold Company. The donor's adjusted basis was $10,000. The fair market value on the date of the gift was $28,000. Rick sells the stock for $40,000 in 1996.
    c. In 1961, he received land worth $12,000. The donor's adjusted basis was $25,000. Rick sells the land for $8,000 in 1996.
    d. In 1993, he received stock worth $30,000. The donor's adjusted basis was $45,000. Rick sells the stock in 1996 for $39,000.

    What is the realized gain or loss from each of the preceding transactions? Assume in each of the gift transactions that no gift tax was paid.

49. Beth received a car from Sam as a gift. Sam paid $7,000 for the car. He had used it for business purposes and had deducted $2,000 for depreciation up to the time he gave the car to Beth. The fair market value of the car is $3,500.
    a. Assuming Beth uses the car for business purposes, what is her basis for depreciation?
    b. If the estimated useful life is two years (from the date of the gift), what is her depreciation deduction for each year? Use the straight-line method.
    c. If Beth sells the car for $800 one year after receiving it, what is her gain or loss?
    d. If Beth sells the car for $4,000 one year after receiving it, what is her gain or loss?

50. In 1991, Ron receives a gift of property that has a fair market value of $100,000 on the date of the gift. The donor's adjusted basis for the property was $40,000. Assume the donor paid gift tax of $15,000 on the gift.
   a. What is Ron's basis for gain and loss and for depreciation?
   b. If Ron had received the gift of property in 1975, what would his basis be for gain and loss and for depreciation?

51. Liz receives a gift of income-producing property that has an adjusted basis of $70,000 on the date of the gift. The fair market value of the property on the date of the gift is $50,000. The donor paid gift tax of $4,000. Liz later sells the property for $54,000. Determine her recognized gain or loss.

52. Ira Cook is planning to make a charitable contribution of Crystal, Inc., stock worth $20,000 to the Boy Scouts. The stock Ira is considering contributing has an adjusted basis of $15,000. A friend has suggested that Ira sell the stock and contribute the $20,000 in proceeds rather than contribute the stock.
   a. Should Ira follow the friend's advice? Why?
   b. Assume the fair market value is only $13,000. In this case, should Ira follow the friend's advice? Why?
   c. Rather than make a charitable contribution to the Boy Scouts, Ira is going to make a gift to Nancy, his niece. Advise Ira regarding (a) and (b).
   d. Write a letter to Ira regarding whether in (a) he should sell the stock and contribute the cash or contribute the stock. He has informed you that he purchased the stock six years ago. Ira's address is 500 Ireland Avenue, De Kalb, IL 60115.

53. Dena inherits property from Mary, her mother. Mary's adjusted basis for the property is $100,000, and the fair market value is $725,000. Six months after Mary's death, the fair market value is $740,000. Dena is the sole beneficiary of Mary's estate.
   a. Can the executor of Mary's estate elect the alternate valuation date?
   b. What is Dena's basis for the property?

54. Earl's estate includes the following assets available for distribution to Robert, one of Earl's beneficiaries:

Asset	Earl's Adjusted Basis	FMV at Date of Death	FMV at Alternate Valuation Date
Cash	$10,000	$ 10,000	$ 10,000
Stock	40,000	125,000	60,000
Apartment building	60,000	300,000	325,000
Land	75,000	100,000	110,000

The fair market value of the stock six months after Earl's death was $60,000. However, believing that the stock would continue to decline in value, the executor of the estate distributed the stock to Robert one month after Earl's death. Robert immediately sold the stock for $85,000.
   a. Determine Robert's basis for the assets if the primary valuation date and amount apply.
   b. Determine Robert's basis for the assets if the executor elects the alternate valuation date and amount.

55. Dan bought a hotel for $720,000 in January 1993. In January 1996, he died and left the hotel to Ed. Dan had deducted $42,000 of cost recovery on the hotel before his death. The fair market value in January 1996 was $780,000.
   a. What is the basis of the property to Ed?
   b. If the land is worth $240,000, what is Ed's basis for cost recovery?

56. Emily makes a gift of 100 shares of appreciated stock to her uncle, George, on January 5, 1996. The basis of the stock is $3,150, and the fair market value is $5,250. George dies on October 8, 1996. During the period that George held the stock, he received a 5% nontaxable stock dividend. Under the provisions of George's will, Emily inherits 100 shares of the stock. The value of the stock for Federal estate tax purposes is $55 per share.
    a. What is the basis of the inherited stock to Emily?
    b. What is the basis of the inherited stock to Emily if she had given the stock to George on January 5, 1995?

57. Larry and Grace live in Louisiana, a community property state. They own land (community property) that has an adjusted basis to them of $100,000. When Grace dies, Larry inherits her share of the land. At the date of Grace's death, the fair market value of the land is $140,000. Six months after Grace's death, the land is worth $150,000.
    a. What is Larry's basis for the land?
    b. What would Larry's basis for the land be if he and Grace lived in Virginia, a common law state, and Larry inherited Grace's share?

58. Joyce owns undeveloped real estate with an adjusted basis of $80,000. She sells the real estate to her sister, Iris, for its fair market value of $65,000.
    a. Calculate Joyce's realized and recognized gain or loss.
    b. If Iris later sells the real estate for $72,000, calculate her realized and recognized gain or loss.
    c. Assume instead that Joyce sold the real estate to Iris for its fair market value of $90,000. Calculate Joyce's realized and recognized gain or loss.
    d. Assume instead that Joyce sold the real estate to Hector, a friend, for its fair market value of $65,000.
    e. Advise Joyce whether she should sell the real estate to Iris or Hector for its fair market value of $65,000.

59. Ted owns a 60% capital and profits interest in TS Partnership, which sells property to Ted for $65,000. The partnership's adjusted basis for the property is $90,000.
    a. Calculate the realized and recognized loss to the partnership.
    b. Calculate the basis of the property to Ted.
    c. If Ted subsequently sells the property for $87,000, calculate his realized and recognized gain or loss.
    d. If Ted gives the property to his daughter, Donna, who subsequently sells it for $87,000, calculate Donna's realized and recognized gain or loss. Assume no gift tax is paid on the gift and the fair market value on the date of the gift is $80,000.
    e. Determine the tax consequences in (a) through (d) if Ted is a shareholder and TS is a corporation.

60. Frank owns 1,000 shares of Amber, Inc., stock with an adjusted basis of $10,000. On December 28, 1996, he sells 400 shares for $3,600. On January 19, 1997, he purchases 300 shares of Amber, Inc., stock for $2,850.
    a. Calculate Frank's realized and recognized loss on the sale of 400 shares on December 28, 1996.
    b. Determine Frank's adjusted basis for the 300 shares purchased on January 19, 1997.

61. Kristy owns 100 shares of stock in Magenta Corporation. Her adjusted basis for the stock is $5,000. On December 21, Kristy sells the stock in the marketplace for $12,000. She purchases 100 shares of Magenta stock in the marketplace on January 5 of the following year for $12,000.
    a. What is Kristy trying to achieve from a tax perspective?
    b. Will she succeed?
    c. Using the same data, except that Kristy's adjusted basis for the stock is $15,000, respond to (a) and (b).
    d. Advise Kristy on how she can avoid any negative tax consequence encountered in (c).

62. James retires from a public accounting firm to enter private practice. He had bought a home two years earlier for $40,000. Upon opening his business, he converts one-fourth

of his home into an office. The fair market value of the home on the date of conversion (January 1, 1991) is $75,000. The adjusted basis is $56,000 (ignore land). James lives and works in the home for six years (after converting it to business use) and sells it at the end of the sixth year. He deducted $6,148 of cost recovery using the statutory percentage method.

a. How much gain or loss is recognized if James sells the property for $44,000?
b. If he sells the property for $70,000?

63. Surendra's personal residence originally cost $180,000 (ignore land). After living in the house for five years, he converts it to rental property. At the date of conversion, the fair market value of the house is $150,000.
a. Calculate Surendra's basis for loss for the rental property.
b. Calculate Surendra's basis for depreciation for the rental property.
c. Calculate Surendra's basis for gain for the rental property.

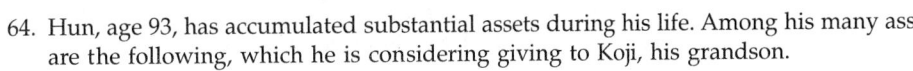

64. Hun, age 93, has accumulated substantial assets during his life. Among his many assets are the following, which he is considering giving to Koji, his grandson.

Assets	Adjusted Basis	Fair Market Value
Red Corporation stock	$ 50,000	$700,000
Silver Corporation stock	70,000	71,000
Emerald Corporation stock	200,000	50,000

Hun has been in ill health for the past five years. His physician has informed him that he probably will not live for more than six months. Advise Hun which of the stocks should be transferred as gifts and which as bequests.

CUMULATIVE PROBLEMS

65. John Custer, age 35, is single. His Social Security number is 443–11–2222, and he resides at 150 Highway 51, Tangipahoa, LA 70443.

John has a two-year-old child, Kendra, who lives with her mother, Katy. John pays alimony of $15,000 per year to Katy and child support of $10,000. The $10,000 of child support covers all of Katy's costs of rearing Kendra. Kendra's Social Security number is 432–60–1000, and Katy's is 444–00–1234.

John's mother, Sally, lived with him until her death in early September 1996. He incurred and paid medical expenses for her of $9,000 and other support payments of $4,000. Sally's only source of income was $2,400 of Social Security benefits, which she spent on her medical expenses and helping to maintain John's household. Sally's Social Security number was 400–10–2000.

John is employed by the Highway Department of the State of Louisiana in an executive position. His salary is $80,000. The appropriate amounts of Social Security and Medicare taxes were withheld. In addition, $15,000 was withheld for Federal income taxes, and $2,200 was withheld for state income taxes.

Upon the death of his Aunt Josie in December 1995, John, her only recognized heir, inherited the following assets:

Asset	Josie's Adjusted Basis	FMV at Date of Death
Car	$ 22,000	$ 15,000
Land—300 acres	150,000	600,000
IBM stock	50,000	125,000
Cash	30,000	30,000

Six months prior to her death, Josie gave John a beachhouse. Her adjusted basis for the beachhouse was $175,000, and the fair market value was $250,000. She paid a gift tax of $18,000.

During the year, John had the following transactions:

- On February 1, 1996, he sold for $40,000 Exxon stock that he inherited from his father four years ago. His father's adjusted basis was $12,000, and the fair market value at the date of the father's death was $35,000.
- The car John inherited from Josie was destroyed in a wreck on October 1, 1996. He had loaned the car to Katy to use for a two-week period while the engine in her car was being replaced. Fortunately, neither Katy nor Kendra was injured. John received insurance proceeds of $14,000, the fair market value of the car on October 1.
- On October 30, 1996, John gambled away the $30,000 he inherited on a riverboat casino in Biloxi. He had hoped this activity would help with the bouts of depression he had been suffering since Sally's death.
- On December 28, John sold the 300 acres of land to his brother, James, for its fair market value of $575,000. James planned on using the land for his dairy farm.
- On December 29, John sold the IBM stock he had inherited for $100,000.

Other sources of income for John were as follows:

Dividend income	$40,000
Interest income:	
Guaranty Bank	9,000
City of Kentwood water bonds	10,000

Potential itemized deductions for John, in addition to items already mentioned, were:

Property taxes paid on real estate	$9,000
Property taxes paid on personalty	2,000
Estimated Federal income taxes paid	8,000
Estimated state income taxes paid	1,500
Charitable contributions	5,000
Mortgage interest on his residence	4,000
Orthodontic and psychiatric expenses for John	3,000

Part 1—Tax Computation
Compute John's net tax payable or refund due for 1996. Suggested software (if available): *TurboTax* or *MacInTax*.

Part 2—Tax Planning
Assume that rather than selling the land to James, John is considering leasing it to him for $30,000 annually with the lease beginning on October 1, 1996. James would prepay the lease payments through December 31, 1996. Thereafter, he would make monthly lease payments at the beginning of each month. What effect would this have on John's 1996 tax liability? What potential problem might John encounter? Write a letter to John in which you advise him of the tax consequences of leasing versus selling. Also, prepare a memo for the tax files.

66. Kenneth Cloud, age 67, is married and files a joint return with his wife, Sarah, age 65. Kenneth and Sarah are both retired. In 1995, they received Social Security benefits of $11,000. Kenneth's Social Security number is 366–55–1111, and Sarah's is 555–66–2222. They reside at 405 College Drive, Hammond, LA 70408.

Kenneth, who retired on January 1, 1995, receives benefits from a qualified pension plan of $600 a month for life. His total contributions to the plan were $62,000. Kenneth's life expectancy at the annuity starting date on January 1, 1995, was 18.4 years. In January 1995, Kenneth received a bonus of $5,000 from his former employer. The bonus related to the performance of the unit he managed in 1994. His former employer accrued the bonus in 1994, but did not pay it until 1995.

Sarah, who retired on December 31, 1994, started receiving benefits of $800 a month on January 1, 1995. Her life expectancy was 20 years from the annuity starting date, and her investment in the qualified pension plan was $57,600.

Kenneth has been paying alimony of $15,000 each year to his former wife, Nancy. Nancy died on October 1, 1995. Thus, Kenneth paid alimony of $11,250 during 1995. Nancy's Social Security number is 400–60–1234.

Sarah enjoyed playing the slot machines at the casino in New Orleans. Her net winnings for the year were $1,000. When Kenneth visited his brother in Richmond, Virginia, he bought a lottery ticket for $1 and won $25,000.

On September 27, 1995, Kenneth and Sarah received a 10% stock dividend on 60 shares of stock they owned. They had paid $12 a share for the stock on March 5, 1976. On December 16, 1995, they sold the 6 shares received as a stock dividend for $40 a share.

On January 10, 1995, Sarah sold the car she had used in commuting to and from work. She paid $5,000 for the car in 1986 and sold it for $4,000.

Kenneth and Sarah received a gift of 100 shares of stock from their son Thomas on July 14, 1978. Thomas's basis in the stock was $30 a share, and the fair market value at the date of gift was $22 a share. No gift tax was paid. Kenneth and Sarah sold the stock on October 8, 1995, for $15 a share.

Sarah's mother died on May 1, 1995. Sarah inherited her mother's personal residence, which had a fair market value of $112,000 on May 1. Her mother's adjusted basis was $130,000. At the end of 1995, Sarah was still listing the house with a realtor. The realtor estimated the house was worth $120,000 at December 31, 1995.

Kenneth and Sarah paid estimated Federal income tax of $3,100 and had itemized deductions of $6,800. If they have overpaid their Federal income tax, they want the amount refunded. Both Kenneth and Sarah wish to have $3 go to the Presidential Election Campaign Fund.

Compute their net tax payable or refund due for 1995. If you use tax forms for your computations, you will need Form 1040 and Schedules A, D, and R. Suggested software (if available): *TurboTax* or *MacInTax*.

RESEARCH PROBLEMS

Note: ***West's Federal Taxation on CD-ROM*** *can be used in preparing solutions to the Research Problems. Alternatively, tax research materials contained in a standard tax library can be used.*

Research Problem 1. On January 1, 1996, Bart, a major shareholder in Copper Corporation, purchases land from the company for $300,000. The fair market value of the land is $1,200,000, and the adjusted basis in the hands of the corporation is $400,000.

a. What are the possible tax consequences to Bart?
b. What is the basis of the land to Bart?
c. What is the tax consequence to Copper Corporation?

Research Problem 2. Terry owns real estate with an adjusted basis of $600,000 and a fair market value of $1,100,000. The amount of the nonrecourse mortgage on the property is $2,500,000. Because of substantial past and projected future losses associated with the real estate development (occupancy rate of only 37% after three years), Terry deeds the property to the creditor.

a. What are the tax consequences to Terry?
b. Assume the data are the same, except the fair market value of the property is $2,525,000. Therefore, when Terry deeds the property to the creditor, she also receives $25,000 from the creditor. What are the tax consequences to Terry?

Partial list of research aids:
Rev.Rul. 76–111, 1976–1 C.B. 214.
Crane v. Comm., 47 USTC ¶9217, 35 AFTR 776, 67 S.Ct. 1047 (USSC, 1947).

Research Problem 3. Olaf gives stock worth $400,000 to Hazel. Olaf's adjusted basis in the stock is $50,000. The gift taxes due are $118,400. As a condition for receiving the gift of stock, Hazel agrees to pay the gift tax. The stock is transferred to Hazel on February 5, 1996.

a. What are the income tax consequences to Olaf?
b. What are the income tax consequences to Olaf if the gift was made on February 5, 1981?

Research Problem 4. As the result of a large inheritance from her grandmother, Beverly has a substantial investment portfolio. The securities are held in street name by her brokerage firm. Beverly's broker, Max, has standing oral instructions from her on sales transactions to sell the shares with the highest cost basis.

In October 1994, Beverly phoned Max and instructed him to sell 6,000 shares of Color, Inc. Her portfolio has 15,000 shares of Color, Inc., which were purchased in several transactions over a three-year period. At the end of each month, the brokerage firm provides Beverly with a monthly statement that includes sales transactions. It does not identify the specific certificates transferred.

In filing her 1994 income tax return, Beverly used the specific identification method to calculate the $90,000 gain on the sale of the Color shares. Now her 1994 return is being audited. The Revenue Agent has taken the position that under Reg. § 1.1012–1(c) Beverly should have used the FIFO method to report the sale of the Color shares. This would result in a recognized gain of $160,000. According to his interpretation of the Regulations, Beverly may not use the specific identification method and must use the FIFO method because the broker did not provide written confirmation of Beverly's sales instructions as required by the Regulations.

Beverly has come to you for tax advice.

Research Problem 5. Ruth died on January 10, 1996. In filing the estate tax return, her executor elects the primary valuation date and amount (fair market value on date of death). On March 12, 1996, the executor invests $30,000 of cash that Ruth had in her money market account in acquiring 1,000 shares of Orange, Inc. ($30 per share). On January 10, 1996, Orange was selling for $29 per share. The stock is distributed to a beneficiary, Annette, on June 1, 1996, when it is selling for $33 per share. The executor would like for you to inform him at what amount the Orange shares should appear on the estate tax return and of Annette's adjusted basis for the stock.

TEAM PROJECT: ARTHUR ANDERSEN TAX CHALLENGE CASES

For more information on the Arthur Andersen Tax Challenge Cases, please refer to Chapter 1, page 1-38.

Information related to tax issues and problems that are discussed in this chapter may be found in the

Fields case on pages 3, 9, 18

Read and analyze the case you have been assigned and *identify* any issues and problems that are related to material covered in this chapter. If the information provided in the case is complete, prepare answers for this part of the case at this time. If you need information that is contained in the later parts of the case, please write a memo summarizing the questions or problems so you can prepare a complete answer at a later date.

CHAPTER

15

Property Transactions: Nontaxable Exchanges

LEARNING OBJECTIVES

After completing Chapter 15, you should be able to:

1. Understand the rationale for nonrecognition (postponement) of gain or loss in certain property transactions.
2. Apply the nonrecognition provisions and basis determination rules for like-kind exchanges.
3. Explain the nonrecognition provisions available on the involuntary conversion of property.
4. Describe the provisions for postponing recognition of gain on the sale and replacement of a personal residence.
5. Discuss the provisions for permanent exclusion of gain on the sale of a personal residence by taxpayers age 55 and older.
6. Identify other nonrecognition provisions contained in the Code.
7. Identify tax planning opportunities related to the nonrecognition provisions discussed in the chapter.

OUTLINE

General Concept of a Nontaxable Exchange

1 Learning Objective
Understand the rationale for nonrecognition (postponement) of gain or loss in certain property transactions.

A taxpayer who is going to replace a productive asset (e.g., machinery) used in a trade or business may structure the transactions as a sale of the old asset and the purchase of a new asset. Using this approach, any realized gain or loss on the asset sale is recognized. The basis of the new asset is its cost. Conversely, the taxpayer may be able to trade the old asset for the new asset. This exchange of assets may produce beneficial tax consequences by qualifying for nontaxable exchange treatment.

The tax law recognizes that nontaxable exchanges result in a change in the *form* but not in the *substance* of the taxpayer's relative economic position. The replacement property received in the exchange is viewed as substantially a continuation of the old investment.[1] Additional justification for nontaxable exchange treatment is that this type of transaction does not provide the taxpayer with the wherewithal to pay the tax on any realized gain.

The nonrecognition provisions for nontaxable exchanges do not apply to realized losses from the sale or exchange of personal use assets. Such losses are not recognized (are disallowed) because they are personal in nature and not because of any nonrecognition provision.

In a **nontaxable exchange,** realized gains or losses are not recognized. However, the nonrecognition is usually temporary. The recognition of gain or loss is *postponed* (deferred) until the property received in the nontaxable exchange is

[1] Reg. § 1.1002-1(c).

subsequently disposed of in a taxable transaction. This is accomplished by assigning a carryover basis to the replacement property.

EXAMPLE 1

Debra exchanges property with an adjusted basis of $10,000 and a fair market value of $12,000 for property with a fair market value of $12,000. The transaction qualifies for nontaxable exchange treatment. Debra has a realized gain of $2,000 ($12,000 amount realized – $10,000 adjusted basis). Her recognized gain is $0. Her basis in the replacement property is a carryover basis of $10,000. Assume the replacement property is nondepreciable. If Debra subsequently sells the replacement property for $12,000, her realized and recognized gain will be the $2,000 gain that was postponed (deferred) in the nontaxable transaction. If the replacement property is depreciable, the carryover basis of $10,000 is used in calculating depreciation. ▼

In some nontaxable exchanges, only part of the property involved in the transaction qualifies for nonrecognition treatment. If the taxpayer receives cash or other nonqualifying property, part or all of the realized gain from the exchange is recognized. In these instances, gain is recognized because the taxpayer has changed or improved his or her relative economic position and has the wherewithal to pay income tax to the extent of cash or other property received.

It is important to distinguish between a nontaxable disposition, as the term is used in the statute, and a tax-free transaction. First, a direct exchange is not required in all circumstances (e.g., replacement of involuntarily converted property or sale and replacement of a personal residence). Second, as previously mentioned, the term *nontaxable* refers to postponement of recognition via a carryover basis. In a *tax-free* transaction, the nonrecognition is permanent (e.g., see the discussion later in the chapter of the § 121 election by a taxpayer age 55 or over to exclude gain on the sale of a residence). Therefore, the basis of any property acquired in a tax-free transaction does not depend on the basis of the property disposed of by the taxpayer.

LIKE-KIND EXCHANGES—§ 1031

2 LEARNING OBJECTIVE
Apply the nonrecognition provisions and basis determination rules for like-kind exchanges.

Section 1031 provides for nontaxable exchange treatment if the following requirements are satisfied:[2]

- The form of the transaction is an exchange.
- Both the property transferred and the property received are held either for productive use in a trade or business or for investment.
- The property is like-kind property.

Like-kind exchanges include business for business, business for investment, investment for business, or investment for investment property. Property held for personal use, inventory, and partnership interests (both limited and general) do not qualify under the like-kind exchange provisions. Securities, even though held for investment, do not qualify for like-kind exchange treatment.

The nonrecognition provision for like-kind exchanges is *mandatory* rather than elective. A taxpayer who wants to recognize a realized gain or loss will have to structure the transaction in a form that does not satisfy the statutory requirements for a like-kind exchange. This topic is discussed further under Tax Planning Considerations.

[2] § 1031(a) and Reg. § 1.1031(a)–1(a).

LIKE-KIND PROPERTY

"The words 'like-kind' refer to the nature or character of the property and not to its grade or quality. One kind or class of property may not . . . be exchanged for property of a different kind or class."[3]

Although the term *like-kind* is intended to be interpreted very broadly, three categories of exchanges are not included. First, livestock of different sexes do not qualify as like-kind property. Second, real estate can be exchanged only for other real estate, and personalty can be exchanged only for other personalty. For example, the exchange of a machine (personalty) for an office building (realty) is not a like-kind exchange. *Real estate* (or realty) includes principally rental buildings, office and store buildings, manufacturing plants, warehouses, and land. It is immaterial whether real estate is improved or unimproved. Thus, unimproved land can be exchanged for an apartment house. Personalty includes principally machines, equipment, trucks, automobiles, furniture, and fixtures. Third, real property located in the United States exchanged for foreign real property (and vice versa) does not qualify as like-kind property.

EXAMPLE 2

Wade made the following exchanges during the taxable year:

a. Inventory for a machine used in business.
b. Land held for investment for a building used in business.
c. Stock held for investment for equipment used in business.
d. A business truck for a business truck.
e. An automobile used for personal transportation for an automobile used in business.
f. Livestock for livestock of a different sex.
g. Land held for investment in New York for land held for investment in London.

Exchanges (b), investment real property for business real property, and (d), business personalty for business personalty, qualify as exchanges of like-kind property. Exchanges (a), inventory; (c), stock; (e), personal use automobile (not held for business or investment purposes); (f), livestock of different sexes; and (g), U.S. and foreign real estate do not qualify. ▼

A special provision applies if the taxpayers involved in the exchange are *related parties* under § 267(b). To qualify for like-kind exchange treatment, the taxpayer and the related party must not dispose of the like-kind property received in the exchange within the two-year period following the date of the exchange. If such an early disposition does occur, the postponed gain is recognized as of the date of the early disposition. Dispositions due to death, involuntary conversions, and certain non-tax avoidance transactions are not treated as early dispositions.

Regulations dealing with § 1031 like-kind exchange treatment provide that if the exchange transaction involves multiple assets of a business (e.g., a television station for another television station), the determination of whether the assets qualify as like-kind property will not be made at the business level.[4] Instead, the underlying assets must be evaluated.

The Regulations also provide for greater specificity in determining whether depreciable tangible personal property is of a like kind or class. Such property held for productive use in a business is of a like class only if the exchanged property is within the same *general business asset class* (as specified by the IRS in Rev.Proc. 87–57 or as subsequently modified) or the same *product class* (as

[3]Reg. § 1.1031(a)–1(b).

[4]Reg. §§ 1.1031(j)–1.

TAX IN THE NEWS

My Land for Your Jail

The Colonial Williamsburg Foundation (CW) has offered to swap 30 acres of undeveloped woodland for the Williamsburg Jail and Courthouse. A few years ago CW built a replica of the eighteenth-century Public Hospital (i.e., insane asylum). Now it is attempting to acquire the adjacent twentieth-century jail and courthouse in a § 1031 trade.

Why does CW want to own a twentieth-century jail and courthouse? It doesn't. CW wants the land for eventual expansion of its DeWitt Wallace Decorative Arts Gallery, which is located behind the Public Hospital. In addition, CW wants to preserve green space in Williamsburg, which would be threatened if a new courthouse and jail are built on land adjacent to the current courthouse and jail in Bicentennial Park.

Although the foundation is tax-exempt, the undeveloped 30 acres are owned by CW's for-profit subsidiary Williamsburg Developments, Inc. Therefore, to avoid recognizing the realized gain on the exchange, the subsidiary needs to avail itself of the § 1031 like-kind exchange provisions. Fortunately, the undeveloped land and the courthouse and jail are like-kind property.

SOURCE: Information from Bentley Boyd, "CW Presses for Moving Courthouse," *Newport News (Virginia) Daily Press,* September 15, 1993, pp. C1, C2; Bentley Boyd, "CW Boosts Proposal for Courthouse," *Newport News (Virginia) Daily Press,* September 29, 1993, pp. B1, B2.

specified by the Department of Commerce). Property included in a general business asset class is evaluated under this system rather than under the product class system.

The following are examples of general business asset classes:

- Office furniture, fixtures, and equipment.
- Information systems (computers and peripheral equipment).
- Airplanes.
- Automobiles and taxis.
- Buses.
- Light general-purpose trucks.
- Heavy general-purpose trucks.

These Regulations have made it more difficult for depreciable tangible personal property to qualify for § 1031 like-kind exchange treatment. For example, the exchange of office equipment for a computer does not qualify as an exchange of like-kind property. Even though both assets are depreciable tangible personal property, they are not like-kind property because they are in different general business asset classes.

EXCHANGE REQUIREMENT

The transaction must actually involve a direct exchange of property to qualify as a like-kind exchange. The sale of old property and the purchase of new property, even though like-kind, is generally not an exchange. However, if the two transactions are mutually dependent, the IRS may treat them as a like-kind exchange. For example, if the taxpayer sells an old business machine to a dealer and purchases a new one from the same dealer, like-kind exchange treatment could result.[5]

The taxpayer may want to avoid nontaxable exchange treatment. Recognition of gain gives the taxpayer a higher basis for depreciation (see Example 31). To the extent that such gains would, if recognized, either receive favorable capital gain treatment or be passive activity income that could offset passive activity losses, it may be preferable to avoid the nonrecognition provisions through an indirect exchange transaction. For example, a taxpayer may sell property to one individual and subsequently purchase similar property from another individual. The taxpayer may also want to avoid nontaxable exchange treatment so that a realized loss can be recognized.

BOOT

If the taxpayer in a like-kind exchange gives or receives some property that is not like-kind property, recognition may occur. Property that is not like-kind property, including cash, is referred to as **boot.** Although the term *boot* does not appear in the Code, tax practitioners commonly use it rather than saying "property that is not like-kind property."

The *receipt* of boot will trigger recognition of gain if there is realized gain. The amount of the recognized gain is the *lesser* of the boot received or the realized gain (realized gain serves as the ceiling on recognition).

EXAMPLE 3

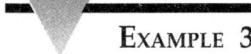

Emily and Fran exchange machinery, and the exchange qualifies as like-kind under § 1031. Since Emily's machinery (adjusted basis of $20,000) is worth $24,000 and Fran's machine has a fair market value of $19,000, Fran also gives Emily cash of $5,000. Emily's recognized gain is $4,000, the lesser of the realized gain ($24,000 amount realized – $20,000 adjusted basis = $4,000) or the fair market value of the boot received ($5,000). ▼

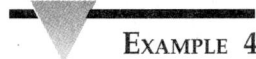

EXAMPLE 4

Assume the same facts as in the previous example, except that Fran's machine is worth $21,000 (not $19,000). Under these circumstances, Fran gives Emily cash of $3,000 to make up the difference. Emily's recognized gain is $3,000, the lesser of the realized gain ($24,000 amount realized – $20,000 adjusted basis = $4,000) or the fair market value of the boot received ($3,000). ▼

The receipt of boot does not result in recognition if there is realized loss.

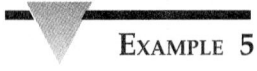

EXAMPLE 5

Assume the same facts as in Example 3, except the adjusted basis of Emily's machine is $30,000. Emily's realized loss is $6,000 ($24,000 amount realized – $30,000 adjusted basis = $6,000 realized loss). The receipt of the boot of $5,000 does not trigger recognition. Therefore, the recognized loss is $0. ▼

The *giving* of boot usually does not trigger recognition. If the boot given is cash, any realized gain or loss is not recognized.

EXAMPLE 6

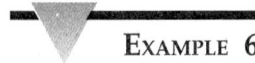

Fred and Gary exchange equipment in a like-kind exchange. Fred receives equipment with a fair market value of $25,000 and Fred transfers equipment worth $21,000 (adjusted basis of $15,000) and cash of $4,000. Fred's realized gain is $6,000 ($25,000 amount realized – $15,000 adjusted basis – $4,000 cash). However, none of the realized gain is recognized. ▼

If, however, the boot given is appreciated or depreciated property, gain or loss is recognized to the extent of the differential between the adjusted basis and the fair

[5] Rev.Rul. 61–119, 1961–1 C.B. 395.

market value of the boot. For this purpose, *appreciated or depreciated property* is defined as property whose adjusted basis is not equal to the fair market value.

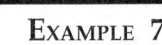

EXAMPLE 7

Assume the same facts as in the previous example, except that Fred transfers equipment worth $10,000 (adjusted basis of $12,000) and boot worth $15,000 (adjusted basis of $9,000). Fred's realized gain appears to be $4,000 ($25,000 amount realized – $21,000 adjusted basis). Since realization previously has served as a ceiling on recognition, it appears that the recognized gain is $4,000 (lower of realized gain of $4,000 or amount of appreciation on boot of $6,000). However, the recognized gain actually is $6,000 (full amount of the appreciation on the boot). In effect, Fred must calculate the like-kind and boot parts of the transaction separately. That is, the realized loss of $2,000 on the like-kind property is not recognized ($10,000 fair market value – $12,000 adjusted basis), and the $6,000 realized gain on the boot is recognized ($15,000 fair market value – $9,000 adjusted basis). ▼

BASIS AND HOLDING PERIOD OF PROPERTY RECEIVED

If an exchange does not qualify as nontaxable under § 1031, gain or loss is recognized, and the basis of property received in the exchange is the property's fair market value. If the exchange qualifies for nonrecognition, the basis of property received must be adjusted to reflect any postponed (deferred) gain or loss. The *basis of like-kind property* received in the exchange is the property's fair market value less postponed gain or plus postponed loss. If the exchange partially qualifies for nonrecognition (if recognition is associated with boot), the basis of like-kind property received in the exchange is the property's fair market value less postponed gain or plus postponed loss. The *basis* of any *boot* received is the boot's fair market value.

If there is a postponed loss, nonrecognition creates a situation in which the taxpayer has recovered *less* than the cost or other basis of the property exchanged in an amount equal to the unrecognized loss. If there is a postponed gain, the taxpayer has recovered *more* than the cost or other basis of the property exchanged in an amount equal to the unrecognized gain.

EXAMPLE 8

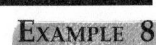

Jaime exchanges a building (used in his business) with an adjusted basis of $30,000 and fair market value of $38,000 for land with a fair market value of $38,000. The land is to be held as an investment. The exchange qualifies as like-kind (an exchange of business real property for investment real property). Thus, the basis of the land is $30,000 (the land's fair market value of $38,000 less the $8,000 postponed gain on the building). If the land is later sold for its fair market value of $38,000, the $8,000 postponed gain is recognized. ▼

EXAMPLE 9

Assume the same facts as in the previous example, except that the building has an adjusted basis of $48,000 and fair market value of only $38,000. The basis in the newly acquired land is $48,000 (fair market value of $38,000 plus the $10,000 postponed loss on the building). If the land is later sold for its fair market value of $38,000, the $10,000 postponed loss is recognized. ▼

The Code provides an alternative approach for determining the basis of like-kind property received:

Adjusted basis of like-kind property surrendered
\+ Adjusted basis of boot given
\+ Gain recognized
− Fair market value of boot received
− Loss recognized
= *Basis of like-kind property received*

This approach is logical in terms of the recovery of capital doctrine. That is, the unrecovered cost or other basis is increased by additional cost (boot given) or decreased by cost recovered (boot received). Any gain recognized is included in the basis of the new property. The taxpayer has been taxed on this amount and is now entitled to recover it tax-free. Any loss recognized is deducted from the basis of the new property. The taxpayer has received a tax benefit on that amount.

The holding period of the property surrendered in the exchange carries over and *tacks on* to the holding period of the like-kind property received.[6] The logic of this rule is derived from the basic concept of the new property as a continuation of the old investment. The boot received has a new holding period (from the date of exchange) rather than a carryover holding period.

Depreciation recapture potential carries over to the property received in a like-kind exchange.[7] See Chapter 17 for a discussion of this topic.

The following comprehensive example illustrates the like-kind exchange rules.

EXAMPLE 10

Vicki exchanged the following old machines for new machines in five independent like-kind exchanges:

Exchange	Adjusted Basis of Old Machine	Fair Market Value of New Machine	Adjusted Basis of Boot Given	Fair Market Value of Boot Received
1	$4,000	$9,000	$ –0–	$ –0–
2	4,000	9,000	3,000	–0–
3	4,000	9,000	6,000	–0–
4	4,000	9,000	–0–	3,000
5	4,000	3,500	–0–	300

Vicki's realized and recognized gains and losses and the basis of each of the like-kind properties received are as follows:

			New Basis Calculation								
Exchange	Realized Gain (Loss)	Recognized Gain (Loss)	Old Adj. Basis	+	Boot Given	+	Gain Recognized	–	Boot Received	=	New Basis
1	$5,000	$ –0–	$ 4,000	+	$ –0–	+	$ –0–	–	$ –0–	=	$ 4,000*
2	2,000	–0–	4,000	+	3,000	+	–0–	–	–0–	=	7,000*
3	(1,000)	–(0)–	4,000	+	6,000	+	–0–	–	–0–	=	10,000**
4	8,000	3,000	4,000	+	–0–	+	3,000	–	3,000	=	4,000*
5	(200)	–(0)–	4,000	+	–0–	+	–0–	–	300	=	3,700**

*Basis may be determined in gain situations under the alternative method by subtracting the gain not recognized from the fair market value of the new property:
$9,000 – $5,000 = $4,000 for exchange 1.
$9,000 – $2,000 = $7,000 for exchange 2.
$9,000 – $5,000 = $4,000 for exchange 4.

**In loss situations, basis may be determined by adding the loss not recognized to the fair market value of the new property:
$9,000 + $1,000 = $10,000 for exchange 3.
$3,500 + $200 = $3,700 for exchange 5.

The basis of the boot received is the boot's fair market value. ▼

[6] § 1223(1) and Reg. § 1.1223–1(a). For this carryover holding period rule to apply to like-kind exchanges after March 1, 1954, the like-kind property surrendered must have been either a capital asset or § 1231 property. See Chapters 16 and 17 for the discussion of capital assets and § 1231 property.

[7] Reg. §§ 1.1245–2(a)(4) and 1.1250–2(d)(1).

If the taxpayer either assumes a liability or takes property subject to a liability, the amount of the liability is treated as boot given. For the taxpayer whose liability is assumed or whose property is taken subject to the liability, the amount of the liability is treated as boot received. Example 11 illustrates the effect of such a liability. In addition, the example illustrates the tax consequences for both parties involved in the like-kind exchange.

EXAMPLE 11

Jane and Leo exchange real estate investments. Jane gives up property with an adjusted basis of $250,000 (fair market value $400,000) that is subject to a mortgage of $75,000 (assumed by Leo). In return for this property, Jane receives property with a fair market value of $300,000 (adjusted basis $200,000) and cash of $25,000.

- Jane's realized gain is $150,000. She gave up property with an adjusted basis of $250,000. Jane received $400,000 from the exchange ($300,000 fair market value of like-kind property plus $100,000 boot received). The boot received consists of the $25,000 cash received from Leo and Jane's mortgage of $75,000 that Leo assumes.
- Jane's recognized gain is $100,000. The realized gain of $150,000 is recognized to the extent of boot received.
- Jane's basis in the real estate received from Leo is $250,000. This basis can be computed by subtracting the postponed gain ($50,000) from the fair market value of the real estate received ($300,000). It can also be computed by adding the recognized gain ($100,000) to the adjusted basis of the real estate given up ($250,000) and subtracting the boot received ($100,000).
- Leo's realized gain is $100,000. Leo gave up property with an adjusted basis of $200,000 plus boot of $100,000 ($75,000 mortgage assumed + $25,000 cash) or a total of $300,000. Leo received $400,000 from the exchange (fair market value of like-kind property received).
- Leo has no recognized gain because he did not receive any boot. The entire realized gain of $100,000 is postponed.
- Leo's basis in the real estate received from Jane is $300,000. This basis can be computed by subtracting the postponed gain ($100,000) from the fair market value of the real estate received ($400,000). It can also be computed by adding the boot given ($75,000 mortgage assumed by Leo + $25,000 cash) to the adjusted basis of the real estate given up ($200,000).[8] ▼

Involuntary Conversions—§ 1033 ✓

3 Learning Objective
Explain the nonrecognition provisions available on the involuntary conversion of property.

Section 1033 provides that a taxpayer who suffers an involuntary conversion of property may postpone recognition of *gain* realized from the conversion. The objective of this provision is to provide relief to the taxpayer who has suffered hardship and does not have the wherewithal to pay the tax on any gain realized from the conversion. Postponement of realized gain is permitted to the extent that the taxpayer *reinvests* the amount realized from the conversion in replacement property. The rules for nonrecognition of gain are as follows:

- If the amount reinvested in replacement property *equals or exceeds* the amount realized, realized gain is *not recognized.*
- If the amount reinvested in replacement property is *less than* the amount realized, realized gain *is recognized* to the extent of the deficiency.

[8] Example (2) of Reg. § 1.1031(d)–2 illustrates a special situation where both the buyer and the seller transfer liabilities that are assumed or property is acquired subject to a liability by the other party.

If a *loss* occurs on an involuntary conversion, § 1033 does not modify the normal rules for loss recognition. That is, if a realized loss would otherwise be recognized, § 1033 does not change the result.

INVOLUNTARY CONVERSION DEFINED ✓

An **involuntary conversion** results from the destruction (complete or partial), theft, seizure, requisition or condemnation, or the sale or exchange under threat or imminence of requisition or condemnation of the taxpayer's property.[9] To prove the existence of a threat or imminence of condemnation, the taxpayer must obtain confirmation that there has been a decision to acquire the property for public use. In addition, the taxpayer must have reasonable grounds to believe the property will be taken.[10] The property does not have to be sold to the authority threatening to condemn it to qualify for § 1033 postponement. If the taxpayer satisfies the confirmation and reasonable grounds requirements, he or she can sell the property to another party.[11] Likewise, the sale of property to a condemning authority by a taxpayer who acquired the property from its former owner with the knowledge that the property was under threat of condemnation also qualifies as an involuntary conversion under § 1033.[12] A voluntary act, such as a taxpayer destroying his or her own property by arson, is not an involuntary conversion.[13]

ETHICAL CONSIDERATIONS

Purchasing Property in Expectation of Condemnation

The city of Richmond is going to condemn some buildings in a run-down section of the city to build a park. Steve's principal residence is one of the dilapidated buildings. His adjusted basis for the house and land is $60,000. The appraised value of the house and land is $52,000.

Steve is unaware of the future condemnation proceedings, but would like for his family to escape from the urban blight in which they are living. Therefore, when Ross, a realtor, mentions that he may have a corporate client who would like to purchase Steve's property for $65,000, Steve is ecstatic and indicates a willingness to sell.

Ross is having some "second thoughts" about his conversation with Steve. The potential corporate purchaser is a corporation owned by Ross and his wife. Unlike Steve, Ross is aware of the forthcoming condemnation proceedings. He considers himself a skilled negotiator and thinks he can obtain a 100 percent return on his investment.

Ross is considering telling Steve that the corporate client has changed his mind. Ross would then explain that in the interim, he has learned that the city will be condemning several buildings in order to create a park, but has not yet established the prices it will pay for the condemned property. He would also tell Steve that because he believes he can get more from the city than Steve would obtain, he is willing to gamble and purchase the property now from Steve for $65,000. Ross would point out that Steve would obtain several benefits from this sale including not having to deal with the city, receiving an amount that exceeds both the appraised value and the original purchase price of the house, and receiving the money now. While admitting that he could reap a substantial profit, Ross

[9] § 1033(a) and Reg. §§ 1.1033(a)–1(a) and –2(a).

[10] Rev.Rul. 63–221, 1963–2 C. B. 332, and *Joseph P. Balistrieri*, 38 TCM 526, T.C.Memo. 1979–115.

[11] Rev.Rul. 81–180, 1981–2 C.B. 161.

[12] Rev.Rul. 81–181, 1981–2 C.B. 162.

[13] Rev.Rul. 82–74, 1982–1 C.B. 110.

would emphasize that he would also be taking on substantial risks. In addition, Ross would explain that when he sells the property to the city, he can defer the taxes by reinvesting the sales proceeds. This deferral is possible because the condemnation is a type of involuntary conversion.

Do you think Ross should make a new proposal to Steve based on his "second thoughts?" How do you think Steve will respond?

COMPUTING THE AMOUNT REALIZED

The amount realized from the condemnation of property usually includes only the amount received as compensation for the property.[14] Any amount received that is designated as severance damages by both the government and the taxpayer is not included in the amount realized. *Severance awards* usually occur when only a portion of the entire property is condemned (e.g., a strip of land is taken to build a highway). Severance damages are awarded because the value of the taxpayer's remaining property has declined as a result of the condemnation. Such damages reduce the basis of the property. However, if either of the following requirements is satisfied, the nonrecognition provision of § 1033 applies to the severance damages.

- Severance damages are used to restore the usability of the remaining property.
- The usefulness of the remaining property is destroyed by the condemnation, and the property is sold and replaced at a cost equal to or exceeding the sum of the condemnation award, severance damages, and sales proceeds.

EXAMPLE 12

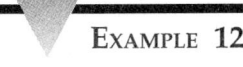

The government condemns a portion of Ron's farmland to build part of an interstate highway. Because the highway denies his cattle access to a pond and some grazing land, Ron receives severance damages in addition to the condemnation proceeds for the land taken. Ron must reduce the basis of the property by the amount of the severance damages. If the amount of the severance damages received exceeds the adjusted basis, Ron recognizes gain. ▼

EXAMPLE 13

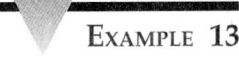

Assume the same facts as in the previous example, except that Ron used the proceeds from the condemnation and the severance damages to build another pond and to clear woodland for grazing. Therefore, all the proceeds are eligible for § 1033 treatment. Thus, there is no possibility of gain recognition as the result of the amount of the severance damages received exceeding the adjusted basis. ▼

REPLACEMENT PROPERTY

The requirements for replacement property generally are more restrictive than those for like-kind property under § 1031. The basic requirement is that the replacement property be similar or related in service or use to the involuntarily converted property.[15]

Different interpretations of the phrase *similar or related in service or use* apply depending on whether the involuntarily converted property is held by an *owner-user* or by an *owner-investor* (e.g., lessor). A taxpayer who uses the property in his or her trade or business is subject to a more restrictive test in terms of

[14] *Pioneer Real Estate Co.*, 47 B.T.A. 886 (1942), *acq.* 1943 C.B. 18.

[15] § 1033(a) and Reg. § 1.1033(a)–1.

acquiring replacement property. For an owner-user, the *functional use test* applies, and for an owner-investor, the *taxpayer use test* applies.

Taxpayer Use Test. The taxpayer use test for owner-investors provides the taxpayer with more flexibility in terms of what qualifies as replacement property than does the functional use test for owner-users. Essentially, the properties must be used by the taxpayer (the owner-investor) in similar endeavors. For example, rental property held by an owner-investor qualifies if replaced by other rental property, regardless of the type of rental property involved. The test is met when an investor replaces a manufacturing plant with a wholesale grocery warehouse if both properties are held for the production of rental income.[16] The replacement of a rental residence with a personal residence does not meet the test.[17]

Functional Use Test. Under this test, the taxpayer's use of the replacement property and of the involuntarily converted property must be the same. Replacing a manufacturing plant with a wholesale grocery warehouse, whether rented or not, does not meet this test. As indicated above, the IRS applies the taxpayer use test to owner-investors. However, the functional use test still applies to owner-users (e.g., a manufacturer whose manufacturing plant is destroyed by fire is required to replace the plant with another facility of similar functional use). Replacing a rental residence with a personal residence does not meet this test.

Special Rules. Under one set of circumstances, the broader replacement rules for like-kind exchanges are substituted for the narrow replacement rules normally used for involuntary conversions. This beneficial provision applies if business real property or investment real property is condemned. Therefore, the taxpayer has substantially more flexibility in selecting replacement property. For example, improved real property can be replaced with unimproved real property.

The rules concerning the nature of replacement property are illustrated in Concept Summary 15–1.

TIME LIMITATION ON REPLACEMENT

The taxpayer normally has a two-year period after the close of the taxable year in which any gain is realized from the involuntary conversion to replace the property (*the latest date*).[18] This rule affords as much as three years from the date of realization of gain to replace the property if the realization of gain took place on the first day of the taxable year.[19] If the involuntary conversion involved the condemnation of real property used in a trade or business or held for investment, a three-year period is substituted for the normal two-year period. In this case, the taxpayer can actually have as much as four years from the date of realization of gain to replace the property.

EXAMPLE 14

Megan's warehouse is destroyed by fire on December 16, 1995. The adjusted basis is $325,000. Megan receives $400,000 from the insurance company on January 10, 1996. She is a calendar year taxpayer. The latest date for replacement is December 31, 1998 (the end of the taxable year in which realized gain occurred plus two years). The critical date is not the date the involuntary conversion occurred, but rather the date of gain realization. ▼

[16] *Loco Realty Co. v. Comm.*, 62–2 USTC ¶9657, 10 AFTR2d 5359, 306 F.2d 207 (CA–8, 1962).

[17] Rev.Rul. 70–466, 1970–2 C.B. 165.

[18] §§ 1033(a)(2)(B) and (g)(4) and Reg. § 1.1033(a)–2(c)(3).

[19] The taxpayer can apply for an extension of this time period anytime before its expiration [Reg. § 1.1033(a)–2(c)(3)]. Also, the period for filing the application for extension can be extended if the taxpayer shows reasonable cause.

CONCEPT SUMMARY 15–1

Replacement Property Tests

Type of Property and User	Like-Kind Test	Taxpayer Use Test	Functional Use Test
Land used by a manufacturing company is condemned by a local government authority.	X		
Apartment and land held by an investor are sold due to the threat or imminence of condemnation.	X		
An investor's rented shopping mall is destroyed by fire; the mall may be replaced by other rental properties (e.g., an apartment building).		X	
A manufacturing plant is destroyed by fire; replacement property must consist of another manufacturing plant that is functionally the same as the property converted.			X
Personal residence of taxpayer is condemned by a local government authority; replacement property must consist of another personal residence.			X

EXAMPLE 15

Assume the same facts as in the previous example, except Megan's warehouse is condemned. The latest date for replacement is December 31, 1999 (the end of the taxable year in which realized gain occurred plus three years). ▼

The *earliest date* for replacement typically is the date the involuntary conversion occurs. However, if the property is condemned, it is possible to replace the condemned property before this date. In this case, the earliest date is the date of the threat or imminence of requisition or condemnation of the property. The purpose of this provision is to enable the taxpayer to make an orderly replacement of the condemned property.

EXAMPLE 16

Assume the same facts as in Example 15. Megan can replace the warehouse before December 16, 1995 (the condemnation date). The earliest date for replacement is the date of the threat or imminence of requisition or condemnation of the warehouse. ▼

ETHICAL CONSIDERATIONS

Postponing Realized Gain from an Involuntary Conversion

Peggy, age 63 and in frail health, owns a furniture store in Petersburg. Due to competition from two large furniture retailers who opened stores in the Petersburg area during the past three years, Peggy's furniture store has been unprofitable.

Due to this lack of profitability as well as her advancing age, Peggy would like to retire. Unfortunately, she has been unable to locate a purchaser for her store. Her prayers seem to be answered when a tornado destroys her building and its contents. Fortunately, no one is injured or killed by the tornado.

Peggy anticipates that she can live on the insurance proceeds of $800,000 for the rest of her life. However, her realized gain on the involuntary conversion would produce a combined state and Federal tax liability of approximately $175,000. In order to forgo paying this amount associated with her 1996 income tax returns, Peggy elects postponement treatment under § 1033, indicating that she intends to replace the involuntarily converted property with similar property even though she does not intend to do so. Her justification, based on her participation in a 12-step program, is that she lives "one day at a time."

Evaluate Peggy's election of § 1033 postponement under these circumstances.

NONRECOGNITION OF GAIN

Nonrecognition of gain can be either mandatory or elective, depending upon whether the conversion is direct (into replacement property) or into money (indirect).

Direct Conversion. If the conversion is directly into replacement property rather than into money, nonrecognition of realized gain is *mandatory.* In this case, the basis of the replacement property is the same as the adjusted basis of the converted property. Direct conversion is rare in practice and usually involves condemnations. The following example illustrates the application of the rules for direct conversions.

EXAMPLE 17

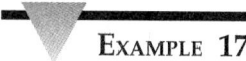

Lupe's property with an adjusted basis of $20,000 is condemned by the state. Lupe receives property with a fair market value of $50,000 as compensation for the property taken. Since the nonrecognition of realized gain is mandatory for direct conversions, Lupe's realized gain of $30,000 is not recognized, and the basis of the replacement property is $20,000 (adjusted basis of the condemned property). ▼

Conversion into Money. If the conversion is into money, at the election of the taxpayer, the realized gain is recognized only to the extent the amount realized from the involuntary conversion exceeds the cost of the qualifying replacement property.[20] This is the usual case, and nonrecognition (postponement) is *elective.* If the election is not made, the realized gain is recognized.

The basis of the replacement property is the property's cost less postponed (deferred) gain.[21] If the election to postpone gain is made, the holding period of the replacement property includes the holding period of the converted property.

Section 1033 applies *only to gains* and *not to losses.* Losses from involuntary conversions are recognized if the property is held for business or income-producing purposes. Personal casualty losses are recognized, but condemnation losses related to personal use assets (e.g., a personal residence) are neither recognized nor postponed.

Examples 18 and 19 illustrate the application of the involuntary conversion provisions.

EXAMPLE 18

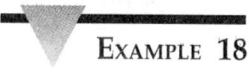

Walt's building (used in his trade or business), with an adjusted basis of $50,000, is destroyed by fire in 1996. Walt is a calendar year taxpayer. In 1996, he receives an insurance reimbursement of $100,000 for the loss. Walt invests $80,000 in a new building.

[20] § 1033(a)(2)(A) and Reg. § 1.1033(a)–2(c)(1).

[21] § 1033(b).

- Walt has until December 31, 1998, to make the new investment and qualify for the nonrecognition election.
- Walt's realized gain is $50,000 ($100,000 insurance proceeds received − $50,000 adjusted basis of old building).
- Assuming the replacement property qualifies as similar or related in service or use, Walt's recognized gain is $20,000. He reinvested $20,000 less than the insurance proceeds received ($100,000 proceeds − $80,000 reinvested). Therefore, his realized gain is recognized to that extent.
- Walt's basis in the new building is $50,000. This is the building's cost of $80,000 less the postponed gain of $30,000 (realized gain of $50,000 − recognized gain of $20,000).
- The computation of realization, recognition, and basis would apply even if Walt was a real estate dealer and the building destroyed by fire was part of his inventory. Unlike § 1031, § 1033 generally does not exclude inventory. ▼

EXAMPLE 19

Assume the same facts as in the previous example, except that Walt receives only $45,000 (instead of $100,000) of insurance proceeds. He has a realized and recognized loss of $5,000. The basis of the new building is the building's cost of $80,000. If the destroyed building was held for personal use, the recognized loss is subject to the following additional limitations.[22] The loss of $5,000 is limited to the decline in fair market value of the property, and the amount of the loss is reduced first by $100 and then by 10% of adjusted gross income (refer to Chapter 7). ▼

INVOLUNTARY CONVERSION OF A PERSONAL RESIDENCE

The tax consequences of the involuntary conversion of a personal residence depend upon whether the conversion is a casualty or condemnation and whether a realized loss or gain results.

Loss Situations. If the conversion is a condemnation, the realized loss is not recognized. Loss from the condemnation of a personal use asset is never recognized. If the conversion is a casualty (a loss from fire, storm, etc.), the loss is recognized subject to the personal casualty loss limitations (refer to Chapter 7).

Gain Situations. If the conversion is a condemnation, the gain may be postponed under either § 1033 or § 1034. That is, the taxpayer may elect to treat the condemnation as a sale under the deferral of gain rules relating to the sale of a personal residence under § 1034 (presented subsequently). If the conversion is a casualty, the gain is postponed only under the involuntary conversion provisions.

REPORTING CONSIDERATIONS

Involuntary conversions from casualty and theft are reported first on Form 4684, Casualties and Thefts. Casualty and theft losses on personal use property for the individual taxpayer are carried from Form 4684 to Schedule A of Form 1040. For other casualty and theft items, the Form 4684 amounts are generally reported on Form 4797, Sales of Business Property, unless Form 4797 is not required. In the latter case, the amounts are reported directly on the tax return involved.

Except for personal use property, recognized gains and losses from involuntary conversions other than by casualty and theft are reported on Form 4797. As stated previously, if the property involved in the involuntary conversion (other

[22] § 165(c)(3) and Reg. § 1.165–7.

than by casualty and theft) is personal use property, any realized loss is not recognized. Any realized gain is treated as gain on a voluntary sale.

Sale of a Residence—§ 1034 ✓

4 Learning Objective
Describe the provisions for postponing recognition of gain on the sale and replacement of a personal residence.

A realized loss from the sale of a **personal residence** is not recognized because the residence is personal use property. A realized gain is subject to taxation, however. The tax law includes two provisions under which all or part of the realized gain is either postponed or excluded from taxation. The first of these, § 1034, is discussed below. The second, § 121, is discussed later in the chapter.

Section 1034 provides for the *mandatory* nonrecognition of gain from the sale or exchange of a personal residence if the sales proceeds are reinvested in a replacement residence within a prescribed time period. Both the old and new residences must qualify as the taxpayer's principal residence. A houseboat or house trailer qualifies if it is used by the taxpayer as a principal residence.[23]

The reason for not recognizing gain when a residence is replaced by a new residence within the prescribed time period (discussed below) is that the new residence is viewed as a continuation of the investment. Also, if the proceeds from the sale are reinvested, the taxpayer does not have the wherewithal to pay tax on the realized gain. Beyond these fundamental concepts, Congress, in enacting § 1034, was concerned with the hardship of involuntary moves and the socially desirable objective of encouraging the mobility of labor.

REPLACEMENT PERIOD

For the nonrecognition treatment to apply, the old residence must be replaced by a new residence within a period *beginning two years before* the sale of the old residence and *ending two years after* the sale. This four-year period applies regardless of whether the new residence is purchased or constructed. The taxpayer must not only *acquire* the new residence during this period, but must *occupy* and use it as well. The occupancy requirement has been strictly construed by both the IRS and the courts, and even circumstances beyond a taxpayer's control do not excuse noncompliance.[24]

Example 20

Gail sells her personal residence from which she realizes a gain of $50,000. She begins constructing a new residence immediately after the sale. However, unstable soil conditions and a trade union strike cause unforeseen delays. The new residence ultimately is completed and occupied by Gail 25 months after the sale of the old residence. Since the occupancy requirement has not been satisfied, § 1034 is inapplicable, and Gail must recognize a gain of $50,000 on the sale of the old residence. ▼

Taxpayers might be inclined to make liberal use of § 1034 as a means of speculating when the price of residential housing is rising. Without any time restriction on its use, § 1034 would permit deferral of gain on multiple sales of principal residences, each of which would result in an economic profit. The Code curbs this approach by precluding the application of § 1034 to any sales occurring within two years of its last use.

[23] Reg. § 1.1034–1(c)(3)(i).

[24] *James A. Henry*, 44 TCM 844, T.C.Memo. 1982–469, and *William F. Peck*, 44 TCM 1030, T.C.Memo. 1982–506.

TAX IN THE NEWS

IRS Continues to Maintain Strict Interpretation of § 1034

Section 1034 permits a taxpayer to postpone the recognition of the realized gain on the sale of his or her residence. To qualify for nonrecognition, the taxpayer must purchase and occupy a replacement residence that costs at least as much as the adjusted sales price of the old residence. In addition, this purchase and occupancy must occur within a four-year window that begins two years prior to the sales date and ends two years after the sales date.

A taxpayer who sold his residence purchased a new residence for an amount in excess of the adjusted sales price of the old residence. He signed the contract to buy the new residence six weeks before the expiration of the two-year period. Prior to the final settlement on the house and before the expiration of the two-year period, he occupied the house. However, the final settlement (signing of deeds, etc.) did not occur until shortly after the expiration of the two-year period.

The IRS has taken the position that it has no authority to ignore the statutory time period requirements. Therefore, the sale of the original residence does not qualify for § 1034 postponement treatment.

EXAMPLE 21

After Seth sells his principal residence (the first residence) in March 1995 for $150,000 (realized gain of $60,000), he buys and sells the following (all of which qualify as principal residences):

	Date of Purchase	Date of Sale	Amount Involved
Second residence	April 1995		$160,000
Second residence		May 1996	180,000
Third residence	June 1996		200,000

Because multiple sales have occurred within a period of two years, § 1034 does not apply to the sale of the second residence. Thus, the realized gain of $20,000 [$180,000 (selling price) – $160,000 (purchase price)] must be recognized. ▼

The two-year rule precluding multiple use of § 1034 could create a hardship where a taxpayer is transferred by his or her employer and has little choice in the matter. For this reason, § 1034 was amended to provide an exception to the two-year rule when the sale results from a change in the location of employment. To qualify for the exception, a taxpayer must meet the distance and length-of-employment requirements specified for the deduction of moving expenses under § 217.[25]

EXAMPLE 22

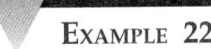

Assume the same facts as in the previous example, except that in February 1996, Seth's employer transfers him to a job in another state. Consequently, the sale of the second residence and the purchase of the third residence were due to the relocation of employ-

[25] Refer to Chapter 9 for the discussion of the rules governing the deduction for moving expenses.

ment. If Seth satisfies the distance and length-of-employment requirements of § 217, no gain is recognized on the sale of the first and second residences. ▼

The running of the time periods specified above (other than the two-year limit on multiple sales) is suspended during any time the taxpayer or spouse is on extended active duty (over 90 days or for an indefinite period) with the U.S. Armed Forces after the date the old residence is sold.[26] This suspension is limited to four years after the date the old residence is sold. A similar suspension is available to U.S. citizens who are employed outside the United States by nongovernmental employers (expatriates).[27]

EXAMPLE 23

Iris, an employee of Blue Corporation, sold her principal residence in Baltimore on July 5, 1996, because she had been transferred to the Berlin office on a one-year assignment. Iris returns to the United States on July 1, 1997, after completing the assignment. The latest date for a qualifying replacement is July 1, 1999 (i.e., two years after the end of the suspension period). ▼

EXAMPLE 24

Assume the same facts as in the previous example, except that the assignment is for a three-year period. Therefore, Iris returns to the United States on July 1, 1999, after completing the assignment. Two years after the end of the suspension period is July 1, 2001. However, since the suspension period exception cannot result in the replacement time period being extended beyond four years after the date the principal residence was sold, the latest date for a qualifying replacement is July 5, 2000. ▼

In one circumstance, the four-year limitation is extended for members of the U.S. Armed Forces. If they are stationed outside the United States or are required thereafter to reside in government quarters at a remote site, the four-year period is replaced with an eight-year period.[28]

PRINCIPAL RESIDENCE

Both the old and new residences must qualify as the taxpayer's principal residence. Whether property is the taxpayer's principal residence depends ". . . upon all the facts and circumstances in each case."[29]

EXAMPLE 25

Mitch sells his principal residence and moves to Norfolk, Virginia, where he is employed. He decides to rent an apartment in Norfolk because of its proximity to his place of employment. He purchases a beach house in Virginia Beach that he occupies most weekends. Mitch does not intend to live in the beach house other than on weekends. The apartment in Norfolk is his principal place of residence. Therefore, the purchase of the beach house does not qualify as an appropriate replacement. ▼

If the old residence ceases to be the taxpayer's principal residence before its sale, the nonrecognition provision does not apply. For example, if the taxpayer abandons the old residence before its sale, the residence no longer qualifies as a principal residence.[30] If the old residence is converted to other than personal use (e.g., rental) before its sale, the nonrecognition provision does not apply. If the residence is only partially converted to business use, gain from the sale of the personal use portion still qualifies for nonrecognition. It is possible to convert part

[26] § 1034(h)(1).
[27] § 1034(k).
[28] § 1034(h)(2).
[29] Reg. § 1.1034–1(c)(3).
[30] *Richard T. Houlette*, 48 T.C. 350 (1967), and *Stolk v. Comm.*, 64–1 USTC ¶9228, 13 AFTR2d 535, 326 F.2d 760 (CA–2, 1964).

of a principal residence to business use and later to convert that part back to being part of the principal residence (e.g., a home office).[31]

Temporarily renting out the old residence before sale does not necessarily terminate its status as the taxpayer's principal residence,[32] nor does temporarily renting out the new residence before it is occupied by the taxpayer. A related issue is whether a taxpayer who temporarily rents out the old residence while attempting to sell it is entitled to deduct expenses in excess of income relating to the rental. That is, is the old residence subject to the loss deduction rules for hobby loss activities? If it is, the deductions associated with the rental activity are limited to the rent income generated. In a divided opinion, the Tax Court concluded that since the property was considered to be the taxpayer's principal residence and as a result qualified for § 1034 postponement of gain, the property was subject to the hobby loss limitations. The Court of Appeals reversed the Tax Court and held that the hobby loss provisions did not apply.[33]

NONRECOGNITION OF GAIN REQUIREMENTS

Realized gain from the sale of the old residence is not recognized if the taxpayer reinvests an amount *at least equal* to the adjusted sales price of the old residence. Realized gain is recognized to the extent the taxpayer does not reinvest an amount at least equal to the adjusted sales price in a new residence. Therefore, the amount not reinvested is treated similarly to boot received in a like-kind exchange.

The **adjusted sales price** is the amount realized from the sale of the old residence less fixing-up expenses. The *amount realized* is the selling price less the selling expenses. *Selling expenses* include items such as the cost of advertising the property for sale, real estate broker commissions, legal fees in connection with the sale, and loan placement fees paid by the taxpayer as a condition of arranging financing for the buyer.

Fixing-up expenses are personal in nature and are incurred by the taxpayer to assist in the sale of the old residence. Fixing-up expenses include such items as ordinary repairs, painting, and wallpapering. To qualify as a fixing-up expense, the expense must (1) be incurred for work performed during the 90-day period ending on the date of the contract of sale, (2) be paid within 30 days after the date of the sale, and (3) not be a capital expenditure.

Although selling expenses are deductible in calculating the amount realized, fixing-up expenses are not. Therefore, fixing-up expenses do not have an impact on the calculation of realized gain or loss. However, since fixing-up expenses are deductible in calculating the adjusted sales price, they do have the potential for producing tax benefit in that they reduce the amount of the reinvestment required to qualify for nonrecognition treatment. Conversely, if a replacement residence is not acquired, the fixing-up expenses produce no tax benefit.

Reducing the amount of the required reinvestment by the amount of fixing-up expenses is another application of the wherewithal to pay concept. To the extent that the taxpayer has expended part of the funds received from the sale in preparing the old residence for sale, he or she does not have the funds available to reinvest in the new residence.

As previously mentioned, fixing-up expenses are not considered in determining realized gain. They are considered only in determining how much realized

[31] Rev.Rul. 82–26, 1982–1 C.B. 114.

[32] *Robert W. Aagaard*, 56 T.C. 191 (1971), *acq*. 1971–2 C.B. 1; *Robert G. Clapham*, 63 T.C. 505 (1975); Rev.Rul. 59–72, 1959–1 C.B. 203; and Rev.Rul. 78–146, 1978–1 C.B. 260.

[33] *Bolaris v. Comm.*, 85–2 USTC ¶9822, 56 AFTR2d 85–6472, 776 F.2d 1428 (CA–9, 1985), *rev'g*. 81 T.C. 840 (1983).

TAX IN THE NEWS

JOINT OWNERSHIP AND A NEW SPOUSE: CAUTION IS NECESSARY

To obtain the full benefits of § 1034 deferral treatment on the sale of a residence, the taxpayer must reinvest in a replacement residence an amount at least equal to the adjusted sales price of the old residence. In a recent Tax Court case, the taxpayer thought she had done so, but the Tax Court disagreed.

The taxpayer and her former spouse, who jointly owned the house with her, sold their residence and calculated their realized gain as follows:

Amount realized	$356,000
Less: Adjusted basis	(216,000)
Realized gain	$140,000

The taxpayer thought that if she reinvested her $178,000 share of the net sales price, she would be able to defer the recognition of her $70,000 share of the realized gain.

She remarried prior to purchasing another residence. She and her new spouse jointly purchased a residence for $180,000. Since the purchase price exceeded her $178,000 share of the net sales price, she concluded that she had made a reinvestment adequate to defer her $70,000 share of the realized gain.

Not so according to the IRS. According to their position, since she purchased the house jointly with her new spouse, she had reinvested only $90,000. Therefore, her realized gain of $70,000 is recognized because this amount was less than her reinvestment deficiency of $88,000. Unfortunately, the Tax Court in *Jeanne G. Snowa*, 70 TCM 163, T.C. Memo. 1995–336, accepted the position of the IRS.

gain is to be postponed. In addition, fixing-up expenses have no direct effect on the basis of the new residence. Indirectly, though, through their effect on postponed gain, they can bring about a lesser basis for the new residence. The effects of fixing-up expenses on the computation of gain realized and recognized and on basis are illustrated in Figure 15–1 and in Example 26.

CAPITAL IMPROVEMENTS

Capital improvements are added to the adjusted basis of a personal residence. The adjusted basis is used in computing gain or loss on a subsequent sale or other disposition of the property. In calculating the cost of a replacement residence (for determining the nonrecognition of gain under § 1034), only capital improvements made during a certain time period are counted. The time period begins two years before the date of sale of the old residence and ends two years after that date (the time period during which the old residence can be replaced).[34]

If the taxpayer receives a residence by gift or inheritance, the residence will not qualify as a replacement residence. However, if the taxpayer makes substantial

[34] *Charles M. Shaw*, 69 T.C. 1034 (1978); Reg. § 1.1034–1(c)(4)(ii); and Rev.Rul. 78–147, 1978–1 C.B. 261.

▼ FIGURE 15–1
Sale-of-Residence Model

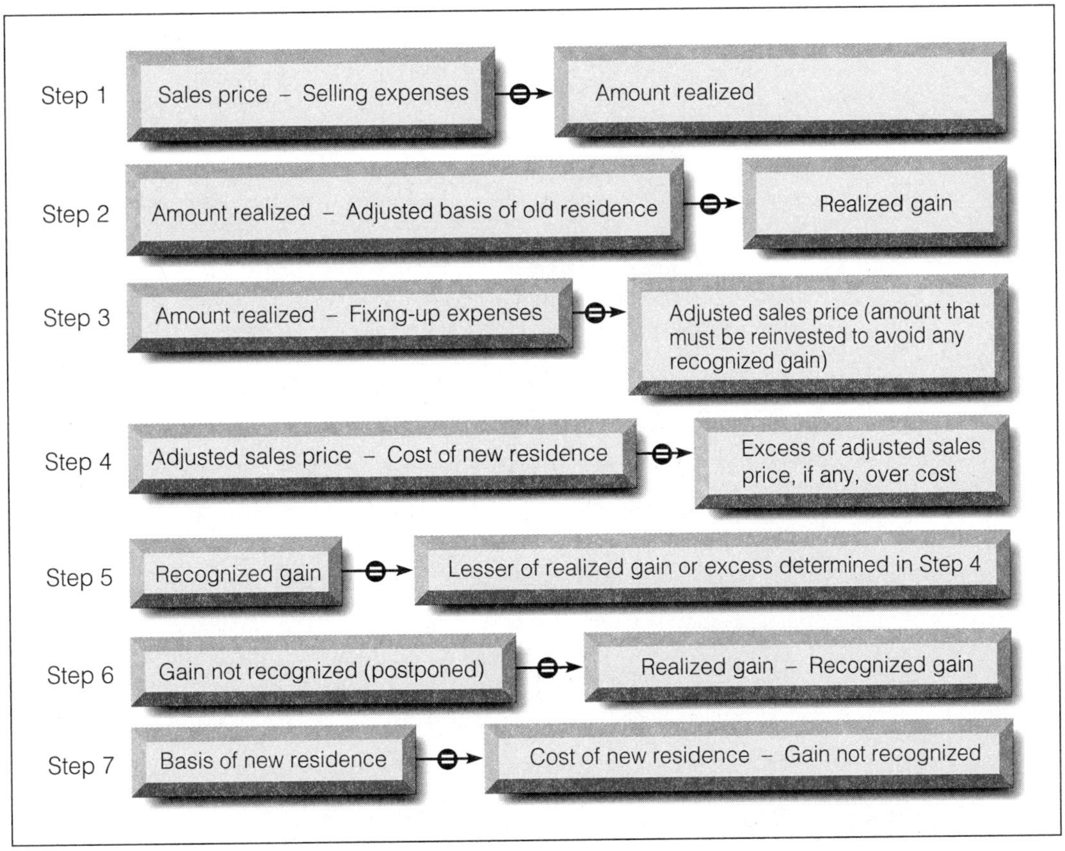

capital expenditures (e.g., reconstruction or additions) to the property within the replacement time period, these expenditures do qualify.[35]

BASIS AND HOLDING PERIOD OF THE NEW RESIDENCE

The *basis* of the new residence is the cost of the new residence less the realized gain not recognized (postponed gain). If there is any postponed gain, the *holding period* of the new residence includes the holding period of the old residence.

Figure 15–1 summarizes the sale-of-residence concepts. Example 26 illustrates these concepts and the application of the nonrecognition provision.

EXAMPLE 26

Veneia, age 47, sells her personal residence (adjusted basis of $136,000) for $244,000. She receives only $229,400 after paying a brokerage fee of $14,600. Ten days before the sale, Veneia incurred and paid for qualified fixing-up expenses of $3,400. Two months later, Veneia acquires a new residence. Determine the gain, if any, she must recognize and the basis of the new residence under each of the following circumstances:

1. The new residence costs $230,000.
2. The new residence costs $210,000.
3. The new residence costs $110,000.

[35] Reg. §§ 1.1034–1(b)(7) and (9) and 1.1034–1(c)(4)(i).

	1	2	3
Step 1: Sales price	$ 244,000	$ 244,000	$ 244,000
–Selling expenses	(14,600)	(14,600)	(14,600)
=Amount realized	$ 229,400	$ 229,400	$ 229,400
Step 2: Amount realized	$ 229,400	$ 229,400	$ 229,400
–Adjusted basis	(136,000)	(136,000)	(136,000)
=Realized gain	$ 93,400	$ 93,400	$ 93,400
Step 3: Amount realized	$ 229,400	$ 229,400	$ 229,400
–Fixing-up expenses	(3,400)	(3,400)	(3,400)
=Adjusted sales price	$ 226,000	$ 226,000	$ 226,000
Step 4: Adjusted sales price	$ 226,000	$ 226,000	$ 226,000
–Cost of new residence	(230,000)	(210,000)	(110,000)
=Excess of ASP over cost	$ –0–	$ 16,000	$ 116,000
Step 5: Recognized gain (lesser of Step 2 or Step 4)	$ –0–	$ 16,000	$ 93,400
Step 6: Realized gain	$ 93,400	$ 93,400	$ 93,400
–Recognized gain	(–0–)	(16,000)	(93,400)
=Postponed gain	$ 93,400	$ 77,400	$ –0–
Step 7: Cost of new residence	$ 230,000	$ 210,000	$ 110,000
–Postponed gain	(93,400)	(77,400)	(–0–)
=Basis of new residence	$ 136,600	$ 132,600	$ 110,000

None of the realized gain of $93,400 is recognized in the first case because the actual reinvestment of $230,000 exceeds the required reinvestment of $226,000. In the second case, the recognized gain is $16,000 because the required reinvestment of $226,000 exceeds the actual reinvestment of $210,000 by this amount. In the third case, the required reinvestment of $226,000 exceeds the actual reinvestment of $110,000 by $116,000. Since this amount is greater than the realized gain of $93,400, the realized gain of $93,400 is recognized, and § 1034 deferral does not apply. ▼

REPORTING PROCEDURES

The taxpayer is required to report the details of the sale of the residence on the tax return for the taxable year in which gain is realized, even if all of the gain is postponed. If a new residence is acquired and occupied before filing, a statement should be attached to the return showing the purchase date, the cost, and date of occupancy. Form 2119, Sale or Exchange of Your Home, is used to show the details of the sale and replacement, and the taxpayer should retain a copy permanently as support for the basis of the new residence. If a replacement residence has not been purchased by the time the return is filed, the taxpayer should submit the details of the purchase on the return of the taxable year during which it occurs. If the old residence is not replaced within the prescribed time period, or if some recognized gain results, the taxpayer must file an amended return for the year in which the sale took place.

SALE OF A RESIDENCE—§ 121 ✓

5 LEARNING OBJECTIVE
Discuss the provisions for permanent exclusion of gain on the sale of a personal residence by taxpayers age 55 and older.

Under the **Section 121 exclusion,** taxpayers age 55 or older who sell or exchange their principal residence may *elect to exclude* up to $125,000 ($62,500 for married individuals filing separate returns) of realized gain from the sale or exchange.[36] The election can be made *only once.*[37] This provision differs from § 1034 where nonrecognition is mandatory and may occur many times during a taxpayer's lifetime. Section 121 also differs from § 1034 in that it does not require the taxpayer to purchase a new residence. The excluded gain is never recognized, whereas the realized gain not recognized under § 1034 is postponed by subtracting it from the cost of the new residence in calculating the adjusted basis.

This provision is the only case in the tax law where a realized gain from the disposition of property that is not recognized is excluded rather than merely postponed. The provision allows the taxpayer a permanent recovery of more than the cost or other basis of the residence tax-free.

Congress enacted § 121 simply to relieve older citizens of the large tax they might incur from the sale of a personal residence. The dollar and age limitations restrict the benefit of § 121 to taxpayers who presumably have a greater need for increased tax-free dollars.

EXCLUSION REQUIREMENTS

The taxpayer must be at least age 55 before the date of the sale and have *owned* and *used* the residence as a principal residence for at least *three years* during the *five-year* period ending on the date of sale. The ownership and use periods do not have to be the same period of time. Short temporary absences (e.g., vacations) count as periods of use. If the residence is owned jointly by husband and wife, only one of the spouses is required to meet these requirements if a joint return is filed for the taxable year in which the sale took place.

In determining whether the ownership and use period requirements are satisfied, transactions affecting prior residences may be relevant. If a former residence is involuntarily converted and any gain is postponed under § 1033, the holding period of the former residence is added to the holding period of the replacement residence for § 121 purposes. However, if the realized gain is postponed under § 1034 (sale-of-residence provision), the holding period of the former residence is not added to the holding period of the replacement residence for § 121 purposes. In this instance, the holding period of the replacement residence begins with the acquisition date of the replacement residence.

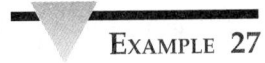

EXAMPLE 27 Cole has lived in his residence since 1986. The residence is involuntarily converted in July 1996. He purchases a replacement residence in August 1996. When the replacement residence is subsequently sold, Cole includes the holding period of the involuntarily converted residence in determining whether he can satisfy the ownership and use requirements. ▼

EXAMPLE 28 Assume the same facts as in the previous example, except that Cole's residence was not involuntarily converted. Instead, he sold it so that he could move into a larger house. When

36 §§ 121(a), (b), and (c). For married taxpayers, each spouse must consent.

37 § 121(b)(2) and Reg. § 1.121–2(b). Only one election may be made by married individuals.

the replacement residence is subsequently sold, Cole is not permitted to include the holding period of the old residence in determining whether he can satisfy the ownership and use requirements. ▼

ETHICAL CONSIDERATIONS

A Couple's Approach to the § 121 Exclusion

Bob and Sandra, both age 67, live in Houston, Texas, where each owns a personal residence on which the realized gain from a sale would be $125,000. They plan to marry and move to Williamsburg, Virginia. Not wanting the burdens of home ownership, they intend to rent a house.

Bob and Sandra both satisfy the requirements for the § 121 exclusion. Because of the soft real estate market in Houston, they have been unsuccessful in selling their personal residences. Being aware that a married couple can qualify only once for the § 121 exclusion, the realtor suggests the following plan. Bob will sell his house to Sandra, and Sandra will sell her house to Bob for the fair market value. Each will elect § 121 exclusion treatment. They will then marry and move to Williamsburg. Upon the subsequent sale of the houses to external buyers, the recognized gain, if any, will be minimal, since the adjusted basis of each house will have stepped up to the fair market value on the prior sale to each other.

Evaluate the realtor's proposal for Bob and Sandra.

RELATIONSHIP TO OTHER PROVISIONS

The taxpayer can treat an involuntary conversion of a principal residence as a sale for purposes of § 121. Any gain not excluded under § 121 is then subject to postponement under § 1033 or § 1034 (condemnation only), assuming the requirements of those provisions are met.

Any gain from the sale of a residence not excluded under § 121 is subject to postponement under § 1034, assuming the requirements of that provision are met. Examples 29 and 30 illustrate this relationship.

MAKING AND REVOKING THE ELECTION

The election not to recognize gain under § 121 may be made or revoked at any time before the statute of limitations expires. Therefore, the taxpayer generally has until the *later* of (1) three years from the due date of the return for the year the gain is realized or (2) two years from the date the tax is paid to make or revoke the election. The election is made by attaching a signed statement (showing all the details of the sale) to the return for the taxable year in which the sale took place. Form 2119 is used for this purpose. The election is revoked by filing a signed statement (showing the taxpayer's name, Social Security number, and taxable year for which the election was made) indicating the revocation.[38]

COMPUTATION PROCEDURE

The following examples illustrate the application of both the § 121 and § 1034 provisions.

[38] Reg. §§ 1.121–4(b) and (c).

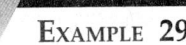

EXAMPLE 29 Keith sells his personal residence (adjusted basis of $32,000) for $205,000, of which he receives only $195,400 after paying the selling expenses of $9,600. Ten days before the sale, he incurred and paid for qualified fixing-up expenses of $6,400. Keith is age 55 and elects the exclusion of gain under § 121. He does not acquire a replacement residence. ▼

EXAMPLE 30 Assume the same facts as in the previous example, except that Keith acquires a new residence for $40,000 within the prescribed time period.

The solutions to Examples 29 and 30 are as follows:

	Example 29	Example 30
Amount realized ($205,000 – $9,600)	$ 195,400	$ 195,400
Adjusted basis	(32,000)	(32,000)
Realized gain	$ 163,400	$ 163,400
§ 121 exclusion	(125,000)	(125,000)
Realized gain after exclusion	$ 38,400	$ 38,400
Amount realized	$ 195,400	$ 195,400
Fixing-up expenses	(6,400)	(6,400)
Adjusted sales price	$ 189,000	$ 189,000
§ 121 exclusion	(125,000)	(125,000)
Adjusted sales price after exclusion	$ 64,000	$ 64,000
Cost of new residence	(–0–)	(40,000)
Excess of adjusted sales price after the exclusion over reinvestment	$ 64,000	$ 24,000
Recognized gain (lower of realized gain after exclusion or above excess)	$ 38,400	$ 24,000
Realized gain after exclusion	$ 38,400	$ 38,400
Recognized gain	(38,400)	(24,000)
Postponed gain	$ –0–	$ 14,400
Cost of new residence	$ –0–	$ 40,000
Postponed gain	(–0–)	(14,400)
Basis of new residence	$ –0–	$ 25,600

▼

Comparing the results of Examples 29 and 30 provides insight into the relationship between § 1034 and § 121. If Keith had not made the election to postpone gain under § 121 in Example 29, his recognized gain would have been $163,400 (the realized gain). Thus, the election resulted in the permanent exclusion of the $125,000 of realized gain by reducing the recognized gain to $38,400. Further documentation of the permanent nature of the § 121 exclusion is provided in the calculation of the basis of the new residence in Example 30. The $40,000 cost of the residence is reduced only by the postponed gain of $14,400. That is, it is not reduced by the § 121 exclusion amount of $125,000. To postpone all of the $38,400 realized gain after the exclusion, Keith would have needed to reinvest $64,000 (the adjusted sales price after the exclusion). Also, note that the Example 29 results demonstrate that the realized gain after the exclusion is the ceiling on recognition.

OTHER NONRECOGNITION PROVISIONS

6 LEARNING OBJECTIVE
Identify other nonrecognition provisions contained in the Code.

The typical taxpayer experiences the sale of a residence or an involuntary conversion more frequently than the other types of nontaxable exchanges. Several additional nonrecognition provisions that are not as common are treated briefly in the remainder of this chapter.

EXCHANGE OF STOCK FOR PROPERTY—§ 1032

Under § 1032, a corporation does not recognize gain or loss on the receipt of money or other property in exchange for its stock (including treasury stock). In other words, a corporation does not recognize gain or loss when it deals in its own stock. This provision is consistent with the accounting treatment of such transactions.

CERTAIN EXCHANGES OF INSURANCE POLICIES—§ 1035

Under this provision, no gain or loss is recognized from the exchange of certain insurance contracts or policies. The rules relating to exchanges not solely in kind and the basis of the property acquired are the same as under § 1031. Exchanges qualifying for nonrecognition include the following:

- The exchange of life insurance contracts.
- The exchange of a life insurance contract for an endowment or annuity contract.
- The exchange of an endowment contract for another endowment contract that provides for regular payments beginning at a date not later than the date payments would have begun under the contract exchanged.
- The exchange of an endowment contract for an annuity contract.
- The exchange of annuity contracts.

EXCHANGE OF STOCK FOR STOCK OF THE SAME CORPORATION—§ 1036

A shareholder does not recognize gain or loss on the exchange of common stock solely for common stock in the same corporation or from the exchange of preferred stock for preferred stock in the same corporation. Exchanges between individual shareholders as well as between a shareholder and the corporation are included. The rules relating to exchanges not solely in kind and the basis of the property acquired are the same as under § 1031. For example, a nonrecognition exchange occurs when common stock with different rights, such as voting for nonvoting, is exchanged. A shareholder usually recognizes gain or loss from the exchange of common for preferred or preferred for common even though the stock exchanged is in the same corporation.

CERTAIN REACQUISITIONS OF REAL PROPERTY—§ 1038

Under this provision, no loss is recognized from the repossession of real property sold on an installment basis. Gain is recognized to a limited extent.

TRANSFERS OF PROPERTY BETWEEN SPOUSES OR INCIDENT TO DIVORCE—§ 1041

Section 1041 provides that transfers of property *between spouses or former spouses incident to divorce* are nontaxable transactions. Therefore, the basis to the recipient is a carryover basis. To be treated as incident to the divorce, the transfer must be related to the cessation of marriage or occur within one year after the date on which the marriage ceases.

Section 1041 also provides for nontaxable exchange treatment on property transfers *between spouses during marriage.* The basis to the recipient spouse is a carryover basis.

ROLLOVERS INTO SPECIALIZED SMALL BUSINESS INVESTMENT COMPANIES—§ 1044

The Revenue Reconciliation Act of 1993 provides a postponement opportunity associated with the sale of publicly traded securities. If the amount realized is reinvested in the common stock or partnership interest of a specialized small business investment company (SSBIC), the realized gain is not recognized. Any amount not reinvested will trigger the recognition of the realized gain on the sale to the extent of the deficiency. The taxpayer must reinvest the proceeds within 60 days of the date of sale in order to qualify. In calculating the basis of the SSBIC stock, the amount of the purchase price is reduced by the amount of the postponed gain.

Statutory ceilings are imposed on the amount of realized gain that can be postponed for any taxable year as follows:

- Individual taxpayer: Lesser of:
  - $50,000 ($25,000 for married filing separately).
  - $500,000 ($250,000 for married filing separately) reduced by the amount of such nonrecognized gain in prior taxable years.
- Corporate taxpayer: Lesser of:
  - $250,000.
  - $1,000,000 reduced by the amount of such nonrecognized gain in prior taxable years.

Investors *ineligible* for this postponement treatment include partnerships, S corporations, estates, and trusts.

Chapter 15 has covered certain situations in which realized gains or losses are not recognized (nontaxable exchanges). Chapters 16 and 17 are concerned with the *classification* of recognized gains and losses. That is, if a gain or loss is recognized, is it an ordinary or capital gain or loss? Chapter 16 discusses the tax consequences of capital gains and losses.

TAX PLANNING CONSIDERATIONS

LIKE-KIND EXCHANGES

7 LEARNING OBJECTIVE
Identify tax planning opportunities related to the nonrecognition provisions discussed in the chapter.

Since application of the like-kind exchange provisions is mandatory rather than elective, in certain instances it may be preferable to avoid qualifying for § 1031 nonrecognition. If the like-kind exchange provisions do not apply, the end result may be the recognition of capital gain in exchange for a higher basis in the newly acquired asset. Also, the immediate recognition of gain may be preferable in certain situations. Examples where immediate recognition is beneficial include the following:

- Taxpayer has unused net operating loss carryovers.
- Taxpayer has unused general business credit carryovers.
- Taxpayer has suspended or current passive activity losses.
- Taxpayer expects his or her effective tax rate to increase in the future.

EXAMPLE 31

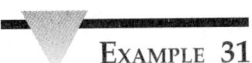

Alicia disposes of a machine (used in her business) with an adjusted basis of $3,000 for $4,000. She also acquires a new business machine for $9,000. If § 1031 applies, the $1,000

realized gain is not recognized, and the basis of the new machine is reduced by $1,000 (from $9,000 to $8,000). If § 1031 does not apply, a $1,000 gain is recognized and may receive favorable capital gain treatment to the extent that the gain is not recognized as ordinary income due to the depreciation recapture provisions (see Chapter 17). In addition, the basis for depreciation on the new machine is $9,000 rather than $8,000 since there is no unrecognized gain. ▼

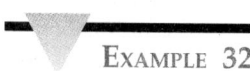

The application of § 1031 nonrecognition treatment should also be avoided when the adjusted basis of the property being disposed of exceeds the fair market value.

EXAMPLE 32

Assume the same facts as in the previous example, except the fair market value of the machine is $2,500. If § 1031 applies, the $500 realized loss is not recognized. To recognize the loss, Alicia should sell the old machine and purchase the new one. The purchase and sale transactions should be with different taxpayers. ▼

On the other hand, the like-kind exchange procedure can be utilized to control the amount of recognized gain.

EXAMPLE 33

Rex has property with an adjusted basis of $40,000 and a fair market value of $100,000. Sandra wants to buy Rex's property, but Rex wants to limit the amount of recognized gain on the proposed transaction. Sandra acquires other like-kind property (from an outside party) for $80,000. She then exchanges this property and $20,000 cash for Rex's property. Rex has a realized gain of $60,000 ($100,000 amount realized – $40,000 adjusted basis). His recognized gain is only $20,000, the lower of the $20,000 boot received or the $60,000 realized gain. Rex's basis for the like-kind property is $40,000 ($40,000 adjusted basis + $20,000 gain recognized – $20,000 boot received). If Rex had sold the property to Sandra for its fair market value of $100,000, the result would have been a $60,000 recognized gain ($100,000 amount realized – $40,000 adjusted basis) to him. It is permissible for Rex to identify the like-kind property that he wants Sandra to purchase.[39] ▼

INVOLUNTARY CONVERSIONS

In certain cases, a taxpayer may prefer to recognize gain from an involuntary conversion. Keep in mind that § 1033, unlike § 1031 (dealing with like-kind exchanges), generally is an elective provision.

EXAMPLE 34

Ahmad has a $40,000 realized gain from the involuntary conversion of an office building. He reinvests the entire proceeds of $450,000 in a new office building. He does not elect to postpone gain under § 1033, however, because of an expiring net operating loss carryover that is offset against the gain. Therefore, none of the realized gain of $40,000 is postponed. By not electing § 1033 postponement, Ahmad's basis in the replacement property is the property's cost of $450,000 rather than $410,000 ($450,000 reduced by the $40,000 realized gain). ▼

SALE OF A PERSONAL RESIDENCE

Replacement Period Requirements. Several problems arise in avoiding the recognition of gain on the sale of a principal residence. Most of these problems can be resolved favorably through appropriate planning procedures. However, a few

[39] *Franklin B. Biggs*, 69 T.C. 905 (1978); Rev.Rul. 57–244, 1957–1 C.B. 247; Rev.Rul. 73–476, 1973–2 C.B. 300; *Starker vs. U.S.*, 79–2 USTC ¶9541, 44 AFTR2d 79–5525, 602 F.2d 1341 (CA–9, 1979); and *Baird Publishing Co.*, 39 T.C. 608 (1962).

represent situations where the taxpayer has to accept the adverse tax consequences and possesses little, if any, planning flexibility. One pitfall concerns the failure to reinvest *all* of the proceeds from the sale of the residence in a new principal residence.

EXAMPLE 35

Rita sells her principal residence in January 1994 for $150,000 (adjusted basis of $40,000). Shortly thereafter, she purchases for $100,000 a 50-year-old house in a historical part of the community and uses it as her principal residence. Rita intends to significantly renovate the property over a period of time and make it more suitable to her living needs. In December 1996, she enters into a contract with a home improvement company to carry out the renovation at a cost of $60,000. It is clear that only $100,000 of the proceeds from the sale of the old residence has been reinvested in a new principal residence on a *timely* basis. Of the realized gain of $110,000, therefore, $50,000 ($150,000 adjusted sales price − $100,000 reinvested) must be recognized.[40] ▼

One problem that a taxpayer may not be in a position to do anything about is the acquisition of property *before* the beginning of the replacement period. Recall that the replacement period begins two years before the sale and ends two years after the sale.

EXAMPLE 36

Tab's employer transfers him to a different city in July 1994, at which time Tab lists his house for sale with a realtor. Tab purchases a principal residence in the city to which he is transferred in September 1994. Because of market conditions, he is unable to sell his original residence until December 1996. Since the sale does not occur within two years of the purchase, the residence Tab bought in September 1994 is not a qualifying replacement residence. ▼

Principal Residence Requirement. Section 1034 will not apply unless the property involved is the taxpayer's principal residence. A potential hurdle arises in cases where the residence has been rented and therefore has not been occupied by the taxpayer for an extended period of time. Depending on the circumstances, the IRS may contend that the taxpayer has abandoned the property as his or her principal residence. The *key* to the abandonment issue is whether or not the taxpayer intended to reoccupy the property and use it as a principal residence upon returning to the locale. If the residence is, in fact, not reoccupied, the taxpayer should have a good reason to explain why it is not.

EXAMPLE 37

Lori's employer transfers her to another office out of the state on a three-year assignment. It is the understanding of the parties that the assignment is temporary, and upon its completion, Lori will return to the original job site. During her absence, she rents her principal residence and lives in an apartment at the new location. Lori has every intention of reoccupying her residence. However, when she returns from the temporary assignment, she finds that the residence no longer suits her needs. Specifically, the public school located nearby where she had planned to send her children has been closed. As a consequence, Lori sells the residence and replaces it with one more conveniently located to a public school. Under these circumstances, it would appear that Lori is in an excellent position to show that she has not abandoned the property as her principal residence. She can satisfactorily explain why she did not reoccupy the residence before its sale.[41] ▼

---

[40] It has been assumed that § 121 did not apply.

[41] Rev.Rul. 78–146, 1978–1 C.B. 260. Compare *Rudolph M. Stucchi*, 35 TCM 1052, T.C.Memo. 1976–242.

The principal residence requirement can cause difficulty when a taxpayer works in two places and maintains more than one household. In such cases, the principal residence will be the location where the taxpayer lives most of the time.[42]

EXAMPLE 38 Hubert is a vice president of Green Corporation and in this capacity spends about an equal amount of time in the company's New York City and Miami offices. He owns a house in each location and expects to retire in about five years. At that time, he plans to sell his New York home and use some of the proceeds to make improvements on the Miami property. Both homes have appreciated in value since their acquisition, and Hubert expects the appreciation to continue. From a tax planning standpoint, Hubert should be looking toward the use of §§ 121 and 1034 to shelter some or all of the gain he will realize on the future sale of the New York City home.[43] To do this, he should arrange his affairs so as to spend more than six months each year at that location. Upon its sale, therefore, the New York home will be his principal residence. ▼

Section 121 Considerations. Older individuals who may be contemplating a move from their home to an apartment should consider the following possibilities for minimizing or deferring taxes:

- Wait until age 55 to sell the residence and elect under § 121 to exclude up to $125,000 of the realized gain.
- Sell the personal residence under an installment contract to spread the gain over several years.[44]
- Sell the personal residence and purchase a condominium instead of renting an apartment, thereby permitting further deferral of the unrecognized gain.

The use of § 121 should be carefully considered. Although the use avoids the immediate recognition of gain, the election expends the full $125,000 allowed.

EXAMPLE 39 In 1996 Kate, age 55, sells her personal residence for an amount that yields a realized gain of $5,000. Presuming Kate does not plan to reinvest the sales proceeds in a new principal residence (take advantage of the deferral possibility of § 1034), should she avoid the recognition of this gain by utilizing § 121? Electing § 121 means that Kate will waste $120,000 of her lifetime exclusion. ▼

In this connection, the use of § 121 by one spouse precludes the other spouse from later taking advantage of the exclusion.

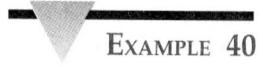

EXAMPLE 40 Assume the same facts as in the previous example, except that Kate was married to Wes at the time of the sale. Later, Kate and Wes are divorced and Wes marries Alice. If Kate has used the § 121 exclusion, it is unavailable to Wes and Alice even though either one of them may otherwise qualify. This result occurs because when Kate made the election for the 1996 sale, it was necessary for Wes to join with her in making the election even though the residence was owned separately by Kate. For Wes and Alice to be able to make the § 121 election, Wes and Kate must revoke their prior election. Another planning approach is for Alice to sell her residence before marrying Wes and to elect the exclusion on that sale. ▼

[42] Rev.Rul. 77–298, 1977–2 C.B. 308.

[43] If Hubert qualifies, § 121 would allow the first $125,000 of gain to be excluded. Further gain might be avoided under § 1034 to the extent the sales proceeds are applied toward improvements on the Miami home.

[44] § 453(a). See the discussion of the installment method in Chapter 18.

A taxpayer who is eligible to elect § 121 exclusion treatment may choose not to do so in order to remain eligible to elect it in the future. In arriving at this decision, consideration must be given to the probability that the taxpayer will satisfy the three-out-of-five-year ownership and use period requirements associated with a residence sale in the future. As previously mentioned, the holding period for the occupancy and use requirements carries over for a § 1033 involuntary conversion but not for a § 1034 sale.

Taxpayers should maintain records of both the purchase and sale of personal residences since the sale of one residence results in an adjustment of the basis of the new residence if the deferral provisions of § 1034 apply. Form 2119 should be filed with the tax return and a copy retained as support for the basis of the new residence. Detailed cost records should be retained for an indefinite period.

KEY TERMS

PROBLEM MATERIALS

DISCUSSION QUESTIONS

1. What is the justification for nontaxable exchange treatment?
2. Distinguish between a loss that is not recognized on a nontaxable exchange and a loss that is not recognized on the sale or exchange of a personal use asset.
3. Distinguish between a nontaxable exchange and a tax-free transaction.
4. Can the exchange of property held for productive use in a trade or business for investment property qualify for like-kind exchange treatment?
5. Can the exchange of personal use property for productive use property qualify for like-kind exchange treatment?
6. Amos owns a lathe that he uses in his trade or business. The adjusted basis is $40,000. Although the lathe is only two years old, Amos needs to replace it due to advances in technology. He exchanges the lathe and $20,000 in cash for a new lathe worth $50,000. May Amos elect not to treat the transaction as a like-kind exchange so that the realized loss of $10,000 can be recognized?
7. Which of the following qualify as like-kind exchanges under § 1031?
   a. Improved for unimproved real estate.
   b. Vending machine (used in business) for inventory.
   c. Rental house for personal residence.
   d. Business equipment for securities.
   e. Warehouse for office building (both used for business).
   f. Truck for computer (both used in business).
   g. Rental house for land (both held for investment).
   h. Ten shares of stock in Blue Corporation for 10 shares of stock in Red Corporation.
   i. Office furniture for office equipment (both used in business).
   j. American automobile for Japanese automobile (both used in business).

8. Under what circumstances can the exchange of partnership interests qualify for like-kind exchange treatment?

9. Ross would like to dispose of some land that he acquired five years ago because he believes that it will not continue to appreciate. Its value has increased by $50,000 during the five-year period. He also intends to sell stock that has declined in value by $50,000 during the eight-month period he has owned it. Ross has four offers to acquire the stock and land:

Buyer number 1:	Exchange land.
Buyer number 2:	Purchase land for cash.
Buyer number 3:	Exchange stock.
Buyer number 4:	Purchase stock for cash.

Identify the tax issues relevant to Ross in disposing of this land and stock.

10. What is boot, and how does it affect the recognition of gain or loss on a like-kind exchange when received by the taxpayer? How is the recognition of gain or loss affected when boot is given?

11. The receipt of boot in a § 1031 exchange triggers the recognition of realized gain. The gain recognition will affect the basis of the property received by the taxpayer.
    a. Discuss the relationship between the realized gain and the boot received if the boot received is greater than the realized gain.
    b. Discuss the relationship between the realized gain and the boot received if the boot received is less than the realized gain.
    c. What effect does the recognition of gain have on the basis of the like-kind property received? Of the boot received?

12. In a like-kind exchange, the basis of the property received is the same as the adjusted basis of the property transferred. If boot is received, what effect does the boot have on the basis of the like-kind property received? If boot is given, what effect does the boot have on the basis of the like-kind property received?

13. In connection with like-kind exchanges, discuss each of the following:
    a. Realized gain.
    b. Realized loss.
    c. Recognized gain.
    d. Recognized loss.
    e. Postponed gain.
    f. Postponed loss.
    g. Basis of like-kind property received.
    h. Basis of boot received.

14. Aaron exchanges a machine used in his business for another machine and stock of Teal, Inc. Explain why the machine has a carryover holding period and the stock has a new (date of exchange) holding period.

15. Mortgaged real estate may be received in a like-kind exchange. If the taxpayer assumes the mortgage, what effect does the mortgage have on the recognition of realized gain? On the basis of the real estate received?

16. A taxpayer's appreciated property is involuntarily converted. She receives insurance proceeds equal to the fair market value of the property. What is the minimum amount the taxpayer must reinvest in qualifying property to defer recognition of realized gain?

17. What constitutes an involuntary conversion?

18. Ed receives severance damages from the state government for a public road built across his property. Under what circumstances can the § 1033 involuntary conversion provision apply to prevent the recognition of gain?

19. Julia owns a shopping mall that she leases to tenants. The shopping mall is destroyed by a tornado. Is the functional use test or the taxpayer use test applied in terms of appropriate replacement property? Explain the differences between the two tests.

20. Rebecca, a calendar year taxpayer, owns an office building that she uses in her business. The building is involuntarily converted on June 15, 1996. On October 5, 1996, Rebecca receives proceeds large enough to produce a realized gain. What is the latest date she can replace the building if the form of the conversion is:
    a. A flood?
    b. A condemnation?
    c. A tornado?

21. What is the earliest date that a taxpayer can replace involuntarily converted property if the form of the conversion is:
    a. A casualty?
    b. A theft?
    c. A condemnation?

22. Bob is notified by the city public housing authority on October 5, 1996, that his apartment building is going to be condemned as part of an urban renewal project. On October 12, 1996, Carol offers to buy the building from Bob. Bob sells the building to Carol on October 30, 1996. Condemnation occurs on February 1, 1997, and Carol receives the condemnation proceeds from the city. Assume both Bob and Carol are calendar year taxpayers.
    a. What is the earliest date that Bob can dispose of the building and qualify for § 1033 postponement treatment?
    b. Does the sale to Carol qualify as a § 1033 involuntary conversion?
    c. What is the latest date that Carol can acquire qualifying replacement property and qualify for postponement of the realized gain?
    d. What type of property will be qualifying replacement property?

23. A warehouse owned by Martha and used in her business (i.e., to store inventory) is being condemned by the city to provide a right of way for a highway. The warehouse has appreciated by $100,000 based on Martha's estimate of fair market value. In the negotiations, the city is offering $40,000 less than what Martha believes the property is worth. Alan, a real estate broker, has offered to purchase Martha's property for $25,000 more than the city's offer. Martha plans to invest the proceeds she will receive in an office building that she will lease to various tenants. Identify the relevant tax issues for Martha.

24. Discuss the justification for nonrecognition of gain on the sale or exchange of a principal residence. Discuss the justification for disallowance of loss.

25. Samantha, who is age 39, would like to quit her job, sell her house, buy a sailboat, and sail the seven seas. The projected realized gain on the sale of her personal residence is $150,000. Is it possible for Samantha to defer the recognition of this gain?

26. What is the earliest date a principal residence that has been sold can be replaced and qualify for postponement treatment? The latest date?

27. Jim sells his principal residence on September 18, 1996. Although he does not replace it until August 19, 2000, the replacement qualifies for postponement treatment under § 1034. Discuss how this replacement could satisfy the residence replacement period requirement.

28. Sandy owns a residence that she acquired 19 months ago. It has appreciated by $40,000 during this period. Now, however, the school board has redrawn the boundaries for the school districts, and her son will have to transfer to a different high school for his senior year. Sandy is considering selling her residence and buying another one that will enable her son to remain in the same high school. Without this reason, she would not sell the house. Identify the relevant tax issues for Sandy.

29. What is a principal residence? Can a taxpayer have more than one principal residence at one point in time?

30. Peggy has owned and occupied a house as her principal residence for 10 years. She purchases a new residence in March 1996. She initially listed her old residence with a realtor in January 1996. Needing the cash flow, she rents the old residence to Joe for a six-month period beginning in March. She sells the old residence to Paul upon the expiration of the rental period in September. Does the sale of the old residence in September qualify as the sale of a principal residence?

31. Define each of the following associated with the sale of a residence:
    a. Amount realized.
    b. Adjusted sales price.
    c. Fixing-up expenses.
    d. Realized gain.
    e. Recognized gain.
    f. Postponed gain.
    g. Basis of new residence.

32. Can capital expenditures made to a house received through inheritance enable the taxpayer to qualify for postponement treatment under § 1034?

33. What does the § 121 exclusion cover? Is it elective? Does the old residence have to be replaced?

34. How many times can § 121 exclusion treatment be elected by a taxpayer? If the taxpayer is filing a joint return with his or her spouse, do both taxpayers have to meet the ownership and use requirements?

35. Can any other provision be applied to any remaining gain that is not excluded under § 121?

PROBLEMS

36. Kay owns undeveloped land with an adjusted basis of $150,000. She exchanges it for other undeveloped land worth $185,000.
    a. What are Kay's realized and recognized gain or loss?
    b. What is Kay's basis in the undeveloped land she receives?

37. Kareem owns an automobile that he uses exclusively in his business. The adjusted basis is $19,000, and the fair market value is $16,000. Kareem exchanges the car for a car that he will use exclusively in his business.
    a. What are Kareem's realized and recognized gain or loss?
    b. What is his basis in the new car?
    c. What are the tax consequences to Kareem in (a) and (b) if he used the old car and will use the new car exclusively for personal purposes?

38. Tex Wall owns undeveloped land that he is holding for investment. His adjusted basis is $175,000. On October 7, 1996, he exchanges the land with his 23-year-old daughter, Paige, for other undeveloped land that he will hold for investment. The appraised value of Paige's land is $250,000.
    a. Calculate Tex's realized and recognized gain or loss from the exchange with Paige and on a subsequent sale of the land by Tex to Baxter, a real estate broker, for $300,000 on February 15, 1997.
    b. Calculate Tex's realized and recognized gain or loss on the exchange with Paige if Tex does not sell the land received from Paige, but Paige sells the land received from Tex on February 15, 1997. Calculate Tex's basis for the land on October 7, 1996, and on February 15, 1997.
    c. Write a letter to Tex advising him on how he could avoid any recognition of gain associated with the October 7, 1996, exchange prior to his actual sale of the land. His address is The Corral, El Paso, TX 79968.

39. Bonnie owns a personal computer that she uses exclusively in her business. The adjusted basis is $5,000. Bonnie transfers the personal computer and cash of $4,000 to Don for a laser printer worth $10,000 that she will use in her business.
    a. Calculate Bonnie's recognized gain or loss on the exchange.
    b. Calculate Bonnie's basis for the printer.

40. Chee exchanges an automobile used exclusively in his business for a light-duty truck that will be used in his business. The adjusted basis for the automobile is $12,000, and the fair market value of the truck is $10,000.
    a. Calculate Chee's recognized gain or loss on the exchange.
    b. Calculate Chee's basis for the truck.

41. Tom owns land and building with an adjusted basis of $125,000 and a fair market value of $275,000. Tom exchanges the land and building for land with a fair market value of $175,000 that he will use as a parking lot. In addition, he receives stock worth $100,000.
    a. What is Tom's realized gain or loss?
    b. His recognized gain or loss?
    c. The basis of the land and the stock received?

42. Olga owns a machine that she uses in her business. The adjusted basis is $60,000, and the fair market value is $90,000. She exchanges it for another machine worth $55,000. Olga also receives cash of $35,000.
    a. Calculate Olga's realized and recognized gain or loss on the exchange.
    b. Calculate Olga's basis for the new machine.

43. Ed owns investment land with an adjusted basis of $35,000. Polly has offered to purchase the land from Ed for $175,000 for use in a real estate development. The amount offered by Polly is $10,000 in excess of what Ed perceives as the fair market value of the land. Ed would like to dispose of the land to Polly but does not want to incur the tax liability that would result. He identifies an office building with a fair market value of $175,000 that he would like to acquire. Polly purchases the office building and then exchanges the office building for Ed's land.
    a. Calculate Ed's realized and recognized gain on the exchange and his basis for the office building.
    b. Calculate Polly's realized and recognized gain on the exchange and her basis in the land.

44. What is the basis of the new property in each of the following exchanges?
    a. Apartment building held for investment (adjusted basis $150,000) for office building to be held for investment (fair market value $200,000).
    b. Land and building used as a barber shop (adjusted basis $30,000) for land and building used as a grocery store (fair market value $350,000).
    c. Office building (adjusted basis $30,000) for bulldozer (fair market value $42,000), both held for business use.
    d. IBM common stock (adjusted basis $14,000) for Exxon common stock (fair market value $18,000).
    e. Rental house (adjusted basis $90,000) for mountain cabin to be held for personal use (fair market value $115,000).

45. Norm owns Machine A, which he uses in his business. The adjusted basis of Machine A is $12,000, and the fair market value is $18,000. Norm is considering two options for the disposal of Machine A. Under the first option, Norm will transfer Machine A and $3,000 cash to Joan, a dealer, in exchange for Machine B, which has a fair market value of $21,000. Under the second option, Norm will sell Machine A for $18,000 to Tim, who is a dealer. Norm will then purchase Machine B from Joan for $21,000. Machine A and Machine B qualify as like-kind property.
    a. Calculate Norm's recognized gain or loss and the basis for Machine B under the first option.
    b. Calculate Norm's recognized gain or loss and the basis for Machine B under the second option.
    c. Advise Norm on which option he should select.

46. Gus exchanges real estate held for investment plus stock for real estate to be held for investment. The stock transferred has an adjusted basis of $15,000 and a fair market value of $10,000. The real estate transferred has an adjusted basis of $15,000 and a fair market value of $45,000. The real estate acquired has a fair market value of $55,000.
    a. What is Gus's realized gain or loss?
    b. His recognized gain or loss?
    c. The basis of the newly acquired real estate?

47. Agnes exchanges a warehouse and the related land with Damon for an office building and the related land. Agnes's adjusted basis for her warehouse and land is $420,000. The fair market value of Damon's office building and land is $410,000. Agnes's property has a $90,000 mortgage that Damon assumes.
    a. Calculate Agnes's realized and recognized gain or loss.
    b. Calculate Agnes's adjusted basis for the office building and land received.
    c. As an alternative, Damon has proposed that rather than assuming the mortgage, he will transfer cash of $90,000 to Agnes. Agnes would use the cash to pay off the mortgage. Advise Agnes on whether this alternative would be beneficial to her from a tax perspective.

48. Determine the realized, recognized, and postponed gain or loss and the new basis for each of the following like-kind exchanges:

	Adjusted Basis of Old Asset	Boot Given	Fair Market Value of New Asset	Boot Received
a.	$ 7,000	$ –0–	$12,000	$4,000
b.	14,000	2,000	15,000	–0–
c.	3,000	7,000	8,000	500
d.	22,000	–0–	32,000	–0–
e.	10,000	–0–	11,000	1,000
f.	10,000	–0–	8,000	–0–

49. Shontelle owns an apartment house that has an adjusted basis of $1,100,000 but is subject to a mortgage of $250,000. She transfers the apartment house to Dave and receives from him $125,000 in cash and an office building with a fair market value of $1,125,000 at the time of the exchange. Dave assumes the $250,000 mortgage on the apartment house.
    a. What is Shontelle's realized gain or loss?
    b. Her recognized gain or loss?
    c. The basis of the newly acquired office building?

50. Carmen's office building, which has an adjusted basis of $200,000, is destroyed by a tornado. Since Carmen's business has excess office space, she decides not to replace the office building, but instead to contribute the proceeds to the working capital of her business.
    a. If the insurance proceeds are $225,000, what is Carmen's recognized gain or loss?
    b. If the insurance proceeds are $180,000, what is Carmen's recognized gain or loss?

51. Albert owns 100 acres of land on which he grows spruce Christmas trees. His adjusted basis for the land is $100,000. He receives condemnation proceeds of $10,000 when the city's new beltway takes 5 acres along the eastern boundary of his property. He also receives a severance award of $6,000 associated with the possible harmful effects of exhaust fumes on his Christmas trees. Albert invests the $16,000 in a growth mutual fund.
    a. Determine the tax consequences to Albert of the condemnation proceeds.
    b. Determine the tax consequences to Albert of the severance award.

52. For each of the following involuntary conversions, indicate whether the property acquired qualifies as replacement property:
    a. Frank owns a shopping mall that is destroyed by a tornado. The space in the mall was rented to various tenants. Frank uses the insurance proceeds to build a shopping mall in a neighboring community where no property has been damaged by tornadoes.
    b. Ivan owns a warehouse that he uses in his business. The warehouse is destroyed by fire. Due to economic conditions in the area, Ivan decides not to rebuild the warehouse. Instead, he uses the insurance proceeds to build a warehouse to be used in his business in another state.
    c. Ridge's personal residence is condemned as part of a local government project to widen the highway from two lanes to four lanes. He uses the condemnation proceeds to purchase another personal residence.
    d. Juanita owns a building that she uses in her retail business. The building is destroyed by a hurricane. Due to an economic downturn in the area caused by the closing of a military base, she decides to rent space for her retail outlet rather than to replace the building. She uses the insurance proceeds to buy a four-unit apartment building in another city. A realtor in that city will handle the rental of the apartments for her.
    e. Susan and Rick's personal residence is destroyed by a tornado. Since they would like to travel, they decide not to acquire a replacement residence. Instead, they invest the insurance proceeds in a duplex that they rent to tenants.

53. The building that houses LaToya's designer clothing store is destroyed in a mud slide associated with a flood on June 27, 1996. LaToya had anticipated the flood and moved her inventory, furniture, and fixtures to a warehouse outside the floodplain on June 20, 1996. Her adjusted basis for the building is $150,000, and she receives insurance proceeds of $160,000 on July 15, 1996. LaToya intends to purchase another building for her store, but would like to have time to locate one in a safer location. Her taxable year ends on June 30.
    a. What are the earliest and latest dates that LaToya can make a qualified replacement?
    b. Assuming LaToya makes a qualified replacement costing $160,000, what are her realized gain, recognized gain, and basis for the replacement property?

54. Lynn's office building, which is used in her business, is destroyed by a hurricane in September 1996. The adjusted basis is $210,000. Lynn receives insurance proceeds of $390,000 in October 1996.
    a. Calculate Lynn's realized gain or loss, recognized gain or loss, and basis for the replacement property if she acquires an office building for $390,000 in October 1996.
    b. Calculate Lynn's realized gain or loss, recognized gain or loss, and basis for the replacement property if she acquires an office building for $350,000 in October 1996.
    c. Calculate Lynn's realized gain or loss and recognized gain or loss if she does not acquire replacement property.

55. Carlos's warehouse, which has an adjusted basis of $325,000 and a fair market value of $490,000, is condemned by an agency of the Federal government to make way for a highway interchange. The initial condemnation offer is $450,000. After substantial negotiations, the agency agrees to transfer to Carlos a surplus warehouse that he believes is worth $490,000.
    a. What are the recognized gain or loss and the basis of the replacement warehouse if Carlos's objective is to recognize as much gain as possible?
    b. Advise Carlos regarding what he needs to do by what date in order to achieve his objective.

56. What are the *maximum* postponed gain or loss and the basis for the replacement property for the following involuntary conversions?

	Property	Type of Conversion	Amount Realized	Adjusted Basis	Amount Reinvested
a.	Drugstore (business)	Condemned	$160,000	$120,000	$100,000
b.	Apartments (investment)	Casualty	100,000	120,000	200,000
c.	Grocery store (business)	Casualty	400,000	300,000	350,000
d.	Residence (personal)	Casualty	16,000	18,000	17,000
e.	Vacant lot (investment)	Condemned	240,000	160,000	240,000
f.	Residence (personal)	Casualty	20,000	18,000	19,000
g.	Residence (personal)	Condemned	18,000	20,000	26,000
h.	Apartments (investment)	Condemned	150,000	100,000	200,000

57. Rental property owned by Freda, a calendar year taxpayer, is destroyed by a tornado on January 1, 1996. Freda had originally paid $150,000 for the property, of which $125,000 was allocated to the building and $25,000 was allocated to the land. During the time Freda owned the property, MACRS deductions of $46,250 were taken. MACRS deductions of $57,500 would have been taken, except that Freda chose to forgo deductions of $11,250 one year when her tax return showed a net operating loss. Freda receives insurance proceeds of $60,000 in November 1996. As a result of continuing negotiations with the insurance company, Freda receives additional proceeds of $35,000 in August 1997.
    a. What is Freda's adjusted basis for the property?
    b. What is Freda's realized gain or loss on the involuntary conversion in 1996? In 1997?
    c. What is the latest date that Freda can replace the involuntarily converted property to qualify for § 1033 postponement?
    d. What is the latest date that Freda can replace the involuntarily converted property to qualify for § 1033 postponement if the form of the involuntary conversion is a condemnation?

58. Cassandra's personal residence is condemned on October 31, 1996, as part of a plan to build a freeway around the city. Her adjusted basis is $125,000. She receives condemnation proceeds of $110,000 on November 19, 1996. Cassandra is a calendar year taxpayer. She purchases another personal residence on November 20, 1996, for $150,000.
    a. What are Cassandra's realized and recognized gain or loss?
    b. What is her adjusted basis for the new residence?

59. Milton listed his personal residence with a realtor on March 3, 1996, at a listed price of $250,000. He rejected several offers in the $200,000 range during the summer. Finally, on August 16, 1996, he and the purchaser signed a contract to sell for $235,000. The sale (i.e., closing) took place on September 7, 1996. The closing statement showed the following disbursements being made:

Realtor's commission	$ 14,000
Appraisal fee	500
Exterminator's certificate	300
Recording fees	400
Mortgage to First Bank	180,000
Cash to seller	39,800

    Milton's adjusted basis for the house is $150,000.
    a. Calculate Milton's realized gain on the sale.
    b. What is the latest date that Milton can acquire a replacement residence in order to postpone any realized gain?

60. Tina, age 42, has lived in her residence for three years. Her adjusted basis is $130,000. In February 1994, she decides to move to another neighborhood to reduce her commuting time and lists her residence for sale for $225,000. In May 1994, she moves to another

residence that she has purchased for $240,000 at the beginning of the month. By April 1996, she has still not sold her old residence due to market conditions. She is becoming concerned that she will not satisfy the two-year replacement provision. Therefore, she is considering moving back into her old residence and selling her new residence. She anticipates no difficulty in selling the new residence for $250,000.

a. Advise Tina regarding whether she should (1) sell her new residence and move back into her old residence or (2) stay in her new residence and continue to try to sell her old residence.
b. If Tina moves back into her old residence, what is her adjusted basis for the old residence?

61. Ted is a colonel in the U.S. Air Force who is stationed in Newport News, Virginia. He is being transferred to Turkey for a three-year tour of duty beginning on September 15, 1996. He sells his principal residence in Newport News on August 25, 1996, for $220,000. His adjusted basis is $120,000. The selling expenses are $12,000, and the fixing-up expenses are $3,000. He returns to the United States on September 15, 1999, and purchases a new residence for $210,000 in San Antonio, Texas, where he is now stationed.
    a. What is Ted's realized gain or loss?
    b. His recognized gain or loss?
    c. The basis of the residence?

62. On January 15, 1996, Kelly, a 48-year-old widow, buys a new residence for $180,000. On March 1, 1996, she sells for an adjusted sales price of $197,000 her old residence, which had an adjusted basis of $110,000. No fixing-up expenses are incurred. Between April 1 and June 30, 1996, she constructs an addition to her new house at a cost of $20,000.
    a. What is Kelly's realized gain or loss?
    b. Kelly's recognized gain or loss?
    c. Kelly's basis for the new residence?

63. What are the realized, recognized, and postponed gain or loss, the new basis, and the adjusted sales price for each of the following? Assume that none of the taxpayers is 55 years of age or older.
    a. Susan sells her residence for $90,000. The adjusted basis was $55,000. The selling expenses were $5,000. The fixing-up expenses were $3,000. She did not reinvest in a new residence.
    b. Rocky sells his residence for $170,000. The adjusted basis was $120,000. The selling expenses were $4,000. The fixing-up expenses were $6,000. Rocky reinvested $160,000 in a new residence.
    c. Veneia sells her residence for $65,000. The adjusted basis was $35,000. The selling expenses were $1,000. The fixing-up expenses were $2,000. She reinvested $40,000.
    d. Barry sells his residence for $70,000. The adjusted basis was $65,000. The selling expenses were $6,000. He reinvested $80,000 in a new residence.
    e. Carl sells his residence for $100,000, and his mortgage is assumed by the buyer. The adjusted basis was $80,000; the mortgage, $50,000. The selling expenses were $4,000. The fixing-up expenses were $2,000. He reinvested $120,000 in a new residence.

64. Ned, age 47, sells his residence in Richmond on May 5, 1996, for $115,000. He incurs realtor's commissions of $6,900 and qualified fixing-up expenses of $2,000. His adjusted basis is $70,000. Ned sells the house because his employer assigns him to a temporary job in another state. Ned moves back to Richmond in December 1997. However, he has decided that he enjoys being relieved of the responsibilities of home ownership. Therefore, he rents an apartment and does not purchase another residence by May 5, 1998.
    a. What should Ned have reported on his 1996 return with respect to the sale of his residence?
    b. What should Ned do in 1998 when he has not replaced the residence within the required two-year period?

65. Pedro, age 57, is the sole owner of his principal residence. He has owned and occupied it for 10 years. Maria, his spouse, refuses to join him in making the § 121 election.

a. Can Pedro elect the § 121 exclusion if he and Maria file a joint return? If so, what is the available amount of the exclusion?
b. Can Pedro elect the § 121 exclusion if he files a separate return? If so, what is the available amount of the exclusion?
c. If Maria joins Pedro in making the election, what is the available amount of the exclusion on a joint return? On a separate return?

66. Pat sold his residence, which he had owned and occupied for 18 years. The adjusted basis was $130,000, and the selling price was $325,000. The selling expenses were $22,000, and the fixing-up expenses were $5,000. He reinvested $132,000 in a new residence. Pat is 57 years old.
   a. What are the realized, recognized, and postponed gain or loss, the new basis, and the adjusted sales price if his objective is to minimize the recognized gain?
   b. Based on the data provided, should Pat elect the § 121 exclusion?

67. Nell, Nina, and Nora Sanders, who are sisters, sell their principal residence in which they have lived for the past 20 years. The youngest of the sisters is age 58. The selling price is $555,000, selling expenses and legal fees are $15,000, and the adjusted basis is $60,000 (the fair market value of the residence when inherited from their parents 20 years ago). Since the sisters are going to live in rental housing, they do not plan to acquire another residence. Nell has contacted you on behalf of the three sisters regarding the tax consequences of the sale.
   a. Write a letter to Nell advising her of the tax consequences and how taxes can be minimized. Nell's address is 100 Oak Avenue, Billings, MT 59101.
   b. Prepare a memo for the tax files.

68. Jeff and Jill are divorced on August 1, 1996. According to the terms of the divorce decree, Jeff's ownership interest in the house is to be transferred to Jill in exchange for the release from marital rights. Before the divorce, the house was jointly owned by Jeff and Jill. The adjusted basis and the fair market value at the date of the transfer are $150,000 and $200,000, respectively.
   a. Does the transfer of the house produce recognized gain to either Jeff or Jill?
   b. What is the basis of the house to Jill?
   c. If the same transfer was made by Jeff to Jill for $100,000 and was not associated with a divorce, would either Jeff or Jill have recognized gain?

69. Sam, age 63, owns a residence in which he has lived for 20 years. The residence is destroyed by fire on August 8, 1996. The adjusted basis is $90,000, and the fair market value is $300,000. Sam receives insurance proceeds of $300,000 for the residence. He is trying to decide whether to purchase a comparable house. He anticipates that he will retire in two years and will move to a warmer climate where he will rent in case he decides to live in different places.
   a. Advise Sam of the tax consequences of replacing versus not replacing the residence.
   b. Which do you recommend to him?

CUMULATIVE PROBLEMS

70. Tammy Walker, age 37, is a self-employed accountant. Tammy's Social Security number is 333–40–1111. Her address is 101 Glass Road, Richmond, VA 23236. Her income and expenses associated with her accounting practice for 1996 are as follows:

Revenues (cash receipts during 1996)	$212,000
Expenses	
Salaries	$ 89,000
Office supplies	2,100
Postage	1,500
Depreciation of equipment	25,000
Telephone	800
	$118,400

Since Tammy is a cash method taxpayer, she does not record her receivables as revenue until she receives cash payment. At the beginning of 1996, her accounts receivable were $20,000, and the balance had decreased to $8,000 by the end of the year. The balance on December 31, 1996, would have been $14,000, except that an account for $6,000 had become uncollectible in November.

Tammy used one room in her 10-room house as the office for her accounting practice (400 square feet out of a total square footage of 4,000). She paid the following expenses related to the house during 1996:

Utilities	$4,000
Insurance	800
Property taxes	4,000
Repairs	1,400

Tammy had purchased the house on September 1, 1995, for $200,000. She sold her previous house on November 15, 1995, for $105,000. Her selling expenses had been $9,000, and qualified fixing-up expenses were $1,100. Tammy and her former husband, Lou, had purchased the house in 1992 for $80,000. Tammy had received Lou's 50% ownership interest as part of their divorce settlement in August 1994. Tammy had not used any part of the former residence as a home office.

Tammy has one child, Thomas, age 17. Thomas lives with his father during the summer and with Tammy for the rest of the year. Tammy can document that she spent $8,000 during 1996 for the child's support. The father normally provides about $2,000 per year, but this year he gave the child a new car for Christmas. The cost of the car was $18,000. The divorce decree is silent regarding the dependency exemption for the child.

Under the terms of the divorce decree, Tammy is to receive alimony of $900 per month. The payments will terminate at Tammy's death or if she should remarry.

Tammy provides part of the support of her mother, age 67. The total support for 1996 for her mother was as follows:

Social Security benefits	$5,300
From Tammy	1,700
From Bob, Tammy's brother	1,200
From Susan, Tammy's sister	1,800

Bob and Susan have both indicated their willingness to sign a multiple support waiver form if it will benefit Tammy.

Tammy's deductible itemized deductions during 1996, excluding any itemized deductions related to the house, were $13,000. She made estimated tax payments of $28,000.

Part 1—Tax Computation
Compute Tammy's lowest net tax payable or refund due for 1996. Suggested software (if available): *TurboTax* or *MacInTax.*

Part 2—Tax Planning
Tammy and her former husband have been discussing the $900 alimony he pays her each month. Due to a health problem of his new wife, he does not feel that he can afford to continue to pay the $900 each month. He is in the 15% tax bracket. If Tammy will agree to decrease the amount by 25%, he will agree that the amount paid is not alimony for tax purposes. Assume that the other data used in calculating Tammy's taxable income for 1996 will apply for her 1997 tax return. Write a letter to Tammy that contains your advice on whether she should agree to her former husband's proposal. Also prepare a memo for the tax files. Suggested software (if available): *TurboTax* or *MacInTax.*

71. Arnold Young, age 39, is single. He lives at 1507 Iris Lane, Tucson, AZ 85721. His Social Security number is 999–55–2000. Arnold does not wish to have $3 go to the Presidential Election Campaign Fund.

Arnold was divorced in 1992 after 15 years of marriage. He pays alimony of $36,000 a year to his former spouse, Carol. Carol's Social Security number is 999–33–3000. Arnold's son, Tom, who is age 13, resides with Carol. Arnold pays child support of $6,000 per year.

Arnold owns a sole proprietorship that is on the accrual method of accounting. His revenues and expenses for 1995 are as follows:

Sales revenue	$688,000
Cost of goods sold	430,000
Salary expense	90,000
Rent expense	24,000
Utilities	12,000
Telephone	3,000
Advertising	4,000
Bad debts	6,000
Depreciation	15,000
Insurance	7,000
Accounting and legal fees	4,000
Supplies	1,000

Other income received by Arnold includes the following:

Dividend income:	
Swan, Inc.	$8,000
Wren, Inc.	3,000
Interest income:	
First Bank	5,000
Second Bank	1,000
Lottery winnings (tickets purchased cost $700)	6,000
Raffle prize (ticket cost $60)	200

During the year, Arnold and his sole proprietorship had the following property transactions:

a. Sold Blue, Inc., stock for $27,000 on March 12, 1995. He had purchased the stock on September 5, 1992, for $3,500.
b. Received an inheritance of $30,000 from his Uncle Steve. Arnold used the $30,000 to purchase Green, Inc., stock on May 15, 1995.
c. Received Orange, Inc., stock worth $7,500 as a gift from his Aunt Jane on June 17, 1995. Her adjusted basis for the stock was $5,000. No gift taxes were paid on the transfer. Aunt Jane had purchased the stock on April 1, 1989. Arnold sold the stock on July 1, 1995, for $7,000.
d. On July 15, 1995, Arnold's sole proprietorship sold land that it had acquired on January 18, 1989, for $75,000. The land was initially acquired with the idea of constructing a building for the sole proprietorship. Arnold has abandoned this idea as the result of the low rental rates he pays and will continue to lease. The sales proceeds are $90,000.
e. Arnold is notified on August 1, 1995, that Yellow, Inc., stock he purchased from a colleague on September 1, 1994, for $18,000 is worthless. While he perceived the investment was risky, he did not anticipate that the corporation would declare bankruptcy.
f. On August 15, 1995, Arnold received a parcel of land in Phoenix worth $200,000 in exchange for a parcel of land he owned in Tucson. Since the Tucson parcel was worth $215,000, he also received $15,000 cash. Arnold's adjusted basis for the Tucson parcel was $205,000. He originally purchased it on September 18, 1992.

g. Sold the condominium in which he had been living for the past 10 years on December 1, 1995. He and Carol had purchased the condominium as joint owners for $120,000. Arnold had received Carol's ownership interest as part of the divorce proceedings. The fair market value at that time was $150,000. The sales price is $225,000, selling expenses are $12,000, and fixing-up expenses are $4,000. Although he has not yet purchased a replacement residence, negotiations are under way and are likely to be concluded during the first half of 1996. Arnold estimates that the purchase price will be about $215,000.

Arnold's itemized deductions are as follows:

Medical expenses (before the 7.5% floor)	$6,000
Property taxes on residence	4,000
State income taxes	5,000
Charitable contributions	10,000
Mortgage interest on residence	7,500

During the year, Arnold makes estimated Federal income tax payments of $29,000.

Compute Arnold's lowest net tax payable or refund due for 1995, assuming he makes any available elections that will reduce the tax. If you use tax forms for your computations, you will need Forms 1040 and 2119, and Schedules A, B, C, D, and SE. Suggested software (if available): *TurboTax* or *MacInTax*.

RESEARCH PROBLEMS

Note: ***West's Federal Taxation on CD-ROM*** *can be used in preparing solutions to the Research Problems. Alternatively, tax research materials contained in a standard tax library can be used.*

Research Problem 1. Ralph and Agnes have lived in the city since their graduation from college more than 20 years ago. They decide to move to the country. The adjusted basis of their residence is $85,000. The amount realized on the sale of the residence in July is $250,000. Also in July, they purchase a farm, which has a residence, a barn, and 60 acres of land, for $300,000. Since the cost of the farm exceeds the amount realized on the sale of their residence, they believe that the realized gain on the sale is postponed under § 1034. Determine if their conclusion is correct.

Research Problem 2. Jeff and Andrea were married in 1980. In 1982, they purchased a residence on Glenn Avenue. In June 1992, in anticipation of a divorce, Jeff moved from the residence to a friend's house. He took personal belongings such as clothes, but left behind tools, heirlooms, and other items that he had acquired before the marriage. In September 1992, he moved into the home of his future wife, Melissa.

Jeff and Andrea were divorced on December 17, 1993, and on December 18, 1993, Jeff married Melissa. Jeff had continued to make the mortgage payments on the Glenn Avenue residence through June 1993. At the time he stopped making the mortgage payments, he started paying alimony and child support. Starting in the summer of 1993, Jeff and Andrea began splitting the cost of incidental expenses relating to the residence including property taxes, insurance, and utilities.

The divorce agreement provided that Andrea would have exclusive use of the residence for a two-year period ending December 17, 1995. The residence would be sold as soon as reasonably possible thereafter with the sales proceeds divided between Jeff and Andrea. Andrea would have exclusive temporary use of the residence until sold.

The Glenn Avenue residence was listed for sale in December 1995 and was sold in March 1996. Jeff's share of the realized gain was $120,000, and his share of the adjusted sales price was $170,000. In May 1996, Jeff and Melissa purchased a residence on Turtle Lane for $400,000. Jeff would like to defer the realized gain on the sale of the Glenn Avenue residence under § 1034. Can he do so?

Research Problem 3. Shelia, age 64, sold her Wren Lane residence in June 1991 for an adjusted sales price of $200,000. Her realized gain was $25,000. On her 1991 tax return, the tax return preparer, a CPA, reflected the exclusion of the $25,000 realized gain under § 121.

Shelia had purchased a smaller residence on First Street in a planned community in December 1990. The cost of this residence was $275,000.

In January 1996, Shelia sells the First Street residence for $360,000. She does not intend to purchase another residence. She would like to use the § 121 election to exclude the realized gain. Since the § 1034 sale-of-residence deferral is mandatory, she believes that the § 121 election on the sale of the Wren Lane residence is invalid. Therefore, Shelia believes that she is eligible to make the § 121 election on the sale of the First Street residence. In defense of her position, she also points out that she was unaware, until recently, that the § 121 election was made on her 1991 tax return.

Is Shelia eligible for the § 121 exclusion on her 1996 tax return?

Partial list of research aids:
§§ 121 and 1034.
Mary K. Robarts, 103 T.C. 72 (1994).

Research Problem 4. You are the new general manager of the Cleveland Indians, Inc. In order for the Indians to become a more serious contender to win the World Series, you believe that player changes are necessary. In particular, you believe that you need to improve your pitching staff. Discussions are in progress with the general manager of the Seattle Mariners. He has offered to trade Randy Johnson (an all-star pitcher) and $5 million to the Indians in exchange for Kenny Lofton (an all-star outfielder) and Carlos Baerga (an all-star second baseman). You have countered by expressing interest in receiving Johnson and Edgar Martinez (an all-star third baseman) rather than cash. You believe that if you are going to give up the speed provided by Lofton and the defensive play of Baerga, you need more than a starting pitcher in return. In addition, you vaguely remember from your MBA days that a player trade with no cash involved will provide better tax results. Before you finalize a trade, you need to know the tax consequences. Obtain a written opinion from your CPA on the way you should structure the trade. The mailing address is Jacobs Field, Cleveland, OH 44118.

Research Problem 5. Greenside Construction, Inc., is in the road construction business. Greenside exchanges a grader used in its road construction business and $20,000 in cash for a scraper to be used in its road construction business. The adjusted basis of the grader is $50,000, and the fair market value of the scraper is $85,000. What are the tax consequences to Greenside of the exchange transaction?

TEAM PROJECT: ARTHUR ANDERSEN TAX CHALLENGE CASES

For more information on the Arthur Andersen Tax Challenge Cases, please refer to Chapter 1, page 1-38.

Information related to tax issues and problems that are discussed in this chapter may be found in the

Fields case on pages 1, 3, 13 -16, 22
Miller case on pages 3, 5, 28

Read and analyze the case you have been assigned and *identify* any issues and problems that are related to material covered in this chapter. If the information provided in the case is complete, prepare answers for this part of the case at this time. If you need information that is contained in the later parts of the case, please write a memo summarizing the questions or problems so you can prepare a complete answer at a later date.

CHAPTER

16

PROPERTY TRANSACTIONS: CAPITAL GAINS AND LOSSES

LEARNING OBJECTIVES

After completing Chapter 16, you should be able to:

1. Understand the rationale for separate reporting of capital gains and losses.
2. Distinguish capital assets from ordinary assets.
3. Understand the relevance of a sale or exchange to classification as a capital gain or loss and apply the special rules for the capital gain or loss treatment of the retirement of corporate obligations, options, patents, franchises, and lease cancellation payments.
4. Determine whether the holding period for a capital asset is long term or short term.
5. Describe the beneficial tax treatment for capital gains and the detrimental tax treatment for capital losses for noncorporate taxpayers.
6. Describe the tax treatment for capital gains and the detrimental tax treatment for capital losses for corporate taxpayers.
7. Identify tax planning opportunities arising from the sale or exchange of capital assets.

OUTLINE

General Considerations

RATIONALE FOR SEPARATE REPORTING OF CAPITAL GAINS AND LOSSES

1 Learning Objective
Understand the rationale for separate reporting of capital gains and losses.

Fourteen years ago, a taxpayer purchased 100 shares of IBM stock for $17 a share. This year the taxpayer sells the shares for $97 a share. Should the $80 per share gain receive any special tax treatment? The $80 gain has built up over 14 years, so it may not be fair to tax it the same as income that was all earned this year.

What if the stock had been purchased for $97 per share and sold for $17 a share? Should the loss be fully deductible? The tax law has an intricate approach to answering these investment activity–related questions.

As you study this chapter, keep in mind that how investment-related gains and losses are taxed can dramatically affect whether taxpayers make investments and which investments are made. Except for a brief discussion in Chapter 3, earlier chapters dwelt on how to determine the amount of gain or loss from a property disposition, but did not discuss the classification of gains and losses. This chapter will focus on that topic.

The tax law requires **capital gains** and **capital losses** to be separated from other types of gains and losses. There are two reasons for this treatment. First, long-term capital gains may be taxed at a lower rate than ordinary gains. An *alternative tax computation* is used to determine the tax when taxable income includes net long-term capital gain. Capital gains and losses must therefore be matched with one another to see if a net long-term capital gain exists. The alternative tax computation is discussed later in the chapter under Tax Treatment of Capital Gains and Losses of Noncorporate Taxpayers.

The second reason the Code requires separate reporting of gains and losses and a determination of their tax character is that a net capital loss is only

TAX IN THE NEWS

Do Lower Capital Gain Tax Rates Encourage the Sale Of Investment Assets?

Tax legislation nearly enacted would have reduced the rate of tax on long-term capital gains. In the debate over this legislation in the House of Representatives, the Democrats contended that reducing the tax rates on long-term capital gains would primarily benefit the rich. The Republicans contended that reducing the tax rates on long-term capital gains would stimulate the economy. The House Ways and Means Committee Report (authored by the Republican majority) says:

> The taxation of capital gains upon realization encourages investors who have accrued past gains to keep their monies "locked in" to such investments even when better investment opportunities present themselves. All economists that testified before the Committee agreed that reducing the rate of taxation of capital gains would encourage investors to unlock many of these gains. This unlocking will permit more monies to flow to new, highly valued uses in the economy.... The Committee rejects the narrow view that reductions in the taxation of capital gains benefit primarily higher-income Americans.... the Committee sees a reduction in the taxation of capital gains as providing potential benefits to all individuals....

SOURCE: Contract With America Tax Relief Act of 1995, H.R. 1215, Report of the House Committee on Ways and Means, pp. 35 and 36, March 21, 1995.

deductible up to $3,000 per year. Excess loss over the annual limit carries over and may be deductible in a future tax year. Capital gains and losses must be matched with one another to see if a net capital loss exists.

For these reasons, capital gains and losses must be distinguished from other types of gains and losses. Most of this chapter and the next chapter describe the intricate rules for determining what type of gains and losses the taxpayer has.

As a result of the need to distinguish and separately match capital gains and losses, the individual tax forms include very extensive reporting requirements for capital gains and losses. This chapter explains the principles underlying the forms. The forms are illustrated with examples at the end of the chapter.

GENERAL SCHEME OF TAXATION

Recognized gains and losses must be properly classified. Proper classification depends upon three characteristics:

- The tax status of the property.
- The manner of the property's disposition.
- The holding period of the property.

The three possible tax statuses are capital asset, § 1231 asset, or ordinary asset. Property disposition may be by sale, exchange, casualty, theft, or condemnation. The two holding periods are one year or less (short term) and more than one year (long term).

The major focus of this chapter is capital gains and losses. Capital gains and losses usually result from the disposition of a capital asset. The most common disposition is a sale of the asset. Capital gains and losses can also result from the disposition of § 1231 assets, which is discussed in Chapter 17.

CAPITAL ASSETS

DEFINITION OF A CAPITAL ASSET

2 LEARNING OBJECTIVE
Distinguish capital assets from ordinary assets.

Personal use assets and investment assets are the most common capital assets owned by individual taxpayers. Personal use assets usually include items such as clothing, recreation equipment, a residence, and automobiles. Investment assets usually include corporate stocks and bonds, government bonds, and vacant land. Remember, however, that losses from the sale or exchange of personal use assets are not recognized. Therefore, the classification of such losses as capital losses can be ignored.

Due to the historical preferential treatment of capital gains, taxpayers have preferred that gains be capital gains rather than ordinary gains. As a result, a great many statutes, cases, and rulings have accumulated in the attempt to define what is and what is not a capital asset.

Capital assets are not directly defined in the Code. Instead, § 1221 defines what is *not* a capital asset. A **capital asset** is property held by the taxpayer (whether or not it is connected with the taxpayer's business) that is *not* any of the following:

- Inventory or property held primarily for sale to customers in the ordinary course of a business. The Supreme Court, in *Malat v. Riddell,* defined *primarily* as meaning *of first importance* or *principally.*[1]
- Accounts and notes receivable acquired from the sale of inventory or acquired for services rendered in the ordinary course of business.
- Depreciable property or real estate used in a business.
- Certain copyrights; literary, musical, or artistic compositions; or letters, memoranda, or similar property held by (1) a taxpayer whose efforts created the property; (2) in the case of a letter, memorandum, or similar property, a taxpayer for whom it was produced; or (3) a taxpayer in whose hands the basis of the property is determined, for purposes of determining gain from a sale or exchange, in whole or in part by reference to the basis of such property in the hands of a taxpayer described in (1) or (2).
- U.S. government publications that are (1) received by a taxpayer from the U.S. government other than by purchase at the price at which they are offered for sale to the public or (2) held by a taxpayer whose basis, for purposes of determining gain from a sale or exchange, is determined by reference to a taxpayer described in (1).

The Code defines what is not a capital asset. From the preceding list, it is apparent that inventory, accounts and notes receivable, and most fixed assets of a business are not capital assets. The following discussion provides further detail on each part of the capital asset definition.

[1] 66–1 USTC ¶9317, 17 AFTR2d 604, 86 S.Ct. 1030 (USSC, 1966).

Inventory. What constitutes inventory is determined by the taxpayer's business.

EXAMPLE 1

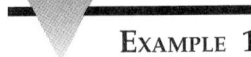

Green Company buys and sells used cars. Its cars are inventory. Its gains from the sale of the cars are ordinary income. ▼

EXAMPLE 2

Soong sells her personal use automobile at a $500 gain. The automobile is a personal use asset and, therefore, a capital asset. The gain is a capital gain. ▼

Accounts and Notes Receivable. Collection of an accrual basis account receivable usually does not result in a gain or loss because the amount collected equals the receivable's basis. The sale of an account or note receivable may generate a gain or loss, and the gain or loss is ordinary because the receivable is not a capital asset. The sale of an accrual basis receivable may result in a gain or loss because it will probably be sold for more or less than its basis. A cash basis account receivable has no basis. Sale of such a receivable generates a gain. Collection of a cash basis receivable generates ordinary income rather than a gain. A gain usually requires a sale of the receivable. See the discussion of Sale or Exchange later in this chapter.

EXAMPLE 3

Oriole Company has accounts receivable of $100,000. Because it needs working capital, it sells the receivables for $83,000 to a financial institution. If Oriole is an accrual basis taxpayer, it has a $17,000 ordinary loss. Revenue of $100,000 would have been recorded and a $100,000 basis would have been established when the receivable was created. If Oriole is a cash basis taxpayer, it has $83,000 of ordinary income because it would not have recorded any revenue earlier; thus, the receivable has no tax basis. ▼

Business Fixed Assets. Depreciable personal property and real estate (both depreciable and nondepreciable) used by a business are not capital assets. Thus, *business fixed assets* are generally not capital assets.

The Code has a very complex set of rules pertaining to such property. One of these rules is discussed under Real Property Subdivided for Sale in this chapter; the remainder of the rules are discussed in Chapter 17. Although business fixed assets are not capital assets, a long-term capital gain can sometimes result from their sale. Chapter 17 discusses the potential capital gain treatment for business fixed assets under § 1231.

Copyrights and Creative Works. Generally, the person whose efforts led to the copyright or creative work has an ordinary asset, not a capital asset. *Creative works* include the works of authors, composers, and artists. Also, the person for whom a letter, memorandum, or other similar property was created has an ordinary asset. Finally, a person receiving a copyright, creative work, letter, memorandum, or similar property by gift from the creator or the person for whom the work was created has an ordinary asset.

EXAMPLE 4

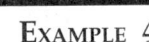

Wanda is a part-time music composer. A music publisher purchases one of her songs for $5,000. Wanda has a $5,000 ordinary gain from the sale of an ordinary asset. ▼

EXAMPLE 5

Ed received a letter from the President of the United States in 1962. In the current year, Ed sells the letter to a collector for $300. Ed has a $300 ordinary gain from the sale of an ordinary asset (because the letter was created for Ed). ▼

EXAMPLE 6 Isabella gives a song she composed to her son. The son sells the song to a music publisher for $5,000. The son has a $5,000 ordinary gain from the sale of an ordinary asset. If the son inherits the song from Isabella, his basis for the song is its fair market value at Isabella's death. The song is a capital asset because the son's basis is not related to Isabella's basis for the song. ▼

(Patents are subject to special statutory rules discussed later in the chapter.)

U.S. Government Publications. U.S. government publications received from the U.S. government (or its agencies) for a reduced price are not capital assets. This prevents a taxpayer from later donating the publications to charity and claiming a charitable contribution equal to the fair market value of the publications. A charitable contribution of a capital asset generally yields a deduction equal to the fair market value. A charitable contribution of an ordinary asset generally yields a deduction equal to less than the fair market value. If such property is received by gift from the original purchaser, the property is not a capital asset to the donee. (For a more comprehensive explanation of charitable contributions of property, refer to Chapter 10.)

EFFECT OF JUDICIAL ACTION

Court decisions play an important role in the definition of capital assets. Because the Code only lists categories of what are *not* capital assets, judicial interpretation is sometimes required to determine whether a specific item fits into one of those categories. The Supreme Court follows a literal interpretation of the categories. For instance, corporate stock is not mentioned in § 1221. Thus, corporate stock is *usually* a capital asset. However, what if corporate stock is purchased for resale to customers? Then it is *inventory* and not a capital asset because inventory is one of the categories in § 1221. (See the discussion of Dealers in Securities below.)

A Supreme Court decision was required to distinguish between capital asset and non-capital asset status when a taxpayer who did not normally acquire stock for resale to customers acquired stock with the intention of resale.[2] The Court decided that since the stock was not acquired primarily for sale to customers (the taxpayer did not sell the stock to its regular customers), the stock was a capital asset.

Often the crux of the capital asset determination hinges on whether the asset is held for investment purposes (capital asset) or business purposes (ordinary asset). The taxpayer's *use* of the property often provides objective evidence.

EXAMPLE 7 Ramon's business buys an expensive painting. If the painting is used to decorate Ramon's office and is not of investment quality, the painting is depreciable and, therefore, not a capital asset. If Ramon's business is buying and selling paintings, the painting is inventory and, therefore, an ordinary asset. If the painting is of investment quality and the business purchased it for investment, the painting is a capital asset, even though it serves a decorative purpose in Ramon's office. *Investment quality* generally means that the painting is expected to appreciate in value. ▼

Because of the uncertainty associated with capital asset status, Congress has enacted several Code Sections to clarify the definition. These statutory expansions of the capital asset definition are discussed in the following section.

[2] *Arkansas Best v. Comm.*, 88–1 USTC ¶9210, 61 AFTR2d 88–655, 108 S.Ct. 971 (USSC, 1988).

STATUTORY EXPANSIONS

Congress has often expanded the § 1221 general definition of what is *not* a capital asset.

Dealers in Securities. As a general rule, securities (stocks, bonds, and other financial instruments) held by a dealer are considered to be inventory and are not, therefore, subject to capital gain or loss treatment. A *dealer in securities* is a merchant (e.g., a brokerage firm) that regularly engages in the purchase and resale of securities to customers. The dealer must identify any securities being held for investment. Generally, if a dealer clearly identifies certain securities as held for investment purposes by the close of business on the acquisition date, gain from the securities' sale will be capital gain. However, the gain will not be capital gain if the dealer ceases to hold the securities for investment prior to the sale. Losses are capital losses if at any time the securities have been clearly identified by the dealer as held for investment.[3]

EXAMPLE 8

Tracy is a securities dealer. She purchases 100 shares of Swan stock. If Tracy takes no further action, the stock is inventory and an ordinary asset. If she designates in her records that the stock is held for investment, the stock is a capital asset. Tracy must designate the investment purpose by the close of business on the acquisition date. If Tracy maintains her investment purpose and later sells the stock, the gain or loss is capital gain or loss. If Tracy redesignates the stock as held for resale (inventory) and then sells it, any gain is ordinary, but any loss is capital loss. Stock designated as held for investment and then sold at a loss always yields a capital loss. ▼

ETHICAL CONSIDERATIONS

Capital Asset Status for Stock Held by Securities Dealers

A securities dealer purchases stock for her own account at 10:00 A.M. At the close of business that day, the stock has dropped slightly in price, so the dealer does not designate it as held for investment. By 10:30 A.M. the next morning, however, the value of the stock has risen substantially above the dealer's purchase price. Using her knowledge of computer programming, the dealer could manipulate the firm's computer records so that the stock will appear to have been designated as held for investment at the end of the previous day. She is absolutely certain that neither the firm nor the IRS will ever discover what she has done. Comment on the securities dealer's potential behavior and the motivation for it.

Real Property Subdivided for Sale. Substantial real property development activities may result in the owner being considered a dealer for tax purposes. Income from the sale of real estate property lots is treated as the sale of inventory (ordinary income) if the owner is considered to be a dealer. However, § 1237 allows real estate investors capital gain treatment if they engage *only* in *limited* development activities. To be eligible for § 1237 treatment, the following requirements must be met:

[3] §§ 1236(a) and (b) and Reg. § 1.1236–1(a).

- The taxpayer may not be a corporation.
- The taxpayer may not be a real estate dealer.
- No substantial improvements may be made to the lots sold. *Substantial* generally means more than a 10 percent increase in the value of a lot. Shopping centers and other commercial or residential buildings are considered substantial, while filling, draining, leveling, and clearing operations are not.
- The taxpayer must have held the lots sold for at least 5 years, except for inherited property. The substantial improvements test is less stringent if the property is held at least 10 years.

If the preceding requirements are met, all gain is capital gain until the tax year in which the *sixth* lot is sold. Sales of contiguous lots to a single buyer in the same transaction count as the sale of one lot. Beginning with the tax year the *sixth* lot is sold, some of the gain may be ordinary income. Five percent of the revenue from lot sales is potential ordinary income. That potential ordinary income is offset by any selling expenses from the lot sales. Practically, sales commissions often are at least 5 percent of the sales price, so none of the gain is treated as ordinary income.

Section 1237 does not apply to losses. A loss from the sale of subdivided real property is an ordinary loss unless the property qualifies as a capital asset under § 1221. The following example illustrates the application of § 1237.

EXAMPLE 9

Ahmed owns a large tract of land and subdivides it for sale. Assume Ahmed meets all the requirements of § 1237 and during the tax year sells the first 10 lots to 10 different buyers for $10,000 each. Ahmed's basis in each lot sold is $3,000, and he incurs total selling expenses of $4,000 on the sales. Ahmed's gain is computed as follows:

Selling price (10 × $10,000)		$100,000	
Basis (10 × $3,000)		(30,000)	
Excess over basis		$ 70,000	
Five percent of selling price	$ 5,000		
Selling expenses	(4,000)		
Amount of ordinary income			$ 1,000
Five percent of selling price	$ 5,000		
Excess of expenses over 5% of selling price	–0–	(5,000)	
Capital gain			65,000
Total gain ($70,000 – $4,000 selling expenses)			$66,000

▼

Lump-Sum Distributions. A *lump-sum distribution* is generally a distribution of an employee's entire qualified pension or profit sharing plan balance within one tax year. The distribution must result from the employee's (1) death, (2) reaching age 59½, or (3) separation from service with an employer. TRA of 1986 repealed a provision that allowed a portion of a lump-sum distribution to be treated as capital gain. However, partial capital gain treatment may still be available because transition rules allow certain taxpayers to continue using prior law. See Chapter 19 for a further discussion of lump-sum distributions.

Nonbusiness Bad Debts. A loan not made in the ordinary course of business is classified as a nonbusiness receivable. In the year the receivable becomes completely worthless, it is a *nonbusiness bad debt,* and the bad debt is treated as a short-term capital loss. Even if the receivable was outstanding for more than one year, the loss is still a short-term capital loss. Chapter 7 discusses nonbusiness bad debts more thoroughly.

SALE OR EXCHANGE

3 LEARNING OBJECTIVE
Understand the relevance of a sale or exchange to classification as a capital gain or loss and apply the special rules for the capital gain or loss treatment of the retirement of corporate obligations, options, patents, franchises, and lease cancellation payments.

Recognition of capital gain or loss usually requires a sale or exchange of a capital asset. The Code uses the term **sale or exchange,** but does not define it. Generally, a property sale involves the receipt of money by the seller and/or the assumption by the purchaser of the seller's liabilities. An exchange involves the transfer of property for other property. Thus, an involuntary conversion (casualty, theft, or condemnation) is not a sale or exchange. In several situations, the determination of whether a sale or exchange has taken place has been clarified by the enactment of Code Sections that specifically provide for sale or exchange treatment.

Recognized gains or losses from the cancellation, lapse, expiration, or any other termination of a right or obligation with respect to personal property (other than stock) that is or would be a capital asset in the hands of the taxpayer are capital gains or losses.[4] See the discussion under Options later in the chapter for more details.

WORTHLESS SECURITIES AND § 1244 STOCK

Occasionally, securities such as stock and, especially, bonds may become worthless due to the insolvency of their issuer. If such a security is a capital asset, the loss is deemed to have occurred as the result of a sale or exchange on the *last day* of the tax year.[5] This last-day rule may have the effect of converting what otherwise would have been a short-term capital loss into a long-term capital loss. See Treatment of Capital Losses later in this chapter.

Section 1244 allows an ordinary deduction on disposition of stock at a loss. The stock must be that of a small business company, and the ordinary deduction is limited to $50,000 ($100,000 for married individuals filing jointly) per year. For a more detailed discussion, refer to Chapter 7.

SPECIAL RULE—RETIREMENT OF CORPORATE OBLIGATIONS

A debt obligation (e.g., a bond or note payable) may have a tax basis in excess of or less than its redemption value because it may have been acquired at a premium or discount. Consequently, the collection of the redemption value may result in a loss or gain. Generally, the collection of a debt obligation is *not* a sale or exchange. Therefore, any loss or gain cannot be a capital loss or gain because no sale or exchange has taken place. However, if the debt obligation was issued by a corporation or certain government agencies, the collection of the redemption value is treated as a sale or exchange.[6]

EXAMPLE 10

Fran acquires $1,000 of Osprey Corporation bonds for $980 in the open market. If the bonds are held to maturity, the $20 difference between Fran's collection of the $1,000 redemption value and her cost of $980 is treated as capital gain. If the obligation had been issued to Fran

[4] § 1234A.
[5] § 165(g)(1).
[6] § 1271.

by an individual instead of by a corporation, her $20 gain would be ordinary, since she did not sell or exchange the debt. ▼

Original Issue Discount. The benefit of the sale or exchange exception that allows a capital gain from the collection of certain obligations is reduced when the obligation has original issue discount. **Original issue discount (OID)** arises when the issue price of a debt obligation is less than the maturity value of the obligation. OID must generally be amortized over the life of the debt obligation using the effective interest method. The OID amortization increases the basis of the bond. Most new publicly traded bond issues do not carry OID since the stated interest rate is set to make the market price on issue the same as the bond's face amount. In addition, even if the issue price is less than the face amount, the difference is not considered to be OID if the difference is less than one-fourth of 1 percent of the redemption price at maturity multiplied by the number of years to maturity.[7]

In the case where OID does exist, it may or may not have to be amortized, depending upon the date the obligation was issued. When OID is amortized, the amount of gain upon collection, sale, or exchange of the obligation is correspondingly reduced. The obligations covered by the OID amortization rules and the method of amortization are presented in §§ 1272–1275. Similar rules for other obligations can be found in §§ 1276–1288.

EXAMPLE 11

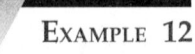

Jerry purchases $10,000 of newly issued White Corporation bonds for $6,000. The bonds have OID of $4,000. Jerry must amortize the discount over the life of the bonds. The OID amortization *increases* his interest income. (The bonds were selling at a discount because the market rate of interest was greater than the bonds' interest rate.) After Jerry has amortized $1,800 of OID, he sells the bonds for $8,000. Jerry has a capital gain of $200 [$8,000 – ($6,000 cost + $1,800 OID amortization)]. The OID amortization rules prevent him from converting ordinary interest income into capital gain. Without the OID amortization, Jerry would have capital gain of $2,000 ($8,000 – $6,000 cost). ▼

OPTIONS

Frequently, a potential buyer of property wants some time to make the purchase decision, but wants to control the sale and/or the sale price in the meantime. **Options** are used to achieve these objectives. The potential purchaser (grantee) pays the property owner (grantor) for an option on the property. The grantee then becomes the option holder. The option usually sets a price at which the grantee can buy the property and expires after a specified period of time.

Sale of an Option. A grantee may sell or exchange the option rather than exercising it or letting it expire. Generally, the grantee's sale or exchange of the option results in capital gain or loss if the option property is (or would be) a capital asset to the grantee.[8]

EXAMPLE 12

Rosa wants to buy some vacant land for investment purposes. She cannot afford the full purchase price. Instead, she convinces the landowner (grantor) to sell her the right to purchase the land for $100,000 anytime in the next two years. Rosa (grantee) pays $3,000 to obtain this option to buy the land. The option is a capital asset for Rosa because if she

[7] § 1273(a)(3).

[8] § 1234(a) and Reg. § 1.1234–1(a)(1). Stock options are discussed in Chapter 19.

actually purchased the land, the land would be a capital asset. Three months after purchasing the option, Rosa sells it for $7,000. She has a $4,000 ($7,000 – $3,000) short-term capital gain on this sale since she held the option for one year or less. ▼

Failure to Exercise Options. If an option holder (grantee) fails to exercise the option, the lapse of the option is considered a sale or exchange on the option expiration date. Thus, the loss is a capital loss if the property subject to the option is (or would be) a capital asset in the hands of the grantee.

The grantor of an option on *stocks, securities, commodities, or commodity futures* receives short-term capital gain treatment upon the expiration of the option. Options on property other than stocks, securities, commodities, or commodity futures result in ordinary income to the grantor when the option expires. For example, an individual investor who owns certain stock (a capital asset) may sell a call option, entitling the buyer of the option to acquire the stock at a specified price higher than the value at the date the option is granted. The writer of the call receives a premium (e.g., 10 percent) for writing the option. If the price of the stock does not increase during the option period, the option will expire unexercised. Upon the expiration of the option, the grantor must recognize short-term capital gain. These provisions do not apply to options held for sale to customers (the inventory of a securities dealer).

Exercise of Options by Grantee. If the option is exercised, the amount paid for the option is added to the optioned property's selling price. This increases the gain (or reduces the loss) to the grantor resulting from the sale of the property. The grantor's gain or loss is capital or ordinary depending on the tax status of the property. The grantee adds the cost of the option to the basis of the property purchased.

EXAMPLE 13

On September 1, 1989, Wes purchases 100 shares of Eagle Company stock for $5,000. On April 1, 1996, he writes a call option on the stock, giving the grantee the right to buy the stock for $6,000 during the following six-month period. Wes (the grantor) receives a call premium of $500 for writing the call.

- If the call is exercised by the grantee on August 1, 1996, Wes has $1,500 ($6,000 + $500 – $5,000) of long-term capital gain from the sale of the stock. The grantee has a $6,500 ($500 option premium + $6,000 purchase price) basis for the stock.
- Assume that Wes decides to sell his stock prior to exercise for $6,000 and enters into a closing transaction by purchasing a call on 100 shares of Eagle Company stock for $5,000. Since the Eagle stock is selling for $6,000, Wes must pay a call premium of $1,000. He recognizes a $500 short-term capital loss [$1,000 (call premium paid) – $500 (call premium received)] on the closing transaction. On the actual sale of the Eagle stock, Wes has a long-term capital gain of $1,000 [$6,000 (selling price) – $5,000 (cost)]. The grantee is not affected by Wes's closing transaction. The original option is still in existence, and the grantee's tax consequences will depend on what action the grantee takes—exercising the option, letting the option expire, or selling the option.
- Assume that the original option expired unexercised. Wes has a $500 short-term capital gain equal to the call premium received for writing the option. This gain is not recognized until the option expires. The grantee has a loss from expiration of the option. The nature of the loss will depend upon whether the option was a capital asset or an ordinary asset. ▼

Concept Summary 16–1 summarizes the rules for options.

Concept Summary 16–1

Options

Event	Effect on Grantor	Effect on Grantee
Option is granted.	Receives value and has a contract obligation (a liability).	Pays value and has a contract right (an asset).
Option expires.	Has a short-term capital gain if the option property is stocks, securities, commodities, or commodity futures. Otherwise, gain is ordinary income.	Has a loss (capital loss if option property would have been a capital asset for the grantee).
Option is exercised.	Amount received for option increases proceeds from sale of the option property.	Amount paid for option becomes part of the basis of the option property purchased.
Option is sold or exchanged by grantee.	Result depends upon whether option later expires or is exercised (see above).	Could have gain or loss (capital gain or loss if option property would have been a capital asset for the grantee).

PATENTS

Transfer of a **patent** is treated as the sale or exchange of a long-term capital asset when all substantial rights to the patent (or an undivided interest that includes all such rights) are transferred by a holder.[9] The transferor/holder may receive payment in virtually any form. Lump-sum or periodic payments are most common. The amount of the payments may also be contingent on the transferee/purchaser's productivity, use, or disposition of the patent. If the transfer meets these requirements, any gain or loss is *automatically a long-term* capital gain or loss. Whether the asset was a capital asset for the transferor, whether a sale or exchange occurred, and how long the transferor held the patent are not relevant.

This special long-term capital gain or loss treatment for patents is intended to encourage technological progress. Ironically, authors, composers, and artists are not eligible for capital gain treatment when their creations are transferred. Books, songs, and artists' works may be copyrighted, but copyrights and the assets they represent are not capital assets. Thus, the disposition of those assets by their creators usually results in ordinary gain or loss. The following example illustrates the special treatment for patents.

Example 14

Mei-Yen, a druggist, invents a pill-counting machine, which she patents. In consideration of a lump-sum payment of $200,000 plus $10 per machine sold, Mei-Yen assigns the patent to Drug Products, Inc. Assuming Mei-Yen has transferred all substantial rights, the question of whether the transfer is a sale or exchange of a capital asset is not relevant. Mei-Yen automatically has a long-term capital gain from both the lump-sum payment and the $10 per machine royalty to the extent these proceeds exceed her basis for the patent. ▼

[9] § 1235.

Substantial Rights. To receive favorable capital gain treatment, all *substantial rights* to the patent (or an undivided interest in it) must be transferred. All substantial rights to a patent means all rights (whether or not then held by the grantor) that are valuable at the time the patent rights (or an undivided interest in the patent) are transferred. All substantial rights have not been transferred when the transfer is limited geographically within the issuing country or when the transfer is for a period less than the remaining life of the patent. The circumstances of the entire transaction, rather than merely the language used in the transfer instrument, are to be considered in deciding whether all substantial rights have been transferred.[10]

EXAMPLE 15

Assume Mei-Yen, the druggist in Example 14, only licensed Drug Products, Inc., to manufacture and sell the invention in Michigan. She retained the right to license the machine elsewhere in the United States. Mei-Yen has retained a substantial right and is not eligible for automatic long-term capital gain treatment. ▼

Holder Defined. The *holder* of a patent must be an *individual* and is usually the invention's creator. A holder may also be an individual who purchases the patent rights from the creator before the patented invention is reduced to practice. However, the creator's employer and certain parties related to the creator do not qualify as holders. Thus, in the common situation where an employer has all rights to an employee's inventions, the employer is not eligible for long-term capital gain treatment. More than likely, the employer will have an ordinary asset because the patent was developed as part of its business.

FRANCHISES, TRADEMARKS, AND TRADE NAMES

A mode of operation, a widely recognized brand name (trade name), and a widely known business symbol (trademark) are all valuable assets. These assets may be licensed (commonly known as franchising) by their owner for use by other businesses. Many fast-food restaurants (such as McDonald's and Taco Bell) are franchises. The franchisee usually pays the owner (franchisor) an initial fee plus a contingent fee. The contingent fee is often based upon the franchisee's sales volume.

For Federal income tax purposes, a **franchise** is an agreement that gives the franchisee the right to distribute, sell, or provide goods, services, or facilities within a specified area.[11] A franchise transfer includes the grant of a franchise, a transfer by one franchisee to another person, or the renewal of a franchise.

A franchise transfer is generally not a sale or exchange of a capital asset. Section 1253 provides that a transfer of a franchise, trademark, or trade name is not a transfer of a capital asset when the transferor retains any significant power, right, or continuing interest in the property transferred.

Significant Power, Right, or Continuing Interest. *Significant powers, rights, or continuing interests* include control over assignment, quality of products and services, sale or advertising of other products or services, and the right to require that substantially all supplies and equipment be purchased from the transferor. Also included are the right to terminate the franchise at will and the right to substantial contingent payments. Most modern franchising operations involve some or all of these powers, rights, or continuing interests.

[10] Reg. § 1.1235–2(b)(1).

[11] § 1253(b)(1).

In the unusual case where no significant power, right, or continuing interest is retained by the transferor, a sale or exchange may occur, and capital gain or loss treatment may be available. For capital gain or loss treatment to be available, the asset transferred must qualify as a capital asset.

EXAMPLE 16

Orange, Inc., a franchisee, sells the franchise to a third party. Payments to Orange are not contingent, and all significant powers, rights, and continuing interests are transferred. The gain (payments – adjusted basis) on the sale is a capital gain to Orange. ▼

Noncontingent Payments. When the transferor retains a significant power, right, or continuing interest, the transferee's noncontingent payments to the transferor are ordinary income to the transferor. The franchisee capitalizes the payments and amortizes them over 15 years. The amortization is subject to recapture under § 1245.[12]

EXAMPLE 17

Grey Company signs a 10-year franchise agreement with DOH Donuts. Grey (the franchisee) makes payments of $3,000 per year for the first 8 years of the franchise agreement—a total of $24,000. Grey cannot deduct $3,000 per year as the payments are made. Instead, Grey may amortize the $24,000 total over 15 years. Thus, Grey may deduct $1,600 per year for each of the 15 years of the amortization period. The same result would occur if Grey made a $24,000 lump-sum payment at the beginning of the franchise period. Assuming DOH Donuts (the franchisor) retains significant powers, rights, or a continuing interest, it will have ordinary income when it receives the payments from Grey. ▼

Contingent Payments. Whether or not the tranferor retains a significant power, right, or continuing interest, contingent franchise payments are ordinary income for the franchisor and an ordinary deduction for the franchisee. For this purpose, a payment qualifies as a contingent payment only if the following requirements are met:

- The contingent amounts are part of a series of payments that are paid at least annually throughout the term of the transfer agreement.
- The payments are substantially equal in amount or are payable under a fixed formula.

EXAMPLE 18

TAK, a spicy chicken franchisor, transfers an eight-year franchise to Otis. TAK retains a significant power, right, or continuing interest. Otis, the franchisee, agrees to pay TAK 15% of sales. This contingent payment is ordinary income to TAK and a business deduction for Otis as the payments are made. ▼

Sports Franchises. Professional sports franchises (e.g., the Detroit Tigers) are not covered by § 1253.[13] However, § 1056 restricts the allocation of sports franchise acquisition costs to player contracts. Player contracts are usually one of the major assets acquired with a sports franchise. These contracts last only for the time stated in the contract. Therefore, owners of sports franchises would like to allocate franchise acquisition costs disproportionately to the contracts so that the acquisition costs will be amortizable over the contracts' lives. Section 1056 prevents this by generally limiting the amount that can be allocated to player contracts to no more than 50 percent of the franchise acquisition cost. In addition, the seller of the

[12] See Chapter 17 for a discussion of the recapture provisions.

[13] § 1253(e).

CONCEPT SUMMARY 16–2

Franchises

	Effect on	
Event	**Franchisor**	**Franchisee**
Franchisor Retains Significant Powers and Rights		
Noncontingent payment	Ordinary income.	Capitalized and amortized over 15 years as an ordinary deduction; if franchise is sold, amortization is subject to recapture under § 1245.
Contingent payment	Ordinary income.	Ordinary deduction.
Franchisor Does *Not* Retain Significant Powers and Rights		
Noncontingent payment	Ordinary income if franchise rights are an ordinary asset; capital gain if franchise rights are a capital asset (unlikely).	Capitalized and amortized over 15 years as an ordinary deduction; if the franchise is sold, amortization is subject to recapture under § 1245.
Contingent payment	Ordinary income.	Ordinary deduction.

sports franchise has ordinary income under § 1245 for the portion of the gain allocable to the disposition of player contracts.[14]

Concept Summary 16–2 summarizes the rules for franchises.

LEASE CANCELLATION PAYMENTS

The tax treatment of payments received for canceling a lease depends on whether the recipient is the **lessor** or the **lessee** and whether the lease is a capital asset or not.

Lessee Treatment. Lease cancellation payments received by a lessee are treated as an exchange.[15] Thus, these payments are capital gains if the lease is a capital asset. Generally, a lessee's lease is a capital asset if the property (either personalty or realty) is used for the lessee's personal use (e.g., his or her residence). A lessee's lease is an ordinary asset if the property is used in the lessee's trade or business.[16]

EXAMPLE 19

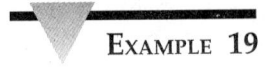

Mark owns an apartment building that he is going to convert into an office building. Vicki is one of the apartment tenants and receives $1,000 from Mark to cancel the lease. Vicki has a capital gain of $1,000 (which is long term or short term depending upon how long she has held the lease). Mark has an ordinary deduction of $1,000. ▼

Lessor Treatment. Payments received by a lessor for a lease cancellation are always ordinary income because they are considered to be in lieu of rental payments.[17]

---

[14] See Chapter 17 for a discussion of the recapture provisions.

[15] § 1241 and Reg. § 1.1241–1(a).

[16] Reg. § 1.1221–1(b).

[17] *Hort v. Comm.*, 41–1 USTC ¶9354, 25 AFTR 1207, 61 S.Ct. 757 (USSC, 1941).

EXAMPLE 20

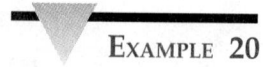

Floyd owns an apartment building near a university campus. Hui-Fen is one of the tenants. Hui-Fen is graduating early and offers Floyd $800 to cancel the apartment lease. Floyd accepts the offer. Floyd has ordinary income of $800. Hui-Fen has a nondeductible payment since the apartment was personal use property. ▼

HOLDING PERIOD

4 LEARNING OBJECTIVE
Determine whether the holding period for a capital asset is long term or short term.

Property must be held more than one year to qualify for long-term capital gain or loss treatment.[18] Property not held for the required long-term period results in short-term capital gain or loss. To compute the **holding period,** start counting on the day after the property was acquired and include the day of disposition.

EXAMPLE 21

Marge purchases a capital asset on January 15, 1995, and sells it on January 16, 1996. Marge's holding period is more than one year. If Marge had sold the asset on January 15, 1996, the holding period would have been exactly one year, and the gain or loss would have been short term. ▼

To be held for more than one year, a capital asset acquired on the last day of any month must not be disposed of until on or after the first day of the thirteenth succeeding month.[19]

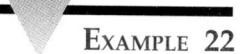

EXAMPLE 22

Leo purchases a capital asset on February 28, 1995. If Leo sells the asset on February 29, 1996, the holding period is one year, and Leo will have a short-term capital gain or loss. If Leo sells the asset on March 1, 1996, the holding period is more than one year, and he will have a long-term capital gain or loss. ▼

REVIEW OF SPECIAL HOLDING PERIOD RULES

There are several special holding period rules.[20] The application of these rules depends on the type of asset and how it was acquired.

Nontaxable Exchanges. The holding period of property received in a like-kind exchange includes the holding period of the former asset if the property that has been exchanged is a capital asset or a § 1231 asset. In certain nontaxable transactions involving a substituted basis, the holding period of the former property is *tacked on* to the holding period of the newly acquired property.

EXAMPLE 23

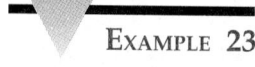

Vern exchanges a business truck for another truck in a like-kind exchange. The holding period of the exchanged truck tacks on to the holding period of the new truck. ▼

EXAMPLE 24

Alicia sells her personal residence and acquires a new residence. If the transaction qualifies for nonrecognition of gain on the sale of a residence, the holding period of the new residence includes the holding period of the former residence. ▼

Certain Nontaxable Transactions Involving a Carryover of Another Taxpayer's Basis. A former owner's holding period is tacked on to the present owner's holding period if the transaction is nontaxable and the former owner's basis carries over to the present owner.

[18] § 1222.
[19] Rev.Rul. 66–7, 1966–1 C.B. 188.
[20] § 1223.

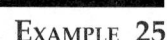

EXAMPLE 25 Kareem acquires 100 shares of Robin Corporation stock for $1,000 on December 31, 1989. He transfers the shares by gift to Megan on December 31, 1995, when the stock is worth $2,000. Kareem's basis of $1,000 becomes the basis for determining gain or loss on a subsequent sale by Megan. Megan's holding period begins with the date the stock was acquired by Kareem. ▼

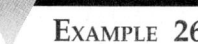

EXAMPLE 26 Assume the same facts as in Example 25, except that the fair market value of the shares is only $800 on the date of the gift. The holding period begins on the date of the gift if Megan sells the stock for a loss. The value of the shares at the date of the gift is used in the determination of her basis for loss. If she sells the shares for $500 on April 1, 1996, Megan has a $300 recognized capital loss, and the holding period is from December 31, 1995, to April 1, 1996 (thus, the loss is short term). ▼

Certain Disallowed Loss Transactions. Under several Code provisions, realized losses are disallowed. When a loss is disallowed, there is no carryover of holding period. Losses can be disallowed under § 267 (sale or exchange between related taxpayers) and § 262 (sale or exchange of personal use assets) as well as other Code Sections. Taxpayers who acquire property in a disallowed loss transaction will have a new holding period begin and will have a basis equal to the purchase price.

EXAMPLE 27 Janet sells her personal automobile at a loss. She may not deduct the loss because it arises from the sale of personal use property. Janet purchases a replacement automobile for more than the selling price of her former automobile. Janet has a basis equal to the cost of the replacement automobile, and her holding period begins when she acquires the replacement automobile. ▼

Inherited Property. The holding period for inherited property is treated as long term no matter how long the property is actually held by the heir. The holding period of the decedent or the decedent's estate is not relevant for the heir's holding period.

EXAMPLE 28 Shonda inherits Blue Company stock from her father. She receives the stock on April 1, 1996, and sells it on November 1, 1996. Even though the stock was not held more than one year by Shonda, she receives long-term capital gain or loss treatment on the sale. ▼

SPECIAL RULES FOR SHORT SALES

The holding period of property sold short is determined under special rules provided in § 1233. A **short sale** occurs when a taxpayer sells borrowed property and repays the lender with substantially identical property either held on the date of the sale or purchased after the sale. Short sales usually involve corporate stock. The seller's objective is to make a profit in anticipation of a decline in the stock's price. If the price declines, the seller in a short sale recognizes a profit equal to the difference between the sales price of the borrowed stock and the price paid for the replacement stock.

A *short sale against the box* occurs when the stock is borrowed from a broker by a seller who already owns the same stock. The box is the safe deposit box where stock owners routinely used to keep stock certificates. Although today stockbrokers generally keep stock certificates for their customers, the terminology short sale against the box is still used.

TAX IN THE NEWS

A Big Short Sale against the Box

Estée Lauder and her son Ronald recently sold stock in Estée Lauder Companies in an initial public offering (IPO) for approximately $340 million. By using the "short sale against the box" technique, their current Federal tax liability associated with the sale is zero. This result occurs because the sales transaction will not close until they repay the borrowed stock that they delivered to the purchasers. Other family members were willing to loan the stock to Estée and Ronald, who pledged an equivalent number of Estée Lauder Companies shares as security.

If the short sale is not closed until after Estée and Ronald die, then neither they nor their heirs will ever pay Federal income tax on the transaction because of the step-up in basis rules associated with inherited property. Estée is said to be at least age 87 and Ronald is age 51.

SOURCE: Information from Allan Sloan, "Passing the Smell Test?" *Newsweek*, December 4, 1995, p. 57.

Example 29

Chris does not own any shares of Brown Corporation. However, Chris sells 30 shares of Brown. The shares are borrowed from Chris's broker and must be replaced within 45 days. Chris has a short sale because he was short the shares he sold. He will *close* the short sale by purchasing Brown shares and delivering them to his broker. If the original 30 shares were sold for $10,000 and Chris later purchases 30 shares for $8,000, he has a gain of $2,000. Chris's hunch that the price of Brown stock would decline was correct. Chris was able to profit from selling high and buying low. If Chris had to purchase Brown shares for $13,000 to close the short sale, he would have a loss of $3,000. In this case, Chris has sold low and bought high—not the result he wanted! Chris would be making a short sale against the box if he borrowed shares from his broker to sell and then closed the short sale by delivering other Brown shares he owned at the time he made the short sale. ▼

A short sale gain or loss is a capital gain or loss to the extent that the short sale property constitutes a capital asset of the taxpayer. The gain or loss is not recognized until the short sale is closed. Generally, the holding period of the short sale property is determined by how long the property used to close the short sale was held. However, if *substantially identical property* (e.g., other shares of the same stock) is held by the taxpayer, the short-term or long-term character of the short sale gain or loss may be affected:

- If substantially identical property has *not* been held for the long-term holding period on the short sale date, the short sale *gain or loss* is short term.
- If substantially identical property has *been* held for the long-term holding period on the short sale date, the short sale *gain* is long term if the substantially identical property is used to close the short sale and short term if it is not used to close the short sale.
- If substantially identical property has *been* held for the long-term holding period on the short sale date, the short sale *loss* is long term whether or not the substantially identical property is used to close the short sale.
- If substantially identical property is acquired *after* the short sale date and on or before the closing date, the short sale *gain or loss* is short term.

CONCEPT SUMMARY 16–3

Short Sales of Securities

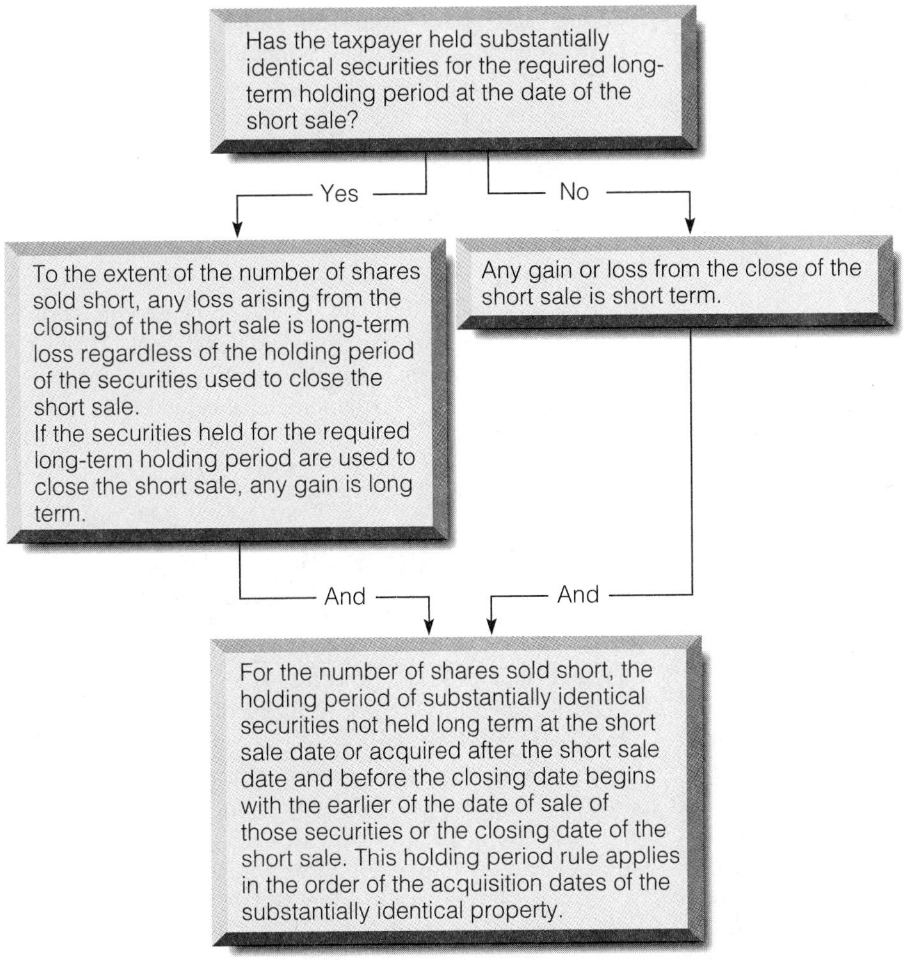

Has the taxpayer held substantially identical securities for the required long-term holding period at the date of the short sale?
Yes
No
To the extent of the number of shares sold short, any loss arising from the closing of the short sale is long-term loss regardless of the holding period of the securities used to close the short sale.
If the securities held for the required long-term holding period are used to close the short sale, any gain is long term.
Any gain or loss from the close of the short sale is short term.
And
And
For the number of shares sold short, the holding period of substantially identical securities not held long term at the short sale date or acquired after the short sale date and before the closing date begins with the earlier of the date of sale of those securities or the closing date of the short sale. This holding period rule applies in the order of the acquisition dates of the substantially identical property.

Concept Summary 16–3 summarizes the short sale rules.

These rules are intended to prevent the conversion of short-term capital gains into long-term capital gains and long-term capital losses into short-term capital losses. The following examples illustrate the application of the short sale rules.

EXAMPLE 30 On January 4, 1996, Donald purchases five shares of Osprey Corporation common stock for $100. On April 14, 1996, he engages in a short sale of five shares of the same stock for $150. On August 15, Donald closes the short sale by repaying the borrowed stock with the five shares purchased on January 4. Donald has a $50 short-term capital gain from the short sale because he had not held substantially identical shares for the long-term holding period on the short sale date. ▼

EXAMPLE 31 Assume the same facts as in the previous example, except that Donald closes the short sale on January 28, 1997, by repaying the borrowed stock with five shares purchased on January

27, 1997, for $200. The stock used to close the short sale was not the property purchased on January 4, 1996, but since Donald held short-term property at the April 14, 1996, short sale date, the gain or loss from closing the short sale is short term. Donald has a $50 short-term capital loss ($200 cost of stock purchased January 27, 1997, and a short sale selling price of $150). ▼

EXAMPLE 32

Assume the same facts as in Example 31. On January 31, 1997, Donald sells for $200 the stock purchased January 4, 1996. Donald's holding period for that stock begins January 28, 1997, because the holding period portion of the short sale rules applies to the substantially identical property in order of acquisition. Donald has a short-term capital gain of $100 ($100 cost of stock purchased January 4, 1996, and a selling price of $200). ▼

EXAMPLE 33

On January 4, 1996, Rita purchases five shares of Owl Corporation common stock for $100. She purchases five more shares of the same stock on April 14, 1996, for $200. On January 17, 1997, she sells short five shares of the same stock for $150. On September 30, 1997, she repays the borrowed stock with the five shares purchased on April 14, 1996, and sells the five shares purchased on January 4, 1996, for $200. Rita has a $50 long-term capital loss from the short sale because she held substantially identical shares for more than one year on the date of the short sale. Rita has a $100 long-term capital gain from the sale of the shares purchased on January 4, 1996. ▼

TAX TREATMENT OF CAPITAL GAINS AND LOSSES OF NONCORPORATE TAXPAYERS

5 LEARNING OBJECTIVE
Describe the beneficial tax treatment for capital gains and the detrimental tax treatment for capital losses for noncorporate taxpayers.

All taxpayers net their capital gains and losses. Short-term gains and losses (if any) are netted against one another, and long-term gains and losses (if any) are netted against one another. The results will be net short-term gain or loss and net long-term gain or loss. If these two net positions are of opposite sign (one is a gain and one is a loss), they are netted against one another.

Six possibilities exist for the result after all possible netting has been completed. Three of these final results are gains, and three are losses. One possible result is a net long-term capital gain (NLTCG). Net long-term capital gains of noncorporate taxpayers are subject to beneficial treatment. A second possibility is a net short-term capital gain (NSTCG). Third, the netting may result in both NLTCG and NSTCG.

The NLTCG portion of these net results is subject to a 28 percent maximum tax rate. Since the maximum individual tax rate on non-NLTCG (ordinary income and NSTCG) income is 39.6 percent, the 28 percent maximum tax rate on NLTCG may reduce the tax rate by as much as 11.6 percentage points. The alternative tax computation (discussed in the next section of this chapter) is used to get this tax saving.

The last three results of the capital gain and loss netting process are losses. Thus, a fourth possibility is a net long-term capital loss (NLTCL). A fifth result is a net short-term capital loss (NSTCL). Finally, a sixth possibility includes both an NLTCL and an NSTCL. Neither NLTCLs nor NSTCLs are treated as ordinary losses. Treatment as an ordinary loss generally is preferable to capital loss treatment since ordinary losses are deductible in full while the deductibility of capital losses is subject to certain limitations. An individual taxpayer may deduct a maximum of $3,000 of net capital losses for a taxable year.[21]

[21] § 1211(b).

TAX IN THE NEWS

Capital Gain in 1979 Leads to Additional Taxes

A capital gain of $6,498 ended up costing President Bill Clinton and First Lady Hillary Rodham Clinton $14,615 in back Federal and state taxes and interest. The gain resulted from Mrs. Clinton's commodity trading that failed to be reported on the Clintons' 1980 tax returns because they did not have a statement on the trade from the brokerage firm.

The Clintons made the payments voluntarily—they could not be required to do so because the statute of limitations had expired. Such problems are not unique to the Clintons. David Kendall, the president's personal attorney, pointed out that three of the last five presidents have paid back taxes and interest to the IRS.

SOURCE: Adapted from Michael K. Frisby and Scott Kilman, "Clintons Pay Back Taxes and Interest of $14,615 Related to 1980 Capital Gain," *Wall Street Journal*, April 12, 1994, p. A20.

TREATMENT OF CAPITAL GAINS

Computation of Net Capital Gain. As just discussed, the *first step* in the computation is to net all long-term capital gains and losses and all short-term capital gains and losses. The result is the taxpayer's net long-term capital gain (NLTCG) or loss (NLTCL) and net short-term capital gain (NSTCG) or loss (NSTCL).

EXAMPLE 34

Some possible results of the first step in netting capital gains and losses are shown below. Assume that each case is independent (assume the taxpayer's only capital gains and losses are those shown in the given case).

Case	STCG	STCL	LTCG	LTCL	Result of Netting	Description of Result
A	$8,000	($5,000)			$ 3,000	NSTCG
B	2,000	(7,000)			(5,000)	NSTCL
C			$9,000	($1,000)	8,000	NLTCG
D			8,800	(9,800)	(1,000)	NLTCL

The *second step* in netting capital gains and losses requires offsetting any positive and negative amounts that remain after the first netting step. This procedure is illustrated in the following examples.

EXAMPLE 35

Assume that Sanjay had all the capital gains and losses specified in Cases B and C in Example 34:

Case C ($9,000 LTCG – $1,000 LTCL)	$ 8,000	NLTCG
Case B ($2,000 STCG – $7,000 STCL)	(5,000)	NSTCL
Excess of NLTCG over NSTCL	$ 3,000	

The excess of NLTCG over NSTCL is defined as **net capital gain (NCG).** The result in Example 35 is a $3,000 NCG. There is an alternative tax computation when taxable income includes a NCG.

The **alternative tax** computation for the individual taxpayer taxes the NCG component of taxable income at a maximum tax rate of 28 percent. When taxable income including the NCG does not put the taxpayer into at least the 31 percent rate bracket, the alternative tax computation does not yield a tax benefit.

The NCG alternative tax is the summation of the following computations. It is illustrated in Example 36.

1. The tax computed using the regular rates on the greater of:
   a. Taxable income less the NCG, or
   b. The amount of taxable income taxed at a rate below 28 percent, plus
2. Twenty-eight percent of taxable income in excess of taxable income used in (1).

EXAMPLE 36

Tim, an unmarried taxpayer, has taxable income (TI) of $175,000. The TI includes NCG of $50,000. Tim's regular tax liability for 1996 is $52,071 [($24,000 × 15%) + 28%($58,150 – $24,000) + 31%($121,300 – $58,150) + 36%($175,000 – $121,300)]. His alternative tax on the NCG is calculated as follows:

1. Tax on greater of:	
a. TI less NCG ($175,000 – $50,000)	
b. TI taxed below 28% ($24,000), plus	$34,071
2. 28% of TI exceeding TI used in (1)	
[28% × ($175,000 – $125,000)]	14,000
Alternative tax on TI including NCG	$48,071

The NCG alternative tax saves Tim $4,000 ($52,071 – $48,071) in 1996. ▼

ETHICAL CONSIDERATIONS

Delaying Stock Sales to Reduce Tax

Jeremy, who is in the 36% tax bracket, had held publicly traded corporate stock for 10 months as of the last day of 1996. The stock was purchased for $3,000 and was worth $13,000. Jeremy needed cash to pay for a trip to his alma mater's football bowl game. He pledged the stock as collateral and borrowed $5,000. He sold the stock on March 1, 1997 and repaid the loan. Consequently, he saved $800 in tax (while having a small amount of nondeductible personal interest expense) by not selling the stock in 1996 or earlier in 1997. Is there anything wrong with what Jeremy did?

There is no special name for the excess of NSTCG over NLTCL, nor is there any special tax treatment. The nature of the gain is short term, and the gain is treated the same as ordinary gain and is included in the taxpayer's gross income.

EXAMPLE 37

Assume that Nora had all the capital gains and losses specified in Cases A and D in Example 34:

Case A ($8,000 STCG – $5,000 STCL)	$ 3,000	NSTCG
Case D ($8,800 LTCG – $9,800 LTCL)	(1,000)	NLTCL
Excess of NSTCG over NLTCL	$ 2,000	

▼

ETHICAL CONSIDERATIONS

Indexing Long-Term Capital Gains for Inflation

Tim, an economist, purchased a lot in a planned community for $100,000 in 1987. His intent at that time was to hold the land for investment. During the period from 1976 to 1986, golf course lots in the planned community had appreciated by 200 percent.

Each year Tim pays real property taxes of $1,000 to the county. In addition, he pays $1,200 annually to the homeowners' association for maintenance of the community, security, and garbage collection. He deducts the property taxes on his Federal income tax return and capitalizes the homeowners' association fee.

Tim sells the lot at the end of 1996 for $160,000. Inflation for the 10-year period has been 30 percent. Tim is aware that the Internal Revenue Code of 1986 includes a number of statutory indexing provisions. Although one is not specifically provided for capital asset transactions, Tim feels that the appropriate way for the sale of the land to be taxed is as follows:

Adjusted basis of land:	
Cost	$100,000
Homeowners' association fees ($1,200 × 10 years)	12,000
Inflation adjustment ($100,000 × 30%)	30,000
	$142,000
Amount realized	$160,000
Adjusted basis	(142,000)
Recognized gain	$ 18,000

Since Tim's marginal tax rate is 28 percent, his tax liability associated with the sales transaction is $5,040 ($18,000 × 28%). What is your reaction to Tim's approach?

TREATMENT OF CAPITAL LOSSES

Computation of Net Capital Loss. A **net capital loss (NCL)** results if capital losses exceed capital gains for the year. An NCL may be all long term, all short term, or part long and part short term.[22] The characterization of an NCL as long or short term is important in determining the capital loss deduction (discussed later in this chapter).

EXAMPLE 38

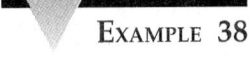

Three different individual taxpayers have the following capital gains and losses during the year:

Taxpayer	LTCG	LTCL	STCG	STCL	Result of Netting	Description of Result
Robert	$1,000	($2,800)	$1,000	($ 500)	($1,300)	NLTCL
Carlos	1,000	(500)	1,000	(2,800)	(1,300)	NSTCL
Troy	400	(1,200)	500	(1,200)	(1,500)	NLTCL ($800) NSTCL ($700)

[22] Section 1222(10) defines a net capital loss as the net loss after the capital loss deduction. However, that definition confuses the discussion of net capital loss. Therefore, net capital loss is used here to mean the result after netting capital gains and losses and before considering the capital loss deduction. The capital loss deduction is discussed under Treatment of Net Capital Loss in this chapter.

Robert's NCL of $1,300 is all long term. Carlos's NCL of $1,300 is all short term. Troy's NCL is $1,500, $800 of which is long term and $700 of which is short term. ▼

Treatment of Net Capital Loss. An NCL is deductible from gross income to the extent of $3,000 per tax year.[23] Capital losses exceeding the loss deduction limits carry forward indefinitely. Thus, although there may or may not be beneficial treatment for capital gains, there is *unfavorable* treatment for capital losses in terms of the $3,000 annual limitation on deducting NCL against ordinary income. If the NCL includes both long-term and short-term capital loss, the short-term capital loss is counted first toward the $3,000 annual limitation.

EXAMPLE 39

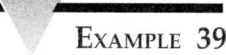

Burt has an NCL of $5,500, of which $2,000 is STCL and $3,500 is LTCL. Burt has a capital loss deduction of $3,000 [$2,000 of STCL and $1,000 of LTCL]. He has an LTCL carryforward of $2,500 ($3,500 – $1,000). ▼

Carryovers. Taxpayers are allowed to carry over unused capital losses indefinitely. The STCL and LTCL carried over retain their character as STCL or LTCL.

EXAMPLE 40

In 1996, Yoon incurred $1,000 of STCL and $11,000 of LTCL. In 1997, Yoon has a $400 LTCG.

- Yoon's NCL for 1996 is $12,000. Yoon deducts $3,000 ($1,000 STCL and $2,000 LTCL). He has $9,000 of LTCL carried forward to 1997.
- Yoon combines the $9,000 LTCL carryforward with the $400 LTCG for 1997. He has an $8,600 NLTCL for 1997. Yoon deducts $3,000 of LTCL in 1997 and carries forward $5,600 of LTCL to 1998. ▼

When a taxpayer has both a capital loss deduction and negative taxable income, a special computation of the capital loss carryover is required.[24] Specifically, the capital loss carryover is the NCL minus the lesser of:

- The capital loss deduction claimed on the return.
- The negative taxable income increased by the capital loss deduction claimed on the return and the personal and dependency exemption deduction.

Without this provision, some of the tax benefit of the capital loss deduction would be wasted when the deduction drives taxable income below zero.

EXAMPLE 41

In 1996, Joanne has a $13,000 NCL (all long term), a $2,550 personal exemption deduction, and $4,000 negative taxable income. The negative taxable income includes a $3,000 capital loss deduction. The capital loss carryover to 1997 is $11,450 computed as follows:

- The $4,000 negative taxable income is treated as a negative number, but the capital loss deduction and personal exemption deduction are treated as positive numbers.
- The normal ceiling on the capital loss deduction is $3,000.
- However, if the $3,000 capital loss deduction and the $2,550 exemption deduction are added back to the $4,000 negative taxable income, only $1,550 of the $3,000 capital loss deduction is needed to make taxable income equal to zero.
- Therefore, this special computation results in only $1,550 of the $13,000 NCL being consumed. The LTCL carryforward is $11,450 ($13,000 – $1,550). ▼

Concept Summary 16–4 summarizes the rules for noncorporate taxpayers' treatment of capital gains and losses.

[23] § 1211(b)(1). Married persons filing separate returns are limited to a $1,500 deduction per tax year.

[24] § 1212(b).

CONCEPT SUMMARY 16–4

Noncorporate Taxpayer's Treatment of Net Capital Gain or Loss

Net Capital Gain Treatment Summarized	
1. All long-term capital gain	28% alternative tax, but it is not always beneficial.
2. All short-term capital gain	Taxable as ordinary income.
3. Part long-term and part short-term capital gain	Short-term capital gain portion taxable as ordinary income. 28% alternative tax is available for long-term capital gain portion, but it is not always beneficial.
Net Capital Loss Treatment Summarized	
4. All long-term capital loss	$1 of loss used to make $1 of deduction. Deduction is *for* AGI and limited to $3,000 per year. Portion of loss not used to make deduction carries forward indefinitely.
5. All short-term capital loss	$1 of loss used to make $1 of deduction. Deduction is *for* AGI and limited to $3,000 per year. Portion of loss not used to make deduction carries forward indefinitely.
6. Part long-term and part short-term capital loss	Short-term losses used first to make $3,000 deduction.

REPORTING PROCEDURES

The following discusses only 1995 tax forms because the 1996 tax forms were not available at the time of this writing.

Capital gains and losses are reported on Schedule D of the 1995 Form 1040 (reproduced on page 16–27). Part I of Schedule D is used to report short-term capital gains and losses. Part II of Schedule D is used to report long-term capital gains and losses. Part III summarizes the results of Parts I and II. Part IV lists additional short-term capital gains and losses. It is a continuation of Part I. Part V lists additional long-term capital gains and losses. It is a continuation of Part II. The Form 1040 instructions have a Schedule D tax worksheet that is used for the alternative tax computation for net long-term capital gains. Parts IV and V of Schedule D and the Schedule D tax worksheet are not reproduced here.

EXAMPLE 42

During 1995, Erlyne Smith (Social Security number, 466–36–4596) had the following sales of capital assets (a 1995 example has been used, since a 1996 form was unavailable):

Description	Date Acquired	Date Sold	Selling Price	Cost Basis*
100 shares of Apple Corp. common stock	10/21/95	12/3/95	$11,000	$10,000
300 shares of Orange Corp. preferred stock	7/29/95	11/25/95	5,000	5,500
2,000 shares of Peach Corp. common stock	1/31/89	12/12/95	8,000	7,000
40 shares of Pear Corp. common stock	6/11/89	12/5/95	16,000	18,800

*Includes selling expenses (e.g., brokerage commissions).

Note that Erlyne's tax position is the same as that of Robert in Example 38. Thus, Erlyne has a NLTCL of $1,800 (Part II of Schedule D) and an NSTCG of $500 (Part I of Schedule D). These amounts are combined (see Part III of Schedule D) for a NLTCL of $1,300. All of the $1,300 is deductible *for* AGI as a capital loss deduction. There is no remaining capital loss to carry over to 1996. In completing a Schedule D for Erlyne Smith, it was assumed that she had no capital loss carryovers from prior years. Her total stock sales of $40,000 ($11,000 + $5,000 + $8,000 + $16,000) were reported to her by her broker on a Form 1099–B. ▼

Tax Treatment of Capital Gains and Losses of Corporate Taxpayers

6 LEARNING OBJECTIVE
Describe the tax treatment for capital gains and the detrimental tax treatment for capital losses for corporate taxpayers.

The treatment of a corporation's net capital gain or loss differs from the rules for individuals. Briefly, the differences are as follows:

- There is an NCG alternative tax rate of 35 percent.[25] However, since the maximum corporate tax rate is 35 percent, the alternative tax is not beneficial.
- Capital losses offset only capital gains. No deduction of capital losses is permitted against ordinary taxable income (whereas a $3,000 deduction is allowed to individuals).[26]
- There is a three-year carryback and a five-year carryover period for net capital losses.[27] Corporate carryovers and carrybacks are always treated as short term, regardless of their original nature.

EXAMPLE 43

Sparrow Corporation has a $15,000 NLTCL for the current year and $57,000 of ordinary taxable income. Sparrow may not offset the $15,000 NLTCL against its ordinary income by taking a capital loss deduction. The $15,000 NLTCL becomes a $15,000 STCL for carryback and carryover purposes. This amount may be offset by capital gains in the three-year carryback period or, if not absorbed there, offset by capital gains in the five-year carryforward period. ▼

The rules applicable to corporations are discussed in greater detail in Chapter 20.

Tax Planning Considerations

IMPORTANCE OF CAPITAL ASSET STATUS

7 LEARNING OBJECTIVE
Identify tax planning opportunities arising from the sale or exchange of capital assets.

Why is capital asset status important when net long-term capital gain is subject to a maximum 28 percent tax rate? The 11.6 percent difference between the maximum 39.6 percent regular tax rate and the maximum 28 percent net long-term capital gain tax rate may generate significant tax savings for taxpayers in the highest regular tax bracket (and to a lesser extent for taxpayers in the 31 percent and 36 percent tax brackets) who can receive income in the form of long-term capital gains. Thus, individuals who can receive income in the form of long-term capital gains have an advantage over taxpayers who cannot receive income in this form.

Capital asset status is also important because capital gains must be offset by capital losses. If a net capital loss results, the maximum deduction is $3,000 per year.

[25] § 1201.
[26] § 1211(a).
[27] § 1212(a)(1).

SCHEDULE D (Form 1040)
Department of the Treasury Internal Revenue Service (99)

Capital Gains and Losses

▶ Attach to Form 1040. ▶ See Instructions for Schedule D (Form 1040).
▶ Use lines 20 and 22 for more space to list transactions for lines 1 and 9.

OMB No. 1545-0074
1995
Attachment Sequence No. **12**

Name(s) shown on Form 1040: *Erlyne Smith*
Your social security number: *466 36 4596*

Part I Short-Term Capital Gains and Losses—Assets Held One Year or Less

(a) Description of property (Example: 100 sh. XYZ Co.)	(b) Date acquired (Mo., day, yr.)	(c) Date sold (Mo., day, yr.)	(d) Sales price (see page D-3)	(e) Cost or other basis (see page D-3)	(f) LOSS If (e) is more than (d), subtract (d) from (e)	(g) GAIN If (d) is more than (e), subtract (e) from (d)
1 *100 shares Apple Corp. common*	*10/21/95*	*12/3/95*	*11,000*	*10,000*		*1,000*
300 shares Orange Corp. preferred	*7/29/95*	*11/25/95*	*5,000*	*5,500*	*500*	
2 Enter your short-term totals, if any, from line 21 . . .		2				
3 **Total short-term sales price amounts.** Add column (d) of lines 1 and 2 . . .		3	*16,000*			
4 Short-term gain from Forms 2119 and 6252, and short-term gain or loss from Forms 4684, 6781, and 8824 . . .				4		
5 Net short-term gain or loss from partnerships, S corporations, estates, and trusts from Schedule(s) K-1 . . .				5		
6 Short-term capital loss carryover. Enter the amount, if any, from line 9 of your 1994 Capital Loss Carryover Worksheet . . .				6		
7 Add lines 1 through 6 in columns (f) and (g) . . .				7	(*500*)	*1,000*
8 **Net short-term capital gain or (loss).** Combine columns (f) and (g) of line 7 . . . ▶					8	*500*

Part II Long-Term Capital Gains and Losses—Assets Held More Than One Year

(a) Description of property	(b) Date acquired	(c) Date sold	(d) Sales price	(e) Cost or other basis	(f) LOSS	(g) GAIN
9 *2,000 shares Peach Corp. common*	*1/31/89*	*12/12/95*	*8,000*	*7,000*		*1,000*
40 shares Pear Corp. preferred	*6/11/89*	*12/5/95*	*16,000*	*18,800*	*2,800*	
10 Enter your long-term totals, if any, from line 23 . . .		10				
11 **Total long-term sales price amounts.** Add column (d) of lines 9 and 10 . . .		11	*24,000*			
12 Gain from Form 4797; long-term gain from Forms 2119, 2439, and 6252; and long-term gain or loss from Forms 4684, 6781, and 8824 . . .				12		
13 Net long-term gain or loss from partnerships, S corporations, estates, and trusts from Schedule(s) K-1 . . .				13		
14 Capital gain distributions . . .				14		
15 Long-term capital loss carryover. Enter the amount, if any, from line 14 of your 1994 Capital Loss Carryover Worksheet . . .				15		
16 Add lines 9 through 15 in columns (f) and (g) . . .				16	(*2,800*)	*1,000*
17 **Net long-term capital gain or (loss).** Combine columns (f) and (g) of line 16 . . . ▶					17	(*1,800*)

Part III Summary of Parts I and II

18 Combine lines 8 and 17. If a loss, go to line 19. If a gain, enter the gain on Form 1040, line 13. **Note:** *If both lines 17 and 18 are gains, see the* ***Capital Gain Tax Worksheet*** *on page 24* . .	18	(*1,300*)
19 If line 18 is a loss, enter here and as a (loss) on Form 1040, line 13, the **smaller** of these losses: a The loss on line 18; **or** b ($3,000) or, if married filing separately, ($1,500) . . .	19	(*1,300*)
Note: *See the* ***Capital Loss Carryover Worksheet*** *on page D-3 if the loss on line 18 exceeds the loss on line 19* ***or*** *if Form 1040, line 35, is a loss.*		

For Paperwork Reduction Act Notice, see Form 1040 instructions. Cat. No. 11338H **Schedule D (Form 1040) 1995**

Consequently, capital gains and losses must be segregated from other types of gains and losses and must be reported separately on Schedule D of Form 1040.

PLANNING FOR CAPITAL ASSET STATUS

It is important to keep in mind that capital asset status often is a question of objective evidence. Thus, property that is not a capital asset to one party may qualify as a capital asset to another party.

EXAMPLE 44 Diane, a real estate dealer, transfers by gift a tract of land to Jeff, her son. The land was recorded as part of Diane's inventory (it was held for resale) and was therefore not a capital asset to her. Jeff, however, treats the land as an investment. The land is a capital asset in Jeff's hands, and any later taxable disposition of the property by him will yield a capital gain or loss. ▼

ETHICAL CONSIDERATIONS

Assuring Capital Asset Status

The taxpayer is an antiques collector and is going to sell an antique purchased many years ago for a very large gain in 1996. The facts and circumstances indicate that the taxpayer might be classified as a dealer rather than an investor in antiques. The taxpayer will save $40,000 in taxes if the gain is treated as a long-term capital gain rather than as an ordinary gain.

The taxpayer is considering the following options as ways to assure the $40,000 tax savings:

- Give the antique to his daughter, who is an investment banker, to sell.
- Merely assume that he has held the antique as an investment.
- Exchange the antique in a like-kind exchange for another antique he wants.

One of the tax preparers the taxpayer has contacted has said he would be willing to prepare the return under the second option. Would you be willing to do so? Why? Evaluate the other options.

If proper planning is carried out, even a dealer may obtain long-term capital gain treatment on the sale of the type of property normally held for resale.

EXAMPLE 45 Jim, a real estate dealer, segregates tract A from the real estate he regularly holds for resale and designates the property as being held for investment purposes. The property is not advertised for sale and is disposed of several years later. The negotiations for the subsequent sale were initiated by the purchaser and not by Jim. Under these circumstances, it would appear that any gain or loss from the sale of tract A should be a capital gain or loss.[28] ▼

When a business is being sold, one of the major decisions usually concerns whether a portion of the sales price is for goodwill. For the seller, goodwill generally represents the disposition of a capital asset. Goodwill has no basis and

[28] *Toledo, Peoria & Western Railroad Co.*, 35 TCM 1663, T.C.Memo. 1976–366.

represents a residual portion of the selling price that cannot be allocated reasonably to the known assets. The amount of goodwill thus represents capital gain. The buyer purchasing goodwill has a capitalizable, 15-year amortizable asset—a disadvantageous situation.

Prior to the Revenue Reconciliation Act (RRA) of 1993, the buyer would prefer that the residual portion of the purchase price be allocated to a covenant not to compete (a promise that the seller will not compete against the buyer by conducting a business similar to the one that the buyer has purchased). Payments for a covenant not to compete are ordinary income to the seller, but were ordinary deductions for the buyer over the life of the covenant. However, § 197 now provides that a covenant is amortized over the same 15-year period as goodwill.

EXAMPLE 46

Marcia is buying Jack's dry cleaning proprietorship. An appraisal of the assets indicates that a reasonable purchase price would exceed the value of the known assets by $30,000. If the purchase contract does not specify the nature of the $30,000, the amount will be for goodwill, and Jack will have a long-term capital gain of $30,000. Marcia will have a 15-year amortizable $30,000 asset. If Marcia is paying the extra $30,000 to prevent Jack from conducting another dry cleaning business in the area (a covenant not to compete), Jack will have $30,000 of ordinary income. Marcia will have a $30,000 deduction over the statutory 15-year amortization period rather than over the actual life of the covenant (e.g., 5 years). ▼

EFFECT OF CAPITAL ASSET STATUS IN TRANSACTIONS OTHER THAN SALES

The nature of an asset (capital or ordinary) is important in determining the tax consequences that result when a sale or exchange occurs. It may, however, be just as significant in circumstances other than a taxable sale or exchange. When a capital asset is disposed of, the result is not always a capital gain or loss. Rather, in general, the disposition must be a sale or exchange. Collection of a debt instrument having a basis less than the face value results in an ordinary gain rather than a capital gain even though the debt instrument is a capital asset. The collection is not a sale or exchange. Sale of the debt shortly before the due date for collection will not produce a capital gain.[29] If selling the debt in such circumstances could produce a capital gain but collecting could not, the narrow interpretation of what constitutes a capital gain or loss would be frustrated. Another illustration of the sale or exchange principle involves a donation of certain appreciated property to a qualified charity. Recall that in certain circumstances, the measure of the charitable contribution is fair market value when the property, if sold, would have yielded a long-term capital gain (refer to Chapter 10 and the discussion of § 170(e)).

EXAMPLE 47

Sharon wants to donate a tract of unimproved land (basis of $40,000 and fair market value of $200,000) held for the required long-term holding period to State University (a qualified charitable organization). However, Sharon currently is under audit by the IRS for capital gains she reported on certain real estate transactions during an earlier tax year. Although Sharon is not a licensed real estate broker, the IRS agent conducting the audit is contending that she has achieved dealer status by virtue of the number and frequency of the real estate transactions she has conducted. Under these circumstances, Sharon would be well-advised to postpone the donation to State University until her status is clarified. If she has achieved dealer status, the unimproved land may be inventory (refer to Example 45 for another

[29] *Comm. v. Percy W. Phillips*, 60–1 USTC ¶9294, 5 AFTR2d 855, 275 F.2d 33 (CA–4, 1960).

possible result), and Sharon's charitable contribution deduction would be limited to $40,000. If not, and if the land is held as an investment, Sharon's deduction is $200,000 (the fair market value of the property). ▼

STOCK SALES

The following rules apply in determining the date of a stock sale:

- The date the sale is executed is the date of the sale. The execution date is the date the broker completes the transaction on the stock exchange.
- The settlement date is the date the cash or other property is paid to the seller of the stock. This date is *not* relevant in determining the date of sale.

EXAMPLE 48 Lupe, a cash basis taxpayer, sells stock that results in a gain. The sale was executed on December 29, 1995. The settlement date is January 4, 1996. The date of sale is December 29, 1995 (the execution date). The holding period for the stock sold ends with the execution date. ▼

MAXIMIZING BENEFITS

Ordinary losses generally are preferable to capital losses because of the limitations imposed on the deductibility of net capital losses and the requirement that capital losses be used to offset capital gains. The taxpayer may be able to convert what would otherwise have been capital loss to ordinary loss. For example, business (but not nonbusiness) bad debts, losses from the sale or exchange of small business investment company stock, and losses from the sale or exchange of small business company stock all result in ordinary losses.[30]

Although capital losses can be carried over indefinitely, *indefinite* becomes definite when a taxpayer dies. Any loss carryovers not used by the taxpayer are permanently lost. That is, no tax benefit can be derived from the carryovers subsequent to death.[31] Therefore, the potential benefit of carrying over capital losses diminishes when dealing with older taxpayers.

It is usually beneficial to spread gains over more than one taxable year. In some cases, this can be accomplished through the installment sales method of accounting.

YEAR-END PLANNING

The following general rules can be applied for timing the recognition of capital gains and losses near the end of a taxable year:

- If the taxpayer already has recognized over $3,000 of capital loss, sell assets to generate capital gain equal to the excess of the capital loss over $3,000.

EXAMPLE 49 Kevin has already incurred a $7,000 STCL. Kevin should generate $4,000 of capital gain. The gain will offset $4,000 of the loss. The remaining loss of $3,000 can be deducted against ordinary income. ▼

- If the taxpayer already has recognized capital gain, sell assets to generate capital loss equal to the capital gain. The gain will not be taxed, and the loss will be fully *deductible* against the gain.

[30] §§ 166(d), 1242, and 1244. Refer to the discussion in Chapter 7.

[31] Rev.Rul. 74–175, 1974–1 C.B. 52.

- If the taxpayer's ordinary taxable income is already in the 28 percent bracket, it would make sense to recognize long-term capital gain rather than ordinary income where the taxpayer has a choice between the two. Such gain is taxed at the alternative rate of 28 percent whereas ordinary income may be taxed under the regular tax rates at 31 percent or more.

KEY TERMS

Alternative tax, 16–22

Capital asset, 16–4

Capital gains, 16–2

Capital losses, 16–2

Franchise, 16–13

Holding period, 16–16

Lessee, 16–15

Lessor, 16–15

Net capital gain (NCG), 16–21

Net capital loss (NCL), 16–23

Options, 16–10

Original issue discount (OID), 16–10

Patent, 16–12

Sale or exchange, 16–9

Short sale, 16–17

PROBLEM MATERIALS

DISCUSSION QUESTIONS

1. What type of gain may be subject to beneficial tax treatment for noncorporate taxpayers?
2. Upon what three characteristics does proper classification of recognized gains and losses depend?
3. Can the sale of personal use assets generally result in capital losses?
4. What broad class of assets is excluded from the capital asset category for tax purposes, but is labeled a capital asset in accounting textbooks for the capital asset budgeting decision?
5. Todd owns the following assets. Which of them are capital assets?
   a. Ten shares of Standard Motors common stock.
   b. A copyright on a song Todd wrote.
   c. A U.S. government savings bond.
   d. A note Todd received when he loaned $100 to a friend.
   e. A very rare copy of "Your Federal Income Tax" (a U.S. government publication that Todd purchased many years ago from the U.S. Government Printing Office).
   f. Todd's personal use automobile.
   g. A letter Todd received from a former U.S. President. Todd received the letter because he had complained to the President about the President's foreign policy.
6. Why doesn't the collection of an accrual basis account receivable usually result in a gain or loss?
7. Joanne purchases song copyrights from composers. What tax issues does Joanne face in determining whether the copyrights are capital assets for her?
8. Why do court decisions play an important role in the definition of capital assets?
9. In what circumstances may real estate held for resale receive capital gain treatment?
10. Jonathan lent $2,000 to a friend who became unemployed unexpectedly. Shortly thereafter, the friend took a new job in another state. After very diligent efforts to locate the friend, Jonathan was unable to find him, and payment of the loan is now 14 months overdue. Assuming the loan is fully noncollectible, what tax issues does Jonathan face?

11. Recognition of capital gain or loss usually requires a sale or exchange of a capital asset. Define "sale" and "exchange."

12. A corporate bond is worthless due to a bankruptcy on May 10. At what date does the tax loss occur? (Assume the bond was held by an individual for investment purposes.)

13. Why does the Code require amortization of original issue discount? What is the effect of this amortization on the interest income of the taxpayer owning the bond? On the adjusted basis?

14. David purchased a one-year option on 40 acres of farmland for $25,000. David's plans for the property did not work out, so he let the option expire unexercised. What tax issues does David face in determining how to treat the $25,000?

15. If a grantee of an option exercises the option, do the grantor's proceeds from the sale of the option property increase? Why?

16. When does the transfer of a patent result in long-term capital gain? Short-term capital gain? Ordinary income?

17. If an inventor's employer automatically has sole patent rights to the inventor's inventions, is the employer a holder of the patent?

18. What is a franchise? In practice, does the transfer of a franchise usually result in capital gain or loss treatment? Why or why not?

19. Under what circumstances is a contingent payment received by a franchise transferor from a transferee a capital gain?

20. When are lease cancellation payments received by a lessee capital in nature? When are lease cancellation payments received by a lessor capital in nature?

21. Taxpayer is the lessee and the lease is on the taxpayer's residence. Taxpayer makes a payment to the lessor to cancel the lease. Why is the payment nondeductible?

22. What does it mean when a capital asset has been held "short term"?

23. In determining the long-term holding period, how is the day of acquisition counted? The day of disposition?

24. Helen exchanges a computer used in her business for another computer that she will use in her business. The transaction qualifies as a like-kind exchange. Helen had held the computer given up in the exchange for four years. The computers are § 1231 assets. What is the holding period of the computer received in the exchange on the day of its acquisition?

25. Juan purchased corporate stock for $10,000 on April 10, 1995. On July 14, 1996, when the stock was worth $17,000, he gave it to his son, Miguel. When does Miguel's holding period for the stock begin?

26. John inherits stock on July 17, 1996. John's father had purchased the stock on April 10, 1995, for $12,000. The stock was worth $15,000 when the father died on December 20, 1995. The stock was worth $18,000 when John received it on July 17, 1996. When does John's holding period for the stock begin?

27. Define a short sale. Why does a seller enter into a short sale?

28. After all possible capital gain and loss netting is complete, what are the possibilities for outcomes that include a net long-term capital gain?

29. After all possible capital gain and loss netting is complete, what are the possibilities for outcomes that include a net long-term capital loss?

30. Sue and Ramon each have gross income of $150,000. Yet Sue contends that her gross income will be taxed at a lesser rate than Ramon's gross income. Assuming she is correct, what could explain this odd result?

31. A noncorporate taxpayer's taxable income, not including a $50,000 long-term capital gain, puts the taxpayer in the 36% bracket. Would all of the long-term capital gain be taxed at 28%?

32. When a noncorporate taxpayer has both a capital loss deduction and negative taxable income, why is a special computation of the capital loss carryover required?

33. Differentiate between the capital loss carryover rules for unused capital losses of individuals and corporations.

PROBLEMS

34. Nancy had three property transactions during the year. She sold a vacation home used for personal purposes at a $21,000 loss. The home had been held for five years and had never been rented. Nancy also sold an antique clock for $3,500 that she had inherited from her grandmother. The clock was valued in Nancy's grandmother's estate at $2,000. Nancy owned the clock for only four months. Nancy sold these assets to finance her full-time occupation as a songwriter. Near the end of the year, Nancy sold one of the songs she had written two years earlier. She received cash of $38,000 and a royalty interest in revenues derived from the merchandising of the song. Nancy had no tax basis for the song. Nancy had no other income and $18,000 in deductible songwriting expenses. Assuming the year is 1996, what is Nancy's adjusted gross income?

35. Revez owns an antique shop. He buys property from estates, often at much less than the retail value of the property. Recently, Revez sold for $4,000 an antique desk for which he had paid $125. Revez had held the desk in his shop for 15 months before selling it. Revez would like the gain on the sale of the desk to be a long-term capital gain. How can he achieve that objective?

36. Gary makes a gift to Barbara of the copyright on his song, "I Love the Spartans." The song has a basis of $20,000 to Gary. Gary had owned the copyright for two years. The copyright has a fair market value of $25,000 at the date of the gift. Three years after receiving the copyright, Barbara sells it to Jim for $30,000.
   a. What is Barbara's recognized gain on the sale?
   b. What is the nature of Barbara's gain?

37. Brenda Reynolds is a dealer in securities. She has spotted a fast-rising company and would like to buy and hold its stock for investment. The stock is currently selling for $45 per share, and Brenda thinks it will climb to $93 a share within two years. Brenda's co-workers have told her that there is "no way" she can get long-term capital gain treatment when she purchases stock because she is a securities dealer. Brenda has asked you to calculate her potential gain and tell her whether her co-workers are right. Draft a letter to Brenda responding to her request. Her address is 200 Morningside Drive, Hattisburg, MS 39406.

38. Abby sells real estate lots, but meets all the conditions of § 1237. In 1996, she sells six lots, one lot each to Betty, Carl, Donna, and Evelyn and two adjacent lots to Frank. The sales price of each lot is $20,000. Abby's basis is $15,000 for each lot. Sales expenses are $500 per lot.
   a. What is the realized and recognized gain?
   b. Explain the nature of the gain (ordinary income or capital gain).
   c. Would your answers change if the two lots sold to Frank were not adjacent? If so, how?

39. Sue has had a bad year with her investments. She lent a friend $3,700; the friend did not repay the loan when it was due, and then declared bankruptcy. The loan is totally uncollectible. Sue also was notified by her broker that the Willow corporate bonds she owned became worthless on October 13, 1996. She had purchased the bonds for $10,000 on October 10, 1995. Sue also had a $20,000 loss on the disposition of § 1244 corporate stock that she purchased several years ago. Sue is single.
   a. What are the nature and amount of Sue's losses?
   b. What is Sue's AGI for 1996 assuming she has $65,000 of ordinary gross income from sources other than those discussed above?
   c. What are the nature and amount of Sue's loss carryforwards?

40. Fred purchases $100,000 of newly issued Gold Corporation bonds for $66,000. The bonds have original issue discount of $34,000. After Fred has held the bonds for two years and has amortized $14,000 of the original issue discount, he sells the bonds for

$98,000. What is Fred's adjusted basis for the bonds when he sells them, and what are the amount and nature of the gain from the disposition of the bonds?

41. Samantha is in the business of buying song copyrights from struggling songwriters, holding those copyrights, and then reselling the songs to major record companies and singers. Samantha has a four-month option to purchase a song copyright. She paid $2,000 for this option. A famous singer has heard the song and is willing to buy the option from Samantha for $10,000. Samantha thinks the song may be worth $35,000 in six months. If Samantha exercises the option, she will have to pay $20,000 for the song. Assuming Samantha is in the 36% tax bracket, which of these alternatives will give her a better after-tax cash flow?

42. Marta is looking for vacant land to buy. She would hold the land as an investment. For $1,000, she is granted an 11-month option on January 1, 1996, to buy 10 acres of vacant land for $25,000. The owner (who is holding the land for investment) paid $10,000 for the land several years ago.
    a. Does the landowner have gross income when $1,000 is received for granting the option?
    b. Does Marta have an asset when the option is granted?
    c. If the option lapses, does the landowner have a recognized gain? If so, what type of gain? Does Marta have a recognized loss? If so, what type of loss?
    d. If the option is exercised and an additional $25,000 is paid for the land, how much recognized gain does the seller have? What type of gain? What is Marta's tax basis for the property?

43. Frank owns a patent on a part that Teal Corporation wishes to use as a component in a product it manufactures. Frank had purchased the patent from the inventor before the inventor reduced the patent to practice. Frank had intended to use the patented part in his business, but found that it was not suitable. Teal is willing to pay Frank $5,000 per month plus 1% of the manufactured cost of the part. How should Frank construct the contract with Teal so that the $5,000 per month and 1% of manufactured cost are long-term capital gain?

44. Susan is the holder of a patent on a corn detassling machine. She sells all substantial rights to the patent for $88,000. Susan had developed the patented machine, but had not yet reduced it to practice. She had spent $43,000 developing the machine and obtaining the patent. What are the nature and amount of Susan's gain?

45. Freys, Inc., sells a 12-year franchise to Reynaldo. The franchise contains many restrictions on how Reynaldo may operate his store. For instance, Reynaldo cannot use less than Grade 10 Idaho potatoes, must fry the potatoes at a constant 410 degrees, dress store personnel in Freys-approved uniforms, and have a Freys sign that meets detailed specifications on size, color, and construction. When the franchise contract is signed, Reynaldo makes a noncontingent $40,000 payment to Freys. During the same year, Reynaldo pays Freys $25,000—14% of Reynaldo's sales. How does Freys treat each of these payments? How does Reynaldo treat each of the payments?

46. Irene lives in an apartment near her college campus. Her lease runs out in July 1997, but her landlord could sell the building if he can convince all the tenants to cancel their leases and move out by the end of 1996. The landlord has offered Irene $1,000 to cancel her lease. Irene's lease began on August 1, 1996. What tax factors should Irene consider in deciding whether to take the landlord's offer?

47. Evelyn acquires 200 Copper Corporation common shares at $10 per share on October 13, 1993. On August 10, 1995, Evelyn gives the shares to her son, Bob. At the time of the gift, the shares are worth $40 each. On May 11, 1996, Bob sells the shares for $45 each. What is Bob's gain? Is it short or long term?

48. Dennis sells short 100 shares of ARC stock at $20 per share on January 15, 1996. He buys 200 shares of ARC stock on April 1, 1996, at $25 per share. On May 2, 1996, he closes the short sale by delivering 100 of the shares purchased on April 1.
    a. What are the amount and nature of Dennis's loss upon closing the short sale?
    b. When does the holding period for the remaining 100 shares begin?

c. If Dennis sells (at $27 per share) the remaining 100 shares on January 20, 1997, what will be the nature of his gain or loss?

49. Elaine Case (single with no dependents) has the following transactions in 1996:

Adjusted gross income (exclusive of capital gains and losses)	$240,000
Long-term capital gain	12,000
Long-term capital loss	(5,000)
Short-term capital gain	19,000
Short-term capital loss	(23,000)

What is Elaine's net capital gain or loss? Draft a letter to Elaine describing how the net capital gain or loss will be treated on her tax return. Assume Elaine's income from other sources puts her in the 36% bracket. Elaine's address is 300 Ireland Avenue, Shepherdstown, WV 25443.

50. In 1996, Betty (head of household with three dependents) had an $18,000 loss from the sale of a personal residence. She also purchased from an individual inventor for $8,000 (and resold in two months for $7,000) a patent on a rubber bonding process. The patent had not yet been reduced to practice. Betty purchased the patent as an investment. Additionally, she had the following capital gains and losses from stock transactions:

Long-term capital loss	($ 3,000)
Long-term capital loss carryover from 1995	(12,000)
Short-term capital gain	21,000
Short-term capital loss	(6,000)

What is Betty's net capital gain or loss? Draft a letter to Betty explaining the tax treatment of the sale of her personal residence. Assume Betty's income from other sources puts her in the 36% bracket.

51. In 1996, Venezia has a $5,800 net short-term capital loss and $9,030 of negative taxable income. She used the standard deduction and has one personal exemption. What is the amount of Venezia's capital loss carryover to 1997?

52. For 1996, Ahmad completes the following stock transactions:

	Date Acquired	**Cost**	**Date Sold**	**Selling Price**
1,000 shares ABC	1/6/96	$4,000	8/2/96	$8,000
200 shares DEF	7/1/82	8,800	9/18/96	9,400
3,500 shares GHI	5/2/96	7,000	11/2/96	8,900
5,000 shares JKL	8/5/96	9,700	12/15/96	5,000

What is Ahmad's includible gain or deductible loss resulting from these stock sales?

53. Consuela, a head of household with two dependents, has the following 1996 transactions:

Adjusted gross income (exclusive of capital gains and losses)	$125,250
Long-term capital loss	(5,000)
Long-term capital gain	20,000
Short-term capital loss carryover	(2,000)

a. What is Consuela's net capital gain or loss?
b. What is Consuela's taxable income assuming she does not itemize?
c. What is Consuela's tax on taxable income?

54. Purple Corporation has $16,800 of long-term capital loss for 1996 and $5,000 of other taxable income. What is its 1996 taxable income and the amount (if any) of its capital loss carryover?

55. June owns a sole proprietorship that Doria is going to purchase. They have agreed on a price for all the assets except goodwill and June's covenant not to compete against Doria. June is willing to give Doria a two-year covenant not to compete for only $1 of compensation, but would like $25,000 for the business goodwill. Doria would like to pay June $25,000 for the covenant not to compete and only $1 for the business goodwill. June is in the 36% tax bracket, and Doria is in the 31% tax bracket. Which of these approaches is better for June? For Doria?

CUMULATIVE PROBLEMS

56. Nikki Hassad is a graduate student at State University. She is single and has no dependents. During 1996, she had $5,500 wages from a full-time job she held until returning to school in August. Nikki received a $3,000 scholarship from State University and used all of the scholarship money to pay for tuition and fees. In June 1996, she won $135,000 with an instant lottery ticket and immediately invested in various stocks. The following table summarizes her stock transactions for 1996:

	Date Acquired	Cost	Date Sold	Selling Price
150 shares Clay	7/2/96	$5,000	12/11/96	$6,200
100 shares Gold	7/2/96	5,000	11/6/96	3,300
120 shares Iron	7/2/96	3,100	10/8/96	8,000
25 shares Sand	7/2/96	1,900		
100 shares Uranium	6/16/91	2,000	12/11/96	9,600

Nikki does not have many itemized deductions, so she will take the standard deduction. Her Social Security number is 393–86–4502, and she lives at 518 Marigold Lane, Okemos, MI 48864. She had $600 of Federal income tax withheld on her wages and $37,000 of Federal income tax withheld on her lottery winnings. She also made Federal estimated income tax payments of $3,500.

Compute Nikki's lowest legal tax liability for 1996. Suggested software (if available): *TurboTax* or *MacInTax*.

Draft a brief letter to Nikki describing (1) how long she must hold the Sand stock for it to become "long term," (2) what the 1997 tax consequences would be if she sold that stock for a $4,000 long-term capital gain, and (3) what would happen if she was eligible for the alternative tax on long-term capital gains. Also, prepare a memo for Nikki's tax file.

57. Margaret Gill, age 33, has two dependents. She does not wish to have $3 go to the Presidential Election Campaign Fund. Margaret is an insurance adjuster. She resides at 2510 Grace Avenue, Richmond, VA 23100. Her Social Security number is 566–88–1000. The following information is for Margaret's 1995 tax year. She earned a $40,000 salary. Margaret received $35,000 of alimony and $40,000 of child support from her former husband. The children are Susan Gill (age 11, Social Security number 396–42–8909) and Jason Gill (age 9, Social Security number 396–43–9090). Both children lived with Margaret all year. On March 1, 1982, she purchased 500 shares of People's Power Company for $10,000. She sold those shares on December 14, 1995, for $8,500 after

receiving nontaxable dividends totaling $2,600 (including $700 in 1995). She also received $300 in taxable dividends in 1995 from People's Power Company. On November 7, 1983, Margaret purchased 1,000 shares of Violet Corporation for $22,000. On February 12, 1995, she received an additional 100 shares in a nontaxable 10% stock dividend. On December 13, 1995, she sold those 100 shares for $2,500. During 1995, she paid $16,000 in deductible home mortgage interest, $7,000 in property taxes, $2,000 in state income taxes, $600 in sales tax, $2,300 in charitable contributions, and $1,500 in professional dues and subscriptions. Her employer withheld Federal income tax of $8,200. Compute Margaret's net tax payable or refund due for 1995. If you use tax forms for your computations, you will need Form 1040 and Schedules A, B, and D. Suggested software (if available): *TurboTax* or *MacInTax*.

RESEARCH PROBLEMS

Note: ***West's Federal Taxation on CD-ROM*** *can be used in preparing solutions to the Research Problems. Alternatively, tax research materials contained in a standard tax library can be used.*

Research Problem 1. The Banc Two Mortgage Company requires a fee of 1% of the remaining mortgage balance when a mortgage is paid off early. In the current year, Banc Two received $760,000 of such fees. What is the nature of the fee: ordinary income or capital gain?

Research Problem 2. Clean Corporation runs a chain of dry cleaners. Borax is used heavily in Clean's dry cleaning process and has been in short supply several times in the past. Clean Corporation buys a controlling interest in Dig Corporation—a borax mining concern. Clean's sole reason for purchasing the Dig stock is to assure Clean of a continuous supply of borax if another shortage develops. Although borax must be refined before it is usable for dry cleaning purposes, a well-established commodities market exists for trading unrefined borax for refined borax. After owning the Dig stock for several years, Clean sells the stock at a loss because Dig is in difficult financial straits. Clean no longer needs to own Dig because Clean has obtained an alternative source of borax. What is the nature of Clean's loss on the disposition of the Dig Corporation stock? Write a letter to the controller, Salvio Guitterez, that contains your advice and prepare a memo for the tax files. The mailing address of Clean Corporation is 4455 Whitman Way, San Mateo, CA 44589.

Research Problem 3. Oak Corporation, a manufacturing company, hired several executives during 1996. The executives had homes in other cities when Oak hired them. If the executives were unable to sell those homes, they would be unable to buy replacement homes in Oak's area. Consequently, if the executives were unable to sell their homes within 30 days of listing them for sale, Oak bought the homes from the executives for 10% less than the list price. Oak immediately put the homes it purchased up for sale. Each home Oak purchased was sold at a loss. By the end of 1996, Oak did not own any homes, but had suffered a loss totaling $125,000. Oak is uncertain how to report the sale of the homes. Oak has a $32,000 short-term capital gain from stock investment transactions during 1996. What is the nature of the $125,000 loss on the sale of the homes? What is Oak's net capital gain or loss for 1996?

Partial list of research aids:
Rev.Rul. 82–204, 1982–2 CB 192.
Azar Nut Co., 91–1 USTC ¶50,257, 67 AFTR2d 91–987, 931 F.2d 314 (CA-5, 1991).

TEAM PROJECT: ARTHUR ANDERSEN TAX CHALLENGE CASES

For more information on the Arthur Andersen Tax Challenge Cases, please refer to Chapter 1, page 1-38.

Information related to tax issues and problems that are discussed in this chapter may be found in the

Miller case on pages 11, 20, 36, 37

Read and analyze the case you have been assigned and *identify* any issues and problems that are related to material covered in this chapter. If the information provided in the case is complete, prepare answers for this part of the case at this time. If you need information that is contained in the later parts of the case, please write a memo summarizing the questions or problems so you can prepare a complete answer at a later date.

CHAPTER

17

PROPERTY TRANSACTIONS: SECTION 1231 AND RECAPTURE PROVISIONS

LEARNING OBJECTIVES

After completing Chapter 17, you should be able to:

1. Understand the rationale for and the nature and treatment of gains and losses from the disposition of business assets.
2. Distinguish § 1231 assets from ordinary assets and capital assets and calculate the § 1231 gain or loss.
3. Determine when § 1245 recapture applies and how it is computed.
4. Determine when § 1250 recapture applies and how it is computed.
5. Understand considerations common to §§ 1245 and 1250.
6. Apply the special recapture provisions for related parties and IDC and be aware of the special recapture provision for corporations.
7. Describe and apply the reporting procedures for §§ 1231, 1245, and 1250.
8. Identify tax planning opportunities associated with §§ 1231, 1245, and 1250.

OUTLINE

Businesses own many assets that are used in the business rather than held for resale. In financial accounting, such assets are known as "fixed assets." For example, a foundry's 30,000-pound stamping machine is a fixed asset. It is also a depreciable asset. The building housing the foundry is another fixed asset. This chapter largely deals with how to *classify* the gains and losses arising from the disposition of fixed assets. Chapter 8 discussed how to depreciate such assets. Chapters 14 and 15 discussed how to determine the adjusted basis and the amount of gain or loss from their disposition.

A long-term capital gain was defined in Chapter 16 as the recognized gain from the sale or exchange of a capital asset held for the required long-term holding period.[1] This chapter is concerned with classification under § 1231, which applies to the sale or exchange of business properties and to certain involuntary conversions. The business properties are not capital assets because they are depreciable and/or are real property used in business or for the production of income. Section 1221(2) provides that such assets are not capital assets. Nonetheless, these business properties may be held for long periods of time and may be sold at a gain. Congress decided many years ago that such assets deserved *limited* capital gain–type treatment. Unfortunately, this limited capital gain–type treatment is very complex and difficult to understand.

Because the limited capital gain–type treatment sometimes gives too much tax advantage if assets are eligible for depreciation (or cost recovery), certain recapture rules may remove the capital gain treatment when depreciation is taken. Thus, this chapter also covers the recapture provisions that tax as ordinary income certain gains that might otherwise qualify for long-term capital gain treatment.

[1] The long-term holding period is more than one year.

TAX IN THE NEWS

"Going Out of Business" Has Tax Implications

Recently, a Western wear store in a midwestern town advertised a "Going Out of Business" sale. All the clothes in the store were sold at heavily reduced prices. At the same time, the store also sold its "store fixtures," such as its clothes racks and display counters. The clothes sold are inventory for the store, but the store fixtures are fixed assets. The store treats the sale of the clothes as a normal sale of inventory, but must calculate a gain or loss on the sale of the store fixtures. While the sale of the clothes will produce ordinary income or loss, the sale of the store fixtures could produce both capital gain/loss and ordinary income/loss.

Section 1231 Assets

RELATIONSHIP TO CAPITAL ASSETS

1 Learning Objective
Understand the rationale for and the nature and treatment of gains and losses from the disposition of business assets.

Depreciable property and real property used in business are not capital assets.[2] Thus, the recognized gains from the disposition of such property (principally machinery, equipment, buildings, and land) would appear to be ordinary income rather than capital gain. Due to § 1231, however, *net gain* from the disposition of such property is sometimes *treated* as *long-term capital gain.* A long-term holding period requirement must be met; the disposition must generally be from a sale, exchange, or involuntary conversion; and certain recapture provisions must be satisfied for this result to occur. Section 1231 may also apply to involuntary conversions of capital assets. Since an involuntary conversion is not a sale or exchange, such a disposition would not normally result in a capital gain.

If the disposition of depreciable property and real property used in business results in a *net loss,* § 1231 *treats* the *loss* as an *ordinary loss* rather than as a capital loss. Ordinary losses are fully deductible *for* adjusted gross income (AGI). Capital losses are offset by capital gains, and, if any loss remains, the loss is deductible to the extent of $3,000 per year for individuals and currently is not deductible at all by regular corporations. It seems, therefore, that § 1231 provides the *best* of both potential results: net gain may be treated as long-term capital gain, and net loss is treated as ordinary loss.

Example 1

Roberto sells business land and building at a $5,000 gain and business equipment at a $3,000 loss. Both properties were held for the long-term holding period. Roberto's net gain is $2,000, and that net gain may (depending on various recapture rules discussed later in this chapter) be treated as a long-term capital gain under § 1231. ▼

Example 2

Samantha sells business equipment at a $10,000 loss and business land at a $2,000 gain. Both properties were held for the long-term holding period. Samantha's net loss is $8,000, and that net loss is an ordinary loss. ▼

---

[2] § 1221(2).

The rules regarding § 1231 treatment do *not* apply to *all* business property. Important in this regard are the holding period requirements and the fact that the property must be either depreciable property or real estate used in business. Nor is § 1231 necessarily limited to business property. Transactions involving certain capital assets may fall into the § 1231 category. Thus, § 1231 singles out only some types of business property.

As discussed in Chapter 16, there is beneficial tax treatment for long-term capital gains. Section 1231 requires netting of **§ 1231 gains and losses.** If the result is a gain, it may be treated as a long-term capital gain. The net gain is added to the "real" long-term capital gains (if any) and netted with capital losses (if any). Thus, the net § 1231 gain may eventually be eligible for beneficial capital gain treatment or help avoid the unfavorable net capital loss result. The § 1231 gain and loss netting may result in a loss. In this case, the loss is an ordinary loss and is deductible *for* AGI. Finally, § 1231 assets are treated the same as capital assets for purposes of the appreciated property charitable contribution provisions (refer to Chapter 10).

JUSTIFICATION FOR FAVORABLE TAX TREATMENT

The favorable capital gain/ordinary loss treatment sanctioned by § 1231 can be explained by examining several historical developments. Before 1938, business property had been included in the definition of capital assets. Thus, if such property was sold for a loss (not an unlikely possibility during the depression years), a capital loss resulted. If, however, the property was depreciable and could be retained for its estimated useful life, much (if not all) of its costs could be recovered in the form of depreciation. Because the allowance for depreciation was fully deductible whereas capital losses were not, the tax law favored those who did not dispose of an asset. Congress recognized this inequity when it removed business property from the capital asset classification. During the period 1938–1942, therefore, all such gains and losses were ordinary gains and losses.

With the advent of World War II, two developments in particular forced Congress to reexamine the situation regarding business assets. First, the sale of business assets at a gain was discouraged because the gain would be ordinary income. Gains were common because the war effort had inflated prices. Second, taxpayers who did not want to sell their assets often were required to because the government acquired them through condemnation. Often, as a result of the condemnation awards, taxpayers who were forced to part with their property experienced large gains and were deprived of the benefits of future depreciation deductions. Of course, the condemnations constituted involuntary conversions, so taxpayers could defer the gain by timely reinvestment in property that was "similar or related in service or use." But where was such property to be found in view of wartime restrictions and other governmental condemnations? The end result did not seem equitable: a large ordinary gain due to government action and no possibility of deferral due to government restrictions.

In recognition of these conditions, in 1942, Congress eased the tax bite on the disposition of some business property by allowing preferential capital gain treatment. Thus, the present scheme of § 1231 and the dichotomy of capital gain/ordinary loss treatment evolved from a combination of economic considerations existing in 1938 and 1942.

PROPERTY INCLUDED

2 LEARNING OBJECTIVE
Distinguish § 1231 assets from ordinary assets and capital assets and calculate the § 1231 gain or loss.

Section 1231 property includes the following:

- Depreciable or real property used in business or for the production of income (principally machinery and equipment, buildings, and land).
- Timber, coal, or domestic iron ore to which § 631 applies.
- Livestock held for draft, breeding, dairy, or sporting purposes.
- Unharvested crops on land used in business.
- Certain *purchased* intangible assets (such as patents and goodwill) that are eligible for amortization.

PROPERTY EXCLUDED

Section 1231 property does *not* include the following:

- Property not held for the long-term holding period. Since the benefit of § 1231 is long-term capital gain treatment, the holding period must correspond to the more-than-one-year holding period that applies to capital assets. Livestock must be held at least 12 months (24 months in some cases). Unharvested crops do not have to be held for the required long-term holding period, but the land must be held for the long-term holding period.
- Property where casualty losses exceed casualty gains for the taxable year. If a taxpayer has a net casualty loss, the individual casualty gains and losses are treated as ordinary gains and losses.
- Inventory and property held primarily for sale to customers.
- Copyrights; literary, musical, or artistic compositions, etc.; and certain U.S. government publications.
- Accounts receivable and notes receivable arising in the ordinary course of the trade or business.

SPECIAL RULES FOR CERTAIN § 1231 ASSETS

A rather diverse group of assets is included under § 1231. The following discussion summarizes the special rules for some of those assets.

Timber. A taxpayer can *elect* to treat the cutting of timber held for sale or for use in business as a sale or exchange.[3] If the taxpayer makes this election, the transaction qualifies under § 1231. The taxpayer must have owned the timber or a contract to cut it on the first day of the year and for the long-term holding period before the date the cutting takes place. The recognized § 1231 gain or loss is determined at the time the timber is cut and is equal to the difference between the timber's fair market value as of the first day of the taxable year and the adjusted basis for depletion. If a taxpayer sells the timber for more or less than the fair market value as of the first day of the taxable year in which it is cut, the difference is ordinary income or loss.

This provision was enacted to provide preferential treatment relative to the natural growth value of timber, which takes a relatively long time to mature. Congress believed this favorable treatment would encourage reforestation of

[3] § 631(a) and Reg. § 1.631–1.

CONCEPT SUMMARY 17–1

Section 1231 Netting Procedure

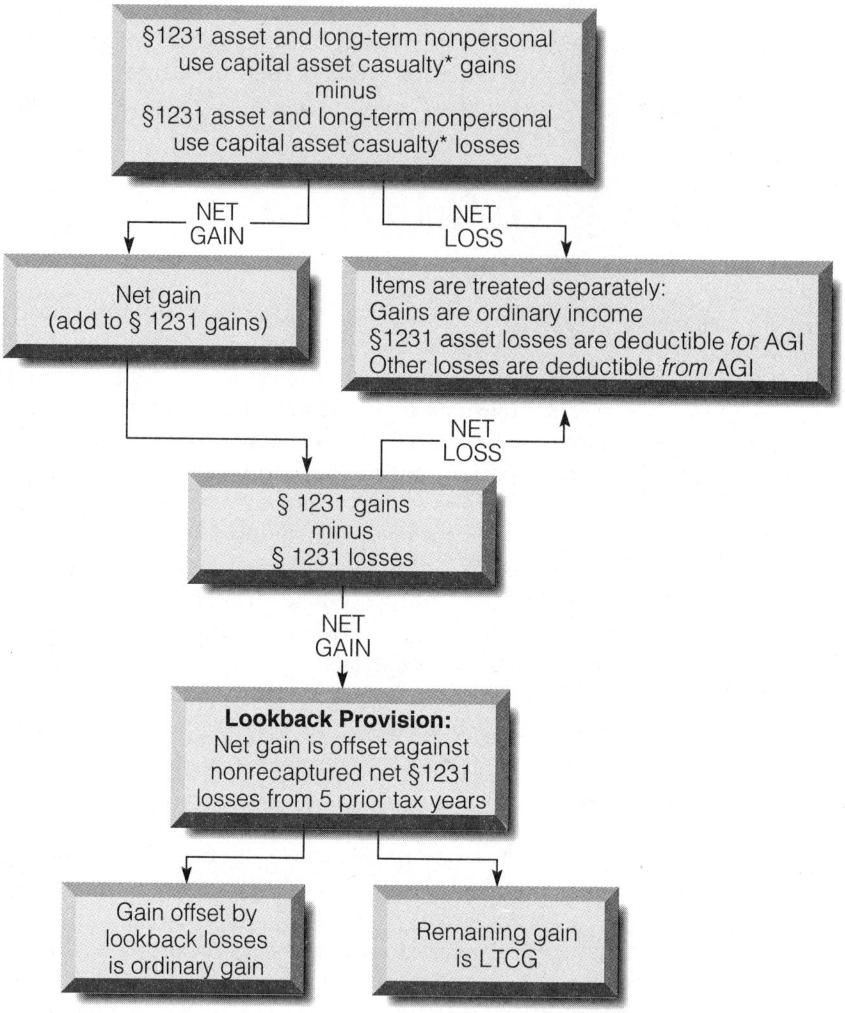
§1231 asset and long-term nonpersonal use capital asset casualty* gains
minus
§1231 asset and long-term nonpersonal use capital asset casualty* losses
NET GAIN
NET LOSS
Net gain (add to § 1231 gains)
Items are treated separately:
Gains are ordinary income
§1231 asset losses are deductible *for* AGI
Other losses are deductible *from* AGI
NET LOSS
§ 1231 gains
minus
§ 1231 losses
NET GAIN
Lookback Provision:
Net gain is offset against nonrecaptured net §1231 losses from 5 prior tax years
Gain offset by lookback losses is ordinary gain
Remaining gain is LTCG

*Includes casualties and thefts.

timber lands. If a taxpayer disposes of timber held for the long-term holding period, either by sale or under a royalty contract (where the taxpayer retains an economic interest in the property), the disposal is treated as a sale of the timber. Therefore, any gain or loss qualifies under § 1231.

EXAMPLE 3

Several years ago, Tom purchased a tract of land with a substantial stand of trees on it. The land cost $40,000, and the timber cost $100,000. On the first day of 1996, the timber was appraised at $250,000. In August 1996, Tom cut the timber and sold it for $265,000. Tom elects to treat the cutting as a sale or exchange under § 1231. He has a $150,000 § 1231 gain ($250,000 – $100,000) and a $15,000 ordinary gain ($265,000 – $250,000).

What if the timber had been sold for $235,000? Tom would still have a $150,000 § 1231 gain, but would also have a $15,000 ordinary loss. The price for computation of § 1231 gain is the price at the beginning of the year. Any difference between that price and the sales price is ordinary gain or loss. Here, since the price declined by $15,000, Tom has an ordinary loss in that amount. ▼

Livestock. Cattle and horses must be held 24 months or more and other livestock must be held 12 months or more to qualify under § 1231.[4] The primary reason for enacting this provision was the considerable amount of litigation over the character of livestock (whether livestock was held primarily for sale to customers [ordinary income] or for use in a trade or business [§ 1231 property]). Poultry is not livestock for purposes of § 1231.

ETHICAL CONSIDERATIONS

Determining How Long an Asset Has Been Held

George, a dairy farmer sells a milk cow for $12,000. Normally, George does not sell his cows, but he received an offer he could not refuse for this "super milker." George is not sure exactly when the cow was born, but he does know that it is the calf of another cow he owns. Consequently, he has a zero tax basis for the cow that was sold. George owns 500 cows.

When George's tax adviser points out that the cow must have been held 24 months to be eligible for § 1231 treatment, George gets very upset. The tax adviser knows that George's records are a mess. George thinks the cow was born "within the last 27 months." After the tax adviser explains the tax benefits of the sale qualifying for § 1231 treatment, George decides the cow was more than 24 months old.

Section 1231 Assets Disposed of by Casualty or Theft. When § 1231 assets are disposed of by casualty or theft, a special netting rule is applied. For simplicity, the term *casualty* is used to mean both casualty and theft dispositions. First, the casualty gains and losses from § 1231 assets *and* the casualty gains and losses from **long-term nonpersonal use capital assets** are determined. A nonpersonal use capital asset might be an investment painting or a baseball card collection held by a nondealer in baseball cards.

Next, the § 1231 asset casualty gains and losses and the nonpersonal use capital asset casualty gains and losses are netted together (see Concept Summary 17–1). If the result is a *net loss,* the § 1231 casualty gains and the nonpersonal use capital asset casualty gains are treated as ordinary gains, the § 1231 casualty losses are deductible *for* AGI, and the nonpersonal use capital asset casualty losses are deductible *from* AGI subject to the 2 percent-of-AGI limitation.

If the result of the netting is a *net gain,* the net gain is treated as a § 1231 gain. Thus, a § 1231 asset disposed of by casualty may or may not get § 1231 treatment, depending on whether the netting process results in a gain or a loss. Also, a nonpersonal use capital asset disposed of by casualty may get § 1231 treatment or ordinary treatment, but will not get capital gain or loss treatment!

Personal use property casualty gains and losses are not subject to the § 1231 rules. If the result of netting these gains and losses is a gain, the net gain is a capital gain. If the netting results in a loss, the net loss is a deduction *from* AGI to the extent it exceeds 10 percent of AGI.

[4] Note that the holding period is "12 months or more" and not "more than 12 months."

TAX IN THE NEWS

Casualties May Not Be "Casualties"

A tornado recently struck southwestern Texas, destroying both the personal home and the ranch buildings on one ranch. The news reports on the tornado emphasized the devastation of the ranch. Although the rancher had suffered a major tragedy, the tax consequences might be quite different than one would expect. If the property was properly insured, the rancher is likely to have at least some gain on the casualty because the insurance proceeds will exceed the adjusted basis of some of the property. If he has a gain on his personal home, it is a capital gain because the home is a capital asset. The ranch buildings are § 1231 assets if they have been held more than one year. The casualty gains and losses from the ranch buildings are subject to a special netting process for tax purposes to determine if they receive capital or ordinary treatment.

Casualties, thefts, and condemnations are *involuntary conversions.* Involuntary conversion gains may be deferred if conversion proceeds are reinvested; involuntary conversion losses are recognized currently (refer to Chapter 15) regardless of whether the conversion proceeds are reinvested. Thus, the special netting process discussed above for casualties and thefts would not include gains that are not currently recognizable because the insurance proceeds are reinvested.

The special netting process for casualties and thefts also does not include condemnation gains and losses. Consequently, a § 1231 asset disposed of by condemnation will receive § 1231 treatment. This variation between recognized casualty and condemnation gains and losses sheds considerable light on what § 1231 is all about. Section 1231 has no effect on whether or not *realized* gain or loss is recognized. Instead, § 1231 merely dictates how such *recognized* gain or loss is *classified* (ordinary, capital, or § 1231) under certain conditions.

Personal use property condemnation gains and losses are not subject to the § 1231 rules. The gains are capital gains (because personal use property is a capital asset), and the losses are nondeductible because they arise from the disposition of personal use property.

GENERAL PROCEDURE FOR § 1231 COMPUTATION

The tax treatment of § 1231 gains and losses depends on the results of a rather complex *netting* procedure. The steps in this netting procedure are as follows.

Step 1: Casualty Netting. Net all recognized long-term gains and losses from casualties of § 1231 assets and nonpersonal use capital assets. Casualty gains result when insurance proceeds exceed the adjusted basis of the property. This casualty netting is beneficial because if there is a net gain, the gain may receive long-term capital gain treatment. If there is a net loss, it receives ordinary loss treatment.

a. If the casualty gains exceed the casualty losses, add the excess to the other § 1231 gains for the taxable year.
b. If the casualty losses exceed the casualty gains, exclude all casualty losses and gains from further § 1231 computation. If this is the case, all casualty gains are ordinary income. Section 1231 asset casualty losses are deductible *for* AGI. Other casualty losses are deductible *from* AGI.

Step 2: § 1231 Netting. After adding any net casualty gain from Step 1a to the other § 1231 gains and losses (including recognized § 1231 asset condemnation gains and losses), net all § 1231 gains and losses.

a. If the gains exceed the losses, the net gain is offset by the "lookback" nonrecaptured § 1231 losses (see below) from the five prior tax years. To the extent of this offset, the net § 1231 gain is classified as ordinary gain. Any remaining gain is long-term capital gain.
b. If the losses exceed the gains, all gains are ordinary income. Section 1231 asset losses are deductible *for* AGI. Other casualty losses are deductible *from* AGI.

Step 3: § 1231 Lookback Provision. The net § 1231 gain from Step 2a is offset by the nonrecaptured net § 1231 losses for the five preceding taxable years. For 1996, the lookback years are 1991, 1992, 1993, 1994, and 1995. To the extent of the nonrecaptured net § 1231 loss, the current year net § 1231 gain is ordinary income. The *nonrecaptured* net § 1231 losses are those that have not already been used to offset net § 1231 gains. Only the net § 1231 gain exceeding this net § 1231 loss carryforward is given long-term capital gain treatment. Concept Summary 17–1 summarizes the § 1231 computational procedure. Examples 6 and 7 illustrate the **§ 1231 lookback** provision.

Examples 4 through 7 illustrate the application of the § 1231 computation procedure.

EXAMPLE 4

During 1996, Ross had $125,000 of AGI before considering the following recognized gains and losses:

Capital Gains and Losses	
Long-term capital gain	$3,000
Long-term capital loss	(400)
Short-term capital gain	1,000
Short-term capital loss	(200)
Casualties	
Theft of diamond ring (owned four months)	($800)*
Fire damage to personal residence (owned 10 years)	(400)*
Gain from insurance recovery on fire loss to business building (owned two years)	200
§ 1231 Gains and Losses from Depreciable Business Assets Held Long Term	
Asset A	$ 300
Asset B	1,100
Asset C	(500)
Gains and Losses from Sale of Depreciable Business Assets Held Short Term	
Asset D	$ 200
Asset E	(300)

*As adjusted for the $100 floor on personal casualty losses.

Ross had no net § 1231 losses in tax years before 1996.

Disregarding the recapture of depreciation (discussed later in the chapter), Ross's gains and losses receive the following tax treatment:

- The diamond ring and the residence are personal use assets. Therefore, these casualties are not § 1231 transactions. The $800 (ring) plus $400 (residence) losses are potentially deductible *from* AGI. However, the total loss of $1,200 does not exceed 10% of AGI. Thus, only the business building (a § 1231 asset) casualty gain remains. The netting of the § 1231 asset and nonpersonal use capital asset casualty gains and losses contains only one item—the $200 gain from the business building. Consequently, there is a net gain and that gain is treated as a § 1231 gain (added to the § 1231 gains).
- The gains from § 1231 transactions (Assets A, B, and C and the § 1231 asset casualty gain) exceed the losses by $1,100 ($1,600 – $500). This excess is a long-term capital gain and is added to Ross's other long-term capital gains.
- Ross's net long-term capital gain is $3,700 ($3,000 + $1,100 from § 1231 transactions – $400 long-term capital loss). Ross's net short-term capital gain is $800 ($1,000 – $200). The result is capital gain net income of $4,500. The $3,700 net long-term capital gain portion is eligible for beneficial capital gain treatment, and the $800 net short-term capital gain is subject to tax as ordinary income.[5]
- Ross treats the gain and loss from Assets D and E (depreciable business assets held for less than the long-term holding period) as ordinary gain and loss.

Results of the Gains and Losses on Ross's Tax Computation

NLTCG	$ 3,700
NSTCG	800
Ordinary gain from sale of Asset D	200
Ordinary loss from sale of Asset E	(300)
AGI from other sources	125,000
AGI	$129,400

- Ross will have personal use property casualty losses of $1,200 [$800 (diamond ring) + $400 (personal residence)]. A personal use property casualty loss is deductible only to the extent it exceeds 10% of AGI. Thus, none of the $1,200 is deductible ($129,400 × 10% = $12,940). ▼

EXAMPLE 5

Assume the same facts as in Example 4, except the loss from Asset C was $1,700 instead of $500.

- The treatment of the casualty losses is the same as in Example 4.
- The losses from § 1231 transactions now exceed the gains by $100 ($1,700 – $1,600). As a result, the gains from Assets A and B and the § 1231 asset casualty gain are ordinary income, and the loss from Asset C is a deduction *for* AGI (a business loss). The same result can be achieved by simply treating the $100 net loss as a deduction *for* AGI.
- Capital gain net income is $3,400 ($2,600 long-term + $800 short-term). The $2,600 net long-term capital gain portion is eligible for beneficial capital gain treatment, and the $800 net short-term capital gain is subject to tax as ordinary income.

[5] Ross's taxable income (unless the itemized deductions and the personal exemption and dependency deductions are extremely large) will put him in at least the 31% bracket. Thus, the 28% alternative tax computation will yield a lower tax. See Example 36 in Chapter 16.

Results of the Gains and Losses on Ross's Tax Computation	
NLTCG	$ 2,600
NSTCG	800
Net ordinary loss on Assets A, B, and C and § 1231 casualty gain	(100)
Ordinary gain from sale of Asset D	200
Ordinary loss from sale of Asset E	(300)
AGI from other sources	125,000
AGI	$128,200

- None of the personal use property casualty losses will be deductible since $1,200 does not exceed 10% of $128,200. ▼

EXAMPLE 6

Assume the same facts as in Example 4, except that Ross has a $700 nonrecaptured net § 1231 loss from 1995.

- The treatment of the casualty losses is the same as in Example 4.
- The 1996 net § 1231 gain of $1,100 is treated as ordinary income to the extent of the 1995 nonrecaptured § 1231 loss of $700. The remaining $400 net § 1231 gain is a long-term capital gain and is added to Ross's other long-term capital gains.
- Ross's net long-term capital gain is $3,000 ($3,000 + $400 from § 1231 transactions – $400 long-term capital loss). Ross's net short-term capital gain is still $800 ($1,000 – $200). The result is capital gain net income of $3,800. The $3,000 net long-term capital gain portion is eligible for beneficial capital gain treatment, and the $800 net short-term capital gain is subject to tax as ordinary income.

Results of the Gains and Losses on Ross's Tax Computation	
NLTCG	$ 3,000
NSTCG	800
Ordinary gain from recapture of § 1231 losses	700
Ordinary gain from sale of Asset D	200
Ordinary loss from sale of Asset E	(300)
AGI from other sources	125,000
AGI	$129,400

- None of the personal use property casualty losses will be deductible since $1,200 does not exceed 10% of $129,400. ▼

EXAMPLE 7

Assume the same facts as in Example 4, except that Ross had a net § 1231 loss of $2,700 in 1994 and a net § 1231 gain of $300 in 1995.

- The treatment of the casualty losses is the same as in Example 4.
- The 1994 net § 1231 loss of $2,700 will have carried over to 1995 and been offset against the 1995 net § 1231 gain of $300. Thus, the $300 gain will have been classified as ordinary income, and $2,400 of nonrecaptured 1994 net § 1231 loss will carry over to 1996. The 1996 net § 1231 gain of $1,100 will be offset against this loss, resulting in $1,100 of ordinary income. The nonrecaptured net § 1231 loss of $1,300 ($2,400 – $1,100) carries over to 1997.

- Capital gain net income is $3,400 ($2,600 net long-term capital gain + $800 net short-term capital gain). The $2,600 net long-term capital gain portion is eligible for beneficial capital gain treatment, and the $800 net short-term capital gain is subject to tax as ordinary income.

Results of the Gains and Losses on Ross's Tax Computation	
NLTCG	$ 2,600
NSTCG	800
Ordinary gain from recapture of § 1231 losses	1,100
Ordinary gain from sale of Asset D	200
Ordinary loss from sale of Asset E	(300)
AGI from other sources	125,000
AGI	$129,400

- None of the personal use property casualty losses will be deductible since $1,200 does not exceed 10% of $129,400. ▼

Section 1245 Recapture

3 Learning Objective
Determine when § 1245 recapture applies and how it is computed.

Now that the basic rules of § 1231 have been introduced, it is time to add some complications. The Code contains two major *recapture* provisions—§§ 1245 and 1250. These provisions cause *gain* to be treated *initially* as ordinary gain. Thus, what may appear to be a § 1231 gain is ordinary gain instead. These recapture provisions may also cause a gain in a nonpersonal use casualty to be *initially* ordinary gain rather than casualty gain. Classifying gains (and losses) properly initially is important because improper initial classification may lead to incorrect mixing and matching of gains and losses. This section discusses the § 1245 recapture rules, and the next section discusses the § 1250 recapture rules.

Ethical Considerations

Does Applying the Recapture Rules Make a Difference?

Due to their complexity, the § 1245 and § 1250 recapture rules require careful study to obtain a complete understanding. It is much easier just to assume that the sale of business fixed assets results in capital gain or loss. Certainly, most taxpayers expect that result. Arnold, an overworked tax practitioner, concluded that quite often, taxable income is the same whether the recapture rules are properly applied or not. Therefore, he hypothesized that if ultimately there is *no difference* between tax liability with proper handling of recapture and tax liability without proper handling of recapture, is it not logical and practical for him simply to ignore the recapture rules?

Section 1245 requires taxpayers to treat all gain as ordinary gain unless the property is disposed of for more than was paid for it. This result is accomplished by requiring that all gain be treated as ordinary gain to the extent of the depreciation taken on the property disposed of. Section 1231 gain results only when the property is disposed of for more than its original cost. The excess of the

TAX IN THE NEWS

Purchase of Assets Creates Potential for Ordinary Income

A recent newspaper article touted the sale of a local software development company to a national company. The national company paid $30 million for the rights to software developed by the local company and $1 million for the local company's office furniture and equipment. The national company acquired two types of assets that would be subject to § 1245 recapture if later resold for a gain. The software is a § 197 asset with a 15-year life and is eligible for straight-line amortization, and the office furniture and equipment are eligible for accelerated depreciation.

sales price over the original cost is § 1231 gain. Section 1245 applies primarily to non-real estate property such as machinery, trucks, and office furniture. Section 1245 does not apply if property is disposed of at a loss. Generally, the loss will be a § 1231 loss unless the form of the disposition is a casualty.

EXAMPLE 8

Alice purchased a $100,000 business machine and deducted $70,000 depreciation before selling it for $80,000. If it were not for § 1245, the $50,000 gain would be § 1231 gain ($80,000 amount realized – $30,000 adjusted basis). Section 1245 prevents this potentially favorable result by treating as ordinary income (not as § 1231 gain) any gain to the extent of depreciation taken. In this example, the entire $50,000 gain would be ordinary income. If Alice had sold the machine for $120,000, she would have a gain of $90,000 ($120,000 amount realized – $30,000 adjusted basis). The § 1245 gain would be $70,000 (equal to the depreciation taken), and the § 1231 gain would be $20,000 (equal to the excess of the sales price over the original cost). ▼

Section 1245 recapture provides, in general, that the portion of recognized gain from the sale or other disposition of § 1245 property that represents depreciation (including § 167 depreciation, § 168 cost recovery, § 179 immediate expensing, and § 197 amortization) is *recaptured* as ordinary income. Thus, in Example 8, $50,000 of the $70,000 depreciation taken is recaptured as ordinary income when the business machine is sold for $80,000. Only $50,000 is recaptured rather than $70,000 because Alice is only required to recognize § 1245 recapture ordinary gain equal to the lower of the depreciation taken or the gain recognized.

The method of depreciation (e.g., accelerated or straight-line) does not matter. All depreciation taken is potentially subject to recapture. Thus, § 1245 recapture is often referred to as *full recapture.* Any remaining gain after subtracting the amount recaptured as ordinary income will usually be § 1231 gain. The remaining gain would be casualty gain if it were disposed of in a casualty event. If the business machine in Example 8 had been disposed of by casualty and the $80,000 received had been an insurance recovery, Alice would still have a gain of $50,000, and the gain would still be recaptured by § 1245 as ordinary gain. The § 1245 recapture rules apply before there is any casualty gain. Since all the $50,000 gain is recaptured, no casualty gain arises from the casualty.

Although § 1245 applies primarily to non-real estate property, it does apply to certain real estate. Nonresidential real estate acquired after 1980 and before 1987 and for which accelerated depreciation (the statutory percentage method of the accelerated cost recovery system) is used is subject to the § 1245 recapture rules. Such property includes 15-year, 18-year, and 19-year nonresidential real estate.

The following examples illustrate the general application of § 1245.

EXAMPLE 9

On January 1, 1996, Gary sold for $13,000 a machine acquired several years ago for $12,000. He had taken $10,000 of depreciation on the machine.

- The recognized gain from the sale is $11,000. This is the amount realized of $13,000 less the adjusted basis of $2,000 ($12,000 cost – $10,000 depreciation taken).
- Depreciation taken is $10,000. Therefore, since § 1245 recapture gain is the lower of depreciation taken or gain recognized, $10,000 of the $11,000 recognized gain is ordinary income, and the remaining $1,000 gain is § 1231 gain.
- The § 1231 gain of $1,000 is also equal to the excess of the sales price over the original cost of the property ($13,000 – $12,000 = $1,000 § 1231 gain). ▼

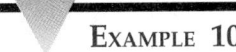

EXAMPLE 10

Assume the same facts as in the previous example, except the asset is sold for $9,000 instead of $13,000.

- The recognized gain from the sale is $7,000. This is the amount realized of $9,000 less the adjusted basis of $2,000.
- Depreciation taken is $10,000. Therefore, since the $10,000 depreciation taken exceeds the recognized gain of $7,000, the entire $7,000 recognized gain is ordinary income.
- The § 1231 gain is zero. There is no § 1231 gain because the selling price ($9,000) does not exceed the original purchase price ($12,000). ▼

EXAMPLE 11

Assume the same facts as in Example 9, except the asset is sold for $1,500 instead of $13,000.

- The recognized loss from the sale is $500. This is the amount realized of $1,500 less the adjusted basis of $2,000.
- Since there is a loss, there is no depreciation recapture. All of the loss is § 1231 loss. ▼

If § 1245 property is disposed of in a transaction other than a sale, exchange, or involuntary conversion, the maximum amount recaptured is the excess of the property's fair market value over its adjusted basis. See the discussion under Considerations Common to §§ 1245 and 1250 later in the chapter.

SECTION 1245 PROPERTY

Generally, **§ 1245 property** includes all depreciable personal property (e.g., machinery and equipment), including livestock. Buildings and their structural components generally are not § 1245 property. The following property is *also* subject to § 1245 treatment:

- Amortizable personal property such as goodwill, patents, copyrights, and leaseholds of § 1245 property. Professional baseball and football player contracts are § 1245 property.
- Amortization of reforestation expenditures.
- Expensing of costs to remove architectural and transportation barriers that restrict the handicapped and/or elderly.
- Section 179 immediate expensing of depreciable tangible personal property costs.
- Elevators and escalators acquired before January 1, 1987.
- Certain depreciable tangible real property (other than buildings and their structural components) employed as an integral part of certain activities such as manufacturing and production. For example, a natural gas storage tank where the gas is used in the manufacturing process is § 1245 property.

- Pollution control facilities, railroad grading and tunnel bores, on-the-job training, and child care facilities on which amortization is taken.
- Single-purpose agricultural and horticultural structures and petroleum storage facilities (e.g., a greenhouse or silo).
- As noted above, 15-year, 18-year, and 19-year nonresidential real estate for which accelerated cost recovery is used is subject to the § 1245 recapture rules, although it is technically not § 1245 property. Such property would have been placed in service after 1980 and before 1987.

EXAMPLE 12

James acquired nonresidential real property on January 1, 1986, for $100,000. He used the statutory percentage method to compute the ACRS cost recovery. He sells the asset on January 15, 1996, for $120,000. The amount and nature of James's gain are computed as follows:

Amount realized			$120,000
Adjusted basis			
Cost		$100,000	
Less cost recovery:	1986	(8,800)	
	1987	(8,400)	
	1988	(7,600)	
	1989	(6,900)	
	1990	(6,300)	
	1991	(5,700)	
	1992	(5,200)	
	1993	(4,700)	
	1994	(4,200)	
	1995	(4,200)	
	1996	(175)	
January 15, 1996, adjusted basis			(37,825)
Gain realized and recognized			$ 82,175

The gain of $82,175 is treated as ordinary income to the extent of *all* depreciation taken because the property is 19-year nonresidential real estate for which accelerated depreciation was used. Thus, James reports ordinary income of $62,175 ($8,800 + $8,400 + $7,600 + $6,900 + $6,300 + $5,700 + $5,200 + 4,700 + $4,200 + $4,200 + $175) and § 1231 gain of $20,000 ($82,175 – $62,175). ▼

OBSERVATIONS ON § 1245

- In most instances, the total depreciation taken will exceed the recognized gain. Therefore, the disposition of § 1245 property usually results in ordinary income rather than § 1231 gain. Thus, generally, no § 1231 gain will occur unless the § 1245 property is disposed of for more than its original cost. Refer to Examples 9 and 10.
- Recapture applies to the total amount of depreciation allowed or allowable regardless of the depreciation method used.
- Recapture applies regardless of the holding period of the property. Of course, the entire recognized gain would be ordinary income if the property were held for less than the long-term holding period because § 1231 would not apply.
- Section 1245 does not apply to losses, which receive § 1231 treatment.
- Gains from the disposition of § 1245 assets may also be treated as passive activity gains (see Chapter 11).

SECTION 1250 RECAPTURE

4 LEARNING OBJECTIVE
Determine when § 1250 recapture applies and how it is computed.

Generally, **§ 1250 property** is depreciable real property (principally buildings and their structural components) that is not subject to § 1245.[6] Intangible real property, such as leaseholds of § 1250 property, is also included.

Section 1250 recapture is substantially less punitive than § 1245 recapture since only the amount of additional depreciation is subject to recapture. To have additional depreciation, accelerated depreciation must have been taken on the asset. Straight-line depreciation (except for property held one year or less) is not recaptured. Since real property placed in service after 1986 can only be depreciated using the straight-line method, there will be *no § 1250 depreciation recapture* on such property.

Section 1250 was enacted in 1964 for depreciable real property and has been revised many times. If straight-line depreciation is taken on the property, § 1250 does not apply. Nor does § 1250 apply if the real property is sold at a loss. The loss will generally be a § 1231 loss unless the property is disposed of by casualty.

Section 1250 as originally enacted required recapture of a percentage of the additional depreciation deducted by the taxpayer. **Additional depreciation** is the excess of accelerated depreciation actually deducted over depreciation that would have been deductible if the straight-line method had been used. Since only the additional depreciation is subject to recapture, § 1250 recapture is often referred to as *partial recapture.*

Post-1969 additional depreciation on nonresidential real property is subject to 100 percent recapture (see Example 13). Post-1969 additional depreciation on residential property may be subject to less than 100 percent recapture (see Example 14).

If § 1250 property is disposed of in a transaction other than a sale, exchange, or involuntary conversion, the maximum amount recaptured is the excess of the property's fair market value over the adjusted basis. For example, if a corporation distributes property to its shareholders as a dividend, the property will have been disposed of at a gain if the fair market value is greater than the adjusted basis. The maximum amount of § 1250 recapture will be the amount of the gain.

The following discussion describes the computational steps prescribed in § 1250 and reflected on Form 4797 (Sales of Business Property).

COMPUTING RECAPTURE ON NONRESIDENTIAL REAL PROPERTY

For § 1250 property other than residential rental property, the potential recapture is equal to the amount of additional depreciation taken since December 31, 1969. This nonresidential real property includes buildings such as offices, warehouses, factories, and stores. (The definition of and rules for residential rental housing are discussed later in the chapter.) The lower of the potential § 1250 recapture amount or the recognized gain is ordinary income. The following general rules apply:

- Post-1969 additional depreciation is depreciation taken in excess of straight-line after December 31, 1969.

[6] As previously discussed, in one limited circumstance, § 1245 does apply to nonresidential real estate. If the nonresidential real estate was placed in service after 1980 and before 1987 and accelerated depreciation was used, the § 1245 recapture rules rather than the § 1250 recapture rules apply.

- If the property is held for one year or less (usually not the case), all depreciation taken, even under the straight-line method, is additional depreciation.

The following procedure is used to compute recapture on nonresidential real property under § 1250:

- Determine the recognized gain from the sale or other disposition of the property.
- Determine post-1969 additional depreciation.
- The lower of the recognized gain or the post-1969 additional depreciation is ordinary income.
- If any recognized gain remains (total recognized gain less recapture), it is § 1231 gain. However, it would be casualty gain if the disposition was by casualty.

The following example shows the application of the § 1250 computational procedure.

EXAMPLE 13

On January 3, 1980, Larry acquired a new building at a cost of $200,000 for use in his business. The building had an estimated useful life of 50 years and no estimated salvage value. Depreciation has been taken under the 150% declining-balance method through December 31, 1995. Pertinent information with respect to depreciation taken follows:

Year	Undepreciated Balance (Beginning of the Year)	Current Depreciation Provision	Straight-Line Depreciation	Additional Depreciation
1980	$200,000	$ 6,000	$ 4,000	$ 2,000
1981	194,000	5,820	4,000	1,820
1982	188,180	5,645	4,000	1,645
1983	182,535	5,476	4,000	1,476
1984	177,059	5,312	4,000	1,312
1985	171,747	5,152	4,000	1,152
1986	166,595	4,998	4,000	998
1987	161,597	4,848	4,000	848
1988	156,749	4,702	4,000	702
1989	152,047	4,561	4,000	561
1990	147,486	4,425	4,000	425
1991	143,061	4,292	4,000	292
1992	138,769	4,163	4,000	163
1993	134,606	4,038	4,000	38
1994	130,568	3,917	4,000	(83)
1995	126,651	3,800	4,000	(200)
Total 1980–1995		$77,149	$64,000	$13,149

On January 2, 1996, Larry sold the building for $180,000. Compute the amount of his § 1250 ordinary income and § 1231 gain.

- Larry's recognized gain from the sale is $57,149. This is the difference between the $180,000 amount realized and the $122,851 adjusted basis ($200,000 cost − $77,149 depreciation taken).

- Post-1969 additional depreciation is $13,149.
- The amount of post-1969 ordinary income is $13,149. Since the post-1969 additional depreciation of $13,149 is less than the recognized gain of $57,149, the entire gain is not recaptured.
- The remaining $44,000 ($57,149 − $13,149) gain is § 1231 gain. ▼

COMPUTING RECAPTURE ON RESIDENTIAL RENTAL HOUSING

Section 1250 recapture applies to the sale or other disposition of residential rental housing. Property qualifies as *residential rental housing* only if at least 80 percent of gross rent income is rent income from dwelling units.[7] The rules are the same as for other § 1250 property, except that only the post-1975 additional depreciation may be recaptured. The post-1969 through 1975 recapture percentage is 100 percent less one percentage point for each full month the property is held over 100 months.[8] Therefore, the additional depreciation for periods after 1975 is initially applied against the recognized gain, and such amounts may be recaptured in full as ordinary income. If any of the recognized gain is not absorbed by the recapture rules pertaining to the post-1975 period, the remaining gain is § 1231 gain.

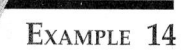

EXAMPLE 14 Assume the same facts as in the previous example, except the building is residential rental housing.

- Post-1975 ordinary income is $13,149 (post-1975 additional depreciation of $13,149).
- The remaining $44,000 ($57,149 − $13,149) gain is § 1231 gain. ▼

Under § 1250, when straight-line depreciation is used, there is no § 1250 recapture potential unless the property is disposed of in the first year of use. Before 1987, accelerated depreciation on real estate generally was available. For real property placed in service after 1986, however, only straight-line depreciation is allowed. Therefore, the § 1250 recapture rules do not apply to such property unless the property is disposed of in the first year of use.

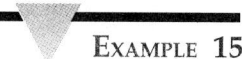

EXAMPLE 15 Sanjay acquires a residential rental building on January 1, 1995, for $300,000. He receives an offer of $450,000 for the building in 1996 and sells it on December 23, 1996.

- Sanjay takes $20,909 [($300,000 × .03485) + ($300,000 × .03636 × 11.5/12) = $20,909] of total depreciation for 1995 and 1996, and the adjusted basis of the property is $279,091 ($300,000 − $20,909).
- Sanjay's recognized gain is $170,909 ($450,000 − $279,091).
- All of the gain is § 1231 gain. ▼

---

[7] § 168(e)(2)(A). Note that there may be residential, nonrental housing (e.g., a bunkhouse on a cattle ranch). Such property is commonly regarded as "nonresidential real estate." The rules for such property were discussed in the previous section.

[8] §§ 1250(a)(1) and (2) and Reg. § 1.1250–1(d)(1)(i)(c). Since the post-1969 through 1975 recapture percentage is 100% less one percentage point for each full month the property is held over 100 months, this approach now yields a zero percentage no matter when the property was acquired in the 1969–1975 period. For instance, if a building was acquired on January 3, 1975, and sold on January 3, 1996, it would have been held 252 months. The recapture percentage is zero because 100% − (252% − 100%) is less than zero.

CONCEPT SUMMARY 17–2

Comparison of § 1245 and § 1250 Depreciation Recapture

	§ 1245	§ 1250
Property affected	All depreciable personal property, but also nonresidential real property acquired after December 31, 1980, and before January 1, 1987, for which accelerated cost recovery was used. Also includes miscellaneous items such as § 179 expense and § 197 amortization of intangibles such as goodwill, patents, and copyrights.	Residential rental real property acquired after December 31, 1980, and before January 1, 1987, on which accelerated cost recovery was taken. Nonresidential real property acquired after December 31, 1969, and before January 1, 1976, on which accelerated depreciation was taken. Residential real and nonresidential real property acquired after December 31, 1975, and before January 1, 1981, on which accelerated depreciation was taken.
Depreciation recaptured	Potentially all depreciation taken. If the selling price is greater than or equal to the original cost, all depreciation is recaptured. If the selling price is between the adjusted basis and the original cost, only some depreciation is recaptured.	Additional depreciation (the excess of accelerated cost recovery over straight-line cost recovery or the excess of accelerated depreciation over straight-line depreciation).
Limit on recapture	Lower of depreciation taken or gain recognized.	Lower of additional depreciation or gain recognized.
Treatment of gain exceeding recapture gain	Usually § 1231 gain.	Usually § 1231 gain.
Treatment of loss	No depreciation recapture; loss is usually § 1231 loss.	No depreciation recapture; loss is usually § 1231 loss.

SECTION 1250 RECAPTURE SITUATIONS

The § 1250 recapture rules apply to the following property for which accelerated depreciation was used:

- Residential rental real estate acquired before 1987.
- Nonresidential real estate acquired before 1981.
- Real property used predominantly outside the United States.
- Certain government-financed or low-income housing.[9]

Concept Summary 17–2 compares and contrasts the § 1245 and § 1250 depreciation recapture rules.

[9] Described in § 1250(a)(1)(B).

Considerations Common to §§ 1245 and 1250

EXCEPTIONS

5 LEARNING OBJECTIVE
Understand considerations common to §§ 1245 and 1250.

Recapture under §§ 1245 and 1250 does not apply to the following transactions.

Gifts. The recapture potential carries over to the donee.[10]

EXAMPLE 16

Wade gives his daughter, Helen, § 1245 property with an adjusted basis of $1,000. The amount of recapture potential is $700. Helen uses the property in her business and claims further depreciation of $100 before selling it for $1,900. Helen's recognized gain is $1,000 ($1,900 amount realized – $900 adjusted basis), of which $800 is recaptured as ordinary income ($100 depreciation taken by Helen + $700 recapture potential carried over from Wade). The remaining gain of $200 is § 1231 gain. Even if Helen used the property for personal purposes, the $700 recapture potential would still be carried over. ▼

Death. Although not a very attractive tax planning approach, death eliminates all recapture potential.[11] In other words, any recapture potential does not carry over from a decedent to an estate or heir.

EXAMPLE 17

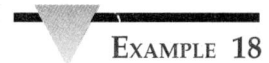

Assume the same facts as in Example 16, except Helen receives the property as a result of Wade's death. The $700 recapture potential from Wade is extinguished. Helen has a basis for the property equal to the property's fair market value (assume $1,700) at Wade's death. She will have a $300 gain when the property is sold because the selling price ($1,900) exceeds the property's adjusted basis of $1,600 ($1,700 original basis to Helen – $100 depreciation) by $300. Because of § 1245, $100 is ordinary income. The remaining gain of $200 is § 1231 gain. ▼

Charitable Transfers. The recapture potential reduces the amount of the charitable contribution deduction under § 170.[12]

EXAMPLE 18

Kanisha donates to her church § 1245 property with a fair market value of $10,000 and an adjusted basis of $7,000. Assume that the amount of recapture potential is $2,000 (the amount of recapture that would occur if the property were sold). Her charitable contribution deduction (subject to the limitations discussed in Chapter 10) is $8,000 ($10,000 fair market value – $2,000 recapture potential). ▼

Certain Nontaxable Transactions. These are transactions in which the transferor's adjusted basis of property carries over to the transferee.[13] The recapture potential also carries over to the transferee.[14] Included in this category are transfers of property pursuant to the following:

- Nontaxable incorporations under § 351.
- Certain liquidations of subsidiary companies under § 332.

---

[10] §§ 1245(b)(1) and 1250(d)(1) and Reg. §§ 1.1245–4(a)(1) and 1.1250–3(a)(1).

[11] §§ 1245(b)(2) and 1250(d)(2).

[12] § 170(e)(1)(A) and Reg. § 1.170A–4(b)(1). In certain circumstances, § 1231 gain also reduces the amount of the charitable contribution. See § 170(e)(1)(B).

[13] §§ 1245(b)(3) and 1250(d)(3) and Reg. §§ 1.1245–4(c) and 1.1250–3(c).

[14] Reg. §§ 1.1245–2(a)(4) and –2(c)(2) and 1.1250–2(d)(1) and (3) and –3(c)(3).

- Nontaxable contributions to a partnership under § 721.
- Nontaxable reorganizations.

Gain may be recognized in these transactions if boot is received. If gain is recognized, it is treated as ordinary income to the extent of the recapture potential or recognized gain, whichever is lower.[15]

Like-Kind Exchanges (§ 1031) and Involuntary Conversions (§ 1033). Realized gain will be recognized to the extent of boot received under § 1031. Realized gain also will be recognized to the extent the proceeds from an involuntary conversion are not reinvested in similar property under § 1033. Such recognized gain is subject to recapture as ordinary income under §§ 1245 and 1250. The remaining recapture potential, if any, carries over to the property received in the exchange.

EXAMPLE 19

Anita exchanges § 1245 property with an adjusted basis of $300 for § 1245 property with a fair market value of $6,000. The exchange qualifies as a like-kind exchange under § 1031. Anita also receives $1,000 cash (boot). Her realized gain is $6,700 ($7,000 amount realized − $300 adjusted basis of property). Assuming the recapture potential is $7,500, Anita recognizes § 1245 gain of $1,000 because she received boot of $1,000. The remaining recapture potential of $6,500 carries over to the like-kind property received. ▼

OTHER APPLICATIONS

Sections 1245 and 1250 apply notwithstanding any other provisions in the Code.[16] That is, the recapture rules under these Sections *override* all other Sections. Special applications include installment sales and property dividends.

Installment Sales. Recapture gain is recognized in the year of the sale regardless of whether gain is otherwise recognized under the installment method.[17] All gain is ordinary income until the recapture potential is fully absorbed. Nonrecapture (§ 1231) gain is recognized under the installment method as cash is received.

EXAMPLE 20

Seth sells § 1245 property for $20,000, to be paid in 10 annual installments of $2,000 each plus interest at 10%. Seth realizes a $6,000 gain from the sale, of which $4,000 is attributable to depreciation taken. If Seth uses the installment method, he recognizes the entire $4,000 of recapture gain as ordinary income in the year of the sale. The $2,000 of nonrecapture (§ 1231) gain will be recognized at the rate of $200 per year for 10 years. ▼

Gain is also recognized on installment sales in the year of sale in an amount equal to the § 179 (immediate expensing) deductions taken with respect to the property sold.

Property Dividends. A corporation generally recognizes gain if it distributes appreciated property as a dividend. Recapture under §§ 1245 and 1250 applies to the extent of the lower of the recapture potential or the excess of the property's fair market value over the adjusted basis.[18]

---

[15] §§ 1245(b)(3) and 1250(d)(3) and Reg. §§ 1.1245–4(c) and 1.1250–3(c). Some of these special corporate problems are discussed in Chapter 20. Partnership contributions are also discussed in Chapter 20.

[16] §§ 1245(d) and 1250(i).

[17] § 453(i). The installment method of reporting gains on the sale of property is discussed in Chapter 18.

[18] § 311(b) and Reg. §§ 1.1245–1(c) and –6(b) and 1.1250–1(a)(4), –1(b)(4), and –1(c)(2).

Concept Summary 17–3

Depreciation Recapture and § 1231 Netting Procedure

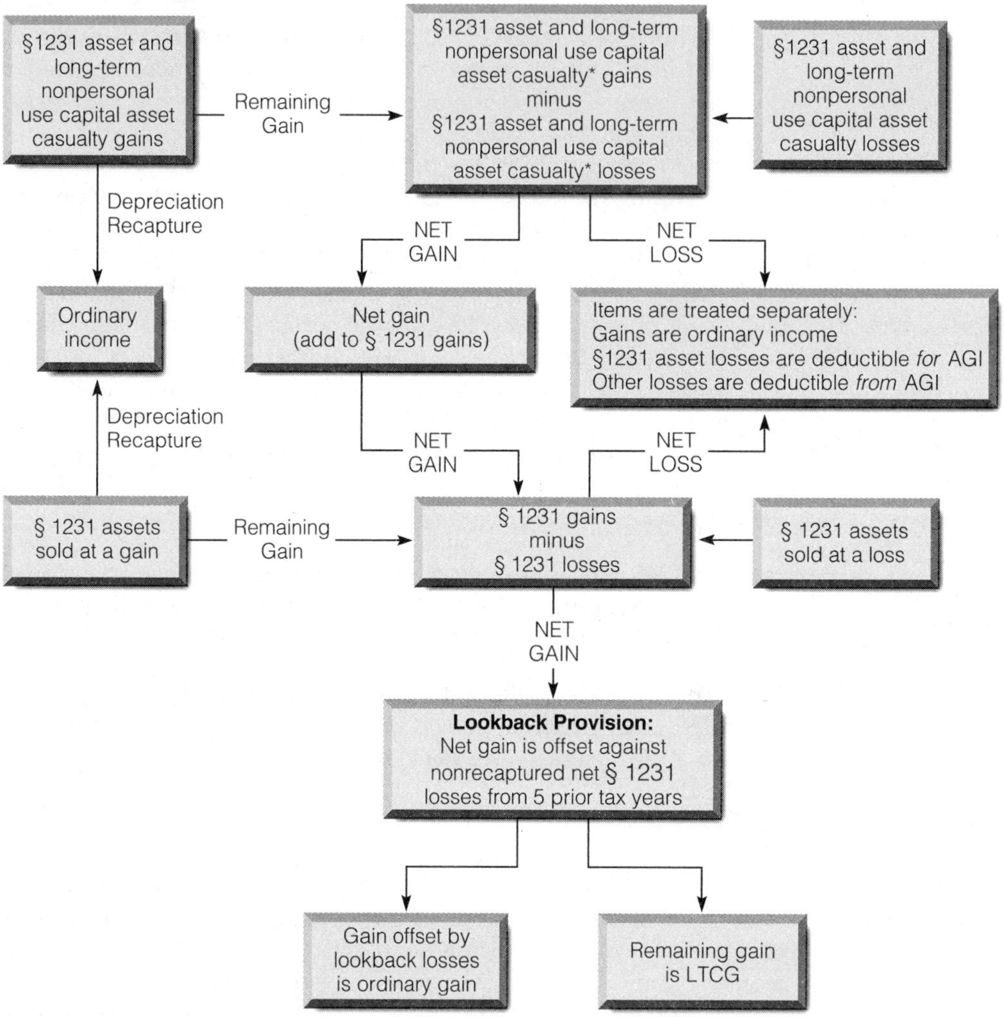

*Includes casualties and thefts.

Example 21 Emerald Corporation distributes § 1245 property as a dividend to its shareholders. The amount of the recapture potential is $300, and the excess of the property's fair market value over the adjusted basis is $800. Emerald recognizes $300 of ordinary income and $500 of § 1231 gain. ▼

Concept Summary 17–3 integrates the depreciation recapture rules with the § 1231 netting process. It is an expanded version of Concept Summary 17–1.

ETHICAL CONSIDERATIONS

To Lookback or Not Lookback

Harold, a CPA, has a new client who recently moved to town. Harold prepares the client's current-year tax return, which shows a net § 1231 gain. Harold calls the client to request copies of the returns for the preceding five years to determine if there are any § 1231 lookback losses. The client says that the returns are "still buried in the moving mess somewhere" and cannot be found. The client also says that he does not remember any § 1231 net losses on the prior-year returns. What should Harold do? Should he complete the current-year return and assume there are no § 1231 lookback losses?

SPECIAL RECAPTURE PROVISIONS

SPECIAL RECAPTURE FOR CORPORATIONS

6 LEARNING OBJECTIVE
Apply the special recapture provisions for related parties and IDC and be aware of the special recapture provision for corporations.

Corporations (other than S corporations) selling depreciable real estate may have ordinary income in addition to that required by § 1250.[19] See the discussion of this topic in Chapter 20.

GAIN FROM SALE OF DEPRECIABLE PROPERTY BETWEEN CERTAIN RELATED PARTIES

When the sale or exchange of property, which in the hands of the *transferee* is depreciable property (principally machinery, equipment, and buildings, but not land), is between certain related parties, any gain recognized is ordinary income.[20] This provision applies to both direct and indirect sales or exchanges. A **related party** is defined as an individual and his or her controlled corporation or partnership or a taxpayer and any trust in which the taxpayer (or the taxpayer's spouse) is a beneficiary.

EXAMPLE 22

Isabella sells a personal use automobile (therefore nondepreciable) to her controlled corporation. The automobile, which was purchased two years ago, originally cost $5,000 and is sold for $7,000. The automobile is to be used in the corporation's business. If the related-party provision did not exist, Isabella would realize a $2,000 long-term capital gain. The income tax consequences would be favorable because Isabella's controlled corporation is entitled to depreciate the automobile based upon the purchase price of $7,000. Under the related-party provision, Isabella's $2,000 gain is ordinary income. ▼

INTANGIBLE DRILLING COSTS

Taxpayers may elect to either *expense or capitalize* intangible drilling and development costs for oil, gas, or geothermal properties.[21] **Intangible drilling and development costs (IDC)** include operator (one who holds a working or operating

[19] § 291(a)(1).
[20] § 1239.
[21] § 263(c).

interest in any tract or parcel of land) expenditures for wages, fuel, repairs, hauling, and supplies. These expenditures must be incident to and necessary for the drilling of wells and preparation of wells for production. In most instances, taxpayers elect to expense IDC to maximize tax deductions during drilling.

Intangible drilling and development costs are subject to § 1254 recapture when the property is disposed of. The gain on the disposition of the property is subject to recapture as ordinary income.

Reporting Procedures

7 Learning Objective
Describe and apply the reporting procedures for §§ 1231, 1245, and 1250.

Noncapital gains and losses are reported on Form 4797, Sales of Business Property. Before filling out Form 4797, however, Form 4684, Casualties and Thefts, Part B, must be completed to determine whether or not any casualties will enter into the § 1231 computation procedure. Recall that gains from § 1231 asset casualties may be recaptured by § 1245 or § 1250. These gains will not appear on Form 4684. The § 1231 gains and nonpersonal use long-term capital gains are netted against § 1231 and nonpersonal use long-term capital losses on Form 4684 to determine if there is a net gain to transfer to Form 4797, Part I.

Because the 1996 tax forms were unavailable at this writing, 1995 tax forms are used in the remainder of the discussion.

Form 4797 is divided into four parts, summarized as follows:

Part	Function
I	To report regular § 1231 gains and losses (including recognized gains and losses from certain involuntary conversions [condemnations]).
II	To report ordinary gains and losses.
III	To determine the portion of the gain that is subject to recapture (e.g., §§ 1245 and 1250 gain).
IV	Computation of recapture amounts under §§ 179 and 280F when business use of depreciable property drops to 50% or less.

Generally, the best approach to completing Form 4797 is to start with Part III. Once the recapture amount has been determined, it is transferred to Part II. The balance of any gain remaining after the recapture has been accounted for is transferred from Part III to Part I. Also transferred to Part I is any net gain from certain casualties and thefts as reported on Form 4684, Part B (refer to above and Chapter 15). If the netting process in Form 4797, Part I, results in a gain, it is reduced by the nonrecaptured net § 1231 losses from prior years (line 9 of Part I). Any remaining gain is shifted to Schedule D, Capital Gains and Losses, of Form 1040. If the netting process in Part I of Form 4797 results in a loss, it goes to Part II to be treated as an ordinary loss.

Example 23

For 1995, Troy Williams (Social Security number 467–85–3036) had the following recognized gains and losses (a 1995 example has been used since 1996 forms were unavailable):

Sale of Depreciable Business Assets Held Long Term	
Asset A (Note 1)	$36,500
Asset B (Note 2)	26,933
Asset C (Note 3)	(880)
Sale of Depreciable Business Assets Held Short Term	
Asset D (Note 4)	$ (600)
Capital Assets	
Long-term gain (Note 5)	$ 3,000
Short-term loss (Note 6)	(200)

Note 1. Asset A was acquired on June 23, 1992, for $50,000. It was five-year MACRS property, and four years' cost recovery allowances totaled $38,480. The property was sold for $48,020 on August 31, 1995.

Note 2. Asset B was purchased on May 10, 1986, for $37,000. It was 19-year ACRS property. Using the statutory percentage method, cost recovery totaled $20,933. The property was sold for $43,000 on January 10, 1995. The building was residential rental property, and straight-line cost recovery for the period of ownership would have totaled $16,991.

Note 3. Asset C was purchased on December 9, 1992, for $16,000. It was five-year MACRS property, and four years' cost recovery totaled $12,314. The property was sold for $2,806 on December 30, 1995.

Note 4. Asset D was purchased for $7,000 on July 27, 1995. It was five-year MACRS property but proved unsuitable to Troy's business. Troy sold it for $6,400 on November 3, 1995.

Note 5. The LTCG resulted from the sale of 100 shares of Orange Corporation stock purchased for $10,000 on April 5, 1986. The shares were sold on October 21, 1995, for $13,223. Expenses of sale were $223.

Note 6. The STCL resulted from the sale of 50 shares of Blue Corporation stock purchased for $350 on March 14, 1995. The shares were sold for $170 on August 20, 1995. Expenses of sale were $20.

The sale of assets A and B at a gain results in the recapture of cost recovery deductions. That recapture is shown in Part III of Form 4797. Some of the gain from the sale of asset B exceeds the recapture amount and is carried from line 34 to Part I, line 6, of Form 4797. On line 2, the loss from asset C appears. Part I is where the § 1231 netting process takes place. Assume Troy Williams has no nonrecaptured net § 1231 losses from prior years. The net gain on line 8 is transferred to Schedule D, line 12. In Part II of Form 4797, the ordinary gains are accumulated. On line 14, the recapture from line 33 (Part III) is shown. On line 11, the loss from asset D is shown. The net gain on line 20 is ordinary income and is transferred to Form 1040, line 14.

Schedule D, Part I, line 1, reports the short-term capital loss from the Blue Corporation stock. Part II of Schedule D has the net § 1231 gain transferred from Form 4797 on line 12 and the Orange Corporation gain on line 9. The net capital gain is determined on line 18, Part III. The capital gain is then carried to line 13 of Form 1040.

Form 4797 and Schedule D (Parts I–III) for Troy Williams are reproduced on the following pages. ▼

The 1995 tax forms solution for Example 23 appear on the following pages.

Form **4797**

Department of the Treasury
Internal Revenue Service (99)

Sales of Business Property
(Also Involuntary Conversions and Recapture Amounts Under Sections 179 and 280F(b)(2))

▶ Attach to your tax return. ▶ See separate instructions.

OMB No. 1545-0184
1995
Attachment Sequence No. **27**

Name(s) shown on return: *Troy Williams*
Identifying number: *467-85-3036*

1 Enter here the gross proceeds from the sale or exchange of real estate reported to you for 1995 on Form(s) 1099-S (or a substitute statement) that you will be including on line 2, 11, or 22 1

Part I Sales or Exchanges of Property Used in a Trade or Business and Involuntary Conversions From Other Than Casualty or Theft—Property Held More Than 1 Year

(a) Description of property	(b) Date acquired (mo., day, yr.)	(c) Date sold (mo., day, yr.)	(d) Gross sales price	(e) Depreciation allowed or allowable since acquisition	(f) Cost or other basis, plus improvements and expense of sale	(g) LOSS ((f) minus the sum of (d) and (e))	(h) GAIN ((d) plus (e) minus (f))
2							
Asset C	*12/9/92*	*12/30/95*	*2,806*	*12,314*	*16,000*	*880*	

	Line	(g) LOSS	(h) GAIN
3 Gain, if any, from Form 4684, line 39	3		
4 Section 1231 gain from installment sales from Form 6252, line 26 or 37	4		
5 Section 1231 gain or (loss) from like-kind exchanges from Form 8824	5		
6 Gain, if any, from line 34, from other than casualty or theft	6		*22,991*
7 Add lines 2 through 6 in columns (g) and (h)	7	(*880*)	*22,991*

8 Combine columns (g) and (h) of line 7. Enter gain or (loss) here, and on the appropriate line as follows: 8 *22,111*

Partnerships—Enter the gain or (loss) on Form 1065, Schedule K, line 6. Skip lines 9, 10, 12, and 13 below.

S corporations—Report the gain or (loss) following the instructions for Form 1120S, Schedule K, lines 5 and 6. Skip lines 9, 10, 12, and 13 below, unless line 8 is a gain and the S corporation is subject to the capital gains tax.

All others—If line 8 is zero or a loss, enter the amount on line 12 below and skip lines 9 and 10. If line 8 is a gain and you did not have any prior year section 1231 losses, or they were recaptured in an earlier year, enter the gain as a long-term capital gain on Schedule D and skip lines 9, 10, and 13 below.

9 Nonrecaptured net section 1231 losses from prior years (see instructions) 9

10 Subtract line 9 from line 8. If zero or less, enter -0-. Also enter on the appropriate line as follows (see instructions): 10

S corporations—Enter this amount on Schedule D (Form 1120S), line 13, and skip lines 12 and 13 below.

All others—If line 10 is zero, enter the amount from line 8 on line 13 below. If line 10 is more than zero, enter the amount from line 9 on line 13 below, and enter the amount from line 10 as a long-term capital gain on Schedule D.

Part II Ordinary Gains and Losses

11 Ordinary gains and losses not included on lines 12 through 18 (include property held 1 year or less):

(a)	(b)	(c)	(d)	(e)	(f)	(g)	(h)
Asset D	*7/27/95*	*11/3/95*	*6,400*	*0*	*7,000*	*600*	

	Line	(g) LOSS	(h) GAIN
12 Loss, if any, from line 8	12		
13 Gain, if any, from line 8, or amount from line 9 if applicable	13		
14 Gain, if any, from line 33	14		*40,442*
15 Net gain or (loss) from Form 4684, lines 31 and 38a	15		
16 Ordinary gain from installment sales from Form 6252, line 25 or 36	16		
17 Ordinary gain or (loss) from like-kind exchanges from Form 8824	17		
18 Recapture of section 179 expense deduction for partners and S corporation shareholders from property dispositions by partnerships and S corporations (see instructions)	18		
19 Add lines 11 through 18 in columns (g) and (h)	19	(*600*)	*40,442*

20 Combine columns (g) and (h) of line 19. Enter gain or (loss) here, and on the appropriate line as follows: . . . 20 *39,842*

a For all except individual returns: Enter the gain or (loss) from line 20 on the return being filed.

b For individual returns:

(1) If the loss on line 12 includes a loss from Form 4684, line 35, column (b)(ii), enter that part of the loss here and on line 22 of Schedule A (Form 1040). Identify as from "Form 4797, line 20b(1)." See instructions . . . . 20b(1)

(2) Redetermine the gain or (loss) on line 20, excluding the loss, if any, on line 20b(1). Enter here and on Form 1040, line 14 . . 20b(2) *39,842*

For Paperwork Reduction Act Notice, see page 1 of separate instructions. Cat. No. 13086I Form **4797** (1995)

Form 4797 (1995) Page **2**

Part III Gain From Disposition of Property Under Sections 1245, 1250, 1252, 1254, and 1255

21 **(a)** Description of section 1245, 1250, 1252, 1254, or 1255 property:	**(b)** Date acquired (mo., day, yr.)	**(c)** Date sold (mo., day, yr.)
A *Asset A*	*6/23/92*	*8/31/95*
B *Asset B*	*5/10/86*	*1/10/95*
C		
D		

Relate lines 21A through 21D to these columns ▶		**Property A**	**Property B**	**Property C**	**Property D**
22 Gross sales price (**Note:** *See line 1 before completing.*)	22	*48,020*	*43,000*		
23 Cost or other basis plus expense of sale	23	*50,000*	*37,000*		
24 Depreciation (or depletion) allowed or allowable	24	*38,480*	*20,933*		
25 Adjusted basis. Subtract line 24 from line 23	25	*11,520*	*16,067*		
26 Total gain. Subtract line 25 from line 22	26	*36,500*	*26,933*		
27 **If section 1245 property:**					
a Depreciation allowed or allowable from line 24	27a	*38,480*			
b Enter the **smaller** of line 26 or 27a	27b	*36,500*			
28 **If section 1250 property:** If straight line depreciation was used, enter -0- on line 28g, except for a corporation subject to section 291.					
a Additional depreciation after 1975 (see instructions)	28a		*3,942*		
b Applicable percentage multiplied by the **smaller** of line 26 or line 28a (see instructions)	28b		*3,942*		
c Subtract line 28a from line 26. If residential rental property or line 26 is not more than line 28a, skip lines 28d and 28e	28c		*22,991*		
d Additional depreciation after 1969 and before 1976	28d		*0*		
e Enter the **smaller** of line 28c or 28d	28e		*0*		
f Section 291 amount (corporations only)	28f		*0*		
g Add lines 28b, 28e, and 28f	28g		*3,942*		
29 **If section 1252 property:** Skip this section if you did not dispose of farmland or if this form is being completed for a partnership.					
a Soil, water, and land clearing expenses	29a				
b Line 29a multiplied by applicable percentage (see instructions)	29b				
c Enter the **smaller** of line 26 or 29b	29c				
30 **If section 1254 property:**					
a Intangible drilling and development costs, expenditures for development of mines and other natural deposits, and mining exploration costs (see instructions)	30a				
b Enter the **smaller** of line 26 or 30a	30b				
31 **If section 1255 property:**					
a Applicable percentage of payments excluded from income under section 126 (see instructions)	31a				
b Enter the **smaller** of line 26 or 31a (see instructions)	31b				

Summary of Part III Gains. Complete property columns A through D, through line 31b before going to line 32.

32 Total gains for all properties. Add property columns A through D, line 26	32	*63,433*
33 Add property columns A through D, lines 27b, 28g, 29c, 30b, and 31b. Enter here and on line 14	33	*40,442*
34 Subtract line 33 from line 32. Enter the portion from casualty or theft on Form 4684, line 33. Enter the portion from other than casualty or theft on Form 4797, line 6	34	*22,991*

Part IV Recapture Amounts Under Sections 179 and 280F(b)(2) When Business Use Drops to 50% or Less

See instructions.

		(a) Section 179	**(b) Section 280F(b)(2)**
35 Section 179 expense deduction or depreciation allowable in prior years	35		
36 Recomputed depreciation. See instructions	36		
37 Recapture amount. Subtract line 36 from line 35. See the instructions for where to report	37		

SCHEDULE D (Form 1040)
Department of the Treasury
Internal Revenue Service (99)

Capital Gains and Losses

▶ Attach to Form 1040. ▶ See Instructions for Schedule D (Form 1040).
▶ Use lines 20 and 22 for more space to list transactions for lines 1 and 9.

OMB No. 1545-0074
1995
Attachment Sequence No. **12**

Name(s) shown on Form 1040: *Troy Williams*
Your social security number: *467 85 3036*

Part I Short-Term Capital Gains and Losses—Assets Held One Year or Less

	(a) Description of property (Example: 100 sh. XYZ Co.)	(b) Date acquired (Mo., day, yr.)	(c) Date sold (Mo., day, yr.)	(d) Sales price (see page D-3)	(e) Cost or other basis (see page D-3)	(f) LOSS If (e) is more than (d), subtract (d) from (e)	(g) GAIN If (d) is more than (e), subtract (e) from (d)
1	*Blue Corp. (50 Shares)*	*3/14/95*	*8/20/95*	*170*	*370*	*200*	
2	Enter your short-term totals, if any, from line 21 2						
3	**Total short-term sales price amounts.** Add column (d) of lines 1 and 2 . . . 3			*170*			
4	Short-term gain from Forms 2119 and 6252, and short-term gain or loss from Forms 4684, 6781, and 8824 4						
5	Net short-term gain or loss from partnerships, S corporations, estates, and trusts from Schedule(s) K-1 5						
6	Short-term capital loss carryover. Enter the amount, if any, from line 9 of your 1994 Capital Loss Carryover Worksheet 6						
7	Add lines 1 through 6 in columns (f) and (g) 7					(*200*)	
8	**Net short-term capital gain or (loss).** Combine columns (f) and (g) of line 7 . . . . . . ▶ 8						(*200*)

Part II Long-Term Capital Gains and Losses—Assets Held More Than One Year

	(a)	(b)	(c)	(d)	(e)	(f)	(g)
9	*Orange Corp. (100 shares)*	*4/5/86*	*10/21/95*	*13,223*	*10,223*		*3,000*
10	Enter your long-term totals, if any, from line 23 10						
11	**Total long-term sales price amounts.** Add column (d) of lines 9 and 10 . . . 11			*13,223*			
12	Gain from Form 4797; long-term gain from Forms 2119, 2439, and 6252; and long-term gain or loss from Forms 4684, 6781, and 8824 12						*22,111*
13	Net long-term gain or loss from partnerships, S corporations, estates, and trusts from Schedule(s) K-1 13						
14	Capital gain distributions 14						
15	Long-term capital loss carryover. Enter the amount, if any, from line 14 of your 1994 Capital Loss Carryover Worksheet 15						
16	Add lines 9 through 15 in columns (f) and (g) 16					( )	*25,111*
17	**Net long-term capital gain or (loss).** Combine columns (f) and (g) of line 16 . . . . . ▶ 17						*25,111*

Part III Summary of Parts I and II

18	Combine lines 8 and 17. If a loss, go to line 19. If a gain, enter the gain on Form 1040, line 13. **Note:** *If both lines 17 and 18 are gains, see the* ***Capital Gain Tax Worksheet*** *on page 24* . .	18	*24,911*
19	If line 18 is a loss, enter here and as a (loss) on Form 1040, line 13, the **smaller** of these losses:		
a	The loss on line 18; **or**		
b	($3,000) or, if married filing separately, ($1,500)	19	( )
	Note: *See the* ***Capital Loss Carryover Worksheet*** *on page D-3 if the loss on line 18 exceeds the loss on line 19* ***or*** *if Form 1040, line 35, is a loss.*		

For Paperwork Reduction Act Notice, see Form 1040 instructions. Cat. No. 11338H **Schedule D (Form 1040) 1995**

TAX PLANNING CONSIDERATIONS

TIMING OF § 1231 GAIN

8 LEARNING OBJECTIVE
Identify tax planning opportunities associated with §§ 1231, 1245, and 1250.

Although §§ 1245 and 1250 recapture much of the gain from the disposition of business property, sometimes § 1231 gain is still substantial. For instance, land held as a business asset will generate either § 1231 gain or § 1231 loss. If the taxpayer already has a capital loss for the year, the sale of land at a gain should be postponed so that the net § 1231 gain is not netted against the capital loss. The capital loss deduction will therefore be maximized for the current tax year, and the capital loss carryforward (if any) may be offset against the gain when the land is sold. If the taxpayer already has a § 1231 loss, § 1231 gains might be postponed to maximize the ordinary loss deduction this year. However, the carryforward of nonrecaptured § 1231 losses will make the § 1231 gain next year an ordinary gain.

EXAMPLE 24

Mark has a $2,000 net STCL for 1996. He could sell business land for a $3,000 § 1231 gain. He will have no other capital gains and losses or § 1231 gains and losses in 1996 or 1997. He has no nonrecaptured § 1231 losses from prior years. Mark is in the 28% tax bracket in 1996 and 1997. If he sells the land in 1996, he will have a $1,000 net LTCG ($3,000 § 1231 gain – $2,000 STCL) and will pay a tax of $280 ($1,000 × 28%). If Mark sells the land in 1997, he will have a 1996 tax savings of $560 ($2,000 capital loss deduction × 28% tax rate on ordinary income). In 1997, he will pay tax of $840 ($3,000 × 28%]. By postponing the sale for a year, Mark will have the use of $840 ($560 + $280). ▼

EXAMPLE 25

Beth has a $15,000 § 1231 loss in 1996. She could sell business equipment for a $20,000 § 1231 gain and a $12,000 § 1245 gain. Beth is in the 28% tax bracket in 1996 and 1997. She has no nonrecaptured § 1231 losses from prior years. If she sells the equipment in 1996, she will have a $5,000 net § 1231 gain and $12,000 of ordinary gain. Her tax would be $4,760 [($5,000 § 1231 gain × 28%) + ($12,000 ordinary gain × 28%)].

If Beth postpones the equipment sale until 1997, she would have a 1996 ordinary loss of $15,000 and tax savings of $4,200 ($15,000 × 28%). In 1997, she would have $5,000 of § 1231 gain (the 1996 § 1231 loss carries over and recaptures $15,000 of the 1997 § 1231 gain as ordinary income) and $27,000 of ordinary gain. Her tax would be $8,960 [($5,000 § 1231 gain × 28%) + ($27,000 ordinary gain × 28%)]. By postponing the equipment sale, Beth has the use of $8,960 ($4,200 + $4,760). ▼

TIMING OF RECAPTURE

Since recapture is usually not triggered until the property is sold or disposed of, it may be possible to plan for recapture in low-bracket or loss years. If a taxpayer has net operating loss carryovers that are about to expire, the recognition of ordinary income from recapture may be advisable to absorb the loss carryovers.

EXAMPLE 26

Ahmad has a $15,000 net operating loss carryover that will expire this year. He owns a machine that he plans to sell in the early part of next year. The expected gain of $17,000 from the sale of the machine will be recaptured as ordinary income under § 1245. Ahmad sells the machine before the end of this year and offsets $15,000 of the ordinary income against the net operating loss carryover. ▼

POSTPONING AND SHIFTING RECAPTURE

It is also possible to postpone recapture or to shift the burden of recapture to others. For example, recapture is avoided upon the disposition of a § 1231 asset if the taxpayer replaces the property by entering into a like-kind exchange. In this instance, recapture potential is merely carried over to the newly acquired property (refer to Example 19).

Recapture can be shifted to others through the gratuitous transfer of § 1245 or § 1250 property to family members. A subsequent sale of such property by the donee will trigger recapture to the donee rather than the donor (refer to Example 16). This procedure would be advisable only if the donee is in a lower income tax bracket than the donor.

AVOIDING RECAPTURE

The immediate expensing election (§ 179) is subject to § 1245 recapture. If the election is not made, the § 1245 recapture potential will accumulate more slowly (refer to Chapter 8). Since using the immediate expense deduction complicates depreciation and book accounting for the affected asset, not taking the deduction may make sense even though the time value of money might indicate it should be taken.

KEY TERMS

Additional depreciation, 17–16

Intangible drilling and development costs (IDC), 17–23

Long-term nonpersonal use capital assets, 17–7

Related party, 17–23

Section 1231 gains and losses, 17–4

Section 1231 lookback, 17–9

Section 1231 property, 17–5

Section 1245 property, 17–14

Section 1245 recapture, 17–13

Section 1250 property, 17–16

Section 1250 recapture, 17–16

PROBLEM MATERIALS

DISCUSSION QUESTIONS

1. What types of transactions involving capital assets are included under § 1231? Why wouldn't they qualify for long-term capital gain treatment without § 1231?
2. Does § 1231 treatment apply to all business property?
3. If depreciable business property is sold at a loss, is the loss an ordinary loss or a capital loss?
4. What two developments near the start of World War II caused Congress to reexamine the tax treatment of business assets?
5. Name two types of assets that are neither § 1231 assets nor capital assets.
6. Does § 1231 property include depreciable business property held for the short-term holding period?
7. Is it possible to recognize both a gain and a loss on the sale of timber in one taxable year? How?
8. Ahmad is a farmer who is thinking about raising ostriches. Ostrich meat is very high in protein, low in calories, and low in fat. Ahmad would like to know what tax issues he would face if he decides to raise ostriches in addition to the cattle he is currently raising.
9. Nonpersonal use property held long term is disposed of by casualty, but the insurance proceeds result in a gain. This is the only nonpersonal use property casualty during the year. How is the gain treated?

10. Sally lives in an area that was hit hard by a hurricane. She has correctly determined that she has a $15,000 business property long-term casualty loss and a $11,000 business property long-term casualty gain. What tax issues must Sally deal with?

11. Are recognized long-term business asset condemnation gains treated as § 1231 gains? (Ignore the possibility of depreciation recapture.)

12. How are personal use property condemnation gains and losses treated?

13. Why is the casualty netting in Step 1 of the general procedure for the § 1231 computation beneficial?

14. How does the *lookback rule* change the character of a current-year net § 1231 gain?

15. Two years ago, Sara had a net § 1231 loss. Last year, she had a net § 1231 gain exceeding that loss. This year, Sara has a net § 1231 gain. Is any of this year's gain treated as ordinary income because of the *lookback rule*?

16. Some of Max's business equipment that had been held long term was stolen in a burglary. The property had been purchased for $80,000, and the insurance company paid Max $33,000. What tax issues do these circumstances present for Max?

17. A business machine held for three years is disposed of at a gain. The cost of the machine was greater than the selling price. What is the nature of the gain?

18. If a farmer buys a pig and uses MACRS, are the cost recovery deductions subject to § 1245 recapture if the pig is sold at a gain?

19. Does § 1245 depreciation recapture apply if depreciable business equipment is sold at a loss?

20. A business machine held for several years is sold at a gain. Part of the gain is § 1245 gain, and part is § 1231 gain. There is no other § 1231 gain or loss this year, but there is a nonrecaptured § 1231 lookback loss that exceeds the current-year § 1231 gain. Describe the treatment of the gain from the disposition of the machine.

21. Differentiate between the types of property covered by §§ 1245 and 1250.

22. In 1984, a warehouse was acquired and depreciated using accelerated depreciation. In 1996, the warehouse is sold for less than was originally paid for it. What is the nature of the gain?

23. Why does § 1250 generally not apply to real estate acquired after 1986?

24. Examine Example 13 in this chapter. Why is the amount in the "additional depreciation" column negative for 1995?

25. Residential rental real estate is acquired and disposed of in 1996. There is a small gain on the disposition of the property. The gain is less than the depreciation taken on the property. What is the nature of that gain?

26. What is the definition of residential rental housing?

27. Death eliminates all recapture potential. Do you agree? Why or why not?

28. Does recapture apply when § 1245 property is donated to charity?

29. What provisions of the Internal Revenue Code do the §§ 1245 and 1250 recapture rules override?

30. May an installment sale trigger § 1245 recapture even though no gain would otherwise be currently recognizable?

31. What happens to depreciation recapture potential under either § 1245 or § 1250 when a corporate taxpayer distributes depreciable equipment as a property dividend? Assume the equipment would have been sold at a gain if it were sold rather than distributed.

32. May corporations transferring real estate have depreciation recapture in addition to § 1250 recapture?

33. In general, how does the related-party ordinary income provision differ from §§ 1245 and 1250?

34. What three tax forms may be required to properly report the gains and losses discussed in Chapter 17?

35. Where in the tax forms is the §§ 1245 and 1250 depreciation recapture shown?

36. On what tax form and where on that form does the § 1231 netting process to determine whether there is a net § 1231 gain or loss take place?

PROBLEMS

37. Sue-Jen purchased a contract to cut timber on a 100-acre tract of land in South Dakota in March 1994 for $20,000. On January 1, 1995, the timber had a fair market value of $50,000. Because of careless cutting in November 1995, when the fair market value was $55,000, the wood was sold on January 30, 1996, for $49,000.
    a. What gain (loss) was realized in 1994, 1995, and 1996? What gain (loss) was recognized in 1994, 1995, and 1996?
    b. What was the nature of the gains (losses) in (a)? What assumption must be made?
    c. Does the answer change if the timber was sold in December 1995? Why?
    d. If the timber was worth only $18,000 on January 1, 1995, was cut in November when worth $21,000, and was sold in December for $19,000, how would the answers to (a) and (b) change?

38. Bob owns a farming sole proprietorship. During the year, Bob sold a milk cow that he had owned for 13 months and a workhorse that he had owned for 56 months. The cow had an adjusted basis of $800 and was sold for $550. The horse had an adjusted basis of $350 and was sold for $1,000. Bob also has a $200 long-term capital loss from the sale of corporate stock. He has $55,000 of other AGI (not associated with the items above) for the year. He has no net § 1231 losses from previous years. What is the nature of the gains or losses from the disposition of the farm animals, and what is Bob's AGI for the year?

39. A painting that Kwan Lee held for investment was destroyed in a flood. The painting was insured, and Kwan had a $10,000 gain from this casualty. He also had a $7,000 loss from an uninsured antique vase that was destroyed by the flood. The vase was also held for investment. Kwan had no other property transactions during the year and has no nonrecaptured § 1231 losses from prior years. Compute his net gain or loss and identify how it would be treated. Also, write a letter to Kwan explaining the nature of the gain or loss. Kwan's address is 2367 Meridian Road, Hannibal Point, MO 34901.

40. Vicki has the following net § 1231 results for each of the years shown. What would be the nature of the net gains in 1995 and 1996?

Tax Year	Net § 1231 Loss	Net § 1231 Gain
1991	$15,000	
1992	17,000	
1993	22,000	
1994		$10,000
1995		20,000
1996		29,000

41. Yoshida owns two parcels of business land (§ 1231 assets). One parcel can be sold at a loss of $30,000, and the other parcel can be sold at a gain of $40,000. Yoshida has no nonrecaptured § 1231 losses from prior years. The parcels could be sold at any time because potential purchasers are abundant. Yoshida has a $25,000 short-term capital loss carryover from a prior tax year and no capital assets that could be sold to generate

long-term capital gains. What should Yoshida do based upon these facts? (Assume tax rates are constant and ignore the present value of future cash flow.)

42. Rose Company owns two lathes. Lathe A was purchased several years ago for $65,000, has a $10,000 adjusted basis, and was sold in 1996 for $17,000. Lathe B was purchased several years ago for $8,000, has a $6,000 adjusted basis, and was sold in 1996 for $2,000. What are the amount and nature of the recognized gain or loss from the disposition of each asset?

43. Tan Corporation sold machines A and B during the current year. The machines had been purchased for $180,000 and $240,000, respectively. The machines were purchased eight years ago and were depreciated to zero. Machine A was sold for $40,000, and machine B for $260,000. What amount of gain is recognized by Tan, and what is the nature of the gain?

44. On March 1, 1992, Cardinal Company bought and placed in service a seven-year MACRS machine for $35,000. Cardinal expensed $10,000 of the machine's cost under § 179 and has also taken $17,841 of cost recovery on the machine. The machine was sold on April 1, 1996, for $32,000.
    a. What is Cardinal's realized and recognized gain?
    b. What is the nature of the gain?
    c. At what point in time did this machine cease being an ordinary asset and become a § 1231 asset?

45. Green Manufacturing purchases a $3,000,000 propane storage tank and places it on a permanent framework outside its plant. The propane is drawn from the tank through a hose and valve system into the burners underneath Green's chemical vats. After $1,800,000 of cost recovery has been taken on the tank, it is sold for $2,300,000. What are the nature and amount of Green's gain or loss from the disposition of the tank?

46. On December 1, 1994, Gray Manufacturing Company (a corporation) purchased another company's assets, including a patent. The patent was used in Gray's manufacturing operations; $40,500 was allocated to the patent, and it was amortized at the rate of $225 per month. On June 30, 1996, Gray sold the patent for $60,000. Nineteen months of amortization had been taken on the patent. What are the amount and nature of the gain Gray recognizes on the disposition of the patent? Write a letter to Gray discussing the treatment of the gain. Gray's address is 6734 Grover Street, Back Bay Harbor, ME 23890. The letter should be addressed to Siddim Sadatha, Controller.

47. On June 1, 1992, Sparrow Enterprises (not a corporation) acquired a retail store for $400,000. The store was 31.5-year real property, and the straight-line cost recovery method was used. The store was sold on June 21, 1996, for $370,000.
    a. Compute the cost recovery and adjusted basis for the store using Table 8–7 from Chapter 8.
    b. What are the amount and nature of Sparrow's gain or loss from disposition of the store?

48. On January 1, 1986, Esteban acquired a $600,000 residential building for use in his rental activity. He took $450,000 of cost recovery on the building before disposing of it for $800,000 on January 1, 1996. For the period Esteban held the building, straight-line cost recovery would have been $400,000. What are the amount and nature of Esteban's gain from the disposition of the property?

49. Dave is the sole proprietor of a trampoline shop. During 1996, the following transactions occurred:

    - Unimproved land adjacent to the store was condemned by the city on February 1. The condemnation proceeds were $25,000. The land, acquired in 1982, had an allocable basis of $15,000. Dave has additional parking across the street and plans to use the condemnation proceeds to build his inventory.

    - A truck used to deliver trampolines was sold on January 2 for $3,500. The truck was purchased on January 2, 1992, for $6,000. On the date of sale, the adjusted basis was $2,509.

- Dave sold an antique rowing machine at an auction. Net proceeds were $3,900. The rowing machine was purchased as used equipment 17 years ago for $5,200 and is fully depreciated.
- Dave sold an apartment building for $200,000 on September 1. The rental property was purchased on September 1, 1993, for $150,000 and was being depreciated over a 27.5-year life using the straight-line method. At the date of sale, the adjusted basis was $124,783.
- Dave's personal yacht was stolen September 5. The yacht had been purchased in August at a cost of $25,000. The fair market value immediately preceding the theft was $20,000. Dave was insured for 50% of the original cost, and he received $12,500 on December 1.
- Dave sold a Buick on May 1 for $9,600. The vehicle had been used exclusively for personal purposes. It was purchased on September 1, 1992, for $20,800.
- An adding machine used by Dave's bookkeeper was sold on June 1. Net proceeds of the sale were $135. The machine was purchased on June 2, 1992, for $350. It was being depreciated over a five-year life employing the straight-line method. The adjusted basis on the date of sale was $95.
- Dave's trampoline stretching machine (owned two years) was stolen on May 5, but the business's insurance company will not pay any of the machine's value because Dave failed to pay the insurance premium. The machine had a fair market value of $8,000 and an adjusted basis of $6,000 at the time of theft.
- Dave had AGI of $4,000 from sources other than those described above.
- Dave has no nonrecaptured § 1231 lookback losses.

a. For each transaction, what are the amount and nature of recognized gain or loss?
b. What is Dave's 1996 AGI?

50. On January 1, 1986, Cora Hassant acquired depreciable real property for $100,000. She used accelerated depreciation to compute the asset's cost recovery. The asset was sold for $89,000 on January 3, 1996, when its adjusted basis was $38,000. Straight-line cost recovery for the period of time the asset was held would have been $52,700.
    a. What are the amount and nature of the gain if the real property was residential?
    b. What are the amount and nature of the gain if the real property was nonresidential?
    c. Cora is curious about how the recapture rules differ for residential rental real estate acquired in 1986 and for residential rental real estate acquired in 1987 and thereafter. Write a letter to Cora explaining the differences. Her address is 2345 Westridge Street #23, Homer, MT 67342.

51. Joanne is in the 39.6% tax bracket and owns depreciable business equipment that she purchased several years ago for $135,000; she has taken $100,000 of depreciation on the equipment, and it is worth $85,000. Joanne's niece, Susan, is starting a new business and is short of cash. Susan has asked Joanne to gift the equipment to her so that Susan can use it in her business. Joanne no longer needs the equipment. Identify the alternatives available to Joanne if she wishes to help Susan and the tax effects of those alternatives. (Assume all alternatives involve the business equipment in one way or another, and ignore the gift tax.)

52. Gregor owns business equipment with a $55,000 adjusted basis; he paid $100,000 for the equipment, and it is currently worth $73,000. Gregor dies suddenly, and his son Adrian inherits the property. What is Adrian's basis for the property, and what happens to the § 1245 depreciation recapture potential?

53. Burt transferred forklifts used in his factory with recapture potential of $6,500 to a dealer in exchange for new forklifts worth $8,000 and $1,500 of marketable securities. The transaction qualified as a § 1031 like-kind exchange. Burt had an adjusted basis of $6,000 in the equipment.

a. What is Burt's realized and recognized gain or loss?
b. What is the nature of the recognized gain or loss?
c. How would your answer to (a) or (b) change if no marketable securities were involved?

54. Cathy sells § 1245 property for $35,000, to be paid in 10 annual installments of $3,500 each plus interest at 8%. Cathy realizes a $12,000 gain from the sale, of which $12,000 is attributable to depreciation taken. Cathy would like to use the installment method to recognize the gain on the sale. May she do so?

55. Ray owns an unimproved parking lot that was used in his parking lot business for 10 years. A real estate developer purchases the lot from Ray for a total of $300,000. Ray receives $50,000 in 1996 and will receive $50,000 (plus 10% interest) each year for the next five years. Ray has a $120,000 adjusted basis for the lot. What are the nature and amount of the gain recognized in 1996?

56. Orange Corporation sells depreciable equipment for $59,000 to its sole shareholder, Jane. Orange had a $45,000 adjusted basis for the equipment and had originally paid $85,000 for it. Jane will use the equipment in her sole proprietorship business. The $59,000 sale price is the property's fair market value at the time of the sale. What are the consequences of this sale for Orange? For Jane?

57. Refer to the sample Form 4797 and Form 1040 Schedule D in the text. Form 4797, Part I, line 2h shows $43,000. Part I, line 9 shows $11,000. What amount should appear on Schedule D, line 12?

58. Refer to the sample Form 4797 and Form 1040 Schedule D in the text. Ernest has the following items on these forms:

Item	Form 4797		Schedule D	
Property A (§ 1245 property)	Line 24	$86,000		
	Line 26	96,000		
Property B (§ 1250 property)	Line 26	34,000		
	Line 28a	32,000		
Property C			Line 9	($3,000)

Ernest has no nonrecaptured § 1231 losses from prior years. What is Ernest's entry on line 12 of Schedule D?

59. Jay sold three items of business equipment for a total of $300,000. None of the equipment was appraised to determine its value. Jay's cost and adjusted basis for the assets are as follows:

Asset	Cost	Adjusted Basis
Skidder	$230,000	$ 40,000
Driller	120,000	60,000
Platform	620,000	–0–
Total	$970,000	$100,000

Jay has been unable to establish the fair market values of the three assets. All he can determine is that combined they were worth $300,000 to the buyer in this arm's length transaction. How should Jay allocate the sales price and figure the gain or loss on the sale of the three assets?

CUMULATIVE PROBLEMS

60. Glen and Diane Okumura are married, file a joint return, and live at 39 Kaloa Street, Honolulu, Hawaii 56790. Glen's Social Security number is 777–88–2000 and Diane's is 888–77–1000. The Okumuras have two dependent children, Amy (age 15) and John (age 9). Glen works for the Hawaii Public Works Department, and Diane owns and materially participates in a retail dress shop. The Okumuras had the following transactions during 1996:
    a. Glen earned $197,000 in wages and had Federal income tax withholding of $15,000.
    b. Diane had a $18,000 profit from the dress shop.
    c. The Okumuras sold a small apartment building for $68,000 on November 15, 1996. The building was acquired in October 1990 for $300,000, cost recovery was $86,820.
    d. Diane sold a delivery truck used in her business. The truck cost $35,000, $21,700 of cost recovery had been taken, and it was sold for $18,000.
    e. The Okumuras received $13,000 in dividends on various domestic corporation stock that they own.
    f. The Okumuras sold stock for a $15,000 long-term capital gain and other stock at a $6,000 short-term capital loss.
    g. The Okumuras had the following itemized deductions: $11,000 unreimbursed medical expenses; $10,500 personal use real property taxes; $7,000 qualified residence interest; $1,500 of Glen's unreimbursed employee business expenses; $535 of investment-related expenses; and $6,300 of state income taxes paid.

    Compute the Okumuras' 1996 net tax payable or refund due. (Ignore self-employment tax.) Suggested software (if available): *TurboTax* or *MacInTax*. Also write a letter to the Okumuras describing how the sale of the apartment building affects their return.

61. Linda Franklin is an attorney. She is single and lives at 1619 Merry Lane, Cantone, TN 16703. Her Social Security number is 345–67–8900. Linda receives a salary of $45,000. During 1995, she had the following property transactions:
    a. Sales of stock held for investment:

Stock	Selling Price	Basis	Date Sold	Date Acquired
Acme Corporation	$2,000	$ 1,400	6/30/1995	12/31/1994
Bareham Corporation	8,000	10,500	12/31/1995	7/15/1995
Cronin, Inc.	9,400	5,400	7/26/1995	5/2/1983
Davis Corporation	1,800	2,900	10/18/1995	10/17/1984

    b. Complete destruction of a personal use travel trailer in a wreck on August 1 (adjusted basis, $6,500; fair market value, $5,000; reimbursement for loss by insurance company, $3,000). Linda had bought the trailer on June 12, 1991.
    c. Sale of photocopying machine used in business for $2,800 on November 6. Linda had acquired the machine on April 29, 1993, for $4,000 and had taken $2,163 of cost recovery on it.
    d. Sale of computer used in business on January 15 for $500. The computer was acquired on May 8, 1993, at a cost of $1,000; cost recovery of $395 had been deducted.
    e. Cash dividends of $5,000 (all from Bareham stock).

    Compute Linda Franklin's AGI from these transactions. If you use tax forms in your computations, you will need Forms 1040, 4684, and 4797 and Schedules B and D. Suggested software (if available): *TurboTax* or *MacInTax*.

RESEARCH PROBLEMS

Note: ***West's Federal Taxation on CD-ROM*** *can be used in preparing solutions to the Research Problems. Alternatively, tax research materials contained in a standard tax library can be used.*

Research Problem 1. Sidney owns a professional football franchise. He has received an offer of $80 million for the franchise, all the football equipment, the rights to concession receipts, the rights to a stadium lease, and the rights to all the player contracts he owns. Most of the players have been with the team for quite a long time and have contracts that were signed several years ago. The contracts have been substantially depreciated. Sidney is concerned about potential § 1245 recapture when the contracts are sold. He has heard about "previously unrecaptured depreciation with respect to initial contracts" and would like to know more about it. Find a definition for that phrase and write an explanation of it.

Research Problem 2. Green Corporation purchased all the assets of Blue Corporation in 1994. In 1996, Green resells all the assets acquired from Blue. Among the assets purchased and then sold is a copyrighted software program. The portion of the cost allocated to the software program was $1,000,000. While Green held this asset, $105,555 of amortization was taken. What is the nature of the gain from the sale of the software copyright if the sale price is $1,456,000?

Research Problem 3. Amata is both a real estate developer and the owner and manager of rental real estate. Amata is retiring and is going to sell both the land he is holding for future development and the rental properties he owns. Straight-line depreciation was used to depreciate the rental real estate. The rental properties will be sold at a substantial loss, and the development property will be sold at a substantial gain. What is the nature of these gains and losses?

Research Problem 4. During 1996, Honest John's Auto Sales, a dealer in new and used cars, sold some new cars, some used cars, some company cars (used in the business to run errands, etc.), and some demonstrators. Since Honest John's is a dealer, can any of these sales be considered sales of § 1231 assets?

Partial list of research aids:
§ 1231(b).
Latimer-Looney Chevrolet, Inc., 19 T.C. 120 (1952), *acq*.

P•A•R•T

VI

Accounting Periods, Accounting Methods, and Deferred Compensation

Part VI provides a more comprehensive examination of the accounting periods and accounting methods that were introduced in Part II. A discussion of special accounting methods is also included. Part VI concludes with an analysis of the tax consequences of deferred compensation transactions.

CHAPTER

18

ACCOUNTING PERIODS AND METHODS

LEARNING OBJECTIVES

After completing Chapter 18, you should be able to:

1. Understand the relevance of the accounting period concept, the different types of accounting periods, and the limitations on their use.
2. Apply the cash method, accrual method, and hybrid method of accounting.
3. Utilize the procedure for changing accounting methods.
4. Determine when the installment method of accounting can be utilized and apply the related calculation techniques.
5. Understand the alternative methods of accounting for long-term contracts (the completed contract method and the percentage of completion method) including the limitations on the use of the completed contract method.
6. Know when accounting for inventories must occur, recognize the types of costs that must be included in inventories, and apply the LIFO method.
7. Identify tax planning opportunities related to accounting periods and accounting methods.

OUTLINE

Tax practitioners must deal with the issue of *when* particular items of income and expense are recognized as well as the basic issue of *whether* the items are includible in taxable income. Earlier chapters discussed the types of income subject to tax (gross income and exclusions) and allowable deductions (the *whether* issue).[1] This chapter focuses on the related issue of the periods in which income and deductions are reported (the *when* issue). Generally, a taxpayer's income and deductions must be assigned to particular 12-month periods—calendar years or fiscal years.

TAX IN THE NEWS

Acceleration of Income

In 1993, the *Wall Street Journal* and various other print and broadcast news sources reported that Hillary Rodham Clinton had the opportunity to receive compensation income in 1992 or 1993. She chose to accelerate the income into 1992. This appears to be at variance with the normal tax planning mode of deferring the reporting of income and accelerating the reporting of deductions.

One possible explanation for reporting the income in 1992 rather than in 1993 is that the family's taxable income was expected to be greater in 1993 than in 1992. However, while the President earns substantially more as President of the United States than as the Governor of Arkansas, the First Lady earns substantially less than she did as a partner in an Arkansas law firm.

Another possible explanation is the expectation that the Revenue Reconciliation Act of 1993 with its retroactive increase in tax rates would be passed by Congress. In any event, the First Lady followed sound tax advice in accelerating the income into 1992.

[1] See Chapters 4, 5, and 6.

Income and deductions are placed within particular years through the use of tax accounting methods. The basic accounting methods are the cash method, accrual method, and hybrid method. Other special purpose methods, such as the installment method and the methods used for long-term construction contracts, are available for specific circumstances or types of transactions.

Over the long run, the accounting period used by a taxpayer will not affect the aggregate amount of reported taxable income. However, taxable income for any particular year may vary significantly due to the use of a particular reporting period. Also, through the choice of accounting methods or accounting periods, it is possible to postpone the recognition of taxable income and to enjoy the benefits from deferring the related tax. This chapter discusses the taxpayer's alternatives for accounting periods and accounting methods.

Accounting Periods

IN GENERAL

1 Learning Objective
Understand the relevance of the accounting period concept, the different types of accounting periods, and the limitations on their use.

A taxpayer who keeps adequate books and records may be permitted to elect a **fiscal year,** a 12-month period ending on the *last day* of a month other than December, for the **accounting period.** Otherwise, a *calendar year* must be used.[2] Frequently, corporations can satisfy the record-keeping requirements and elect to use a fiscal year.[3] Often the fiscal year conforms to a natural business year (e.g., a summer resort's fiscal year may end on September 30, after the close of the season). Individuals seldom use a fiscal year because they do not maintain the necessary books and records and because complications can arise as a result of changes in the tax law (e.g., often the transition rules and effective dates differ for fiscal year taxpayers).

Generally, a taxable year may not exceed 12 calendar months. However, if certain requirements are met, a taxpayer may elect to use an annual period that varies from 52 to 53 weeks.[4] In that case, the year-end must be on the same day of the week (e.g., the Tuesday falling closest to October 31 or the last Tuesday in October). The day of the week selected for ending the year will depend upon business considerations. For example, a retail business that is not open on Sundays may end its tax year on a Sunday so that it can take an inventory without interrupting business operations.

Example 1

Wade is in the business of selling farm supplies. His natural business year terminates at the end of October with the completion of harvesting. At the end of the fiscal year, Wade must take an inventory, which is most easily accomplished on a Tuesday. Therefore, Wade could adopt a 52–53 week tax year ending on the Tuesday closest to October 31. If Wade selects this method, the year-end date may fall in the following month if that Tuesday is closer to October 31. The tax year ending in 1996 will contain 52 weeks beginning on Wednesday, November 1, 1995, and ending on Tuesday, October 29, 1996. The tax year ending in 1997 will have 52 weeks beginning on Wednesday, October 30, 1996, and ending on Tuesday, October 28, 1997. ▼

---

[2] § 441(c) and Reg. § 1.441–1(b)(1)(ii).
[3] Reg. § 1.441–1(e)(2).
[4] § 441(f).

SPECIFIC PROVISIONS FOR PARTNERSHIPS, S CORPORATIONS, AND PERSONAL SERVICE CORPORATIONS

Partnerships and S Corporations. When a partner's tax year and the partnership's tax year differ, the partner will enjoy a deferral of income. This results because the partner reports his or her share of the partnership's income and deductions for the partnership's tax year ending within or with the partner's tax year.[5] For example, if the tax year of the partnership ends on January 31, a calendar year partner will not report partnership profits for the first 11 months of the partnership tax year until the following year. Therefore, partnerships are subject to special tax year requirements.

In general, the partnership tax year must be the same as the tax year of the majority interest partners. The **majority interest partners** are the partners who own a greater than 50 percent interest in the partnership capital and profits. If the majority owners do not have the same tax year, the partnership must adopt the same tax year as its principal partners. A **principal partner** is a partner with a 5 percent or more interest in the partnership capital or profits.[6]

EXAMPLE 2

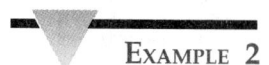

The RST Partnership is owned equally by Rose Corporation, Silver Corporation, and Tom. The partners have the following tax years.

	Partner's Tax Year Ending
Rose	June 30
Silver	June 30
Tom	December 31

The partnership's tax year must end on June 30. If Silver Corporation's as well as Tom's year ended on December 31, the partnership would be required to adopt a calendar year. ▼

If the principal partners do not all have the same tax year and no majority of partners have the same tax year, the partnership must use a year that results in the *least aggregate deferral* of income.[7] Under the **least aggregate deferral method,** the different tax years of the principal partners are tested to determine which produces the least aggregate deferral. This is calculated by first multiplying the combined percentages of the principal partners with the same tax year by the months of deferral for the test year. Once this is done for each set of principal partners with the same tax year, the resulting products are summed to produce the aggregate deferral. After calculating the aggregate deferral for each of the test years, the test year with the smallest summation (the least aggregate deferral) is the tax year for the partnership.

EXAMPLE 3

The DE Partnership is owned equally by Diane and Emily. Diane's fiscal year ends on March 31, and Emily's fiscal year ends on August 31. The partnership must use the partner's fiscal year that will result in the least aggregate deferral of income. Therefore, the fiscal years ending March 31 and August 31 must both be tested.

5 Reg. § 1.706–1(a).

6 §§ 706(b)(1)(B) and 706(b)(3).

7 Temp.Reg. § 1.706–1T(a)(2).

Test for Fiscal Year Ending March 31

Partner	Year Ends	Profit %	Months of Deferral	Product
Diane	3–31	50	0	0
Emily	8–31	50	5	2.5
Aggregate deferral months				2.5

Thus, with a year ending March 31, Emily would be able to defer her half of the income for five months. That is, Emily's share of the partnership income for the fiscal year ending March 31, 1997, would not be included in her income until August 31, 1997.

Test for Fiscal Year Ending August 31

Partner	Year Ends	Profit %	Months of Deferral	Product
Diane	3–31	50	7	3.5
Emily	8–31	50	0	0
Aggregate deferral months				3.5

Thus, with a year ending August 31, Diane would be able to defer her half of the income for seven months. That is, Diane's share of the partnership income for the fiscal year ending August 31, 1997, would not be included in her income until March 31, 1998.

The year ending March 31 must be used because it results in the least aggregate deferral of income. ▼

Generally, S corporations must adopt a calendar year.[8] However, partnerships and S corporations may *elect* an otherwise *impermissible year* under any of the following conditions:

- A business purpose for the year can be demonstrated.[9]
- The partnership's or S corporation's year results in a deferral of not more than three months' income, and the entity agrees to make required tax payments.[10]
- The entity retains the same year as was used for the fiscal year ending in 1987, provided the entity agrees to make required tax payments.

Business Purpose. The only business purpose for a fiscal year that the IRS has acknowledged is the need to conform the tax year to the natural business year of a business.[11] Generally, only seasonal businesses have a natural business year. For example, the natural business year for a department store may end on January 31, after Christmas returns have been processed and clearance sales have been completed.

Required Tax Payments. Under the required payments system, tax payments are due from a fiscal year partnership or S corporation by April 15 of each tax

[8] §§ 1378(a) and (b).

[9] §§ 706(b)(1)(C) and 1378(b)(2).

[10] § 444.

[11] Rev.Rul. 87–57, 1987–2 C.B. 117.

year.[12] The amount due is computed by applying the highest individual tax rate plus 1 percent to an estimate of the deferral period income. The deferral period runs from the close of the fiscal year to the end of the calendar year. Estimated income for this period is based on the average monthly earnings for the previous fiscal year. The amount due is reduced by the amount of required tax payments for the previous year.[13]

EXAMPLE 4

Brown, Inc., an S corporation, elected a fiscal year ending September 30. Bob is the only shareholder. For the fiscal year ending September 30, 1996, Brown earned $100,000. The required tax payment for the previous year was $5,000. The corporation must pay $5,150 by April 15, 1997, calculated as follows:

$$(\$100{,}000 \times 3/12 \times 40.6\%^*) - \$5{,}000 = \$5{,}150$$

*Maximum § 1 rate of 39.6% + 1%. ▼

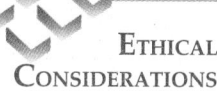

ETHICAL CONSIDERATIONS

Required Tax Years

Before 1987, partnerships could generally use a fiscal year ending September 30, and S corporations could use any fiscal year. With this latitude, accountants often recommended that their partnership and S corporation clients not use a calendar year. This enabled the accountants to spread their work throughout the year and created a tax deferral for the clients.

Members of the accounting profession argued vociferously against the calendar year requirement that was included in the Tax Reform Act of 1986. The choice Congress had to make was whether some groups should be allowed to benefit (i.e., the accountants and their clients) at the expense of the rest of the general public. Of course, the accounting profession viewed the choices differently: Should some groups be burdened (i.e., the accounting profession) for little benefit to the remaining taxpayers?

The compromise reached was the required payments scheme, whereby the burden was lifted from the accounting profession without the clients enjoying tax deferrals. Was this an acceptable compromise?

Personal Service Corporations. A **personal service corporation (PSC)** is a corporation whose shareholder-employees provide personal services (e.g., medical, dental, legal, accounting, engineering, actuarial, consulting, or performing arts). Generally, a PSC must use a calendar year.[14] However, a PSC can *elect* a fiscal year under any of the following conditions:

- A business purpose for the year can be demonstrated.
- The PSC year results in a deferral of not more than three months' income, the corporation pays the shareholder-employee's salary during the portion of the calendar year after the close of the fiscal year, and the salary for that period is at least proportionate to the shareholder-employee's salary received for the preceding fiscal year.[15]
- The PSC retains the same year it used for the fiscal year ending in 1987, provided it satisfies the latter two requirements in the preceding option.

[12] §§ 444(c) and 7519. No payment is required if the calculated amount is $500 or less.

[13] § 7519(b).

[14] § 441(i).

[15] §§ 444 and 280H.

EXAMPLE 5 Nancy's corporation paid Nancy a salary of $120,000 during its fiscal year ending September 30, 1996. The corporation cannot satisfy the business purpose test for a fiscal year. The corporation can continue to use its fiscal year without any negative tax effects, provided Nancy receives at least $30,000 (3 months/12 months × $120,000) as salary during the period October 1 through December 31, 1996. ▼

If the salary test is not satisfied, the PSC can retain the fiscal year, but the corporation's deduction for salary for the fiscal year is limited to the following:

$$A + A(F/N)$$

Where A = Amount paid after the close of the fiscal year

F = Number of months in fiscal year minus number of months from the end of the fiscal year to the end of the ongoing calendar year

N = Number of months from the end of the fiscal year to the end of the ongoing calendar year

EXAMPLE 6 Assume the corporation in the previous example paid Nancy $10,000 of salary during the period October 1 through December 31, 1996. The deduction for Nancy's salary for the corporation's fiscal year ending September 30, 1997, is thus limited to $40,000 calculated as follows:

$$\$10{,}000 + \left[\$10{,}000\left(\frac{12-3}{3}\right)\right] = \$10{,}000 + \$30{,}000 = \$40{,}000$$

▼

MAKING THE ELECTION

A taxpayer elects to use a calendar or fiscal year by the timely filing of his or her initial tax return. For all subsequent years, the taxpayer must use this same period unless approval for change is obtained from the IRS.[16]

CHANGES IN THE ACCOUNTING PERIOD

A taxpayer must obtain consent from the IRS before changing the tax year.[17] This power to approve or not to approve a change is significant in that it permits the IRS to issue authoritative administrative guidelines that must be met by taxpayers who wish to change their accounting period. An application for permission to change tax years must be made on Form 1128, Application for Change in Accounting Period. The application must be filed on or before the fifteenth day of the second calendar month following the close of the short period that results from the change in accounting period.[18]

EXAMPLE 7 Beginning in 1996, Gold Corporation, a calendar year taxpayer, would like to switch to a fiscal year ending March 31. The corporation must file Form 1128 by May 15, 1996. ▼

IRS Requirements. The IRS will not grant permission for the change unless the taxpayer can establish a substantial business purpose for the request. One substantial business purpose is to change to a tax year that coincides with the *natural business year* (the completion of an annual business cycle). The IRS applies

[16] Reg. §§ 1.441–1(b)(3) and 1.441–1(b)(4).

[17] § 442. Under certain conditions, corporations are allowed to change tax years without obtaining IRS approval. See Reg. § 1.442–1(c)(1).

[18] Reg. § 1.442–1(b)(1). In Example 7, the first period after the change in accounting period (January 1, 1996 through March 31, 1996) is less than a 12-month period and is referred to as a *short period*.

an objective gross receipts test to determine if the entity has a natural business year. At least 25 percent of the entity's gross receipts for the 12-month period must be realized in the final 2 months of the 12-month period for three consecutive years.[19]

EXAMPLE 8

A Virginia Beach motel had gross receipts as follows:

	1994	1995	1996
July–August receipts	$ 300,000	$250,000	$ 325,000
September 1–August 31 receipts	1,000,000	900,000	1,250,000
Receipts for 2 months divided by receipts for 12 months	30.0%	27.8%	26.0%

Since it satisfies the natural business year test, the motel will be allowed to use a fiscal year ending August 31. ▼

The IRS usually establishes certain conditions that the taxpayer must accept if the approval for change is to be granted. In particular, if the taxpayer has a net operating loss for the short period, the IRS may require that the loss be carried forward and allocated equally over the 6 following years.[20] As you may recall (refer to Chapter 7), net operating losses are ordinarily carried back for 3 years and forward for 15 years.

EXAMPLE 9

Parrot Corporation changed from a calendar year to a fiscal year ending September 30. The short-period return for the nine months ending September 30, 1996, reflected a $60,000 net operating loss. The corporation had taxable income for 1993, 1994, and 1995. As a condition for granting approval, the IRS requires Parrot to allocate the $60,000 loss over the next six years, rather than carrying the loss back to the three preceding years (the usual order for applying a net operating loss). Thus, Parrot Corporation will reduce its taxable income by $10,000 each year ending September 30, 1997, through September 30, 2002. ▼

TAXABLE PERIODS OF LESS THAN ONE YEAR

A **short taxable year** (or **short period**) is a period of less than 12 calendar months. A taxpayer may have a short year for (1) the first income tax return, (2) the final income tax return, or (3) a change in the tax year. If the short period results from a change in the taxpayer's annual accounting period, the taxable income for the period must be annualized. Due to the progressive tax rate structure, taxpayers could reap benefits from a short-period return if some adjustments were not required. Thus, the taxpayer is required to do the following:

1. Annualize the short-period income.

$$\text{Annualized income} = \text{Short-period income} \times \frac{12}{\text{Number of months in the short period}}$$

2. Compute the tax on the annualized income.

[19] Rev.Proc. 87–32, 1987–1 C.B. 131, and Rev.Rul. 87–57, 1987–2 C.B. 117.

[20] Rev.Proc. 85–16, 1985–1 C.B. 517.

3. Convert the tax on the annualized income to a short-period tax.

$$\text{Short-period tax} = \text{Tax on annualized income} \times \frac{\text{Number of months in the short period}}{12}$$

EXAMPLE 10

Gray Corporation obtained permission to change from a calendar year to a fiscal year ending September 30, beginning in 1996. For the short period January 1 through September 30, 1996, the corporation's taxable income was $48,000. The relevant tax rates and the resultant short-period tax are as follows:

Amount of Taxable Income	Tax Rates
$1–$50,000	15% of taxable income
$50,001–$75,000	$7,500 plus 25% of taxable income in excess of $50,000

Calculation of Short-Period Tax	
Annualized income	
($48,000 × 12⁄9) = $64,000	
Tax on annualized income	
$7,500 + .25($64,000 – $50,000) =	
$7,500 + $3,500 = $11,000	
Short-period tax = ($11,000 × 9⁄12) = $8,250	
Annualizing the income increased the tax by $1,050:	
Tax with annualizing	$ 8,250
Tax without annualizing (.15 × $48,000)	(7,200)
	$ 1,050

▼

Rather than annualize the short-period income, the taxpayer can (1) elect to calculate the tax for a 12-month period beginning on the first day of the short period and (2) convert the tax in (1) to a short-period tax as follows:[21]

$$\frac{\text{Taxable income for short period}}{\text{Taxable income for the 12-month period}} \times \text{Tax on the 12 months of income}$$

EXAMPLE 11

Assume Gray Corporation's taxable income for the calendar year 1996 was $60,000. The tax on the full 12 months of income would have been $10,000 [$7,500 + .25($60,000 – $50,000)]. The short-period tax would be $8,000 [($48,000/$60,000) × $10,000]. Thus, if the corporation utilized this option, the tax for the short period would be $8,000 (rather than $8,250, as calculated in Example 10). ▼

For individuals, annualizing requires some special adjustments:[22]

---

[21] § 443(b)(1).

[22] § 443(b)(2) and Reg. § 1.443–1(a)(2).

- Deductions must be itemized for the short period (the standard deduction is not allowed).
- Personal and dependency exemptions must be prorated.

Fortunately, individuals rarely change tax years.

MITIGATION OF THE ANNUAL ACCOUNTING PERIOD CONCEPT

Several provisions in the Code are designed to give the taxpayer relief from the seemingly harsh results that may be produced by the combined effects of an arbitrary accounting period and a progressive rate structure. For example, under the net operating loss carryback and carryover rules, a loss in one year can be carried back and offset against taxable income for the preceding 3 years. Unused net operating losses are then carried over for 15 years.[23] In addition, the Code provides special relief provisions for casualty losses pursuant to a disaster and for the reporting of insurance proceeds from destruction of crops.[24]

Restoration of Amounts Received under a Claim of Right.

The court-made **claim of right doctrine** applies when the taxpayer receives property as income and treats it as his or her own but a dispute arises over the taxpayer's rights to the income.[25] According to the doctrine, the taxpayer must include the amount as income in the year of receipt. The rationale for the doctrine is that the Federal government cannot await the resolution of all disputes before exacting a tax. As a corollary to the doctrine, if the taxpayer is later required to repay the funds, generally a deduction is allowed in the year of repayment.[26]

EXAMPLE 12

In 1996, Pedro received a $5,000 bonus computed as a percentage of profits. In 1997, Pedro's employer determined that the 1996 profits had been incorrectly computed, and Pedro had to refund the $5,000 in 1997. Pedro was required to include the $5,000 in his 1996 income, but he can claim a $5,000 deduction in 1997. ▼

In Example 12 the transactions were a wash; that is, the income and deduction were the same ($5,000). Suppose, however, Pedro was in the 36 percent tax bracket in 1996 but in the 15 percent bracket in 1997. Without some relief provision, the mistake would be costly to Pedro. He paid $1,800 tax in 1996 (.36 × $5,000), but the deduction reduced his tax liability in 1997 by only $750 (.15 × $5,000). The Code does provide the needed relief in such cases. Under § 1341, when income that has been taxed under the claim of right doctrine must later be repaid, in effect, the taxpayer gets to apply to the deduction the tax rate of the year that will produce the greatest tax benefit. Thus, in Example 12, the repayment in 1997 would reduce Pedro's 1997 tax liability by the greater 1996 rate (.36) applied to the $5,000. However, relief is provided only in cases where the tax is significantly different; that is, when the deduction for the amount previously included in income exceeds $3,000.

[23] § 172. Refer to Chapter 7.

[24] §§ 165(i) and 451(d). Refer to Chapter 7.

[25] *North American Consolidated Oil Co. v. Burnet,* 3 USTC ¶943, 11 AFTR 16, 52 S.Ct. 613 (USSC, 1932).

[26] *U.S. v. Lewis,* 51–1 USTC ¶9211, 40 AFTR 258, 71 S.Ct. 522 (USSC, 1951).

ACCOUNTING METHODS

PERMISSIBLE METHODS

2 LEARNING OBJECTIVE
Apply the cash method, accrual method, and hybrid method of accounting.

Section 446 requires the taxpayer to compute taxable income using the method of accounting regularly employed in keeping his or her books, provided the method clearly reflects income. The Code recognizes the following as generally permissible **accounting methods:**

- The cash receipts and disbursements method.
- The accrual method.
- A hybrid method (a combination of cash and accrual).

The Regulations refer to these alternatives as *overall methods* and add that the term *method of accounting* includes not only the overall method of accounting of the taxpayer but also the accounting treatment of any item.[27]

Generally, any of the three methods of accounting may be used if the method is consistently employed and clearly reflects income. However, the taxpayer is required to use the accrual method for sales and costs of goods sold if inventories are an income-producing factor to the business.[28] Other situations in which the accrual method is required are discussed later. Special methods are also permitted for installment sales, long-term construction contracts, and farmers.

A taxpayer who has more than one trade or business may use a different method of accounting for each trade or business activity.[29] Furthermore, a different method of accounting may be used to determine income from a trade or business than is used to compute nonbusiness items of income and deductions.[30]

EXAMPLE 13

Linda operates a grocery store and owns stock and bonds. The sales and cost of goods sold from the grocery store must be computed by the accrual method because inventories are material. However, Linda can report her dividends and interest under the cash method. ▼

The Code grants the IRS broad powers to determine whether the taxpayer's accounting method *clearly reflects income.* Thus, if the method employed does not clearly reflect income, the IRS has the power to prescribe the method to be used by the taxpayer.[31]

CASH RECEIPTS AND DISBURSEMENTS METHOD—CASH BASIS

Most individuals and many businesses use the cash basis to report income and deductions. The popularity of this method can largely be attributed to its simplicity and flexibility.

Under the **cash method,** income is not recognized until the taxpayer actually receives, or constructively receives, cash or its equivalent. Cash is constructively received if it is available to the taxpayer.[32] Deductions are generally permitted in the year of payment. Thus, year-end accounts receivable, accounts payable, and accrued income and deductions are not included in the determination of taxable income.

27 Reg. § 1.446–1(a)(1).
28 Reg. § 1.446–1(a)(4)(i).
29 § 446(d).
30 Reg. § 1.446–1(c)(1)(iv)(b).
31 § 446(b).
32 Reg. § 1.451–1(a). Refer to Chapter 4 for a discussion of constructive receipt.

TAX IN THE NEWS

The Cash Basis Constructive Receipt Doctrine Requires Factual Inquiry

Julian Block recounted the story of Beatrice Davis (T.C.Memo. 78–012), a cash basis taxpayer who was able to refute the IRS's argument that she was in constructive receipt of a large severance bonus from her former employer. Ms. Davis's former employer had previously told her that she would not receive the severance pay until early in the following year. However, the former employer sent the check earlier than expected, and the post office attempted to deliver the certified letter on December 31. Ms. Davis was not at home, but a notice of attempted delivery was left at her door. She arrived home after the post office closed and did not open the notice until January 2 of the following year because she thought it was a notice of rent increase by her landlord. On January 2, she went to the post office and claimed her check for $17,000.

The IRS contended that Ms. Davis constructively received the check on December 31, when it was made available to her. The Tax Court disagreed, concluding that although the former employer had committed the funds as of December 31, Ms. Davis did not have notice until January of the following year. This was not a case of Ms. Davis unilaterally deferring the receipt of the income. Therefore, she did not constructively receive the bonus income in December.

SOURCE: Information from "Constructive Hints on Receipt of Income," *Chicago Tribune*, December 11, 1994, p. C10 reprinted by permission: Tribune Media services.

In many cases, a taxpayer using the cash method can choose the year in which a deduction is claimed simply by postponing or accelerating the payment of expenses. For fixed assets, however, the cash basis taxpayer claims deductions through depreciation or amortization, the same as an accrual basis taxpayer does. In addition, prepaid expenses must be capitalized and amortized if the life of the asset extends substantially beyond the end of the tax year.[33] Most courts have applied the one-year rule (**one-year rule for prepaid expenses**) to determine whether capitalization and amortization are required. According to this rule, capitalization is required only if the asset has a life that extends beyond the tax year following the year of payment.[34]

Restrictions on Use of the Cash Method. Using the cash method to measure income from a merchandising or manufacturing operation would often yield a distorted picture of the results of operations. Income for the period would largely be a function of when payments were made for goods or materials. Thus, the Regulations prohibit the use of the cash method (and require the accrual method) to measure sales and cost of goods sold if inventories are material to the business.[35]

The prohibition on the use of the cash method if inventories are material and the rules regarding prepaid expenses (discussed above) are intended to assure that annual income is clearly reflected. However, certain taxpayers may not use the

[33] Reg. § 1.461–1(a)(1).

[34] *Zaninovich v. Comm.*, 80–1 USTC ¶9342, 45 AFTR2d 80–1442, 616 F.2d 429 (CA–9, 1980), *rev'g* 69 T.C. 605 (1978). Refer to Chapter 6 for further discussion of the one-year rule.

[35] Reg. § 1.446–1(a)(4)(i).

cash method of accounting for Federal income tax purposes regardless of whether inventories are material. The accrual basis must be used to report the income earned by (1) a corporation (other than an S corporation), (2) a partnership with a corporate partner, and (3) a tax shelter.[36] This accrual basis requirement has three exceptions:[37]

- A farming business.
- A qualified personal service corporation (e.g., a corporation performing services in health, law, engineering, architecture, accounting, actuarial science, performing arts, or consulting).
- An entity that is not a tax shelter whose average annual gross receipts for the most recent three-year period are $5 million or less.

Farming. Although inventories are material to farming operations, the IRS long ago created an exception to the general rule that allows farmers to use the cash method of accounting.[38] The purpose of the exception is to relieve the small farmer from the bookkeeping burden of accrual accounting. However, tax shelter promoters recognized, for example, that by deducting the costs of a crop in one tax year and harvesting the crop in a later year, income could be deferred from tax. Thus, §§ 447 and 464 were enacted to prevent certain farming corporations and limited partnerships (farming syndicates) from using the cash method.[39]

Farmers who are allowed to use the cash method of accounting must nevertheless capitalize their costs of raising trees when the preproduction period is greater than two years.[40] Thus, a cash basis apple farmer must capitalize the cost of raising trees until the trees produce in merchantable quantities. Cash basis farmers can elect not to capitalize these costs, but if the election is made, the alternative depreciation system (refer to Chapter 8) must be used for all farming property.

Generally, the cost of purchasing an animal must be capitalized. However, the cash basis farmer's cost of raising the animal can be expensed.[41]

ACCRUAL METHOD

All Events Test for Income. Under the **accrual method,** an item is generally included in gross income for the year in which it is earned, regardless of when the income is collected. An item of income is earned when (1) all the events have occurred to fix the taxpayer's right to receive the income and (2) the amount of income (the amount the taxpayer has a right to receive) can be determined with reasonable accuracy.[42]

EXAMPLE 14

Andre, a calendar year taxpayer who uses the accrual basis of accounting, was to receive a bonus equal to 6% of Blue Corporation's net income for its fiscal year ending each June 30. For the fiscal year ending June 30, 1996, Blue Corporation had net income of $240,000, and for the six months ending December 31, 1996, the corporation's net income was $150,000. Andre will report $14,400 (.06 × $240,000) for 1996 because his rights to the amount became fixed when Blue Corporation's year closed. However, Andre would not accrue income

[36] § 448(a). For this purpose, the hybrid method of accounting is considered the same as the cash method.

[37] § 448(b).

[38] Reg. § 1.471–6(a).

[39] Section 447(c) contains counterexceptions that allow certain closely held corporations to use the cash method. See also § 464(c).

[40] § 263A(d).

[41] Reg. § 1.162–12(a).

[42] Reg. § 1.451–1(a). Refer to Chapter 4 for further discussion of the accrual basis.

based on the corporation's profits for the last six months of 1996 since his right to the income does not accrue until the close of the corporation's tax year. ▼

In a situation where the accrual basis taxpayer's right to income is being contested and the income has not yet been collected, generally no income is recognized until the dispute has been settled.[43] Before the settlement, "all of the events have not occurred that fix the right to receive the income."

All Events and Economic Performance Tests for Deductions. An **all events test** applies to accrual basis deductions. A deduction cannot be claimed until (1) all the events have occurred to create the taxpayer's liability and (2) the amount of the liability can be determined with reasonable accuracy.[44] Once these requirements are satisfied, the deduction will be permitted only if economic performance has occurred.[45]

The **economic performance test** addresses situations in which the taxpayer has either of the following obligations:

1. To pay for services or property to be provided in the future.
2. To provide services or property (other than money) in the future.

When services or property are to be provided to the taxpayer in the future (situation 1), economic performance occurs when the property or services are actually provided by the other party.

EXAMPLE 15

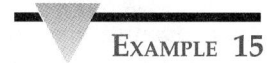

An accrual basis calendar year taxpayer, JAB, Inc., promoted a boxing match held in the company's arena on December 31, 1996. CLN, Inc., had contracted to clean the arena for $5,000, but did not actually perform the work until January 1, 1997. JAB, Inc., did not pay the $5,000 until 1998. Although financial accounting would require JAB, Inc., to accrue the $5,000 cleaning expense in 1996 to match the revenues from the fight, the economic performance test was not satisfied until 1997, when CLN, Inc., performed the service. Thus, JAB, Inc., must deduct the expense in 1997. ▼

If the taxpayer is obligated to provide property or services (situation 2), economic performance occurs (and thus the deduction is allowed) in the year the taxpayer provides the property or services.

EXAMPLE 16

Copper Corporation, an accrual basis taxpayer, is in the strip mining business. According to the contract with the landowner, the company must reclaim the land. The estimated cost of reclaiming land mined in 1996 was $500,000, but the land was not actually reclaimed until 1998. The all events test was satisfied in 1996. The obligation existed, and the amount of the liability could be determined with reasonable accuracy. However, the economic performance test was not satisfied until 1998. Therefore, the deduction is not allowed until 1998.[46] ▼

The economic performance test is waived, and thus year-end accruals can be deducted, if all the following conditions (*recurring item exception*) are met:

- The obligation exists and the amount of the liability can be reasonably estimated.
- Economic performance occurs within a reasonable period (but not later than 8½ months after the close of the taxable year).

[43] *Burnet v. Sanford & Brooks Co.*, 2 USTC ¶636, 9 AFTR 603, 51 S.Ct. 150 (USSC, 1931).

[44] § 461(h)(4).

[45] § 461(h).

[46] See § 468 for an elective method for reporting reclamation costs.

- The item is recurring in nature and is treated consistently by the taxpayer.
- Either the accrued item is not material, or accruing it results in a better matching of revenues and expenses.

EXAMPLE 17

Green Corporation often sells goods that are on hand but cannot be shipped for another week. Thus, the sales account usually includes revenues for some items that have not been shipped at year-end. Green Corporation is obligated to pay shipping costs. Although the company's obligation for shipping costs can be determined with reasonable accuracy, economic performance is not satisfied until Green (or its agent) actually delivers the goods. However, accruing shipping costs on sold items will better match expenses with revenues for the period. Therefore, the company should be allowed to accrue the shipping costs on items sold but not shipped at year-end. ▼

The economic performance test as set forth in the Code does not address all possible accrued expenses. That is, in some cases, the taxpayer incurs cost even though no property or services were received. In these instances, according to Regulations, economic performance generally is not satisfied until the liability is paid. The following liabilities are cases in which payment is generally the only means of satisfying economic performance:[47]

1. Workers' compensation.
2. Torts.
3. Breach of contract.
4. Violation of law.
5. Rebates and refunds.
6. Awards, prizes, and jackpots.
7. Insurance, warranty, and service contracts.[48]
8. Taxes.

EXAMPLE 18

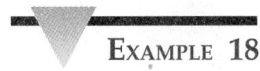

Yellow Corporation sold defective merchandise that injured a customer. Yellow admitted liability in 1996, but did not pay the claim until January 1997. The customer's tort claim cannot be deducted until it is paid. ▼

However, items (5) through (8) above are eligible for the aforementioned recurring item exception.

EXAMPLE 19

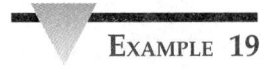

Pelican Corporation filed its 1996 state income tax return in March 1997. At the time the return was filed, Pelican was required to pay an additional $5,000. The state taxes are eligible for the recurring item exception. Thus, the $5,000 of state income taxes can be deducted on the corporation's 1996 Federal tax return. The deduction is allowed because all the events had occurred to fix the liability as of the end of 1996, the payment was made within 8½ months after the end of the tax year, the item is recurring in nature, and allowing the deduction in 1996 produces a good matching of revenues and expenses. ▼

Reserves. Generally, the all events and economic performance tests will prevent the use of reserves (e.g., for product warranty expense) frequently used in financial accounting to match expenses with revenues. However, small banks are allowed to use a bad debt reserve.[49] Furthermore, an accrual basis taxpayer in a

[47] Reg. §§ 1.461–4(g)(2)–(6) and 1.461–5(c).

[48] This item applies to contracts the taxpayer enters into for his or her own protection, rather than the taxpayer's liability as insurer, warrantor, or service provider.

[49] § 585.

service business is permitted to not accrue revenue that appears uncollectible based on experience. In effect, this approach indirectly allows a reserve.[50]

ETHICAL CONSIDERATIONS

Prepaid Income and Deductions

Your client, Hometown Motors Company, is a new automobile dealer and reports its taxable income by the accrual method. The company also sells service contracts on the new automobiles. A customer who buys the contract can have the work performed by any authorized dealer. If someone other than Hometown does the work, the bill is nevertheless paid by Hometown. Typically, a contract sells for $1,000 and provides protection for five years. When Hometown sells the contract to the customer, the company also purchases an insurance contract (for $800) that reimburses Hometown for any cost it incurs under the service contract. In addition, if Hometown actually performs the service, the insurance company pays Hometown its normal charge.

Hometown is caught between two tax accounting rules. Under the rule for prepaid income (discussed in Chapter 4), the entire $1,000 revenue from a service contract must be included in gross income for the year the contract is sold. On the other hand, the cost of the insurance contract must be amortized over its five-year life ($800/5 years = $160 per year). Thus, in the year a contract is sold, Hometown must recognize $840 ($1,000 – $160) of income when the company has received a net amount of only $200 ($1,000 – $800).

Should you suggest that the terms of the service and insurance contracts be changed so that (1) Hometown sells the insurance to the customer and receives a $200 commission, and (2) Hometown agrees to pay the customer if the insurance company goes out of existence or is otherwise unable to pay when the customer requires service? How do you respond if Hometown rejects this proposal, but suggests that since the two forms of transactions produce basically the same economic results, you account for the current transactions as you suggested in your proposal?

HYBRID METHOD

A **hybrid method** of accounting involves the use of more than one method. For example, a taxpayer who uses the accrual basis to report sales and cost of goods sold but uses the cash basis to report other items of income and expense is employing a hybrid method. The Code permits the use of a hybrid method provided the taxpayer's income is clearly reflected.[51] A taxpayer who uses the accrual method for business expenses must also use the accrual method for business income (a cash method may not be used for income items if the taxpayer's expenses are accounted for under the accrual method).

It may be preferable for a business that is required to report sales and cost of goods sold on the accrual method to report other items of income and expense under the cash method. The cash method permits greater flexibility in the timing of income and expense recognition.

[50] § 448(d)(5).

[51] § 446(c).

3 LEARNING OBJECTIVE
Utilize the procedure for changing accounting methods.

CHANGE OF METHOD

The taxpayer, in effect, makes an election to use a particular accounting method when an initial tax return is filed using that method. If a subsequent change in method is desired, the taxpayer must obtain the permission of the IRS. The request for change is made on Form 3115, Application for Change in Accounting Method. Generally, the form must be filed within the first 180 days of the taxable year of the desired change.[52]

As previously mentioned, the term *accounting method* encompasses not only the overall accounting method used by the taxpayer (the cash or accrual method) but also the treatment of any material item of income or deduction.[53] Thus, a change in the method of deducting property taxes from a cash basis to an accrual basis that results in a deduction for taxes in a different year constitutes a change in an accounting method. Another example of accounting method change is a change involving the method or basis used in the valuation of inventories. However, a change in treatment resulting from a change in underlying facts does not constitute a change in the taxpayer's method of accounting.[54] For example, a change in employment contracts so that an employee accrues one day of vacation pay for each month of service rather than 12 days of vacation pay for a full year of service is a change in the underlying facts and is therefore not an accounting method change.

Correction of an Error. A change in accounting method should be distinguished from the *correction of an error.* The taxpayer can correct an error (by filing amended returns) without permission, and the IRS can simply adjust the taxpayer's liability if an error is discovered on audit of the return. Some examples of errors are incorrect postings, errors in the calculation of tax liability or tax credits, deductions of business expense items that are actually personal, and omissions of income and deductions.[55] Unless the taxpayer or the IRS corrects the error within the statute of limitations, the taxpayer's total lifetime taxable income will be overstated or understated by the amount of the error.

Change from an Incorrect Method. An *incorrect accounting method* is the consistent (year-after-year) use of an incorrect rule to report an item of income or expense. The incorrect accounting method generally will not affect the taxpayer's total lifetime income (unlike the error). That is, an incorrect method has a self-balancing mechanism. For example, deducting freight on inventory in the year the goods are purchased, rather than when the inventory is sold, is an incorrect accounting method. The total cost of goods sold over the life of the business is not affected, but the year-to-year income is incorrect.[56]

If a taxpayer is employing an incorrect method of accounting, permission must be obtained from the IRS to change to a correct method. An incorrect method is not treated as a mechanical error that can be corrected by merely filing an amended tax return.

The tax return preparer as well as the taxpayer will be subject to penalties if the tax return is prepared using an incorrect method of accounting and permission for a change to a correct method has not been requested.[57]

[52] Reg. § 1.446–1(e)(3). The deadline may be extended to within the first nine months of the year of the change if the taxpayer can show good cause for the delay in filing the request.

[53] Reg. § 1.446–1(a)(1).

[54] Reg. § 1.446–1(e)(2)(ii).

[55] Reg. § 1.446–1(e)(2)(ii)(b).

[56] But see *Korn Industries v. U.S.*, 76–1 USTC ¶9354, 37 AFTR2d 76–1228, 532 F.2d 1352 (Ct.Cls., 1976).

[57] § 446(f). See *West's Federal Taxation: Corporations, Partnerships, Estates, and Trusts,* Chapter 16.

ETHICAL CONSIDERATIONS

A Change in Accounting Method

Tom, a CPA, recently obtained a new client, the Egret Engineering Corporation (annual gross receipts of $2 million). The company's previous accountant had filed all returns by the accrual method of accounting, the same method that was used to prepare financial statements submitted when the company applied for a loan in its first year of operation. Tom recognizes that under the accrual method of accounting the company is paying tax on its accounts receivable, whereas under the cash method of accounting the income could be deferred until the cash is collected. In many cases, it takes the company three months to collect a receivable. Tom also recognizes that the IRS will not allow the corporation to change to the cash method.

Therefore, Tom is considering the following plan: A new corporation would be formed. Each shareholder in Egret would own the same percentage of stock in the new corporation. The key element of the plan is that the new corporation would elect the cash method of accounting. Egret would complete its contracts in progress, collect its receivables, and gradually be liquidated. Meanwhile all new business would be channeled into the new corporation. Evaluate Tom's plan.

Net Adjustments Due to Change in Accounting Method. In the year of a change in accounting method, some items of income and expense may have to be adjusted to prevent the change from distorting taxable income.

EXAMPLE 20

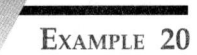

In 1996, White Corporation, with consent from the IRS, switched from the cash to the accrual basis for reporting sales and cost of goods sold. The corporation's accrual basis gross profit for the year was computed as follows:

Sales		$100,000
Beginning inventory	$ 15,000	
Purchases	60,000	
Less: Ending inventory	(10,000)	
Cost of goods sold		(65,000)
Gross profit		$ 35,000

At the end of the previous year, White Corporation had accounts receivable of $25,000 and accounts payable for merchandise of $34,000. The accounts receivable from the previous year in the amount of $25,000 were never included in gross income since White was on the cash basis and did not recognize the uncollected receivables. In the current year, the $25,000 was not included in the accrual basis sales since the sales were made in a prior year. Therefore, a $25,000 adjustment to income is required to prevent the receivables from being omitted from income.

The corollary of the failure to recognize a prior year's receivables is the failure to recognize a prior year's accounts payable. The beginning of the year's accounts payable was not included in the current or prior year's purchases. Thus, a deduction for the $34,000 was not taken in either year and is therefore included as an adjustment to income for the period of change.

An adjustment is also required to reflect the $15,000 beginning inventory that White deducted (due to the use of a cash method of accounting) in the previous year. In this instance, the cost of goods sold during the year of change was increased by the beginning inventory and resulted in a double deduction.

Concept Summary 18–1

Adjustment Periods for Voluntary Changes in Accounting Method

Change	Type of Adjustment	Allocation Period
Incorrect to correct method	Positive	Three years—year of change and the two succeeding years
Incorrect to correct method	Negative	Year of change
Correct to correct	Positive	Six years—year of change and the five succeeding years
Correct to correct	Negative	Six years—year of change and the five succeeding years

The net adjustment due to the change in accounting method is computed as follows:

Beginning inventory (deducted in prior and current year)	$ 15,000
Beginning accounts receivable (omitted from income)	25,000
Beginning accounts payable (omitted from deductions)	(34,000)
Net increase in taxable income	$ 6,000

▼

Disposition of the Net Adjustment. Generally, if the IRS *requires* the taxpayer to change an accounting method, the net adjustment is added to or subtracted from the income for the year of the change. In cases of positive (an increase in income) adjustments in excess of $3,000, the taxpayer is allowed to calculate the tax by spreading the adjustment over one or more previous years.[58]

To encourage taxpayers to *voluntarily* change from incorrect methods and to facilitate changes from one correct method to another, the IRS generally allows the taxpayer to spread the adjustment into future years. Assuming the taxpayer files a timely request for change (Form 3115), the allocation periods in Concept Summary 18–1 generally apply.[59]

Example 21 White Corporation in Example 20 voluntarily changed from an incorrect method (the cash basis was incorrect because inventories were material to the business) to a correct method. The company must add $2,000 (⅓ × $6,000 positive adjustment) to its 1996, 1997, and 1998 income. ▼

Special Accounting Methods

Generally, accrual basis taxpayers recognize income when goods are sold and shipped to the customer. Cash basis taxpayers generally recognize income from a sale on the collection of cash from the customer. The tax law provides special accounting methods for certain installment sales and long-term contracts. These special methods were enacted, in part, to assure that the tax will be due when the taxpayer is best able to pay the tax.

58 § 481(b).
59 Rev.Proc. 92–20, 1992–1 C.B. 301.

INSTALLMENT METHOD

4 LEARNING OBJECTIVE
Determine when the installment method of accounting can be utilized and apply the related calculation techniques.

Under the general rule for computing the gain or loss from the sale of property, the taxpayer recognizes the entire amount of gain or loss upon the sale or other disposition of the property.

EXAMPLE 22

Mark sells property to Fran for $10,000 cash plus Fran's note (fair market value and face amount of $90,000). Mark's basis for the property was $15,000. Gain or loss is computed under either the cash or accrual basis as follows:

Amount realized	
Cash down payment	$ 10,000
Note receivable	90,000
	$100,000
Basis in the property	(15,000)
Realized gain	$ 85,000

In Example 22, the general rule for recognizing gain or loss requires Mark to pay a substantial amount of tax on the gain in the year of sale even though he received only $10,000 cash. Congress enacted the installment sales provisions to prevent this sort of hardship by allowing the taxpayer to spread the gain from installment sales over the collection period. The installment method is a very important planning tool because of the tax deferral possibilities.

Eligibility and Calculations. The **installment method** applies to *gains* (but not losses) from the sale of property where the seller will receive at least one payment *after* the year of sale. For many years, practically all gains from the sale of property were eligible for the installment method. However, over the years, the Code has been amended to *deny* the use of the installment method for the following:[60]

- Gains on property held for sale in the ordinary course of business.
- Depreciation recapture under § 1245 or § 1250.
- Gains on stocks or securities traded on an established market.

As an exception to the first item, the installment method may be used to report gains from sales of the following:[61]

- Time-share units (e.g., the right to use real property for two weeks each year).
- Residential lots (if the seller is not to make any improvements).
- Any property used or produced in the trade or business of farming.

The Nonelective Aspect. Regardless of the taxpayer's method of accounting, as a general rule, eligible sales *must* be reported by the installment method.[62] A special election is required to report the gain by any other method of accounting (see the discussion in a subsequent section of this chapter).

Computing the Gain for the Period. The gain reported on each sale is computed by the following formula:

$$\frac{\text{Total gain}}{\text{Contract price}} \times \text{Payments received} = \text{Recognized gain}$$

[60] §§ 453(b), (i), and (l).
[61] § 453(l)(2).
[62] § 453(a).

The taxpayer must compute each variable as follows:

1. *Total gain* is the selling price reduced by selling expenses and the adjusted basis of the property. The selling price is the total consideration received by the seller, including notes receivable from the buyer and the seller's liabilities assumed by the buyer.
2. *Contract price* is the selling price less the seller's liabilities that are assumed by the buyer. Generally, the contract price is the amount, other than interest, the seller will receive from the purchaser.
3. *Payments received* are the collections on the contract price received in the tax year. This generally is equal to the cash received less the interest income collected for the period. If the buyer pays any of the seller's expenses, the seller regards the amount paid as a payment received.

EXAMPLE 23

The seller is not a dealer, and the facts are as follows:

Sales price		
Cash down payment	$ 1,000	
Seller's mortgage assumed	3,000	
Notes payable to the seller	13,000	$ 17,000
Selling expenses		(500)
Seller's basis		(10,000)
Total gain		$ 6,500

The contract price is $14,000 ($17,000 – $3,000). Assuming the $1,000 is the only payment in the year of sale, the recognized gain in that year is computed as follows:

$$\frac{\$6{,}500 \text{ (total gain)}}{\$14{,}000 \text{ (contract price)}} \times \$1{,}000 = \$464 \text{ (gain recognized in year of sale)}$$

If the sum of the seller's basis and selling expenses is less than the liabilities assumed by the buyer, the difference must be added to the contract price and to the payments (treated as *deemed payments*) received in the year of sale.[63] This adjustment to the contract price is required so that the ratio of total gain to contract price will not be greater than one. The adjustment also accelerates the reporting of income from the deemed payments.

EXAMPLE 24

Assume the same facts as in Example 23, except that the seller's basis in the property is only $2,000. The total gain, therefore, is $14,500 [$17,000 – ($2,000 + $500)]. Payments in the year of sale are $1,500 and are calculated as follows:

Down payment	$1,000
Excess of mortgage assumed over seller's basis and expenses ($3,000 – $2,000 – $500)	500
	$1,500

The contract price is $14,500 [$17,000 (selling price) – $3,000 (seller's mortgage assumed) + $500 (excess of mortgage assumed over seller's basis and selling expenses)]. The gain recognized in the year of sale is computed as follows:

$$\frac{\$14{,}500 \text{ (total gain)}}{\$14{,}500 \text{ (contract price)}} \times \$1{,}500 = \$1{,}500$$

[63] Temp.Reg. § 15a.453–1(b)(2)(iii).

In subsequent years, all amounts the seller collects on the note principal ($13,000) will be recognized gain ($13,000 × 100%). ▼

As previously discussed, gains attributable to ordinary income recapture under §§ 1245 and 1250 are *ineligible* for installment reporting. Therefore, the § 1245 or § 1250 gain realized must be recognized in the year of sale, and the installment sale gain is the remaining gain.

EXAMPLE 25

Olaf sold an apartment building for $50,000 cash and a $75,000 note due in two years. Olaf's basis in the property was $25,000, and he recaptured $40,000 ordinary income under § 1250.

Olaf's realized gain is $100,000 ($125,000 – $25,000), and the $40,000 recapture must be recognized in the year of sale. Of the $60,000 remaining § 1231 gain, $24,000 must be recognized in the year of sale:

$$\frac{\text{§ 1231 gain}}{\text{Contract price}} \times \text{Payments received} = \frac{\$125{,}000 - \$25{,}000 - \$40{,}000}{\$125{,}000} \times \$50{,}000$$

$$= \frac{\$60{,}000}{\$125{,}000} \times \$50{,}000 = \$24{,}000$$

The remaining realized gain of $36,000 ($60,000 – $24,000) will be recognized as the $75,000 note is collected. ▼

Imputed Interest. If a deferred payment contract for the sale of property with a selling price greater than $3,000 does not contain a reasonable interest rate, a reasonable rate is imputed.[64] The imputing of interest effectively restates the selling price of the property to equal the sum of the payments at the date of the sale and the discounted present value of the future payments. The difference between the present value of a future payment and the payment's face amount is taxed as interest income, as discussed in the following paragraphs. Thus, the **imputed interest** rules prevent sellers of capital assets from increasing the selling price to reflect the equivalent of unstated interest on deferred payments and thereby converting ordinary (interest) income into long-term capital gains. In addition, the imputed interest rules are important because they affect the timing of income recognition.

Generally, if the contract does not charge at least the Federal rate, interest will be imputed at the Federal rate. The Federal rate is the interest rate the Federal government pays on new borrowing and is published monthly by the IRS.[65]

As a general rule, the buyer and seller must account for interest on the accrual basis with semiannual compounding.[66] Requiring the use of the accrual basis assures that the seller's interest income and the buyer's interest expense are reported in the same tax year. Under pre-1984 law, the cash basis seller did not report interest income until it was actually collected, but an accrual basis buyer could deduct the interest as it accrued. The following example illustrates the calculation and amortization of imputed interest.

EXAMPLE 26

Peggy, a cash basis taxpayer, sold land on January 1, 1996, for $200,000 cash and $6 million due on December 31, 1997, with 5% interest payable December 31, 1996, and December 31,

[64] §§ 483 and 1274.

[65] § 1274(d)(1). There are three Federal rates: short-term (not over three years), mid-term (over three years but not over nine years), and long-term (over nine years).

[66] §§ 1274(a), 1273(a), and 1272(a).

1997. At the time of the sale, the Federal rate was 8% (compounded semiannually). Because Peggy did not charge at least the Federal rate, interest will be imputed at 8% (compounded semiannually).

Date	Payment	Present Value (at 8%) on 1/1/1996	Imputed Interest
12/31/1996	$ 300,000	$ 277,500	$ 22,500
12/31/1997	6,300,000	5,386,500	913,500
	$6,600,000	$5,664,000	$936,000

Thus, the selling price will be restated to $5,864,000 ($200,000 + $5,664,000) rather than $6,200,000 ($200,000 + $6,000,000), and Peggy will recognize interest income in accordance with the following amortization schedule:

	Beginning Balance	Interest Income (at 8%)*	Received	Ending Balance
1996	$5,664,000	$462,182	$ 300,000	$5,826,182
1997	5,826,182	473,818	6,300,000	-0-

*Compounded semiannually.

▼

Congress has created several exceptions regarding the rate at which interest is imputed and the method of accounting for the interest income and expense. The general rules and exceptions are summarized in Concept Summary 18–2.

Related-Party Sales of Nondepreciable Property. If the Code did not contain special rules, a taxpayer could make an installment sale of property to a related party (e.g., a family member) who would obtain a basis in the property equal to the purchase price (the fair market value of the property). Then, the purchasing family member could immediately sell the property to an unrelated party for cash with no recognized gain or loss (the amount realized would equal the basis). The related-party purchaser would not pay the installment note to the selling family member until a later year or years. The net result would be that the family has the cash, but no taxable gain is recognized until the intrafamily transfer of the cash (the purchasing family member makes payments on the installment note).

Under special rules designed to combat the scheme described above, the proceeds from the subsequent sale (the second sale) by the purchasing family member are treated as though they were used to pay the installment note due the selling family member (the first sale). As a result, the recognition of gain from the original sale between the related parties is accelerated.[67]

However, even with these special rules, Congress did not eliminate the benefits of all related-party installment sales.

[67] § 453(e).

CONCEPT SUMMARY 18–2

Interest on Installment Sales

	Imputed Interest Rate
General rule	Federal rate
Exceptions:	
• Principal amount not over $2.8 million.[1]	Lesser of Federal rate or 9%
• Sale of land (with a calendar year ceiling of $500,000) between family members (the seller's spouse, brothers, sisters, ancestors, or lineal descendants).[2]	Lesser of Federal rate or 6%

	Method of Accounting for Interest	
	Seller's Interest Income	Buyer's Interest Expense
General rule[3]	Accrual	Accrual
Exceptions:		
• Total payments under the contract are $250,000 or less.[4]	Taxpayer's overall method	Taxpayer's overall method
• Sale of a farm (sales price of $1 million or less).[5]	Taxpayer's overall method	Taxpayer's overall method
• Sale of a principal residence.[6]	Taxpayer's overall method	Taxpayer's overall method
• Sale for a note with a principal amount of not over $2 million, the seller is on the cash basis, the property sold is not inventory, and the buyer agrees to report expense by the cash method.[7]	Cash	Cash

[1] § 1274A. This amount is adjusted annually for inflation. For 1996, the amount is $3,622,500.
[2] §§ 1274(c)(3)(F) and 483(e).
[3] §§ 1274(a) and 1272(a)(3).
[4] §§ 1274(c)(3)(C) and 483.
[5] §§ 1274(c)(3)(A) and 483.
[6] §§ 1274(c)(3)(B) and 483.
[7] § 1274A(c). This amount is adjusted annually for inflation. For 1996, the amount is $2,587,500.

- Related parties include the first seller's brothers, sisters, ancestors, lineal descendants, controlled corporations, and partnerships, trusts, and estates in which the seller has an interest.[68]
- There is no acceleration if the second disposition occurs more than two years after the first sale.[69]

[68] § 453(f)(1), cross-referencing §§ 267(b) and 318(a). Although spouses are related parties, the exemption of gain between spouses (§ 1041) makes the second-disposition rules inapplicable when the first sale was between spouses.

[69] § 453(e)(2). But see § 453(e)(2)(B) for extensions of the two-year period.

Thus, if the taxpayer can sell the property to an unrelated party (not a related party) or patient family member, the intrafamily installment sale is still a powerful tax planning tool. Other exceptions also can be applied in some circumstances.[70]

ETHICAL CONSIDERATIONS

A Related-Party Installment Sale Has Unexpected Results

Amos has been in the farming business for over 40 years. Since he is nearing retirement age—although he will never retire—he would like to slow down. He decides to sell 300 acres of his land to his 26-year-old son, Chuck, for $465,000 so Chuck can go into the farming business. Amos's basis for the land is $50,000. Since Chuck does not have much equity and Amos would like to keep the financing of the land in the family, the sales contract calls for a $15,000 down payment and annual payments of $30,000 for 15 years plus interest at 8 percent. Amos anticipates Chuck's profit from the farm will be adequate to cover these payments and provide Chuck with a decent living.

Chuck makes the payment for the first year. Unfortunately, he then gets involved with some young people from a nearby city and develops a drug problem. To finance his drug dependency, 14 months after acquiring the farm, he sells it for $500,000 cash to a real estate developer who intends to build 1,000 tract houses on the land.

When Amos learns of this, he is furious. He disowns Chuck and vows never to speak to him again.

Now Amos's CPA tells him that he has another problem. The sale of the land by Chuck should be treated as if Chuck had paid Amos the remaining balance on the installment sale. The CPA explains to Amos that this result occurs because his original sale to Chuck was a related-party transaction. Amos finds this ridiculous and says he no longer has a son.

Who is correct, Amos or the CPA? Evaluate the equity of the related-party provision.

Related-Party Sales of Depreciable Property. The installment method cannot be used to report a gain on the sale of depreciable property to a controlled entity. The purpose of this rule is to prevent the seller from deferring gain (until collections are received) while the related purchaser is enjoying a stepped-up basis for depreciation purposes.[71]

The prohibition on the use of the installment method applies to sales between the taxpayer and a partnership or corporation in which the taxpayer holds a more-than-50 percent interest. Constructive ownership rules are used in applying the ownership test (e.g., the taxpayer is considered to own stock owned by a spouse and certain other family members).[72] However, if the taxpayer can establish that tax avoidance was not a principal purpose of the transaction, the installment method can be used to report the gain.

EXAMPLE 27

Ali purchased an apartment building from his controlled corporation, Emerald Corporation. Ali was short of cash at the time of the purchase (December 1996), but was to collect a large cash payment in January 1997. The agreement required Ali to pay the entire arm's length price in January 1997. Ali had good business reasons for acquiring the building. Emerald

[70] See §§ 453(e)(6) and (7).

[71] § 453(g).

[72] §§ 1239(b) and (c).

Corporation should be able to convince the IRS that tax avoidance was not a principal purpose for the installment sale because the tax benefits are not overwhelming. The corporation will report all of the gain in the year following the year of sale, and the building must be expensed over 27.5 years (the cost recovery period). ▼

DISPOSITION OF INSTALLMENT OBLIGATIONS

Generally, a taxpayer must recognize the deferred profit from an installment sale when the obligation is transferred to another party or otherwise relinquished. The rationale for accelerating the gain is that the deferral should continue for no longer than the taxpayer owns the installment obligation.[73]

The gift or cancellation of an installment note is treated as a taxable disposition by the donor. The amount realized from the cancellation is the face amount of the note if the parties (obligor and obligee) are related to each other.[74]

EXAMPLE 28

Liz cancels a note issued by Tina (Liz's daughter) that arose in connection with the sale of property. At the time of the cancellation, the note had a basis to Liz of $10,000, a face amount of $25,000, and a fair market value of $20,000. Presuming the initial sale by Liz qualified as an installment sale, the cancellation results in gain of $15,000 ($25,000 – $10,000) to Liz. ▼

Certain exceptions to the recognition of gain provisions are provided for transfers of installment obligations pursuant to tax-free incorporations under § 351, contributions of capital to a partnership, certain corporate liquidations, transfers due to the taxpayer's death, and transfers between spouses or incident to divorce.[75] In such instances, the deferred profit is merely shifted to the transferee, who is responsible for the payment of tax on the subsequent collections of the installment obligations.

INTEREST ON DEFERRED TAXES

With the installment method, the seller earns interest on the receivable. The receivable includes the deferred gain. Thus, one could argue that the seller is earning interest on the deferred taxes. Some commentators reason that the government is, in effect, making interest-free loans to taxpayers who report gains by the installment method. Following the argument that the amount of the deferred taxes is a loan, the taxpayer is required to pay interest on the deferred taxes in some situations.[76]

The taxpayer is required to pay interest on the deferred taxes only if *both* of the following requirements are met:

- The installment obligation arises from the sale of property (other than farming property) for more than $150,000.
- Such installment obligations outstanding at the close of the tax year exceed $5 million.

Interest on the deferred taxes is payable only for the portion of the taxes that relates to the installment obligations in *excess* of $5 million. The interest is calculated using the underpayment rate in § 6621.

---

[73] § 453B(a).

[74] § 453B(f)(2).

[75] §§ 453B(c), (d), and (g). See Chapter 20 for a discussion of some of these subjects.

[76] § 453A.

ELECTING OUT OF THE INSTALLMENT METHOD

A taxpayer can *elect not to use* the installment method. The election is made by reporting on a timely filed return the gain computed by the taxpayer's usual method of accounting (cash or accrual).[77] However, the Regulations provide that the amount realized by a cash basis taxpayer cannot be less than the value of the property sold. This rule differs from the usual cash basis accounting rules (discussed earlier),[78] which measure the amount realized in terms of the fair market value of the property received. The net effect of the Regulations is to allow the cash basis taxpayer to report his or her gain as an accrual basis taxpayer. The election is frequently applied to year-end sales by taxpayers who expect to be in a higher tax bracket in the following year.

EXAMPLE 29

On December 31, 1996, Jaime sold land to Veneia for $20,000 (fair market value). The cash was to be paid on January 4, 1997. Jaime is a cash basis taxpayer, and his basis in the land is $8,000. Jaime has a large casualty loss and very little other income in 1996. Thus, his marginal tax rate in 1996 is 15%. He expects his rate to increase to 36% in 1997.

The transaction constitutes an installment sale because a payment will be received in a tax year after the tax year of disposition. Veneia's promise to pay Jaime is an installment obligation, and under the Regulations, the value of the installment obligation is equal to the value of the property sold ($20,000). If Jaime elects out of the installment method, he would shift $12,000 of gain ($20,000 – $8,000) from the expected higher rate in 1997 to the 15% rate in 1996. The expected tax savings based on the rate differentials may exceed the benefit of the tax deferral available with the installment method. ▼

Revocation of the Election. Permission of the IRS is required to revoke an election not to use the installment method.[79] The stickiness of the election is an added peril.

LONG-TERM CONTRACTS

5 LEARNING OBJECTIVE
Understand the alternative methods of accounting for long-term contracts (the completed contract method and the percentage of completion method) including the limitations on the use of the completed contract method.

A **long-term contract** is a building, installation, construction, or manufacturing contract that is entered into but not completed within the same tax year. However, a *manufacturing* contract is long term *only* if the contract is to manufacture (1) a unique item not normally carried in finished goods inventory or (2) items that normally require more than 12 calendar months to complete.[80] An item is *unique* if it is designed to meet the customer's particular needs and is not suitable for use by others. A contract to perform services (e.g., auditing or legal services) is not considered a contract for this purpose and thus cannot qualify as a long-term contract.

EXAMPLE 30

Rocky, a calendar year taxpayer, entered into two contracts during the year. One contract was to construct a building foundation. Work was to begin in October 1996 and was to be completed by June 1997. The contract is long term because it will not be entered into and completed in the same tax year. The fact that the contract requires less than 12 calendar months to complete is not relevant because the contract is not for manufacturing. The second contract was for architectural services to be performed over two years. These services will not qualify for long-term contract treatment because the taxpayer will not build, install, construct, or manufacture a product. ▼

[77] § 453(d) and Temp.Reg. § 15a.453–1(d). See also Rev.Rul. 82–227, 1982–2 C.B. 89.

[78] Refer to Chapter 4, Example 5.

[79] § 453(d)(3) and Temp.Reg. § 15a.453–1(d)(4).

[80] § 460(f) and Reg. § 1.451–3(b).

Generally, the taxpayer must accumulate all of the direct and indirect costs incurred under a contract. This means the production costs must be accumulated and allocated to individual contracts. Furthermore, mixed services costs, costs that benefit contracts as well as the general administrative operations of the business, must be allocated to production. Exhibit 18–1 lists the types of costs that must be accumulated and allocated to contracts. The taxpayer must develop reasonable bases for cost allocations.[81]

EXAMPLE 31

Falcon, Inc., uses detailed cost accumulation records to assign labor and materials to its contracts in progress. The total cost of fringe benefits is allocated to a contract on the following basis:

$$\frac{\text{Labor on the contract}}{\text{Total salaries and labor}} \times \text{Total cost of fringe benefits}$$

Similarly, storage and handling costs for materials are allocated to contracts on the following basis:

$$\frac{\text{Contract materials}}{\text{Materials purchases}} \times \text{Storage and handling costs}$$

The cost of the personnel operations, a mixed services cost, is allocated between production and general administration based on the number of employees in each function. The personnel cost allocated to production is allocated to individual contracts on the basis of the formula used to allocate fringe benefits. ▼

The accumulated costs are deducted when the revenue from the contract is recognized. Generally, two methods of accounting are used in varying circumstances to determine when the revenue from a contract is recognized:[82]

- The completed contract method.
- The percentage of completion method.

The *completed contract method may be used* for (1) home construction contracts (contracts in which at least 80 percent of the estimated costs are for dwelling units in buildings with four or fewer units) and (2) certain other real estate construction contracts. Other real estate contracts can qualify for the completed contract method if the following requirements are satisfied:

- The contract is expected to be completed within the two-year period beginning on the commencement date of the contract.
- The contract is performed by a taxpayer whose average annual gross receipts for the three taxable years preceding the taxable year in which the contract is entered into do not exceed $10 million.

All other contractors must use the percentage of completion method.

Completed Contract Method. Under the **completed contract method,** no revenue from the contract is recognized until the contract is completed and accepted. However, a taxpayer may not delay completion of a contract for the principal purpose of deferring tax.[83]

In some instances, the original contract price may be disputed, or the buyer may want additional work to be done on a long-term contract. If the disputed

[81] Reg. §§ 1.263A–1T(b)(3)(iii)(A)(1) and 1.451–3(d)(9).
[82] § 460.
[83] Reg. § 1.451–3(b)(2).

▼ EXHIBIT 18–1
Contract Costs, Mixed Services Costs, and Current Expense Items for Contracts

	Contracts Eligible for the Completed Contract Method	Other Contracts
Contract costs:		
Direct materials (a part of the finished product).	Capital	Capital
Indirect materials (consumed in production but not in the finished product, e.g., grease and oil for equipment).	Capital	Capital
Storage, handling, and insurance on materials.	Expense	Capital
Direct labor (worked on the product).	Capital	Capital
Indirect labor (worked in the production process but not directly on the product, e.g., a construction supervisor).	Capital	Capital
Fringe benefits for direct and indirect labor (e.g., vacation, sick pay, unemployment, and other insurance).	Capital	Capital
Pension costs for direct and indirect labor:		
• Current cost.	Expense	Capital
• Past service costs.	Expense	Capital
Depreciation on production facilities:		
• For financial statements.	Capital	Capital
• Tax depreciation in excess of financial statements.	Expense	Capital
Depreciation on idle facilities.	Expense	Expense
Property taxes, insurance, rent, and maintenance on production facilities.	Capital	Capital
Bidding expenses—successful.	Expense	Capital
Bidding expenses—unsuccessful.	Expense	Expense
Interest to finance real estate construction.	Capital	Capital
Interest to finance personal property:		
• Production period of one year or less.	Expense	Expense
• Production period exceeds one year and costs exceed $1 million.	Capital	Capital
• Production period exceeds two years.	Capital	Capital
Mixed services costs:		
• Personnel operations.	Expense	Allocate
• Data processing.	Expense	Allocate
• Purchasing.	Expense	Allocate
Selling, general, and administrative expenses (including an allocated share of mixed services)	Expense	Expense
Losses	Expense	Expense

TAX IN THE NEWS

IRS SAYS THE CASH METHOD DOES NOT CLEARLY REFLECT THE INCOME OF SMALL CONTRACTORS

In a 1980 Tax Court decision, *Raymond Magnon*, 73 T.C. 980, the Court ruled that a small contractor could use the cash method of accounting. More recently, the IRS was unsuccessful in attempting to require a contractor to change from the cash method to the percentage of completion method. The IRS argued that the cash method did not clearly reflect income, but the Tax Court disagreed [*Ansley-Sheppard-Burgess Company*, 104 T.C. No. 17 (1995)].

In other recent cases, however, the IRS has been successful in requiring small contractors to change from the cash method to the accrual method (*Thompson Electric Inc.*, T.C. Memo 1995–292 and *J. P. Sheahan Associates*, T.C. Memo 1995–239). The IRS has successfully argued that the accumulated costs for materials and labor, whether incurred by the contractor or its subcontractors, are subject to the inventory rules. Because inventories are a material income-producing factor, the cash method does not clearly reflect income, and the IRS can require the contractor to employ the accrual method.

SOURCE: "The IRS Insists General Contractor Use Inventories and Change to Accrual Method," *Journal of Taxation* (September 1995): 180.

amount is substantial (it is not possible to determine whether a profit or loss will ultimately be realized on the contract), the Regulations provide that no amount of income or loss is recognized until the dispute is resolved. In all other cases, the profit or loss (reduced by the amount in dispute) is recognized in the current period on completion of the contract. However, additional work may need to be performed with respect to the disputed contract. In this case, the difference between the amount in dispute and the actual cost of the additional work is recognized in the year the work is completed rather than in the year in which the dispute is resolved.[84]

EXAMPLE 32

Ted, a calendar year taxpayer utilizing the completed contract method of accounting, constructed a building for Khalid under a long-term contract. The gross contract price was $500,000. Ted finished construction in 1996 at a cost of $475,000. When Khalid examined the building, he insisted that the building be repainted or the contract price be reduced. The estimated cost of repainting is $10,000. Since under the terms of the contract, Ted is assured of a profit of at least $15,000 ($500,000 – $475,000 – $10,000) even if the dispute is ultimately resolved in Khalid's favor, Ted must include $490,000 ($500,000 – $10,000) in gross income and is allowed deductions of $475,000 for 1996.

In 1997, Ted and Khalid resolve the dispute, and Ted repaints certain portions of the building at a cost of $6,000. Ted must include $10,000 in 1997 gross income and may deduct the $6,000 expense in that year. ▼

EXAMPLE 33

Assume the same facts as in the previous example, except the estimated cost of repainting the building is $50,000. Since the resolution of the dispute completely in Khalid's favor

[84] Reg. § 1.451–3(d)(2)(ii)–(vii), Example (2).

would mean a net loss on the contract for Ted ($500,000 – $475,000 – $50,000 = $25,000 loss), Ted does not recognize any income or loss until the year the dispute is resolved. ▼

Frequently, a contractor receives payment at various stages of completion. For example, when the contract is 50 percent complete, the contractor may receive 50 percent of the contract price less a retainage. The taxation of these payments is generally governed by Regulation § 1.451–5 "advance payments for goods and long-term contracts" (discussed in Chapter 4). Generally, contractors are permitted to defer the advance payments until the payments are recognized as income under the taxpayer's method of accounting.

Percentage of Completion Method. The percentage of completion method must be used to account for long-term contracts unless the taxpayer qualifies for one of the two exceptions that permit the completed contract method to be used (home construction contracts and certain other real estate construction contracts).[85] Under the **percentage of completion method,** a portion of the gross contract price is included in income during each period as the work progresses. The revenue accrued each period (except for the final period) is computed as follows:[86]

$$\frac{C}{T} \times P$$

Where C = Contract costs incurred during the period

T = Estimated total cost of the contract

P = Contract price

All of the costs allocated to the contract during the period are deductible from the accrued revenue.[87] The revenue reported in the final period is simply the unreported revenue from the contract. Because T in this formula is an estimate that frequently differs from total actual costs, which are not known until the contract has been completed, the profit on a contract for a particular period may be overstated or understated.

EXAMPLE 34

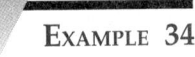

Tan, Inc., entered into a contract that was to take two years to complete, with an estimated cost of $2,250,000. The contract price was $3,000,000. Costs of the contract for 1996, the first year, totaled $1,350,000. The gross profit reported by the percentage of completion method for 1996 was $450,000 [($1,350,000/$2,250,000 × $3,000,000) – $1,350,000]. The contract was completed at the end of 1997 at a total cost of $2,700,000. In retrospect, 1996 profit should have been $150,000 [($1,350,000/$2,700,000 × $3,000,000) – $1,350,000]. Thus, taxes were overpaid for 1996. ▼

A *de minimis* rule enables the contractor to delay the recognition of income for a particular contract under the percentage of completion method. If less than 10 percent of the estimated contract costs have been incurred by the end of the taxable year, the taxpayer can elect to defer the recognition of income and the related costs until the taxable year in which cumulative contract costs are at least 10 percent of the estimated contract costs.[88]

[85] Certain residential construction contracts that do not qualify for the completed contract method may nevertheless use that method to account for 30% of the profit from the contract, with the remaining 70% reported by the percentage of completion method.

[86] § 460(b)(1)(A).

[87] Reg. § 1.451–3(c)(3).

[88] § 460(b)(5).

Lookback Provisions. In the year a contract is completed, a *lookback* provision requires the recalculation of annual profits reported on the contract under the percentage of completion method. Interest is paid to the taxpayer if taxes were overpaid, and interest is payable by the taxpayer if there was an underpayment.[89] For a corporate taxpayer, the lookback interest paid by the taxpayer is deductible, but for an individual taxpayer, it is nondeductible personal interest associated with a tax liability.

EXAMPLE 35

Assume Tan, Inc., in Example 34, was in the 35% tax bracket in both years and the relevant interest rate was 10%. For 1996, the company paid excess taxes of $105,000 [($450,000 – $150,000) × .35]. When the contract is completed at the end of 1997, Tan, Inc., should receive interest of $10,500 for one year on the tax overpayment ($105,000 × .10). ▼

INVENTORIES

6 LEARNING OBJECTIVE
Know when accounting for inventories must occur, recognize the types of costs that must be included in inventories, and apply the LIFO method.

Generally, tax accounting and financial accounting for inventories are much the same:

- The use of inventories is necessary to clearly reflect the income of any business engaged in the production and sale or purchase and sale of goods.[90]
- The inventories should include all finished goods, goods in process, and raw materials and supplies that will become part of the product (including containers).
- Inventory rules must give effect to the *best* accounting practice of a particular trade or business, and the taxpayer's method should be consistently followed from year to year.
- All items included in inventory should be valued at either (1) cost or (2) the lower of cost or market value.

The following are *not* acceptable methods or practices in valuing inventories:

- A deduction for a reserve for anticipated price changes.
- The use of a constant price or nominal value for a so-called normal quantity of materials or goods in stock (e.g., the base stock method).
- The inclusion in inventory of stock in transit to which title is not vested in the taxpayer.
- The direct costing approach (excluding fixed indirect production costs from inventory).
- The prime costing approach (excluding all indirect production costs from inventory).

The reason for the similarities between tax and financial accounting for inventories is that § 471 sets forth what appears to be a two-prong test. Under this provision "inventories shall be taken . . . on such basis . . . as conforming as nearly as may be to the *best accounting practice* in the trade or business and as most *clearly reflecting the income*." The best accounting practice is synonymous with generally accepted accounting principles (hereafter referred to as GAAP). However, the IRS determines whether an inventory method clearly reflects income.

[89] § 460(b)(2).

[90] § 471(a) and Reg. §§ 1.471–1 and –2.

TAX IN THE NEWS

Inventory Valuation Results in Fraud Charges

Robert Perlman, the owner of a chain of appliance and electronics stores, was charged with fraud by the IRS. The Service contended that Mr. Perlman had evaded more than $1 million in taxes by undervaluing the inventories in his stores. Mr. Perlman's accountant testified that the inventories were not undervalued; rather, the IRS was not aware of the actual inventory method used by Perlman. That is, although the tax return said that the inventory was valued at weighted average cost, in fact the inventories had been consistently reported at the lower of cost or market. Four former employees testified that Mr. Perlman frequently made adjustments to computerized inventory. However, according to Mr. Perlman, these adjustments were to hide the true cost of the goods from his competitors, and the adjustments were not made to the inventories used for tax purposes.

The case resulted in a hung jury. The jury was unable to decide whether the taxpayer was guilty of fraud or was simply a sloppy record-keeper.

SOURCE: Reprinted with permission from the *Sun-Sentinel*, Fort Lauderdale, Florida.

In *Thor Power Tool Co. v. Comm.*, there was a conflict between the two tests.[91] The taxpayer's method of valuing obsolete parts was in conformity with GAAP. The IRS, however, successfully argued that the clear reflection of income test was not satisfied because the taxpayer's procedures for valuing its inventories were contrary to the Regulations. Under the taxpayer's method, inventories for parts in excess of estimated future sales were written off (expensed), although the parts were kept on hand and their asking prices were not reduced. [Under Regulation § 1.471–4(b), inventories cannot be written down unless the selling prices also are reduced.] The taxpayer contended that conformity to GAAP creates a presumption that the method clearly reflects income. The Supreme Court disagreed, concluding that the clear reflection of income test was *paramount*. Moreover, it is the opinion of the IRS that controls in determining whether the method of inventory clearly reflects income. Thus, the best accounting practice test was rendered practically meaningless. It follows that the taxpayer's method of inventory must strictly conform to the Regulations regardless of what GAAP may require.

DETERMINING INVENTORY COST

For merchandise purchased, cost is the invoice price less trade discounts plus freight and other handling charges.[92] Cash discounts approximating a fair interest rate can be deducted or capitalized at the taxpayer's option, providing the method used is consistently applied.

Uniform Capitalization. In 1986, Congress added § 263A, which significantly affects the inventory rules, to the Code. Section 263A provides that for inventory

[91] 79–1 USTC ¶9139, 43 AFTR2d 79–362, 99 S.Ct. 773 (USSC, 1979).

[92] Reg. § 1.471–3(b).

and property produced by the taxpayer, "... (A) the direct cost of such property, and (B) such property's share of those indirect costs (including taxes) part or all of which are allocable to such property" must be capitalized. The Committee Reports observe that Congress is attempting to achieve a set of capitalization rules that will apply to all types of businesses: contractors, manufacturers, farmers, wholesalers, and retailers.[93] Congress has labeled the system the **uniform capitalization rules,** and practitioners refer to the rules as a *super-full absorption costing system.*

To value inventory under the uniform capitalization rules, a *producer* must apply the following steps:

- Classify all costs into three categories: (1) production, (2) general administrative expense, and (3) mixed services.
- Allocate mixed services costs to production and general administrative expenses.[94]
- Allocate the production costs between the cost of goods sold and the ending inventory.

Exhibit 18–1 (see the "Other Contracts" column) lists typical items that are included in the three classes of costs. The mixed services costs should be allocated to production on a rational basis. For example, the costs of operating the personnel department may be allocated between production and general administration based on the number of applications processed or the number of employees. In lieu of allocating each mixed services cost, the taxpayer can elect a *simplified method* whereby the total of all mixed services costs is allocated to production as follows:[95]

$$MSP = \frac{TP}{TC} \times TMS$$

Where MSP = Mixed services costs allocated to production

TP = Total production costs, other than interest and mixed services

TC = Total costs, other than interest, state, local or foreign income taxes, and mixed services costs

TMS = Total mixed services costs

The usual cost accounting techniques (e.g., average cost per equivalent unit) can be used to allocate the costs between the cost of goods sold and the ending inventory.

Alternatively, the producer can elect to allocate mixed services costs to production on the basis of labor charges only (production labor as a percentage of total labor costs).

The costs included in the inventory of *wholesalers and retailers* are comparable to those of the producer. However, many of these costs are captured in the price these taxpayers pay for the goods. The following additional costs must be capitalized by these taxpayers:

- All storage costs for wholesalers.
- Offsite storage costs for retailers.
- Purchasing costs (e.g., buyers' wages or salaries).
- Handling, processing, assembly, and repackaging.
- The portion of mixed services costs allocable to these functions.

---

[93] H. Rep. 99–841, 99th Cong., 2nd Sess., 1986, pp. 302–309. See also Reg. § 1.263A–1(a).

[94] Producers with mixed services costs of less than $200,000 for the year are not required to allocate mixed services costs if the simplified method is used to allocate their production costs. Reg. § 1.263A–1(b)(12).

[95] Reg. § 1.263A–1(h)(5).

Mixed services costs must be allocated to offsite storage, purchasing, and packaging on the basis of direct labor costs of these departments as a percentage of total payroll. Thus, the storage, purchasing, and packaging costs allocated to ending inventory include some mixed services costs.

The uniform capitalization rules may result in some costs being capitalized for tax purposes but not for financial accounting purposes. For example, a wholesaler's or a manufacturer's storage costs are generally expensed for financial reporting purposes, but are capitalized for tax purposes. Also, the taxpayer may capitalize straight-line depreciation of production equipment for financial accounting purposes, but the total tax depreciation must be capitalized under uniform capitalization.

Lower of Cost or Market. Except for those taxpayers who use the LIFO method, inventories may be valued at the **lower of cost or market (replacement cost).**[96] Taxpayers using LIFO must value inventory at cost. However, the write-down of damaged or shopworn merchandise and goods that are otherwise unsalable at normal prices is not considered to be an application of the lower of cost or market method. Such items should be valued at bona fide selling price less direct cost of disposal.[97]

In the case of excess inventories (as in *Thor Power Tool Co.*, discussed above), the goods can be written down only to the taxpayer's offering price. If the offering price on the goods is not reduced, the goods must be valued at cost.

EXAMPLE 36

The Cardinal Publishing Company invested $50,000 in printing 10,000 copies of a book. Although only 7,000 copies were sold in the first 3 years and none in the next 5 years, management is convinced that the book will become a classic in 20 years. Cardinal leaves the price the same as it was when the book was first distributed ($15 per copy). The remaining 3,000 books must be valued at cost ($15,000). Note that the tax law provides an incentive for the taxpayer to destroy or abandon its excess inventory and obtain an immediate deduction rather than wait for the event of future sales. ▼

In applying the lower of cost or market method, *each* item included in the inventory must be valued at the lower of its cost or market value.[98]

EXAMPLE 37

The taxpayer's ending inventory is valued as follows:

Item	Cost	Market	Lower of Cost or Market
A	$5,000	$ 4,000	$4,000
B	3,000	2,000	2,000
C	1,500	6,000	1,500
	$9,500	$12,000	$7,500

Under the lower of cost or market method, the taxpayer's inventory is valued at $7,500 rather than $9,500. ▼

Determining Cost—Specific Identification, FIFO, and LIFO. In some cases, it is feasible to determine the cost of the particular item sold. For example,

[96] Reg. § 1.472–4

[97] Reg. § 1.471–2(c).

[98] Reg. § 1.471–4(c).

an automobile dealer can easily determine the specific cost of each automobile that has been sold. However, in most businesses it is necessary to resort to a flow of goods assumption such as *first in, first out* (*FIFO*), *last in, first out* (*LIFO*), or an *average cost* method. A taxpayer may use any of these methods, provided the method selected is consistently applied from year to year.

During a period of rising prices, LIFO will generally produce a lower ending inventory valuation and will result in a greater cost of goods sold than would be obtained under the FIFO method. The following example illustrates how LIFO and FIFO affect the computation of the cost of goods sold.

EXAMPLE 38

On January 1, 1996, the taxpayer opened a retail store to sell refrigerators. At least 10 refrigerators must be carried in inventory to satisfy customer demands. The initial investment in the 10 refrigerators is $5,000. During the year, 10 refrigerators were sold at $750 each and were replaced at a cost of $6,000 ($600 each). Gross profit under the LIFO and FIFO methods is computed as follows:

		FIFO		LIFO
Sales (10 × $750)		$ 7,500		$ 7,500
Beginning inventory	$ 5,000		$ 5,000	
Purchases	6,000		6,000	
	$11,000		$11,000	
Ending inventory				
10 × $600	(6,000)			
10 × $500			(5,000)	
Cost of goods sold		(5,000)		(6,000)
Gross profit		$ 2,500		$ 1,500

Dollar-Value LIFO. In the previous example, the taxpayer was buying and selling a single product, a particular model of a refrigerator. The taxpayer employed the specific goods LIFO technique. Under the specific goods approach, if the identical items are not on hand at the end of the period, the LIFO inventory is depleted, and all of the deferred profit must be recaptured. Thus, taxpayers who frequently change the items carried in inventory would realize little benefit from LIFO. However, the dollar-value LIFO technique avoids the LIFO depletion problem associated with the specific goods technique.

Under **dollar-value LIFO,** each inventory item is assigned to a pool. A *pool* is a collection of similar items and is treated as a separate inventory. Determining whether items are similar involves considerable judgment. In general, however, the taxpayer would prefer broad pools so that when a particular item is sold out, it can be replaced by increases in other items in the same pool. Generally, all products manufactured at a particular plant can be treated as a pool.[99] A department store may have a separate pool for each department. An automobile dealer may have separate pools for new cars, lightweight trucks, heavy-duty trucks, and car and truck parts.

At the end of the period, the ending inventory must be valued at the current year prices and then at the LIFO base period (the year LIFO was adopted). The ratio of the ending inventory at current prices to the ending inventory at base

[99] See, generally, Reg. § 1.472–8.

period prices is the *LIFO index*. If the total current inventory at base period prices is greater than the base period inventory at base period prices, a LIFO layer must be added. The LIFO index is applied to the LIFO layer to convert it to current prices.

EXAMPLE 39

Black Company adopted LIFO effective January 1, 1996. The base LIFO inventory (from December 31, 1995) was $1,000,000. On December 31, 1996, the inventory was $1,320,000 at end-of-1996 prices and $1,200,000 at end-of-1995 (the base period) prices. Thus, Black added a 1996 layer of $200,000 ($1,200,000 – $1,000,000) at base period prices. The layer must be converted to 1996 prices as follows:

$$\text{LIFO index} = \$1{,}320{,}000/\$1{,}200{,}000 = 1.10$$

$$\text{1996 layer} \times \text{LIFO index} = \$200{,}000 \times 1.10 = \$220{,}000$$

Therefore, the 1996 ending inventory is $1,000,000 + $220,000 = $1,220,000.

The inventory on December 31, 1997, is $1,325,000 using 1997 prices and $1,250,000 using base period prices. Thus, the LIFO index for 1997 is $1,325,000/$1,250,000 = 1.06. The LIFO inventory is $1,273,000, computed as follows:

BLACK COMPANY
LIFO Inventory
December 31, 1997

	Base Period Cost	LIFO Index	LIFO Layers
Base inventory	$1,000,000	1.00	$1,000,000
1996 layer	200,000	1.10	220,000
1997 layer	50,000	1.06	53,000
	$1,250,000		$1,273,000

ETHICAL CONSIDERATIONS

Protecting the LIFO Reserve

The Swan Company has been using the LIFO inventory method for the past 20 years and has accumulated a substantial LIFO reserve. During the current year, the company's employees went on strike. By early December, all of the inventories had been depleted. Sugar is the major raw material used in the company's product. The company is considering the following plan to avoid depletion of the LIFO reserve. In late December, the company will purchase a large quantity of sugar. Also, in December, the company will enter into a contract to sell the sugar to a broker. The sugar purchased will not actually be delivered to Swan. Instead, the seller will hold the sugar until early January and then deliver it directly to the broker.

Evaluate Swan's plan.

THE LIFO ELECTION

A taxpayer may adopt LIFO by merely using the method in the tax return for the year of the change and by attaching Form 970 (Application to Use LIFO Inventory Method) to the tax return. Thus, a taxpayer does not have to request approval for changes within the first 180 days of the tax year. Once the election is made, it cannot be revoked. However, a prospective change from LIFO to any other inventory method can be made only if the consent of the IRS is obtained.[100]

The beginning inventory valuation for the first year LIFO is used is computed by the costing method employed in the preceding year. Thus, the beginning LIFO inventory is generally the same as the closing inventory for the preceding year. However, since lower of cost or market cannot be used in conjunction with LIFO, previous write-downs to market for items included in the beginning inventory must be restored to income. The amount the inventories are written up is an adjustment due to a change in accounting method.[101] However, the usual rules for disposition of the adjustments under Revenue Procedure 92–20 are not applicable.[102] The taxpayer is allowed to spread the adjustment ratably over the year of the change and the two succeeding years.

EXAMPLE 40

In 1995, Chee used the lower of cost or market FIFO inventory method. The FIFO cost of his ending inventory was $30,000, and the market value of the inventory was $24,000. Therefore, the ending inventory for 1995 was $24,000. Chee switched to LIFO in 1996 and was required to write up the beginning inventory to $30,000. Chee must add $2,000 ($6,000 ÷ 3) to his income for each of the years 1996, 1997, and 1998. ▼

Congress added this provision to the Code to overrule the previous IRS policy of requiring the taxpayer to include the entire adjustment in income for the year preceding the change to LIFO.[103]

Once the LIFO election is made for tax purposes, the taxpayer's financial reports to owners and creditors must also be prepared on the basis of LIFO.[104] The *conformity* of financial reports to tax reporting is specifically required by the Code and is strictly enforced by the IRS. However, the Regulations permit the taxpayer to make a footnote disclosure of the net income computed by another method of inventory valuation (e.g., FIFO).[105]

TAX PLANNING CONSIDERATIONS

7 LEARNING OBJECTIVE

Identify tax planning opportunities related to accounting periods and accounting methods.

TAXABLE YEAR

Under the general rules for tax years, partnerships and S corporations frequently will be required to use a calendar year. However, if the partnership or S corporation can demonstrate a business purpose for a fiscal year, the IRS will allow the entity to use the requested year. The advantage to a fiscal year is that the calendar year partners and S corporation shareholders may be able to defer from tax the income earned from the close of the fiscal year until the end of the calendar year. Tax advisers for these entities should apply the IRS's gross receipts test described in Revenue Procedure 87–32 to determine if permission for the fiscal year will be granted.

CASH METHOD OF ACCOUNTING

The cash method of accounting gives the taxpayer considerable control over the recognition of expenses and some control over the recognition of income. This

---

[100] Reg. §§ 1.472–3(a) and 1.472–5 and Rev.Proc. 84–74, 1984–2 C.B. 736 at 742.

[101] Reg. § 1.472–2(c). In Rev.Rul. 76–282, 1976–2 C.B. 137, the IRS required the restoration of write-downs for damaged and shop-worn goods when the taxpayer switched to LIFO.

[102] 1992–1 C.B. 301.

[103] § 472(d), overruling the IRS position cited in Footnote 101.

[104] § 472(c).

[105] Reg. § 1.472–2(e).

method can be used by proprietorships, partnerships, and small corporations (gross receipts of $5 million or less) that provide services (inventories are not material to the service business). Farmers (except certain farming corporations) can also use the cash method.

INSTALLMENT METHOD

Unlike the cash and accrual methods, the installment method often results in an interest-free loan (of deferred taxes) from the government. The installment method is not available for the sale of inventory. Nevertheless, the installment method is an important tax planning technique and should be considered when a sale of eligible property is being planned. That is, if the taxpayer can benefit from deferring the tax, the terms of sale can be arranged so that the installment method rules apply. If, on the other hand, the taxpayer expects to be in a higher tax bracket when the payments will be received, he or she can elect to not use the installment method.

Related Parties. Intrafamily installment sales can still be a useful family tax planning tool. If the related party holds the property more than two years, a subsequent sale will not accelerate the gain from the first disposition. Patience and forethought are rewarded.

The 6 percent limitation on imputed interest on sales of land between family members enables the seller to convert ordinary income into capital gain or make what is, in effect, a nontaxable gift. If the selling price is raised to adjust for the low interest rate charges on an installment sale, the seller has more capital gain but less ordinary income than would be realized from a sale to an unrelated party. If the selling price is not raised and the specified interest of 6 percent is charged, the seller enables the relative to have the use of the property without having to pay for its full market value. As an additional benefit, the bargain sale is not a taxable gift.

Disposition of Installment Obligations. A disposition of an installment obligation is also a serious matter. Gifts of the obligations will accelerate income to the seller. The list of taxable and nontaxable dispositions of installment obligations should not be trusted to memory. In each instance where transfers of installment obligations are contemplated, the practitioner should conduct research to be sure he or she knows the consequences.

COMPLETED CONTRACT METHOD

Generally, large contractors must use the percentage of completion method of accounting for reporting the income from long-term contracts. Under the percentage of completion method, the taxpayer must recognize profit in each period costs are incurred. Profit is reported in proportion to the cost incurred for the period as a proportion of the total contract cost. However, small contractors (average annual gross receipts do not exceed $10 million) working on contracts that are completed within a two-year period can elect to use the completed contract method and defer profit until the year in which the contract is completed.

INVENTORIES

Lower of Cost or Market. Generally, under tax accounting rules, a deduction cannot be taken for a loss before the loss is realized. Inventories with a replacement cost below their original cost are the major exception to this rule. The rationale for the lower of cost or market method is that when the replacement cost of the goods has decreased, the taxpayer's selling price must likewise be reduced. Under the lower of cost or market method, the taxpayer is allowed to anticipate a reduction in the expected selling price of the goods by taking a deduction in the period the replacement cost decreases, rather than waiting until the goods are actually sold. Thus, the lower of cost or market method is a tax deferral technique.

LIFO. While the lower of cost or market method defers tax when replacement costs are declining, LIFO defers tax when prices are rising. However, when some goods are increasing in value while others are deceasing, the taxpayer cannot use the lower of cost or market method for the goods declining in value and LIFO for the goods whose replacement costs are rising. That is, LIFO cannot be used in conjunction with the lower of cost or market method. Assuming that prices generally are rising, the taxpayer generally should elect LIFO. The only major disadvantage to LIFO is the financial-tax conformity requirement. However, even this disadvantage can be overcome through footnote disclosure of earnings as computed under FIFO.

KEY TERMS

Accounting methods, 18–11

Accounting period, 18–3

Accrual method, 18–13

All events test, 18–14

Cash method, 18–11

Claim of right doctrine, 18–10

Completed contract method, 18–28

Dollar-value LIFO, 18–36

Economic performance test, 18–14

Fiscal year, 18–3

Hybrid method, 18–16

Imputed interest, 18–22

Installment method, 18–20

Least aggregate deferral method, 18–4

Long-term contract, 18–27

Lower of cost or market (replacement cost), 18–35

Majority interest partners, 18–4

One-year rule for prepaid expenses, 18–12

Percentage of completion method, 18–31

Personal service corporation (PSC), 18–6

Principal partner, 18–4

Short taxable year (short period), 18–8

Uniform capitalization rules, 18–34

PROBLEM MATERIALS

DISCUSSION QUESTIONS

1. Why would a C corporation want to use a tax year other than a calendar year?
2. Megan recently began conducting an office supply business as a corporation. Vito began conducting his law practice through a corporation. Neither corporation has made an S election. What tax year alternatives are available to Megan's business that are not available to Vito's business?

3. Debra is a practicing accountant. Over 90% of her work is done for individuals and S corporations. In the tax season just ended, Debra found that she could not continue to provide high-quality services for so many calendar year clients. Therefore, she plans to propose to some of her S corporation clients that the corporation change to a fiscal year ending September 30. What problems will Debra encounter in getting her clients to agree to a change in tax year?

4. How does a partnership establish a business purpose for a tax year that differs from its partners' tax years?

5. Dan, a calendar year taxpayer, recently became a licensed orthopedic surgeon. He has incorporated his practice. Dan's brother suggested that the corporation's tax year should end on September 30 and thus avoid the end-of-the-calendar-year rush. What complications could result from the corporation filing its return on the basis of a fiscal year ending September 30?

6. Amber Corporation changed its tax year from a fiscal year ending in September to the calendar year, effective in 1996. For what period is the income subject to annualization?

7. Jack is a cash basis taxpayer. In 1995, when Jack was in the 31% marginal tax bracket, he received $25,000 for services provided for Jane. In 1996, Jack discovered that he had overcharged Jane by $4,000 in 1995. Therefore, he immediately refunded Jane the $4,000. As a result of some unusually large expenses in 1996, Jack's taxable income for the year was only $5,000. What special tax treatment is afforded the $4,000 payment?

8. Quinn is the sole shareholder of an accrual basis S corporation, Red, Inc. If Quinn forms another S corporation, Purple, Inc., does the fact that Red uses the accrual method mean that Purple is required to use the accrual method?

9. The Cardinal Insurance Agency is a newly formed corporation, and its gross receipts will probably never exceed $2 million in a year. Generally, it takes approximately two months to collect accounts receivable. Accounts payable generally equal expenses for one month. Cardinal does not expect accounts payable and accounts receivable to increase significantly. It prepares monthly financial statements using the accrual method of accounting. Given that the accounts receivable and accounts payable will not significantly change, would Cardinal derive any benefit from filing its tax return using the cash method of accounting?

10. Rita buys and sells produce. Her annual gross receipts are less than $5 million. Approximately 30% of her sales are on account. Rita sells all of her inventory each day. Thus, she has no beginning or ending inventory each year. Is Rita required to use the accrual method of accounting?

11. Earl, a certified public accountant, recently obtained a new client. The client is a retail grocery store that has used the cash method to report its income since it began doing business. Will Earl incur any liability if he prepares the tax return in accordance with the cash method and does not advise the client of the necessity of seeking the IRS's permission to change to the accrual method?

12. In December 1996, a cash basis taxpayer paid January through June 1997 management fees in connection with his rental properties. The fees were $4,000 per month. Compute the 1996 expense under the following assumptions:
    a. The fees were paid by an individual who derived substantially all of his income from the properties.
    b. The fees were paid by a tax-shelter partnership.

13. Osprey Corporation, an accrual basis taxpayer, had taxable income for 1996. However, Osprey's accountant was ill, and the taxable income for 1996 was not computed until July 1997. The state income tax return for 1996 was filed on August 13, 1997, and $3,000 in state income taxes were paid at that time. Can the 1996 state income taxes be deducted in calculating the corporation's 1996 Federal taxable income?

14. Compare the cash basis and accrual basis of accounting as applied to the following:

a. Fixed assets.
b. Prepaid rent income.
c. Prepaid interest expense.
d. A note received for services performed if the market value and face amount of the note differ.

15. Salmon Corporation and Betty have formed a partnership to rent real estate and operate a coal mine. Salmon uses the accrual method of accounting, and the company's tax year ends March 31. Betty is a cash basis, calendar year taxpayer. What are the tax accounting issues that the partnership must address?

16. Teal Company sells goods under terms that allow the customer to return the goods within 30 days of the sale. At the end of 1996 (as the company has done for all years since it started in business), Teal estimated the returns that it would receive in January 1997 from December 1996 sales. It then subtracted the estimated returns from the gross sales to arrive at net sales. Estimated returns and actual returns were the same amount. Can Teal's method be used for tax purposes?

17. Generally, what is the deadline for a taxpayer filing a request for a change from an incorrect accounting method?

18. What difference does it make whether the taxpayer or the IRS initiates the change in accounting method?

19. Generally, what incentives are provided to encourage a taxpayer to change voluntarily from an incorrect method of accounting?

20. Irene has made Sara an offer on the purchase of a capital asset. Irene will pay (1) $200,000 cash or (2) $50,000 cash and a 9% installment note for $150,000 guaranteed by City Bank of New York. If Sara sells for $200,000 cash, she will invest the after-tax proceeds in certificates of deposit yielding 9% interest. Sara's cost of the asset is $25,000. Why would Sara prefer the installment sale?

21. How does the buyer's assumption of the seller's liabilities in an installment sale affect the following?
    a. Selling price.
    b. Contract price.
    c. Buyer's payments in the year of sale.

22. Sally sold an apartment building to Leroy for a stated selling price of $100,000. She received $20,000 cash and a note for $80,000 due in two years, bearing interest at the rate of 4%. At the time of the sale, the applicable Federal rate was 8%. What effects will the imputed interest rules have on the selling price and the amount of interest that Sally will report?

23. On June 1, 1994, Father sold land to Son for $100,000. Father reported the gain by the installment method, with the gain to be spread over five years. In May 1996, Son received an offer of $150,000 for the land, to be paid over three years. What would be the tax consequences of Son's sale? How could the tax consequences be improved?

24. In 1996, Bhaskar sold a building to his 100% controlled corporation. The entire purchase price is to be paid in 1997. When should Bhaskar report the gain on the sale of the building?

25. What is the tax effect of a gift of an installment obligation?

26. Why does the tax law require the seller to pay interest on the deferred taxes from certain installment sales?

27. Juan, a cash basis taxpayer, sold land in December 1996. At the time of the sale, Juan received $10,000 cash and a note for $90,000 due in 90 days. Juan expects to be in a much higher tax bracket in 1997. Should Juan report the sale in 1996 or 1997?

28. Who may use the completed contract method to report income?

29. What is the purpose of the lookback rules applicable to long-term contracts reported by the percentage of completion method?

30. What are the implications of underestimating the costs of a contract whose income is reported by the percentage of completion method?

31. The Eagle Construction Company began business on April 1 this year. The company erects prefabricated steel buildings and operates as follows. After the customer selects a building model, Eagle orders the materials from the manufacturer. Eagle then erects the building on the customer's property. Eagle prices the contract at 150% of the cost of the prefabricated building. The customer pays 70% of the price at the time the materials are ordered and the balance of the original price when the building is completed. If Eagle buys more than $1 million in materials during the year, the manufacturer will give Eagle a 2% rebate the following February. Several buildings were under construction at the end of the year. Eagle had ordered more than $1 million in materials during the year, but had paid for only about $989,000 through December. What issues involving Eagle's accounting methods are raised by these facts?

32. What costs must a retailer include in inventory in addition to the invoice price of the goods?

33. Brown, Inc., a wholesaler and retailer of building materials, accounted for storage costs as a current expense. What tax accounting issues are raised by Brown's error?

34. What is *market* for purposes of applying the lower of cost or market inventory method?

35. During a period of rising prices, is the LIFO or FIFO cost determination method more likely to produce a smaller profit?

36. Egret, Inc., uses the LIFO method for tax purposes. However, Egret is about to make a public offering of its stock and would like to communicate to potential investors the company's income as computed by the FIFO inventory method. How can this be done without violating the LIFO conformity provisions?

PROBLEMS

37. Red, White, and Blue are unrelated corporations engaged in real estate development. The three corporations formed a joint venture (treated as a partnership) to develop a tract of land. Assuming the venture does not have a natural business year, what tax year must the joint venture adopt under the following circumstances?

		Tax Year Ending	Interest in Joint Venture
a.	Red	Sept. 30	60%
	White	June 30	20%
	Blue	March 31	20%
b.	Red	Sept. 30	30%
	White	June 30	40%
	Blue	January 31	30%

38. The Cardinal Wholesale Company is an S corporation that began business on March 1, 1996. Robert, a calendar year taxpayer, owns 100% of the Cardinal stock. He has $400,000 taxable income from other sources each year. Robert will work approximately 30 hours a week for the corporation. Cardinal sells swimming pool supplies, and its natural business year ends in September. Approximately 80% of Cardinal's gross receipts occur in June through September.

a. What tax year should Cardinal elect, assuming that Robert anticipates the company will produce a net profit for all years?
b. What tax year should Cardinal elect, assuming it will lose $10,000 a month for the first 12 months and an average of $5,000 a month for the next 12 months? In the third year, the corporation will earn taxable income.

39. Zack conducted his professional practice through Zack, Inc. The corporation uses a fiscal year ending September 30 even though the business purpose test for a fiscal year cannot be satisfied. For the year ending September 30, 1996, the corporation paid Zack a salary of $150,000, and during the period January through September 1996, the corporation paid him a salary of $120,000.
    a. How much salary should Zack receive during the period October 1 through December 31, 1996?
    b. Assume Zack received only $30,000 salary during the period October 1 through December 31, 1996. What would be the consequences to Zack, Inc.?

40. Owl Corporation is in the business of sales and home deliveries of fuel oil and currently uses a calendar year for reporting its taxable income. However, Owl's natural business year ends May 31. For the short period, January 1, 1996, through May 31, 1996, the corporation earned $31,500. Assume the corporate tax rates are as follows: 15% on taxable income of $50,000 or less, 25% on taxable income over $50,000 but not over $75,000, and 34% on taxable income over $75,000.
    a. What must Owl Corporation do to change its taxable year?
    b. Compute Owl Corporation's tax for the short period.

41. Gold, Inc., is an accrual basis taxpayer. In 1996, an employee accidentally spilled hazardous chemicals on leased property. The chemicals destroyed trees on neighboring property, resulting in $30,000 damages. In 1996, the owner of the property sued Gold, Inc., for the $30,000. Gold's attorney feels that it is liable and the only issue is whether the neighbor will also seek punitive damages that could be as much as three times the actual damages. In addition, as a result of the spill, Gold was in violation of its lease and was therefore required to pay the landlord $15,000. However, the amount due for the lease violation was not payable until the termination of the lease in 1999. None of these costs were covered by insurance. Jeff Stuart, the president of Gold, Inc., is generally familiar with the accrual basis tax accounting rules and is concerned about when the company will be allowed to deduct the amounts the company is required to pay as a result of this environmental disaster. Write Mr. Stuart a letter explaining these issues. Gold's address is 200 Elm Avenue, San Jose, CA 95192.

42. Compute the taxpayer's income or deductions for 1996 using (1) the cash basis and (2) the accrual basis for each of the following:
    a. In 1996, the taxpayer purchased new equipment for $100,000. The taxpayer paid $25,000 in cash and gave a $75,000 interest-bearing note for the balance. The equipment has a MACRS life of five years, the mid-year convention applies, and the § 179 election was not made.
    b. In December 1996, the taxpayer collected $10,000 for January rents. In January 1997, the taxpayer collected $2,000 for December 1996 rents.
    c. In December 1996, the taxpayer paid office equipment insurance premiums of $30,000 for January–June 1997.

43. Which of the following businesses must use the accrual method of accounting?
    a. A corporation with annual gross receipts of $12 million from equipment rentals.
    b. A partnership (not a tax shelter) engaged in farming and with annual gross receipts of $8 million.
    c. A corporation that acts as an insurance agent, with annual gross receipts of $1 million.
    d. A manufacturer with annual gross receipts of $600,000.
    e. A retailer with annual gross receipts of $250,000.

44. Pink Company calculated its accrual basis income for its first year of operations. Net income before tax was $30,000. For tax purposes, the company would like to elect the method that will minimize its taxable income for the year. Compute Pink's minimum taxable income, given the following information at the end of the first year:

Inventory	$47,000
Accounts receivable	25,000
Office supplies	2,700
Prepaid insurance (6 months)	1,200
Accounts payable (merchandise)	16,000

45. Ron receives appliances on consignment from the manufacturer and collects a 5% commission on any sales made during the year. Ron is an accrual basis taxpayer and made total sales of $750,000 during the year. However, the manufacturer is usually a few weeks behind in recording Ron's sales and at the end of the year recorded only $600,000 in sales. Ron argues that he should report income for the year of only $30,000 (5% × $600,000), since that was all he had a right to receive for the year. Ron had no right to the commissions on the other $150,000 sales until the manufacturer reported them in the following year. What is Ron's correct taxable income for the year? Explain.

46. In 1996, the taxpayer was required to switch from the cash to the accrual basis of accounting for sales and cost of goods sold. Taxable income for 1996 computed under the cash basis was $40,000. Relevant account balances were as follows:

	Beginning of the Year	**End of the Year**
Accounts receivable	$36,000	$30,000
Accounts payable	9,000	8,000
Inventory	7,000	10,000

Compute the following:
a. The adjustment due to the change in accounting method.
b. The accrual basis taxable income for 1996.

47. In 1996, the taxpayer changed from the cash to the accrual basis of accounting for sales, cost of goods sold, and accrued expenses. Taxable income for 1996 computed under the cash method was $45,000. Relevant account balances are as follows:

	Beginning of the Year	**End of the Year**
Accounts receivable	$ 5,000	$13,000
Accounts payable	–0–	–0–
Accrued expenses	5,000	6,000
Inventory	10,000	9,000

a. Compute the accrual basis taxable income for 1996 and the adjustment due to the change in accounting method.
b. Assuming the change was voluntary, how will the adjustment due to the change be treated?

48. Crow Finance Company experiences bad debts of about 5% of its outstanding loans. At the end of the year, the company had outstanding receivables of $18 million. This balance included $3 million of accrued interest receivable. Crow's loan loss reserve for the year was computed as follows:

Balance, January 1, 1996	$750,000
Accounts written off as uncollectible	
Loans made in 1996	(10,000)
Loans made in prior years	(35,000)
Collections on loans previously written off	9,000
Adjustment to required balance	186,000
Balance, December 31, 1996	$900,000

a. Determine the effects of the above on Crow's taxable income for 1996.
b. Assume that Crow has used the reserve method to compute its taxable income for the 10 years the company has been in existence. In 1996, you begin preparing Crow's tax return. What should be done with regard to the reserve?

49. Jeffrey Robin, the president of Robin Furniture Corporation (average annual gross receipts of $4 million), has prepared the company's financial statements and income tax return for the past 25 years. However, in July 1997, after Jeffrey had filed the 1996 return, he hired you to prepare the 1997 corporate tax return because he has not studied taxes for over 20 years and suspects that the rules may have changed. Based upon an initial examination of his trial balance and some account analyses, you have determined that the following items may require adjustments:

- The company uses the LIFO inventory method, as valued at cost. At the end of 1996, the company has written off $25,000 for inventory items that were still on hand but probably were not marketable (because the products are obsolete). No such write-off had been taken in prior years.
- The company expenses all freight on merchandise when the goods are received. The expensed freight allocable to the beginning inventory for 1997 was $12,000.
- The company accrues salaries and commissions, but expenses payroll taxes in the year paid. Because of large 1996 year-end bonuses that were not paid until the beginning of 1997, the company had $24,000 in accrued payroll taxes at the beginning of 1997.
- The company uses the accrual method and has a reserve for bad debts equal to 3% of accounts receivable, which is an accurate percentage. The balance in the account at the beginning of the year is $15,000.

Write a letter to Mr. Robin explaining the adjustments that will be required and how the changes will be implemented. The address of Robin Furniture Corporation is 1000 East Maryland, Evansville, IL 47722.

50. Floyd, a cash basis taxpayer, has agreed to sell land to Beige, Inc., a well-established and highly profitable company. Beige is willing to (1) pay $100,000 cash or (2) pay $25,000 cash and the balance ($75,000) plus interest at 10% (the Federal rate) in two years. Floyd is in the 35% marginal tax bracket (combined Federal and state) for all years and believes he can reinvest the sales proceeds and earn a 14% before-tax rate of return.
a. Should Floyd accept the deferred payments option if his basis in the land is $10,000?
b. Do you think your results would change if Floyd's basis in the land is $90,000?

51. Kay, who is not a dealer, sold an apartment house to Polly during the current year (1996). The closing statement for the sale is as follows:

Total selling price		$100,000
Add: Polly's share of property taxes (6 months) paid by Kay		2,500
Less: Kay's 11% mortgage assumed by Polly	$55,000	
Polly's refundable binder ("earnest money") paid in 1995	1,000	
Polly's 11% installment note given to Kay	30,000	
Kay's real estate commissions and attorney's fees	7,500	(93,500)
Cash paid to Kay at closing		$ 9,000
Cash due from Polly = $9,000 + $7,500 expenses		$ 16,500

During 1996, Kay collected $4,000 in principal on the installment note and $2,000 interest. Kay's basis in the property was $70,000 [$85,000 – $15,000 (depreciation)], and there was $9,000 in potential depreciation recapture under § 1250. The Federal rate is 9%.

a. Compute the following:
   1. Total gain.
   2. Contract price.
   3. Payments received in the year of sale.
   4. Recognized gain in the year of sale and the character of such gain.

(*Hint:* Think carefully about the manner in which the property taxes are handled before you begin your computations.)

b. Same as (a)(2) and (3), except Kay's basis in the property was $45,000.

52. On June 30, 1996, Kelly sold property for $250,000 cash on the date of sale and a $750,000 note due on September 30, 1997. No interest was stated in the contract. The present value of the note (using 13.2%, which was the Federal rate) was $640,000. Kelly's basis in the property was $400,000, and $40,000 of the gain was depreciation recapture under § 1245. Expenses of the sale totaled $10,000, and Kelly was not a dealer in the property sold.
    a. Compute Kelly's gain to be reported in 1996.
    b. Compute Kelly's interest income for 1997.

53. On July 1, 1995, a cash basis taxpayer sold land for $800,000 due on the date of the sale and $6 million principal and $741,600 interest (6%) due on June 30, 1997. The seller's basis in the land was $1 million. The Federal short-term rate was 8%, compounded semiannually.
    a. Compute the seller's interest income and gain in 1995, 1996, and 1997.
    b. Same as (a), except that the amount due in two years was $2 million principal and $508,800 interest and the purchaser will use the cash method to account for interest.

54. Maria made an installment sale of land and a building to Ned. There was no ordinary income recapture on the building. At the time of the sale, the Federal rate was 8%, and the market rate on similar contracts was 10%. Under the contract, Ned would make payments as follows:

Cash at closing, July 1, 1996	$ 50,000
Interest at 9%, due June 30, 1997*	27,607
Interest at 9%, due June 30, 1998*	27,607
Principal due June 30, 1998	300,000

*Interest is compounded semiannually.

    a. Will interest be imputed on the contract?
    b. Assuming Maria is a cash basis taxpayer, what is her interest income for 1996 under the contract?
    c. Assuming Ned is an accrual basis taxpayer, what is his interest expense for 1996 under the contract?

55. On December 30, 1996, Father sold land to Son for $10,000 cash and a 7% installment note with a face amount of $190,000. In 1997, after paying $30,000 on the principal of the note, Son sold the land. In 1998, Son paid Father $25,000 on the note principal. Father's basis in the land was $50,000. Assuming Son sold the land for $250,000, compute Father's taxable gain in 1997.

56. George sold land to an unrelated party in 1995. His basis in the land was $40,000, and the selling price was $100,000—$25,000 payable at closing and $25,000 (plus 10% interest) due January 1, 1996, 1997, and 1998. What would be the tax consequences of the following? [Treat each part independently and assume (1) George did not elect out of the installment method and (2) the installment obligations have values equal to their face amounts.]

a. In 1996, George gave to his daughter the right to collect all future payments on the installment obligations.
b. In 1996, after collecting the payment due on January 1, George transferred the installment obligation to his 100% controlled corporation in exchange for additional shares of stock.
c. On December 31, 1996, George received the payment due on January 1, 1997. On December 15, 1997, George died, and the remaining installment obligation was transferred to his estate. The estate collected the amount due on January 1, 1998.

57. The Dove Construction Company reports its income by the completed contract method. At the end of 1996, the company completed a contract to construct a building at a total cost of $980,000. The contract price was $1,200,000. However, the customer refused to accept the work and would not pay anything on the contract because he claimed the roof did not meet specifications. Dove's engineers estimated it would cost $140,000 to bring the roof up to the customer's standards. In 1997, the dispute was settled in the customer's favor; the roof was improved at a cost of $170,000, and the customer accepted the building and paid the $1,200,000.
a. What would be the effects of the above on Dove's taxable income for 1996 and 1997?
b. Same as (a), except Dove had $1,100,000 accumulated cost under the contract at the end of 1996.

58. Rust Company is a real estate construction company with average annual gross receipts of $4 million. Rust uses the completed contract method, and the contracts require 18 months to complete.
a. Which of the following costs would be allocated to construction in progress by Rust?
1. The payroll taxes on direct labor.
2. The current services pension costs for employees whose wages are included in direct labor.
3. Accelerated depreciation on equipment used on contracts.
4. Sales tax on materials assigned to contracts.
5. The past service costs for employees whose wages are included in direct labor.
6. Bidding expenses for contracts awarded.
b. Assume that Rust generally builds commercial buildings under contracts with the owners and reports the income by the completed contract method. The company is considering building a series of similar stores for a retail chain. The gross profit margin would be a low percentage, but the company's gross receipts would triple. Write a letter to your client, Rust Company, explaining the tax accounting implications of entering into these contracts. Rust's mailing address is P.O. Box 1000, Harrisonburg, VA 22807.

59. Indicate the accounting method that should be used to compute the income from the following contracts:
a. A contract to build six jet aircraft.
b. A contract to build a new home. The contractor's average annual gross receipts are $15 million.
c. A contract to manufacture 3,000 pairs of boots for a large retail chain. The manufacturer has several contracts to produce the same boot for other retailers.
d. A contract to pave a parking lot. The contractor's average annual gross receipts are $2 million.

60. Ostrich Company makes gasoline storage tanks. Everything produced is under contract (that is, the company does not produce until it gets a contract for a product). Ostrich makes three basic models. However, the tanks must be adapted to each individual customer's location and needs (e.g., the location of the valves, the quality of the materials and insulation). Discuss the following issues relative to Ostrich's operations:
a. An examining IRS agent contends that each of the company's contracts is to produce a "unique product." What difference does it make whether the product is unique or a "shelf item"?

b. Producing one of the tanks takes over one year from start to completion, and the total cost is in excess of $1 million. What costs must be capitalized for this contract that are not subject to capitalization for a contract with a shorter duration and lower cost?
c. What must Ostrich do with the costs of bidding on contracts?
d. Ostrich frequently makes several cost estimates for a contract, using various estimates of materials costs. These costs fluctuate almost daily. Assuming Ostrich must use the percentage of completion method to report the income from the contract, what will be the consequence if the company uses the highest estimate of a contract's cost and the actual cost is closer to the lowest estimated cost?

61. Swallow Company is a large real estate construction company that reports its income by the percentage of completion method. In 1997, the company completed a contract at a total cost of $1,960,000. The contract price was $2,400,000. At the end of 1996, the year the contract was begun, Swallow estimated the total cost of the contract would be $2,100,000, and total accumulated costs on the contract at the end of 1996 were $1,400,000. The relevant tax rate is 34%, and the relevant Federal interest rate is 7%. Assume that all returns were filed and taxes were paid on March 15 following the close of the calendar tax year.
a. Compute the gross profit on the contract for 1996 and 1997.
b. Compute the lookback interest due with the 1997 return.
c. Before bidding on a contract, Swallow generally makes three estimates of total contract costs: (1) optimistic, (2) pessimistic, and (3) most likely (based on a blending of optimistic and pessimistic assumptions). The company has asked you to write a letter explaining which of these estimates should be used for percentage of completion purposes. In writing your letter, you should consider the fact that Swallow is incorporated and has made an S corporation election; therefore, the income and deductions flow through to the shareholders who are all individuals in the 36% marginal tax bracket. The relevant Federal interest rate is 8%. Swallow's mailing address is 400 Front Avenue, Ashland, OR 97520.

62. In 1996, Quail Construction Company began two contracts that were completed in 1997:

- Contract #1. The company reported $300,000 cost and $150,000 profit on the contract. In 1997, the company completed the contract, incurring additional cost of $200,000 and reporting an additional $50,000 profit on the contract.
- Contract #2. The company reported $500,000 cost and $100,000 profit on the contract. In 1997, the company incurred an additional $200,000 to complete the contract. The contract price was $650,000.

Quail is a large real estate contractor and reports its profits by the percentage of completion method. The company's marginal tax rate in all relevant years was 34%, and the relevant Federal interest rate was 7%.
a. Compute the lookback interest payable or receivable by Quail.
b. Write a letter to Amos Brown, the president of Quail Construction Company, explaining to him the consequences of the company's errors in estimating contract costs. Quail's mailing address is 200 Country Road, Orono, ME 04469.

63. Bluebird Company, a furniture retailer, is adding a new line of merchandise. In the current year, the company purchased merchandise with an invoice price of $700,000, less a 2% discount for early payment. Freight and handling charges totaled $60,000. The company had to lease additional storage space in a warehouse three blocks from the store. The lease on the storage space was $30,000 for the year. A buyer was added to handle the new line of merchandise, and her salary was $35,000 for the year. Also, as a result of the increase in inventory of goods on hand, the company's insurance increased by $5,000. The invoice cost of the goods on hand at the end of the year was $105,000. Compute the company's ending inventory under the FIFO method.

64. Lavender Manufacturing Company began business in the current year. The company uses the simplified method to allocate mixed services costs to production. The company's costs and expenses for the year were as follows:

Direct labor	$1,250,000
Direct materials	2,000,000
Factory supervision	200,000
Personnel department	100,000
Computer operations	50,000
General administration	150,000
Marketing	100,000
Interest	25,000
	$3,875,000

a. Determine Lavender's total production costs for the year.
b. What suggestions can you offer regarding the allocation of the company's mixed services costs?

65. Flamingo Company produces small machinery. The company also produces parts used to repair the machinery. The parts may be sold for several years after the company has discontinued the product. Flamingo has on hand parts with an original cost of $600,000. The total offering price on these goods is $960,000. However, the company expects to sell only 80% of the parts on hand. The excess parts are kept in case the estimates are incorrect.
a. Can Flamingo deduct the excess inventory under the lower of cost or market rule?
b. Assume that Flamingo deducted the cost of the excess parts on hand. While the parts were still on hand, the company elected LIFO. What are the implications of the change in inventory method?

66. In 1996, Gail changed from the use of the lower of cost or market FIFO method to the LIFO method. The ending inventory for 1995 was computed as follows:

Item	FIFO Cost	Replacement Cost	Lower of Cost or Market
A	$10,000	$ 9,000	$ 9,000
B	25,000	30,000	25,000
			$34,000

a. What is the correct beginning inventory in 1996 under the LIFO method?
b. What immediate tax consequences (if any) would result from the switch to LIFO?

67. Amber Company has used the dollar-value LIFO technique for the past three years. The company has only one inventory pool. Its beginning inventory for the current year was computed as follows:

	Base Period Cost	LIFO Index	LIFO Layer
Base inventory	$1,250,000	1.0	$1,250,000
Year 1 layer	450,000	1.15	517,500
Year 2 layer	100,000	1.05	105,000
	$1,800,000		$1,872,500

The ending inventory is $1,955,000 at current period prices and $1,700,000 at base period prices. Determine the company's LIFO inventory value as of the end of the current year.

68. Your client, Bob Young, is negotiating a sale of investment real estate for $12 million. Bob believes that the buyer would pay cash of $8 million and a note for $4 million, or $3 million cash and a note for $9 million. The notes will pay interest at slightly above the market rate. Bob realizes that the second option involves more risks of collection, but he is willing to accept that risk if the tax benefits of the installment sale are substantial. Write a letter to Bob advising him of the tax consequences of choosing the lower down payment and larger note option, assuming he has no other installment receivables. Bob's address is 200 Jerdone, Gettysburg, PA 17325.

RESEARCH PROBLEMS

Note: ***West's Federal Taxation on CD-ROM*** *can be used in preparing solutions to the Research Problems. Alternatively, tax research materials contained in a standard tax library can be used.*

Research Problem 1. White Electric Company generates electricity that it sells to residential, commercial, and industrial customers. The company uses coal to generate the electricity and accounts for the cost of the coal on a LIFO basis. That is, the coal on hand at the end of the year is deemed to be from the earliest purchases. This LIFO assumption is generally consistent with how the coal is actually used because newly purchased coal is placed on top of the coal on hand at the time of the delivery. The IRS agent contends that LIFO cannot be used to account for the coal because it is a supply rather than inventory. You concede that the coal is not inventory; however, you contend that because the LIFO assumption accurately depicts the cost of the coal used, the method used clearly reflects income, and therefore the IRS cannot change the method. Help your client resolve this issue with the IRS agent.

Research Problem 2. Violet Company discovered certain equipment used in its repair operations had been accounted for as inventory rather than as fixed assets. This incorrect treatment applied to all years in which the equipment had been used, and all of those years are open under the statute of limitations. Violet filed amended returns for all years affected by the incorrect treatment to obtain a refund of overpayments of taxes for the years affected. The IRS refused to accept the amended returns. The IRS reasoned that Violet was actually changing accounting methods and this can only be accomplished through a request for change in methods. In addition, the IRS concluded that an adjustment due to a voluntary change in accounting method must be taken into income for the year of the change. Is the IRS correct? Write a letter to Agnes Boyd, the president of Violet Company, that contains your advice and prepare a memo for the tax files. Violet's address is 100 Whitaker's Mill, Fargo, ND 58105.

Research Problem 3. Rex Custer has incorporated his insurance agency. Rex is the only shareholder, and he handles all of the company's cash receipts and disbursements. In 1996, Rex did not take any salary from the corporation because he had substantial income from other sources. The corporation earned $50,000 for the year, and the corporate tax rate was far lower than Rex's personal tax rate. The IRS contends that Rex constructively received the $50,000 because he had the power to withdraw the funds from the corporation and did not take the money out of the corporation (as salary) solely to avoid his higher marginal tax rate. Is the IRS correct in its application of the constructive receipt doctrine?

Partial list of research aids:
William A. Carahan, 67 TCM 2689, T.C.Memo. 94–163 (1994).

Research Problem 4. You recently contracted to perform tax services for a new funeral home. In preparing the initial tax return, you must decide whether the funeral home can use the cash method of accounting. When discussing this issue with the manager, the manager points out that the company is actually a service business and that the only materials involved are caskets, which average only 15% of the price of a funeral. Is the funeral home required to use the accrual method of accounting?

Research Problem 5. State law requires Clear Cola Company to sell its beverages in returnable bottles. Customers pay a deposit for the bottles, and Clear is required to refund the deposit to anyone who returns the bottles. Grocery stores collect the deposits and pay the customers for returned bottles and then are reimbursed by Clear. The company unsuccessfully argued that the collections of the deposits should not be treated as income. Subsequently, the company argued that if income must be recognized from the receipt of a deposit, a deduction should be allowed for the estimated amounts that must be paid to the customers. Clear estimates that 80% of all bottles are returned. Can Clear accrue a deduction for the estimated cost of bottles that will be returned and thus accurately match revenue and expenses?

CHAPTER

19

DEFERRED COMPENSATION

LEARNING OBJECTIVES

After completing Chapter 19, you should be able to:

1. Distinguish between qualified (defined contribution and defined benefit) and nonqualified compensation arrangements.
2. Identify the qualification requirements for qualified plans.
3. Discuss the tax consequences of qualified plans.
4. Calculate the limitations on contributions to and benefits from qualified plans.
5. Understand the qualified plan (Keogh plan) available to a self-employed person.
6. Describe the benefits of an Individual Retirement Account (IRA).
7. Understand the rationale for nonqualified deferred compensation plans and the related tax treatment.
8. Explain the value of restricted property plans.
9. Differentiate the tax treatment of qualified and nonqualified stock options.
10. Identify tax planning opportunities available with deferred compensation.

OUTLINE

Compensation is important in any type of organization. For example, during the 1992 annual baseball winter meeting, the "meat market" produced $258 million in salary commitments. The San Francisco Giants paid $43.75 million to left-fielder Barry Bonds, and Greg Maddux turned down a reported $34 million from the New York Yankees to pitch for the Atlanta Braves for only $28 million. Apparently, the Yankees were prepared to go to $39 million. Compare these salaries to the approximately $22,000 paid to a new second lieutenant in the U.S. Army or the approximately $30,000 paid to an entry-level accountant.

These record deals caused the mayor of Chicago, Richard J. Daley, to suggest that the city of Chicago should tax the salaries of the Chicago Cubs players directly, rather than impose an entertainment tax on tickets sold at the Chicago baseball park. Obviously, such a tax would punish the players, rather than the ticket holders.

If you have not yet chosen a profession, consider becoming a major league baseball player. The minimum salary in 1995 was $109,000, and the average salary was $1.1 million, up from $329,000 in 1984. For 1995, players for the New York Yankees are the highest paid in major league baseball with an average paycheck of $2.08 million per year. Next are the Atlanta Braves and Chicago White Sox at $1.89 million and $1.63 million per player, respectively. But consider the plight of Roberto Bonilla, who at age 28 received a five-year $28.5 million contract from the New York Mets—$5.7 million per year. Bonilla had spent six years with the Pittsburgh Pirates, with a batting average of .302. Unfortunately, after the Mets paid him that princely sum, he went into a batting slump. The Mets' fans booed him so loudly that he wore ear plugs. For 1995, he received a salary of $5 million from the Baltimore Orioles. The lowest paid team is the Montreal Expos (average player salary of $410,000).

At the same time, consider the tax consequences. A professional athlete's lifetime sports income is compressed into about 10 years. Yet income averaging is not allowed for Federal income tax purposes. As a result, the athlete will lose a larger portion of lifetime earned income in the form of taxes than someone with a comparable amount of earned income over a typical worklife cycle. The athlete does, however, have a method available for reducing the Federal income tax liability in the form of deferred compensation.

This chapter discusses the various types of deferred compensation arrangements available to employees and self-employed individuals. With **deferred compensation,** an employee receives compensation for services after the period when the services were performed. The tax law encourages employers to offer deferred compensation plans to their employees to supplement the Federal Social Security retirement system. Contributions to qualified pension, profit sharing, or stock bonus plans offer three major advantages:

- Contributions are immediately deductible by the employer.
- Employees are not taxed until these funds are made available to them.
- Income earned by the plan trust, which has received the contributions, is not subject to tax until made available to the employees.

A variety of deferred compensation arrangements are being offered to employees, including the following:

- Qualified profit sharing plans.
- Qualified pension plans.
- Employee stock ownership plans.
- Cash or deferred arrangement plans.
- Tax-deferred annuities.
- Incentive stock option plans.
- Nonqualified deferred compensation plans.
- Restricted property plans.
- Cafeteria benefit plans.

In a 1995 survey, KPMG Peat Marwick found that 91 percent of employers with 200 or more employees offer some kind of retirement plan, up from 89 percent in 1994. At least 56 percent of the employers offer two different types of retirement plans. The § 401(k) plan (a defined contribution plan) is the most popular, but the KPMG survey found an increase in the traditional defined benefit pension plan. However, these defined benefit pension plans were less generous than the older plans of this type.

In addition to the various types of deferred compensation, employees may receive other valuable fringe benefits, some of which may be tax-free. Examples of such benefits include group term life insurance, medical reimbursement plans, company-supplied automobiles, education expense reimbursement plans, and group legal services.[1]

The Code, in certain circumstances, prohibits a deduction for certain types of fringe benefits such as a golden parachute payment. Refer to the subsequent discussion under Nonqualified Deferred Compensation Plans.

Qualified Pension, Profit Sharing, and Stock Bonus Plans

1 Learning Objective
Distinguish between qualified (defined contribution and defined benefit) and nonqualified compensation arrangements.

The Federal government has encouraged private pension and profit sharing plans to keep retired people from becoming dependent on the government. Therefore, the Federal tax law provides substantial tax benefits for plans that meet certain

[1] Refer to the discussions in Chapters 4 and 5.

requirements. The major requirement for qualification is that a plan not discriminate in favor of highly compensated employees.

TYPES OF PLANS

There are three types of qualified plans: pension, profit sharing, and stock bonus plans.

Pension Plans. A **pension plan** is a deferred compensation arrangement that provides for systematic payments of definitely determinable retirement benefits to employees who meet the requirements set forth in the plan. Benefits are generally measured by and based on such factors as years of service and employee compensation. Employer contributions under a qualified pension plan must *not* depend on profits. In addition, they must be sufficient to provide definitely determinable benefits on some actuarial basis (except for a defined contribution pension plan).

There are basically two types of qualified pension plans: defined benefit plans and defined contribution plans.

A **defined benefit plan** includes a formula that defines the benefits employees are to receive.[2] Under such a plan, an employer must make annual contributions based upon actuarial computations that will be sufficient to pay the vested retirement benefits. If a plan document permits, employees may make contributions to the pension fund. Separate accounts are not maintained for each participant. A defined benefit plan provides some sense of security for employees since the benefits may be expressed in fixed dollar amounts.

Under a **defined contribution pension plan** (or money purchase plan), a separate account must be maintained for each participant. Benefits are based solely on (1) the amount contributed and (2) income from the fund that accrues to the participant's account.[3] In essence, the plan defines the amount the employer is required to contribute (e.g., a flat dollar amount, an amount based on a special formula, or an amount equal to a certain percentage of compensation). Consequently, actuarial calculations are not required to determine the employer's annual contribution. Upon retirement, an employee's pension amount depends on the value of his or her account. Although it is not mandatory, a plan may require or permit employee contributions to the pension fund.

EXAMPLE 1

The qualified pension plan of Rose Company calls for both the employer and employee to contribute annually to the pension trust an amount equal to 5% of the employee's compensation. Since the employer's rate of contribution is fixed, this pension plan is a defined contribution plan. If the plan called for contributions sufficient to provide retirement benefits equal to 30% of the employee's average salary for the last five years of employment, it would be a defined benefit plan. ▼

Concept Summary 19–1 compares and contrasts a defined benefit plan and a defined contribution plan.

Profit Sharing Plans. A **profit sharing plan** is a deferred compensation arrangement established and maintained by an employer to provide for employee participation in the company's profits. Contributions are paid from the employer's current or accumulated profits to a trustee and are commingled in a single trust

[2] § 414(j).

[3] § 414(i).

CONCEPT SUMMARY 19–1

Defined Benefit Plan and Defined Contribution Plan Compared

Defined Benefit Plan	Defined Contribution Plan
Includes a pension plan.	Includes profit sharing, stock bonus, money purchase, target benefit, qualified cash or deferred compensation, and employee stock ownership plans.
Determinable benefits based upon years of service and average compensation. Benefits calculated by a formula.	An account for each participant. Ultimate benefits depend upon contributions and investment performance.
Maximum annual *benefits* payable may not exceed the smaller of (1) $120,000 (in 1996)* or (2) 100% of the participant's average earnings in the three highest years of employment.	Maximum annual *contribution* to an account may not exceed the smaller of (1) $30,000* or (2) 25% of the participant's compensation (15% for a profit sharing plan).
Forfeitures must reduce subsequent funding costs and cannot increase the benefits any participant can receive under the plan.	Forfeitures may be allocated to the accounts of remaining participants.
Subject to minimum funding requirement in order to avoid penalties.	Exempt from funding requirements.
Greater administrative and actuarial costs and greater reporting requirements.	Costs and reporting requirements less burdensome.
Subject to plan termination insurance.	Not subject to plan termination insurance.
More favorable to employees who are older when plan is adopted since it is possible to fund higher benefits over a shorter period.	More favorable to younger employees since, over a longer period, higher benefits may result.

*This amount is subject to indexing annually in $5,000 increments.

fund. Thus, an employer does not have to have a profit for the current year to make a contribution (the contribution can be from accumulated profits).

In a profit sharing plan, separate accounts are maintained for each participant. The plan must provide a definite, predetermined formula for allocating the contributions (made to the trustee) among the participants. Likewise, it must include a definite, predetermined formula for distributing the accumulated funds after a fixed number of years, on the attainment of a stated age, or on the occurrence of certain events such as illness, layoff, or retirement. A company is not required to contribute a definite, predetermined amount to the plan, although substantial and recurring contributions must be made to meet the permanency requirement. Forfeitures arising under this plan do not have to be used to reduce the employer's contribution. Instead, forfeitures may be used to increase the individual accounts of the remaining participants as long as these increases do not result in prohibited discrimination.[4] Since a profit sharing plan does not necessarily emphasize retirement income, benefits to employees may normally be distributed through lump-sum payouts.

[4] Reg. §§ 1.401–1(b) and 1.401–4(a)(1)(iii).

Stock Bonus Plans. A **stock bonus plan** is another form of deferred compensation. In this case, an employer establishes and maintains the plan in order to contribute shares of its stock. The contributions need not be dependent on the employer's profits. A stock bonus plan is subject to the same requirements as a profit sharing plan for purposes of allocating and distributing the stock among the employees.[5] Any benefits of the plan are distributable in the form of stock of the employer company, except that distributable fractional shares may be paid in cash.

Employee Stock Ownership Plans. An **employee stock ownership plan (ESOP)** is a stock bonus trust that qualifies as a tax-exempt employee trust under § 401(a). Technically, an ESOP is a defined contribution plan that is either a qualified stock bonus plan or a stock bonus and a money purchase plan, each of which is qualified under § 401(a). An ESOP must invest primarily in qualifying employer securities.[6]

Since the corporation can contribute stock rather than cash, there is no cash-flow drain. If stock is contributed, no cash outlay is required, and the corporation receives a tax deduction equal to the fair market value of the stock. Under § 1032, the employer-corporation does not recognize a gain or loss on the contributed stock. The corporation may deduct dividends paid in cash (or dividends used to repay certain ESOP loans) on shares held by an ESOP. The tax savings accruing under the plan may have a favorable impact on the company's working capital. An ESOP also provides flexibility, since contributions may vary from year to year and, in fact, may be omitted in any one year.[7]

A company can fund the ESOP by acquiring outstanding shares of stock from its shareholders, who receive capital gain treatment upon the sale of their stock. Owners of small closely held corporations may elect nonrecognition treatment for any gain realized on the sale of securities to an ESOP where qualified replacement property is purchased during a 15-month period.[8] This 15-month period begins 3 months before the date of the sale and ends 12 months after that date. Nonrecognition treatment is permitted only if the seller has held the securities for at least three years prior to the sale to the ESOP.

Employees are not subject to tax until they receive a distribution of stock or cash from the trust. Distributions to employees may be made entirely in cash or partly in cash and partly in employer securities. A participant must have the right to demand the entire distribution in the form of employer securities.[9]

EXAMPLE 2

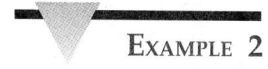

Gray Company establishes an ESOP for its employees and contributes unissued stock to the ESOP trust. The company receives a deduction for the contribution, and there is no cash-flow drain. The employees are not subject to tax until a subsequent stock or cash distribution from the trust. ▼

EXAMPLE 3

The ESOP of Gray Company borrows $100,000 from City Bank in January 1996. The loan is secured by the stock interest and is guaranteed by the company. The ESOP buys stock for the trust from a shareholder of Gray Company for $100,000. The shareholder has owned the stock for four years. The shares are then allocated among the employees' retirement accounts. The shareholder obtains capital gain treatment on the sale or can elect nonrecognition treatment if qualified replacement securities are purchased during a 15-month period. Gray Company makes deductible contributions to the ESOP, which, in turn, pays off the loan. ▼

[5] Reg. § 1.401–1(b)(1)(iii).
[6] § 4975(e)(7).
[7] Reg. § 1.401–1(b)(2).
[8] Qualified replacement property is defined in § 1042(c)(4).
[9] § 409(h)(1).

QUALIFICATION REQUIREMENTS

2 LEARNING OBJECTIVE
Identify the qualification requirements for qualified plans.

To be *qualified*, and thereby to receive favorable tax treatment, a plan must satisfy the following requirements:

- Exclusive benefit requirement.
- Nondiscrimination requirements.
- Participation and coverage requirements.
- Vesting requirements.
- Distribution requirements.

These qualification rules are highly technical and numerous. Thus, an employer should submit a retirement plan to the IRS for a determination letter regarding the qualified status of the plan and trust. A favorable determination letter may be expected within 6 to 12 months, indicating that the plan meets the qualification requirements and that the trust is tax-exempt. However, the continued qualification of the plan depends upon its actual operations. Therefore, the operations of the plan should be reviewed periodically.

Exclusive Benefit Requirement. A pension, profit sharing, or stock bonus trust must be created by an employer for the exclusive benefit of employees or their beneficiaries. Under a prudent person concept, the IRS specifies four investment conditions for meeting the *exclusive benefit* requirement:[10]

- The cost of the investment must not exceed the fair market value at the time of purchase.
- A fair return commensurate with prevailing rates must be provided.
- Sufficient liquidity must be maintained to permit distributions in accordance with the terms of the qualified plan.
- The safeguards and diversity that a prudent investor would adhere to must be present.

Nondiscrimination Requirements. The contributions and benefits under a plan must *not discriminate* in favor of highly compensated employees. A plan is not considered discriminatory merely because the contributions and benefits on behalf of the employees are uniformly related to their compensation.[11] For example, a pension plan that provides for the allocation of employer contributions based upon a flat 3 percent of each employee's compensation would not be discriminatory even though highly paid employees receive greater benefits.

Qualified plans may be *integrated* with Social Security (employer FICA contributions for covered employees may be taken into account) to avoid giving lower-level employees proportionately greater benefits or contributions. Integrated plans may not reduce a participant's benefits or contributions to less than one-half of what they would have been without integration.

Participation and Coverage Requirements. A qualified plan must provide, at a minimum, that all employees in the covered group who are 21 years of age are eligible to participate after completing one year of service. A year of service is generally defined as the completion of 1,000 hours of service within a measuring period of 12 consecutive months. As an alternative, where the plan provides that 100 percent of an employee's accrued benefits will be vested upon entering the

[10] § 401(a); Rev.Rul. 65–178, 1965–2 C.B. 94, and Rev.Rul. 73–380, 1973–2 C.B. 124.

[11] §§ 401(a)(4) and (5).

plan, the employee's participation may be postponed until the later of age 21 or two years from the date of employment.[12] Once the age and service requirements are met, an employee must begin participating no later than the *earlier* of the following:

- The first day of the first plan year beginning after the date upon which the requirements were satisfied.
- Six months after the date on which the requirements were satisfied.[13]

EXAMPLE 4

Coffee Corporation has a calendar year retirement plan covering its employees. The corporation adopts the most restrictive eligibility rules permitted. Wilma, age 21, is hired on January 31, 1995, and meets the service requirement over the next 12 months (completes at least 1,000 hours by January 31, 1996). Wilma must be included in this plan no later than July 31, 1996, because the 6-month limitation would be applicable. If the company had adopted the two-year participation rule, Wilma must be included in the plan no later than July 31, 1997. ▼

Since a qualified plan must be primarily for the benefit of employees and be nondiscriminatory, the plan has to cover a reasonable percentage of the company employees. A plan will be qualified only if it satisfies one of the following tests:[14]

- The plan benefits at least 70 percent of all non-highly compensated employees (the *percentage test*).
- The plan benefits a percentage of non-highly compensated employees equal to at least 70 percent of the percentage of highly compensated employees benefiting under the plan (the *ratio test*).
- The plan meets the *average benefits test.*

If a company has no highly compensated employees, the retirement plan will automatically satisfy the coverage rules.

To satisfy the *average benefits test,* the plan must benefit any employees who qualify under a classification set up by the employer and found by the Secretary of the Treasury not to be discriminatory in favor of highly compensated employees (the classification test). In addition, the average benefit percentage for non-highly compensated employees must be at least 70 percent of the average benefit percentage for highly compensated employees. The *average benefit percentage* means, with respect to any group of employees, the average of the benefit percentages calculated separately for each employee in the group. The term *benefit percentage* means the employer-provided contributions (including forfeitures) or benefits of an employee under all qualified plans of the employer, expressed as a percentage of that employee's compensation.

An employee is a **highly compensated employee** if, at any time during the year or the preceding year, the employee satisfies *any* of the following:[15]

- Was a 5 percent owner of the company.
- Received more than $100,000 (in 1996) in annual compensation from the employer.
- Received more than $66,000 (in 1996) in annual compensation from the employer *and* was a member of the top-paid group of the employer.
- Was an officer of the company and received compensation greater than 150 percent of the maximum statutory dollar amount of the annual addition to a defined contribution plan ($30,000 × 150% = $45,000).

[12] §§ 410(a)(1)(A) and (B).
[13] § 410(a)(4).
[14] § 410(b).
[15] §§ 401(a)(4) and 414(q).

▼ TABLE 19–1
Three-to-Seven-Year Vesting

Years of Service	Nonforfeitable Percentage
3	20%
4	40%
5	60%
6	80%
7 or more	100%

An employee who is among the top 20 percent of the employees on the basis of compensation paid during the year is a member of the top-paid group. The $66,000 and $100,000 amounts are indexed annually.[16]

An additional *minimum participation* test must also be met. A plan must cover at least 40 percent of all employees or, if fewer, at least 50 employees on one representative day of the plan year. In determining all employees, nonresident aliens, certain union members, and employees not fulfilling the minimum age or years-of-service requirement of the plan may be excluded.[17]

EXAMPLE 5

Rust Corporation's retirement plan meets the 70% test (the percentage test) because 70% of all non-highly compensated employees are benefited. The company has 100 employees, but only 38 of these employees are covered by the plan. Therefore, this retirement plan does not meet the minimum participation requirement. ▼

Vesting Requirements. An employee's right to accrued benefits derived from his or her own contributions must be nonforfeitable from the date of contribution. The accrued benefits derived from employer contributions must be nonforfeitable in accordance with one of two alternative minimum vesting schedules. The purpose of the **vesting requirements** is to protect an employee who has worked a reasonable period of time for an employer from losing employer contributions because of being fired or changing jobs.

A plan will not be a qualified plan unless a participant's employer-provided benefits vest at least as rapidly as under one of *two alternative minimum vesting schedules.* To satisfy the *first alternative,* a participant must have a nonforfeitable right to 100 percent of his or her accrued benefits derived from employer contributions upon completion of five years of service (five-year or cliff vesting). The *second alternative* is satisfied if a participant has a nonforfeitable right at least equal to a percentage of the accrued benefits derived from employer contributions as depicted in Table 19–1 (graded vesting). Of the two alternatives, cliff vesting minimizes administration expenses for a company and provides more vesting for a long-term employee. Neither vesting schedule applies to top-heavy plans.

EXAMPLE 6

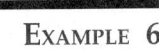

Mitch has six years of service completed as of February 2, 1996, his employment anniversary date. If his defined benefit plan has a five-year (cliff) vesting schedule, 100% of Mitch's accrued benefits are vested. If, however, the plan uses the graded vesting rule, Mitch's nonforfeitable percentage is 80%. ▼

Distribution Requirements. Uniform *minimum distribution rules* exist for all qualified defined benefit and defined contribution plans, Individual Retirement

[16] The indexed amounts for 1996 are provided.

[17] §§ 401(a)(26) and 410(b)(3) and (4).

Accounts (IRAs) and annuities, unfunded deferred compensation plans of state and local governments and tax-exempt employers, and tax-sheltered custodial accounts and annuities. Distributions must begin no later than April 1 of the calendar year *following* the calendar year in which the participant attains age 70½. This commencement date is not affected by the actual date of retirement or termination.[18]

Once age 70½ is reached, minimum annual distributions must be made over the life of the participant or the lives of the participant and a designated individual beneficiary. The amount of the required minimum distribution for a particular year is determined by dividing the account balance as of December 31 of the prior year by the applicable life expectancy. The life expectancy of the owner and his or her beneficiary is based upon the expected return multiples in the Regulations, using ages attained within the calendar year the participant reaches age 70½.[19]

EXAMPLE 7

Beth reaches age 70½ in 1996, and she will also be age 71 in 1996. Her retirement account (an IRA) has a balance of $120,000 on December 31, 1995. Beth must withdraw $7,843 for the 1996 calendar year, assuming her multiple is 15.3 ($120,000 ÷ 15.3). This distribution need not be made until April 1, 1997, but a second distribution must be made by December 31, 1997. ▼

Failure to make a minimum required distribution to a particular participant results in a 50 percent nondeductible excise tax on the excess in any taxable year of the amount that should have been distributed over the amount that actually was distributed. The tax is imposed on the individual required to take the distribution (the payee).[20] The Secretary of the Treasury is authorized to waive the tax for a given taxpayer year if the taxpayer is able to establish that the shortfall is due to reasonable error and that reasonable steps are being taken to remedy the shortfall.

If a taxpayer receives an *early distribution* from a qualified retirement plan, a 10 percent additional tax is levied on the full amount of any distribution includible in gross income.[21] For this purpose, the term qualified retirement plan includes a qualified defined benefit plan or defined contribution plan, a tax-sheltered annuity or custodial account, or an IRA. Certain distributions, however, are *not* treated as early distributions:

- Made on or after the date the employee attains age 59½.
- Made to a beneficiary (or the estate of an employee) on or after the death of the employee.
- Attributable to the employee's being disabled.
- Made as part of a scheduled series of substantially equal periodic payments (made not less frequently than annually) for the life of the participant (or the joint lives of the participant and the participant's beneficiary).
- Made to an employee after separation from service because of early retirement under the plan after attaining age 55. This exception to early distribution treatment does not apply to an IRA.
- Used to pay medical expenses to the extent that the expenses are deductible under § 213 (determined regardless of whether or not the taxpayer itemizes deductions). This exception to early distribution treatment does not apply to an IRA.

[18] § 401(a)(9).
[19] Reg. § 1.72–9. Refer to Chapter 4.
[20] § 4974(a).
[21] § 72(t). See Ltr.Rul. 8837071.

A 15 percent excise tax is imposed on excess distributions from qualified plans.[22] The tax is levied on the individual with respect to whom the excess distribution is made and is reduced by the amount of the tax imposed on early distributions (to the extent attributable to the excess distribution). An *excess distribution* is the aggregate amount of the retirement distributions during the taxable year for an individual to the extent that amount exceeds the greater of $150,000 or $112,500 (1996 indexed amount is $155,000). Thus, for 1996 the annual limitation is $155,000. Since the indexed $112,500 amount now exceeds the $150,000, the indexed amount is now the annual limit. The following distributions are *not* subject to this limitation:

- Any retirement distribution made after the death of the individual.
- Any retirement distribution payable to an alternate payee in conformance with a qualified domestic relations order.
- Any retirement distribution attributable to the employee's investment in the contract (after-tax contributions).
- Any retirement distribution not included in gross income by reason of a rollover contribution.

If the taxpayer elects lump-sum distribution treatment, the $155,000 limit is applied separately to the lump-sum distribution and is increased to five times the generally applicable limit with respect to that distribution (to $775,000).

EXAMPLE 8

Emily, age 65, has accumulated $960,000 in a defined contribution plan, $105,000 of which represents her own after-tax contributions. Receiving a lump-sum distribution would result in an excise tax of $12,000.

Account balance	$ 960,000
Less after-tax contributions	(105,000)
Less lump-sum limitation	(775,000)
Amount subject to tax	$ 80,000
15% excise tax	× .15
Excise tax due	$ 12,000

If Emily receives the distribution in the form of an annuity over her expected lifetime of 20 years, her yearly distributions of $48,000 *plus* related interest would probably be less than the $155,000 annual distribution limit. ▼

TAX CONSEQUENCES TO THE EMPLOYEE AND EMPLOYER

3 LEARNING OBJECTIVE
Discuss the tax consequences of qualified plans.

In General. Although employer contributions to qualified plans are generally deductible immediately (subject to contribution and deductibility rules), these amounts are not subject to taxation until distributed to employees.[23] If benefits are paid with respect to an employee (to a creditor of the employee, a child of the employee, etc.), the benefits paid are treated as if paid to the employee. When benefits are distributed to employees, or paid with respect to an employee, the employer does not receive another deduction.

The tax benefit to the employee amounts to a substantial tax deferral and may be viewed as an interest-free loan from the government to the trust fund. Another advantage of a qualified plan is that any income earned by the trust is not taxable

[22] § 4981A.

[23] § 402(a)(1).

to the trust.[24] Employees, in effect, are taxed on such earnings when they receive the retirement benefits.

The taxation of amounts received by employees in periodic or installment payments is generally subject to the annuity rules in § 72 (refer to Chapter 4). Employee contributions have previously been subject to tax and are therefore included in the employee's *investment in the contract.* Two other alternative options are available for benefit distributions. A taxpayer may roll over the benefits into an IRA or another qualified employer retirement plan.[25] A taxpayer also may receive the distribution in a lump-sum payment.

Lump-Sum Distributions from Qualified Plans. The annuity rules do not apply to a **lump-sum distribution.** All such payments are taxed in one year. Since lump-sum payments have been accumulated over a number of years, bunching retirement benefits into one taxable year may impose a high tax burden because of progressive rates. To overcome this bunching effect, for many years the tax law has provided favorable treatment for certain lump-sum distributions. Major changes were made in the lump-sum distribution rules by TRA of 1986. Transitional provisions allow a participant who reached age 50 before January 1, 1986 (born before 1936) to elect the pre-1987 rules on a limited basis.

Under the pre-1987 rules, the taxable amount is allocated between a capital gain portion and an ordinary income portion (which may be subject to a special 10-year averaging treatment).[26] That portion attributable to the employee's service before 1974 qualifies for capital gain treatment. That portion attributable to the employee's service after 1973 is included as ordinary income when received and may be taxed under the 10-year averaging provision. An employee must be a plan participant for at least five years to take advantage of the 10-year averaging option. It is possible to defer tax on some or all of the distribution, provided that the employee elects to roll over the distribution by transferring the proceeds to an IRA or another qualified employer retirement plan.[27]

An employee may *elect* to treat all of the distribution as ordinary income subject to the 10-year forward averaging provision.[28] In some instances, ordinary income treatment is preferable to long-term capital gain treatment because of the favorable averaging technique.

Special preferential averaging treatment of qualified lump-sum distributions can be used only once during a recipient's lifetime. In the case of a small lump-sum distribution, a recipient may prefer to pay ordinary income tax on the amount and save the averaging election for a larger lump-sum distribution in the future.

To determine the tax on a lump-sum distribution, it is necessary to compute the taxable portion of the distribution by subtracting employee contributions and the net unrealized appreciation in the value of any distributed securities of the employer corporation.[29] The taxable amount is then reduced by a minimum distribution allowance to arrive at the amount that is eligible for the 10-year income averaging provisions.[30] The following portion of the lump-sum distribution is treated as a long-term capital gain:

[24] § 501(a).

[25] Refer to the subsequent discussion in this chapter under Individual Retirement Accounts (IRAs).

[26] § 402(e)(1)(C) of the IRC of 1954.

[27] § 402(a)(5).

[28] § 402(e)(4)(L).

[29] Section 402(e)(4)(J) provides that before any distribution a taxpayer may elect not to have this subtraction associated with employer securities apply.

[30] Section 402(e)(1)(D) defines the *minimum distribution allowance* as the smaller of $10,000 or one-half of the total taxable amount of the lump-sum distribution, reduced by 20% of the amount, if any, by which such total taxable amount exceeds $20,000. Thus, for lump-sum distributions of $70,000 or more, there will be no minimum distribution allowance.

$$\text{Taxable amount} \times \frac{\text{Years of service before 1974}}{\text{Total years of service}}$$

(computed without being reduced by the minimum distribution allowance)

The applicable capital gain rate is 20 percent.

After 1986, subject to the transition rule for recipients born before 1936 mentioned earlier, the 10-year forward averaging rule for lump-sum distributions is replaced by a 5-year forward averaging rule.[31] Only one lump-sum distribution received after age 59½ is eligible for the averaging treatment. Furthermore, capital gain treatment for lump-sum distributions (associated with participation before 1974) is repealed.

EXAMPLE 9 Esteban, age 65 and married, retires at the end of 1996 and receives a lump-sum distribution of $100,000 from his company's profit sharing plan. This plan includes $5,000 of his own contributions and $10,000 of unrealized appreciation on his employer's common stock. Esteban was a participant in the plan for 25 years. Since Esteban attained age 50 before January 1, 1986, he is eligible to elect the pre-1987 10-year forward averaging technique (using 1986 rates and the **zero bracket amount**). Refer to the computation model in Concept Summary 19–2.

Taxable portion of the lump-sum distribution		$85,000
Less: Minimum distribution allowance (½ of the taxable amount up to $20,000)	$ 10,000	
Less: 20% of the taxable amount in excess of $20,000: 20% × ($85,000 – $20,000)	(13,000)	
Minimum distribution allowance		–0–
Taxable amount		$85,000
Computation of tax under 10-year averaging:		
Long-term capital gain portion:		
$\$85{,}000 \times \frac{2\ (\textit{service before } 1974)}{25\ (\textit{total service years})} = \$6{,}800 \times .20 =$		$ 1,360
Ordinary income portion:		
10 times the tax on $10,300[32] [1⁄10 ($85,000 – $6,800) + $2,480]		10,817
Tax on lump-sum distribution		$12,177

Thus, Esteban's capital gain on the distribution is $6,800 and is subject to a 20% capital gain rate. Here Esteban may wish to elect to treat the entire distribution as ordinary income using the 10-year forward averaging approach rather than taxing the capital gain portion at the 20% capital gain rate. The tax liability of $11,905 would be less than the previously calculated tax liability of $12,177. The capital gain on the unrealized appreciation in the employer's common stock is not taxable until Esteban sells the stock. In essence, the cost basis of the securities to the trust becomes the tax basis to the employee.[33] If Esteban keeps the securities until he dies, there may be some income tax savings on this gain to the extent his estate or heirs obtain a step-up in basis. ▼

---

[31] § 402(e)(1).

[32] In making this tax computation, it is necessary to use the 1986 Tax Rate Schedule for single taxpayers and to add $2,480 (the zero bracket amount) to the taxable income. Thus, the tax was computed on $10,300, which is $7,820 (1⁄10 of $78,200) plus $2,480. Note that the tax rates provided in the instructions for Form 4972 (Tax on Lump-Sum Distributions) have already been adjusted for the zero bracket amount (i.e., it is not necessary to add the zero bracket amount in making the calculation).

[33] § 402(e)(4)(J).

CONCEPT SUMMARY 19–2

Model for Lump-Sum Distribution Computation

1. Start with the total lump-sum distribution and deduct any employee contributions and unrealized appreciation in employer securities.
2. Divide the result into the capital gain portion and the ordinary income portion.*
3. Multiply the capital gain portion by the capital gain rate of 20%.
4. Reduce the ordinary income portion by the minimum distribution allowance.
5. Divide the ordinary income portion into 5 or 10 equal portions, whichever is appropriate.
6. Compute the tax on the result in step 5 using the 1986 or current rate schedules (whichever is appropriate) for single taxpayers.
7. Multiply the resulting tax by 5 or 10, whichever is appropriate.
8. Add the results in steps 3 and 7.

*In certain circumstances, none of the taxable amount of the distribution will be eligible for capital gain treatment. In other circumstances, the taxpayer may choose to treat none of the taxable amount as capital gain even though part could qualify.

If Esteban (in Example 9) uses the 5-year forward averaging provision instead, the following results are produced:

Taxable amount	$85,000
Computation of tax under 5-year averaging:	
Long-term capital gain portion:	
$\$85{,}000 \times \frac{2 \text{ (service before 1974)}}{25 \text{ (total service years)}} = \$6{,}800 \times .20 =$	$ 1,360
Ordinary income portion:	
5 times the tax on $15,640[34][⅕ ($85,000 – $6,800)]	11,730
Tax on lump-sum distribution	$13,090

Thus, Esteban's capital gain on the distribution is $6,800 (the same as in the 10-year averaging calculation). The capital gain is subject to a 20 percent capital gain rate.[35] Once again the taxpayer may wish to elect to treat the entire distribution as ordinary income using the 5-year forward averaging approach rather than taxing the capital gain portion at the 20 percent capital gain rate. The tax liability of $12,750 would be less than the previously calculated tax liability of $13,090. Since the ordinary income tax under 10-year forward averaging is less than the ordinary income tax under 5-year forward averaging, it appears that Esteban's best alternative is to use the 10-year forward averaging provision and treat the capital gain as ordinary income.

[34] In making the tax computation, it is necessary to use the 1996 Tax Rate Schedule for single taxpayers.

[35] Note that since Esteban qualifies under the transition rules (attained age 50 before January 1, 1986), he is eligible to elect capital gain treatment in conjunction with 5-year forward averaging.

LIMITATIONS ON CONTRIBUTIONS TO AND BENEFITS FROM QUALIFIED PLANS

4 **LEARNING OBJECTIVE**
Calculate the limitations on contributions to and benefits from qualified plans.

In General. The limitations on contributions to and benefits from qualified plans appearing in § 415 must be written into a qualified plan. The plan terminates if these limits are exceeded. Section 404 sets the limits on deductibility applicable to the employer. The limit on the amount deductible under § 404 may have an impact on the amount the employer is willing to contribute. In fact, a defined benefit plan or defined contribution plan is not allowed a deduction for the amount that exceeds the § 415 limitations.[36]

Defined Contribution Plans. Under a *defined contribution plan* (money purchase pension, profit sharing, or stock bonus plan), the annual addition to an employee's account cannot exceed the smaller of $30,000 or 25 percent of the employee's compensation.[37] The $30,000 amount is to be indexed (in $5,000 increments).

Defined Benefit Plans. Under a *defined benefit plan,* the annual benefit payable to an employee is limited to the smaller of $120,000 (in 1996)[38] or 100 percent of the employee's average compensation for the highest three years of employment. This benefit limit is subject to a $10,000 *de minimis* floor. The $120,000 limitation is reduced actuarially if the benefits begin before the Social Security normal retirement age (currently age 65). The $120,000 amount is increased actuarially if the benefits begin after the Social Security normal retirement age. The dollar limit on annual benefits ($120,000) is reduced by one-tenth for each year of *participation* under 10 years by the employee. Furthermore, the 100 percent of compensation limitation and the $10,000 *de minimis* floor are reduced proportionately for a participant who has less than 10 years of *service* with the employer.[39]

EXAMPLE 10

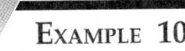

Adam's average compensation for the highest three years of employment is $87,000. Although the § 415(b)(1) limitation does not limit the deduction, the defined benefit plan would not qualify if the plan provides for benefits in excess of the smaller of (1) $87,000 or (2) $120,000 for Adam in 1996 (assuming retirement age of 65). ▼

EXAMPLE 11

Peggy has participated for four years in a defined benefit plan and has six years of service with her employer. Her average compensation for the three highest years is $50,000. Her four years of participation reduce her dollar limitation to $48,000 ($120,000 × 4/10). Her six years of service reduce her 100% of compensation limitation to 60%. Therefore, her limit on annual benefits is $30,000 ($50,000 × 60%). ▼

For collectively bargained plans with at least 100 participants, the annual dollar limitation is the greater of $68,212 or one-half of the $120,000 monetary limit.

The amount of compensation that may be taken into account under any plan is limited to $150,000 (in 1996).[40] Thus, the benefits highly compensated individuals receive may be smaller as a percentage of their pay than those received by non-highly compensated employees.

EXAMPLE 12

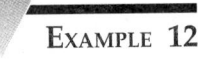

Swan Corporation has a defined contribution plan with a 10% contribution formula. An employee earning less than $150,000 in 1996 would not be affected by this includible

[36] § 404(j).
[37] §§ 415(c) and (d).
[38] This amount is indexed annually.
[39] § 415(b).
[40] §§ 401(a)(17) and 404(l). This amount is to be indexed annually.

compensation limitation. However, an employee earning $300,000 in 1996 would have only 5% of compensation allocated to his or her account because of the $150,000 limit on includible compensation. ▼

Two methods can be used to determine the maximum deduction a corporation is permitted for contributions to pension plans. First, an aggregate cost method allows an actuarially determined deduction based on a level amount, or a level percentage, of compensation over the remaining future service of covered participants. Second, the employer is permitted to deduct the so-called normal cost plus no more than 10 percent of the past service costs.

The employer's contribution is deductible in the tax year such amounts are paid to the pension trust. However, both cash and accrual basis employers may defer the payment of contributions with respect to any tax year until the date fixed for filing the taxpayer's Federal income tax return for that year (including extensions).[41] In effect, the corporation is allowed a deduction to the extent it is compelled to make such contributions to satisfy the funding requirement. If an amount in excess of the allowable amount is contributed in any tax year, the excess may be carried forward and deducted in succeeding tax years (to the extent the carryover plus the succeeding year's contribution does not exceed the deductible limitation for that year).[42]

EXAMPLE 13

During 1996, Green Corporation contributes $17,500 to its qualified pension plan. Normal cost for this year is $7,200, and the amount necessary to pay retirement benefits on behalf of employee services before 1996 is $82,000 (past service costs). The corporation's maximum deduction would be $15,400. This amount consists of the $7,200 normal cost plus 10% ($8,200) of the past service costs. The corporation would have a $2,100 [$17,500 (contribution) − $15,400 (deduction)] contribution carryover. ▼

EXAMPLE 14

Assume in the previous example that Green Corporation has normal cost of $7,200 in 1997 and contributes $10,000 to the pension trust. The corporation's maximum deduction would be $15,400. Green Corporation may deduct $12,100, composed of this year's contribution ($10,000) plus the $2,100 contribution carryover. ▼

A 10 percent excise tax is imposed on nondeductible contributions. The tax is levied on the employer making the contribution. The tax applies to nondeductible contributions for the current year and any nondeductible contributions for the preceding year that have not been eliminated by the end of the current year (as a carryover or by being returned to the employer in the current year).[43]

Profit Sharing and Stock Bonus Plan Limitations. The maximum deduction permitted to an employer each year for contributions to profit sharing and stock bonus plans is 15 percent of the compensation paid or accrued with respect to plan participants. The amount of compensation that may be taken into account under a plan for an employee is $150,000 (in 1996). Any nondeductible excess, a so-called contribution carryover, may be carried forward indefinitely and deducted in subsequent years. The maximum deduction in any succeeding year is 15 percent of all compensation paid or accrued during that taxable year. An employer can circumvent the 15 percent limitation by establishing a money purchase pension plan as a supplement to the profit sharing or stock bonus plan. When

[41] §§ 404(a)(1) and (6).
[42] § 404(a)(1)(D).
[43] § 4972.

there are two or more plans, a maximum deduction of 25 percent of the compensation paid is allowable.[44]

ETHICAL CONSIDERATIONS

Personal Benefit versus Employees' Benefit

As an owner of a small business, Brotherhood, Inc., you are interested when your insurance adviser tells you about a new age-weighted and cross-tested profit sharing plan that satisfies the nondiscrimination requirements of Code § 401(a)(4). He points out that currently only $150,000 of your $250,000 salary is used to calculate your 15 percent annual contribution (e.g., limited to $22,500). Under the new plan, your limit will be 25 percent, up to $30,000.

By changing to this age-weighted and cross-tested plan, you can keep much of the annual contributions you currently make to the business retirement plan for your employees. You will be able to exclude many lower-paid employees and reduce the annual contributions made to the plan on behalf of rank-and-file employees.

Should you agree to this tax shelter, which blends rules for retirement savings plans with rules applicable to pension plans? Most of the affected employees are your friends, and you play softball with them on your company's team.

TOP-HEAVY PLANS

A special set of rules is imposed upon so-called top-heavy plans to discourage retirement plans from conferring disproportionate benefits upon key employees. Top-heaviness is determined on an annual basis.

In general, a **top-heavy plan** allocates more than 60 percent of the cumulative benefits to key employees; a plan may also be part of a top-heavy plan. *Key employees* are defined as follows:

- Officers. However, for purposes of this definition, only the smaller of (1) 50 officers or (2) three employees or 10 percent of all employees (whichever is greater) may be considered officers.
- The 10 employees owning the largest interest in the employer (using the constructive ownership rules of § 318).
- A greater-than-5 percent owner of the employer.
- A greater-than-1 percent owner of the employer with annual compensation in excess of $150,000.[45]

An employee need fall within only one of these categories to be classified as a key employee. However, a key employee does not include officers paid $45,000 or less a year. In addition, for purposes of the 10-employees provision, a key employee does not include an employee whose annual compensation from the employer is $30,000 or less. Employees receiving no compensation for five years are disregarded in testing for top-heavy status.

A top-heavy plan must provide for greater portability for participants who are non-key employees. An employee's right to the accrued benefits derived from employer contributions must become nonforfeitable under either of two vesting

[44] §§ 404(a)(3)(A) and (a)(7).

[45] § 416(i)(1).

▼ TABLE 19–2
Top-Heavy Graded Vesting

Years of Service	Vested Percentage
2	20%
3	40%
4	60%
5	80%
6 or more	100%

schedules. Under the first schedule, an employee who has at least three years of service with the employer must have a nonforfeitable right to 100 percent of his or her accrued benefits derived from employer contributions. Under the second schedule, a six-year graded vesting schedule must be met (see Table 19–2).[46]

To prevent an employer from avoiding the top-heavy rules by establishing a one-person corporate shell, § 269A allows the IRS to allocate any income or deductions between a personal service corporation and its employee-owner. An employee-owner is any employee who owns more than 10 percent of the outstanding stock of the personal service corporation on any day during the tax year.

CASH OR DEFERRED ARRANGEMENT PLANS

A *cash or deferred arrangement plan,* hereafter referred to as a **§ 401(k) plan,** allows participants to elect either to receive up to $9,500 (in 1996)[47] in cash (taxed currently) or to have a contribution made on their behalf to a profit sharing or stock bonus plan. The plan may also be in the form of a salary-reduction agreement between an eligible participant and an employer under which a contribution will be made only if the participant elects to reduce his or her compensation or to forgo an increase in compensation.

Any pretax amount elected by the employee as a plan contribution is not includible in gross income and is 100 percent vested. Any employer contributions are tax deferred, as are earnings on contributions in the plan.

EXAMPLE 15

Sam participates in a § 401(k) plan of his employer. The plan permits the participants to choose between a full salary or a reduced salary where the reduction becomes a before-tax contribution to a retirement plan. Sam elects to contribute 10% of his annual compensation of $30,000 to the plan. Income taxes are paid on only $27,000. No income taxes are paid on the $3,000—or on any earnings—until it is distributed from the plan to Sam. The main benefit of a § 401(k) plan is that Sam can shift a portion of his income to a later taxable year. ▼

The maximum employee annual elective contribution to a § 401(k) plan is $9,500 (in 1996), but that amount is reduced dollar for dollar by other salary-reduction contributions to tax-sheltered annuities and simplified employee pension plans. Elective contributions in excess of the maximum limitation are taxable in the year of deferral. These amounts may be distributed from the plan tax-free before April 15 of the following year. Excess amounts not timely distributed will be taxable in the year of distribution, even though they were included in income

[46] § 416(b).

[47] This amount is indexed annually. For 1995, the amount was $9,240.

in the year of deferral. Annual elective contributions are also limited by complicated nondiscrimination requirements and the defined contribution plan limitations.

A 10 percent excise tax is imposed on the employer for excess contributions not withdrawn from the plan within 2½ months after the close of the plan year. The plan will lose its qualified status if these excess contributions (and any related income) are not withdrawn by the end of the plan year following the plan year in which the excess contributions were made.[48]

EXAMPLE 16

Carmen, an employee of a manufacturing corporation, defers $11,500 in a § 401(k) plan in 1996. The $2,000 excess deferral, along with the appropriate earnings, must be returned to Carmen by April 15, 1997. This $2,000 excess amount plus related income is taxable to her in 1996 and will be taxed again upon distribution (if made after April 15, 1997). There will be a 10% tax on Carmen's employer on any excess contributions not returned within 2½ months after the close of the plan year. ▼

RETIREMENT PLANS FOR SELF-EMPLOYED INDIVIDUALS

5 LEARNING OBJECTIVE
Understand the qualified plan (Keogh plan) available to a self-employed person.

Self-employed individuals (e.g., partners and sole proprietors) and their employees are eligible to receive qualified retirement benefits under what are known as **H.R. 10 (Keogh) plans.** Because of contribution limitations and other restrictions, self-employed plans previously were less attractive than corporate plans. Contributions and benefits of a self-employed person now are subject to the general corporate provisions. Basically, self-employed persons are on a parity with corporate employees. Consequently, Keogh plans can provide a self-employed person with an adequate retirement base.

A variety of funding vehicles can be used for Keogh investments, such as mutual funds, annuities, real estate shares, certificates of deposit, debt instruments, commodities, securities, and personal properties. Investment in most collectibles is not allowed in a self-directed plan. When an individual decides to make all investment decisions, a self-directed retirement plan is established. Otherwise the individual may prefer to invest the funds with a financial institution such as a broker, a bank, or a savings and loan institution.

COVERAGE REQUIREMENTS

Generally, the corporate coverage rules apply to Keogh plans. Thus, the percentage, ratio, and average benefits tests previously discussed also apply to self-employed plans. In addition, the more restrictive top-heavy plan rules apply to Keogh plans.[49] An individual covered under a qualified corporate plan as an employee may also establish a Keogh plan for earnings from self-employment.

CONTRIBUTION LIMITATIONS

A self-employed individual may annually contribute the smaller of $30,000 or 25 percent of earned income to a *defined contribution* Keogh plan.[50] However, if the

[48] § 4979(a).

[49] § 401(d).

[50] § 415(c)(1).

defined contribution plan is a profit sharing plan, a 15 percent deduction limit applies. Under a *defined benefit* Keogh plan, the annual benefit payable to an employee is limited to the smaller of $120,000 (in 1996) or 100 percent of the employee's average compensation for the three highest years of employment.[51] An employee includes a self-employed person. More restrictive rules apply to a top-heavy plan.

Earned income refers to net earnings from self-employment as defined in § 1402(a).[52] Net earnings from self-employment means the gross income derived by an individual from any trade or business carried on by that individual, less appropriate deductions, plus the distributive share of income or loss from a partnership.[53] Earned income is reduced by contributions to a Keogh plan on the individual's behalf and by 50 percent of any self-employment tax.[54]

EXAMPLE 17

Pat, a partner, has earned income of $130,000 in 1996 (after the deduction for one-half of self-employment tax, but before any Keogh contribution). The maximum contribution to a defined contribution plan is $26,000, calculated from the following formula: $\$130{,}000 - .25X = X$, where X is earned income reduced by Pat's Keogh contribution. Solving this equation, $X = \$104{,}000$; thus, the contribution limit is $.25 \times \$104{,}000 = \$26{,}000$. To achieve the maximum contribution of $30,000, Pat would have to earn at least $150,000. In essence, a self-employed individual can contribute 20% of *gross* earned income. (Pat could contribute only 13.043% of self-employment gross earned income if this were a profit sharing plan.) ▼

Many Keogh plans will be considered top-heavy plans (refer to the previous discussion). For nondiscrimination purposes, the 25 percent limitation on the employee contribution is computed on the first $150,000 (in 1996) of earned income.

EXAMPLE 18

Terry, a self-employed accountant, has a money purchase plan with a contribution rate of 15% of compensation. Terry's earned income after the deduction for one-half of self-employment tax, but before the retirement contribution is $250,000. Terry's contribution would be limited to $19,565 ($\$150{,}000 - .15X = X$), since $X = \$130{,}435$ and $.15 \times \$130{,}435 = \$19{,}565$. ▼

Although a Keogh plan must be established before the end of the year in question, contributions may be made up to the normal filing date for that year.

INDIVIDUAL RETIREMENT ACCOUNTS (IRAS)

GENERAL RULES

6 LEARNING OBJECTIVE
Describe the benefits of an Individual Retirement Account (IRA).

Employees not covered by another qualified plan can establish their own tax-deductible **Individual Retirement Accounts (IRAs).** The contribution ceiling is the smaller of $2,000 (or $2,250 for spousal IRAs) or 100 percent of compensation.[55] If the taxpayer or spouse is an active participant in another qualified plan, the IRA

[51] § 415(b)(1). This amount is indexed annually.
[52] § 401(c)(2).
[53] § 1402(a).
[54] §§ 401(c)(2)(A)(v) and 164(f).
[55] §§ 219(b)(1) and (c)(2).

▼ **TABLE 19–3**
Phase-Out of IRA Deduction

AGI Filing Status	Phase-Out Begins	Phase-Out Ends
Single and head of household	$25,000	$35,000
Married, filing joint return	40,000	50,000
Married, filing separate return	–0–	10,000

deduction limitation is phased out *proportionately* between certain adjusted gross income (AGI) ranges, as shown in Table 19–3.[56]

AGI is calculated taking into account any § 469 passive losses and § 86 taxable Social Security benefits and ignoring any § 911 foreign income exclusion, § 135 savings bonds interest exclusion, and the IRA deduction. There is a $200 floor on the IRA deduction limitation for individuals whose AGI is not above the phase-out range.

EXAMPLE 19

In 1996, Mr. and Mrs. Smith had compensation income of $27,000 and $20,000, respectively. Their AGI for 1996 was $47,000. Mr. Smith was an active participant in his employer's qualified retirement plan. Mr. and Mrs. Smith may *each* contribute $600 to an IRA. The deductible amount for each is reduced from $2,000 by $1,400 because of the phase-out mechanism:

$$\frac{\$7{,}000}{\$10{,}000} \times \$2{,}000 = \$1{,}400 \text{ reduction}$$

▼

EXAMPLE 20

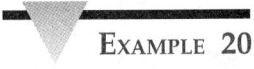

An unmarried individual is an active participant in his employer's qualified retirement plan. With AGI of $34,500, he would normally have an IRA deduction limit of $100 {$2,000 – [($34,500 – $25,000)/$10,000 × $2,000]}. However, because of the special floor provision, a $200 IRA deduction is allowable. ▼

To the extent that an individual is ineligible to make a deductible contribution to an IRA, *nondeductible contributions* can be made to separate accounts.[57] The nondeductible contribution will be subject to the same dollar limits for deductible contributions of $2,000 of earned income ($2,250 for a spousal IRA). Income in the account accumulates tax-free until distributed. Only the account earnings will be taxed (account basis equals the contributions made by the taxpayer) upon distribution. A taxpayer may elect to treat deductible IRA contributions as nondeductible. If an individual has no taxable income for the year after taking into account other deductions, the election would be beneficial. The election is made on the individual's tax return for the taxable year to which the designation relates.

Simplified Employee Pension Plans. An employer may contribute to an IRA covering an employee an amount equal to the lesser of $30,000 or 15 percent of the employee's earned income.[58] In such a plan, the corporation must make contributions for *each* employee who has reached age 21, has performed service for the employer during the calendar year and at least three of the five preceding calendar years, and has received at least $400 (in 1996) in compensation from the employer for the year.[59] Known as **simplified employee pension (SEP) plans,**

[56] § 219(g). However, a special rule in § 219(g)(4) allows a married person filing a separate return to avoid the phase-out rules even though the spouse is an active participant. The individual must live apart from the spouse at all times during the taxable year and must not be an active participant in another qualified plan.

[57] § 408(o).

[58] § 408(j).

[59] § 408(k)(2). This amount is indexed annually. For 1995, the amount also was $400.

TAX IN THE NEWS

SHOULD YOU CONTRIBUTE TO AN IRA

Everyone should have an Individual Retirement Account—at least that's the conventional wisdom you hear from retirement planners. But is an IRA really such a good deal? Some people are beginning to question whether the tax-deferred advantages of IRAs are worth the drawbacks.

For one thing, people who have made both deductible and nondeductible contributions to their IRAs will face a host of calculations when they begin to withdraw their funds. They will owe tax on their deductible contributions, but not on the nondeductible ones, and sorting out which is which will be an onerous task—especially if they have not kept extensive records over the 30 to 40 years they have contributed to their IRA.

Another potential problem is the 10 percent penalty that is usually imposed when funds are withdrawn before the contributor reaches age 59½. Although there are a few exceptions, anyone who loses their job or has their house demolished by a hurricane and needs emergency funds will have to pay dearly for the privilege of getting their money—it is much easier to borrow from a § 401(k) plan.

Then there are the extra taxes that may be owed. People who are congratulating themselves for investing their IRA dollars in small growth stocks that have already appreciated 500 percent should not be so quick to celebrate. When they withdraw that money, it will be taxed at the ordinary income rate, not at the capital gains rate as it would be if they had purchased the stock outside their IRA. For someone in the highest tax bracket, that means paying 39.6 percent instead of receiving beneficial capital gain treatment. Furthermore, if they withdraw more than $155,000 in one year, they may have to pay a 15 percent penalty tax.

Finally, if an individual dies leaving $1 million or more in an IRA, as much as 70 to 80 percent of the money may go for taxes. The government not only imposes estate tax, but also collects all the income tax due on the IRA funds and may levy a 15 percent penalty tax as well.

Contributing to a deductible IRA may make sense (and "dollars"). Think twice before you contribute to a nondeductible IRA.

Source: Adapted from Jonathan Clements, "Here's an Unconventional Idea: Don't Fund Your IRA This Year," *Wall Street Journal*, March 14, 1995, p. C1.

these plans are subject to many of the same restrictions applicable to qualified plans (e.g., age and period-of-service requirements, top-heavy rules, and nondiscrimination limitations). Concept Summary 19–3 compares a SEP with a Keogh plan.

Employees who participate in salary-reduction SEPs may elect to have contributions made to the SEP or to receive contributions in cash.[60] If an employee elects to have contributions made on his or her behalf to the SEP, the contribution is not treated as having been distributed or made available to the employee (i.e., no constructive receipt). The election to have amounts contributed to a SEP or received in cash is available only if at least 50 percent of the employees eligible to

[60] § 408(k)(6).

CONCEPT SUMMARY 19–3

Keogh Plan and SEP Compared

	Keogh	SEP
Form	Trust.	IRA.
Establishment	By end of year.	By extension due date of employer.
Type of plan	Qualified.	Qualified.
Contributions to plan	By extension due date.	By extension due date of employer.
Vesting rules	Qualified plan rules.	100% immediately.
Participants' rules	Flexible.	Stricter.
Lump-sum distributions and averaging	Yes, favorable 5-year or 10-year forward averaging.	No, ordinary income.
$5,000 death benefit exclusion	Yes.	No.
Deduction limitation	Varies.*	Smaller of $30,000** or 15% of earned income.
Self as trustee	Yes.	No.

*For a defined contribution pension plan, the limit is the smaller of $30,000 or 20% of self-employment income (after one-half of self-employment tax is deducted). A defined contribution profit sharing plan has a 13.043% deduction limit. A defined benefit Keogh plan's limit is the smaller of $120,000 (in 1996) or 100% of the employee's average compensation for the highest three years of employment.

**Since only $150,000 of income can be taken into consideration, the dollar limitation is effectively $22,500 ($150,000 × 15%).

participate elect to have amounts contributed to the SEP. This exception to the constructive receipt principle is available only in a taxable year in which the employer maintaining the SEP has 25 or fewer employees eligible to participate at all times during the preceding year.

The amounts contributed to a SEP by an employer on behalf of an employee and the elective deferrals under a SEP are excludible from gross income. Elective deferrals under a SEP are subject to a statutory ceiling of $9,500 (in 1996). Only $150,000 (in 1996) in compensation may be taken into account in making the SEP computation. An employer is permitted to elect to use its taxable year rather than the calendar year for purposes of determining contributions to a SEP.[61]

Spousal IRA. If both spouses work, each can individually establish an IRA. When only one spouse is employed, an IRA can be established for the nonemployed spouse if the employed spouse is eligible to establish an IRA. The maximum deduction for the individual and spouse is the lesser of 100 percent of the compensation income of the working spouse or $2,250. One spouse is permitted to elect to be treated, for this purpose, as having no earned income, thus allowing the contributing spouse to make the additional $250 contribution to an IRA. The contribution may be allocated to either spouse in any amount up to $2,000, and a joint return must be filed. The spousal IRA deduction is also

[61] § 404(h)(1)(A). The $9,500 and $150,000 amounts are indexed annually.

proportionately reduced for active participants whose AGI exceeds the above target ranges.

EXAMPLE 21

Tony, who is married, is eligible to establish an IRA. He received $30,000 in compensation in 1996. Tony can contribute a total of $2,250 to a spousal IRA, to be divided in any manner between the two spouses, except that no more than $2,000 can be allocated to either spouse. ▼

EXAMPLE 22

Assume the same facts as in the previous example, except that Tony's wife has earned income of $100. Absent the election to treat the wife's earned income as zero, the maximum IRA contribution is $2,100 ($2,000 for Tony and $100 for Tony's wife). With the election, $2,250 can be contributed under the spousal IRA provision. ▼

Alimony is considered to be earned income for purposes of IRA contributions. Thus, a person whose only income is alimony can contribute to an IRA.[62]

Timing of Contributions. Contributions (both deductible and nondeductible) can be made to an IRA anytime before the due date of the individual's tax return.[63] For example, an individual can establish and contribute to an IRA through April 15, 1997 (the return due date), and deduct this amount on his or her tax return for 1996. IRA contributions that are made during a tax return extension period do not satisfy the requirement of being made by the return due date. An employer can make contributions up until the time of the due date for filing the return (including extensions) and treat those amounts as a deduction for the prior year.[64] As noted earlier, a similar rule applies to Keogh plans. However, the Keogh plan must be established before the end of the tax year. Contributions to the Keogh plan may then be made anytime before the due date of the individual's tax return.

PENALTY TAXES FOR EXCESS CONTRIBUTIONS

A cumulative, nondeductible 6 percent excise penalty tax is imposed on the smaller of (1) any excess contributions or (2) the market value of the plan assets determined as of the close of the tax year. *Excess contributions* are any contributions that exceed the maximum limitation and contributions that are made during or after the tax year in which the individual reaches age 70½.[65] A taxpayer is not allowed a deduction for excess contributions. If the excess is corrected by contributing less than the deductible amount for a later year, a deduction then is allowable in the later year as a *makeup* deduction.

An excess contribution is taxable annually until returned to the taxpayer or reduced by the underutilization of the maximum contribution limitation in a subsequent year. The 6 percent penalty tax can be avoided if the excess amounts are returned.[66]

EXAMPLE 23

Nancy, age 55, establishes an IRA in 1996 and contributes $2,300 in cash to the plan. She has earned income of $22,000. Nancy is allowed a $2,000 deduction *for* AGI for 1996. Assuming the market value of the plan assets is at least $300, there is a nondeductible 6% excise penalty tax of $18 ($300 × 6%). The $300 may be subject to an additional penalty tax in future years if it is not returned to Nancy or reduced by underutilization of the $2,000 maximum contribution limitation. ▼

[62] § 219(f)(1).
[63] § 219(f)(3).
[64] § 404(h)(1)(B).
[65] §§ 4973(a)(1) and (b).
[66] §§ 408(d)(4) and 4973(b)(2).

TAXATION OF BENEFITS

A participant has a zero basis in the *deductible* contributions to an IRA because such contributions are not taxed currently.[67] Once retirement payments are received, they are ordinary income and are not subject to the 5-year or 10-year averaging allowed for lump-sum distributions. Payments made to a participant from *deductible* IRAs before age 59½ are subject to a nondeductible 10 percent penalty tax on such actual, or constructive, payments.[68]

All IRAs of an individual are treated as one contract, and all distributions during a taxable year are treated as one distribution. If an individual who previously has made both deductible and nondeductible IRA contributions makes a withdrawal from an IRA during a taxable year, the excludible amount must be calculated. The amount excludible from gross income for the taxable year is calculated by multiplying the amount withdrawn by a percentage. The percentage is calculated by dividing the individual's aggregate nondeductible IRA contributions by the aggregate balance of all his or her IRAs (including rollover IRAs and SEPs).[69]

EXAMPLE 24

Carl, age 59, has a $12,000 deductible IRA and a $2,000 nondeductible IRA (without any earnings). Carl withdraws $1,000 from the nondeductible IRA. The excludible portion is $143 ($2,000/$14,000 × $1,000), and the includible portion is $857 ($12,000/$14,000 × $1,000). Carl must pay a 10% penalty tax on a prorated portion considered withdrawn from the deductible IRA and earnings in either type of IRA. Thus, the 10% penalty tax is $85.70 (10% × $857). ▼

Rollovers. An IRA may be the recipient of a rollover from another qualified plan, including another IRA. Such a distribution from a qualified plan is not included in gross income if it is transferred within 60 days of receipt to an IRA or another qualified plan. For a series of distributions that constitute a lump-sum distribution, the 60-day period does not begin until the last distribution. Amounts received from IRAs may be rolled over tax-free only once in a 12-month period. If a person has more than one IRA, the one-year waiting period applies separately to each IRA.[70]

EXAMPLE 25

Nonemployer stock worth $60,000 is distributed to an employee from a qualified retirement plan. Hubert, the employee, sells the stock within 60 days for $60,000 and transfers one-half of the proceeds to an IRA. Hubert will have $30,000 of ordinary income, which is not eligible for 5-year or 10-year forward averaging or for the capital gain treatment for pre-1974 contributions. One-half of the distribution, or $30,000, does escape taxation because of the rollover. ▼

A tax-free rollover for distributions from qualified plans is an alternative to the taxable 5-year or 10-year forward averaging techniques. Any rollover amount in an IRA may later be rolled over into another qualified plan if the IRA consists of only the amounts from the original plan. The amount of nondeductible employee contributions included in a distribution may not be rolled over, but that amount is tax-free because the contributions were made with after-tax dollars. Partial rollovers are allowed, but the maximum amount that may be rolled over may not exceed the portion of the distribution that is otherwise includible in gross income. Rollovers are not available for required distributions under the minimum distribution rules once age 70½ is reached.

---

[67] § 408(d)(1).

[68] § 72(t). There are limited exceptions to the penalty on early distributions.

[69] § 408(d)(2).

[70] § 408(d)(3)(B) and Prop.Reg. 1.408–4(b)(4).

EXAMPLE 26

Jane withdraws $1,500 from her IRA on May 2, 1996, but she redeposits it in the same IRA on June 28, 1996. Although the withdrawal and redeposit was a partial rollover and Jane may have used the funds for a limited time, this is a tax-free rollover.[71] ▼

A rollover is different from a direct transfer of funds from a qualified plan to an IRA or another qualified plan by a trustee or issuer. A direct transfer is not subject to the one-year waiting period and the withholding rules.[72] Further, in many states, IRA amounts are subject to claims of creditors, which is not the case for employer plans.

An employer must withhold 20 percent of any lump-sum distributions unless the transfer is a direct transfer to an IRA or another qualified plan.[73]

EXAMPLE 27

Kay receives a distribution from a qualified retirement plan. The amount of the distribution would have been $20,000, but Kay receives only $16,000 ($20,000 – $4,000) as a result of the 20% withholding provision. After several weeks, Kay decides to contribute $20,000 (the gross amount of the distribution) to her IRA. Since she received only $16,000, she will need to contribute $4,000 from another source in order to make a $20,000 contribution. Kay will be able to claim a refund for the $4,000 that was withheld when she files her tax return for the year. ▼

Distributions to an IRA are generally not eligible for 5- or 10-year averaging or capital gain treatment. An exception applies in the case of a *conduit IRA*, where the sole assets of a plan are rolled over into an IRA, and the assets are then rolled into a qualified plan. With a conduit IRA, the lump-sum distribution from the original plan is still eligible for the special tax treatments.

NONQUALIFIED DEFERRED COMPENSATION PLANS

UNDERLYING RATIONALE FOR TAX TREATMENT

7 LEARNING OBJECTIVE
Understand the rationale for nonqualified deferred compensation plans and the related tax treatment.

Nonqualified deferred compensation (NQDC) plans provide a flexible way for taxpayers, particularly those in the 36 or 39.6 percent tax brackets, to defer income taxes on income payments until a possible lower tax bracket year. Where the deferred compensation is credited with annual earnings until payment, the entire deferred compensation, not the after-tax amount, is generating investment income. Also, most NQDC plans do not have to meet the discrimination, funding, coverage, and other requirements of qualified plans. In addition to these advantages for the employee, the employer may not have a current cash outflow.

The doctrine of constructive receipt is an important concept relating to the taxability of nonqualified deferred compensation.[74] In essence, if a taxpayer irrevocably earns income but may elect to receive it now or at a later date, the income is constructively received and is immediately taxed. Income is not constructively received, however, if the taxpayer's control over the amounts earned is subject to substantial limitations or restrictions.

Another important concept is the economic benefit theory. Although a taxpayer does not have a present right to income, the income will be taxable if a right in the form of a negotiable promissory note exists. Notes and other evidences

[71] Ltr.Rul. 9010007.
[72] Temp.Reg. 35.3405–1.
[73] § 3405(c).
[74] § 451(a) and Reg. § 1.451–2.

of indebtedness received in payment for services constitute income to the extent of their fair market value at the time of the transfer.[75]

EXAMPLE 28

Eagle Corporation and Bill, a cash basis employee, enter into an employment agreement that provides an annual salary of $120,000 to Bill. Of this amount, $100,000 is to be paid in current monthly installments, and $20,000 is to be paid in 10 annual installments beginning at Bill's retirement or death. Although Eagle Corporation maintains a separate account for Bill, that account is not funded (Bill is merely an unsecured creditor of the corporation). The $20,000 is not considered constructively received and is deferred. Compensation of $100,000 is currently taxable to Bill and deductible to Eagle. The other $20,000 will be taxable and deductible when paid in future years. ▼

TAX TREATMENT TO THE EMPLOYER AND EMPLOYEE

The tax treatment of an NQDC plan depends on whether it is *funded* or *unfunded* and whether it is *forfeitable* or *nonforfeitable.* In an unfunded NQDC plan, the employee relies upon the company's mere promise to make the compensation payment in the future. An unfunded, unsecured promise to pay, not represented by a negotiable note, effectively defers the recognition of income. Thus, the employee is taxed later when the compensation is actually paid or made available.[76] Similarly, the employer is allowed a deduction when the employee recognizes income.[77]

The employer can set up an escrow account to accumulate deferred payments on behalf of the employee. These funds may be invested by the escrow agent for the benefit of the employee.[78] By avoiding income recognition until the benefits from the escrow custodial account are received, the employee postpones the tax. An escrow arrangement can be appropriate for a professional athlete or entertainer whose income is earned in a few peak years.

EXAMPLE 29

Ted, a professional athlete, is to receive a bonus for signing an employment contract. An NQDC plan is established to defer the income beyond Ted's peak income years. His employer transfers the bonus to an escrow agent who invests the funds in securities, etc., which may act as a hedge against inflation. The bonus is deferred for 10 years and becomes payable gradually in years 11 through 15. The bonus is taxable to Ted and deductible by his employer when Ted receives the payments in years 11 through 15. ▼

Generally, funded NQDC plans must be forfeitable to keep the compensation payments from being taxable immediately. In most instances, employees prefer to have some assurance that they will ultimately receive benefits from the NQDC (that the plan provides for nonforfeitable benefits). In such instances, the plan will have to be unfunded to prevent immediate taxation to the employee. Note that most funded NQDC plans are subject to many of the provisions that apply to qualified plans.

When to Use an NQDC Arrangement. As a general rule, NQDC plans are more appropriate for executives in a financially secure company. Because of the need for currently disposable income, such plans are usually not appropriate for young employees.

---

[75] Reg. § 1.61–2(d)(4).

[76] Rev.Rul. 60–31, 1960–1 C.B. 174; Reg. § 1.451–2(a); *U.S. v. Basye*, 73–1 USTC ¶9250, 31 AFTR2d 73–802, 93 S.Ct. 1080 (USSC, 1973).

[77] §§ 404(a) and (d).

[78] Rev.Rul. 55–525, 1955–2 C.B. 543.

An NQDC plan can reduce an employee's overall tax payments by deferring the taxation of income to later years (possibly when the employee is in a lower tax bracket). In effect, these plans may produce a form of income averaging. Further, NQDC plans may discriminate in favor of shareholders, officers, specific highly compensated key employees, or a single individual.

Certain disadvantages should be noted. Nonqualified plans are usually required to be unfunded, which means that an employee is not assured that funds ultimately will be available to pay the benefits. Also, the employer's tax deduction is postponed until the employee is taxed on those payments.

Golden Parachute Arrangements. Certain excessive severance payments to employees may be penalized. The Code denies a deduction to an employer who makes a payment of cash or property to an employee or independent contractor that satisfies both of the following conditions:

- The payment is contingent on a change of ownership of a corporation through a stock or asset acquisition.
- The aggregate present value of the payment equals or exceeds three times the employee's (or independent contractor's) average annual compensation.[79]

The law recognizes that a corporation may provide monetary benefits to key employees if those employees lose their jobs as a result of a change in ownership of the corporation. These payments may be unreasonable or not really for services rendered. The Code refers to such payments as **golden parachute payments,** a term that, in essence, means *excess severance pay.* The disallowed amount is the excess of the payment over a statutory base amount (a five-year average of compensation if the taxpayer was an employee for the entire five-year period). Further, a 20 percent excise tax is imposed on the recipient on the receipt of these parachute payments, to be withheld at the time of payment.[80]

EXAMPLE 30

Irene, an executive, receives a golden parachute payment of $380,000 from her employer. Her average annual compensation for the most recent five tax years is $120,000. The corporation will be denied a deduction for $260,000 ($380,000 payment – $120,000 base amount). Irene's excise tax is $52,000 ($260,000 × 20%). ▼

Golden parachute payments do not include payments to or from qualified pension, profit sharing, stock bonus, annuity, or simplified employee pension plans. Also excluded is the amount of the payment that, in fact, represents reasonable compensation for personal services actually rendered or to be rendered. S corporations are not subject to the golden parachute rules. Generally, corporations that do not have stock that is readily tradable on an established securities market or elsewhere are also exempt. Such excluded payments are not taken into account when determining whether the threshold (the aggregate present value calculation) is exceeded.

Publicly Held Companies' Compensation Limitation. For purposes of both the regular income tax and the alternative minimum tax, the deductible compensation for the top five executives of publicly traded companies is limited to $1 million for each executive. A company is publicly held if the corporation has common stock listed on a national securities exchange.[81] This $1 million deduction

[79] § 280G.

[80] § 4999.

[81] § 162(m).

limitation is decreased by any nondeductible golden parachute payments made to the employee during the same year.

This deduction limitation applies when the compensation deduction would otherwise be taken. For example, in the case of a nonqualified stock option (NQSO), which is discussed later in this chapter, the deduction is normally taken in the year the NQSO is exercised, even though the option was granted with respect to services performed in a prior year.

Certain types of compensation are *not* subject to this new deduction limit and are not taken into account in determining whether other compensation exceeds $1 million:

- Compensation payable on a commission basis.
- Compensation payable solely on account of the attainment of one or more performance goals when certain requirements involving the approval of outside directors and shareholders are met.
- Payments to a tax-qualified retirement plan (including salary reduction contributions).
- Amounts that are excludible from an executive's gross income (such as employer-provided health benefits and miscellaneous fringe benefits).

The most important exception is performance-based compensation. Compensation qualifies for this exception only if the following conditions are satisfied:

- The compensation is paid solely on account of the attainment of one or more performance goals.
- The performance goals are established by a compensation committee consisting solely of two or more outside directors.
- The material terms under which the compensation is to be paid (including the performance goals) are disclosed to and approved by the shareholders in a separate vote prior to payment.
- Prior to payment, the compensation committee certifies that the performance goals and any other material terms were in fact satisfied.

Compensation (other than stock options or other stock appreciation rights) is not treated as paid solely on account of the attainment of one or more performance goals unless the compensation is paid to the particular executive under a preestablished objective performance formula or standard that precludes discretion. In essence, a third party with knowledge of the relevant performance results could calculate the amount to be paid to the particular executive. A performance goal is broadly defined and includes, for example, any objective performance standard that is applied to the individual executive, a business unit (e.g., a division or a line of business), or the corporation as a whole. Performance standards could include increases in stock price, market share, sales, or earnings per share.

ETHICAL CONSIDERATIONS

Limiting Compensation for Executives But Not for Other Highly Paid Employees

The top five executives of publicly traded corporations have a $1 million limit on deductible compensation. During 1992, the average compensation for two hundred of the highest-paid chief financial officers was $458,636. However, many of these CFOs had salaries ranging as high as $3 million. During 1991, Leon Hirsch at U.S. Surgical was paid $118 million, Anthony O'Reilly at H. J. Heinz was paid $75 million, and Martin Wygod at Medco Containment received $33.7 million.

The average salary for a player in the American League or National League on the opening day of the 1995 baseball season was $1.1 million. Top salaries for 1995 include Detroit's Cecil Fielder ($9.2 million), New York Yankees' David Cone ($8 million), San Francisco's Barry Bonds ($8 million), Seattle's Ken Griffey, Jr. ($7.55 million), and Toronto's Joe Carter ($7.5 million). In football in 1995, the Dallas Cowboys enticed Deion Sanders from the San Francisco Forty-Niners for a five-year, $35 million contract, including a $13 million bonus. Sanders joined quarterback Troy Aikman who has a $50 million deal with the Cowboys. In basketball, David Robinson of the San Antonio Spurs was the highest paid basketball player for the 1993–94 season with a $5.74 million salary, which was 30 percent of the Spurs' $19.3 million total payroll. For 1995, Robinson's salary was $7.9 million.

Similarly, many television and movie performers are receiving huge salaries (e.g., David Letterman at $14 million). Yet these entertainers and professional sports players are not subject to the $1 million compensation cap. Some question the fairness of a policy that subjects business executives to a compensation limitation while allowing entertainers and sports stars to be exempt.

Restricted Property Plans

GENERAL PROVISIONS

8 LEARNING OBJECTIVE
Explain the value of restricted property plans.

A **restricted property plan** is an arrangement whereby an employer transfers property (e.g., stock of the employer-corporation) to a provider of services at no cost or at a bargain price. The purpose of a restricted stock plan is to retain the services of key employees who might otherwise leave. The employer hopes that such compensation arrangements will encourage company growth and attainment of performance objectives. Section 83 was enacted in 1969 to provide rules for the taxation of incentive compensation arrangements, which previously were governed by judicial and administrative interpretations. Although the following discussion refers to an employee as the provider of the services, the services need not be performed by an employee (§ 83 also applies to independent contractors).

As a general rule, if an employee performs services and receives property (e.g., stock), the fair market value of that property in excess of any amount paid by the employee is includible in his or her gross income. The time for inclusion is the earlier of (1) the time the property is no longer subject to a substantial risk of forfeiture or (2) the time the property is transferable by the employee. The fair market value of the property is determined without regard to any restriction, except a restriction that by its terms will never lapse.[82] Since the amount of the compensation is determined at the date that the restrictions lapse or when the property is transferable, the opportunity to generate capital gain treatment on the property is denied during a period when the ordinary income element is being deferred.

EXAMPLE 31

On October 1, 1992, Blue Corporation sold 100 shares of its stock to Ahmad, an employee, for $10 per share. At the time of the sale, the fair market value of the stock was $100 per share. Under the terms of the sale, each share of stock was nontransferable and subject to a substantial risk of forfeiture (which was not to lapse until October 1, 1996). Evidence of these restrictions was stamped on the face of the stock certificates. On October 1, 1996, the

[82] § 83(a)(1); *Miriam Sakol*, 67 T.C. 986 (1977); *T. M. Horwith*, 71 T.C. 932 (1979).

fair market value of the stock was $250 per share. Since the stock was nontransferable and was subject to a substantial risk of forfeiture, Ahmad did not include any compensation in gross income during 1992 (assuming no special election was made). Instead, Ahmad was required to include $24,000 of compensation in gross income [100 shares × ($250 – $10 per share)] during 1996. If for some reason the substantial risk of forfeiture had occurred (e.g., the plan required Ahmad to surrender the stock to the corporation if he voluntarily terminated his employment with the company before October 1, 1996) and Ahmad never received the stock certificates, he would have been allowed a capital loss of $1,000 (the extent of his investment). ▼

SUBSTANTIAL RISK OF FORFEITURE

A **substantial risk of forfeiture** exists if a person's rights to full enjoyment of property are conditioned upon the future performance, or the refraining from the performance, of substantial services by that individual.[83] For example, if an employee must return the property (receiving only his or her original cost, if any) should there be a failure to complete a substantial period of service (for any reason), the property is subject to a substantial risk of forfeiture. Another such situation exists when an employer can compel an employee to return the property due to a breach of a substantial covenant not to compete. Any substantial risk of forfeiture should be stated on the face of the stock certificates. Assuming that a substantial risk of forfeiture does not exist, the property received is valued at its fair market value, ignoring any restrictions, except for one instance dealing with closely held stock.

SPECIAL ELECTION AVAILABLE

An employee may elect within 30 days after the receipt of restricted property to recognize immediately as ordinary income the fair market value in excess of the amount paid for the property. Any appreciation in the value of the property after receipt is classified as capital gain instead of ordinary income. No deduction is allowed to the employee for taxes paid on the original amount included in income if the property is subsequently forfeited.[84] The employee is permitted to take a capital loss for any amounts that were actually paid for the property. Furthermore, in such a case, the employer must repay taxes saved by any compensation deduction taken in the earlier year.[85]

Any increase in value between the time the property is received and the time it becomes either nonforfeitable or transferable is taxed as ordinary income if the employee does not make a special election. However, if the employee elects to be taxed immediately on the difference between the cost and fair market value on the date of issue, any future appreciation is treated as capital gain. In determining whether the gain is long term or short term, the holding period starts when the employee is taxed on the ordinary income.[86]

EXAMPLE 32

On July 1, 1986, Sparrow Company sold 100 shares of its preferred stock, worth $15 per share, to Diane (an employee) for $5 per share. The sale was subject to Diane's agreement to resell the preferred shares to the company for $5 per share if she terminated her employment during the following 10 years. Assume that the stock had a value of $25 per share on July 1, 1996, and Diane sold the stock for $30 per share on October 10, 1996. Diane made the special election to include the original spread (between the value of $15 in 1986

[83] § 83(c); Regulation § 1.83–3(c)(2) includes several examples of restricted property arrangements.

[84] § 83(b).

[85] Reg. §§ 1.83–6(c) and 2(a).

[86] § 1223(6).

and the amount paid of $5) in income for 1986. Diane was required to recognize $1,000 of compensation income in 1986 ($15 – $5 = $10 × 100 shares), at which time her holding period in her stock began. Diane's tax basis in the stock was $1,500 ($1,000 + $500). When the preferred stock was sold in 1996, Diane recognized a $1,500 long-term capital gain ($30 × 100 shares – $1,500). ▼

EXAMPLE 33

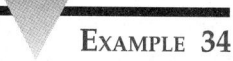

Assume the same facts as in Example 32, except that Diane sells the stock in 1997 (rather than 1996). She would not recognize any gain in 1996 when the substantial risk of forfeiture lapses. Instead, Diane would recognize the $1,500 long-term capital gain in 1997. ▼

This special provision is usually not elected since it results in an immediate recognition of income and adverse tax consequences result from a subsequent forfeiture. However, the special election may be attractive in the following situations:

- The bargain element is relatively small.
- Substantial appreciation is expected in the future.
- A high probability exists that the restrictions will be met.

EMPLOYER DEDUCTIONS

At the time the employee is required to include the compensation in income, the employer is allowed a tax deduction for the same amount. The employer must withhold on this amount in accordance with § 3402. In the no-election situation, the deduction is limited to the fair market value of the restricted property (without regard to the restrictions) at the time the restrictions lapse, reduced by the amount originally paid for the property by the employee.[87] When the employee elects to be taxed immediately, the corporate deduction also is accelerated and deductible in like amount. In cases of deferred income recognition, the employer can receive a very sizable deduction if the property has appreciated.

EXAMPLE 34

On March 14, 1994, Gold Corporation sold to Harry, an employee, 10 shares of Gold common stock for $100 per share. Both the corporation and Harry were calendar year taxpayers. The common stock was subject to a substantial risk of forfeiture and was nontransferable; both conditions were to lapse on March 14, 1996. At the time of the sale, the fair market value of the common stock (without considering the restrictions) was $1,000 per share. On March 14, 1996, when the fair market value of the stock was $2,000 per share, the restrictions lapsed. Harry did not make a special election. In 1996, Harry realized ordinary income of $19,000 (10 shares at $2,000 per share less the $100 per share he had paid). Likewise, Gold Corporation was allowed a $19,000 compensation deduction in 1996. ▼

EXAMPLE 35

In the previous example, assume that Harry had made the special election. Since he was taxed on $9,000 in 1994, the corporation was allowed to deduct a like amount in 1994. No deduction would be available in 1996. ▼

STOCK OPTIONS

9 LEARNING OBJECTIVE
Differentiate the tax treatment of qualified and nonqualified stock options.

IN GENERAL

Various equity types of stock option programs are available for an employee's compensation package. Some authorities believe that some form of *equity kicker* is

[87] Reg. § 1.83–6(a).

TAX IN THE NEWS

Stock Options for Senior Officers

Stock options are becoming an increasingly popular means of rewarding top executives. In 1995, for instance, U.S. corporations reserved 10 percent of their stock for options and outright grants to senior officers—three times as much as in the 1970s.

From a CEO's perspective, stock options have much to recommend them. If the company prospers, the options can be a bonanza, and even if the company's earnings and stock price plummet, none of the CEO's own money is at risk. Such opportunities are available only to CEO's and a handful of other top managers. According to Institutional Shareholder Services, an investment research firm, the top 15 executives in a company generally receive 97 percent of the options.

As some commentators are pointing out, however, the benefits of stock options do not extend to the common shareholders. While they risk their own money to buy the company's stock, stock options are diluting their equity. As for the argument that large stock option awards are necessary to lure and keep quality executives, one might consider the case of Westinghouse, which reportedly offered Michael Jordan a million share option to become CEO. So far, under Jordan's leadership, the price of Westinghouse stock has languished. While Jordan has not made any money on his options, he has not lost any either, and unlike many Westinghouse employees, he still has his job. Accordingly, the commentators suggest that if stock options are to be an inducement to performance, executives should buy them with their own money.

SOURCE: Adapted from Robert A. G. Monks, "Stock Options Don't Work. If CEOs Want Shares, Let'Em Buy Some," *Fortune*, September 18, 1995, pp. 230-31.

needed to attract new management, convert key officers into *partners* by giving them a share of the business, and retain the services of executives who might otherwise leave. Encouraging the managers of a business to have a proprietary interest in its successful operation should provide executives with a key motive to expand the company and improve its profits. In addition, under certain conditions, stock options may fall outside the $1 million limitation on the salaries of the top five executives of publicly traded companies.

A **stock option** gives an individual the right to purchase a stated number of shares of stock from a corporation at a certain price within a specified period of time. The optionee must be under no obligation to purchase the stock, and the option may be revocable by the corporation. The option must be in writing, and its terms must be clearly expressed.[88]

INCENTIVE STOCK OPTIONS

An equity type of stock option called an *incentive stock options (ISO)* is available for options granted after 1975 and exercised after 1980.[89] An ISO arrangement receives much the same tax treatment previously accorded to restricted and qualified stock

[88] Reg. §§ 1.421–1(a)(1) and –7(a)(1).

[89] Qualified stock options were available under § 422 (prior to repeal by the Revenue Reconciliation Act of 1990) for certain qualified options granted before May 21, 1976. These qualified stock options had many of the statutory requirements of ISOs, but ISOs have a more favorable tax treatment.

option plans. There are no tax consequences when the option is granted, but the *spread* (the excess of the fair market value of the share at the date of exercise over the option price)[90] is a tax preference item for purposes of the alternative minimum tax. The determination of fair market value is made without regard to any lapse restrictions (a restriction that will expire after a period of time). After the option is exercised and when the stock is sold, any gain from the sale is taxed as a long-term capital gain if certain holding period requirements are met. To qualify as a long-term capital gain, the employee must not dispose of the stock within two years after the option is granted or within one year after acquiring the stock.[91] If the employee meets the holding period requirements, none of these transactions generates any business deduction for the employer.[92]

Since some beneficial treatment for long-term capital gains for the individual was restored beginning in 1991 and tax rates were increased in 1993, ISOs have regained some of their tax appeal on the gain side. In addition, an employee who has capital losses would prefer capital gain treatment.

EXAMPLE 36

Wren Corporation granted an ISO for 100 shares of its stock to Rocky, an employee, on March 18, 1993. The option price was $100, and the fair market value was $100 on the date of the grant. Rocky exercised the option on April 1, 1995, when the market value of the stock was $200 per share. He sells the stock on April 6, 1996, for $300 per share. Rocky did not recognize any ordinary income on the date of the grant or the exercise date since the option qualified as an ISO. Wren received no compensation deduction. Rocky has a $10,000 tax preference item on the exercise date. He has a long-term capital gain of $20,000 [($300 – $100) × 100] upon the sale of the stock in 1996, because the one-year and two-year holding periods and other requirements have been met. ▼

As a further requirement for ISO treatment, the option holder must be an employee of the issuing corporation from the date the option is granted until 3 months (12 months if disabled) before the date of exercise. The holding period and the employee-status rules just described (the one-year, two-year, and three-month requirements) are waived in the case of the death of an employee.[93]

EXAMPLE 37

Assume the same facts as in the previous example, except that Rocky was not employed by Wren Corporation for six months before the date he exercised the options. Rocky must recognize ordinary income to the extent of the spread, assuming there was no substantial risk of forfeiture. Thus, Rocky recognizes $10,000 [($200 – $100) × 100] of ordinary income on the exercise date, because he was not an employee of Wren Corporation at all times during the period beginning on the grant date and ending three months before the exercise date. Wren is allowed a deduction at the same time that Rocky reports the ordinary income. ▼

If the holding period requirements are not satisfied but all other conditions are met, the tax is still deferred to the point of the sale. However, the difference between the option price and the value of the stock at the date the option was exercised is treated as ordinary income. The difference between the amount realized for the stock and the value of the stock at the date of exercise is short-term or long-term capital gain, depending on the holding period of the stock itself. The employer is allowed a deduction equal to the amount recognized by the employee

[90] §§ 422(a), 421(a)(1), and 57(a)(3).

[91] § 422(a)(1).

[92] § 421(a)(2).

[93] §§ 422(a)(2) and (c)(3). Exceptions are made for parent and subsidiary situations, corporate reorganizations, and liquidations. Also, in certain situations involving an insolvent employee, the holding period rules are modified.

as ordinary income. The employee does not have a tax preference for alternative minimum tax purposes.

EXAMPLE 38

Assume the same facts as in Example 36, except that Rocky sells the stock on March 22, 1996, for $290 per share. Since Rocky did not hold the stock itself for at least one year, $10,000 of the gain is treated as ordinary income in 1996, and Wren Corporation is allowed a $10,000 compensation deduction in 1996. The remaining $9,000 is a short-term capital gain ($29,000 – $20,000). ▼

Qualification Requirements for Incentive Stock Option Plans. An **incentive stock option (ISO)** is an option to purchase stock of a corporation granted to an individual for any reason connected with his or her employment.[94] The option is granted by the employer-corporation or by a parent or subsidiary corporation of the employer-corporation. An employee can use company stock to pay for the stock when exercising an option without disqualifying the ISO plan.

For an option to qualify as an ISO, the terms of the option itself must meet the following conditions:

- The option must be granted under a plan specifying the number of shares of stock to be issued and the employees or class of employees eligible to receive the options. The plan must be approved by the shareholders of the corporation within 12 months before or after the plan is adopted.
- The option must be granted within 10 years of the date the plan is adopted or of the date the plan is approved by the shareholders, whichever date is earlier.
- The option must by its terms be exercisable only within 10 years of the date it is granted.
- The option price must equal or exceed the fair market value of the stock at the time the option is granted. This requirement is deemed satisfied if there has been a good faith attempt to value the stock accurately, even if the option price is less than the stock value.
- The option by its terms must be nontransferable other than at death and must be exercisable during the employee's lifetime only by the employee.
- The employee must not, immediately before the option is granted, own stock representing more than 10 percent of the voting power or value of all classes of stock in the employer-corporation or its parent or subsidiary. (Here, the attribution rules of § 267 are applied in modified form.) However, the stock ownership limitation will be waived if the option price is at least 110 percent of the fair market value (at the time the option is granted) of the stock subject to the option and the option by its terms is not exercisable more than five years from the date it is granted.[95]

An overall limitation is imposed on the amount of ISOs that can be exercised in one year. This limit is set at $100,000 per year (based on the value of the stock determined at the time the option is granted) per employee.

NONQUALIFIED STOCK OPTIONS

A **nonqualified stock option (NQSO)** does not satisfy the statutory requirements for ISOs. In addition, a stock option that otherwise would qualify as an ISO will be treated as an NQSO if the terms of the stock option provide that it is not an ISO. If the NQSO has a readily ascertainable fair market value (e.g., the option is traded

[94] § 422(b).

[95] § 422(c)(5).

on an established exchange), the value of the option must be included in the employee's income at the date of grant. Thereafter, capital gain or loss is recognized only upon the disposal of the optioned stock. The employee's basis is the amount paid for the stock plus any amount reported as ordinary income. The employer obtains a corresponding tax deduction at the same time and to the extent that ordinary income is recognized by the employee.[96]

EXAMPLE 39

On February 1, 1995, Janet was granted an NQSO to purchase 100 shares of stock from her employer at $10 per share. On this date, the option was selling for $2 on an established exchange. Janet exercised the option on March 30, 1996, when the stock was worth $20 per share. On June 5, 1996, Janet sold the optioned stock for $22 per share.

- Janet must report ordinary income of $200 ($2 × 100 shares) on the date of grant (February 1, 1995), because the option has a readily ascertainable fair market value.
- Upon the sale of the stock (June 5, 1996), Janet must report a long-term capital gain of $1,000 [($22 – $12) × 100 shares].
- At the date of grant (February 1, 1995), the employer receives a tax deduction of $200, the amount of income reported by Janet. ▼

If an NQSO does not have a readily ascertainable fair market value, an employee does not recognize income at the grant date. However, as a general rule, ordinary income must be reported in the year of exercise (the difference between the fair market value of the stock at the exercise date and the option price).[97] The amount paid by the employee for the stock plus the amount reported as ordinary income becomes the basis. Any appreciation above that basis is taxed as a long-term capital gain upon disposition (assuming the stock is held for the required long-term holding period after exercise). The corporation receives a corresponding tax deduction at the same time and to the extent that ordinary income is recognized by the employee.

EXAMPLE 40

On February 3, 1994, Maria was granted an NQSO for 100 shares of common stock at $10 per share. On the date of the grant, there was no readily ascertainable fair market value for the option. Maria exercised the options on January 3, 1995, when the stock was selling for $15 per share. She sold one-half of the shares on April 15, 1995, and the other half on September 17, 1996. The sale price on both dates was $21 per share. Maria would not recognize any income on the grant date (February 3, 1994) but would recognize $500 ($1,500 – $1,000) of ordinary income on the exercise date (January 3, 1995). She would recognize a short-term capital gain of $300 on the sale of the first half in 1995 and a $300 long-term capital gain on the sale of the second batch of stock in 1996 [½($2,100 – $1,500)]. ▼

The major *advantages* of NQSOs can be summarized as follows:

- A tax deduction is available to the corporation without a cash outlay.
- The employee receives capital gain treatment on any appreciation in the stock starting either at the exercise date if the option does not have a readily ascertainable fair market value or at the date of grant if the option has a readily ascertainable fair market value.
- Options can be issued at more flexible terms than under ISO plans (e.g., longer exercise period and discount on exercise price).

A major *disadvantage* is that the employee must recognize ordinary income on the exercise of the option or at the date of grant without receiving cash to pay the tax.

[96] Reg. §§ 1.421–6(c), (d), (e), and (f); Reg. § 1.83–7.

[97] Reg. § 1.83–7(a); Reg. § 1.421–6(d).

TAX PLANNING CONSIDERATIONS

10 LEARNING OBJECTIVE
Identify tax planning opportunities available with deferred compensation.

DEFERRED COMPENSATION

With the higher 39.6 percent individual tax rate, taxpayers may try to lower their tax burden by participating in more deferred compensation arrangements. The $1 million annual limit on the compensation deduction for the top five executives of publicly traded companies may cause a shift into § 401(k) plans, qualified retirement plans, and especially nonqualified deferred compensation arrangements. However, the amount of compensation that can be taken into consideration for purposes of calculating contributions or benefits under a qualified pension or profit sharing plan has been reduced to $150,000.

The tightening of the antidiscrimination rules may increase the costs to the employer of providing deferred compensation. Restrictions upon the deductibility of interest expense make it more costly for an employee to borrow money as part of a compensation program. Payment of compensation in cash in 1996 still may be beneficial, however, especially if individual tax rates continue to increase in future years.

QUALIFIED PLANS

Qualified plans provide maximum tax benefits for employers, because the employer receives an immediate tax deduction for contributions to such plans and the income that is earned on the contributions is not taxable to the employer. The employer contributions and the trust earnings are not taxed to the employees until those funds are made available to them.

Qualified plans are most appropriate where it is desirable to provide benefits for a cross section of employees. In some closely held corporations, the primary objective is to provide benefits for the officer-shareholder group and other highly paid personnel. The nondiscrimination requirements that must be met in a qualified plan may prevent such companies from attaining these objectives. Thus, a nonqualified arrangement may be needed as a supplement to, or used in lieu of, the qualified plan.

SELF-EMPLOYED RETIREMENT PLANS

A Keogh or IRA participant may make a deductible contribution for a tax year up to the time prescribed for filing the individual's tax return. A Keogh plan must have been established by the end of the tax year (e.g., December 31) to obtain a current deduction for the contribution made in the subsequent year. An individual can establish an IRA after the end of the tax year and still receive a current deduction for the contribution made in the subsequent year. However, since the deductibility of contributions to IRAs has been restricted for many middle-income and upper-income taxpayers, Keogh plans are likely to become more important.

INDIVIDUAL RETIREMENT ACCOUNTS

Fewer taxpayers are now allowed to make deductible contributions to IRAs. A working taxpayer not covered by another qualified plan may still deduct IRA contributions up to the smaller of $2,000 or 100 percent of earned income. If both spouses work, each may individually establish an IRA. Where only one spouse has earned income, an IRA may be established for the nonworking spouse. A total of $2,250 may then be contributed to the two IRAs. If the nonworking spouse has a small amount of income (e.g., jury duty), an election may be made to ignore such income for spousal IRA purposes.

A married couple may put $4,000 into an IRA when one spouse works for the other spouse. This requires paying the *employee spouse* at least $2,000 in salary and having him or her make an independent contribution to an IRA. This extra amount (at least $2,000) is subject to FICA, however.

A single working taxpayer covered by another retirement plan may deduct a $2,000 IRA contribution only if AGI is less than $25,000 a year. For married couples filing jointly, the ceiling is $40,000. The IRA deduction is reduced proportionately as AGI increases within a $10,000 phase-out range above the $25,000 and $40,000 ceilings.

IRA and Keogh participants can self-direct their investments into a wide variety of assets. The participant self-directs the investments into various assets even though the assets are under the control of a trustee or custodian. The acquisition of collectibles (e.g., art, gems, metals) by an IRA or self-directed Keogh or corporate plan is treated as a distribution (taxed). For an IRA or Keogh participant under age 59½, there is also a 10 percent premature distribution penalty.

COMPARISON OF § 401(k) PLAN WITH IRA

Most employees will find a § 401(k) plan more attractive than an IRA. Probably the biggest limitation of an IRA is the $2,000 maximum shelter. Under § 401(k), employees are permitted to shelter compensation up to $9,500 (in 1996).[98] The restrictions on deducting contributions to IRAs for many middle-income and upper-income taxpayers may cause many employees to utilize § 401(k) plans more frequently.

Another difference between § 401(k) plans and IRAs is the manner in which the money is treated. Money placed in an IRA may be tax deductible, whereas dollars placed in a § 401(k) plan are considered to be deferred compensation. Thus, a § 401(k) reduction may reduce profit sharing payments, group life insurance, and Social Security benefits. Concept Summary 19–4 compares a § 401(k) plan with an IRA.

NONQUALIFIED DEFERRED COMPENSATION (NQDC) PLANS

Nonqualified deferred compensation arrangements such as restricted property plans can be useful to attract executive talent or to provide substantial retirement benefits for executives. A restricted property plan may be used to retain a key employee of a closely held company when management continuity problems are anticipated. Without such employees, the untimely death or disability of one of the owners might cause a disruption of the business with an attendant loss in value for his or her heirs. Such plans may discriminate in favor of officers and other highly paid employees. The employer, however, does not receive a tax deduction until the employee is required to include the deferred compensation in income (upon the lapse of the restrictions).

The principal advantage of NQDC plans is that the employee can defer the recognition of income to future periods when his or her income tax bracket may be lower (e.g., during retirement years). The time value benefits from the deferral of income should also be considered. However, with the trend toward increasing rates, an executive with a deferred compensation arrangement entered into in a

[98] This amount is indexed annually.

CONCEPT SUMMARY 19–4

Section 401(k) Plan and IRA Compared

	§ 401(k) Plan	IRA
Deduction limitation	Smaller of $9,500 (in 1996) or approximately 25% of total earnings. Limited by antidiscrimination requirements of § 401(k)(3).	$2,000 or 100% of compensation.
Distributions	Early withdrawal possible if for early retirement (55 or over) or to pay medical expenses.	10% penalty for early withdrawals.
Effect on gross earnings	Gross salary reduction, which may reduce profit sharing contributions, Social Security benefits, and group life insurance.	No effect.
Employer involvement	Must keep records; monitor for compliance with antidiscrimination test.	Minimal.
Lump-sum distributions	Favorable 5-year or 10-year forward averaging.	Ordinary income.
Timing of contribution	Within 30 days of plan year-end or due date of employer's return.*	Grace period up to due date of tax return (not including extensions).
Loans from plan	Yes.	No.

*Elective contributions must be made to the plan no later than 30 days after the end of the plan year, and nonelective contributions no later than the due date of the tax return (including extensions).

prior year may wish to accelerate the income into 1996 since individual tax rates in future years may be even higher.

The principal disadvantage of NQDC plans could be the bunching effect that takes place on the expiration of the period of deferral. In some cases, planning can alleviate this result.

EXAMPLE 41

During 1996, Kelly, an executive, enters into an agreement to postpone a portion of her payment for current services until retirement. The deferred amount is not segregated from the company's general assets and is subject to normal business risk. The entire payment, not the after-tax amount, is invested in securities and variable annuity contracts. Kelly is not taxed on the payment in 1996, and the company receives no deduction in 1996. If Kelly receives the deferred payment in a lump sum when she retires, the tax rates may be higher and more progressive than in 1996. Thus, Kelly may wish to arrange for a number of payments to be made to her or a designated beneficiary over a number of years. ▼

STOCK OPTIONS

Rather than paying compensation in the form of corporate stock, an alternative approach is to issue options to purchase stock at a specific price to an employee.

CONCEPT SUMMARY 19–5

Incentive Stock Options and Nonqualified Stock Options Compared

	ISO	NQSO
Granted at any price	No	Yes
May have any duration	No	Yes
Governing Code Section	§ 422	§ 83
Spread subject to alternative minimum tax	Yes	No
Deduction to employer for spread	No	Yes
Type of gain/loss on disposal	Capital	Capital
Statutory amount ($100,000) limitation	Yes	No

Stock option plans are used more frequently by publicly traded companies than by closely held companies. This difference is due to the problems of determining the value of the stock of a company that is not publicly held.

Nonqualified stock options (NQSOs) are more flexible and less restrictive than incentive stock options (ISOs). For example, the holding period for an NQSO is not as long as that for an ISO. Further, the option price of an NQSO may be less than the fair market value of the stock at the time the option is granted. An NQSO creates an employer deduction that lowers the cost of the NQSO to the employer. The employer may pass along this tax savings to the employee in the form of a cash payment. Both the employer and the employee may be better off by combining NQSOs with additional cash payments rather than using ISOs. See Concept Summary 19–5.

FLEXIBLE BENEFIT PLANS

Employees may be permitted to choose from a package of employer-provided fringe benefits.[99] In these so-called **cafeteria benefit plans,** some of the benefits chosen by an employee may be taxable, and some may be statutory nontaxable benefits (e.g., health and accident insurance and group term life insurance).

Employer contributions made to a flexible plan are included in an employee's gross income only to the extent that the employee actually elects the taxable benefits. Certain nondiscrimination standards with respect to coverage, eligibility for participation, contributions, and benefits must be met. Thus, such a plan must cover a fair cross section of employees. Also, a flexible plan cannot include an election to defer compensation, and a key employee is not exempt from taxation on the taxable benefits made available where more than 25 percent of the statutory nontaxable benefits are provided to key employees.

[99] § 125.

KEY TERMS

PROBLEM MATERIALS

DISCUSSION QUESTIONS

1. Describe the three basic types of qualified plans.
2. Compare and contrast qualified pension and profit sharing plans.
3. Determine whether each of the following independent statements best applies to a defined contribution plan (DCP), defined benefit plan (DBP), both (B), or neither (N):
   a. Includes an employee stock ownership plan (ESOP).
   b. Forfeitures can be allocated to the remaining participants' accounts.
   c. Requires greater reporting requirements and more actuarial and administrative costs.
   d. Forfeitures can revert to the employer.
   e. More favorable to employees who are older at the time the plan is adopted.
   f. Employee forfeitures can be used to reduce future contributions by the employer.
   g. May exclude employees who begin employment within five years of normal retirement age.
   h. Annual addition to each employee's account may not exceed the smaller of $30,000 or 25% of the employee's salary.
   i. The final benefit to a participant depends upon investment performance.
   j. To avoid penalties, the amount of annual contributions must meet minimum funding requirements.
4. Indicate whether the following statements apply to a pension plan (P), a profit sharing plan (PS), both (B), or neither (N):
   a. Forfeited amounts can be used to reduce future contributions by the employer.
   b. Allocation of forfeitures may discriminate in favor of the prohibited group (highly compensated employees).
   c. Forfeitures can revert to the employer.

d. Forfeitures can increase plan benefits by allocating the forfeitures to participants.
e. An annual benefit of $60,000 could be payable on behalf of a participant.
f. More favorable to employees who are older at the time the qualified plan is adopted.

5. When will the $30,000 maximum annual contribution to a defined contribution plan be indexed?

6. What are the tax and financial advantages accruing to a company that adopts an employee stock ownership plan (ESOP) for employees?

7. List the qualification requirements that must be satisfied in order for a qualified plan to receive favorable tax treatment.

8. Is it possible to provide greater vested benefits for highly paid employees and still meet the nondiscrimination requirements under a qualified pension plan? Explain.

9. Once the age and service requirements are met, when must an employee begin participating in a qualified plan?

10. What is vesting, and how will vesting requirements help employees who do not remain with one employer during their working years?

11. Discuss the penalty for excess distributions from qualified plans.

12. Manuel plans to retire in 1996 at age 68. Identify any issues facing Manuel with respect to distributions from his qualified retirement plans.

13. Discuss the tax consequences to employee, employer, and the trust of a qualified pension or profit sharing plan.

14. Harvey Maxwell, who is age 66, is going to receive a lump-sum distribution from a qualified plan. He has asked you to provide him with a description of the alternatives available to him for taxing the lump-sum distribution. Draft a letter to Harvey in which you respond. He resides at 3000 East Glenn, Tulsa, OK 74104.

15. Which of the following would be considered a tax benefit or advantage of a qualified retirement plan?
    a. Certain lump-sum distributions may be subject to capital gain treatment.
    b. Employer contributions are currently deductible.
    c. Employee contributions are currently deductible.
    d. The qualified trust is tax-exempt as to all income (other than unrelated business income).
    e. In a lump-sum distribution, any capital gain tax on the portion attributable to any unrealized appreciation in the stock of the employer at the time of distribution is deferred until the time the employee disposes of the stock in a taxable transaction.
    f. Election may be made to allow a lump-sum distribution to be subject to a 5-year or 10-year forward averaging technique.

16. What ceiling limitations have been placed on employer contributions (relative to individual employees) to defined contribution and defined benefit plans?

17. What is the maximum deduction permitted to an employer each year for contributions to a profit sharing plan and a stock bonus plan?

18. Define the term *key employee* for purposes of a top-heavy plan.

19. Determine the 1996 indexed amounts for the following items:
    a. Maximum annual contribution to a defined contribution plan.
    b. Maximum annual benefits payable by a defined benefit plan.
    c. The $150,000 or $112,500 amounts for calculating the 15% excise tax imposed on excess distributions.
    d. The maximum amount of the annual contribution to a cash or deferred arrangement plan.

20. Frank Paterson calls you and asks about the differences between Keogh plans and Individual Retirement Accounts. Prepare a memo for the files about your discussion.

21. What tax-free alternative is available for the 5-year or 10-year forward averaging techniques for lump-sum distributions?

22. For which of the following situations is a nonqualified deferred compensation plan taxable under the constructive receipt doctrine?
    a. The contract is funded, and there is no substantial risk of forfeiture.
    b. Same as (a), except the employee must work for three years.
    c. An agreement to defer payment is entered into after compensation is earned.
    d. The agreement is entered into before services are rendered.
    e. In (a), the contract is not funded.

23. During his senior year in college, Mark is drafted by the Los Angeles Dodgers. When he graduates, he expects to sign a five-year contract in the range of $1.8 million per year. Mark plans to marry his girlfriend before he reports to the Dodger farm team in California. Identify the relevant tax issues facing this left-handed pitcher.

24. List some payments to employees that would not be considered golden parachute payments.

25. Currently, there is an absolute maximum limit of $1 million on the deductible compensation for each of the top five executives of publicly traded companies. Discuss the accuracy of this statement.

26. What is a substantial risk of forfeiture? Why is it necessary to impose this restriction on the transfer of restricted property?

27. Determine which of the following conditions would cause options to fall *outside* the qualification requirements for incentive stock options:
    a. The employee disposes of his stock within 15 months from the date of the granting of the options.
    b. The employee is allowed to exercise the options up to 12 years from the date the options are granted.
    c. The employee is transferred to the parent of the corporation six months before he exercises the options.
    d. The option price is 112% of the fair market value of the stock on the grant date, and the shareholder owns 15% of the stock.
    e. The option may be exercised by the employee's spouse in the event of the employee's death.

28. Would a 30-year-old corporate executive in the 39.6% tax bracket prefer an extra $20,000 bonus or the option to purchase $20,000 worth of securities for $8,000 from the employer under a nonqualified stock option plan in the current year?

29. Compare and contrast an IRA and a § 401(k) plan.

30. Amanda is the major owner and employee of a closely held corporation. She is in the 39.6% tax bracket, living in a state with a 6% income tax rate, and has a 7.65% FICA tax rate. She needs to determine how to receive compensation from her corporation. Identify relevant tax issues facing Amanda.

31. Indicate whether each of the following items is considered a nonqualified compensation plan (N), a qualified compensation plan (Q), or both (B):
    a. Individual Retirement Account.
    b. Incentive stock option.
    c. Group term life insurance.
    d. Cafeteria plan.
    e. Pension plan.
    f. Employee stock ownership plan.
    g. Nonqualified stock option.
    h. Keogh plan.
    i. Simplified employee pension plan.

PROBLEMS

32. Red Corporation has a total of 1,000 employees, of whom 700 are non-highly compensated. The retirement plan covers 300 non-highly compensated employees and 200 highly compensated employees. Does this plan satisfy the minimum coverage test?

33. Cardinal Corporation's pension plan benefits 620 of its 1,000 highly compensated employees. How many of its 620 non-highly compensated employees must benefit to meet the ratio test for the minimum coverage requirement?

34. A retirement plan covers 72% of the non-highly compensated individuals. The plan benefits 49 of the 131 employees. Determine if the participation requirement is met.

35. Robin, Inc., uses the three-to-seven-year graded vesting approach in its retirement plan. Calculate the nonforfeitable percentage for each of the following employees based on the years of service completed:

Participant	Years of Service
Sandy	2
Rod	4
Tony	6
Heather	8

36. Tyronne, age 46, is the sole remaining participant of a money purchase pension plan. The plan is terminated, and a $180,000 taxable distribution is made to Tyronne. Calculate the amount of any early distribution penalty tax.

37. Cheryl receives a $190,000 distribution from her qualified retirement plan. If this amount is not a lump-sum distribution, calculate the amount of any excess distribution penalty tax. Cheryl made no after-tax contributions to the plan.

38. George received a distribution from a qualified plan that was entitled to capital gain treatment under § 402(a)(2). The 100 shares of the employer company stock received have a tax basis of $20 per share and a fair market value of $85 per share. George sold this stock five months after the distribution for $120 per share. Calculate the amount and character of any gain to George.

39. When Leif retires in 1996, he receives a lump-sum distribution of $50,000 from a noncontributory qualified pension plan. His active period of participation was from January 1, 1971, through December 31, 1978. Assume that Leif attained age 50 before January 1, 1986. If Leif files a joint return with his wife in 1996 and elects to use the 10-year forward averaging provision, calculate (a) his separate tax on this distribution and (b) the capital gain portion.

40. Yvonne Blair receives a $165,000 lump-sum distribution from a contributory pension plan in 1996; the distribution includes employer common stock with net unrealized appreciation of $30,000. Yvonne contributed $25,000 to the qualified plan while she was an active participant from February 10, 1973, to February 10, 1978. Yvonne attained age 50 before January 1, 1986. Yvonne wishes to know her tax consequences with respect to the lump-sum distribution. Write a letter to Yvonne that includes your calculations. Her address is 209 Barrett Street, Laramie, WY 82071.

41. Wade has been an active participant in a defined benefit plan for 17 years. During his last 5 years of employment, Wade earned $20,000, $30,000, $45,000, $50,000, and $60,000, respectively (representing his highest income years).
    a. Calculate Wade's maximum allowable benefits from this qualified plan (assume there are fewer than 100 participants).
    b. Assume that Wade's average compensation for his three high years is $132,000. Calculate Wade's maximum allowable benefits.

42. Determine the maximum annual benefits payable to an employee from a defined benefit plan in the following independent situations:
    a. Quincy, age 65, has been a participant for 12 years, and his highest average compensation for 3 years is $85,000.
    b. Wendy, age 66, has been a participant for 8 years (11 years of service), and her highest average compensation for 3 years is $86,000.
    c. Paul, age 67, has been a participant for 11 years in a collectively bargained plan with 238 participants. His highest average compensation for 3 years is $70,300.

43. The compensation paid by Orange Corporation to the plan participants of a profit sharing plan in 1996 was $33,300. During 1996, Orange Corporation contributed $10,000 to the plan.
    a. Calculate Orange Corporation's deductible amount for 1996.
    b. Calculate the amount of the contribution carryover from 1996.

44. A money purchase plan covers three employees: Samuel (who has annual compensation of $310,000), Mary (who has annual compensation of $160,000), and Larry (who has annual compensation of $40,000). If the contribution rate is 15%, what amount can be contributed to these employees' accounts?

45. During 1996, Keith is a key employee of a top-heavy pension plan. His salary is $275,000. Calculate Keith's maximum contribution to such a defined benefit plan.

46. Autumn Company's defined benefit plan allocates $300,000 of the $410,000 of cumulative benefits to key employees. The company has contacted you asking if the plan is in danger of being labeled a top-heavy plan. Prepare a memo for the tax files that includes your analysis and conclusions.

47. Blue, Inc., uses the six-year graded vesting schedule for its top-heavy retirement plan. Calculate the nonforfeitable percentage for each of the following non-key employees based on the years of service completed:

Participant	Years of Service
Dana	2
Gene	4
Samuel	5
Janet	7

48. Miguel, a single individual, participates in a § 401(k) plan of his employer. The plan permits participants to choose between a full salary or a reduced salary where the reduction becomes a before-tax contribution to a retirement plan. Miguel elects to contribute 10% of his annual compensation of $86,000 to the plan. On what amount of his salary are income taxes paid in 1996?

49. Susan earns $220,000 of self-employment net income (after the deduction for one-half of self-employment tax) in 1996 in a sole proprietorship.
    a. Calculate the maximum amount that Susan can deduct for contributions to a defined contribution Keogh plan.
    b. Suppose Susan contributes more than the allowable amount to the Keogh plan. What are the consequences to her?
    c. Can Susan retire and begin receiving Keogh payments at age 55?

50. Dawn is unmarried and is an active participant in a qualified IRA plan. Her modified AGI is $33,000. Calculate the amount that Dawn can contribute to the IRA and the amount she can deduct.

51. Answer the following independent questions with respect to IRA contributions:

a. Juan earns a salary of $25,000 and is not an active participant in any other qualified plan. His wife has no earned income. What is the maximum total deductible contribution to their IRAs? Juan wishes to contribute as much as possible to his own IRA.
b. Abby has earned income of $23,000, and her husband has earned income of $1,900. They are not active participants in any other qualified plan. What is the maximum contribution to their IRAs?
c. Leo's employer makes a contribution of $3,500 to Leo's simplified employee pension plan. If Leo's earned income is $27,000 and AGI is $24,000, what amount, if any, can he also contribute to an IRA?

52. Spring, Inc., pays bonuses to its key employees each year. The specific employees to receive bonuses and the amount of bonus for each recipient are determined on December 1 of each year. An employee eligible for a bonus may decide on or before November 15 of each year to postpone the receipt of the bonus until retirement or death. An employee electing to postpone receipt of a bonus is allowed to designate, at any time before retirement, the time and manner of the postretirement payments and to designate the persons to receive any amount payable after death. Separate accounts are not maintained for each employee. Under this compensation plan, Heather may elect to receive her $90,000 bonus in cash, or she may elect to defer the receipt of the bonus until 2001. Recommend to Heather which alternative to accept.

53. Lori is a disqualifying individual, as defined under § 280G, who receives a possible golden parachute payment of $580,000 from her employer. Her base amount (average annual compensation for the most recent five tax years) is $200,000.
a. Calculate the amount deductible by Lori's employer and any excise tax payable by Lori.
b. Assume that Lori's base amount is $110,000 and she receives $390,000. Calculate the employer's deduction and Lori's excise tax.

54. James, an executive, receives a $600,000 payment under a golden parachute agreement. James's base amount from Silver Corporation is $140,000.
a. What amount is not deductible to Silver Corporation under § 280G?
b. What total tax must James pay, assuming a 39.6% tax rate?
c. Answer (a) and (b) assuming the payment is $400,000.

55. On February 20, 1996, Tim (an executive of Hawk Corporation) purchased 100 shares of Hawk stock (selling at $20 a share) for $10. A condition of the transaction was that Tim must resell the stock to Hawk at cost if he voluntarily leaves the company within five years of receiving the stock (assume this represents a substantial risk of forfeiture).
a. Assuming that no special election is made under § 83(b), what amount, if any, is taxable to Tim in 1996?
b. Five years later when the stock is selling for $40 a share, Tim is still employed by Hawk. What amount of ordinary income, if any, is taxable to Tim?
c. What amount, if any, is deductible by Hawk as compensation expense five years later?
d. Should Tim make the § 83(b) special election in 1996? What amount would be taxable in 1996 if he makes the special election?
e. In (d), what amount would be deductible by Hawk five years later?
f. Under (d), assume Tim sold all the stock six years later for $65 per share. How much capital gain is included in his gross income?
g. In (d), what loss is available to Tim if he voluntarily resigns in 2000 before the five-year period and does not sell the stock back to the corporation?
h. In (g), in the year Tim resigns, what amount, if any, would be taxable to Hawk Corporation?

56. On July 2, 1992, Black Corporation sold 1,000 of its common shares (worth $14 per share) to Earl, an employee, for $5 per share. The sale was subject to Earl's agreement to

resell the shares to the corporation for $5 per share if his employment is terminated within the following four years. The shares had a value of $24 per share on July 2, 1996. Earl sells the shares for $31 per share on September 16, 1996. No special election under § 83(b) is made.

a. What amount, if any, will be taxed to Earl on July 2, 1992?
b. On July 2, 1996?
c. On September 16, 1996?
d. What deduction, if any, will Black Corporation obtain?
e. Assume the same facts but that Earl makes the election under § 83(b). What amount, if any, will be taxed to Earl on July 2, 1992?
f. Will the assumption made in (e) have any effect on any deduction Black Corporation will receive? Explain.

57. Rosa exercises incentive stock options for 100 shares of Copper Corporation stock at the option price of $100 per share on May 21, 1996, when the fair market value is $120 per share. She sells the 100 shares of common stock three and one-half years later for $140.
    a. Calculate the total long-term capital gain on this sale.
    b. Assume Rosa holds the stock seven months and sells the shares for $140 per share. Calculate any ordinary income on the sale.
    c. In (b), what amount can Copper Corporation deduct?
    d. Suppose Rosa holds the stock for two years and sells the shares for $115 per share. Calculate any capital gain on this transaction.
    e. In (a), assume the options are nonqualified options with a nonascertainable fair market value on the date of the grant. Calculate total long-term capital gain, if any, in the year of sale.
    f. In (e), assume that each option has an ascertainable fair market value of $10 on the date of the grant and no substantial risk of forfeiture exists. Calculate total long-term capital gain, if any, on the date of the sale.

58. On November 19, 1994, Rex is granted a nonqualified stock option to purchase 100 shares of Tan Company (on that date the stock is selling for $8 per share and the option price is $9 per share). Rex exercises the option on August 21, 1995, when the stock is selling for $10 per share. Five months later, Rex sells the shares for $11.50 per share.
    a. What amount is taxable to Rex in 1994?
    b. What amount is taxable to Rex in 1995?
    c. What amount and type of gain are taxable to Rex in 1996?
    d. What amount, if any, is deductible by Tan Company in 1995?
    e. What amount, if any, is recognized in 1996 if the stock is sold for $9.50 per share?

59. Sara Reid, the owner of a small business, is trying to decide whether to have a § 401(k) plan or a simplified employee pension plan. Her salary will be approximately $45,000, and she will have no employees. She asks you to provide her with information on the advantages and disadvantages of both types of plans and your recommendation. Draft a letter to Sara that contains your response. Her address is 1000 Canal Avenue, New Orleans, LA 70148.

60. Lou's employer provides a qualified cafeteria plan under which he can choose cash of $6,000 or health and accident insurance premiums worth approximately $6,000. If Lou is in the 39.6% tax bracket, advise him of his tax alternatives.

RESEARCH PROBLEMS

Note: ***West's Federal Taxation on CD-ROM*** *can be used in preparing solutions to the Research Problems. Alternatively, tax research materials contained in a standard tax library can be used.*

Research Problem 1. Mr. Sanjay Baker and his sister owned and operated a mail-order business in corporate form. The corporation used the homes of Mr. Baker and his sister for corporate mail-order activities (assembling, storing inventory, etc.). The corporation paid Mr. Baker and the sister rent for the use of the homes. The payments were deducted as rent and reported by the two parties on their tax returns. The IRS disallowed most of the deduction, contending that the rent was excessive. Is the excessive rent deductible as compensation? Write a letter to Mr. Baker that contains your advice and prepare a memo for the tax files. His address is 63 Rose Avenue, San Francisco, CA 94117.

Partial list of research aids:
Multnomah Operating Co., 57–2 USTC ¶9979, 52 AFTR 672, 248 F.2d 661 (CA–9, 1957).

Research Problem 2. Frank and Polly were married, but Frank died on February 25, 1996. During 1996, Frank earned $5,226 in wages, but Polly had no earned income. Neither had contributed any money to an IRA during 1996. What amount, if any, can be contributed to Frank's IRA and/or Polly's spousal IRA?

Research Problem 3. Six executives entered into elective deferred compensation agreements whereby, after rendering the necessary services, they are entitled to be paid deferred compensation plus incremental amounts designated as "interest." This "interest" is calculated by reference to a predetermined formula. On their retirement, the executives are entitled to receive the deferred compensation plus the incremental "interest" amounts. During 1996, the accrual method employer put $929,000 of deferred compensation into the deferred compensation accounts (DCAs) along with $177,500 of "interest." The DCAs were unfunded and unsecured. The employer intends to deduct the $177,500 as interest within the meaning of § 163. Is this the appropriate tax treatment?

Research Problem 4. What is a phantom stock plan? Outline the tax treatment. Could a phantom stock payment be considered performance-based compensation for purposes of the $1 million deduction limitation on executive pay?

Research Problem 5. What are stock appreciation rights? Outline the tax treatment.

TEAM PROJECT: ARTHUR ANDERSEN TAX CHALLENGE CASES

For more information on the Arthur Andersen Tax Challenge Cases, please refer to Chapter 1, page 1-38.

Information related to tax issues and problems that are discussed in this chapter may be found in the

Fields case on page 19
Miller case on pages 2, 4, 5, 12-15, 18-20

Read and analyze the case you have been assigned and *identify* any issues and problems that are related to material covered in this chapter. If the information provided in the case is complete, prepare answers for this part of the case at this time. If you need information that is contained in the later parts of the case, please write a memo summarizing the questions or problems so you can prepare a complete answer at a later date.

P • A • R • T

VII

Corporations and Partnerships

The primary orientation of this text is toward basic tax concepts and the individual taxpayer. Although many of these tax concepts also apply to corporations and partnerships, numerous tax concepts apply specifically to corporations or partnerships. An overview of these provisions is presented in Part VII. Comprehensive coverage of these topics appears in *West's Federal Taxation: Corporations, Partnerships, Estates, and Trusts.*

CHAPTER

20

CORPORATIONS AND PARTNERSHIPS

LEARNING OBJECTIVES

After completing Chapter 20, you should be able to:

1. Identify those entities that are treated as corporations for Federal income tax purposes.
2. Contrast the income tax treatment of individuals with that applicable to corporations.
3. Recognize and calculate the tax deductions available only to corporations.
4. Determine the corporate tax liability and comply with various procedural and reporting requirements.
5. Understand the tax rules governing the formation of corporations.
6. Work with the tax rules governing the operation of corporations.
7. Recognize the tax rules governing the liquidation of corporations.
8. Appreciate the utility and effect of the Subchapter S election.
9. Understand the tax consequences of forming and operating a partnership.
10. Evaluate the advantages and disadvantages of the various forms for conducting a business.

OUTLINE

Until now this text has concentrated on the Federal income taxation of individual taxpayers. However, even the most basic business decisions require some awareness of the tax implications of other business forms.

EXAMPLE 1

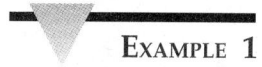

Gina and Tom are contemplating entering into a new business venture that will require additional capital investment by other parties. As the venture will involve financial risk, both Gina and Tom are concerned about personal liability. Further, they would prefer to avoid any income taxes at the entity level. Both Gina and Tom would like to take advantage of any losses the venture may generate during its formative period. ▼

In choosing the form for the venture, Gina and Tom will have to consider using a corporation. The corporate form limits a shareholder's liability to the amount invested in the stock. Regular corporations, however, are subject to the corporate income tax. Furthermore, losses incurred by corporations do not pass through to the shareholders. Perhaps the ideal solution would be to use the corporate form and elect to be taxed as an S corporation. The election would avoid the corporate income tax and permit the pass-through of losses while providing limited liability for the shareholders.

Although the resolution of the problem posed by Example 1 seems simple enough, it did not consider the possible use of a partnership. More important, the decision required *some* knowledge of corporations and the S corporation election. This chapter is intended to provide such knowledge by briefly reviewing the tax consequences of the various forms of business organization.

What Is a Corporation?

COMPLIANCE WITH STATE LAW

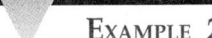

1 LEARNING OBJECTIVE
Identify those entities that are treated as corporations for Federal income tax purposes.

A company must comply with the specific requirements for corporate status under state law. For example, it is necessary to draft and file articles of incorporation with the state regulatory agency, be granted a charter, and issue stock to shareholders.

Compliance with state law, although important, is not the only requirement that must be met to qualify for corporate *tax* status. For example, a corporation qualifying under state law may be disregarded as a taxable entity if it is a mere sham lacking in economic substance. The key consideration is the degree of business activity conducted at the corporate level.

EXAMPLE 2

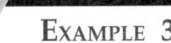

Gene and Mike are joint owners of a tract of unimproved real estate that they wish to protect from future creditors. Gene and Mike form Falcon Corporation, to which they transfer the land in return for all of the corporation's stock. The corporation merely holds title to the land and conducts no other activities. In all respects, Falcon Corporation meets the legal requirements of a corporation under applicable state law. Nevertheless, Falcon might not be recognized as a separate entity for corporate tax purposes under these facts.[1] ▼

EXAMPLE 3

Assume the same facts as in Example 2. In addition to holding title to the land, Falcon Corporation leases the property, collects rents, and pays the property taxes. Falcon probably would be treated as a corporation for Federal income tax purposes because of the scope of its activities. ▼

In some instances, the IRS has attempted to disregard (or collapse) a corporation in order to make the income taxable directly to the shareholders.[2] In other cases, the IRS has asserted that the corporation is a separate taxable entity so as to assess tax at the corporate level and to tax corporate distributions to shareholders as dividend income (double taxation).[3]

THE ASSOCIATION APPROACH

An organization not qualifying as a regular corporation under state law may nevertheless be taxed as a corporation under the association approach. The designation given to an entity under the state law is not controlling. For example, a partnership of physicians has been treated as an association even though state law prohibited the practice of medicine in the corporate form. The partnership thus was subject to the Federal income tax rules applicable to corporations.[4] Another sensitive area involves limited partnerships where the only general partner is a corporation. Unless certain prescribed guidelines are carefully followed, the IRS will treat the partnership as an association.[5]

Whether or not an entity will be considered an **association** for Federal income tax purposes depends upon the number of corporate characteristics it possesses.

[1] See *Paymer v. Comm.*, 45–2 USTC ¶9353, 33 AFTR 1536, 150 F.2d 334 (CA–2, 1945).

[2] *Floyd Patterson*, 25 TCM 1230, T.C.Memo. 1966–239, *aff'd.* in 68–2 USTC ¶9471, 22 AFTR2d 5810 (CA–2, 1968).

[3] *Raffety Farms Inc. v. U.S.*, 75–1 USTC ¶9271, 35 AFTR2d 75–811, 511 F.2d 1234 (CA–8, 1975).

[4] *U.S. v. Kintner*, 54–2 USTC ¶9626, 46 AFTR 995, 216 F.2d 418 (CA–5, 1954).

[5] Rev.Proc. 89–12, 1989–1 C.B. 798.

TAX IN THE NEWS

WHO IS TAXED ON A BASKETBALL STAR'S SALARY?

When he signed with the Houston Rockets, Allen Leavell agreed to be under their direction and control in carrying out all athletic activities required of him. Immediately after signing and upon the advice of his tax adviser, Allen formed the Leavell Corporation. Allen and Leavell Corporation contracted for the exclusive right to his services. Under the arrangement, all income Allen earned would belong to the corporation, and he would receive an annual salary. The amount of the salary was far less than the Rockets were paying Allen for playing point guard on the team.

During the years Allen played for the Rockets, his paychecks were turned over to the corporation, which reported those amounts on the Forms 1120 it filed. Upon audit by the IRS, Allen's pay from the Rockets was deemed taxed to him and not to Leavell Corporation.

In *Allen Leavell* [104 T.C. 140 (1995)], the Tax Court sided with the IRS. Income is taxed to whoever earns it. In this case, Allen (and not the corporation) earned the amounts paid by the Rockets. The Rockets were paying for services performed by Allen and not by his corporation.

According to court decisions and the Regulations, corporate characteristics include the following:[6]

1. Associates.
2. An objective to carry on a business and divide the gains therefrom.
3. Continuity of life.
4. Centralized management.
5. Limited liability.
6. Free transferability of interests.

The Regulations state that an unincorporated organization shall not be classified as an association unless it possesses *more* corporate than noncorporate characteristics. In making this determination, the characteristics common to both corporate and noncorporate business organizations are to be disregarded. Both corporations and partnerships generally have associates (shareholders and partners) and an objective to carry on a business and divide the gains. Therefore, only if a partnership has at least three of attributes 3 through 6 will it be treated as an association (taxable as a corporation).

EXAMPLE 4

The Green Partnership agreement provides for the following: the partnership terminates with the withdrawal of a partner; all of the partners have authority to participate in the management of the partnership; all of the partners are individually liable for the debts of the partnership; and a partner may not freely transfer his or her interest in the partnership to another. None of corporate attributes 3 through 6 are present. Since the majority requirement of the Regulations is not satisfied, Green is not taxable as an association. ▼

[6] Reg. § 301.7701–2(a).

LIMITED LIABILITY COMPANIES

All U. S. states have adopted statutes allowing **limited liability companies.** These organizations have the corporate feature of limited liability, so the owners have no personal liability for the debts of the business. This type of organization is becoming increasingly popular for professional groups. In most cases, the owners want the organization to be treated as a partnership for Federal income tax purposes, so as to avoid the double tax resulting from operating as a corporation. Often, centralized management is present, but the other key corporate characteristics (i.e., continuity of life and free transferability of interests) are absent.[7]

INCOME TAX CONSIDERATIONS

GENERAL TAX CONSEQUENCES OF DIFFERENT FORMS OF BUSINESS ENTITIES

2 LEARNING OBJECTIVE
Contrast the income tax treatment of individuals with that applicable to corporations.

A business operation may be conducted as a sole proprietorship, as a partnership, or in corporate form.

- Sole proprietorships are not separate taxable entities. The owner of the business reports all business transactions on his or her individual income tax return.
- Partnerships are not subject to the income tax. Under the *conduit* concept, the various tax attributes of the partnership's operations flow through to the individual partners to be reported on their personal income tax returns.
- The regular corporate form of doing business carries with it the imposition of the corporate income tax. The corporation is recognized as a separate taxpaying entity. Income is taxed to the corporation as earned and taxed again to the shareholders as dividends when distributed.
- A regular corporation may elect to be taxed as an S corporation. This special treatment is similar (although not identical) to the partnership rules. Income tax is generally avoided at the corporate level, and shareholders are taxed currently on the taxable income of the S corporation.

INDIVIDUALS AND CORPORATIONS COMPARED—AN OVERVIEW

Similarities between Corporate and Individual Tax Rules. The gross income of a corporation is determined in much the same manner as for individuals. Both individuals and corporations are entitled to exclusions from gross income, such as interest on municipal bonds. Gains and losses from property transactions are also treated similarly. For example, whether a gain or loss is capital or ordinary depends on the nature and use of the asset rather than the type of taxpayer. Upon the sale or other taxable disposition of depreciable personalty, the recapture rules of § 1245 make no distinction between corporate and noncorporate taxpayers. In the case of the recapture of depreciation on real property (§ 1250), however, corporate taxpayers experience more severe tax consequences.

[7] See Chapter 13 of *West's Federal Taxation: Corporations, Partnerships, Estates, and Trusts.*

As illustrated later, corporations must recognize as additional ordinary income 20 percent of the excess of the amount that would be recaptured under § 1245 over the amount recaptured under § 1250.

The business deductions of corporations parallel those available to individuals. Corporate deductions are allowed for all ordinary and necessary expenses paid or incurred in carrying on a trade or business. Corporations may also deduct interest, certain taxes, losses, bad debts, depreciation, cost recovery, charitable contributions subject to corporate limitation rules, net operating losses, research and experimental expenditures, and other less common deductions.

Many of the tax credits available to individuals, such as the foreign tax credit, can be claimed by corporations. Not available to corporations are certain credits that are personal in nature. Examples of credits not available to corporations include the credit for child and dependent care expenses, the credit for the elderly or disabled, and the earned income credit.

Corporations usually have the same choices of accounting periods as do individuals. Like an individual, a corporation may choose a calendar year or a fiscal year for reporting purposes. Corporations do enjoy greater flexibility in the election of a tax year. For example, corporations usually can have different tax years from those of their shareholders. Also, a newly formed corporation generally has a free choice of any approved accounting period without having to obtain the consent of the IRS. As noted in Chapter 18, however, personal service corporations are subject to severe restrictions on the use of a fiscal year.

The use of the cash method of accounting is denied to large corporations (those with average annual gross receipts in excess of $5 million). Smaller corporations as well as qualified personal service corporations and other corporations engaged in the trade or business of farming have a choice between the cash or accrual method of accounting for tax purposes. Both individuals and corporations that maintain inventory for sale to customers are required to use the accrual method of accounting for determining sales and cost of goods sold.

Dissimilarities. Both noncorporate and corporate taxpayers are subject to progressive income tax rates. For individuals, the rates are 15, 28, 31, 36, and 39.6 percent. For corporations, the rates are 15, 25, 34, and 35 percent. Corporate taxpayers lose the benefits of the lower brackets (using a phase-out approach) once taxable income reaches a certain level. Noncorporate taxpayers, however, continue to enjoy the benefits of the lower brackets even though they have reached the higher taxable income levels.

Both corporate and noncorporate taxpayers are subject to the alternative minimum tax (AMT). For AMT purposes, many adjustments and tax preference items are the same for both, but other adjustments and tax preferences apply only to corporations or only to individuals. Corporate tax rates are discussed later in the chapter. The AMT is discussed at length in Chapter 12. See also the coverage in *West's Federal Taxation: Corporations, Partnerships, Estates, and Trusts.*

All allowable corporate deductions are treated as business expenses. The determination of adjusted gross income, so essential for individuals, has no relevance to corporations. Corporations need not be concerned with classifying deductions into *deduction for* and *deduction from* categories.[8]

[8] The standard deduction, itemized deductions, and personal and dependency exemptions are not available to corporations.

SPECIFIC PROVISIONS COMPARED

Corporate and individual tax rules also differ in the following areas:

- Capital gains and losses.
- Recapture of depreciation.
- Charitable contributions.
- Net operating losses.
- Special deductions for corporations.

Capital Gains and Losses. Both corporate and noncorporate taxpayers are required to aggregate gains and losses from the taxable sale or exchange of capital assets. (Refer to Chapter 16 for a description of the netting process that takes place after the aggregation has been completed.) For net long-term capital gains, individual taxpayers enjoy an advantage (the alternative tax). In no event will the gains be taxed at a rate in excess of 28 percent. In the case of corporations, all capital gains are taxed using the rates for ordinary income. Therefore, the net long-term capital gains of a corporation could be taxed at a rate of 35 percent (the highest rate applicable to corporations).

Significant differences exist in the treatment of capital losses for income tax purposes. Individuals, for example, can annually deduct up to $3,000 of net capital losses against ordinary income. Corporations are not permitted to use net capital losses to offset ordinary income. Net capital losses can be used only to offset past or future capital gains.[9] Unlike individuals, corporations are not allowed an unlimited carryover period for capital losses. Instead, they may carry back excess capital losses to the three preceding years, applying them initially to the earliest year. If not exhausted by the carryback, remaining unused capital losses may be carried forward for a period of five years from the year of the loss.[10]

When carried back or forward, *both* short-term capital losses and long-term capital losses are treated as short-term capital losses by corporate taxpayers. For noncorporate taxpayers, a capital loss does not lose its identity. Thus, long-term capital losses of noncorporate taxpayers are carried forward as long-term capital losses, and short-term capital losses are carried forward as short-term capital losses.

EXAMPLE 5

Hawk Corporation, a calendar year taxpayer, incurs a long-term net capital loss of $5,000 for 1996. None of the capital loss may be deducted in 1996. Hawk may, however, carry the loss back to years 1993, 1994, and 1995 (in this order) and offset any capital gains recognized in these years. If the carryback does not exhaust the loss, the loss may be carried forward to 1997, 1998, 1999, 2000, and 2001 (in this order). Such capital loss carrybacks or carryovers are treated as short-term capital losses. ▼

Recapture of Depreciation. Corporations selling depreciable real estate may have ordinary income in addition to that required by § 1250. Under § 291, the additional ordinary income element is 20 percent of the excess of the § 1245 recapture potential over the § 1250 recapture. As a result, the § 1231 gain is correspondingly decreased by the additional recapture.

EXAMPLE 6

Condor Corporation purchases residential real property on January 3, 1984, for $300,000. Accelerated cost recovery is taken in the amount of $256,250 before the property is sold on

[9] §§ 1211(a) and (b).

[10] § 1212(a).

February 5, 1996, for $250,000. Straight-line cost recovery would have been $241,667 (using a 15-year recovery period under ACRS).

First, determine realized gain:

Sales price		$250,000
Less adjusted basis:		
Cost of property	$ 300,000	
Less cost recovery	(256,250)	(43,750)
Realized gain		$206,250

Second, determine § 1245 recapture potential. This is the lesser of $206,250 (realized gain) or $256,250 (cost recovery claimed), or $206,250. Third, determine § 1250 recapture amount:

Cost recovery taken	$ 256,250
Less straight-line cost recovery	(241,667)
§ 1250 ordinary income	$ 14,583

Fourth, because the taxpayer is a corporation, determine the additional § 291 amount:

§ 1245 recapture potential	$206,250
Less § 1250 recapture amount	(14,583)
Excess § 1245 recapture potential	$191,667
Apply § 291 percentage	× 20%
Additional ordinary income under § 291	$ 38,333

Condor Corporation's realized and recognized gain of $206,250 is accounted for as follows:

Ordinary income under § 1250	$ 14,583
Ordinary income under § 291	38,333
§ 1231 gain	153,334
Total recognized gain	$206,250

▼

Charitable Contributions. Generally, a charitable contribution deduction is allowed only for the tax year in which the payment is made. However, an important exception is made for accrual basis corporations. The deduction may be claimed in the tax year *preceding* payment if the following conditions are satisfied:

- The contribution is authorized by the board of directors by the end of that tax year *and*
- The contribution is paid on or before the fifteenth day of the third month of the next tax year.[11]

EXAMPLE 7

On December 28, 1996, the board of directors of Dove Corporation, a calendar year, accrual basis taxpayer, authorizes a $5,000 donation to a qualified charity. The donation is paid on March 14, 1997. Dove Corporation may claim the $5,000 donation as a deduction for 1996. As an alternative, Dove may claim the deduction in 1997 (the year of payment). ▼

Like individuals, corporations are not permitted an unlimited charitable contribution deduction. In any one year, a corporate taxpayer is limited to 10

[11] § 170(a)(2).

percent of taxable income. For this purpose, taxable income is computed without regard to the charitable contribution deduction, any net operating loss carryback or capital loss carryback, or the dividends received deduction.[12] Any contributions in excess of the 10 percent limitation are carried forward to the five succeeding tax years. Any carryover must be added to subsequent contributions and is subject to the 10 percent limitation. In applying the limitation, the most recent contributions must be deducted first.[13]

EXAMPLE 8

During 1996, Eagle Corporation (a calendar year taxpayer) had the following income and expenses:

Income from operations	$140,000
Expenses from operations	110,000
Dividends received	10,000
Charitable contributions made in 1996	5,000

For purposes of the 10% limitation only, Eagle's taxable income is $40,000 ($140,000 – $110,000 + $10,000). Consequently, the allowable charitable contribution deduction for 1996 is $4,000 (10% × $40,000). The $1,000 unused portion of the contribution is carried forward to 1997, 1998, 1999, 2000, and 2001 (in that order) until exhausted. ▼

EXAMPLE 9

Assume the same facts as in Example 8. In 1997, Eagle Corporation has taxable income (after adjustments) of $50,000 and makes a charitable contribution of $4,800. The maximum deduction allowed for 1997 is $5,000 (10% × $50,000). The first $4,800 of the allowed deduction must be allocated to the 1997 contributions, and the $200 excess is carried over from 1996. The remaining $800 of the 1996 contribution is carried over to 1998, etc. ▼

As noted in Chapter 10, the deduction for charitable contributions of ordinary income property is limited to the lesser of the fair market value or the adjusted basis of the property. A special rule permits a corporation to contribute inventory (ordinary income property) to certain charitable organizations and receive a deduction equal to the adjusted basis plus one-half of the difference between the fair market value and the adjusted basis of the property.[14] In no event, however, may the deduction exceed twice the adjusted basis of the property. To qualify for this exception, the inventory must be used by the charity in its exempt purpose for the care of *children*, the *ill*, or the *needy*.

EXAMPLE 10

In the current year, Robin Company (a retail clothier) donates sweaters and overcoats to Sheltering Arms (a qualified charity caring for the homeless). The clothing is inventory and has a basis of $10,000 and a fair market value of $14,000. If Robin is a corporation, the charitable contribution that results is $12,000 [$10,000 (basis) + $2,000 (50% of the appreciation of $4,000)]. In contrast, if Robin is not a corporation, the charitable contribution is limited to $10,000 (basis). ▼

Net Operating Losses. The computation of a net operating loss (NOL) for individuals was discussed in Chapter 7. Corporations are not subject to the complex adjustments required for individuals (e.g., a corporation has no adjustments for nonbusiness deductions or capital gains and losses). Corporations are subject to fewer adjustments than individuals are because a corporation's loss

[12] § 170(b)(2).
[13] § 170(d)(2).
[14] § 170(e)(3).

more clearly approximates a true economic loss. Artificial deductions (e.g., personal and dependency exemptions) that merely generate paper losses are not permitted for corporations.

In computing the NOL of a corporation, the dividends received deduction (discussed below) can be claimed in determining the amount of the loss.[15] Corporate NOLs may be carried back 3 years and forward 15 years (or taxpayers may elect to forgo the carryback period) to offset taxable income for those years.

EXAMPLE 11

In 1996, Wren Corporation has gross income of $200,000 and deductions of $300,000, excluding the dividends received deduction. Wren received taxable dividends of $100,000 from Exxon stock. Wren has an NOL of $170,000, computed as follows:

Gross income (including Exxon dividends)		$ 200,000
Less: Business deductions	$300,000	
Dividends received deduction (70% × $100,000)	70,000	(370,000)
Taxable income (loss)		($ 170,000)

EXAMPLE 12

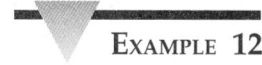

Assume the same facts as in Example 11 and that Wren Corporation had taxable income of $40,000 in 1993. The NOL of $170,000 is carried back to 1993 (unless Wren elects not to carry back the loss to that year). The carryover to 1994 is $130,000, computed as follows:

Taxable income for 1993	$ 40,000
Less: NOL carryback from 1996	(170,000)
Carryover of unabsorbed 1996 loss	($ 130,000)

In Example 12, the carryback to 1993 might have been ill-advised if Wren Corporation had little, if any, taxable income in 1994 and 1995 and if it anticipated large amounts of taxable income in the immediate future. In that case, the *election to forgo* the carryback might generate greater tax savings. In this regard, three points should be considered. First, the time value of the tax refund that is lost by not using the carryback procedure must be considered. Second, the election to forgo an NOL carryback is irrevocable. Thus, it cannot be changed later if the future high profits do not materialize. Third, future increases or decreases in corporate income tax rates that can reasonably be anticipated should be considered.

DEDUCTIONS AVAILABLE ONLY TO CORPORATIONS

3 LEARNING OBJECTIVE
Recognize and calculate the tax deductions available only to corporations.

Dividends Received Deduction. The purpose of the **dividends received deduction** is to prevent triple taxation. Without the deduction, income paid to a corporation in the form of a dividend would be subject to taxation for a second time (once to the distributing corporation) with no corresponding deduction to the distributing corporation. A third level of tax would be assessed on the shareholders when the recipient corporation distributed the income to its shareholders. Since the dividends received deduction may be less than 100 percent, the law provides only partial relief.

The amount of the dividends received deduction depends upon the percentage of ownership the recipient corporate shareholder holds in the corporation making the dividend distribution.[16] For dividends received or accrued, the *deduction percentage* is summarized as follows:

[15] § 172(d).

[16] § 243(a).

Percentage of Ownership by Corporate Shareholder	Deduction Percentage
Less than 20%	70%
20% or more (but less than 80%)	80%
80% or more	100%

The dividends received deduction may be limited to a percentage of the taxable income of a corporation computed without regard to the NOL deduction, the dividends received deduction, or any capital loss carryback to the current tax year. The percentage of taxable income limitation corresponds to the deduction percentage. Thus, if a corporate shareholder owns less than 20 percent of the stock in the distributing corporation, the dividends received deduction is limited to 70 percent of taxable income (as previously defined). However, this limitation does not apply if the corporation has an NOL for the current taxable year.[17]

In working with these myriad rules, the following steps need to be taken:

1. Multiply the dividends received by the deduction percentage.
2. Multiply the taxable income (as previously defined) by the deduction percentage.
3. The deduction is limited to the lesser of Step 1 or Step 2, unless subtracting the amount derived from Step 1 from taxable income (as previously defined) generates a negative number. If so, the amount derived in Step 1 should be used.

EXAMPLE 13 Crane, Osprey, and Gull Corporations, three unrelated calendar year corporations, have the following transactions for 1996:

	Crane Corporation	Osprey Corporation	Gull Corporation
Gross income from operations	$ 400,000	$ 320,000	$ 260,000
Expenses from operations	(340,000)	(340,000)	(340,000)
Dividends received from domestic corporations (less than 20% ownership)	200,000	200,000	200,000
Taxable income before the dividends received deduction	$ 260,000	$ 180,000	$ 120,000

In determining the dividends received deduction, use the step procedure just described:

	Crane Corporation	Osprey Corporation	Gull Corporation
Step 1: (70% × $200,000)	$140,000	$140,000	$140,000
Step 2:			
70% × $260,000 (taxable income)	$182,000		
70% × $180,000 (taxable income)		$126,000	
70% × $120,000 (taxable income)			$ 84,000

[17] § 246(b).

Step 3:			
Lesser of Step 1 or Step 2	$140,000	$126,000	
Generates an NOL			$140,000

Osprey Corporation is subject to the 70 percent of taxable income limitation. It does not qualify for the loss rule treatment, since subtracting $140,000 (Step 1) from $180,000 does not yield a loss. Gull Corporation qualifies for the loss rule treatment because subtracting $140,000 (Step 1) from $120,000 does yield a loss. In summary, each corporation has the following dividends received deduction for 1996: $140,000 for Crane, $126,000 for Osprey, and $140,000 for Gull. If a corporation already has an NOL before any dividends received deduction is claimed, the full dividends received deduction (as calculated in Step 1) is allowed.

Deduction of Organizational Expenditures. Under § 248, a corporation may elect to amortize organizational expenses over a period of 60 months or more. If the election is not made on a timely basis, the expenditures cannot be deducted until the corporation ceases to conduct business and liquidates. The election is made in a statement attached to the corporation's return for its first taxable year. The election covers all qualifying expenses *incurred* in the corporation's first year.[18]

Organizational expenditures include the following:

- Legal services incident to organization (e.g., drafting the corporate charter, bylaws, minutes of organizational meetings, terms of original stock certificates).
- Necessary accounting services.
- Expenses of temporary directors and of organizational meetings of directors and shareholders.
- Fees paid to the state of incorporation.

Expenditures connected with issuing or selling shares of stock or other securities (e.g., commissions, professional fees, and printing costs) or with the transfer of assets to a corporation do not qualify. These expenditures are generally added to the capital account and are not subject to amortization.

DETERMINATION OF CORPORATE TAX LIABILITY

4 LEARNING OBJECTIVE
Determine the corporate tax liability and comply with various procedural and reporting requirements.

Income Tax Rates. The Revenue Reconciliation Act of 1993 revised the corporate rate schedule for tax years beginning after 1992. The rates *were not changed for taxable income of $10 million or less.* For corporations with taxable income in excess of $10 million, a rate of 35 percent applies to the excess. An additional tax at the rate of 3 percent (not to exceed $100,000) is imposed on taxable income in excess of $15 million.[19] In effect, the rate brackets on corporations are as follows:

[18] A cash basis taxpayer need not have paid the expenses as long as they were incurred.

[19] § 11(b).

Taxable Income	Tax Rate
Not over $50,000	15%
Over $50,000 but not over $75,000	25%
Over $75,000 but not over $100,000	34%
Over $100,000 but not over $335,000	39%*
Over $335,000 but not over $10,000,000	34%
Over $10,000,000 but not over $15,000,000	35%
Over $15,000,000 but not over $18,333,333	38%**
Over $18,333,333	35%

*Five percent of this rate represents a phase-out of the benefits of the lower tax rates on the first $75,000 of taxable income.
**Three percent of this rate represents a phase-out of the benefits of the lower tax rate (34% rather than 35%) on the first $10 million of taxable income.

EXAMPLE 14

A calendar year corporation has taxable income of $90,000 for 1996. The income tax liability is $18,850, determined as follows: $7,500 (15% × $50,000) + $6,250 (25% × $25,000) + $5,100 (34% × $15,000). ▼

Qualified personal service corporations are taxed at a flat 35 percent rate on all taxable income. They do not enjoy the tax savings of the lower brackets. For this purpose, a *qualified* **personal service corporation** is one that is substantially employee owned and engages in one of the following activities: health, law, engineering, architecture, accounting, actuarial science, performing arts, or consulting.

Alternative Minimum Tax. Corporations are subject to an alternative minimum tax (AMT) that is structured in the same manner as that applicable to individuals. The AMT for corporations, as for individuals, defines a more expansive tax base than for the regular tax. Like individuals, corporations are required to apply a minimum tax rate to the expanded base and pay the difference between the tentative AMT liability and the regular tax. Many of the adjustments and tax preference items necessary to arrive at alternative minimum taxable income (AMTI) are the same for individuals and corporations. Although the objective of the AMT is the same for individuals and for corporations, the rate and exemptions are different. Computation of the AMT is discussed in Chapter 12.

CORPORATE FILING REQUIREMENTS

A corporation must file a return whether it has taxable income or not.[20] A corporation that was not in existence throughout an entire annual accounting period is required to file a return for the fraction of the year during which it was in existence. In addition, the corporation must file a return even though it has ceased to do business if it has valuable claims for which it will bring suit. It is relieved of filing returns once it ceases business and dissolves.

The corporate return is filed on Form 1120 unless the corporation is a small corporation entitled to file the shorter Form 1120–A. Among the *several* require-

[20] § 6012(a)(2).

ments for filing Form 1120–A are gross receipts (or sales) of less than $500,000 and total assets of less than $500,000. Corporations making the S corporation election (discussed later in the chapter) file on Form 1120S.

The return must be filed on or before the fifteenth day of the third month following the close of the corporation's tax year. Corporations can receive an automatic extension of six months for filing the corporate return by filing Form 7004 by the due date of the return. However, the IRS may terminate an extension by mailing a 10-day notice to the taxpayer corporation.[21]

A corporation must make payments of estimated tax unless its tax liability can reasonably be expected to be less than $500.[22] For 1996, the payments must equal 100 percent of the corporation's final tax. These payments may be made in four installments due on or before the fifteenth day of the fourth, sixth, ninth, and twelfth months of the corporate taxable year. The full amount of the unpaid tax is due on the date of the return. Failure to make the required estimated tax prepayments will result in a nondeductible penalty being imposed on the corporation. The penalty can be avoided, however, if any of various exceptions apply.[23]

RECONCILIATION OF CORPORATE TAXABLE INCOME AND ACCOUNTING INCOME

Taxable income and accounting net income are seldom the same amount. For example, a difference may arise if the corporation uses accelerated depreciation for tax purposes and straight-line depreciation for accounting purposes.

Many items of income for accounting purposes, such as proceeds from a life insurance policy on the death of a corporate officer and interest on municipal bonds, may not be includible in calculating taxable income. Some expense items for accounting purposes, such as expenses to produce tax-exempt income, estimated warranty reserves, a net capital loss, and Federal income taxes, are not deductible for tax purposes.

Schedule M–1 on the last page of Form 1120 is used to reconcile accounting net income (net income after Federal income taxes) with taxable income (as computed on the corporate tax return before the deduction for a net operating loss and the dividends received deduction). In the left-hand column of Schedule M–1, net income per books is added to the following: the Federal income tax liability for the year, the excess of capital losses over capital gains (which cannot be deducted in the current year), income for tax purposes that is not income in the current year for accounting purposes, and expenses recorded on the books that are not deductible on the tax return. In the right-hand column, income recorded on the books that is not currently taxable or is tax-exempt and deductions for tax purposes that are not expenses for accounting purposes are totaled and subtracted from the left-hand column total to arrive at taxable income (before the net operating loss or dividends received deductions).

EXAMPLE 15

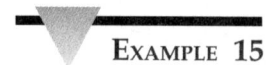

During 1996, Crow Corporation had the following transactions:

Net income per books (after tax)	$92,400
Taxable income	50,000
Federal income tax liability (15% × $50,000)	7,500

[21] § 6081.

[22] § 6655(f).

[23] See § 6655 for the penalty involved and the various exceptions.

Interest income from tax-exempt bonds	5,000
Interest paid on loan, the proceeds of which were used to purchase the tax-exempt bonds	500
Life insurance proceeds received as a result of the death of a key employee	50,000
Premiums paid on key employee life insurance policy	2,600
Excess of capital losses over capital gains	2,000

For book and tax purposes, Crow determines depreciation under the straight-line method. Crow's Schedule M–1 for the current year follows.

Schedule M-1 **Reconciliation of Income (Loss) per Books With Income per Return** (See page 18 of instructions.)

1	Net income (loss) per books	*92,400*	7	Income recorded on books this year not included on this return (itemize): Tax-exempt interest $ 5,000 Life insurance proceeds on key employee $50,000	*55,000*
2	Federal income tax	*7,500*	8	Deductions on this return not charged against book income this year (itemize):	
3	Excess of capital losses over capital gains	*2,000*	a	Depreciation $	
4	Income subject to tax not recorded on books this year (itemize):		b	Contributions carryover $	
5	Expenses recorded on books this year not deducted on this return (itemize):				
a	Depreciation $				
b	Contributions carryover $				
c	Travel and entertainment $ Int. on tax-exempt bonds $500, Prem. on key employee ins. $2,600	*3,100*	9	Add lines 7 and 8	*55,000*
6	Add lines 1 through 5	*105,000*	10	Income (line 28, page 1)—line 6 less line 9	*50,000*

▼

Schedule M–2 reconciles unappropriated retained earnings at the beginning of the year with unappropriated retained earnings at year-end. Beginning balance plus net income per books, as entered on line 1 of Schedule M–1, less dividend distributions during the year equals ending retained earnings. Other sources of increases or decreases in retained earnings are also listed on Schedule M–2.

EXAMPLE 16

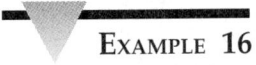

Assume the same facts as in Example 15. Crow Corporation's beginning balance in unappropriated retained earnings is $125,000, and Crow distributed a cash dividend of $30,000 to its shareholders during the year. Based on these further assumptions, Crow has the following Schedule M–2 for the current year.

Schedule M-2 **Analysis of Unappropriated Retained Earnings per Books (Line 25, Schedule L)**

1	Balance at beginning of year	*125,000*	5	Distributions: a Cash	*30,000*
2	Net income (loss) per books	*92,400*		b Stock	
3	Other increases (itemize):			c Property	
			6	Other decreases (itemize):	
			7	Add lines 5 and 6	*30,000*
4	Add lines 1, 2, and 3	*217,400*	8	Balance at end of year (line 4 less line 7)	*187,400*

Printed on recycled paper

▼

CONCEPT SUMMARY 20-1

Summary of Income Tax Consequences

	Individuals	Corporations
Computation of gross income	§ 61.	§ 61.
Computation of taxable income	§§ 62, 63(b) through (h).	§ 63(a). Concept of AGI has no relevance.
Deductions	Trade or business (§ 162); nonbusiness (§ 212); some personal and employee expenses (generally deductible as itemized deductions).	Trade or business (§ 162).
Charitable contributions	Limited in any tax year to 50% of AGI; 30% for long-term capital gain property unless election is made to reduce fair market value of gift; 20% for long-term capital gain property contributed to private nonoperating foundations.	Limited in any tax year to 10% of taxable income computed without regard to the charitable contribution deduction, net operating loss or capital loss carryback, and dividends received deduction.
	Time of deduction—year in which payment is made.	Time of deduction—year in which payment is made unless accrual basis taxpayer. Accrual basis corporation may take deduction in year preceding payment if contribution was authorized by board of directors by end of that year and contribution is paid by fifteenth day of third month of following year.
Casualty losses	$100 floor on nonbusiness casualty and theft losses; nonbusiness casualty and theft losses deductible only to extent losses exceed 10% of AGI.	Deductible in full.
Depreciation recapture for § 1250 property	Recaptured to extent accelerated depreciation exceeds straight-line.	20% of excess of amount that would be recaptured under § 1245 over amount recaptured under § 1250 is additional ordinary income under § 291.
Net operating loss	Adjusted for nonbusiness deductions over nonbusiness income and for personal and dependency exemptions.	Generally no adjustments.
Dividend exclusion or deduction	None.	Generally 70% of dividends received.
Long-term capital gains	Taxed at a rate no higher than 28%.	Taxed using regular corporate rates.
Capital losses	Only $3,000 of capital loss can offset ordinary income; loss is carried forward indefinitely to offset capital gains or ordinary income up to $3,000; carryovers remain long term or short term (as the case may be).	Can offset only capital gains; carried back three years and forward five years; carrybacks and carryovers are treated as short-term losses.
Passive activity losses	Generally deductible only against income from passive activities.	For regular corporations, no limitation on deductibility. Personal service corporations and certain closely held corporations, however, are subject to same limitations as imposed on individuals. A closely held corporation is one where 5 or fewer individuals own more than 50% of the stock either directly or indirectly.

	Individuals	Corporations
Alternative minimum tax	Applied at a graduated rate schedule of 26% and 28% to AMT base (taxable income as modified by certain adjustments plus preference items minus exemption amount); exemption allowed depending on filing status (e.g., $45,000 for married filing jointly); exemption phase-out begins when AMTI reaches a certain amount (e.g., $150,000 for married filing jointly).	Applied at a 20% rate to AMT base (taxable income as modified by certain adjustments plus preference items minus exemption amount); $40,000 exemption allowed but phase-out begins once AMTI reaches $150,000; adjustments and tax preference items similar to those applicable to individuals but also include 75% of adjusted current earnings (ACE) over AMTI.
Tax rates	Progressive with five rates (15%, 28%, 31%, 36%, and 39.6%).	Progressive with four rates (15%, 25%, 34%, and 35%); lower brackets phased out at higher levels.

FORMING THE CORPORATION

CAPITAL CONTRIBUTIONS

5 LEARNING OBJECTIVE
Understand the tax rules governing the formation of corporations.

The receipt of money or property in exchange for capital stock produces neither recognized gain nor loss to the recipient corporation.[24] Gross income of a corporation does not include shareholders' contributions of money or property to the capital of the corporation.[25] Contributions by nonshareholders are also excluded from the gross income of a corporation.[26] The basis of the property (capital transfers by nonshareholders) to the corporation is zero.

EXAMPLE 17

A city donates land worth $200,000 to Cardinal Corporation as an inducement for it to locate in the city. The receipt of the land does not represent gross income. The land's basis to the corporation is zero. ▼

Thin Capitalization. The advantages of capitalizing a corporation with debt may be substantial. Interest on debt is deductible by the corporation, while dividend payments are not. Further, the shareholders are not taxed on loan repayments unless the payments exceed basis. If a company is capitalized solely with common stock, subsequent repayments of such capital contributions are likely to be treated as dividends to the shareholders.

In certain instances, the IRS will contend that debt is really an equity interest (**thin capitalization**) and will deny the shareholders the tax advantages of debt financing. If the debt instrument has too many features of stock, it may be treated as a form of stock, and principal and interest payments are treated as dividends.[27]

The form of the instrument will not assure debt treatment, but failure to observe certain formalities in creating the debt may lead to an assumption that the purported debt is a form of stock. The debt should be in proper legal form, bear a

[24] § 1032.
[25] § 118.
[26] *Edwards v. Cuba Railroad Co.*, 1 USTC ¶139, 5 AFTR 5398, 45 S.Ct. 614 (USSC, 1925).
[27] Section 385 lists several factors that might be used to determine whether a debtor-creditor relationship or a shareholder-corporation relationship exists.

legitimate rate of interest, have a definite maturity date, and be repaid on a timely basis. Payments should not be contingent upon earnings. Further, the debt should not be subordinated to other liabilities, and proportionate holdings of stock and debt should be avoided or minimized.

TRANSFERS TO CONTROLLED CORPORATIONS

Without special provisions in the Code, a transfer of property to a corporation in exchange for its stock would be a sale or exchange of property and would constitute a taxable transaction to the transferor shareholder. Section 351 provides for the nonrecognition of gain or loss upon such transfers of property if the transferors are in control of the corporation immediately after the transfer. Gain or loss is merely postponed in a manner similar to a like-kind exchange.[28] The following requirements must be met to qualify under § 351:

- The transferors must be in control of the corporation immediately after the exchange. *Control* is defined as ownership of at least 80 percent of the total combined voting power of all classes of stock entitled to vote and at least 80 percent of the total number of shares of all other classes of stock.[29]
- Realized gain (but not loss) is recognized to the extent that the transferors receive property other than stock. Such nonqualifying property is commonly referred to as *boot*.

If the requirements of § 351 are satisfied and no boot is involved, nonrecognition of gain or loss is *mandatory*.

Basis Considerations and Computation of Gain. The nonrecognition of gain or loss is accompanied by a carryover of basis. The basis of stock received in a § 351 transfer is determined as follows:

- Start with the adjusted basis of the property transferred by the shareholder.
- Add any gain recognized by the shareholder as a result of the transfer.
- Subtract the fair market value of any boot received by the shareholder from the corporation.[30]

Shareholders who receive noncash boot have a basis in the property equal to the fair market value.

The basis of properties received by the corporation is the basis in the hands of the transferor increased by the amount of any gain recognized to the transferor shareholder.[31]

EXAMPLE 18

Ann and Lori form Bluejay Corporation. Ann transfers property with an adjusted basis of $30,000 and a fair market value of $60,000 for 50% of the stock. Lori transfers property with an adjusted basis of $40,000 and a fair market value of $60,000 for the remaining 50% of the stock. The realized gain ($30,000 for Ann and $20,000 for Lori) is not recognized on the transfer because the transfer qualifies under § 351. The basis of the stock to Ann is $30,000, and the basis of the stock to Lori is $40,000. Bluejay Corporation has a basis of $30,000 in the property transferred by Ann and a basis of $40,000 in the property transferred by Lori. ▼

EXAMPLE 19

Mike and John form Condor Corporation with the following investments: Mike transfers property (adjusted basis of $30,000 and fair market value of $70,000), and John transfers cash of $60,000. Each receives 50 shares of the Condor stock, but Mike also receives $10,000

[28] Refer to the discussion in Chapter 15.
[29] § 368(c).
[30] § 358(a).
[31] § 362(a).

in cash. Assume each share of the Condor stock is worth $1,200. Mike's realized gain is $40,000, determined as follows:

Value of the Condor stock received [50 (shares) × $1,200 (value per share)]	$ 60,000
Cash received	10,000
Amount realized	$ 70,000
Less basis of property transferred	(30,000)
Realized gain	$ 40,000

Mike's recognized gain is $10,000, the lesser of the realized gain ($40,000) or the fair market value of the boot received ($10,000). Mike's basis in the Condor stock is $30,000, computed as follows:

Basis in the property transferred	$ 30,000
Plus recognized gain	10,000
	$ 40,000
Less boot received	(10,000)
Basis to Mike of the Condor stock	$ 30,000

Condor Corporation's basis in the property transferred by Mike is $40,000 [$30,000 (basis of the property to Mike) + $10,000 (gain recognized by Mike)]. John neither realizes nor recognizes gain or loss and will have a basis of $60,000 in the Condor stock. ▼

The receipt of stock for the performance of *services* always results in ordinary income to the transferor shareholder. An example might be an attorney who does not charge a fee for incorporating a business but instead receives the value equivalent in stock of the newly formed corporation. The basis of stock received for the performance of services is equal to the fair market value of the services.

OPERATING THE CORPORATION

DIVIDEND DISTRIBUTIONS

6 LEARNING OBJECTIVE
Work with the tax rules governing the operation of corporations.

Corporate distributions of cash or property to shareholders are treated as ordinary dividend income to the extent the corporation has accumulated *or* current earnings and profits (E & P).[32] In determining the source of the distribution, a dividend is deemed to have been made initially from current E & P.

EXAMPLE 20

As of January 1, 1996, Teal Corporation has a deficit in accumulated E & P of $30,000. For tax year 1996, it has current E & P of $10,000. In 1996, the corporation distributes $5,000 to its shareholders. The $5,000 distribution is treated as a taxable dividend, since it is deemed to have been made from current E & P. This is the case even though Teal still has a deficit in its accumulated E & P at the end of 1996. ▼

If a corporate distribution is not covered by E & P (either current or past), it is treated as a return of capital (refer to the discussion of the recovery of capital doctrine in Chapter 4). This treatment allows the shareholder to apply the amount

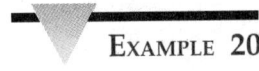

[32] § 316.

of the distribution against the basis of the stock investment and therefore represents a nontaxable return of capital. Any amount received in excess of the stock basis is classified as a capital gain (if the stock is a capital asset in the hands of the shareholder).

EXAMPLE 21

When Mallard Corporation has no E & P (either current or accumulated), it distributes cash of $30,000 to its sole shareholder, Helen. The basis of Helen's stock investment is $20,000. Based on these facts, the $30,000 distribution Helen receives is accounted for as follows:

Return of capital (nontaxable)	$20,000
Capital gain	10,000
Total amount of distribution	$30,000

After the distribution, Helen has a basis of zero in her stock investment. ▼

Concept of Earnings and Profits. The term **earnings and profits** is not defined in the Code, although § 312 does include certain transactions that affect E & P. Although E & P and the accounting concept of retained earnings have certain similarities, they differ in numerous respects. For example, although a nontaxable stock dividend is treated as a capitalization of retained earnings for accounting purposes, it does not decrease E & P for tax purposes. Taxable dividends do reduce E & P but cannot yield a deficit. Referring to Example 21, after the distribution, Mallard Corporation's E & P remains zero rather than being a negative amount.

Generally, *current E & P* for a taxable year is taxable income plus or minus certain adjustments (e.g., an addition is made for tax-exempt income). Federal income taxes are subtracted from taxable income in arriving at current E & P. *Accumulated E & P* is the sum of the corporation's past current E & P that has not been distributed as dividends. A detailed discussion of the concept of E & P is beyond the scope of this chapter.

Property Dividends. A distribution of property to a shareholder is measured by the fair market value of the property on the date of distribution. The shareholder's basis in the property received is also the fair market value.[33]

EXAMPLE 22

Drake Corporation has E & P of $60,000. It distributes land with a fair market value of $50,000 (adjusted basis of $30,000) to its sole shareholder, Art. Art has a taxable dividend of $50,000 and a basis in the land of $50,000. ▼

A corporation that distributes appreciated property to its shareholders as a dividend must recognize the amount of the appreciation as gain.[34]

EXAMPLE 23

Assume the same facts as in Example 22. Drake Corporation must recognize a gain of $20,000 on the distribution it made to Art. ▼

However, if the property distributed has a basis in excess of its fair market value, the distributing corporation cannot recognize any loss.

Constructive Dividends. Many taxpayers mistakenly assume that dividend consequences do not take place unless the distribution carries the formalities of a

[33] § 301.

[34] The tax consequences to a corporation of nonliquidating distributions to shareholders are covered in § 311.

dividend (declaration date, record date, payment date). They further assume that dividends must be paid out to all shareholders on a pro rata basis. This may not be the case when closely held corporations are involved. Here, the key to dividend treatment depends upon whether the shareholders derive a benefit from the corporation that cannot be otherwise classified (e.g., reasonable salary). The following are examples of **constructive dividends**:

- Salaries paid to shareholder-employees that are not reasonable (refer to Example 6 in Chapter 6).
- Interest on debt owed by the corporation to shareholders that is reclassified as equity because the corporation is thinly capitalized (refer to the earlier discussion in this chapter).
- Excessive rent paid by a corporation for the use of shareholder property. The arm's length standard is used to test whether the rent is excessive (refer to Example 23 in Chapter 1).
- Advances to shareholders that are not bona fide loans.
- Interest-free (or below-market) loans to shareholders. In this situation, the dividend component is the difference between the interest provided for, if any, and that calculated using the market rate.
- Shareholder use of corporate property for less than an arm's length rate.
- Absorption by the corporation of a shareholder's personal expenses.
- Bargain purchase of corporate property by shareholders.

Like regular dividends, constructive dividends must be covered by E & P to carry dividend income consequences to the shareholders. As noted above, however, constructive dividends need not be available to all shareholders on a pro rata basis.

Although dividends reduce the E & P of a corporation, they are not deductible for income tax purposes. In this regard, certain constructive dividends could have subtle tax consequences for all parties concerned.

EXAMPLE 24

Grouse Corporation makes a loan to one of its shareholders, Hal. No interest is provided for, but application of the market rate would produce $20,000 of interest for the term of the loan. Presuming the loan is bona fide, the following results occur:

- Hal has dividend income of $20,000.
- Grouse Corporation has interest income of $20,000.
- Hal might obtain an interest deduction of $20,000.

Not only does Grouse Corporation have to recognize income of $20,000, but it also obtains no income tax deduction for the $20,000 constructive dividend. ▼

EXAMPLE 25

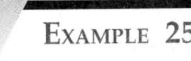

Assume the same facts as in Example 24, except that the loan to Hal was not bona fide. In this event, the full amount of the loan is regarded as a dividend to Hal. Therefore, the interest element is not a factor, since no bona fide loan ever existed. ▼

STOCK REDEMPTIONS

If a corporation redeems a shareholder's stock (a **stock redemption**), one of two possible outcomes occurs:

- The redemption may qualify as a sale or exchange under § 302 or § 303. In that case, capital gain or loss treatment usually applies to the qualifying shareholders.
- The redemption will be treated as a dividend under § 301, provided the distributing corporation has E & P.

EXAMPLE 26

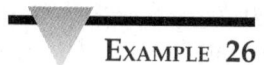

Reba owns 300 shares of Snipe Corporation stock as an investment. The shares have a basis to Reba of $100 each, for a total of $30,000. When the fair market value of a share is $200, Snipe redeems 200 of Reba's shares. If the redemption qualifies for sale or exchange treatment, the result is a capital gain to Reba of $20,000 [$40,000 (redemption price) – $20,000 (basis in 200 shares)]. Reba's basis in the remaining 100 shares is $10,000 [$30,000 (basis in the original shares) – $20,000 (basis in the shares redeemed)]. ▼

EXAMPLE 27

Assume the same facts as in Example 26, except that the redemption does not qualify for sale or exchange treatment. Presuming adequate E & P, the redemption results in $40,000 dividend income. Reba's basis in the remaining 100 shares now becomes $30,000, or $300 per share. ▼

A stock redemption qualifies as a sale or exchange if it meets any of the safe harbors of § 302 or § 303.

LIQUIDATING THE CORPORATION

7 LEARNING OBJECTIVE
Recognize the tax rules governing the liquidation of corporations.

Unlike dividend distributions or stock redemptions, where the distributing corporation continues its operations, **liquidating distributions** occur during the termination of the business. All debts are paid, and any remaining corporate assets are distributed pro rata to the shareholders in exchange for their stock. Once these distributions are completed, the corporation undergoing liquidation will cease to be a separate tax entity.

GENERAL RULE OF § 331

Under the general rule, the shareholders recognize gain or loss in a corporate liquidation. The amount of recognized gain or loss is measured by the difference between the fair market value of the assets received from the corporation and the adjusted basis of the stock surrendered. The shareholders recognize capital gain or loss if the stock is a capital asset.[35]

EXAMPLE 28

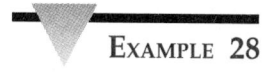

Pursuant to a complete liquidation, Starling Corporation distributes $100,000 in cash to Edna, one of its shareholders. If Edna's basis in the stock surrendered is $40,000, she must recognize a gain of $60,000. If Edna held the stock as an investment, the $60,000 gain is capital gain—either short term or long term (depending on the holding period). ▼

EXCEPTION TO THE GENERAL RULE

Section 332 is an exception to the general rule that the shareholder recognizes gain or loss on a corporate liquidation. If a parent corporation liquidates a subsidiary corporation in which it owns at least 80 percent of the voting power and value of the stock, no gain or loss is recognized by the parent company. The subsidiary must distribute all of its property in complete liquidation of all of its stock within the taxable year or within three years from the close of the tax year in which the first distribution occurred.

[35] If the stock is held as an investment, which is usually the case, gain or loss will be capital. Stock owned by a broker probably will be inventory and therefore will not constitute a capital asset. Thus, the gain or loss on this type of stock is ordinary and not capital.

BASIS DETERMINATION—§§ 334 AND 338

General Rule. Where gain or loss is recognized upon the complete liquidation of a corporation, the basis of the property received by the shareholders is the property's fair market value.[36]

Subsidiary Liquidation Basis Rules. The general rule is that the property received by the parent corporation in a complete liquidation of its subsidiary under § 332 has the same basis it had in the hands of the subsidiary (a carryover basis).[37] The parent's basis in the stock of the liquidated subsidiary disappears.

EXAMPLE 29

Swallow, the parent corporation, has a basis of $20,000 in the stock of Shrike Corporation, a subsidiary in which it owns 85% of all classes of stock. Swallow purchased the stock of Shrike Corporation 10 years ago. In the current year, Swallow liquidates Shrike Corporation and receives assets worth $50,000 with a tax basis to Shrike of $40,000. Swallow Corporation would have a basis of $40,000 in the assets, with a potential gain upon sale of $10,000. Swallow's original $20,000 basis in the Shrike stock disappears. ▼

An exception to the carryover of basis rule is provided in § 338. Under this exception, the parent company may elect to receive a basis for the assets equal to the adjusted basis of the stock of the subsidiary. In effect, the initial acquisition of the subsidiary is treated as if the parent company had acquired the assets (rather than the stock) of the subsidiary.

EFFECT OF THE LIQUIDATION ON THE CORPORATION

Having examined what happens to the shareholder upon the liquidation of a corporation, what happens at the corporate level? Here, § 336 applies to dictate the tax consequences to the corporation being liquidated.

Under § 336, the distributing corporation recognizes gain or loss upon complete liquidation. In this regard, it does not matter whether the corporation distributes the property in-kind (*as is*) to the shareholders or first sells the property and then distributes the proceeds.

EXAMPLE 30

Pursuant to a complete liquidation, Grackle Corporation distributes the following assets to its shareholders: undeveloped land held as an investment (basis of $150,000 and fair market value of $140,000) and marketable securities (basis of $160,000 and fair market value of $200,000). Since Grackle is treated as if it had sold the property, a gain of $40,000 results from the securities, and a loss of $10,000 results from the land. ▼

ETHICAL CONSIDERATIONS

Necessity for Filing a Corporate Tax Return

For many years, Hanna has owned and operated several apartment buildings. In 1990 and upon the advice of her attorney, Hanna transferred the apartment buildings to a newly formed corporation. Her main reason for incorporating the business was to achieve limited liability.

[36] § 334(a).

[37] § 334(b)(1).

Every year since 1990, Hanna has prepared and filed a Form 1120 for the corporation. No corporate income tax has been paid because, after the deduction of various expenses (including Hanna's salary), the corporation has zero taxable income.

In 1996, Hanna decides that filing Form 1120 is a waste of time. Instead, she will report all of the financial activities of the apartment business on her own individual Form 1040.

Has Hanna acted properly or should she first liquidate the corporation?

The deductibility of losses may be restricted by the related-party rules (refer to Chapter 6) if certain conditions exist (e.g., the distributions are not pro rata).[38]

A wholly owned subsidiary corporation does not recognize gain or loss when the parent corporation uses the carryover basis option of § 334(b)(1). The reason for the special treatment is that the subsidiary's basis (and all other tax attributes) in the assets carries over to the parent corporation.

THE S ELECTION

JUSTIFICATION FOR THE ELECTION

8 LEARNING OBJECTIVE
Appreciate the utility and effect of the Subchapter S election.

Numerous nontax reasons exist for operating a business in the corporate form (e.g., limited liability). Consequently, the existence of income tax disadvantages (e.g., double taxation of corporate income and shareholder dividends) should not deter business people from using the corporate form. To prevent tax considerations from interfering with the exercise of sound business judgment, Congress enacted Subchapter S of the Code.

To qualify for **S corporation** status, the corporation must be a **small business corporation.**[39] This includes any corporation that has the following characteristics:

- Is a domestic corporation.
- Is not a member of an affiliated group.
- Has no more than 35 shareholders.
- Has as its shareholders only individuals, estates, and certain trusts.
- Does not have a nonresident alien as a shareholder.
- Has only one class of stock outstanding.

These characteristics must continue to exist if an electing S corporation is to maintain S status.

Making the Election. The election is made by filing Form 2553, and *all* shareholders must consent. For this purpose, husbands and wives are counted as a single shareholder.

To be effective for the current year, the election must be filed anytime during the preceding taxable year or on or before the fifteenth day of the third month of the current year.[40]

EXAMPLE 31

Heron, a calendar year taxpayer, is a regular corporation that wishes to elect S status for 1996. If the election is filed anytime from January 1, 1995, through March 15, 1996, it will be effective for 1996. ▼

---

[38] § 336(d).
[39] § 1361(b).
[40] § 1362.

TAX IN THE NEWS

S Corporations Can Get Better

Currently, approximately one-half of U.S. corporations have elected S status. The election is highly attractive because it avoids the double tax that results from operating as a C (i.e., regular) corporation. Evidence indicates that the election would be even more popular if S status were easier to live with.

In 1995, legislation was introduced in both the House of Representatives and the Senate that would significantly change current S corporation rules. These proposed changes include the following:

- Increase in the number of shareholders allowed.
- Expansion of who can be shareholders (e.g., trusts, nonresident aliens, charitable organizations).
- Second class of stock (e.g., preferred) allowed to be issued.
- Invalid elections correctible on an "after-the-fact" basis.

Of course, no one can predict which, if any, of these changes will be enacted into law.

ETHICAL CONSIDERATIONS

Can a Past Error Be Overlooked?

In 1991, Canary Corporation was formed, and a Form 2553 was timely filed with the IRS to elect S status. Since then, the corporation has filed a Form 1120S each year and treated itself as an S corporation for income tax purposes.

Canary Corporation's regular CPA dies in January of 1996. Canary's management has asked you to assume the former CPA's duties, which include preparing and filing Form 1120S for calendar year 1995. In connection with the new engagement, you review Canary's past tax files. Among other things, you find a copy of the Form 2553 that was filed with the IRS in 1991. You are somewhat shocked to discover that one of the shareholders failed to sign the form. When you question management about this oversight, you are told that "George was sick at the time, and we didn't want to bother him!"

Do you have a problem with continuing this new engagement? Why or why not? What do you suggest?

Loss of the Election. The S election may be terminated *voluntarily* (a majority of the shareholders file to revoke the election) or *involuntarily*. An involuntary termination may occur in *any* of the following ways:

- The corporation ceases to qualify as a small business corporation (e.g., the number of shareholders exceeds 35, or a partnership becomes a shareholder).
- The corporation has passive investment income (e.g., interest, dividends) in excess of 25 percent of gross receipts for a period of three consecutive years. This possibility applies only if the corporation was previously a regular corporation and has earnings and profits from that period.

If the holders of a *majority* of the shares consent to a voluntary revocation of S status, the election to revoke must be made on or before the fifteenth day of the third month of the tax year to be effective for that year.

EXAMPLE 32 The shareholders of Stork Corporation, a calendar year S corporation, elect to revoke the election on January 4, 1996. Assuming the election is duly executed and timely filed, Stork will become a regular corporation for calendar year 1996. If the election to revoke is not made until June 1996, Stork will not become a regular corporation until calendar year 1997. ▼

Suppose the shareholders in Example 32 file the election to revoke on January 4, 1996, but do not want the revocation to take place until 1997. If the election so specifies, Stork Corporation will cease to have S status as of January 1, 1997.

In the case where S status is lost because of a disqualifying act (involuntarily), the loss of the election takes effect as of the date on which the event occurs.

EXAMPLE 33 Crow Corporation has been a calendar year S corporation for several years. On August 13, 1996, one of its shareholders sells her stock to Kite Corporation. Since Crow Corporation no longer satisfies the definition of a small business corporation (it has another corporation as a shareholder), the election has been involuntarily terminated. For calendar year 1996, therefore, Crow will be an S corporation through August 12 and a regular corporation from August 13 through December 31, 1996. ▼

In the event the election is lost through a violation of the passive investment income limitation, the loss of S status starts at the beginning of the next tax year.

Barring certain exceptions, the loss of the election places the corporation in a five-year holding period before S status can be reelected.

OPERATIONAL RULES

The S corporation is primarily a tax-reporting rather than a taxpaying entity. In this respect, the entity is taxed much like a partnership.[41] Under the conduit concept, the taxable income and losses of an S corporation flow through to the shareholders who report them on their personal income tax returns.

To ascertain the annual tax consequences to each shareholder, it is necessary to carry out two steps at the S corporation level. First, all corporate transactions that will flow through to the shareholders on an *as is* basis under the conduit approach must be set aside. Second, what remains is aggregated as the taxable income of the S corporation and is allocated to each shareholder on a per-share and per-day of stock ownership basis.[42]

Separately Stated Items. The following are some of the items that do not lose their identity as they pass through the S corporation and are therefore picked up by each shareholder on an *as is* basis:

- Tax-exempt income.
- Long-term and short-term capital gains and losses.
- Section 1231 gains and losses.
- Charitable contributions.
- Foreign tax credits.

[41] This is not to imply that an S corporation is always free from the income tax. For example, a tax may be imposed on certain built-in gains or certain excessive passive investment income.

[42] § 1366.

- Depletion.
- Nonbusiness income or loss under § 212.
- Intangible drilling costs.
- Investment interest, income, and expenses covered under § 163(d).
- Certain portfolio income.
- Passive activity gains, losses, and credits under § 469.
- AMT adjustments and tax preference items.

These items are separately stated because each may lead to a different tax result when combined with a particular shareholder's other transactions.

EXAMPLE 34

Arnold and Jean are equal shareholders in Lark Corporation (an S corporation). For calendar year 1996, each must account for one-half of a corporate short-term capital gain of $6,000. Arnold has no other capital asset transactions, and Jean has a short-term capital loss of $3,000 from the sale of stock in IBM Corporation. In terms of overall effect, the difference between the two taxpayers is significant. Although both must report the short-term capital gain pass-through, Jean will neutralize its inclusion in gross income by offsetting it with the $3,000 short-term capital loss from the sale of the IBM stock. For Arnold, the short-term capital gain pass-through results in a $3,000 increase in his taxable income. ▼

Taxable Income. After the separately stated items have been removed, the balance represents the taxable income of the S corporation. In arriving at taxable income, the dividends received deduction and the net operating loss deduction are not allowed. An S corporation does come under the regular corporate rules, however, for purposes of amortization of organizational expenditures.

Once taxable income has been determined, it passes through to each shareholder as of the last day of the S corporation's tax year.

EXAMPLE 35

Harrier Corporation, a calendar year S corporation, had the following transactions during the current year:

Sales		$ 40,000
Cost of goods sold		(23,000)
Other income		
*Tax-exempt interest	$ 300	
*Long-term capital gain	500	800
Other expenses		
*Charitable contributions	$ 400	
Advertising expense	1,500	
Other operating expenses	2,000	
*Short-term capital loss	150	(4,050)
Net income per books		$ 13,750

When the items that are to be separately stated (those preceded by an asterisk [*]) and shown *as is* by each shareholder are withdrawn, Harrier has the following taxable income:

Sales		$ 40,000
Cost of goods sold		(23,000)
Other expenses		
Advertising expense	$1,500	
Other operating expenses	2,000	(3,500)
Taxable income		$ 13,500

▼

EXAMPLE 36

If Oscar owned 10% of the stock in Harrier Corporation (refer to Example 35) during all of the current year, he must account for the following:

Separately stated items	
Tax-exempt interest	$ 30
Long-term capital gain	50
Charitable contributions	40
Short-term capital loss	15
Taxable income (10% of $13,500)	1,350

Some of the separately stated items need not be reported on Oscar's individual income tax return (e.g., the tax-exempt interest). Others must be reported but may not lead to tax consequences. Oscar picks up his share of Harrier's taxable income ($1,350) as ordinary income. ▼

Treatment of Losses. As previously noted, separately stated loss items (e.g., capital losses, § 1231 losses) flow through to the shareholders on an *as is* basis. Their treatment by a shareholder depends on the shareholder's individual income tax position. If the S corporation's taxable income determination results in an operating loss, it also passes through to the shareholders. As is the case with separately stated items, the amount of the loss each shareholder receives depends on the stock ownership during the year.

EXAMPLE 37

In 1996, Oriole Corporation (a calendar year S corporation) incurred an operating loss of $36,600. During 1996, Jason's ownership in Oriole was as follows: 20% for 200 days and 30% for 166 days. Jason's share of the loss is determined as follows:

[$36,600 × (200/366)] × 20% =	$4,000
[$36,600 × (166/366)] × 30% =	4,980
Total loss for Jason	$8,980

Presuming the basis limitation does not come into play (see the following discussion), Jason deducts $8,980 in arriving at adjusted gross income. ▼

Basis Determination. A shareholder's *basis* in the stock of an S corporation, like that of a regular corporation, is the original investment plus additional capital contributions less return of capital distributions. At this point, however, the symmetry disappears. Generally, basis is increased by the pass-through of income items (including those separately stated) and decreased by the loss items (including those separately stated).[43]

EXAMPLE 38

In 1996, Warbler Corporation is formed with an investment of $100,000, of which Janice contributed $20,000 for a 20% stock interest. A timely S election is made, and for 1996, Warbler earns taxable income of $15,000. Janice's basis in her stock investment now becomes $23,000 [$20,000 (original capital contribution) + $3,000 (the 20% share of the corporation's taxable income assigned to Janice)]. ▼

Distributions by an S corporation reduce the basis of a shareholder's stock investment. However, if the amount of the distribution exceeds basis, the excess normally receives capital gain treatment.

As previously noted, operating losses of an S corporation pass through to the shareholders and reduce the basis in their stock investment. Because the basis of

[43] § 1367.

the stock cannot fall below zero, an excess loss is then applied against the basis of any loans the shareholder may have made to the corporation.

EXAMPLE 39

Flamingo Corporation, a calendar year S corporation, has an operating loss of $60,000 for 1996. Norman, a 50% shareholder, has an adjusted basis of $25,000 in his stock investment and has made loans to the corporation of $5,000. Based on these facts, Norman may take full advantage of the $30,000 loss (50% of $60,000) on his 1996 individual income tax return. Norman's basis in the stock and the loans must be reduced accordingly, and both will be zero after the pass-through. ▼

In the event the basis limitation precludes an operating loss from being absorbed, the loss can be carried forward and deducted when and if it is covered by basis.

EXAMPLE 40

Assume the same facts as in Example 39, except that Norman had not made any loans to Flamingo Corporation. Further assume that Flamingo has taxable income of $15,000 in the following year (1997). Norman's tax situation for 1996 and 1997 is summarized as follows:

Ordinary loss for 1996	$25,000
Income to be reported in 1997 (50% of $15,000)	7,500
Restoration of stock basis in 1997 (50% of $15,000)	7,500
Loss allowed for 1997 ($30,000 – $25,000)	5,000
Basis in stock account after 1997 ($7,500 – $5,000)	2,500

Thus, Norman's unabsorbed loss of $5,000 from 1996 carries over to 1997 and is applied against the $7,500 of ordinary income for that year. ▼

PARTNERSHIPS

NATURE OF PARTNERSHIP TAXATION

9 LEARNING OBJECTIVE
Understand the tax consequences of forming and operating a partnership.

Unlike corporations, partnerships are not considered separate taxable entities. Each member of a partnership is subject to income tax on his or her distributive share of the partnership's income, even if an actual distribution is not made. The tax return (Form 1065) required of a partnership serves only to provide information necessary in determining the character and amount of each partner's distributive share of the partnership's income and expense. Because a partnership acts as a conduit, items that pass through to the partners do not lose their identity. For example, tax-exempt income earned by a partnership is picked up by the partners as tax-exempt income. In this regard, partnerships function in much the same fashion as S corporations, which also serve as conduits.

A partnership is considered a separate taxable entity for purposes of making various elections and selecting its taxable year, method of depreciation, and accounting method. A partnership is also treated as a separate legal entity under civil law with the right to own property in its own name and to transact business free from the personal debts of its partners.

PARTNERSHIP FORMATION

Recognition of Gain or Loss. The general rule is that no gain or loss is recognized by a partnership or any of its partners on the contribution of property in exchange for a capital interest in the partnership.[44] The general rule also applies to all subsequent contributions of property.

There are certain exceptions to the nonrecognition of gain or loss rule including the following:

- If a partner transfers property to the partnership and receives money or other consideration (boot) as a result, the transaction will be treated as a sale or exchange rather than as a contribution of capital. Realized gain is recognized to the extent of the fair market value of the boot received.
- If a partnership interest is received in exchange for services rendered or to be rendered by the partner to the partnership, the fair market value of the transferred capital interest is regarded as compensation for services rendered. In such cases, the recipient of the capital interest must recognize the amount as ordinary income in the year actually or constructively received.
- If property that is subject to a liability in excess of its basis is contributed to a partnership, the contributing partner may recognize gain.

Basis of a Partnership Interest. The contributing *partner's basis* in the partnership interest received is the sum of money contributed plus the adjusted basis of any other property transferred to the partnership.[45]

EXAMPLE 41

In return for the contribution of property (with a basis of $50,000 and a fair market value of $80,000) and cash of $10,000 to the Brown Partnership, Marcia receives a 10% capital interest worth $90,000. Although Marcia has a realized gain of $30,000 ($90,000 – $60,000) on the transfer, none of the gain is recognized. The basis of her interest in the Brown Partnership is $60,000 [$50,000 (basis of property contributed) + $10,000 (cash contribution)]. ▼

A partner's basis in the partnership interest is determined without regard to any amount reflected on the partnership's books as capital, equity, or a similar account.

EXAMPLE 42

Marge and Clyde form the equal Blue Partnership with a cash contribution of $30,000 from Marge and a property contribution (adjusted basis of $18,000 and fair market value of $30,000) from Clyde. Although the books of the Blue Partnership may reflect a credit of $30,000 to each partner's capital account, only Marge has a tax basis of $30,000 in her partnership interest. Clyde's tax basis in his partnership interest is $18,000, the amount of his tax basis in the property contributed to the partnership. ▼

After its initial determination, the basis of a partnership interest is subject to continuous fluctuations. A partner's basis is increased by additional contributions and the sum of his or her current and prior years' distributive share of the following:

- Taxable income of the partnership, including capital gains.
- Tax-exempt income of the partnership.
- The excess of the deductions for depletion over the basis of the partnership's property subject to depletion.[46]

Similarly, the basis of a partner's interest is decreased, but not below zero, by distributions of partnership property and by the sum of the current and prior years' distributive share of the following:

[44] § 721.
[45] § 722.
[46] § 705(a).

- Partnership losses, including capital losses.
- Partnership expenditures that are not deductible in computing taxable income or loss and that are not capital expenditures.

Changes in the liabilities (including trade accounts payable, bank loans, etc.) of a partnership also affect the basis of a partnership interest. A partner's basis is increased by his or her assumption of partnership liabilities and by his or her pro rata share of liabilities incurred by the partnership. Likewise, the partner's basis is decreased by the amount of any personal liabilities assumed by the partnership and by the pro rata share of any decreases in the liabilities of the partnership.

EXAMPLE 43

Tony, Martha, and Carolyn form the Orange Partnership with the following contributions: cash of $50,000 from Tony for a 50% interest in capital and profits, cash of $25,000 from Martha for a 25% interest, and property valued at $33,000 from Carolyn for a 25% interest. The property contributed by Carolyn has an adjusted basis of $15,000 and is subject to a mortgage of $8,000, which is assumed by the partnership. Carolyn's basis in her interest in the Orange Partnership is $9,000, determined as follows:

Adjusted basis of Carolyn's contributed property	$15,000
Less portion of mortgage assumed by Tony and Martha and treated as a distribution of money to Carolyn (75% of $8,000)	(6,000)
Basis of Carolyn's interest in Orange Partnership	$ 9,000

▼

EXAMPLE 44

Assuming the same facts as in Example 43, Tony and Martha have a basis in their partnership interests of $54,000 and $27,000, respectively.

	Tony	Martha
Cash contribution	$50,000	$25,000
Plus portion of mortgage assumed and treated as an additional cash contribution:		
(50% of $8,000)	4,000	
(25% of $8,000)		2,000
Basis of interest in Orange Partnership	$54,000	$27,000

▼

Partnership's Basis in Contributed Property. The *basis of property* contributed to a partnership by a partner is the adjusted basis of the property to the contributing partner at the time of the contribution.[47] Additionally, the holding period of the property for the partnership includes the period during which the property was held by the contributing partner. This is logical, since the partnership's basis in the property is the same basis the property had in the hands of the partner.[48]

EXAMPLE 45

In 1996, Roger contributed equipment with an adjusted basis of $10,000 and fair market value of $30,000 to the Red Partnership in exchange for a one-third interest in the partnership. No gain or loss is recognized by Roger. The basis in the equipment is $10,000 to the Red Partnership. If Roger had acquired the equipment in 1986, the holding period for the Red Partnership would include the period from 1986 through 1996. ▼

[47] § 723.

[48] § 1223(2).

PARTNERSHIP OPERATION

Measuring and Reporting Partnership Income. Although a partnership is not subject to Federal income taxation, it is required to determine its taxable income and file an income tax return for information purposes.[49] The tax return, Form 1065, is due on the fifteenth day of the fourth month following the close of the taxable year of the partnership.

In measuring and reporting partnership income, certain transactions must be segregated and reported separately on the partnership return. Items such as charitable contributions, capital gains and losses, and foreign taxes are excluded from partnership taxable income and are allocated separately to the partners.[50] These items must be segregated and allocated separately because they affect the computation of various exclusions, deductions, and credits at the individual partner level. For example, one of the partners may have made personal charitable contributions in excess of the ceiling limitations on his or her individual tax return. Therefore, partnership charitable contributions are excluded from partnership taxable income and are reported separately on the partnership return.

A second step in the measurement and reporting process is the computation of the partnership's ordinary income or loss. The taxable income of a partnership is computed in the same manner as the taxable income of an individual taxpayer. However, a partnership is not allowed the following deductions:[51]

- The deduction for personal and dependency exemptions.
- The deduction for taxes paid to foreign countries or possessions of the United States.
- The deduction for charitable contributions.
- The deduction for net operating losses.
- The additional itemized deductions allowed individuals in §§ 211 through 219.

The partnership's ordinary income or loss and each of the items requiring separate treatment are reported in the partnership's information return and allocated to the partners in accordance with their distributive shares.

Limitation on Partner's Share of Losses. A partner's deduction of the distributive share of partnership losses (including capital losses) could be limited. The limitation is the adjusted basis of the partnership interest at the end of the partnership year in which the losses were incurred.

The limitation for partnership loss deductions is similar to that applicable to losses of S corporations. Like S corporation losses, partnership losses may be carried forward by the partner and utilized against future increases in the basis of the partnership interest. Such increases might result from additional capital contributions to the partnership, from additional partnership liabilities, or from future partnership income.

EXAMPLE 46

Florence and Donald do business as the Green Partnership, sharing profits and losses equally. All parties use the calendar year for tax purposes. As of January 1, 1996, Florence's basis in her partnership interest is $25,000. The partnership sustained an operating loss of $80,000 in 1996 and earned a profit of $70,000 in 1997. For the calendar year 1996, Florence may claim only $25,000 of her $40,000 distributive share of the partnership loss (one-half of the $80,000

[49] § 6031.
[50] § 702(a).
[51] § 703(a).

loss). As a result, the basis in her partnership interest is reduced to zero as of January 1, 1997, and she must carry forward the remaining $15,000 of partnership losses. ▼

EXAMPLE 47

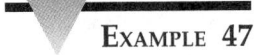

Assuming the same facts as in Example 46, what are the income tax consequences for Florence in 1997? Since the partnership earned a profit of $70,000 for the calendar year 1997, Florence reports income from the partnership of $20,000 ($35,000 distributive share of income for 1997 less the $15,000 loss not allowed for 1996). The adjusted basis of her partnership interest now becomes $20,000. ▼

Transactions between Partner and Partnership. A partner engaging in a transaction with the partnership is generally regarded as a nonpartner or outsider. However, the Code includes certain exceptions to prevent unwarranted tax avoidance. For instance, losses from the sale or exchange of property are disallowed if they arise in either of the following cases:

- Between a partnership and a person whose direct or indirect interest in the capital or profits of the partnership is more than 50 percent.
- Between two partnerships in which the same persons own more than a 50 percent interest in the capital or profits.[52]

If one of the purchasers later sells the property, any gain realized will be recognized only to the extent that it exceeds the loss previously disallowed.

EXAMPLE 48

Pat owns a 60% interest in the capital and profits of the Rose Partnership. In the current year, Pat sells property with an adjusted basis of $50,000 to the partnership for its fair market value of $35,000. The $15,000 loss is not deductible since Pat's ownership interest is more than 50%. If the Rose Partnership later sells the property for $40,000, none of the $5,000 (sale price of $40,000 less adjusted basis to partnership of $35,000) gain will be recognized since it is offset by $5,000 of the previously disallowed loss of $15,000. The unused loss of $10,000, however, is of no tax benefit either to the partnership or to Pat. ▼

Payments made by a partnership to one of its partners for services rendered or for the use of capital, to the extent they are determined without regard to the income of the partnership, are treated by the partnership in the same manner as payments made to a person who is not a partner. Referred to as **guaranteed payments,** these are generally deductible by the partnership as a business expense.[53] The payments must be reported as ordinary income by the receiving partner. Their deductibility distinguishes guaranteed payments from a partner's distributive share of income that is not deductible by the partnership.

EXAMPLE 49

Under the terms of the Silver Partnership agreement, Kim is entitled to a fixed annual salary of $18,000 without regard to the income of the partnership. He is also to share in the profits and losses of the partnership as a one-third partner. After deducting the guaranteed payment, the partnership has $36,000 of ordinary income. Kim must include $30,000 as ordinary income on his income tax return for his tax year with or within which the partnership tax year ends ($18,000 guaranteed payment + $12,000 one-third distributive share of partnership income). ▼

Other Partnership Considerations. Complex tax provisions involving liquidating and nonliquidating distributions and the sale of a partnership interest are

[52] § 707(b)(1).

[53] § 707(c).

beyond the scope of this text and are discussed in depth in *West's Federal Taxation: Corporations, Partnerships, Estates, and Trusts.*

Tax Planning Considerations

10 Learning Objective
Evaluate the advantages and disadvantages of the various forms for conducting a business.

CORPORATE VERSUS NONCORPORATE FORMS OF BUSINESS ORGANIZATION

The decision to use the corporate form in conducting a trade or business must be weighed carefully. Besides the nontax aspects of the corporate form (limited liability, continuity of life, free transferability of interests, centralized management), tax ramifications play an important role in any such decision. Close attention should be paid to the following:

1. The corporate form means the imposition of the corporate income tax. Corporate-source income will be taxed twice—once as earned by the corporation and again when distributed to the shareholders. Since dividends are not deductible, a strong incentive exists in a closely held corporation to structure corporate distributions in a deductible form. The shareholders may bail out profits in the form of salaries, interest, or rents. These procedures lead to a multitude of problems, one of which, the reclassification of debt as equity, has been discussed. The problems of unreasonable salaries and rents were discussed in Chapter 6.
2. The applicable income tax rates also affect the choice of the form for doing business. Unfortunately, because of the wide range of possibilities involved (15 to 39.6 percent for individuals and 15 to 35 percent for corporations), this factor must be considered on a case-by-case basis. For example, the corporate form is very appealing if the anticipated taxable income falls within the 25 percent bracket while the shareholder's individual bracket is 39.6 percent. Here, the time value of the taxes saved (by not distributing dividends and postponing the effect of the double tax) could make operating a business in the corporate form advantageous.
3. Corporate-source income loses its identity as it passes through the corporation to the shareholders. Thus, items possessing preferential tax treatment (e.g., interest on municipal bonds) are not taxed as such to the shareholders.
4. As noted earlier, it may be difficult for shareholders to recover some or all of their investment in the corporation without an ordinary income result. Recall that most corporate distributions are treated as dividends to the extent of the corporation's earnings and profits. Structuring the capital of the corporation to include debt is a partial solution to this problem. Thus, the shareholder-creditor could recoup part of his or her investment through the tax-free payment of principal. Too much debt, however, may lead to the debt being reclassified as equity.
5. Corporate losses cannot be passed through to the shareholders.
6. The liquidation of a corporation may generate tax consequences to both the corporation and its shareholders.
7. The corporate form provides the shareholders with the opportunity to be treated as employees for tax purposes if they render services to the corporation. This status makes a number of attractive tax-sheltered fringe benefits available (e.g., group term life insurance). These benefits are not available to partners and sole proprietors.

REGULAR CORPORATION VERSUS S STATUS

Due to the pass-through concept, the use of S status generally avoids the income tax at the corporate level, bringing the individual income tax into play. As noted in item 2 in the previous section, the differential between the rates applicable to noncorporate and corporate taxpayers makes this a factor to be considered. The S election enables a business to operate in the corporate form, avoid the corporate income tax, and, depending on taxable income, possibly take advantage of the lower rates usually applicable to individuals. Also, losses incurred at the corporate level pass through to the shareholders, who will utilize them on their individual returns (compare with item 5).

Electing S status can present several problems. First, the election is available only to small business corporations. Consequently, many corporations will not qualify for the election. Second, S corporations are subject to the rules governing regular corporations unless otherwise specified in the Code. For example, if an S corporation carries out a stock redemption or is liquidated, the rules covering regular corporations apply. Third, some states do not recognize S status for purposes of state and local taxation. Therefore, an S corporation might be subject to a state franchise tax (refer to Chapter 1) or a state or local income tax.

USE OF AN ENTITY TO REDUCE THE FAMILY INCOME TAX BURDEN

One objective of tax planning is to keep the income from a business within the family unit but to disperse the income in such a manner as to minimize the overall tax burden. To the extent feasible, therefore, income should be shifted from higher-bracket to lower-bracket family members.

Unfortunately, the income from property (a business) cannot be shifted to another without also transferring an interest in the property. If, for example, a father wants to assign income from his sole proprietorship to his children, he must form a partnership or incorporate the business.[54] In either case, the transfer of the interest may be subject to the Federal gift tax. But any potential gift tax can be eliminated or controlled through judicious use of the annual exclusion, the election to split gifts (for married donors), and the unified tax credit (refer to the discussion of the Federal gift tax in Chapter 1).

Consequently, the first problem to be resolved becomes which form of business organization will best fit the objective of income shifting. For the partnership form, one major obstacle arises. Family partnership rules preclude the assignment of income to a family member unless capital is a material income-producing factor.[55] If not, the family member must contribute substantial or vital services. Ordinarily, capital is not a material income-producing factor if the income of the business consists principally of compensation for personal services performed by members or employees of the partnership. Conversely, capital is a material income-producing factor if the operation of the business entails a substantial investment in physical assets (e.g., inventory, plant, machinery, or equipment).

Income shifting through the use of a partnership, therefore, may be ineffectual if a personal service business is involved. In fact, it could be hopeless if the assignees are minors. The use of the corporate form usually involves no such impediment. Regardless of the nature of the business, a gift of stock carries with it the attributes of ownership. Thus, dividends paid on stock are taxed to the owner of the stock.

But what if the corporate form is utilized and the S election is made? A new hurdle arises. The Code authorizes the IRS to make adjustments in situations where

[54] Income shifting will not work, however, if the minor is under 14 years of age. In such cases, net unearned income (refer to the discussion in Chapter 3) of the child is taxed at the parents' tax rate. § 1(g).

[55] § 704(e).

shareholders are not being adequately compensated for the value of their services or capital provided to an S corporation in a family setting.[56] Thus, an S corporation suffers from the same vulnerability that exists with family partnerships.

ETHICAL CONSIDERATIONS

Does a Shifting of Income Occur?

Several years ago, Roy incorporated his sole proprietorship and made an election under Subchapter S. Since then, Roy has been paying himself an annual salary of $90,000. In 1996, Roy makes a gift of 10 percent of the stock to each of his four children. All of the children are over 13 but less than 21 years of age, and none work in the business. For 1996 and subsequent years, Roy reduces his salary to $50,000.

What is Roy trying to accomplish? Will it work?

A further factor that favors the corporate form (either a regular or an S corporation) as a device for income splitting is the ease with which it can be carried out. Presuming the entity already exists, the transfer of stock merely requires an entry in the corporation's stock ledger account. In contrast, a gift of a partnership interest probably requires an amendment to the articles of copartnership. If minors are to be the assignees (donees), a state's Uniform Gifts to Minors Act provides a useful and flexible means of holding a stock interest until the assignees become adults.[57] In the case of a partnership interest, however, a guardianship may have to be set up to achieve the same flexibility. In summary, the transfer of stock is more convenient and, since it usually avoids legal problems, can be less expensive.

Regardless of the form of organization used for the business, income shifting will not take place unless the transfer is complete.[58] If the donor continues to exercise control over the interest transferred and does not recognize and protect the ownership rights of the donee, the IRS may argue that the transfer is ineffective for tax purposes. In that case, the income from the transferred interest continues to be taxed to the donor.

KEY TERMS

Association, 20–3

Constructive dividends, 20–21

Dividends received deduction, 20–10

Earnings and profits, 20–20

Guaranteed payments, 20–33

Limited liability companies, 20–5

Liquidating distribution, 20–22

Organizational expenditures, 20–12

Personal service corporation, 20–13

S corporation, 20–24

Small business corporation, 20–24

Stock redemption, 20–21

Thin capitalization, 20–17

[56] § 1366(e).

[57] The Uniform Gifts to Minors Act is explained in Chapter 4.

[58] *Ginsberg v. Comm.*, 74–2 USTC ¶9660, 34 AFTR2d 74–5760, 502 F.2d 965 (CA–6, 1974), and *Michael F. Beirne*, 61 T.C. 268 (1973).

PROBLEM MATERIALS

DISCUSSION QUESTIONS

1. What is the role of state law in determining whether or not an entity will be classified as a corporation for Federal income tax purposes?

2. Under what circumstances might the disregard of the corporate entity produce a favorable result for the IRS?

3. When will an entity be classified as a corporation under the association approach?

4. Why are limited liability companies advantageous?

5. When contrasted with the partnership, the corporate form of doing business results in another layer of Federal income tax. Explain.

6. Must all corporations use the accrual method of accounting? Explain.

7. Are the tax brackets applied differently in any way to individuals and corporations in higher taxable income levels?

8. Are the net long-term capital gains of individual taxpayers taxed in the same manner as those of corporate taxpayers? Explain.

9. Contrast the corporate tax rules for deducting net capital losses with the rules for individuals. Are the corporate capital loss rules *more or less* favorable than the capital loss provisions for individuals? Why?

10. Do corporations have to recapture more depreciation than noncorporate taxpayers? Explain.

11. How do the tax rules applicable to the charitable contribution deduction differ for individuals and corporations?

12. In computing an NOL, corporations are subject to fewer adjustments than are individuals. Explain.

13. Why would a corporation elect not to carry back an NOL to a particular year?

14. What is the rationale for the dividends received deduction for corporate shareholders?

15. Are any limitations placed on the amount of the dividends received deduction that can be claimed? Explain.

16. Mallard Corporation was formed in December 1995 and plans to use the cash basis of accounting. Mallard incurred one-half of its organizational expenses in December 1995 and one-half in January 1996. The payment of these expenses also occurred in these two months. Do you recognize any income tax problem?

17. Snipe Corporation is wholly owned by Regis, who is its CEO. For the past several years, Snipe has reported taxable income as follows: $75,100 (1994), $74,900 (1995), and $74,800 (1996). Snipe has a policy of paying its CEO a year-end bonus that varies in amount. Do you discern any potential income tax problems?

18. What purpose does the Schedule M–1 reconciliation of Form 1120 serve for the taxpayer? For the IRS?

19. To encourage a corporation to open a manufacturing facility in the community, a city donates land to the corporation. Does the donation generate income to the corporation? What basis will the corporation have in the land?

20. Why is it usually advantageous to capitalize a corporation by using debt? Is it possible that the debt will be reclassified as equity? Why?

21. Several persons plan to start a business that will be conducted by a newly formed corporation. One of the organizers, however, desires to recognize gain on the appreciated property he transfers to the corporation. What do you suggest?

22. When a corporation receives property in a nontaxable exchange under § 351, what is its income tax basis in the property?

23. Does it matter to a corporation whether a shareholder-transferor has recognized gain on a § 351 transfer? Why or why not?

24. In return for the performance of legal services, Imelda receives stock in newly formed Swallow Corporation. What is Imelda's income tax situation for this stock?

25. How do the following transactions affect the earnings and profits of a corporation?
    a. A nontaxable stock dividend issued to the shareholders.
    b. Receipt of interest on municipal bonds.
    c. Federal corporate income tax liability.

26. When is a distribution by a corporation to its shareholders treated by the shareholders as a return of capital? When can a shareholder have a capital gain on a distribution received from a corporation?

27. A corporation distributes a property dividend to its shareholders.
    a. Is any gain or loss recognized by the distributing corporation?
    b. What basis will the shareholders have in the property?

28. The stock of Loon Corporation is owned equally by a brother and two sisters: Cole, Alma, and Kara. During the year, the following transactions occur.
    a. Cole buys property from Loon Corporation.
    b. Alma rents property to Loon Corporation.
    c. Kara borrows money from Loon Corporation.
    d. Loon Corporation pays interest on bonds it sold to Cole, Alma, and Kara.

    Discuss any potential tax problems that these transactions might involve.

29. What difference does it make whether a corporation's redemption of its stock qualifies as a sale or exchange?

30. What is the usual tax effect to a shareholder when the corporation liquidates?

31. Why did Congress enact Subchapter S of the Code?

32. In the case of S corporations, what is the difference between the treatment of capital losses and operating losses? Why does the difference exist?

33. Compare the nonrecognition of gain or loss on contributions to a partnership with the similar provision found in corporate formation (§ 351). What are the major differences and similarities?

34. Under what circumstances does the receipt of a partnership interest result in the recognition of ordinary income? What is the effect of this on the partnership and the other partners?

35. How is a contributing partner's basis in a partnership interest determined?

36. What transactions or events will cause a partner's basis in his or her partnership interest to fluctuate continuously?

37. Describe the two-step approach used in determining partnership income. Why is the computation necessary?

38. To what extent can a partner deduct his or her distributive share of partnership losses? What happens to any unused losses?

39. What are guaranteed payments? When might such payments be used?

40. Cecil is the sole shareholder of Stilt Corporation (an S corporation). In order to shift income to lower-bracket family members, Cecil gives 40% of the stock in Stilt to his four children. Cecil's children are all minors, and none of them works for the corporation. Do you see any potential tax problems?

PROBLEMS

41. Canary Corporation has net short-term capital gains of $10,000 and net long-term capital losses of $90,000 during 1996. Taxable income from other sources is $400,000.

Prior years' transactions included the following:

1992	Net short-term capital gains	$40,000
1993	Net long-term capital gains	20,000
1994	Net short-term capital gains	30,000
1995	Net long-term capital gains	20,000

a. How are the capital gains and losses treated on the 1996 tax return?
b. Compute the capital loss carryback to the carryback years.
c. Compute the amount of capital loss carryover, if any, and designate the years to which the loss may be carried.

42. Starling Corporation acquired residential rental property on January 3, 1986, for $100,000. The property was depreciated using the accelerated method and a 19-year recovery period under ACRS. Depreciation in the amount of $57,975 was claimed. Straight-line depreciation for the period would have been $47,586. Starling sold the property on January 1, 1996, for $110,000. What is the gain on the sale, and how is it taxed?

43. Assume the property in Problem 42 was a commercial building and Starling Corporation used the straight-line method of depreciation with a 19-year recovery period under ACRS. What would be the gain on the sale, and how would it be taxed?

44. During 1996, Warbler Corporation, a calendar year taxpayer, had the following income and expenses:

Income from operations	$450,000
Expenses from operations	330,000
Dividends from domestic corporations	30,000
NOL carryover from 1995	9,000

On May 1, 1996, Warbler made a contribution to a qualified charitable organization of $21,000 in cash (not included in any of the items listed above).
a. Determine Warbler's deduction for charitable contributions for 1996.
b. What happens to any portion of the contribution not deductible in 1996?

45. Grackle Company is a wholesale grocery business. During 1996, it donated canned and dried food (held as inventory) to the local Salvation Army. The basis of the food is $25,000, and it has a fair market value of $26,000. Based on the following assumptions, what amount qualifies as a charitable contribution?
a. Grackle Company is a sole proprietorship.
b. Grackle Company is a regular corporation.

46. During 1996, Raven Corporation had net income from operations of $200,000. In addition, Raven received dividends in the following amounts: $10,000 from Flicker Corporation and $20,000 from Blackbird Corporation. Raven owns 14% of the stock of Flicker and 40% of the stock of Blackbird. Determine Raven Corporation's dividends received deduction for 1996.

47. In each of the following independent situations, determine the dividends received deduction. Assume that none of the corporate shareholders owns 20% or more of the stock in the corporation paying the dividends.

	Lark Corporation	**Crow Corporation**	**Bluebird Corporation**
Income from operations	$ 350,000	$ 400,000	$ 350,000
Expenses of operations	(300,000)	(450,000)	(370,000)
Qualifying dividends	50,000	100,000	100,000

48. In each of the following independent situations, determine the corporation's income tax liability. Assume that all corporations use a calendar year for tax purposes, and that the tax year involved is 1996.

	Taxable Income
Cardinal Corporation	$ 30,000
Sparrow Corporation	105,000
Robin Corporation	300,000
Nighthawk Corporation	10,000,000
Jay Corporation (a qualified personal service corporation)	50,000

49. Using the following legend, classify each statement accordingly:

Legend
I = Applies to the income taxation of individuals.
C = Applies to the income taxation of regular corporations.
B = Applies to the income taxation of both individuals and regular corporations.
N = Applies to the income taxation of neither individuals nor regular corporations.

a. Net capital losses can be carried back.
b. Net capital losses can be carried over indefinitely.
c. Net capital losses can offset other income.
d. Net long-term capital gains can be taxed at a rate in excess of 28%.
e. A cash basis taxpayer cannot deduct charitable contributions until the year of payment.
f. A dividends received deduction may be available.
g. The application of § 1250 (the recapture of depreciation claimed on certain real property) may yield less ordinary income.
h. The concept of adjusted gross income (AGI) is relevant.
i. Percentage limitations do not restrict the amount of charitable deductions that can be claimed in any one tax year.
j. Casualty losses are deductible in full.
k. Tax rates are progressive.

50. Pam, Gail, and Wyatt form the Godwit Corporation with the following investments:

	Basis	Fair Market Value	Number of Shares Issued
From Pam—			
Cash	$50,000	$50,000	50
From Gail—			
Land	50,000	60,000	45
From Wyatt—			
Services		5,000	5

In addition to stock, Gail received $15,000 in cash from the corporation. Wyatt received his 5 shares for performing legal and accounting services in forming the corporation. Assume each share of Godwit Stock is worth $1,000.

a. How much gain (or loss) must Gail recognize?
b. What basis will Gail have in the stock?
c. What basis will Godwit Corporation have in the land?
d. How much gain, if any, must Wyatt recognize?
e. What basis will he have in the stock?

51. Joanne and Tab form the Vireo Corporation with the following investments:

	Basis	Fair Market Value	Number of Shares Issued
From Joanne—			
Cash	$60,000	$60,000	60
From Tab—			
Land	65,000	50,000	40

In addition to stock, Tab received $10,000 in cash. Assume each share of Vireo stock is worth $1,000.
a. How much gain (or loss) must Tab recognize?
b. What basis will Tab have in the stock?
c. What basis will Vireo Corporation have in the land?

52. Jane, the sole shareholder of Plover Corporation, has a basis of $20,000 in her stock investment. At a time when Plover Corporation has E & P of $14,000, it distributes cash of $30,000 to Jane. What are the tax consequences to Jane of the $30,000 distribution?

53. The stock of Sandpiper Corporation is held equally by Russ and Erlyne. The shareholders would like to receive, as a dividend, value of $100,000 each. The corporation has the following assets it can spare:

Asset	Adjusted Basis to Sandpiper Corporation	Fair Market Value
Land (parcel A)	$ 60,000	$100,000
Land (parcel B)	130,000	100,000

Both assets are held as investments. Sandpiper Corporation has a capital loss carryover from the previous year of $10,000 and has accumulated E & P in excess of $1 million.

Russ and Erlyne have come to you for advice. Suggest an attractive tax plan to carry out what the parties want. Write a letter (addressed to Sandpiper Corporation at P.O. Box 1150, St. Louis, MO 63130) describing your plan and its tax consequences.

54. At a time when Longspur Corporation has ample E & P, it redeems 500 of Cynthia's 1,500 shares for their fair market value of $500,000 ($1,000 for each share). All of Cynthia's shares were acquired 10 years ago as an investment and have an adjusted basis of $150,000 ($100 for each share).
a. Describe the tax effect of the redemption if it qualifies for sale or exchange treatment.
b. Describe the tax effect of the redemption if it does not qualify for sale or exchange treatment.

55. In the current year, Shearwater Corporation is liquidated under the general rules of § 331. The company distributes its only asset (land with a fair market value of $100,000 and adjusted basis of $20,000) to Oscar, who holds all of the Shearwater stock as an investment. Oscar's basis in the Shearwater stock is $60,000. Shearwater Corporation has E & P of $10,000.
a. What are the amount and character of the gain or loss recognized by Oscar upon receiving the land in exchange for the stock?
b. What is Oscar's basis in the land?
c. Is there any tax effect to Shearwater Corporation? Explain.

56. Ten years ago, Albatross Corporation purchased all of the stock of Kingbird Corporation for $100,000. In the current year, Kingbird has a basis in its assets of $300,000 and a fair market value of $400,000. Albatross liquidates Kingbird Corporation and receives all of its assets. The exception to the carryover basis rule does not apply.
   a. Does Albatross Corporation recognize any gain as a result of the liquidation?
   b. What is Albatross Corporation's basis for the assets it receives from Kingbird Corporation?

57. During 1996, Crossbill Corporation (a calendar year, accrual basis S corporation) had the following transactions:

Sales	$300,000
Cost of goods sold	120,000
Salaries	150,000
Charitable contributions	20,000
Capital losses (short term)	15,000
Advertising	12,000
Interest on City of Tulsa bonds	3,000

   a. Determine Crossbill Corporation's separately stated items for 1996.
   b. Determine Crossbill Corporation's taxable income for 1996.

58. Julius Walker owns all of the stock of Mockingbird Corporation, a calendar year S corporation. For calendar year 1996, Mockingbird anticipates an operating loss of $20,000 and could, if deemed worthwhile, sell a stock investment that would generate a $3,000 long-term capital loss. Julius has an adjusted basis of $5,000 in the Mockingbird stock. He anticipates no capital asset transactions and expects to be in the 36% tax bracket in 1996.
   a. Can you recommend a course of action that can save Julius taxes for 1996?
   b. Write a letter to Julius explaining your recommendations. Julius's address is Box 429, Normal, AL 35762.

59. In 1996, Heron Corporation (a calendar year S corporation) had an NOL of $73,200. Otto, a calendar year individual, held stock in Heron Corporation as follows: 40% for 200 days and 60% for 166 days. Based on these facts, what is Otto's loss pass-through for 1996?

60. Sam, Bob, and Clara form the Beige Partnership on January 1, 1996. In exchange for a 30% capital interest, Sam transfers property (basis of $14,000, fair market value of $25,000) subject to a liability of $10,000. The liability is assumed by the partnership. Bob transfers property (basis of $24,000, fair market value of $15,000) for a 30% capital interest, and Clara transfers cash of $20,000 for the remaining 40% capital interest.
   a. How much gain must Sam recognize on the transfer?
   b. What is Sam's basis in his partnership interest?
   c. How much loss may Bob recognize on the transfer?
   d. What is Bob's basis in his partnership interest?
   e. What is Clara's basis in her partnership interest?
   f. What basis will the Beige Partnership have in the property transferred by Sam? The property transferred by Bob?
   g. What would be the tax consequences to Sam if the basis of the property he contributed is only $9,000?

61. As of January 1, 1995, Victor had a basis of $26,000 in his 25% capital interest in the Gray Partnership. He and the partnership use the calendar year for tax purposes. The partnership incurred an operating loss of $120,000 for 1995 and a profit of $80,000 for 1996.
   a. How much, if any, loss may Victor recognize for 1995?
   b. How much income must Victor recognize for 1996?
   c. What basis will Victor have in his partnership interest as of January 1, 1996?

d. What basis will Victor have in his partnership interest as of January 1, 1997?
e. What year-end tax planning would you suggest to ensure that a partner could deduct all of his or her share of any partnership losses?

62. Sarah owns a 51% interest in the capital and profits of the Rose Partnership. In 1995, Sarah sells property (adjusted basis of $120,000) to the partnership for the property's fair market value of $109,000. In 1996, Rose Partnership sells the same property to an outsider for $112,000.
 a. What are Sarah's tax consequences on the 1995 sale?
 b. What are Rose Partnership's tax consequences on the 1996 sale?

RESEARCH PROBLEMS

Note: ***West's Federal Taxation on CD-ROM*** *can be used in preparing solutions to the Research Problems. Alternatively, tax research materials contained in a standard tax library can be used.*

Research Problem 1. Roland and Peter are brothers and equal shareholders in Condor Corporation, a calendar year taxpayer. In 1996, as employees, they incurred certain travel and entertainment expenditures on behalf of Condor Corporation. Because Condor was in a precarious financial condition, Roland and Peter decided not to seek reimbursement for these expenditures. Instead, on his own individual return (Form 1040), each brother deducted what he had spent. Upon audit of the returns filed by Roland and Peter for 1996, the IRS disallowed these expenditures. Do you agree? Why or why not?

Partial list of research aids:
Roy L. Harding, 29 TCM 789, T.C.Memo. 1970–179.

Research Problem 2. Leonora incorporates her retail clothing business. She transfers all her business assets (total basis of $100,000 and fair market value of $95,000) along with business liabilities of $10,000 and a personal note in the amount of $15,000 to the corporation for 100% of its stock. The note is for money borrowed from the bank six months before incorporation to finance improvements on her home. What are the tax consequences of the transfer?

Research Problem 3. Several years ago, Mike Dalton incorporated his sole proprietorship and immediately made an election under Subchapter S. Mike lives in El Paso, Texas, and is married to Consuela, a citizen of Mexico. Since Consuela's father is ill and requires constant care, she lives with him across the border in Ciudad Juarez.

This year, the IRS audits the Forms 1120S filed by Mike's corporation and disallows its Subchapter S status. What could be the cause of the disallowance?

Research Problem 4. Ms. Marge Bland and a number of her friends want to diversify their investment portfolios. With this in mind, they form a partnership to which they transfer appreciated securities. Each transferor receives an interest in the new partnership proportionate to the value of the securities transferred. Will the creation of the partnership be tax-free? Why or why not?
 a. Prepare a letter to Ms. Bland giving your advice. Ms. Bland's address is 349 Azalea Drive, Athens, GA 30602.
 b. Prepare a memo for your firm's client files.

APPENDIX A
Tax Rate Schedules and Tables

1995 Tax Rate Schedules

Single—Schedule X

If taxable income is: *Over—*	*But not over—*	The tax is:	*of the amount over—*
$0	$ 23,350	................**15%**	**$0**
23,350	56,550	**$3,502.50 + 28%**	**23,350**
56,550	117,950	**12,798.50 + 31%**	**56,550**
117,950	256,500	**31,832.50 + 36%**	**117,950**
256,500	....	**81,710.50 + 39.6%**	**256,500**

Head of household—Schedule Z

If taxable income is: *Over—*	*But not over—*	The tax is:	*of the amount over—*
$0	$ 31,250	................**15%**	**$0**
31,250	80,750	**$4,687.50 + 28%**	**31,250**
80,750	130,800	**18,547.50 + 31%**	**80,750**
130,800	256,500	**34,063.00 + 36%**	**130,800**
256,500	....	**79,315.00 + 39.6%**	**256,500**

Married filing jointly or Qualifying widow(er)—Schedule Y-1

If taxable income is: *Over—*	*But not over—*	The tax is:	*of the amount over—*
$0	$ 39,000	................**15%**	**$0**
39,000	94,250	**$5,850.00 + 28%**	**39,000**
94,250	143,600	**21,320.00 + 31%**	**94,250**
143,600	256,500	**36,618.50 + 36%**	**143,600**
256,500	....	**77,262.50 + 39.6%**	**256,500**

Married filing separately—Schedule Y-2

If taxable income is: *Over—*	*But not over—*	The tax is:	*of the amount over—*
$0	$ 19,500	................**15%**	**$0**
19,500	47,125	**$2,925.00 + 28%**	**19,500**
47,125	71,800	**10,660.00 + 31%**	**47,125**
71,800	128,250	**18,309.25 + 36%**	**71,800**
128,250	....	**38,631.25 + 39.6%**	**128,250**

1995 Tax Table

Use if your taxable income is less than $100,000. If $100,000 or more, use the Tax Rate Schedules.

Example. Mr. and Mrs. Brown are filing a joint return. Their taxable income on line 37 of Form 1040 is $25,300. First, they find the $25,300–25,350 income line. Next, they find the column for married filing jointly and read down the column. The amount shown where the income line and filing status column meet is $3,799. This is the tax amount they must enter on line 38 of their Form 1040.

Sample Table

At least	But less than	Single	Married filing jointly *	Married filing separately	Head of a household
		Your tax is—			
25,200	**25,250**	4,028	3,784	4,528	3,784
25,250	**25,300**	4,042	3,791	4,542	3,791
25,300	**25,350**	4,056	(3,799)	4,556	3,799
25,350	**25,400**	4,070	3,806	4,570	3,806

If line 37 (taxable income) is—		And you are—			
At least	But less than	Single	Married filing jointly *	Married filing separately	Head of a household
		Your tax is—			
0	**5**	0	0	0	0
5	**15**	2	2	2	2
15	**25**	3	3	3	3
25	**50**	6	6	6	6
50	**75**	9	9	9	9
75	**100**	13	13	13	13
100	**125**	17	17	17	17
125	**150**	21	21	21	21
150	**175**	24	24	24	24
175	**200**	28	28	28	28
200	**225**	32	32	32	32
225	**250**	36	36	36	36
250	**275**	39	39	39	39
275	**300**	43	43	43	43
300	**325**	47	47	47	47
325	**350**	51	51	51	51
350	**375**	54	54	54	54
375	**400**	58	58	58	58
400	**425**	62	62	62	62
425	**450**	66	66	66	66
450	**475**	69	69	69	69
475	**500**	73	73	73	73
500	**525**	77	77	77	77
525	**550**	81	81	81	81
550	**575**	84	84	84	84
575	**600**	88	88	88	88
600	**625**	92	92	92	92
625	**650**	96	96	96	96
650	**675**	99	99	99	99
675	**700**	103	103	103	103
700	**725**	107	107	107	107
725	**750**	111	111	111	111
750	**775**	114	114	114	114
775	**800**	118	118	118	118
800	**825**	122	122	122	122
825	**850**	126	126	126	126
850	**875**	129	129	129	129
875	**900**	133	133	133	133
900	**925**	137	137	137	137
925	**950**	141	141	141	141
950	**975**	144	144	144	144
975	**1,000**	148	148	148	148
1,000					
1,000	**1,025**	152	152	152	152
1,025	**1,050**	156	156	156	156
1,050	**1,075**	159	159	159	159
1,075	**1,100**	163	163	163	163
1,100	**1,125**	167	167	167	167
1,125	**1,150**	171	171	171	171
1,150	**1,175**	174	174	174	174
1,175	**1,200**	178	178	178	178
1,200	**1,225**	182	182	182	182
1,225	**1,250**	186	186	186	186
1,250	**1,275**	189	189	189	189
1,275	**1,300**	193	193	193	193
1,300	**1,325**	197	197	197	197
1,325	**1,350**	201	201	201	201
1,350	**1,375**	204	204	204	204
1,375	**1,400**	208	208	208	208
1,400	**1,425**	212	212	212	212
1,425	**1,450**	216	216	216	216
1,450	**1,475**	219	219	219	219
1,475	**1,500**	223	223	223	223
1,500	**1,525**	227	227	227	227
1,525	**1,550**	231	231	231	231
1,550	**1,575**	234	234	234	234
1,575	**1,600**	238	238	238	238
1,600	**1,625**	242	242	242	242
1,625	**1,650**	246	246	246	246
1,650	**1,675**	249	249	249	249
1,675	**1,700**	253	253	253	253
1,700	**1,725**	257	257	257	257
1,725	**1,750**	261	261	261	261
1,750	**1,775**	264	264	264	264
1,775	**1,800**	268	268	268	268
1,800	**1,825**	272	272	272	272
1,825	**1,850**	276	276	276	276
1,850	**1,875**	279	279	279	279
1,875	**1,900**	283	283	283	283
1,900	**1,925**	287	287	287	287
1,925	**1,950**	291	291	291	291
1,950	**1,975**	294	294	294	294
1,975	**2,000**	298	298	298	298
2,000					
2,000	**2,025**	302	302	302	302
2,025	**2,050**	306	306	306	306
2,050	**2,075**	309	309	309	309
2,075	**2,100**	313	313	313	313
2,100	**2,125**	317	317	317	317
2,125	**2,150**	321	321	321	321
2,150	**2,175**	324	324	324	324
2,175	**2,200**	328	328	328	328
2,200	**2,225**	332	332	332	332
2,225	**2,250**	336	336	336	336
2,250	**2,275**	339	339	339	339
2,275	**2,300**	343	343	343	343
2,300	**2,325**	347	347	347	347
2,325	**2,350**	351	351	351	351
2,350	**2,375**	354	354	354	354
2,375	**2,400**	358	358	358	358
2,400	**2,425**	362	362	362	362
2,425	**2,450**	366	366	366	366
2,450	**2,475**	369	369	369	369
2,475	**2,500**	373	373	373	373
2,500	**2,525**	377	377	377	377
2,525	**2,550**	381	381	381	381
2,550	**2,575**	384	384	384	384
2,575	**2,600**	388	388	388	388
2,600	**2,625**	392	392	392	392
2,625	**2,650**	396	396	396	396
2,650	**2,675**	399	399	399	399
2,675	**2,700**	403	403	403	403
2,700	**2,725**	407	407	407	407
2,725	**2,750**	411	411	411	411
2,750	**2,775**	414	414	414	414
2,775	**2,800**	418	418	418	418
2,800	**2,825**	422	422	422	422
2,825	**2,850**	426	426	426	426
2,850	**2,875**	429	429	429	429
2,875	**2,900**	433	433	433	433
2,900	**2,925**	437	437	437	437
2,925	**2,950**	441	441	441	441
2,950	**2,975**	444	444	444	444
2,975	**3,000**	448	448	448	448
3,000					
3,000	**3,050**	454	454	454	454
3,050	**3,100**	461	461	461	461
3,100	**3,150**	469	469	469	469
3,150	**3,200**	476	476	476	476
3,200	**3,250**	484	484	484	484
3,250	**3,300**	491	491	491	491
3,300	**3,350**	499	499	499	499
3,350	**3,400**	506	506	506	506
3,400	**3,450**	514	514	514	514
3,450	**3,500**	521	521	521	521
3,500	**3,550**	529	529	529	529
3,550	**3,600**	536	536	536	536
3,600	**3,650**	544	544	544	544
3,650	**3,700**	551	551	551	551
3,700	**3,750**	559	559	559	559
3,750	**3,800**	566	566	566	566
3,800	**3,850**	574	574	574	574
3,850	**3,900**	581	581	581	581
3,900	**3,950**	589	589	589	589
3,950	**4,000**	596	596	596	596
4,000					
4,000	**4,050**	604	604	604	604
4,050	**4,100**	611	611	611	611
4,100	**4,150**	619	619	619	619
4,150	**4,200**	626	626	626	626
4,200	**4,250**	634	634	634	634
4,250	**4,300**	641	641	641	641
4,300	**4,350**	649	649	649	649
4,350	**4,400**	656	656	656	656
4,400	**4,450**	664	664	664	664
4,450	**4,500**	671	671	671	671
4,500	**4,550**	679	679	679	679
4,550	**4,600**	686	686	686	686
4,600	**4,650**	694	694	694	694
4,650	**4,700**	701	701	701	701
4,700	**4,750**	709	709	709	709
4,750	**4,800**	716	716	716	716
4,800	**4,850**	724	724	724	724
4,850	**4,900**	731	731	731	731
4,900	**4,950**	739	739	739	739
4,950	**5,000**	746	746	746	746

Continued on next page

* This column must also be used by a qualifying widow(er).

1995 Tax Table—*Continued*

If line 37 (taxable income) is— At least	But less than	Single	Married filing jointly *	Married filing separately	Head of a household
		Your tax is—			
5,000					
5,000	5,050	754	754	754	754
5,050	5,100	761	761	761	761
5,100	5,150	769	769	769	769
5,150	5,200	776	776	776	776
5,200	5,250	784	784	784	784
5,250	5,300	791	791	791	791
5,300	5,350	799	799	799	799
5,350	5,400	806	806	806	806
5,400	5,450	814	814	814	814
5,450	5,500	821	821	821	821
5,500	5,550	829	829	829	829
5,550	5,600	836	836	836	836
5,600	5,650	844	844	844	844
5,650	5,700	851	851	851	851
5,700	5,750	859	859	859	859
5,750	5,800	866	866	866	866
5,800	5,850	874	874	874	874
5,850	5,900	881	881	881	881
5,900	5,950	889	889	889	889
5,950	6,000	896	896	896	896
6,000					
6,000	6,050	904	904	904	904
6,050	6,100	911	911	911	911
6,100	6,150	919	919	919	919
6,150	6,200	926	926	926	926
6,200	6,250	934	934	934	934
6,250	6,300	941	941	941	941
6,300	6,350	949	949	949	949
6,350	6,400	956	956	956	956
6,400	6,450	964	964	964	964
6,450	6,500	971	971	971	971
6,500	6,550	979	979	979	979
6,550	6,600	986	986	986	986
6,600	6,650	994	994	994	994
6,650	6,700	1,001	1,001	1,001	1,001
6,700	6,750	1,009	1,009	1,009	1,009
6,750	6,800	1,016	1,016	1,016	1,016
6,800	6,850	1,024	1,024	1,024	1,024
6,850	6,900	1,031	1,031	1,031	1,031
6,900	6,950	1,039	1,039	1,039	1,039
6,950	7,000	1,046	1,046	1,046	1,046
7,000					
7,000	7,050	1,054	1,054	1,054	1,054
7,050	7,100	1,061	1,061	1,061	1,061
7,100	7,150	1,069	1,069	1,069	1,069
7,150	7,200	1,076	1,076	1,076	1,076
7,200	7,250	1,084	1,084	1,084	1,084
7,250	7,300	1,091	1,091	1,091	1,091
7,300	7,350	1,099	1,099	1,099	1,099
7,350	7,400	1,106	1,106	1,106	1,106
7,400	7,450	1,114	1,114	1,114	1,114
7,450	7,500	1,121	1,121	1,121	1,121
7,500	7,550	1,129	1,129	1,129	1,129
7,550	7,600	1,136	1,136	1,136	1,136
7,600	7,650	1,144	1,144	1,144	1,144
7,650	7,700	1,151	1,151	1,151	1,151
7,700	7,750	1,159	1,159	1,159	1,159
7,750	7,800	1,166	1,166	1,166	1,166
7,800	7,850	1,174	1,174	1,174	1,174
7,850	7,900	1,181	1,181	1,181	1,181
7,900	7,950	1,189	1,189	1,189	1,189
7,950	8,000	1,196	1,196	1,196	1,196

If line 37 (taxable income) is— At least	But less than	Single	Married filing jointly *	Married filing separately	Head of a household
		Your tax is—			
8,000					
8,000	8,050	1,204	1,204	1,204	1,204
8,050	8,100	1,211	1,211	1,211	1,211
8,100	8,150	1,219	1,219	1,219	1,219
8,150	8,200	1,226	1,226	1,226	1,226
8,200	8,250	1,234	1,234	1,234	1,234
8,250	8,300	1,241	1,241	1,241	1,241
8,300	8,350	1,249	1,249	1,249	1,249
8,350	8,400	1,256	1,256	1,256	1,256
8,400	8,450	1,264	1,264	1,264	1,264
8,450	8,500	1,271	1,271	1,271	1,271
8,500	8,550	1,279	1,279	1,279	1,279
8,550	8,600	1,286	1,286	1,286	1,286
8,600	8,650	1,294	1,294	1,294	1,294
8,650	8,700	1,301	1,301	1,301	1,301
8,700	8,750	1,309	1,309	1,309	1,309
8,750	8,800	1,316	1,316	1,316	1,316
8,800	8,850	1,324	1,324	1,324	1,324
8,850	8,900	1,331	1,331	1,331	1,331
8,900	8,950	1,339	1,339	1,339	1,339
8,950	9,000	1,346	1,346	1,346	1,346
9,000					
9,000	9,050	1,354	1,354	1,354	1,354
9,050	9,100	1,361	1,361	1,361	1,361
9,100	9,150	1,369	1,369	1,369	1,369
9,150	9,200	1,376	1,376	1,376	1,376
9,200	9,250	1,384	1,384	1,384	1,384
9,250	9,300	1,391	1,391	1,391	1,391
9,300	9,350	1,399	1,399	1,399	1,399
9,350	9,400	1,406	1,406	1,406	1,406
9,400	9,450	1,414	1,414	1,414	1,414
9,450	9,500	1,421	1,421	1,421	1,421
9,500	9,550	1,429	1,429	1,429	1,429
9,550	9,600	1,436	1,436	1,436	1,436
9,600	9,650	1,444	1,444	1,444	1,444
9,650	9,700	1,451	1,451	1,451	1,451
9,700	9,750	1,459	1,459	1,459	1,459
9,750	9,800	1,466	1,466	1,466	1,466
9,800	9,850	1,474	1,474	1,474	1,474
9,850	9,900	1,481	1,481	1,481	1,481
9,900	9,950	1,489	1,489	1,489	1,489
9,950	10,000	1,496	1,496	1,496	1,496
10,000					
10,000	10,050	1,504	1,504	1,504	1,504
10,050	10,100	1,511	1,511	1,511	1,511
10,100	10,150	1,519	1,519	1,519	1,519
10,150	10,200	1,526	1,526	1,526	1,526
10,200	10,250	1,534	1,534	1,534	1,534
10,250	10,300	1,541	1,541	1,541	1,541
10,300	10,350	1,549	1,549	1,549	1,549
10,350	10,400	1,556	1,556	1,556	1,556
10,400	10,450	1,564	1,564	1,564	1,564
10,450	10,500	1,571	1,571	1,571	1,571
10,500	10,550	1,579	1,579	1,579	1,579
10,550	10,600	1,586	1,586	1,586	1,586
10,600	10,650	1,594	1,594	1,594	1,594
10,650	10,700	1,601	1,601	1,601	1,601
10,700	10,750	1,609	1,609	1,609	1,609
10,750	10,800	1,616	1,616	1,616	1,616
10,800	10,850	1,624	1,624	1,624	1,624
10,850	10,900	1,631	1,631	1,631	1,631
10,900	10,950	1,639	1,639	1,639	1,639
10,950	11,000	1,646	1,646	1,646	1,646

If line 37 (taxable income) is— At least	But less than	Single	Married filing jointly *	Married filing separately	Head of a household
		Your tax is—			
11,000					
11,000	11,050	1,654	1,654	1,654	1,654
11,050	11,100	1,661	1,661	1,661	1,661
11,100	11,150	1,669	1,669	1,669	1,669
11,150	11,200	1,676	1,676	1,676	1,676
11,200	11,250	1,684	1,684	1,684	1,684
11,250	11,300	1,691	1,691	1,691	1,691
11,300	11,350	1,699	1,699	1,699	1,699
11,350	11,400	1,706	1,706	1,706	1,706
11,400	11,450	1,714	1,714	1,714	1,714
11,450	11,500	1,721	1,721	1,721	1,721
11,500	11,550	1,729	1,729	1,729	1,729
11,550	11,600	1,736	1,736	1,736	1,736
11,600	11,650	1,744	1,744	1,744	1,744
11,650	11,700	1,751	1,751	1,751	1,751
11,700	11,750	1,759	1,759	1,759	1,759
11,750	11,800	1,766	1,766	1,766	1,766
11,800	11,850	1,774	1,774	1,774	1,774
11,850	11,900	1,781	1,781	1,781	1,781
11,900	11,950	1,789	1,789	1,789	1,789
11,950	12,000	1,796	1,796	1,796	1,796
12,000					
12,000	12,050	1,804	1,804	1,804	1,804
12,050	12,100	1,811	1,811	1,811	1,811
12,100	12,150	1,819	1,819	1,819	1,819
12,150	12,200	1,826	1,826	1,826	1,826
12,200	12,250	1,834	1,834	1,834	1,834
12,250	12,300	1,841	1,841	1,841	1,841
12,300	12,350	1,849	1,849	1,849	1,849
12,350	12,400	1,856	1,856	1,856	1,856
12,400	12,450	1,864	1,864	1,864	1,864
12,450	12,500	1,871	1,871	1,871	1,871
12,500	12,550	1,879	1,879	1,879	1,879
12,550	12,600	1,886	1,886	1,886	1,886
12,600	12,650	1,894	1,894	1,894	1,894
12,650	12,700	1,901	1,901	1,901	1,901
12,700	12,750	1,909	1,909	1,909	1,909
12,750	12,800	1,916	1,916	1,916	1,916
12,800	12,850	1,924	1,924	1,924	1,924
12,850	12,900	1,931	1,931	1,931	1,931
12,900	12,950	1,939	1,939	1,939	1,939
12,950	13,000	1,946	1,946	1,946	1,946
13,000					
13,000	13,050	1,954	1,954	1,954	1,954
13,050	13,100	1,961	1,961	1,961	1,961
13,100	13,150	1,969	1,969	1,969	1,969
13,150	13,200	1,976	1,976	1,976	1,976
13,200	13,250	1,984	1,984	1,984	1,984
13,250	13,300	1,991	1,991	1,991	1,991
13,300	13,350	1,999	1,999	1,999	1,999
13,350	13,400	2,006	2,006	2,006	2,006
13,400	13,450	2,014	2,014	2,014	2,014
13,450	13,500	2,021	2,021	2,021	2,021
13,500	13,550	2,029	2,029	2,029	2,029
13,550	13,600	2,036	2,036	2,036	2,036
13,600	13,650	2,044	2,044	2,044	2,044
13,650	13,700	2,051	2,051	2,051	2,051
13,700	13,750	2,059	2,059	2,059	2,059
13,750	13,800	2,066	2,066	2,066	2,066
13,800	13,850	2,074	2,074	2,074	2,074
13,850	13,900	2,081	2,081	2,081	2,081
13,900	13,950	2,089	2,089	2,089	2,089
13,950	14,000	2,096	2,096	2,096	2,096

* This column must also be used by a qualifying widow(er).

Continued on next page

1995 Tax Table—*Continued*

If line 37 (taxable income) is— At least	But less than	And you are— Single	Married filing jointly *	Married filing separately	Head of a household
		Your tax is—			
14,000					
14,000	**14,050**	2,104	2,104	2,104	2,104
14,050	**14,100**	2,111	2,111	2,111	2,111
14,100	**14,150**	2,119	2,119	2,119	2,119
14,150	**14,200**	2,126	2,126	2,126	2,126
14,200	**14,250**	2,134	2,134	2,134	2,134
14,250	**14,300**	2,141	2,141	2,141	2,141
14,300	**14,350**	2,149	2,149	2,149	2,149
14,350	**14,400**	2,156	2,156	2,156	2,156
14,400	**14,450**	2,164	2,164	2,164	2,164
14,450	**14,500**	2,171	2,171	2,171	2,171
14,500	**14,550**	2,179	2,179	2,179	2,179
14,550	**14,600**	2,186	2,186	2,186	2,186
14,600	**14,650**	2,194	2,194	2,194	2,194
14,650	**14,700**	2,201	2,201	2,201	2,201
14,700	**14,750**	2,209	2,209	2,209	2,209
14,750	**14,800**	2,216	2,216	2,216	2,216
14,800	**14,850**	2,224	2,224	2,224	2,224
14,850	**14,900**	2,231	2,231	2,231	2,231
14,900	**14,950**	2,239	2,239	2,239	2,239
14,950	**15,000**	2,246	2,246	2,246	2,246
15,000					
15,000	**15,050**	2,254	2,254	2,254	2,254
15,050	**15,100**	2,261	2,261	2,261	2,261
15,100	**15,150**	2,269	2,269	2,269	2,269
15,150	**15,200**	2,276	2,276	2,276	2,276
15,200	**15,250**	2,284	2,284	2,284	2,284
15,250	**15,300**	2,291	2,291	2,291	2,291
15,300	**15,350**	2,299	2,299	2,299	2,299
15,350	**15,400**	2,306	2,306	2,306	2,306
15,400	**15,450**	2,314	2,314	2,314	2,314
15,450	**15,500**	2,321	2,321	2,321	2,321
15,500	**15,550**	2,329	2,329	2,329	2,329
15,550	**15,600**	2,336	2,336	2,336	2,336
15,600	**15,650**	2,344	2,344	2,344	2,344
15,650	**15,700**	2,351	2,351	2,351	2,351
15,700	**15,750**	2,359	2,359	2,359	2,359
15,750	**15,800**	2,366	2,366	2,366	2,366
15,800	**15,850**	2,374	2,374	2,374	2,374
15,850	**15,900**	2,381	2,381	2,381	2,381
15,900	**15,950**	2,389	2,389	2,389	2,389
15,950	**16,000**	2,396	2,396	2,396	2,396
16,000					
16,000	**16,050**	2,404	2,404	2,404	2,404
16,050	**16,100**	2,411	2,411	2,411	2,411
16,100	**16,150**	2,419	2,419	2,419	2,419
16,150	**16,200**	2,426	2,426	2,426	2,426
16,200	**16,250**	2,434	2,434	2,434	2,434
16,250	**16,300**	2,441	2,441	2,441	2,441
16,300	**16,350**	2,449	2,449	2,449	2,449
16,350	**16,400**	2,456	2,456	2,456	2,456
16,400	**16,450**	2,464	2,464	2,464	2,464
16,450	**16,500**	2,471	2,471	2,471	2,471
16,500	**16,550**	2,479	2,479	2,479	2,479
16,550	**16,600**	2,486	2,486	2,486	2,486
16,600	**16,650**	2,494	2,494	2,494	2,494
16,650	**16,700**	2,501	2,501	2,501	2,501
16,700	**16,750**	2,509	2,509	2,509	2,509
16,750	**16,800**	2,516	2,516	2,516	2,516
16,800	**16,850**	2,524	2,524	2,524	2,524
16,850	**16,900**	2,531	2,531	2,531	2,531
16,900	**16,950**	2,539	2,539	2,539	2,539
16,950	**17,000**	2,546	2,546	2,546	2,546

If line 37 (taxable income) is— At least	But less than	And you are— Single	Married filing jointly *	Married filing separately	Head of a household
		Your tax is—			
17,000					
17,000	**17,050**	2,554	2,554	2,554	2,554
17,050	**17,100**	2,561	2,561	2,561	2,561
17,100	**17,150**	2,569	2,569	2,569	2,569
17,150	**17,200**	2,576	2,576	2,576	2,576
17,200	**17,250**	2,584	2,584	2,584	2,584
17,250	**17,300**	2,591	2,591	2,591	2,591
17,300	**17,350**	2,599	2,599	2,599	2,599
17,350	**17,400**	2,606	2,606	2,606	2,606
17,400	**17,450**	2,614	2,614	2,614	2,614
17,450	**17,500**	2,621	2,621	2,621	2,621
17,500	**17,550**	2,629	2,629	2,629	2,629
17,550	**17,600**	2,636	2,636	2,636	2,636
17,600	**17,650**	2,644	2,644	2,644	2,644
17,650	**17,700**	2,651	2,651	2,651	2,651
17,700	**17,750**	2,659	2,659	2,659	2,659
17,750	**17,800**	2,666	2,666	2,666	2,666
17,800	**17,850**	2,674	2,674	2,674	2,674
17,850	**17,900**	2,681	2,681	2,681	2,681
17,900	**17,950**	2,689	2,689	2,689	2,689
17,950	**18,000**	2,696	2,696	2,696	2,696
18,000					
18,000	**18,050**	2,704	2,704	2,704	2,704
18,050	**18,100**	2,711	2,711	2,711	2,711
18,100	**18,150**	2,719	2,719	2,719	2,719
18,150	**18,200**	2,726	2,726	2,726	2,726
18,200	**18,250**	2,734	2,734	2,734	2,734
18,250	**18,300**	2,741	2,741	2,741	2,741
18,300	**18,350**	2,749	2,749	2,749	2,749
18,350	**18,400**	2,756	2,756	2,756	2,756
18,400	**18,450**	2,764	2,764	2,764	2,764
18,450	**18,500**	2,771	2,771	2,771	2,771
18,500	**18,550**	2,779	2,779	2,779	2,779
18,550	**18,600**	2,786	2,786	2,786	2,786
18,600	**18,650**	2,794	2,794	2,794	2,794
18,650	**18,700**	2,801	2,801	2,801	2,801
18,700	**18,750**	2,809	2,809	2,809	2,809
18,750	**18,800**	2,816	2,816	2,816	2,816
18,800	**18,850**	2,824	2,824	2,824	2,824
18,850	**18,900**	2,831	2,831	2,831	2,831
18,900	**18,950**	2,839	2,839	2,839	2,839
18,950	**19,000**	2,846	2,846	2,846	2,846
19,000					
19,000	**19,050**	2,854	2,854	2,854	2,854
19,050	**19,100**	2,861	2,861	2,861	2,861
19,100	**19,150**	2,869	2,869	2,869	2,869
19,150	**19,200**	2,876	2,876	2,876	2,876
19,200	**19,250**	2,884	2,884	2,884	2,884
19,250	**19,300**	2,891	2,891	2,891	2,891
19,300	**19,350**	2,899	2,899	2,899	2,899
19,350	**19,400**	2,906	2,906	2,906	2,906
19,400	**19,450**	2,914	2,914	2,914	2,914
19,450	**19,500**	2,921	2,921	2,921	2,921
19,500	**19,550**	2,929	2,929	2,932	2,929
19,550	**19,600**	2,936	2,936	2,946	2,936
19,600	**19,650**	2,944	2,944	2,960	2,944
19,650	**19,700**	2,951	2,951	2,974	2,951
19,700	**19,750**	2,959	2,959	2,988	2,959
19,750	**19,800**	2,966	2,966	3,002	2,966
19,800	**19,850**	2,974	2,974	3,016	2,974
19,850	**19,900**	2,981	2,981	3,030	2,981
19,900	**19,950**	2,989	2,989	3,044	2,989
19,950	**20,000**	2,996	2,996	3,058	2,996

If line 37 (taxable income) is— At least	But less than	And you are— Single	Married filing jointly *	Married filing separately	Head of a household
		Your tax is—			
20,000					
20,000	**20,050**	3,004	3,004	3,072	3,004
20,050	**20,100**	3,011	3,011	3,086	3,011
20,100	**20,150**	3,019	3,019	3,100	3,019
20,150	**20,200**	3,026	3,026	3,114	3,026
20,200	**20,250**	3,034	3,034	3,128	3,034
20,250	**20,300**	3,041	3,041	3,142	3,041
20,300	**20,350**	3,049	3,049	3,156	3,049
20,350	**20,400**	3,056	3,056	3,170	3,056
20,400	**20,450**	3,064	3,064	3,184	3,064
20,450	**20,500**	3,071	3,071	3,198	3,071
20,500	**20,550**	3,079	3,079	3,212	3,079
20,550	**20,600**	3,086	3,086	3,226	3,086
20,600	**20,650**	3,094	3,094	3,240	3,094
20,650	**20,700**	3,101	3,101	3,254	3,101
20,700	**20,750**	3,109	3,109	3,268	3,109
20,750	**20,800**	3,116	3,116	3,282	3,116
20,800	**20,850**	3,124	3,124	3,296	3,124
20,850	**20,900**	3,131	3,131	3,310	3,131
20,900	**20,950**	3,139	3,139	3,324	3,139
20,950	**21,000**	3,146	3,146	3,338	3,146
21,000					
21,000	**21,050**	3,154	3,154	3,352	3,154
21,050	**21,100**	3,161	3,161	3,366	3,161
21,100	**21,150**	3,169	3,169	3,380	3,169
21,150	**21,200**	3,176	3,176	3,394	3,176
21,200	**21,250**	3,184	3,184	3,408	3,184
21,250	**21,300**	3,191	3,191	3,422	3,191
21,300	**21,350**	3,199	3,199	3,436	3,199
21,350	**21,400**	3,206	3,206	3,450	3,206
21,400	**21,450**	3,214	3,214	3,464	3,214
21,450	**21,500**	3,221	3,221	3,478	3,221
21,500	**21,550**	3,229	3,229	3,492	3,229
21,550	**21,600**	3,236	3,236	3,506	3,236
21,600	**21,650**	3,244	3,244	3,520	3,244
21,650	**21,700**	3,251	3,251	3,534	3,251
21,700	**21,750**	3,259	3,259	3,548	3,259
21,750	**21,800**	3,266	3,266	3,562	3,266
21,800	**21,850**	3,274	3,274	3,576	3,274
21,850	**21,900**	3,281	3,281	3,590	3,281
21,900	**21,950**	3,289	3,289	3,604	3,289
21,950	**22,000**	3,296	3,296	3,618	3,296
22,000					
22,000	**22,050**	3,304	3,304	3,632	3,304
22,050	**22,100**	3,311	3,311	3,646	3,311
22,100	**22,150**	3,319	3,319	3,660	3,319
22,150	**22,200**	3,326	3,326	3,674	3,326
22,200	**22,250**	3,334	3,334	3,688	3,334
22,250	**22,300**	3,341	3,341	3,702	3,341
22,300	**22,350**	3,349	3,349	3,716	3,349
22,350	**22,400**	3,356	3,356	3,730	3,356
22,400	**22,450**	3,364	3,364	3,744	3,364
22,450	**22,500**	3,371	3,371	3,758	3,371
22,500	**22,550**	3,379	3,379	3,772	3,379
22,550	**22,600**	3,386	3,386	3,786	3,386
22,600	**22,650**	3,394	3,394	3,800	3,394
22,650	**22,700**	3,401	3,401	3,814	3,401
22,700	**22,750**	3,409	3,409	3,828	3,409
22,750	**22,800**	3,416	3,416	3,842	3,416
22,800	**22,850**	3,424	3,424	3,856	3,424
22,850	**22,900**	3,431	3,431	3,870	3,431
22,900	**22,950**	3,439	3,439	3,884	3,439
22,950	**23,000**	3,446	3,446	3,898	3,446

* This column must also be used by a qualifying widow(er).

Continued on next page

1995 Tax Table—*Continued*

If line 37 (taxable income) is—		And you are—			
At least	But less than	Single	Married filing jointly *	Married filing separately	Head of a household
		Your tax is—			
23,000					
23,000	**23,050**	3,454	3,454	3,912	3,454
23,050	**23,100**	3,461	3,461	3,926	3,461
23,100	**23,150**	3,469	3,469	3,940	3,469
23,150	**23,200**	3,476	3,476	3,954	3,476
23,200	**23,250**	3,484	3,484	3,968	3,484
23,250	**23,300**	3,491	3,491	3,982	3,491
23,300	**23,350**	3,499	3,499	3,996	3,499
23,350	**23,400**	3,510	3,506	4,010	3,506
23,400	**23,450**	3,524	3,514	4,024	3,514
23,450	**23,500**	3,538	3,521	4,038	3,521
23,500	**23,550**	3,552	3,529	4,052	3,529
23,550	**23,600**	3,566	3,536	4,066	3,536
23,600	**23,650**	3,580	3,544	4,080	3,544
23,650	**23,700**	3,594	3,551	4,094	3,551
23,700	**23,750**	3,608	3,559	4,108	3,559
23,750	**23,800**	3,622	3,566	4,122	3,566
23,800	**23,850**	3,636	3,574	4,136	3,574
23,850	**23,900**	3,650	3,581	4,150	3,581
23,900	**23,950**	3,664	3,589	4,164	3,589
23,950	**24,000**	3,678	3,596	4,178	3,596
24,000					
24,000	**24,050**	3,692	3,604	4,192	3,604
24,050	**24,100**	3,706	3,611	4,206	3,611
24,100	**24,150**	3,720	3,619	4,220	3,619
24,150	**24,200**	3,734	3,626	4,234	3,626
24,200	**24,250**	3,748	3,634	4,248	3,634
24,250	**24,300**	3,762	3,641	4,262	3,641
24,300	**24,350**	3,776	3,649	4,276	3,649
24,350	**24,400**	3,790	3,656	4,290	3,656
24,400	**24,450**	3,804	3,664	4,304	3,664
24,450	**24,500**	3,818	3,671	4,318	3,671
24,500	**24,550**	3,832	3,679	4,332	3,679
24,550	**24,600**	3,846	3,686	4,346	3,686
24,600	**24,650**	3,860	3,694	4,360	3,694
24,650	**24,700**	3,874	3,701	4,374	3,701
24,700	**24,750**	3,888	3,709	4,388	3,709
24,750	**24,800**	3,902	3,716	4,402	3,716
24,800	**24,850**	3,916	3,724	4,416	3,724
24,850	**24,900**	3,930	3,731	4,430	3,731
24,900	**24,950**	3,944	3,739	4,444	3,739
24,950	**25,000**	3,958	3,746	4,458	3,746
25,000					
25,000	**25,050**	3,972	3,754	4,472	3,754
25,050	**25,100**	3,986	3,761	4,486	3,761
25,100	**25,150**	4,000	3,769	4,500	3,769
25,150	**25,200**	4,014	3,776	4,514	3,776
25,200	**25,250**	4,028	3,784	4,528	3,784
25,250	**25,300**	4,042	3,791	4,542	3,791
25,300	**25,350**	4,056	3,799	4,556	3,799
25,350	**25,400**	4,070	3,806	4,570	3,806
25,400	**25,450**	4,084	3,814	4,584	3,814
25,450	**25,500**	4,098	3,821	4,598	3,821
25,500	**25,550**	4,112	3,829	4,612	3,829
25,550	**25,600**	4,126	3,836	4,626	3,836
25,600	**25,650**	4,140	3,844	4,640	3,844
25,650	**25,700**	4,154	3,851	4,654	3,851
25,700	**25,750**	4,168	3,859	4,668	3,859
25,750	**25,800**	4,182	3,866	4,682	3,866
25,800	**25,850**	4,196	3,874	4,696	3,874
25,850	**25,900**	4,210	3,881	4,710	3,881
25,900	**25,950**	4,224	3,889	4,724	3,889
25,950	**26,000**	4,238	3,896	4,738	3,896
26,000					
26,000	**26,050**	4,252	3,904	4,752	3,904
26,050	**26,100**	4,266	3,911	4,766	3,911
26,100	**26,150**	4,280	3,919	4,780	3,919
26,150	**26,200**	4,294	3,926	4,794	3,926
26,200	**26,250**	4,308	3,934	4,808	3,934
26,250	**26,300**	4,322	3,941	4,822	3,941
26,300	**26,350**	4,336	3,949	4,836	3,949
26,350	**26,400**	4,350	3,956	4,850	3,956
26,400	**26,450**	4,364	3,964	4,864	3,964
26,450	**26,500**	4,378	3,971	4,878	3,971
26,500	**26,550**	4,392	3,979	4,892	3,979
26,550	**26,600**	4,406	3,986	4,906	3,986
26,600	**26,650**	4,420	3,994	4,920	3,994
26,650	**26,700**	4,434	4,001	4,934	4,001
26,700	**26,750**	4,448	4,009	4,948	4,009
26,750	**26,800**	4,462	4,016	4,962	4,016
26,800	**26,850**	4,476	4,024	4,976	4,024
26,850	**26,900**	4,490	4,031	4,990	4,031
26,900	**26,950**	4,504	4,039	5,004	4,039
26,950	**27,000**	4,518	4,046	5,018	4,046
27,000					
27,000	**27,050**	4,532	4,054	5,032	4,054
27,050	**27,100**	4,546	4,061	5,046	4,061
27,100	**27,150**	4,560	4,069	5,060	4,069
27,150	**27,200**	4,574	4,076	5,074	4,076
27,200	**27,250**	4,588	4,084	5,088	4,084
27,250	**27,300**	4,602	4,091	5,102	4,091
27,300	**27,350**	4,616	4,099	5,116	4,099
27,350	**27,400**	4,630	4,106	5,130	4,106
27,400	**27,450**	4,644	4,114	5,144	4,114
27,450	**27,500**	4,658	4,121	5,158	4,121
27,500	**27,550**	4,672	4,129	5,172	4,129
27,550	**27,600**	4,686	4,136	5,186	4,136
27,600	**27,650**	4,700	4,144	5,200	4,144
27,650	**27,700**	4,714	4,151	5,214	4,151
27,700	**27,750**	4,728	4,159	5,228	4,159
27,750	**27,800**	4,742	4,166	5,242	4,166
27,800	**27,850**	4,756	4,174	5,256	4,174
27,850	**27,900**	4,770	4,181	5,270	4,181
27,900	**27,950**	4,784	4,189	5,284	4,189
27,950	**28,000**	4,798	4,196	5,298	4,196
28,000					
28,000	**28,050**	4,812	4,204	5,312	4,204
28,050	**28,100**	4,826	4,211	5,326	4,211
28,100	**28,150**	4,840	4,219	5,340	4,219
28,150	**28,200**	4,854	4,226	5,354	4,226
28,200	**28,250**	4,868	4,234	5,368	4,234
28,250	**28,300**	4,882	4,241	5,382	4,241
28,300	**28,350**	4,896	4,249	5,396	4,249
28,350	**28,400**	4,910	4,256	5,410	4,256
28,400	**28,450**	4,924	4,264	5,424	4,264
28,450	**28,500**	4,938	4,271	5,438	4,271
28,500	**28,550**	4,952	4,279	5,452	4,279
28,550	**28,600**	4,966	4,286	5,466	4,286
28,600	**28,650**	4,980	4,294	5,480	4,294
28,650	**28,700**	4,994	4,301	5,494	4,301
28,700	**28,750**	5,008	4,309	5,508	4,309
28,750	**28,800**	5,022	4,316	5,522	4,316
28,800	**28,850**	5,036	4,324	5,536	4,324
28,850	**28,900**	5,050	4,331	5,550	4,331
28,900	**28,950**	5,064	4,339	5,564	4,339
28,950	**29,000**	5,078	4,346	5,578	4,346
29,000					
29,000	**29,050**	5,092	4,354	5,592	4,354
29,050	**29,100**	5,106	4,361	5,606	4,361
29,100	**29,150**	5,120	4,369	5,620	4,369
29,150	**29,200**	5,134	4,376	5,634	4,376
29,200	**29,250**	5,148	4,384	5,648	4,384
29,250	**29,300**	5,162	4,391	5,662	4,391
29,300	**29,350**	5,176	4,399	5,676	4,399
29,350	**29,400**	5,190	4,406	5,690	4,406
29,400	**29,450**	5,204	4,414	5,704	4,414
29,450	**29,500**	5,218	4,421	5,718	4,421
29,500	**29,550**	5,232	4,429	5,732	4,429
29,550	**29,600**	5,246	4,436	5,746	4,436
29,600	**29,650**	5,260	4,444	5,760	4,444
29,650	**29,700**	5,274	4,451	5,774	4,451
29,700	**29,750**	5,288	4,459	5,788	4,459
29,750	**29,800**	5,302	4,466	5,802	4,466
29,800	**29,850**	5,316	4,474	5,816	4,474
29,850	**29,900**	5,330	4,481	5,830	4,481
29,900	**29,950**	5,344	4,489	5,844	4,489
29,950	**30,000**	5,358	4,496	5,858	4,496
30,000					
30,000	**30,050**	5,372	4,504	5,872	4,504
30,050	**30,100**	5,386	4,511	5,886	4,511
30,100	**30,150**	5,400	4,519	5,900	4,519
30,150	**30,200**	5,414	4,526	5,914	4,526
30,200	**30,250**	5,428	4,534	5,928	4,534
30,250	**30,300**	5,442	4,541	5,942	4,541
30,300	**30,350**	5,456	4,549	5,956	4,549
30,350	**30,400**	5,470	4,556	5,970	4,556
30,400	**30,450**	5,484	4,564	5,984	4,564
30,450	**30,500**	5,498	4,571	5,998	4,571
30,500	**30,550**	5,512	4,579	6,012	4,579
30,550	**30,600**	5,526	4,586	6,026	4,586
30,600	**30,650**	5,540	4,594	6,040	4,594
30,650	**30,700**	5,554	4,601	6,054	4,601
30,700	**30,750**	5,568	4,609	6,068	4,609
30,750	**30,800**	5,582	4,616	6,082	4,616
30,800	**30,850**	5,596	4,624	6,096	4,624
30,850	**30,900**	5,610	4,631	6,110	4,631
30,900	**30,950**	5,624	4,639	6,124	4,639
30,950	**31,000**	5,638	4,646	6,138	4,646
31,000					
31,000	**31,050**	5,652	4,654	6,152	4,654
31,050	**31,100**	5,666	4,661	6,166	4,661
31,100	**31,150**	5,680	4,669	6,180	4,669
31,150	**31,200**	5,694	4,676	6,194	4,676
31,200	**31,250**	5,708	4,684	6,208	4,684
31,250	**31,300**	5,722	4,691	6,222	4,695
31,300	**31,350**	5,736	4,699	6,236	4,709
31,350	**31,400**	5,750	4,706	6,250	4,723
31,400	**31,450**	5,764	4,714	6,264	4,737
31,450	**31,500**	5,778	4,721	6,278	4,751
31,500	**31,550**	5,792	4,729	6,292	4,765
31,550	**31,600**	5,806	4,736	6,306	4,779
31,600	**31,650**	5,820	4,744	6,320	4,793
31,650	**31,700**	5,834	4,751	6,334	4,807
31,700	**31,750**	5,848	4,759	6,348	4,821
31,750	**31,800**	5,862	4,766	6,362	4,835
31,800	**31,850**	5,876	4,774	6,376	4,849
31,850	**31,900**	5,890	4,781	6,390	4,863
31,900	**31,950**	5,904	4,789	6,404	4,877
31,950	**32,000**	5,918	4,796	6,418	4,891

* This column must also be used by a qualifying widow(er).

Continued on next page

1995 Tax Table—*Continued*

If line 37 (taxable income) is— At least	But less than	And you are— Single	Married filing jointly *	Married filing separately	Head of a household
		Your tax is—			
32,000					
32,000	**32,050**	5,932	4,804	6,432	4,905
32,050	**32,100**	5,946	4,811	6,446	4,919
32,100	**32,150**	5,960	4,819	6,460	4,933
32,150	**32,200**	5,974	4,826	6,474	4,947
32,200	**32,250**	5,988	4,834	6,488	4,961
32,250	**32,300**	6,002	4,841	6,502	4,975
32,300	**32,350**	6,016	4,849	6,516	4,989
32,350	**32,400**	6,030	4,856	6,530	5,003
32,400	**32,450**	6,044	4,864	6,544	5,017
32,450	**32,500**	6,058	4,871	6,558	5,031
32,500	**32,550**	6,072	4,879	6,572	5,045
32,550	**32,600**	6,086	4,886	6,586	5,059
32,600	**32,650**	6,100	4,894	6,600	5,073
32,650	**32,700**	6,114	4,901	6,614	5,087
32,700	**32,750**	6,128	4,909	6,628	5,101
32,750	**32,800**	6,142	4,916	6,642	5,115
32,800	**32,850**	6,156	4,924	6,656	5,129
32,850	**32,900**	6,170	4,931	6,670	5,143
32,900	**32,950**	6,184	4,939	6,684	5,157
32,950	**33,000**	6,198	4,946	6,698	5,171
33,000					
33,000	**33,050**	6,212	4,954	6,712	5,185
33,050	**33,100**	6,226	4,961	6,726	5,199
33,100	**33,150**	6,240	4,969	6,740	5,213
33,150	**33,200**	6,254	4,976	6,754	5,227
33,200	**33,250**	6,268	4,984	6,768	5,241
33,250	**33,300**	6,282	4,991	6,782	5,255
33,300	**33,350**	6,296	4,999	6,796	5,269
33,350	**33,400**	6,310	5,006	6,810	5,283
33,400	**33,450**	6,324	5,014	6,824	5,297
33,450	**33,500**	6,338	5,021	6,838	5,311
33,500	**33,550**	6,352	5,029	6,852	5,325
33,550	**33,600**	6,366	5,036	6,866	5,339
33,600	**33,650**	6,380	5,044	6,880	5,353
33,650	**33,700**	6,394	5,051	6,894	5,367
33,700	**33,750**	6,408	5,059	6,908	5,381
33,750	**33,800**	6,422	5,066	6,922	5,395
33,800	**33,850**	6,436	5,074	6,936	5,409
33,850	**33,900**	6,450	5,081	6,950	5,423
33,900	**33,950**	6,464	5,089	6,964	5,437
33,950	**34,000**	6,478	5,096	6,978	5,451
34,000					
34,000	**34,050**	6,492	5,104	6,992	5,465
34,050	**34,100**	6,506	5,111	7,006	5,479
34,100	**34,150**	6,520	5,119	7,020	5,493
34,150	**34,200**	6,534	5,126	7,034	5,507
34,200	**34,250**	6,548	5,134	7,048	5,521
34,250	**34,300**	6,562	5,141	7,062	5,535
34,300	**34,350**	6,576	5,149	7,076	5,549
34,350	**34,400**	6,590	5,156	7,090	5,563
34,400	**34,450**	6,604	5,164	7,104	5,577
34,450	**34,500**	6,618	5,171	7,118	5,591
34,500	**34,550**	6,632	5,179	7,132	5,605
34,550	**34,600**	6,646	5,186	7,146	5,619
34,600	**34,650**	6,660	5,194	7,160	5,633
34,650	**34,700**	6,674	5,201	7,174	5,647
34,700	**34,750**	6,688	5,209	7,188	5,661
34,750	**34,800**	6,702	5,216	7,202	5,675
34,800	**34,850**	6,716	5,224	7,216	5,689
34,850	**34,900**	6,730	5,231	7,230	5,703
34,900	**34,950**	6,744	5,239	7,244	5,717
34,950	**35,000**	6,758	5,246	7,258	5,731

If line 37 (taxable income) is— At least	But less than	And you are— Single	Married filing jointly *	Married filing separately	Head of a household
		Your tax is—			
35,000					
35,000	**35,050**	6,772	5,254	7,272	5,745
35,050	**35,100**	6,786	5,261	7,286	5,759
35,100	**35,150**	6,800	5,269	7,300	5,773
35,150	**35,200**	6,814	5,276	7,314	5,787
35,200	**35,250**	6,828	5,284	7,328	5,801
35,250	**35,300**	6,842	5,291	7,342	5,815
35,300	**35,350**	6,856	5,299	7,356	5,829
35,350	**35,400**	6,870	5,306	7,370	5,843
35,400	**35,450**	6,884	5,314	7,384	5,857
35,450	**35,500**	6,898	5,321	7,398	5,871
35,500	**35,550**	6,912	5,329	7,412	5,885
35,550	**35,600**	6,926	5,336	7,426	5,899
35,600	**35,650**	6,940	5,344	7,440	5,913
35,650	**35,700**	6,954	5,351	7,454	5,927
35,700	**35,750**	6,968	5,359	7,468	5,941
35,750	**35,800**	6,982	5,366	7,482	5,955
35,800	**35,850**	6,996	5,374	7,496	5,969
35,850	**35,900**	7,010	5,381	7,510	5,983
35,900	**35,950**	7,024	5,389	7,524	5,997
35,950	**36,000**	7,038	5,396	7,538	6,011
36,000					
36,000	**36,050**	7,052	5,404	7,552	6,025
36,050	**36,100**	7,066	5,411	7,566	6,039
36,100	**36,150**	7,080	5,419	7,580	6,053
36,150	**36,200**	7,094	5,426	7,594	6,067
36,200	**36,250**	7,108	5,434	7,608	6,081
36,250	**36,300**	7,122	5,441	7,622	6,095
36,300	**36,350**	7,136	5,449	7,636	6,109
36,350	**36,400**	7,150	5,456	7,650	6,123
36,400	**36,450**	7,164	5,464	7,664	6,137
36,450	**36,500**	7,178	5,471	7,678	6,151
36,500	**36,550**	7,192	5,479	7,692	6,165
36,550	**36,600**	7,206	5,486	7,706	6,179
36,600	**36,650**	7,220	5,494	7,720	6,193
36,650	**36,700**	7,234	5,501	7,734	6,207
36,700	**36,750**	7,248	5,509	7,748	6,221
36,750	**36,800**	7,262	5,516	7,762	6,235
36,800	**36,850**	7,276	5,524	7,776	6,249
36,850	**36,900**	7,290	5,531	7,790	6,263
36,900	**36,950**	7,304	5,539	7,804	6,277
36,950	**37,000**	7,318	5,546	7,818	6,291
37,000					
37,000	**37,050**	7,332	5,554	7,832	6,305
37,050	**37,100**	7,346	5,561	7,846	6,319
37,100	**37,150**	7,360	5,569	7,860	6,333
37,150	**37,200**	7,374	5,576	7,874	6,347
37,200	**37,250**	7,388	5,584	7,888	6,361
37,250	**37,300**	7,402	5,591	7,902	6,375
37,300	**37,350**	7,416	5,599	7,916	6,389
37,350	**37,400**	7,430	5,606	7,930	6,403
37,400	**37,450**	7,444	5,614	7,944	6,417
37,450	**37,500**	7,458	5,621	7,958	6,431
37,500	**37,550**	7,472	5,629	7,972	6,445
37,550	**37,600**	7,486	5,636	7,986	6,459
37,600	**37,650**	7,500	5,644	8,000	6,473
37,650	**37,700**	7,514	5,651	8,014	6,487
37,700	**37,750**	7,528	5,659	8,028	6,501
37,750	**37,800**	7,542	5,666	8,042	6,515
37,800	**37,850**	7,556	5,674	8,056	6,529
37,850	**37,900**	7,570	5,681	8,070	6,543
37,900	**37,950**	7,584	5,689	8,084	6,557
37,950	**38,000**	7,598	5,696	8,098	6,571

If line 37 (taxable income) is— At least	But less than	And you are— Single	Married filing jointly *	Married filing separately	Head of a household
		Your tax is—			
38,000					
38,000	**38,050**	7,612	5,704	8,112	6,585
38,050	**38,100**	7,626	5,711	8,126	6,599
38,100	**38,150**	7,640	5,719	8,140	6,613
38,150	**38,200**	7,654	5,726	8,154	6,627
38,200	**38,250**	7,668	5,734	8,168	6,641
38,250	**38,300**	7,682	5,741	8,182	6,655
38,300	**38,350**	7,696	5,749	8,196	6,669
38,350	**38,400**	7,710	5,756	8,210	6,683
38,400	**38,450**	7,724	5,764	8,224	6,697
38,450	**38,500**	7,738	5,771	8,238	6,711
38,500	**38,550**	7,752	5,779	8,252	6,725
38,550	**38,600**	7,766	5,786	8,266	6,739
38,600	**38,650**	7,780	5,794	8,280	6,753
38,650	**38,700**	7,794	5,801	8,294	6,767
38,700	**38,750**	7,808	5,809	8,308	6,781
38,750	**38,800**	7,822	5,816	8,322	6,795
38,800	**38,850**	7,836	5,824	8,336	6,809
38,850	**38,900**	7,850	5,831	8,350	6,823
38,900	**38,950**	7,864	5,839	8,364	6,837
38,950	**39,000**	7,878	5,846	8,378	6,851
39,000					
39,000	**39,050**	7,892	5,857	8,392	6,865
39,050	**39,100**	7,906	5,871	8,406	6,879
39,100	**39,150**	7,920	5,885	8,420	6,893
39,150	**39,200**	7,934	5,899	8,434	6,907
39,200	**39,250**	7,948	5,913	8,448	6,921
39,250	**39,300**	7,962	5,927	8,462	6,935
39,300	**39,350**	7,976	5,941	8,476	6,949
39,350	**39,400**	7,990	5,955	8,490	6,963
39,400	**39,450**	8,004	5,969	8,504	6,977
39,450	**39,500**	8,018	5,983	8,518	6,991
39,500	**39,550**	8,032	5,997	8,532	7,005
39,550	**39,600**	8,046	6,011	8,546	7,019
39,600	**39,650**	8,060	6,025	8,560	7,033
39,650	**39,700**	8,074	6,039	8,574	7,047
39,700	**39,750**	8,088	6,053	8,588	7,061
39,750	**39,800**	8,102	6,067	8,602	7,075
39,800	**39,850**	8,116	6,081	8,616	7,089
39,850	**39,900**	8,130	6,095	8,630	7,103
39,900	**39,950**	8,144	6,109	8,644	7,117
39,950	**40,000**	8,158	6,123	8,658	7,131
40,000					
40,000	**40,050**	8,172	6,137	8,672	7,145
40,050	**40,100**	8,186	6,151	8,686	7,159
40,100	**40,150**	8,200	6,165	8,700	7,173
40,150	**40,200**	8,214	6,179	8,714	7,187
40,200	**40,250**	8,228	6,193	8,728	7,201
40,250	**40,300**	8,242	6,207	8,742	7,215
40,300	**40,350**	8,256	6,221	8,756	7,229
40,350	**40,400**	8,270	6,235	8,770	7,243
40,400	**40,450**	8,284	6,249	8,784	7,257
40,450	**40,500**	8,298	6,263	8,798	7,271
40,500	**40,550**	8,312	6,277	8,812	7,285
40,550	**40,600**	8,326	6,291	8,826	7,299
40,600	**40,650**	8,340	6,305	8,840	7,313
40,650	**40,700**	8,354	6,319	8,854	7,327
40,700	**40,750**	8,368	6,333	8,868	7,341
40,750	**40,800**	8,382	6,347	8,882	7,355
40,800	**40,850**	8,396	6,361	8,896	7,369
40,850	**40,900**	8,410	6,375	8,910	7,383
40,900	**40,950**	8,424	6,389	8,924	7,397
40,950	**41,000**	8,438	6,403	8,938	7,411

* This column must also be used by a qualifying widow(er).

Continued on next page

1995 Tax Table—*Continued*

If line 37 (taxable income) is— At least	But less than	And you are— Single	Married filing jointly *	Married filing separately	Head of a household
		Your tax is—			
41,000					
41,000	41,050	8,452	6,417	8,952	7,425
41,050	41,100	8,466	6,431	8,966	7,439
41,100	41,150	8,480	6,445	8,980	7,453
41,150	41,200	8,494	6,459	8,994	7,467
41,200	41,250	8,508	6,473	9,008	7,481
41,250	41,300	8,522	6,487	9,022	7,495
41,300	41,350	8,536	6,501	9,036	7,509
41,350	41,400	8,550	6,515	9,050	7,523
41,400	41,450	8,564	6,529	9,064	7,537
41,450	41,500	8,578	6,543	9,078	7,551
41,500	41,550	8,592	6,557	9,092	7,565
41,550	41,600	8,606	6,571	9,106	7,579
41,600	41,650	8,620	6,585	9,120	7,593
41,650	41,700	8,634	6,599	9,134	7,607
41,700	41,750	8,648	6,613	9,148	7,621
41,750	41,800	8,662	6,627	9,162	7,635
41,800	41,850	8,676	6,641	9,176	7,649
41,850	41,900	8,690	6,655	9,190	7,663
41,900	41,950	8,704	6,669	9,204	7,677
41,950	42,000	8,718	6,683	9,218	7,691
42,000					
42,000	42,050	8,732	6,697	9,232	7,705
42,050	42,100	8,746	6,711	9,246	7,719
42,100	42,150	8,760	6,725	9,260	7,733
42,150	42,200	8,774	6,739	9,274	7,747
42,200	42,250	8,788	6,753	9,288	7,761
42,250	42,300	8,802	6,767	9,302	7,775
42,300	42,350	8,816	6,781	9,316	7,789
42,350	42,400	8,830	6,795	9,330	7,803
42,400	42,450	8,844	6,809	9,344	7,817
42,450	42,500	8,858	6,823	9,358	7,831
42,500	42,550	8,872	6,837	9,372	7,845
42,550	42,600	8,886	6,851	9,386	7,859
42,600	42,650	8,900	6,865	9,400	7,873
42,650	42,700	8,914	6,879	9,414	7,887
42,700	42,750	8,928	6,893	9,428	7,901
42,750	42,800	8,942	6,907	9,442	7,915
42,800	42,850	8,956	6,921	9,456	7,929
42,850	42,900	8,970	6,935	9,470	7,943
42,900	42,950	8,984	6,949	9,484	7,957
42,950	43,000	8,998	6,963	9,498	7,971
43,000					
43,000	43,050	9,012	6,977	9,512	7,985
43,050	43,100	9,026	6,991	9,526	7,999
43,100	43,150	9,040	7,005	9,540	8,013
43,150	43,200	9,054	7,019	9,554	8,027
43,200	43,250	9,068	7,033	9,568	8,041
43,250	43,300	9,082	7,047	9,582	8,055
43,300	43,350	9,096	7,061	9,596	8,069
43,350	43,400	9,110	7,075	9,610	8,083
43,400	43,450	9,124	7,089	9,624	8,097
43,450	43,500	9,138	7,103	9,638	8,111
43,500	43,550	9,152	7,117	9,652	8,125
43,550	43,600	9,166	7,131	9,666	8,139
43,600	43,650	9,180	7,145	9,680	8,153
43,650	43,700	9,194	7,159	9,694	8,167
43,700	43,750	9,208	7,173	9,708	8,181
43,750	43,800	9,222	7,187	9,722	8,195
43,800	43,850	9,236	7,201	9,736	8,209
43,850	43,900	9,250	7,215	9,750	8,223
43,900	43,950	9,264	7,229	9,764	8,237
43,950	44,000	9,278	7,243	9,778	8,251
44,000					
44,000	44,050	9,292	7,257	9,792	8,265
44,050	44,100	9,306	7,271	9,806	8,279
44,100	44,150	9,320	7,285	9,820	8,293
44,150	44,200	9,334	7,299	9,834	8,307
44,200	44,250	9,348	7,313	9,848	8,321
44,250	44,300	9,362	7,327	9,862	8,335
44,300	44,350	9,376	7,341	9,876	8,349
44,350	44,400	9,390	7,355	9,890	8,363
44,400	44,450	9,404	7,369	9,904	8,377
44,450	44,500	9,418	7,383	9,918	8,391
44,500	44,550	9,432	7,397	9,932	8,405
44,550	44,600	9,446	7,411	9,946	8,419
44,600	44,650	9,460	7,425	9,960	8,433
44,650	44,700	9,474	7,439	9,974	8,447
44,700	44,750	9,488	7,453	9,988	8,461
44,750	44,800	9,502	7,467	10,002	8,475
44,800	44,850	9,516	7,481	10,016	8,489
44,850	44,900	9,530	7,495	10,030	8,503
44,900	44,950	9,544	7,509	10,044	8,517
44,950	45,000	9,558	7,523	10,058	8,531
45,000					
45,000	45,050	9,572	7,537	10,072	8,545
45,050	45,100	9,586	7,551	10,086	8,559
45,100	45,150	9,600	7,565	10,100	8,573
45,150	45,200	9,614	7,579	10,114	8,587
45,200	45,250	9,628	7,593	10,128	8,601
45,250	45,300	9,642	7,607	10,142	8,615
45,300	45,350	9,656	7,621	10,156	8,629
45,350	45,400	9,670	7,635	10,170	8,643
45,400	45,450	9,684	7,649	10,184	8,657
45,450	45,500	9,698	7,663	10,198	8,671
45,500	45,550	9,712	7,677	10,212	8,685
45,550	45,600	9,726	7,691	10,226	8,699
45,600	45,650	9,740	7,705	10,240	8,713
45,650	45,700	9,754	7,719	10,254	8,727
45,700	45,750	9,768	7,733	10,268	8,741
45,750	45,800	9,782	7,747	10,282	8,755
45,800	45,850	9,796	7,761	10,296	8,769
45,850	45,900	9,810	7,775	10,310	8,783
45,900	45,950	9,824	7,789	10,324	8,797
45,950	46,000	9,838	7,803	10,338	8,811
46,000					
46,000	46,050	9,852	7,817	10,352	8,825
46,050	46,100	9,866	7,831	10,366	8,839
46,100	46,150	9,880	7,845	10,380	8,853
46,150	46,200	9,894	7,859	10,394	8,867
46,200	46,250	9,908	7,873	10,408	8,881
46,250	46,300	9,922	7,887	10,422	8,895
46,300	46,350	9,936	7,901	10,436	8,909
46,350	46,400	9,950	7,915	10,450	8,923
46,400	46,450	9,964	7,929	10,464	8,937
46,450	46,500	9,978	7,943	10,478	8,951
46,500	46,550	9,992	7,957	10,492	8,965
46,550	46,600	10,006	7,971	10,506	8,979
46,600	46,650	10,020	7,985	10,520	8,993
46,650	46,700	10,034	7,999	10,534	9,007
46,700	46,750	10,048	8,013	10,548	9,021
46,750	46,800	10,062	8,027	10,562	9,035
46,800	46,850	10,076	8,041	10,576	9,049
46,850	46,900	10,090	8,055	10,590	9,063
46,900	46,950	10,104	8,069	10,604	9,077
46,950	47,000	10,118	8,083	10,618	9,091
47,000					
47,000	47,050	10,132	8,097	10,632	9,105
47,050	47,100	10,146	8,111	10,646	9,119
47,100	47,150	10,160	8,125	10,660	9,133
47,150	47,200	10,174	8,139	10,676	9,147
47,200	47,250	10,188	8,153	10,691	9,161
47,250	47,300	10,202	8,167	10,707	9,175
47,300	47,350	10,216	8,181	10,722	9,189
47,350	47,400	10,230	8,195	10,738	9,203
47,400	47,450	10,244	8,209	10,753	9,217
47,450	47,500	10,258	8,223	10,769	9,231
47,500	47,550	10,272	8,237	10,784	9,245
47,550	47,600	10,286	8,251	10,800	9,259
47,600	47,650	10,300	8,265	10,815	9,273
47,650	47,700	10,314	8,279	10,831	9,287
47,700	47,750	10,328	8,293	10,846	9,301
47,750	47,800	10,342	8,307	10,862	9,315
47,800	47,850	10,356	8,321	10,877	9,329
47,850	47,900	10,370	8,335	10,893	9,343
47,900	47,950	10,384	8,349	10,908	9,357
47,950	48,000	10,398	8,363	10,924	9,371
48,000					
48,000	48,050	10,412	8,377	10,939	9,385
48,050	48,100	10,426	8,391	10,955	9,399
48,100	48,150	10,440	8,405	10,970	9,413
48,150	48,200	10,454	8,419	10,986	9,427
48,200	48,250	10,468	8,433	11,001	9,441
48,250	48,300	10,482	8,447	11,017	9,455
48,300	48,350	10,496	8,461	11,032	9,469
48,350	48,400	10,510	8,475	11,048	9,483
48,400	48,450	10,524	8,489	11,063	9,497
48,450	48,500	10,538	8,503	11,079	9,511
48,500	48,550	10,552	8,517	11,094	9,525
48,550	48,600	10,566	8,531	11,110	9,539
48,600	48,650	10,580	8,545	11,125	9,553
48,650	48,700	10,594	8,559	11,141	9,567
48,700	48,750	10,608	8,573	11,156	9,581
48,750	48,800	10,622	8,587	11,172	9,595
48,800	48,850	10,636	8,601	11,187	9,609
48,850	48,900	10,650	8,615	11,203	9,623
48,900	48,950	10,664	8,629	11,218	9,637
48,950	49,000	10,678	8,643	11,234	9,651
49,000					
49,000	49,050	10,692	8,657	11,249	9,665
49,050	49,100	10,706	8,671	11,265	9,679
49,100	49,150	10,720	8,685	11,280	9,693
49,150	49,200	10,734	8,699	11,296	9,707
49,200	49,250	10,748	8,713	11,311	9,721
49,250	49,300	10,762	8,727	11,327	9,735
49,300	49,350	10,776	8,741	11,342	9,749
49,350	49,400	10,790	8,755	11,358	9,763
49,400	49,450	10,804	8,769	11,373	9,777
49,450	49,500	10,818	8,783	11,389	9,791
49,500	49,550	10,832	8,797	11,404	9,805
49,550	49,600	10,846	8,811	11,420	9,819
49,600	49,650	10,860	8,825	11,435	9,833
49,650	49,700	10,874	8,839	11,451	9,847
49,700	49,750	10,888	8,853	11,466	9,861
49,750	49,800	10,902	8,867	11,482	9,875
49,800	49,850	10,916	8,881	11,497	9,889
49,850	49,900	10,930	8,895	11,513	9,903
49,900	49,950	10,944	8,909	11,528	9,917
49,950	50,000	10,958	8,923	11,544	9,931

* This column must also be used by a qualifying widow(er).

Continued on next page

1995 Tax Table—*Continued*

If line 37 (taxable income) is—		And you are—			
At least	But less than	Single	Married filing jointly *	Married filing sepa-rately	Head of a house-hold
		Your tax is—			
50,000					
50,000	**50,050**	10,972	8,937	11,559	9,945
50,050	**50,100**	10,986	8,951	11,575	9,959
50,100	**50,150**	11,000	8,965	11,590	9,973
50,150	**50,200**	11,014	8,979	11,606	9,987
50,200	**50,250**	11,028	8,993	11,621	10,001
50,250	**50,300**	11,042	9,007	11,637	10,015
50,300	**50,350**	11,056	9,021	11,652	10,029
50,350	**50,400**	11,070	9,035	11,668	10,043
50,400	**50,450**	11,084	9,049	11,683	10,057
50,450	**50,500**	11,098	9,063	11,699	10,071
50,500	**50,550**	11,112	9,077	11,714	10,085
50,550	**50,600**	11,126	9,091	11,730	10,099
50,600	**50,650**	11,140	9,105	11,745	10,113
50,650	**50,700**	11,154	9,119	11,761	10,127
50,700	**50,750**	11,168	9,133	11,776	10,141
50,750	**50,800**	11,182	9,147	11,792	10,155
50,800	**50,850**	11,196	9,161	11,807	10,169
50,850	**50,900**	11,210	9,175	11,823	10,183
50,900	**50,950**	11,224	9,189	11,838	10,197
50,950	**51,000**	11,238	9,203	11,854	10,211
51,000					
51,000	**51,050**	11,252	9,217	11,869	10,225
51,050	**51,100**	11,266	9,231	11,885	10,239
51,100	**51,150**	11,280	9,245	11,900	10,253
51,150	**51,200**	11,294	9,259	11,916	10,267
51,200	**51,250**	11,308	9,273	11,931	10,281
51,250	**51,300**	11,322	9,287	11,947	10,295
51,300	**51,350**	11,336	9,301	11,962	10,309
51,350	**51,400**	11,350	9,315	11,978	10,323
51,400	**51,450**	11,364	9,329	11,993	10,337
51,450	**51,500**	11,378	9,343	12,009	10,351
51,500	**51,550**	11,392	9,357	12,024	10,365
51,550	**51,600**	11,406	9,371	12,040	10,379
51,600	**51,650**	11,420	9,385	12,055	10,393
51,650	**51,700**	11,434	9,399	12,071	10,407
51,700	**51,750**	11,448	9,413	12,086	10,421
51,750	**51,800**	11,462	9,427	12,102	10,435
51,800	**51,850**	11,476	9,441	12,117	10,449
51,850	**51,900**	11,490	9,455	12,133	10,463
51,900	**51,950**	11,504	9,469	12,148	10,477
51,950	**52,000**	11,518	9,483	12,164	10,491
52,000					
52,000	**52,050**	11,532	9,497	12,179	10,505
52,050	**52,100**	11,546	9,511	12,195	10,519
52,100	**52,150**	11,560	9,525	12,210	10,533
52,150	**52,200**	11,574	9,539	12,226	10,547
52,200	**52,250**	11,588	9,553	12,241	10,561
52,250	**52,300**	11,602	9,567	12,257	10,575
52,300	**52,350**	11,616	9,581	12,272	10,589
52,350	**52,400**	11,630	9,595	12,288	10,603
52,400	**52,450**	11,644	9,609	12,303	10,617
52,450	**52,500**	11,658	9,623	12,319	10,631
52,500	**52,550**	11,672	9,637	12,334	10,645
52,550	**52,600**	11,686	9,651	12,350	10,659
52,600	**52,650**	11,700	9,665	12,365	10,673
52,650	**52,700**	11,714	9,679	12,381	10,687
52,700	**52,750**	11,728	9,693	12,396	10,701
52,750	**52,800**	11,742	9,707	12,412	10,715
52,800	**52,850**	11,756	9,721	12,427	10,729
52,850	**52,900**	11,770	9,735	12,443	10,743
52,900	**52,950**	11,784	9,749	12,458	10,757
52,950	**53,000**	11,798	9,763	12,474	10,771

If line 37 (taxable income) is—		And you are—			
At least	But less than	Single	Married filing jointly *	Married filing sepa-rately	Head of a house-hold
		Your tax is—			
53,000					
53,000	**53,050**	11,812	9,777	12,489	10,785
53,050	**53,100**	11,826	9,791	12,505	10,799
53,100	**53,150**	11,840	9,805	12,520	10,813
53,150	**53,200**	11,854	9,819	12,536	10,827
53,200	**53,250**	11,868	9,833	12,551	10,841
53,250	**53,300**	11,882	9,847	12,567	10,855
53,300	**53,350**	11,896	9,861	12,582	10,869
53,350	**53,400**	11,910	9,875	12,598	10,883
53,400	**53,450**	11,924	9,889	12,613	10,897
53,450	**53,500**	11,938	9,903	12,629	10,911
53,500	**53,550**	11,952	9,917	12,644	10,925
53,550	**53,600**	11,966	9,931	12,660	10,939
53,600	**53,650**	11,980	9,945	12,675	10,953
53,650	**53,700**	11,994	9,959	12,691	10,967
53,700	**53,750**	12,008	9,973	12,706	10,981
53,750	**53,800**	12,022	9,987	12,722	10,995
53,800	**53,850**	12,036	10,001	12,737	11,009
53,850	**53,900**	12,050	10,015	12,753	11,023
53,900	**53,950**	12,064	10,029	12,768	11,037
53,950	**54,000**	12,078	10,043	12,784	11,051
54,000					
54,000	**54,050**	12,092	10,057	12,799	11,065
54,050	**54,100**	12,106	10,071	12,815	11,079
54,100	**54,150**	12,120	10,085	12,830	11,093
54,150	**54,200**	12,134	10,099	12,846	11,107
54,200	**54,250**	12,148	10,113	12,861	11,121
54,250	**54,300**	12,162	10,127	12,877	11,135
54,300	**54,350**	12,176	10,141	12,892	11,149
54,350	**54,400**	12,190	10,155	12,908	11,163
54,400	**54,450**	12,204	10,169	12,923	11,177
54,450	**54,500**	12,218	10,183	12,939	11,191
54,500	**54,550**	12,232	10,197	12,954	11,205
54,550	**54,600**	12,246	10,211	12,970	11,219
54,600	**54,650**	12,260	10,225	12,985	11,233
54,650	**54,700**	12,274	10,239	13,001	11,247
54,700	**54,750**	12,288	10,253	13,016	11,261
54,750	**54,800**	12,302	10,267	13,032	11,275
54,800	**54,850**	12,316	10,281	13,047	11,289
54,850	**54,900**	12,330	10,295	13,063	11,303
54,900	**54,950**	12,344	10,309	13,078	11,317
54,950	**55,000**	12,358	10,323	13,094	11,331
55,000					
55,000	**55,050**	12,372	10,337	13,109	11,345
55,050	**55,100**	12,386	10,351	13,125	11,359
55,100	**55,150**	12,400	10,365	13,140	11,373
55,150	**55,200**	12,414	10,379	13,156	11,387
55,200	**55,250**	12,428	10,393	13,171	11,401
55,250	**55,300**	12,442	10,407	13,187	11,415
55,300	**55,350**	12,456	10,421	13,202	11,429
55,350	**55,400**	12,470	10,435	13,218	11,443
55,400	**55,450**	12,484	10,449	13,233	11,457
55,450	**55,500**	12,498	10,463	13,249	11,471
55,500	**55,550**	12,512	10,477	13,264	11,485
55,550	**55,600**	12,526	10,491	13,280	11,499
55,600	**55,650**	12,540	10,505	13,295	11,513
55,650	**55,700**	12,554	10,519	13,311	11,527
55,700	**55,750**	12,568	10,533	13,326	11,541
55,750	**55,800**	12,582	10,547	13,342	11,555
55,800	**55,850**	12,596	10,561	13,357	11,569
55,850	**55,900**	12,610	10,575	13,373	11,583
55,900	**55,950**	12,624	10,589	13,388	11,597
55,950	**56,000**	12,638	10,603	13,404	11,611

If line 37 (taxable income) is—		And you are—			
At least	But less than	Single	Married filing jointly *	Married filing sepa-rately	Head of a house-hold
		Your tax is—			
56,000					
56,000	**56,050**	12,652	10,617	13,419	11,625
56,050	**56,100**	12,666	10,631	13,435	11,639
56,100	**56,150**	12,680	10,645	13,450	11,653
56,150	**56,200**	12,694	10,659	13,466	11,667
56,200	**56,250**	12,708	10,673	13,481	11,681
56,250	**56,300**	12,722	10,687	13,497	11,695
56,300	**56,350**	12,736	10,701	13,512	11,709
56,350	**56,400**	12,750	10,715	13,528	11,723
56,400	**56,450**	12,764	10,729	13,543	11,737
56,450	**56,500**	12,778	10,743	13,559	11,751
56,500	**56,550**	12,792	10,757	13,574	11,765
56,550	**56,600**	12,806	10,771	13,590	11,779
56,600	**56,650**	12,822	10,785	13,605	11,793
56,650	**56,700**	12,837	10,799	13,621	11,807
56,700	**56,750**	12,853	10,813	13,636	11,821
56,750	**56,800**	12,868	10,827	13,652	11,835
56,800	**56,850**	12,884	10,841	13,667	11,849
56,850	**56,900**	12,899	10,855	13,683	11,863
56,900	**56,950**	12,915	10,869	13,698	11,877
56,950	**57,000**	12,930	10,883	13,714	11,891
57,000					
57,000	**57,050**	12,946	10,897	13,729	11,905
57,050	**57,100**	12,961	10,911	13,745	11,919
57,100	**57,150**	12,977	10,925	13,760	11,933
57,150	**57,200**	12,992	10,939	13,776	11,947
57,200	**57,250**	13,008	10,953	13,791	11,961
57,250	**57,300**	13,023	10,967	13,807	11,975
57,300	**57,350**	13,039	10,981	13,822	11,989
57,350	**57,400**	13,054	10,995	13,838	12,003
57,400	**57,450**	13,070	11,009	13,853	12,017
57,450	**57,500**	13,085	11,023	13,869	12,031
57,500	**57,550**	13,101	11,037	13,884	12,045
57,550	**57,600**	13,116	11,051	13,900	12,059
57,600	**57,650**	13,132	11,065	13,915	12,073
57,650	**57,700**	13,147	11,079	13,931	12,087
57,700	**57,750**	13,163	11,093	13,946	12,101
57,750	**57,800**	13,178	11,107	13,962	12,115
57,800	**57,850**	13,194	11,121	13,977	12,129
57,850	**57,900**	13,209	11,135	13,993	12,143
57,900	**57,950**	13,225	11,149	14,008	12,157
57,950	**58,000**	13,240	11,163	14,024	12,171
58,000					
58,000	**58,050**	13,256	11,177	14,039	12,185
58,050	**58,100**	13,271	11,191	14,055	12,199
58,100	**58,150**	13,287	11,205	14,070	12,213
58,150	**58,200**	13,302	11,219	14,086	12,227
58,200	**58,250**	13,318	11,233	14,101	12,241
58,250	**58,300**	13,333	11,247	14,117	12,255
58,300	**58,350**	13,349	11,261	14,132	12,269
58,350	**58,400**	13,364	11,275	14,148	12,283
58,400	**58,450**	13,380	11,289	14,163	12,297
58,450	**58,500**	13,395	11,303	14,179	12,311
58,500	**58,550**	13,411	11,317	14,194	12,325
58,550	**58,600**	13,426	11,331	14,210	12,339
58,600	**58,650**	13,442	11,345	14,225	12,353
58,650	**58,700**	13,457	11,359	14,241	12,367
58,700	**58,750**	13,473	11,373	14,256	12,381
58,750	**58,800**	13,488	11,387	14,272	12,395
58,800	**58,850**	13,504	11,401	14,287	12,409
58,850	**58,900**	13,519	11,415	14,303	12,423
58,900	**58,950**	13,535	11,429	14,318	12,437
58,950	**59,000**	13,550	11,443	14,334	12,451

* This column must also be used by a qualifying widow(er).

Continued on next page

1995 Tax Table—*Continued*

If line 37 (taxable income) is— At least	But less than	And you are— Single	Married filing jointly *	Married filing sepa-rately	Head of a house-hold
		Your tax is—			
59,000					
59,000	**59,050**	13,566	11,457	14,349	12,465
59,050	**59,100**	13,581	11,471	14,365	12,479
59,100	**59,150**	13,597	11,485	14,380	12,493
59,150	**59,200**	13,612	11,499	14,396	12,507
59,200	**59,250**	13,628	11,513	14,411	12,521
59,250	**59,300**	13,643	11,527	14,427	12,535
59,300	**59,350**	13,659	11,541	14,442	12,549
59,350	**59,400**	13,674	11,555	14,458	12,563
59,400	**59,450**	13,690	11,569	14,473	12,577
59,450	**59,500**	13,705	11,583	14,489	12,591
59,500	**59,550**	13,721	11,597	14,504	12,605
59,550	**59,600**	13,736	11,611	14,520	12,619
59,600	**59,650**	13,752	11,625	14,535	12,633
59,650	**59,700**	13,767	11,639	14,551	12,647
59,700	**59,750**	13,783	11,653	14,566	12,661
59,750	**59,800**	13,798	11,667	14,582	12,675
59,800	**59,850**	13,814	11,681	14,597	12,689
59,850	**59,900**	13,829	11,695	14,613	12,703
59,900	**59,950**	13,845	11,709	14,628	12,717
59,950	**60,000**	13,860	11,723	14,644	12,731
60,000					
60,000	**60,050**	13,876	11,737	14,659	12,745
60,050	**60,100**	13,891	11,751	14,675	12,759
60,100	**60,150**	13,907	11,765	14,690	12,773
60,150	**60,200**	13,922	11,779	14,706	12,787
60,200	**60,250**	13,938	11,793	14,721	12,801
60,250	**60,300**	13,953	11,807	14,737	12,815
60,300	**60,350**	13,969	11,821	14,752	12,829
60,350	**60,400**	13,984	11,835	14,768	12,843
60,400	**60,450**	14,000	11,849	14,783	12,857
60,450	**60,500**	14,015	11,863	14,799	12,871
60,500	**60,550**	14,031	11,877	14,814	12,885
60,550	**60,600**	14,046	11,891	14,830	12,899
60,600	**60,650**	14,062	11,905	14,845	12,913
60,650	**60,700**	14,077	11,919	14,861	12,927
60,700	**60,750**	14,093	11,933	14,876	12,941
60,750	**60,800**	14,108	11,947	14,892	12,955
60,800	**60,850**	14,124	11,961	14,907	12,969
60,850	**60,900**	14,139	11,975	14,923	12,983
60,900	**60,950**	14,155	11,989	14,938	12,997
60,950	**61,000**	14,170	12,003	14,954	13,011
61,000					
61,000	**61,050**	14,186	12,017	14,969	13,025
61,050	**61,100**	14,201	12,031	14,985	13,039
61,100	**61,150**	14,217	12,045	15,000	13,053
61,150	**61,200**	14,232	12,059	15,016	13,067
61,200	**61,250**	14,248	12,073	15,031	13,081
61,250	**61,300**	14,263	12,087	15,047	13,095
61,300	**61,350**	14,279	12,101	15,062	13,109
61,350	**61,400**	14,294	12,115	15,078	13,123
61,400	**61,450**	14,310	12,129	15,093	13,137
61,450	**61,500**	14,325	12,143	15,109	13,151
61,500	**61,550**	14,341	12,157	15,124	13,165
61,550	**61,600**	14,356	12,171	15,140	13,179
61,600	**61,650**	14,372	12,185	15,155	13,193
61,650	**61,700**	14,387	12,199	15,171	13,207
61,700	**61,750**	14,403	12,213	15,186	13,221
61,750	**61,800**	14,418	12,227	15,202	13,235
61,800	**61,850**	14,434	12,241	15,217	13,249
61,850	**61,900**	14,449	12,255	15,233	13,263
61,900	**61,950**	14,465	12,269	15,248	13,277
61,950	**62,000**	14,480	12,283	15,264	13,291

If line 37 (taxable income) is— At least	But less than	And you are— Single	Married filing jointly *	Married filing sepa-rately	Head of a house-hold
		Your tax is—			
62,000					
62,000	**62,050**	14,496	12,297	15,279	13,305
62,050	**62,100**	14,511	12,311	15,295	13,319
62,100	**62,150**	14,527	12,325	15,310	13,333
62,150	**62,200**	14,542	12,339	15,326	13,347
62,200	**62,250**	14,558	12,353	15,341	13,361
62,250	**62,300**	14,573	12,367	15,357	13,375
62,300	**62,350**	14,589	12,381	15,372	13,389
62,350	**62,400**	14,604	12,395	15,388	13,403
62,400	**62,450**	14,620	12,409	15,403	13,417
62,450	**62,500**	14,635	12,423	15,419	13,431
62,500	**62,550**	14,651	12,437	15,434	13,445
62,550	**62,600**	14,666	12,451	15,450	13,459
62,600	**62,650**	14,682	12,465	15,465	13,473
62,650	**62,700**	14,697	12,479	15,481	13,487
62,700	**62,750**	14,713	12,493	15,496	13,501
62,750	**62,800**	14,728	12,507	15,512	13,515
62,800	**62,850**	14,744	12,521	15,527	13,529
62,850	**62,900**	14,759	12,535	15,543	13,543
62,900	**62,950**	14,775	12,549	15,558	13,557
62,950	**63,000**	14,790	12,563	15,574	13,571
63,000					
63,000	**63,050**	14,806	12,577	15,589	13,585
63,050	**63,100**	14,821	12,591	15,605	13,599
63,100	**63,150**	14,837	12,605	15,620	13,613
63,150	**63,200**	14,852	12,619	15,636	13,627
63,200	**63,250**	14,868	12,633	15,651	13,641
63,250	**63,300**	14,883	12,647	15,667	13,655
63,300	**63,350**	14,899	12,661	15,682	13,669
63,350	**63,400**	14,914	12,675	15,698	13,683
63,400	**63,450**	14,930	12,689	15,713	13,697
63,450	**63,500**	14,945	12,703	15,729	13,711
63,500	**63,550**	14,961	12,717	15,744	13,725
63,550	**63,600**	14,976	12,731	15,760	13,739
63,600	**63,650**	14,992	12,745	15,775	13,753
63,650	**63,700**	15,007	12,759	15,791	13,767
63,700	**63,750**	15,023	12,773	15,806	13,781
63,750	**63,800**	15,038	12,787	15,822	13,795
63,800	**63,850**	15,054	12,801	15,837	13,809
63,850	**63,900**	15,069	12,815	15,853	13,823
63,900	**63,950**	15,085	12,829	15,868	13,837
63,950	**64,000**	15,100	12,843	15,884	13,851
64,000					
64,000	**64,050**	15,116	12,857	15,899	13,865
64,050	**64,100**	15,131	12,871	15,915	13,879
64,100	**64,150**	15,147	12,885	15,930	13,893
64,150	**64,200**	15,162	12,899	15,946	13,907
64,200	**64,250**	15,178	12,913	15,961	13,921
64,250	**64,300**	15,193	12,927	15,977	13,935
64,300	**64,350**	15,209	12,941	15,992	13,949
64,350	**64,400**	15,224	12,955	16,008	13,963
64,400	**64,450**	15,240	12,969	16,023	13,977
64,450	**64,500**	15,255	12,983	16,039	13,991
64,500	**64,550**	15,271	12,997	16,054	14,005
64,550	**64,600**	15,286	13,011	16,070	14,019
64,600	**64,650**	15,302	13,025	16,085	14,033
64,650	**64,700**	15,317	13,039	16,101	14,047
64,700	**64,750**	15,333	13,053	16,116	14,061
64,750	**64,800**	15,348	13,067	16,132	14,075
64,800	**64,850**	15,364	13,081	16,147	14,089
64,850	**64,900**	15,379	13,095	16,163	14,103
64,900	**64,950**	15,395	13,109	16,178	14,117
64,950	**65,000**	15,410	13,123	16,194	14,131

If line 37 (taxable income) is— At least	But less than	And you are— Single	Married filing jointly *	Married filing sepa-rately	Head of a house-hold
		Your tax is—			
65,000					
65,000	**65,050**	15,426	13,137	16,209	14,145
65,050	**65,100**	15,441	13,151	16,225	14,159
65,100	**65,150**	15,457	13,165	16,240	14,173
65,150	**65,200**	15,472	13,179	16,256	14,187
65,200	**65,250**	15,488	13,193	16,271	14,201
65,250	**65,300**	15,503	13,207	16,287	14,215
65,300	**65,350**	15,519	13,221	16,302	14,229
65,350	**65,400**	15,534	13,235	16,318	14,243
65,400	**65,450**	15,550	13,249	16,333	14,257
65,450	**65,500**	15,565	13,263	16,349	14,271
65,500	**65,550**	15,581	13,277	16,364	14,285
65,550	**65,600**	15,596	13,291	16,380	14,299
65,600	**65,650**	15,612	13,305	16,395	14,313
65,650	**65,700**	15,627	13,319	16,411	14,327
65,700	**65,750**	15,643	13,333	16,426	14,341
65,750	**65,800**	15,658	13,347	16,442	14,355
65,800	**65,850**	15,674	13,361	16,457	14,369
65,850	**65,900**	15,689	13,375	16,473	14,383
65,900	**65,950**	15,705	13,389	16,488	14,397
65,950	**66,000**	15,720	13,403	16,504	14,411
66,000					
66,000	**66,050**	15,736	13,417	16,519	14,425
66,050	**66,100**	15,751	13,431	16,535	14,439
66,100	**66,150**	15,767	13,445	16,550	14,453
66,150	**66,200**	15,782	13,459	16,566	14,467
66,200	**66,250**	15,798	13,473	16,581	14,481
66,250	**66,300**	15,813	13,487	16,597	14,495
66,300	**66,350**	15,829	13,501	16,612	14,509
66,350	**66,400**	15,844	13,515	16,628	14,523
66,400	**66,450**	15,860	13,529	16,643	14,537
66,450	**66,500**	15,875	13,543	16,659	14,551
66,500	**66,550**	15,891	13,557	16,674	14,565
66,550	**66,600**	15,906	13,571	16,690	14,579
66,600	**66,650**	15,922	13,585	16,705	14,593
66,650	**66,700**	15,937	13,599	16,721	14,607
66,700	**66,750**	15,953	13,613	16,736	14,621
66,750	**66,800**	15,968	13,627	16,752	14,635
66,800	**66,850**	15,984	13,641	16,767	14,649
66,850	**66,900**	15,999	13,655	16,783	14,663
66,900	**66,950**	16,015	13,669	16,798	14,677
66,950	**67,000**	16,030	13,683	16,814	14,691
67,000					
67,000	**67,050**	16,046	13,697	16,829	14,705
67,050	**67,100**	16,061	13,711	16,845	14,719
67,100	**67,150**	16,077	13,725	16,860	14,733
67,150	**67,200**	16,092	13,739	16,876	14,747
67,200	**67,250**	16,108	13,753	16,891	14,761
67,250	**67,300**	16,123	13,767	16,907	14,775
67,300	**67,350**	16,139	13,781	16,922	14,789
67,350	**67,400**	16,154	13,795	16,938	14,803
67,400	**67,450**	16,170	13,809	16,953	14,817
67,450	**67,500**	16,185	13,823	16,969	14,831
67,500	**67,550**	16,201	13,837	16,984	14,845
67,550	**67,600**	16,216	13,851	17,000	14,859
67,600	**67,650**	16,232	13,865	17,015	14,873
67,650	**67,700**	16,247	13,879	17,031	14,887
67,700	**67,750**	16,263	13,893	17,046	14,901
67,750	**67,800**	16,278	13,907	17,062	14,915
67,800	**67,850**	16,294	13,921	17,077	14,929
67,850	**67,900**	16,309	13,935	17,093	14,943
67,900	**67,950**	16,325	13,949	17,108	14,957
67,950	**68,000**	16,340	13,963	17,124	14,971

* This column must also be used by a qualifying widow(er).

Continued on next page

1995 Tax Table—*Continued*

If line 37 (taxable income) is— At least	But less than	And you are— Single	Married filing jointly *	Married filing separately	Head of a household
		Your tax is—			
68,000					
68,000	**68,050**	16,356	13,977	17,139	14,985
68,050	**68,100**	16,371	13,991	17,155	14,999
68,100	**68,150**	16,387	14,005	17,170	15,013
68,150	**68,200**	16,402	14,019	17,186	15,027
68,200	**68,250**	16,418	14,033	17,201	15,041
68,250	**68,300**	16,433	14,047	17,217	15,055
68,300	**68,350**	16,449	14,061	17,232	15,069
68,350	**68,400**	16,464	14,075	17,248	15,083
68,400	**68,450**	16,480	14,089	17,263	15,097
68,450	**68,500**	16,495	14,103	17,279	15,111
68,500	**68,550**	16,511	14,117	17,294	15,125
68,550	**68,600**	16,526	14,131	17,310	15,139
68,600	**68,650**	16,542	14,145	17,325	15,153
68,650	**68,700**	16,557	14,159	17,341	15,167
68,700	**68,750**	16,573	14,173	17,356	15,181
68,750	**68,800**	16,588	14,187	17,372	15,195
68,800	**68,850**	16,604	14,201	17,387	15,209
68,850	**68,900**	16,619	14,215	17,403	15,223
68,900	**68,950**	16,635	14,229	17,418	15,237
68,950	**69,000**	16,650	14,243	17,434	15,251
69,000					
69,000	**69,050**	16,666	14,257	17,449	15,265
69,050	**69,100**	16,681	14,271	17,465	15,279
69,100	**69,150**	16,697	14,285	17,480	15,293
69,150	**69,200**	16,712	14,299	17,496	15,307
69,200	**69,250**	16,728	14,313	17,511	15,321
69,250	**69,300**	16,743	14,327	17,527	15,335
69,300	**69,350**	16,759	14,341	17,542	15,349
69,350	**69,400**	16,774	14,355	17,558	15,363
69,400	**69,450**	16,790	14,369	17,573	15,377
69,450	**69,500**	16,805	14,383	17,589	15,391
69,500	**69,550**	16,821	14,397	17,604	15,405
69,550	**69,600**	16,836	14,411	17,620	15,419
69,600	**69,650**	16,852	14,425	17,635	15,433
69,650	**69,700**	16,867	14,439	17,651	15,447
69,700	**69,750**	16,883	14,453	17,666	15,461
69,750	**69,800**	16,898	14,467	17,682	15,475
69,800	**69,850**	16,914	14,481	17,697	15,489
69,850	**69,900**	16,929	14,495	17,713	15,503
69,900	**69,950**	16,945	14,509	17,728	15,517
69,950	**70,000**	16,960	14,523	17,744	15,531
70,000					
70,000	**70,050**	16,976	14,537	17,759	15,545
70,050	**70,100**	16,991	14,551	17,775	15,559
70,100	**70,150**	17,007	14,565	17,790	15,573
70,150	**70,200**	17,022	14,579	17,806	15,587
70,200	**70,250**	17,038	14,593	17,821	15,601
70,250	**70,300**	17,053	14,607	17,837	15,615
70,300	**70,350**	17,069	14,621	17,852	15,629
70,350	**70,400**	17,084	14,635	17,868	15,643
70,400	**70,450**	17,100	14,649	17,883	15,657
70,450	**70,500**	17,115	14,663	17,899	15,671
70,500	**70,550**	17,131	14,677	17,914	15,685
70,550	**70,600**	17,146	14,691	17,930	15,699
70,600	**70,650**	17,162	14,705	17,945	15,713
70,650	**70,700**	17,177	14,719	17,961	15,727
70,700	**70,750**	17,193	14,733	17,976	15,741
70,750	**70,800**	17,208	14,747	17,992	15,755
70,800	**70,850**	17,224	14,761	18,007	15,769
70,850	**70,900**	17,239	14,775	18,023	15,783
70,900	**70,950**	17,255	14,789	18,038	15,797
70,950	**71,000**	17,270	14,803	18,054	15,811
71,000					
71,000	**71,050**	17,286	14,817	18,069	15,825
71,050	**71,100**	17,301	14,831	18,085	15,839
71,100	**71,150**	17,317	14,845	18,100	15,853
71,150	**71,200**	17,332	14,859	18,116	15,867
71,200	**71,250**	17,348	14,873	18,131	15,881
71,250	**71,300**	17,363	14,887	18,147	15,895
71,300	**71,350**	17,379	14,901	18,162	15,909
71,350	**71,400**	17,394	14,915	18,178	15,923
71,400	**71,450**	17,410	14,929	18,193	15,937
71,450	**71,500**	17,425	14,943	18,209	15,951
71,500	**71,550**	17,441	14,957	18,224	15,965
71,550	**71,600**	17,456	14,971	18,240	15,979
71,600	**71,650**	17,472	14,985	18,255	15,993
71,650	**71,700**	17,487	14,999	18,271	16,007
71,700	**71,750**	17,503	15,013	18,286	16,021
71,750	**71,800**	17,518	15,027	18,302	16,035
71,800	**71,850**	17,534	15,041	18,318	16,049
71,850	**71,900**	17,549	15,055	18,336	16,063
71,900	**71,950**	17,565	15,069	18,354	16,077
71,950	**72,000**	17,580	15,083	18,372	16,091
72,000					
72,000	**72,050**	17,596	15,097	18,390	16,105
72,050	**72,100**	17,611	15,111	18,408	16,119
72,100	**72,150**	17,627	15,125	18,426	16,133
72,150	**72,200**	17,642	15,139	18,444	16,147
72,200	**72,250**	17,658	15,153	18,462	16,161
72,250	**72,300**	17,673	15,167	18,480	16,175
72,300	**72,350**	17,689	15,181	18,498	16,189
72,350	**72,400**	17,704	15,195	18,516	16,203
72,400	**72,450**	17,720	15,209	18,534	16,217
72,450	**72,500**	17,735	15,223	18,552	16,231
72,500	**72,550**	17,751	15,237	18,570	16,245
72,550	**72,600**	17,766	15,251	18,588	16,259
72,600	**72,650**	17,782	15,265	18,606	16,273
72,650	**72,700**	17,797	15,279	18,624	16,287
72,700	**72,750**	17,813	15,293	18,642	16,301
72,750	**72,800**	17,828	15,307	18,660	16,315
72,800	**72,850**	17,844	15,321	18,678	16,329
72,850	**72,900**	17,859	15,335	18,696	16,343
72,900	**72,950**	17,875	15,349	18,714	16,357
72,950	**73,000**	17,890	15,363	18,732	16,371
73,000					
73,000	**73,050**	17,906	15,377	18,750	16,385
73,050	**73,100**	17,921	15,391	18,768	16,399
73,100	**73,150**	17,937	15,405	18,786	16,413
73,150	**73,200**	17,952	15,419	18,804	16,427
73,200	**73,250**	17,968	15,433	18,822	16,441
73,250	**73,300**	17,983	15,447	18,840	16,455
73,300	**73,350**	17,999	15,461	18,858	16,469
73,350	**73,400**	18,014	15,475	18,876	16,483
73,400	**73,450**	18,030	15,489	18,894	16,497
73,450	**73,500**	18,045	15,503	18,912	16,511
73,500	**73,550**	18,061	15,517	18,930	16,525
73,550	**73,600**	18,076	15,531	18,948	16,539
73,600	**73,650**	18,092	15,545	18,966	16,553
73,650	**73,700**	18,107	15,559	18,984	16,567
73,700	**73,750**	18,123	15,573	19,002	16,581
73,750	**73,800**	18,138	15,587	19,020	16,595
73,800	**73,850**	18,154	15,601	19,038	16,609
73,850	**73,900**	18,169	15,615	19,056	16,623
73,900	**73,950**	18,185	15,629	19,074	16,637
73,950	**74,000**	18,200	15,643	19,092	16,651
74,000					
74,000	**74,050**	18,216	15,657	19,110	16,665
74,050	**74,100**	18,231	15,671	19,128	16,679
74,100	**74,150**	18,247	15,685	19,146	16,693
74,150	**74,200**	18,262	15,699	19,164	16,707
74,200	**74,250**	18,278	15,713	19,182	16,721
74,250	**74,300**	18,293	15,727	19,200	16,735
74,300	**74,350**	18,309	15,741	19,218	16,749
74,350	**74,400**	18,324	15,755	19,236	16,763
74,400	**74,450**	18,340	15,769	19,254	16,777
74,450	**74,500**	18,355	15,783	19,272	16,791
74,500	**74,550**	18,371	15,797	19,290	16,805
74,550	**74,600**	18,386	15,811	19,308	16,819
74,600	**74,650**	18,402	15,825	19,326	16,833
74,650	**74,700**	18,417	15,839	19,344	16,847
74,700	**74,750**	18,433	15,853	19,362	16,861
74,750	**74,800**	18,448	15,867	19,380	16,875
74,800	**74,850**	18,464	15,881	19,398	16,889
74,850	**74,900**	18,479	15,895	19,416	16,903
74,900	**74,950**	18,495	15,909	19,434	16,917
74,950	**75,000**	18,510	15,923	19,452	16,931
75,000					
75,000	**75,050**	18,526	15,937	19,470	16,945
75,050	**75,100**	18,541	15,951	19,488	16,959
75,100	**75,150**	18,557	15,965	19,506	16,973
75,150	**75,200**	18,572	15,979	19,524	16,987
75,200	**75,250**	18,588	15,993	19,542	17,001
75,250	**75,300**	18,603	16,007	19,560	17,015
75,300	**75,350**	18,619	16,021	19,578	17,029
75,350	**75,400**	18,634	16,035	19,596	17,043
75,400	**75,450**	18,650	16,049	19,614	17,057
75,450	**75,500**	18,665	16,063	19,632	17,071
75,500	**75,550**	18,681	16,077	19,650	17,085
75,550	**75,600**	18,696	16,091	19,668	17,099
75,600	**75,650**	18,712	16,105	19,686	17,113
75,650	**75,700**	18,727	16,119	19,704	17,127
75,700	**75,750**	18,743	16,133	19,722	17,141
75,750	**75,800**	18,758	16,147	19,740	17,155
75,800	**75,850**	18,774	16,161	19,758	17,169
75,850	**75,900**	18,789	16,175	19,776	17,183
75,900	**75,950**	18,805	16,189	19,794	17,197
75,950	**76,000**	18,820	16,203	19,812	17,211
76,000					
76,000	**76,050**	18,836	16,217	19,830	17,225
76,050	**76,100**	18,851	16,231	19,848	17,239
76,100	**76,150**	18,867	16,245	19,866	17,253
76,150	**76,200**	18,882	16,259	19,884	17,267
76,200	**76,250**	18,898	16,273	19,902	17,281
76,250	**76,300**	18,913	16,287	19,920	17,295
76,300	**76,350**	18,929	16,301	19,938	17,309
76,350	**76,400**	18,944	16,315	19,956	17,323
76,400	**76,450**	18,960	16,329	19,974	17,337
76,450	**76,500**	18,975	16,343	19,992	17,351
76,500	**76,550**	18,991	16,357	20,010	17,365
76,550	**76,600**	19,006	16,371	20,028	17,379
76,600	**76,650**	19,022	16,385	20,046	17,393
76,650	**76,700**	19,037	16,399	20,064	17,407
76,700	**76,750**	19,053	16,413	20,082	17,421
76,750	**76,800**	19,068	16,427	20,100	17,435
76,800	**76,850**	19,084	16,441	20,118	17,449
76,850	**76,900**	19,099	16,455	20,136	17,463
76,900	**76,950**	19,115	16,469	20,154	17,477
76,950	**77,000**	19,130	16,483	20,172	17,491

* This column must also be used by a qualifying widow(er).

Continued on next page

1995 Tax Table—*Continued*

If line 37 (taxable income) is— At least	But less than	And you are— Single	Married filing jointly *	Married filing sepa-rately	Head of a house-hold
		Your tax is—			
77,000					
77,000	**77,050**	19,146	16,497	20,190	17,505
77,050	**77,100**	19,161	16,511	20,208	17,519
77,100	**77,150**	19,177	16,525	20,226	17,533
77,150	**77,200**	19,192	16,539	20,244	17,547
77,200	**77,250**	19,208	16,553	20,262	17,561
77,250	**77,300**	19,223	16,567	20,280	17,575
77,300	**77,350**	19,239	16,581	20,298	17,589
77,350	**77,400**	19,254	16,595	20,316	17,603
77,400	**77,450**	19,270	16,609	20,334	17,617
77,450	**77,500**	19,285	16,623	20,352	17,631
77,500	**77,550**	19,301	16,637	20,370	17,645
77,550	**77,600**	19,316	16,651	20,388	17,659
77,600	**77,650**	19,332	16,665	20,406	17,673
77,650	**77,700**	19,347	16,679	20,424	17,687
77,700	**77,750**	19,363	16,693	20,442	17,701
77,750	**77,800**	19,378	16,707	20,460	17,715
77,800	**77,850**	19,394	16,721	20,478	17,729
77,850	**77,900**	19,409	16,735	20,496	17,743
77,900	**77,950**	19,425	16,749	20,514	17,757
77,950	**78,000**	19,440	16,763	20,532	17,771
78,000					
78,000	**78,050**	19,456	16,777	20,550	17,785
78,050	**78,100**	19,471	16,791	20,568	17,799
78,100	**78,150**	19,487	16,805	20,586	17,813
78,150	**78,200**	19,502	16,819	20,604	17,827
78,200	**78,250**	19,518	16,833	20,622	17,841
78,250	**78,300**	19,533	16,847	20,640	17,855
78,300	**78,350**	19,549	16,861	20,658	17,869
78,350	**78,400**	19,564	16,875	20,676	17,883
78,400	**78,450**	19,580	16,889	20,694	17,897
78,450	**78,500**	19,595	16,903	20,712	17,911
78,500	**78,550**	19,611	16,917	20,730	17,925
78,550	**78,600**	19,626	16,931	20,748	17,939
78,600	**78,650**	19,642	16,945	20,766	17,953
78,650	**78,700**	19,657	16,959	20,784	17,967
78,700	**78,750**	19,673	16,973	20,802	17,981
78,750	**78,800**	19,688	16,987	20,820	17,995
78,800	**78,850**	19,704	17,001	20,838	18,009
78,850	**78,900**	19,719	17,015	20,856	18,023
78,900	**78,950**	19,735	17,029	20,874	18,037
78,950	**79,000**	19,750	17,043	20,892	18,051
79,000					
79,000	**79,050**	19,766	17,057	20,910	18,065
79,050	**79,100**	19,781	17,071	20,928	18,079
79,100	**79,150**	19,797	17,085	20,946	18,093
79,150	**79,200**	19,812	17,099	20,964	18,107
79,200	**79,250**	19,828	17,113	20,982	18,121
79,250	**79,300**	19,843	17,127	21,000	18,135
79,300	**79,350**	19,859	17,141	21,018	18,149
79,350	**79,400**	19,874	17,155	21,036	18,163
79,400	**79,450**	19,890	17,169	21,054	18,177
79,450	**79,500**	19,905	17,183	21,072	18,191
79,500	**79,550**	19,921	17,197	21,090	18,205
79,550	**79,600**	19,936	17,211	21,108	18,219
79,600	**79,650**	19,952	17,225	21,126	18,233
79,650	**79,700**	19,967	17,239	21,144	18,247
79,700	**79,750**	19,983	17,253	21,162	18,261
79,750	**79,800**	19,998	17,267	21,180	18,275
79,800	**79,850**	20,014	17,281	21,198	18,289
79,850	**79,900**	20,029	17,295	21,216	18,303
79,900	**79,950**	20,045	17,309	21,234	18,317
79,950	**80,000**	20,060	17,323	21,252	18,331

If line 37 (taxable income) is— At least	But less than	And you are— Single	Married filing jointly *	Married filing sepa-rately	Head of a house-hold
		Your tax is—			
80,000					
80,000	**80,050**	20,076	17,337	21,270	18,345
80,050	**80,100**	20,091	17,351	21,288	18,359
80,100	**80,150**	20,107	17,365	21,306	18,373
80,150	**80,200**	20,122	17,379	21,324	18,387
80,200	**80,250**	20,138	17,393	21,342	18,401
80,250	**80,300**	20,153	17,407	21,360	18,415
80,300	**80,350**	20,169	17,421	21,378	18,429
80,350	**80,400**	20,184	17,435	21,396	18,443
80,400	**80,450**	20,200	17,449	21,414	18,457
80,450	**80,500**	20,215	17,463	21,432	18,471
80,500	**80,550**	20,231	17,477	21,450	18,485
80,550	**80,600**	20,246	17,491	21,468	18,499
80,600	**80,650**	20,262	17,505	21,486	18,513
80,650	**80,700**	20,277	17,519	21,504	18,527
80,700	**80,750**	20,293	17,533	21,522	18,541
80,750	**80,800**	20,308	17,547	21,540	18,555
80,800	**80,850**	20,324	17,561	21,558	18,571
80,850	**80,900**	20,339	17,575	21,576	18,586
80,900	**80,950**	20,355	17,589	21,594	18,602
80,950	**81,000**	20,370	17,603	21,612	18,617
81,000					
81,000	**81,050**	20,386	17,617	21,630	18,633
81,050	**81,100**	20,401	17,631	21,648	18,648
81,100	**81,150**	20,417	17,645	21,666	18,664
81,150	**81,200**	20,432	17,659	21,684	18,679
81,200	**81,250**	20,448	17,673	21,702	18,695
81,250	**81,300**	20,463	17,687	21,720	18,710
81,300	**81,350**	20,479	17,701	21,738	18,726
81,350	**81,400**	20,494	17,715	21,756	18,741
81,400	**81,450**	20,510	17,729	21,774	18,757
81,450	**81,500**	20,525	17,743	21,792	18,772
81,500	**81,550**	20,541	17,757	21,810	18,788
81,550	**81,600**	20,556	17,771	21,828	18,803
81,600	**81,650**	20,572	17,785	21,846	18,819
81,650	**81,700**	20,587	17,799	21,864	18,834
81,700	**81,750**	20,603	17,813	21,882	18,850
81,750	**81,800**	20,618	17,827	21,900	18,865
81,800	**81,850**	20,634	17,841	21,918	18,881
81,850	**81,900**	20,649	17,855	21,936	18,896
81,900	**81,950**	20,665	17,869	21,954	18,912
81,950	**82,000**	20,680	17,883	21,972	18,927
82,000					
82,000	**82,050**	20,696	17,897	21,990	18,943
82,050	**82,100**	20,711	17,911	22,008	18,958
82,100	**82,150**	20,727	17,925	22,026	18,974
82,150	**82,200**	20,742	17,939	22,044	18,989
82,200	**82,250**	20,758	17,953	22,062	19,005
82,250	**82,300**	20,773	17,967	22,080	19,020
82,300	**82,350**	20,789	17,981	22,098	19,036
82,350	**82,400**	20,804	17,995	22,116	19,051
82,400	**82,450**	20,820	18,009	22,134	19,067
82,450	**82,500**	20,835	18,023	22,152	19,082
82,500	**82,550**	20,851	18,037	22,170	19,098
82,550	**82,600**	20,866	18,051	22,188	19,113
82,600	**82,650**	20,882	18,065	22,206	19,129
82,650	**82,700**	20,897	18,079	22,224	19,144
82,700	**82,750**	20,913	18,093	22,242	19,160
82,750	**82,800**	20,928	18,107	22,260	19,175
82,800	**82,850**	20,944	18,121	22,278	19,191
82,850	**82,900**	20,959	18,135	22,296	19,206
82,900	**82,950**	20,975	18,149	22,314	19,222
82,950	**83,000**	20,990	18,163	22,332	19,237

If line 37 (taxable income) is— At least	But less than	And you are— Single	Married filing jointly *	Married filing sepa-rately	Head of a house-hold
		Your tax is—			
83,000					
83,000	**83,050**	21,006	18,177	22,350	19,253
83,050	**83,100**	21,021	18,191	22,368	19,268
83,100	**83,150**	21,037	18,205	22,386	19,284
83,150	**83,200**	21,052	18,219	22,404	19,299
83,200	**83,250**	21,068	18,233	22,422	19,315
83,250	**83,300**	21,083	18,247	22,440	19,330
83,300	**83,350**	21,099	18,261	22,458	19,346
83,350	**83,400**	21,114	18,275	22,476	19,361
83,400	**83,450**	21,130	18,289	22,494	19,377
83,450	**83,500**	21,145	18,303	22,512	19,392
83,500	**83,550**	21,161	18,317	22,530	19,408
83,550	**83,600**	21,176	18,331	22,548	19,423
83,600	**83,650**	21,192	18,345	22,566	19,439
83,650	**83,700**	21,207	18,359	22,584	19,454
83,700	**83,750**	21,223	18,373	22,602	19,470
83,750	**83,800**	21,238	18,387	22,620	19,485
83,800	**83,850**	21,254	18,401	22,638	19,501
83,850	**83,900**	21,269	18,415	22,656	19,516
83,900	**83,950**	21,285	18,429	22,674	19,532
83,950	**84,000**	21,300	18,443	22,692	19,547
84,000					
84,000	**84,050**	21,316	18,457	22,710	19,563
84,050	**84,100**	21,331	18,471	22,728	19,578
84,100	**84,150**	21,347	18,485	22,746	19,594
84,150	**84,200**	21,362	18,499	22,764	19,609
84,200	**84,250**	21,378	18,513	22,782	19,625
84,250	**84,300**	21,393	18,527	22,800	19,640
84,300	**84,350**	21,409	18,541	22,818	19,656
84,350	**84,400**	21,424	18,555	22,836	19,671
84,400	**84,450**	21,440	18,569	22,854	19,687
84,450	**84,500**	21,455	18,583	22,872	19,702
84,500	**84,550**	21,471	18,597	22,890	19,718
84,550	**84,600**	21,486	18,611	22,908	19,733
84,600	**84,650**	21,502	18,625	22,926	19,749
84,650	**84,700**	21,517	18,639	22,944	19,764
84,700	**84,750**	21,533	18,653	22,962	19,780
84,750	**84,800**	21,548	18,667	22,980	19,795
84,800	**84,850**	21,564	18,681	22,998	19,811
84,850	**84,900**	21,579	18,695	23,016	19,826
84,900	**84,950**	21,595	18,709	23,034	19,842
84,950	**85,000**	21,610	18,723	23,052	19,857
85,000					
85,000	**85,050**	21,626	18,737	23,070	19,873
85,050	**85,100**	21,641	18,751	23,088	19,888
85,100	**85,150**	21,657	18,765	23,106	19,904
85,150	**85,200**	21,672	18,779	23,124	19,919
85,200	**85,250**	21,688	18,793	23,142	19,935
85,250	**85,300**	21,703	18,807	23,160	19,950
85,300	**85,350**	21,719	18,821	23,178	19,966
85,350	**85,400**	21,734	18,835	23,196	19,981
85,400	**85,450**	21,750	18,849	23,214	19,997
85,450	**85,500**	21,765	18,863	23,232	20,012
85,500	**85,550**	21,781	18,877	23,250	20,028
85,550	**85,600**	21,796	18,891	23,268	20,043
85,600	**85,650**	21,812	18,905	23,286	20,059
85,650	**85,700**	21,827	18,919	23,304	20,074
85,700	**85,750**	21,843	18,933	23,322	20,090
85,750	**85,800**	21,858	18,947	23,340	20,105
85,800	**85,850**	21,874	18,961	23,358	20,121
85,850	**85,900**	21,889	18,975	23,376	20,136
85,900	**85,950**	21,905	18,989	23,394	20,152
85,950	**86,000**	21,920	19,003	23,412	20,167

* This column must also be used by a qualifying widow(er).

Continued on next page

1995 Tax Table—*Continued*

If line 37 (taxable income) is— At least	But less than	And you are— Single	Married filing jointly *	Married filing sepa-rately	Head of a house-hold
		Your tax is—			
86,000					
86,000	**86,050**	21,936	19,017	23,430	20,183
86,050	**86,100**	21,951	19,031	23,448	20,198
86,100	**86,150**	21,967	19,045	23,466	20,214
86,150	**86,200**	21,982	19,059	23,484	20,229
86,200	**86,250**	21,998	19,073	23,502	20,245
86,250	**86,300**	22,013	19,087	23,520	20,260
86,300	**86,350**	22,029	19,101	23,538	20,276
86,350	**86,400**	22,044	19,115	23,556	20,291
86,400	**86,450**	22,060	19,129	23,574	20,307
86,450	**86,500**	22,075	19,143	23,592	20,322
86,500	**86,550**	22,091	19,157	23,610	20,338
86,550	**86,600**	22,106	19,171	23,628	20,353
86,600	**86,650**	22,122	19,185	23,646	20,369
86,650	**86,700**	22,137	19,199	23,664	20,384
86,700	**86,750**	22,153	19,213	23,682	20,400
86,750	**86,800**	22,168	19,227	23,700	20,415
86,800	**86,850**	22,184	19,241	23,718	20,431
86,850	**86,900**	22,199	19,255	23,736	20,446
86,900	**86,950**	22,215	19,269	23,754	20,462
86,950	**87,000**	22,230	19,283	23,772	20,477
87,000					
87,000	**87,050**	22,246	19,297	23,790	20,493
87,050	**87,100**	22,261	19,311	23,808	20,508
87,100	**87,150**	22,277	19,325	23,826	20,524
87,150	**87,200**	22,292	19,339	23,844	20,539
87,200	**87,250**	22,308	19,353	23,862	20,555
87,250	**87,300**	22,323	19,367	23,880	20,570
87,300	**87,350**	22,339	19,381	23,898	20,586
87,350	**87,400**	22,354	19,395	23,916	20,601
87,400	**87,450**	22,370	19,409	23,934	20,617
87,450	**87,500**	22,385	19,423	23,952	20,632
87,500	**87,550**	22,401	19,437	23,970	20,648
87,550	**87,600**	22,416	19,451	23,988	20,663
87,600	**87,650**	22,432	19,465	24,006	20,679
87,650	**87,700**	22,447	19,479	24,024	20,694
87,700	**87,750**	22,463	19,493	24,042	20,710
87,750	**87,800**	22,478	19,507	24,060	20,725
87,800	**87,850**	22,494	19,521	24,078	20,741
87,850	**87,900**	22,509	19,535	24,096	20,756
87,900	**87,950**	22,525	19,549	24,114	20,772
87,950	**88,000**	22,540	19,563	24,132	20,787
88,000					
88,000	**88,050**	22,556	19,577	24,150	20,803
88,050	**88,100**	22,571	19,591	24,168	20,818
88,100	**88,150**	22,587	19,605	24,186	20,834
88,150	**88,200**	22,602	19,619	24,204	20,849
88,200	**88,250**	22,618	19,633	24,222	20,865
88,250	**88,300**	22,633	19,647	24,240	20,880
88,300	**88,350**	22,649	19,661	24,258	20,896
88,350	**88,400**	22,664	19,675	24,276	20,911
88,400	**88,450**	22,680	19,689	24,294	20,927
88,450	**88,500**	22,695	19,703	24,312	20,942
88,500	**88,550**	22,711	19,717	24,330	20,958
88,550	**88,600**	22,726	19,731	24,348	20,973
88,600	**88,650**	22,742	19,745	24,366	20,989
88,650	**88,700**	22,757	19,759	24,384	21,004
88,700	**88,750**	22,773	19,773	24,402	21,020
88,750	**88,800**	22,788	19,787	24,420	21,035
88,800	**88,850**	22,804	19,801	24,438	21,051
88,850	**88,900**	22,819	19,815	24,456	21,066
88,900	**88,950**	22,835	19,829	24,474	21,082
88,950	**89,000**	22,850	19,843	24,492	21,097
89,000					
89,000	**89,050**	22,866	19,857	24,510	21,113
89,050	**89,100**	22,881	19,871	24,528	21,128
89,100	**89,150**	22,897	19,885	24,546	21,144
89,150	**89,200**	22,912	19,899	24,564	21,159
89,200	**89,250**	22,928	19,913	24,582	21,175
89,250	**89,300**	22,943	19,927	24,600	21,190
89,300	**89,350**	22,959	19,941	24,618	21,206
89,350	**89,400**	22,974	19,955	24,636	21,221
89,400	**89,450**	22,990	19,969	24,654	21,237
89,450	**89,500**	23,005	19,983	24,672	21,252
89,500	**89,550**	23,021	19,997	24,690	21,268
89,550	**89,600**	23,036	20,011	24,708	21,283
89,600	**89,650**	23,052	20,025	24,726	21,299
89,650	**89,700**	23,067	20,039	24,744	21,314
89,700	**89,750**	23,083	20,053	24,762	21,330
89,750	**89,800**	23,098	20,067	24,780	21,345
89,800	**89,850**	23,114	20,081	24,798	21,361
89,850	**89,900**	23,129	20,095	24,816	21,376
89,900	**89,950**	23,145	20,109	24,834	21,392
89,950	**90,000**	23,160	20,123	24,852	21,407
90,000					
90,000	**90,050**	23,176	20,137	24,870	21,423
90,050	**90,100**	23,191	20,151	24,888	21,438
90,100	**90,150**	23,207	20,165	24,906	21,454
90,150	**90,200**	23,222	20,179	24,924	21,469
90,200	**90,250**	23,238	20,193	24,942	21,485
90,250	**90,300**	23,253	20,207	24,960	21,500
90,300	**90,350**	23,269	20,221	24,978	21,516
90,350	**90,400**	23,284	20,235	24,996	21,531
90,400	**90,450**	23,300	20,249	25,014	21,547
90,450	**90,500**	23,315	20,263	25,032	21,562
90,500	**90,550**	23,331	20,277	25,050	21,578
90,550	**90,600**	23,346	20,291	25,068	21,593
90,600	**90,650**	23,362	20,305	25,086	21,609
90,650	**90,700**	23,377	20,319	25,104	21,624
90,700	**90,750**	23,393	20,333	25,122	21,640
90,750	**90,800**	23,408	20,347	25,140	21,655
90,800	**90,850**	23,424	20,361	25,158	21,671
90,850	**90,900**	23,439	20,375	25,176	21,686
90,900	**90,950**	23,455	20,389	25,194	21,702
90,950	**91,000**	23,470	20,403	25,212	21,717
91,000					
91,000	**91,050**	23,486	20,417	25,230	21,733
91,050	**91,100**	23,501	20,431	25,248	21,748
91,100	**91,150**	23,517	20,445	25,266	21,764
91,150	**91,200**	23,532	20,459	25,284	21,779
91,200	**91,250**	23,548	20,473	25,302	21,795
91,250	**91,300**	23,563	20,487	25,320	21,810
91,300	**91,350**	23,579	20,501	25,338	21,826
91,350	**91,400**	23,594	20,515	25,356	21,841
91,400	**91,450**	23,610	20,529	25,374	21,857
91,450	**91,500**	23,625	20,543	25,392	21,872
91,500	**91,550**	23,641	20,557	25,410	21,888
91,550	**91,600**	23,656	20,571	25,428	21,903
91,600	**91,650**	23,672	20,585	25,446	21,919
91,650	**91,700**	23,687	20,599	25,464	21,934
91,700	**91,750**	23,703	20,613	25,482	21,950
91,750	**91,800**	23,718	20,627	25,500	21,965
91,800	**91,850**	23,734	20,641	25,518	21,981
91,850	**91,900**	23,749	20,655	25,536	21,996
91,900	**91,950**	23,765	20,669	25,554	22,012
91,950	**92,000**	23,780	20,683	25,572	22,027
92,000					
92,000	**92,050**	23,796	20,697	25,590	22,043
92,050	**92,100**	23,811	20,711	25,608	22,058
92,100	**92,150**	23,827	20,725	25,626	22,074
92,150	**92,200**	23,842	20,739	25,644	22,089
92,200	**92,250**	23,858	20,753	25,662	22,105
92,250	**92,300**	23,873	20,767	25,680	22,120
92,300	**92,350**	23,889	20,781	25,698	22,136
92,350	**92,400**	23,904	20,795	25,716	22,151
92,400	**92,450**	23,920	20,809	25,734	22,167
92,450	**92,500**	23,935	20,823	25,752	22,182
92,500	**92,550**	23,951	20,837	25,770	22,198
92,550	**92,600**	23,966	20,851	25,788	22,213
92,600	**92,650**	23,982	20,865	25,806	22,229
92,650	**92,700**	23,997	20,879	25,824	22,244
92,700	**92,750**	24,013	20,893	25,842	22,260
92,750	**92,800**	24,028	20,907	25,860	22,275
92,800	**92,850**	24,044	20,921	25,878	22,291
92,850	**92,900**	24,059	20,935	25,896	22,306
92,900	**92,950**	24,075	20,949	25,914	22,322
92,950	**93,000**	24,090	20,963	25,932	22,337
93,000					
93,000	**93,050**	24,106	20,977	25,950	22,353
93,050	**93,100**	24,121	20,991	25,968	22,368
93,100	**93,150**	24,137	21,005	25,986	22,384
93,150	**93,200**	24,152	21,019	26,004	22,399
93,200	**93,250**	24,168	21,033	26,022	22,415
93,250	**93,300**	24,183	21,047	26,040	22,430
93,300	**93,350**	24,199	21,061	26,058	22,446
93,350	**93,400**	24,214	21,075	26,076	22,461
93,400	**93,450**	24,230	21,089	26,094	22,477
93,450	**93,500**	24,245	21,103	26,112	22,492
93,500	**93,550**	24,261	21,117	26,130	22,508
93,550	**93,600**	24,276	21,131	26,148	22,523
93,600	**93,650**	24,292	21,145	26,166	22,539
93,650	**93,700**	24,307	21,159	26,184	22,554
93,700	**93,750**	24,323	21,173	26,202	22,570
93,750	**93,800**	24,338	21,187	26,220	22,585
93,800	**93,850**	24,354	21,201	26,238	22,601
93,850	**93,900**	24,369	21,215	26,256	22,616
93,900	**93,950**	24,385	21,229	26,274	22,632
93,950	**94,000**	24,400	21,243	26,292	22,647
94,000					
94,000	**94,050**	24,416	21,257	26,310	22,663
94,050	**94,100**	24,431	21,271	26,328	22,678
94,100	**94,150**	24,447	21,285	26,346	22,694
94,150	**94,200**	24,462	21,299	26,364	22,709
94,200	**94,250**	24,478	21,313	26,382	22,725
94,250	**94,300**	24,493	21,328	26,400	22,740
94,300	**94,350**	24,509	21,343	26,418	22,756
94,350	**94,400**	24,524	21,359	26,436	22,771
94,400	**94,450**	24,540	21,374	26,454	22,787
94,450	**94,500**	24,555	21,390	26,472	22,802
94,500	**94,550**	24,571	21,405	26,490	22,818
94,550	**94,600**	24,586	21,421	26,508	22,833
94,600	**94,650**	24,602	21,436	26,526	22,849
94,650	**94,700**	24,617	21,452	26,544	22,864
94,700	**94,750**	24,633	21,467	26,562	22,880
94,750	**94,800**	24,648	21,483	26,580	22,895
94,800	**94,850**	24,664	21,498	26,598	22,911
94,850	**94,900**	24,679	21,514	26,616	22,926
94,900	**94,950**	24,695	21,529	26,634	22,942
94,950	**95,000**	24,710	21,545	26,652	22,957

* This column must also be used by a qualifying widow(er).

Continued on next page

1995 Tax Table—*Continued*

If line 37 (taxable income) is—		And you are—			
At least	But less than	Single	Married filing jointly *	Married filing separately	Head of a household
		Your tax is—			
95,000					
95,000	**95,050**	24,726	21,560	26,670	22,973
95,050	**95,100**	24,741	21,576	26,688	22,988
95,100	**95,150**	24,757	21,591	26,706	23,004
95,150	**95,200**	24,772	21,607	26,724	23,019
95,200	**95,250**	24,788	21,622	26,742	23,035
95,250	**95,300**	24,803	21,638	26,760	23,050
95,300	**95,350**	24,819	21,653	26,778	23,066
95,350	**95,400**	24,834	21,669	26,796	23,081
95,400	**95,450**	24,850	21,684	26,814	23,097
95,450	**95,500**	24,865	21,700	26,832	23,112
95,500	**95,550**	24,881	21,715	26,850	23,128
95,550	**95,600**	24,896	21,731	26,868	23,143
95,600	**95,650**	24,912	21,746	26,886	23,159
95,650	**95,700**	24,927	21,762	26,904	23,174
95,700	**95,750**	24,943	21,777	26,922	23,190
95,750	**95,800**	24,958	21,793	26,940	23,205
95,800	**95,850**	24,974	21,808	26,958	23,221
95,850	**95,900**	24,989	21,824	26,976	23,236
95,900	**95,950**	25,005	21,839	26,994	23,252
95,950	**96,000**	25,020	21,855	27,012	23,267
96,000					
96,000	**96,050**	25,036	21,870	27,030	23,283
96,050	**96,100**	25,051	21,886	27,048	23,298
96,100	**96,150**	25,067	21,901	27,066	23,314
96,150	**96,200**	25,082	21,917	27,084	23,329
96,200	**96,250**	25,098	21,932	27,102	23,345
96,250	**96,300**	25,113	21,948	27,120	23,360
96,300	**96,350**	25,129	21,963	27,138	23,376
96,350	**96,400**	25,144	21,979	27,156	23,391
96,400	**96,450**	25,160	21,994	27,174	23,407
96,450	**96,500**	25,175	22,010	27,192	23,422
96,500	**96,550**	25,191	22,025	27,210	23,438
96,550	**96,600**	25,206	22,041	27,228	23,453
96,600	**96,650**	25,222	22,056	27,246	23,469
96,650	**96,700**	25,237	22,072	27,264	23,484
96,700	**96,750**	25,253	22,087	27,282	23,500
96,750	**96,800**	25,268	22,103	27,300	23,515
96,800	**96,850**	25,284	22,118	27,318	23,531
96,850	**96,900**	25,299	22,134	27,336	23,546
96,900	**96,950**	25,315	22,149	27,354	23,562
96,950	**97,000**	25,330	22,165	27,372	23,577
97,000					
97,000	**97,050**	25,346	22,180	27,390	23,593
97,050	**97,100**	25,361	22,196	27,408	23,608
97,100	**97,150**	25,377	22,211	27,426	23,624
97,150	**97,200**	25,392	22,227	27,444	23,639
97,200	**97,250**	25,408	22,242	27,462	23,655
97,250	**97,300**	25,423	22,258	27,480	23,670
97,300	**97,350**	25,439	22,273	27,498	23,686
97,350	**97,400**	25,454	22,289	27,516	23,701
97,400	**97,450**	25,470	22,304	27,534	23,717
97,450	**97,500**	25,485	22,320	27,552	23,732
97,500	**97,550**	25,501	22,335	27,570	23,748
97,550	**97,600**	25,516	22,351	27,588	23,763
97,600	**97,650**	25,532	22,366	27,606	23,779
97,650	**97,700**	25,547	22,382	27,624	23,794
97,700	**97,750**	25,563	22,397	27,642	23,810
97,750	**97,800**	25,578	22,413	27,660	23,825
97,800	**97,850**	25,594	22,428	27,678	23,841
97,850	**97,900**	25,609	22,444	27,696	23,856
97,900	**97,950**	25,625	22,459	27,714	23,872
97,950	**98,000**	25,640	22,475	27,732	23,887
98,000					
98,000	**98,050**	25,656	22,490	27,750	23,903
98,050	**98,100**	25,671	22,506	27,768	23,918
98,100	**98,150**	25,687	22,521	27,786	23,934
98,150	**98,200**	25,702	22,537	27,804	23,949
98,200	**98,250**	25,718	22,552	27,822	23,965
98,250	**98,300**	25,733	22,568	27,840	23,980
98,300	**98,350**	25,749	22,583	27,858	23,996
98,350	**98,400**	25,764	22,599	27,876	24,011
98,400	**98,450**	25,780	22,614	27,894	24,027
98,450	**98,500**	25,795	22,630	27,912	24,042
98,500	**98,550**	25,811	22,645	27,930	24,058
98,550	**98,600**	25,826	22,661	27,948	24,073
98,600	**98,650**	25,842	22,676	27,966	24,089
98,650	**98,700**	25,857	22,692	27,984	24,104
98,700	**98,750**	25,873	22,707	28,002	24,120
98,750	**98,800**	25,888	22,723	28,020	24,135
98,800	**98,850**	25,904	22,738	28,038	24,151
98,850	**98,900**	25,919	22,754	28,056	24,166
98,900	**98,950**	25,935	22,769	28,074	24,182
98,950	**99,000**	25,950	22,785	28,092	24,197
99,000					
99,000	**99,050**	25,966	22,800	28,110	24,213
99,050	**99,100**	25,981	22,816	28,128	24,228
99,100	**99,150**	25,997	22,831	28,146	24,244
99,150	**99,200**	26,012	22,847	28,164	24,259
99,200	**99,250**	26,028	22,862	28,182	24,275
99,250	**99,300**	26,043	22,878	28,200	24,290
99,300	**99,350**	26,059	22,893	28,218	24,306
99,350	**99,400**	26,074	22,909	28,236	24,321
99,400	**99,450**	26,090	22,924	28,254	24,337
99,450	**99,500**	26,105	22,940	28,272	24,352
99,500	**99,550**	26,121	22,955	28,290	24,368
99,550	**99,600**	26,136	22,971	28,308	24,383
99,600	**99,650**	26,152	22,986	28,326	24,399
99,650	**99,700**	26,167	23,002	28,344	24,414
99,700	**99,750**	26,183	23,017	28,362	24,430
99,750	**99,800**	26,198	23,033	28,380	24,445
99,800	**99,850**	26,214	23,048	28,398	24,461
99,850	**99,900**	26,229	23,064	28,416	24,476
99,900	**99,950**	26,245	23,079	28,434	24,492
99,950	**100,000**	26,260	23,095	28,452	24,507

$100,000 or over — use the Tax Rate Schedules on page A-2

* This column must also be used by a qualifying widow(er).

1996 Tax Rate Schedules

Single—Schedule X

If taxable income is: *Over—*	*But not over—*	The tax is:		*of the amount over—*
$0	$ 24,000	....	15%	$0
24,000	58,150	$3,600.00 +	28%	24,000
58,150	121,300	13,162.00 +	31%	58,150
121,300	263,750	32,738.50 +	36%	121,300
263,750	....	84,020.50 +	39.6%	263,750

Head of household—Schedule Z

If taxable income is: *Over—*	*But not over—*	The tax is:		*of the amount over—*
$0	$ 32,150	....	15%	$0
32,150	83,050	$4,822.50 +	28%	32,150
83,050	134,500	19,074.50 +	31%	83,050
134,500	263,750	35,024.00 +	36%	134,500
263,750	....	81,554.00 +	39.6%	263,750

Married filing jointly or Qualifying widow(er)—Schedule Y-1

If taxable income is: *Over—*	*But not over—*	The tax is:		*of the amount over—*
$0	$ 40,100	....	15%	$0
40,100	96,900	$6,015.00 +	28%	40,100
96,900	147,700	21,919.00 +	31%	96,900
147,700	263,750	37,667.00 +	36%	147,700
263,750	....	79,445.00 +	39.6%	263,750

Married filing separately—Schedule Y-2

If taxable income is: *Over—*	*But not over—*	The tax is:		*of the amount over—*
$0	$ 20,050	....	15%	$0
20,050	48,450	$3,007.50 +	28%	20,050
48,450	73,850	10,959.50 +	31%	48,450
73,850	131,875	18,833.50 +	36%	73,850
131,875	....	39,722.50 +	39.6%	131,875

Appendix B
Tax Forms

Form **1040EZ**

Department of the Treasury—Internal Revenue Service

Income Tax Return for Single and Joint Filers With No Dependents 1995

OMB No. 1545-0675

Use the IRS label here

Your first name and initial | Last name

If a joint return, spouse's first name and initial | Last name

Home address (number and street). If you have a P.O. box, see page 11. | Apt. no.

City, town or post office, state, and ZIP code. If you have a foreign address, see page 11.

Your social security number

Spouse's social security number

See instructions on back and in Form 1040EZ booklet.

Presidential Election Campaign (See page 11.)

Note: *Checking "Yes" will not change your tax or reduce your refund.*

Do you want $3 to go to this fund? ▶ Yes No

If a joint return, does your spouse want $3 to go to this fund? ▶ Yes No

Dollars Cents

Income

Attach Copy B of Form(s) W-2 here. Enclose, but do not attach, any payment with your return.

1 Total wages, salaries, and tips. This should be shown in box 1 of your W-2 form(s). Attach your W-2 form(s). 1

2 Taxable interest income of $400 or less. If the total is over $400, you cannot use Form 1040EZ. 2

3 Unemployment compensation (see page 14). 3

4 Add lines 1, 2, and 3. This is your **adjusted gross income.** If less than $9,230, see page 15 to find out if you can claim the earned income credit on line 8. 4

Note: *You must check Yes or No.*

5 Can your parents (or someone else) claim you on their return?

☐ **Yes.** Do worksheet on back; enter amount from line G here.

☐ **No.** If **single,** enter 6,400.00. If **married,** enter 11,550.00. For an explanation of these amounts, see back of form. 5

6 Subtract line 5 from line 4. If line 5 is larger than line 4, enter 0. This is your **taxable income.** ▶ 6

Payments and tax

7 Enter your Federal income tax withheld from box 2 of your W-2 form(s). 7

8 **Earned income credit** (see page 15). Enter type and amount of nontaxable earned income below.

Type | $ 8

9 Add lines 7 and 8 (don't include nontaxable earned income). These are your **total payments.** 9

10 **Tax.** Use the amount on **line 6** to find your tax in the tax table on pages 29–33 of the booklet. Then, enter the tax from the table on this line. 10

Refund or amount you owe

11 If line 9 is larger than line 10, subtract line 10 from line 9. This is your **refund.** 11

12 If line 10 is larger than line 9, subtract line 9 from line 10. This is the **amount you owe.** See page 22 for details on how to pay and what to write on your payment. 12

I have read this return. Under penalties of perjury, I declare that to the best of my knowledge and belief, the return is true, correct, and accurately lists all amounts and sources of income I received during the tax year.

Sign your return

Keep a copy of this form for your records.

Your signature | Spouse's signature if joint return

Date | Your occupation | Date | Spouse's occupation

For IRS Use Only — Please do not write in boxes below.

1 2 3 4 5

6 7 8 9 10

1995 Instructions for Form 1040EZ

Use this form if

- Your filing status is single or married filing jointly.
- You do not claim any dependents.
- You (and your spouse if married) were under 65 on January 1, 1996, and not blind at the end of 1995.
- Your taxable income (line 6) is less than $50,000.
- You had **only** wages, salaries, tips, taxable scholarship or fellowship grants, or unemployment compensation, and your taxable interest income was $400 or less. **But** if you earned tips, including allocated tips, that are not included in box 5 and box 7 of your W-2, you may not be able to use Form 1040EZ. See page 13.
- You did not receive any advance earned income credit payments.

Caution: *If married and either you or your spouse had total wages of over $61,200, you may not be able to use this form. See page 9.*

If you are not sure about your filing status, see page 10. If you have questions about dependents, call Tele-Tax (see page 27) and listen to topic 354. If you **can't use this form**, call Tele-Tax (see page 27) and listen to topic 352.

Filling in your return

Because this form is read by a machine, please print your numbers inside the boxes like this:

9	8	7	6	5	4	3	2	1	0

Do not type your numbers. Do not use dollar signs.

If you received a scholarship or fellowship grant or tax-exempt interest income, such as on municipal bonds, see the booklet before filling in the form. Also, see the booklet if you received a Form 1099-INT showing income tax withheld.

Remember, you must report all wages, salaries, and tips even if you don't get a W-2 form from your employer. You must also report all your taxable interest income, including interest from banks, savings and loans, credit unions, etc., even if you don't get a Form 1099-INT.

If you paid someone to prepare your return, see page 22.

Worksheet for dependents who checked "Yes" on line 5

Use this worksheet to figure the amount to enter on line 5 if someone can claim you (or your spouse if married) as a dependent, even if that person chooses not to do so. To find out if someone can claim you as a dependent, call Tele-Tax (see page 27) and listen to topic 354.

A. Enter the amount from line 1 on the front.	**A.**	______
B. Minimum standard deduction.	**B.**	650.00
C. Enter the LARGER of line A or line B here.	**C.**	______
D. Maximum standard deduction. If single, enter 3,900.00; if married, enter 6,550.00.	**D.**	______
E. Enter the SMALLER of line C or line D here. This is your standard deduction.	**E.**	______
F. Exemption amount. • If single, enter 0. • If married and both you and your spouse can be claimed as dependents, enter 0. • If married and only one of you can be claimed as a dependent, enter 2,500.00.	**F.**	______
G. Add lines E and F. Enter the total here and on line 5 on the front.	**G.**	______

If you checked "No" on line 5 because no one can claim you (or your spouse if married) as a dependent, enter on line 5 the amount shown below that applies to you.

- Single, enter 6,400.00. This is the total of your standard deduction (3,900.00) and personal exemption (2,500.00).
- Married, enter 11,550.00. This is the total of your standard deduction (6,550.00), exemption for yourself (2,500.00), and exemption for your spouse (2,500.00).

Avoid mistakes

See page 5 of the Form 1040EZ booklet for a list of common mistakes to avoid. Errors will delay your refund.

Mailing your return

Mail your return by **April 15, 1996**. Use the envelope that came with your booklet. If you don't have that envelope, see page 36 for the address to use.

Form **1040A** (99) Department of the Treasury—Internal Revenue Service
U.S. Individual Income Tax Return 1995
IRS Use Only—Do not write or staple in this space.

OMB No. 1545-0085

Label (See page 19.)

Use the IRS label. Otherwise, please print or type.

LABEL HERE

Your first name and initial	Last name	**Your social security number**
If a joint return, spouse's first name and initial	Last name	**Spouse's social security number**
Home address (number and street). If you have a P.O. box, see page 19.	Apt. no.	
City, town or post office, state, and ZIP code. If you have a foreign address, see page 19.		

For Privacy Act and Paperwork Reduction Act Notice, see page 11.

Presidential Election Campaign Fund (See page 19.) | Yes | No
Do you want $3 to go to this fund? . . . .
If a joint return, does your spouse want $3 to go to this fund?

Note: *Checking "Yes" will not change your tax or reduce your refund.*

Check the box for your filing status (See page 20.) Check only one box.

1 ☐ Single
2 ☐ Married filing joint return (even if only one had income)
3 ☐ Married filing separate return. Enter spouse's social security number above and full name here. ▶ ______
4 ☐ Head of household (with qualifying person). (See page 21.) If the qualifying person is a child but not your dependent, enter this child's name here. ▶ ______
5 ☐ Qualifying widow(er) with dependent child (year spouse died ▶ 19). (See page 22.)

Figure your exemptions (See page 22.)

If more than seven dependents, see page 25.

6a ☐ **Yourself.** If your parent (or someone else) can claim you as a dependent on his or her tax return, **do not** check box 6a. But be sure to check the box on line 18b on page 2.

b ☐ **Spouse**

No. of boxes checked on 6a and 6b ____

c **Dependents:**

(1) First name Last name	(2) Dependent's social security number. If born in 1995, see page 25.	(3) Dependent's relationship to you	(4) No. of months lived in your home in 1995

No. of your children on 6c who:
• lived with you ____
• didn't live with you due to divorce or separation (see page 26) ____
Dependents on 6c not entered above ____

d If your child didn't live with you but is claimed as your dependent under a pre-1985 agreement, check here . . . . ▶ ☐

e Total number of exemptions claimed.

Add numbers entered on lines above ☐

Figure your adjusted gross income

Attach Copy B of your Forms W-2 and 1099-R here.
If you didn't get a W-2, see page 27.
Enclose, but do not attach, any payment.

Line	Description		Line	Amount
7	Wages, salaries, tips, etc. This should be shown in box 1 of your W-2 form(s). Attach Form(s) W-2.		7	
8a	**Taxable** interest income (see page 28). If over $400, attach Schedule 1.		8a	
b	**Tax-exempt** interest. DO NOT include on line 8a.	8b		
9	Dividends. If over $400, attach Schedule 1.		9	
10a	Total IRA distributions. 10a	**10b** Taxable amount (see page 29).	10b	
11a	Total pensions and annuities. 11a	**11b** Taxable amount (see page 29).	11b	
12	Unemployment compensation (see page 32).		12	
13a	Social security benefits. 13a	**13b** Taxable amount (see page 33).	13b	
14	Add lines 7 through 13b (far right column). This is your **total income.** ▶		14	
15a	Your IRA deduction (see page 35).	15a		
b	Spouse's IRA deduction (see page 35).	15b		
c	Add lines 15a and 15b. These are your **total adjustments.**		15c	
16	Subtract line 15c from line 14. This is your **adjusted gross income.** If less than $26,673 and a child lived with you (less than $9,230 if a child didn't live with you), see "Earned income credit" on page 47. ▶		16	

51A5AAA

Cat. No. 11327A

1995 Form 1040A page 2

Figure your standard deduction, exemption amount, and taxable income

17 Enter the amount from line 16. — 17

18a Check if: ☐ **You** were 65 or older ☐ Blind; ☐ **Spouse** was 65 or older ☐ Blind } **Enter number of boxes checked** ▶ 18a ☐

b If your parent (or someone else) can claim you as a dependent, check here . . . . . ▶ 18b ☐

c If you are married filing separately and your spouse itemizes deductions, see page 40 and check here. . . . . ▶ 18c ☐

19 Enter the **standard deduction** shown below for your filing status. **But if you checked any box on line 18a or b,** go to page 40 to find your standard deduction. **If you checked box 18c,** enter -0-.

- Single—$3,900
- Married filing jointly or Qualifying widow(er)—$6,550
- Head of household—$5,750
- Married filing separately—$3,275 — 19

20 Subtract line 19 from line 17. If line 19 is more than line 17, enter -0-. — 20

21 Multiply $2,500 by the total number of exemptions claimed on line 6e. — 21

22 Subtract line 21 from line 20. If line 21 is more than line 20, enter -0-. This is your **taxable income.** ▶ 22

Figure your tax, credits, and payments

If you want the IRS to figure your tax, see the instructions for line 22 on page 41.

23 Find the tax on the amount on line 22. Check if from: ☐ Tax Table (pages 65–70) or ☐ Form 8615 (see page 42). — 23

24a Credit for child and dependent care expenses. Attach Schedule 2. — 24a

b Credit for the elderly or the disabled. Attach Schedule 3. — 24b

c Add lines 24a and 24b. These are your **total credits.** — 24c

25 Subtract line 24c from line 23. If line 24c is more than line 23, enter -0-. — 25

26 Advance earned income credit payments from Form W-2. — 26

27 Household employment taxes. Attach Schedule H. — 27

28 Add lines 25, 26, and 27. This is your **total tax.** ▶ 28

29a Total Federal income tax withheld. If any is from Form(s) 1099, check here. ▶ ☐ — 29a

b 1995 estimated tax payments and amount applied from 1994 return. — 29b

c **Earned income credit.** Attach Schedule EIC if you have a qualifying child. — 29c

Nontaxable earned income: amount ▶ and type ▶

d Add lines 29a, 29b, and 29c (don't include nontaxable earned income). These are your **total payments.** ▶ 29d

Figure your refund or amount you owe

30 If line 29d is more than line 28, subtract line 28 from line 29d. This is the amount you **overpaid.** — 30

31 Amount of line 30 you want **refunded to you.** — 31

32 Amount of line 30 you want **applied to your 1996 estimated tax.** — 32

33 If line 28 is more than line 29d, subtract line 29d from line 28. This is the **amount you owe.** For details on how to pay, including what to write on your payment, see page 55. — 33

34 Estimated tax penalty (see page 55). Also, include on line 33. — 34

Sign your return

Keep a copy of this return for your records.

Under penalties of perjury, I declare that I have examined this return and accompanying schedules and statements, and to the best of my knowledge and belief, they are true, correct, and accurately list all amounts and sources of income I received during the tax year. Declaration of preparer (other than the taxpayer) is based on all information of which the preparer has any knowledge.

Your signature	Date	Your occupation
Spouse's signature. If joint return, BOTH must sign.	Date	Spouse's occupation

Paid preparer's use only

Preparer's signature	Date	Check if self-employed ☐	Preparer's SSN
Firm's name (or yours if self-employed) and address		EIN	
		ZIP code	

N1A5AAA

Schedule 1 (Form 1040A)

Department of the Treasury—Internal Revenue Service

Interest and Dividend Income for Form 1040A Filers (99) 1995

OMB No. 1545-0085

Name(s) shown on Form 1040A | Your social security number

Part I
Interest income

(See pages 28 and 71.)

Note: *If you received a Form 1099–INT, Form 1099–OID, or substitute statement from a brokerage firm, enter the firm's name and the total interest shown on that form.*

		Amount
1 List name of payer. If any interest is from a seller-financed mortgage and the buyer used the property as a personal residence, see page 71 and list this interest first. Also, show that buyer's social security number and address.	1	
2 Add the amounts on line 1.	2	
3 Excludable interest on series EE U.S. savings bonds issued after 1989 from Form 8815, line 14. You **must** attach Form 8815 to Form 1040A.	3	
4 Subtract line 3 from line 2. Enter the result here and on Form 1040A, line 8a.	4	

Part II
Dividend income

(See pages 28 and 72.)

Note: *If you received a Form 1099–DIV or substitute statement from a brokerage firm, enter the firm's name and the total dividends shown on that form.*

		Amount
5 List name of payer	5	
6 Add the amounts on line 5. Enter the total here and on Form 1040A, line 9.	6	

5/15AAA

For Paperwork Reduction Act Notice, see Form 1040A instructions. Cat. No. 12075R **1995 Schedule 1 (Form 1040A) page 1**

Printed on recycled paper

Form **1040** Department of the Treasury—Internal Revenue Service
U.S. Individual Income Tax Return 1995

(99) IRS Use Only—Do not write or staple in this space.

For the year Jan. 1–Dec. 31, 1995, or other tax year beginning , 1995, ending , 19 OMB No. 1545-0074

Label (See instructions on page 11.)
Use the IRS label. Otherwise, please print or type.

LABEL HERE

Your first name and initial | Last name | Your social security number

If a joint return, spouse's first name and initial | Last name | Spouse's social security number

Home address (number and street). If you have a P.O. box, see page 11. | Apt. no.

City, town or post office, state, and ZIP code. If you have a foreign address, see page 11.

For Privacy Act and Paperwork Reduction Act Notice, see page 7.

Presidential Election Campaign (See page 11.)

	Yes	No
Do you want $3 to go to this fund?		
If a joint return, does your spouse want $3 to go to this fund?		

Note: *Checking "Yes" will not change your tax or reduce your refund.*

Filing Status (See page 11.)

Check only one box.

1 ☐ Single
2 ☐ Married filing joint return (even if only one had income)
3 ☐ Married filing separate return. Enter spouse's social security no. above and full name here. ▶
4 ☐ Head of household (with qualifying person). (See page 12.) If the qualifying person is a child but not your dependent, enter this child's name here. ▶
5 ☐ Qualifying widow(er) with dependent child (year spouse died ▶ 19). (See page 12.)

Exemptions (See page 12.)

6a ☐ **Yourself.** If your parent (or someone else) can claim you as a dependent on his or her tax return, **do not** check box 6a. But be sure to check the box on line 33b on page 2

b ☐ **Spouse**

No. of boxes checked on 6a and 6b ____

c **Dependents:**

(1) First name Last name	(2) Dependent's social security number. If born in 1995, see page 13.	(3) Dependent's relationship to you	(4) No. of months lived in your home in 1995

If more than six dependents, see page 13.

No. of your children on 6c who:
- lived with you ____
- didn't live with you due to divorce or separation (see page 14) ____

Dependents on 6c not entered above ____

d If your child didn't live with you but is claimed as your dependent under a pre-1985 agreement, check here ▶ ☐
e Total number of exemptions claimed

Add numbers entered on lines above ▶ ☐

Income

Attach Copy B of your Forms W-2, W-2G, and 1099-R here.

If you did not get a W-2, see page 14.

Enclose, but do not attach, your payment and payment voucher. See page 33.

7	Wages, salaries, tips, etc. Attach Form(s) W-2	7	
8a	**Taxable** interest income (see page 15). Attach Schedule B if over $400	8a	
b	**Tax-exempt** interest (see page 15). DON'T include on line 8a 8b		
9	Dividend income. Attach Schedule B if over $400	9	
10	Taxable refunds, credits, or offsets of state and local income taxes (see page 15)	10	
11	Alimony received	11	
12	Business income or (loss). Attach Schedule C or C-EZ	12	
13	Capital gain or (loss). If required, attach Schedule D (see page 16)	13	
14	Other gains or (losses). Attach Form 4797	14	
15a	Total IRA distributions 15a ; **b** Taxable amount (see page 16)	15b	
16a	Total pensions and annuities 16a ; **b** Taxable amount (see page 16)	16b	
17	Rental real estate, royalties, partnerships, S corporations, trusts, etc. Attach Schedule E	17	
18	Farm income or (loss). Attach Schedule F	18	
19	Unemployment compensation (see page 17)	19	
20a	Social security benefits 20a ; **b** Taxable amount (see page 18)	20b	
21	Other income. List type and amount—see page 18	21	
22	Add the amounts in the far right column for lines 7 through 21. This is your **total income** ▶	22	

GI concept

Adjustments to Income

23a	Your IRA deduction (see page 19)	23a	
b	Spouse's IRA deduction (see page 19)	23b	
24	Moving expenses. Attach Form 3903 or 3903-F	24	
25	One-half of self-employment tax	25	
26	Self-employed health insurance deduction (see page 21)	26	
27	Keogh & self-employed SEP plans. If SEP, check ▶ ☐	27	
28	Penalty on early withdrawal of savings	28	
29	Alimony paid. Recipient's SSN ▶	29	
30	Add lines 23a through 29. These are your **total adjustments** ▶	30	

same as S.S. → 25
30% premium 26

Adjusted Gross Income

31 Subtract line 30 from line 22. This is your **adjusted gross income**. If less than $26,673 and a child lived with you (less than $9,230 if a child didn't live with you), see "Earned Income Credit" on page 27 ▶ 31

Form 1040 (1995) Page **2**

Tax Computation

(See page 23.)

32	Amount from line 31 (adjusted gross income)	32
33a	Check if: ☐ **You** were 65 or older, ☐ Blind; ☐ **Spouse** was 65 or older, ☐ Blind. Add the number of boxes checked above and enter the total here ▶ 33a	
b	If your parent (or someone else) can claim you as a dependent, check here ▶ 33b ☐	
c	If you are married filing separately and your spouse itemizes deductions or you are a dual-status alien, see page 23 and check here ▶ 33c ☐	
34	Enter the **larger** of your: **Itemized deductions** from Schedule A, line 28, **OR** **Standard deduction** shown below for your filing status. **But if you checked any box on line 33a or b,** go to page 23 to find your standard deduction. If you checked **box 33c,** your standard deduction is zero. • Single—$3,900 • Married filing jointly or Qualifying widow(er)—$6,550 • Head of household—$5,750 • Married filing separately—$3,275	34
35	Subtract line 34 from line 32	35
36	If line 32 is $86,025 or less, multiply $2,500 by the total number of exemptions claimed on line 6e. If line 32 is over $86,025, see the worksheet on page 23 for the amount to enter	36
37	**Taxable income.** Subtract line 36 from line 35. If line 36 is more than line 35, enter -0-	37
38	Tax. Check if from a ☐ Tax Table, b ☐ Tax Rate Schedules, c ☐ Capital Gain Tax Worksheet, or d ☐ Form 8615 (see page 24). Amount from Form(s) 8814 ▶ e	38
39	Additional taxes. Check if from a ☐ Form 4970 b ☐ Form 4972	39
40	Add lines 38 and 39 ▶	40

If you want the IRS to figure your tax, see page 35.

Credits

(See page 24.)

41	Credit for child and dependent care expenses. Attach Form 2441	41	
42	Credit for the elderly or the disabled. Attach Schedule R	42	
43	Foreign tax credit. Attach Form 1116	43	
44	Other credits (see page 25). Check if from a ☐ Form 3800 b ☐ Form 8396 c ☐ Form 8801 d ☐ Form (specify) ____	44	
45	Add lines 41 through 44		45
46	Subtract line 45 from line 40. If line 45 is more than line 40, enter -0- ▶		46

Other Taxes

(See page 25.)

47	Self-employment tax. Attach Schedule SE	47
48	Alternative minimum tax. Attach Form 6251	48
49	Recapture taxes. Check if from a ☐ Form 4255 b ☐ Form 8611 c ☐ Form 8828	49
50	Social security and Medicare tax on tip income not reported to employer. Attach Form 4137	50
51	Tax on qualified retirement plans, including IRAs. If required, attach Form 5329	51
52	Advance earned income credit payments from Form W-2	52
53	Household employment taxes. Attach Schedule H	53
54	Add lines 46 through 53. This is your **total tax** ▶	54

Payments

Attach Forms W-2, W-2G, and 1099-R on the front.

55	Federal income tax withheld. If any is from Form(s) 1099, check ▶ ☐	55	
56	1995 estimated tax payments and amount applied from 1994 return	56	
57	**Earned income credit.** Attach Schedule EIC if you have a qualifying child. Nontaxable earned income: amount ▶ ____ and type ▶ ____	57	
58	Amount paid with Form 4868 (extension request)	58	
59	Excess social security and RRTA tax withheld (see page 32)	59	
60	Other payments. Check if from a ☐ Form 2439 b ☐ Form 4136	60	
61	Add lines 55 through 60. These are your **total payments** ▶		61

Refund or Amount You Owe

62	If line 61 is more than line 54, subtract line 54 from line 61. This is the amount you **OVERPAID**		62
63	Amount of line 62 you want **REFUNDED TO YOU** ▶		63
64	Amount of line 62 you want **APPLIED TO YOUR 1996 ESTIMATED TAX** ▶	64	
65	If line 54 is more than line 61, subtract line 61 from line 54. This is the **AMOUNT YOU OWE.** For details on how to pay and use **Form 1040-V,** Payment Voucher, see page 33 ▶		65
66	Estimated tax penalty (see page 33). Also include on line 65	66	

Sign Here

Keep a copy of this return for your records.

Under penalties of perjury, I declare that I have examined this return and accompanying schedules and statements, and to the best of my knowledge and belief, they are true, correct, and complete. Declaration of preparer (other than taxpayer) is based on all information of which preparer has any knowledge.

▶ Your signature	Date	Your occupation
▶ Spouse's signature. If a joint return, BOTH must sign.	Date	Spouse's occupation

Paid Preparer's Use Only

Preparer's signature ▶	Date	Check if self-employed ☐	Preparer's social security no.
Firm's name (or yours if self-employed) and address ▶			EIN
			ZIP code

from AGI

SCHEDULES A&B (Form 1040)

Department of the Treasury Internal Revenue Service (99)

Schedule A—Itemized Deductions

(Schedule B is on back)

▶ **Attach to Form 1040.** ▶ **See Instructions for Schedules A and B (Form 1040).**

OMB No. 1545-0074

1995

Attachment Sequence No. **07**

Name(s) shown on Form 1040 | **Your social security number**

Medical and Dental Expenses		**Caution:** *Do not include expenses reimbursed or paid by others.*			
	1	Medical and dental expenses (see page A-1) 7 7.5%	1		
	2	Enter amount from Form 1040, line 32. [2] AGI			
	3	Multiply line 2 above by 7.5% (.075)	3		
	4	Subtract line 3 from line 1. If line 3 is more than line 1, enter -0-		4	
Taxes You Paid	5	State and local income taxes	5		
	6	Real estate taxes (see page A-2)	6		
(See page A-1.) DMV	7	Personal property taxes	7		
	8	Other taxes. List type and amount ▶	8		
	9	Add lines 5 through 8		9	
Interest You Paid (See page A-2.)	10	Home mortgage interest and points reported to you on Form 1098	10		
	11	Home mortgage interest not reported to you on Form 1098. If paid to the person from whom you bought the home, see page A-3 and show that person's name, identifying no., and address ▶	11		
Note: Personal interest is not deductible.	12	Points not reported to you on Form 1098. See page A-3 for special rules	12		
	13	Investment interest. If required, attach Form 4952. (See page A-3.) – somebody who borrowed money	13		
	14	Add lines 10 through 13		14	
Gifts to Charity	15	Gifts by cash or check. If you made any gift of $250 or more, see page A-3	15		
If you made a gift and got a benefit for it, see page A-3.	16	Other than by cash or check. If any gift of $250 or more, see page A-3. If over $500, you **MUST** attach Form 8283	16		
	17	Carryover from prior year	17		
	18	Add lines 15 through 17		18	
Casualty and Theft Losses	19	Casualty or theft loss(es). Attach Form 4684. (See page A-4.)		19	
Job Expenses and Most Other Miscellaneous Deductions	20	Unreimbursed employee expenses—job travel, union dues, job education, etc. If required, you **MUST** attach Form 2106 or 2106-EZ. (See page A-5.) ▶	20		
	21	Tax preparation fees	21		
(See page A-5 for expenses to deduct here.)	22	Other expenses—investment, safe deposit box, etc. List type and amount ▶ Sec. 212	22		
	23	Add lines 20 through 22	23		
	24	Enter amount from Form 1040, line 32. [24]			
	25	Multiply line 24 above by 2% (.02)	25		
	26	Subtract line 25 from line 23. If line 25 is more than line 23, enter -0-		26	
Other Miscellaneous Deductions	27	Other—from list on page A-5. List type and amount ▶		27	
Total Itemized Deductions	28	Is Form 1040, line 32, over $114,700 (over $57,350 if married filing separately)? **NO.** Your deduction is not limited. Add the amounts in the far right column for lines 4 through 27. Also, enter on Form 1040, line 34, the **larger** of this amount or your standard deduction. **YES.** Your deduction may be limited. See page A-5 for the amount to enter. ▶		28	

For Paperwork Reduction Act Notice, see Form 1040 instructions. Cat. No. 11330X **Schedule A (Form 1040) 1995**

Schedules A&B (Form 1040) 1995 — OMB No. 1545-0074 — Page 2

Name(s) shown on Form 1040. Do not enter name and social security number if shown on other side. | **Your social security number**

Schedule B—Interest and Dividend Income

Attachment Sequence No. **08**

Part I Interest Income

(See pages 15 and B-1.)

Note: If you received a Form 1099-INT, Form 1099-OID, or substitute statement from a brokerage firm, list the firm's name as the payer and enter the total interest shown on that form.

Note: *If you had over $400 in taxable interest income, you must also complete Part III.*

			Amount
1	List name of payer. If any interest is from a seller-financed mortgage and the buyer used the property as a personal residence, see page B-1 and list this interest first. Also, show that buyer's social security number and address ▶	1	
2	Add the amounts on line 1	2	
3	Excludable interest on series EE U.S. savings bonds issued after 1989 from Form 8815, line 14. You MUST attach Form 8815 to Form 1040	3	
4	Subtract line 3 from line 2. Enter the result here and on Form 1040, line 8a ▶	4	

Part II Dividend Income

(See pages 15 and B-1.)

Note: If you received a Form 1099-DIV or substitute statement from a brokerage firm, list the firm's name as the payer and enter the total dividends shown on that form.

Note: *If you had over $400 in gross dividends and/or other distributions on stock, you must also complete Part III.*

			Amount
5	List name of payer. Include gross dividends and/or other distributions on stock here. Any capital gain distributions and nontaxable distributions will be deducted on lines 7 and 8 ▶	5	
6	Add the amounts on line 5	6	
7	Capital gain distributions. Enter here and on Schedule D* . | 7 |		
8	Nontaxable distributions. (See the inst. for Form 1040, line 9.) | 8 |		
9	Add lines 7 and 8	9	
10	Subtract line 9 from line 6. Enter the result here and on Form 1040, line 9 . ▶	10	

**If you do not need Schedule D to report any other gains or losses, see the instructions for Form 1040, line 13, on page 16.*

Part III Foreign Accounts and Trusts

(See page B-2.)

If you had over $400 of interest or dividends **or** had a foreign account or were a grantor of, or a transferor to, a foreign trust, you must complete this part.

		Yes	No
11a	At any time during 1995, did you have an interest in or a signature or other authority over a financial account in a foreign country, such as a bank account, securities account, or other financial account? See page B-2 for exceptions and filing requirements for Form TD F 90-22.1		
b	If "Yes," enter the name of the foreign country ▶		
12	Were you the grantor of, or transferor to, a foreign trust that existed during 1995, whether or not you have any beneficial interest in it? If "Yes," you may have to file Form 3520, 3520-A, or 926 .		

SCHEDULE C (Form 1040)

Department of the Treasury
Internal Revenue Service (99)

Profit or Loss From Business

(Sole Proprietorship)

▶ Partnerships, joint ventures, etc., must file Form 1065.

▶ Attach to Form 1040 or Form 1041. ▶ See Instructions for Schedule C (Form 1040).

OMB No. 1545-0074

1995

Attachment Sequence No. **09**

Name of proprietor | **Social security number (SSN)**

A Principal business or profession, including product or service (see page C-1) | **B Enter principal business code** (see page C-6) ▶

C Business name. If no separate business name, leave blank. | **D Employer ID number (EIN), if any**

E Business address (including suite or room no.) ▶
City, town or post office, state, and ZIP code

F Accounting method: **(1)** ☐ Cash **(2)** ☐ Accrual **(3)** ☐ Other (specify) ▶

G Method(s) used to value closing inventory: **(1)** ☐ Cost **(2)** ☐ Lower of cost or market **(3)** ☐ Other (attach explanation) **(4)** ☐ Does not apply (if checked, skip line H) | **Yes** | **No**

H Was there any change in determining quantities, costs, or valuations between opening and closing inventory? If "Yes," attach explanation

I Did you "materially participate" in the operation of this business during 1995? If "No," see page C-2 for limit on losses.

J If you started or acquired this business during 1995, check here ▶ ☐

Part I Income

1	Gross receipts or sales. **Caution:** *If this income was reported to you on Form W-2 and the "Statutory employee" box on that form was checked, see page C-2 and check here* ▶ ☐	1	
2	Returns and allowances	2	
3	Subtract line 2 from line 1	3	
4	Cost of goods sold (from line 40 on page 2)	4	
5	**Gross profit.** Subtract line 4 from line 3	5	
6	Other income, including Federal and state gasoline or fuel tax credit or refund (see page C-2)	6	
7	**Gross income.** Add lines 5 and 6 ▶	7	

Part II Expenses. Enter expenses for business use of your home **only** on line 30.

8	Advertising	8		19	Pension and profit-sharing plans	19	
9	Bad debts from sales or services (see page C-3)	9		20	Rent or lease (see page C-4):		
				a	Vehicles, machinery, and equipment	20a	
10	Car and truck expenses (see page C-3)	10		b	Other business property	20b	
				21	Repairs and maintenance	21	
11	Commissions and fees	11		22	Supplies (not included in Part III)	22	
12	Depletion	12		23	Taxes and licenses	23	
13	Depreciation and section 179 expense deduction (not included in Part III) (see page C-3)	13		24	Travel, meals, and entertainment:		
				a	Travel	24a	
14	Employee benefit programs (other than on line 19)	14		b	Meals and entertainment		
15	Insurance (other than health)	15		c	Enter 50% of line 24b subject to limitations (see page C-4)		
16	Interest:						
a	Mortgage (paid to banks, etc.)	16a		d	Subtract line 24c from line 24b	24d	
b	Other	16b		25	Utilities	25	
17	Legal and professional services	17		26	Wages (less employment credits)	26	
18	Office expense	18		27	Other expenses (from line 46 on page 2)	27	

28	**Total expenses** before expenses for business use of home. Add lines 8 through 27 in columns ▶	28	
29	Tentative profit (loss). Subtract line 28 from line 7	29	
30	Expenses for business use of your home. Attach **Form 8829**	30	
31	**Net profit or (loss).** Subtract line 30 from line 29. • If a profit, enter on **Form 1040, line 12,** and ALSO on **Schedule SE, line 2** (statutory employees, see page C-5). Estates and trusts, enter on Form 1041, line 3. • If a loss, you MUST go on to line 32.	31	
32	If you have a loss, check the box that describes your investment in this activity (see page C-5). • If you checked 32a, enter the loss on **Form 1040, line 12,** and ALSO on **Schedule SE, line 2** (statutory employees, see page C-5). Estates and trusts, enter on Form 1041, line 3. • If you checked 32b, you MUST attach **Form 6198.**		**32a** ☐ All investment is at risk. **32b** ☐ Some investment is not at risk.

For Paperwork Reduction Act Notice, see Form 1040 instructions. Cat. No. 11334P **Schedule C (Form 1040) 1995**

Schedule C (Form 1040) 1995 Page **2**

Part III **Cost of Goods Sold** (see page C-5)

33	Inventory at beginning of year. If different from last year's closing inventory, attach explanation	33		
34	Purchases less cost of items withdrawn for personal use	34		
35	Cost of labor. Do not include salary paid to yourself	35		
36	Materials and supplies	36		
37	Other costs	37		
38	Add lines 33 through 37	38		
39	Inventory at end of year	39		
40	**Cost of goods sold.** Subtract line 39 from line 38. Enter the result here and on page 1, line 4	40		

Part IV **Information on Your Vehicle.** Complete this part **ONLY** if you are claiming car or truck expenses on line 10 and are not required to file Form 4562 for this business. See the instructions for line 13 on page C-3 to find out if you must file.

41 When did you place your vehicle in service for business purposes? (month, day, year) ▶ ..../........../...... .

42 Of the total number of miles you drove your vehicle during 1995, enter the number of miles you used your vehicle for:

a Business .... b Commuting .... c Other ....

43 Do you (or your spouse) have another vehicle available for personal use? ☐ **Yes** ☐ **No**

44 Was your vehicle available for use during off-duty hours? ☐ **Yes** ☐ **No**

45a Do you have evidence to support your deduction? ☐ **Yes** ☐ **No**

b If "Yes," is the evidence written? ☐ **Yes** ☐ **No**

Part V **Other Expenses.** List below business expenses not included on lines 8–26 or line 30.

46 Total other expenses. Enter here and on page 1, line 27	46	

Printed on recycled paper

SCHEDULE D (Form 1040)

Department of the Treasury
Internal Revenue Service (99)

Capital Gains and Losses

▶ Attach to Form 1040. ▶ See Instructions for Schedule D (Form 1040).

▶ Use lines 20 and 22 for more space to list transactions for lines 1 and 9.

OMB No. 1545-0074

1995

Attachment Sequence No. **12**

Name(s) shown on Form 1040 | **Your social security number**

Part I Short-Term Capital Gains and Losses—Assets Held One Year or Less

	(a) Description of property (Example: 100 sh. XYZ Co.)	(b) Date acquired (Mo., day, yr.)	(c) Date sold (Mo., day, yr.)	(d) Sales price (see page D-3)	(e) Cost or other basis (see page D-3)		(f) LOSS If (e) is more than (d), subtract (d) from (e)	(g) GAIN If (d) is more than (e), subtract (e) from (d)
1								
2	Enter your short-term totals, if any, from line 21		2					
3	**Total short-term sales price amounts.** Add column (d) of lines 1 and 2 . . .		3					
4	Short-term gain from Forms 2119 and 6252, and short-term gain or loss from Forms 4684, 6781, and 8824					4		
5	Net short-term gain or loss from partnerships, S corporations, estates, and trusts from Schedule(s) K-1					5		
6	Short-term capital loss carryover. Enter the amount, if any, from line 9 of your 1994 Capital Loss Carryover Worksheet					6		
7	Add lines 1 through 6 in columns (f) and (g)					7	( )	
8	**Net short-term capital gain or (loss).** Combine columns (f) and (g) of line 7 . . . . . ▶						8	

Part II Long-Term Capital Gains and Losses—Assets Held More Than One Year

	(a)	(b)	(c)	(d)	(e)		(f)	(g)
9								
10	Enter your long-term totals, if any, from line 23		10					
11	**Total long-term sales price amounts.** Add column (d) of lines 9 and 10 . . .		11					
12	Gain from Form 4797; long-term gain from Forms 2119, 2439, and 6252; and long-term gain or loss from Forms 4684, 6781, and 8824					12		
13	Net long-term gain or loss from partnerships, S corporations, estates, and trusts from Schedule(s) K-1					13		
14	Capital gain distributions					14		
15	Long-term capital loss carryover. Enter the amount, if any, from line 14 of your 1994 Capital Loss Carryover Worksheet					15		
16	Add lines 9 through 15 in columns (f) and (g)					16	( )	
17	**Net long-term capital gain or (loss).** Combine columns (f) and (g) of line 16 . . . . . ▶						17	

Part III Summary of Parts I and II

18	Combine lines 8 and 17. If a loss, go to line 19. If a gain, enter the gain on Form 1040, line 13. **Note:** *If both lines 17 and 18 are gains, see the* ***Capital Gain Tax Worksheet*** *on page 24* . .	18	
19	If line 18 is a loss, enter here and as a (loss) on Form 1040, line 13, the **smaller** of these losses:		
a	The loss on line 18; **or**		
b	($3,000) or, if married filing separately, ($1,500)	19	( )
	Note: *See the* ***Capital Loss Carryover Worksheet*** *on page D-3 if the loss on line 18 exceeds the loss on line 19* ***or*** *if Form 1040, line 35, is a loss.*		

For Paperwork Reduction Act Notice, see Form 1040 instructions. Cat. No. 11338H **Schedule D (Form 1040) 1995**

Schedule D (Form 1040) 1995 Attachment Sequence No. **12** Page **2**

Name(s) shown on Form 1040. Do not enter name and social security number if shown on other side.	**Your social security number**

Part IV **Short-Term Capital Gains and Losses—Assets Held One Year or Less** *(Continuation of Part I)*

	(a) Description of property (Example: 100 sh. XYZ Co.)	**(b)** Date acquired (Mo., day, yr.)	**(c)** Date sold (Mo., day, yr.)	**(d)** Sales price (see page D-3)	**(e)** Cost or other basis (see page D-3)	**(f) LOSS** If (e) is more than (d), subtract (d) from (e)	**(g) GAIN** If (d) is more than (e), subtract (e) from (d)
20							
21	Short-term totals. Add columns (d), (f), and (g) of line 20. Enter here and on line 2 .		21				

Part V **Long-Term Capital Gains and Losses—Assets Held More Than One Year** *(Continuation of Part II)*

22							
23	Long-term totals. Add columns (d), (f), and (g) of line 22. Enter here and on line 10 .		23				

Printed on recycled paper

SCHEDULE E (Form 1040)

Department of the Treasury
Internal Revenue Service (99)

Supplemental Income and Loss

(From rental real estate, royalties, partnerships, S corporations, estates, trusts, REMICs, etc.)

▶ **Attach to Form 1040 or Form 1041.** ▶ **See Instructions for Schedule E (Form 1040).**

OMB No. 1545-0074

1995

Attachment Sequence No. **13**

Name(s) shown on return | **Your social security number**

Part I **Income or Loss From Rental Real Estate and Royalties** **Note:** *Report income and expenses from your business of renting personal property on* ***Schedule C*** *or* ***C-EZ*** *(see page E-1). Report farm rental income or loss from* ***Form 4835*** *on page 2, line 39.*

1	Show the kind and location of each **rental real estate property:**	2 For each rental real estate property listed on line 1, did you or your family use it for personal purposes for more than the greater of 14 days or 10% of the total days rented at fair rental value during the tax year? (See page E-1.)		Yes	No
A			A		
B			B		
C			C		

Income:		Properties A	Properties B	Properties C		**Totals** (Add columns A, B, and C.)
3 Rents received	3				3	
4 Royalties received	4				4	
Expenses:						
5 Advertising	5					
6 Auto and travel (see page E-2)	6					
7 Cleaning and maintenance	7					
8 Commissions	8					
9 Insurance	9					
10 Legal and other professional fees	10					
11 Management fees	11					
12 Mortgage interest paid to banks, etc. (see page E-2)	12				12	
13 Other interest	13					
14 Repairs	14					
15 Supplies	15					
16 Taxes	16					
17 Utilities	17					
18 Other (list) ▶	18					
19 Add lines 5 through 18	19				19	
20 Depreciation expense or depletion (see page E-2)	20				20	
21 Total expenses. Add lines 19 and 20	21					
22 Income or (loss) from rental real estate or royalty properties. Subtract line 21 from line 3 (rents) or line 4 (royalties). If the result is a (loss), see page E-2 to find out if you must file **Form 6198**	22					
23 Deductible rental real estate loss. **Caution:** *Your rental real estate loss on line 22 may be limited. See page E-3 to find out if you must file* ***Form 8582****. Real estate professionals must complete line 42 on page 2*	23	( )	( )	( )		
24 **Income.** Add positive amounts shown on line 22. **Do not** include any losses					24	
25 **Losses.** Add royalty losses from line 22 and rental real estate losses from line 23. Enter the total losses here					25	( )
26 Total rental real estate and royalty income or (loss). Combine lines 24 and 25. Enter the result here. If Parts II, III, IV, and line 39 on page 2 do not apply to you, also enter this amount on Form 1040, line 17. Otherwise, include this amount in the total on line 40 on page 2					26	

For Paperwork Reduction Act Notice, see Form 1040 instructions. Cat. No. 11344L **Schedule E (Form 1040) 1995**

Schedule E (Form 1040) 1995 Attachment Sequence No. **13** Page **2**

Name(s) shown on return. Do not enter name and social security number if shown on other side. | **Your social security number**

Note: *If you report amounts from farming or fishing on Schedule E, you must enter your gross income from those activities on line 41 below. Real estate professionals must complete line 42 below.*

Part II Income or Loss From Partnerships and S Corporations

Note: *If you report a loss from an at-risk activity, you MUST check either column **(e)** or **(f)** of line 27 to describe your investment in the activity. See page E-4. If you check column **(f)**, you must attach **Form 6198**.*

27	**(a)** Name	**(b)** Enter **P** for partnership; **S** for S corporation	**(c)** Check if foreign partnership	**(d)** Employer identification number	Investment At Risk? **(e)** All is at risk	**(f)** Some is not at risk
A						
B						
C						
D						
E						

	Passive Income and Loss		Nonpassive Income and Loss		
	(g) Passive loss allowed (attach **Form 8582** if required)	**(h)** Passive income from **Schedule K–1**	**(i)** Nonpassive loss from **Schedule K–1**	**(j)** Section 179 expense deduction from **Form 4562**	**(k)** Nonpassive income from **Schedule K–1**
A					
B					
C					
D					
E					
28a Totals					
b Totals					

29	Add columns (h) and (k) of line 28a	29	
30	Add columns (g), (i), and (j) of line 28b	30	( )
31	Total partnership and S corporation income or (loss). Combine lines 29 and 30. Enter the result here and include in the total on line 40 below	31	

Part III Income or Loss From Estates and Trusts

32	**(a)** Name	**(b)** Employer identification number
A		
B		

	Passive Income and Loss		Nonpassive Income and Loss	
	(c) Passive deduction or loss allowed (attach **Form 8582** if required)	**(d)** Passive income from **Schedule K–1**	**(e)** Deduction or loss from **Schedule K–1**	**(f)** Other income from **Schedule K–1**
A				
B				
33a Totals				
b Totals				

34	Add columns (d) and (f) of line 33a	34	
35	Add columns (c) and (e) of line 33b	35	( )
36	Total estate and trust income or (loss). Combine lines 34 and 35. Enter the result here and include in the total on line 40 below	36	

Part IV Income or Loss From Real Estate Mortgage Investment Conduits (REMICs)—Residual Holder

37	**(a)** Name	**(b)** Employer identification number	**(c)** Excess inclusion from **Schedules Q,** line 2c (see page E-4)	**(d)** Taxable income (net loss) from **Schedules Q,** line 1b	**(e)** Income from **Schedules Q,** line 3b

38	Combine columns (d) and (e) only. Enter the result here and include in the total on line 40 below	38	

Part V Summary

39	Net farm rental income or (loss) from **Form 4835**. Also, complete line 41 below	39	
40	TOTAL income or (loss). Combine lines 26, 31, 36, 38, and 39. Enter the result here and on Form 1040, line 17 ▶	40	
41	**Reconciliation of Farming and Fishing Income.** Enter your **gross** farming and fishing income reported on Form 4835, line 7; Schedule K-1 (Form 1065), line 15b; Schedule K-1 (Form 1120S), line 23; and Schedule K-1 (Form 1041), line 13 (see page E-4)	41	
42	**Reconciliation for Real Estate Professionals.** If you were a real estate professional (see page E-3), enter the net income or (loss) you reported anywhere on Form 1040 from all rental real estate activities in which you materially participated under the passive activity loss rules	42	

SCHEDULE EIC
(Form 1040A or 1040)
Department of the Treasury
Internal Revenue Service (99)

Earned Income Credit
(Qualifying Child Information)

▶ Attach to Form 1040A or 1040.
▶ See instructions on back.

OMB No. 1545-0074
1995
Attachment Sequence No. **43**

Name(s) shown on return | **Your social security number**

Before You Begin . . .

- Answer the questions on page 47 of the Form 1040A instructions or page 27 of the Form 1040 instructions to see if you can take this credit.
- If you can take the credit, fill in the worksheet on page 48 (1040A) or page 28 (1040) to figure your credit. **But if you want the IRS to figure it for you, see page 42 (1040A) or page 35 (1040).**

Then, you **must** complete and attach Schedule EIC only if you have a qualifying child (see boxes on back).

Information About Your Qualifying Child or Children

If you have more than two qualifying children, you only have to list two to get the maximum credit.

Caution: *If you don't attach Schedule EIC and fill in all the lines that apply, it will take us longer to process your return and issue your refund.*	**(a) Child 1**	**(b) Child 2**
	First name Last name	First name Last name
1 Child's name		
2 Child's year of birth	19___	19___
3 If the child was born **before 1977** AND—		
a was **under age 24** at the end of 1995 **and** a student, check the "Yes" box, **OR**	☐ Yes	☐ Yes
b was permanently and totally disabled (see back), check the "Yes" box	☐ Yes	☐ Yes
4 Enter the child's social security number. If born in 1995, see instructions on back		
5 Child's relationship to you (for example, son, grandchild, etc.) .		
6 Number of months child lived with you in the United States in 1995	months	months

5/E5AAA

TIP: Do you want the earned income credit added to your take-home pay in 1996? To see if you qualify, get **Form W-5** from your employer or by calling the IRS at 1-800-TAX-FORM (1-800-829-3676).

Instructions

Purpose of Schedule

If you can take the earned income credit and have a qualifying child, use Schedule EIC to give information about that child. To figure the amount of your credit, use the worksheet on page 48 of the Form 1040A instructions or page 28 of the Form 1040 instructions.

Line 1

Enter each qualifying child's name.

Line 3a

If your child was born **before 1977** but was under age 24 at the end of 1995 and a student, put a checkmark in the "Yes" box.

Your child was a **student** if he or she—

- Was enrolled as a full-time student at a school during any 5 months of 1995, or
- Took a full-time, on-farm training course during any 5 months of 1995. The course had to be given by a school or a state, county, or local government agency.

A **school** includes technical, trade, and mechanical schools. It does not include on-the-job training courses or correspondence schools.

Line 3b

If your child was born **before 1977** and was permanently and totally disabled during any part of 1995, put a checkmark in the "Yes" box.

A person is **permanently and totally disabled** if **both** of the following apply.

1. He or she cannot engage in any substantial gainful activity because of a physical or mental condition.

2. A doctor determines the condition has lasted or can be expected to last continuously for at least a year or can lead to death.

Line 4

If your child was born **before November 1, 1995,** you **must** enter his or her social security number (SSN) on line 4. If you don't enter an SSN or if the SSN you enter is incorrect, it will take us longer to issue any refund shown on your return. If your child doesn't have a number, apply for one by filing **Form SS-5** with your local Social Security Administration (SSA) office. It usually takes about 2 weeks to get a number. If your child won't have an SSN by April 15, 1996, you can get an automatic 4-month extension by filing Form 4868 with the IRS by that date.

If your child was born **after October 31, 1995,** you don't have to enter his or her SSN on line 4. Instead, enter the month and year your child was born. For example, your child was born on December 1, 1995. You should enter "12/95" on line 4.

Line 6

Enter the number of months your child lived with you in your home in the United States during 1995. (If you were in the military on extended active duty outside the United States, your home is considered to be in the United States during that duty period.) Do not enter more than 12. Count temporary absences, such as for school, vacation, or medical care, as time lived in your home. If the child lived with you for more than half of 1995 but less than 7 months, enter "7" on this line.

Exception. If your child, including a foster child, was born or died in 1995 and your home was the child's home for the entire time he or she was alive during 1995, enter "12" on line 6.

Qualifying Child

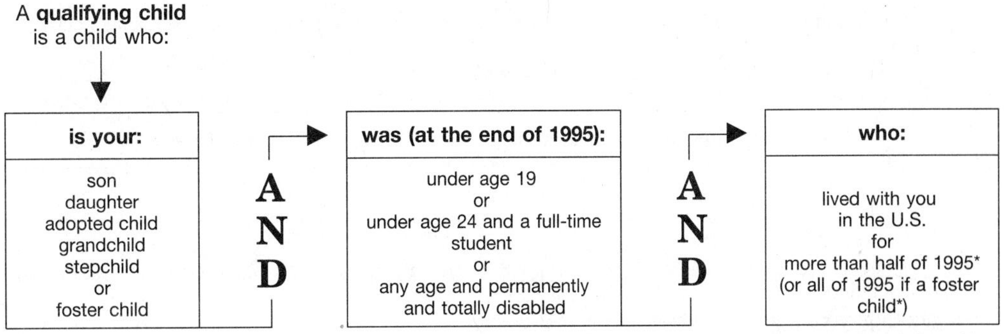

*If the child didn't live with you for the required time (for example, was born in 1995), see the **Line 6** instructions above.

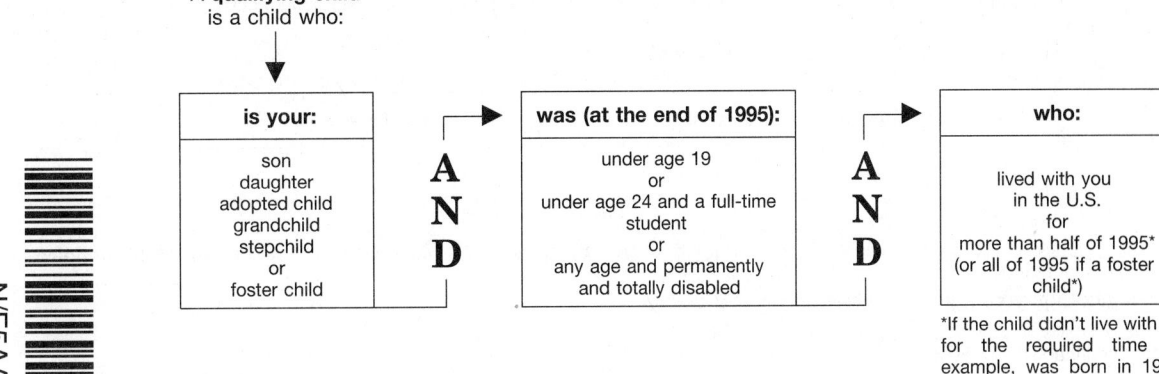

If the child was married or is also a qualifying child of another person (other than your spouse if filing a joint return), special rules apply. For details, see page 50 of the Form 1040A instructions or page 28 of the Form 1040 instructions.

N/E5AAA

Printed on recycled paper

Schedule R (Form 1040)

Department of the Treasury
Internal Revenue Service (99)

Credit for the Elderly or the Disabled

▶ Attach to Form 1040. ▶ See separate instructions for Schedule R.

OMB No. 1545-0074

1995

Attachment Sequence No. **16**

Name(s) shown on Form 1040 | **Your social security number**

You may be able to take this credit and reduce your tax if by the end of 1995:

- You were age 65 or older, **OR** • You were under age 65, you retired on **permanent and total** disability, and you received taxable disability income.

But you must also meet other tests. See the separate instructions for Schedule R.

Note: *In most cases, the IRS can figure the credit for you. See page 35 of the Form 1040 instructions.*

Part I Check the Box for Your Filing Status and Age

If your filing status is:	And by the end of 1995:		Check only one box:
Single, Head of household, or Qualifying widow(er) with dependent child	1 You were 65 or older	1	☐
	2 You were under 65 and you retired on permanent and total disability . . .	2	☐
Married filing a joint return	3 Both spouses were 65 or older	3	☐
	4 Both spouses were under 65, but only one spouse retired on permanent and total disability	4	☐
	5 Both spouses were under 65, and both retired on permanent and total disability	5	☐
	6 One spouse was 65 or older, and the other spouse was under 65 and retired on permanent and total disability	6	☐
	7 One spouse was 65 or older, and the other spouse was under 65 and **NOT** retired on permanent and total disability	7	☐
Married filing a separate return	8 You were 65 or older and you lived apart from your spouse for all of 1995 . .	8	☐
	9 You were under 65, you retired on permanent and total disability, and you lived apart from your spouse for all of 1995.	9	☐

Did you check box 1, 3, 7, or 8?
- **Yes** ▶ Skip Part II and complete Part III on back.
- **No** ▶ Complete Parts II and III.

Part II Statement of Permanent and Total Disability (Complete **only** if you checked box 2, 4, 5, 6, or 9 above.)

IF: 1 You filed a physician's statement for this disability for 1983 or an earlier year, or you filed a statement for tax years after 1983 and your physician signed line B on the statement, **AND**

2 Due to your continued disabled condition, you were unable to engage in any substantial gainful activity in 1995, check this box . . . . ▶ ☐

- If you checked this box, you do not have to file another statement for 1995.
- If you **did not** check this box, have your physician complete the statement below.

Physician's Statement (See instructions at bottom of page 2.)

I certify that ______________________________
Name of disabled person

was permanently and totally disabled on January 1, 1976, or January 1, 1977, **OR** was permanently and totally disabled on the date he or she retired. If retired after 1976, enter the date retired. ▶ ____________

Physician: Sign your name on **either** line A or B below.

A The disability has lasted or can be expected to last continuously for at least a year . . . . ______________________
Physician's signature Date

B There is no reasonable probability that the disabled condition will ever improve . . . . ______________________
Physician's signature Date

Physician's name	Physician's address

Schedule R (Form 1040) 1995 Page **2**

Part III **Figure Your Credit**

10 **If you checked (in Part I):** **Enter:**

Box 1, 2, 4, or 7 . . . . $5,000
Box 3, 5, or 6 . . . . $7,500
Box 8 or 9 . . . . $3,750 } **10**

Did you check box 2, 4, 5, 6, or 9 in Part I?
Yes ▶ You **must** complete line 11.
No ▶ Enter the amount from line 10 on line 12 and go to line 13.

11 **If you checked:**

- Box 6 in Part I, add $5,000 to the taxable disability income of the spouse who was under age 65. Enter the total.
- Box 2, 4, or 9 in Part I, enter your taxable disability income.
- Box 5 in Part I, add your taxable disability income to your spouse's taxable disability income. Enter the total.

} **11**

TIP: For more details on what to include on line 11, see the instructions.

12 If you completed line 11, enter the **smaller** of line 10 or line 11; **all others,** enter the amount from line 10 . . . . **12**

13 Enter the following pensions, annuities, or disability income that you (and your spouse if filing a joint return) received in 1995.

a Nontaxable part of social security benefits, and Nontaxable part of railroad retirement benefits treated as social security. See instructions. } . . . **13a**

b Nontaxable veterans' pensions, and Any other pension, annuity, or disability benefit that is excluded from income under any other provision of law. See instructions. } . . . **13b**

c Add lines 13a and 13b. (Even though these income items are not taxable, they **must** be included here to figure your credit.) If you did not receive any of the types of nontaxable income listed on line 13a or 13b, enter -0- on line 13c **13c**

14 Enter the amount from Form 1040, line 32 **14**

15 **If you checked (in Part I):** **Enter:**

Box 1 or 2 . . . . $7,500
Box 3, 4, 5, 6, or 7 . . . . $10,000
Box 8 or 9 . . . . $5,000 } **15**

16 Subtract line 15 from line 14. If zero or less, enter -0- **16**

17 Enter one-half of line 16 . . . . **17**

18 Add lines 13c and 17 . . . . **18**

19 Subtract line 18 from line 12. If zero or less, **stop;** you **cannot** take the credit. Otherwise, go to line 20 . . . . **19**

20 Multiply line 19 by 15% (.15). Enter the result here and on Form 1040, line 42. **Caution:** *If you file Schedule C, C-EZ, D, E, or F (Form 1040), your credit may be limited. See the instructions for line 20 for the amount of credit you can claim* **20**

Instructions for Physician's Statement

Taxpayer

If you retired after 1976, enter the date you retired in the space provided in Part II.

Physician

A person is permanently and totally disabled if **both** of the following apply:

1. He or she cannot engage in any substantial gainful activity because of a physical or mental condition, and

2. A physician determines that the disability has lasted or can be expected to last continuously for at least a year or can lead to death.

Printed on recycled paper

SCHEDULE SE (Form 1040)

Department of the Treasury
Internal Revenue Service (99)

Self-Employment Tax

▶ See Instructions for Schedule SE (Form 1040).

▶ Attach to Form 1040.

OMB No. 1545-0074

1995

Attachment Sequence No. **17**

Name of person with **self-employment** income (as shown on Form 1040)	Social security number of person with **self-employment** income ▶	

Who Must File Schedule SE

You must file Schedule SE if:

- You had net earnings from self-employment from **other than** church employee income (line 4 of Short Schedule SE or line 4c of Long Schedule SE) of $400 or more, **OR**
- You had church employee income of $108.28 or more. Income from services you performed as a minister or a member of a religious order **is not** church employee income. See page SE-1.

Note: *Even if you have a loss or a small amount of income from self-employment, it may be to your benefit to file Schedule SE and use either "optional method" in Part II of Long Schedule SE. See page SE-3.*

Exception. If your only self-employment income was from earnings as a minister, member of a religious order, or Christian Science practitioner **and** you filed Form 4361 and received IRS approval not to be taxed on those earnings, **do not** file Schedule SE. Instead, write "Exempt–Form 4361" on Form 1040, line 47.

May I Use Short Schedule SE or MUST I Use Long Schedule SE?

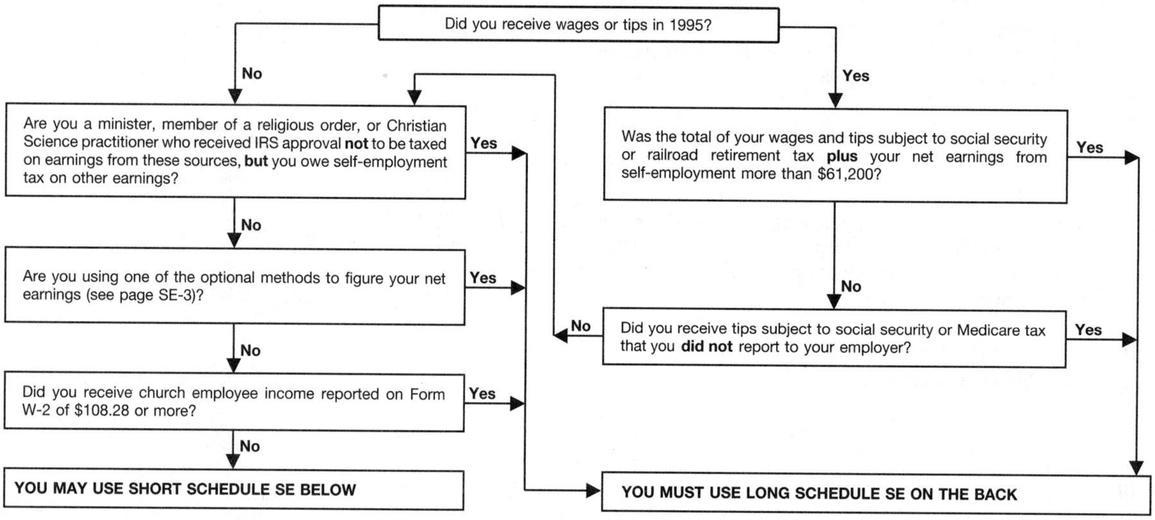

Section A—Short Schedule SE. Caution: *Read above to see if you can use Short Schedule SE.*

1	Net farm profit or (loss) from Schedule F, line 36, and farm partnerships, Schedule K-1 (Form 1065), line 15a	1	
2	Net profit or (loss) from Schedule C, line 31; Schedule C-EZ, line 3; and Schedule K-1 (Form 1065), line 15a (other than farming). Ministers and members of religious orders see page SE-1 for amounts to report on this line. See page SE-2 for other income to report	2	
3	Combine lines 1 and 2	3	
4	**Net earnings from self-employment.** Multiply line 3 by 92.35% (.9235). If less than $400, **do not** file this schedule; you do not owe self-employment tax ▶	4	
5	**Self-employment tax.** If the amount on line 4 is: • $61,200 or less, multiply line 4 by 15.3% (.153). Enter the result here and on **Form 1040, line 47.** • More than $61,200, multiply line 4 by 2.9% (.029). Then, add $7,588.80 to the result. Enter the total here and on **Form 1040, line 47.**	5	
6	**Deduction for one-half of self-employment tax.** Multiply line 5 by 50% (.5). Enter the result here and on **Form 1040, line 25** 6		

For Paperwork Reduction Act Notice, see Form 1040 instructions. Cat. No. 11358Z **Schedule SE (Form 1040) 1995**

Schedule SE (Form 1040) 1995 Attachment Sequence No. 17 Page 2

Name of person with **self-employment** income (as shown on Form 1040)	Social security number of person with **self-employment** income ▶

Section B—Long Schedule SE

Part I Self-Employment Tax

Note: *If your only income subject to self-employment tax is* ***church employee income,*** *skip lines 1 through 4b. Enter -0- on line 4c and go to line 5a. Income from services you performed as a minister or a member of a religious order* ***is not*** *church employee income. See page SE-1.*

A If you are a minister, member of a religious order, or Christian Science practitioner **and** you filed Form 4361, but you had $400 or more of **other** net earnings from self-employment, check here and continue with Part I . . . . . . ▶ ☐

Line	Description	Box	Amount
1	Net farm profit or (loss) from Schedule F, line 36, and farm partnerships, Schedule K-1 (Form 1065), line 15a. **Note:** *Skip this line if you use the farm optional method. See page SE-3*	1	
2	Net profit or (loss) from Schedule C, line 31; Schedule C-EZ, line 3; and Schedule K-1 (Form 1065), line 15a (other than farming). Ministers and members of religious orders see page SE-1 for amounts to report on this line. See page SE-2 for other income to report. **Note:** *Skip this line if you use the nonfarm optional method. See page SE-3.*	2	
3	Combine lines 1 and 2	3	
4a	If line 3 is more than zero, multiply line 3 by 92.35% (.9235). Otherwise, enter amount from line 3	4a	
b	If you elected one or both of the optional methods, enter the total of lines 15 and 17 here	4b	
c	Combine lines 4a and 4b. If less than $400, **do not** file this schedule; you do not owe self-employment tax. **Exception.** If less than $400 and you had **church employee income,** enter -0- and continue ▶	4c	
5a	Enter your **church employee income** from Form W-2. **Caution:** *See page SE-1 for definition of church employee income* 5a		
b	Multiply line 5a by 92.35% (.9235). If less than $100, enter -0-	5b	
6	**Net earnings from self-employment.** Add lines 4c and 5b	6	
7	Maximum amount of combined wages and self-employment earnings subject to social security tax or the 6.2% portion of the 7.65% railroad retirement (tier 1) tax for 1995	7	61,200 00
8a	Total social security wages and tips (total of boxes 3 and 7 on Form(s) W-2) and railroad retirement (tier 1) compensation 8a		
b	Unreported tips subject to social security tax (from Form 4137, line 9) 8b		
c	Add lines 8a and 8b	8c	
9	Subtract line 8c from line 7. If zero or less, enter -0- here and on line 10 and go to line 11 . ▶	9	
10	Multiply the **smaller** of line 6 or line 9 by 12.4% (.124)	10	
11	Multiply line 6 by 2.9% (.029)	11	
12	**Self-employment tax.** Add lines 10 and 11. Enter here and on **Form 1040, line 47**	12	
13	**Deduction for one-half of self-employment tax.** Multiply line 12 by 50% (.5). Enter the result here and on **Form 1040, line 25** 13		

Part II Optional Methods To Figure Net Earnings (See page SE-3.)

Farm Optional Method. You may use this method **only** if:

- Your gross farm income[1] was not more than $2,400, **or**
- Your gross farm income[1] was more than $2,400 and your net farm profits[2] were less than $1,733.

Line	Description	Box	Amount
14	Maximum income for optional methods	14	1,600 00
15	Enter the **smaller** of: two-thirds (⅔) of gross farm income[1] (not less than zero) **or** $1,600. Also, include this amount on line 4b above	15	

Nonfarm Optional Method. You may use this method **only** if:

- Your net nonfarm profits[3] were less than $1,733 and also less than 72.189% of your gross nonfarm income,[4] **and**
- You had net earnings from self-employment of at least $400 in 2 of the prior 3 years.

Caution: *You may use this method no more than five times.*

Line	Description	Box	Amount
16	Subtract line 15 from line 14	16	
17	Enter the **smaller** of: two-thirds (⅔) of gross nonfarm income[4] (not less than zero) **or** the amount on line 16. Also, include this amount on line 4b above	17	

[1]From Schedule F, line 11, and Schedule K-1 (Form 1065), line 15b.
[2]From Schedule F, line 36, and Schedule K-1 (Form 1065), line 15a.
[3]From Schedule C, line 31; Schedule C-EZ, line 3; and Schedule K-1 (Form 1065), line 15a.
[4]From Schedule C, line 7; Schedule C-EZ, line 1; and Schedule K-1 (Form 1065), line 15c.

Form **1040-ES**

Department of the Treasury
Internal Revenue Service

Estimated Tax for Individuals

This package is primarily for first-time filers of estimated tax.

OMB No. 1545-0087

1996

Paperwork Reduction Act Notice

We ask for the information on the payment vouchers to carry out the Internal Revenue laws of the United States. You are required to give us the information. We need it to ensure that you are complying with these laws and to allow us to figure and collect the right amount of tax.

The time needed to complete the worksheets and prepare and file the payment vouchers will vary depending on individual circumstances. The estimated average time is: **Recordkeeping,** 1 hr., 19 min.; **Learning about the law,** 18 min.; **Preparing the worksheets and payment vouchers,** 49 min.; **Copying, assembling, and sending the payment voucher to the IRS,** 10 min. If you have comments concerning the accuracy of these time estimates or suggestions for making this package simpler, we would be happy to hear from you. You can write to the Tax Forms Committee, Western Area Distribution Center, Rancho Cordova, CA 95743-0001. **DO NOT** send the payment vouchers to this address. Instead, see **Where To File Your Payment Voucher** on page 5.

Purpose of This Package

Use this package to figure and pay your estimated tax. Estimated tax is the method used to pay tax on income that is not subject to withholding; for example, earnings from self-employment, interest, dividends, rents, alimony, unemployment compensation, etc.

This package is primarily for first-time filers who are or may be subject to paying estimated tax. This package can also be used if you did not receive or have lost your preprinted 1040-ES package. The estimated tax worksheet on page 3 will help you figure the correct amount to pay. The payment vouchers in this package are for crediting your estimated tax payments to your account correctly. Use the **Record of Estimated Tax Payments** on page 5 to keep track of the payments you have made and the number and amount of your remaining payments.

After we receive your first payment voucher from this package, we will mail you a 1040-ES package with your name, address, and social security number preprinted on each payment voucher. Use the preprinted vouchers to make your **remaining** estimated tax payments for the year. This will speed processing, reduce processing costs, and reduce the chance of errors.

Do not use the vouchers in this package to notify the IRS of a **change of address.** If you have a new address, get **Form 8822,** Change of Address, by calling 1-800-TAX-FORM (1-800-829-3676). Send the completed form to the Internal Revenue Service Center where you filed your last tax return. The Service Center will update your record and send you new preprinted payment vouchers.

Note: *Continue to use your old preprinted payment vouchers to make payments of estimated tax until you receive the new vouchers.*

Who Must Make Estimated Tax Payments

In most cases, you must make estimated tax payments if you expect to owe, after subtracting your withholding and credits, at least $500 in tax for 1996, and you expect your withholding and credits to be less than the **smaller** of:

1. 90% of the tax shown on your 1996 tax return, or

2. The tax shown on your 1995 tax return (110% of that amount if you are not a farmer or a fisherman and the adjusted gross income shown on that return is more than $150,000 or, if married filing separately for 1996, more than $75,000).

However, if you did not file a 1995 tax return or that return did not cover all 12 months, item 2 above does not apply.

For this purpose, household employment taxes are not included when figuring the tax shown on your tax return and are not required to be included when figuring your estimated tax payments. However, you may choose to include these taxes when paying estimated tax to avoid a large balance due at the time your tax return is due.

Exception. You do not have to pay estimated tax if you were a U.S. citizen or resident alien for all of 1995 and you had no tax liability for the full 12-month 1995 tax year.

The estimated tax rules apply to:

- U.S. citizens and residents,
- Residents of Puerto Rico, the Virgin Islands, Guam, the Commonwealth of the Northern Mariana Islands, and American Samoa, and
- Nonresident aliens (use Form 1040-ES (NR)).

If you also receive salaries and wages, you may be able to avoid having to make estimated tax payments by asking your employer to take more tax out of your earnings. To do this, file a new **Form W-4,** Employee's Withholding Allowance Certificate, with your employer.

Caution: You may not make joint estimated tax payments if you or your spouse is a nonresident alien, you are separated under a decree of divorce or separate maintenance, or you and your spouse have different tax years.

Additional Information You May Need

Most of the information you will need can be found in:

Pub. 505, Tax Withholding and Estimated Tax.

Other available information:

Pub. 553, Highlights of 1995 Tax Changes, and

Instructions for the 1995 Form 1040, 1040A, or 1040-T.

To order forms and publications, call 1-800-TAX-FORM (1-800-829-3676). If you have a personal computer and a modem, you can also get forms and publications electronically. For details, see page 34 of the Instructions for Form 1040, page 58 of the Instructions for Form 1040A, or page 41 of the Instructions for Form 1040-T.

If you have tax questions, call 1-800-829-1040 for assistance.

Tax Law Changes Effective for 1996

Use your 1995 tax return as a guide in figuring your 1996 estimated tax, but be sure to consider the changes noted in this section.

Earned Income Credit. You will not be eligible for the credit if your total income from interest (including tax-exempt interest), dividends, and net income from rents and royalties not received in the ordinary course of a trade or business exceeds $2,350 in 1996.

(Continued on page 2)

Standard Deduction for 1996. If you do not itemize your deductions, you may take the 1996 standard deduction listed below:

Filing Status	Standard Deduction
Married filing jointly or Qualifying widow(er)	$6,700
Head of household	$5,900
Single	$4,000
Married filing separately	$3,350

Caution: If you can be claimed as a dependent on another person's 1996 return, your standard deduction is the greater of $650 or your earned income, up to the standard deduction amount.

An additional amount is added to the standard deduction if:

1. You are an unmarried individual (single or head of household) and are:

65 or older or blind	$1,000
65 or older and blind	$2,000

2. You are a married individual (filing jointly or separately) or a qualifying widow(er) and are:

65 or older or blind	$800
65 or older and blind	$1,600
Both spouses 65 or older	$1,600 *
Both spouses 65 or older and blind	$3,200 *

* If married filing separately, these amounts apply only if you can claim an exemption for your spouse.

Pending Legislation

At the time these instructions were printed, Congress was considering major tax legislation. Among the proposed changes are provisions that would:

- Allow a tax credit of up to $500 for each qualifying dependent child under 18 for taxpayers whose adjusted gross income does not exceed certain threshold amounts.
- Change the tax treatment of capital gains.
- Treat a loss on the sale or exchange of a main home as a deductible capital loss.

For further developments on these and other changes that may affect your 1996 estimated tax, see Pub. 553.

To Figure Your Estimated Tax Use

- The **1996 Estimated Tax Worksheet** on page 3.
- The instructions on page 4 for the worksheet on page 3.
- The **1996 Tax Rate Schedules** below.
- Your 1995 tax return and instructions as a guide to figuring your income, deductions, and credits (but be sure to consider the tax law changes noted earlier).

If you receive your income unevenly throughout the year (e.g., you operate your business on a seasonal basis), you may be able to lower or eliminate the amount of your required estimated tax payment for one or more periods by using the annualized income installment method. See Pub. 505 for details.

To amend or correct your estimated tax, see **Amending Estimated Tax Payments** on page 4.

1996 Tax Rate Schedules

Caution: *Do not use these Tax Rate Schedules to figure your 1995 taxes. Use only to figure your 1996 estimated taxes.*

Single—Schedule X

If line 5 is: Over—	*But not over—*	The tax is:	*of the amount over—*
$0	$24,000	..........15%	**$0**
24,000	58,150	**$3,600.00 + 28%**	**24,000**
58,150	121,300	**13,162.00 + 31%**	**58,150**
121,300	263,750	**32,738.50 + 36%**	**121,300**
263,750	....	**84,020.50 + 39.6%**	**263,750**

Head of household—Schedule Z

If line 5 is: Over—	*But not over—*	The tax is:	*of the amount over—*
$0	$32,150	..........15%	**$0**
32,150	83,050	**$4,822.50 + 28%**	**32,150**
83,050	134,500	**19,074.50 + 31%**	**83,050**
134,500	263,750	**35,024.00 + 36%**	**134,500**
263,750	....	**81,554.00 + 39.6%**	**263,750**

Married filing jointly or Qualifying widow(er)—Schedule Y-1

If line 5 is: Over—	*But not over—*	The tax is:	*of the amount over—*
$0	$40,100	..........15%	**$0**
40,100	96,900	**$6,015.00 + 28%**	**40,100**
96,900	147,700	**21,919.00 + 31%**	**96,900**
147,700	263,750	**37,667.00 + 36%**	**147,700**
263,750	....	**79,445.00 + 39.6%**	**263,750**

Married filing separately—Schedule Y-2

If line 5 is: Over—	*But not over—*	The tax is:	*of the amount over—*
$0	$20,050	..........15%	**$0**
20,050	48,450	**$3,007.50 + 28%**	**20,050**
48,450	73,850	**10,959.50 + 31%**	**48,450**
73,850	131,875	**18,833.50 + 36%**	**73,850**
131,875	....	**39,722.50 + 39.6%**	**131,875**

1996 Estimated Tax Worksheet (keep for your records)

1	Enter amount of adjusted gross income you expect in 1996 (see instructions)	1	
2	• If you plan to itemize deductions, enter the estimated total of your itemized deductions. **Caution:** If line 1 above is over $117,950 ($58,975 if married filing separately), your deduction may be reduced. See Pub. 505 for details. • If you do not plan to itemize deductions, see **Standard Deduction for 1996** on page 2, and enter your standard deduction here.	2	
3	Subtract line 2 from line 1	3	
4	Exemptions. Multiply $2,550 by the number of personal exemptions. If you can be claimed as a dependent on another person's 1996 return, your personal exemption is not allowed. **Caution:** If line 1 above is over $176,950 ($147,450 if head of household; $117,950 if single; $88,475 if married filing separately), get Pub. 505 to figure the amount to enter	4	
5	Subtract line 4 from line 3	5	
6	**Tax.** Figure your tax on the amount on line 5 by using the 1996 Tax Rate Schedules on page 2. DO NOT use the Tax Table or the Tax Rate Schedules in the 1995 Form 1040, Form 1040A, or Form 1040-T instructions. **Caution:** If you have a net capital gain and line 5 is over $96,900 ($83,050 if head of household; $58,150 if single; $48,450 if married filing separately), get Pub. 505 to figure the tax	6	
7	Additional taxes (see instructions)	7	
8	Add lines 6 and 7	8	
9	Credits (see instructions). Do not include any income tax withholding on this line	9	
10	Subtract line 9 from line 8. Enter the result, but not less than zero	10	
11	Self-employment tax (see instructions). Estimate of 1996 net earnings from self-employment $.................. ; if **$62,700 or less,** multiply the amount by 15.3%; if **more than $62,700,** multiply the amount by 2.9%, add $7,774.80 to the result, and enter the total. **Caution:** If you also have wages subject to social security tax, get Pub. 505 to figure the amount to enter	11	
12	Other taxes (see instructions)	12	
13a	Add lines 10 through 12	13a	
b	Earned income credit and credit from **Form 4136**	13b	
c	Subtract line 13b from line 13a. Enter the result, but not less than zero. **THIS IS YOUR TOTAL 1996 ESTIMATED TAX** ▶	13c	
14a	Multiply line 13c by 90% (66⅔% for farmers and fishermen) — 14a		
b	Enter the tax shown on your 1995 tax return (110% of that amount if you are not a farmer or a fisherman and the adjusted gross income shown on that return is more than $150,000 or, if married filing separately for 1996, more than $75,000) — 14b		
c	Enter the **smaller** of line 14a or 14b. **THIS IS YOUR REQUIRED ANNUAL PAYMENT TO AVOID A PENALTY** ▶ **Caution:** Generally, if you do not prepay (through income tax withholding and estimated tax payments) at least the amount on line 14c, you may owe a penalty for not paying enough estimated tax. To avoid a penalty, make sure your estimate on line 13c is as accurate as possible. Even if you pay the required annual payment, you may still owe tax when you file your return. If you prefer, you may pay the amount shown on line 13c. For more details, get Pub. 505.	14c	
15	Income tax withheld and estimated to be withheld during 1996 (including income tax withholding on pensions, annuities, certain deferred income, etc.)	15	
16	Subtract line 15 from line 14c. (**Note:** *If zero or less, or line 13c minus line 15 is less than $500, stop here. You are not required to make estimated tax payments.*)	16	
17	If the first payment you are required to make is due April 15, 1996, enter ¼ of line 16 (minus any 1995 overpayment that you are applying to this installment) here and on your payment voucher(s)	17	

Instructions for Worksheet on Page 3

Line 1—If you are self-employed, be sure to take into account the deduction for one-half of your self-employment tax. For details on figuring your adjusted gross income, see **Expected Adjusted Gross Income** in Pub. 505.

Line 7—Additional Taxes. Enter the additional taxes from **Form 4970,** Tax on Accumulation Distribution of Trusts, or **Form 4972,** Tax on Lump-Sum Distributions.

Line 9—Credits. See the 1995 Form 1040, lines 41 through 45; Form 1040A, lines 24a and 24b; or Form 1040-T, line 27; and the related instructions.

Line 11—Self-Employment Tax. If you and your spouse make joint estimated tax payments and you both have self-employment income, figure the self-employment tax for each of you separately. Enter the total on line 11. When figuring your estimate of 1996 net earnings from self-employment, be sure to use only 92.35% of your total net profit from self-employment.

Line 12—Other Taxes. Except as noted below, enter any other taxes, such as alternative minimum tax and the tax on early distributions from a qualified retirement plan (including your IRA), annuity, or modified endowment contract (entered into after June 20, 1988).

Do not include tax on recapture of a Federal mortgage subsidy, social security and Medicare tax on unreported tip income, household employment taxes, or uncollected employee social security and Medicare or RRTA tax on tips or group-term life insurance. These taxes are not required to be paid until your income tax return is due (not including extensions).

Payment Due Dates

You may pay all of your estimated tax by April 15, 1996, or in four equal amounts by the dates shown below:

1st payment	April 15, 1996
2nd payment	June 17, 1996
3rd payment	Sept. 16, 1996
4th payment	Jan. 15, 1997*

*You do not have to make the payment due January 15, 1997, if you file your 1996 tax return by January 31, 1997, **AND** pay the entire balance due with your return.

Note: *Payments are due by the dates indicated whether or not you are outside the United States and Puerto Rico.*

If, after March 31, 1996, you have a large change in income, deductions, additional taxes, or credits that requires you to start making estimated tax payments, you should figure the amount of your estimated tax payments by using the annualized income installment method, as explained in Pub. 505. Although your payment due dates will be the same as shown above, the payment amounts will vary based on your income, deductions, additional taxes, and credits for the months ending before each payment due date. As a result, this method may allow you to skip or lower the amount due for one or more payments. If you use the annualized income installment method, be sure to file **Form 2210,** Underpayment of Estimated Tax by Individuals, Estates, and Trusts, with your 1996 tax return, even if no penalty is owed.

Farmers and Fishermen. If at least two-thirds of your gross income for 1995 or 1996 is from farming or fishing, you may do one of the following:

- Pay all of your estimated tax by January 15, 1997, or
- File your 1996 Form 1040 by March 3, 1997, and pay the total tax due. In this case, 1996 estimated payments are not required.

Fiscal Year Taxpayers. You are on a fiscal year if your 12-month tax period ends on any day except December 31. Due dates for fiscal year taxpayers are the 15th day of the 4th, 6th, and 9th months for your current fiscal year and the 1st month of the following fiscal year. If any payment date falls on a Saturday, Sunday, or legal holiday, use the next business day.

Amending Estimated Tax Payments

To change or amend your estimated payments, refigure your total estimated payments due (line 16 of the worksheet on page 3). Then use the worksheets under **Amended estimated tax** in Chapter 2 of Pub. 505 to figure the payment due for each remaining payment period. If an estimated tax payment for a previous period is less than one-fourth of your amended estimated tax, you may owe a penalty when you file your return.

When a Penalty Is Applied

In some cases, you may owe a penalty when you file your return. The penalty is imposed on each underpayment for the number of days it remains unpaid. A penalty may be applied if you did not pay enough estimated tax or you did not make the payments on time or in the required amount. A penalty may apply even if you have an overpayment on your tax return.

The penalty may be waived under certain conditions. See Pub. 505 for details.

How To Complete and Use the Payment Voucher

There is a separate payment voucher for each due date. Please be sure you use the voucher with the correct due date shown in the upper right corner. Complete and send in the voucher **only** if you are making a payment. To complete your voucher:

- Type or print your name, address, and social security number in the space provided on the voucher. If filing a joint voucher, also enter your spouse's name and social security number. List the names and social security numbers in the same order on the joint voucher as you will on your joint return. If you and your spouse plan to file separate returns, file separate vouchers instead of a joint voucher.
- Enter on the payment line of the voucher only the amount you are sending in. When making payments of estimated tax, be sure to take into account any 1995 overpayment that you choose to credit against your 1996 tax, but do not include the overpayment amount on this line.
- Enclose your payment, making the check or money order payable to: "Internal Revenue Service" (not "IRS").
- Write your social security number and "1996 Form 1040-ES" on your check or money order.
- Do not staple or attach your payment to the voucher.
- Mail your payment voucher to the address shown on page 5 for the place where you live.
- Fill in the **Record of Estimated Tax Payments** on page 5 for your files.

If you changed your name and made estimated tax payments using your old name, attach a statement to the front of your 1996 tax return. List all of the estimated tax payments you and your spouse made for 1996, the address where you made the payments, and the name(s) and social security number(s) under which you made the payments.

Record of Estimated Tax Payments (see page 4 for correct payment due dates)

Payment number	(a) Date	(b) Check or money order number	(c) Amount paid	(d) 1995 overpayment credit applied	(e) Total amount paid and credited (add (c) and (d))
1					
2					
3					
4					
Total. . . . . ▶					

Where To File Your Payment Voucher

Mail your payment voucher to the Internal Revenue Service at the address shown below for the place where you live. **Do not** mail your tax return to this address. Also, do not mail your estimated tax payments to the address shown in the Form 1040, 1040A, or 1040-T instructions.

Note: *For proper delivery of your estimated tax payment to a P.O. box, you must include the box number in the address. Also, note that only the U.S. Postal Service can deliver to P.O. boxes.*

If you live in:	Use this address:
New Jersey, New York (New York City and counties of Nassau, Rockland, Suffolk, and Westchester)	P.O. Box 162, Newark, NJ 07101-0162
New York (all other counties), Connecticut, Maine, Massachusetts, New Hampshire, Rhode Island, Vermont	P.O. Box 371999, Pittsburgh, PA 15250-7999
Delaware, District of Columbia, Maryland, Pennsylvania, Virginia	P.O. Box 8318, Philadelphia, PA 19162-8318
Florida, Georgia, South Carolina	P.O. Box 105900, Atlanta, GA 30348-5900
Indiana, Kentucky, Michigan, Ohio, West Virginia	P.O. Box 7422, Chicago, IL 60680-7422
Alabama, Arkansas, Louisiana, Mississippi, North Carolina, Tennessee	P.O. Box 1219, Charlotte, NC 28201-1219
Illinois, Iowa, Minnesota, Missouri, Wisconsin	P.O. Box 970006, St. Louis, MO 63197-0006
Kansas, New Mexico, Oklahoma, Texas	P.O. Box 970001, St. Louis, MO 63197-0001
Alaska, Arizona, California (counties of Alpine, Amador, Butte, Calaveras, Colusa, Contra Costa, Del Norte, El Dorado, Glenn, Humboldt, Lake, Lassen, Marin, Mendocino, Modoc, Napa, Nevada, Placer, Plumas, Sacramento, San Joaquin, Shasta, Sierra, Siskiyou, Solano, Sonoma, Sutter, Tehama, Trinity, Yolo, and Yuba), Colorado, Idaho, Montana, Nebraska, Nevada, North Dakota, Oregon, South Dakota, Utah, Washington, Wyoming	P.O. Box 510000, San Francisco, CA 94151-5100
California (all other counties), Hawaii	P.O. Box 54030, Los Angeles, CA 90054-0030
American Samoa	P.O. Box 8318, Philadelphia, PA 19162-8318
The Commonwealth of the Northern Mariana Islands	P.O. Box 8318, Philadelphia, PA 19162-8318
Puerto Rico (or if excluding income under section 933)	P.O. Box 8318, Philadelphia, PA 19162-8318
Guam: Nonpermanent residents	P.O. Box 8318, Philadelphia, PA 19162-8318
Guam: Permanent residents*	Department of Revenue and Taxation, Government of Guam, Building 13-1 Mariner Avenue, Tiyjan Barrigada, GU 96913

* You must prepare separate vouchers for estimated income tax and self-employment tax payments. Send the income tax vouchers to the Guam address and the self-employment tax vouchers to the address for Guam nonpermanent residents shown above.

If you live in:	Use this address:
Virgin Islands: Nonpermanent residents	P.O. Box 8318, Philadelphia, PA 19162-8318
Virgin Islands: Permanent residents*	V.I. Bureau of Internal Revenue, 9601 Estate Thomas, Charlotte Amalie, St. Thomas, VI 00802

* You must prepare separate vouchers for estimated income tax and self-employment tax payments. Send the income tax vouchers to the Virgin Islands address and the self-employment tax vouchers to the address for Virgin Islands nonpermanent residents shown above.

If you live in:	Use this address:
All APO and FPO addresses	P.O. Box 8318, Philadelphia, PA 19162-8318
Foreign country: U.S. citizens and those filing Form 2555, Form 2555-EZ, or Form 4563	P.O. Box 8318, Philadelphia, PA 19162-8318

Tear off here

Form **1040-ES** Department of the Treasury Internal Revenue Service

1996 Payment Voucher 4

OMB No. 1545-0087

File only if you are making a payment of estimated tax. Return this voucher with check or money order payable to the **"Internal Revenue Service."** Please write your social security number and "1996 Form 1040-ES" on your check or money order. Do not send cash. Enclose, but do not staple or attach, your payment with this voucher.

Calendar year—Due Jan. 15, 1997

Amount of payment

$............................

Please type or print

Your first name and initial	Your last name	Your social security number
If joint payment, complete for spouse		
Spouse's first name and initial	Spouse's last name	Spouse's social security number
Address (number, street, and apt. no.)		
City, state, and ZIP code. (If a foreign address, enter city, province or state, postal code, and country.)		

For Paperwork Reduction Act Notice, see instructions on page 1.

Form **1040-ES** Department of the Treasury Internal Revenue Service | **1996 Payment Voucher 3** | OMB No. 1545-0087

Calendar year—Due Sept. 16, 1996

File only if you are making a payment of estimated tax. Return this voucher with check or money order payable to the **"Internal Revenue Service."** Please write your social security number and "1996 Form 1040-ES" on your check or money order. Do not send cash. Enclose, but do not staple or attach, your payment with this voucher.

Amount of payment	Please type or print			
		Your first name and initial	Your last name	Your social security number
		If joint payment, complete for spouse		
		Spouse's first name and initial	Spouse's last name	Spouse's social security number
		Address (number, street, and apt. no.)		
$		City, state, and ZIP code. (If a foreign address, enter city, province or state, postal code, and country.)		

For Paperwork Reduction Act Notice, see instructions on page 1.

Tear off here

Form **1040-ES** Department of the Treasury Internal Revenue Service | **1996 Payment Voucher 2** | OMB No. 1545-0087

Calendar year—Due June 17, 1996

File only if you are making a payment of estimated tax. Return this voucher with check or money order payable to the **"Internal Revenue Service."** Please write your social security number and "1996 Form 1040-ES" on your check or money order. Do not send cash. Enclose, but do not staple or attach, your payment with this voucher.

Amount of payment	Please type or print			
		Your first name and initial	Your last name	Your social security number
		If joint payment, complete for spouse		
		Spouse's first name and initial	Spouse's last name	Spouse's social security number
		Address (number, street, and apt. no.)		
$		City, state, and ZIP code. (If a foreign address, enter city, province or state, postal code, and country.)		

For Paperwork Reduction Act Notice, see instructions on page 1.

Tear off here

Form **1040-ES** Department of the Treasury Internal Revenue Service | **1996 Payment Voucher 1** | OMB No. 1545-0087

Calendar year—Due April 15, 1996

File only if you are making a payment of estimated tax. Return this voucher with check or money order payable to the **"Internal Revenue Service."** Please write your social security number and "1996 Form 1040-ES" on your check or money order. Do not send cash. Enclose, but do not staple or attach, your payment with this voucher.

Amount of payment	Please type or print			
		Your first name and initial	Your last name	Your social security number
		If joint payment, complete for spouse		
		Spouse's first name and initial	Spouse's last name	Spouse's social security number
		Address (number, street, and apt. no.)		
$		City, state, and ZIP code. (If a foreign address, enter city, province or state, postal code, and country.)		

For Paperwork Reduction Act Notice, see instructions on page 1.

Form **2106** — Department of the Treasury, Internal Revenue Service (99)

Employee Business Expenses

▶ See separate instructions.

▶ Attach to Form 1040 or Form 1040-T.

OMB No. 1545-0139 — **1995** — Attachment Sequence No. **54**

Your name	Social security number	Occupation in which expenses were incurred

Part I Employee Business Expenses and Reimbursements

STEP 1 Enter Your Expenses		Column A Other Than Meals and Entertainment	Column B Meals and Entertainment
1 Vehicle expense from line 22 or line 29	1		
2 Parking fees, tolls, and transportation, including train, bus, etc., that **did not** involve overnight travel	2		
3 Travel expense while away from home overnight, including lodging, airplane, car rental, etc. **Do not** include meals and entertainment	3		
4 Business expenses not included on lines 1 through 3. **Do not** include meals and entertainment	4		
5 Meals and entertainment expenses (see instructions)	5		
6 **Total expenses.** In Column A, add lines 1 through 4 and enter the result. In Column B, enter the amount from line 5	6		

Note: *If you were not reimbursed for any expenses in Step 1, skip line 7 and enter the amount from line 6 on line 8.*

STEP 2 Enter Amounts Your Employer Gave You for Expenses Listed in STEP 1

		Column A	Column B
7 Enter amounts your employer gave you that were **not** reported to you in box 1 of Form W-2. Include any amount reported under code "L" in box 13 of your Form W-2 (see instructions) . . .	7		

STEP 3 Figure Expenses To Deduct on Schedule A (Form 1040) or Form 1040-T, Section B

		Column A	Column B
8 Subtract line 7 from line 6	8		
Note: *If* ***both columns*** *of line 8 are zero,* ***stop here.*** *If Column A is less than zero, report the amount as income on Form 1040, line 7, or Form 1040-T, line 1.*			
9 In Column A, enter the amount from line 8 (if zero or less, enter -0-). In Column B, multiply the amount on line 8 by 50% (.50) .	9		

10 Add the amounts on line 9 of both columns and enter the total here. **Also, enter the total on Schedule A (Form 1040), line 20, or Form 1040-T, Section B, line n.** (Qualified performing artists and individuals with disabilities, see the instructions for special rules on where to enter the total.) . . . . ▶	10	

For Paperwork Reduction Act Notice, see instructions. Cat. No. 11700N Form **2106** (1995)

Form 2106 (1995) Page 2

Part II **Vehicle Expenses** (See instructions to find out which sections to complete.)

Section A.—General Information

			(a) Vehicle 1	(b) Vehicle 2
11	Enter the date vehicle was placed in service	11	/ /	/ /
12	Total miles vehicle was driven during 1995	12	miles	miles
13	Business miles included on line 12	13	miles	miles
14	Percent of business use. Divide line 13 by line 12	14	%	%
15	Average daily round trip commuting distance	15	miles	miles
16	Commuting miles included on line 12	16	miles	miles
17	Other personal miles. Add lines 13 and 16 and subtract the total from line 12	17	miles	miles

18 Do you (or your spouse) have another vehicle available for personal purposes? ☐ Yes ☐ No

19 If your employer provided you with a vehicle, is personal use during off-duty hours permitted? ☐ Yes ☐ No ☐ Not applicable

20 Do you have evidence to support your deduction? ☐ Yes ☐ No

21 If "Yes," is the evidence written? ☐ Yes ☐ No

Section B.—Standard Mileage Rate (Use this section only if you own the vehicle.)

22	Multiply line 13 by 30¢ (.30). Enter the result here and on line 1. (Rural mail carriers, see instructions.)	22	

Section C.—Actual Expenses

			(a) Vehicle 1	(b) Vehicle 2
23	Gasoline, oil, repairs, vehicle insurance, etc.	23		
24a	Vehicle rentals	24a		
b	Inclusion amount (see instructions)	24b		
c	Subtract line 24b from line 24a	24c		
25	Value of employer-provided vehicle (applies only if 100% of annual lease value was included on Form W-2—see instructions)	25		
26	Add lines 23, 24c, and 25	26		
27	Multiply line 26 by the percentage on line 14	27		
28	Depreciation. Enter amount from line 38 below	28		
29	Add lines 27 and 28. Enter total here and on line 1	29		

Section D.—Depreciation of Vehicles (Use this section only if you own the vehicle.)

			(a) Vehicle 1	(b) Vehicle 2
30	Enter cost or other basis (see instructions)	30		
31	Enter amount of section 179 deduction (see instructions)	31		
32	Multiply line 30 by line 14 (see instructions if you elected the section 179 deduction)	32		
33	Enter depreciation method and percentage (see instructions)	33		
34	Multiply line 32 by the percentage on line 33 (see instructions)	34		
35	Add lines 31 and 34	35		
36	Enter the limitation amount from the table in the line 36 instructions	36		
37	Multiply line 36 by the percentage on line 14	37		
38	Enter the **smaller** of line 35 or line 37. Also, enter this amount on line 28 above	38		

Form **2106-EZ**

Department of the Treasury
Internal Revenue Service (99)

Unreimbursed Employee Business Expenses

▶ See instructions on back.

▶ Attach to Form 1040 or Form 1040-T.

OMB No. 1545-1441

1995

Attachment Sequence No. **54A**

Your name	Social security number	Occupation in which expenses were incurred
	: :	

Part I **General Information**

You May Use This Form ONLY if All of the Following Apply:

- You are an employee deducting expenses attributable to your job.
- You **do not** get reimbursed by your employer for any expenses (amounts your employer included in box 1 of your Form W-2 are not considered reimbursements).
- If you are claiming vehicle expense,
  - **a** You own your vehicle, and
  - **b** You are using the standard mileage rate for 1995 **and** also used it for the year you first placed the vehicle in service.

Part II **Figure Your Expenses**

1	Vehicle expense using the standard mileage rate. Complete Part III and multiply line 8a by 30¢ (.30)	1		
2	Parking fees, tolls, and transportation, including train, bus, etc., that **did not** involve overnight travel	2		
3	Travel expense while away from home overnight, including lodging, airplane, car rental, etc. **Do not** include meals and entertainment	3		
4	Business expenses not included on lines 1 through 3. **Do not** include meals and entertainment	4		
5	Meals and entertainment expenses: $ ________ x 50% (.50)	5		
6	**Total expenses.** Add lines 1 through 5. Enter here and **on line 20 of Schedule A (Form 1040), or Form 1040-T, Section B, line n.** (Qualified performing artists and individuals with disabilities, see the instructions for special rules on where to enter this amount.)	6		

Part III **Information on Your Vehicle.** Complete this part **ONLY** if you are claiming vehicle expense on line 1.

7 When did you place your vehicle in service for business purposes? (month, day, year) ▶ ...... / ...... / ......

8 Of the total number of miles you drove your vehicle during 1995, enter the number of miles you used your vehicle for:

a Business .... **b** Commuting .... **c** Other ....

9 Do you (or your spouse) have another vehicle available for personal use? ☐ **Yes** ☐ **No**

10 Was your vehicle available for use during off-duty hours? ☐ **Yes** ☐ **No**

11a Do you have evidence to support your deduction? ☐ **Yes** ☐ **No**

b If "Yes," is the evidence written? ☐ **Yes** ☐ **No**

For Paperwork Reduction Act Notice, see back of form. Cat. No. 20604Q Form **2106-EZ** (1995)

Form **2119**

Department of the Treasury
Internal Revenue Service

Sale of Your Home

▶ Attach to Form 1040 for year of sale.

▶ See separate instructions. ▶ Please print or type.

OMB No. 1545-0072

1995

Attachment Sequence No. **20**

Your first name and initial. If a joint return, also give spouse's name and initial.	Last name	Your social security number
Fill in Your Address Only If You Are Filing This Form by Itself and Not With Your Tax Return	Present address (no., street, and apt. no., rural route, or P.O. box no. if mail is not delivered to street address)	Spouse's social security number
	City, town or post office, state, and ZIP code	

Part I Gain on Sale

1 Date your former main home was sold (month, day, year) . . . . . ▶ | 1 | / / |

2 Have you bought or built a new main home? . . . . . ☐ Yes ☐ No

3 If any part of either main home was ever rented out or used for business, check here ▶ ☐ and see page 3.

4 Selling price of home. Do not include personal property items you sold with your home . .	4	
5 Expense of sale (see page 3)	5	
6 Subtract line 5 from line 4	6	
7 Adjusted basis of home sold (see page 3)	7	
8 **Gain on sale.** Subtract line 7 from line 6	8	

Is line 8 more than zero?
- Yes ⟶ If line 2 is "Yes," you **must** go to Part II or Part III, whichever applies. If line 2 is "No," go to line 9.
- No ⟶ **Stop;** see **Loss on the Sale of Your Home** on page 1.

9 If you haven't replaced your home, do you plan to do so within the **replacement period** (see page 1)? . ☐ Yes ☐ No
- If line 9 is "Yes," stop here, attach this form to your return, and see **Additional Filing Requirements** on page 1.
- If line 9 is "No," you **must** go to Part II or Part III, whichever applies.

Part II One-Time Exclusion of Gain for People Age 55 or Older—By completing this part, you are electing to take the one-time exclusion (see page 2). If you are not electing to take the exclusion, go to Part III now.

10 Who was age 55 or older on the date of sale? . . . . . ☐ You ☐ Your spouse ☐ Both of you

11 Did the person who was 55 or older own and use the property as his or her main home for a total of at least 3 years of the 5-year period before the sale? See page 2 for exceptions. If "No," go to Part III now . . . ☐ Yes ☐ No

12 At the time of sale, who owned the home? . . . . . ☐ You ☐ Your spouse ☐ Both of you

13 Social security number of spouse at the time of sale if you had a different spouse from the one above. If you were not married at the time of sale, enter "None" . . . . ▶	13	
14 **Exclusion.** Enter the **smaller** of line 8 or $125,000 ($62,500 if married filing separate return). Then, go to line 15	14	

Part III Adjusted Sales Price, Taxable Gain, and Adjusted Basis of New Home

15 If line 14 is blank, enter the amount from line 8. Otherwise, subtract line 14 from line 8 . . | 15 | |
- If line 15 is zero, stop and attach this form to your return.
- If line 15 is more than zero and line 2 is "Yes," go to line 16 now.
- If you are reporting this sale on the installment method, stop and see page 4.
- All others, stop and **enter the amount from line 15 on Schedule D, col. (g), line 4 or line 12.**

16 Fixing-up expenses (see page 4 for time limits)	16	
17 If line 14 is blank, enter amount from line 16. Otherwise, add lines 14 and 16	17	
18 **Adjusted sales price.** Subtract line 17 from line 6	18	
19a Date you moved into new home ▶ / / **b** Cost of new home (see page 4)	19b	
20 Subtract line 19b from line 18. If zero or less, enter -0-	20	
21 **Taxable gain.** Enter the **smaller** of line 15 or line 20	21	

- If line 21 is zero, go to line 22 and attach this form to your return.
- If you are reporting this sale on the installment method, see the line 15 instructions and go to line 22.
- All others, **enter the amount from line 21 on Schedule D, col. (g), line 4 or line 12,** and go to line 22.

22 Postponed gain. Subtract line 21 from line 15	22	
23 **Adjusted basis of new home.** Subtract line 22 from line 19b	23	

Sign Here Only If You Are Filing This Form by Itself and Not With Your Tax Return

Under penalties of perjury, I declare that I have examined this form, including attachments, and to the best of my knowledge and belief, it is true, correct, and complete.

Your signature ▶ ______ Date ______ Spouse's signature ▶ ______ Date ______

If a joint return, both must sign.

For Paperwork Reduction Act Notice, see separate instructions. Cat. No. 11710J Form **2119** (1995)

Printed on recycled paper

Form **2120**
(Rev. January 1994)
Department of the Treasury
Internal Revenue Service

Multiple Support Declaration

▶ **Attach to Form 1040 or Form 1040A of Person Claiming the Dependent.**

OMB No. 1545-0071
Expires 1-31-97

Attachment Sequence No. **50**

Name of person claiming the dependent | **Social security number**

During the calendar year 19 ...., I paid over 10% of the support of

....
Name of person

I could have claimed this person as a dependent except that I did not pay over 50% of his or her support. I understand that this person named above is being claimed as a dependent on the income tax return of

....
Name

....
Address

I agree not to claim this person as a dependent on my Federal income tax return for any tax year that began in this calendar year.

....
Your signature Your social security number

....
Date Address (number, street, apt. no.)

....
City, state, and ZIP code

Instructions

Paperwork Reduction Act Notice

We ask for the information on this form to carry out the Internal Revenue laws of the United States. You are required to give us the information. We need it to ensure that you are complying with these laws and to allow us to figure and collect the right amount of tax.

The time needed to complete and file this form will vary depending on individual circumstances. The estimated average time is: **Recordkeeping**, 7 minutes; **Learning about the law or the form**, 2 minutes; **Preparing the form**, 7 minutes; and **Copying, assembling, and sending the form to the IRS**, 10 minutes.

If you have comments concerning the accuracy of these time estimates or suggestions for making this form more simple, we would be happy to hear from you. You can write to both the IRS and the Office of Management and Budget at the addresses listed in the instructions of the tax return with which this form is filed.

Purpose of Form

When two or more individuals together pay over 50% of another person's support, Form 2120 or a similar statement is used to allow one of them to claim the person as a dependent for tax purposes.

The similar statement must contain the same information that is required by this form.

Who Can Claim the Dependent

To claim someone as a dependent, you must pay over 50% of that person's living expenses (support).

If no one meets this support test, but two or more of you together provide over 50% of a person's support, then one of you can claim that person as a dependent.

To claim the dependent, you must meet **all three** of the following requirements:

1. You paid over 10% of the support, and

2. All others who paid over 10% agree not to claim the person as a dependent, and

3. The other four dependency tests are met. See **Dependents** in the Form 1040 or Form 1040A instructions.

All contributors who provided over 10% support must choose which one of them will claim the dependent. If you will be claiming the dependent, see **How To File** below.

If you are a 10% contributor but **will not** be claiming the dependent, complete and sign a Form 2120 or similar statement. Give it to the person claiming the dependent.

How To File

If you are claiming the dependent, you must attach to your tax return a Form 2120 or similar statement that is completed and signed by each of the 10% contributors who are not claiming the dependent for the tax year. Be sure your name and social security number are at the top of each Form 2120 or similar statement.

Additional Information

See **Pub. 501,** Exemptions, Standard Deduction, and Filing Information, for more information.

Form **2210**

Department of the Treasury
Internal Revenue Service

Underpayment of Estimated Tax by Individuals, Estates, and Trusts

▶ See separate instructions.

▶ Attach to Form 1040, 1040A, 1040-T, 1040NR, 1040NR-EZ, or 1041.

OMB No. 1545-0140

1995

Attachment Sequence No. **06A**

Name(s) shown on tax return | **Identifying number**

Note: *In most cases, you* **do not** *need to file Form 2210. The IRS will figure any penalty you owe and send you a bill. File Form 2210* **only** *if one or more boxes in Part I apply to you. If you do not need to file Form 2210, you still may use it to figure your penalty. Enter the amount from line 20 or line 36 on the penalty line of your return, but do not attach Form 2210.*

Part I **Reasons For Filing—**If 1a, b, or c below applies to you, you may be able to lower or eliminate your penalty. But you MUST check the boxes that apply and file Form 2210 with your tax return. If 1d below applies to you, check that box and file Form 2210 with your tax return.

1 Check whichever boxes apply (if none apply, see the **Note** above):

a ☐ You request a **waiver.** In certain circumstances, the IRS will waive all or part of the penalty. See **Waiver of Penalty** on page 1 of the instructions.

b ☐ You use the **annualized income installment method.** If your income varied during the year, this method may reduce the amount of one or more required installments. See page 4 of the instructions.

c ☐ You had Federal income tax withheld from wages and you treat it as paid for estimated tax purposes when it was **actually** withheld instead of in equal amounts on the payment due dates. See the instructions for line 22.

d ☐ Your required annual payment (line 13 below) is based on your 1994 tax and you filed or are filing a joint return for either 1994 or 1995 but not for both years.

Part II **Required Annual Payment**

2	Enter your 1995 tax after credits (see instructions)		2
3	Other taxes (see instructions)		3
4	Add lines 2 and 3		4
5	Earned income credit	5	
6	Credit for Federal tax paid on fuels	6	
7	Add lines 5 and 6		7
8	Current year tax. Subtract line 7 from line 4		8
9	Multiply line 8 by 90% (.90)	9	
10	Withholding taxes. **Do not** include any estimated tax payments on this line (see instructions)		10
11	Subtract line 10 from line 8. If less than $500, stop here; **do not** complete or file this form. You do not owe the penalty		11
12	Enter the tax shown on your 1994 tax return (110% of that amount if the adjusted gross income shown on that return is more than $150,000, or if married filing separately for 1995, more than $75,000). **Caution:** *See instructions*		12
13	**Required annual payment.** Enter the **smaller** of line 9 or line 12		13

Note: *If line 10 is equal to or more than line 13, stop here; you do not owe the penalty. Do not file Form 2210 unless you checked box 1d above.*

Part III **Short Method (Caution:** *Read the instructions to see if you can use the short method. If you checked box* **1b** *or* **c** *in Part I, skip this part and go to Part IV.***)**

14	Enter the amount, if any, from line 10 above	14	
15	Enter the total amount, if any, of estimated tax payments you made	15	
16	Add lines 14 and 15		16
17	**Total underpayment for year.** Subtract line 16 from line 13. If zero or less, stop here; you do not owe the penalty. Do not file Form 2210 unless you checked box 1d above		17
18	Multiply line 17 by .06066		18
19	• If the amount on line 17 was paid **on or after** 4/15/96, enter -0-. • If the amount on line 17 was paid **before** 4/15/96, make the following computation to find the amount to enter on line 19. Amount on line 17 × Number of days paid before 4/15/96 × .00025		19
20	**PENALTY.** Subtract line 19 from line 18. Enter the result here and on Form 1040, line 66; Form 1040A, line 34; Form 1040-T, line 42; Form 1040NR, line 66; Form 1040NR-EZ, line 26; or Form 1041, line 26 ▶		20

For Paperwork Reduction Act Notice, see page 1 of separate instructions. Cat. No. 11744P Form **2210** (1995)

Form 2210 (1995) Page **2**

Part IV **Regular Method** (See the instructions if you are filing Form 1040NR or 1040NR-EZ.)

Section A—Figure Your Underpayment		**Payment Due Dates** (a) 4/15/95	(b) 6/15/95	(c) 9/15/95	(d) 1/15/96
21 **Required installments.** If box 1b applies, enter the amounts from Schedule AI, line 26. Otherwise, enter ¼ of line 13, Form 2210, in each column	21				
22 Estimated tax paid and tax withheld (see instructions). For column (a) only, also enter the amount from line 22 on line 26. If line 22 is equal to or more than line 21 for all payment periods, stop here; you do not owe the penalty. Do not file Form 2210 unless you checked a box in Part I	22				
Complete lines 23 through 29 of one column before going to the next column. 23 Enter amount, if any, from line 29 of previous column	23				
24 Add lines 22 and 23	24				
25 Add amounts on lines 27 and 28 of the previous column	25				
26 Subtract line 25 from line 24. If zero or less, enter -0-. For column (a) only, enter the amount from line 22 .	26				
27 If the amount on line 26 is zero, subtract line 24 from line 25. Otherwise, enter -0-	27				
28 **Underpayment.** If line 21 is equal to or more than line 26, subtract line 26 from line 21. Then go to line 23 of next column. Otherwise, go to line 29 . . ▶	28				
29 Overpayment. If line 26 is more than line 21, subtract line 21 from line 26. Then go to line 23 of next column	29				

Section B—Figure the Penalty (Complete lines 30 through 35 of one column before going to the next column.)

Rate Period			(a)	(b)	(c)	(d)
Rate Period 1	**April 16, 1995—June 30, 1995**		4/15/95	6/15/95		
	30 Number of days FROM the date shown above line 30 TO the date the amount on line 28 was paid **or** 6/30/95, whichever is earlier	30	*Days:*	*Days:*		
	31 $\frac{\text{Underpayment on line 28 (see instructions)}}{} \times \frac{\text{Number of days on line 30}}{365} \times .10$ ▶	31	$	$		
Rate Period 2	**July 1, 1995—December 31, 1995**		6/30/95	6/30/95	9/15/95	
	32 Number of days FROM the date shown above line 32 TO the date the amount on line 28 was paid **or** 12/31/95, whichever is earlier	32	*Days:*	*Days:*	*Days:*	
	33 $\frac{\text{Underpayment on line 28 (see instructions)}}{} \times \frac{\text{Number of days on line 32}}{365} \times .09$ ▶	33	$	$	$	
Rate Period 3	**January 1, 1996—April 15, 1996**		12/31/95	12/31/95	12/31/95	1/15/96
	34 Number of days FROM the date shown above line 34 TO the date the amount on line 28 was paid **or** 4/15/96, whichever is earlier	34	*Days:*	*Days:*	*Days:*	*Days:*
	35 $\frac{\text{Underpayment on line 28 (see instructions)}}{} \times \frac{\text{Number of days on line 34}}{366} \times .09$ ▶	35	$	$	$	$

36 **PENALTY.** Add all amounts on lines 31, 33, and 35 in all columns. Enter the total here and on Form 1040, line 66; Form 1040A, line 34; Form 1040-T, line 42; Form 1040NR, line 66; Form 1040NR-EZ, line 26; or Form 1041, line 26 . . . . ▶ | 36 | $

Form 2210 (1995) Page 3

Schedule AI—Annualized Income Installment Method (see instructions)

Estates and trusts, **do not** use the period ending dates shown to the right. Instead, use the following: 2/28/95, 4/30/95, 7/31/95, and 11/30/95.

Part I Annualized Income Installments

Caution: *Complete lines 20–26 of one column before going to the next column.*

			(a) 1/1/95–3/31/95	(b) 1/1/95–5/31/95	(c) 1/1/95–8/31/95	(d) 1/1/95–12/31/95
1	Enter your adjusted gross income for each period (see instructions). (Estates and trusts, enter your taxable income without your exemption for each period.)	1				
2	Annualization amounts. (Estates and trusts, see instructions.)	2	4	2.4	1.5	1
3	Annualized income. Multiply line 1 by line 2	3				
4	Enter your itemized deductions for the period shown in each column. If you do not itemize, enter -0- and skip to line 7. (Estates and trusts, enter -0-, skip to line 9, and enter the amount from line 3 on line 9.)	4				
5	Annualization amounts	5	4	2.4	1.5	1
6	Multiply line 4 by line 5 (see instructions if line 3 is more than $57,350)	6				
7	In each column, enter the full amount of your standard deduction from Form 1040, line 34; Form 1040A, line 19; or Form 1040-T, line 20 (Form 1040NR or 1040NR-EZ filers, enter -0-. **Exception:** Indian students and business apprentices, enter standard deduction from Form 1040NR, line 33 or Form 1040NR-EZ, line 10.)	7				
8	Enter the **larger** of line 6 or line 7	8				
9	Subtract line 8 from line 3	9				
10	In each column, multiply $2,500 by the total number of exemptions claimed (see instructions if line 3 is more than $86,025). (Estates and trusts and Form 1040NR or 1040NR-EZ filers, enter the exemption amount shown on your tax return.)	10				
11	Subtract line 10 from line 9	11				
12	Figure your tax on the amount on line 11 (see instructions)	12				
13	Form 1040 filers only, enter your self-employment tax from line 35 below	13				
14	Enter other taxes for each payment period (see instructions)	14				
15	Total tax. Add lines 12, 13, and 14	15				
16	For each period, enter the same type of credits as allowed on Form 2210, lines 2, 5, and 6 (see instructions)	16				
17	Subtract line 16 from line 15. If zero or less, enter -0-	17				
18	Applicable percentage	18	22.5%	45%	67.5%	90%
19	Multiply line 17 by line 18	19				
20	Add the amounts in all preceding columns of line 26	20				
21	Subtract line 20 from line 19. If zero or less, enter -0-	21				
22	Enter ¼ of line 13 on page 1 of Form 2210 in each column	22				
23	Enter amount from line 25 of the preceding column of this schedule	23				
24	Add lines 22 and 23 and enter the total	24				
25	Subtract line 21 from line 24. If zero or less, enter -0-	25				
26	Enter the **smaller** of line 21 or line 24 here and on Form 2210, line 21 ▶	26				

Part II Annualized Self-Employment Tax

			(a)	(b)	(c)	(d)
27a	Net earnings from self-employment for the period (see instructions)	27a				
b	Annualization amounts	27b	4	2.4	1.5	1
c	Multiply line 27a by line 27b	27c				
28	Social security tax limit	28	$61,200	$61,200	$61,200	$61,200
29	Enter actual wages subject to social security tax or the 6.2% portion of the 7.65% railroad retirement (tier 1) tax	29				
30	Annualization amounts	30	4	2.4	1.5	1
31	Multiply line 29 by line 30	31				
32	Subtract line 31 from line 28. If zero or less, enter -0-	32				
33	Multiply the smaller of line 27c or line 32 by .124	33				
34	Multiply line 27c by .029	34				
35	Add lines 33 and 34. Enter the result here and on line 13 above ▶	35				

Printed on recycled paper

Form **2441**

Department of the Treasury
Internal Revenue Service (99)

Child and Dependent Care Expenses

▶ **Attach to Form 1040.**

▶ **See separate instructions.**

OMB No. 1545-0068

1995

Attachment Sequence No. **21**

Name(s) shown on Form 1040 | **Your social security number**

You need to understand the following terms to complete this form: **Qualifying Person(s), Dependent Care Benefits, Qualified Expenses,** and **Earned Income.** See **Important Terms** on page 1 of the Form 2441 instructions.

Part I **Persons or Organizations Who Provided the Care**—You **must** complete this part. (If you need more space, use the bottom of page 2.)

1 **(a)** Care provider's name	**(b)** Address (number, street, apt. no., city, state, and ZIP code)	**(c)** Identifying number (SSN or EIN)	**(d)** Amount paid (see instructions)

2 Add the amounts in column (d) of line 1 . . . . **2**

3 Enter the number of **qualifying persons** cared for in 1995 . . . . ▶ ☐

Did you receive **dependent care benefits?**
- **NO** ⟶ Complete only Part II below.
- **YES** ⟶ Complete Part III on the back now.

Part II **Credit for Child and Dependent Care Expenses**

4 Enter the amount of **qualified expenses** you incurred and paid in 1995. DO NOT enter more than $2,400 for one qualifying person or $4,800 for two or more persons. If you completed Part III, enter the amount from line 25 . . . . **4**

5 Enter YOUR **earned income** **5**

6 If married filing a joint return, enter YOUR SPOUSE'S earned income (if student or disabled, see the instructions); **all others,** enter the amount from line 5 . . . . **6**

7 Enter the **smallest** of line 4, 5, or 6 . . . . **7**

8 Enter the amount from Form 1040, line 32 . . . . **8**

9 Enter on line 9 the decimal amount shown below that applies to the amount on line 8

If line 8 is— Over—But not over	Decimal amount is	If line 8 is— Over—But not over	Decimal amount is
$0—10,000	.30	$20,000—22,000	.24
10,000—12,000	.29	22,000—24,000	.23
12,000—14,000	.28	24,000—26,000	.22
14,000—16,000	.27	26,000—28,000	.21
16,000—18,000	.26	28,000—No limit	.20
18,000—20,000	.25		

9 × .

10 Multiply **line 7** by the decimal amount on line 9. Enter the result. Then, see the instructions for the amount of credit to enter on Form 1040, line 41 . . . . **10**

Caution: *If you paid a person who worked in your home, you may have to pay employment taxes. See the instructions for Form 1040, line 53, on page 26.*

For Paperwork Reduction Act Notice, see separate instructions. Cat. No. 11862M Form **2441** (1995)

Form 2441 (1995) Page **2**

Part III **Dependent Care Benefits—**Complete this part **only** if you received these benefits.

11	Enter the total amount of **dependent care benefits** you received for 1995. This amount should be shown in box 10 of your W-2 form(s). DO NOT include amounts that were reported to you as wages in box 1 of Form(s) W-2		11	
12	Enter the amount forfeited, if any. See the instructions		12	
13	Subtract line 12 from line 11		13	
14	Enter the total amount of **qualified expenses** incurred in 1995 for the care of the qualifying person(s)	14		
15	Enter the **smaller** of line 13 or 14	15		
16	Enter YOUR **earned income**	16		
17	If married filing a joint return, enter YOUR SPOUSE'S earned income (if student or disabled, see the line 6 instructions); if married filing a separate return, see the instructions for the amount to enter; **all others,** enter the amount from line 16	17		
18	Enter the **smallest** of line 15, 16, or 17	18		
19	**Excluded benefits.** Enter here the **smaller** of the following: • The amount from line 18, or • $5,000 ($2,500 if married filing a separate return **and** you were required to enter your spouse's earned income on line 17).		19	
20	**Taxable benefits.** Subtract line 19 from line 13. Also, include this amount on Form 1040, line 7. On the dotted line next to line 7, write "DCB"		20	

To claim the child and dependent care credit, complete lines 21–25 below, and lines 4–10 on the front of this form.

21	Enter the amount of qualified expenses you incurred and paid in 1995. DO NOT include on this line any excluded benefits shown on line 19		21	
22	Enter $2,400 ($4,800 if two or more qualifying persons)	22		
23	Enter the amount from line 19	23		
24	Subtract line 23 from line 22. If zero or less, **STOP**. You cannot take the credit. **Exception.** If you paid 1994 expenses in 1995, see the line 10 instructions		24	
25	Enter the **smaller** of line 21 or 24 here **and** on line 4 on the front of this form		25	

Printed on recycled paper

Form **3800**

Department of the Treasury
Internal Revenue Service

General Business Credit

▶ Attach to your tax return.

▶ See separate instructions.

OMB No. 1545–0895

1995

Attachment Sequence No. **22**

Name(s) shown on return | Identifying number

Part I **Tentative Credit**

1a	Current year investment credit (Form 3468, Part I)	1a	
b	Current year jobs credit (Form 5884, Part I)	1b	
c	Current year credit for alcohol used as fuel (Form 6478)	1c	
d	Current year credit for increasing research activities (Form 6765, Part I)	1d	
e	Current year low-income housing credit (Form 8586, Part I)	1e	
f	Current year enhanced oil recovery credit (Form 8830, Part I)	1f	
g	Current year disabled access credit (Form 8826, Part I)	1g	
h	Current year renewable electricity production credit (Form 8835, Part I)	1h	
i	Current year Indian employment credit (Form 8845, Part I)	1i	
j	Current year credit for employer social security and Medicare taxes paid on certain employee tips (Form 8846, Part I)	1j	
k	Current year credit for contributions to selected community development corporations (Form 8847, Part I)	1k	
l	Current year trans-Alaska pipeline liability fund credit (see instructions)	1l	
m	**Current year general business credit.** Add lines 1a through 1l	1m	
2	Passive activity credits included on line 1m (see instructions)	2	
3	Subtract line 2 from line 1m	3	
4	Passive activity credits allowed for 1995 (see instructions)	4	
5	Carryforward of general business, WIN, or ESOP credit to 1995 (see instructions for the schedule to attach)	5	
6	Carryback of general business credit to 1995 (see instructions)	6	
7	**Tentative general business credit.** Add lines 3 through 6	7	

Part II **General Business Credit Limitation Based on Amount of Tax**

8a	Individuals. Enter amount from Form 1040, line 40				
b	Corporations. Enter amount from Form 1120, Schedule J, line 3 (or Form 1120-A, Part I, line 1)			8	
c	Other filers. Enter regular tax before credits from your return				
9a	Credit for child and dependent care expenses (Form 2441, line 10)	9a			
b	Credit for the elderly or the disabled (Schedule R (Form 1040), line 20)	9b			
c	Mortgage interest credit (Form 8396, line 11)	9c			
d	Foreign tax credit (Form 1116, line 32, or Form 1118, Sch. B, line 12)	9d			
e	Possessions tax credit (Form 5735)	9e			
f	Orphan drug credit (Form 6765)	9f			
g	Credit for fuel from a nonconventional source	9g			
h	Qualified electric vehicle credit (Form 8834, line 19)	9h			
i	Add lines 9a through 9h			9i	
10	Net regular tax. Subtract line 9i from line 8			10	
11	Tentative minimum tax (see instructions):				
a	Individuals. Enter amount from Form 6251, line 26				
b	Corporations. Enter amount from Form 4626, line 13			11	
c	Estates and trusts. Enter amount from Form 1041, Schedule I, line 37				
12	Net income tax:				
a	Individuals. Add line 10 above and line 28 of Form 6251				
b	Corporations. Add line 10 above and line 15 of Form 4626			12	
c	Estates and trusts. Add line 10 above and line 41 of Form 1041, Schedule I				
13	If line 10 is more than $25,000, enter 25% (.25) of the excess (see instructions)			13	
14	Subtract line 11 or line 13, whichever is greater, from line 12. If zero or less, enter -0-			14	
15	**General business credit allowed for current year.** Enter the **smaller** of line 7 or line 14. Enter here and on Form 1040, line 44; Form 1120, Schedule J, line 4d; Form 1120-A, Part I, line 2a; or the appropriate line of your tax return. (Individuals, estates, and trusts, see instructions if the credit for increasing research activities is claimed. C corporations, see instructions for Schedule A if any regular investment credit carryforward is claimed. See the instructions if the corporation has undergone a post-1986 "ownership change.")			15	

For Paperwork Reduction Act Notice, see page 2 of this form. Cat. No. 12392F Form **3800** (1995)

Form 3800 (1995) Page 2

Schedule A—Additional General Business Credit Allowed By Section 38(c)(2) (Before Repeal by the Revenue Reconciliation Act of 1990)—Only Applicable to C Corporations

16	Enter the portion of the credit shown on line 5, page 1, that is attributable to the regular investment credit under section 46 (before amendment by the Revenue Reconciliation Act of 1990)			16	
17	Tentative minimum tax (from line 11, page 1)	17			
18	Multiply line 17 by 25% (.25)			18	
19	Enter the amount from line 14, page 1.	19			
20	Enter the portion of the credit shown on line 7, page 1, that is NOT attributable to the regular investment credit under section 46 (before amendment by the Revenue Reconciliation Act of 1990).	20			
21	Subtract line 20 from line 19 (if zero or less, enter -0-)			21	
22	Subtract line 21 from line 16 (if zero or less, enter -0-)			22	
23	For purposes of this line only, refigure the amount on line 11, Form 4626, by using zero on line 6, Form 4626, and enter the result here.	23			
24	Multiply line 23 by 10% (.10)			24	
25	Net income tax (from line 12, page 1)			25	
26	General business credit (from line 15, page 1)			26	
27	Subtract line 26 from line 25			27	
28	Subtract line 24 from line 27			28	
29	Enter the smallest of line 18, line 22, or line 28.			29	
30	Subtract line 29 from line 17			30	
31	Enter the greater of line 30 or line 13, page 1			31	
32	Subtract line 31 from line 25			32	
33	Enter the smaller of line 32 or line 10, page 1. Enter this amount also on line 15, page 1, instead of the amount previously figured on that line. Write "Sec. 38(c)(2)" in the margin next to your entry on line 15, page 1			33	
34	If line 32 is greater than line 33, enter the excess here and see the instructions on how to claim the additional credit			34	

Paperwork Reduction Act Notice

We ask for the information on this form to carry out the Internal Revenue laws of the United States. You are required to give us the information. We need it to ensure that you are complying with these laws and to allow us to figure and collect the right amount of tax.

The time needed to complete and file this form will vary depending on individual circumstances. The estimated average time is:

Recordkeeping . . . 11 hr., 43 min.

Learning about the law or the form . . . 1 hr.

Preparing and sending the form to the IRS . . 1 hr., 14 min.

If you have comments concerning the accuracy of these time estimates or suggestions for making this form simpler, we would be happy to hear from you. You can write to the IRS at the address listed in the instructions for the tax return with which this form is filed.

Form **3903**

Department of the Treasury
Internal Revenue Service

Moving Expenses

▶ **Attach to Form 1040.**

▶ **See instructions on back.**

OMB No. 1545-0062

1995

Attachment Sequence No. **62**

Name(s) shown on Form 1040

Your social security number

Caution: *If you are a member of the armed forces, see the instructions before completing this form.*

1	Enter the number of miles from your **old home** to your **new workplace** . .	1	miles		
2	Enter the number of miles from your **old home** to your **old workplace** . . .	2	miles		
3	Subtract line 2 from line 1. Enter the result but not less than zero	3	miles		
	Is line 3 at least 50 miles?				
	Yes ▶ Go to line 4. Also, see **Time Test** in the instructions.				
	No ▶ You **cannot** deduct your moving expenses. Do not complete the rest of this form.				
4	Transportation and storage of household goods and personal effects			4	
5	Travel and lodging expenses of moving from your old home to your new home. **Do not** include meals			5	
6	Add lines 4 and 5			6	
7	Enter the total amount your employer paid for your move (including the value of services furnished in kind) that is **not** included in the wages box (box 1) of your W-2 form. This amount should be identified with code **P** in box 13 of your W-2 form.			7	
	Is line 6 more than line 7?				
	Yes ▶ Go to line 8.				
	No ▶ You **cannot** deduct your moving expenses. If line 6 is less than line 7, subtract line 6 from line 7 and include the result in income on Form 1040, line 7.				
8	Subtract line 7 from line 6. Enter the result here and on Form 1040, line 24. This is your **moving expense deduction**			8	

For Paperwork Reduction Act Notice, see back of form. Cat. No. 12490K Form **3903** (1995)

Paperwork Reduction Act Notice

We ask for the information on this form to carry out the Internal Revenue laws of the United States. You are required to give us the information. We need it to ensure that you are complying with these laws and to allow us to figure and collect the right amount of tax.

The time needed to complete and file this form will vary depending on individual circumstances. The estimated average time is:

Recordkeeping	33 min.
Learning about the law or the form	3 min.
Preparing the form	13 min.
Copying, assembling, and sending the form to the IRS	20 min.

If you have comments concerning the accuracy of these time estimates or suggestions for making this form simpler, we would be happy to hear from you. You can write or call the IRS. See the Instructions for Form 1040.

General Instructions

Purpose of Form

Use Form 3903 to figure your moving expense deduction if you moved to a new principal place of work (workplace) within the United States or its possessions. If you qualify to deduct expenses for more than one move, use a separate Form 3903 for each move.

Note: *Use* ***Form 3903-F,*** *Foreign Moving Expenses, instead of this form if you are a U.S. citizen or resident alien who moved to a new principal workplace outside the United States or its possessions.*

Additional Information

For more details, get **Pub. 521,** Moving Expenses.

Other Forms You May Have To File

If you sold your main home in 1995, you must file **Form 2119,** Sale of Your Home, to report the sale.

Who May Deduct Moving Expenses

If you moved to a different home because of a change in job location, you may be able to deduct your moving expenses. You may be able to take the deduction whether you are self-employed or an employee. But you must meet certain tests explained next.

Distance Test.—Your new principal workplace must be at least 50 miles farther from your old home than your old workplace was. For example, if your old workplace was 3 miles from your old home, your new workplace must be at least 53 miles from that home. If you did not have an old workplace, your new workplace must be at least 50 miles from your old home. The distance between the two points is the shortest of the more commonly traveled routes between them.

Time Test.—If you are an employee, you must work full time in the general area of your new workplace for at least 39 weeks during the 12 months right after you move. If you are self-employed, you must work full time in the general area of your new workplace for at least 39 weeks during the first 12 months and a total of at least 78 weeks during the 24 months right after you move.

You may deduct your moving expenses even if you have not met the time test before your return is due. You may do this if you expect to meet the 39-week test by the end of 1996 or the 78-week test by the end of 1997. If you deduct your moving expenses on your 1995 return but do not meet the time test, you will have to either:

- Amend your 1995 tax return by filing **Form 1040X,** Amended U.S. Individual Income Tax Return, or
- Report the amount of your 1995 moving expense deduction that reduced your 1995 income tax as income in the year you cannot meet the test. For more details, see **Time Test** in Pub. 521.

If you do not deduct your moving expenses on your 1995 return and you later meet the time test, you may take the deduction by filing an amended return for 1995. To do this, use Form 1040X.

Exceptions to the Time Test.—The time test does not have to be met if any of the following apply:

- Your job ends because of disability.
- You are transferred for your employer's benefit.
- You are laid off or discharged for a reason other than willful misconduct.
- You meet the requirements (explained later) for retirees or survivors living outside the United States.
- You are filing this form for a decedent.

Members of the Armed Forces

If you are in the armed forces, you do not have to meet the **distance and time tests** if the move is due to a permanent change of station. A permanent change of station includes a move in connection with and within 1 year of retirement or other termination of active duty.

How To Complete the Form.—First, complete lines 4 through 6 using your actual expenses. **Do not** reduce your expenses by any reimbursements or allowances you received from the government in connection with the move. Also, do not include any expenses for moving services that were provided by the government. If you and your spouse and dependents are moved to or from different locations, treat the moves as a single move.

Next, enter on line 7 the total reimbursements and allowances you received from the government in connection with the expenses you claimed on lines 4 and 5. **Do not** include the value of moving services provided by the government. Then, complete line 8 if applicable.

Retirees or Survivors Living Outside the United States

If you are a retiree or survivor who moved to a home in the United States or its possessions and you meet the following requirements, you are treated as if you moved to a new workplace located in the United States. You are subject to the distance test. Use this form instead of Form 3903-F to figure your moving expense deduction.

Retirees.—You may deduct moving expenses for a move to a new home in the United States when you actually retire if both your old principal workplace and your old home were outside the United States.

Survivors.—You may deduct moving expenses for a move to a home in the United States if you are the spouse or dependent of a person whose principal workplace at the time of death was outside the United States. In addition, the expenses must be for a move (1) that begins within 6 months after the decedent's death, and (2) from a former home outside the United States that you lived in with the decedent at the time of death.

Reimbursements

If your employer paid for any part of your move, your employer must give you a statement showing a detailed breakdown of reimbursements or payments for moving expenses. Your employer may use **Form 4782,** Employee Moving Expense Information, or his or her own form.

You may choose to deduct moving expenses in the year you are reimbursed by your employer, even though you paid the expenses in a different year. However, special rules apply. See **How To Report** in Pub. 521.

Moving Expenses Incurred Before 1994.—If you were reimbursed for moving expenses incurred before 1994 and you did not deduct those expenses on a prior year's return, you may be able to deduct them on **Schedule A,** Itemized Deductions. But you must use the **1994** Form 3903 to do so. You can get the 1994 Form 3903 by calling 1-800-TAX-FORM (1-800-829-3676).

Specific Instructions

You may deduct the following expenses you incurred in moving your family and dependent household members. Do not deduct expenses for employees such as a maid, nanny, or nurse.

Line 4.—Enter the actual cost to pack, crate, and move your household goods and personal effects. You may also include the cost to store and insure household goods and personal effects within any period of 30 days in a row after the items were moved from your old home and before they were delivered to your new home.

Line 5.—Enter the costs of travel from your old home to your new home. These include transportation and lodging on the way. Include costs for the day you arrive. Although not all the members of your household have to travel together or at the same time, you may only include expenses for one trip per person.

If you use your own car(s), you may figure the expenses by using either:

- Actual out-of-pocket expenses for gas and oil, or
- Mileage at the rate of 9 cents a mile.

You may add parking fees and tolls to the amount claimed under either method. Keep records to verify your expenses.

Form **4255** (Rev. April 1994) Department of the Treasury Internal Revenue Service

Recapture of Investment Credit

▶ Attach to your income tax return.

OMB No. 1545-0166 Expires 4-30-97

Attachment Sequence No. **65**

Name(s) as shown on return | **Identifying number**

Properties	Type of property—State whether rehabilitation, energy, reforestation, or transition property. (See the Instructions for Form 3468 for the year the investment credit property was placed in service for definitions.) If rehabilitation property, also show type of building. If energy property, show type.
A	
B	
C	
D	

Original Investment Credit

	Computation Steps: (See Specific Instructions)	**Properties** A	B	C	D
1	Original rate of credit				
2	Date property was placed in service				
3	Cost or other basis				
4	Original estimated useful life or class of property				
5	Applicable percentage				
6	Original qualified investment (Multiply line 3 by the percentage on line 5.)				
7	Original credit (Multiply line 6 by the percentage on line 1.)				
8	Date property ceased to be qualified investment credit property				
9	Number of full years between the date on line 2 and the date on line 8				

Computation of Recapture Tax

		A	B	C	D
10	Recapture percentage (from instructions)				
11	Tentative recapture tax (Multiply line 7 by the percentage on line 10.)				
12	Add line 11, columns A through D				
13	Enter the recapture tax from property ceasing to be at risk, or for which there was an increase in nonqualified-nonrecourse financing (Attach separate computation.)				
14	Add lines 12 and 13				
15	Portion of original credit (line 7) not used to offset tax in any year, plus any carryback and carryforward of credits you can now apply to the original credit year because you have freed up tax liability in the amount of the tax recaptured (Do not enter more than line 14—see instructions.)				
16	Total increase in tax. Subtract line 15 from line 14. Enter here and on the appropriate line of your tax return				

Paperwork Reduction Act Notice

We ask for the information on this form to carry out the Internal Revenue laws of the United States. You are required to give us the information. We need it to ensure that you are complying with these laws and to allow us to figure and collect the right amount of tax.

The time needed to complete and file this form will vary depending on individual circumstances. The estimated average time is:

Recordkeeping	7 hr., 53 min.
Learning about the law or the form	2 hr., 23 min.
Preparing, copying, assembling, and sending the form to the IRS	2 hr., 37 min.

If you have comments concerning the accuracy of these time estimates or suggestions for making this form more simple, we would be happy to hear from you. You can write to both the IRS and the Office of Management and Budget at the addresses listed in the instructions for the tax return with which this form is filed.

General Instructions

Section references are to the Internal Revenue Code before amendment by the Revenue Reconciliation Act of 1990 (RRA of 1990), unless otherwise noted.

Purpose of Form

Use Form 4255 to figure the increase in tax for the recapture of investment credit claimed.

You must refigure the credit if you claimed it in an earlier year, but disposed of the property before the end of the recapture period or the useful life you used to figure the original credit, whichever applies. Refigure the credit for all property (except nonrecovery placed in service before 1991) when the property ceases to be investment credit property before the end of 5 full years after the property is placed in service (recapture period). For nonrecovery property placed in service before 1991, refigure the credit when the property ceases to be investment credit property before the end of the useful life used to figure the credit. See the line 10 instructions for details.

You must also refigure the credit if you returned leased property (on which you had taken a credit) to the lessor before the end of the recapture period or useful life.

If you claim investment credit for property and the percentage of business use in a later year falls below the percentage for the year the property was placed in service, you are treated as having disposed of part of the property and may have to recapture part of the investment credit.

You must refigure the credit if you changed the use of property so that it no longer qualifies as investment credit property. For example, you must refigure the credit if you change the use of property from business use to personal use, or if there is any decrease in the percentage of business use of investment credit property. See sections 50(a)(2) (as amended by the RRA of 1990), 47(a)(3), 47(a)(5)(C), and 49(e)(2) for information on recapture for progress expenditure property. Also, see the instructions for line 13 regarding recapture if property ceases to be at risk, or if there is an increase in nonqualified-nonrecourse financing related to certain at-risk property.

An election to be treated as an S corporation does not automatically trigger recapture of investment credit taken before the election was effective. However, the S corporation is liable for any recapture of investment credit taken before the election.

If property on which you took both regular and energy investment credit ceases to be energy credit property but still qualifies as regular investment credit property, only refigure the energy investment credit. However, if you took both credits, and you dispose of the property, or the property ceases to be both energy and regular investment credit property, you must refigure both credits.

If you are an S corporation, a partnership, or an estate or trust that allocated any or all of the investment credit to your shareholders, partners, or beneficiaries, you must provide the information they need to refigure the credit. See Regulations sections 1.47-4, 1.47-5, and 1.47-6.

Partners, shareholders, and beneficiaries.—If your Schedule K-1 shows recapture of investment credit claimed in an earlier year, you will need your copy of the original Form 3468 to complete lines 1 through 9 of this Form 4255.

Special rules.—If you claimed a credit on the following kinds of property, see the sections listed below before you complete Form 4255:

Property	Section
Motion picture films and video tapes .	47(a)(8)
Ships	46(g)(4)

If you took any nonconventional source fuel credit, see section 29(b)(4).

Note: *The RRA of 1990 changed the rules for property eligible for the rehabilitation credit under section 47, as amended by the RRA of 1990. Increase the basis of this property by 100% of the recapture amount. For details, see sections 50(c)(2) and 50(c)(3), as amended by the RRA of 1990.*

Specific Instructions

Note: *Do not figure the recapture tax on lines 1 through 12 for property ceasing to be at risk, or if there is an increase in nonqualified-nonrecourse financing related to certain at-risk property. Figure the recapture tax for these properties on separate schedules and enter the recapture tax on line 13. Include any unused credit for these properties on line 15.*

Lines A through D.—Describe the property for which you must refigure the credit.

Complete lines 1 through 11 for each property on which you are refiguring the credit. Use a separate column for each item. If you must recapture both the energy investment credit and the regular investment credit for the same item, use a separate column for each credit. If you need more columns, use additional Forms 4255, or other schedules that include all the information shown on Form 4255. Enter the total from the separate sheets on line 12.

Line 1.—Enter the rate you used to figure the original credit from the Form 3468 that you filed.

See section 46(b)(4) for the rates for qualified rehabilitation expenditures made after 1981.

Line 2.—Enter the day, month, and year that the property was available for service.

Line 3.—Enter the cost or other basis that you used to figure the original credit.

Line 4.—Enter the estimated useful life that you used to figure the original credit for the property.

Line 5.—Enter the applicable percentage that you used to figure the original qualified investment from the Form 3468 that you filed.

Generally, the applicable percentage will be 100% for property eligible for the investment credit under section 46, as amended by the RRA of 1990.

Line 8.—Generally, this will be the date you disposed of the property. See Regulations section 1.47-1(c) for more information.

Line 9.—Do not enter partial years. If the property was held less than 12 months, enter zero.

Line 10.—Enter the recapture percentage from the following tables:

Property placed in service after 12/31/90 and recovery property

If number of full years on line 9 of Form 4255 is:	The recapture percentage is:
0	100
1	80
2	60
3	40
4	20
5 or more	0

Nonrecovery property placed in service before 1991

If number of full years on line 9 of Form 4255 is:	The recapture percentage for property with an original useful life of: 5 or more but less than 7 years is:	7 or more years is:
4	50	66.6
5	0	33.3
6	0	33.3
7 or more	0	0

Line 12.—If you have used more than one Form 4255, or separate sheets to list additional items on which you figured an increase in tax, write to the left of the entry space "Tax from attached, $ ...." Include the amount in the total for line 12.

Line 13.—For certain taxpayers, the basis or cost of property is limited to the amount the taxpayer is at risk for the property at yearend. The basis or cost must be reduced by the amount of any "nonqualified-nonrecourse financing" related to the property at yearend. If property ceases to be at risk in a later year, or if there is an increase in nonqualified-nonrecourse financing, recapture may be required. See section 49(b), as amended by the RRA of 1990, for details. Attach a separate computation schedule to figure the recapture tax and enter the total tax on line 13.

Line 15.—If you did not use all the credit you originally figured, either in the year you figured it or in a carryback or carryforward year, you do not have to recapture the amount of the credit you did not use. In refiguring the credit for the original credit year, be sure to include any carryforwards from previous years, plus any carrybacks arising within the 3 taxable years after the original credit year that are now allowed because the recapture and recomputation of the original credit made available some additional tax liability in that year. See Regulations section 1.47-1(d) and Rev. Rul. 72-221 1972-1 C.B. 15, for details.

Note: *You must also take into account any applicable 35% reduction in credit under section 49(c)(2) when computing the amount to enter on line 15.*

Figure the unused portion on a separate sheet and enter it on this line. Do not enter more than the recapture tax on line 14.

Note: *Be sure to adjust your current unused credit to reflect any unused portion of the original credit that was entered on line 15 of this form.*

Form **4562**

Department of the Treasury
Internal Revenue Service (99)

Depreciation and Amortization
(Including Information on Listed Property)

▶ See separate instructions. ▶ Attach this form to your return.

OMB No. 1545-0172

1995

Attachment Sequence No. **67**

Name(s) shown on return	Business or activity to which this form relates	Identifying number

Part I **Election To Expense Certain Tangible Property (Section 179) (Note:** *If you have any "Listed Property," complete Part V before you complete Part I.*)

1	Maximum dollar limitation. If an enterprise zone business, see page 1 of the instructions	1	$17,500
2	Total cost of section 179 property placed in service during the tax year. See page 2 of the instructions	2	
3	Threshold cost of section 179 property before reduction in limitation	3	$200,000
4	Reduction in limitation. Subtract line 3 from line 2. If zero or less, enter -0-	4	
5	Dollar limitation for tax year. Subtract line 4 from line 1. If zero or less, enter -0-. If married filing separately, see page 2 of the instructions	5	

	(a) Description of property	(b) Cost	(c) Elected cost
6			
7	Listed property. Enter amount from line 27	7	

8	Total elected cost of section 179 property. Add amounts in column (c), lines 6 and 7	8	
9	Tentative deduction. Enter the smaller of line 5 or line 8	9	
10	Carryover of disallowed deduction from 1994. See page 2 of the instructions	10	
11	Taxable income limitation. Enter the smaller of taxable income (not less than zero) or line 5 (see instructions)	11	
12	Section 179 expense deduction. Add lines 9 and 10, but do not enter more than line 11	12	
13	Carryover of disallowed deduction to 1996. Add lines 9 and 10, less line 12 ▶	13	

Note: *Do not use Part II or Part III below for listed property (automobiles, certain other vehicles, cellular telephones, certain computers, or property used for entertainment, recreation, or amusement). Instead, use Part V for listed property.*

Part II **MACRS Depreciation For Assets Placed in Service ONLY During Your 1995 Tax Year (Do Not Include Listed Property.)**

Section A—General Asset Account Election

14 If you are making the election under section 168(i)(4) to group any assets placed in service during the tax year into one or more general asset accounts, check this box. See page 2 of the instructions ▶ ☐

	(a) Classification of property	(b) Month and year placed in service	(c) Basis for depreciation (business/investment use only—see instructions)	(d) Recovery period	(e) Convention	(f) Method	(g) Depreciation deduction
	Section B—General Depreciation System (GDS) (See page 2 of the instructions.)						
15a	3-year property						
b	5-year property						
c	7-year property						
d	10-year property						
e	15-year property						
f	20-year property						
g	Residential rental property			27.5 yrs.	MM	S/L	
				27.5 yrs.	MM	S/L	
h	Nonresidential real property			39 yrs.	MM	S/L	
					MM	S/L	
	Section C—Alternative Depreciation System (ADS) (See page 4 of the instructions.)						
16a	Class life					S/L	
b	12-year			12 yrs.		S/L	
c	40-year			40 yrs.	MM	S/L	

Part III **Other Depreciation (Do Not Include Listed Property.)** (See page 4 of the instructions.)

17	GDS and ADS deductions for assets placed in service in tax years beginning before 1995	17	
18	Property subject to section 168(f)(1) election	18	
19	ACRS and other depreciation	19	

Part IV **Summary** (See page 4 of the instructions.)

20	Listed property. Enter amount from line 26	20	
21	**Total.** Add deductions on line 12, lines 15 and 16 in column (g), and lines 17 through 20. Enter here and on the appropriate lines of your return. Partnerships and S corporations—see instructions	21	
22	For assets shown above and placed in service during the current year, enter the portion of the basis attributable to section 263A costs	22	

For Paperwork Reduction Act Notice, see page 1 of the separate instructions. Cat. No. 12906N Form **4562** (1995)

Form 4562 (1995) Page 2

Part V **Listed Property—Automobiles, Certain Other Vehicles, Cellular Telephones, Certain Computers, and Property Used for Entertainment, Recreation, or Amusement**

Note: *For any vehicle for which you are using the standard mileage rate or deducting lease expense, complete* ***only*** *23a, 23b, columns (a) through (c) of Section A, all of Section B, and Section C if applicable.*

Section A—Depreciation and Other Information (Caution: *See page 5 of the instructions for limitations for automobiles.)*

23a Do you have evidence to support the business/investment use claimed? ☐ **Yes** ☐ **No** **23b** If "Yes," is the evidence written? ☐ **Yes** ☐ **No**

(a) Type of property (list vehicles first)	(b) Date placed in service	(c) Business/ investment use percentage	(d) Cost or other basis	(e) Basis for depreciation (business/investment use only)	(f) Recovery period	(g) Method/ Convention	(h) Depreciation deduction	(i) Elected section 179 cost
24 Property used more than 50% in a qualified business use (See page 5 of the instructions.):								
		%						
		%						
		%						
25 Property used 50% or less in a qualified business use (See page 5 of the instructions.):								
		%				S/L –		
		%				S/L –		
		%				S/L –		

26 Add amounts in column (h). Enter the total here and on line 20, page 1 . . . . . . **26**

27 Add amounts in column (i). Enter the total here and on line 7, page 1 . . . . **27**

Section B—Information on Use of Vehicles

Complete this section for vehicles used by a sole proprietor, partner, or other "more than 5% owner," or related person.

If you provided vehicles to your employees, first answer the questions in Section C to see if you meet an exception to completing this section for those vehicles.

	(a) Vehicle 1		(b) Vehicle 2		(c) Vehicle 3		(d) Vehicle 4		(e) Vehicle 5		(f) Vehicle 6	
28 Total business/investment miles driven during the year (DO NOT include commuting miles)												
29 Total commuting miles driven during the year												
30 Total other personal (noncommuting) miles driven												
31 Total miles driven during the year. Add lines 28 through 30.												
	Yes	**No**	**Yes**	**No**	**Yes**	**No**	**Yes**	**No**	**Yes**	**No**	**Yes**	**No**
32 Was the vehicle available for personal use during off-duty hours?												
33 Was the vehicle used primarily by a more than 5% owner or related person?												
34 Is another vehicle available for personal use?												

Section C—Questions for Employers Who Provide Vehicles for Use by Their Employees

Answer these questions to determine if you meet an exception to completing Section B for vehicles used by employees who ***are not*** *more than 5% owners or related persons.*

	Yes	**No**
35 Do you maintain a written policy statement that prohibits all personal use of vehicles, including commuting, by your employees?		
36 Do you maintain a written policy statement that prohibits personal use of vehicles, except commuting, by your employees? See page 6 of the instructions for vehicles used by corporate officers, directors, or 1% or more owners		
37 Do you treat all use of vehicles by employees as personal use?		
38 Do you provide more than five vehicles to your employees, obtain information from your employees about the use of the vehicles, and retain the information received?		
39 Do you meet the requirements concerning qualified automobile demonstration use? See page 6 of the instructions . .		

Note: *If your answer to 35, 36, 37, 38, or 39 is "Yes," you need not complete Section B for the covered vehicles.*

Part VI **Amortization**

(a) Description of costs	(b) Date amortization begins	(c) Amortizable amount	(d) Code section	(e) Amortization period or percentage	(f) Amortization for this year
40 Amortization of costs that begins during your 1995 tax year:					

41 Amortization of costs that began before 1995 . . . . **41**

42 **Total.** Enter here and on "Other Deductions" or "Other Expenses" line of your return . . . **42**

Printed on recycled paper

Form **4684**

Department of the Treasury
Internal Revenue Service

Casualties and Thefts

▶ See separate instructions.
▶ Attach to your tax return.
▶ Use a separate Form 4684 for each different casualty or theft.

OMB No. 1545-0177
1995
Attachment Sequence No. **26**

Name(s) shown on tax return | **Identifying number**

SECTION A—Personal Use Property (Use this section to report casualties and thefts of property **not** used in a trade or business or for income-producing purposes.)

1 Description of properties (show type, location, and date acquired for each):
Property **A** ....
Property **B** ....
Property **C** ....
Property **D** ....

		Properties (Use a separate column for each property lost or damaged from one casualty or theft.)			
		A	B	C	D
2 Cost or other basis of each property	2				
3 Insurance or other reimbursement (whether or not you filed a claim). See instructions	3				
Note: *If line 2 is* ***more than*** *line 3, skip line 4.*					
4 Gain from casualty or theft. If line 3 is **more than** line 2, enter the difference here and skip lines 5 through 9 for that column. See instructions if line 3 includes insurance or other reimbursement you did not claim, or you received payment for your loss in a later tax year	4				
5 Fair market value **before** casualty or theft	5				
6 Fair market value **after** casualty or theft	6				
7 Subtract line 6 from line 5	7				
8 Enter the **smaller** of line 2 or line 7	8				
9 Subtract line 3 from line 8. If zero or less, enter -0-	9				

10 Casualty or theft loss. Add the amounts on line 9. Enter the total	10	
11 Enter the amount from line 10 or $100, whichever is **smaller**	11	
12 Subtract line 11 from line 10	12	
Caution: *Use only one Form 4684 for lines 13 through 18.*		
13 Add the amounts on line 12 of all Forms 4684	13	
14 Combine the amounts from line 4 of all Forms 4684	14	
15 • If line 14 is **more than** line 13, enter the difference here and on Schedule D. Do not complete the rest of this section (see instructions). • If line 14 is **less than** line 13, enter -0- here and continue with the form. • If line 14 is **equal to** line 13, enter -0- here. Do not complete the rest of this section.	15	
16 If line 14 is **less than** line 13, enter the difference	16	
17 Enter 10% of your adjusted gross income (Form 1040, line 32). Estates and trusts, see instructions	17	
18 Subtract line 17 from line 16. If zero or less, enter -0-. Also enter result on Schedule A (Form 1040), line 19. Estates and trusts, enter on the "Other deductions" line of your tax return	18	

For Paperwork Reduction Act Notice, see page 1 of separate instructions. Cat. No. 12997O Form **4684** (1995)

Form 4684 (1995) Attachment Sequence No. **26** Page **2**

Name(s) shown on tax return. Do not enter name and identifying number if shown on other side. | **Identifying number**

SECTION B—Business and Income-Producing Property (Use this section to report casualties and thefts of property used in a trade or business or for income-producing purposes.)

Part I Casualty or Theft Gain or Loss (Use a separate Part I for each casualty or theft.)

19 Description of properties (show type, location, and date acquired for each):

Property **A** ....

Property **B** ....

Property **C** ....

Property **D** ....

		Properties (Use a separate column for each property lost or damaged from one casualty or theft.) A	B	C	D
20 Cost or adjusted basis of each property	20				
21 Insurance or other reimbursement (whether or not you filed a claim). See the instructions for line 3 . **Note:** *If line 20 is* ***more than*** *line 21, skip line 22.*	21				
22 Gain from casualty or theft. If line 21 is **more than** line 20, enter the difference here and on line 29 or line 34, column (**c**), except as provided in the instructions for line 33. Also, skip lines 23 through 27 for that column. See the instructions for line 4 if line 21 includes insurance or other reimbursement you did not claim, or you received payment for your loss in a later tax year	22				
23 Fair market value **before** casualty or theft . . .	23				
24 Fair market value **after** casualty or theft	24				
25 Subtract line 24 from line 23	25				
26 Enter the **smaller** of line 20 or line 25 . . . . **Note:** *If the property was totally destroyed by casualty or lost from theft, enter on line 26 the amount from line 20.*	26				
27 Subtract line 21 from line 26. If zero or less, enter -0-	27				

28 Casualty or theft loss. Add the amounts on line 27. Enter the total here and on line 29 **or** line 34 (see instructions). | 28 |

Part II Summary of Gains and Losses (from separate Parts I)

(a) Identify casualty or theft		(b) Losses from casualties or thefts (i) Trade, business, rental or royalty property	(ii) Income-producing property		(c) Gains from casualties or thefts includible in income
Casualty or Theft of Property Held One Year or Less					
29		( )	( )		
		( )	( )		
30 Totals. Add the amounts on line 29	30	( )	( )		
31 Combine line 30, columns (b)(i) and (c). Enter the net gain or (loss) here and on Form 4797, line 15. If Form 4797 is not otherwise required, see instructions				31	
32 Enter the amount from line 30, column (b)(ii) here and on Schedule A (Form 1040), line 22. Partnerships, S corporations, estates and trusts, see instructions				32	
Casualty or Theft of Property Held More Than One Year					
33 Casualty or theft gains from Form 4797, line 34				33	
34		( )	( )		
		( )	( )		
35 Total losses. Add amounts on line 34, columns (b)(i) and (b)(ii) . . .	35	( )	( )		
36 Total gains. Add lines 33 and 34, column (c)				36	
37 Add amounts on line 35, columns (b)(i) and (b)(ii)				37	
38 If the loss on line 37 is **more than** the gain on line 36:					
a Combine line 35, column (b)(i) and line 36, and enter the net gain or (loss) here. Partnerships and S corporations see the note below. All others enter this amount on Form 4797, line 15. If Form 4797 is not otherwise required, see instructions				38a	
b Enter the amount from line 35, column (b)(ii) here. Partnerships and S corporations see the note below. Individuals enter this amount on Schedule A (Form 1040), line 22. Estates and trusts, enter on the "Other deductions" line of your tax return				38b	
39 If the loss on line 37 is **equal to** or **less than** the gain on line 36, combine these lines and enter here. Partnerships, see the note below. All others, enter this amount on Form 4797, line 3				39	

Note: *Partnerships, enter the amount from line 38a, 38b, or line 39 on Form 1065, Schedule K, line 7. S corporations, enter the amount from line 38a or 38b on Form 1120S, Schedule K, line 6.*

Form **4797**

Department of the Treasury
Internal Revenue Service (99)

Sales of Business Property

(Also Involuntary Conversions and Recapture Amounts Under Sections 179 and 280F(b)(2))

▶ **Attach to your tax return.** ▶ **See separate instructions.**

OMB No. 1545-0184

1995

Attachment Sequence No. **27**

Name(s) shown on return | **Identifying number**

1 Enter here the gross proceeds from the sale or exchange of real estate reported to you for 1995 on Form(s) 1099-S (or a substitute statement) that you will be including on line 2, 11, or 22 . . . . **1**

Part I Sales or Exchanges of Property Used in a Trade or Business and Involuntary Conversions From Other Than Casualty or Theft—Property Held More Than 1 Year

	(a) Description of property	**(b)** Date acquired (mo., day, yr.)	**(c)** Date sold (mo., day, yr.)	**(d)** Gross sales price	**(e)** Depreciation allowed or allowable since acquisition	**(f)** Cost or other basis, plus improvements and expense of sale	**(g)** LOSS ((f) minus the sum of (d) and (e))	**(h)** GAIN ((d) plus (e) minus (f))
2								

3 Gain, if any, from Form 4684, line 39 . . . . **3**

4 Section 1231 gain from installment sales from Form 6252, line 26 or 37 . . . . **4**

5 Section 1231 gain or (loss) from like-kind exchanges from Form 8824 . . . . **5**

6 Gain, if any, from line 34, from other than casualty or theft **6**

7 Add lines 2 through 6 in columns (g) and (h) . . . . **7** ( )

8 Combine columns (g) and (h) of line 7. Enter gain or (loss) here, and on the appropriate line as follows: **8**

Partnerships—Enter the gain or (loss) on Form 1065, Schedule K, line 6. Skip lines 9, 10, 12, and 13 below.

S corporations—Report the gain or (loss) following the instructions for Form 1120S, Schedule K, lines 5 and 6. Skip lines 9, 10, 12, and 13 below, unless line 8 is a gain and the S corporation is subject to the capital gains tax.

All others—If line 8 is zero or a loss, enter the amount on line 12 below and skip lines 9 and 10. If line 8 is a gain and you did not have any prior year section 1231 losses, or they were recaptured in an earlier year, enter the gain as a long-term capital gain on Schedule D and skip lines 9, 10, and 13 below.

9 Nonrecaptured net section 1231 losses from prior years (see instructions) **9**

10 Subtract line 9 from line 8. If zero or less, enter -0-. Also enter on the appropriate line as follows (see instructions): **10**

S corporations—Enter this amount on Schedule D (Form 1120S), line 13, and skip lines 12 and 13 below.

All others—If line 10 is zero, enter the amount from line 8 on line 13 below. If line 10 is more than zero, enter the amount from line 9 on line 13 below, and enter the amount from line 10 as a long-term capital gain on Schedule D.

Part II Ordinary Gains and Losses

11 Ordinary gains and losses not included on lines 12 through 18 (include property held 1 year or less):

12 Loss, if any, from line 8 . . . . **12**

13 Gain, if any, from line 8, or amount from line 9 if applicable **13**

14 Gain, if any, from line 33 . . . . **14**

15 Net gain or (loss) from Form 4684, lines 31 and 38a **15**

16 Ordinary gain from installment sales from Form 6252, line 25 or 36 . . . . **16**

17 Ordinary gain or (loss) from like-kind exchanges from Form 8824 . . . . **17**

18 Recapture of section 179 expense deduction for partners and S corporation shareholders from property dispositions by partnerships and S corporations (see instructions) **18**

19 Add lines 11 through 18 in columns (g) and (h) . . . . **19** ( )

20 Combine columns (g) and (h) of line 19. Enter gain or (loss) here, and on the appropriate line as follows: . . . **20**

a For all except individual returns: Enter the gain or (loss) from line 20 on the return being filed.

b For individual returns:

(1) If the loss on line 12 includes a loss from Form 4684, line 35, column (b)(ii), enter that part of the loss here and on line 22 of Schedule A (Form 1040). Identify as from "Form 4797, line 20b(1)." See instructions . . . . **20b(1)**

(2) Redetermine the gain or (loss) on line 20, excluding the loss, if any, on line 20b(1). Enter here and on Form 1040, line 14 . . **20b(2)**

Part III Gain From Disposition of Property Under Sections 1245, 1250, 1252, 1254, and 1255

21 **(a)** Description of section 1245, 1250, 1252, 1254, or 1255 property:	**(b)** Date acquired (mo., day, yr.)	**(c)** Date sold (mo., day, yr.)
A		
B		
C		
D		

	Relate lines 21A through 21D to these columns	▶	Property A	Property B	Property C	Property D
22	Gross sales price (**Note:** *See line 1 before completing.*)	22				
23	Cost or other basis plus expense of sale	23				
24	Depreciation (or depletion) allowed or allowable	24				
25	Adjusted basis. Subtract line 24 from line 23	25				
26	Total gain. Subtract line 25 from line 22	26				
27	**If section 1245 property:**					
a	Depreciation allowed or allowable from line 24	27a				
b	Enter the **smaller** of line 26 or 27a	27b				
28	**If section 1250 property:** If straight line depreciation was used, enter -0- on line 28g, except for a corporation subject to section 291.					
a	Additional depreciation after 1975 (see instructions)	28a				
b	Applicable percentage multiplied by the **smaller** of line 26 or line 28a (see instructions)	28b				
c	Subtract line 28a from line 26. If residential rental property or line 26 is not more than line 28a, skip lines 28d and 28e	28c				
d	Additional depreciation after 1969 and before 1976	28d				
e	Enter the **smaller** of line 28c or 28d	28e				
f	Section 291 amount (corporations only)	28f				
g	Add lines 28b, 28e, and 28f	28g				
29	**If section 1252 property:** Skip this section if you did not dispose of farmland or if this form is being completed for a partnership.					
a	Soil, water, and land clearing expenses	29a				
b	Line 29a multiplied by applicable percentage (see instructions)	29b				
c	Enter the **smaller** of line 26 or 29b	29c				
30	**If section 1254 property:**					
a	Intangible drilling and development costs, expenditures for development of mines and other natural deposits, and mining exploration costs (see instructions)	30a				
b	Enter the **smaller** of line 26 or 30a	30b				
31	**If section 1255 property:**					
a	Applicable percentage of payments excluded from income under section 126 (see instructions)	31a				
b	Enter the **smaller** of line 26 or 31a (see instructions)	31b				

Summary of Part III Gains. Complete property columns A through D, through line 31b before going to line 32.

32	Total gains for all properties. Add property columns A through D, line 26	32	
33	Add property columns A through D, lines 27b, 28g, 29c, 30b, and 31b. Enter here and on line 14	33	
34	Subtract line 33 from line 32. Enter the portion from casualty or theft on Form 4684, line 33. Enter the portion from other than casualty or theft on Form 4797, line 6	34	

Part IV Recapture Amounts Under Sections 179 and 280F(b)(2) When Business Use Drops to 50% or Less

See instructions.

			(a) Section 179	**(b)** Section 280F(b)(2)
35	Section 179 expense deduction or depreciation allowable in prior years	35		
36	Recomputed depreciation. See instructions	36		
37	Recapture amount. Subtract line 36 from line 35. See the instructions for where to report	37		

Printed on recycled paper

1995 Form 4868

Department of the Treasury
Internal Revenue Service

General Instructions

Note: *Form 1040-T references are to a new form sent to certain individuals on a test basis.*

A Change To Note

We have combined Form 4868-V (payment voucher) and Form 4868 into one, smaller, detachable Form 4868. The form is at the bottom of this page.

Purpose of Form

Use Form 4868 to apply for 4 more months to file **Form 1040EZ, Form 1040A, Form 1040,** or **Form 1040-T.**

To get the extra time you **MUST:**

- Properly estimate your 1995 tax liability using the information available to you,
- Enter your tax liability on line 6a of Form 4868,
- Sign your Form 4868, **AND**
- File Form 4868 by the regular due date of your return.

If you cannot pay the entire balance due, see the instructions for line 6c.

You do not have to explain why you are asking for the extension. We will contact you only if your request is denied.

Do not file Form 4868 if you want the IRS to figure your tax or you are under a court order to file your return by the regular due date.

If you need an additional extension, see **Additional Time** on page 3.

Note: *An extension of time to file your 1995* ***calendar year*** *income tax return also extends the time to file a gift or generation-skipping transfer (GST) tax return* ***(Form 709 or 709-A)*** *for 1995.*

Out of the Country

If you already had 2 extra months to file because you were a U.S. citizen or resident and were out of the country, use this form to obtain an additional 2 months to file. Write "Taxpayer Abroad" across the top of Form 4868. "Out of the country" means either **(a)** you live outside the United States and Puerto Rico **and** your main place of work is outside the United States and Puerto Rico, **or (b)** you are in military or naval service outside the United States and Puerto Rico.

When To File Form 4868

File Form 4868 by April 15, 1996. If you are filing a fiscal year return, file Form 4868 by the regular due date of your return.

If you had 2 extra months to file your return because you were out of the country, file Form 4868 by June 17, 1996, for a 1995 calendar year return.

For Paperwork Reduction Act Notice, see page 3. Cat. No. 13141W Form **4868** (1995)

▼ DETACH HERE ▼

Form **4868**
Department of the Treasury
Internal Revenue Service

Application for Automatic Extension of Time To File U.S. Individual Income Tax Return

OMB No. 1545-0188
1995

1 Your name(s) (see instructions)

Address (see instructions)

City, town or post office, state, and ZIP code

3 **Your social security number**

4 **Spouse's social security no.**

2a **Amount due—** Add lines 6c, d, and e . ▶ $ ____________

b **Amount you are paying** ▶ $

5 I request an automatic 4-month extension of time to August 15, 1996, to file my individual tax return for the calendar year 1995 or to , 19 , for the fiscal tax year ending , 19 .

6 **Individual Income Tax—**See instructions.

a Total tax liability for 1995 . . . . . . $ ____________
b Total payments for 1995. . . . . . . $ ____________
c **Balance due.** Subtract 6b from 6a . . $

Gift or GST Tax Return(s)—See instructions.

Check here **ONLY** if filing a gift or GST tax return . . . . } Yourself ▶ ☐ Spouse ▶ ☐
d Amount of gift or GST tax **you** are paying $ ____________
e **Your spouse's** gift/GST tax payment $

Under penalties of perjury, I declare that I have examined this form, including accompanying schedules and statements, and to the best of my knowledge and belief, it is true, correct, and complete; and, if prepared by someone other than the taxpayer, that I am authorized to prepare this form.

▶ Your signature ____________ Date ____________ ▶ Spouse's signature, if filing jointly ____________ Date ____________

▶ Preparer's signature (other than taxpayer) ____________ Date ____________

Form 4868 (1995) Page 2

Where To File

If you live in:	And you are making a payment, send Form 4868 with your payment to IRS:	And you are NOT making a payment, send Form 4868 to Internal Revenue Service Center:
Florida, Georgia, South Carolina	P.O. Box 105073 Atlanta, GA 30348-5073	Atlanta, GA 39901
New Jersey, New York (New York City and counties of Nassau, Rockland, Suffolk, and Westchester)	P.O. Box 22423 Newark, NJ 07101-2423	Holtsville, NY 00501
New York (all other counties), Connecticut, Maine, Massachusetts, New Hampshire, Rhode Island, Vermont	P.O. Box 371410 Pittsburgh, PA 15250-7410	Andover, MA 05501
Illinois, Iowa, Minnesota, Missouri, Wisconsin	P.O. Box 970028 St. Louis, MO 63197-0028	Kansas City, MO 64999
Delaware, District of Columbia, Maryland, Pennsylvania, Virginia	P.O. Box 7990 Philadelphia, PA 19162-7990	Philadelphia, PA 19255
Indiana, Kentucky, Michigan, Ohio, West Virginia	P.O. Box 6252 Chicago, IL 60680-6252	Cincinnati, OH 45999
Kansas, New Mexico, Oklahoma, Texas	P.O. Box 970027 St. Louis, MO 63197-0027	Austin, TX 73301
Alaska, Arizona, California (counties of Alpine, Amador, Butte, Calaveras, Colusa, Contra Costa, Del Norte, El Dorado, Glenn, Humboldt, Lake, Lassen, Marin, Mendocino, Modoc, Napa, Nevada, Placer, Plumas, Sacramento, San Joaquin, Shasta, Sierra, Siskiyou, Solano, Sonoma, Sutter, Tehama, Trinity, Yolo, and Yuba), Colorado, Idaho, Montana, Nebraska, Nevada, North Dakota, Oregon, South Dakota, Utah, Washington, Wyoming	P.O. Box 7122 San Francisco, CA 94120-7122	Ogden, UT 84201
California (all other counties), Hawaii	P.O. Box 54916 Los Angeles, CA 90054-0916	Fresno, CA 93888
Alabama, Arkansas, Louisiana, Mississippi, North Carolina, Tennessee	P.O. Box 1236 Charlotte, NC 28201-1236	Memphis, TN 37501
All APO and FPO addresses, American Samoa, Puerto Rico (or if excluding income under section 933), nonpermanent residents of Guam or the Virgin Islands, foreign addresses (or if a dual status alien) if a U.S. citizen or if filing Form 2555, Form 2555-EZ, or Form 4563	P.O. Box 7990 Philadelphia, PA 19162-7990	Philadelphia, PA 19255
Guam: Permanent residents	Send Form 4868 and payments to:	Department of Revenue and Taxation Government of Guam Building 13-1 Mariner Avenue Tiyjan Barrigada, GU 96913
Virgin Islands: Permanent residents	Send Form 4868 and payments to:	V.I. Bureau of Internal Revenue 9601 Estate Thomas Charlotte Amalie St. Thomas, VI 00802

How To Send In Your Payment

- When sending a payment with Form 4868, use the addresses in the middle column under **Where To File** on page 2.
- Make your check or money order payable to "Internal Revenue Service" (not "IRS"). Do not send cash.
- Write your social security number, daytime phone number, and "1995 Form 4868" on your check or money order.
- Do not staple or attach your payment to the form.

If You Need Additional Time

If the automatic extension does not give you enough time, you can ask for additional time later. But you'll have to give a good reason, and it must be approved by the IRS. To ask for the additional time, you must do **either** of the following:

1. File **Form 2688,** Application for Additional Extension of Time To File U.S. Individual Income Tax Return, or

2. Explain your reason in a letter. Mail it to the address in the right column under **Where To File** on page 2.

File Form 4868 **before** you file Form 2688 or write a letter asking for more time. Only in cases of undue hardship will the IRS approve your request for an additional extension without receiving Form 4868 first. Ask early for this extra time. Then, you can still file your return on time if your request is not approved.

Filing Your Tax Return

You may file your tax return any time before the extension expires. But remember, Form 4868 does not extend the time to pay taxes. If you do not pay the amount due by the regular due date, you will owe interest. You may also be charged penalties.

Do not attach a copy of Form 4868 to your return.

Interest

You will owe interest on any tax not paid by the regular due date of your return. The interest runs until you pay the tax. Even if you had a good reason for not paying on time, you will still owe interest.

Late Payment Penalty

The penalty is usually ½ of 1% of any tax (other than estimated tax) not paid by the regular due date. It is charged for each month or part of a month the tax is unpaid. The maximum penalty is 25%.

The late payment penalty will not be charged if you can show reasonable cause for not paying on time. Attach a statement to your return fully explaining the reason. **Do not** attach the statement to Form 4868.

You are considered to have "reasonable cause" for the period covered by this automatic extension if at least 90% of your actual 1995 tax liability is paid before the regular due date of your return through withholding, estimated tax payments, or with Form 4868.

Late Filing Penalty

A penalty is usually charged if your return is filed after the due date (including extensions). It is usually 5% of the tax not paid by the regular due date for each month or part of a month your return is late. Generally, the maximum penalty is 25%. If your return is more than 60 days late, the minimum penalty is $100 or the balance of the tax due on your return, whichever is smaller. You might not owe the penalty if you have a good reason for filing late. Attach a statement to your return fully explaining the reason. **Do not** attach the statement to Form 4868.

How To Claim Credit for Payment Made With This Form

When you file your return, include the amount of any payment you sent with Form 4868 on the appropriate line of your tax return. If you file Form 1040EZ, the instructions for line 9 of that form will tell you how to report the payment. If you file Form 1040A, see the instructions for line 29d. If you file Form 1040, enter the payment on line 58. If you file Form 1040-T, enter the payment on line 35.

If you and your spouse each filed a separate Form 4868 but later file a joint return for 1995, enter the total paid with both Forms 4868 on the appropriate line of your joint return.

If you and your spouse jointly filed Form 4868 but later file separate returns for 1995, you may enter the total amount paid with Form 4868 on either of your separate returns. Or you and your spouse may divide the payment in any agreed amounts. Be sure each separate return has the social security numbers of both spouses.

Paperwork Reduction Act Notice

We ask for the information on this form to carry out the Internal Revenue laws of the United States. You are required to give us the information. We need it to ensure that you are complying with these laws and to allow us to figure and collect the right amount of tax.

The time needed to complete and file this form will vary depending on individual circumstances. The estimated average time is: **Recordkeeping,** 26 min.; **Learning about the law or the form,** 13 min.; **Preparing the form,** 17 min.; and **Copying, assembling, and sending the form to the IRS,** 10 min.

If you have comments concerning the accuracy of these time estimates or suggestions for making this form simpler, we would be happy to hear from you. You can write to the Tax Forms Committee, Western Area Distribution Center, Rancho Cordova, CA 95743-0001. **DO NOT** send the form to this address. Instead, see **Where To File** on page 2.

Specific Instructions

How To Complete Form 4868

Box 1

Enter your name(s) and address. If you plan to file a joint return, include both spouses' names in the order in which they will appear on the return.

If you want correspondence regarding this extension to be sent to you at an address other than your own or to an agent acting for you, include the agent's name, (if any), and enter that address instead.

If you changed your name after you filed your last return because of marriage, divorce, etc., be sure to report this to your local Social Security Administration office before filing Form 4868. This prevents delays in processing your extension request.

If you changed your mailing address after you filed your last return, you should use **Form 8822,** Change of Address, to notify the IRS of the change. Showing a new address on Form 4868 will not update your record. You can get Form 8822 by calling 1-800-TAX-FORM (1-800-829-3676).

Line 2

Enter the total of lines 6c, d, and e on line 2a. On line 2b, enter the amount of your check or money order. If you are paying your entire estimate of tax liability, both lines should be the same.

Lines 3 and 4

If you plan to file jointly, enter the SSN on line 3 that you will show first on your return. Enter your spouse's SSN on line 4.

Line 6a—Total Tax Liability for 1995

This is the amount you expect to enter on Form 1040EZ, line 10; Form 1040A, line 28; Form 1040, line 54; or Form 1040-T, line 31. If you expect this amount to be zero, enter zero.

Caution: *You can estimate this amount, but be as exact as you can with the information you have. If we later find that your estimate was not reasonable, the extension will be null and void.*

Line 6b—Total Payments for 1995

This is the amount you expect to enter on Form 1040EZ, line 9; Form 1040A, line 29d; Form 1040, line 61 (excluding line 58); or Form 1040-T, line 37 (excluding line 35).

Line 6c—Balance Due

Subtract line 6b from line 6a. If line 6b is more than line 6a, enter zero.

If you find you can't pay the full amount shown on line 6c, you can still get the extension. But you should pay as much as you can to limit the amount of interest you will owe. Also, you may be charged the late payment penalty on the unpaid tax from the regular due date of your return. See **Late Payment Penalty** on page 3.

Lines 6d and 6e—Gift or GST Tax

Fill in this part only if you or your spouse plan to file Form 709 or 709-A **and** you are also using Form 4868 to apply for an extension of time to file your 1995 **calendar year** income tax return. **Do not** include income tax on lines 6d and 6e.

Enter the amount of gift and GST tax you (or your spouse) expect to owe on these lines. If your spouse files a **separate** Form 4868, **do not** check the box for your spouse; enter on your form only the total gift and GST tax **you** expect to owe. Pay in full with this form to avoid interest and penalties. If paying gift and GST taxes on time would cause you undue hardship (not just inconvenience), attach an explanation to Form 4868.

Signature

Form 4868 must be signed or your extension will be denied. If you plan to file a joint return, both of you should sign. If there is a good reason why one of you cannot, the other spouse may sign for both. Attach a statement explaining why the other spouse cannot sign.

Anyone with a power of attorney can also sign. But the following can sign for you without a power of attorney:

- Attorneys, CPAs, and enrolled agents.
- A person in close personal or business relationship to you who is signing because you cannot. There must be a good reason why you cannot sign, such as illness or absence. Attach an explanation.

Printed on recycled paper

Form **4952**

Department of the Treasury
Internal Revenue Service (99)

Investment Interest Expense Deduction

► **Attach to your tax return.**

OMB No. 1545-0191

1995

Attachment Sequence No. **12A**

Name(s) shown on return	**Identifying number**

Part I **Total Investment Interest Expense**

1	Investment interest expense paid or accrued in 1995. See instructions	1	
2	Disallowed investment interest expense from 1994 Form 4952, line 7	2	
3	**Total investment interest expense.** Add lines 1 and 2	3	

Part II **Net Investment Income**

4a	Gross income from property held for investment (excluding any net gain from the disposition of property held for investment)			4a	
b	Net gain from the disposition of property held for investment	4b			
c	Net capital gain from the disposition of property held for investment	4c			
d	Subtract line 4c from line 4b. If zero or less, enter -0-			4d	
e	Enter all or part of the amount on line 4c that you elect to include in investment income. Do not enter more than the amount on line 4b. See instructions ►			4e	
f	Investment income. Add lines 4a, 4d, and 4e. See instructions			4f	
5	Investment expenses. See instructions			5	
6	**Net investment income.** Subtract line 5 from line 4f. If zero or less, enter -0-			6	

Part III **Investment Interest Expense Deduction**

7	Disallowed investment interest expense to be carried forward to 1996. Subtract line 6 from line 3. If zero or less, enter -0-	7	
8	**Investment interest expense deduction.** Enter the smaller of line 3 or 6. See instructions	8	

Paperwork Reduction Act Notice

We ask for the information on this form to carry out the Internal Revenue laws of the United States. You are required to give us the information. We need it to ensure that you are complying with these laws and to allow us to figure and collect the right amount of tax.

The time needed to complete and file this form will vary depending on individual circumstances. The estimated average time is:

Recordkeeping	13 min.
Learning about the law or the form	15 min.
Preparing the form	21 min.
Copying, assembling, and sending the form to the IRS	10 min.

If you have comments concerning the accuracy of these time estimates or suggestions for making this form simpler, we would be happy to hear from you. See the instructions for the tax return with which this form is filed.

General Instructions

Section references are to the Internal Revenue Code unless otherwise noted. Form 1040-T references are to a new form sent to certain individuals on a test basis.

A Change To Note

If you had a carryover of disallowed interest expense from 1983, 1984, 1985, or 1986, that carryover may need to be refigured based on Rev. Rul. 95-16, 1995-1 C.B. 9. Under Rev. Rul. 95-16, the carryover of disallowed investment interest expense from any tax year is not limited by the taxable income for that year. The amount you enter on line 2 of the 1995 Form 4952 could be affected by this change.

Purpose of Form

Interest expense paid by an individual, estate, or trust on a loan allocable to property held for investment may not be fully deductible in the current year. Use Form 4952 to figure the amount of investment interest expense deductible for the current year and the amount, if any, to carry forward to future years.

For more details, get **Pub. 550,** Investment Income and Expenses.

Who Must File

If you are an individual, estate, or a trust, and you claim a deduction for investment interest expense, you must complete and attach Form 4952 to your tax return, unless **all** the following apply.

- Your only investment income was from interest or dividends.
- You have no other deductible expenses connected with the production of interest or dividends.
- Your investment interest expense is not more than your investment income.
- You have no disallowed investment interest expense from 1994.

Allocation of Interest Expense Under Temporary Regulations Section 1.163-8T

If you paid or accrued interest on a loan and used the loan proceeds for more than one purpose, you may have to allocate the interest paid. This is necessary because different rules apply to investment interest, personal interest, trade or business interest, home mortgage interest, and passive activity interest. See Pub. 550.

Specific Instructions

Part I—Total Investment Interest Expense

Line 1

Enter the investment interest paid or accrued during the tax year, regardless of when you incurred the indebtedness. Investment interest is interest paid or accrued on a loan (or part of a loan) that is allocable to property held for investment (as defined below).

Include investment interest expense reported to you on Schedule K-1 from a partnership or an S corporation. Include amortization of bond premium on taxable bonds purchased after October 22, 1986, but before January 1, 1988, unless you elected to offset amortizable bond premium against the interest payments on the bond. A taxable bond is a bond on which the interest is includible in gross income.

Investment interest expense does not include the following:

- Home mortgage interest.
- Interest expense that is properly allocable to a passive activity. Generally, a passive activity is any business activity in which you **do not** materially participate and any rental activity. See the separate instructions for **Form 8582,** Passive Activity Loss Limitations, for more details.
- Any interest expense that is capitalized, such as construction interest subject to section 263A.
- Interest expense related to tax-exempt interest income under section 265.

Property held for investment.—Property held for investment includes property that produces income (unless derived in the ordinary course of a trade or business) from interest, dividends, annuities, or royalties; and gains from the disposition of property that produces those types of income or is held for investment. However, it does not include an interest in a passive activity.

Property held for investment also includes an interest in an activity of conducting a trade or business in which you did not materially participate and that is not a passive activity. For example, a working interest in an oil or gas property that you held directly or through an entity that did not limit your liability is property held for investment if you did not materially participate in the activity.

Part II—Net Investment Income

Line 4a

Gross income from property held for investment to enter on line 4a includes income (unless derived in the ordinary course of a trade or business) from:

- Interest,
- Dividends (except Alaska Permanent Fund dividends),
- Annuities, and
- Royalties.

If you are filing **Form 8814,** Parents' Election To Report Child's Interest and Dividends, part or all of your child's income may be included on line 4a. See Form 8814 for details.

Also, include on line 4a net income from the following passive activities:

- Rental of substantially nondepreciable property,
- Equity-financed lending activities, and
- Acquisition of certain interests in a pass-through entity licensing intangible property.

See Regulations section 1.469-2(f)(10) for details.

Also include on line 4a (or 4b, if applicable) net passive income from a passive activity of a publicly traded partnership (as defined in section 469(k)(2)). See Notice 88-75, 1988-2 C.B. 386, for details.

Include investment income reported to you on Schedule K-1 from a partnership or an S corporation. Also include net investment income from an estate or a trust.

Do not include on line 4a any net gain from the disposition of property held for investment. Instead, enter this amount on line 4b.

Line 4b

Net gain from the disposition of property held for investment is the excess, if any, of total gains over total losses from the disposition of property held for investment. When figuring this amount, include capital gain distributions from mutual funds.

Line 4c

Net capital gain from the disposition of property held for investment is the excess, if any, of net long-term capital gain over net short-term capital loss from the disposition of property held for investment. When figuring this amount, include capital gain distributions from mutual funds.

Line 4e

Net capital gain from the disposition of property held for investment is excluded from investment income. However, you may elect to include in investment income all or part of the net capital gain from the disposition of property held for investment. If you make the election, you also must reduce the amount of net capital gain eligible for the 28% maximum capital gains rate by the amount of net capital gain you included in investment income. Therefore, you should consider the effect on your tax using the maximum capital gains rate before making this election. You must make the election no later than the due date (including extensions) of your income tax return. Once made, the election may not be revoked without IRS consent.

To make the election, enter all or part of the amount on line 4c, but not more than the amount on line 4b, that you elect to include in investment income. Also enter this amount on line 3 of the **Capital Gain Tax Worksheet** in the Form 1040 (or Form 1040-T) instructions, or on line 37b of Schedule D (Form 1041), if applicable.

Line 5

Investment expenses are your allowed deductions, other than interest expense, directly connected with the production of investment income. For example, depreciation or depletion allowed on assets that produce investment income is an investment expense.

Include investment expenses reported to you on Schedule K-1 from a partnership or an S corporation.

Investment expenses do not include any deductions taken into account in determining your income or loss from a passive activity.

If you have investment expenses that are included as a miscellaneous itemized deduction on Schedule A (Form 1040), line 22 (or Form 1040-T, Section B, line o), you may not have to use the entire amount for purposes of Form 4952, line 5. The 2% adjusted gross income limitation on Schedule A (Form 1040), line 25 (or Form 1040-T, Section B, line q) may reduce the amount you must enter on Form 4952, line 5.

To figure the amount to use, compare the amount of the investment expenses included on Schedule A (Form 1040), line 22 (or Form 1040-T, Section B, line o), with the total miscellaneous expenses on Schedule A (Form 1040), line 26 (or Form 1040-T, Section B, line r). The smaller of (a) the investment expenses included on Schedule A (Form 1040), line 22 (or Form 1040-T, Section B, line o), or (b) the total on Schedule A (Form 1040), line 26 (or Form 1040-T, Section B, line r) is the amount of investment expenses included as a miscellaneous itemized deduction to use when figuring Form 4952, line 5.

Example for Form 1040. Assume Schedule A, line 22, includes investment expenses of $3,000, and line 26 is $1,300 after the 2% adjusted gross income limitation. Investment expenses from Schedule A of $1,300 are used to figure the amount of investment expenses for line 5. If investment expenses of $800 were included on line 22 and line 26 was $1,300, investment expenses from Schedule A of $800 would be used.

Part III—Investment Interest Expense Deduction

Line 8

This is the amount you may deduct as investment interest expense.

Individuals.—Generally, enter the amount from line 8 on Schedule A (Form 1040), line 13 (or Form 1040-T, Section B, line j), even if all or part of it is attributable to a partnership or an S corporation. If any portion of this amount is attributable to royalties, enter that part of the interest expense on Schedule E (Form 1040). If any portion is attributable to a trade or business in which you did not materially participate and that is not a passive activity, enter that part of the interest expense on the schedule where you report other expenses for that trade or business.

Estates and trusts.—Enter the amount from line 8 on Form 1041, line 10.

Form 6198.—If any portion of the deductible investment interest expense is attributable to an activity for which you are not at risk, you must also use **Form 6198,** At-Risk Limitations, to figure your deductible investment interest expense. Enter the portion attributable to the at-risk activity on Form 6198, line 4. Reduce Form 4952, line 8, by the amount entered on Form 6198. See Form 6198 and its instructions for more details, especially the instructions for line 4 of that form.

Alternative minimum tax (AMT).—Deductible interest expense is an adjustment for the AMT. Get **Form 6251,** Alternative Minimum Tax—Individuals, or Form 1041, Schedule I, for estates and trusts.

Printed on recycled paper

Form **4972**

Department of the Treasury
Internal Revenue Service

Tax on Lump-Sum Distributions

From Qualified Retirement Plans

▶ **Attach to Form 1040 or Form 1041.** ▶ **See separate instructions.**

OMB No. 1545-0193

1995

Attachment Sequence No. **28**

Name of recipient of distribution | **Identifying number**

Part I Complete this part to see if you qualify to use Form 4972

			Yes	No
1	Did you roll over any part of the distribution? If "Yes," do not use this form . . .	1		
2	Was the retirement plan participant born before 1936 OR was he or she at least age 59½ on the date of the distribution? If "No," do not use this form . . .	2		
3	Was this a lump-sum distribution from a qualified pension, profit-sharing, or stock bonus plan? (See **What Is A Qualified Lump-Sum Distribution?** in the instructions.) If "No," do not use this form . . .	3		
4	Was the participant in the plan for at least 5 years before the year of the distribution? . . .	4		
5	Was this distribution paid to you as a beneficiary of a plan participant who died? . . . If you answered "No" to both questions 4 **and** 5, do not use this form.	5		
6	Was the plan participant:			
a	An employee who received the distribution because he or she quit, retired, was laid off, or was fired? . .	6a		
b	Self-employed or an owner-employee who became permanently and totally disabled before the distribution?	6b		
c	Age 59½ or older at the time of the distribution? (**Caution:** *If "No," you may owe an additional tax. Get Form 5329 and its instructions for details.*) . . . If you answered "No" to question 5 and **all** parts of question 6, do not use this form.	6c		
7a	Did you use Form 4972 after 1986 for a previous distribution from your own plan? If "Yes," do not use this form for a 1995 distribution from your own plan . . .	7a		
b	If you are receiving this distribution as a beneficiary of a plan participant who died, did you use Form 4972 for a previous distribution received for that plan participant after 1986? If "Yes," you may not use the form for this distribution . . .	7b		

Part II Complete this part to choose the 20% capital gain election (See instructions.) Do not complete this part unless the participant was born **before** 1936.

8	Capital gain part from box 3 of Form 1099-R . . .	8	
9	Multiply line 8 by 20% (.20) . . . If you also choose to use Part III, go to line 10. Otherwise, enter the amount from line 9 on Form 1040, line 39, or Form 1041, Schedule G, line 1b, whichever applies.	9	

Part III Complete this part to choose the 5- or 10-year tax option (See instructions.)

10	Ordinary income from Form 1099-R, box 2a minus box 3. If you did not complete Part II, enter the taxable amount from box 2a of Form 1099-R . . .	10	
11	Death benefit exclusion . . .	11	
12	Total taxable amount. Subtract line 11 from line 10 . . .	12	
13	Current actuarial value of annuity (from Form 1099-R, box 8) . . .	13	
14	Adjusted total taxable amount. Add lines 12 and 13. If this amount is $70,000 or more, **skip** lines 15 through 18, and enter this amount on line 19 . . .	14	
15	Multiply line 14 by 50% (.50), but **do not** enter more than $10,000 — 15		
16	Subtract $20,000 from line 14. If the result is less than zero, enter -0- . . . — 16		
17	Multiply line 16 by 20% (.20) . . . — 17		
18	Minimum distribution allowance. Subtract line 17 from line 15 . . .	18	
19	Subtract line 18 from line 14 . . .	19	
20	Federal estate tax attributable to lump-sum distribution . . .	20	
21	Subtract line 20 from line 19 . . .	21	
	If line 13 is blank, skip lines 22 through 24 and go to line 25.		
22	Divide line 13 by line 14 and enter the result as a decimal . . .	22	.
23	Multiply line 18 by the decimal on line 22 . . .	23	
24	Subtract line 23 from line 13 . . .	24	

For Paperwork Reduction Act Notice, see separate instructions. Cat. No. 13187U Form **4972** (1995)

Form 4972 (1995) Page 2

Part III **5- or 10-year tax option—CONTINUED**

5-year tax option	25	Multiply line 21 by 20% (.20)		25	
	26	Tax on amount on line 25. Use the Tax Rate Schedule for the 5-Year Tax Option in the instructions		26	
	27	Multiply line 26 by five (5). If line 13 is blank, skip lines 28 through 30, and enter this amount on line 31		27	
	28	Multiply line 24 by 20% (.20)	28		
	29	Tax on amount on line 28. Use the Tax Rate Schedule for the 5-Year Tax Option in the instructions	29		
	30	Multiply line 29 by five (5)		30	
	31	Subtract line 30 from line 27. (Multiple recipients, see page 4 of the instructions.)		31	
10-year tax option		**Note:** *Complete lines 32 through 38 ONLY if the participant was born before 1936. Otherwise, enter the amount from line 31 on line 39.*			
	32	Multiply line 21 by 10% (.10)		32	
	33	Tax on amount on line 32. Use the Tax Rate Schedule for the 10-Year Tax Option in the instructions		33	
	34	Multiply line 33 by ten (10). If line 13 is blank, skip lines 35 through 37, and enter this amount on line 38		34	
	35	Multiply line 24 by 10% (.10)	35		
	36	Tax on amount on line 35. Use the Tax Rate Schedule for the 10-Year Tax Option in the instructions	36		
	37	Multiply line 36 by ten (10)		37	
	38	Subtract line 37 from line 34. (Multiple recipients, see page 4 of the instructions.)		38	
	39	Compare lines 31 and 38. Enter the **smaller** amount here. ▶		39	
	40	Tax on lump-sum distribution. Add line 9 and line 39. Also, enter this amount on Form 1040, line 39, or Form 1041, Schedule G, line 1b, whichever applies ▶		40	

Printed on recycled paper

Form **6251**

Department of the Treasury
Internal Revenue Service

Alternative Minimum Tax—Individuals

▶ See separate instructions.

▶ Attach to Form 1040, Form 1040NR, or Form 1040-T.

OMB No. 1545-0227

1995

Attachment Sequence No. **32**

Name(s) shown on Form 1040 | **Your social security number**

Part I Adjustments and Preferences

1	If you itemized deductions on Schedule A (Form 1040) (or you entered the amount from Form 1040-T, Section B, line t, on Form 1040-T, line 20), go to line 2. Otherwise, enter your standard deduction from Form 1040, line 34 (or Form 1040-T, line 20), and go to line 6	1	
2	Medical and dental. Enter the smaller of Schedule A (Form 1040), line 4 **or** 2½% of Form 1040, line 32 (Form 1040-T filers, enter the smaller of Section B, line c **or** 2½% of Form 1040-T, line 16)	2	
3	Taxes. Enter the amount from Schedule A (Form 1040), line 9 (or the total of lines d through g of Form 1040-T, Section B)	3	
4	Certain interest on a home mortgage not used to buy, build, or improve your home	4	
5	Miscellaneous itemized deductions. Enter the amount from Schedule A (Form 1040), line 26 (or Form 1040-T, Section B, line r)	5	
6	Refund of taxes. Enter any tax refund from Form 1040, line 10 or line 21 (or Form 1040-T, line 4 or line 9)	6	( )
7	Investment interest. Enter difference between regular tax and AMT deduction	7	
8	Post-1986 depreciation. Enter difference between regular tax and AMT depreciation	8	
9	Adjusted gain or loss. Enter difference between AMT and regular tax gain or loss	9	
10	Incentive stock options. Enter excess of AMT income over regular tax income	10	
11	Passive activities. Enter difference between AMT and regular tax income or loss	11	
12	Beneficiaries of estates and trusts. Enter the amount from Schedule K-1 (Form 1041), line 8	12	
13	Tax-exempt interest from private activity bonds issued after 8/7/86	13	
14	Other. Enter the amount, if any, for each item and enter the total on line 14.		

a Charitable contributions		h Loss limitations	
b Circulation expenditures		i Mining costs	
c Depletion		j Patron's adjustment	
d Depreciation (pre-1987)		k Pollution control facilities	
e Installment sales		l Research and experimental	
f Intangible drilling costs		m Tax shelter farm activities	
g Long-term contracts		n Related adjustments	

		14	
15	**Total Adjustments and Preferences.** Combine lines 1 through 14 ▶	15	

Part II Alternative Minimum Taxable Income

16	Enter the amount from **Form 1040, line 35 (or Form 1040-T, line 21).** If less than zero, enter as a (loss) ▶	16	
17	Net operating loss deduction, if any, from Form 1040, line 21. Enter as a positive amount	17	
18	If Form 1040, line 32 (or Form 1040-T, line 16), is over $114,700 (over $57,350 if married filing separately), and you itemized deductions, enter the amount, if any, from line 9 of the worksheet for Schedule A (Form 1040), line 28 (or line 9 of the worksheet for Section B, line t, of Form 1040-T)	18	( )
19	Combine lines 15 through 18 ▶	19	
20	Alternative tax net operating loss deduction. See page 5 of the instructions	20	
21	**Alternative Minimum Taxable Income.** Subtract line 20 from line 19. (If married filing separately and line 21 is more than $165,000, see page 5 of the instructions.) ▶	21	

Part III Exemption Amount and Alternative Minimum Tax

22 **Exemption Amount.** (If this form is for a child under age 14, see page 6 of the instructions.)

If your filing status is:	**And line 21 is not over:**	**Enter on line 22:**
Single or head of household	$112,500	$33,750
Married filing jointly or qualifying widow(er)	150,000	45,000
Married filing separately	75,000	22,500

If line 21 is **over** the amount shown above for your filing status, see page 6 of the instructions. — 22

23	Subtract line 22 from line 21. If zero or less, enter -0- here and on lines 26 and 28 ▶	23	
24	If line 23 is $175,000 or less ($87,500 or less if married filing separately), multiply line 23 by 26% (.26). Otherwise, multiply line 23 by 28% (.28) and subtract $3,500 ($1,750 if married filing separately) from the result	24	
25	Alternative minimum tax foreign tax credit. See page 6 of the instructions	25	
26	Tentative minimum tax. Subtract line 25 from line 24 ▶	26	
27	Enter your tax from Form 1040, line 38 (plus any amount from Form 4970 included on Form 1040, line 39), minus any foreign tax credit from Form 1040, line 43 (Form 1040-T filers, enter the amount from Form 1040-T, line 26)	27	
28	**Alternative Minimum Tax.** (If this form is for a child under age 14, see page 7 of the instructions.) Subtract line 27 from line 26. If zero or less, enter -0-. Enter here and on Form 1040, line 48 (or Form 1040-T, line 31) ▶	28	

Form **6252**

Department of the Treasury
Internal Revenue Service

Installment Sale Income

▶ See separate instructions. ▶ Attach to your tax return.
▶ Use a separate form for each sale or other disposition of property on the installment method.

OMB No. 1545-0228

1995

Attachment Sequence No. **79**

Name(s) shown on return | **Identifying number**

1 Description of property ▶ ....

2a Date acquired (month, day, year) ▶ / / **b** Date sold (month, day, year) ▶ / /

3 Was the property sold to a related party after May 14, 1980? See instructions . . . ☐ Yes ☐ No

4 If the answer to question 3 is "Yes," was the property a marketable security? If "Yes," complete Part III. If "No," complete Part III for the year of sale and for 2 years after the year of sale. . . . ☐ Yes ☐ No

Part I Gross Profit and Contract Price. Complete this part for the year of sale only.

5	Selling price including mortgages and other debts. Do not include interest whether stated or unstated		5
6	Mortgages and other debts the buyer assumed or took the property subject to, but not new mortgages the buyer got from a bank or other source	6	
7	Subtract line 6 from line 5	7	
8	Cost or other basis of property sold	8	
9	Depreciation allowed or allowable	9	
10	Adjusted basis. Subtract line 9 from line 8	10	
11	Commissions and other expenses of sale	11	
12	Income recapture from Form 4797, Part III. See instructions	12	
13	Add lines 10, 11, and 12		13
14	Subtract line 13 from line 5. If zero or less, **stop here.** Do not complete the rest of this form		14
15	If the property described on line 1 above was your main home, enter the total of lines 14 and 22 from Form 2119. Otherwise, enter -0-		15
16	**Gross profit.** Subtract line 15 from line 14		16
17	Subtract line 13 from line 6. If zero or less, enter -0-		17
18	**Contract price.** Add line 7 and line 17		18

Part II Installment Sale Income. Complete this part for the year of sale and any year you receive a payment or have certain debts you must treat as a payment on installment obligations.

19	Gross profit percentage. Divide line 16 by line 18. For years after the year of sale, see instructions		19
20	**For year of sale only**—Enter amount from line 17 above; otherwise, enter -0-		20
21	Payments received during year. See instructions. Do not include interest whether stated or unstated		21
22	Add lines 20 and 21		22
23	Payments received in prior years. See instructions. Do not include interest whether stated or unstated	23	
24	**Installment sale income.** Multiply line 22 by line 19		24
25	Part of line 24 that is ordinary income under recapture rules. See instructions		25
26	Subtract line 25 from line 24. Enter here and on Schedule D or Form 4797. See instructions		26

Part III Related Party Installment Sale Income. Do not complete if you received the final payment this tax year.

27 Name, address, and taxpayer identifying number of related party ....

28 Did the related party, during this tax year, resell or dispose of the property ("second disposition")? . . . ☐ Yes ☐ No

29 **If the answer to question 28 is "Yes," complete lines 30 through 37 below unless one of the following conditions is met. Check only the box that applies.**

a ☐ The second disposition was more than 2 years after the first disposition (other than dispositions of marketable securities). If this box is checked, enter the date of disposition (month, day, year) ▶ / /

b ☐ The first disposition was a sale or exchange of stock to the issuing corporation.

c ☐ The second disposition was an involuntary conversion where the threat of conversion occurred after the first disposition.

d ☐ The second disposition occurred after the death of the original seller or buyer.

e ☐ It can be established to the satisfaction of the Internal Revenue Service that tax avoidance was not a principal purpose for either of the dispositions. If this box is checked, attach an explanation. See instructions.

30	Selling price of property sold by related party	30
31	Enter contract price from line 18 for year of first sale	31
32	Enter the **smaller** of line 30 or line 31	32
33	Total payments received by the end of your 1995 tax year. See instructions	33
34	Subtract line 33 from line 32. If zero or less, enter -0-	34
35	Multiply line 34 by the gross profit percentage on line 19 for year of first sale	35
36	Part of line 35 that is ordinary income under recapture rules. See instructions	36
37	Subtract line 36 from line 35. Enter here and on Schedule D or Form 4797. See instructions	37

For Paperwork Reduction Act Notice, see separate instructions. Cat. No. 13601R Form **6252** (1995)

Printed on recycled paper

Form **8283** (Rev. October 1995)
Department of the Treasury
Internal Revenue Service

Noncash Charitable Contributions

▶ **Attach to your tax return if you claimed a total deduction of over $500 for all contributed property.**

▶ **See separate instructions.**

OMB No. 1545-0908

Attachment Sequence No. **55**

Name(s) shown on your income tax return | **Identifying number**

Note: *Figure the amount of your contribution deduction before completing this form. See your tax return instructions.*

Section A—List in this section **only** items (or groups of similar items) for which you claimed a deduction of $5,000 or less. Also, list certain publicly traded securities even if the deduction is over $5,000 (see instructions).

Part I **Information on Donated Property—**If you need more space, attach a statement.

1	**(a)** Name and address of the donee organization	**(b)** Description of donated property
A		
B		
C		
D		
E		

Note: *If the amount you claimed as a deduction for an item is $500 or less, you do not have to complete columns (d), (e), and (f).*

	(c) Date of the contribution	**(d)** Date acquired by donor (mo., yr.)	**(e)** How acquired by donor	**(f)** Donor's cost or adjusted basis	**(g)** Fair market value	**(h)** Method used to determine the fair market value
A						
B						
C						
D						
E						

Part II **Other Information—**Complete line 2 if you gave less than an entire interest in property listed in Part I. Complete line 3 if restrictions were attached to a contribution listed in Part I.

2 If, during the year, you contributed less than the entire interest in the property, complete lines a – e.

a Enter the letter from Part I that identifies the property ▶ ________ . If Part II applies to more than one property, attach a separate statement.

b Total amount claimed as a deduction for the property listed in Part I: **(1)** For this tax year ▶ ________________ **(2)** For any prior tax years ▶ ________________ .

c Name and address of each organization to which any such contribution was made in a prior year (complete only if different than the donee organization above):

Name of charitable organization (donee)

Address (number, street, and room or suite no.)

City or town, state, and ZIP code

d For tangible property, enter the place where the property is located or kept ▶ ________________

e Name of any person, other than the donee organization, having actual possession of the property ▶ ________________

3 If conditions were attached to any contribution listed in Part I, answer questions a – c and attach the required statement (see instructions).	**Yes**	**No**
a Is there a restriction, either temporary or permanent, on the donee's right to use or dispose of the donated property?		
b Did you give to anyone (other than the donee organization or another organization participating with the donee organization in cooperative fundraising) the right to the income from the donated property or to the possession of the property, including the right to vote donated securities, to acquire the property by purchase or otherwise, or to designate the person having such income, possession, or right to acquire?		
c Is there a restriction limiting the donated property for a particular use?		

Form 8283 (Rev. 10-95) Page **2**

Name(s) shown on your income tax return	**Identifying number**

Section B—Appraisal Summary—List in this section only items (or groups of similar items) for which you claimed a deduction of more than $5,000 per item or group. **Exception.** Report contributions of certain publicly traded securities only in Section A.

If you donated art, you may have to attach the complete appraisal. See the **Note** in Part I below.

Part I **Information on Donated Property**—To be completed by the taxpayer and/or appraiser.

4 Check type of property:

☐ Art* (contribution of $20,000 or more) ☐ Real Estate ☐ Gems/Jewelry ☐ Stamp Collections
☐ Art* (contribution of less than $20,000) ☐ Coin Collections ☐ Books ☐ Other

*Art includes paintings, sculptures, watercolors, prints, drawings, ceramics, antique furniture, decorative arts, textiles, carpets, silver, rare manuscripts, historical memorabilia, and other similar objects.

Note: *If your total art contribution deduction was $20,000 or more, you must attach a complete copy of the signed appraisal. See instructions.*

5	**(a)** Description of donated property (if you need more space, attach a separate statement)	**(b)** If tangible property was donated, give a brief summary of the overall physical condition at the time of the gift	**(c)** Appraised fair market value
A			
B			
C			
D			

	(d) Date acquired by donor (mo., yr.)	**(e)** How acquired by donor	**(f)** Donor's cost or adjusted basis	**(g)** For bargain sales, enter amount received	See instructions: **(h)** Amount claimed as a deduction	See instructions: **(i)** Average trading price of securities
A						
B						
C						
D						

Part II **Taxpayer (Donor) Statement**—List each item included in Part I above that is separately identified in the appraisal as having a value of $500 or less. See instructions.

I declare that the following item(s) included in Part I above has to the best of my knowledge and belief an appraised value of not more than $500 (per item). Enter identifying letter from Part I and describe the specific item. See instructions. ▶ ____________

Signature of taxpayer (donor) ▶ Date ▶

Part III **Declaration of Appraiser**

I declare that I am not the donor, the donee, a party to the transaction in which the donor acquired the property, employed by, or related to any of the foregoing persons, or married to any person who is related to any of the foregoing persons. And, if regularly used by the donor, donee, or party to the transaction, I performed the majority of my appraisals during my tax year for other persons.

Also, I declare that I hold myself out to the public as an appraiser or perform appraisals on a regular basis; and that because of my qualifications as described in the appraisal, I am qualified to make appraisals of the type of property being valued. I certify that the appraisal fees were not based on a percentage of the appraised property value. Furthermore, I understand that a false or fraudulent overstatement of the property value as described in the qualified appraisal or this appraisal summary may subject me to the penalty under section 6701(a) (aiding and abetting the understatement of tax liability). I affirm that I have not been barred from presenting evidence or testimony by the Director of Practice.

Sign Here Signature ▶ Title ▶ Date of appraisal ▶

Business address (including room or suite no.)	**Identifying number**
City or town, state, and ZIP code	

Part IV **Donee Acknowledgment**—To be completed by the charitable organization.

This charitable organization acknowledges that it is a qualified organization under section 170(c) and that it received the donated property as described in Section B, Part I, above on ▶ ____________ (Date)

Furthermore, this organization affirms that in the event it sells, exchanges, or otherwise disposes of the property described in Section B, Part I (or any portion thereof) within 2 years after the date of receipt, it will file **Form 8282,** Donee Information Return, with the IRS and give the donor a copy of that form. This acknowledgment does not represent agreement with the claimed fair market value.

Name of charitable organization (donee)	**Employer identification number**	
Address (number, street, and room or suite no.)	City or town, state, and ZIP code	
Authorized signature	Title	Date

Printed on recycled paper

Form **8332**
(Rev. March 1993)
Department of the Treasury
Internal Revenue Service

Release of Claim to Exemption for Child of Divorced or Separated Parents

ATTACH to noncustodial parent's return each year exemption claimed.

OMB No. 1545-0915
Expires 3-31-96

Attachment
Sequence No. **51**

Name(s) of parent claiming exemption

Social security number

Part I **Release of Claim to Exemption for Current Year**

I agree not to claim an exemption for ______________________
Name(s) of child (or children)

for the tax year 19_____.

______________________ Signature of parent releasing claim to exemption

______________________ Social security number

__________ Date

If you choose not to claim an exemption for this child (or children) for future tax years, complete Part II.

Part II **Release of Claim to Exemption for Future Years** *(If completed, see* ***Noncustodial Parent*** *below.)*

I agree not to claim an exemption for ______________________
Name(s) of child (or children)

for the tax year(s)______________________.
(Specify. See instructions.)

______________________ Signature of parent releasing claim to exemption

______________________ Social security number

__________ Date

General Instructions

Paperwork Reduction Act Notice.—We ask for the information on this form to carry out the Internal Revenue laws of the United States. You are required to give us the information. We need it to ensure that you are complying with these laws and to allow us to figure and collect the right amount of tax.

The time needed to complete and file this form will vary depending on individual circumstances. The estimated average time is: **Recordkeeping,** 7 min.; **Learning about the law or the form,** 5 min.; **Preparing the form,** 7 min.; and **Copying, assembling, and sending the form to the IRS,** 14 min.

If you have comments concerning the accuracy of these time estimates or suggestions for making this form more simple, we would be happy to hear from you. You can write to both the IRS and the Office of Management and Budget at the addresses listed in the instructions for the return with which this form is filed.

Purpose of Form.—If you are a **custodial parent,** you may use this form to release your claim to your child's exemption. To do so, complete this form and give it to the **noncustodial parent** who will claim the child's exemption. Then, the noncustodial parent must attach this form or a similar statement to his or her tax return each year the exemption is claimed.

You are the **custodial parent** if you had custody of the child for most of the year. You are the **noncustodial parent** if you had custody for a shorter period of time or did not have custody at all.

Instead of using this form, you (the custodial parent) may use a similar statement as long as it contains the same information required by this form.

Children of Divorced or Separated Parents.—Special rules apply to determine if the support test is met for children of parents who are divorced or legally separated under a decree of divorce or separate maintenance or separated under a written separation agreement. The rules also apply to children of parents who did not live together at any time during the last 6 months of the year, even if they do not have a separation agreement.

The general rule is that the custodial parent is treated as having provided over half of the child's support if:

1. The child received over half of his or her total support for the year from both of the parents, **AND**

2. The child was in the custody of one or both of his or her parents for more than half of the year.

Note: *Public assistance payments, such as Aid to Families with Dependent Children, are not support provided by the parents.*

If both **1** and **2** above apply, and the other four dependency tests in the instructions for Form 1040 or Form 1040A are also met, the custodial parent can claim the child's exemption.

Exception. The general rule does not apply if **any** of the following applies:

- The custodial parent agrees not to claim the child's exemption by signing this form or similar statement. The noncustodial parent **must** attach this form or similar statement to his or her tax return for the tax year. See **Custodial Parent** later.
- The child is treated as having received over half of his or her total support from a person under a multiple support agreement **(Form 2120,** Multiple Support Declaration**).**
- A pre-1985 divorce decree or written separation agreement states that the noncustodial parent can claim the child as a dependent. But the noncustodial parent must provide at least $600 for the child's support during the year. The noncustodial parent must also check the box on line 6d of Form 1040 or Form 1040A. This rule does not apply if the decree or agreement was changed after 1984 to say that the noncustodial parent cannot claim the child as a dependent.

Additional Information.—For more details, get **Pub. 504,** Divorced or Separated Individuals.

Specific Instructions

Custodial Parent.—You may agree to release your claim to the child's exemption for the current tax year or for future years, or both.

- Complete **Part I** if you agree to release your claim to the child's exemption for the current tax year.
- Complete **Part II** if you agree to release your claim to the child's exemption for any or all future years. If you do, write the specific future year(s) or "all future years" in the space provided in Part II.

Noncustodial Parent.—Attach Form 8332 or a similar statement to your tax return for the tax year in which you claim the child's exemption. You may claim the exemption **only** if the other four dependency tests in the Form 1040 or Form 1040A instructions are met.

Note: *If the custodial parent completed Part II, you* ***must*** *attach a copy of this form to your tax return for each future year in which you claim the exemption.*

Form **8582**

Department of the Treasury
Internal Revenue Service

Passive Activity Loss Limitations

▶ See separate instructions.
▶ Attach to Form 1040 or Form 1041.

OMB No. 1545-1008
1995
Attachment Sequence No. 88

Name(s) shown on return | Identifying number

Part I 1995 Passive Activity Loss
Caution: *See the instructions for Worksheets 1 and 2 on page 8 before completing Part I.*

Rental Real Estate Activities With Active Participation (For the definition of active participation see **Active Participation in a Rental Real Estate Activity** on page 4 of the instructions.)

1a Activities with net income (from Worksheet 1, column (a)) . . .	1a			
b Activities with net loss (from Worksheet 1, column (b))	1b	( )		
c Prior year unallowed losses (from Worksheet 1, column (c)) . .	1c	( )		
d Combine lines 1a, 1b, and 1c			1d	

All Other Passive Activities

2a Activities with net income (from Worksheet 2, column (a)) . . .	2a			
b Activities with net loss (from Worksheet 2, column (b))	2b	( )		
c Prior year unallowed losses (from Worksheet 2, column (c)) . .	2c	( )		
d Combine lines 2a, 2b, and 2c			2d	
3 Combine lines 1d and 2d. If the result is net income or zero, see the instructions for line 3 on page 8. If this line and line 1d are losses, go to line 4. Otherwise, enter -0- on line 9 and go to line 10.			3	

Part II Special Allowance for Rental Real Estate With Active Participation
Note: *Enter all numbers in Part II as positive amounts. See page 8 of the instructions for examples.*

4 Enter the **smaller** of the loss on line 1d or the loss on line 3			4	
5 Enter $150,000. If married filing separately, see page 8 of the instructions	5			
6 Enter modified adjusted gross income, but not less than zero (see page 8 of the instructions)	6			
Note: *If line 6 is equal to or greater than line 5, skip lines 7 and 8, enter -0- on line 9, and then go to line 10. Otherwise, go to line 7.*				
7 Subtract line 6 from line 5	7			
8 Multiply line 7 by 50% (.5). **Do not** enter more than $25,000. If married filing separately, see page 9 of the instructions			8	
9 Enter the **smaller** of line 4 or line 8			9	

Part III Total Losses Allowed

10 Add the income, if any, on lines 1a and 2a and enter the total	10	
11 **Total losses allowed from all passive activities for 1995.** Add lines 9 and 10. See pages 10 and 11 of the instructions to find out how to report the losses on your tax return	11	

Form 8582 (1995) Page **2**

Caution: *The worksheets are not required to be filed with your tax return and may be detached before filing Form 8582. Keep a copy of the worksheets for your records.*

Worksheet 1—For Form 8582, Lines 1a, 1b, and 1c (See page 8 of the instructions.)

Name of activity	Current year		Prior year	Overall gain or loss	
	(a) Net income (line 1a)	(b) Net loss (line 1b)	(c) Unallowed loss (line 1c)	(d) Gain	(e) Loss
Total. Enter on Form 8582, lines 1a, 1b, and 1c. . . . . ▶					

Worksheet 2—For Form 8582, Lines 2a, 2b, and 2c (See page 8 of the instructions.)

Name of activity	Current year		Prior year	Overall gain or loss	
	(a) Net income (line 2a)	(b) Net loss (line 2b)	(c) Unallowed loss (line 2c)	(d) Gain	(e) Loss
Total. Enter on Form 8582, lines 2a, 2b, and 2c. . . . . ▶					

Worksheet 3—Use this worksheet if an amount is shown on Form 8582, line 9 (See page 9 of the instructions.)

Name of activity	Form or schedule to be reported on	(a) Loss	(b) Ratio	(c) Special allowance	(d) Subtract column (c) from column (a)
Total . . . . ▶			1.00		

Worksheet 4—Allocation of Unallowed Losses (See page 9 of the instructions.)

Name of activity	Form or schedule to be reported on	(a) Loss	(b) Ratio	(c) Unallowed loss
Total . . . . ▶			1.00	

Worksheet 5—Allowed Losses (See page 9 of the instructions.)

Name of activity	Form or schedule to be reported on	(a) Loss	(b) Unallowed loss	(c) Allowed loss
Total . . . . ▶				

Worksheet 6—Activities With Losses Reported on Two or More Different Forms or Schedules (See page 9 of the instructions.)

Name of Activity:	(a)	(b)	(c) Ratio	(d) Unallowed loss	(e) Allowed loss
Form or Schedule To Be Reported on:					
1a Net loss plus prior year unallowed loss from form or schedule . ▶					
b Net income from form or schedule . . . . ▶					
c Subtract line 1b from line 1a. If zero or less, enter -0- ▶					
Form or Schedule To Be Reported on:					
1a Net loss plus prior year unallowed loss from form or schedule . ▶					
b Net income from form or schedule . . . . ▶					
c Subtract line 1b from line 1a. If zero or less, enter -0- ▶					
Form or Schedule To Be Reported on:					
1a Net loss plus prior year unallowed loss from form or schedule . ▶					
b Net income from form or schedule . . . . ▶					
c Subtract line 1b from line 1a. If zero or less, enter -0- ▶					
Total . . . . ▶			1.00		

Printed on recycled paper

Form **8606**

Department of the Treasury
Internal Revenue Service

Nondeductible IRAs (Contributions, Distributions, and Basis)

▶ Please see What Records Must I Keep? on page 2.
▶ Attach to Form 1040, Form 1040A, or Form 1040NR.

OMB No. 1545-1007

1995

Attachment Sequence No. **47**

Name. If married, file a separate Form 8606 for each spouse. See instructions. | **Your social security number**

Fill in Your Address Only If You Are Filing This Form by Itself and Not With Your Tax Return

Home address (number and street, or P.O. box if mail is not delivered to your home) | Apt. no.

City, town or post office, state, and ZIP code

Contributions, Nontaxable Distributions, and Basis

1	Enter your IRA contributions for 1995 that you choose to be nondeductible. Include those made during 1/1/96-4/15/96 that were for 1995. See instructions	1	
2	Enter your total IRA basis for 1994 and earlier years. See instructions	2	
3	Add lines 1 and 2	3	

Did you receive any IRA distributions (withdrawals) in 1995?
- No ▶ Enter the amount from line 3 on line 12. Then, **stop** and read **When and Where To File** on page 2.
- Yes ▶ Go to line 4.

4	Enter only those contributions included on line 1 that were made during 1/1/96-4/15/96. This amount will be the same as line 1 if all of your nondeductible contributions for 1995 were made in 1996 by 4/15/96. See instructions	4	
5	Subtract line 4 from line 3	5	
6	Enter the total value of **ALL** your IRAs as of 12/31/95 plus any outstanding rollovers. See instructions — 6		
7	Enter the total IRA distributions received during 1995. Do not include amounts rolled over before 1/1/96. See instructions — 7		
8	Add lines 6 and 7 — 8		
9	Divide line 5 by line 8 and enter the result as a decimal (to at least two places). Do not enter more than "1.00" — 9 × .		
10	Multiply line 7 by line 9. This is the amount of your **nontaxable distributions for 1995**	10	
11	Subtract line 10 from line 5. This is the **basis in your IRA(s) as of 12/31/95**	11	
12	Add lines 4 and 11. This is your **total IRA basis for 1995 and earlier years**	12	

Taxable Distributions for 1995

13	Subtract line 10 from line 7. Enter the result here and on Form 1040, line 15b; Form 1040A, line 10b; or Form 1040NR, line 16b, whichever applies	13	

Sign Here Only If You Are Filing This Form by Itself and Not With Your Tax Return

Under penalties of perjury, I declare that I have examined this form, including accompanying attachments, and to the best of my knowledge and belief, it is true, correct, and complete.

▶ Your signature ▶ Date

Paperwork Reduction Act Notice

We ask for the information on this form to carry out the Internal Revenue laws of the United States. You are required to give us the information. We need it to ensure that you are complying with these laws and to allow us to figure and collect the right amount of tax.

The time needed to complete and file this form will vary depending on individual circumstances. The estimated average time is: **Recordkeeping,** 26 min.; **Learning about the law or the form,** 7 min.; **Preparing the form,** 21 min.; and **Copying, assembling, and sending the form to the IRS,** 20 min.

If you have comments concerning the accuracy of these time estimates or suggestions for making this form more simple, we would be happy to hear from you. You can write to both the IRS and the Office of Management and Budget at the addresses listed in the Instructions for Form 1040, Form 1040A, or Form 1040NR.

General Instructions

Section references are to the Internal Revenue Code.

Purpose of Form

Use Form 8606 to report your IRA contributions that you choose to be nondeductible. For example, if you cannot deduct all of your contributions because of the income limits for IRAs, you may want to make nondeductible contributions.

Also use Form 8606 to figure the basis in your IRA(s) and the taxable part of any distributions you received in 1995 if you have ever made nondeductible contributions.

Your **basis** is the total of all your nondeductible IRA contributions minus the total of all nontaxable IRA distributions received. It is to your advantage to keep track of your basis because it is used to figure the nontaxable part of future distributions.

Note: *To figure your deductible IRA contributions, use the Instructions for Form 1040 or Form 1040A, whichever applies.*

Who Must File

You must file Form 8606 for 1995 if:

- You made nondeductible contributions to your IRA for 1995, **or**
- You received IRA distributions in 1995 **and** you have ever made nondeductible contributions to any of your IRAs.

Cat.No. 63966F

What Records Must I Keep?

To verify the nontaxable part of distributions from your IRA, keep a copy of this form together with copies of the following forms and records until all distributions are made from your IRA(s):

- Page 1 of Forms 1040 (or Forms 1040A or Forms 1040NR) filed for each year you make a nondeductible contribution.
- Forms 5498 or similar statements received each year showing contributions you made.
- Forms 5498 or similar statements received showing the value of your IRA(s) for each year you received a distribution.
- Forms 1099-R and W-2P received for each year you received a distribution.

When and Where To File

Attach Form 8606 to your 1995 Form 1040, Form 1040A, or Form 1040NR.

If you are required to file Form 8606 but do not have to file an income tax return because you do not meet the requirements for filing a return, you still **must** file Form 8606 with the Internal Revenue Service at the same time and place you would be required to file Form 1040, Form 1040A, or Form 1040NR.

Penalty for Not Filing

If you are required to file Form 8606 but do not do so, you will have to pay a $50 penalty for each failure to file this form unless you can show reasonable cause.

Penalty for Overstatement

If you overstate your nondeductible contributions for any tax year, you must pay a $100 penalty for each overstatement unless it was due to reasonable cause.

Additional Information

For more details on nondeductible contributions, IRA basis, and distributions, get **Pub. 590,** Individual Retirement Arrangements (IRAs).

Amending Form 8606

After you file your return, you may change a nondeductible contribution made on a prior year's return to a deductible contribution or vice versa. To do this, complete a new Form 8606 showing the revised information and attach it to **Form 1040X,** Amended U.S. Individual Income Tax Return. Send both of these forms to the Internal Revenue Service Center shown in the Form 1040X instructions for your area.

Specific Instructions

Note: *If you received an IRA distribution in 1995 and you also made IRA contributions for 1995 that may not be fully deductible because of the income limits, you need to make a special computation before completing this form. For details, including how to complete Form 8606, see **Tax Treatment of Distributions** in Chapter 6 of Pub. 590.*

Name and Social Security Number

If you file a joint return on Form 1040 or Form 1040A, enter the name and social security number of the spouse whose IRA information is shown.

Line 1

If you used IRA Worksheet 2 in the Form 1040 or Form 1040A instructions, include the following on line 1 of Form 8606:

- The amount shown on line 10 of IRA Worksheet 2 (Form 1040) or line 8 of IRA Worksheet 2 (Form 1040A) that you choose to make nondeductible.
- The part, if any, of the amount shown on line 9 of IRA Worksheet 2 (Form 1040) or line 7 of IRA Worksheet 2 (Form 1040A) that you choose to make nondeductible. You cannot take a deduction for the part included on line 1.

Note: *Enter any nondeductible contributions for your **nonworking spouse** from the appropriate lines of IRA Worksheet 2 on line 1 of your spouse's **separate** Form 8606.*

If none of your contributions are deductible, you may choose to make up to $2,000 (but not more than your earned income) of your contributions nondeductible. Enter on line 1 of Form 8606 your contributions that you choose to make nondeductible.

If contributions were also made to your nonworking spouse's IRA, you may choose to make nondeductible contributions up to $2,250 (but not more than your earned income). Enter on line 1 of your Form 8606 the total nondeductible contributions you are making to your IRA. Enter the balance on line 1 of your nonworking spouse's Form 8606. Do not enter more than $2,000 on either your or your spouse's Form 8606. Also, the total of the two amounts cannot be more than $2,250.

If you used IRA Worksheet 1 in the Form 1040 or Form 1040A instructions but choose not to deduct the full amount shown on line 3 of that worksheet, subtract the amount you are deducting from the amount on line 3. Enter the result on line 1 of your Form 8606.

If contributions were made to your nonworking spouse's IRA but you choose not to deduct the full amount shown on line 8 of IRA Worksheet 1, subtract the amount you are deducting for your nonworking spouse from the amount on line 8. Enter the result on line 1 of your nonworking spouse's Form 8606.

Line 2

If this is the first year you are required to file Form 8606, enter zero. If you filed a **1994 or 1993** Form 8606, enter the amount from line 12 of the last Form 8606 you filed. If you did not file a 1994 or 1993 Form 8606 but you filed a Form 8606 for any year after **1988**, enter the amount from line 14 of the **last** Form 8606 you filed. Otherwise, enter the total of the amounts from lines 7 and 16 of your **1988** Form 8606. Or, if you didn't file a 1988 Form 8606, enter the total of the amounts from lines 4 and 13 of your **1987** Form 8606.

Line 4

If you made contributions in 1995 and 1996 that are for 1995, you may choose to apply the contributions made in 1995 first to nondeductible contributions and then to deductible contributions, or vice versa. But the amount on line 1 minus the amount on line 4 cannot be more than the IRA contributions you actually made in 1995.

Example. You made contributions of $1,000 in 1995 and $1,000 in 1996 of which $1,500 are deductible and $500 are nondeductible. You choose $500 of your contribution in 1995 to be nondeductible. In this case, the $500 would be entered on line 1, but not on line 4, and would become part of your basis for 1995.

Line 5

Although the 1995 IRA contributions you made during 1/1/96–4/15/96 (line 4) can be treated as nondeductible for purposes of line 1, they are not included in your basis for purposes of figuring the nontaxable part of any distributions you received in 1995. This is why you subtract line 4 from line 3.

Line 6

Enter the total value of **ALL** your IRAs as of 12/31/95 **plus** any outstanding rollovers. You should receive a statement by 1/31/96 for each IRA account showing the value on 12/31/95. A **rollover** is a tax-free distribution from one IRA that is contributed to another IRA. The rollover must be completed within 60 days of receiving the distribution from the first IRA. An **outstanding rollover** is any amount distributed to you from one IRA within 60 days of the end of 1995 (between Nov. 2 and Dec. 31) that you did not roll over to another IRA by 12/31/95, but that you roll over to another IRA in 1996 within the normal 60-day rollover period.

Line 7

Do not include on line 7:

- Distributions received in 1995 and rolled over to another IRA by 12/31/95,
- Outstanding rollovers included on line 6,
- Contributions under section 408(d)(4) returned to you on or before the due date of the return, or
- Excess contributions under section 408(d)(5) returned to you after the due date of the return.

Line 11

This is the total of your nondeductible IRA contributions made in 1995 and earlier years minus the total of any nontaxable IRA distributions received in those years.

Line 12

This is the total of your IRA basis as of 12/31/95 and any nondeductible IRA contributions for 1995 that you made in 1996 by 4/15/96.

This amount will be used on Form 8606 in future years if you make nondeductible IRA contributions or receive distributions.

Printed on recycled paper

Form **8615**

Department of the Treasury
Internal Revenue Service

Tax for Children Under Age 14 Who Have Investment Income of More Than $1,300

▶ **Attach ONLY to the child's Form 1040, Form 1040A, Form 1040NR, or Form 1040-T.**

OMB No. 1545-0998

1995

Attachment Sequence No. **33**

Child's name shown on return | **Child's social security number**

A Parent's name (first, initial, and last). **Caution:** *See instructions on back before completing.* | **B Parent's social security number**

C Parent's filing status (check one):
☐ Single ☐ Married filing jointly ☐ Married filing separately ☐ Head of household ☐ Qualifying widow(er)

Step 1 Figure child's net investment income

1	Enter child's investment income, such as taxable interest and dividend income. See instructions. If this amount is $1,300 or less, **stop;** do not file this form	1	
2	If the child DID NOT itemize deductions on Schedule A (Form 1040 or Form 1040NR) or Section B (Form 1040-T), enter $1,300. If the child ITEMIZED deductions, see instructions	2	
3	Subtract line 2 from line 1. If the result is zero or less, **stop;** do not complete the rest of this form but ATTACH it to the child's return	3	
4	Enter child's **taxable** income from Form 1040, line 37; Form 1040A, line 22; Form 1040NR, line 36; or Form 1040-T, line 25	4	
5	Enter the **smaller** of line 3 or line 4 ▶	5	

Step 2 Figure tentative tax based on the tax rate of the parent listed on line A

6	Enter parent's **taxable** income from Form 1040, line 37; Form 1040A, line 22; Form 1040EZ, line 6; Form 1040NR, line 36; Form 1040NR-EZ, line 13; or Form 1040-T, line 25. If the parent transferred property to a trust, see instructions	6	
7	Enter the total net investment income, if any, from Forms 8615, line 5, of ALL OTHER children of the parent identified above. **Do not** include the amount from line 5 above	7	
8	Add lines 5, 6, and 7	8	
9	Tax on line 8 based on the **parent's** filing status. See instructions. If from Capital Gain Tax Worksheet, enter amount from line 4 of that worksheet here ▶ ______	9	
10	Enter parent's tax from Form 1040, line 38; Form 1040A, line 23; Form 1040EZ, line 10; Form 1040NR, line 37; Form 1040NR-EZ, line 14; or Form 1040-T, line 26. If from **Capital Gain Tax Worksheet,** enter amount from line 4 of that worksheet here ▶ ______	10	
11	Subtract line 10 from line 9. If line 7 is blank, enter on line 13 the amount from line 11; skip lines 12a and 12b	11	
12a	Add lines 5 and 7 — 12a ______		
b	Divide line 5 by line 12a. Enter the result as a decimal (rounded to two places)	12b	× .
13	Multiply line 11 by line 12b ▶	13	

Step 3 Figure child's tax—If lines 4 and 5 above are the same, enter -0- on line 15 and go to line 16.

14	Subtract line 5 from line 4 — 14 ______		
15	Tax on line 14 based on the **child's** filing status. See instructions. If from Capital Gain Tax Worksheet, enter amount from line 4 of that worksheet here ▶ ______	15	
16	Add lines 13 and 15	16	
17	Tax on line 4 based on the **child's** filing status. See instructions. If from Capital Gain Tax Worksheet, check here ▶ ☐	17	
18	Enter the **larger** of line 16 or line 17 here and on Form 1040, line 38; Form 1040A, line 23; Form 1040NR, line 37; or Form 1040-T, line 26. Be sure to check the box (or, on Form 1040-T, fill in the space) for "Form 8615" even if line 17 is more than line 16 ▶	18	

General Instructions

Caution: *At the time this form was printed, Congress was considering legislation that would change the tax treatment of capital gains. For information on the changes, get* ***Pub. 553,*** *Highlights of 1995 Tax Changes.*

Purpose of Form.—For children under age 14, investment income over $1,300 is taxed at the parent's rate if the parent's rate is higher than the child's rate. If the child's investment income is more than $1,300, use this form to figure the child's tax.

Investment Income.—As used on this form, "investment income" includes all taxable income other than earned income as defined on page 2. It includes taxable interest, dividends, capital gains, rents, royalties, etc. It also includes pension and annuity income and income (other than earned income) received as the beneficiary of a trust.

Who Must File.—Generally, Form 8615 must be filed for any child who was under age 14 on January 1, 1996, had more than $1,300 of investment income, and is required to file a tax return. If neither parent was alive on December 31, 1995, do not use Form 8615. Instead, figure the child's tax in the normal manner.

Note: *The parent may be able to elect to report the child's interest and dividends on his or her return. If the parent makes this election, the child will not have to file a return or Form 8615. For more details, see the child's tax return instruction booklet or get* ***Form 8814,*** *Parents' Election To Report Child's Interest and Dividends.*

Additional Information.—For more details, get **Pub. 929,** Tax Rules for Children and Dependents.

Incomplete Information for Parent.—If the parent's taxable income or filing status or the net investment income of the parent's other children is not known by the due date of the child's return, reasonable estimates may be used. Write "Estimated" on the appropriate line(s) of Form 8615. For more details, see Pub. 929.

Amended Return.—If after the child's return is filed the parent's taxable income is changed or the net investment income of any of the parent's other children is changed, the child's tax must be refigured using the adjusted amounts. If the child's tax is changed as a result of the adjustment(s), file **Form 1040X,** Amended U.S. Individual Income Tax Return, to correct the child's tax.

Alternative Minimum Tax.—A child whose tax is figured on Form 8615 may owe the alternative minimum tax. For details, get **Form 6251,** Alternative Minimum Tax—Individuals, and its instructions.

Line Instructions

Section references are to the Internal Revenue Code. Form 1040-T references are to a new form sent to certain individuals on a test basis.

Lines A and B.—If the child's parents were married to each other and filed a joint return, enter the name and social security number (SSN) of the parent who is listed first on the joint return. For example, if the father's name is listed first on the return and his SSN is entered in the block labeled "Your social security number," enter his name on line A and his SSN on line B.

If the parents were married but filed separate returns, enter the name and SSN of the parent who had the **higher** taxable income. If you do not know which parent had the higher taxable income, see Pub. 929.

If the parents were unmarried, treated as unmarried for Federal income tax purposes, or separated either by a divorce or separate maintenance decree, enter the name and SSN of the parent who had custody of the child for most of the year (the custodial parent).

Exception. If the custodial parent remarried and filed a joint return with his or her new spouse, enter the name and SSN of the person listed first on the joint return, even if that person is not the child's parent. If the custodial parent and his or her new spouse filed separate returns, enter the name and SSN of the person with the **higher** taxable income, even if that person is not the child's parent.

Note: *If the parents were unmarried but lived together during the year with the child, enter the name and SSN of the parent who had the* ***higher*** *taxable income.*

Line 1.—If the child had no earned income (defined later), enter the child's adjusted gross income from Form 1040, line 32; Form 1040A, line 17; Form 1040NR, line 32; or Form 1040-T, line 16.

If the child had earned income, use the following worksheet to figure the amount to enter on line 1. But if the child files **Form 2555,** Foreign Earned Income, or **Form 2555-EZ,** Foreign Earned Income Exclusion, has a net loss from self-employment, or claims a net operating loss deduction, **do not** use the worksheet below. Instead, use the worksheet in Pub. 929 to figure the amount to enter on line 1.

Worksheet (keep a copy for your records)

1. Enter the amount from the child's Form 1040, line 22; Form 1040A, line 14; Form 1040NR, line 23; or Form 1040-T, line 10, whichever applies . . . . ______
2. Enter the child's **earned income** (defined below) plus any deduction the child claims on Form 1040, line 28; Form 1040NR, line 28; or Form 1040-T, line 13, whichever applies . . ______
3. Subtract line 2 from line 1. Enter the result here and on Form 8615, line 1 . . ______

Earned income includes wages, tips, and other payments received for personal services performed. Generally, it is the total of the amounts reported on Form 1040, lines 7, 12, and 18; Form 1040A, line 7; Form 1040NR, lines 8, 13, and 19; or Form 1040-T, line 1.

Line 2.—If the child itemized deductions, enter the **greater** of:

- $650 plus the portion of the amount on Schedule A (Form 1040), line 28, Schedule A (Form 1040NR), line 17, or Section B (Form 1040-T), line t, that is directly connected with the production of the investment income on Form 8615, line 1;

OR

- $1,300.

Line 6.—If the parent's taxable income is less than zero, enter zero on line 6. If the parent filed a joint return, enter the taxable income shown on that return even if the parent's spouse is not the child's parent. If the parent transferred property to a trust that sold or exchanged the property during the year at a gain, include any gain that was taxed to the trust under section 644 in the amount entered on line 6. Enter "Section 644" and the amount to the right of the line 6 entry. Also, see the instructions for line 10.

Line 9.—Figure the tax using the Tax Table, Tax Rate Schedules, or the Capital Gain Tax Worksheet, whichever applies. If any net capital gain is included on lines 5, 6, and/or 7, the tax on the amount on line 8 may be less if the Capital Gain Tax Worksheet can be used to figure the tax. See Pub. 929 for details on how to figure the net capital gain included on line 8 and how to complete the worksheet. The Capital Gain Tax Worksheet should be used if:

the parent's filing status is:	AND	the amount on Form 8615, line 8, is over:
• Single		$56,550
• Married filing jointly or Qualifying widow(er)		$94,250
• Married filing separately		$47,125
• Head of household		$80,750

If the Capital Gain Tax Worksheet is used to figure the tax, enter on Form 8615, line 9, the amount from line 13 of that worksheet. Also, enter the amount from line 4 of that worksheet in the space next to line 9 of Form 8615.

Line 10.—If the parent filed a joint return, enter the tax shown on that return even if the parent's spouse is not the child's parent. If the parent filed Form 8814, enter "Form 8814" and the total tax from line 8 of Form(s) 8814 in the space next to line 10 of Form 8615.

If line 6 includes any gain taxed to a trust under section 644, add the tax imposed under section 644(a)(2)(A) to the tax shown on the parent's return and enter the total on line 10. Also, enter "Section 644" next to line 10.

Line 15.—Figure the tax using the Tax Table, Tax Rate Schedule X, or the Capital Gain Tax Worksheet, whichever applies. If line 14 is more than $56,550 and includes any net capital gain, the tax may be less if the Capital Gain Tax Worksheet is used to figure the tax. See Pub. 929 for details on how to figure the net capital gain included on line 14 and how to complete the worksheet.

Line 17.—Figure the tax as if these rules did not apply. For example, if the child can use the Capital Gain Tax Worksheet to figure his or her tax, complete that worksheet.

Paperwork Reduction Act Notice.—We ask for the information on this form to carry out the Internal Revenue laws of the United States. You are required to give us the information. We need it to ensure that you are complying with these laws and to allow us to figure and collect the right amount of tax.

The time needed to complete and file this form will vary depending on individual circumstances. The estimated average time is: **Recordkeeping,** 13 min.; **Learning about the law or the form,** 12 min.; **Preparing the form,** 45 min.; and **Copying, assembling, and sending the form to the IRS,** 17 min.

If you have comments concerning the accuracy of these time estimates or suggestions for making this form simpler, we would be happy to hear from you. See the instructions for the tax return with which this form is filed.

Form **8824**

Department of the Treasury
Internal Revenue Service

Like-Kind Exchanges

(and nonrecognition of gain from conflict-of-interest sales)

▶ **See separate instructions.** ▶ **Attach to your tax return.**

▶ **Use a separate form for each like-kind exchange.**

OMB No. 1545-1190

1995

Attachment Sequence No. **49**

Name(s) shown on tax return | **Identifying number**

Part I Information on the Like-Kind Exchange

Note: *If the property described on line 1 or line 2 is real property located outside the United States, indicate the country.*

1 Description of like-kind property given up ▶ ....

2 Description of like-kind property received ▶ ....

3	Date like-kind property given up was originally acquired (month, day, year)	3	/ /
4	Date you actually transferred your property to other party (month, day, year)	4	/ /
5	Date the like-kind property you received was identified (month, day, year). See instructions	5	/ /
6	Date you actually received the like-kind property from other party (month, day, year)	6	/ /

7 Was the exchange made with a related party? If "Yes," complete Part II. If "No," go to Part III. See instructions.

a ☐ Yes, in this tax year **b** ☐ Yes, in a prior tax year **c** ☐ No.

Part II Related Party Exchange Information

8 Name of related party | Related party's identifying number

Address (no., street, and apt., room, or suite no.)

City or town, state, and ZIP code | Relationship to you

9 During this tax year (and before the date that is 2 years after the last transfer of property that was part of the exchange), did the related party sell or dispose of the like-kind property received from you in the exchange? ☐ **Yes** ☐ **No**

10 During this tax year (and before the date that is 2 years after the last transfer of property that was part of the exchange), did you sell or dispose of the like-kind property you received? . . . ☐ **Yes** ☐ **No**

If both lines 9 and 10 are "No" and this is the year of the exchange, go to Part III. If either line 9 or line 10 is "Yes," the deferred gain or (loss) from line 24 ***must*** *be reported on your return this tax year,* ***unless*** *one of the exceptions on line 11 applies. See* ***Related Party Exchanges*** *in the instructions.*

11 If one of the exceptions below applies to the disposition, check the applicable box:

a ☐ The disposition was after the death of either of the related parties.

b ☐ The disposition was an involuntary conversion, and the threat of conversion occurred after the exchange.

c ☐ You can establish to the satisfaction of the IRS that neither the exchange nor the disposition had tax avoidance as its principal purpose. If this box is checked, attach an explanation. See instructions.

Part III Realized Gain or (Loss), Recognized Gain, and Basis of Like-Kind Property Received

Caution: *If you transferred* ***and*** *received* ***(a)*** *more than one group of like-kind properties, or* ***(b)*** *cash or other (not like-kind) property, see instructions under* ***Multi-Asset Exchanges.***

Note: *Complete lines 12 through 14 ONLY if you gave up property that was not like-kind. Otherwise, go to line 15.*

12	Fair market value (FMV) of other property given up	12			
13	Adjusted basis of other property given up	13			
14	Gain or (loss) recognized on other property given up. Subtract line 13 from line 12. Report the gain or (loss) in the same manner as if the exchange had been a sale			14	
15	Cash received, FMV of other property received, plus net liabilities assumed by other party, reduced (but not below zero) by any exchange expenses you incurred. See instructions			15	
16	FMV of like-kind property you received			16	
17	Add lines 15 and 16			17	
18	Adjusted basis of like-kind property you gave up, net amounts paid to other party, plus any exchange expenses **not** used on line 15. See instructions			18	
19	**Realized gain or (loss).** Subtract line 18 from line 17			19	
20	Enter the smaller of line 15 or line 19, but not less than zero			20	
21	Ordinary income under recapture rules. Enter here and on Form 4797, line 17. See instructions			21	
22	Subtract line 21 from line 20. If zero or less, enter -0-. If more than zero, enter here and on Schedule D or Form 4797, unless the installment method applies. See instructions			22	
23	**Recognized gain.** Add lines 21 and 22			23	
24	Deferred gain or (loss). Subtract line 23 from line 19. If a related party exchange, see instructions			24	
25	**Basis of like-kind property received.** Subtract line 15 from the sum of lines 18 and 23			25	

For Paperwork Reduction Act Notice, see separate instructions. Cat. No. 12311A Form **8824** (1995)

Form 8824 (1995) Page 2

Name(s) shown on tax return. Do not enter name and social security number if shown on other side.	Your social security number
	: :

Part IV **Section 1043 Conflict-of-Interest Sales.** See instructions. Attach a copy of your certificate of divestiture.

Note: *This part is only to be used by officers or employees of the executive branch of the Federal Government for reporting nonrecognition of gain under section 1043 on the sale of property to comply with the conflict-of-interest requirements. This part can be used only if the cost of the replacement property exceeds the basis of the divested property.*

26 Description of divested property ▶ ....

27 Description of replacement property ▶ ....

28	Date divested property was sold (month, day, year)			28	/ /
29	Sales price of divested property. See instructions	29			
30	Basis of divested property	30			
31	**Realized gain.** Subtract line 30 from line 29			31	
32	Cost of replacement property purchased within 60 days after date of sale	32			
33	Subtract line 32 from line 29. If zero or less, enter -0-			33	
34	Ordinary income under recapture rules. Enter here and on Form 4797, line 11. See instructions			34	
35	Subtract line 34 from line 33. If zero or less, enter -0-. If more than zero, enter here and on Schedule D or Form 4797. See instructions			35	
36	**Recognized gain.** Add lines 34 and 35			36	
37	Deferred gain. Subtract line 36 from line 31			37	
38	**Basis of replacement property.** Subtract line 37 from line 32			38	

Form **8829**

Department of the Treasury
Internal Revenue Service (99)

Expenses for Business Use of Your Home

► File only with Schedule C (Form 1040). Use a separate Form 8829 for each home you used for business during the year.

► See separate instructions.

OMB No. 1545-1266

1995

Attachment Sequence No. **66**

Name(s) of proprietor(s) | Your social security number

Part I Part of Your Home Used for Business

1	Area used regularly and exclusively for business, regularly for day care, or for inventory storage. See instructions	1	
2	Total area of home	2	
3	Divide line 1 by line 2. Enter the result as a percentage	3	%
	• **For day-care facilities not used exclusively for business, also complete lines 4–6.**		
	• **All others, skip lines 4–6 and enter the amount from line 3 on line 7.**		
4	Multiply days used for day care during year by hours used per day — 4: hr.		
5	Total hours available for use during the year (365 days × 24 hours). See instructions — 5: 8,760 hr.		
6	Divide line 4 by line 5. Enter the result as a decimal amount — 6: .		
7	Business percentage. For day-care facilities not used exclusively for business, multiply line 6 by line 3 (enter the result as a percentage). All others, enter the amount from line 3 ►	7	%

Part II Figure Your Allowable Deduction

			(a) Direct expenses	(b) Indirect expenses		
8	Enter the amount from Schedule C, line 29, **plus** any net gain or (loss) derived from the business use of your home and shown on Schedule D or Form 4797. If more than one place of business, see instructions				8	
	See instructions for columns (a) and (b) before completing lines 9–20.					
9	Casualty losses. See instructions	9				
10	Deductible mortgage interest. See instructions	10				
11	Real estate taxes. See instructions	11				
12	Add lines 9, 10, and 11	12				
13	Multiply line 12, column (b) by line 7		13			
14	Add line 12, column (a) and line 13				14	
15	Subtract line 14 from line 8. If zero or less, enter -0-				15	
16	Excess mortgage interest. See instructions	16				
17	Insurance	17				
18	Repairs and maintenance	18				
19	Utilities	19				
20	Other expenses. See instructions	20				
21	Add lines 16 through 20	21				
22	Multiply line 21, column (b) by line 7		22			
23	Carryover of operating expenses from 1994 Form 8829, line 41		23			
24	Add line 21 in column (a), line 22, and line 23				24	
25	Allowable operating expenses. Enter the **smaller** of line 15 or line 24				25	
26	Limit on excess casualty losses and depreciation. Subtract line 25 from line 15				26	
27	Excess casualty losses. See instructions		27			
28	Depreciation of your home from Part III below		28			
29	Carryover of excess casualty losses and depreciation from 1994 Form 8829, line 42		29			
30	Add lines 27 through 29				30	
31	Allowable excess casualty losses and depreciation. Enter the **smaller** of line 26 or line 30				31	
32	Add lines 14, 25, and 31				32	
33	Casualty loss portion, if any, from lines 14 and 31. Carry amount to **Form 4684,** Section B				33	
34	Allowable expenses for business use of your home. Subtract line 33 from line 32. Enter here and on Schedule C, line 30. If your home was used for more than one business, see instructions ►				34	

Part III Depreciation of Your Home

35	Enter the **smaller** of your home's adjusted basis or its fair market value. See instructions	35	
36	Value of land included on line 35	36	
37	Basis of building. Subtract line 36 from line 35	37	
38	Business basis of building. Multiply line 37 by line 7	38	
39	Depreciation percentage. See instructions	39	%
40	Depreciation allowable. Multiply line 38 by line 39. Enter here and on line 28 above. See instructions	40	

Part IV Carryover of Unallowed Expenses to 1996

41	Operating expenses. Subtract line 25 from line 24. If less than zero, enter -0-	41	
42	Excess casualty losses and depreciation. Subtract line 31 from line 30. If less than zero, enter -0-	42	

Appendix C
Glossary of Tax Terms

The words and phrases in this glossary have been defined to reflect their conventional use in the field of taxation. The definitions may therefore be incomplete for other purposes.

A

Abandoned spouse. The abandoned spouse provision enables a married taxpayer with a dependent child whose spouse did not live in the taxpayer's home during the last six months of the tax year to file as a head of household rather than as married filing separately.

Accelerated cost recovery system (ACRS). A method in which the cost of tangible property is recovered over a prescribed period of time. Enacted by the Economic Recovery Tax Act (ERTA) of 1981 and substantially modified by the Tax Reform Act (TRA) of 1986 (the modified system is referred to as MACRS), the approach disregards salvage value, imposes a period of cost recovery that depends upon the classification of the asset into one of various recovery periods, and prescribes the applicable percentage of cost that can be deducted each year. § 168.

Accelerated depreciation. Various methods of depreciation that yield larger deductions in the earlier years of the life of an asset than the straight-line method. Examples include the double declining-balance and the sum-of-the-years' digits methods of depreciation. § 167.

Accident and health benefits. Employee fringe benefits provided by employers through the payment of health and accident insurance premiums or the establishment of employer-funded medical reimbursement plans. Employers generally are entitled to a deduction for such payments, whereas employees generally exclude the fringe benefits from gross income. §§ 105 and 106.

Accountable plan. An accountable plan is a type of expense reimbursement plan that requires an employee to render an adequate accounting to the employer and return any excess reimbursement or allowance. If the expense qualifies, it will be treated a deduction *for* AGI.

Accounting income. The accountant's concept of income is generally based upon the realization principle. Financial accounting income may differ from taxable income (e.g., accelerated depreciation might be used for Federal income tax and straight-line depreciation for financial accounting purposes). Differences are included in a reconciliation of taxable and accounting income on Schedule M–1 of Form 1120 for corporations. Seventy-five percent of the excess of adjusted current earnings over alternative minimum taxable income is an adjustment for alternative minimum tax purposes for a corporation. See *alternative minimum tax* and *economic income.*

Accounting method. The method under which income and expenses are determined for tax purposes. Major accounting methods are the cash basis and the accrual basis. Special methods are available for the reporting of gain on installment sales, recognition of income on construction projects (the completed contract and percentage of completion methods), and the valuation of inventories (last-in, first-out and first-in, first-out). §§ 446–474. See also *accrual method, cash receipts method, completed contract method, percentage of completion method,* etc.

Accounting period. The period of time, usually a year, used by a taxpayer for the determination of tax liability. Unless a fiscal year is chosen, taxpayers must determine and pay their income tax liability by using the calendar year (January 1 through December 31) as the period of measurement. An example of a fiscal year is July 1 through June 30. A change in accounting period (e.g., from a calendar year to a fiscal year) generally requires the consent of the IRS. A new taxpayer, such as a newly formed corporation or an estate created upon the death of an individual taxpayer, is free to select either a calendar or a fiscal year without the consent of the IRS. Limitations exist on the accounting period that may be selected by a partnership, an S corporation, and a personal service corporation. §§ 441–444.

Accrual basis. See *accrual method.*

Accrual method. A method of accounting that reflects expenses incurred and income earned for any one tax year. In contrast to the cash basis of accounting, expenses do not have to be paid to be deductible nor does income have to be received to be taxable. Unearned income (e.g., prepaid interest and rent) generally is taxed in the year of receipt regardless of the method of accounting used by the taxpayer. § 446(c)(2). See also *accounting method, cash receipts method,* and *unearned income.*

Accumulated earnings tax. A special tax imposed on corporations that accumulate (rather than distribute) their earnings beyond the reasonable needs of the business. The tax is imposed on accumulated taxable income and is imposed in addition to the corporate income tax. §§ 531–537.

ACE adjustment. See *adjusted current earnings (ACE) adjustment* and *business untaxed reported profits.*

Acquiescence. In agreement with the result reached. The IRS follows a policy of either acquiescing (*A, Acq.*) or nonacquiescing (*NA, Nonacq.*) in the results reached in certain judicial decisions.

Acquisition indebtedness. Debt incurred in acquiring, constructing, or substantially improving a qualified residence of the taxpayer. The interest on such loans is deductible as *qualified residence interest.* However, interest on such debt is deductible only on the portion of the indebtedness that does not exceed $1,000,000 ($500,000 for married persons filing separate returns). § 163(h)(3). See also *home equity loans.*

ACRS. See *accelerated cost recovery system.*

Active income. Active income includes wages, salary, commissions, bonuses, profits from a trade or business in which the taxpayer is a material participant, gain on the sale or other disposition of assets used in an active trade or business, and income from intangible property if the taxpayer's personal efforts significantly contributed to the creation of the property. The passive activity loss rules require classification of income and losses into three categories with active income being one of them.

Active participation. A term that is relevant for both the at-risk rules and the passive activity loss rules associated with rental real estate activities. For the at-risk rules, the following factors indicate active participation: (1) making decisions involving the operation or management of the activity, (2) performing services for the activity, and (3) hiring and discharging employees. For the passive activity loss rules, the taxpayer must participate in the making of management decisions in a significant and bona fide sense.

Additional depreciation. The excess of the amount of depreciation actually deducted over the amount that would have been deducted had the straight-line method been used. § 1250(b). See also *Section 1250 recapture.*

Adjusted basis. The cost or other basis of property reduced by depreciation (cost recovery) allowed or allowable and increased by capital improvements. See also *basis* and *realized gain or loss.*

Adjusted current earnings (ACE) adjustment. An adjustment in computing corporate alternative minimum taxable income (AMTI), computed at 75 percent of the excess of adjusted current earnings and profits computations over unadjusted AMTI. ACE computations reflect longer and slower cost recovery deductions and other restrictions on the timing of certain recognition events. Exempt interest, life insurance proceeds, and other receipts that are included in earnings and profits but not in taxable income also increase the ACE adjustment. If unadjusted AMTI exceeds adjusted current earnings and profits, the ACE adjustment is negative. The negative adjustment is limited to the aggregate of the positive adjustments under ACE for prior years, reduced by any previously claimed negative adjustments. See also *alternative minimum tax, business untaxed reported profits,* and *earnings and profits.*

Adjusted gross income (AGI). A determination peculiar to individual taxpayers. Generally, it represents gross income less business expenses, expenses attributable to the production of rent or royalty income, the allowed capital loss deduction, and certain personal expenses (deductions *for* AGI). § 62. See also *gross income.*

Adjusted sales price. The amount realized from the sale of a residence reduced by the fixing-up expenses is the adjusted sales price. An amount equal to the adjusted sales price must be reinvested in a replacement residence to defer the recognition of the realized gain on the sale of a residence. See also *amount realized, fixing-up expense,* and *realized gain or loss.*

Ad valorem tax. A tax imposed on the value of property. The most familiar ad valorem tax is that imposed by states, counties, and cities on real estate. Ad valorem taxes can, however, be imposed upon personal property (e.g., a motor vehicle tax based on the value of an automobile). §§ 164(a)(1) and (2).

Advance payments. In general, prepayments for services or goods are includible in gross income upon receipt of the advance payments (for both accrual and cash basis taxpayers). However, Rev.Proc. 71–21 (1971–2 C.B. 549) provides guidelines for the deferral of tax on certain advance payments providing specific conditions are met.

AFTR. Published by Research Institute of America (formerly by Prentice-Hall), *American Federal Tax Reports* contains all of the Federal tax decisions issued by the U.S. District Courts, U.S. Court of Federal Claims, U.S. Courts of Appeals, and U.S. Supreme Court.

AFTR2d. The second series of the *American Federal Tax Reports.*

Alimony and separate maintenance payments. Alimony and separate maintenance payments are includible in the gross income of the recipient and are deductible by the payor. The payments must be made in discharge of a legal obligation arising from a marital or family relationship. Child support and voluntary payments are not treated as alimony. Alimony is deductible *for* AGI. §§ 62(10), 71, and 215. See also *child support payments.*

Alimony recapture. The amount of alimony that previously has been included in the gross income of the recipient and deducted by the payor that now is deducted by the recipient and included in the gross income of the payor as the result of front-loading. § 71(f).

All events test. For accrual method taxpayers, income is earned when (1) all the events have occurred that fix the right to receive the income and (2) the amount can be determined with reasonable accuracy. Accrual of income cannot be postponed simply because a portion of the income may have to be returned in a subsequent period. The all events test also is utilized to determine when expenses can be deducted by an accrual basis taxpayer. The application of the test could cause a variation between the treatment of an item for accounting and for tax purposes. For example, a reserve for warranty expense may be properly accruable under generally accepted accounting principles but not be deductible under the Federal income tax law. Because of the application of the all events test, the deduction becomes available in the year the warranty obligation becomes fixed and the amount is determinable with reasonable certainty. See also *economic performance test.* Reg. §§ 1.446–1(c)(1)(ii) and 1.461–1(a)(2).

Alternate valuation date. Property passing from a person by reason of death may be valued for death tax purposes as of the date of death or the alternate valuation date. The alternate valuation date is six months from the date of death or the date the property is disposed of by the estate, whichever comes first. To use the alternate valuation date, the executor or administrator of the estate must make an affirmative election. The election of the alternate valuation date is not available unless it decreases both the amount of the gross estate *and* the estate tax liability. §§ 1014(a) and 2032.

Alternative depreciation system (ADS). A cost recovery system that produces a smaller deduction than would be calculated under ACRS or MACRS. The alternative system must be used in certain instances and can be elected in other instances. § 168(g). See also *cost recovery allowance.*

Alternative minimum tax (AMT). The alternative minimum tax is imposed only to the extent it exceeds the regular income tax (in effect, the tax liability is the greater of the tax liability calculated using the AMT rules and that calculated using the regular income tax rules). The AMT rates (26 and 28 percent for the individual taxpayer and 20 percent for the corporate taxpayer) are applied to the AMT base. The AMT base is calculated by modifying taxable income as follows: (1) add tax preferences, (2) add certain adjustments, (3) deduct certain adjustments, and (4) deduct the exemption amount. §§ 55–59. See also *adjusted current earnings (ACE) adjustment* and *business untaxed reported profits.*

Alternative minimum tax credit. The AMT can result from timing differences that give rise to positive adjustments in calculating the AMT base. To provide equity for the taxpayer when these timing differences reverse, the regular tax liability may be reduced by a tax credit for prior year's minimum tax liability attributable to timing differences. § 53.

Alternative tax. An option that is allowed in computing the tax on net capital gain. The rate is 35 percent of net capital gain for corporations and 28 percent for noncorporate taxpayers. For 1988 through 1990, the alternative tax did not produce a beneficial result. For 1991 and thereafter, the alternative tax can produce beneficial results for the noncorporate taxpayer because the regular tax rates can be as high as 39.6 percent. §§ 1(h) and 1201. See also *net capital gain.*

Alternative tax NOL deduction (ATNOLD). In calculating the AMT, the taxpayer is allowed to deduct NOL carryovers and carrybacks. A special calculation, referred to as the ATNOLD, is required for this purpose. The regular income tax is modified for AMT adjustments and preferences to produce the ATNOLD. § 56(d).

Amortization. The allocation (and charge to expense) of the cost or other basis of an intangible asset over a statutory period of 15 years. Examples of amortizable intangibles include patents, copyrights, covenants not to compete, acquired goodwill, and leasehold interests. See also *estimated useful life* and *goodwill.*

Amount realized. The amount received by a taxpayer on the sale or other disposition of property. The amount realized is the sum of the cash and the fair market value of any property or services received, plus any related debt assumed by the buyer. Determining the amount realized is the starting point for arriving at realized gain or loss. The amount realized is defined in § 1001(b) and the related Regulations. See also *realized gain or loss* and *recognized gain or loss.*

AMT adjustments. In calculating AMTI, certain adjustments are added to or deducted from taxable income. These adjustments generally reflect timing differences. § 56.

AMT exclusions. A credit that can be used to reduce the regular tax liability in future tax years is available in connection with the AMT (*AMT credit*). The credit is applicable only with respect to the AMT that results from timing differences. It is not available in connection with AMT exclusions, which include the standard deduction, personal exemptions, medical expenses deductible in calculating the regular income tax that are not deductible in computing the AMT, other itemized deductions that are not allowable for AMT purposes, excess percentage depletion, and tax-exempt interest on specified private activity bonds.

Annuity. A fixed sum payable to a person at specified intervals for a specific period of time or for life. Payments represent a partial return of capital and a return (interest) on the capital investment. Therefore, an exclusion ratio must be used to compute the amount of nontaxable income. The exclusion ratio is used until the annuitant has recovered his or her investment in the annuity contract. Thereafter, all of the annuity payments received are included in gross income. If the annuitant dies before his or her investment is recovered, a deduction is allowed. § 72. See also *qualified pension or profit sharing plan.*

Appellate court. For Federal tax purposes, appellate courts include the Courts of Appeals and the Supreme

Court. If the party losing in the trial (or lower) court is dissatisfied with the result, the dispute may be carried to the appropriate appellate court. See also *Court of Appeals* and *trial court.*

Arm's length transaction. The standard under which unrelated parties would determine an exchange price for a transaction. Suppose, for example, Cardinal Corporation sells property to its sole shareholder for $10,000. In testing whether the $10,000 is an "arm's length" price, one would ascertain the price that would have been negotiated between the corporation and an unrelated party in a bargained exchange.

Asset Depreciation Range (ADR) system. A system of estimated useful lives for categories of tangible assets prescribed by the IRS. The system provides a range for each category that extends from 20 percent above to 20 percent below the guideline class lives prescribed by the IRS.

Assignment of income. A procedure whereby a taxpayer attempts to avoid the recognition of income by assigning the property that generates the income to another. Such a procedure will not avoid the recognition of income by the taxpayer making the assignment if it can be said that the income was earned at the point of the transfer. In this case, usually referred to as an anticipatory assignment of income, the income will be taxed to the person who earns it.

Association. An organization treated as a corporation for Federal tax purposes even though it may not qualify as such under applicable state law. An entity designated as a trust or a partnership, for example, may be classified as an association if it clearly possesses corporate attributes. Corporate attributes include centralized management, continuity of life, free transferability of interests, and limited liability. § 7701(a)(3).

At-risk limitation. Under the at-risk rules, a taxpayer's deductible losses from an activity for any taxable year are limited to the amount the taxpayer has at risk at the end of the taxable year. The initial amount considered at risk is generally the sum of the amount of cash and the adjusted basis of property contributed to the activity and amounts borrowed for use in the activity for which the taxpayer is personally liable or has pledged as security property not used in the activity.

Attribution. Under certain circumstances, the tax law applies attribution (construction ownership) rules to assign to one taxpayer the ownership interest of another taxpayer. If, for example, the stock of Gold Corporation is held 60 percent by Marsha and 40 percent by Sid, Marsha may be deemed to own 100 percent of Gold Corporation if she and Sid are mother and son. In that case, the stock owned by Sid is attributed to Marsha. See, for example, §§ 267 and 318.

Audit. Inspection and verification of a taxpayer's return or other transactions possessing tax consequences. See also *correspondence audit, field audit,* and *office audit.*

Automatic mileage method. See *automobile expenses.*

Automobile expenses. Automobile expenses are generally deductible only to the extent the automobile is used in business or for the production of income. Personal commuting expenses are not deductible. The taxpayer may deduct actual expenses (including depreciation and insurance), or the standard (automatic) mileage rate may be used (27.5 cents per mile for 1991, 28 cents per mile for 1992, 28 cents per mile for 1993, 29 cents per mile for 1994, 30 cents per mile for 1995, and 31 cents per mile for 1996) during any one year. Automobile expenses incurred for medical purposes or in connection with job-related moving expenses are deductible to the extent of actual out-of-pocket expenses or at the rate of 10 cents per mile (12 cents for charitable activities). See also *transportation expenses.*

B

Bad debts. A deduction is permitted if a business account receivable subsequently becomes partially or completely worthless, providing the income arising from the debt previously was included in income. Available methods are the specific charge-off method and the reserve method. However, except for certain financial institutions, TRA of 1986 repealed the use of the reserve method for 1987 and thereafter. If the reserve method is used, partially or totally worthless accounts are charged to the reserve. A nonbusiness bad debt deduction is allowed as a short-term capital loss if the loan did not arise in connection with the creditor's trade or business activities. Loans between related parties (family members) generally are classified as nonbusiness. § 166. See also *nonbusiness bad debts.*

Basis. The acquisition cost assigned to an asset for income tax purposes. For assets acquired by purchase, the basis is the cost (§ 1012). Special rules govern the basis of property received by virtue of another's death (§ 1014) or by gift (§ 1015), the basis of stock received on a transfer of property to a controlled corporation (§ 358), the basis of the property transferred to the corporation (§ 362), and the basis of property received upon the liquidation of a corporation (§§ 334 and 338). See also *adjusted basis.*

Book value. The net amount of an asset after reduction by a related reserve. The book value of accounts receivable, for example, is the face amount of the receivables less the reserve for bad debts. The book value of a building is the cost less the accumulated depreciation.

Boot. Cash or property of a type not included in the definition of a nontaxable exchange. The receipt of boot will cause an otherwise nontaxable transfer to become taxable to the extent of the lesser of the fair market value of such boot or the realized gain on the transfer. Examples of nontaxable exchanges that could be partially or completely taxable due to the receipt of boot include transfers to controlled corporations [§ 351(b)] and like-kind exchanges [§ 1031(b)]. See also *realized gain or loss* and *recognized gain or loss.*

Bribes and illegal payments. Section 162 denies a deduction for bribes or kickbacks, fines and penalties paid to a government official or employee for violation of law, and two-thirds of the treble damage payments made to claimants for violation of the antitrust law. Denial of a deduction for bribes and illegal payments is based upon the judicially established principle that allowing such payments would be contrary to public policy.

B.T.A. The Board of Tax Appeals was a trial court that considered Federal tax matters. This court is now the U.S. Tax Court.

Burden of proof. The requirement in a lawsuit to show the weight of evidence and thereby gain a favorable decision. Except in cases of tax fraud, the burden of proof in a tax case generally is on the taxpayer.

Business bad debt. A debt created or acquired in connection with a trade or business of the taxpayer, or a debt the loss from the worthlessness of which is incurred in the taxpayer's trade or business. A business bad debt is deducted as an ordinary deduction.

Business energy credit. See *energy tax credit—business property.*

Business expenses. See *trade or business expenses.*

Business gifts. Business gifts are deductible only to the extent that each gift does not exceed $25 per person per year. Exceptions are made for gifts costing $4 or less and for certain employee awards. § 274(b).

Business untaxed reported profits. Such profits are a positive adjustment for purposes of the corporate alternative minimum tax. For taxable years beginning after 1989, the amount is 75 percent of the excess of adjusted current earnings over the alternative minimum taxable income (AMTI). This adjustment was replaced in 1990 with the ACE adjustment. §§ 56(c)(1) and (g). See also *adjusted current earnings (ACE) adjustment* and *alternative minimum tax.*

C

Cafeteria benefit plan. An employee benefit plan under which an employee is allowed to select from among a variety of employer-provided fringe benefits. Some of the benefits may be taxable and some may be statutory nontaxable benefits (e.g., health and accident insurance and group term life insurance). The employee is taxed only on the taxable benefits selected. A cafeteria benefit plan is also referred to as a flexible benefit plan.

Cafeteria plan. See *cafeteria benefit plan.*

Canons of taxation. Criteria used in the selection of a tax base that were originally discussed by Adam Smith in *The Wealth of Nations.* Canons of taxation include equality, convenience, certainty, and economy.

Capital asset. Broadly speaking, all assets are capital except those specifically excluded by the Code. Major categories of noncapital assets include property held for resale in the normal course of business (inventory), trade accounts and notes receivable, and depreciable property and real estate used in a trade or business (§ 1231 assets). § 1221. See also *capital gain* and *capital loss.*

Capital contributions. Various means by which a shareholder makes additional funds available to the corporation (placed at the risk of the business) without the receipt of additional stock. Such contributions are added to the basis of the shareholder's existing stock investment and do not generate income to the corporation. § 118.

Capital expenditure. An expenditure that should be added to the basis of the property improved. For income tax purposes, this generally precludes a full deduction for the expenditure in the year paid or incurred. Any capital recovery in the form of a tax deduction must come in the form of depreciation. § 263.

Capital gain. The gain from the sale or exchange of a capital asset. See also *capital asset* and *net capital gain.*

Capital gain net income. If the total capital gains for the tax year exceed the total capital losses, the result is capital gain net income. Note that the term does not distinguish between the long-term and short-term gains. § 1222(9). See also *net capital gain.*

Capital gain or loss holding period. The period of time that a capital asset is held by the taxpayer. To qualify for long-term treatment, the asset must be held for more than one year. See also *holding period.*

Capital gain property. Property contributed to a charitable organization that, if sold rather than contributed, would have resulted in long-term capital gain to the donor. See also *ordinary income property.*

Capital loss. The loss from the sale or exchange of a capital asset. See also *capital asset.*

Cash basis. See *accounting method* and *cash receipts method.*

Cash equivalent doctrine. Generally, a cash basis taxpayer does not report income until cash is constructively or actually received. Under the cash equivalent doctrine, cash basis taxpayers are required to report income if they receive the equivalent of cash (e.g., property is received) in a taxable transaction.

Cash method. See *cash receipts method.*

Cash receipts method. A method of accounting under which the taxpayer generally reports income when cash is collected and reports expenses when cash payments are made. However, for fixed assets, the cash basis taxpayer claims deductions through depreciation or amortization in the same manner as an accrual basis taxpayer. Prepaid expenses must be capitalized and amortized if the life of the asset extends "substantially beyond" the end of the tax year. See also *constructive receipt.*

Casualty loss. A casualty is defined as "the complete or partial destruction of property resulting from an identifiable event of a sudden, unexpected or unusual nature" (e.g., floods, storms, fires, auto accidents). Individuals may deduct a casualty loss only if the loss is incurred in a trade or business or in a transaction entered into for profit or arises from fire, storm, shipwreck, or other casualty or from theft. Individuals usually deduct personal casualty losses as itemized deductions subject to a $100 nondeductible amount and to an annual floor equal to 10 percent of adjusted gross income that applies after the $100 per casualty floor has been applied. Special rules are provided for the netting of certain casualty gains and losses. See also *disaster area loss* and *Section 1231 gains and losses.*

C corporation. A corporation that has not elected conduit treatment under § 1361. See also *S corporation status.*

Cert. den. By denying the Writ of Certiorari, the U.S. Supreme Court refuses to accept an appeal from a U.S. Court of Appeals. The denial of certiorari does not, however, mean that the U.S. Supreme Court agrees with the result reached by the lower court.

Certiorari. Appeal from a U.S. Court of Appeals to the U.S. Supreme Court is by Writ of Certiorari. The Supreme Court does not have to accept the appeal and usually does not (*cert. den.*) unless there is a conflict among the lower courts that needs to be resolved or a constitutional issue is involved.

Change in accounting method. A change in the taxpayer's method of accounting (e.g., from FIFO to LIFO) generally requires prior approval from the IRS. Generally, a request must be filed within 180 days after the beginning of the taxable year of the desired change. In some instances, the permission for change will not be granted unless the taxpayer agrees to certain adjustments prescribed by the IRS.

Change in accounting period. A taxpayer must obtain the consent of the IRS before changing his or her tax year. Income for the short period created by the change must be annualized.

Charitable contributions. Contributions are deductible (subject to various restrictions and ceiling limitations) if made to qualified nonprofit charitable organizations. A cash basis taxpayer is entitled to a deduction solely in the year of payment. Accrual basis corporations may accrue contributions at year-end if payment is properly authorized before the end of the year and payment is made within two and one-half months after the end of the year. § 170.

Child and dependent care expenses credit. A tax credit ranging from 20 percent to 30 percent of employment-related expenses (child and dependent care expenses) for amounts of up to $4,800 is available to individuals who are employed (or deemed to be employed) and maintain a household for a dependent child under age 13, disabled spouse, or disabled dependent. § 21.

Child support payments. Payments for child support do not constitute alimony and are therefore not includible in gross income by the recipient or deductible as alimony by the payor. Generally, none of the amounts paid are regarded as child support unless the divorce decree or separation agreement specifically calls for child support payments. However, if the amount of the payment to the former spouse would be reduced upon the happening of a contingency related to a child (e.g., the child attains age 21 or dies), the amount of the future reduction in the payment will be deemed child support for post-1984 agreements and decrees. § 71(c). See also *alimony and separate maintenance payments.*

Circuit Court of Appeals. See *Court of Appeals.*

Circulation expenditures. Expenditures of establishing or increasing the circulation of a periodical that may be either expensed or capitalized. If such expenses are expensed, an adjustment will occur for AMT purposes, since the expenses are deducted over a three-year period for AMT purposes. Over the three-year period, both positive and negative AMT adjustments will be produced. § 173. See also *AMT adjustments.*

Claim of right doctrine. A judicially imposed doctrine applicable to both cash and accrual basis taxpayers that holds that an amount is includible in income upon actual or constructive receipt if the taxpayer has an unrestricted claim to the payment. For the tax treatment of amounts repaid when previously included in income under the claim of right doctrine, see § 1341.

Claims Court. One of three Federal trial courts that consider Federal tax controversy. Now known as the U.S. Court of Federal Claims, appeal from this court (formerly to the U.S. Supreme Court) now goes to the Court of Appeals for the Federal Circuit. See also *trial court.*

Clear reflection of income. The IRS has the authority to redetermine a taxpayer's income using a method that clearly reflects income if the taxpayer's method does not do so. § 446(b). In addition, the IRS may apportion or allocate income among various related businesses if income is not "clearly reflected." § 482.

Closely held corporation. A corporation where the stock ownership is not widely dispersed. Instead, a few shareholders are in control of corporate policy and are in a position to benefit personally from that policy.

Community property. Louisiana, Texas, New Mexico, Arizona, California, Washington, Idaho, Nevada, and Wisconsin have community property systems. The rest of the states are classified as common law jurisdictions. The difference between common law and community property systems centers around the property rights possessed by married persons. In a common law system, each spouse owns whatever he or she earns. Under a community property system, one-half of the earnings of each spouse is considered owned by the other spouse. Assume, for example, Alice and Jeff are husband and wife and their only income is the $50,000 annual salary Jeff receives. If they live in New York (a common law state), the $50,000 salary belongs to

Jeff. If, however, they live in Texas (a community property state), the $50,000 salary is divided equally, in terms of ownership, between Jeff and Alice. See also *separate property.*

Compensatory damages. Damages received or paid by the taxpayer can be classified as compensatory damages or as punitive damages. Compensatory damages are those paid to compensate one for harm caused by another. Compensatory damages are excludible from the recipient's gross income. See also *punitive damages.*

Completed contract method. A method of reporting gain or loss on certain long-term contracts. Under this method of accounting, gross income and expenses are recognized in the tax year in which the contract is completed. Reg. § 1.451–3. Limitations exist on a taxpayer's ability to use the completed contract method. § 460. See also *long-term contract* and *percentage of completion method.*

Component depreciation. The process of dividing an asset (e.g., a building) into separate components or parts for the purpose of calculating depreciation. The advantage of dividing an asset into components is to use shorter depreciation lives for selected components under § 167. Generally, the same cost recovery period must be used for all the components of an asset under § 168.

Condemnation. The taking of property by a public authority. The property is condemned as the result of legal action, and the owner is compensated by the public authority. The power to condemn property is known as the right of eminent domain.

Conduit concept. An approach assumed by the tax law in the treatment of certain entities and their owners. Specific tax characteristics pass through the entity without losing their identity. For example, items of income and expense, capital gains and losses, tax credits, etc., realized by a partnership pass through the partnership (a conduit) and are subject to taxation at the partner level. Also, in an S corporation, certain items pass through and are reported on the returns of the shareholders.

Constructive dividends. In addition to dividends formally declared by the board of directors of a corporation (i.e., declaration date, record date, and payment date), a shareholder may receive a distribution that does not have the formalities of a dividend but is treated as a dividend. Examples include salaries paid to shareholder-employees that are not reasonable and the shareholder use of corporate property for less than an arm's length rate.

Constructive ownership. See *attribution.*

Constructive receipt. If income is unqualifiedly available, it will be subject to the income tax even though it is not physically in the taxpayer's possession. An example is accrued interest on a savings account. Under the constructive receipt of income concept, the interest will be taxed to a depositor in the year it is available rather than the year actually withdrawn. The fact that the depositor uses the cash basis of accounting for tax purposes is irrelevant. See Reg. § 1.451–2.

Consumer interest. Interest expense of the taxpayer of a personal nature (not trade or business interest, investment interest, qualified residence interest, or passive activity interest). TRA of 1986 provided that no deduction is permitted for consumer interest. However, the provision was not fully effective until 1991. § 163(h). See also *qualified residence interest.*

Contributions to the capital of a corporation. See *capital contributions.*

Convention expenses. Travel expenses incurred in attending a convention are deductible if the meetings are related to a taxpayer's trade or business or job-related activities. If, however, the convention trip is primarily for pleasure, no deduction is permitted for transportation expenses. Likewise, if the expenses are for attending a convention related to the production of income (§ 212), no deduction is permitted. Specific limitations are provided for foreign convention expenses. See § 274(n) for the limitations on the deductions for meals. § 274(h).

Correspondence audit. An audit conducted by the IRS by mail. Typically, the IRS writes to the taxpayer requesting the verification of a particular deduction, exemption, or credit. The completion of a special form or the remittance of copies of records or other support is all that is requested of the taxpayer. To be distinguished from a *field audit* or an *office audit.*

Cost depletion. Depletion that is calculated based on the adjusted basis of the asset. The adjusted basis is divided by the expected recoverable units to determine the depletion per unit. The depletion per unit is multiplied by the units sold during the tax year to calculate cost depletion. See also *percentage depletion.*

Cost recovery allowance. The portion of the cost of an asset written off under ACRS (or MACRS), which replaced the depreciation system as a method for writing off the cost of an asset for most assets placed in service after 1980 (after 1986 for MACRS). § 168. See also *alternative depreciation system.*

Cost recovery period. A period specified in the Code for writing off the cost of an asset under ACRS or MACRS.

Court of Appeals. Any of 13 Federal courts that consider tax matters appealed from the U.S. Tax Court, U.S. Court of Federal Claims, or a U.S. District Court. Appeal from a U.S. Court of Appeals is to the U.S. Supreme Court by Writ of Certiorari. See also *appellate court.*

Court of Federal Claims. See *Claims Court.*

Court of original jurisdiction. The Federal courts are divided into courts of original jurisdiction and appellate courts. The dispute between the taxpayer and the IRS is first considered by a court of original jurisdiction (i.e., a trial court). The four Federal courts of original jurisdiction are the U.S. Tax Court, U.S. District Court, the Court of Federal Claims, and the Small Cases Division of the U.S. Tax Court. See *Court of Appeals.*

Credit for child and dependent care expenses. See *child and dependent care expenses credit.*

D

Death benefit. A payment made by an employer to the beneficiary or beneficiaries of a deceased employee on account of the death of the employee. Under certain conditions, the first $5,000 of the payment is exempt from the income tax. § 101(b)(1).

Death tax. See *estate tax.*

Declaration of estimated tax. A procedure whereby individuals and corporations are required to make quarterly installment payments of estimated tax. Individuals are required to make the declaration and file quarterly payments of the estimated tax if certain requirements are met. In 1996, a declaration is not required for an individual whose estimated tax is reasonably expected to be less than $500.

Deductions for adjusted gross income. See *adjusted gross income.*

Deductions from adjusted gross income. See *itemized deductions.*

Deferred compensation. Compensation that will be taxed when received or upon the removal of certain restrictions on receipt and not when earned. Contributions by an employer to a qualified pension or profit sharing plan on behalf of an employee are an example. The contributions will not be taxed to the employee until the funds are made available or distributed to the employee (e.g., upon retirement). See also *qualified pension or profit sharing plan.*

Deficiency. Additional tax liability owed by a taxpayer and assessed by the IRS. See also *statutory notice of deficiency.*

Defined benefit plan. Qualified plans can be dichotimized into defined benefit plans and defined contribution plans. Under a defined benefit plan, a formula defines the benefits employees are to receive. The formula usually includes years of service, employee compensation, and some stated percentage. The employer must make annual contributions based on actuarial computations that will be sufficient to pay the vested retirement benefits. See also *defined contribution plan* and *pension plan.*

Defined contribution plan. Qualified plans can be dichotimized into defined benefit plans and defined contribution plans. Under a defined contribution plan, a separate account is maintained for each covered employee. The employee's benefits under the plan are based solely on (1) the amount contributed and (2) income from the fund that accrues to the employee's account. The plan defines the amount the employer is required to contribute (e.g., a flat dollar amount, an amount based on a special formula, or an amount equal to a certain percentage of compensation). See also *defined benefit plan* and *pension plan.*

Defined contribution pension plan. See *defined contribution plan.*

***De minimis* fringe.** Benefits provided to employees that are too insignificant to warrant the time and effort required to account for the benefits received by each employee and the value of those benefits. Such amounts are excludible from the employee's gross income. § 132.

Dependency exemption. See *personal and dependency exemptions.*

Depletion. The process by which the cost or other basis of a natural resource (e.g., an oil or gas interest) is recovered upon extraction and sale of the resource. The two ways to determine the depletion allowance are the cost and percentage (or statutory) methods. Under the cost method, each unit of production sold is assigned a portion of the cost or other basis of the interest. This is determined by dividing the cost or other basis by the total units expected to be recovered. Under the percentage (or statutory) method, the tax law provides a special percentage factor for different types of minerals and other natural resources. This percentage is multiplied by the gross income from the interest to arrive at the depletion allowance. §§ 613 and 613A.

Depreciation. The deduction of the cost or other basis of a tangible asset over the asset's estimated useful life. § 167. For intangible assets, see *amortization.* For natural resources, see *depletion.* Also see *estimated useful life.* The depreciation system was replaced by ACRS for most assets placed in service after 1980 (by MACRS for most assets placed in service after 1986) but still applies for assets placed in service before 1981. See also *recapture of depreciation.*

Determination letter. Upon the request of a taxpayer, a District Director will comment on the tax status of a completed transaction. Determination letters are most frequently used to clarify employee versus self-employed status, to determine whether a pension or profit sharing plan qualifies under the Code, and to determine the tax-exempt status of certain nonprofit organizations.

Direct charge-off method. See *specific charge-off method.*

Disabled access credit. A tax credit whose purpose is to encourage small businesses to make their businesses more accessible to disabled individuals. The credit is equal to 50 percent of the eligible expenditures that exceed $250 but do not exceed $10,250. Thus, the maximum amount for the credit is $5,000. The adjusted basis for depreciation is reduced by the amount of the credit. To qualify, the facility must have been placed in service before November 6, 1990. § 44. See also *general business credit.*

Disaster area loss. A casualty sustained in an area designated as a disaster area by the President of the United States. In such an event, the disaster loss may be treated as having occurred in the taxable year immediately preceding the year in which the disaster actually occurred. Thus, immediate tax benefits are provided to victims of a disaster. § 165(i). See also *casualty loss.*

Dissent. To disagree with the majority. If, for example, Judge Brown disagrees with the result reached by Judges

Charles and Davis (all of whom are members of the same court), Judge Brown could issue a dissenting opinion.

District Court. A Federal District Court is a trial court for purposes of litigating (among others) Federal tax matters. It is the only trial court where a jury trial can be obtained. See also *trial court.*

Dividends received deduction. A deduction allowed a shareholder that is a corporation for dividends received from a domestic corporation. The percentage applied in calculating the dividends received deduction varies according to the percentage of stock ownership. If the stock ownership percentage is less than 20 percent, the percentage is 70 percent of the dividends received. If the stock ownership percentage is at least 20 percent but less than 80 percent, the percentage is 80 percent. If the stock ownership percentage is at least 80 percent, the percentage is 100 percent. §§ 243–246A.

Dollar value LIFO. An inventory technique that focuses on the dollars invested in the inventory rather than the particular items on hand each period. Each inventory item is assigned to a pool. A pool is a collection of similar items and is treated as a separate inventory. At the end of the period, each pool is valued in terms of prices at the time LIFO was adopted (base period prices), whether or not the particular items were actually on hand in the year LIFO was adopted, to compare with current prices to determine if there has been an increase or decrease in inventories.

E

Earned income. Income from personal services as distinguished from income generated by property. See §§ 32 and 911 and the related Regulations.

Earned income credit. A refundable tax credit whose purpose is to provide assistance to certain low-income individuals. To receive the most beneficial treatment, the taxpayer must have qualifying children. However, it is possible to qualify for the credit without having a child. To calculate the credit for a taxpayer with one or more children for 1996, a statutory rate of 34.0 percent for one child (40.0 percent for two or more children) is multiplied by the earned income (subject to a statutory maximum of $6,330 with one qualifying child or $8,890 with two or more qualifying children). Once the earned income exceeds $11,610, the credit is phased out using a 15.98 percent rate for one qualifying child and a 21.06 percent rate for two or more qualifying children. For the qualifying taxpayer without children, the credit is calculated on a maximum earned income of $4,220 applying a 7.65 percent rate with the phaseout beginning at $5,280 applying the same rate. § 32.

Earnings and profits. A tax concept peculiar to corporate taxpayers that measures economic capacity to make a distribution to shareholders that is not a return of capital. Such a distribution will result in dividend income to the shareholders to the extent of the corporation's current and accumulated earnings and profits.

Economic income. The change in the taxpayer's net worth, as measured in terms of market values, plus the value of the assets the taxpayer consumed during the year. Because of the impracticality of this income model, it is not used for tax purposes. See also *accounting income.*

Economic performance test. One of the requirements that must be satisfied in order for an accrual basis taxpayer to deduct an expense. The accrual basis taxpayer first must satisfy the all events test. That test is not deemed satisfied until economic performance occurs. This occurs, when property or services are provided to the taxpayer or, in the case in which the taxpayer is required to provide property or services, whenever the property or services are actually provided by the taxpayer. See also *all events test.*

Education expenses. Employees may deduct education expenses if such items are incurred either (1) to maintain or improve existing job-related skills or (2) to meet the express requirements of the employer or the requirements imposed by law to retain employment status. The expenses are not deductible if the education is required to meet the minimum educational standards for the taxpayer's job or if the education qualifies the individual for a new trade or business. Reg. § 1.162–5.

Educational savings bonds. United States Series EE bonds whose proceeds are used for qualified higher educational expenses for the taxpayer, the taxpayer's spouse, or a dependent. The interest may be excluded from gross income, provided the taxpayer's adjusted gross income does not exceed certain amounts. § 135.

Employee expenses. The deductions *for* adjusted gross income include reimbursed expenses and certain expenses of performing artists. All other employee expenses are deductible *from* adjusted gross income. § 62. See also *trade or business expenses.*

Employee stock ownership plan (ESOP). A type of defined contribution plan that qualifies as a tax-exempt employee trust. The ESOP must invest primarily in qualifying employer securities. A major benefit of an ESOP to the employer corporation is that it can contribute stock rather than cash and receive a tax deduction equal to the fair market value of the stock.

Employment taxes. Employment taxes are those taxes that an employer must pay on account of its employees. Employment taxes include FICA (Federal Insurance Contributions Act) and FUTA (Federal Unemployment Tax Act) taxes. Employment taxes are paid to the IRS in addition to income tax withholdings at specified intervals. Such taxes can be levied on the employees, the employer, or both. See also *FICA tax* and *FUTA tax.*

Energy tax credit—business property. A 10 percent tax credit is available to businesses that invest in certain energy property. The purpose of the credit is to create incentives for conservation and to penalize the increased use of oil and gas. The business energy tax credit applies to equipment with an estimated useful life of at least three years that uses fuel or feedstock other than oil or natural gas (e.g., solar, geothermal). §§ 46(2) and 48(a). See also *estimated useful life* and *investment tax credit*.

Entertainment expenses. These expenses are deductible only if they are directly related to or associated with a trade or business. Various restrictions and documentation requirements have been imposed upon the deductibility of entertainment expenses to prevent abuses by taxpayers. See, for example, the provision contained in § 274(n) that disallows 50 percent of entertainment expenses. § 274.

Estate tax. A tax imposed on the right to transfer property by reason of death. Thus, an estate tax is levied on the decedent's estate and not on the heir receiving the property. §§ 2001 and 2002. See also *inheritance tax*.

Estimated tax. The amount of tax (including alternative minimum tax and self-employment tax) an individual expects to owe for the year after subtracting tax credits and income tax withheld. The estimated tax must be paid in installments at designated intervals (e.g. for the individual taxpayer, by April 15, June 15, September 15, and January 15 of the following year).

Estimated useful life. The period over which an asset will be used by a particular taxpayer. Although the period cannot be longer than the estimated physical life of an asset, it could be shorter if the taxpayer does not intend to keep the asset until it wears out. Assets such as goodwill do not have an estimated useful life. The estimated useful life of an asset is essential to measuring the annual tax deduction for depreciation and amortization. An asset subject to ACRS or MACRS is written off over a specified cost recovery period rather than over its estimated useful life. In addition, most intangibles are now amortized over a 15-year statutory period.

Excise tax. A tax on the manufacture, sale, or use of goods or on the carrying on of an occupation or activity. Also a tax on the transfer of property. Thus, the Federal estate and gift taxes are, theoretically, excise taxes.

Extraordinary personal services. These are services provided by individuals where the customers' use of the property is incidental to their receipt of the services. For example, a patient's use of a hospital bed is incidental to his or her receipt of medical services. This is one of the six exceptions to determine whether an activity is a passive rental activity.

F

Fair market value. The amount at which property would change hands between a willing buyer and a willing seller, neither being under any compulsion to buy or sell and both having reasonable knowledge of the relevant facts. Reg. § 20.2031–1(b).

F.3d. An abbreviation for the Third Series of the *Federal Reporter*, the official series where decisions of the U.S. Claims Court (before October 1982) and the U.S. Courts of Appeals are published.

F.Supp. The abbreviation for the *Federal Supplement*, the official series where the reported decisions of the U.S. District Courts are published.

Federal district court. See *district court*.

FICA tax. An abbreviation for Federal Insurance Contributions Act, commonly referred to as the Social Security tax. The FICA tax is comprised of the Social Security tax (old age, survivors, and disability insurance) and the Medicare tax (hospital insurance) and is imposed on both employers and employees. The employer is responsible for withholding from the employee's wages the Social Security tax at a rate of 6.2 percent on a maximum wage base of $62,700 (for 1996) and the Medicare tax at a rate of 1.45 percent (no maximum wage base). The employer is required to match the employee's contribution. See also *employment taxes*.

Field audit. An audit by the IRS conducted on the business premises of the taxpayer or in the office of the tax practitioner representing the taxpayer. To be distinguished from a *correspondence audit* or an *office audit*.

Finalized regulation. See *regulations*.

First-in, first-out (FIFO). An accounting method for determining the cost of inventories. Under this method, the inventory on hand is deemed to be the sum of the cost of the most recently acquired units. See also *last-in, first-out (LIFO)*.

Fiscal year. A fiscal year is a 12-month period ending on the last day of a month other than December. In certain circumstances, a taxpayer is permitted to elect a fiscal year instead of being required to use a calendar year. See also *accounting period* and *taxable year*.

Fixing-up expense. An expense that is incurred to assist in the sale of a residence and is deductible in calculating the adjusted sales price. Fixing-up expenses include such items as ordinary repairs, painting, and wallpapering. To qualify, the expense must (1) be incurred on work performed during the 90-day period ending on the date of the contract of sale, (2) be paid within 30 days after the date of the sale, and (3) not be a capital expenditure. § 1034. See also *adjusted sales price*.

Flat tax. In its pure form, it would replace the graduated income tax rates with a single rate (e.g., 17 percent). All deductions are eliminated, and a large personal exemption is allowed to remove low-income and many middle-income taxpayers from the application of the tax.

Foreign earned income exclusion. The foreign earned income exclusion is a relief provision that applies to U.S. citizens working in a foreign country. To qualify for the exclusion, the taxpayer must be either a bona fide resident of the foreign country or present in the country for 330 days during any 12 consecutive months. The exclusion is limited to $70,000 per year. § 911.

Foreign tax credit or deduction. Both individual taxpayers and corporations may claim a foreign tax credit on income earned and subject to tax in a foreign country or U.S. possession. As an alternative to the credit, a deduction may be taken for the foreign taxes paid. §§ 27, 164, and 901–905.

Franchise. An agreement that gives the transferee the right to distribute, sell, or provide goods, services, or facilities within a specified area. The cost of obtaining a franchise may be amortized over a statutory period of 15 years. In general, the franchisor's gain on the sale of franchise rights is an ordinary gain because the franchisor retains a significant power, right, or continuing interest in the subject of the franchise. §§ 197 and 1253.

Franchise tax. A tax levied on the right to do business in a state as a corporation. Although income considerations may come into play, the tax usually is based on the capitalization of the corporation.

Fringe benefits. Compensation or other benefits received by an employee that are not in the form of cash. Some fringe benefits (e.g., accident and health plans, group term life insurance) may be excluded from the employee's gross income and therefore are not subject to the Federal income tax.

Fruit and tree metaphor. The courts have held that an individual who earns income from property or services cannot assign that income to another. For example, a father cannot assign his earnings from commissions to his child and escape income tax on those amounts.

FUTA tax. An employment tax levied on employers. Jointly administered by the Federal and state governments, the tax provides funding for unemployment benefits. FUTA applies at a rate of 6.2 percent in 1996 on the first $7,000 of covered wages paid during the year for each employee. The Federal government allows a credit for FUTA paid (or allowed under a merit rating system) to the state. The credit cannot exceed 5.4 percent of the covered wages. See also *employment taxes.*

G

General business credit. The summation of various nonrefundable business credits, including the investment tax credit, jobs credit, research activities credit, low-income housing credit, and disabled access credit. The amount of general business credit that can be used to reduce the tax liability is limited to the taxpayer's net income tax reduced by the greater of (1) the tentative minimum tax or (2) 25 percent of the net regular tax liability that exceeds $25,000. Unused general business credits can be carried back 3 years and forward 15 years. § 38.

Gift. A transfer of property for less than adequate consideration. Gifts usually occur in a personal setting (such as between members of the same family). Gifts are excluded from the income tax but may be subject to the *gift tax.*

Gift tax. A tax imposed on the transfer of property by gift. The tax is imposed upon the donor of a gift and is based upon the fair market value of the property on the date of the gift. §§ 2501–2524.

Golden parachute payments. A severance payment to employees that meets the following requirements: (1) the payment is contingent on a change of ownership of a corporation through a stock or asset acquisition and (2) the aggregate present value of the payment equals or exceeds three times the employee's average annual compensation. To the extent the severance payment meets these conditions, a deduction is disallowed to the employer for the excess of the payment over a statutory base amount (a five-year average of compensation if the taxpayer was an employee for the entire five-year period). In addition, a 20 percent excise tax is imposed on the employee who receives the excess severance pay. §§ 280G and 4999.

Goodwill. The ability of a business to generate income in excess of a normal rate on assets due to superior managerial skills, market position, new product technology, etc. In the purchase of a business, goodwill represents the difference between the purchase price and the fair market value of the net assets acquired. Goodwill is an intangible asset that possesses an indefinite life. However, since acquired goodwill is a § 197 intangible asset, it is amortized over a 15-year statutory period. Self-created goodwill cannot be amortized. Reg. § 1.167(a)–3. See also *amortization.*

Government bonds issued at a discount. Certain U.S. government bonds (Series E and EE) are issued at a discount and do not pay interest during the life of the bonds. Instead, the bonds are redeemable at increasing fixed amounts. Thus, the difference between the purchase price and the amount received upon redemption represents interest income to the holder. A cash basis taxpayer may defer recognition of gross income until the bonds are redeemed. For Series EE savings bonds issued after 1989, the interest otherwise taxable at redemption can be excluded if the bonds are qualified educational savings bonds. As an alternative to deferring recognition of gross income until the bonds are redeemed, the taxpayer may elect to include in gross income on an annual basis the annual increase in the value of the bonds. § 454.

Gross income. Income subject to the Federal income tax. Gross income does not include income for which the Code permits exclusion treatment (e.g., interest on municipal bonds). For a manufacturing or merchandising business, gross income means gross profit (gross sales or gross receipts less cost of goods sold). § 61 and Reg. § 1.61–3(a).

Group term life insurance. Life insurance coverage permitted by an employer for a group of employees. Such insurance is renewable on a year-to-year basis and does not accumulate in value (i.e., no cash surrender value is built up). The premiums paid by the employer on the insurance are not taxed to an employee on coverage of up to $50,000 per person. § 79 and Reg. § 1.79–1(a).

Guaranteed payments. Payments made by a partnership to one of its partners for services rendered or for the use of capital, to the extent the payments are determined without regard to the income of the partnership. Such payments generally are deductible by the partnership as a business expense and are reported as ordinary income by the recipient partner. § 707(c).

H

Half-year convention. The half-year convention is a cost recovery convention that assumes all property is placed in service at mid-year and thus provides for a half-year's cost recovery for that year.

Head of household. An unmarried individual who maintains a household for another and satisfies certain conditions set forth in § 2(b). Such status enables the taxpayer to use a set of income tax rates [see § 1(b)] that are lower than those applicable to other unmarried individuals [§ 1(c)] but higher than those applicable to surviving spouses and married persons filing a joint return [§ 1(a)]. See also *tax rate schedules.*

Highly compensated employee. The employee group is generally divided into two categories for fringe benefit (including pension and profit sharing plans) purposes. These are (1) highly compensated employees and (2) non-highly compensated employees. For most fringe benefits, if the fringe benefit plan discriminates in favor of highly compensated employees, it will not be a qualified plan with respect, at a minimum, to the highly compensated employees.

Hobby loss. A nondeductible loss arising from a personal hobby as contrasted with an activity engaged in for profit. Generally, the law provides a rebuttable presumption that an activity is engaged in for profit if profits are earned during any three or more years during a five-year period. § 183. See also *vacation home.*

Holding period. The period of time property has been held for income tax purposes. The holding period is crucial in determining whether gain or loss from the sale or exchange of a capital asset is long term or short term. § 1223. See also *capital gain or loss holding period.*

Home equity loans. Loans that utilize the personal residence of the taxpayer as security. The interest on such loans is deductible as *qualified residence interest.* However, interest is deductible only on the portion of the loan that does not exceed the lesser of (1) the fair market value of the residence, reduced by the *acquisition indebtedness,* or (2) $100,000 ($50,000 for married persons filing separate returns). A major benefit of a home equity loan is that there are no tracing rules regarding the use of the loan proceeds. § 163(h)(3).

Home office expenses. See *office-in-the-home expenses.*

H.R. 10 (Keogh) plan. See *self-employment retirement plan.*

Hybrid method. A combination of the accrual and cash methods of accounting. That is, the taxpayer may account for some items of income on the accrual method (e.g., sales and cost of goods sold) and other items (e.g., interest income) on the cash method.

I

Imputed interest. For certain long-term sales of property, the IRS can convert some of the gain from the sale into interest income if the contract does not provide for a minimum rate of interest to be paid by the purchaser. The application of this procedure has the effect of forcing the seller to recognize less long-term capital gain and more ordinary income (interest income). §§ 483 and 1274 and the Regulations thereunder. In addition, interest income and interest expense are imputed (deemed to exist) on interest-free or below-market rate loans between certain related parties. § 7872. See also *interest-free loans.*

Incentive stock option (ISO). A type of stock option that receives favorable tax treatment. If various qualification requirements can be satisfied, there are no recognition tax consequences when the stock option is granted. However, the spread (the excess of the fair market value at the date of exercise over the option price) is a tax preference item for purposes of the alternative minimum tax. The gain on disposition of the stock resulting from the exercise of the stock option will be classified as long-term capital gain if certain holding period requirements are met (the employee must not dispose of the stock within two years after the option is granted or within one year after acquiring the stock). § 422. See *nonqualified stock option (NQSO).*

Income. For tax purposes, an increase in wealth that has been realized.

Independent contractor. A self-employed person as distinguished from one who is employed as an employee.

Individual retirement account (IRA). Individuals with earned income who are not active participants in qualified retirement plans are permitted to set aside up to 100 percent of their salary per year (generally not to exceed $2,000 or $2,250 for a spousal IRA) for a retirement account. The amount set aside can be deducted by the taxpayer and will be subject to income tax only upon withdrawal. Specific requirements are established for the withdrawal of such funds, and penalties are provided for failure to comply. If the employee is an active participant in a qualified retirement plan, the IRA deduction is phased out once adjusted gross income exceeds certain amounts. Even if the IRA deduction has been completely phased out, the taxpayer can still make a nondeductible contribution. § 219. See also *simplified employee pension plan.*

Inheritance tax. An excise tax levied on the heir based on the value of property received from a decedent. See also *estate tax.*

Installment method. A method of accounting enabling a taxpayer to spread the recognition of gain on the sale of property over the payout period. Under this procedure, the seller computes the gross profit percentage from the sale (the gain divided by the contract price) and applies it to each payment received to arrive at the gain to be recognized. §§ 453 and 453A.

Intangible drilling and development costs (IDC). Taxpayers may elect to expense or capitalize (subject to amortization) intangible drilling and development costs. However, ordinary income recapture provisions apply to oil and gas properties on a sale or other disposition if the expense method is elected. §§ 263(c) and 1254(a).

Interest-free loans. Bona fide loans that carry no interest (or a below-market rate). If made in a nonbusiness setting, the imputed interest element is treated as a gift from the lender to the borrower. If made by a corporation to a shareholder, a constructive dividend could result. In either event, the lender may recognize interest income, and the borrower may be able to deduct interest expense. § 7872.

Interpretive regulation. A Regulation issued by the Treasury Department that purports to explain the meaning of a particular Code Section. An interpretive Regulation is given less deference than a legislative Regulation. See also *legislative regulation* and *procedural regulation.* § 7805.

Investigation of a new business. Expenditures by taxpayers who are not engaged in a trade or business incurred in the evaluation of prospective business activities (acquiring an existing business or entering into a new trade or business). If the expenditures are general, it is the position of the IRS that no deduction is permitted even if the investigation is abandoned because the taxpayer is not engaged in a trade or business. The courts, however, have permitted a loss deduction providing the expenditures were specific.

Investment income. Gross income from interest, dividends, annuities, and royalties not derived in the ordinary course of a trade or business. Net capital gain attributable to the disposition of property producing these types of income normally is not included in investment income. However, a taxpayer may elect to include the capital gains as investment income if the net capital gain qualifying for the *alternative tax* is reduced by an equivalent amount. See also *investment interest.*

Investment indebtedness. If funds are borrowed by noncorporate taxpayers for the purpose of purchasing or continuing to hold investment property, some portion of the interest expense deduction may be disallowed. The interest deduction is generally limited to net investment income. Amounts that are disallowed may be carried forward and treated as investment interest of the succeeding year. § 163(d).

Investment interest. Payment for the use of funds used to acquire assets that produce investment income. The deduction for investment interest is limited to *net investment income* for the tax year. See also *investment income.*

Investment tax credit (ITC). A tax credit that usually was equal to 10 percent (unless a reduced credit was elected) of the qualified investment in tangible personalty used in a trade or business. If the tangible personalty had a recovery period of five years or more, the full cost of the property qualified for the credit. Only 60 percent of cost qualified for property with a recovery period of three years. However, the regular investment tax credit was repealed by TRA of 1986 for property placed in service after December 31, 1985. §§ 46–48. See also *general business credit, recapture of investment tax credit,* and *Section 38 property.*

Involuntary conversion. The loss or destruction of property through theft, casualty, or condemnation. Any gain realized on an involuntary conversion can, at the taxpayer's election, be postponed (deferred) for Federal income tax purposes if the owner reinvests the proceeds within a prescribed period of time in property that is similar or related in service or use. § 1033. See also *nontaxable exchange.*

IRA. See *individual retirement account.*

Itemized deductions. Certain personal expenditures allowed by the Code as deductions *from* adjusted gross income. Examples include certain medical expenses, interest on home mortgages, state income taxes, and charitable contributions. Itemized deductions are reported on Schedule A of Form 1040. Certain miscellaneous itemized deductions are reduced by 2 percent of the taxpayer's adjusted gross income. In addition, a taxpayer whose adjusted gross income exceeds $100,000 ($50,000 for married filing separately) must reduce the itemized deductions by 3 percent of the excess of adjusted gross income over $100,000. For 1996, the indexed amount for the $100,000 is $117,950, and the indexed amount for the $50,000 is $58,975. Medical, casualty and theft, and investment interest deductions are not subject to the 3 percent reduction. The 3 percent reduction may not reduce itemized deductions that are subject to the reduction to below 20 percent of their initial amount. §§ 63(d), 67, and 68.

J

Jobs credit. Employers are allowed a tax credit equal to 40 percent of the first $6,000 of wages (per eligible employee) for the first year of employment. Eligible employees include certain hard-to-employ individuals (e.g., youths from low-income families, handicapped persons). The employer's deduction for wages is reduced by the amount of the credit taken. For qualified summer youth employees, the 40 percent rate is applied to the first $3,000 of qualified wages. The credit is available for wages paid to employees in their first year of service if they begin working for their employer before 1995. §§ 51 and 52.

K

Keogh plan. See *self-employment retirement plan.*

Kiddie tax. To reduce the tax savings that result from shifting income from parents to children, the net unearned income of a child under age 14 is taxed at the marginal tax rate of the parent(s). For the provision to apply, the child must have at least one living parent and unearned income of more than $1,300 for the tax year. § 1(g). See also *unearned income.*

L

Last-in, first-out (LIFO). An accounting method for valuing inventories for tax purposes. Under this method, it is assumed that the inventory on hand is valued at the cost of the earliest acquired units. § 472 and the related Regulations. See also *first-in, first-out (FIFO).*

Least aggregate deferral method. An algorithm set forth in the Regulations to determine the tax year for a partnership with partners whose tax years differ. The tax year that produces the least aggregate deferral of income for the partners is selected.

Legislative regulation. Some Code Sections give the Secretary of the Treasury or his delegate the authority to prescribe Regulations to carry out the details of administration or to otherwise complete the operating rules. Regulations issued pursuant to this type of authority truly possess the force and effect of law. In effect, Congress is almost delegating its legislative powers to the Treasury Department. See also *interpretive regulation* and *procedural regulation.*

Lessee. One who rents property from another. In the case of real estate, the lessee is also known as the tenant.

Lessor. One who rents property to another. In the case of real estate, the lessor is also known as the landlord.

Letter rulings. Issued upon a taxpayer's request, by the National Office of the IRS, they describe how the IRS will treat a proposed transaction for tax purposes. They apply only to the taxpayer who asks for and obtains the ruling, but post-1984 rulings may be substantial authority for purposes of avoiding the accuracy-related penalties. The IRS limits the issuance of letter rulings to restricted, preannounced areas of taxation.

Life insurance proceeds. Generally, life insurance proceeds paid to a beneficiary upon the death of the insured are exempt from Federal income tax. An exception is provided when a life insurance contract has been transferred for valuable consideration to another individual who assumes ownership rights. In that case, the proceeds are income to the assignee to the extent that the proceeds exceed the amount paid for the policy plus any subsequent premiums paid. Insurance proceeds may be subject to the Federal estate tax if the decedent retained any incidents of ownership in the policy before death or if the proceeds are payable to the decedent's estate. §§ 101 and 2042.

Like-kind exchange. An exchange of property held for productive use in a trade or business or for investment (except inventory, stocks and bonds, and partnership interests) for other investment or trade or business property. Unless non-like-kind property is received (boot), the exchange will be nontaxable. § 1031. See also *boot* and *nontaxable exchange.*

Limited expensing. See *Section 179 expensing.*

Limited liability company. An organization that combines the corporate characteristic of limited liability with treatment as a partnership for Federal income tax purposes.

Liquidating distribution. A distribution of assets by a corporation associated with the termination of the business. See also *liquidation of a corporation.*

Liquidation of a corporation. In a complete or partial liquidation of a corporation, amounts received by the shareholders in exchange for their stock are usually treated as a sale or exchange of the stock resulting in capital gain or loss treatment. § 331. Special rules apply to the liquidation of a subsidiary under § 332. Generally, a liquidation is a taxable event to the corporation. § 336. Special rules apply to a parent corporation that is liquidating a subsidiary. § 337.

Listed property. The term listed property includes (1) any passenger automobile, (2) any other property used as a means of transportation, (3) any property of a type generally used for purposes of entertainment, recreation, or amusement, (4) any computer or peripheral equipment (with an exception for exclusive business use), (5) any cellular telephone (or other similar telecommunications equipment), and (6) any other property of a type specified in the Regulations. If listed property is predominantly used for business, the taxpayer is allowed to use the statutory percentage method of cost recovery. Otherwise, the straight-line cost recovery method must be used. § 280F.

Long-term contract. A building, installation, construction, or manufacturing contract that is entered into but not completed within the same tax year. A manufacturing contract is a long-term contract only if the contract is to manufacture (1) a unique item not normally carried in finished goods inventory or (2) items that normally require more than 12 calendar months to complete. The two available methods to account for long-term contracts are the percentage of completion method and the completed contract method. The completed contract method can be used only in limited circumstances. § 460. See also *completed contract method* and *percentage of completion method.*

Long-term nonpersonal use capital assets. Includes investment property with a long-term holding period. Such property disposed of by casualty or theft may receive § 1231 treatment. See also *Section 1231 gains and losses.*

Lower of cost or market. An elective inventory method, whereby the taxpayer may value inventories at the lower of the taxpayer's actual cost or the current replacement cost of the goods. This method cannot be used in conjunction with the LIFO inventory method.

Low-income housing. Low-income housing is rental housing that is a dwelling unit for low- or moderate-income individuals or families. Beneficial tax treatment is in the form of the *low-income housing credit*. § 42. See also *accelerated cost recovery system (ACRS)*.

Low-income housing credit. Beneficial treatment to owners of low-income housing is provided in the form of a tax credit. The calculated credit is claimed in the year the building is placed in service and in the following nine years. § 42. See also *general business credit*.

Lump-sum distribution. Payment of the entire amount due at one time rather than in installments. Such distributions often occur from qualified pension or profit sharing plans upon the retirement or death of a covered employee. The recipient of a lump-sum distribution may recognize both long-term capital gain and ordinary income upon the receipt of the distribution. The ordinary income portion may be subject to a special 5-year or 10-year income averaging provision. § 402(e).

M

MACRS. See *accelerated cost recovery system (ACRS)*.

Majority interest partners. Partners who have more than a 50 percent interest in partnership profits and capital, counting only those partners who have the same taxable year, are referred to as majority interest partners. The term is of significance in determining the appropriate taxable year of a partnership. § 706(b). See also *accounting period* and *principal partner*.

Marital deduction. A deduction allowed upon the transfer of property from one spouse to another. The deduction is allowed under the Federal gift tax for lifetime (inter vivos) transfers or under the Federal estate tax for death (testamentary) transfers. §§ 2056 and 2523.

Marriage penalty. The additional tax liability that results for a married couple compared with what their tax liability would be if they were not married and filed separate returns.

Material participation. If an individual taxpayer materially participates in a nonrental trade or business activity, any loss from that activity is treated as an active loss that can be offset against active income. Material participation is achieved by meeting any one of seven tests provided in the Regulations.

Medical expenses. Medical expenses of an individual, spouse, and dependents are allowed as an itemized deduction to the extent that such amounts (less insurance reimbursements) exceed 7.5 percent of adjusted gross income. § 213.

Mid-month convention. The mid-month convention is a cost recovery convention that assumes property is placed in service in the middle of the month that it is actually placed in service.

Mid-quarter convention. The mid-quarter convention is a cost recovery convention that assumes property placed in service during the year is placed in service at the middle of the quarter in which it is actually placed in service. The mid-quarter convention applies if more than 40 percent of the value of property (other than eligible real estate) is placed in service during the last quarter of the year.

Miscellaneous itemized deductions. A special category of itemized deductions that includes such expenses as professional dues, tax return preparation fees, job-hunting costs, unreimbursed employee business expenses, and certain investment expenses. Such expenses are deductible only to the extent they exceed 2 percent of adjusted gross income. § 67. See also *itemized deductions*.

Mitigation of the annual accounting period concept. Various tax provisions that provide relief from the effect of the finality of the annual accounting period concept. For example, the *net operating loss* provisions provide relief to a taxpayer whose business profits and losses for different taxable years fluctuate. See also *accounting period*.

Modified accelerated cost recovery system (MACRS). See *accelerated cost recovery system (ACRS)*.

Moving expenses. A deduction *for* AGI is permitted to employees and self-employed individuals provided certain tests are met. The taxpayer's new job must be at least 50 miles farther from the old residence than the old residence was from the former place of work. In addition, an employee must be employed on a full-time basis at the new location for 39 weeks in the 12-month period following the move. Deductible moving expenses include the cost of moving the household and personal effects, transportation, and lodging expenses during the move. The cost of meals during the move are not deductible. Qualified moving expenses that are paid (or reimbursed) by the employer can be excluded from the employee's gross income. In this case, the related deduction by the employee is not permitted. §§ 62(a)(15), 132(a)(6), and 217.

Multiple support agreement. To qualify for a dependency exemption, the support test must be satisfied. This requires that over 50 percent of the support of the potential dependent be provided by the taxpayer. Where no one person provides more than 50 percent of the support, a multiple support agreement enables a taxpayer to still qualify for the dependency exemption. Any person who contributed more than 10 percent of the support is entitled to claim the exemption if each person in the group who contributed more than 10 percent files a written consent (Form 2120). Each person who is a party to the multiple support agreement must meet all the other requirements for claiming the dependency exemption. § 152(c). See also *personal and dependency exemptions*.

N

National sales tax. Intended as a replacement for the current Federal income tax. Unlike a value added tax (VAT), which is levied on the manufacturer, it would be imposed on the consumer upon the final sale of goods and services. To keep the tax from being regressive, low-income taxpayers would be granted some kind of credit or exemption.

Necessary. Appropriate and helpful in furthering the taxpayer's business or income-producing activity. §§ 162(a) and 212. See also *ordinary.*

Net capital gain. The excess of the net long-term capital gain for the tax year over the net short-term capital loss. The net capital gain of an individual taxpayer is eligible for the alternative tax. § 1222(11). See also *alternative tax.*

Net capital loss. The excess of the losses from sales or exchanges of capital assets over the gains from sales or exchanges of such assets. Up to $3,000 per year of the net capital loss may be deductible by noncorporate taxpayers against ordinary income. The excess net capital loss carries over to future tax years. For corporate taxpayers, the net capital loss cannot be offset against ordinary income, but it can be carried back 3 years and forward 5 years to offset net capital gains. §§ 1211, 1212, and 1221(10).

Net investment income. The excess of *investment income* over investment expenses. Investment expenses are those deductible expenses directly connected with the production of investment income. Investment expenses do not include investment interest. The deduction for *investment interest* for the tax year is limited to net investment income. § 163(d).

Net operating loss. To mitigate the effect of the annual accounting period concept, § 172 allows taxpayers to use an excess loss of one year as a deduction for certain past or future years. In this regard, a carryback period of 3 years and a carryforward period of 15 years are allowed. See also *mitigation of the annual accounting period concept.*

Net worth method. An approach used by the IRS to reconstruct the income of a taxpayer who fails to maintain adequate records. Under this approach, the gross income for the year is the increase in net worth of the taxpayer (assets in excess of liabilities) with appropriate adjustment for nontaxable receipts and nondeductible expenditures. The net worth method often is used when tax fraud is suspected.

Ninety-day letter. See *statutory notice of deficiency.*

No-additional-cost services. Services that the employer may provide the employee at no additional cost to the employer. Generally, the benefit is the ability to utilize the employer's excess capacity (vacant seats on an airliner). Such amounts are excludible from the recipient's gross income. § 132.

Nonaccountable plan. An expense reimbursement plan that does not have an accountability feature. The result is that employee expenses must be claimed as deductions *from* AGI. An exception is moving expenses, which are deductions *for* AGI. See also *accountable plan.*

Nonacquiescence. Announcement of disagreement by the IRS on the result reached in certain judicial decisions. Sometimes abbreviated *Nonacq.* or *NA.* See also *acquiescence.*

Nonbusiness bad debts. A bad debt loss not incurred in connection with a creditor's trade or business. The loss is deductible as a short-term capital loss and is allowed only in the year the debt becomes entirely worthless. In addition to family loans, many investor losses fall into the classification of nonbusiness bad debts. § 166(d). See also *bad debts.*

Nonqualified deferred compensation (NQDC) plans. Compensation arrangements that are frequently offered to executives. Such plans may include stock options, restricted stock, etc. Often, an executive may defer the recognition of taxable income. The employer, however, does not receive a tax deduction until the employee is required to include the compensation in income. See also *restricted property plan.*

Nonqualified stock option (NQSO). A type of stock option that does not satisfy the statutory requirements of an incentive stock option. If the NQSO has a readily ascertainable fair market value (e.g., the option is traded on an established exchange), the value of the option must be included in the employee's gross income at the date of the grant. Otherwise, the employee does not recognize income at the grant date. Instead, ordinary income is recognized in the year of exercise of the option. See also *incentive stock option (ISO).*

Nonrecourse debt. An obligation on which the endorser is not personally liable. An example of a nonrecourse debt is a mortgage on real estate acquired by a partnership without the assumption of any liability on the mortgage by the partnership or any of the partners. The acquired property generally is pledged as collateral for the loan.

Nonrefundable credit. A nonrefundable credit is a credit that is not paid if it exceeds the taxpayer's tax liability. Some nonrefundable credits qualify for carryback and carryover treatment. See also *refundable credit.*

Nontaxable exchange. A transaction in which realized gains or losses are not recognized. The recognition of gain or loss is postponed (deferred) until the property received in the nontaxable exchange is subsequently disposed of in a taxable transaction. Examples are § 1031 like-kind exchanges, § 1033 involuntary conversions, and § 1034 sale of a residence. See also *involuntary conversion* and *like-kind exchange.*

O

Occupational tax. A tax imposed on various trades or businesses. A license fee that enables a taxpayer to engage in a particular occupation.

Office audit. An audit by the IRS of a taxpayer's return that is conducted in the agent's office. To be distinguished from a *correspondence audit* or a *field audit.*

Office-in-the-home expenses. Employment and business-related expenses attributable to the use of a residence (e.g., den or office) are allowed only if the portion of the residence is exclusively used on a regular basis as a principal place of business of the taxpayer or as a place of business that is used by patients, clients, or customers. If the expenses are incurred by an employee, the use must be for the convenience of the employer as opposed to being merely appropriate and helpful. § 280A.

One-year rule for prepaid expenses. Taxpayers who use the cash method are required to use the accrual method for deducting certain prepaid expenses (i.e., must capitalize the item and can deduct only when used). If a prepayment will not be consumed or expire by the end of the tax year following the year of payment, the prepayment must be capitalized and prorated over the benefit period. Conversely, if the prepayment will be consumed by the end of the tax year following the year of payment, it can be expensed when paid. To obtain the current deduction under the one-year rule, the payment must be a required payment rather than a voluntary payment.

Open transaction. A judicially imposed doctrine that allows the taxpayer to defer all gain until he or she has collected an amount equal to the adjusted basis of assets transferred pursuant to an exchange transaction. This doctrine has been applied where the property received in an exchange has no ascertainable fair market value due to the existence of contingencies. The method is permitted only in very limited circumstances. See also *recovery of capital doctrine.*

Options. The sale or exchange of an option to buy or sell property results in capital gain or loss if the property is a capital asset. Generally, the closing of an option transaction results in short-term capital gain or loss to the writer of the call and the purchaser of the call option. § 1234.

Ordinary. Common and accepted in the general industry or type of activity in which the taxpayer is engaged. It comprises one of the tests for the deductibility of expenses incurred or paid in connection with a trade or business; for the production or collection of income; for the management, conservation, or maintenance of property held for the production of income; or in connection with the determination, collection, or refund of any tax. §§ 162(a) and 212. See also *necessary.*

Ordinary and necessary. See *necessary* and *ordinary.*

Ordinary income property. Property contributed to a charitable organization that, if sold rather than contributed, would have resulted in other than long-term capital gain to the donor (i.e., ordinary income property and short-term capital gain property). Examples are inventory and capital assets held for less than the long-term holding period.

Organizational expenses. A corporation may elect to amortize organizational expenses over a period of 60 months or more. Certain expenses of organizing a company do not qualify for amortization (e.g., expenditures connected with issuing or selling stock or other securities). § 248.

Original issue discount (OID). The difference between the issue price of a debt obligation (e.g., a corporate bond) and the maturity value of the obligation when the issue price is *less than* the maturity value. OID represents interest and must be amortized over the life of the debt obligation using the effective interest method. The difference is not considered to be original issue discount for tax purposes when it is less than one-fourth of 1 percent of the redemption price at maturity multiplied by the number of years to maturity. §§ 1272 and 1273(a)(3).

Outside salesperson. An outside salesperson solicits business away from the employer's place of business on a full-time basis. The employment-related expenses of an outside salesperson are itemized deductions unless reimbursed by the employer. If reimbursed, such expenses are deductible *for* AGI.

P

Partnerships. A partnership is treated as a conduit and is not subject to taxation. Various items of partnership income, expenses, gains, and losses flow through to the individual partners and are reported on the partners' personal income tax returns.

Passive activity. A trade or business activity in which the taxpayer does not materially participate is subject to limitations on the deduction of losses and credits. Rental activities (subject to exceptions) and limited partnership interests are inherently passive. Relief from passive activity limitation treatment is provided in certain situations, such as for certain rental real estate if the taxpayer actively participates in the activity. The annual ceiling on the relief is $25,000. § 469. See also *portfolio income.*

Passive investment income. As defined in § 1362(d)(3)(D), passive investment income means gross receipts from royalties, certain rents, dividends, interest, annuities, and gains from the sale or exchange of stock and securities. Revocation of the S corporation election may occur in certain cases when the S corporation has passive investment income in excess of 25 percent of gross receipts for a period of three consecutive years.

Passive loss. Any loss from (1) activities in which the taxpayer does not materially participate or (2) rental activities (subject to certain exceptions). Net passive losses cannot be used to offset income from nonpassive sources. Rather, they are suspended until the taxpayer either generates net passive income (and a deduction of the losses is allowed) or disposes of the underlying property (at which time the loss deductions are allowed in full). One relief provision allows landlords who actively participate in the rental activities to deduct up to $25,000 of passive losses annually. However, a phaseout of the $25,000 amount commences when the landlord's AGI exceeds $100,000. See also *portfolio income.*

Patent. A patent is an intangible asset that may be amortized over a statutory 15-year period as a § 197 intangible. The sale of a patent usually results in favorable long-term capital gain treatment. §§ 197 and 1235.

Pension plan. A type of deferred compensation arrangement that provides for systematic payments of definitely determinable retirement benefits to employees who meet the requirements set forth in the plan. See also *defined benefit plan* and *defined contribution plan.*

Percentage depletion. Percentage depletion is depletion based on a statutory percentage applied to the gross income from the property. The taxpayer deducts the greater of cost depletion or percentage depletion. § 613. See also *cost depletion.*

Percentage of completion method. A method of reporting gain or loss on certain long-term contracts. Under this method of accounting, the gross contract price is included in income as the contract is being completed. § 460 and Reg. § 1.451–3. See also *completed contract method* and *long-term contract.*

Personal and dependency exemptions. The tax law provides an exemption for each individual taxpayer and an additional exemption for the taxpayer's spouse if a joint return is filed. An individual may also claim a dependency exemption for each dependent, provided certain tests are met. The amount of the personal and dependency exemptions is $2,500 in 1995 and $2,550 in 1996. The amount is indexed for inflation. The exemption is subject to phaseout once adjusted gross income exceeds certain statutory threshold amounts. §§ 151 and 152.

Personal casualty gain. The recognized gain from any involuntary conversion of personal use property arising from fire, storm, shipwreck, or other casualty, or from theft. See also *personal casualty loss.*

Personal casualty loss. The recognized loss from any involuntary conversion of personal use property arising from fire, storm, shipwreck, or other casualty, or from theft. See also *personal casualty gain.*

Personal exemption. See *personal and dependency exemptions.*

Personal expenses. Expenses of an individual for personal reasons that are not deductible unless specifically provided for under the tax law. § 262.

Personal property. Generally, all property other than real estate. It is sometimes referred to as personalty when real estate is termed realty. Personal property also can refer to property that is not used in a taxpayer's trade or business or held for the production or collection of income. When used in this sense, personal property can include both realty (e.g., a personal residence) and personalty (e.g., personal effects such as clothing and furniture).

Personal residence. The sale of a personal residence generally results in the recognition of capital gain (but not loss). However, the gain may be deferred if the adjusted sales price of the old residence is reinvested in the purchase of a new residence within certain prescribed time periods. Also, taxpayers age 55 or older may exclude $125,000 of the gain from tax, provided certain requirements are met. §§ 1034 and 121. See also *Section 121 exclusion.*

Personal service corporation (PSC). A corporation the principal activity of which is the performance of personal services (e.g., health, law, engineering, architecture, accounting, actuarial science, performing arts, or consulting), with such services being substantially performed by the employee-owners.

Personalty. All property other than realty (real estate). Personalty usually is categorized as tangible or intangible property. Tangible personalty includes such assets as machinery and equipment, automobiles and trucks, and office equipment. Intangible personalty includes stocks and bonds, goodwill, patents, trademarks, and copyrights. See also *personal property.*

Points. Loan origination fees that may be deductible as interest by a buyer of property. A seller of property who pays points reduces the selling price by the amount of the points paid for the buyer. While the seller is not permitted to deduct this amount as interest, the buyer may do so. See *prepaid interest* for the timing of the interest deduction.

Pollution control facilities. A certified pollution control facility, the cost of which may be amortized over a 60-month period if the taxpayer elects. § 169.

Portfolio income. The term is relevant in applying the limitation on passive activity losses and credits. Although normally considered passive in nature, for this purpose portfolio income is treated as nonpassive. Therefore, net passive losses and credits cannot be offset against portfolio income. Examples of portfolio income are interest, dividends, annuities, and certain royalties. § 469. See also *passive activity.*

Precedent. A previously decided court decision that is recognized as authority for the disposition of future decisions.

Prepaid expenses. Cash basis as well as accrual basis taxpayers usually are required to capitalize prepayments for rent, insurance, etc., that cover more than one year. Deductions are taken during the period the benefits are received.

Prepaid interest. In effect, the Code places cash basis taxpayers on an accrual basis for purposes of recognizing a deduction for prepaid interest. Thus, interest paid in advance is deductible as an interest expense only as it accrues. The one exception to this rule involves the interest element when a cash basis taxpayer pays points to obtain financing for the purchase of a principal residence (or to make improvements thereto) if the payment of points is an established business practice in the area in which the indebtedness is incurred and the amount involved is not excessive. § 461(g). See also *points.*

Principal partner. A partner with a 5 percent or greater interest in partnership capital or profits. § 706(b)(3). See also *majority interest partners.*

Private activity bond. Interest on state and local bonds is excludible from gross income. § 103. Certain such bonds are labeled private activity bonds. Although the interest on such bonds is excludible for regular income tax purposes, it is treated as a tax preference in calculating the AMT. See also *alternative minimum tax (AMT).*

Prizes and awards. The fair market value of a prize or award generally is includible in gross income. However, exclusion is permitted if the prize or award is made in recognition of religious, charitable, scientific, educational, artistic, literary, or civic achievement, and the recipient transfers the award to a qualified governmental unit or a nonprofit organization. In that case, the recipient must be selected without any action on his or her part to enter a contest or proceeding, and the recipient must not be required to render substantial future services as a condition of receiving the prize or award. § 74.

Procedural regulation. A Regulation issued by the Treasury Department that is a housekeeping-type instruction indicating information that taxpayers should provide the IRS as well as information about the internal management and conduct of the IRS itself. See also *interpretive regulation* and *legislative regulation.*

Profit sharing plan. A deferred compensation plan established and maintained by an employer to provide for employee participation in the company's profits. Contributions are paid from the employer's current or accumulated profits to a trustee. Separate accounts are maintained for each participant employee. The plan must provide a definite, predetermined formula for allocating the contributions among the participants. It also must include a definite, predetermined formula for distributing the accumulated funds after a fixed number of years, on the attainment of a stated age, or on the occurrence of certain events such as illness, layoff, or retirement.

Proposed regulation. A Regulation issued by the Treasury Department in proposed, rather than final, form. The interval between the proposal of a Regulation and its finalization permits taxpayers and other interested parties to comment on the propriety of the proposal. See also *regulations* and *temporary regulation.*

Public policy limitation. See *bribes and illegal payments.*

Punitive damages. Damages received or paid by the taxpayer can be classified as compensatory damages or as punitive damages. Punitive damages are those awarded to punish the defendant for gross negligence or the intentional infliction of harm. Such damages are includible in gross income unless the claim arises out of physical injury or physical sickness. See also *compensatory damages.*

Q

Qualified employee discounts. Discounts offered employees on merchandise or services that the employer ordinarily sells or provides to customers. The discounts must be generally available to all employees. In the case of property, the discount cannot exceed the employer's gross profit (the sales price cannot be less than the employer's cost). In the case of services, the discounts cannot exceed 20 percent of the normal sales price. § 132.

Qualified pension or profit sharing plan. An employer-sponsored plan that meets the requirements of § 401. If these requirements are met, none of the employer's contributions to the plan will be taxed to the employee until distributed to him or her (§ 402). The employer will be allowed a deduction in the year the contributions are made (§ 404). See also *annuity* and *deferred compensation.*

Qualified real property business indebtedness. Indebtedness that was incurred or assumed by the taxpayer in connection with real property used in a trade or business and is secured by such real property. The taxpayer must not be a C corporation. For qualified real property business indebtedness, the taxpayer may elect to exclude some or all of the income realized from cancellation of debt on qualified real property. If the election is made, the basis of the property must be reduced by the amount excluded. The amount excluded cannot be greater than the excess of the principal amount of the outstanding debt over the fair market value (net of any other debt outstanding on the property) of the property securing the debt.

Qualified residence interest. A term relevant in determining the amount of interest expense the individual taxpayer may deduct as an itemized deduction for what otherwise would be disallowed as a component of personal interest (consumer interest). Qualified residence interest consists of interest paid on qualified residences (principal residence and one other residence) of the taxpayer. Debt that qualifies as qualified residence interest is limited to $1 million of debt to acquire, construct, or substantially improve qualified residences (acquisition indebtedness) plus $100,000 of other debt secured by qualified residences (home equity indebtedness). The home equity indebtedness may not exceed the fair market value of a qualified residence reduced by the acquisition indebtedness for that residence. § 163(h)(3). See also *consumer interest* and *home equity loans.*

Qualified transportation fringes. Transportation benefits provided by the employer to the employee. Such benefits include (1) transportation in a commuter highway vehicle between the employee's residence and the place of employment, (2) a transit pass, and (3) qualified parking. Qualified transportation fringes are excludible from the employee's gross income to the extent categories (1) and (2) above do not exceed $65 per month and category (3) does not exceed $165 per month. These amounts are indexed annually for inflation. § 132.

Qualified tuition reduction plan. A type of fringe benefit plan that is available to employees of nonprofit educational institutions. Such employees (and the spouse and dependent children) are allowed to exclude a tuition waiver pursuant to a qualified tuition reduction plan from gross income. The exclusion applies to undergraduate tuition. In limited circumstances, the exclusion also applies to the graduate tuition of teaching and research assistants. § 117(d).

R

RAR. A Revenue Agent's Report, which reflects any adjustments made by the agent as a result of an audit of the taxpayer. The RAR is mailed to the taxpayer along with the 30-day letter, which outlines the appellate procedures available to the taxpayer.

Realized gain or loss. The difference between the amount realized upon the sale or other disposition of property and the adjusted basis of the property. § 1001. See also *adjusted basis* and *recognized gain or loss.*

Realty. All real estate, including land and buildings. Permanent improvements to a building (fixtures) become realty if their removal would cause significant damage to the property. An example of a fixture is the installation of a central air conditioning or heating system to a building. Thus, personalty can become realty through the fixture reclassification.

Reasonable needs of the business. See *accumulated earnings tax.*

Reasonableness. The Code includes a reasonableness requirement with respect to the deduction of salaries and other compensation for services. What constitutes reasonableness is a question of fact. If an expense is unreasonable, the amount that is classified as unreasonable is not allowed as a deduction. The question of reasonableness generally arises with respect to closely held corporations where there is no separation of ownership and management. § 162(a)(1).

Recapture. To recover the tax benefit of a deduction or a credit previously taken.

Recapture of depreciation. Upon the disposition of depreciable property used in a trade or business, gain or loss is determined measured by the difference between the consideration received (the amount realized) and the adjusted basis of the property. Before the enactment of the recapture of depreciation provisions of the Code, any such gain recognized could be § 1231 gain and usually qualified for long-term capital gain treatment. The recapture provisions of the Code (e.g., §§ 1245 and 1250) may operate to convert some or all of the previous § 1231 gain into ordinary income. The justification for recapture of depreciation is that it prevents a taxpayer from deducting depreciation at ordinary income rates and having the related gain on disposition taxed at capital gain rates. The recapture of depreciation rules do not apply when the property is disposed of at a loss. See also *residential rental property, Section 1231 gains and losses, Section 1245 recapture,* and *Section 1250 recapture.*

Recapture of investment tax credit. When investment tax credit property is disposed of or ceases to be used in the trade or business of the taxpayer, some or all of the investment tax credit claimed on the property may be recaptured as additional tax liability. The amount of the recapture is the difference between the amount of the credit originally claimed and what should have been claimed in light of the length of time the property was actually held or used for qualifying purposes. § 50. See also *investment tax credit.*

Recapture potential. Reference is to property that, if disposed of in a taxable transaction, would result in the recapture of depreciation (§§ 1245 or 1250) and/or of the investment tax credit (§ 50).

Recognized gain or loss. The portion of realized gain or loss that is considered in computing taxable income. See also *realized gain or loss.*

Recovery of capital doctrine. When a taxable sale or exchange occurs, the seller may be permitted to recover his or her investment (or other adjusted basis) in the property before gain or loss is recognized. See also *open transaction.*

Refundable credit. A refundable credit is a credit that is paid to the taxpayer even if the amount of the credit (or credits) exceeds the taxpayer's tax liability. See also *nonrefundable credit.*

Regulations. Treasury Department Regulations represent the position of the IRS as to how the Internal Revenue Code is to be interpreted. Their purpose is to provide taxpayers and IRS personnel with rules of general and specific application to the various provisions of the tax law. Regulations are published in the *Federal Register* and in all tax services. See also *interpretive regulation, legislative regulation, procedural regulation,* and *proposed regulation.*

Rehabilitation expenditures credit. A credit that is based on expenditures incurred to rehabilitate industrial and commercial buildings and certified historic structures. The credit, an extension of the regular investment tax credit, is intended to discourage businesses from moving from older, economically distressed areas to newer locations and to encourage the preservation of historic structures. § 47. See *rehabilitation expenditures credit recapture.*

Rehabilitation expenditures credit recapture. When property that qualifies for the rehabilitation expenditures credit is disposed of or ceases to be used in the trade or business of the taxpayer, some or all of the tax credit claimed on the property may be recaptured as additional tax liability. The amount of the recapture is the difference between the amount of the credit claimed originally and what should have been claimed in light of the length of time the property was actually held or used for qualifying purposes. § 50. See *rehabilitation expenditures credit.*

Related party. Includes certain family members and controlled entities (i.e., partnerships and corporations). §§ 267, 707(b), and 1239. See also *related-party transactions.*

Related-party transactions. The tax law places restrictions upon the recognition of gains and losses between related parties because of the potential for abuse. For example, restrictions are placed on the deduction of losses from the sale or exchange of property between related parties. In addition, under certain circumstances, related-party gains that would otherwise be classified as capital gain are classified as ordinary income. §§ 267, 707(b), and 1239. See also *related party.*

Rental activity. Any activity where payments are received principally for the use of tangible property is a rental activity. Temporary Regulations provide that in certain circumstances activities involving rentals of real and personal property are not to be *treated* as rental activities. The Temporary Regulations list six exceptions.

Research activities credit. A tax credit whose purpose is to encourage research and development. It consists of two components: the incremental research activities credit and the basic research credit. The incremental research activities credit is equal to 20 percent of the excess of qualified research expenditures over the base amount. The basic research credit is equal to 20 percent of the excess of basic research payments over the base amount. § 41. See also *general business credit.*

Research and experimental expenditures. The Code provides three alternatives for the tax treatment of research and experimentation expenditures. They may be expensed in the year paid or incurred, deferred subject to amortization, or capitalized. If the taxpayer does not elect to expense such costs or to defer them subject to amortization (over 60 months), the expenditures must be capitalized. § 174. Two types of research activities credits are available: the basic research credit and the incremental research activities credit. The rate for each type is 20 percent. § 41. See also *research activities credit.*

Reserve for bad debts. A method of accounting whereby an allowance is permitted for estimated uncollectible accounts. Actual write-offs are charged to the reserve, and recoveries of amounts previously written off are credited to the reserve. The Code permits only certain financial institutions to use the reserve method. § 166. See also *specific charge-off method.*

Reserve method. See *reserve for bad debts.*

Reserves for estimated expenses. Except in the limited case for bad debts, reserves for estimated expenses (e.g., warranty service costs) are not permitted for tax purposes even though such reserves are appropriate for financial accounting purposes. See also *all events test.*

Residential rental property. Buildings for which at least 80 percent of the gross rents are from dwelling units (e.g., an apartment building). This type of building is distinguished from nonresidential (commercial or industrial) buildings in applying the recapture of depreciation provisions. The term also is relevant in distinguishing between buildings that are eligible for a 27.5-year life versus a 39-year (or 31.5-year) life for MACRS purposes. Generally, residential buildings receive preferential treatment. §§ 168(e)(2) and 1250. See also *recapture of depreciation.*

Residential rental real estate. See *residential rental property.*

Restricted property plan. An arrangement whereby an employer transfers property (usually stock) to an employee at a bargain price (for less than the fair market value). If the transfer is accompanied by a substantial risk of forfeiture and the property is not transferable, no compensation results to the employee until the restrictions disappear. An example of a substantial risk of forfeiture would be a requirement that the employee return the property if his or her employment is terminated within a specified period of time. § 83. See also *nonqualified deferred compensation (NQDC) plans* and *substantial risk of forfeiture.*

Retirement of corporate obligations. The retirement of corporate and certain government obligations is considered to be a sale or exchange. Gain or loss, upon the retirement of a corporate obligation, therefore, is treated as capital gain or loss rather than as ordinary income or loss. §§ 1271–1275.

Return of capital doctrine. See *recovery of capital doctrine.*

Revenue neutrality. A description that characterizes tax legislation when it neither increases nor decreases the revenue result. Thus, any tax revenue losses are offset by tax revenue gains.

Revenue Procedure. A matter of procedural importance to both taxpayers and the IRS concerning the administration of the tax law is issued by the National Office of the IRS as a Revenue Procedure (abbreviated Rev.Proc.). A Revenue Procedure is first published in an *Internal Revenue Bulletin* (I.R.B.) and later transferred to the appropriate *Cumulative Bulletin* (C.B.). Both the *Internal Revenue Bulletin* and the *Cumulative Bulletin* are published by the U.S. Government Printing Office.

Revenue Ruling. A Revenue Ruling (abbreviated Rev.Rul.) is issued by the National Office of the IRS to express an official interpretation of the tax law as applied to specific transactions. It is more limited in application than a Regulation. A Revenue Ruling is first published in an *Internal Revenue Bulletin* (I.R.B.) and later transferred to the appropriate *Cumulative Bulletin* (C.B.). Both the *Internal Revenue Bulletin* and the *Cumulative Bulletin* are published by the U.S. Government Printing Office.

S

Sale or exchange. A requirement for the recognition of capital gain or loss. Generally, the seller of property must receive money or relief from debt in order to have sold the property. An exchange involves the transfer of property for other property. Thus, *collection* of a debt is neither a sale nor an exchange. The term *sale or exchange* is not defined by the Code.

Sales tax. A transaction tax imposed upon the sale of goods. It usually is based on a specified percentage of the value of the property sold. A sales tax is to be distinguished from an excise tax, since a sales tax applies to a broad variety of commodities.

Salvage value. The estimated amount a taxpayer will receive upon the disposition of an asset used in the taxpayer's trade or business. Salvage value is relevant in calculating depreciation under § 167, but is not relevant in calculating cost recovery under § 168.

Scholarships. Scholarships are generally excluded from the gross income of the recipient unless the payments are a disguised form of compensation for services rendered. However, the Code imposes restrictions on the exclusion. The recipient must be a degree candidate. The excluded amount is limited to amounts used for tuition, fees, books, supplies, and equipment required for courses of instruction. Amounts received for room and board are not eligible for the exclusion. § 117.

S corporation. See *S corporation status.*

S corporation status. An elective provision permitting certain small business corporations (§ 1361) and their shareholders to elect (§ 1362) to be treated for income tax purposes in accordance with the operating rules of §§ 1363–1379. Of major significance are the facts that S status avoids the corporate income tax and corporate losses can be claimed by the shareholders. See also *C corporation.*

Section 38 property. Property that qualified for the investment tax credit. Generally, this included all tangible property (other than real estate) used in a trade or business. § 48 prior to repeal by the Revenue Reconciliation Act of 1990. See also *investment tax credit.*

Section 121 exclusion. An exclusion of $125,000 of realized gain available to taxpayers who are age 55 or over associated with the sale of their principal residence. The taxpayer must have owned and occupied the residence for at least three years during the five-year period ending on the date of sale. The exclusion treatment is elective, and the election can be made only once. If married, both spouses must consent to the election. § 121. See also *personal residence.*

Section 179 expensing. The ability to deduct a capital expenditure in the year an asset is placed in service rather than over the asset's useful life or cost recovery period. The annual ceiling on the deduction is $17,500. However, the deduction is reduced dollar for dollar when § 179 property placed in service during the taxable year exceeds $200,000. In addition, the amount expensed under § 179 cannot exceed the aggregate amount of taxable income derived from the conduct of any trade or business by the taxpayer.

Section 401(k) plan. A cash or deferred arrangement plan that allows participants to elect to receive up to $9,500 in 1996 in cash (taxed currently) or to have a contribution made on their behalf to a profit sharing or stock bonus plan (excludible from gross income). The plan may also be in the form of a salary reduction agreement between the participant and the employer.

Section 1231 assets. Depreciable assets and real estate used in a trade or business and held for the required long-term holding period. Under certain circumstances, the classification also includes timber, coal, domestic iron ore, livestock (held for draft, breeding, dairy, or sporting purposes), and unharvested crops. § 1231(b).

Section 1231 gains and losses. If the net result of the combined gains and losses from the taxable dispositions of § 1231 assets plus the net gain from the involuntary conversion of nonpersonal use assets is a gain, the gains and losses from § 1231 assets are treated as long-term capital gains and losses. In arriving at § 1231 gains, however, the depreciation recapture provisions (e.g., §§ 1245 and 1250) are first applied to produce ordinary income. If the net result of the combination is a loss, the gains and losses from § 1231 assets are treated as ordinary gains and losses. § 1231(a). See also *recapture of depreciation.*

Section 1231 lookback. In order for gain to be classified as § 1231 gain, the gain must survive the § 1231 lookback. To the extent of nonrecaptured § 1231 losses for the five prior tax years, the gain is classified as ordinary income. § 1231(c).

Section 1231 property. See *Section 1231 assets.*

Section 1244 stock. Stock issued under § 1244 by qualifying small business corporations. If § 1244 stock is disposed of at a loss or becomes worthless, the shareholders may claim an ordinary loss rather than the usual capital loss. The annual ceiling on the ordinary loss treatment is $50,000 ($100,000 for married individuals filing jointly). See also *worthless securities.*

Section 1245 property. Property that is subject to the recapture of depreciation under § 1245. For a definition of § 1245 property, see § 1245(a)(3). See also *Section 1245 recapture.*

Section 1245 recapture. Upon a taxable disposition of § 1245 property, all depreciation claimed on the property after 1961 is recaptured as ordinary income (but not to exceed the recognized gain from the disposition). See also *recapture of depreciation.*

Section 1250 property. Real estate that is subject to the recapture of depreciation under § 1250. For a definition of § 1250 property, see § 1250(c). See also *Section 1250 recapture.*

Section 1250 recapture. Upon a taxable disposition of § 1250 property, some or all of the additional depreciation claimed on the property may be recaptured as ordinary income. Various recapture rules apply depending upon the type of property (residential or nonresidential real estate) and the date acquired. Generally, the additional depreciation is recaptured in full to the extent of the gain recognized. See also *additional depreciation* and *recapture of depreciation.*

Self-employment retirement plan. A designation for retirement plans available to self-employed taxpayers. Also referred to as H.R. 10 and Keogh plans. Under such plans, a taxpayer may deduct each year up to either 20 percent of net earnings from self-employment or $30,000, whichever is less. If the plan is a profit sharing plan, the percentage is 13.043 percent.

Self-employment tax. In 1996, a tax of 12.4 percent is levied on individuals with net earnings from self-employment (up to $62,700) to provide Social Security benefits (i.e., the old age, survivors, and disability insurance portion) for such individuals. In addition, in 1996, a tax of 2.9 percent is levied on individuals with net earnings from self-employment (with no statutory ceiling) to provide Medicare benefits (i.e., the hospital insurance portion) for such individuals. If a self-employed individual also receives wages from an employer that are subject to FICA, the self-employment tax will be reduced if total income subject to Social Security is more than $62,700. A partial deduction is allowed in calculating the self-employment tax. Individuals with net earnings of $400 or more from self-employment are subject to this tax.

Separate property. In a community property jurisdiction, separate property is the property that belongs entirely to one of the spouses. Generally, it is property acquired before marriage or acquired after marriage by gift or inheritance. See also *community property.*

Severance tax. A tax imposed upon the extraction of natural resources.

Short sale. A short sale occurs when a taxpayer sells borrowed property (usually stock) and repays the lender with substantially identical property either held on the date of the short sale or purchased after the sale. No gain or loss is recognized until the short sale is closed, and such gain or loss is generally short term. § 1233.

Short taxable year (short period). A tax year that is less than 12 months. A short taxable year may occur in the initial reporting period, in the final tax year, or when the taxpayer changes tax years.

Significant participation activity. There are seven tests to determine whether an individual has achieved material participation in an activity, one of which is based on more than 500 hours of participation in significant participation activities. A significant participation activity is one in which the individual's participation exceeds 100 hours during the year.

Simplified employee pension (SEP) plan. An employer may make contributions to an employee's IRA in amounts not exceeding the lesser of 15 percent of compensation or $30,000 per individual. These employer-sponsored simplified employee pensions are permitted only if the contributions are nondiscriminatory and are made on behalf of all employees who have attained age 21 and have worked for the employer during at least three of the five preceding calendar years. § 219(b). See also *individual retirement account (IRA).*

Small business corporation. A corporation that satisfies the definition of § 1361(b), § 1244(c)(3), or both. Satisfaction of § 1361(b) permits an S corporation election, and satisfaction of § 1244 enables the shareholders of the corporation to claim an ordinary loss. See also *S corporation status* and *Section 1244 stock.*

Small business stock. See *small business corporation.*

Small cases division. A subsidiary division of the U.S. Tax Court. The jurisdiction of the Small Cases division is limited to small claims (i.e., claims of $10,000 or less). The proceedings of the Small Cases Division are informal, and the findings cannot be appealed.

Specific charge-off method. A method of accounting for bad debts in which a deduction is permitted only when an account becomes partially or completely worthless. See also *reserve for bad debts.*

Standard deduction. The individual taxpayer can either itemize deductions or take the standard deduction. The amount of the standard deduction depends on the taxpayer's filing status (single, head of household, married filing jointly, surviving spouse, or married filing separately). For 1996, the amount of the standard deduction ranges from $3,350 to $6,700. Additional standard deductions of either $800 (for married taxpayers) or $1,000 (for single taxpayers) are available if the taxpayer is either blind or age 65 or over. Limitations exist on the amount of the standard deduction of a taxpayer who is another taxpayer's dependent. Beginning in 1989, the standard deduction amounts are adjusted for inflation each year. § 63(c). See also *zero bracket amount.*

Statute of limitations. Provisions of the law that specify the maximum period of time in which action may be taken on a past event. Code §§ 6501–6504 contain the limitation periods applicable to the IRS for additional assessments, and §§ 6511–6515 relate to refund claims by taxpayers.

Statutory employee. Statutory employees are considered self-employed independent contractors for purposes of reporting income and expenses on their tax returns. Generally, a statutory employee must meet three tests:

- It is understood from a service contract that the services will be performed by the person.
- The person does not have a substantial investment in facilities (other than transportation) used to perform the services.
- The services involve a continuing relationship with the person for whom they are performed.

For further information on statutory employees, see Circular E *Employer's Tax Guide* (IRS Publication 15).

Statutory notice of deficiency. Commonly referred to as the 90-day letter, this notice is sent to a taxpayer upon request, upon the expiration of the 30-day letter, or upon exhaustion by the taxpayer of his or her administrative remedies before the IRS. The notice gives the taxpayer 90 days in which to file a petition with the U.S. Tax Court. If a petition is not filed, the IRS will issue a demand for payment of the assessed deficiency. §§ 6211–6216. See also *thirty-day letter.*

Stock bonus plan. A type of deferred compensation plan in which the employer establishes and maintains the plan and contributes employer stock to the plan for the benefit of employees. The contributions need not be dependent on the employer's profits. Any benefits of the plan are distributable in the form of employer stock, except that distributable fractional shares may be paid in cash.

Stock option. The right to purchase a stated number of shares of stock from a corporation at a certain price within a specified period of time. §§ 421 and 422. See also *incentive stock option (ISO)* and *nonqualified stock option (NQSO).*

Stock redemption. The redemption of the stock of a shareholder by the issuing corporation is treated as a sale or exchange of the stock if the redemption is not a dividend. §§ 301 and 302.

Substantial risk of forfeiture. A term that is associated with a restricted property plan. Generally, an employee who receives property (e.g., stock of the employer-corporation) from the employer at a bargain price or at no cost must include the bargain element in gross income. However, the employee currently does not have to do so if there is a substantial risk of forfeiture. A substantial risk of forfeiture exists if a person's rights to full enjoyment of property are conditioned upon the future performance, or the refraining from the performance, of substantial services by the individual. § 83. See also *restricted property plan.*

Super-full absorption costing rules. See *uniform capitalization rules.*

Surviving spouse. The joint return tax rates apply for a surviving spouse. Such rates apply for the two tax years after the tax year of the death of the spouse. To qualify as a surviving spouse, the taxpayer must maintain a household for a dependent child. § 2.

T

Targeted jobs tax credit. See *jobs credit.*

Taxable year. The annual period over which income is measured for income tax purposes. Most individuals use a calendar year, but many businesses use a fiscal year based on the natural business year. See also *accounting period* and *fiscal year.*

Tax avoidance. The minimization of one's tax liability by taking advantage of legally available tax planning opportunities. Tax avoidance can be contrasted with tax evasion, which entails the reduction of tax liability by illegal means.

Tax benefit rule. A provision that limits the recognition of income from the recovery of an expense or loss properly deducted in a prior tax year to the amount of the deduction that generated a tax benefit. § 111.

Tax Court. The U.S. Tax Court is one of three trial courts of original jurisdiction that decide litigation involving Federal income, estate, or gift taxes. It is the only trial court where the taxpayer need not first pay the deficiency assessed by the IRS. The Tax Court will not have jurisdiction over a case unless the statutory notice of deficiency (90-day letter) has been issued by the IRS and the taxpayer files the petition for hearing within the time prescribed.

Tax credits. Tax credits are amounts that directly reduce a taxpayer's tax liability. The tax benefit received from a tax credit is not dependent on the taxpayer's marginal tax rate, whereas the benefit of a tax deduction or exclusion is dependent on the taxpayer's tax bracket.

Tax credit for the elderly or disabled. An elderly (age 65 and over) or disabled taxpayer may receive a tax credit amounting to 15 percent of $5,000 ($7,500 for qualified married individuals filing jointly). This amount is reduced by Social Security benefits, excluded pension benefits, and one-half of the taxpayer's adjusted gross income in excess of $7,500 ($10,000 for married taxpayers filing jointly). § 22.

Tax-free exchange. Transfers of property specifically exempted from Federal income tax consequences. Examples are a transfer of property to a controlled corporation under § 351(a) and a like-kind exchange under § 1031(a). The recognition of gain or loss is postponed, rather than being permanently excluded, through the assignment of a carryover basis to the replacement property. See also *nontaxable exchange.*

Tax home. Since travel expenses of an employee are deductible only if the taxpayer is away from home, the deductibility of such expenses rests upon the definition of tax home. The IRS position is that tax home is the business location, post, or station of the taxpayer. If an employee is temporarily reassigned to a new post for a period of one year or less, the taxpayer's home should be his or her personal residence, and the travel expenses should be deductible. If the assignment is for more than two years, the IRS position is that it is indefinite or permanent and the taxpayer is therefore not in travel status. If the assignment is for between one and two years, the IRS position is that the location of the tax home will be determined on the basis of the facts and circumstances. The courts are in conflict regarding what constitutes a person's home for tax purposes. For such costs paid or incurred after December 31, 1992, the Energy Policy Act of 1992 provides that the taxpayer shall not be treated as temporarily away from home if the employment period exceeds one year. Thus, in this situation, the tax home will be the place of employment. See also *travel expenses.*

Tax preferences. Those items set forth in § 57 that may result in the imposition of the alternative minimum tax. See also *alternative minimum tax (AMT).*

Tax rate schedules. Rate schedules appearing in Appendix A that are used by upper-income taxpayers and those not permitted to use the tax table. Separate rate schedules are provided for married individuals filing jointly, head of household, single taxpayers, estates and trusts, and married individuals filing separate returns. § 1.

Tax research. The method used to determine the best available solution to a situation that possesses tax consequences. Both tax and nontax factors are considered.

Tax shelters. The typical tax shelter generated large losses in the early years of the activity. Investors would offset these losses against other types of income and, therefore, avoid paying income taxes on this income. These tax shelter investments could then be sold after a few years and produce capital gain income, which is taxed at a lower rate than ordinary income. The passive activity loss rules and the at-risk rules now limit tax shelter deductions.

Tax table. A tax table appearing in Appendix A that is provided for taxpayers with less than $100,000 of taxable income. Separate columns are provided for single taxpayers, married taxpayers filing jointly, head of household, and married taxpayers filing separately. § 3.

Technical advice memoranda (TAMs). TAMs are issued by the National Office of the IRS in response to questions raised by IRS field personnel during audits. They deal with completed rather than proposed transactions and are often requested for questions related to exempt organizations and employee plans.

Temporary regulation. A Regulation issued by the Treasury Department in temporary form. When speed is critical, the Treasury Department issues Temporary Regulations, which take effect immediately. These Regulations have the same authoritative value as final Regulations and may be cited as precedent for three years. Temporary Regulations are also issued as Proposed Regulations. See also *proposed regulation* and *regulations.*

Theft loss. A loss from larceny, embezzlement, and robbery. It does not include misplacement of items. See also *casualty loss.*

Thin capitalization. When debt owed by a corporation to its shareholders is large relative to its capital structure (stock and shareholder equity), the IRS may contend that the corporation is thinly capitalized. In effect, this means that some or all of the debt will be reclassified as equity. The immediate result is to disallow any interest deduction to the corporation on the reclassified debt. To the extent of the corporation's earnings and profits, interest payments and loan repayments on the reclassified debt are treated as dividends to the shareholders. § 385.

Thirty-day letter. A letter that accompanies a Revenue Agent's Report (RAR) issued as a result of an IRS audit of a taxpayer (or the rejection of a taxpayer's claim for refund). The letter outlines the taxpayer's appeal procedure before the IRS. If the taxpayer does not request any such procedures within the 30-day period, the IRS will issue a *statutory notice of deficiency* (the 90-day letter).

Timber. Special rules apply to the recognition of gain from the sale of timber. A taxpayer may elect to treat the cutting of timber that is held for sale or use in a trade or business as a sale or exchange. If the holding period requirements are met, the gain is recognized as § 1231 gain and may therefore receive long-term capital gain treatment. § 631.

Top-heavy plan. A type of retirement plan that primarily benefits key employees. Such plans allocate more than 60 percent of the cumulative benefits to key employees. Special rules are imposed to discourage retirement plans from conferring disproportionate benefits on key employees.

Trade or business expenses. Deductions *for* AGI that are attributable to a taxpayer's business or profession. Some employee expenses may also be treated as trade or business expenses. See also *employee expenses.*

Transportation expenses. Transportation expenses for an employee include only the cost of transportation (taxi fares, automobile expenses, etc.) in the course of employment when the employee is not away from home in travel status. Commuting expenses are not deductible. See also *automobile expenses.*

Travel expenses. Travel expenses include meals (subject to a 50 percent disallowance) and lodging and transportation expenses while away from home in the pursuit of a trade or business (including that of an employee). See also *tax home.*

Trial court. The court of original jurisdiction; the first court to consider litigation. In Federal tax controversies, trial courts include U.S. District Courts, the U.S. Tax Court, and the U.S. Court of Federal Claims. See also *appellate court.*

U

Unearned income. Also referred to as investment income, it includes such income as interest, dividends, capital gains, rents, royalties, and pension and annuity income. See also *kiddie tax.*

Unearned (prepaid) income. For tax purposes, prepaid income (e.g., rent) is taxable in the year of receipt. In certain cases involving advance payments for goods and services, income may be deferred. See Rev.Proc. 71–21 (1971–2 C.B. 549) and Reg. § 1.451–5. See also *accrual method.*

Uniform capitalization rules. Under § 263A, the Regulations provide a set of rules that all taxpayers (regardless of the particular industry) can use to determine the items of cost (and means of allocating those costs) that must be capitalized with respect to the production of tangible property.

Unreasonable compensation. Under § 162(a)(1), a deduction is allowed for "reasonable" salaries or other compensation for personal services actually rendered. To the extent compensation is excessive ("unreasonable"), no deduction will be allowed. The problem of unreasonable compensation usually is limited to closely held corporations where the motivation is to pay out profits in some form deductible to the corporation. Deductible compensation, therefore, becomes an attractive substitute for nondeductible dividends when the shareholders are also employees of the corporation.

U.S. Court of Federal Claims. See *Claims Court.*

Use tax. A use tax is an ad valorem tax, usually at the same rate as the sales tax, on the use or consumption of tangible personalty. The purpose of a use tax is to prevent the avoidance of a sales tax.

U.S. Supreme Court. The highest appellate court or the court of last resort in the Federal court system and in most states. Only a small number of tax decisions of the U.S. Courts of Appeal are reviewed by the U.S. Supreme Court under its certiorari procedure. The Supreme Court usually grants certiorari to resolve a conflict among the Courts of Appeal (e.g., two or more appellate courts have assumed opposing positions on a particular issue) or when the tax issue is extremely important (e.g., size of the revenue loss to the Federal government).

U.S. Tax Court. See *Tax Court.*

USTC. Published by Commerce Clearing House, *U.S. Tax Cases* contain all of the Federal tax decisions issued by the U.S. District Courts, U.S. Court of Federal Claims, U.S. Courts of Appeals, and the U.S. Supreme Court.

V

Vacation home. The Code places restrictions upon taxpayers who rent their residences or vacation homes for part of the tax year. The restrictions may result in a scaling down of expense deductions for the taxpayers. § 280A. See also *hobby loss.*

Value added tax (VAT). A national sales tax that taxes the increment in value as goods move through the production process. A VAT is much used in other countries, but has not yet been incorporated as part of the U.S. Federal tax structure.

Vesting requirements. A qualified deferred compensation arrangement must satisfy a vesting requirement. Under this provision, an employee's right to accrued plan benefits derived from employer contributions must be nonforfeitable in accordance with one of two vesting time period schedules.

W

Wash sale. A loss from the sale of stock or securities that is disallowed because the taxpayer within 30 days before or after the sale has acquired stock or securities that are substantially identical to those sold. § 1091.

Wherewithal to pay. This concept recognizes the inequity of taxing a transaction when the taxpayer lacks the means with which to pay the tax. Under it, there is a correlation between the imposition of the tax and the ability to pay the tax. It is particularly suited to situations in which the taxpayer's economic position has not changed significantly as a result of the transaction.

Withholding allowances. The number of withholding allowances serves as the basis for determining the amount of income taxes withheld from an employee's salary or wages. The more withholding allowances claimed, the less income tax withheld by an employer. An employee may claim withholding allowances for personal exemptions for self and spouse (unless claimed as a dependent of another person), dependency exemptions, and special withholding allowances.

Working condition fringe. A type of fringe benefit received by the employee that is excludible from the employee's gross income. It consists of property or services provided (paid or reimbursed) by the employer for which the employee could take a tax deduction if the employee had paid for them. § 132.

Worthless securities. A loss (usually capital) is allowed for a security that becomes worthless during the year. The loss is deemed to have occurred on the last day of the year. Special rules apply to securities of affiliated companies and small business stock. § 165. See also *Section 1244 stock.*

Writ of certiorari. See *certiorari.*

Z

Zero bracket amount. A deduction that was generally available to all individual taxpayers in arriving at taxable income. It represented the equivalent of the standard deduction for taxable years before 1987. The taxpayer did not take a deduction for the zero bracket amount because it was built into the tax tables and tax rate schedules. Because the amount was built in, if the taxpayer itemized deductions, only the excess itemized deductions (amount of the itemized deductions in excess of the zero bracket amount) were deductible. TRA of 1986 repealed the zero bracket amount and replaced it with the standard deduction for 1987 and thereafter. The zero bracket amount for 1986 is presently used in the 10-year forward averaging calculation for lump-sum distributions. § 63(c). See also *standard deduction.*

APPENDIX D-1

Table of Code Sections Cited

[See Title 26 U.S.C.A.]

Appendix D-2

Table of Regulations Cited

Temporary Treasury Regulations

Proposed Treasury Regulations

Proposed Treasury Regulations

Proposed Treasury Regulations

Proposed Treasury Regulations

Proposed Treasury Regulations

APPENDIX D-3

Table of Revenue Procedures and Revenue Rulings Cited

Revenue Procedure

Rev.Proc.	This Work Page
71-21	4-13, 4-14, 4-40
83-35	8-6
83-78	2-44
84-74	18-38
85-16	18-8
87-1	2-29
87-32	18-8, 18-38
87-56	2-37, 8-8, 8-23, 8-49, 12-11
87-57	8-37, 8-42, 15-4
89-12	20-3
92-20	18-19, 18-38
92-71	6-29
94-27	10-16, 10-33
94-73	10-7
95-73	9-5
96-3	2-10

Revenue Rulings

Rev.Rul.	This Work Page
53-61	4-4
53-190	9-5
54-567	2-30
55-261	10-6
55-525	19-27
56-60	14-15
56-406	14-20
57-244	15-27
57-344	3-11
57-345	10-10
57-418	6-17
57-502	9-36
58-419	3-11
59-72	15-19
59-86	14-13

Revenue Rulings

Rev.Rul.	This Work Page
60-31	19-27
61-119	15-6
61-186	3-42
62-102	5-7
63-221	15-10
63-232	7-9
64-221	3-42
65-34	2-30
65-178	19-7
65-235	2-37
66-7	16-16
67-297	10-16
68-99	4-55
68-212	10-6
68-579	5-47
68-662	6-13
69-185	2-44
69-292	9-13
70-466	15-12
70-558	9-36
70-622	10-10
71-190	10-12
71-425	5-3
72-25	4-55
72-312	4-15
72-545	6-26
72-592	7-9
73-380	19-7
73-476	15-28
74-78	9-13
74-175	16-30
75-14	6-19
75-168	9-7
75-380	9-4
75-448	5-10
76-111	14-40
76-282	18-38

Revenue Rulings

APPENDIX E
Citator Example

ILLUSTRATION OF THE USE OF THE CITATOR

BACKGROUND

The *Federal Tax Citator* is a separate multivolume service with monthly supplements.[1] Cases reported by the *Citator* are divided into the various issues involved. Since the researcher may be interested in only one or two issues, only those cases involving the particular issue need to be checked.

The *Federal Tax Citator* includes the following volumes, each of which covers a particular period of time:

- Volume 1 (1863–1941)
- Volume 2 (1942–1948)
- Volume 3 (1948–1954)
- Volume 1, Second Series (1954–1977)
- Volume 2, Second Series (1978–1989)
- Cumulative supplement (1990–1995)
- Monthly cumulative supplements (paperback)

Through the use of symbols, the *Citator* indicates whether a decision has been followed, explained, criticized, questioned, or overruled by a later court decision. These symbols are reproduced in Figure E–1.

EXAMPLE

Determine the background and validity of *Adda v. Comm.*, 37 AFTR 654, 171 F.2d 457 (CA–4, 1948).

SOLUTION

Turning directly to the case itself (reproduced as Figure E–2), note the two issues involved (issues 1 and 2). For purposes of emphasis, these issues have been bracketed and identified by a marginal notation in the figure. The reason for the division of the issues becomes apparent when the case is traced through the *Citator.*

Refer to Volume 3 of the First Series (covering the period from October 7, 1948, through July 29, 1954) of the *Federal Tax Citator.* The case reference is located on page 5505, which is reproduced in Figure E–3.

Correlating the symbols in Figure E–1 with the shaded portion of Figure E–3 reveals the following information about *Adda v. Comm.:*

[1] Features in the *Federal Tax Citator* that do not appear in the CCH *Citator* include the following: (1) distinguishes between the various issues in the case, (2) lists all court decisions that cite the court decision being researched, (3) indicates the relationship (e.g., explained, criticized, followed, or overruled) between the court decision being researched and subsequent decisions, and (4) pinpoints the exact page on which one court decision is cited by another court decision. Prior to the acquisition of Prentice-Hall Information Services, the *Federal Tax Citator* was published by Prentice-Hall. The *Federal Tax Citator* is now published by Research Institute of America.

▼ FIGURE E–1

Citator Symbols*
COURT DECISIONS
Judicial History of the Case

a	affirmed (by decision of a higher court)
d	dismissed (appeal to a higher court dismissed)
m	modified (decision modified by a higher court, or on rehearing)
r	reversed (by a decision of a higher court)
s	same case (e.g., on rehearing)
rc	related case (companion cases and other cases arising out of the same subject matter are so designated)
x	certiorari denied (by the Supreme Court of the United States)
(C or G)	The Commissioner or Solicitor General has made the appeal
(T)	Taxpayer has made the appeal
(A)	Tax Court's decision acquiesced in by Commissioner
(NA)	Tax Court's decision nonacquiesced in by Commissioner
sa	same case affirmed (by the cited case)
sd	same case dismissed (by the cited case)
sm	same case modified (by the cited case)
sr	same case reversed (by the cited case)
sx	same case—certiorari denied

Syllabus of the Cited Case

iv	four (on all fours with the cited case)
f	followed (the cited case followed)
e	explained (comment generally favorable, but not to a degree that indicates the cited case is followed)
k	reconciled (the cited case reconciled)
n	dissenting opinion (cited in a dissenting opinion)
g	distinguished (the cited case distinguished either in law or on the facts)
l	limited (the cited case limited to its facts. Used when an appellate court so limits a prior decision, or a lower court states that in its opinion the cited case should be so limited)
c	criticized (adverse comment on the cited case)
q	questioned (the cited case not only criticized, but its correctness questioned)
o	overruled

*Reproduced from the *Federal Tax 2nd Citator* with the permission of the publisher, Research Institute of America, Englewood Cliffs, NJ 07632.

- Application for certiorari (appeal to the U.S. Supreme Court) filed by the taxpayer (T) on March 1, 1949.
- Certiorari was denied (x) by the U.S. Supreme Court on April 18, 1949.
- The trial court decision is reported in 10 T.C. 273 and was affirmed on appeal (sa) to the Fourth Court of Appeals.
- During the time frame of Volume 3 of the *Citator* (October 7, 1948, through July 29, 1954), one decision (*Milner Hotels, Inc.*) has agreed "on all fours with the cited case" (iv). One decision (*Comm. v. Nubar*) has limited the cited case

▼ FIGURE E–2

ADDA v. COMMISSIONER OF INTERNAL REVENUE 457
Cite as 171 F.2d 457

ADDA v. COMMISSIONER OF INTERNAL REVENUE.
No. 5796.

United States Court of Appeals
Fourth Circuit.
Dec. 3, 1948.

ISSUE 1

1. Internal revenue ⚷792

Where nonresident alien's brother residing in United States traded for alien's benefit on commodity exchanges in United States at authorization of alien, who vested full discretion in brother with regard thereto, and many transactions were effected through different brokers, several accounts were maintained, and substantial gains and losses realized, transactions constituted a "trade or business," profits of which were "capital gains" taxable as income to the alien. 26 U.S.C.A. § 211(b).

See Words and Phrases, Permanent Edition, for other judicial constructions and definitions of "Capital Gains" and "Trade or Business".

ISSUE 2

2. Internal revenue ⚷792

The exemption of a nonresident alien's commodity transactions in the United States provided for by the Internal Revenue Code does not apply where alien has agent in United States using his own discretion in effecting transactions for alien's account. 26 U.S.C.A. § 211(b).

On Petition to Review the Decision of The Tax Court of the United States.

Petition by Fernand C. A. Adda to review a decision of the Tax Court redetermining a deficiency in income tax imposed by the Commissioner of Internal Revenue.

Decision affirmed.

Rollin Browne and Mitchell B. Carroll, both of New York City, for petitioner.

Irving I. Axelrad, Sp. Asst. to Atty. Gen. (Theron Lamar Caudle, Asst. Atty. Gen., and Ellis N. Slack and A. F. Prescott, Sp. Assts. to Atty. Gen., on the brief), for respondent.

Before PARKER, Chief Judge, and SOPER and DOBIE, Circuit Judges.

PER CURIAM.

[1, 2] This is a petition by a non-resident alien to review a decision of the Tax Court. Petitioner is a national of Egypt, who in the year 1941 was residing in France. He had a brother who at that time was residing in the United States and who traded for petitioner's benefit on commodity exchanges in the United States in cotton, wool, grains, silk, hides and copper. This trading was authorized by petitioner who vested full discretion in his brother with regard thereto, and it resulted in profits in the sum of $193,857.14. The Tax Court said: "While the number of transactions or the total amount of money involved in them has not been stated, it is apparent that many transactions were effected through different brokers, several accounts were maintained, and gains and losses in substantial amounts were realized. This evidence shows that the trading was extensive enough to amount to a trade or business, and the petitioner does not contend, nor has he shown, that the transactions were so infrequent or inconsequential as not to amount to a trade or business." We agree with the Tax Court that, for reasons adequately set forth in its opinion, this income was subject to taxation, and that the exemption of a non-resident alien's commodity transactions in the United States, provided by section 211(b) of the Internal Revenue Code, 26 U.S.C.A. § 211(b), does not apply to a case where the alien has an agent in the United States using his own discretion in effecting the transactions for the alien's account. As said by the Tax Court, "Through such transactions the alien is engaging in trade or business within the United States, and the profits on these transactions are capital gains taxable to him." Nothing need be added to the reasoning of the Tax Court in this connection, and the decision will be affirmed on its opinion.

Affirmed.

to its facts (1) and two decisions (*The Scottish American Investment Co., Ltd.* and *Zareh Nubar*) have distinguished the cited case on issue number one (g-1).

Reference to Volume 1 of the *Citator* Second Series (covering the period from 1954 through 1977) shows the *Adda v. Comm.* case on page 25, which is reproduced in Figure E–4.

▼ FIGURE E–3

ADAMSON, JAMES H. & MARION C. v U. S., — F Supp —, 36 AFTR 1529, 1946 P.-H. ¶ 72,418 (DC Calif) (See Adamson v U. S.)

ADAMSON, R. R., MRS., — BTA —, 1934 (P.-H.) BTA Memo. Dec. ¶ 34,370

ADAMSON v U. S., 26 AFTR 1188 (DC Calif, Sept 8, 1939)
iv—Coggan, Linus C., 1939 (P.-H.) BTA Memo. Dec. page 39—806

ADAMSON; U. S. v, 161 F(2d) 942, 35 AFTR 1404 (CCA 9)
1—Lazier v U. S., 170 F(2d) 524, 37 AFTR 545, 1948 P.-H. page 73,174 (CCA 8)
1—Grace Bros., Inc. v Comm., 173 F(2d) 178, 37 AFTR 1014, 1949 P.-H. page 72,433 (CCA 9)
1—Briggs; Hofferbert v, 178 F(2d) 744, 38 AFTR 1219, 1950 P.-H. page 72,267 (CCA 4)
1—Rogers v Comm., 180 F(2d) 722, 39 AFTR 115, 1950 P.-H. page 72,531 (CCA 3)
1—Lamar v Granger, 99 F Supp 41, 40 AFTR 270, 1951 P.-H. page 72,945 (DC Pa)
1—Herbert v Riddell, 103 F Supp 383, 41 AFTR 975, 1952 P.-H. page 72,383 (DC Calif)
1—Hudson, Galvin, 20 TC 737, 20-1953 P.-H. TC 418

ADAMSON v U. S., — F Supp —, 36 AFTR 1529, 1946 P.-H. ¶ 72,418 (DC Calif, Jan 28, 1946)

ADAMS-ROTH BAKING CO., 8 BTA 458
1—Gunderson Bros. Engineering Corp., 16 TC 129, 16-1951 P.-H. TC 72

ADAMSTON FLAT GLASS CO. v COMM., 162 F(2d) 875, 35 AFTR 1579 (CCA 6)
4—Forrest Hotel Corp. v. Fly, 112 F Supp 789, 43 AFTR 1080, 1953 P.-H. page 72,856 (DC Miss)

ADDA v COMM., 171 F(2d) 457, 37 AFTR 654, 1948 P.-H. ¶ 72,655 (CCA 4, Dec 3, 1948)
Cert. filed, March 1, 1949 (T)
No cert. (G) 1949 P-H ¶ 71,050
x—Adda v Comm., 336 US 952, 69 S Ct 883, 93 L Ed 1107, April 18, 1949 (T)
sa—Adda, Fernand C. A., 10 TC 273 (No. 33), ¶ 10.33 P.-H. TC 1948
iv—Milner Hotels, Inc., N. Y., 173 F (2d) 567, 37 AFTR 1170, 1949 P.-H. page 72,528 (CCA 6)
1—Nubar; Comm. v, 185 F(2d) 588, 39 AFTR 1315, 1950 P.-H. page 73,423 (CCA 4)
g-1—Scottish Amer. Invest. Co., Ltd., The, 12 TC 59, 12-1949 P.-H. TC 32
g-1—Nubar, Zareh, 13 TC 579, 13-1949 P.-H. TC 318

ADDA, FERNAND C. A., 10 TC 273 (No. 33), ¶ 10.33 P.-H. TC 1948 (A) 1948-2 CB 1
a—Adda v Comm., 171 F(2d) 457, 37 AFTR 654, 1948 P.-H. ¶ 72,655 (CCA 4)
1—Nubar; Comm. v, 185 F(2d) 588, 39 AFTR 1315, 1950 P.-H. page 73,423 (CCA 4)
g-1—Scottish Amer. Invest. Co., Ltd., The, 12 TC 59, 12-1949 P.-H. TC 32
g-1—Nubar, Zareh, 13 TC 579, 13-1949 P.-H. TC 318

ADDA, FERNAND C. A., 10 TC 1291 (No. 168), ¶ 10.168 P.-H. TC 1948 (A) 1953-1 CB 3, 1953 P.-H. ¶ 76,453 (NA) 1948-2 CB 5, 1948 P.-H. ¶ 76,434 withdrawn
1—Scottish Amer. Invest. Co., Ltd., The, 12 TC 59, 12-1949 P.-H. TC 32

ADDA INC., 9 TC 199 (A) 1949-1 CB 1, 1949 P.-H. ¶ 76,260 (NA) 1947-2 CB 6 withdrawn
a—Adda, Inc.; Comm. v, 171 F(2d) 367, 37 AFTR 641, 1948 P.-H. ¶ 72,654 (CCA 2)
a—Adda, Inc.; Comm. v, 171 F(2d) 367, 37 AFTR 641, 1949 P.-H. ¶ 72,303 (CCA 2)
e-1—G.C.M. 26069, 1949-2 CB 38, 1949 P.-H. page 76,226
3—Koshland, Execx.; U.S. v, 208 F(2d) 640, — AFTR —, 1953 P.-H. page 73,597 (CCA 9)
4—Kent, Otis Beall, 1954 (P. H.) TC Memo. Dec page 54—47

ADDA, INC.; COMM. v, 171 F(2d) 367, 37 AFTR 641, 1948 P.-H. ¶ 72,654 (CCA 2, Dec 6, 1948)
sa—Adda, Inc., 9 TC 199
s—Adda, Inc.; Comm. v, 171 F(2d) 367, 37 AFTR 641, 1949 P.-H. ¶ 72,303 (CCA 2) reh. den.
e-1—G.C.M. 26069, 1949-2 CB 39, 1949 P.-H. page 76,227
e-2—G.C.M. 26069, 1949-2 CB 39, 1949 P.-H. page 76,227

ADDA, INC.; COMM. v, 171 F(2d) 367, 37 AFTR 641, 1949 P.-H. ¶ 72,303 (CCA 2, Dec 6, 1948) reh. den.
sa—Adda, Inc., 9 TC 199
s—Adda, Inc.; Comm. v, 171 F(2d) 367, 37 AFTR 641, 1948 P.-H. ¶ 72,654 (CCA 2)

ADDISON-CHEVROLET SALES, INC. v CHAMBERLAIN, L. A. & NAT. BANK OF WASH., THE, — F Supp —, — AFTR —, 1954 P.-H. ¶ 72,550 (DC DC) (See Campbell v Chamberlain)

ADDISON v COMM., 177 F(2d) 521, 38 AFTR 821, 1949 P.-H. ¶ 72,637 (CCA 8, Nov 3, 1949)
sa—Addison, Irene D., — TC —, 1948 (P.-H.) TC Memo. Dec. ¶ 48,177
1—Roberts, Supt. v U. S., 115 Ct Cl 439, 87 F Supp 937, 38 AFTR 1314, 1950 P.-H. page 72,292
1—Cold Metal Process Co., The, 17 TC 934, 17-1951 P.-H. TC 512
1—Berger, Samuel & Lillian, 1954 (P.-H.) TC Memo. Dec. page 54—232
2—Urquhart, George Gordon & Mary F., 20 TC 948, 20-1953 P.-H. TC 536

ADDISON, IRENE D., — TC —, 1948 (P.-H.) TC Memo. Dec. ¶ 48,177
App (T) Jan 14. 1949 (CCA 8)
a—Addison v Comm., 177 F(2d) 521, 38 AFTR 821, 1949 P.-H. ¶ 72,637 (CCA 8)
1—Urquhart, George Gordon & Mary F., 20 TC 948, 20-1953 P.-H. TC 536

ADDITON, HARRY L. & ANNIE S., 3 TC 427
1—Lum, Ralph E., 12 TC 379, 12-1949 P.-H. TC 204
1—Christie, John A. & Elizabeth H., — TC —, 1949 (P.-H.) TC Memo. Dec. page 49—795

ADDRESSOGRAPH - MULTIGRAPH CORP., 1945 (P.-H.) TC Memo. Dec. ¶ 45,058
f-10—Rev. Rul. 54-71, 1954 P.-H. page 76,453

ADDRESSOGRAPH-MULTIGRAPH CORP. v U. S., 112 Ct Cl 201, 78 F Supp 111, 37 AFTR 53, 1948 P.-H. ¶ 72,504 (June 1, 1948)
No cert (G) 1949 P.-H. ¶ 71,041
1—New Oakmont Corp., The v U. S., 114 Ct Cl 686, 86 F Supp 901, 38 AFTR 924, 1949 P.-H. page 73,181

ADELAIDE PARK LAND, 25 BTA 211
g—Amer. Security & Fidelity Corp., — BTA —, 1940 (P.-H.) BTA Memo. Dec. page 40—571

ADELPHI PAINT & COLOR WORKS, INC., 18 BTA 436
1—Neracher, William A., — BTA —, 1939 (P.-H.) BTA Memo. Dec. page 39—69
1—Lyman-Hawkins Lumber Co., — BTA —, 1939 (P.-H.) BTA Memo. Dec. page 39—350

ADEMAN v U. S., 174 F(2d) 283, 37 AFTR 1406 (CCA 9, April 25, 1949)

ADICONIS, NOELLA L. (PATNAUDE), 1953 (P.-H.) TC Memo. Dec. ¶ 53,305

ADJUSTMENT BUREAU OF ST. LOUIS ASSN., OF CREDIT MEN, 21 BTA 232
1—Cook County Loss Adjustment Bureau, — BTA —, 1940 (P.-H.) BTA Memo. Dec. page 40—331

ADKINS, CHARLES I., — BTA —, 1933 (P.-H.) BTA Memo. Dec. ¶ 33,457

ADLER v COMM., 77 F(2d) 733, 16 AFTR 162 (CCA 5)
g-2—McEuen v Comm., 196 F(2d) 130, 41 AFTR 1172, 1952 P.-H. page 72,604 (CCA 5)

Reproduced from the *Federal Taxes 2nd Citator* with permission of the publisher, Research Institute of America, Englewood Cliffs, N.J. 07632.

▼ FIGURE E–4

ADASKAVICH, STEPHEN A. v U.S., 39 AFTR2d 77-517, 422 F Supp 276 (DC Mont) (See Wiegand, Charles J., Jr v U.S.)

AD. AURIEMA, INC., 1943 P-H TC Memo ¶ 43,422
e-1—Miller v U.S., 13 AFTR2d 1515, 166 Ct Cl 257, 331 F2d 859

ADAY v SUPERIOR CT. OF ALAMEDA COUNTY, 8 AFTR2d 5367, 13 Cal Reptr 415, 362 P2d 47 (Calif, 5-11-61)

ADCO SERVICE, INC., ASSIGNEE v CYBERMATICS, INC., 36 AFTR2d 75-6342 (NJ) (See Adco Service, Inc., Assignee v Graphic Color Plate)

ADCO SERVICE, INC., ASSIGNEE v GRAPHIC COLOR PLATE, 36 AFTR2d 75-6342 (NJ, Supr Ct, 11-10-75)

ADCO SERVICE, INC., ASSIGNEE v GRAPHIC COLOR PLATE, INC., 36 AFTR2d 75-6342 (NJ) (See Adco Service, Inc., Assignee v Graphic Color Plate)

ADDA v COMM., 171 F2d 457, 37 AFTR 654 (USCA 4)
Rev. Rul. 56-145, 1956-1 CB 613
1—Balanovski; U.S. v, 236 F2d 304, 49 AFTR 2013 (USCA 2)
1—Liang, Chang Hsiao, 23 TC 1045, 23-1955 P-H TC 624
f-1—Asthmanefrin Co., Inc., 25 TC 1141, 25-1956 P-H TC 639
g-1—de Vegvar, Edward A. Neuman, 28 TC 1061, 28-1957 P-H TC 599
g-1—Purvis, Ralph E. & Patricia Lee, 1974 P-H TC Memo 74-669
k-1—deKrause, Piedad Alvarado, 1974 P-H TC Memo 74-1291
1—Rev. Rul. 56-392, 1956-2 CB 971

ADDA, FERNAND C.A., 10 TC 273, ¶ 10,133 P-H TC 1948
1—Balanovski; U.S. v, 236 F2d 303, 49 AFTR 2012 (USCA 2)
1—Liang, Chang Hsiao, 23 TC 1045, 23-1955 P-H TC 624
g-1—de Vegvar, Edward A. Neuman, 28 TC 1061, 28-1957 P-H TC 599
g-1—Purvis, Ralph E. & Patricia Lee, 1974 P-H TC Memo 74-669
k-1—deKrause, Piedad Alvarado, 1974 P-H TC Memo 74-1291

ADDA, INC., 9 TC 199
Pardee, Marvin L., Est. of, 49 TC 152, 49 P-H TC 107 [See 9 TC 206-208]
f-1—Asthmanefrin Co., Inc., 25 TC 1141, 25-1956 P-H TC 639
1—Keil Properties, Inc. (Dela), 24 TC 1117, 24-1955 P-H TC 615
1—Saffan, Samuel, 1957 P-H TC Memo 57—701
1—Rev. Rul. 56-145, 1956-1 CB 613
1—Rev. Rul. 56-392, 1956-2 CB 971
4— Midler Court Realty, Inc., 61 TC 597, 61 P-H TC 368

ADDA, INC.; COMM. v, 171 F2d 367, 37 AFTR 641 (USCA 2)
1—Pardee, Marvin L., Est. of, 49 TC 152, 49 P-H TC 107
1—Saffan, Samuel, 1957 P-H TC Memo 57-701
2—Midler Court Realty, Inc., 61 TC 597, 61 P-H TC 368

ADDELSTON, ALBERT A. & SARAH M., 1965 P-H TC Memo ¶ 65,215

ADDISON v COMM., 177 F2d 521, 38 AFTR 821 (USCA 8)
g-1—Industrial Aggregate Co. v U.S., 6 AFTR2d 5963, 284 F2d 645 (USCA 8)
1—Sturgeon v McMahon, 155 F Supp 630, 52 AFTR 789 (DC NY)
1—Gilmore v U.S., 16 AFTR2d 5211, 5213, 245 F Supp 384, 386 (DC Calif)
1—Waldheim & Co., Inc., 25 TC 599, 25-1955 P-H TC 332
g-1—Galewitz, Samuel & Marian, 50 TC 113, 50 P-H TC 79
1—Buder, G. A., Est. of, 1963 P-H TC Memo 63-345
e-1—Rhodes, Lynn E. & Martha E., 1963 P-H TC Memo 63-1374
2—Shipp v Comm., 217 F2d 402, 46 AFTR 1170 (USCA 9)

ADDISON—Contd.
g-2—Industrial Aggregate Co. v U.S., 6 AFTR2d 5964, 284 F2d 645 (USCA 8)
e-2—Buder, Est. of v Comm., 13 AFTR2d 1238, 330 F2d 443 (USCA 8)
2—Iowa Southern Utilities Co. v Comm., 14 AFTR2d 5063, 333 F2d 385 (USCA 8)
2—Kelly, Daniel, S.W., 23 TC 687, 23-1955 P-H TC 422
f-2—Morgan, Joseph P., Est. of, 37 TC 36, 37, 37-1961 P-H TC 26, 27
n-2—Woodward, Fred W. & Elsie M., 49 TC 385, 49 P-H TC 270

ADDISON, IRENE D., 1948 P-H TC Memo ¶ 48,177
1—Waldheim & Co., Inc., 25 TC 599, 25-1955 P-H TC 332
f-1—Morgan, Joseph P., Est. of, 37 TC 36, 37, 37-1961 P-H TC 26, 27
1—Buder, G. A., Est. of, 1963 P-H TC Memo 63-345
e-1—Rhodes, Lynn E. & Martha E., 1963 P-H TC Memo 63-1374

ADDISON, JOHN MILTON, BKPT; U.S. v, 20 AFTR2d 5630, 384 F2d 748 (USCA 5) (See Rochelle Jr., Trtee; U.S. v)

ADDRESSOGRAPH - MULTIGRAPH CORP., 1945 P-H TC Memo ¶ 45,058
Conn. L. & P. Co., The v U.S., 9 AFTR2d 679, 156 Ct Cl 312, 314, 299 F2d 264
Copperhead Coal Co., Inc., 1958 P-H TC Memo 58-33
1—Seas Shipping Co., Inc. v Comm., 19 AFTR2d 596, 371 F2d 529 (USCA 2)
e-1—Hitchcock, E. R., Co., The v U.S., 35 AFTR2d 75-1207, 514 F2d 487 (USCA 2)
f-2—Vulcan Materials Co. v U.S., 25 AFTR2d 70-446, 308 F Supp 57 (DC Ala)
f-3—Marlo Coil Co. v U.S., 1969 P-H 58,133 (Ct Cl Comr Rep)
4—United Gas Improvement Co. v Comm., 240 F2d 318, 50 AFTR 1354 (USCA 3)
10—St. Louis Co. (Del) (in Dissolution) v U.S., 237 F2d 156, 50 AFTR 257 (USCA 3)

ADDRESSOGRAPH - MULTIGRAPH CORP. v U.S., 112 Ct Cl 201, 78 F Supp 111, 37 AFTR 53
f-1—St. Joseph Lead Co. v U.S., 9 AFTR2d 712, 299 F2d 350 (USCA 2)
e-1—Central & South West Corp. v U.S., 1968 P-H 58,175 (Ct Cl Comr Rep)
1—Smale & Robinson, Inc. v U.S., 123 F Supp 469, 46 AFTR 375 (DC Calif)
1—St. Joseph Lead Co. v U.S., 7 AFTR2d 401, 190 F Supp 640 (DC NY)
1—Eisenstadt Mfg. Co., 28 TC 230, 28-1957 P-H TC 132
f-2—St. Joseph Lead Co. v U.S., 9 AFTR2d 712, 299 F2d 350 (USCA 2)
f-3—Consol. Coppermines Corp. v U.S., 8 AFTR2d 5873, 155 Ct Cl 736, 296 F2d 745

ADELAIDE PARK LAND, 25 BTA 211
g—Custom Component Switches, Inc. v U.S., 19 AFTR2d 560 (DC Calif) [See 25 BTA 215]
O'Connor, John C., 1957 P-H TC Memo 57-190

ADELBERG, MARVIN & HELEN, 1971 P-H TC Memo ¶ 71,015

ADELMAN v U.S., 27 AFTR2d 71-1464, 440 F2d 991 (USCA 9, 5-3-71)
sa—Adelman v U.S., 24 AFTR2d 69-5769, 304 F Supp 599 (DC Calif)

ADELMAN v U.S., 24 AFTR2d 69-5769, 304 F Supp 599 (DC Calif, 9-30-69)
a—Adelman v U.S., 27 AFTR2d 71-1464, 440 F2d 991 (USCA 9)

ADELSON, SAMUEL; U.S. v, 52 AFTR 1798 (DC RI) (See Sullivan Co., Inc.: U.S. v)

ADELSON v U.S., 15 AFTR2d 246, 342 F2d 332 (USCA 9, 1-13-65)
sa—Adelson v U.S., 12 AFTR2d 5010, 221 F Supp 31 (DC Calif)
g-1—Greenlee, L. C. & Gladys M., 1966 P-H TC Memo 66-985
f-1—Cochran, Carol J., 1973 P-H TC Memo 73-459
f-1—Marchionni, Siro L., 1976 P-H TC Memo 76-1321
f-2—Krist, Edwin F. v Comm., 32 AFTR2d 73-5663, 483 F2d 1351 (USCA 2)
f-2—Fugate v U.S., 18 AFTR2d 5607, 259 F Supp 401 (DC Tex) [See 15 AFTR2d 249, 342 F2d 335]

Correlating the symbols in Figure E–1 with the shaded portion of Figure E–4 reveals the following additional information about *Adda v. Comm.*:

- The case was cited without comment in two rulings and two cases: Rev.Rul. 56–145 , Rev.Rul. 56–392 , *Balanovski,* and *Liang.*
- It was followed in *Asthmanefrin Co.* (f-1).
- It was distinguished in *de Vegvar* and *Purvis* (g-1).
- It was reconciled in *deKrause* (k-1).

Reference to the "Court Decisions" section of Volume 2, Second Series of the *Citator* (covering the period from 1978 through 1989) shows that *Adda v. Comm.* was cited in *Judith C. Connelly* and *Robert E. Cleveland,* with each case limited to its facts (1). This page (22) is reproduced in Figure E–5.

The *Citator* includes a cumulative supplement (i.e., 1990–1995), and a cumulative monthly supplement is published each month. Be sure to refer to these supplements, or very recent citations might be overlooked. No citations appear in the supplements for *Adda v. Comm.*

Except as otherwise noted, it appears that *Adda v. Comm.* has withstood the test of time.

▼ FIGURE E–5

22 **ADAMSON—ADELSON**

ADAMSON, LEE A., 1981 PH TC Memo ¶ 81,285 (See Petty, R. M. & Allene A.)

ADAMSON, RAY P., 1981 PH TC Memo ¶ 81,285 (See Petty, R. M. & Allene A.)

ADAMSON, ROY & CATHERINE, 1986 PH TC Memo ¶ 86,489
f-1—Dew, James Edward, 91 TC 626, 91 PH TC 310
e-1—Telfeyan, Louis & Lynn, 1988 PH TC Memo 88-2146
e-1—Bullock, Kenneth & Gail, 1988 PH TC Memo 88-2706

ADAMSON, SANDRA L., 1981 PH TC Memo ¶ 81,285 (See Petty, R. M. & Allene A.)

ADAMSON; U.S. v, 161 F2d 942, 35 AFTR 1404 (USCA 9)
e-1—Inco Electroenergy Corp., 1987 PH TC Memo 87-2295

ADAMUCCI, RICHARD, 1987 PH TC Memo ¶ 87,378 (See Batastini, Paul J. & Amelia)

ADCOCK, HOMER & DOROTHY, 1982 PH TC Memo ¶ 82,206
e-1—Kauffman, Wilma G., 1982 PH TC Memo 82-2193
e-1—Scallen, Stephen B. & Chacke Y., 1987 PH TC Memo 87-2134

ADDA v COMM., 171 F2d 457, 37 AFTR 654 (USCA 4)
1—Connelly, Judith C., 1982 PH TC Memo 82-2866
1—Cleveland, Robert E., 1983 PH TC Memo 83-1223

ADDA, FERNAND C.A., 10 TC 273, ¶ 10.133 PH TC 1948
1—Connelly, Judith C., 1982 PH TC Memo 82-2866
1—Cleveland, Robert E., 1983 PH TC Memo 83-1223

ADDA, INC., 9 TC 199
e—Hodges, Irene McLaughlin & Thomas Lyman, 1985 PH TC Memo 85-2062 [See 9 TC 210-211]
1—Security Bancorp, Inc. v U.S., 48 AFTR2d 81-5514 (DC Mich)
4—Watson Land Co., 1983 PH TC Memo 83-744

ADDA, INC.; COMM. v, 171 F2d 367, 37 AFTR 641 (USCA 2)
Security Bancorp, Inc. v U.S., 48 AFTR2d 81-5514 (DC Mich)
Watson Land Co., 1983 PH TC Memo 83-744
e—Hodges, Irene McLaughlin & Thomas Lyman, 1985 PH TC Memo 85-2062

ADDEO, ARTHUR J., Jr. & MARY, 1984 PH TC Memo ¶ 84,493
e-1—Brown, Stewart L., 1986 PH TC Memo 86-1153

ADDINGTON, DOUGLAS F., 1986 PH TC Memo ¶ 86,358 (See Hoak, Roderick C. & Cornelia)

ADDINGTON, WILLIAM H. & DONNA L., 1980 PH TC Memo ¶ 80,046
a—Court Order, 10-20-81, 663 F2d 104 (USCA 5)
d—1981 PH 61,000 (USCA 10)

ADDISON, ALBERT I., 1979 PH TC Memo ¶ 79,317
e-1—Ridenour, Harry P., Jr. v U.S., 52 AFTR2d 83-5589, 3 Cl Ct 134
e-1—Reinhardt, Jules & Marilyn D., 85 TC 526, 85 PH TC 299

ADDISON INTERNAT., INC., 90 TC 1207, ¶ 90.78 PH TC
a—Addison Internat., Inc. v Comm., 64 AFTR2d 89-5747, 887 F2d 660 (USCA 6)
rc—Rocky Mountain Associates Internat., Inc., 90 TC 1241, 1242, 90 PH TC 637, 638
g-1—Butka, David J. & Sabine I., 91 TC 130, 91 PH TC 66

ADDISON INTERNAT., INC. v COMM., 64 AFTR2d 89-5747, 887 F2d 660 (USCA 6, 10-10-89)
sa—Addison Internat., Inc., 90 TC 1207, ¶ 90.78 PH TC

ADDRESSOGRAPH-MULTIGRAPH CORP., 1945 PH TC Memo ¶ 45,058
1—Buffalo Wire Works Co., Inc., 74 TC 938, 74 PH TC 509
g-1—Maier Brewing Co., 1987 PH TC Memo 87-1978

ADEE, ALLEN R., TRUST NO. 1 v U.S., 52 AFTR2d 83-6437 (DC Kan, 7-19-83)

ADEE, DONALD P., TRUSTEE v U.S., 52 AFTR2d 83-6437 (DC Kan) (See Adee, Allen R., Trust No. 1 v U.S.)

ADEE, JACK R., TRUSTEE v U.S., 52 AFTR2d 83-6437 (DC Kan) (See Adee, Allen R., Trust No. 1 v U.S.)

ADELBERG, MARVIN & HELEN M., 1985 PH TC Memo ¶ 85,597
a—Court Order, 1-21-87, 811 F2d 1507 (USCA 9)
e-1—Chao, Wen Y. & Ching J., 92 TC 1144, 92 PH TC 577
e-1—Nicklo, Joseph J., 1988 PH TC Memo 88-1199

ADELEKE, JOEL & CATHERINE A., 1980 PH TC Memo ¶ 80,479
e-1—Pike-Biegunski, Maciej Jan & Denise Nadine, 1984 PH TC Memo 84-1123

ADELMAN v U.S., 27 AFTR2d 71-1464, 440 F2d 991 (USCA 9)
e-1—Barbados #7 Ltd., 92 TC 813, 92 PH TC 409

ADELMAN v U.S., 24 AFTR2d 69-5769, 304 F Supp 599 (DC Calif)
e-2—Barbados #7 Ltd., 92 TC 813, 92 PH TC 409

ADELSON, SHELDON G. v U.S., 54 AFTR2d 84-5428, 737 F2d 1569 (USCA Fed, 6-28-84)
remg—Adelson, Sheldon G. v U.S., 52 AFTR2d 83-5211 (Cl Ct)
s—Adelson, Sheldon G. v U.S., 51 AFTR2d 83-574 (Cl Ct) 535 F Supp 1082
s—Adelson, Sheldon G. v U.S., 54 AFTR2d 84-5959, 6 Cl Ct 102
rc—Adelson, Sheldon G. v U.S., 57 AFTR2d 86-736, 782 F2d 1010 (USCA Fed)
rc—Adelson, Sheldon G. v U.S., 59 AFTR2d 87-993, 12 Cl Ct 231
e-1—Larson, Roger Roy, In re, 62 AFTR2d 88-5801, 862 F2d 117 (USCA 7)
e-1—Raab, George S. v I.R.S., 57 AFTR2d 86-715, 86-716 (DC Pa)

ADELSON, SHELDON G. v U.S., 57 AFTR2d 86-736, 782 F2d 1010 (USCA Fed, 1-29-86)
remg—Adelson, Sheldon G. v U.S., 54 AFTR2d 84-5959, 6 Cl Ct 102
rc—Adelson, Sheldon G. v U.S., 54 AFTR2d 84-5428, 737 F2d 1569 (USCA Fed)
rc—Adelson, Sheldon G. v U.S., 52 AFTR2d 83-5211, 2 Cl Ct 591
rc—Adelson, Sheldon G. v U.S., 51 AFTR2d 83-574, 1 Cl Ct 61, 553 F Supp 1082
rc—Adelson, Sheldon G. v U.S., 59 AFTR2d 87-993, 12 Cl Ct 231

ADELSON, SHELDON G. v U.S., 51 AFTR2d 83-574, 1 Cl Ct 61, 553 F Supp 1082 (12-27-82)
s—Adelson, Sheldon G. v U.S., 54 AFTR2d 84-5428, 737 F2d 1569 (USCA Fed)
s—Adelson, Sheldon G. v U.S., 52 AFTR2d 83-5211, 2 Cl Ct 591
rc—Adelson, Sheldon G. v U.S., 57 AFTR2d 86-736, 782 F2d 1010 (USCA Fed)
rc—Adelson, Sheldon G. v U.S., 54 AFTR2d 84-5959, 6 Cl Ct 102
rc—Adelson, Sheldon G. v U.S., 59 AFTR2d 87-993, 12 Cl Ct 231
e-1—Mann, Guy L. Est. of, 53 AFTR2d 84-1304, 731 F2d 273 (USCA 5)

ADELSON, SHELDON G. v U.S., 52 AFTR2d 83-5211, 2 Cl Ct 591 (6-14-83)
remd—Adelson, Sheldon G. v U.S., 54 AFTR2d 84-5428, 737 F2d 1569 (USCA Fed)
s—Adelson, Sheldon G. v U.S., 51 AFTR2d 83-574 (Cl Ct) 553 F Supp 1082
rc—Adelson, Sheldon G. v U.S., 57 AFTR2d 86-736, 782 F2d 1010 (USCA Fed)
rc—Adelson, Sheldon G. v U.S., 54 AFTR2d 84-5959, 6 Cl Ct 102
rc—Adelson, Sheldon G. v U.S., 59 AFTR2d 87-993, 12 Cl Ct 231

ADELSON, SHELDON G. v U.S., 54 AFTR2d 84-5959, 6 Cl Ct 102 (9-12-84)
remd—Adelson, Sheldon G. v U.S., 57 AFTR2d 86-736, 782 F2d 1010 (USCA Fed)
s—Adelson, Sheldon G. v U.S., 54 AFTR2d 84-5428, 737 F2d 1569 (USCA Fed)
rc—Adelson, Sheldon G. v U.S., 51 AFTR2d 83-574, 1 Cl Ct 61, 553 F Supp 1082
rc—Adelson, Sheldon G. v U.S., 52 AFTR2d 83-5211, 2 Cl Ct 591
rc—Adelson, Sheldon G. v U.S., 59 AFTR2d 87-993, 12 Cl Ct 231

Reproduced from the *Federal Tax 2nd Citator* with the permission of the publisher, Research Institute of America, Englewood Cliffs, NJ 07632.

APPENDIX F
Comprehensive Tax Return Problems

PROBLEM 1

1. Ely R. and Cora M. Taylor, ages 45 and 43, are married and file a joint income tax return. Ely is a specialist in horticulture and is employed by the Parker Seed Corporation as director of their research activities. Cora is a school teacher and is employed by St. Luke's Middle School, a private institution owned and operated by a religious group. Salary and tax withholdings for 1995 were:

	Salary	Federal	State
Ely	$71,000	$6,380	$2,780
Cora	32,000	4,100	1,450

2. The Taylors have always lived and worked in Des Moines, IA. They reside at 312 Drake Avenue, Des Moines, IA 50312. Living with them are their three children, Nancy (age 14), Martin (age 16), and Irene (age 21). Also living with the Taylors is Ely's widower father, Paul (age 71). Irene is a full-time student at Drake University. During the year, she earned $3,000 from a part-time job. Paul received $9,000 in Social Security benefits, which he deposited in his savings account. The Taylors contributed more than 50% of the support of their children and of Paul.

3. The Taylors contribute 25% of the support of Cora's aunt, Martha Bates, who lives with Cora's sister. The remainder of Martha's support is received from Cora's sister and two brothers, 25% each. Cora's sister and brothers have signed a multiple support agreement allowing Cora to claim the dependency exemption for Martha. As noted below, the Taylors have provided their share of support by paying Martha's medical expenses.

4. Relevant Social Security numbers are:

Ely	478-12-6024
Cora	477-19-1002
Nancy	479-22-6018
Martin	479-29-5025
Irene	479-31-4129
Paul	481-15-6113
Martha	480-42-1266

5. Because Paul is confined to a wheelchair due to a stroke he suffered several years ago, the Taylors spent $7,300 during the year adding impairment-related improvements to their personal residence (e.g., wheelchair ramps, widening of hallways, bathtub railings). A friend who is in the real estate business estimates that these changes increased the value of the residence by $2,500.

6. During 1995, the Taylors had water damage to their personal residence. They purchased this house on June 15, 1972, and paid $65,000 for it. A professional appraisal, for which

the Taylors paid $400, reflects that the value of the residence decreased by $15,000 ($110,000 before and $95,000 after) due to the storm causing the water damage. The Taylor's homeowner's insurance policy does not cover water damage.

7. On June 1, 1991, and as a favor to a former college roommate, Ely lent $3,200 to Lyle Petit. Lyle signed a note, maturity date of June 1, 1995, with annual interest of 10%. Ely has never recovered any of the loan or received any interest. Lyle was declared bankrupt in April 1995 and is currently under investigation for mail fraud.

8. Cora has a Bachelor of Education degree which she received many years ago. Recently, the directors at St. Luke's School resolved that all of its teachers must earn a Master of Education degree in order to continue in their present jobs. The teachers were allowed ten years in which to satisfy this new requirement. During the summer of 1995, Cora enrolled at a local university and took several graduate courses in education. Cora lived at home and commuted to her classes. Her expenses were as follows:

Books and tuition	$1,800
Transportation	
Bus fares	75
Personal auto mileage (150) miles	?
Meals while on campus (between classes)	92
Parking charges	51

When Cora did not take the bus, usually on rainy days, she drove the family auto (use the automatic mileage method—30 cents for 1995). When Cora drove, she had to pay for on-campus parking.

9. During 1995, the Taylors sold the following stocks:

Robin Corporation	
(400 shares common) July 5	$33,000
Canary Corporation	
(300 shares preferred) August 10	16,000

The Robin Corporation stock had been received from Cora's mother as a gift on January 2, 1995, when it had a fair market value of $31,000. Her mother had purchased the stock on June 1, 1994, for $30,500. No gift tax was due or paid on the mother's gift.

The Canary Corporation stock was inherited by Ely from his mother. The mother died on December 10, 1994, and her estate was settled on March 3, 1995 (the day Ely received the stock). The stock was worth $14,600 on December 10, 1994, and $14,900 on March 3, 1995. Ely has found a broker's statement that shows his mother purchased the stock on September 9, 1994, for $14,100 (including brokerage fee).

10. Besides any other items mentioned eleswhere, the Taylors had the following receipts for 1995:

Interest on CD (Iowa State Bank)		$1,920
Interest on city of Des Moines general purpose bonds		1,700
Dividends		
Robin Corporation stock	$1,250	
Canary Corporation stock	950	2,200
Riverboat casino winnings		1,300
Garage sale of old clothes and household goods (reasonable cost estimate of items sold $6,500)		1,100

11. As to medical expenses, the Taylors had the following during 1995:

Hospital and doctor bills for Martha	$3,100
Ely's contribution toward the cost of his employer's medical insurance premiums	2,900
Insurance recovery for 1994 expenses under employment medical policy	820
Orthodontia expenses for children	3,600
Prescription drugs	1,400
Doctor bills for family	1,250
Tonsillectomy for Nancy (surgeon and hospital)	1,800
Wheelchair and hearing aid for Paul	2,150

The $820 insurance recovery for the year 1994 was for medical expenses the Taylors deducted on their 1994 Federal income tax return.

The Taylors have not yet submitted any claims to the insurance company for their 1995 medical expenses. They estimate that, after the required deductible, the reimbursed amount will be $1,700.

12. Other expenditures for 1995 are summarized below:

Interest on home mortgage	$5,100
Property taxes on home	3,150
Payment of church pledge ($200 was for the 1994 remaining balance)	2,800
Additional state income tax due for 1994	230
School supplies Cora uses for her classes (not provided by St. Luke's School)	305
Professional dues (Ely and Cora)	405
Professional journals (Ely and Cora)	300
Lab coats (used by Ely at work)	340
Laundry of lab coats	105
Safety goggles and shoes (used by Ely at work)	190
Riverboat casino losses (supported by adequate records)	1,600

13. The Taylors do not wish to designate a contribution to the presidential Election Campaign Fund. If they have overpaid, any refund is to be applied toward the 1996 Federal income tax liability.

Requirements

You are to prepare a joint Federal income tax return for the Taylors for 1995.

PROBLEM 2

1. Al P. Hart, age 44, is divorced and lives alone at 426 Lantern Lane, Cincinnati, OH 45221. He provides more than half of the cost of maintaining a household for Norma Hart, who lives in an apartment nearby. Norma, age 68, is Al's widowed mother and qualifies as his dependent.

2. Al and Leona were married eighteen years ago and were divorced in 1992. Leona was awarded custody of their only child, Peter, now twelve years old. Under the divorce decree, Al must pay Leona $450 each month until Peter reaches age 21 or dies (whichever occurs first). Upon the occurrence of either event, the monthly payment

becomes $100. Since Al and Leona have been alternating claiming Peter as a dependent, Leona did not waive the dependency exemption for Peter for 1995. Al sent Leona the required $5,400 ($450 x 12 months) for 1995. Furthermore, he sent Leona an additional $900 for dental work she had done on her teeth. He also paid an optometrist/optician $350 for Peter's eye exams and prescription glasses.

3. Al is a licensed hair stylist and beautician and operates his own salon under the business name of "Al's Creations." Although it varies as to number, Al's business consists of four to six stations operated by himself and other licensed beauticians. The beauticians who work in the salon are treated as independent contractors. In this regard, each has his or her own telephone line. They maintain their own appointment books, have their own customers, and collect and keep the fees charged. For the use of the work stations and various facilities (e.g., hair dryers, shampoo sinks, waiting area), each pays Al a monthly rental. Al does not control their work hours, although most choose to follow Al's own work schedule.

4. Al's Creations is well-known for its selection and quality of men's hairpieces (i.e., toupees) and women's wigs. The business also sells a considerable quantity of beauty products (e.g., conditioners, shampoos, curling irons). Some of these items are sold to other beauticians but most are sold to regular patrons and walk in customers.

5. Al's Creations is located at 6194 Taft Street, Cincinnati, OH 45221. The employer identification number is 31-0009521; the professional activity code for beauticians is 8110.

6. The building in which the business is located is rented under a long-term lease for $1,200 each month. Al pays his own utilities. Before Al moved in, the landlord customized the facilities so as to be suited for its intended use. The only employee Al has is a shampoo person, who also performs light janitorial services. Al hires an outside service to do the heavier janitorial duties. Likewise, a local accounting group is on retainer to keep the financial records and prepare the tax returns for the business.

7. Al's Creations had the following receipts for 1995:

Sales of cosmetics	$16,525
Sales of hairpieces, wigs	28,100
Fees received from patrons by Al (including tips received)	32,350
Rent charged other beauticians	23,050

The amounts shown for the retail sales of cosmetics, hairpieces, and wigs, include state sales tax.

8. Al's Creations has the following expenses for 1995:

Purchases of cosmetics	$ 8,990
Purchases of hairpieces, wigs	13,150
Operating supplies (shampoo, permanent wave solution, color, etc.)	5,210
Rent for building	14,400
Utilities and telephone	6,020
Payroll expense	4,950
Payroll taxes (FICA, FUTA, state unemployment)	610
Sales taxes remitted to state	2,350
Health insurance coverage for employee	290
City of Cincinnati occupation permit for 1995	500
State beautician license fee	380
Liability insurance premiums (coverage is for calendar years 1995-1997)	6,000

Casualty insurance on business furnishings and equipment for 1995	1,400
Janitorial services	2,290
Accounting services ($550 was for preparation of personal tax return)	3,900
Waiting room furniture	3,200
Magazine subscriptions for waiting room	220
Advertising	950
Fine paid to City of Cincinnati	300

9. Al decided to completely renovate the furnishings in his waiting room. Consequently, he spent $3,200 for chairs, sofa, lamps, coffee table, etc., all placed in service on April 20, 1995. The old furnishings were given to patrons or thrown away. The old furniture was completely depreciated and had a zero tax basis. Al has always followed a policy of claiming as much depreciation as soon as possible. All of his other business assets (e.g., hair driers, work-station chairs) have been fully depreciated by 1995.

10. The fine paid to the city was assessed by the Sanitation Department. Al had failed, in accordance with a city ordinance, to separate the trash of the business into recyclable and nonrecyclable bins.

11. In late 1994, a transient customer visiting the city had purchased a hairpiece from the business for $190. The customer's check was not deposited until early 1995 and ultimately proved fraudulent. The sale was reported on Al's 1994 tax return. Al has no doubt that he will never collect the $190 due him.

12. Al maintains an inventory as to the merchandise he sells. The business inventories (based on the lower of cost or market) are as follows:

	12/31/94	**12/31/95**
Hairpieces and wigs	$ 3,200	$ 2,700
Cosmetics	1,900	2,100

13. In 1995, Al was audited by both the city and the state as to his 1994 income tax returns. As a result of the audit, he had to pay the city an additional $180 but he received a refund from the state of $110.

14. Except for the inventory and purchases accounts, Al operates the business on a cash method. Customers pay for services as rendered. Sales income is recorded when the merchandise is sold. Al does not extend credit but does accept payment by charge card and check (see item 11 above).

15. Al's medical expenses for 1995, and not mentioned elsewhere, included the following:

Gall bladder operation (includes hospital and surgeon's charges) for Norma	$2,100
Annual physical for Al	390
Dentists charges for Al (includes crown, bridges, fillings, etc.)	4,300
Hernia operation (includes hospital and surgeon's charges)	2,100
Prescription medicines	800
Medical insurance premiums	800

In November of 1995, Al purchased a medical insurance policy. The policy does not cover anyone but Al and his one employee (see item 6 above). The premium for the employee coverage is stated separately at item 8. Also, the policy does not apply to dental bills. Al filed a claim with the insurance company in late December. He received a check in January of 1996 which, after the appropriate deductible, was for $300.

16. Al's other expenses are listed below:

Property taxes on residence	$3,800
Interest on home mortgage	5,200
Annual dues for membership in the American Association of Beauticians	150
Professional journals	190

17. Al has always itemized his deductions because even without substantial medical expenses, his deductions from adjusted gross income have exceeded the standard deduction.

18. Al had no stock transactions in 1995 but he does have a $5,000 long-term capital loss carryover from 1994.

19. Al's other income for 1995 is summarized below:

Interest income from a savings account at Enterprise Bank	$6,800
Cash dividend from P&G common stock	6,100

20. Al made estimated tax payments for 1995 as follows:

City income tax	$ 700
Ohio income tax	2,500
Federal income and self-employment taxes (paid $1,400 quarterly)	5,600

21. Relevant social security numbers are—

Al Hart	268-01-5869
Norma Hart	301-42-2657
Leona Hart	300-52-7981
Peter Hart	302-64-1826

Requirements

You are to prepare Al's Federal income tax return for 1995. Al wants to designate that $3 he directed to the Presidential Election Campaign fund. If he has overpaid his 1995 taxes, he wants to have the amount applied to his 1996 estimated taxes.

Appendix G
Table of Cases Cited

APPENDIX H
Depreciation

INTRODUCTION

Cost recovery, amortization, and depletion are presented in Chapter 8. For most fixed assets (e.g., machinery, equipment, furniture, fixtures, buildings) placed in service after December 31, 1980, the Economic Recovery Tax Act of 1981 (ERTA) has replaced the depreciation system with the cost recovery system.[1] The general relationship between the depreciation system and the cost recovery system is summarized in Exhibit H–1.

Despite ERTA, a discussion of § 167 depreciation is still relevant for two reasons. First, assets that were placed in service prior to 1981 are still in use. Second, certain assets placed in service after 1980 are not eligible to use the cost recovery system (ACRS and MACRS) and therefore must be depreciated. They include property placed in service after 1980 whose life is not based on years (e.g., units-of-production method).

DEPRECIATION

Section 167 permits a depreciation deduction in the form of a reasonable allowance for the exhaustion, wear and tear, and obsolescence of business property and property held for the production of income (e.g., rental property held by an investor).[2] Obsolescence refers to normal technological change due to reasonably foreseeable economic conditions. If rapid or abnormal obsolescence occurs, a taxpayer may change to a shorter estimated useful life if there is a "clear and

▼ EXHIBIT H–1
Depreciation and Cost Recovery: Relevant Time Periods

System	Date Property Is Placed in Service
§ 167 depreciation	Before January 1, 1981, and *certain* property placed in service after December 31, 1980.
Original accelerated cost recovery system (ACRS)	After December 31, 1980, and before January 1, 1987.
Modified accelerated cost recovery system (MACRS)	After December 31, 1986.

[1] Depreciation is covered in § 167, and cost recovery (ACRS and MACRS) is covered in § 168.

[2] § 167(a) and Reg. § 1.167(a)–1.

convincing basis for the redetermination." Depreciation deductions are *not* permitted for personal use property.

The taxpayer must adopt a reasonable and consistent plan for depreciating the cost or other basis of assets over the estimated useful life of the property (e.g., the taxpayer cannot arbitrarily defer or accelerate the amount of depreciation from one year to another). The basis of the depreciable property must be reduced by the depreciation allowed and by not less than the allowable amount.[3] The *allowed* depreciation is the depreciation actually taken, whereas the *allowable* depreciation is the amount that could have been taken under the applicable depreciation method. If the taxpayer does not claim any depreciation on property during a particular year, the basis of the property still must be reduced by the amount of depreciation that should have been deducted (the allowable depreciation).

EXAMPLE 1

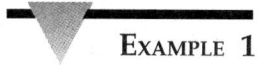

On January 1, Ted paid $7,500 for a truck to be used in his business. He chose a five-year estimated useful life, no salvage value, and straight-line depreciation. Thus, the allowable depreciation deduction was $1,500 per year. However, depreciation actually taken (allowed) was as follows:

Year 1	$1,500
Year 2	–0–
Year 3	–0–
Year 4	1,500
Year 5	1,500

The adjusted basis of the truck must be reduced by the amount of allowable depreciation of $7,500 ($1,500 × 5 years) even though Ted claimed only $4,500 depreciation during the five-year period. Therefore, if Ted sold the truck at the end of Year 5 for $1,000, he would recognize a $1,000 gain, since the adjusted basis of the truck is zero. ▼

QUALIFYING PROPERTY AND BASIS FOR DEPRECIATION

The use rather than the character of property determines whether a depreciation deduction is permitted. Property must be used in a trade or business or held for the production of income to qualify as depreciable.

EXAMPLE 2

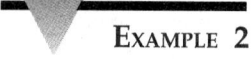

Carol is a self-employed CPA who maintains her office in a room in her home. The room, which is used exclusively for her business, comprises 20% of the square footage of her house. Carol is permitted a depreciation deduction only for the business use part of the house. No depreciation deduction is permitted for the 80% of the square footage of her house that is used as her residence. ▼

The basis for depreciation generally is the adjusted cost basis used to determine gain if the property is sold or otherwise disposed of.[4] However, if personal use assets are converted to business or income-producing use, the basis for depreciation *and* for loss is the *lower* of the adjusted basis or fair market value at the time of the conversion of the property.[5] As a result of this lower of basis

[3] § 1016(a)(2) and Reg. § 1.167(a)–10(a).
[4] § 167(c).
[5] Reg. § 1.167(g)–1.

rule, losses that occurred while the property was personal use property will not be recognized for tax purposes through the depreciation of the property.

EXAMPLE 3

Hans acquires a personal residence for $130,000. Four years later, when the fair market value is only $125,000, he converts the property to rental use. The basis for depreciation is $125,000, since the fair market value is less than the adjusted basis. The $5,000 decline in value is deemed to be personal (since it occurred while the property was held for personal use) and therefore nondeductible. ▼

The Regulations provide that tangible property is depreciable only to the extent that the property is subject to wear and tear, decay or decline from natural causes, exhaustion, and obsolescence.[6] Thus, land and inventory are not depreciable, but land improvements are depreciable (e.g., paved surfaces, fences, landscaping).

OTHER DEPRECIATION CONSIDERATIONS

In determining the amount of the depreciation deduction, the following additional considerations need to be addressed:

- The salvage value of the asset.
- The choice of depreciation methods.
- The useful life of the asset.

For property subject to depreciation under § 167, taxpayers generally must take into account the **salvage value** (assuming there is a salvage value) of an asset in calculating depreciation. An asset cannot be depreciated below its salvage value. However, the Code permits a taxpayer to disregard salvage value for amounts up to 10 percent of the basis in the property. This provision applies to tangible personal property (other than livestock) with an estimated useful life of three years or more.[7]

EXAMPLE 4

Green Company acquired a machine for $10,000 in 1980 with an estimated salvage value of $3,000 after 17 years. The company may disregard salvage value to the extent of $1,000 and compute the machine's depreciation based upon a cost of $10,000 less $2,000 salvage value. The adjusted basis may be reduced to $2,000 (depreciation of $8,000 may be taken) even though the actual salvage value is $3,000. ▼

This provision was incorporated into the law to reduce the number of IRS-taxpayer disputes over the amount of the salvage value that should be used.

Another consideration is the *choice of depreciation methods* from among the several allowed. The following alternative depreciation methods are permitted for property placed into service before January 1, 1981, and for the aforementioned property placed in service after December 31, 1980, for which cost recovery is not permitted:

- The straight-line (SL) method (cost basis less salvage value ÷ estimated useful life).
- The declining-balance method (DB) using a rate not to exceed twice the straight-line rate. Common methods include 200 percent DB (double-declining balance), 150 percent DB, and 125 percent DB. Salvage value is not taken into account under any of the declining-balance methods. However,

[6] Reg. § 1.167(a)–2.

[7] Reg. §§ 1.167(a)–1(c) and (f)–1.

no further depreciation can be claimed once net book value (cost minus depreciation) and salvage value are the same.

- The sum-of-the-years' digits method (SYD).
- Any other consistent method that does not result in greater total depreciation being claimed during the first two-thirds of the useful life than would have been allowable under the double-declining balance method. Permissible methods include machine hours and the units-of-production method.

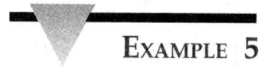

EXAMPLE 5 On January 1, 1980, Diego acquired a new machine to be used in his business. The asset cost $10,000 with an estimated salvage value of $2,000 and a four-year estimated useful life.[8] The following amounts of depreciation could be deducted, depending on the method of depreciation used:

	1980	1981	1982	1983
1. Straight-line: $10,000 cost less ($2,000 salvage value reduced by 10% of cost) ÷ 4 years	$2,250	$2,250	$2,250	$2,250
2. Double-declining balance:				
a. $10,000 × 50% (twice the straight-line rate)	5,000			
b. ($10,000 – $5,000) × 50%		2,500		
c. ($10,000 – $5,000 – $2,500) × 50%			1,250	
d. ($10,000 – $5,000 – $2,500 – $1,250) ×50%				250[9]
3. Sum-of-the-years' digits:* $10,000 cost less ($2,000 salvage value reduced by 10% of cost) or $9,000				
a. $9,000 × 4/10	3,600			
b. $9,000 × 3/10		2,700		
c. $9,000 × 2/10			1,800	
d. $9,000 × 1/10				900

*The formula for the sum-of-the-years' digits (SYD) method is

$$\text{Cost} - \text{Salvage value} \times \frac{\text{Remaining life at the beginning of the year}}{\text{Sum-of-the-years' digits of the estimated life}}$$

In this example, the denominator for SYD is 1 + 2 + 3 + 4, or 10. The numerator is 4 for Year 1 (the number of years left at the beginning of Year 1), 3 for Year 2, etc. The denominator can be calculated by the following formula:

$$S = \frac{Y(Y+1)}{2} \quad \text{where } Y = \text{estimated useful life}$$

$$S = \frac{4(4+1)}{2} = 10$$

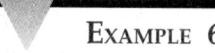

EXAMPLE 6 Using the depreciation calculations in Example 5, the depreciation reserve (accumulated depreciation) and net book value at the end of 1983 are as follows:

	Cost	–	Depreciation	=	Net Book Value*
Straight-line	$10,000		$9,000		$1,000
Double-declining balance	10,000		9,000		1,000
Sum-of-the-years' digits	10,000		9,000		1,000

*Note that an asset may not be depreciated below its salvage value even when a declining-balance method is used.

[8] A four-year life is used to illustrate the different depreciation methods. Note that an asset placed in service in 1980 must have a useful life of at least 17 years in order for depreciation to be deducted in 1996.

[9] Total depreciation taken cannot exceed cost minus estimated salvage value ($1,000 in this example).

In 1969, Congress placed certain restrictions on the use of accelerated methods for new and used realty that are subject to the depreciation rules under § 167. These restrictions were imposed to reduce the opportunities for using real estate investments as tax shelters. The use of accelerated depreciation frequently resulted in the recognition of ordinary tax losses on economically profitable real estate ventures.

The following methods were permitted for residential and nonresidential real property:

	Nonresidential Real Property (Commercial and Industrial Buildings, Etc.)	**Residential Real Property (Apartment Buildings, Etc.)**
New property acquired after July 24, 1969, and generally before January 1, 1981	150% DB, SL	200% DB, SYD, 150% DB, or SL
Used property acquired after July 24, 1969, and generally before January 1, 1981	SL	125% DB (if estimated useful life is 20 years or greater) or SL

Congress chose to permit accelerated methods (200 percent declining-balance and sum-of-the-years' digits) for new residential rental property. Presumably, the desire to stimulate construction of new housing units justified the need for such accelerated methods.

Restrictions on the use of accelerated methods were not imposed on new tangible personalty (e.g., machinery, equipment, and automobiles). However, the 200 percent declining-balance and sum-of-the-years' digits methods were not permitted for used tangible personal property. The depreciation methods permitted for *used* tangible personal property were as follows:

	Useful Life of Three Years or More	**Useful Life of Less Than Three Years**
Used tangible personal property acquired after July 24, 1969, and generally before January 1, 1981	150% DB, SL	SL

Since the acquisition of used property does not result in any net addition to gross private investment in our economy, Congress chose not to provide as rapid accelerated depreciation for used property.

The determination of a *useful life* for a depreciable asset often led to disagreement between taxpayers and the IRS. One source of information was the company's previous experience and policy with respect to asset maintenance and utilization. Another source was the guideline lives issued by the IRS.[10] In 1971, the IRS guideline life system was modified and liberalized by the enactment of the **Asset Depreciation Range (ADR) system.**[11]

10 Rev.Proc. 72–10, 1972–1 C.B. 721, superseded by Rev.Proc. 83–35, 1983–1 C.B. 745.

11 Reg. § 1.167(a)–11.

KEY TERMS

INDEX

A

H

I

J

K

L

U

V

W

Z